LANCHESTER LIBRARY

3 8001 00784 0550

WITHDRAWN

Praise for *Family Law*

"… an excellent all-round textbook for this area of law. It is written in an accessible style that is appealing to students; yet it also manages to draw out the complexities of the subject. It is always a popular choice!"
Dr Caroline Jones, Associate Professor, Swansea University

"Placing Family law in a wider social context, Herring's 'Family Law' is essential reading for all involved in studying and teaching the subject."
Richard Collier, Professor, Newcastle University

"This is one of the most comprehensive textbooks in family law. It is very thorough, yet student friendly. A distinctive feature of Herring is that it places the law in its social context: it almost reads as a novel and you want to know how it ends!"
Dr Eugenia Caracciolo di Torella, Associate Professor, Leicester Law School

"This textbook provides an accessible and comprehensive account of contemporary family law, allowing students to navigate essential legal information, whilst providing clear signposts for critical thinking and engagement with matters of socio-legal debate. It is an essential read for those new to the study of family law."
Hannah Gibbons-Jones, Lecturer in Law, School of Law, Keele University

"…provides all the legal knowledge required in an interesting and accessible way — introducing diverse and respected critical views, highlighting controversial and emerging issues, and weaving through the ethical, philosophical, sociological backgrounds."
Fiona Buchanan, Co-Programme Leader LLB, University of Cumbria

D1627797

P Pearson

At Pearson, we have a simple mission: to help people make more of their lives through learning.

We combine innovative learning technology with trusted content and educational expertise to provide engaging and effective learning experiences that serve people wherever and whenever they are learning.

From classroom to boardroom, our curriculum materials, digital learning tools and testing programmes help to educate millions of people worldwide – more than any other private enterprise.

Every day our work helps learning flourish, and wherever learning flourishes, so do people.

To learn more, please visit us at **www.pearson.com/uk**

Family Law

Tenth edition

Jonathan Herring

Exeter College
University of Oxford

Pearson

Harlow, England • London • New York • Boston • San Francisco • Toronto • Sydney • Dubai • Singapore • Hong Kong
Tokyo • Seoul • Taipei • New Delhi • Cape Town • São Paulo • Mexico City • Madrid • Amsterdam • Munich • Paris • Milan

PEARSON EDUCATION LIMITED
KAO Two
KAO Park
Harlow
CM17 9NA
United Kingdom
Tel: +44 (0)1279 623623
Web: www.pearson.com/uk

First published 2001 (print)
Ninth edition published 2019 (print and electronic)
Tenth edition published 2021 (print and electronic)

© Pearson Education Limited 2001, 2004, 2007, 2009, 2011 (print)
© Pearson Education Limited 2013, 2015, 2017, 2019, 2021 (print and electronic)

The right of Jonathan Herring to be identified as author of this work has been asserted by him in accordance with the Copyright, Designs and Patents Act 1988.

The print publication is protected by copyright. Prior to any prohibited reproduction, storage in a retrieval system, distribution or transmission in any form or by any means, electronic, mechanical, recording or otherwise, permission should be obtained from the publisher or, where applicable, a licence permitting restricted copying in the United Kingdom should be obtained from the Copyright Licensing Agency Ltd, Barnard's Inn, 86 Fetter Lane, London EC4A 1EN.

The ePublication is protected by copyright and must not be copied, reproduced, transferred, distributed, leased, licensed or publicly performed or used in any way except as specifically permitted in writing by the publishers, as allowed under the terms and conditions under which it was purchased, or as strictly permitted by applicable copyright law. Any unauthorised distribution or use of this text may be a direct infringement of the author's and the publisher's rights and those responsible may be liable in law accordingly.

All trademarks used herein are the property of their respective owners. The use of any trademark in this text does not vest in the author or publisher any trademark ownership rights in such trademarks, nor does the use of such trademarks imply any affiliation with or endorsement of this book by such owners.

Contains public sector information licensed under the Open Government Licence (OGL) v3.0.
http://www.nationalarchives.gov.uk/doc/open-government-licence/version/3/.

Contains Parliamentary information licensed under the Open Parliament Licence (OPL) v3.0.
http://www.parliament.uk/site-information/copyright/open-parliament-licence/.

Pearson Education is not responsible for the content of third-party internet sites.

ISBN: 978-1-292-34325-9 (print)
     978-1-292-34326-6 (PDF)
     978-1-292-34327-3 (ePub)

British Library Cataloguing-in-Publication Data
A catalogue record for the print edition is available from the British Library

Library of Congress Cataloging-in-Publication Data
Names: Herring, Jonathan, author.
Title: Family law / Jonathan Herring, Exeter College, University of Oxford.
Other titles: Family law (Treatise)
Description: Tenth edition. | Harlow, England ; New York : Pearson, 2021. |
  Includes bibliographical references and index. | Summary: "Family Law,
  10th edition, by Jonathan Herring, is the best-selling textbook that's
  loved by students and lecturers alike. Offering exceptional coverage of
  all key family law principles, this book explores the theories, debates
  and ethical dilemmas that underpin the subject, ensuring you have the
  knowledge required to critique the existing law and evaluate reform
  options. The tenth edition has been fully updated with all significant
  legal developments in the area of family law"– Provided by publisher.
Identifiers: LCCN 2020058298 (print) | LCCN 2020058299 (ebook) | ISBN
  9781292343259 (paperback) | ISBN 9781292343266 (PDF) | ISBN
  9781292343273 (epub)
Subjects: LCSH: Domestic relations–England.
Classification: LCC KD750 .H47 2021 (print) | LCC KD750 (ebook) | DDC
  346.4201/5–dc23
LC record available at https://lccn.loc.gov/2020058298
LC ebook record available at https://lccn.loc.gov/2020058299

10 9 8 7 6 5 4 3 2 1
25 24 23 22 21

Front cover image: Superstock/Alamy Stock Photo
Cover designed by Kelly Miller

Print edition typeset in 9/12 ITC Giovanni Std by SPi Global
Printed in Slovakia by Neografia

NOTE THAT ANY PAGE CROSS REFERENCES REFER TO THE PRINT EDITION

Coventry University Library

To Kirsten, Laurel, Jo and Darcy

Brief contents

Contents

6 Property on separation   207

Preface

This text tries to present family law in its context. I hope readers will gain not only an understanding of what the law actually is, but also an awareness of the complex tensions in social, philosophical and political forces which surround 'family life'. This means the text not only contains much law, but also a little sociology, political theory and philosophy. Of course, a little of anything might be said to be a bad thing and the text can only give a flavour of the wide-ranging issues surrounding family life and its regulation. Still, it is hoped the reader can see that family law is not simply a set of rules cast down from up on high, but rules that have to operate in the messy world of personal relations where many people do not know what the law says, and even if they do, do not care very much about it.

I am extremely grateful for the support of the team at Pearson Education, particularly Akanksha Marwah and Hemalatha Loganathan who oversaw the project; Stephen Pepper for his outstanding editing; and Gavin Parish for the excellent proofreading. I am also grateful for the support and help of colleagues and friends while writing *Family Law*, and in particular Alan Bogg, Bev Clough, Shazia Choudhry, Charlotte Elves, John Eekelaar, Michelle Madden Dempsey, Stephen Gilmore, Imogen Goold, Rebecca Probert, George P. Smith, Rachel Taylor and Julie Wallbank. In all sorts of ways they have helped with the text. Of course, my wife Kirsten and children Laurel, Joanna and Darcy have been a constant source of fun, laughs and encouragement.

The text seeks to present the law as at 1 September 2020.

Jonathan Herring
Exeter College, University of Oxford
September 2020

Table of cases

Table of statutes

Table of statutory instruments

Table of European and International legislation

1   What is family law?

Learning objectives

When you finish reading this chapter you will be able to:

1. Explain and evaluate how different theories seek to define a 'family'
2. Discuss the arguments for and against family life and its alternatives
3. Explain and evaluate how different theories seek to define 'family law'
4. Summarise the broad issues which underpin family law
5. Describe how the Human Rights Act 1998 affects family law
6. Consider the impact of COVID-19 on family law

1 Introduction

Families can be the scenes of some of the greatest joys, as well as some of the greatest sadnesses, that life can bring. Studies suggest that for a substantial majority of people families are more important to them than jobs or status.[1] The interaction of law and the family therefore gives rise to questions of enormous importance to the individuals who appear before the courts and to society at large.[2] In *Huang v Secretary of State for the Home Department*[3] the House of Lords emphasised the importance of families to individuals:

> Human beings are social animals. They depend on others. Their family, or extended family, is the group on which many people most heavily depend, socially, emotionally and often financially. There comes a point at which, for some, prolonged and unavoidable separation from this group seriously inhibits their ability to live full and fulfilling lives.

The importance of families to the general social good was recognised by the Government in 2014 when it announced a 'family test' for all new policies and legislation.[4] This requires

---

[1] Future Foundation (1999).
[2] For a remarkable history of family law during the twentieth century, see Cretney (2003a).
[3] [2007] 2 AC 167.
[4] Department for Work and Pensions (2014a).

Government departments to assess the impact of proposed reforms on families. That is because the Government states that:

> Strong and stable families, in all their forms, play an important role in our society. Families have a major impact on the life chances of individuals and strong family relationships are recognised as an important component of individual, community and national wellbeing.[5]

However, a report in 2019 by the Centre for Social Justice[6] concluded that engagement with the 'family test' was 'superficial' and that none of the Government departments had records as to the number of times the test had been used.

Not only are family law cases important for the individual, but they can also be stressful for judges. In a, perhaps surprisingly honest, comment, Jackson LJ in *LL v Lord Chancellor*[7] explained that family law judges:

> undertake some of the most arduous and emotionally draining cases that come before the courts. Their task can be a lonely one. Feelings run high in many family cases. People who are otherwise entirely reasonable may become aggressive or obstructive litigants when contesting the future arrangements for their children. These are the conditions under which the judge in this case was seeking, in good faith, to discharge her duties.

This chapter will consider some key questions about families: What is family law? Is family life in crisis? It will also highlight some of the most controversial issues which face family lawyers today and which will appear throughout the text. First, it is necessary to attempt a definition of a family.

2 Seeking a definition of the family

Learning objective 1

Explain and evaluate how different theories seek to define a 'family'

The notion of a 'family' is notoriously difficult to define.[8] Traditionally, people have a stereotypical image of what the 'ideal family' is like – a mother, a father and two children. Yet this family composition is not the family form that most people will have experienced. In 2019, there were 27.8 million households, but just under seven million of those had a child aged 14 or under.[9] So the image of two parents and two children as the ideal family is just that, an ideal; a powerful ideal, but not the most common household form.

It is possible to distinguish families (a group of people related by blood, marriage or adoption); a nuclear family (parents and their dependent children); extended families (the nuclear family plus the wider kin, e.g. grandparents); kinships (the larger family groups related by blood or marriage); and households (a group of people sharing accommodation).[10] David Archard suggests a family is 'that group of individuals whose adults take primary custodial roles in respect of its dependent children'.[11] But his requirement that a family must contain children is controversial. Does a child cease to be a member of a family once they leave home? Are a couple who cannot have a child not, therefore, a family? One of the difficulties in defining

---

[5] Department for Work and Pensions (2014a).
[6] Centre for Social Justice (2019).
[7] [2017] EWCA Civ 237, para 9.
[8] Herring, Probert and Gilmore (2015: ch. 1).
[9] National Statistics (2020).
[10] See Archard (2003: ch. 2) for further discussion.
[11] Archard (2012 and 2018).

'family' is the power of the definition and especially the stigma that follows from denying that a certain group of people is a family.[12] Hence the extensive campaigning over the past few decades to have gay and lesbian relationships recognised as family.

'Family' is presently a term that is of limited legal significance. As we shall see in this text, much effort has been made in attempting a legal definition of 'marriage', 'parent' and 'parenthood', but relatively few cases have defined a 'family'. How might the law define a family?[13]

A The person in the street's definition

In an attempt to define a 'family', the law could rely on common usage: how would the person in the street define a family? The difficulty with this is that although there may be some cases where everyone would agree that a particular group of people is a family, there are many other cases where, when asked, people would answer 'I don't know', or there would be conflicting answers, reflecting different values, religious beliefs or cultural perspectives. When children have been asked to define families, they have revealed a broad understanding of the term, including those people they feel close to and even included pets.[14]

B A formalistic definition

The law could rely upon a formalistic approach.[15] Such definitions would focus on whether the group of individuals in question has certain observable traits that can be objectively proved. These definitions often focus on criteria such as marriage or the existence of children. The benefit of formalistic definitions is their clarity and ease of proof. The approach therefore has a strong appeal to lawyers. The definitions avoid involving the court in time-consuming or unnecessarily controversial questions.

The main disadvantage is that the approach can be rather technical. If the group of people failed to meet the formal requirements of the definition even though they functioned as a family, should they be denied the status of family? For example, some people argue that it would be bizarre if the law treated an unmarried couple who had lived together for 20 years and raised children together any differently from a married couple who had been married 20 years. Should the fact that the married couple undertook a short ceremony 20 years previously make a difference? Those who take such a view may prefer a definition that considers the lived reality of the relationship, rather than its technical nature.

C A lived reality-based definition

A lived reality-based definition suggests that if a group of people live together in a certain way then the law can term them a family. In other words, the approach focuses on what they do, rather than what they are. This has led David Morgan to argue that although we may not be able to define what a family is, we can identify what 'family practices' are.[16] If such an approach were to be adopted, the law might describe the functions of a family as: providing security and care for its members; producing children; socialising and raising of children; and providing economically for its members. However, whether a family needs to fulfil all or only some of

---

[12] Douglas (2005: 3).
[13] See Diduck (2005) for an excellent discussion of the changing legal understanding of families.
[14] Smart, Neale and Wade (2001: 52).
[15] See Glennon (2008) and Leckey (2008) for an informative analysis.
[16] Morgan (2011).

these functions is controversial. Some have argued that a family's existence should be focused around children.[17] Others suggest that a sexual relationship, or a potential sexual relationship is essential if families are to be distinguished from friendship.[18] Still others have argued that caring is what is central to a family.[19] Alison Diduck has written:

> 'family' is one way to describe forms or expressions of intimate or private living based upon care and interdependence. And so, family could include a couple, of the same or different sexes with or without children, co-habiting with or without legal formality, or, indeed not co-habiting at all. Family also means an adult caring for a child or other dependent relative. What makes a relationship familial to me then is not necessarily a biological, legal, or conjugal connection, rather it is what people do in it, it is a relationship characterized by some degree of intimacy, interdependence, and care.[20]

Opponents of a lived reality-based approach claim that it presupposes a particular role for a family, but not everyone will agree on what that role is. Hence, it is argued that it is only because of the dominant position religion has held in our society that a sexual element is seen as important to the definition of marriage.[21] There is also the problem of proof. Determining what the group of people does is normally far harder than determining whether or not they have undergone a formal ceremony of some kind. Others complain that a lived reality-based approach ignores some of the things that hold families together, such as shared values, memories, and a sense of identity, which are not captured by the 'doings' of a family.[22]

D An idealised definition

Another approach suggests that a workable definition of what a family is does not exist, but that a definition of an idealised family can be provided. In our society traditionally this would be seen as a married couple with children.[23] The difficulty is that this idealised picture has become tarnished through evidence of domestic violence; abuse of children within the home; and the oppression of women within marriage. Further, the approach also assumes that what is the ideal family for one person must be the ideal for all. What might be a good family for you might not be a good family for someone else. Perhaps, rather than the law promoting a particular ideal of family life, we should let each person work out for themselves what family form works for them. Further, in a culturally diverse nation such as ours it would be impossible to agree on an idealised family form that would be acceptable to everyone.

E A self-definition approach

This approach would state 'you are a family if you say you are'. Eekelaar and Nhlapo[24] have suggested that societies are gradually accepting an increasing variety of family forms and are reaching the position that a family is any group of people who regard themselves as a family. The benefit of such an approach is that it does not stigmatise people as 'not family' unless they

---

[17] Archard (2012 and 2018).
[18] See Lord Clyde in *Fitzpatrick v Sterling Housing Association* [2000] 1 FCR 21 at p. 35. But see Lind (2011) for an excellent discussion of how friendship needs to be taken more seriously.
[19] See Herring (2013a).
[20] Diduck (2011).
[21] Herring (2014a).
[22] McKie and Callan (2012).
[23] Morgan (2007).
[24] Eekelaar and Nhlapo (1998: ix).

do not wish to be regarded as a family. The problem with it is that it becomes difficult to use the concept to promote particular policies or legal responses as it loses any objective meaning.

F Do we give up?

So, there are severe difficulties in defining families. There is little agreement within society over exactly what constitutes family or what the purposes of a family are. Does this lead us to throw up our hands and say there is no such thing as a family, as so many sociologists do? The argument for not doing so is that most people regard their family (whatever they mean by that) as of enormous importance, and indeed families are seen as having great social significance. Promoting the family is one of the few political ideals with which most people agree.[25]

What this demonstrates is that there are dangers in seeking to promote family life or talk about family law unless we are clear what it is we mean by families. We need to be precise about what aspect of the family a law is seeking to promote, or which group of people is intended to be covered by a particular law. Indeed, it may be that some parts of family law will apply to some families and not to others. It is not that some groups are family and some are not, but that some family groups may need the benefits of a particular law and others not. What is clear is that the definition of a family may change over time.

G Discussion of how the law defines families

The legal definition of families has changed over the decades. In 1950 in *Gammans v Ekins*,[26] talking of an unmarried couple, it was stated: 'to say of two people masquerading as these two were as husband and wife, that they were members of the same family, seems to be an abuse of the English Language'. This approach would no longer represent the law.

Lady Hale in *Whittington Hospital NHS Trust v XX*[27] stated:

> More dramatic still have been the developments in the law's ideas of what constitutes a family. Traditionally, families were limited to those related by consanguinity (blood) or affinity (marriage). Hence at first only opposite sex married couples could apply for parental orders. Now they have been joined by same sex married couples, by same sex and opposite sex civil partners, and by couples, whether of the same or opposite sexes, who are neither married nor civil partners, but are living together in an enduring family relationship. They have also been joined by single applicants. All of these would be regarded as family relationships within the meaning of article 8 of the ECHR.

Ms Justice Russell in *Re B (A Child) (No 2) (Welfare: Child Arrangements Order)*[28] explained that now the focus is on the everyday nature of the relationship, rather than its formal nature:

> The family courts are familiar with many kinds of families including those that might have once been considered unconventional and take a broad and purposive approach both to families and to family life; family life is a matter of fact, one of substance, not form.

It is noticeable that such statements avoid a precise definition of a family.

The European Court of Human Rights has had to consider the definition of a family because Article 8 of the European Convention on Human Rights requires a right to respect

---

[25] Edwards and Gillies (2012).
[26] [1950] 2 KB 328 at p. 331.
[27] [2020] UKSC 14, para 30.
[28] [2017] EWHC 488 (Fam).

for family life. The European Court has determined that family ties can emerge from a biological link (especially between a parent and child) or from a sustained relationship. In *Paradiso and Campanelli v Italy*[29] a couple who had asked a woman to carry a child for them as a surrogate mother were not held to have a right to family life in respect of the child. There was no biological link between them and the child, and they had not actively cared for the child. We will return to this issue when we look at surrogacy in Chapter 8.

So, to summarise, in defining a family, the law does not restrict the definition of family life to those who are married or those who are related by blood. It is willing to accept that other less formal relations can be family if they can demonstrate a sharing of lives and degree of intimacy and stability. However, it would be wrong to say that the law takes a pure lived reality-based approach because if a couple are married then they will be regarded as a family, even if their relationship is not a loving, committed or stable one. Further, the European Court of Human Rights particularly considers that close blood ties are often seen as generating a claim to family life, even without much social interaction.

H The Government's definition of family

The Government's 'family test',[30] which was mentioned in the previous section, has a very broad understanding of families as including:

- couple relationships (including same-sex couples) including marriage, civil partnerships, co-habitation and those living apart together;
- relationships in lone parent families, including relationships between the parent and children with a non-resident parent, and with extended family;
- parent and step-parent to child relationships;
- relationships with foster children and adopted children;
- sibling relationships;
- children's relationship with their grandparents;
- kinship carers; and
- extended families, particularly where they are playing a role in raising children or caring for older or disabled family members.

In producing this list, the Government has avoided using a single criterion (e.g. blood ties) and seems to have relied on a broad range of different ways of understanding the family. This recognises the diverse range of being and doing family life in Britain today.

I New families?

Some commentators believe that in the past few decades we have witnessed some fundamental changes in the nature of families. Others argue that family life has been in constant flux across the centuries and contemporary changes are no different from the changes in centuries past.[31] Certainly some current statistics make dramatic reading.[32]

---

[29] App. No. 25358/12.
[30] Department for Work and Pensions (2014b).
[31] See the detailed discussion in Brown (2019).
[32] These statistics are all taken from Office for National Statistics (2020a).

KEY STATISTICS

- People are now marrying at an older age; the rate of marriage is dropping; and there are projections that fewer and fewer people will marry. In 2019, 66.8% of families in the United Kingdom involved a married couple or civil partners. That is a drop from 68.6% in 2009.
- Increasingly people are co-habiting outside of marriage. In 2019 in the United Kingdom 18.4% of families involved co-habiting couples.
- Living alone is an increasingly popular option, with 8.2 million people living on their own, 29.5% of all households.
- In 1971, 91.6% of births in England and Wales were within marriage or civil partnership; by 2019 this had decreased to 51.5%. In 2019, 14.9% of families were headed by a single parent, while 86% of lone parents were women.
- Same-sex relationships are increasingly acceptable. In 2019 it was estimated there were 212,000 families consisting of same-sex couples, a 40% increase from 2015.
- In the 1970s and 1980s there were sharp increases in the rate of divorce. In recent years the divorce rate appears to have levelled off, and even slightly declined. However, current estimates are that 42% of marriages end in divorce.

There are some who believe that such statistics indicate that families are in crisis. Typical of such a view is the following statement of the Conservative Party's Centre for Social Justice:[33]

> A strong, successful and cohesive Britain needs strong families. Family stability in Britain has been in continuous decline for four decades. Since the 1970s there has been a decline in marriage. Over the same period there has been a marked increase in the number of lone parents, with a quarter of all children now growing up in single parent households. A further one in four children are born to cohabiting couples. Around one in ten families with dependent children are stepfamilies. Sadly, 15 per cent of all babies are born and grow up without a resident biological father, and seven per cent are born without a registered father on their birth certificate. Britain has the highest divorce rate and highest teenage pregnancy rate in Europe, with the teenage pregnancy rate actually rising between 2006 and 2007 . . . Tragically, at least one in three children will experience family breakdown, in the form of parental separation, by age 16.

To many, however, such views are 'old fashioned'. Certainly, there has been a notable shift in public attitudes in these areas. In the British Social Attitudes Survey 2020[34] 74 per cent of people thought that sex outside of marriage was not wrong at all; the figure in 1984 had been 42 per cent. Two-thirds of people thought sex between people of the same sex was not wrong at all. Contrast that with the one-fifth who took that view in 1984 and you can see the huge shift in attitudes. The figures on these issues, as you might expect, depend significantly on age and among younger people the 'liberal' approach is even higher than these averages. However, it would be wrong to assume that in all areas of family life there has been a liberalisation of attitudes. When asked if it was wrong for a married person to have sexual relations with someone other than their partner, 63 per cent say that it is 'always wrong'. That is an increase from the 58 per cent who thought this in 1984.

---

[33] Centre for Social Justice (2010).
[34] National Centre for Social Research (2020).

Those dismayed at these statistics commonly refer to the need to promote 'family values'.[35] But that term is normally used to promote a particular agenda: stable marriages; gendered division of roles; the confinement of sexuality to the married heterosexual unit; and the support of these patterns through government policy.[36] Alison Diduck has questioned that claim and suggested that when people mourn the loss of the traditional family they are in fact grieving for the loss of the values of loyalty, stability, cooperation, love and respect, rather than the traditional image of the married couple with children.[37]

Anthony Giddens[38] suggests that there has been a fundamental shift in the nature of intimate relationships. He suggests that today the typical relationship is one:

> entered into for its own sake, for what can be derived by each person from a sustained association with another; and which is continued only in so far as it is thought by both parties to deliver enough satisfaction for each individual to stay within it.

He describes this as a 'pure relationship'. This is a highly individualised concept of relationships in which relationships are appreciated by people only in so far as they give them what they want.[39] This, if it is correct, can be regarded as a symptom of individualism.

TOPICAL ISSUE

The growth of individualism

Some sociologists believe family life is being affected by an increase in individualisation, with personal development being a key aspect of people's lives.[40] Elisabeth Beck-Gernsheim explains the individualisation thesis in this way:

> On the one hand, the traditional social relationships, bonds and belief systems that used to determine people's lives in the narrowest detail have been losing more and more of their meaning . . . New space and new options have thereby opened up for individuals. Now men and women can and should, may and must, decide for themselves how to shape their lives – within certain limits, at least.
>
> On the other hand, individualization means that people are linked into [social] institutions . . . these institutions produce various regulations . . . that are typically addressed to individuals rather than the family as a whole. And the crucial feature of these new regulations is that they enjoin the individual to lead a life of his or her own beyond any ties to the family or other groups – or sometimes even to shake off such ties and to act without referring to them.[41]

She argues that individualism has led to a 'detraditionalization' of family life with people abandoning the traditional obligations to one's family or spouse and taking on informal relationships which have looser obligations. People value being free to move away from relationships they no longer find fruitful and to move on to new relationships. In the past it might have been possible to predict, with a degree of certainty, a person's life course: they would grow up with their parents; find a job; get married; have children; and retire. There would be

---

[35] For a discussion of the difficulty in finding agreed 'family values' in today's society, see Carbone (2000).
[36] Diduck (2003).
[37] Diduck (2003: 23).
[38] Giddens (1992: 58).
[39] For arguments against such increased individualism, see Eekelaar and Maclean (2004).
[40] Beck (2002); Daly and Scheiwe (2010).
[41] Beck (2002: ix).

a strong expectation that this was followed. However, increasingly, people are breaking free from this standard model and wanting to choose their own version of the life course.[42] This, it is said, explains why we have fewer people wishing to be tied into marriage; higher rates of divorce; and less family care for older people. Individualisation also enables people to move on from the assumptions about the roles of husband, wife, father or mother and develop their own understandings of their relationships.

Not everyone accepts the individualisation argument.[43] To some, such as Neil Gross, the thesis fails to acknowledge that many people still do feel obligations to their family and spend much time caring for them.[44] This is shown in the way people still leave their money on death primarily to family members, rather than close friends.[45] Most notably parents feel strong obligations to care for their children and do not feel free to move on if the relationship is not working out.[46] People are profoundly committed to their children and those they are close to. Lewis has argued that although individualism is a significant influence in many people's lives, it should not be thought that this means that people do not value commitment. Rather, this commitment is negotiated and the result of 'give and take' within a relationship. This means that the value of the relationship is found by the couple themselves, rather than in the form it takes. In other words, people no longer feel there are social expectations on how relationships should develop (e.g. that they should lead to marriage).[47] Rather, people develop their own relationships in their own way. Although, as we shall see shortly, despite people's purported views, it seems the traditional models of male and female roles in relationships still have a strong hold, at least in heterosexual relationships.

As the statistics indicate, the nature of family life is certainly undergoing a change. Julia Brannen[48] suggests we are moving towards 'beanpole' families, with people having few children, fewer siblings and living longer. Geoff Dench and Jim Ogg have suggested that we are experiencing a dramatic shift from the traditional model of 'mother–father–child' family to one based on 'mother–grandmother–child', with fathers (and fathers' sides of the family) becoming irrelevant for many children. They argue:

> We can see a clear tendency at the moment for matrilineal ties (through the mother) to become the more active, while patrilineal, through the father, may often be very tenuous or even non-existent . . . [There is now] a growing frailty in ties between parents . . . an increasing marginalisation of men, and of ties traced through men, and a stronger focusing of families around women.[49]

Certainly, there has been a dramatic increase in the extent to which childcare is undertaken by grandparents, so that now four in five pre-school children are to some extent cared for by grandparents.[50] Also there has been an increasing number of children living apart from their fathers. As the Centre for Social Justice[51] notes:

> A teenager sitting their GCSEs is more likely to own a smart phone than live with their father.

[42] Herring (2021).
[43] Chambers (2014: 38).
[44] Gross (2005).
[45] Douglas (2015).
[46] Smart (2007a) and Eekelaar (2009).
[47] Lewis (2001b); Eekelaar and Maclean (2004).
[48] Brannen (2003).
[49] Dench and Ogg (2002: x–xiii).
[50] For further discussion see Chapter 12.
[51] Centre for Social Justice (2016).

Contrary to the views of Dench and Ogg, others have argued we are witnessing a significant change in family life because fathers are seeking to play an increasing role in the lives of their children.[52]

TOPICAL ISSUE

New men, old fathers?

The role of fathers today has become a major issue.[53] Traditionally the family could be seen as a central way in which sex roles were created and reinforced.[54] Women were to be bearers and carers of children and other dependants. Men were to be providers of money and food. The woman's role and place were in the home. The man's domain was in the 'real world' of commerce and business.[55]

This is now changing, although quite how is unclear.[56] There certainly appears to be an increased acceptance that the traditional model of the family is not how things should be. In the British Social Attitudes Survey 2017 only 8 per cent agreed that 'a man's job is to earn money; a woman's job is to look after the home and family'; 43 per cent of people had agreed with that statement in 1984.[57] In the 2019 version of the survey, when asked the best way to care for a pre-school child, of those who expressed a view 72.9 suggested it was best if the father worked full time and the mother did not work or had only a part-time job.

Most people accept that there has been a change in public perception about what is expected of a 'good father'. Even though attitudes have changed[58] it is unclear how much this has affected the practice of fathering.[59] Indeed, it seems many men *increase* their hours at work on becoming a father.[60] Looking at the new paternity leave of two weeks given to fathers following the birth of a child, a study found that only 50 per cent of fathers took the full two weeks of fully paid leave available.[61] Less than 20 per cent took up the right to claim more than that. Similarly, couples are now permitted to share their parental leave, but between 2 and 8 per cent have done so.[62] Perhaps surprisingly, the 2019 British Attitudes Survey found that only 34 per cent of respondents thought that couples should share their parental leave.[63] Busby and Weldon-Jones[64] argue that the Government sends mixed messages on sharing care in using rhetoric to promote shared care, but not doing enough to facilitate it:

> The UK's law and policy framework . . . seeks, on the one hand, to reorient men's engagement through notions of shared care but does little to incentivise or enable men and women to actually participate in this ideal whilst, on the other hand, providing reduced or restricted rights to fathers in comparison to those available to mothers.

---

[52] Collier (2010); Fatherhood Institute (2008).
[53] Collier (2005 and 2007); Jordan (2009).
[54] Collier and Sheldon (2008).
[55] Collier (2010).
[56] Featherstone (2009 and 2010a).
[57] National Centre for Social Research (2018).
[58] National Centre for Social Research (2013).
[59] Featherstone (2009).
[60] McGill (2014).
[61] Smeaton (2006). See further Weldon-Johns (2011).
[62] National Centre for Social Research (2019).
[63] National Centre for Social Research (2019).
[64] Busby and Weldon-Jones (2019).

The TUC[65] found in 2016 that on average just 64 per cent of mothers with children aged up to the age of four were in paid employment, compared to 93 per cent of fathers with pre-school age children. Further, only 50.5 per cent of mothers had full-time jobs, as compared to 93.2 per cent of fathers.[66] This is not solely down to 'ideological reasons' based on the 'natural role' of the mother. The income of men in employment typically exceeds that of women and so it makes 'economic sense' for the woman to reduce her employment hours.

Many couples seek to ensure that there is an equal sharing of household tasks and child-care. However, most fail, and in heterosexual couples women still end up performing the clear majority of household labour and childcare.[67] Even in cases where both partners work more than 48 hours a week, only 20 per cent of women said their partner had the main responsibility for the washing and the cooking.[68] Each month women in heterosexual relationships work two days more than men on housework and childcare.[69] Women spend 28 per cent more time on housework than men and 31 per cent more on childcare.

Another study in the role of the modern father found that, although the majority of fathers were spending more time with their children, their care was often mediated through the mother. In other words, the mother enabled the care, for example by supervising it or suggesting what the father might do with the child.[70] Further, there is good evidence of many fathers 'cherry picking' the fun parts of childcare (e.g. playing with the child), leaving the more mundane roles to mothers.[71] Perhaps this is indicated by a survey of children who were asked 'Who understands you best?': 53 per cent said 'mum'; 19 per cent said a best friend and only 13 per cent said 'dad'.[72] In any event, an optimist may hope that we are seeing the start of an acceptance that the raising of children should be undertaken equally by men and women. The image of fathers in the law has certainly changed, with Sheldon and Collier noting that:

> the image of unmarried fathers as unworthy, irresponsible and disengaged has been increasingly supplemented, if not entirely supplanted, by a very different depiction of unmarried fathers: as a discriminated group who are often deeply committed to their children yet find themselves denied access to them, being left unfairly dependent on the whims of sometimes hostile mothers.[73]

Not only has the image of what makes a 'good father' changed, so too has the notion of what makes a 'good mother'.[74] There has been an increased responsibility placed on parents if their children behave badly[75] and it has been mothers in particular who have been penalised for the misbehaviour of their children.[76] Certainly the acceptability, and even necessity, of 'working mothers'[77] has increased.[78] During the last few years we have seen significant steps being taken by the Government to facilitate 'working motherhood': improvements in the provision of childcare (although it is still inadequate in many areas); an increase in provision

[65] Trades Union Congress (2015).
[66] National Centre for Social Research (2019).
[67] Van Hooff (2013); Herring (2013: ch. 4).
[68] Family and Parenting Institute (2009).
[69] Oxfam (2017).
[70] Lewis and Welsh (2006); Welsh et al. (2004).
[71] Sullivan (2013); Featherstone (2009: 34).
[72] ICM (2004).
[73] Collier and Sheldon (2008: ch. 6).
[74] For a discussion of the idealisation of mothers, see Cain (2011); Herring (2008a).
[75] Kaganas (2010a).
[76] Featherstone (2010a). See Hale (2011b) for an excellent discussion of responsibilities and families.
[77] The idea that mothers who are not in paid employment are not working is, of course, false.
[78] See the discussion in Churchill (2008).

for maternity leave;[79] much effort to encourage lone parents to take up employment; and the development by companies of 'family friendly policies' for their staff.[80] Despite this, there are enormous pressures on mothers seeking to combine their paid and caring work.[81] Especially so, now that we live in the era of the 'domestic goddess'.

Sylvia Hewlett[82] argues there is a battle for motherhood. Mothers are finding the tension between a desire to maintain a career and to have children complex. She notes that 59 per cent of Britain's top female executives do not have children. Among professional women in the US 42 per cent do not have children. One study estimated that in the UK a third of graduate women will not have children.[83] The 'work–life balance' is seen as an enormous tension for many women especially.[84] Women balancing work and care face the danger of only just coping to do both. They manage just to keep their jobs, while struggling to put in the expected hours and being overlooked for promotion due to their other commitments, while also feeling that the care provided to their children is only just good enough.[85] These issues are made all the harder for the 'sandwich generation', a term used to refer to those who are caring for their children and parents at the same time.[86]

3 Should family life be encouraged?

Learning objective 2

Discuss the arguments for and against family life and its alternatives

Most people regard families as beneficial. Indeed, the Universal Declaration of Human Rights proclaims that the family is 'the natural and fundamental group unit of society'. However, there are those who oppose families. The benefits and disadvantages of family life will now be briefly summarised.

DEBATE

Is family life good?

Arguments in favour of family life

1. Emotional security. Family members can provide crucial emotional support and care for each other. Parents can furnish the love and security that children need as they are growing up. Several studies have sought to ascertain whether there are links between a happy family life and well-being. It is difficult to establish this. It does seem that being in a stable relationship is linked to good health. Men in particular do less well on well-being standards if they are single, as compared with if they are in a relationship.[87]

---

[79] See Work and Families Act 2006. However, there is still ample evidence of discrimination against workers who become pregnant: Adams, McAndrew and Winterbotham (2005).
[80] Lewis (2009); James (2009).
[81] Gatrell (2005).
[82] Hewlett (2003).
[83] Leapman (2007).
[84] James and Busby (2011).
[85] Golynker, O. (2015).
[86] Grundy and Henretta (2006).
[87] Ploubidis et al. (2015).

2. The advantages of family life are not limited to the benefits received by the members themselves. Families benefit the state. The Government's 'family test' is an acknowledgement of the importance to the state of family life. Families are seen as promoting social cohesion and having a stake in education and public services.

3. The family can also be supported as an institution which protects people from powerful organisations within the state.[88] It is harder for the state to misuse its powers against groups of people living together than to oppress individuals living alone.

4. While not, perhaps, the most ringing endorsement of families, David Archard in his analysis concludes: 'In favour of the family is the simple and undeniable fact that it is impossibly hard to think of any other social institution that could do as good a job of protecting children from their natural vulnerability and dependence on adults.'[89]

Arguments against families

1. A major concern over families is the level of abuse that takes place against the weakest members. Levels of domestic violence and familial child abuse are strikingly high.[90] Certainly, behind the screen of 'respectable family life' appalling abuse of children and women has occurred. Whether the amount of interpersonal violence would decrease if there were no families may be open to doubt.

2. There is a major concern that families are a means of oppression of women. Delphy and Leonard argue:

   > We see men and women as economic classes with one category/class subordinating the other and exploiting its work. Within the family system specifically, we see men exploiting women's practical, emotional, sexual and reproductive labour. For us 'men' and 'women' are not two naturally given groups, which at some point in history fell into a hierarchical relationship. Rather the reason the two groups are distinguished socially is because one dominates the other in order to use its labour.[91]

   The argument is not necessarily that every family involves oppression, but that the structure of family life too readily enables oppression to occur.

3. Families can reinforce social inequality. Daniel Engster[92] writes:

   > The family is widely recognised as one of the most important obstacles to fair equality of opportunity. Because different parents have different capacities and resources for raising children, children tend to have widely different opportunities to pursue their interests and achieve goods as adults. Children raised by more educated, wealthy, loving, emotionally stable, and supportive parents typically enjoy more opportunities to develop their capabilities during childhood and obtain socially valuable goods as adults (including meaningful and high-paying jobs, nice homes in safe neighbourhoods, and stable relationships) than children raised by less advantaged or supportive parents.

   He goes on to accept that it is not inevitable that families create these inequalities, but without state intervention families can perpetuate social advantage and disadvantage.

---

[88] Mount (1982: 1).
[89] Archard (2010: 100).
[90] See Chapter 7.
[91] Delphy and Leonard (1992: 258).
[92] Engster (2018).

4. Barrett and MacIntosh[93] argue that families encourage the values of selfishness, exclusiveness and the pursuit of private interest, which undermine those of altruism, community and the pursuit of the public good. They insist: 'The world around the family is not a pre-existing harsh climate against which the family offers protection and warmth. It is as if the family has drawn comfort and security into itself and left the outside world bereft. As a bastion against a bleak society it has made that society bleak.'[94] If, rather than spending time on DIY and gardening, family members spent time on community projects, would society be a better place?

5. The breakdown of family life carries major social costs. In 2020 it was estimated that the collapse of family relationships cost £51 billion.[95] However, if there were no families there would be added expense for the state of having to care for those currently cared for by families.

Questions

1. *What, if anything, is good about family life? Are those goods found in all families?*

2. *Imagine we had a completely different society. What forms and structures of intimate relationships could be possible? Would they be better or worse than we currently have?*

Further reading

Read **Herring** (2010c) and **Fineman** (2004) for a discussion of whether family law should be arranged around caring relationships rather than sexual ones.

A Proposing new visions for families

If the law and society were to attempt to promote a radically different form of family life, what might that be?

1. Martha Fineman has suggested that we should view the carer–dependant[96] relationship as the core element of a family.[97] She is therefore seeking to move away from seeing the sexual relationship between a man and a woman as the core element of family life and instead is focusing on dependent relationships.[98] It is these caring relationships which are of real value to society, certainly more so than a couple having just a sexual relationship. Adopting such an approach I have argued in favour of a 'sexless family law':[99]

> The way ahead is to focus on care, rather than sex. Caring relationships are the ones that need promoting through family law, because they are the relationships that are key to the well-being of society. Caring relationships are the ones that can create vulnerability to abuse and should be the focus of protection. It is in caring relationships that the law is [needed] to remedy the disadvantages that flow from [them] . . . In short, family law needs to be less sexy and more careful.[100]

---

[93] Barrett and MacIntosh (1991).
[94] Barrett and MacIntosh (1991: 80).
[95] Relationships Foundation (2020).
[96] Although see Herring (2007a) for an argument that the distinction between carer and cared for is not straightforward.
[97] Fineman (2004 and 2011).
[98] See also Deech (2010a).
[99] Herring (2010c: 16).
[100] Herring (2014a: 40).

This kind of approach would include relationships which are not currently covered by family law, such as a daughter caring for her elderly father. It might also mean that some relationships currently within family law, a married couple with no children for example, would fall outside it.[101] It would also change the nature of family law; indeed, maybe it would no longer be family law. Sara Cantillon and Kathleen Lynch[102] give an indication of the kind of law that would be required:

> [I]t would include at a minimum, maternity, paternity, and parental leave that recognizes the nurturing needs of children and the emotional needs of parents; it would involve the provision of accessible, affordable public childcare and elder/vulnerable adult-care supports for carers. It would also involve changing the 24/7 work culture that has become synonymous with many career-led white collar jobs; shortening the working day so everyone has quality time to give love and to receive love; setting wages at levels that are sustainable for a dignified, economically secure life; taxing excessive wealth globally; and limiting income differentials between top and bottom earners. Mobilizing the revolutionary potential of love would also mean making education about love, care, and solidarity central to all forms of education.

Such approaches, however, face the difficulty in defining what a 'caring relationship' is. Is a person who helps out an elderly neighbour now and then to become subject to family rights and responsibilities?[103] And if the law starts to regulate caring relationships, will that rob them of their informal intimate nature?

2. Barrett and MacIntosh argue that society should move away from small units towards collectivism. They would like to see a range of favoured patterns of family life, involving larger groups of people living together in a variety of relationship forms.[104] This could involve acknowledging that many people have a range of friends, relatives and neighbours to whom they feel, in different ways, attached. One consequence of this could be to acknowledge we should not assume that family members have to live together. Sociologists have recognised 'living apart together relationships', where a couple have a monogamous sexual relationship, but live in separate places.[105] Levin suggests three conditions to be regarded as a couple who are 'living apart together' (LAT): that the couple agree they are a couple; others see them as such; and they live in separate houses.[106] Online communication makes such relationships easier to maintain. A device that allows couples who are separated by distance to have long-distance sex by drawing in light on each other's bodies may be of assistance too![107] It has been estimated that around 10 per cent of the population are LAT.[108] It should not be assumed that LATs are less dedicated to each other than cohabiting partners. Duncan et al.[109] found a significant proportion of LAT partners provided substantial levels of care and support to each other.

3. Weeks et al., looking at the meaning of 'family' within the LGBTQI+ community, talk of 'families of choice'. Family is seen as 'an affinity circle which may or may not involve children which has cultural and symbolic meaning for the subjects that participate or feel a sense of belonging in and through it'.[110] Family in this definition are those people to whom a person feels particularly close, rather than those with whom there is a blood tie.[111]

---

[101] For further discussion see Herring (2014d); Brake (2012); Scott and Scott (2014).
[102] Cantillon and Lynch (2017).
[103] For a powerful critique of care-based approaches see Barker (2014).
[104] Barrett and MacIntosh (1991: 134).
[105] Duncan et al. (2012); Duncan and Phillips (2010); Haskey and Lewis (2006).
[106] Levin (2004: 227).
[107] BBC News Online (2009c).
[108] Duncan and Phillips (2010).
[109] Duncan et al. (2012).
[110] Weeks, Donovan and Heaphy (2001: 86).
[111] See also Ellickson (2010) who focuses on the notion of a household.

4 Approaches to family law

Learning objective 3

Explain and evaluate how different theories seek to define 'family law'

A What is family law?

There is no accepted definition of family law. Family law is usually seen as the law governing the relationships between children and parents, and between adults in close emotional relationships.

Many areas of law can have an impact on family life: from taxation to immigration law; from insurance to social security. Therefore, any text that attempts to state all the laws which might affect family life would be enormous, and inevitably texts have to be selective in what material is presented. Conventions have built up over the kinds of topics usually covered, but these are in many ways arbitrary decisions. For example, the laws on social security benefits and taxation can have a powerful effect on family life, but they are usually avoided in family law courses. This text has a section on family issues surrounding older people, but this topic is not included in many family law courses.

B How to examine family law

There has been much debate over how to assess family law. What makes good family law? How do we know if the law is working well? This section will now consider some of the approaches that are taken to answer these questions, although no one approach is necessarily the correct one and perhaps it is best to be willing to look at the law from a number of these perspectives.

(i) A functionalist approach

This approach regards family law as having a series of goals to be fulfilled. We can then assess family law by judging how well it succeeds in reaching those goals.[112] For example, if we decide that the aim of a particular law has the purpose of increasing the number of couples who marry, then we can look at the rate of marriages to see if the law has succeeded in its aim. So, what might be the objectives of family law?

Eekelaar[113] has suggested that, broadly speaking, family law seeks to pursue three goals:

1. Protective – to guard members of a family from physical, emotional or economic harm.

2. Adjustive – to help families which have broken down to adjust to new lives apart.

3. Supportive – to encourage and support family life.

More recently he has presented another way of thinking about the purpose of family law:

> It might be possible to see its purpose as to uphold the view of the 'common good' taken by those in power. But Finnis adds a crucial qualification: that a fundamental component of the common good is 'respect for the equal right of all to respectful consideration'.[114]

It is interesting to contrast Eekelaar's two formulations. The second seems to emphasise family law as a vehicle for promoting the public good, rather than for the benefit of the particular parties. Also, the second seems to recognise the power dynamics in family law as the common good is that defined 'by those in power'.

---

[112] Millbank (2008b).
[113] Eekelaar (1984: 24–6); Eekelaar (1987b). Developed in George (2012b: ch. 1).
[114] Eekelaar (2018).

It might be thought that functionalism is such a straightforward approach that it would be uncontroversial. However, there are difficulties with the functionalist approach:

1. One difficulty is that a law rarely has a single clearly identified goal. More often it is attempting a compromise between competing claims. A 1996 Act on divorce claims that it is seeking both to uphold marriage and to make it possible to divorce with as little bitterness or expense as possible.[115] These are contradictory aims. The Act may or may not strike an appropriate balance between them, but we cannot judge the success of the Act by deciding whether or not it reaches a particular goal, because it has several.

2. Another problem with the functionalist approach is that the law is only one of the influences on the way that people act in their family life. So, an Act designed to reduce the divorce rate may have little effect if other social influences cause an increase in the divorce rate. The fact that the divorce rate has not fallen may not be the fault of the Act. The rise might be the result of a complex interaction between the law and all sorts of other influences on family life.

3. With the functionalist approach there is a danger of not questioning whether the aims of the law are the correct ones to pursue. So, just asking whether an Act designed to reduce the divorce rate has actually helped reduce divorce sidesteps asking whether we want to reduce the divorce rate. It is even a little more complex than this because sometimes the law appears to create the very problem it is seeking to fix. For example, it is only because we have legal marriage that we have 'a problem' with divorce.

4. A further difficulty with functionalism is that it overlooks what the law does not try to do. The fact that the law does not regulate a particular area can be as significant as a decision of the law to regulate.

These are powerful criticisms of the functionalist perspective, but do not render it invalid. The approach is so tied to common sense that it cannot be denied as a useful method. However, as the criticisms demonstrate, it does have serious limitations.

(ii) Feminist perspectives

Feminist contributions to family law have been invaluable.[116] At the heart of feminist approaches is the consideration of how the law impacts on both men and women; in particular, how the law is and has been used to enable men to exercise power over women.[117] Gone are the days when a judge could say what a family law judge said as recently as 1911:

> Some people think that . . . you must treat men and women on the same footing. But this Court has not taken, and, I hope, never will take, that view. I trust that, in dealing with these cases, it will ever be remembered that the woman is the weaker vessel: that her habits of thought and feminine weaknesses are different from those of the man.[118]

Nevertheless, feminist commentators seek to highlight some of the less obvious ways the law disadvantages women. Linda McKie and Samantha Callan explain:

> Feminist explanations of families and family life are generally based on the notion of patriarchy, namely, that women are undervalued, denied aspects of their rights and are thus oppressed.

---

[115] Family Law Act 1996, s. 1.
[116] For excellent discussions of family law from feminist perspectives, see Diduck and O'Donovan (2007); Diduck (2003); Fineman (2004: ch. 6); Munro (2007) and Herring (2013a).
[117] Rhode (2014).
[118] *Pretty v Pretty* [1911] P 83.

Further, it is argued that the power resources of societies favour men, and women are exploited in numerous ways, including, the division of domestic labour, access to higher paid jobs and ensuring equal pay for work of equal value. Women are persecuted for being women through various forms of violence and violation, including rape, domestic abuse, sexualized stereotypes in advertising and media, so called 'honour' killings, female circumcision and female infanticide. With the family, gendered oppressive power dynamics are sustained, learnt and evolved.[119]

It is important to appreciate the richness of the feminist perspectives:

1. At a basic level, feminist writers point to ways in which the law directly discriminates against women. For example, at one point in history a husband could divorce his wife on the ground of adultery, but a wife could only divorce her husband on the adultery ground if there was also some aggravating feature, for example that the adultery was incestuous. Nowadays there are relatively few provisions that discriminate in such an overt way.[120] Munby LJ in *Re G (Education: Religious Upbringing)*[121] insisted there was now equality before the law:

   [M]en and women, husbands and wives, fathers and mothers . . . come before the family courts . . . on an exactly equal footing. The voice of the father carries no more weight because he is the father, nor does the mother's because she is the mother.

2. Feminist writers also highlight aspects of family law which are indirectly discriminatory: that is, laws which on face value do not appear to discriminate against women, but in effect work against women's interests. An example is the rule that financial contributions to a household are far more likely to give rise to a share of ownership in the house than non-financial ones through housework.[122] This indirectly discriminates against women because it is far more likely that women provide only non-financial contributions to a household than men. A central theme of much feminist writing on families is the way that caring has been devalued and ignored by family law and law more generally.[123]

3. Feminists have also sought to challenge the norms that form the foundation of the law. Terms which the law might regard as having a given meaning, such as 'family', 'marriage', 'work' and 'mother', have been shown in fact to be 'constructs', images which the law has wished to present as uncontroversial, but which are in fact value-laden.[124] Feminists argue that the law has a construct of what is a 'good mother' and penalises those who are not regarded as 'proper mothers', such as lone parents.[125] Rather less work has been done on the way the law constructs men and what makes a good father.[126]

4. Some feminist perspectives have also challenged what are sometimes called 'male' forms of reasoning. These feminists have categorised reasoning which focuses on individual rights as 'male' and as undermining the values that women prize, such as relationship and inter-dependency.[127] Gilligan has written of a distinction between the ethic of care (which rests on responsibilities, relationships and flexible solutions rather than on fixed long-term solutions)

---

[119] McKie and Callan (2012: 60).
[120] See *Runkee v UK* [2007] 2 FCR 178 where a challenge to the payment to widows but not widowers failed. Now the benefits for widows and widowers are the same.
[121] [2012] EWCA Civ 1233, para 24.
[122] See Chapter 5.
[123] Herring (2013a).
[124] See e.g. Herring (2012h) on the law and use of surnames.
[125] See e.g. Herring (2008a).
[126] But see Collier (2000; 2003; 2008).
[127] Gilligan (1982).

and the ethic of justice (which focuses on abstract principles from an impartial stance and stresses the consistency and predictability of results).[128] This has led to much dispute over whether rights or ethic of care are a more appropriate way to develop feminist thought.[129]

An approach based on an ethic of care would promote laws which recognised the value and importance of caring relationships. Rather than emphasising rights which promote independence, such as autonomy and privacy, it would prioritise the responsibilities that tie us together and the legal response that promotes care. A central part of that would be ensuring there was effective protection from abuse within relationships.[130] As Ferguson and Brake[131] have identified, there is a potential tension within writings on the ethic of care. They ask:

> If 'intimacy' or 'caring' are taken as the focus of family law, is this because care and intimacy are values which the law should protect and promote—or because care and intimacy create vulnerabilities against which the law should protect?

It may be the correct answer is both. Or it may be to challenge the view that vulnerability is a bad thing from which we need protection. Daniel Bedford, for example, has written of the benefits of vulnerabilities.[132]

5. Feminists have also been concerned with how the law operates in practice and not just with what the law says.[133] For example, although the law might try to pretend that both parents have equal parental rights and responsibilities,[134] in real life it is mothers who carry out the vast majority of the tasks of parenthood.[135] So, it is argued, the legal picture of shared parental roles does not match the reality.[136]

There are, of course, divisions among feminist commentators and there are dangers in referring to 'the feminist response' to a question. Most notably for family law there is a disagreement between those who espouse feminism of difference and those who endorse feminism of equality. Feminism of equality (sometimes called liberal feminism) argues that women and men should be treated identically. Okin,[137] for example, would like to see a world where gender matters as little as eye colour.[138] Feminism of difference argues that the law should accept that men and women are different, but should ensure that no disadvantages follow from the differences. The issue of childcare is revealing.[139] Feminists of equality might argue that we should seek to encourage men and women to have an equal role in child rearing so that they also have an equal role in the workforce. Feminists of difference would contend that we need to ensure that child rearing is valued within society and recompensed financially.[140] Society needs to esteem the nurturing work traditionally carried out by women, rather than forcing women to have to adopt traditionally male roles if they are to receive financial reward.

[128] For further elaboration on the ethics of care, see Held (2006) and Herring (2007a, 2013a, 2017).
[129] Wallbank, Choudhry and Herring (2009).
[130] See further Herring (2013a and 2014d).
[131] Ferguson and Brake (2018).
[132] Bedford (2017) and Bedford and Herring (2019).
[133] Wallbank (2009).
[134] This is only true if both have parental responsibility. (See Chapter 8.)
[135] Aassve, Fuochi and Mencarini (2014).
[136] Wallbank (2009). See Mitchell (2019) on how parental leave could more effectively be used.
[137] Okin (1992: 171).
[138] For an argument for gender neutrality in family law from a perspective which is not explicitly feminist, see Bainham (2000c).
[139] See Boyd (2008) for an excellent discussion of the uses of equality made by fathers' groups and feminists.
[140] Laufer-Ukeles (2008).

The root problem with these approaches is that they can both work against some women. Feminism of equality might work to the disadvantage of the woman who does not want to enter the world of employment but wants to work at home childcaring and homemaking. Indeed, arguably, middle-class women have only felt able to go out to work because they have been able to employ other women to provide housework and childcare services. The difficulty with feminism of difference is that, by stressing differences, it can be seen as exacerbating and reinforcing the traditional roles that men and women play and so can limit the options for women. Much work is therefore being done to produce a third model which values the caring and nurturing work traditionally carried out by women, but at the same time protects the position of women in the workforce.[141] Dunn[142] argues there is a need for:

> recognising and celebrating the value of women's traditional areas of work and influence rather than accepting a masculine and capitalist hierarchy of value which can lead to women passing on their responsibilities to less powerful women. In conjunction with this would be the view that this valuable work is something that male peers can and should do, the aim being to facilitate and insist upon change in men's lives – enabling them to become more like women to the same degree that women have become more like men.

But until men are more willing to embrace this change and value the caring work women do, women are left to carry on their caring work unvalued. As should be clear, the law can only supply part of the impetus for equality for women. Political, cultural and psychological changes are necessary if there is ever to be an end to disadvantages for women.[143]

There are also fierce debates over the category of 'women' and trans rights. The debate was sparked by the suggestion that one should be able to self-declare one's gender for legal purposes.[144] This has led some to express concerns. From a practical point of view that men could claim to be trans and access women's changing areas and prisons, for example, and thereby abuse women. And from a theoretical angle there were concerns that if being a woman is simply a matter of self-identification then the category of women loses its meaning. Those with these concerns often seek to emphasise the distinction between sex, which is a biological given and cannot be changed, and gender, the male or female (or other) role adopted by a person in society. So, sex, it is said, is a fixed fact, while gender reflects the wishes of a person and the norms of a society. On the other side there are those who argue that it is important to stand up for trans rights. Someone who identifies as a woman should be accepted as such, as that is core to their identity. The practical concerns can be easily overcome with appropriate measures (e.g. offering individual closed stalls in changing areas). Further, the practical issues facing trans women excluded from women's spaces or being required to prove they have undergone surgery would be extremely harsh. On the theoretical side it is denied that sex is a biological given, but rather society influences which biological characteristics are accepted as markers of biological sex. So, both sex and gender are a construction of society.[145] Being a woman is about an identity, not having particular body parts.

Of course, there are those who fiercely reject the feminist agenda, arguing nowadays it is men, rather than women, who are disadvantaged. Peter Lloyd argues:

> Rubbishing the male of the species and everything he stands for is a disturbing – and growing – 21st century phenomenon. It is the fashionable fascism of millions of women – and many, many

---

[141] For an excellent discussion of equality and discrimination generally, see Fredman (2002).
[142] Dunn (1999: 94).
[143] Lewis and Campbell (2007).
[144] This raises issues for those classified as female but wishing to identify as male, but the debate has primary centered on the category of women.
[145] See Sharpe (2020) for an excellent discussion

men, too. Instead of feeling proud of our achievements, we men are forced to spend our time apologising for them. When people chide us for not being able to multi-task or use a washing machine we join in the mocking laughter – even though we invented the damned thing in the first place.[146]

Such a view is rarely articulated in the academic literature.

(iii) The public/private divide

Traditionally it has been thought appropriate to divide life into public and private arenas. Family law has been seen as the protector of private life. Notably, the European Convention on Human Rights upholds 'a right to respect for private and family life'.[147] The significance of this distinction between public and private life is twofold. First, the traditional liberal position is that there are some areas of our lives that are so intimate that it is inappropriate for the state to intervene.[148] It is argued that it is quite proper for the law to regulate aspects of public life, such as contracts, commercial dealings and governments, but that other areas of life are so private that they are not the state's business. Goldstein *et al.* argue that protection of family privacy is essential to promote the welfare of the child because state intrusion undermines the child's trust in their parents.[149]

Not only, it is contended, should the state not intervene in private areas, it cannot. Imagine a law that makes adultery illegal. This might be opposed on the basis that it infringes people's privacy. It might also be argued that it would be unfeasible. The police cannot keep an eye on the nation's bedrooms and hotels[150] to monitor whether adultery is taking place!

Secondly, it is maintained that where it does intervene in the public arena, the law seeks to promote different kinds of values than it does on the rare occasions when it deals with private law issues. In the public law sector people are presumed to be self-sufficient and able to look after themselves, whereas in the private arena the law stresses mutual cooperation and dependency.[151]

The distinction between private areas of life (into which the law should not intervene) and public areas of life (where the law may intervene) is deeply embedded in many people's thinking and much liberal political philosophy. The differentiation is particularly important in family life, although it is far from straightforward. The following are some of the difficulties with the distinction:

1. Is there really a difference between intervention and non-intervention? Imagine a family where the husband regularly abuses his wife. The law might take the view that this is a private matter and that it should not intervene. But, with this approach, what is the law doing? It could be argued that by choosing not to intrude, the law has permitted the existing power structure to be reinforced. In other words, the husband's power can be exercised by him only because of the state's decision not to step in. So, a decision not to intervene should not be seen in a neutral light, but as a decision to accept the status quo.[152] This makes the distinction between intervention and non-intervention more complex than at first appears.

---

[146] Lloyd (2014).

[147] *Nazarenko v Russia* (App. No. 39438/13).

[148] See Herring (2009b and 2014f) for a discussion of the role played by autonomy.

[149] Goldstein *et al.* (1996: 90).

[150] To make a rather conservative selection of venues.

[151] A distinction is sometimes drawn between *Gemeinshaft*: the values of love, duty and common purpose (private values); and *Geschellshaft*: the values of individualism, competition and formality (public values).

[152] This may be because the law is happy with the status quo or because the law is concerned that legal intervention would cause even more harm. See further Eekelaar (2000a).

2. Can we distinguish the public and the private? Take the example of child abuse. Although this takes place within the home, the consequences of it can affect all of society. The state will have the cost of providing alternative care for the child and of dealing with the social harms that flow from child abuse. This indicates that although the conduct takes place in private it has public consequences. Who changes the nappies and boils the pasta is, in fact, a matter of huge public importance because it can impact on equality between men and women.[153]

3. Why exactly might we want to protect the private? The argument for respecting private life is that it enables people to make decisions about how to live their lives free from state intervention. The traditional liberal approach is that each person should be able to develop his or her own beliefs and personality, free from state intervention unless there is a very good reason for the state to intrude.[154] However, this argument does not necessarily support a neutral stance from the state. A woman being regularly assaulted by her partner may not be able to develop her own beliefs and personality without the intervention of the law.

4. What is private and public may be a matter of class. The image of the home and family as a private place is an ideal that may be true for some middle-class couples, but for those reliant on social housing and benefits the home can be seen as replete with social intrusion. In fact, the state may police families in a less obvious way than direct legal intervention: health visitors,[155] teachers, neighbourhood watch schemes and social workers could all be thought a form of policing of families outside formal legal regulation. The argument here is that to regard legal intervention in family life as the only form of state intervention is unduly narrow.

(iv) Autopoietic theory

Autopoietic theory has been developed from the ideas of Gunther Teubner. Its main proponent in the family law arena is Michael King.[156] He argues that society is made up of systems of discourse, and that law is but one system of communication within society.[157] One significance of the theory is that it recognises that there are difficulties in one system of communication working with another. In other words, the law has a certain way of looking at the world and interacting with it. The law classifies people and disputes in particular ways ('a mother'; 'a father'; 'a contact dispute'; 'a child abuse case'), applies the legal rules to it, and produces the appropriate legal response. This process may transform the problem, as the parties understood it, into a quite different form of dispute and then produce an answer inappropriate to the parties' actual needs. Further, when other systems of communication attempt to interact with the legal system, unless they are able to put their arguments into the form of legal communication, the legal system cannot deal with them. For example, when social workers or psychologists are called upon by the courts to advise on what is in the best interests of the child, their evidence will be transformed into a legal communication. This may not be easy for lawyers. The law tends to concentrate on sharp conclusions: guilty or not guilty; abuse or no abuse. Social workers, by contrast, concentrate on ongoing relationships and working in flexible methods over time, rather than setting down in a written order what should happen to children for the future.

[153] Maclean (2007: 77).
[154] Herring (2009b).
[155] Health visitors regularly visit a mother in her house following the birth of a child.
[156] King (2000). See Newnham (2015) for a recent excellent use of the approach. For a more critical discussion see Eekelaar (1995).
[157] E.g. King (2000).

5 Current issues in family law

Learning objective 4

Summarise the broad issues
which underpin family law

Some of the general issues that affect family law will now be considered.

A How the state interacts with families

Fox Harding has suggested seven ways in which the state could interact with families.[158] Although only sketched here at a superficial level, they demonstrate the variety of attitudes the state could have towards families.

1. *An authoritarian model.* Under this approach the state would set out to enforce preferred family behaviour and prohibit other conduct. The law could rely on both criminal sanctions and informal means of social exclusion and stigmatisation. This approach would severely limit personal freedom.

2. *The enforcement of responsibilities in specific areas.* This model would choose the most important family obligations which the state would then seek to enforce. It is similar to the authoritarian model, but recognises that some family obligations are unenforceable.

3. *The manipulation of incentives.* Here the aim is to encourage certain forms of family behaviour through use of rewards (for example, tax advantages), rather than discourage undesirable behaviour through punishment.[159]

4. *Working within constraining assumptions.* Here the state does not overtly advocate particular family forms, but bases social resources on presumptions of certain styles of family life. For example, especially in the past, benefit and tax laws were based on the presumption that the wife was financially dependent on her husband.

5. *Substituting for and supporting families.* In this model the state's role is limited to supporting or substituting for families if they fail. In other words, the state does not seek to influence the running of the family until the family breaks down, but if it does then the state will intervene.

6. *Responding to needs and demands.* Here the law intervenes only when requested to do so by family members. Apart from responding to such requests, the state does not intrude in family life.

7. *Laissez-faire model.* Under this approach the state would seek to exercise minimal control of family life, which would be regarded as a private matter, unsuitable for legal intervention.

B Privatisation of family law

There is much debate over whether there is a lessening of the legal regulation of family life. Some believe that we are witnessing the privatisation of family life, with the law regulating it less and less.[160] For example, the Government has attempted to encourage couples who are divorcing to use mediation to resolve financial disputes and disagreements about what

---

[158] Fox Harding (1996).
[159] See further Roberts (2001).
[160] Herring (2009b). Fink and Carbone (2003) foresee a form of family law based on contracts agreed by the parties.

should happen to the children after divorce, rather than using lawyers and court procedures (see Chapter 2). Strikingly, the current Government has said:

> The court's role should be focused on protecting the vulnerable from abuse, victimisation and exploitation and should avoid intervening in family life except where there is clear benefit to children or vulnerable adults in doing so.[161]

On the other hand, there are other areas of family law where the law appears more interventionist. There has, for example, been an increased use of the criminal law against parents whose children misbehave.[162] So, the picture is not a straightforward one of intervention or deregulation. Dewar has argued that, rather than experiencing deregulation, the law is focusing its resources on cases where there is a need for legal intervention.[163] An example to illustrate his argument concerns parental arrangements for children on divorce. Previously, in divorce cases involving children there would be a hearing where a judge would meet the parties and consider the arrangements for the children. However, now there is no such hearing and, unless either party applies for a court order, the judge will not consider the arrangements for the children in depth. This could be seen as privatisation of family law, but it could also be seen as focusing judicial time on those cases which need it – those where the parents cannot agree what should happen to the child.

Certainly, the role played by families is an important political issue. This is well captured by Martha Fineman's comment on a particular political approach to families:

> Right-wing politicians also have a view of the family as isolated, which produces their demand that it be self-contained and self-sufficient – wholly independent from state and market (and not requiring public resources). Domestic arrangements that fail to live up to these conservative expectations are deemed failures and relegated to a 'public' and punitive status, rather than a private and protected order to be shielded from regulation and intervention.[164]

As she notes, the roles families play and are expected to play reflect important political assumptions and ideals.

The law does seem more ready to intervene in family life once the family has broken up. For example, while the family is together there is no direct attempt to ensure that a child is receiving a reasonable level of financial support from his or her parents. However, once the couple separate, the child support legislation and the Matrimonial Causes Act 1973 come into operation to ensure that a wage-earning parent financially supports the child at a suitable level. The law appears to assume that where a family lives together any difficulties can be resolved by the parties themselves within the ongoing relationship; the law is only needed when the parents separate.[165] Some academics have complained that this non-interventionist stance has undermined family life. Clare Huntington has argued that family law responds to the breakdown of a family but does nothing to foster strong relationships.[166] She argues for a more active state involvement which is designed to support and enable families to flourish.

It is perhaps ironic that at the same time as many call for family law to become increasingly privatised, there has been increasing pressure on the Government to open up the family courts.[167] Traditionally, family cases, especially those involving children, have been held in

---

[161] Norgrave (2012: annex A).
[162] See Keating (2008).
[163] Dewar (1992: 6–7).
[164] Fineman (2018).
[165] Eekelaar and Maclean (1997: 2).
[166] Huntington (2014).
[167] E.g. Munby J (2005).

private, and publication is not permitted without the express permission of the judge. This has enabled some to say that the family law courts are secretive and are able to pass judgments free of public scrutiny and accountability. Behind closed doors judges and social workers conspired to remove children from their parents and make judgments which were anti-fathers, it was alleged. Cynics might argue that the press were frustrated in not being able to report sordid tales of child abuse and family breakdown which would sell newspapers. Increasing pressure led to a change in the law.[168] The Family Proceedings (Amendment) (No. 2) Rules[169] and the President of the Family Division have issued guidance[170] on publication of judgment. These permit accredited members of the press to attend most proceedings in family courts. This includes ancillary relief proceedings as well as disputes over children.[171] The press can be excluded to protect the privacy of the parties, especially children,[172] or where their presence will impact on the evidence given to the court.[173] Those seeking to exclude the press must offer very strong justifications for doing so.[174] Court judgments can be anonymised to ensure that the identity of the child cannot be discovered.[175] The courts will attach weight to the fact that excluding the press can stoke conspiracy theories and confidence in the family courts will be upheld if they are seen to be open to public scrutiny.[176] In *Fields v Fields*[177] Holman J explained:

> There is considerable current, legitimate public interest in the way the family courts daily operate, and that cannot be shut out simply on an argument that the affairs of the parties are private or personal. Precisely because I am a public court and not a private arbitrator, I must be subject to public scrutiny and gaze. But the exposure is very avoidable by the parties themselves.

The last sentence suggests that parties cannot object to their family lives being made public because they can avoid a court hearing through mediation or arbitration. Even if convincing, that argument does not deal with any breach of privacy which relates to children. It is clearly not their fault that the matter is before the court. Certainly, there is some concern that the current law fails to protect children's privacy.[178]

C Autonomy

Linked to the public–private debate is the role attached to autonomy. Autonomy has become a major theme in family law in recent years.[179] In basic terms, autonomy is the principle that people should be able to make their own decisions about how to live their lives, as long as in doing so they do not harm others. Joseph Raz defines it in this way:

> The ruling idea behind the ideal of personal autonomy is that people should make their own lives. The autonomous person is a (part) author of his own life. The ideal of personal autonomy

---

[168] Crawford and Pierce (2010) and George and Roberts (2009) provide useful discussion of the issues.

[169] SI 2009/857.

[170] McFarlane (2020).

[171] Although it seems less likely that cases involving financial issues are made public: *Cooper-Hohn v Hohn* [2014] EWHC 2314 (Fam); *Appleton and Gallagher v Newsgroup Newspapers Ltd and The Press Association* [2015] EWHC 2689 (Fam).

[172] *Re C (Publication of Judgment)* [2015] EWCA Civ 500.

[173] *Spencer v Spencer* [2009] EWHC 1529 (Fam).

[174] *A v BBC* [2014] UKSC 25.

[175] Although see *H v A (No. 2)* [2015] EWHC 2630 (Fam) on the problem of 'jigsaw' identification from bits of information, even where the names of those involved is not disclosed.

[176] *Haringey LBC v Musa* [2014] EWHC 1200 (Fam).

[177] [2015] EWHC 1670 (Fam).

[178] Brophy (2014).

[179] Herring (2014f).

is the vision of people controlling, to some degree, their own destiny, fashioning it through successive decisions throughout their lives.[180]

In terms of family law, this means that we should respect individual's decisions about how they wish to live their family lives, and the state should not interfere. This ties in with the theme of individualism, mentioned earlier. People should be free to leave relationships without undue hardship. Similarly, in the case of disputes between the parties, we should respect their decisions about how to resolve them. The state should not be telling people how to run their families, or imposing solutions on their disputes. Autonomy appears to be playing a more prominent role in family law with increasing weight being placed on enabling couples to resolve disputes themselves and with the law taking a less interventionist stance.[181] This emphasis on autonomy could be explained in part by it falling in with Government attempts to reduce legal aid and general legal expenditure. It might also reflect the fact that the issues raised in family cases are often contentious: relying on autonomy avoids the Government having to take sides. However, not everyone supports the emphasis on autonomy. I have argued that the image of individuals making choices to pursue their goals in life is anathema to family life:

> Individualism ignores the complex web of relations and connections which make up most people's lives. The reality for everyone, but in our society particularly women, is that it is the values of inter-dependence and connection, rather than self-sufficiency and independence, which reflect their reality. People do not understand their family lives as involving clashes of individual rights or interests, but rather as a working through of relationships. The muddled give and take of everyday family life where sacrifices are made, and benefits gained, without them being totted up on some giant familial star chart, chimes more with everyday family life than the image of independent interests and rights.[182]

Autonomy presupposes that people are competent independent individuals who are in a position to make decisions for themselves. For some commentators this overlooks the vulnerability that many face.[183] However, there are dangers here. The emphasis on autonomy can lead to a distinction being drawn between those who are vulnerable and those who are not. Those who are vulnerable are seen by some as in need of protection and that can lead to paternalistic interventions.[184] Alison Diduck warns that if autonomy is seen as the ideal then carers and women generally can be seen to suffer the 'unfortunate condition of vulnerability' and need protection. The idea of universal vulnerability,[185] namely that everyone is vulnerable and needs help from others, is one way of responding to that concern.[186] Anne Barlow[187] decries the shift away from 'solidarity' to the emphasis on autonomy. She argues in favour of solidarity as capturing 'the collective nature of the enterprise in family life'.

---

[180] Raz (1986: 369). For further discussion see Fleming and McClain (2013).
[181] Scherpe and Sloane (2014).
[182] Herring (2010b: 266). See also Rhoades (2010a and b); Nedelsky, J. (2011) and Herring (2014f).
[183] Bedford and Herring (2019); Collins (2014); Diduck (2014b).
[184] Fineman and Grear (2013).
[185] Foster, Herring and Doran (2014).
[186] But see Collins (2014) for a critique.
[187] Barlow (2015).

D The decline in 'moral judgements'

It is arguable that the law is increasingly reluctant to make what some see as moral judge-ments.[188] At one time the courts were happy to state what had caused the breakdown of a marriage; who was a good mother or a good father; or what was the best way to raise a child.[189] Stirling LJ once explained the function of the judges was 'to promote virtue and morality and to discourage vice and immorality'.[190] However, increasingly the courts have been unwilling to do this, and have accepted that there is not necessarily one right answer in difficult cases.[191] In particular, the courts are more and more reluctant to accept that a party's bad conduct should affect the outcome of a case. At one time the question of whether a party had engaged in improper conduct was highly relevant in divorce cases, custody disputes and financial cases. Nowadays behaviour is rarely relevant, unless it can be shown to have an impact on the future welfare of the child.[192]

It may be that the law's increasing reluctance to make moral judgements represents increas-ing uncertainty over moral absolutes in society at large.[193] Bainham[194] questions the assump-tion that there is a shared body of common values about family life and the role of family in society. He even questions whether it can be said that society accepts that adultery is morally wrong. He argues: 'It seems likely that if we were to concentrate on the practice rather than the theory of matrimonial obligations, at least as strong a case could be made for identifying a community norm of marital infidelity.' If we cannot even agree that adultery is wrong, there are few areas indeed where the law could set down moral judgements. However, Regan has argued that the law cannot avoid making moral judgements.[195] Even declining to express a moral judgement is in a way expressing a moral view. Also, the courts are willing to use bad behaviour as evidence of how an individual may behave in the future. So, although a father who has been violent may not be denied contact with his child on the basis that he has behaved immorally, he might be denied contact on the basis that his past bad conduct indicates that he might pose a risk to the child in the future.[196] This means that it is wrong to think bad conduct is no longer relevant.

Some have criticised the reluctance of the law to impose moral judgement and confirm the importance of family responsibilities.[197] Baroness Deech[198] makes the interesting point that we are happy to attach responsibilities and make moral judgements about some areas of life – the environment, diet or smoking – but not in relation to intimate family life.

While there has been a decline in the talk of imposing moral values, the concept of obliga-tion still has a role in family law. Gillian Douglas has suggested a helpful distinction between commitments, which are voluntarily chosen and involve a degree of mutual reciprocity, and obligations, which need not be voluntarily undertaken.[199] Using this distinction the

---

[188] For a discussion of the interaction between legal and social norms, see Eekelaar (2000a).
[189] For a wide-ranging discussion on the role of fault in family law, see Bainham (2001a).
[190] *Constantinidi v Constantinidi and Lance* [1905] P 253, 278, per Stirling LJ.
[191] *Piglowska v Piglowski* [1999] 2 FLR 763.
[192] Bainham (2001a).
[193] Munby J (2005: 502); Bainham (2000c).
[194] Bainham (1995b: 239).
[195] Regan (2000).
[196] Bainham (2001a).
[197] Bridgeman, Keating and Lind (2008; 2011) and Lind, Keating and Bridgeman (2011).
[198] Deech (2010d).
[199] Douglas (2018).

obligations of parenthood, especially, in child support are obligations (you cannot opt out of them) whereas obligations to financially support a partner are commitments (undertaken if you decide to marry your partner).

E Sending messages through the law

The number of cases where the courts actually decide what happens to a family is small. Of far more importance is the general message that the law sends to individuals and to the solicitors who advise them.[200] The ability of the law to send messages has been recognised by the Law Commission, which concluded, in a discussion on the law of divorce, that: 'for some of our respondents, as for our predecessors, it was important that divorce law should send the right messages, to the married and the marrying, about the seriousness and the permanence of the commitment involved. We agree.'[201] The law can also send messages through the language it uses.[202] For example, judges have said that it is no longer appropriate in legal terms to speak of illegitimacy, because whether a child's parents are married or not does not affect the child's status.

The problem with using the law as a means of sending messages is that, as regards the general public, the message that the law wishes to send is transmitted by the news media. The reliability of the media as conveyors of legal messages is certainly open to doubt. The Government, of course, can send messages of its own about family life outside the context of the law.

An interesting development is judges seeking to write judgments in a way which could be understood easily by the parties and the general public. In *Re Jack (A Child: care and placement orders)*[203] DDJ Reed wrote a judgment concerning the son of a father with learning difficulties. He wrote it 'using simple words' so that D, with support, could understand it. Similarly, Jackson LJ in *Re A (Letter to a Young Person)*[204] wrote the judgment in the form of a letter to the young man at the centre of the case, which opened:

> Dear Sam,
> It was a pleasure to meet you on Monday and I hope your camp this week went well.
> This case is about you and your future, so I am writing this letter as a way of giving my decision to you and to your parents . . .

F Non-legal responses to family problems

No family lawyer would claim that the law provides the solutions to all problems that families might face.[205] The importance of the role played by social workers, psychiatrists, psychologists and mediators in resolving difficulties families face should not be underestimated. Thorpe LJ,[206] in an important case concerning disputes over contact with children, stated:

> The disputes are often driven by personality disorders, unresolved adult conflicts or egocentricity. These originating or contributing factors would generally be better treated therapeutically, where at least there would be some prospect of beneficial change, rather than given vent in the family justice system.

---

[200] Garrison (2015); Dewar (2010).
[201] Law Commission Report 192 (1990: para 3.4).
[202] Bainham (1998b).
[203] Law Commission Report 192 (1990: para 3.4).
[204] Bainham (1998b).
[205] Wall LJ (2009).
[206] *Re L (A Child) (Contact: Domestic Violence)* [2000] 2 FCR 404 at p. 439. See further Smart (2007a).

It is notable that solicitors are being expected not only to provide legal advice, but also point clients in the direction of other sources of help.[207] In part this is in response to recognition that litigation can be distressing for the child.[208] There has been an increasing emphasis on keeping family cases out of court (see Chapter 2). We are also seeing the development of specialist courts which seek to recognise that a family case may raise a host of complex issues. For example, Family Drug and Alcohol Courts have opened in some areas which seek to draw on a wide range of professional expertise for families affected by drugs and alcohol.

G Rules or discretion

There is a debate over the extent to which family law cases should be resolved by relying on rules and the extent to which they should be decided on a discretionary basis. Put simply, should a judge decide each case on its merits and be given a wide discretion in reaching a solution appropriate to a particular case or should we have rules to ensure consistency,[209] save costs, and protect the rights of individual family members?[210] In fact, the distinction is not that sharp because there is a continuum between wide discretion and inflexible rules. The more family law is seen as a set of fixed rights and responsibilities, the more likely it is for a rule-based system to be used; but if family law is seen as being about achieving justice for the particular individuals involved, it is more likely that a discretionary-based system will be employed. With a discretionary-based system, if the case is going to be decided on its own special facts, the court will require all the relevant evidence to be heard, and this creates more costs in both the preparation of and hearing of a case. So, the expense involved is another important factor in deciding the balance between the two regimes.[211]

H Multiculturalism and religious diversity

To what extent should family law take into account the variety of cultural practices in British society?[212] The question can be framed as how to balance the desire to protect the values of the dominant culture with a need to recognise and respect the values of minority cultures. For example, in relation to marriage, should the law permit polygamous marriages out of respect for minority cultures which may encourage polygamy, or should it rather reflect the disapproval of the majority culture towards polygamy? Corporal punishment of children is another issue over which different cultures may have different practices. Alternatively, the issue can be seen as this: does the law believe that people have rights which should be protected, regardless of their cultural background, or does the law encourage cultural groups to adopt different practices, regardless of whether the majority approves of them?

There are various strategies that could be adopted, including the following:[213]

1. **Absolutism.** This view is that the values of the majority are the only correct values. Absolutism would lead to a strategy of complete non-recognition of the values of minority cultures.

---

[207] Melville and Laing (2010).

[208] *Re N (Section 91(14))* [2010] 1 FLR 1110.

[209] As Dewar (2000b) points out, clear rules would ensure that there is consistency between decisions reached not only in the courtroom but also between settlements negotiated by the parties and their lawyers.

[210] Dewar (1997).

[211] For further discussion, see Dewar and Parker (2000).

[212] For some useful discussions, see Barton (2009); Banda (2005 and 2003); Brophy (2000); Khaliq and Young (2001) and Malik (2007).

[213] For a thorough discussion, see Freeman (2002b).

Minority cultures would have to adopt the values of the majority. This is not an approach that would be acceptable to most western democracies.

2. **Pluralism.** This approach recognises that there are some issues where minority values should be protected, but others where the majority's values must be preserved.[214] In England, female genital mutilation is unlawful and the courts will seek to make it unlawful,[215] while minority religious celebrations are, of course, permitted. Poulter argues that minority cultural values should be restricted in instances where human rights as set out in international agreements must be protected.[216] For example, if the practices of a minority culture infringe children's rights, the law is permitted to outlaw those practices. Parkinson suggests that 'the importance of preserving the inherited cultural values of the majority must be balanced against the effects of such laws on the minority's capacity for cultural expression'. Parkinson insists, in reference to Australia, that there are some aspects of the majority's culture which are fundamental and should be fixed.[217] He refers to the minimum age of marriage, to laws prohibiting incest, and to the need for consent for marriage as being some of the fundamental values. On these issues, minority family practices which contravened these principles could be outlawed. However, on less fundamental values, the minority practices should be respected, even if the majority found them distasteful.

3. **Relativism.** This view states that there are no moral absolutes; that different values may be acceptable for particular cultures at particular times.[218] Therefore, if a form of conduct is accepted in a minority culture, the majority has no ground upon which to forbid it. If this approach were adopted, there might be difficulties over issues where the minority practice is based on a mistaken factual premise. For example, if female circumcision was acceptable in a minority culture because it was thought to provide medical benefits, would the majority be entitled to forbid it because they 'know' that it has no medical benefits? In a more positive light, relativism claims that society benefits from there being a wide variety of different cultural practices and beliefs – it creates a richer and more diverse society.[219] However, most relativists accept that there might be some forms of cultural practice that so infringe the rights of others to live their lives as they wish that they should be prohibited.[220] Opponents of relativism argue that once society accepts that people have certain rights, these rights should not be lost simply because a citizen is from a minority culture. If, for example, children's rights require that the law forbids corporal punishment, children should not lose those rights because they belong to a culture which accepts corporal punishment.

Freeman has argued that a degree of scepticism is justifiable when considering cultural practices:

> Many cultural practices when critically examined turn upon the interpretation of a male elite (an oligarchy, clergy or judiciary): if there is now consensus, this was engineered, an ideology construction to cloak the interests of only one section of society.[221]

---

[214] For further discussion, see Raz (1994).
[215] *Suffolk CC v RD* [2020] EWHC 323 (Fam).
[216] Poulter (1987).
[217] Parkinson (1996: 148).
[218] See the discussion in Tilley (2000).
[219] Raz (1994).
[220] Raz (1994).
[221] Freeman (2000d: 13).

He stated that the way ahead is to develop, through dialogues across communities, versions of 'common sense' values.[222]

An interesting example of the issue was *A v T (Ancillary Relief: Cultural Factors)*[223] which involved a divorce between an Iranian couple, who had recently moved to England. On their divorce the husband was refusing to grant his wife a *talaq* divorce, which meant that even though the couple might be divorced in the eyes of the law, they remained married in the eyes of their religion. Baron J ordered that if the husband did not provide the wife with the talaq divorce he was to pay her an extra £25,000. He did this having heard evidence that this was the approach that Sharia courts would have taken, arguing that where the spouses have only a 'secondary attachment' to English jurisdiction and culture, then due weight could be given to factors relevant to their 'primary culture'. It will be interesting to see whether courts in other cases will accept an argument that a different family law might apply to different cultures. In Chapter 2 we will consider the role that religious 'courts' can play in resolving family disputes.

In recent times it seems that there is particularly a tension between religion and family law.[224] For those with conservative religious values many of the developments in family law are antagonistic to fundamental beliefs, particularly in the area of same-sex relationships.[225] Among some Christians, evangelicals and Roman Catholics, in particular, there is a perception that their faith is 'under attack'. Lord Carey, the former Archbishop of Canterbury, is reported to have said:

> It is now Christians who are persecuted; often sought out and framed by homosexual activists . . . Christians are driven underground. There appears to be a clear animus to the Christian faith and to Judaeo-Christian values. Clearly the courts of the United Kingdom require guidance.[226]

In *R (Johns and Johns) v Derby City Council (Equality and Human Rights Commission Intervening)*[227] a barrister, Mr Diamond, representing a couple who claimed their religious views on homosexuality had meant they were not approved as foster carers, argued that 'something is very wrong with the legal, moral and ethical compass of our country' and that 'gay rights advocates construe religious protection down to vanishing point'. He submitted that the state 'should not use its coercive powers to de-legitimise Christian belief'. Munby J provided a trenchant reply. He rejected claims that Christians were treated unequally before the law. He went on to explain that Britain was 'a democratic and pluralistic society, in a secular state not a theocracy', adding:

> Although historically this country is part of the Christian west, and although it has an established church which is Christian, there have been enormous changes in the social and religious life of our country over the last century. Our society is now pluralistic and largely secular. But one aspect of its pluralism is that we also now live in a multi-cultural community of many faiths. One of the paradoxes of our lives is that we live in a society which has at one and the same time become both increasingly secular but also increasingly diverse in religious affiliation . . . Religion – whatever the particular believer's faith – is no doubt something to be encouraged but it is not the business of government or of the secular courts, though the courts will, of course, pay every respect and give great weight to the individual's religious principles.

---

[222] Freeman (2002b).
[223] [2004] 1 FLR 977. See also S. Edwards (2004).
[224] Cahn and Carbone (2010).
[225] See e.g. *Islington LBC v Ladele* [2009] EWCA Civ 1357 where a registrar refused on religious grounds to conduct a civil partnership and was sacked.
[226] Bingham (2012).
[227] [2011] EWHC 375 (Admin).

There is no denying that Christianity has been highly influential on the development of the law and culture in England and Wales. However, the courts have made it clear that they do not see it as their role to ensure the law reflects the teaching of the Church.

At the root of the tension between law and religion is that many of the terms and concepts that family lawyers use has religious significance. Words such as marriage, father and child have religious connotations to some. Changes to the legal definition of marriage, for example, were seen by some as a challenge to the religious concept. It may be that now religious and legal understandings of these terms are diverging and, if so, we need a new kind of language, and better appreciation, if we are to separate the religious and legal understandings of terms like marriage.

Racism and family law

Racism infects society. For children, while 17 per cent of white children live below the poverty line, it is 47 per cent of children in Pakistani heritage households, 41 per cent Bangladeshi and 30 per cent from Black households.[228] That means that, for example, a child of Pakistani heritage is 2.8 times more likely to live in poverty than a White child. A recent survey[229] found that 43 per cent of those from a minority ethnic background reported they had been unfairly overlooked for promotion at work, as compared with 18 per cent of White people who reported the same. Those from ethnic minorities were three times as likely to be thrown out of or denied entrance to a restaurant, bar or club in the last five years. Two-thirds of those questioned thought Britain had a problem with racism.

The employment gap, as measured between the BME and White British population, was 11 per cent in 2016.[230] While 76 per cent of White adults were employed in 2016, only 54 per cent Pakistani/Bangladeshi and 67 per cent of Black people were employed. Around 18 per cent of Bangladeshi workers are paid below the National Minimum Wage, compared to only 3 per cent of White workers and 5 per cent of Black African population. These economic disadvantages can all be connected to disadvantages for children from minority ethnic backgrounds. It is a major issue of children's rights that affects one's upbringing and economic prospects. There are also strong links between poverty and engagement with the care system and the need for legal aid. As we shall in Chapter 2, the lack of access to legal aid has had a profound impact on how family law operates for those who are not well off.

There are also issues about racial diversity within the judiciary. Ekaney[231] sums up the issue:

The 2019 Judicial Diversity Statistics show that all the judges of the Supreme Court are white. BAME people make up 6% of Court of Appeal judges and 3% of High Court judges. No fulltime Family Division judge is of a BAME background. Of all the judges appointed last year in the High Court, all but one of the nine were Oxbridge educated. People with BAME heritage make up 4% of Circuit Judges, 9% of District Judges (County Courts) and 9% of Deputy District Judges (County Courts). Under-representation of BAME people in the judiciary is real and may feed into a sense of inevitable structural disadvantages for BAME participants in the FJS.

---

[228] Office for National Statistics (2020b).
[229] Booth, R and Mohdin, A (2019) 'Revealed: the stark evidence of everyday racial bias in Britain', *The Guardian*, 2 December.
[230] Khan, O. (2019) *Economic inequality and racial inequalities in the UK: Current evidence and the possible effects of systemic economic change.* London: Runnymede Trust.
[231] Ekaney (2020).

J The Human Rights Act 1998 and family law

Learning objective 5

Describe how the Human Rights Act 1998 affects family law

The Human Rights Act 1998 protects individuals' rights under the European Convention on Human Rights.[232] That Convention sets out the minimum standards of treatment under the law that people are entitled to expect.[233] There are two important aspects of the Human Rights Act. First, the rights in the Act (which are essentially the rights protected in the European Convention on Human Rights) are directly enforceable against public authorities (e.g. local authorities) and all public authorities must act in a way that is compatible with these rights unless required not to do so by other legislation.[234] Secondly, under s. 3 of the Human Rights Act all legislation is to be interpreted, if at all possible, in line with the Convention rights. If it is not possible to interpret the legislation in accordance with these rights, then the legislation should be enforced as it stands and a declaration of incompatibility issued: this requires Parliament to confirm or amend the offending legislation.[235] In interpreting the extent of the rights protected in the Human Rights Act, the decisions of the European Court of Human Rights and European Commission will be taken into account by the courts.[236] The possible relevance of rights under the Act will be considered at the relevant points throughout this text. However, the impact has been less in family law than in other areas. Sonia Harris-Short[237] suggests two reasons why family law judges have taken a 'minimalist' approach to the use of the Act. First, there is a long-standing suspicion of rights among family lawyers, especially because the notion of parental rights might be used to usurp the fundamental principle that the welfare of the child should be the law's paramount concern. Secondly, many family law cases involve complex issues of moral, social and political significance and the courts wish to avoid being brought into such disputes. Hence, we will see (in Chapter 12) that courts are very reluctant to use the Human Rights Act to order local authorities to provide children in care with particular services. Indeed, a recurrent theme in the way courts have dealt with the common law or Children Act 1989 is to protect the interests of children and adults to the same extent as the Human Rights Act 1998 does. This means that if the Human Rights Act 1998 were repealed, it is unlikely to make a huge difference to English family law.

K Brexit and family law

At the time of writing, it is still not absolutely clear in what form Brexit will take. It is international family law that will be most seriously affected.[238] There are a host of treaties and procedures dealing with transnational families and the recognition of international judgments which will potentially be significantly changed. As this book does not cover international aspects of family law, whether Brexit occurs or not will not hugely impact on its contents. However, for lawyers advising international couples it is clear we are in for a time of considerable uncertainty.

---

[232] See Choudhry and Herring (2010) for a detailed examination of human rights and family law.
[233] This point is emphasised in Bainham (2000c).
[234] Human Rights Act 1998, s. 6.
[235] Secondary legislation which does not comply with the Human Rights Act can be disapplied: *Re P* [2008] UKHL 38, discussed in Herring (2009a).
[236] Human Rights Act 1998, s. 2.
[237] Human Rights Act 1998, s. 2.
[238] Dutta (2017); Beaumont (2017); Carruthers and Crawford (2017); Lowe (2017) and Lamont (2017).

6 The coronavirus and family law

Learning objective 6

Consider the impact of COVID-19 on family law

The coronavirus has, of course, had a huge impact upon national and international life. It has created practical and theoretical challenges to the operation of family law and family life. Here are the main problems that have arisen for the family courts from COVID:

1. Face-to-face hearings have become challenging and at times impossible, given lockdown restrictions. Remote hearings are commonly being used, but there are serious questions about whether these can achieve justice. We will explore this further in Chapter 2.

2. As a result of the difficulties in holding face-to-face hearings, long delays have built up. Particularly where children are involved this can lead to uncertainty and distress. Shortages in family law judiciary and legal practitioners mean that a system already under strain is severely pressurised.

3. It is important to appreciate that people who come to family court often face a host of problems. Specialist Family Drug and Alcohol Courts have been set up to deal with cases where the family dispute also raises issues of substance misuse. These courts can provide an invaluable service, opening doors to non-legal services which can help people address their broader issues. Such courts have been severely impacted by COVID.[239]

4. There have been disputes over contact sessions during the lockdown. If a child is living with, say, their mother, but seeing their father once a week, should the child still see the father if that increases the risk of COVID? Or is doing that just a way that mothers might stop fathers seeing their children? Guidance issued by the President of Family Division says that if parents are worried that contact may not be safe 'the best way to deal with these difficult times will be for parents to communicate with one another about their worries, and what they think would be a good, practical solution.'[240] The difficulty is that, as the guidance acknowledges, the couple may not agree and the only solution is then to seek a court order. But access to the courts is currently very limited.

5. COVID has meant that it has proved difficult to follow the normal guidance on adoption, with children meeting and staying with prospective adopters before full adoption. Also, the kinds of face-to-face meetings involved in assessing potential adopters may not be possible. New regulations[241] have tried to utilise online meetings, but for the kind of assessments that take place prior to adoption these may not be adequate alternatives.

6. COVID has raised issues around financial orders on divorce. What if a financial order was made based on the assumption that one or both spouses would continue working, but COVID means that someone has lost their job. Can the order be re-opened?[242] The courts could be inundated with applications if they can. But to say they cannot will mean an order was made based on a false assumption. This issue will be explored further in Chapter 6.

As well as such practical issues raised by COVID, there have been some interesting theoretical ones. Especially in the lockdown, homes and families were seen as places of safety, with people being recommended to stay with their households and mixing with other households not permitted. However, as we shall see in Chapter 6, the issues of domestic abuse and child abuse mean the home is by no means necessarily a safe place. COVID showed powerfully the conflicting images as the place of security and safety; and as a place of imprisonment and torture.

---

[239] Stanley (2020).
[240] McFarlane (2020).
[241] Adoption and Children (Coronavirus) (Amendment) Regulations 2020.
[242] Chandler (2020).

It was notable too how the lockdown highlighted the importance to people of their relationships. The difficulty in maintaining relationships and limiting social interaction was widely seen as a cause of stress and unhappiness. The dating app Tinder saw its busiest ever day in March 2020 during the pandemic.[243]

During three months at the start of COVID, the Government issued advice for those who were 'clinically especially vulnerable'. It required them to shield: 'You're strongly advised to stay at home at all times and avoid any face-to-face contact.' Those who were self-isolating should sleep alone in a separate bedroom and not use the same bathroom as anyone else; and were encouraged to have meals in their own room and to eat alone. If they had to be in a room with someone they were advised to keep two meters apart and keep time spent together to a minimum.

This was remarkably strict advice. It was a bit like house arrest, but worse. The guidance offered was premised on the assumption you had lavish accommodation, including a spare bedroom; a spare bathroom; and rooms with what estate agents call generous dimensions. It had scant regard for family life. Partners may not sleep together and should minimise time spent together. Parents should not cuddle their children or hold their hands. Comfort must be offered at a two-meter distance. Mealtimes should be solitary. The lifestyle promoted was starkly monastic. It also had no regard for the possibility that the clinically vulnerable may need to care for family members. It did accept that 'you may find that shielding and distancing can be boring or frustrating' and recommended to combat such feelings by finding a room with a nice view. It is notable that this advice seemed to ignore the importance of relationships to people's well-being and the caring obligations they have. Family lawyers will never do that. For them, appreciating the importance of relationships and acknowledging the obligations that can flow from them are paramount.

7 Conclusion

This chapter has considered the nature of families and family law. One point that has emerged is that the terms 'family' and 'law' do not have fixed meanings. The understanding of a family has changed over time. For example, although at one point a family would have been defined as an opposite-sex married couple with children, now a same-sex couple can marry and few would deny that a gay couple can be a family.[244] John Eekelaar has even suggested that rather than talking about family law it would be more appropriate to talk about the 'personal law'.[245] He uses this term to 'refer to laws, whether applicable on the basis of an individual's communal allegiance or not, which purport directly to regulate their private life'.

This recognises that increasingly it is intimate caring relationships, rather than traditional family ones, which are the focus of the law's attention. Despite the lack of clarity over what a family is, it is clear that it is a powerful ideal: no major political party would openly advocate 'family unfriendly policies'. The chapter has also noted the diversity of ways that family law can be approached. There is no one correct way of viewing the law, and each approach has its benefits and limitations. However, the discussion demonstrates that the interaction between families, law and socio-political forces is complex. The tensions between the traditional ideal of what a family should be like and the realities of family life today are revealed in the topical issues discussed throughout the chapter.

---

[243] Bruce and Verdan (2020).
[244] *Fitzpatrick v Sterling Housing Association Ltd* [2000] 1 FCR 21.
[245] Eekelaar (2006b: 31). Although his use of this phrase is potentially misleading because by 'personal' he means 'personal relationships with others'. It is not, therefore, as individualistic a concept as at first appears. See further the discussion in Diduck (2008).

Further reading

Archard, D. (2010) *The Family: A Liberal Defence,* Basingstoke: Palgrave.

Archard, D. (2012) 'The future of the family', *Ethics and Social Welfare* 6: 132.

Barlow, A. (2015) 'Solidarity, autonomy and equality: mixed messages for the family?' *Child and Family Law Quarterly* 223.

Bedford, D. and Herring, J. (eds) (2019) *Embracing Vulnerability,* London: Routledge.

Brake, E. and Ferguson, L. (eds) (2018) *Philosophical Foundations of Children's and Family Law,* Oxford: OUP.

Bridgeman, J., Keating, H. and Lind, C. (2008) *Responsibility, Law and the Family,* Aldershot: Ashgate.

Bridgeman, J., Keating, H. and Lind, C. (2011) *Regulating Family Responsibilities,* Aldershot: Ashgate.

Brown, A. (2019) *What is the Family of Law? The Influence of the Nuclear Family,* Oxford: Hart.

Brunning, L. (2018) 'The distinctiveness of polyamory', *Journal of Applied Philosophy* 35: 513.

Busby, N. and Weldon-Johns, M. (2019) 'Fathers as carers in UK law and policy: dominant ideologies and lived experience', *Journal of Social Welfare and Family Law* 41: 280.

Chambers, D. (2014) *A Sociology of Family Life,* Bristol: Polity.

Choudhry, S. and Herring, J. (eds) (2019) *Comparative Family Law,* Cambridge: Cambridge University Press.

Collier, R. and Sheldon, S. (2008) *Fragmenting Fatherhood,* Oxford: Hart.

Diduck, A. (2003) *Law's Families,* London: LexisNexis Butterworths.

Diduck, A. (2011) 'What is family law for?' *Current Legal Problems* 64: 287.

Diduck, A. (2014b) 'Autonomy and vulnerability in family law: the missing link', in J. Wallbank and J. Herring (eds) *Vulnerabilities, Care and Family Law,* London: Routledge.

Diduck, A. and O'Donovan, K. (eds) (2007) *Feminist Perspectives on Family Law,* London: Routledge.

Douglas, G. (2018) *Obligation and Commitment in Family Law,* Oxford: Hart.

Eekelaar, J. (2006b) *Family Life and Personal Life,* Oxford: OUP.

Eekelaar, J. (2012b) 'Rights and obligations in the contemporary family: retheorizing individualism, families and the state', *Theoretical Inquiries in Law* 13: 75.

Ekaney, N. (2020) 'Equal family justice – its pursuit in a pandemic', *Family Law* 50: 959

Fineman, M. (2004) *The Autonomy Myth,* New York: The New Press.

George, R.H. (2012b) *Ideas and Debates in Family Law,* Oxford: Hart.

Glennon, L. (2008) 'Obligations between adult partners: moving from form to function?' *International Journal of Law Policy and the Family* 22: 22.

Golombok, S. (2015) *Modern Families: Parents and Children in New Family Forms,* Cambridge: CUP.

Grillo, R. (2014) *Muslim Families, Politics and the Law,* Aldershot: Ashgate.

Herring, J. (2014a) 'Making family law less sexy and more careful', in R. Leckey (ed) *After Legal Equality,* Abingdon: Routledge.

Herring, J. (2014f) *Relational Autonomy and Family Law,* Amsterdam: Springer.

Herring, J. (2017) 'Compassion, ethics of care and legal rights', *International Journal of Law in Context* 13: 158.

Herring, J. (2019) *Law and the Relational Self*, Cambridge: CUP.

Herring, J. (2021) *Law through the Life Course*, Bristol: BUP.

Herring, J., Probert, R. and Gilmore, S. (2015) *Great Debates: Family Law,* Basingstoke: Palgrave.

Huntington, C. (2014) *Failure to Flourish: How Law Undermines Family Relationships*, Oxford: OUP.

Lind, C., Keating, H. and Bridgeman, J. (2011) *Taking Responsibility, Law and the Changing Family,* Aldershot: Ashgate.

Malik, M. (2014) 'Family law in diverse societies', in J. Eekelaar and R. George (eds) *Routledge Handbook of Family Law and Policy,* Abingdon: Routledge.

Smart, C. (2007a) *Personal Life,* Bristol: Polity Press.

Wallbank, J., Choudhry, S. and Herring, J. (eds) (2009) *Rights, Gender and Family Law,* London: Routledge.

Wallbank, J. and Herring, J. (2014) *Vulnerabilities, Care and Family Law,* London: Routledge.

Visit **go.pearson.com/uk/he/resources** to access **resources** specifically written to complement this text.

Family justice

Learning objectives

When you finish reading this chapter you will be able to:

1. Explain the nature of the legal aid reforms
2. Discuss the impact of the legal aid reforms
3. Examine the impact of COVID on family court hearings
4. Describe the nature of mediation
5. Explore the arguments for and against mediation
6. Consider the issues around the use of religious tribunals

---

1 Introduction

This chapter is about the family justice system. At first that may sound like a rather dry subject. But English family law has undergone a profound revolution in the past few years, which has had an enormous impact on the way family law disputes are dealt with. This chapter will focus on three major issues. First, the consequences of the withdrawal of legal aid from many family law cases. Second, the use of remote hearings as a result of COVID. Third, the move towards mediation and other out of court-based forms of dispute resolution.

2 The Family Justice Review and reform of legal aid

In late 2011 the Family Justice Review was published.[1] This involved a major examination of the family justice system. It identified two major problems with the family justice system. The first was delay:

> Delay blights lives. It is a troubling statistic that every 2 month delay for a young child represents 1% of their whole childhood. Yet the average care case now takes 55 weeks to complete – and many cases take a good deal longer. These are some of the most vulnerable children in our society. It is absolutely unacceptable that delay is common in so many areas.[2]

---

[1] Norgrave (2012).
[2] Ministry of Justice (2012a: 2).

The second was the adversarial nature of proceedings:

> Too often, divorcing couples end up arguing over deeply sensitive and emotional issues in the adversarial environment of the courtroom, when they might have resolved their disputes more quickly, simply and consensually outside it. And when judges do hand down judgments – particularly decisions which determine how separated parents share responsibility for their children – compliance is too low and enforcement ineffective.[3]

The Government accepted the proposals in the Review and implemented a series of reforms. It set out the following key principles to govern its approach to family justice:

- that the welfare of the child remains the paramount consideration in any proceedings determining the upbringing of the child;
- that the family is nearly always the best place for bringing up children, except where there is a risk of significant harm;
- that in private law, specifically, problems should be resolved out of court, and the courts will only become involved where it is really necessary;
- where court is the right option, that children deserve a family court in which their needs come first;
- that both in public and private law cases children must be given an opportunity to have their voices heard in the decisions that affect them;
- that the process must protect vulnerable children, and their families;
- that this is a task not limited in responsibility to one organisation or another, but something we must all work on together; and
- that judicial independence must be upheld as the system is made more coherent and managed more effectively.

A major part of the response to the Family Justice Review was a series of procedural reforms designed to speed up the family justice system. One of the most significant is s. 17(3) of the Crime and Courts Act 2013 which creates a single family court. It will mean that a single court building will deal with all family cases in a particular area, rather than the work being spread across magistrates' courts, county courts and high courts.[4] That should make the maintenance of files easier and provide a more coordinated service. Although the creation of family courts is generally welcomed, the difficulty is that this has been matched by a dramatic cut in the number of courts. The Government has explained that 'over 95% of citizens will be able to reach their required court within an hour by car'.[5] The problem is that those without cars, or with childcare responsibilities, may find such lengthy journeys a real impediment to accessing justice. However, an even greater impediment to accessing justice is the cutbacks to legal aid.

3 Legal Aid, Sentencing and Punishment of Offenders Act 2012

Learning objective 1

Explain the nature of the legal aid reforms

The Legal Aid, Sentencing and Punishment of Offenders Act 2012 (LASPO) has drastically restricted access to legal aid in family law cases. There is no legal aid in private cases (e.g. disputes between parents over children and financial disputes) with two exceptions:

---

[3] Ministry of Justice (2012a: 2).
[4] They do not deal with cases under the inherent jurisdiction or international cases.
[5] Ministry of Justice (2015a).

(i) Applications for protective orders in relation to domestic violence, such as occupation orders, non-molestation orders or injunctions.[6]

(ii) Cases where the applicant falls into one of the exceptional categories, to be discussed shortly.

In public law cases (e.g. where a local authority wants to take a child into care), legal aid will be available for parties to the proceedings, but this will be restricted to a fixed fee. The Act has also restricted legal aid to cases involving welfare benefits, debt cases, employment tribunals and immigration claims. This chapter will focus on the impact on family law cases, although there are significant issues raised in other areas of the law.

A The exceptional categories

Those seeking legal aid in family cases will need to show that they fall within an exceptional category to be entitled to legal aid. There are five of them:

- the applicant is the victim of domestic violence;
- the case involves a forced marriage injunction;
- the case involves allegations of child abuse;
- a child who is party to proceedings; or
- there are exceptional circumstances.[7]

This means, for example, that if a father is seeking contact with his child or a wife is seeking financial support following divorce, while in the past (subject to their means) they could have obtained legal aid to obtain legal advice and representation, this will not now be available, unless they are the victim of domestic violence. They will need to negotiate the issue with their partner or represent themselves in court. The most they might get is £150 for mediation and legal help. Jess Mant and Julie Wallbank[8] explain:

> Those falling outside the [exceptional] rule – people bringing all kinds of private family law problems – will be funnelled away from formal law and towards informal processes such as relying on Internet-based sources of advice and other information packs. It will be argued that these sources are wildly inappropriate for a vast number of people, as many are dealing with very difficult personal circumstances, which are often compounded by factors such as socio-economic disadvantage, abusive relationships, mental health issues and learning difficulties. Consequently, many are left in an empty space between the formal and informal scales of family law, within which they are unable to make use of either formal or informal sources.

We need to explore in more detail the rare cases when legal aid will be available in family law cases.

B Domestic violence

One exception is where the applicant 'has been, or is at risk of, domestic violence'.[9] The definitions of domestic abuse are explored later (in Chapter 7).

---

[6] Section 9.
[7] See Legal Aid, Sentencing and Punishment of Offenders Act 2012, Sched. 1; discussed in Hunter (2011).
[8] Mant and Wallbank (2017). See also Mant (2019).
[9] Legal Aid, Sentencing and Punishment of Offenders Act 2012, Sched. 1, para 12(1).

There are, however, significant limitations on the restrictions on how one can prove one has been or is at risk of domestic violence. The Civil Legal Aid (Procedure) Regulations 2012, reg. 33 lists how one can prove one has been or is at risk of domestic violence.[10] This includes a conviction or caution or bail or bind over for a domestic violence offence; a protective injunction or undertaking; a letter from a member of a multi-agency risk assessment conference confirming the applicant was referred to the conference as a victim of domestic abuse and has been considered by them; a finding of fact in court proceedings that there has been domestic violence; or a letter from a health care professional or social services department or a domestic violence support organisation confirming they are satisfied the victim has been or is at risk of domestic violence.[11] The list of acceptable evidence is closed and so if one does not have one of the listed documents one cannot fall into the exemption.

Under the old version of the regulations Women's Aid[12] found that 39 per cent of women who had been affected by domestic violence were not able to provide the necessary forms of evidence. That is because, as explained in Chapter 7, many victims of domestic violence do not report the violence to the authorities. The courts have now ruled the 24-month limitation unlawful.

CASE: R (Rights of Women) v The Lord Chancellor and Secretary of State for Justice [2016] EWCA Civ 91

Rights of Women challenged the lawfulness of the regulations about what evidence could be introduced to show that an applicant was a victim of domestic violence and so fell into the exception entitling them to legal aid. The regulation limited the evidence to documents that showed that within the previous 24 months there was domestic abuse. The claim was successful, with particular weight being placed on two actual cases and seven hypothetical cases where the applicants were undoubtedly at risk of being the victims of domestic violence, but were not able to produce the precise information required which related to the past 24 months. This showed the strict regulations had 'no rational connection with the statutory purpose' of ensuring victims of domestic violence had access to legal aid and the 24-month time limit was therefore unlawful.

As a result of this decision new regulations[13] have removed the time limit altogether for criminal convictions, but for the others increased it to 60 months. The fact the original regulations had such a strict time limit reveals fully the failure of the Government to appreciate the significance of the impact of domestic violence and the remarkable implication that two years after an incident of domestic violence, a victim should be in a position to represent themselves. Despite the reforms, real difficulties remain for those victims of domestic abuse who did not report the incident to the police at the time, through fear. And there are other difficulties.

The option of obtaining medical reports is not as straightforward as may be thought. Doctors are required to sign a form which states:

> I can confirm that the [injuries/condition] that I presented to you with on [insert date when you were examined by the health professional if known] were caused by domestic violence.[14]

---

[10] As amended by the Civil Legal Aid (Procedure) (Amendment) Regulations 2016 (SI 2016/516).

[11] Legal Aid Agency (2014) has set further detailed guidance on what evidence is required to demonstrate these grounds.

[12] Women's Aid (2014 and 2015).

[13] As amended by the Civil Legal Aid (Procedure) (Amendment) Regulations 2016 (SI 2016/516).

[14] Ministry of Justice (2015a).

Medical professionals may find it difficult to sign this form. The injuries may be consistent with domestic violence, but they are not in a position to confirm the injuries were caused by domestic violence. Even if the doctor or nurse is willing to sign the form, Women's Aid[15] reported 22.2 per cent of women in their survey had been asked to pay for the reports, with 7.4 per cent having to pay over £50. There are reports of the police charging £85 for letters confirming there are ongoing proceedings.[16] These sums are likely to be beyond the reach of claimants on benefits, who are those most likely to be seeking legal aid.[17] Women's Aid found that 28 per cent of respondents had to wait more than seven days to receive the evidence from official bodies. In cases where an application is in relation to an urgent matter this may cause applicants to proceed without legal aid. The Ministry of Justice[18] undertook a review of the evidence required to show one had been a victim of domestic abuse and accepted it showed there were still:

> Difficulties in accessing certain pieces of evidence: such as the cost of acquiring it; the unwillingness of organisations, and health professionals in particular, to write letters; data protection issues when attempting to access evidence from the police; language barriers or other vulnerabilities experienced by victims that prevent them from obtaining the necessary evidence.

A further difficulty is that the Government intends the assessment of legal aid to be made by a helpline operator over a telephone service. The idea that a victim of domestic abuse will be able to provide evidence to a helpline operator displays a complete failure to appreciate the impact and nature of domestic abuse. It will work in a particularly harsh way for women from cultures where claiming domestic violence is 'dishonouring' to the family.[19] It is hard to see how the domestic violence exception is going to be policed in a way which is fair to claimants or does not get so broad as to mean the savings made are very limited.[20]

With many victims of domestic violence being unable to prove what has happened they are left with the unpalatable alternative of navigating the court procedures themselves to bring proceedings against their abusers in court or having no legal protection against the violence. And, as Rosemary Hunter has pointed out, there is strong evidence that victims who try to put up with the violence are likely to find it escalates to ever more serious levels.[21]

Critics suggest the need for 'objective evidence' perpetuates a culture of disbelief of victims of domestic violence. However, in fairness the Government could not grant legal aid to everyone who claims to be the victim of domestic violence. That would leave the system open to abuse. A further issue is that the difficulty in proof may encourage some to apply for non-molestation orders primarily in order to obtain legal aid.[22] Indeed between July and September 2013 when the reforms were introduced domestic violence applications rose by 21 per cent in the same period compared to the previous year.[23]

Some critics have complained that while the victim of domestic violence will be entitled to receive legal aid, the alleged abuser will not.[24] The personal and social impact of a finding of domestic violence is considerable and John Eekelaar argues that such a person should be

---

[15] Women's Aid (2014).
[16] Blacklaws (2014).
[17] Platt and Emmerson (2013).
[18] Ministry of Justice (2018).
[19] For broader concerns on the use of telephone advice on legal aid see Smith *et al.* (2014).
[20] Hunter (2014b).
[21] Hunter (2014b).
[22] Emmerson and Platt (2014).
[23] Hunter (2014b).
[24] Ministry of Justice (2011: para 45).

regarded as entitled to legal aid.[25] Even from the point of view of victims the issue is troubling because it means the alleged abuser will be representing themselves in court and may, therefore, be involved in cross-examining.

C Children at risk

A second exemption category is where there is evidence that children are at risk of harm from someone other than the applicant and the proceedings are designed to protect the child.[26] Regulation 34 sets out the evidence that is required to establish that children are at risk. This is similar to the grounds for proof of domestic violence and include, for example, that there is an unspent conviction for a child abuse offence.

D Exceptional funding

Even if the case does not fall into one of these two categories, under s. 10 of LASPO the Legal Aid Agency can still grant legal aid to a financially eligible person where there are exceptional circumstances set out in ss. 10(3):

(a) that it is necessary to make the services available to the individual under this Part because failure to do so would be a breach of—

    (i) the individual's Convention rights (within the meaning of the Human Rights Act 1998), or

    (ii) any rights of the individual to the provision of legal services that are enforceable EU rights, or

(b) that it is appropriate to do so, in the particular circumstances of the case, having regard to any risk that failure to do so would be such a breach.

It had been thought that extensive use would be made of this facility. However, in the first 10 months only eight family applications were granted following 601 applications.[27] For the year 2019–20 for all family law legal aid claims there were only 4,391 applications of which 187 were granted.[28] The judiciary have been surprisingly unrestrained in expressing their concern. In *MG v JG*[29] Mostyn J stated:

14. As the President explained in *Q v Q* the number of annual cases where the safety net has been applied can be counted on the fingers of two hands. In the year to March 2014 there were 9. Indeed between December 2013 and March 2014 one solitary case was caught by the safety net. The President stated at para 14 'if the scheme is indeed working effectively, then it might be thought that the scheme is inadequate, for the proper demand is surely at a level very significantly greater than 8 or 9 cases a year.' Thus it would be perfectly reasonable to describe this 'safety net' as a fig leaf. MG and JG have not applied for exceptional funding under section 10(3)(b), no doubt taking the realistic view that any such application would be rejected summarily.

The number of successful applications is astonishingly few because, as shall be discussed shortly, it might be thought that the right to a fair hearing given protection by the Human Rights Act would apply in many cases where a person was denied legal aid. It suggests the Agency is being extremely strict about when exceptional funding is available. A report from

---

[25] Eekelaar (2011b).
[26] Civil Legal Aid (Procedure) Regulations 2012, reg. 34.
[27] Mourby (2014); Emmerson and Platt (2014).
[28] Office for National Statistics (2020c).
[29] [2015] EWHC 564 (Fam).

the Coram Children's Legal Centre concludes that the exceptional funding scheme is 'woefully inadequate and does not provide the promised safety net for vulnerable or disadvantaged people who are struggling to navigate complex legal processes and effectively advocate for their rights'.

4 The impact of the legal aid cuts

Learning objective 2

Discuss the impact of the legal aid reforms

In relation to family matters there has been a dramatic cut in the number of certificates for legal help. For 2011 there were 64,507 certificates; for the first quarter of 2020 it was 7,250.[30] It is beyond doubt that there are many people with family law cases who would prior to LASPO have received legal aid, but who as a result of the legislation are not.[31] By April 2020, in 39 per cent of family cases neither party was represented and in only 18 per cent of cases were both parties represented.[32]

As legal aid is only available for the poorest people, we must assume that nearly all of those who would previously have obtained legal aid will be denied access to lawyers. Those seeking legal aid will be among the most vulnerable people in society and lack the skills or knowledge to represent themselves. These problems are exacerbated by the fact that one consequence of the cutbacks in family legal aid is that many firms of solicitors are stopping doing family law work.[33] Even if a client is entitled to legal aid, they may find it difficult to find a solicitor close by who can deal with their case on a legal aid basis. Women's Aid found that 33 per cent of women had to travel between 5 and 15 miles to find a legal aid solicitor.[34] It is understandable that the Law Society[35] has argued that LASPO is 'damaging to the very foundation of our justice system'. Even Justices of the Supreme Court have weighed in, with Lord Wilson stating the Act placed access to justice under threat.[36] Mr Justice Bodey spoke at his retirement of the difficulties for litigants that the cuts had caused: 'I find it shaming that in this country, with its fine record of justice and fairness, that I should be presiding over such cases'.[37]

5 The justification for the cuts

The legal aid cuts have generated ferocious debate. Although it is fair to say that in the academic and professional literature it has been a rather one-sided debate. It is hard to find any family lawyer who supports them. Perhaps that is not surprising.

The cuts in legal aid have been described by leading experts of family law and policy as 'savage'[38] and 'breathtaking'.[39] What could justify them?

Undoubtedly, the primary justification is money. The Government hopes the reforms will lead to a saving of £450 million annually; from a legal aid bill which in total was £2 billion

[30] Office for National Statistics (2020c).
[31] The Judicial Working Group on Litigants in Person (2013).
[32] Ministry of Justice (2020).
[33] Lloyd Platt (2014) fears some firms have delegated family law work to very junior staff.
[34] Women's Aid (2014).
[35] Law Society (2017).
[36] Bowcott (2018).
[37] Bowcott (2017).
[38] Maclean (2011).
[39] Hunter (2011).

each year at the time of LASPO. These claims have been challenged. One commentator claims only 40 per cent of the hoped-for savings will be achieved.[40] First, the Government may have underestimated the number of people who, even under its proposals, will be entitled to claim legal aid. In particular, there may be significant numbers of people who are victims of domestic violence or are vulnerable and so entitled to be regarded as exceptional. Second, the cutbacks in legal aid have led to more people representing themselves in court.[41] Cases which might have been negotiated by lawyers are now going to court. And at court such cases are not presented in concise arguments, but in a less focused and more emotional manner.[42] The former President of the Family Division[43] has claimed that cases that could be resolved in an hour with legal representation take a day or longer with litigants in person. The savings to legal aid must be balanced with the increased costs in terms of running the courts, judicial time and increased delay. Third, there may be 'knock on costs'.[44] For example, if separating parents do not receive the financial orders they are entitled to there may be increased claims on benefits or social housing. Ongoing disputes over contact may increase stress and illness for partners and their children. Baroness Hale has suggested LASPO may be a 'false economy'.[45] In *Lindner v Rawlins*[46], Aikens LJ recounted the knock-on effect of these entirely predictable problems:

> Yet again, the court was without any legal assistance and had to spend time researching the law for itself then attempting to apply it to the relevant facts in order to arrive at the correct legal answer. To do the latter exercise meant that the court itself had to trawl through a large amount of documents in the file. All this involves an expensive use of judicial time, which is in short supply as it is. Money may have been saved from the legal aid funds, but an equal amount of expense, if not more, has been incurred in terms of the costs of judges' and court time. The result is that there is, in fact, no economy at all.

It is difficult to assess overall what the financial position is. While there has certainly been, as mentioned earlier, a dramatic cut in the number of certificates granted and that will have saved significant sums, the knock-on costs are hard to assess.

It would, however, be wrong to think the cutbacks in legal aid are solely motivated by a desire to save money. The Government thinks that it is beneficial for couples to avoid using courts and instead use mediation. This is a controversial claim and is discussed later in this chapter. Two other reasons appear in the Government's justification for the cutbacks. One is that litigation should not be available for things that are a result of a personal choice.[47] The argument appears to be that if someone chooses to divorce, they cannot expect the state to fund the litigation that results from their decision. John Eekelaar argues the reasoning is 'bizarre to the point of incoherence'.[48] As he points out, a person may be a victim of fraud as a result of their choice, but that is no reason for not giving legal aid to protect their rights. In any event, many family disputes are not a result of a choice. For example, a parent seeking a contact order because they are being prevented from seeing their children by the other parent is not acting as a result of her choice.

Another justification for the restriction on legal aid is that 'it is not the case that everyone is entitled to legal representation, funded by the taxpayer, for any dispute or to a particular

---

[40] Cookson (2013).
[41] Ministry of Justice (2011: para 45).
[42] Williams (2011).
[43] Wall (2012).
[44] Cookson (2011).
[45] Bowcott (2017).
[46] [2015] EWCA Civ 61 at [34].
[47] Ministry of Justice (2010: para 4.19).
[48] Eekelaar (2011b).

outcome in litigation'.[49] This quotation has been challenged by several commentators.[50] Surely people are entitled to a particular outcome in litigation: they are entitled to have their human rights upheld or the welfare of their children protected. If they need legal aid to do that, they should be entitled to it.

One of the most striking things about the Government's justifications for the cutbacks in legal aid is its failure to appreciate what legal aid in family law cases is actually spent on. The Government's justifications give the impression that family lawyers spend their time litigating cases. In fact, very few family law cases are resolved through the courts. Less than 10 per cent of disputes end up in court. Only the most complex of cases reach the courts. Joan Hunt,[51] looking at contact disputes, notes that even looking at cases where there are concerns over child abuse or neglect, domestic violence, substance abuse or mental illness, only 51 per cent had been to court. Among those where the non-resident parent complained that the resident parent had prevented contact, only 19 per cent litigated. So, litigation is already very rare. The contact cases that will be shifted from the courts to mediation by the reforms are not trivial cases where couples have litigated for fun, but are the most serious of an already serious category of cases. As Hunt puts it: 'Parents go to court, therefore, not because they see this as a simple way of dealing with contact difficulties, but because, in most cases, they are desperate and cannot think what else to do'.[52] Telling them they should mediate will not do much good.

6 The objections to LASPO

The primary objections to LASPO can be put as follows:

A Human rights

Opponents to the new legislation argue that the cutbacks in legal aid will cause real injustice. It is easy to imagine we are talking about couples disputing trivial issues. However, the cutbacks will affect major claims. A good example of the difficulties with withdrawal of legal aid was *Re T (Children)*[53] where there were claims that the grandparents were involved in the abuse of their grandchild. They were a retired fisherman and bookkeeper with a modest income, but not enough for legal aid. They were joined as parties to care proceedings and borrowed £55,000 to fund their defence of the allegations. At the hearings it was found that the allegations were entirely without foundation and the grandparents were completely exonerated. They were left with a legal bill which it would take over 15 years to pay off. The Supreme Court, while sympathising with the grandparents' position, held that the local authority (who had acted appropriately) could not be ordered to pay their costs. The fact that couples of very modest circumstances will have to go into great debt, or be simply unable, to defend themselves against allegations of child abuse is hard to justify. The Supreme Court rightly raised Article 6 of the European Convention on Human Rights (ECHR) which guarantees a right to a fair trial.

As that case hints, future litigation may centre on the extent to which the restrictions on legal aid infringe people's human rights.[54] The European Court of Human Rights (ECtHR) has

---

[49] Ministry of Justice (2011: para 140, emphasis supplied).
[50] Eekelaar (2011b); George (2012c).
[51] Hunt (2012).
[52] Hunt (2012).
[53] [2012] UKSC 36.
[54] Miles (2011a).

made it clear that the right to fair trial in Article 6 does not mean that someone is automatically entitled to legal aid. However, access to legal aid may be needed to ensure there is 'equality of arms' and therefore a fair trial. In *Airey v Ireland*[55] the court explained in deciding whether a denial of legal aid breached Article 6 the court would take into account:

(i)   the complexity of the case, including procedural and legal issues

(ii) the need to present evidence and examine witnesses and use expert evidence; and

(iii) the person's own capacity and circumstances.[56]

In *P, C and S v United Kingdom*[57] the court emphasised that fairness was key to deciding if there was a breach of Article 6:

> [T]here is the importance of ensuring the appearance of the fair administration of justice and a party in civil proceedings must be able to participate effectively, *inter alia*, by being able to put forward the matters in support of his or her claims. Here, as in other aspects of Art 6, the seriousness of what is at stake for the applicant will be of relevance to assessing the adequacy and fairness of the procedures. (at para [91])

As that quote indicates, if the court is satisfied that a person can appropriately represent their own interests or that pro bono representation is adequate, there is no breach of Article 6.[58]

The ECtHR may be particularly concerned in cases involving children. The Children's Commissioner has expressed grave concerns that restrictions on legal aid will impact negatively on children. As she points out, even if children are not parties to litigation, parents are often relied upon to represent children's interests.[59] It is interesting to note that Parliament's Joint Committee on Human Rights, in a recent review of the impact of the legal aid cuts, concluded that the Government 'cannot rely upon this scheme as it currently operates in order to avoid breaches of access to justice rights'.[60]

English judges too have become increasingly aware of the significance of Article 6. The Judicial Working Group on Litigants in Person[61] reports that: 'A withdrawal of funding of this magnitude has the potential to undermine the right to access to justice and as a result the rule of law itself.' In *Kinderis v Kineriene*[62] Holman J refused to continue with a child abduction case where a mother was representing herself with no knowledge of the law and very limited English. He allowed an adjournment to allow her to appeal against the refusal to grant her legal aid, suggesting that to continue the case could risk unfairness under Article 6. In *Re L (Application Hearing: Legal Representation)*[63] it was accepted that a father with a history of mental disorder was a 'vulnerable litigant' and it would breach his Article 6 rights to require him to represent himself. In *RP and others v United Kingdom*[64] a mother with learning difficulties, who lacked capacity to litigate, was denied legal representation in a public law case. This was found to breach her Article 6 rights. In the following case Munby P made it clear the breach of human rights is not just a matter of technical law, but of basic humanity and fairness:

---

[55] (1979) 2 EHRR 305.
[56] *NJDB v The United Kingdom* (App. No. 76760/12).
[57] Judgment of 16 July 2002.
[58] *NJDB v The United Kingdom* (App. No. 76760/12).
[59] Office of the Children's Commissioner (2012).
[60] Joint Committee on Human Rights (2014: para 142).
[61] Judicial Working Group on Litigants in Person (2013).
[62] [2013] EWHC 4139 (Fam).
[63] [2013] EWCA Civ 267.
[64] [2013] 1 FLR 744.

> **CASE:** *Re D (Non-Availability of Legal Aid) (No. 2)* [2015] EWFC 2
>
> The President of the Family Division (Munby P) heard a case involving the removal of children from parents so they could be placed with prospective adopters. Both parents had learning difficulties, but were not eligible for legal aid. He was concerned this might breach their Article 6 and 8 rights and continued:
>
> > A parent facing the permanent removal of their child must be entitled to put their case to the court, however seemingly forlorn, and that must surely be as much the right of a parent with learning disabilities (as in the case of the mother) or a parent who lacks capacity (as in the case of the father) as of any other parent. It is one of the oldest principles of our law – it goes back over 400 centuries to the earliest years of the seventeenth century – that no-one is to be condemned unheard. I trust that all involved will bear this in mind.
> >
> > This is a case about three human beings. It is a case which raises the most profound issues for each of these three people. The outcome will affect each of them for the rest of their lives. Even those of us who spend our lives in the family courts can have but a dim awareness of the agony these parents must be going through as they wait, and wait, and wait, and wait, to learn whether or not their child is to be returned to them. Yet for much of the time since their son was taken from them – for far too much of that time – the focus of the proceedings has had to be on the issue of funding, which has indeed been the primary focus of the last three hearings. The parents can be forgiven for thinking that they are trapped in a system which is neither compassionate nor even humane.[65]

Cases of denial of access to justice are not limited to those where legal aid is denied. Even if legal aid is granted there can still be difficulties in finding a lawyer who will deal with a legal aid family law case. The House of Commons Justice Committee[66] found 14 local authorities for which there were no lawyers taking on civil legal aid cases. The Women's Aid[67] survey identified 71 per cent of respondents who found it difficult or very difficult to find legal aid solicitors; 23 per cent had to travel more than 15 miles to access legal advice and an additional 34 per cent between 6 and 15 miles. As the number of legal aid cases reduces it becomes harder for firms to make the work worthwhile given the bureaucracy in accessing the legal aid and dealing with the legal aid authorities. That paperwork may be justifiable for a firm dealing with a large quantity of work; with a smaller number of cases it becomes less worth the effort and expense.

Article 6 may not be the only relevant human right in the debate. Shazia Choudhry and I[68] have argued that the state has an obligation to protect victims of domestic abuse from behaviour which interferes with their rights under Article 3 and 8. Where the LASPO reforms lead to victims being denied protection or where it requires them to be questioned by their abuser in court, this may infringe those rights.

B Litigants in person

One might have confidently predicted that following the implementation of the 2012 Act we would have seen a sharp decrease in court hearings and a greater use of mediation or other 'self-help' remedies for people with family problems. However, surprisingly, the number of

---

[65] Paras 21 and 22.
[66] House of Commons Justice Committee (2015).
[67] (2015).
[68] Choudhry and Herring (2017).

applications to the family courts has, in many areas of work, increased. Following LASPO there was an increase in the number of family law cases, to a total of 57,757 in the second quarter of 2013 and 65,553 in the first quarter of 2020.[69] Why has this happened?

The explanation seems to be that couples with disputes over their family issues are representing themselves. In the past a person with a family dispute may have consulted a solicitor who might have been able to negotiate a settlement, deal with the matter with a formal letter or advise that the case had no merit. All of these would have avoided a hearing. As there is no legal aid to provide these services people simply turn straight to the court and hence the increase in the number of applications.

The belief that individuals denied legal aid will be able to mediate their disputes or litigate in person may be based on false assumptions about the kind of people currently receiving legal aid who end up in bitter legal disputes.[70] Jo Miles and colleagues[71] point out that such cases are not rare. They note that 71 per cent of those eligible for legal aid for family problems reported mental health problems. Liz Trinder[72] notes in her international analysis of litigants in person (LIPs) that they are often people who are highly vulnerable, possess limited abilities to communicate, and are victims of domestic abuse.[73] She concludes:

> The international evidence is clear that LIPs have a wide range of support needs, but that it is very difficult to provide accessible, consistent and effective support for all LIPs that will enable them to put their case forward effectively whilst at the same time not disadvantaging represented parties or overburdening already stretched judges and court staff.

The idea that those with mental health problems, addictions or limited English should represent themselves or use mediation is bizarre.[74]

The dramatic increase in the numbers of litigants in person has put judges in a difficult position. They must engage directly with people who in the emotion of the situation may be ill placed to understand what is being said.[75] Judges who are used to being presented with finely honed arguments by experienced lawyers must now face long rambling speeches from fraught individuals. Cases that used to commence with the paperwork in place and the arguments well articulated must now start with little or no paperwork and no agreement on any issues.

A flavour of some of the problems is caught in this quote by Black LJ in *Re R (Care Proceedings: Welfare Analysis of Changed Circumstances)*.[76] She explained:

> More and more litigants appear in front of us in person. Where, as here, the appellant is unrepresented, this requires all those involved in the appeal process to take on burdens that they would not normally have to bear. The court office finds itself having to attempt to make sure that the parties to the litigation are notified of the appeal because litigants in person do not always know who should be served; the only respondent named by M here was LA. The bundles that the court requires in order to determine the appeal are often not provided by the litigant, or are incomplete, and proper papers have to be assembled by the court, not infrequently at the request of the judges allocated to hear the case when they embark upon their preparation for the hearing just days before it is due to start. The grounds of appeal that can properly be advanced have to be identified by the judge hearing the permission application and the arguments in support of them may have to be pinpointed by the court hearing the appeal.

[69] Ministry of Justice (2020). Especially given COVID, one might have expected this number to have dropped.
[70] Hunter (2014a).
[71] Miles, Balmer and Smith (2012).
[72] Trinder (2014a).
[73] See also Kaganas (2017).
[74] House of Commons Justice Committee (2011).
[75] Lethem (2014).
[76] [2014] EWCA Civ 597.

> The court has no extra resources to respond to these added challenges . . . Everyone involved in public and private law children cases is attempting to achieve the best possible result for the children whose welfare is at the heart of the proceedings and, without legal representatives for the parties, that task is infinitely more difficult.

It is not surprising that extreme concern is being expressed by the judiciary.[77] Sir James Munby, the President of the Family Division, in September 2016 claimed there was a 'clear and imminent crisis' facing the Family Division due to the workload on the courts.[78]

Hunter and Trinder[79] in their study found only a tiny minority of litigants in person were able to competently deal with all matters of litigation. They go on to explain:

> Many LIPs did not grasp foundational legal principles or concepts such as the importance of disclosure or the expectation of negotiation or settlement to forestall contested hearings. Two key 'legal' tasks – the preparation of bundles and cross-examination – were beyond the capacity of most LIPs. The legally aided group had higher levels of drug, alcohol and mental health problems, and a higher proportion of non-English speakers requiring interpreters.

In *Azizi v Aghaty*[80] Holman J bemoaned the lot of a district court judge who was expected to deal with a case involving complex issues of international family law with two unrepresented litigants both of whom had limited English, but had been denied legal aid.

The National Audit Office[81] has also expressed concern at the financial costs that LIPs are causing the court system. The legal aid budget may be falling, but that must be weighed against the increased costs for the court services.

There is now a long list of cases[82] where the judges have spoken strongly about the problems caused to the courts from LIPs and the 'gross unfairness'.[83] The House of Commons Justice Committee (2015: para 107) explained:

> The family courts make decisions which often have life-long consequences for the children involved. The courts need the best evidence possible to make the right decisions; this will not be achieved by putting vulnerable witnesses through cross-examination by their abuser.

Not only can LIPs cause problems for the courts, they also can be their own worst enemy. They may fail to present to court their strongest arguments in the clearest way, and their presentation itself may harm the case. In *Re W (A Child)*[84] a mother whose child had been abused by her paternal grandfather opposed the father having contact and was representing herself in court. Despite the court ordering that the father should have contact, she persisted in refusing to allow it. The Court of Appeal ordered that the child should now live with the father. The Court justified this on the basis that the mother was 'obsessed' with the earlier child abuse and had persisted in not allowing contact. No doubt the case involved complex issues, but one wonders whether the fact the mother had to represent herself meant she came across as more emotionally vulnerable than would have been the case had she been represented by a lawyer. Further, that had she been represented, her lawyer would have strongly advised her against taking such

---

[77] Judicial Executive Board to the Justice Select Committee Inquiry on Civil Legal Aid (2013).

[78] Bowcott (2016).

[79] Hunter and Trinder (2015).

[80] [2016] EWHC 110 (Fam).

[81] National Audit Office (2014).

[82] E.g. *Kinderis v Kineriene* [2013] EWHC 4139 (Fam); *Re B (A Child) (Private Law Fact Finding – Unrepresented Father)* [2014] EWHC 700 (Fam); *Q v Q* [2014] EWFC 7; *Q v Q (No. 2)* [2014] EWFC 31; *Re H* [2014] EWFC B127; *Re D (A Child)* [2014] EWFC 39; *CD v ED* [2014] EWFC B153; *Re D (A Child) (No. 2)* [2015] EWFC 2; and *Re K & H (Children: Unrepresented Father: Cross-Examination of Child)* [2015] EWFC 1.

[83] *MG v JG* [2015] EWHC 564.

[84] [2014] EWCA Civ 772.

a stark line against contact. Those without legal representation lose out not only on a source of information, but also on having a counsellor who can guide and warn them on issues arising from the case. Perhaps even more seriously there are reports of violence breaking out between parties in courts, without lawyers being there to lower the emotional temperature.[85]

Another alternative to being a LIP is to find someone who will represent you for free. Unless you have a friend willing to do this, you could seek to use 'McKenzie friends' who will offer you free services, or at a rate significantly lower than solicitors.[86] Recent research indicated there were around 100 McKenzie Friends offering to work for fees.[87] It is difficult to determine how many there are working for free. The problem is that these people may well not be legally qualified and may have a particular agenda in mind. For example, they are fathers' rights advocates or have religious motivations. While there are undoubtedly some who offer a good service, the lack of regulation or proper training can be concerning.

C Parties facing litigants in person

While the potential unfairness to those who must represent themselves is obvious, what is less obvious is the harm to those who must face a litigant in person. This is particularly problematic in a case of a victim of domestic violence. Imagine a dispute over child arrangements, with a mother who has been able to prove that the father was abusive towards her. She is able to obtain legal aid. However, he cannot and is representing himself. He may well wish to challenge her allegations of domestic abuse in court and he will be required to cross-examine her. As Coy et al.[88] found in their survey, that can be highly traumatic for the victim. One woman said that 'it's like going through the abuse again'. They found women being emotionally and psychologically ground down; panic, depression and sleeplessness being caused by having to litigate against their former abuser without legal representation.[89] This seems to be a serious breach of the human rights of victims of domestic abuse.[90]

In *Re K and H (Private Law: Public Funding)*[91] a father, who had been denied legal aid and was representing himself, was accused by a girl of sexual abuse. The father denied it. The judge found it would be utterly improper for the father to cross-examine the girl. The Court of Appeal thought the judge should conduct the cross-examination or a justice's clerk or a guardian appointed for the children. It was not possible to require the Lord Chancellor to fund legal representation for the cross-examination. The problem is that none of the alternative suggestions of the Court of Appeal seem entirely satisfactory, especially given the gravity of the issue.

Nothing has been done to resolve this issue and the judiciary are becoming increasingly vocal about it. In *Re A (A minor: Fact Finding: Unrepresented Party)*[92] Hayden J said:

> It is a stain on the reputation of our family justice system that a judge can still not prevent a victim being cross-examined by an alleged perpetrator. This may not have been the worst or most extreme example but it serves only to underscore that the process is inherently and profoundly unfair. I would go further it is, in itself, abusive. For my part, I am simply not prepared to hear a case in this way again. I cannot regard it as consistent with my judicial oath and my responsibility to ensure fairness between the parties.

[85] Holt and Kelly (2014).
[86] Barry (2019).
[87] Smith, Hitchings, and Sefton (2017).
[88] Coy, Scott, Tweedale and Perks (2015).
[89] See also All-Party Parliamentary Group on Domestic Violence (2016).
[90] Choudhry and Herring (2017).
[91] [2015] EWCA Civ 543.
[92] [2017] EWHC 1195 (Fam).

In *Re J (Children)*[93] the Court of Appeal agreed with these concerns and quoted with approval from a Women's Aid publication:

> Allowing a perpetrator of domestic abuse who is controlling, bullying and intimidating to question their victim when in the family court regarding child arrangement orders is a clear disregard for the impact of domestic abuse, and offers perpetrators of abuse another opportunity to wield power and control.

The Court of Appeal accepted that in these cases the alternative was stark: 'Either the alleged abuser conducts the cross examination himself (possibly with the assistance of a McKenzie Friend) or questions are put on his behalf to the witness by the judge.' After discussion they indicated that of these two options 'the least worst is likely to be that of the judge assuming the role of questioner'. The Domestic Abuse Bill 2020, when enacted will prevent a victim of domestic abuse being cross-examined by an alleged abuser.

D Expert witnesses

In many complex cases an expert report is required if the court is to make an effective assessment of what is in the child's welfare. A court has the power under s. 13(6) to require a report from an expert if necessary to assist the court to resolve the proceedings justly. The difficulty arises as to who will pay for the expert. If the parties are representing themselves, they are unlikely to be able to provide the funding. Even if legal aid is awarded to a client there may be great difficulty in persuading the legal aid agency to fund expert witnesses. In *JG v Lord Chancellor*[94] it was held that the decision not to provide legal aid to fund an expert in a private law case under the Children Act was unlawful.[95]

E LASPO: the future

In 2019 the Ministry of Justice undertook a post-implementation review of LASPO. The Review[96] praised the saving created by LASPO, stating that: 'In 2017-18, the scope of the changes saw legal aid spending fall by approximately £90m in civil cases and £160m in family cases.' It acknowledged that there were problems with 'legal aid deserts' where no firms took on legal aid work, and in people struggling to access legal advice. This led to further proposals based on this premise:

> For too long our approach to supporting access to justice has been concentrated on funding for court disputes. There are too many people entangled in the justice system for a variety of issues, and some may not necessarily need to be there. Our ambition must be to give people the tools to resolve their problems well before this point, before they become legal problems that require a court visit and a lawyer. Early intervention is key and it is upon this that our new vision for legal support is founded.[97]

The proposals state the Government will review the financial thresholds for legal aid entitlement; simplify the exceptional funding scheme; and enhance the support for litigants in person. However, the bulk of the proposals is to promote ways for people to access information online, rather than directly through lawyers:

---

[93] [2018] EWCA Civ 115.
[94] [2014] EWCA Civ 656.
[95] *Q v Q* [2014] EWFC 31.
[96] Ministry of Justice (2019).
[97] Ministry of Justice (2019b).

- We will work collaboratively with providers to develop web based products which bring a range of legal support tools together in one place.

- We will improve the signposting advice and support available from our specialist telephone service and test enhancements to this service.

- We will use funding to encourage the delivery of legal support through technology.

- Recognising that a comprehensive service may offer people an opportunity to support themselves, we will work collaboratively with the legal and advice sector to evaluate the impact of legal support hubs.

Clearly the aim is to divert people away from the court process. Such efforts have not worked to date and it is unclear they will in the future. The faith in online services may be misplaced in family law cases where there are no 'hard and fast' rules which can be stated and so much depends on the particular circumstances of the case. It is hard enough for an experienced lawyer to advise on the outcome of a case, let alone an algorithm. The online system will also only work for those with the language, intellectual and social skills to engage with such products.[98]

In 2019 the former President of the Family Division gave a devastating critique of the family justice system and it is unlikely the reforms will do much to improve it:

> The shocking condition of the court estate today reflects decades of neglect, under-spending and penny-pinching cost-cutting . . . The truth, though those in power will never admit it, is that there is inadequate recognition both of the vital importance of the rule of law and of the equally vital need to ensure that our justice system is properly funded and resourced. Without the rule of law, and without a properly resourced justice system, there can be no democracy, no fair and stable civil society, and, indeed, no thriving economy. The rule of law, and its essential concomitant, a properly resourced justice system, is not some optional extra; at root, the first two responsibilities of any government must be defence – protection from our external enemies – and a justice system adequately resourced to maintain and enhance the rule of law.[99]

7 COVID and family courts

Learning objective 3

Examine the impact of COVID on family court hearings

The lockdown and restrictions on social distancing have had a severe impact on the operation of family justice. During lockdown face-to-face hearings were impossible and online hearings were the only possibility, and after lockdown when face-to-face hearings were permitted, the capacity for courts to conduct these safely were highly limited.

In the early days there were examples of deeply concerning issues around online hearings. One report records a judge saying of one remote hearing:

> [In] a case involving a Polish mother and Egyptian father—both needing interpreters . . . the mother had severe mental health issues such that she now does not have litigation capacity, and at that remote hearing she was screaming constantly throughout the call. It was impossible to manage the hearing and even when she stayed calm the interpreters had to take turns to translate. It just was impossible for anyone to get any flow in their submission. The parents were at

---

[98] For an excellent discussion of online legal resources see Maclean and Dijksterhuis (2019).
[99] Munby (2019); MacFarlane (2020) and MacDonald (2020).

the same venue and her father could be heard whispering or muffling the sound—it felt as if he was trying to tell the mother what to say. In court you would be able to pick up on that, but it felt very uncomfortable to me.[100]

Another judge reported:

The mother, who was at risk of having her four children removed, gave evidence by telephone from her garden shed as there was nowhere else private she could go as she was self-isolating due to COVID-19 and the children were in the house, being cared for by their grandmother. It was unsatisfactory to make any decision without being able to assess the evidence in the round, and unsatisfactory for the mother to give such important evidence in these circumstances. The likelihood of parents involved in care proceedings having a private space from which to attend remote hearings seems low.

Those examples were from the early days of COVID. There is now much greater awareness about the pitfalls of remote hearings, and how to deal with them. Judges have been given a broad discretion to decide whether a remote hearing is appropriate.[101] This has led to a distinction to a range of views being expressed, particularly on the need to see witnesses in person. In *Re P (A Child: Remote Hearing)*[102] McFarlane J thought that in a case where it was alleged that a mother had fabricated (or even induced) illness in her child, the need to see the mother's reaction was a significant factor against a remote hearing. By contrast, Lieven J in *A Local Authority v Mother*[103] stated:

. . . my own view is that is not possible to say as a generality whether it is easier to tell whether a witness is telling the truth in court rather than remotely . . . I agree with Leggatt LJ that demeanour will often not be a good guide to truthfulness. Some people are much better at lying than others and that will be no different whether they do so remotely or in court. Certainly, in court the demeanour of a witness, or anyone else in court, will often be more obvious to the judge, but that does not mean it will be more illuminating.

In *A Local Authority v The mother*[104] Williams J stated:

I should observe that the advantages of physical attendance of a party at court are not confined to the perceived, but perhaps in reality limited, advantage to the judge of being able to look the witness in the eye and assess their demeanour and thus credibility.

Williams J recognised that in the 'vast majority of cases' the credibility of the witness relies 'principally upon the evaluation of the content of their evidence rather than the evaluation of their demeanour'.

The Court of Appeal in *Re A (Children) (Remote Hearing: Care and Placement Orders)*[105] and MacDonald J in *Lancashire County Council v M (COVID-19 Adjournment Application)*[106] stated some further factors to be considered when deciding whether a remote hearing is appropriate:

---

[100] Ryan, Harker, and Rothera (2020).
[101] *Re A (Children) (Remote Hearing: Care and Placement Orders)* [2020] EWCA Civ 583; MacFarlane (2020); Phillimore (2020).
[102] [2020] EWFC 32.
[103] [2020] EWHC 1086 (Fam).
[104] [2020] EWHC 1233 (Fam).
[105] [2020] EWCA Civ 583.
[106] [2020] EWFC 43.

1. The ability of the parties to engage with remote evidence. This might be particularly relevant if one of the parties has a learning difficulty or otherwise finds online material difficult to engage with.

2. The need for an urgent hearing. If a remote hearing is not possible there will almost inevitably be a delay and where a child is, for example, subject to care proceedings it may be an important factor. The Guidance from the President of the Family Division[107] states:

> Whilst a court is not required to hold the child's welfare as the paramount consideration when making case management decisions, the child's welfare and the need to avoid delay will always be a most important factor and may well be determinative in many cases. Making a timely decision as to the child's further care is in essence what each case is about. The child's welfare should be in the forefront of the court's mind throughout the process.

3. The need for a fair and just process for all the parties.

4. The view of the parties on whether a remote hearing is suitable.

5. 'The statutory requirement that all public law children cases are to be completed within 26 weeks and that any extension to the 26 week timetable must be necessary to enable the court to resolve the proceedings justly.'[108]

6. 'Whether there is a special need for urgency, or whether the decision could await a later hearing without causing significant disadvantage to the child or the other parties.'[109]

One option that courts can use is to have hybrid hearings, partly online and partly in person.[110] This might mean that, for example, the evidence of an expert is heard online, while that of a parent is heard in person.

The courts are right to highlight the concern that some litigants will find online proceedings a challenge.[111] The Equality and Human Rights Commission's[112] interim evidence report, *Inclusive Justice, a system designed for all* (released shortly after *Re P* was decided) states:

> We found that video hearings can significantly impede communication and understanding for disabled people with certain impairments, such as a learning disability, autism spectrum disorders and mental health conditions. People with these conditions are significantly over represented in the criminal justice system.

There are also very practical concerns, with reports of individuals running out of data on their mobile phone or not being able to afford to top up data to participate in the process. There are clearly no easy answers to finding a way to deal justly with intense disputes in a way which is timely and COVID-safe. Further issues involve the management of the technology. In *Re C (A Child)*[113] a judge closed her laptop and believed that severed the link with parties, but in fact they were able to continue hearing her making disparaging remarks about one party. A rehearing was required.

[107] McFarlane (2020).
[108] *Lancashire County Council v M (COVID-19 Adjournment Application)* [2020] EWFC 43.
[109] *Lancashire County Council v M (COVID-19 Adjournment Application)* [2020] EWFC 43.
[110] MacDonald (2020).
[111] Munroe and Tautz (2020).
[112] Equality and Human Rights Commission (2020).
[113] [2020] EWCA 987.

8 Mediation

A Introduction

One key principle runs through the Family Justice Review:

> Generally it seems better that parents resolve things for themselves if they can. They are then more likely to come to an understanding that will allow arrangements to change as they and their children change. Most people could do with better information to help this happen. Others need to be helped to find routes to resolve their disputes short of court proceedings.[114]

This shift towards encouraging mediation, rather than the use of lawyers and courts, has been effected through the Legal Aid, Sentencing and Punishment of Offenders Act 2012 and the restrictions on access to legal aid; and the Children and Families Act 2014, which, as we shall see, requires all applicants in family cases to attend a meeting to learn more about mediation.

The Legal Aid Agency will pay for a MIAM (Mediation Information & Assessment Meeting), lasting up to two hours.[115] The MIAM will inform the couple about the availability of mediation and provide funding for those who are eligible.[116] Practice Direction 3A explains:

> Attendance at a MIAM provides an opportunity for the parties to a dispute to receive information about the process of mediation and to understand the benefits it can offer as a way to resolve disputes. At that meeting, a trained mediator will discuss with the parties the nature of their dispute and will explore with them whether mediation would be a suitable way to resolve the issues on which there is disagreement.[117]

As already mentioned, although it was expected that the cutbacks in legal aid would increase, in fact the number of publicly funded mediation cases dropped by 32 per cent in the year following the restrictions and there was a 51 per cent reduction in the number of couples attending meetings to learn about mediation. In 2012–13, the year before LASPO, there were 31,000 mediation assessments and 14,000 mediation starts. By 2019–20, the numbers had dramatically fallen to 12,175 mediation assessments and 7,557 mediation starts.[118]

It has been suggested that lawyers were a significant cause of referrals for mediation, and this source has been lost.[119] This seems a very plausible explanation as prior to LASPO 80 per cent of publicly funded MIAMs were referred by legal aid lawyers and post-LASPO this dropped to 10 per cent. In a review undertaken in 2017 the Ministry of Justice accepted that LASPO has not had the intended effect of encouraging couples to use mediation.[120]

Perhaps in response to such figures the Children and Families Act 2014 now requires parties to attend a MIAM before making an application for 'family proceedings'.[121] These include applications for a child arrangements order, a parental responsibility order, a special guardianship order and financial orders. Consent orders are not included so if the couple have reached an agreement over the issue through negotiation or mediation, they are not required to attend a MIAM but can apply to have an order of the court in line with the terms of the agreement. Although that is the formal picture, one survey found 31 per cent of respondent lawyers saying

---

[114] Norgrave (2012: para 104).
[115] Morris (2013).
[116] Morris (2013).
[117] Para 10.
[118] Ministry of Justice (2020c).
[119] Hunter (2017); Emmerson and Platt (2014).
[120] Dugan (2017).
[121] Para 12 and 13 define these in detail.

that in their courts applicants were permitted to make applications even though they had not attended a MIAM.[122] Some 45 per cent reported no change in the number of MIAMs since they became compulsory. Indeed, in 2019–20 successfully completed MIAMs numbering 4,557 were recorded out of a total of 54,930 private law applications, suggesting that the attempt to require people to consider alternatives to court proceedings has had little success.

Before issuing a family proceeding an applicant must show that they have attended a MIAM, have been issued a 'mediation confirmation' from a mediator, stating the couple have received information and advice about mediation, or that a 'mediator's exemption' applies because the case is not suitable for mediation, or the couple fall within an exemption.[123] The exemptions are found in Family Proceedings Rules, para 8(1):

Domestic violence

(a) there is evidence of domestic violence, as specified in Practice Direction 3A; or Child protection concerns

(b) –

   (i) a child would be the subject of the application; and

   (ii) that child or another child of the family who is living with that child is currently –

      (aa) the subject of enquiries by a local authority under section 47 of the 1989 Act; or

      (ab) the subject of a child protection plan put in place by a local authority; or

Urgency

(c) the application must be made urgently because –

   (i) there is risk to the life, liberty or physical safety of the prospective applicant or his or her family or his or her home; or

   (ii) any delay caused by attending a MIAM would cause—

      (aa) a risk of harm to a child;

      (ab) a risk of unlawful removal of a child from the United Kingdom, or a risk of unlawful retention of a child who is currently outside England and Wales;

      (ac) a significant risk of a miscarriage of justice;

      (ad) unreasonable hardship to the prospective applicant; or

      (ae) irretrievable problems in dealing with the dispute (including the irretrievable loss of significant evidence); or

   (iii) there is a significant risk that in the period necessary to schedule and attend a MIAM, proceedings relating to the dispute will be brought in another state in which a valid claim to jurisdiction may exist, such that a court in that other State would be seised of the dispute before a court in England and Wales.

Other exemptions include the bankruptcy of the party or that the parties have a certificate from a mediator confirming the case is inappropriate for the couple to attend.

It is important to appreciate the somewhat limited nature of the requirement to attend a MIAM. First, only the applicant needs to attend.[124] Second, the requirement is to attend the information session. It does not require the parties to undertake mediation. In **Rosalba Alassini**

---

[122] Blacklaws (2014).

[123] Practice Direction 3a – Family Mediation Information & Assessment Meetings (MIAMS).

[124] Practice Direction 3a – Family Mediation Information & Assessment Meetings (MIAMS). See Relate (2014) for an argument that both parties should be required to attend, although it is hard to see what punishment could be imposed on the respondent who failed to attend.

and Others[125] it was held by the European Court of Justice that forcing people to use mediation rather than courts interfered with their human rights. Given the low take up of mediation it might be argued that the requirement to attend a MIAM does little more than inconvenience the parties, delay the case and increase costs.

Before considering whether the shift to mediation is to be welcomed, mediation must be defined.

B What is mediation?

Learning objective 4

Describe the nature of mediation

It is important to distinguish between reconciliation and mediation. The aim of reconciliation is to encourage the parties to abandon the divorce petition and to rescue their marriage. Mediation, however, accepts the fact of breakdown and attempts to assist the parties in deciding what should happen in the future.[126] It may happen that in the course of working together to arrange their life post-divorce, the parties become reconciled, but that is not the purpose of mediation. The core goal in mediation is 'to help separating and divorcing couples to reach their own agreed joint decisions about future arrangements; to improve communications between them; and to help couples work together on the practical consequences of divorce with particular emphasis on their joint responsibilities to cooperate as parents in bringing up their children'.[127]

C The role of the mediator

Here are four models a mediator could use:[128]

1. *Minimal intervention.* This model requires the mediator to ensure there is effective communication between the parties, but it is not the job of the mediator to influence the content of the agreement.[129] So even if the mediator believes that the parties are reaching an agreement that is wholly unfair to one side, the mediator should not try to correct the balance. At the heart of this model is the notion that the agreement should be the parties' own decision. If the agreement seems fair to them, then it is not for anyone else to declare it unfair. Marion Stevenson has called this the 'client self-determination model'.[130]

2. *Directive intervention.* Under this model the mediator might provide additional information and seek to influence the content of the agreement if the proposed agreement is clearly unfair to one side or the other. He or she may try to persuade one or both parties to change their views, and may attempt to persuade the parties to agree to the arrangements the mediator believes are most suitable. One trainer of mediators encourages them to 'take their gloves off' and fight for the interests of children, ensuring that the parents reach agreements in the child's best interests.[131] However, most mediators accept that ultimately the decision is for the parties to reach themselves and the parties are free under this model to reject the views of the mediator.[132]

---

[125] Joined Cases C-317/08, C-318/08, C-319/08 and C-320/08, 18 March 2010.
[126] See Leach (2005) for a discussion of what mediation is.
[127] Lord Chancellor's Department (1995: para 6.17).
[128] Roberts (1988).
[129] Stylianou (2011).
[130] Stevenson (2015).
[131] Schaffer (2007).
[132] Hitchings and Miles (2016).

3. **Therapeutic intervention.** Here the mediator focuses on the relationship between the parties. This model promotes the belief that the dispute is merely a symptom of a broken relationship. The time spent in mediation may not therefore focus on the actual issues in dispute, but on trying to improve the parties' relationship generally.

4. **'Med-Arb'.** The couple agree to mediate, but if they cannot reach agreement the mediator becomes an arbitrator and determines a solution, based on the parties' discussions, and the parties agree to be bound by their decision.[133] This is a radical change in the traditional model of mediation and it has few proponents to date, although a notable supporter of a version of this is Peter Harris.[134] He proposes separating couples meet a 'lawyer commissioner' who would discuss the case with the parties. The first aim would be to facilitate an agreement. If that was not possible, the commissioner would decide what order would be appropriate and recommend it to the court. Unless the court objected to it, an order would be made in these terms.

In the UK the model of minimalist intervention is one which is generally promoted.[135] But this model does not render the mediator powerless. Most mediators hold a screening meeting before starting mediation and if, for example, it becomes clear that there has been serious violence in the past, they will refuse to go ahead with the mediation. Further, if during the course of the mediation the mediator is concerned that one party is being taken advantage of, it is always open to the mediator to stop the mediation and suggest that the parties seek legal advice.[136]

Maclean and Eekelaar[137] in their study found that in fact there were numerous examples of mediators giving advice to the parties about the best process for the discussion and the outcome. As they go on to argue, the distinction between providing information, but not advice, which is often relied upon by mediators to explain their neutral role, is not a firm distinction. For example, is the statement 'normally children who are 10 years old are allowed to decide which parent to live with' advice or information?

Rachel Blakey[138] in her study found that mediators did regularly intervene and were required to do so by their professional guidance. This is most notable where there are issues of domestic abuse; where one party is seen to be unfairly pressurising the others; and where the interests of children are at stake. We need, she suggests, to acknowledge that the mediator neutrality model is outdated and be more explicit about when and how mediators should intervene.

Marion Stevenson, a prominent British mediator, sees three key elements for a mediator: empathy, impartiality and questioning.[139] Empathy requires the mediator to be aware of the emotions that may underpin the views of the parties. Impartiality means 'mediation is a problem-solving activity in which the impartiality of the mediator enables people to seek and find the solutions that are going to fit the situation best. Mediators need to be scrupulous about not advising or pressurising towards any outcomes: if not they risk getting drawn into disputes as judges of rights and wrongs and losing the trust of one or both parties. They also risk

---

[133] Hitchings and Miles (2016).

[134] Harris (2016).

[135] UK College of Mediators (2000: para 42). But see S. Roberts (2000) who suggests there is variation in practice over the style of mediation used.

[136] The contents of mediation are to be kept privileged and cannot usually be referred to in later proceedings: *DB v PO* [2004] EWHC 2064 (Fam).

[137] Maclean and Eekelaar (2016).

[138] Blakey (2020).

[139] Stevenson (2013).

disempowering people in terms of responsibility for decision-making.' Questioning requires that mediators keep asking questions about what is the best approach.

A further distinction in styles of mediation is referred to by Maclean and Eekelaar.[140] They note that some mediators use 'structured mediation', where the mediator seeks to find an agreement which meets as many of the preferred outcomes of each party as possible. Others use 'transformative mediation', which 'is designed to enhance the participants' appreciation of each other's feelings and perspectives'. This might lead to the parties changing their preferences. Co-mediation is possible where two mediators are used, perhaps with one being a lawyer and the other trained in therapeutic approaches.[141]

It may be that there is a changing attitude to this issue[142] and that increasingly mediators in England are being interventionist. All mediators would encourage parties to have good relationships with each other and to put the interests of their children first.[143] But that is seeking to influence the parties' agreements, albeit in a relatively uncontroversial way. It may simply be impossible for a mediator not to rely on norms of some kind.[144] Some mediators claim that it is permissible to seek to persuade the parties to adopt current societal or cultural norms, such as that the interests of children should come first.[145] What is not permissible is for the mediator to seek to impose his or her own norms on the couple.[146] However, this view is based on being able to draw a reasonably clear line between which norms are social and which are personal. One suggestion is that as long as the mediator is open about what norms he or she is bringing to the discussion, and the couple accept this, the mediator is acting appropriately.[147]

There is a fierce debate over whether mediation is desirable. It is important to separate out two distinct arguments in favour of mediation. First there is the claim that mediation produces better outcomes for families in dispute. Second, there is the argument in favour of mediation as a way of reducing the costs to the state. Both of these are disputed. There is no doubt that in the future mediation is going to play a central role in family justice. Notably, many family solicitors are now training to be mediators, accepting that there may be less work for lawyers and more for mediators in the years ahead.[148]

Now the arguments over the benefits and disadvantages of mediation must be considered.[149]

D The benefits of mediation

Learning objective 5

Explore the arguments for and against mediation

The following are some of the possible benefits of mediation:

1. Central to the arguments in favour of mediation is the idea that there is no 'right answer' to a particular dispute. If the parties reach a solution which is right for them, no one else should be able to regard their agreement as the wrong one. It could be said to be none of the state's business to seek to interfere in the arrangement the parties have reached. In part, mediation is fuelled by a belief that the court cannot claim that there is a particular solution

---

[140] Maclean and Eekelaar (2016).
[141] Hope (2019).
[142] Wilson (2009).
[143] Stepan (2010).
[144] MacFarlane (2002).
[145] Belhorn (2005).
[146] See the discussion in Stepan (2010).
[147] Irvine (2009).
[148] Stevenson (2012a).
[149] As Mantle (2001: 151) argues, much more research is required before it is possible properly to assess the advantages of mediation.

that is 'just' or 'in the best interests of the child' because there are no agreed community values the law could use as a basis for such a solution. Indeed, the House of Lords itself has accepted that in many cases a variety of solutions could be appropriate and there is not necessarily a right or wrong one.[150]

There are three key issues here. The first is whether it is correct that there is no right answer for a court to declare. If there is not, then the solution reached by the parties is likely to be as good as the solution reached by anyone else. If, however, you do not accept this and believe that it is possible to state that some solutions are better than others, then the second key issue is whether there is a good reason to believe that the court is more likely to find a better solution than the parties in mediation. Thirdly, even if you accept that some solutions are better than others and that the court is more likely than the parties to find a better solution, there is still the issue of whether the state, through the courts, should be able to impose the right answer (or *a* right answer) on the parties. The law might want to set down a right answer on the divorcing couple because there are interests of either third parties or of the state which justify forcing a solution on the parties.[151] So, for example, many argue that mediation is not acceptable because it does not adequately protect the interests of the child. There is nothing to prevent the parents reaching an agreement in mediation which does not promote the interests of the child. However, such an argument would need to demonstrate that allowing judges to resolve disputes over children has a better chance of promoting children's interests than letting parents reach the decision.

2. Supporters of mediation claim that the solutions agreed by the parties are more effective than court orders in the long term,[152] although one study found that only one half of all mediated agreements were intact six months after they were reached.[153] There are three aspects to the argument that mediation produces more effective results. The first is that because the parties have reached the agreement themselves, they will more easily be able to renegotiate it together if difficulties with the agreement subsequently arise. Secondly, the solution reached through mediation will be one which the parties can tailor to their particular lifestyles rather than being a formula applied by lawyers or judges to deal with 'these kinds of cases'. Thirdly, it is argued that, as mediation can be hard work and emotionally exhausting, the parties will therefore feel more committed to the agreement than if it had been given to them by a judge.

3. Mediation enables the parties to communicate more effectively. The White Paper on mediation criticises the use of lawyers as detrimental to communication:

> Marriage breakdown and divorce are . . . intimate processes, and negotiating at arm's length through lawyers can result in misunderstandings and reduction in communication between spouses. Lawyers have to translate what their clients say and pass it on to the other side. The other party's lawyers then translate again and pass this on to his or her client. There can thus be a good deal of misunderstanding and a good deal of anger about what is said and how it is said.[154]

---

[150] *Piglowska v Piglowski* [1999] 2 FLR 763 HL

[151] Or even that there are rights that the divorcing couple have themselves which they should not be permitted to negotiate away in the process of mediation.

[152] HM Government (2004: para 2). For a discussion of the evidence against this proposition, see Eekelaar, Maclean and Beinart (2000: 16) and Wright (2007).

[153] Mantle (2001: 141). He regards this rate as impressive, given the level of conflict between many parties in court cases. For other studies finding no evidence that mediated agreements were longer lasting than court orders, see Davis *et al.* (2000: 101) and Walker (2004a: 142).

[154] Lord Chancellor's Department (1995: para 5.19).

Opponents of mediation argue that lawyers can filter out particularly offensive communications and so in fact reduce bitterness, while mediation, by contrast, can increase bitterness. It is said that placing people whose relationship is breaking down in a room together is bound to generate animosity and discord. Despite these arguments, it must be agreed that if mediation enables the parties to talk to each other effectively, it has given them an invaluable gift. The question is: how many couples are helped and how many might find that the process of mediation exacerbates bitterness? To this we have no clear answer.

Another aspect of this argument is that supporters of mediation claim that family disputes are unsuitable for court hearings. It is argued that court hearings work reasonably well in finding out past facts: 'who did what to whom and when'; but are less effective in building up ongoing relationships. In other words, the court procedure works best if the parties are never going to have to see one another again. Mediation, it is claimed, is a more suitable basis for a long-term relationship.

4. A linked argument to the one made above is that mediation is a better forum for resolving the emotional issues involved in divorce. The mediation process can not only help to resolve the dispute but perhaps also help the parties to come to terms with their feelings about the other person and begin the post-breakdown healing process. One mediator claims that mediation enables parties to express their anger and notions of blame more effectively than the legal process.[155] This might be why, on successful mediation, parties report high levels of satisfaction with the result. While this is true where the procedure is successful, where it is unsuccessful the failure might simply increase the emotional anguish. Indeed, one psychologist has warned of the dangers of encouraging parties to put their anger to one side 'for the sake of the children', as mediators often encourage parties to do.[156]

5. Mediation gives time for all issues which are important to the parties to be discussed. It has been a complaint of the legal process that it 'transforms' the parties' disputes. Their arguments are put into legal terminology and some issues that might be of concern to them are ignored. For example, if a husband and wife were using lawyers and wanted help in resolving a dispute over who should keep their goldfish, lawyers would refuse to spend much time on this, regarding it as a trivial issue. Certainly, a judge would not be impressed if asked to rule on who should keep the goldfish. By contrast, in mediation any matter which is important to the parties can be discussed and they can put their arguments in the language they wish to use rather than transforming the issue through legal terminology. Perhaps the real concern here is public funding. Should public funds be used to resolve what appear to be trivial issues, whether in mediation or the courts? It could also be argued that the use of formal lawyer's language helps avoid antagonism between the parties, which might occur if more open language was used.

6. Mediation saves costs, or at least the Government certainly hoped that mediation would save costs. By using just one mediator rather than two lawyers, and with the hourly rate for mediators being generally less than that for lawyers, savings could be made. The Law Commission suggested that the average mediation was £550 per case, while £1,565 was the average legal aid bill per case using lawyers.[157] In fact, whether or not mediation saves money depends on the success rate of mediation. The present research indicates that if all

---

[155] Richards (2001).
[156] Day Sclater (1999: 180).
[157] Law Commission Report 192 (1990).

couples were required to attend state-subsidised mediation it would be likely to lead to increased, not reduced, costs.[158] This is because of the extra costs involved when mediation fails. The Newcastle study (based on people volunteering for mediation) suggested that only about 39 per cent of mediations were wholly successful, 41 per cent were partially successful and 20 per cent failed.[159] Preliminary findings of a more recent study found that 56 per cent of referrals to mediation (which included couples who had not chosen mediation) went no further than the initial meetings.[160] For the totally failed mediations[161] there are inevitably greater costs than if the parties had gone to lawyers to begin with, without using mediation. If mediation is partly successful, the parties still need to consult lawyers to resolve the remaining issues. But asking a lawyer to resolve 50 per cent of a dispute does not mean incurring only 50 per cent of what the cost would have been had he or she been asked to resolve the whole of the dispute. This is because it is the gathering together of all the facts and information that takes up most of a lawyer's time and this will need to be done whether the lawyer is resolving all or only a part of a dispute. So, resolving 50 per cent of a dispute may cost 75 per cent of what the fee would have been for resolving all of a dispute, in which case it is not clear that mediation actually saves costs.[162] Even if the mediation is completely successful, there are some who believe the costs will be greater.[163]

An important study looking at the comparative costs of mediation and solicitor-based negotiation found that mediation could cost between 65 per cent and 115 per cent of the solicitor-based negotiation.[164] The study suggested that if the success rate for mediation fell below 60 per cent (which the evidence suggests it would be very likely to do), there would be no savings. The success rate of mediation for couples who sought mediation after attending an information meeting under the study for the Legal Services Commission was only 34 per cent for financial cases and 45 per cent for children cases.[165] A subsequent study found that 59 per cent of cases were wholly or partially successful for mediation.[166] A study[167] found that the modal costs for not-for-profit mediators was £700; and £1,200 for solicitor-mediators. However, it is impossible to know how much these would have cost had lawyers dealt with these cases. Another survey[168] found that on average a referral to court funded by legal aid cost £930 more than a mediated case. Such statistics are of limited use because it cannot be assumed that the cases that went to court could have been successfully mediated. More importantly, it should not just be a question of whether mediation is cheaper, but whether its benefits (or disadvantages) are worth the expenditure (or savings).[169]

---

[158] Walker (2004a: 134).
[159] In Davis's (2000) research there was 45 per cent agreement on all issues and 24 per cent on some. In Walker (2004a) only 25 per cent reached agreement on all issues.
[160] Parkinson (2013).
[161] The success rate would be likely to be significantly lower if mediation were forced on all divorcing couples, as the survey covered those who had volunteered to participate in mediation.
[162] Davis, Clisby, Cumming et al. (2003: 5) found that 57 per cent of their sample stated that their partner was not keen to resolve the legal disputes and compromise.
[163] Davis, Clisby, Cumming et al. (2003: 5).
[164] Bevan and Davis (1999).
[165] Davis, Finch and Barnham (2003: 9). See similar figures for the success rate for mediation in the pilot studies: Walker (2001b: 3).
[166] House of Commons Public Accounts Committee (2007).
[167] Davis, Finch and Barnham (2003).
[168] Walker (2004a).
[169] Reid (2009).

E The disadvantages of mediation

1. Some opponents of mediation argue that it is in fact impossible for a mediator to be purely impartial.[170] A mediator can influence the content of the agreement, through explicit as well as indirect means, such as body language or the way a mediator responds to one party's proposal.[171] Marion Stevenson gives an example of a mediator who, on hearing the father describe the circumstances in which he visited his children said 'that must be tough'. That was taken by the mother as an indication the mediator supported the husband's view, even though the mediator was probably trying to be empathetic.[172] Piper,[173] in her study of mediation, notes that a mediator's summaries of what has been said to date play a crucial role in the mediation and yet often exclude what the mediator believes to be 'non-relevant matters'. Dingwall and Greatbatch found that mediators had 'the parameters of the permissible',[174] in other words, a band of orders they thought acceptable. There would be no intervention as long as the negotiations were within that band, but if the mediation appeared to be going beyond that band the mediator would seek to influence the discussion.[175]

   If the mediator does directly or indirectly affect the content of the agreement, then there are concerns that mediation will become, in effect, adjudication in secret. The mediator will act like a judge but without having to give any reasons or be publicly accountable for the outcome. For example, one recent study suggested that mediators often spoke of a father's right of contact with his children, even though the courts have expressly denied such a right.[176]

2. One powerful criticism of mediation is that it can work against the interests of the weaker party.[177] Weakness in the bargaining position may stem from three sources: first, a lack of information, coupled with the inability to verify presented information. Every family lawyer would say that it is common for rich spouses to portray themselves as impoverished. As mediation has a less effective method of checking levels of wealth compared with disclosure mechanisms used by lawyers,[178] it is likely to work against the interests of the less-well-off spouse.[179] A party's lack of personal expert knowledge may also impede their bargaining position. For example, if one party is a trained accountant and the other has an aversion to figures then when the parties discuss what should happen to the pension or the endowment mortgage there might be an inequality of power. The second weakness in the bargaining process may result from a lack of negotiation skills. One party may regularly take part in negotiations in the course of his or her work and may be trained to push for an agreement, while the other may not. The third weakness can be psychological. Women, it is argued by

---

[170] As Wilson (2004: 685) points out, a mediator needs to 'connect' with clients and it is difficult to do this without becoming involved.
[171] See Richards (2005: 390) where a mediator discusses the techniques used by mediators if the negotiations are going to lead to what is thought by the mediator to be an inappropriate result.
[172] Stevenson *et al.* (2015).
[173] Piper (1996).
[174] Dingwall and Greatbatch (2001).
[175] One example given was that the mediator did not mind whether the father saw the children one weekend in three or four, but would not be happy if the father was to have no contact.
[176] Davis, Pearce, Bird *et al.* (2000).
[177] See *SA v FA* [2017] EWHC 1731 (Fam) where a woman agreed to a consent order after threats her children would be abducted.
[178] Parkinson (2012).
[179] In their sample, Davis, Clisby, Cumming *et al.* (2003: 5) found high levels of mistrust among those who were mediating.

some, are, in general, by nature conflict-averse.[180] They may more readily agree rather than argue, partly as a result of being socially conditioned to avoid conflict.[181] There is also an argument that women generally may put greater value on things that are not material in value and/or they may have lower self-esteem. It may well be that the wife's primary concern is that she keeps the children, and is willing to agree to anything in order to achieve that goal. One survey of the research concluded that generally women were not putting their own interests first in mediation and therefore were losing out to men, who were.[182] However, these points are controversial and there is in fact much debate over whether women do better or worse using mediation.

There are particular concerns about using mediation where the relationship has been characterised by violence.[183] In such cases mediators themselves accept that mediation is unsuitable because cooperation and proper negotiations can only take place where there is no abuse or fear.[184] The concern is whether the mediators can always ascertain those cases where there has been domestic violence.[185] Particularly difficult are cases where the parties do not regard themselves as victims of domestic violence.[186] In a recent study of mediation it was found that mediators used a variety of techniques to put domestic violence issues to one side.[187] It may be that increased awareness of domestic violence issues and improved training can improve the response to violence among mediators.[188] However, at least one recent study complains that mediators lack the time and training to properly assess for domestic violence.[189] Ann Barlow[190] quotes one abused woman's report of mediation: 'it was just another arena in which he could bully me'.

Perhaps most fundamentally there is an issue about whether, if you believe that people have legal rights, we should have a system which does not guarantee their enforcement. Lord Dyson, a Supreme Court Judge has asked:

> Can it be right that parties who have exercised their right to go to court can be forced to sit down with the individual they believe to have wronged them to try to find a compromise which would probably leave them worse off than had they had their day in court? Leaving aside any human rights issues then, in my view, this simply cannot be right . . . [191]

The Code of Practice states that mediators:

> must advise participants that it is in their own interests to seek independent legal (or other appropriate) advice before reaching any final agreement and warn them of the risks and disadvantages if they do not do so.

---

[180] Doughty (2009). One does not have to accept the gendered way the argument is presented in order to appreciate its weight. For example, if one party is conflict-averse, regardless of whether they are a man or a woman, they may be at a disadvantage.

[181] Walker (2004a: 138) argues that women are more concerned than men with keeping the relationship amicable.

[182] Tilley (2007).

[183] Kaganas and Piper (1994).

[184] Where mediators detect a clear imbalance of power which they cannot counter they should terminate the mediation: Leach (2005).

[185] Barlow *et al.* (2014).

[186] Davis, Clisby, Cumming *et al.* (2003: 5) found that 41 per cent of women and 21 per cent of men in their sample stated that fear of violence made it difficult to resolve issues in their case.

[187] Trinder, Firth and Jenks (2010); Dingwall (2010).

[188] Parkinson (2011).

[189] Morris (2013).

[190] Barlow *et al.* (2014).

[191] Dyson, Lord (2010).

However, the problem is that given the cutbacks in legal aid that legal advice may not be available to less-well-off clients.[192]

3. Mediation can be skewed by the norms of society. Neale and Smart have argued that even if one accepts that the mediators and the law are not influencing the agreement, it is wrong to believe that the values of the parties are the only ones that shape the agreement. The norms of society (which may not be legal norms) will predominate.[193] Researchers have found that 'folk myths' concerning what should happen on divorce can play an important part in the mediation.[194] Specifically, Neale and Smart are concerned that if the parties focus on protecting the children's welfare, then the burden of caring for the children will fall mostly on mothers, based on the common assumption that the woman should look after the children. Further, Neale and Smart are concerned that the money and property will be seen as belonging to the wage earner, most often the husband. So the wife will be in the weaker position of arguing for some of 'his' money, rather than discussing how to distribute 'their' money.[195] Similarly, it might be assumed by the parties that it is best for the child to spend an equal amount of time with each parent, although the empirical data is disputed on that (see Chapter 10). This may be partly circumvented by allowing the parties to receive legal advice before or during mediation, although the more legal advice is used, the greater the costs.

4. As already mentioned, there are concerns over whether mediation affects children's interests. As Richards explains:

> [W]hile mediation may do much to help parents reach agreements and set up workable arrangements for children, it cannot protect children's interests. It must rely on the information about children that the parties bring to the sessions. Necessarily this information will be presented in the light of parental perceptions, hopes, fears, anxieties, and guilt. In most cases this will serve children's interests well enough, but it cannot be termed protection as it is not based on an independent view.[196]

The autonomy argument, which is at the heart of the mediation claim, in one sense privatises the dispute. It is presented as belonging to the couple and is for them to set out. Not everyone agrees that family disputes are simply private matters. As Diduck explains:

> Yet the current zeal for autonomous dispute resolution represents an unproblematic pursuit of a non-relational form of autonomy that uncritically accepts presumptions which separate personal relations from public ones and isolate the autonomous will or interests of individuals from the interests of others.

Diduck argues that the choices we make about family life cannot be detached from the public and social consequences they are made in and produce. A good example is gender expectations and roles in family life which can have a profound impact on gender equality. If, for example, mediated settlements exacerbate women's poverty following relationship breakdown; provide a disincentive to undertake care of children or other dependants; or reward domestic abuse, all of these will have profound impacts on the kind of society we live in.[197]

---

[192] Parkinson (2013).
[193] Neale and Smart (1997).
[194] Piper (1996).
[195] Neale and Smart (1997).
[196] Richards (1995b: 225).
[197] Herring (2013a).

Certainly, there seems little in mediation that will ensure the rights of children are protected.[198] Janet Walker[199] suggests that children's rights under Article 6 to a fair hearing may be infringed if competent children are not heard in mediation. As well as the question of whether mediation will protect the interests of children, there is also the question of whether children should be involved in the proceedings.[200] Many think that children should not be involved in the process, especially given the tension that is often felt early on in a mediation.[201] A middle route is that the mediator should at least meet the child so their voice can be taken into account. Indeed, the Ministry of Justice has indicated support for the principle:

> of child inclusive practice and the adoption of a non-legal presumption that all children and young people aged 10 and above should be offered the opportunity to have their voices heard during dispute resolution processes, including mediation, if they wish.[202]

That is only a recommendation and is not a legal requirement. If it becomes widespread, it will mean the cost of mediation will go up and mediators will need training on dealing with children.

Involving the child in mediation may help repair damaged parental–child relationships.[203] On the other hand, bringing the children into what may be a heated exchange of views may cause distress. Further, it should be noted that encouraging the parties to consider the interests of the children is quite different from a legal system which requires that the interests of the children are paramount.

5. There are doubts whether mediators have the expertise to consider the complex tax and financial issues which may have to be dealt with on divorce.[204] For example, even experienced solicitors struggle with the valuation and sharing of pensions on divorce and most seek expert advice. To expect mediators and the couple to deal with such issues is to expect too much.

6. An argument can be made that mediation does not acknowledge the psychological realities of many divorces. Although it would be nice if every divorcing couple amicably reached an agreement over their children and finances, and that would reassure us that all was well with 'the family', the anger, fear and bitterness mean such a pleasant picture is for the few. It is anger, bitterness and fear that dominate, rather than a desire to sit down and talk the matter out. In a recent study, 25 per cent of those involved in mediation were dissatisfied with the mediation they received.[205] This was of those who had chosen to receive mediation. Mavis Maclean argues that: 'At a time of stress, men and women seek information, advice and support from someone who is committed to helping them, in preference to an impartial facilitator whose primary task is to promote an agreement rather than meet the needs of the individual client.'

7. Even if an agreement is mediated it may still be necessary to obtain a court order to ensure there is no possible legal proceeding later on. However, this may put a lawyer in a

---

198 Dennison (2010).
199 Walker (2013).
200 Voice of the Child Dispute Resolution Advisory Group (2015); Walker and Lake-Carroll (2014 and 2015).
201 Henry and Hamilton (2012), looking at the Australian system, reported some children found being involved in mediation distressing, especially in cases where there had been violence or abuse. They noted most children were positive about their experiences, however.
202 Ministry of Justice (2015b).
203 Bell et al. (2013).
204 Dingwall and Greatbatch (2001).
205 House of Commons Public Accounts Committee (2007).

difficult position. Is the lawyer liable in negligence if they do not point out potential prob-lems with the mediated agreement? The issue was raised **Minkin v Landsberg**[206] where a lawyer put a negotiated agreement into a consent order, but did not point out the disadvan-tages to the wife of the agreement. The wife's claim in negligence failed for several reasons: the lawyer had made it clear that he was simply putting the agreement into the form of a consent order and not offering advice on it; the client was a professional accountant who understood the nature of the agreement; and that even if the solicitor had highlighted the problems the client would have instructed the solicitor to proceed nonetheless. Although that claim failed it does highlight the dangers for a lawyer in such a case. Indeed, it may well be that many lawyers would rather not handle such cases (especially as they will not be well paid) and if so that will cause problems for mediated agreements.

A study by a group based at Exeter University[207] found far higher rates of satisfaction with clients who used negotiation through solicitors or collaborative family law (to be discussed shortly) over mediation. Lisa Parkinson[208] thinks we cannot read too much into such findings:

> This is hardly surprising, since solicitors are partisan even when they work collaboratively, whereas in mediation, divorcing couples and separated parents face each other with an impar-tial mediator who does not support either of them individually. Comparing satisfaction rates of clients who used negotiations via solicitors or collaborative law with satisfaction rates of mediation participants could be described, simplistically, as comparing apples with lemons.

However, others will reply that the fact that solicitors are partisan is a point in favour of solicitor-led negotiation: it means that clients are protected from an inequality in the parties.

F The false dichotomy of mediation and litigation

In considering the benefits and disadvantages of mediation it is important to stress that the choice is not between mediation and litigation in the courtroom, but rather between media-tion and negotiation between lawyers.[209] The image of lawyers aggressively fighting cases out in the courtroom is exceptional.[210] In fact, few cases actually reach the courts for settlement. Davis *et al.* noted:

> . . . some solicitors gave us the impression that they regarded trials of the ancillary relief issue in much the same light as they viewed the white rhino – a possibly mythical creature which was outside their immediate experience.[211]

A recent study of clients' experiences of solicitors found no evidence of lawyers as 'aggressive troublemakers'.[212] A cynical response is to suggest the mediators' profession has worked effec-tively to present lawyers as aggressive litigators to encourage the Government to give them more work.[213]

Supporters of a lawyer-based approach argue that negotiations between lawyers ensure that the bargaining process is on an equal footing and that values which the law wishes to promote

---

[206] [2015] EWCA Civ 1152.
[207] Barlow *et al.* (2014).
[208] Parkinson (2013).
[209] Eekelaar, Maclean and Beinart (2000).
[210] Davis (2000).
[211] Davis, Cretney and Collins (1994: 40).
[212] Davis, Finch and Fitzgerald (2001).
[213] Dingwall (2010).

can infiltrate the negotiations. The lawyer also plays an important role in being partisan: being on the side of the client.[214] It is, of course, possible to go through the divorce procedure without using lawyers and mediators. To many clients, having someone to take their side and fight their corner is of great psychological benefit during the trauma of divorce. Interestingly, of clients who had used both lawyers and mediators in one study, 60 per cent stated that their lawyers had been helpful, but only 35 per cent their mediators.[215] In a later study[216] 67 per cent of those who had divorced said they were satisfied or fairly satisfied with their solicitors; 22 per cent were dissatisfied or very dissatisfied. The complaints particularly centred on the failure of solicitors to take account of the stressful and emotional aspects of the divorce. Satisfaction with solicitors was notably higher than with mediators.[217]

G Collaborative family law

Collaborative law is an approach which has been adopted and developed by quite a number of firms of solicitors.[218] At its heart is a rejection of litigation as a helpful way of resolving financial disputes and the development of five principles:

- There is to be an open but privileged sharing with the other participants of advice and information.
- There is to be a face-to-face, four-way meeting (two clients, each with their lawyer) designed to reach an agreement.[219] They may also be assisted by other professionals, such as an accountant.
- The negotiations are interest-based. This means that the process begins by identifying the interests of the parties and then negotiations seek to find a solution to meet those interests. This differs from the orthodox approach of each party setting out what they want.
- The clients and lawyers commit to resolving issues without the court.
- Participants sign a formal participation agreement, including that the lawyers will not represent the parties in any litigation if the negotiations break down.

Users claim a success rate of over 85 per cent and increased rates of satisfaction from clients.[220] There is much that is attractive about this model, which in a way formalises what was common practice in the past. It has received support from the judiciary, being described in *S v P (Settlement by Collaborative Law Process)*[221] as designed 'to provide as much encouragement as possible to people to resolve their difficulties in this civilised and sensible way'.[222] Supporters claim it can be significantly cheaper than court-based remedies. Of course, it is of no assistance for those who cannot afford legal advice.

Collaborative family law is not without its critics. There have been concerns that people feel under considerable pressure to reach an agreement. The process is about putting the client in charge of the settlement, with the lawyers being facilitators of that. If a party is particularly

---

[214] Davis, Finch and Fitzgerald (2001).
[215] Davis, Clisby, Cumming *et al.* (2003: 11).
[216] Newcastle Centre for Family Studies (2004).
[217] For a more negative view of the relationship between solicitors and clients, see C. Wright (2006) who finds that clients and solicitors face difficulties in communicating.
[218] See Healy (2015) for a helpful analysis.
[219] Bishop *et al.* (2011); Wright (2011).
[220] Bishop *et al.* (2011).
[221] [2008] 2 FLR 2040.
[222] Thompson (2013).

meek or attaches great significance to one issue and is willing to sacrifice anything for one issue, their interests may not be adequately protected. Katherine Wright's study[223] found cases where agreements were reached which the lawyers agreed they would have urged their clients not to agree to in a traditional negotiation approach. Solicitors using collaborative family law can be put in a difficult position if they feel their clients are not negotiating effectively or are agreeing to a settlement which is much to their disadvantage.

A more recent development is 'collaborative law lite'.[224] This is similar to collaborative law but does not have the requirement that lawyers cannot act for the parties if the negotiations break down. To opponents this means the lawyers have no incentive to ensure agreement is reached and that there is a danger that openness does not take place as the risk of litigation hangs large over the meeting. The benefit to the lawyers is that if the collaborative system does not work, they do not lose the clients.

Another model is to have a single lawyer who acts for both of the clients.[225] This has clear advantages for the parties in halving legal costs. It will require the lawyers to depart from their more adversarial role. This approach is best suited to where it is expected the parties will mediate their dispute.

9 Arbitration

An alternative to mediation is arbitration.[226] This involves the parties asking an arbitrator, normally an experienced family lawyer, to resolve their dispute.[227] Arbitrators need to be paid and normally the parties will be legally represented, and so this is an option for the wealthy. The parties may seek to involve a member of the Institute of Family Law Arbitrators (IFLA), but there is no requirement to do this. The arbitrator will hear the evidence and arguments of both parties and resolve the issue, very much as a judge would. Normally the arbitrator will agree to apply the law in England and Wales, although there is nothing to stop the parties agreeing to the law of some other jurisdiction being used.

The primary appeal of arbitration is likely to be privacy.[228] Arbitration might also appeal to the parties because it tends to be slightly cheaper than a full court hearing. It can also operate more quickly in some cases. There can be flexibility over the timings and structure of the hearing. The parties can also ask the arbitrator to rule on matters on which a judge would be reluctant to do so, such as who should keep a pet.

Typically, the parties will agree to be bound by the ruling of the arbitrator. Once the arbitrator has made an award, they cannot revisit it, save to correct any clerical errors.[229] However, in many cases it will be necessary for the parties to obtain a consent order from a court to approve the agreement, particularly if the parties want to obtain a clean break (see Chapter 6). This means that the arbitrator will seek to make an award which they believe is in line with legal principles and will be accepted by the court.

---

[223] Wright (2011).
[224] Bishop *et al.* (2011).
[225] Skinner (2019).
[226] Practice Guidance, Arbitration in the Family Court (2015) governs the procedural aspects.
[227] Bennett (2014).
[228] Singer (2012). Practice Guidance, Arbitration in the Family Court (2015) provides for ensuring confidentiality is maintained even if the parties require a consent order.
[229] *H v W (Arbitration Award: Power to Correct)* [2019] EWHC 1897 (Fam).

There has been judicial approval of the use of arbitration in *S v S (Financial Remedies: Arbitral Award)*.[230] Sir James Munby heard a case where the couple had arbitrated their financial dispute under an IFLA scheme. The parties presented the award of the arbitrator for the approval of the court and to be made into a court order. Sir James Munby stated:

> Where the consent order which the judge is being asked to approve is founded on an arbitral award under the IFLA Scheme or something similar (and the judge will, of course, need to check that the order does indeed give effect to the arbitral award and is workable) the judge's role will be simple. The judge will not need to play the detective unless something leaps off the page to indicate that something has gone so seriously wrong in the arbitral process as fundamentally to vitiate the arbitral award. Although recognising that the judge is not a rubber stamp, the combination of (a) the fact that the parties have agreed to be bound by the arbitral award, (b) the fact of the arbitral award (which the judge will of course be able to study) and (c) the fact that the parties are putting the matter before the court by consent, means that it can only be in the rarest of cases that it will be appropriate for the judge to do other than approve the order. With a process as sophisticated as that embodied in the IFLA scheme it is difficult to contemplate such a case.[231]

He accepted it was always open to a party to seek to persuade a court to reject the award of the arbitrator but indicated that very compelling reasons would be required to do so. Only in the 'rarest of cases' would a court decline to follow the proposed award.

There are three primary routes that could be used to challenge an award. The first is under the Arbitration Act 1996, s. 69. In such a case Ambrose QC in *R v K*[232] held it would need to be shown 'either (i) that the arbitrator misdirected himself in point of law, or (ii) the decision was such that no reasonable arbitrator could reach'. It would be very difficult to show a decision relating to a financial order under the Matrimonial Causes Act 1973 contained an error of law as the scheme is such a discretionary one.

The second route to challenge an arbitration award is under s. 68 of the Arbitration Act 1996. There it would need to be shown that there was a serious irregularity in the arbitration proceedings. It would need to be shown that 'the tribunal has gone so wrong in its conduct that justice calls out for it to be corrected'.[233]

The third route would be ask the court to refuse to make the award into a consent order. In *DB v DLJ (Challenge to Arbitral Award)*[234] Mostyn J warned that 'almost never' will a court decline to follow an arbitrator's award because it is 'wrong' or 'unjust'. Only where there is a vitiating mistake or supervening event might a court intervene.[235] This restrictive approach was explained by Ambrose QC in *R v K*[236] in this way:

> The parties have elected to have their 'day in court' before their chosen arbitrator and the 1996 Act deals with procedural irregularity and errors of law. Arbitration is not a dress rehearsal enabling a dissatisfied party to re-open and improve his evidence on appeal in the High Court.

That quote could be applied to the general approach of the courts to attempts to set aside arbitration awards. It is clear that only in extreme cases will the court want to reopen the case.

---

[230] [2014] EWHC 7 (Fam).
[231] Para 21.
[232] [2020] EWHC 841 (Fam).
[233] *R v K* [2020] EWHC 841 (Fam).
[234] [2016] EWHC 324 (Fam).
[235] *BC v BG (Financial Remedies)* [2019] EWFC 7.
[236] [2020] EWHC 841 (Fam).

The argument used in *S v S*[237] for giving weight to the arbitration award was autonomy. Indeed, Munby P seems to suggest that the case for giving weight to an arbitration award is even stronger than the case for a pre-nup. This has been questioned by Lucinda Ferguson[238] who argues:

> In relation to nuptial agreements, the parties thus understand the nature of any proposed final outcome before they agree to restrict their future choices, whereas parties agreeing to arbitration do not. When contrasted in that light, there may be a good case for arguing that, to the extent that one is 'of its nature even stronger' than the other, it is in fact nuptial agreements that are a greater expression of the parties' autonomy than arbitral awards.

Arbitration does offer some advantages over mediation. The vulnerable party has the reassurance that they will not be pressurised into agreeing to something which is disastrous for them. An experienced professional (the arbitrator) will determine what is fair and one can assume that the result will, at least, not be manifestly unfair. However, the agreement is imposed from 'outside' on the couple. They are not in control of its content in a way the parties are in mediation. Shiva Ancliffe[239] sums up the benefits of arbitration:

> Arbitration offers a markedly less stressful, less expensive, bespoke alternative to the court system. There is a greater degree of informality which clients find more comfortable but there is some formality in keeping with the nature of the decision-making process. The arbitration can be tailored to each case and certain straightforward matters can be dealt with swiftly whereas in proceedings, they would have required endless email correspondence, applications and further case management hearings.

It may be that the delays and pressure on the current court system caused by COVID will result in arbitration being seen as a more attractive option. Although traditionally arbitration has been used for adult matters, the current delays in the court process could lead to arbitrators being used in some children's cases, such as contact or relocation disputes.[240]

The primary disadvantage of arbitration is its costs. Not only must the lawyers' costs be met, so too must the payment of the arbitrator, the venue and the costs of the court hearing approving the order. It might, therefore, be more costly than a court resolved dispute.[241] Even the advantage of privacy may not really be a benefit because as Lucinda Ferguson put it 'confidentiality may hide potential injustice to one party'.[242] Despite these points, especially among wealthier clients, arbitration appears to be becoming an increasingly popular option for resolving family law disputes. Arbitrators seem to be keen to ensure their fees are competitive and being able to offer weekend and expedited hearing may increase the overall perception as to value for money.[243]

10 Religious tribunals

Learning objective 6

Consider the issues around the use of religious tribunals

One form of arbitration which has attracted considerable public attention is a couple applying to a religious court to resolve their family dispute. To some the use of religious tribunals should be no different from the use of any arbitrator scheme. If the couple

---

[237] [2014] EWHC 7 (Fam).
[238] Ferguson (2015a).
[239] Ancliffe (2019).
[240] Ancliffe (2019).
[241] Ferguson (2013a).
[242] Ferguson (2013a).
[243] Ancliffe (2019).

feel that the religious court will deal fairly with their dispute, we should respect their decision. Should it really matter whether the person they ask to help them resolve their dispute is a retired judge, a friend or a religious cleric?

Penny Booth voices the concerns of others with such recognition of these courts: 'The danger is in the development of a parallel system of (any) law where the choice as to which system or principle is used is determined not by the individual or the issue but by the group bullies. In family law this danger could arise where the determination of system and approach is not made by the woman but the man: not through the female but through the male-dominated system.'[244] In particular there are concerns that the Sharia councils work in a way which fails to protect the rights of women and at worst condone domestic abuse.[245]

John Eekelaar has suggested that giving effect to agreements reached following an order of a religious court should be made, as long as the agreement was genuine, followed independent advice, and was consistent with 'overriding policy goals', such as the best interests of children.[246]

The issue came to a head with the Arbitration and Mediation Services (Equality) Bills of 2011, 2013 and 2015. These Bills, which have repeatedly failed in Parliament, are designed to ensure that Sharia courts or other religious courts or bodies do not claim legal jurisdiction over family law. There is a particular concern that religious courts would not protect the fundamental rights of women. The Bills failed but they would have created a criminal offence of falsely claiming jurisdiction of a criminal or family matter. They would also have stated that the sex discrimination provisions of the Equality Act 2010 apply to tribunals.

Many people were unconvinced that this was an appropriate way to deal with the issue. John Eekelaar has written:

> It is a mistake to think of Sharia as a monolithic system, impervious to change. In fact the bodies apply it in different ways, and it is subject to internal arguments and contestation. Might it be better to allow it to develop within its communities, responding to its internal critiques and influenced by the culture around it?[247]

A helpful study of the work of religious tribunals has indicated that the tribunals were aware of the limits of their jurisdiction and tended to focus on religious issues flowing from relationship breakdown.[248] This suggests the fear that religious courts will take over the work of family courts is misguided.

A Home Office independent review into the operation of Sharia courts[249] had three primary recommendations. The first two primarily related to marriage and will be discussed in Chapter 3: to compel civil registration of religious marriages and increase awareness of the lack of legal recognition given to religious-only marriages. The third was that Sharia Councils be subject to regulation. The Review proposed the Government create a code of practice for Sharia Councils to accept and adopt. A body containing Sharia Council members and specialist family lawyers would monitor and audit compliance with the code. The primary aim of the regulation would be to ensure that there was no discrimination before Sharia Councils and that similar standards used by the secular courts were adopted by the Councils. However, such regulation would not restrict the work of the Council on purely religious issues. There

---

[244] Booth (2008: 395). For further discussion, see Ahmed (2010).
[245] Zee (2016) is a powerful and critical account.
[246] Eekelaar (2011a).
[247] Eekelaar (2011a).
[248] Douglas *et al.* (2012).
[249] Home Office (2018).

is a difficulty balance here because neither the Council nor the Government would wish the state to become involved in determining issues of religious disagreement. On the other hand, the State does not want citizens losing legal rights through the decisions of a Council; or Councils being set up as rival alternatives to secular courts. The difficulty is that drawing a sharp line between what is a religious matter and what is a matter of secular legal rights is difficult, particularly in the area of family law.

The issue has been addressed by the court.

CASE: AI v MT (Alternative Dispute Resolution) [2013] EWHC 100 (Fam)

The case involved a couple who wished to refer their dispute over children to a religious court, the New York Beth Din. They were Orthodox Jews with an international lifestyle and wanted the issue resolved by the New York Beth Din. Baker J made it clear that the agreement could not remove the court's jurisdiction and so only a non-binding process could be accepted. He received confirmation from the rabbi arbitrator that the court would apply the principle that the interests of the children were paramount and would take all the material information into account. He therefore endorsed the proposal to refer the dispute for non-binding arbitration. Subsequently he approved of the agreements reached by the court in relation to financial order and children. He emphasised that in doing so he was not departing from the welfare principle or undermining the role of the court. The court could never be bound to depart from that principle through respect of the religion. However, it was in the interests of parties to resolve dispute by agreement and to avoid court proceedings if possible.

It is important to stress a number of crucial aspects of this case.[250] It came before the court with the agreement of all the parties, who had received full legal advice. Also, the religious court was able to confirm the welfare of the child would be paramount. Further, the agreement was still subject to the endorsement by the court and it will be open to a court to decide not to give effect to the ruling reached by the religious court. In other jurisdictions where a similar route has been adopted it seems that the secular courts nearly always do give effect to the decision of the religious tribunal once it has been approved by the court.[251]

Making the determination of the religious tribunal non-binding goes some way towards mitigating the concerns of those who are worried that the decisions of the religious tribunals will undermine the rights of the family members (especially women) or fail to protect the interests of children. It manages to convey a recognition for the validity of those tribunals while retaining the final say for the courts. Of course, this all depends on the extent to which the courts are seen as providing a 'double check' on the decision of the tribunal. If the courts are seen to rubber stamp the decisions of religious courts then the concerns over women and children become greater. One issue that the courts will be particularly aware of is that the phrase 'children's welfare' can be understood in a range of ways. A religious court could, for example, claim to put the children's welfare first, but then determine that it is always in the welfare of the child to be raised by the father. In *AI v MT (Alternative Dispute Resolution)*[252]

---

[250] See the discussion in Pearce (2013) and Tolley (2013).
[251] Tolley (2013).
[252] [2013] EWHC 100 (Fam).

Baker J was satisfied that the understanding of children's welfare taken by the tribunal would match that of the law.

There are other concerns over the use of religious tribunals. One is whether there is a genuine consent to the process. It was key in *AI v MT (Alternative Dispute Resolution)*[253] that the parties both received extensive independent legal advice. However, it is not difficult to imagine cases where familial and cultural pressure is such that a person will feel they have no choice but to accede to the religious court of their culture, even if they are provided legal advice.

In a positive light it might be argued that the procedure adopted in *AI v MT (Alternative Dispute Resolution)*[254] will mean that the law can exert a positive influence on religious tribunals. In order to promote their recognition and standing the tribunals will want to have their validity accepted by the courts. This means they will ensure that their judgments reflect basic principles of human rights and the welfare of the child.[255]

11 Conclusion

A recent study of over 100 family law practitioners found that around half believed that in the future lawyers will not be the first port of call for divorcing couples.[256] Increasingly, it seems, people will resolve issues on family breakdown without any legal involvement and rely on mediation.

It is generally accepted that the state has a responsibility to ensure there is a fair and effective means of resolving family legal disputes.[257] The question is how the state meets that responsibility. The issue facing family law currently is whether mediation or self-represented legal proceedings are adequate. It may be that a model which combines legal advice and mediation will be developed further in the future.[258] At the moment, mediation in part moves the disputes beyond the reach of the state. This can be seen in some of the rhetoric of describing disputes as 'relationship problems' rather than legal disputes. This implies that family disputes should be seen as more of a personal emotional problem, rather than one involving legal rights. Their solution is more about emotional intelligence and therapy than with justice or legal rights.[259] However, as we have seen, plenty of commentators believe that the resolution of family disputes has a profound impact upon society more generally and they cannot be categorised as simply private squabbles.

It is already clear that the cutbacks in legal aid mean that many people who would previously have had access to legal advice to deal with their family disputes will no longer have the benefit of that. Christine Piper argues that the cutbacks in legal aid will particularly affect women, ethnic minorities and people with disabilities.[260] The legal aid reductions will lead to a radical shift in the work of family law solicitors. Many will have to move to other areas of work. Far more important is that without access to legal advice and courts people will be left to fend for themselves through mediation. Some, the rich and the strong, will do so without undue difficulty. Others, the weak and poor, will not.[261] Their rights will go unprotected; their children will be ignored by the law; justice will not be done.

[253] [2013] EWHC 100 (Fam).
[254] [2013] EWHC 100 (Fam).
[255] Tolley (2013) and Eekelaar (2013c).
[256] Mills and Reeve (2015).
[257] Diduck (2014a).
[258] Maclean and Eekelaar (2016).
[259] Doughty and Murch (2012).
[260] Piper (2014); Diduck (2014b); Cobb (2013).
[261] Wong and Cain (2019).

Further reading

Ahmed, F. and Calderwood Norton, J. (2012) 'Religious tribunals, religious freedom, and concern for vulnerable women', *Child and Family Law Quarterly* 24: 363.

Akhtar, R. (2019) 'Plural approaches to faith-based dispute resolution by Britain's Muslim communities', *Child and Family Law Quarterly* 189.

Ali, S. (2013) 'Authority and authenticity: Sharia councils, Muslim women's rights, and the English courts', *Child and Family Law Quarterly* 25: 133.

Barlow, A. (2017) 'Rising to the post-LASPO challenge: How should mediation respond?' *Journal of Social Welfare and Family Law* 39: 20.

Barlow, A., Hunter R., Smithson, J. and Ewing, J. (2017) *Mapping paths to family justice: resolving family disputes in neo-liberal times,* London: Palgrave.

Barnett, A. (2017) 'Family law without lawyers – A systems theory perspective', *Journal of Social Welfare and Family Law* 39: 22.

Barry, K-A. (2019) 'McKenzie Friends and litigants in person: widening access to justice or foes in disguise?' *Child and Family Law Quarterly* 31.

Blakey, R. (2020) 'Cracking the code: the role of mediators and flexibility post-LASPO', *Child and Family Law Quarterly* 53.

Choudhry, S. and Herring, J. (2017) 'A human right to legal aid? – The implications of changes to the legal aid scheme for victims of domestic abuse', *Journal of Social Welfare and Family Law* 39: 152.

Coy, M., Scott, E., Tweedale, R. and Perks, K. (2015) '"It's like going through the abuse again": domestic violence and women and children's (un)safety in private law contact proceedings', *Journal of Social Welfare and Family Law* 37: 53.

Diduck, A. (2014a) 'Justice by ADR in private family matters: is it fair and is it possible?' *Family Law* 44: 616.

Eekelaar, J. and Maclean, M. (2013) *Family Justice: The Work of Family Judges in Uncertain Times,* Oxford: Hart.

Ferguson, L. (2013) 'Arbitration in financial dispute resolution: the final step to reconstructing the default(s) and exception(s)?' *Journal of Social Welfare and Family Law* 35: 115.

Hunter, R. (2017) 'Inducing demand for family mediation – before and after LASPO', *Journal of Social Welfare and Family Law* 39: 189.

Kaganas, F. (2017) 'Justifying the LASPO Act: authenticity, necessity, suitability, responsibility and autonomy', *Journal of Social Welfare and Family Law* 39: 168.

Kennett, W. (2016) 'It's arbitration, but not as we know it: reflections on family law dispute resolution', *International Journal of Law, Policy and the Family* 16: 1.

Luk, S. (2012) 'How religious arbitration could enhance personal autonomy', *Oxford Journal of Legal Studies* 424.

Maclean, M. and Dijksterhuis, B. (eds) (2019) *Digital Family Justice: From Alternative Dispute Resolution to Online Dispute Resolution?* Oxford: Hart.

Maclean, M. and Eekelaar, J. (2016) *Lawyers and Mediators,* Oxford: Hart.

Maclean, M. and Eekelaar, J. (2019) *Act the Act: Access to Family Justice after LASPO,* Oxford: Hart.

Mant, J. (2017) 'Neoliberalism, family law and the cost of access to justice', *Journal of Social Welfare and Family Law* 39: 246.

Mant, J. (2019) 'Litigants' experiences of the post-LASPO family court: key findings from recent research', *Family Law* 49: 300.

Mant, J. and Wallbank, J. (2018) 'The mysterious case of disappearing family law and the shrinking vulnerable subject: the shifting sands of family law's jurisdiction', *Social and Legal Studies* 26: 629.

Munroe, A. and Tautz, W. (2020) 'Not remotely fair: an analysis of *Re P* and remote hearings in the family courts', *Family Law* 59: 643.

Parkinson, L. (2013) 'The Place of Mediation in the Family Justice System', *Child and Family Law Quarterly* 300.

Piper, C. (2014) 'Mediation and vulnerable parents', in J. Wallbank and J. Herring (eds) (2014) *Vulnerabilities, Care and Family Law,* London: Routledge.

Richardson, K. and Speed, A. (2019) 'Restrictions on legal aid in family law cases in England and Wales: creating a necessary barrier to public funding or simply increasing the burden on the family courts?' *Journal of Social Welfare and Family Law* 41: 135.

Roberts, M. and Moscati, M. (eds) (2020) *Family Mediation: Contemporary Issues*, London: Bloomsbury.

Ryan, M., Harker, L., Rothera, S. (2020) *Remote Hearings in the Family Justice System*, London: Nuffield Family Justice Observatory.

Smith, L., Hitchings, E. and Sefton, M. (2017) 'Fee-charging McKenzie Friends in private family law cases: key findings from the research report', *Family Law* 971.

Tamanna, N. (2013) 'Recognition of "difference" in Shari'a: a feminist scrutiny through the lens of substantive equality', *Journal of Social Welfare and Family Law* 35: 3.

Trinder, L., Hunter, R., Hitchings, E., Miles, J., Moorhead, R., Smith, L., Sefton, M., Hinchly, V., Bader, K. and Pearce, J. (2014) *Litigants in person in private family law cases,* London: Ministry of Justice.

Wong, S. and Cain, R. (2019) 'The impact of cuts in legal aid funding of private family law cases', *Journal of Social Welfare and Family Law* 41: 3.

Visit **go.pearson.com/uk/he/resources** to access **resources** specifically written to complement this text.

3 Marriage, civil partnership and cohabitation

Learning objectives

When you finish reading this chapter you will be able to:

1. Recall key statistics on marriage
2. Explain and evaluate how different theories define marriage
3. Appreciate why people marry
4. Contrast the status and contract views of marriage and understand the implications of each
5. Explain how a presumption of marriage can arise and how it can be rebutted
6. Differentiate between divorce, nullity, a void marriage, a voidable marriage and a non-qualifying ceremony
7. Explain the grounds on which a marriage is void
8. Explain the grounds on which a marriage is voidable
9. Explain and evaluate the law relating to civil partnerships
10. Explain how the law has defined cohabitation
11. Compare and contrast the legal position of spouses and civil partners with unmarried couples
12. Appreciate potential reform options for marriage

1 Introduction

In most societies around the world it is widely accepted that it is best for children to be brought up in 'stable intimate partnerships' and that such partnerships can provide adults with much personal fulfilment. The regularisation of these stable relationships has in England and Wales been channelled through marriage, but marriage worldwide is a hugely varied phenomenon.[1] For example, there is no agreement over whether marriage is polygamous or

---

[1] For a wonderful history of marriage, see Probert (2009a).

monogamous (i.e. how many parties there should be to a marriage); whether or not the upbringing and/or nurturing of children is central to the concept of marriage; whether marriage partners should be chosen by the parties themselves or by their wider family; whether marriage should be restricted to couples of the opposite sex; or at what age marriage is appropriate. In Britain, in our culturally diverse society, it would be difficult to say anything about the nature of marriage that would be true for all married couples. Traditionally, it has been the Christian conception of marriage which has been dominant, although it is far from clear exactly what that conception is, with considerable debate within churches over what marriage should mean.[2] This was particularly evident in the debates surrounding the Marriage (Same Sex Couples) Act 2013.

Increasingly there is a tension between religious and legal conceptions of marriage.[3] England is unusual in allowing some religious ceremonies of marriage to also be legal marriages. However, legal marriages can take place in circumstances which would not be approved by many churches.[4] Most notably while marriage between those of the same sex is permitted in law, only a few Christian denominations currently permit same-sex marriage.[5] The Church of England does not. It is interesting that some religious groups have even seen the need for legal marriages to be bolstered by special religious pledges, involving commitments beyond the legal obligations of marriage.[6] We are gradually moving to the position where legal and religious marriages are seen as being different things, which is the position in most countries.

Marriage used to be the main focus of family law. Textbooks would concentrate on discussion of the formalities of marriage, the consequences of marriage, and its dissolution. However, today, many commentators on family law feel that parenthood is the core concept in family law[7] and that marriage is of limited legal significance. Alison Diduck and Felicity Kaganas have suggested that 'marriage is both central and peripheral to family law but arguably remains at the heart of family ideology'.[8] Their argument is that, while the legal consequences of marriage are limited, the symbolic nature of marriage still plays an important part as providing an image of what the ideal family should be.[9] That said, marriage still creates some important legal consequences – it would not be possible for a lawyer to advise a client over a family matter unless the lawyer knew whether the couple were married. For example, marriage still plays a role in determining who is the parent of a child (see Chapter 8).

There are two particular challenges that threaten to limit the legal significance of marriage even further. First, as marriage has become easier to enter and to exit, any claim that it is a special relationship deserving of particular respect becomes harder to maintain. Secondly, there are arguments that those who are unmarried but live together in many ways like a traditionally married couple should be treated in the same way as a married couple.[10] These pressures make it harder to claim a unique status for marriage.

[2] Thatcher (2011).
[3] Edge (2016).
[4] National Statistics (2008d) records that 68 per cent of all marriages were civil ceremonies (i.e. not in a church or other religious building).
[5] E.g. the Quakers, the United Reformed Church.
[6] E.g. the Promise Keepers movement in the US, discussed critically in Fineman (2004: 130–1).
[7] Parkinson (2011) emphasises that parenthood, unlike marriage, is indissoluble.
[8] Diduck and Kaganas (2006: 30).
[9] Leckey (2018b).
[10] Thornton, Azinn and Xie (2007).

2 Statistics on marriage

KEY STATISTICS

There were 24.1 million people who were married in 2017.[11] This was 50.9% of the population aged 16 and over. Just under 39% of the adult population are single (i.e. not living as a couple). The percentage of the population who are married has been gradually falling and it has been estimated that it will fall to 42% by 2033. Of those born in 1930, 90% of men and 94% of women had married by age 40. In contrast, of those born in 1970, 63% of men and 71% of women had married by the same age. Of those age 16 to 29, the majority of males and females were 'not living in a couple: never married or civil partnered', at 77.4% and 66.9% respectively.

In 2017, there were 242,842 marriages, a decrease of 2.8% compared with 2016 and 1.1% lower than 2015; 97% of those marriages were to opposite-sex couples. A better picture of the popularity of marriage is gained by the rate of marriage, because the number of marriages can depend on the size of the population. In 2017, the number of men marrying per 1,000 unmarried men aged 16 or over was 21.1; for women the number was 19.5. These rates were a significant drop from the rates in the year 2000, which were 29.5 for men and 25.7 for women. Indeed, even between 2016 and 2017 there was a 3.2% drop in the marriage rate for men and 3.0% for women. They are the lowest marriage rates on record, although it should be noted that these figures do not take account of people who marry abroad. The Office for National Statistics explains:

> This long-term decline in the number of marriages and marriage rates is a likely consequence of increasing numbers of men and women delaying marriage, or couples choosing to cohabit rather than marry, either as a precursor to marriage or as an alternative.

Significantly, in 2017, 23% of opposite-sex marriages were second or further marriages for at least one of the parties. This suggests that there are numbers of people marrying, divorcing and remarrying who are keeping the numbers of marriages at their present rate. Also of note is the fact that only 23% of marriages between opposite-sex couples were religious ceremonies. The majority were civil ceremonies (i.e. did not contain a religious element). Civil marriages first exceeded religious ceremonies in 1976, and have consistently outnumbered religious marriages every year since 1992. Indeed, there was a 9.1% decrease in the number of religious marriages in 2017, as compared with 2016. Only 0.6% of same-sex marriages were religious, reflecting the relatively small number of religious groups who support same-sex marriage. It seems, therefore, for only a minority of people is marriage a particularly religious matter.

The number of people who choose not to marry at all has greatly increased. Soon we will be in the position of marriage not being the norm for adults in the United Kingdom. Barlow *et al.* suggest that we are at a time 'where unmarried cohabitation is quite normal and where marriage is more of a lifestyle choice rather than an expected part of life'.[12] In fact, as the statistics above suggest, it is living as a single person[13] which is becoming increasingly common.

Levels of wealth can significantly affect the likelihood of marriage. Benson[14] notes that 'of mothers with children under five, 87% of those in higher income groups are married compared to just 24% of those in lower income groups'.

---

[11] The statistics in this box are taken from Office for National Statistics (2020e). The statistics always relate to a couple of years behind the date of publication.

[12] Barlow *et al.* (2005: 49).

[13] Even though in a relationship.

[14] Benson (2015).

Learning objective 1

Recall key statistics on marriage

Whether or not marriage is in terminal decline remains to be seen. It is clear that the nature of marriage is changing. Two points in particular are worth noting. First, the average age of first marriage in England and Wales has changed – the average age of marriage has risen from 23 for men and 21.4 for women in 1975 to 38.0 for men and 35.7 for women in 2017.[15] Secondly, it is now commonplace for a couple to cohabit before marriage. In 2017, 88 per cent of married opposite-sex couples cohabited prior to marriage. So, marriage does not indicate the start of an intimate relationship, but normally a serious commitment to it.

3 What is marriage?

A The meaning of marriage

Learning objective 2

Explain and evaluate how different theories define marriage

It is impossible to provide a single definition of marriage. Marriage involves a complex mix of social, legal, religious and personal issues. Indeed, one approach is to say that one cannot define marriage because marriage is whatever the parties to a marriage take it to mean. Thus, a Christian couple seeking to base their marriage on biblical principles may well see their marriage in very different terms from a couple who understand their marriage to be open and short term, entered into for tax purposes. Further, the wife's experience and understanding of marriage may be very different from the husband's. At one time a common marriage vow of a wife was that she be 'bonny and buxom in bed and board'![16] As this indicates, expectations of the obligations of marriage have changed over time. Martha Fineman has written:

> Marriage, to those involved in one, can mean a legal tie, a symbol of commitment, a privileged sexual affiliation, a relationship of hierarchy and subordination, a means of self-fulfilment, a social construct, a cultural phenomenon, a religious mandate, an economic relationship, the preferred unit for reproduction, a way to ensure against poverty and dependence on the state, a way out of the birth family, the realization of a romantic ideal, a natural or divine connection, a commitment to traditional notions of morality, a desired status that communicates one's sexual desirability to the world, or a purely contractual relationship in which each term is based on bargaining.[17]

And this, she suggests, is not an exhaustive list. The lack of a clear definition of marriage may be a sign of the times. It reflects the religious, cultural and ethnic diversity within our society.[18] As Glendon writes:

> [T]he lack of firm and fixed ideas about what marriage is and should be is but an aspect of the alienation of modern man. And in this respect the law seems truly to reflect the fact that in modern society more and more is expected of human relationships while at the same time social changes have rendered those relationships increasingly fragile.[19]

---

[15] Office for National Statistics (2020e).
[16] Iknstone-Brewer (2002: 231).
[17] Fineman (2004: 99).
[18] Eekelaar (2007).
[19] Glendon (1989).

But it would be too easy to see marriage as simply being whatever the parties want it to be, because this denies the power of the idealised image of marriage within society. In a study of 14- to 18-year-olds, a remarkable 78 per cent stated they would like to get married.[20] Not everyone agrees that marriage is still something aspired to. Rosemary Auchmuty suggests it is generally regarded as old-fashioned and based on sexist assumptions. People feel they need to justify why they are getting married these days, rather than having to explain why they are not.[21] Marriage can be examined from a number of perspectives:

(i) Functional

From a functionalist approach it would be necessary to decide what the purpose of marriage is. Some insist that children are at the heart of marriage. Hoggett *et al.* suggest: 'If nothing else, then, marriage is about the licence to beget children.'[22] However, given nearly as many children are born to unmarried couples as are born to married ones that appears a little outdated. Engels,[23] on the other hand, saw the role of marriage and family as an integral part of the regulation of private property and the creation of legitimate heirs. Others would emphasise the role of creating an environment of love and comfort for the spouses and any children.

(ii) Psychological

Others analyse marriage by considering the psychological need to marry and the psychological interactions between the two marriage partners. Anthony Giddens, developing the concept of the 'pure relationship' has argued that modern intimate relations are entered into 'for what can be derived by each person from a sustained association with another; and . . . is continued only in so far as it is thought by both parties to deliver enough satisfaction for each individual to stay within it'.[24] In other words, people are now more individualistic and are only willing to stay in relationships so long as they feel they personally are benefiting from them.[25]

(iii) Political

It is also possible to consider the role marriage plays in wider society. Some see the subjugation of women as the essence of marriage. Marriage has been described as 'a public form of labour relationship between men and women, whereby a women pledges for life (with limited rights to quit) her labour, sexuality and reproductive capacity, and receives protection, upkeep and certain rights to children'.[26] Baroness Hale, however, has rejected the argument that there should nowadays be a feminist objection to marriage: 'These are not the olden days when the husband and wife were one person in law and that person was the husband. A desire to reject legal patriarchy is no longer a rational reason to reject marriage.'[27]

---

[20] Brown (2020).
[21] Auchmuty (2009).
[22] Hoggett *et al.* (2003).
[23] Engels (1978).
[24] Giddens (1992: 58).
[25] Lewis (2001a; 2001b). See Bettle and Herring (2014) for a tongue in cheek response that marrying a robot may be appropriate for the 'pure relationship'.
[26] Lenard (1980).
[27] *Re G (Adoption: Unmarried Couple)* [2009] AC 173.

(iv) Religious

There is a wide variety of religious understandings of marriage.[28] Some religions teach of a spiritual union between spouses on marriage, with the spouses' love reflecting God's love.[29] Some religions regard marriage as indissoluble, although others do not take a hard line on divorce. Some religious groups teach that marriage must be between an opposite-sex couple; others are very open to same-sex marriage. In England and Wales the law's understanding of marriage has historically been strongly influenced by Christian theology.[30] In *Sheffield CC v E and S*, Munby J stated that 'although we live in a multi-cultural society of many faiths, it must not be forgotten that as a secular judge my concern . . . is with marriage as a civil contract, not a religious vow'.[31] This is hardly controversial, but the fact that Munby J felt it was necessary to say what he did indicates the hold of religion over the notion of marriage.[32]

B The legal definition of marriage

The most commonly cited definition of marriage in the law is that in *Hyde v Hyde and Woodhouse*:[33] 'the voluntary union for life of one man and one woman to the exclusion of all others'. This is perhaps better understood as an ideal promoted by the law rather than a definition as such. As we shall see, it is quite possible to have a legally valid marriage which is entered into involuntarily,[34] is characterised by sexual unfaithfulness, and is ended by divorce. Contrast the *Hyde* definition with the more recent definition of marriage provided by Thorpe LJ: 'a contract for which the parties elect but which is regulated by the state, both in its formation and in its termination by divorce because it affects status upon which depend a variety of entitlements, benefits and obligations'.[35] Notably, this has no requirement that the parties are opposite sex; that the marriage is for life; or monogamous. Indeed, it seems only the 'voluntariness' element of the *Hyde* definition remains in his formulation. It should not, however, be thought that Thorpe LJ's definition represents the current law. Lord Millet demonstrated that some members of the judiciary have a more traditional understanding of the concept when he stated in a dissenting judgment:

> Marriage is the lawful union of a man and a woman. It is a legal relationship between persons of the opposite sex. A man's spouse must be a woman; a woman's spouse must be a man. This is of the very essence of the relationship, which need not be loving, sexual, stable, faithful, long-lasting, or contented.[36]

Lord Wilson, a Justice of the Supreme Court, writing extra-judicially in 2017 has suggested: 'My own view is that we have now reached the stage in which, if acting with appropriate care and understanding, parties should be allowed to elect the sort of marriage which they want.' That is a radical shift in the understanding of the nature of marriage from a status defined by the law, to contract defined by the parties.

---

[28] Thatcher (2011).
[29] Pontifical Council for the Family (2000).
[30] Scott and Warren (2001).
[31] [2004] EWHC 2808 (Fam), para 116.
[32] See Probert (2012a) and Douglas (2015) for a helpful discussion on the links between civil and religious marriage.
[33] (1866) LR 1 PD 130 at p. 133, per Lord Penzance. This definition is discussed in Probert (2007e).
[34] If a marriage is not entered into voluntarily, the marriage will be voidable, which will mean that it is a legally valid marriage, but can still be set aside if the pressurised party wishes to have the marriage annulled.
[35] *Bellinger v Bellinger* [2001] 2 FLR 1048, at para 128.
[36] *Ghaidan v Godin-Mendoza* [2004] 2 AC 557.

In *Re X*[37] Munby J strongly rejected an argument that a couple who had gone through a ceremony of marriage but had never engaged in sexual relations were not married. He said:

> The fact that it is platonic, and without a sexual component, is, as a matter of long-established law, neither here nor there and in truth no concern of the judges or of the State. One needs look no further than Nigel Nicolson's *Portrait of a Marriage*, his acclaimed account of the unusual marriage of his parents, Vita Sackville-West and Harold Nicolson, to see how happy and fulfilling a marriage, more or less conventional, more or less unconventional, can be. But it is really none of our business. As the first Elizabeth put it, we should not make windows into people's souls.

In fact, as that quote indicates, it is probably most accurate to say the law does not attempt to define marriage as such. The law has had much to say about who can marry whom and how the relationship can be ended, but says very little explicitly about the content of the relationship itself. In fact, it would be possible for a couple to be legally married but never to have lived together or had any kind of relationship.[38] In *R (on the Application of the Crown Prosecution Service) v Registrar General of Births, Deaths and Marriages*[39] the Crown Prosecution Service sought an order preventing a marriage between a man charged with murder and the woman intended to be the main prosecution witness at his trial. It was argued that the marriage was being entered into so that she would not be a compellable witness against him. However, the Court of Appeal refused to grant the order. It would not examine the reason why the couple wanted to marry and consider if it was a valid one.[40] This is not surprising because the law cannot force a married couple to live in any particular relationship. The law on marriage merely provides parameters within which the couple are free to develop the content of their marriage as they wish.

C Why do people marry?

Learning objective 3

Appreciate why people marry

Several studies have sought to discover why people marry.[41] Of course, the decision is rarely made entirely on rational grounds.[42] Hibbs *et al.*[43] carried out an interesting study into why people married. Forty-two per cent of those engaged people questioned gave 'love' or 'love and . . .' as the reason for marriage. A further 13 per cent stated the reason for marriage as being a sign of commitment and 9 per cent as marriage being a sign of progression of their relationship. Three per cent said they did not know why they were getting married! Three factors which might have been expected to appear were rarely mentioned: only 4 per cent mentioned children being a reason to marry; less than 1 per cent mentioned religion;[44] and none gave legal reasons for getting married.[45] A study by Eekelaar and Maclean[46] emphasised that different ethnic groups gave different reasons for marriage. They found that among some communities religious reasons and a desire to please parents constituted an important reason for marrying. They suggested that reasons for marrying could be divided into three categories: pragmatic

---

[37] [2018] EWFC 15.
[38] *Vervaeke v Smith* [1983] 1 AC 145.
[39] [2003] 1 FCR 110; [2003] QB 1222.
[40] See also *M v H* [1996] NZFLR 241 where the New Zealand court upheld the marriage of two students entered into solely so that their parents' wealth would not be taken into account in calculating the level of their grant.
[41] Much less research has been carried out on why people cohabit, but see Smart (2000a) and Barlow *et al.* (2005).
[42] Barlow (2009a).
[43] Hibbs, Barton and Beswick (2001). See also Barlow *et al.* (2003).
[44] Kiernan (2001) found a strong link between marriage rates and religious belief.
[45] Although 3 per cent stated that legal considerations had influenced their decision to get married. In fact, 41 per cent of those questioned thought (quite incorrectly) that marriage would not change their legal rights and responsibilities towards each other. See also Barlow *et al.* (2005: 56).
[46] Eekelaar and Maclean (2004).

(e.g. for legal reasons); conventional (e.g. pressure from parents, religious belief); or internal (e.g. to affirm their commitment to each other).[47] They found that the vast majority of their respondents referred to conventional or internal reasons in explaining their decision to marry.

We have certainly seen a decrease in the practical significance of marriage in recent decades and a couple choosing not to marry are very unlikely to face social criticism or huge practical problems. So, as Cherlin argues:

> if marriage is now optional, it remains highly valued. As the practical importance of marriage has declined, its symbolic importance has remained high and may even have increased.

Indeed, there is now strong evidence that decisions to marry are based on emotions and upbringing, rather than rational thought.[48]

Alissa Goodman and Ellen Greaves[49] in a survey of the evidence concluded that a couple are more likely to marry rather than cohabit if:

- the mother is of Indian, Pakistani or Bangladeshi ethnicity;
- the mother is religious;
- the mother's parents did not separate;
- there are no children of previous partners in the household;
- the mother and father have high levels of education;
- the parents own their own home;
- the couple lived together for longer prior to the child's birth;
- the pregnancy was planned;
- the mother was 20 or older when her first child was born;
- there is more than one child in the household;
- the parents have a higher relationship quality when the baby is nine months old.

Another study, looking at why people did not marry, found that the most common reason given was that people could not afford it (21.8 per cent of those questioned).[50] The cost of marriage is also sometimes given as a reason for delaying marriage. It has been claimed that the average cost of marriage in 2018 was £30,355.[51] This will represent many years' savings for most couples. A marriage need cost only £47 (the registry office fees), but the reception, honeymoon, etc. that go along with the modern wedding create significant additional expense.

4 Marriage as a status or contract

Learning objective 4

Contrast the status and contract views of marriage and understand the implications of each

Marriage could be regarded as either a status or a contract.[52] In law, a status is regarded as a relationship which has a set of legal consequences flowing automatically from that relationship, regardless of the intentions of the parties. A status has been defined as 'the condition of belonging to a class in society to

---

[47] See Douglas (2016) for an interesting discussion of the nature of commitment.
[48] Billari and Liefbroer (2016).
[49] Goodman and Greaves (2010b: 5).
[50] Lewis (2001b: 135).
[51] Hosie (2018).
[52] See Brake (2012) for a powerful argument that marriage should be 'minimised' to a contract between the parties.

which the law ascribes peculiar rights and duties, capacities and incapacities'.[53] So, the status view of marriage would suggest that, if a couple marry, then they are subject to the laws governing marriage, regardless of their intentions or choices. The alternative approach would be to regard contract as governing marriage. The legal consequences of marriage would then flow from the intentions of the parties as set out in an agreement rather than any given rules set down by the law. In English law marriage is best understood as a mixture of a contract and a status.

Baroness Hale has explained:

> Marriage is, of course, a contract, in the sense that each party must agree to enter into it and once entered both are bound by its legal consequences. But it is also a status. This means two things. First, the parties are not entirely free to determine all its legal consequences for themselves. They contract into the package which the law of the land lays down. Secondly, their marriage also has legal consequences for other people and for the state.[54]

Rob George,[55] arguing for a status understanding of marriage puts the point like this:

> Entering a marriage is, in some ways, more like joining a club. If you meet the entry requirements, you may become a member, but it does not entitle you to alter the club's rules unilaterally. You can join the club or not, and you can campaign to change the rules of the club whether you are a member or not; but you cannot both be a member of the club and refuse to abide by its current rules.

Dewar and Parker have suggested marriage should be regarded as 'a contractually acquired status'.[56] There are some legal consequences which flow automatically from marriage, and other consequences which depend on the agreement of the parties. The law sets out: who can marry; when the relationship can be ended; and what are the consequences for the parties of being married. However, increasing emphasis is placed on encouraging the parties to resolve their disputes at the end of their relationship themselves without referring them to court (see Chapter 2). Further, in ***Radmacher v Granatino***[57] the Supreme Court has given legal weight to pre-nuptial contracts, suggesting a greater willingness to allow people to decide for themselves the legal consequences of their relationship. The case produced a rather hysterical reaction with one commentator suggesting it was the 'death knell of marriage'[58] because if couples could choose what marriage meant for them then marriage would lose all its meaning. As there are severe restrictions on what obligations a married couple can contract out of, this was an exaggeration. History will tell, however, whether the case was the first step towards a wholly contractualised vision of marriage.[59]

Some have argued that it would be preferable to move towards a more contractarian view of marriage. The law could require each couple wishing to marry to decide for themselves exactly what the legal consequences of their marriage would be in a pre-marriage contract. If necessary, the law could produce some sample contracts that people might choose to use. The supporters of such a proposal tend to fall within three camps. First, some feminists argue that a contractarian view of marriage would enable women to avoid the traditional marital roles that are disadvantageous to them. Secondly, from a libertarian perspective some argue that the

---

[53] *The Ampthill Peerage Case* [1977] AC 547.
[54] *Radmacher v Granatino* [2010] UKSC 42, para 132.
[55] (2012b: 83).
[56] Dewar and Parker (2000: 125).
[57] [2010] UKSC 42.
[58] Herring (2010i).
[59] Vardag and Miles (2016).

law should not impose upon people any regulation of their intimate lives. Spouses should choose their own form of regulation[60] rather than there being one kind of marriage sanctioned by the state. After all, there are many different kinds and understandings of marriage and a contractual-based approach can recognise those differences. Thirdly, there are traditionalists who believe that the present law on marriage is too liberal and that a couple should be allowed to contract to enter a 'traditional' marriage, for example severely restricting access to divorce.[61]

Opponents of contractual marriage argue that pre-marriage contracts are unpopular among the general public because they are 'not very romantic'.[62] They implicitly accept that marriage may not be for life. Perhaps more significantly, it is argued that entering a fair contract is only possible if the parties are fully aware of each other's financial position, are independently advised and have equality of bargaining power.[63] In only a few cases will this be so. Even if the parties do have full information and equality of bargaining power, the parties cannot foresee the future, and so the contract may rapidly become outdated and need to be continually renegotiated. Other opponents argue that the contract approach overlooks the interests the state might have in the marriage: the state might wish to support marriage because it has benefits for society as a whole; or the state may have an interest in ensuring that people are not taken advantage of within intimate relationships.[64] If this is so, the state will not want to leave the law of marriage entirely up to the parties themselves. Mary Lyndon Shanley has suggested that the contractual view of marriage 'fails to take into account the ideal of marriage as a relationship that transcends the individual lives of the parties'.[65] Margaret Brinig[66] argues that marriage represents public support and reinforcement for relationships that enable trust to be built up because they rest on a long-term commitment. A compromise solution would be for the state to offer people who wish to marry a range of alternative forms of marriage from which they can choose. For example, some US states offer, as an alternative to the standard marriage, 'covenant' marriage, which permits divorce in limited circumstances only.[67]

5 The presumption of marriage

Learning objective 5

Explain how a presumption of marriage can arise and how it can be rebutted

If a couple live together, believe themselves to be married, and present themselves as married, the law sometimes presumes that they are legally married.[68] Where the presumption applies, anyone who seeks to claim that the couple are not married must introduce evidence to rebut this presumption. The policy behind this is that a couple who believe themselves to be married should not suffer the disadvantages that would follow from being found not to be married without there being clear evidence.[69] In many cases the presumption can be rebutted by showing that they do not appear on the register of marriage.

[60] McLellan (1996).
[61] See Chapter 4 for a discussion of these arguments.
[62] Bridge (2001: 27).
[63] McLellan (1996).
[64] Herring (2009b).
[65] Lyndon Shanley (2004: 6).
[66] Brinig (2010).
[67] Waddington (2000: 251–2). Fineman (2004: 133) reports that where these are available only 1.5 per cent of marriages have been covenant marriages.
[68] The presumption was preserved by s. 7(3)(b)(i) of the Civil Evidence Act 1995.
[69] Borkowski (2002).

The presumption is most often used where the marriage took place a long time ago or abroad[70] and so official records are not available. In *Hayatleh v Mofdy*[71] the couple had married in Syria and there was conflicting evidence as to whether they had married. The couple had lived as a married couple and regarded themselves as such and this was sufficient to create a presumption of marriage. By contrast, in **Martin v Myers**,[72] where the couple had never travelled abroad, the court held that as there was no record of their marriage in the register of marriage this was sufficient evidence to rebut the presumption. The presumption will only arise if there is a consistent and lengthy period of cohabitation. The court appears to be taking a strict approach. Eight years was said to be insufficient in **Dukali v Lamrani**.[73] In **Al-Saedy v Musawi (Presumption of Marriage)**[74] it was found there had been cohabitation 'for periods of time from time to time', but there was insufficient consistency to raise the presumption. It might be questioned how relevant the period of cohabitation should be.[75] Remember the presumption is that there has been a valid ceremony of marriage. The length of cohabitation (certainly once it is longer than a few months) is not a very reliable indicator of whether the couple underwent a ceremony of marriage. Even then much will depend on the cultural and religious beliefs of the couple.

The presumption can be rebutted if it can be shown that the parties did not undergo a legal marriage.[76] However, the longer the parties have cohabited, the stronger the presumption is that they are legally married.[77] In order to rebut the presumption of marriage, clear and positive evidence must be introduced.[78] In *Pazpena de Vire v Pazpena de Vire*[79] a distinction was drawn between cases where the couple have cohabited following a ceremony but there are doubts whether the ceremony is valid, and cases where there is no evidence of a ceremony but there has been a lengthy cohabitation, with the couple believing themselves to be, and being regarded by others as being, married. Where there has been some kind of ceremony, it must be shown beyond reasonable doubt that the ceremony was an invalid marriage; otherwise the presumption will apply.[80] Where there is no evidence of a ceremony, there must be firm evidence that there was no marriage. It is important to appreciate that the law is not saying that couples who live together are married because they cohabit, but that there is a presumption that they have undergone a ceremony of marriage unless proved otherwise. In **Al-Saedy v Musawi (Presumption of Marriage)**[81] Bodey J warned against:

> . . . elevating a presumption born of common sense into the status of a rule of substance, whereby long cohabitation plus a reputation of marriage would establish marriage, even where all the identified evidence showed that no valid or even void marriage took place.

If the validity of a marriage is ambiguous, there is power under s. 55 of the Family Law Act 1986 for a court to make a declaration clarifying the status of the marriage.

---

[70] *A-M v A-M (Divorce: Jurisdiction: Validity of Marriage)* [2001] 2 FLR 6.
[71] [2017] EWCA Civ 70. See Probert (2018).
[72] [2004] EWHC 1947 (Ch).
[73] [2012] EWHC 1748 (Fam). *A v H (Registrar General for England and Wales and another intervening)* [2009] 3 FCR 95 said a year and a half was insufficient.
[74] [2010] EWHC 3293 (Fam).
[75] Probert (2018).
[76] *Asaad v Kurter* [2013] EWHC 3852 (Fam); *Akhter v Khan* [2018] EWFC 54.
[77] *Chief Adjudication Officer v Bath* [2000] 1 FLR 8.
[78] *Chief Adjudication Officer v Bath* [2000] 1 FLR 8; *Hayatleh v Mofdy* [2017] EWCA Civ 70.
[79] [2001] 1 FLR 460.
[80] But where it is shown that that marriage was void, the presumption cannot be relied upon: *MA v JA* [2012] EWHC 2219 (Fam).
[81] [2010] EWHC 3293 (Fam).

6 Non-qualifying ceremony, void marriages and voidable marriages

Learning objective 6

Differentiate between divorce, nullity, a void marriage, a voidable marriage and a non-qualifying ceremony

Although it is relatively rare for a party to seek to have a marriage annulled in law, nullity is particularly important because, in effect, it defines who may or may not marry and reveals what the law sees as the essential ingredients of marriage. What might appear to be a ceremony of marriage can either be:

- a valid marriage;
- a voidable marriage;
- a void marriage; or
- a non-qualifying ceremony (previously known as a non-marriage), which is of no legal effect.[82]

It is necessary to draw some important distinctions at this point.

A The difference between divorce and nullity

The law relating to marriage draws an important distinction between those marriages which are annulled (void or voidable marriage) and those which are ended by divorce. Where the marriage is annulled the law recognises that there has been some flaw in the establishment of the marriage, rendering it ineffective. Where there is a divorce the creation of the marriage is considered proper but subsequent events demonstrate that the marriage should be brought to an end.

B The difference between a void marriage and non-qualifying ceremony

In both a void marriage and a non-qualifying ceremony (NQC) there is a significant breach of the marriage requirements. If the parties were unaware of the breach then the marriage may still be valid. Where the couple were aware of the breach the ceremony will be a void marriage or an NQC. A void marriage is one where, although there may have been some semblance of a marriage, there is in fact a fundamental flaw in the marriage which means that it is not recognised in the law as valid. This needs to be distinguished from an NQC, where the ceremony that the parties undertook was nothing like a marriage and so is of no legal consequence.[83] In short, a void marriage is a flawed and unsuccessful attempt to marry; an NQC does not even constitute an attempt at a marriage. An example might be a 'marriage' during a theatrical performance or some friends having a 'marriage' in a park for a laugh. An NQC is a nothing in the eyes of the law. The distinction is of great practical significance because if it is a void marriage then the court has the power to make financial orders, redistributing property between the couple. If the ceremony is an NQC the court has no power to redistribute property and the couple will be treated as an unmarried couple.

The distinction between void marriages and NQCs has proved complex. One important factor is whether an onlooker would think the ceremony was a marriage. In *Gereis v Yagoub*[84]

---

[82] See the useful discussion on the distinction between these in Probert (2002b and 2013b).
[83] *Dukali v Lamrani* [2012] EWHC 1748 (Fam).
[84] [1997] 1 FLR 854, [1997] 3 FCR 755.

the couple went through a purported marriage at a Coptic Orthodox Church without going through the legal formalities. Although the priest had encouraged the parties to have a civil ceremony of marriage, they had not done so. Judge Aglionby decided that the marriage was void because the parties had knowingly and wilfully intermarried in disregard of the formalities under the Marriage Act 1949. He held that the ceremony should be regarded as a void marriage rather than an NQC because of the following factors: the ceremony had the 'hallmarks of an ordinary Christian marriage'; the parties regarded themselves as married (they had sexual intercourse only after the service); the couple held themselves out as a married couple by, for example, claiming married couple's tax allowance.

It could be argued that the case law is discriminating against ethnic minorities because their ceremonies do not 'bear the hallmarks of a marriage' as understood in a Christian context.[85] Indeed, an Islamic ceremony in a private flat[86] and a Hindu ceremony in a restaurant[87] have been held to be NQCs, being too far distant from what one would expect from a marriage ceremony. Care must be taken in these judgments not to impose cultural norms about what marriages are meant to look like.

It is also clear the court will focus on the intents of the parties. So, in **Hudson v Leigh (Status of Non-Marriage)**[88] the parties had a ceremony using an amended version of a marriage service. But the amendments made it clear the parties did not intend to get married, because the promises related to marriage in the future. That was strong evidence this was an NQC.

In **Galloway v Goldstein**[89] a couple who had married in America went through a ceremony in England. The English ceremony was held to be an NQC. The couple could not have intended the ceremony to be a marriage, as they were already married. That case should be contrasted with **K v K**[90] where, similarly, the husband was married to someone else, but here the evidence indicated the couple did intend to enter a (polygamous) marriage. Although as a polygamous marriage entered into in the UK it could not be a valid marriage, the fact the parties intended it to be a marriage rendered it a void marriage (rather than an NQC). In **Galloway v Goldstein**[91] there had been no suggestion the parties wanted to create a polygamous marriage.

The leading case on the distinction between void marriages and NQCs is the following.

KEY CASE: *Her Majesty's Attorney General v Akhter and Khan* [2020] EWCA Civ 122

The couple undertook a Muslim Nikah marriage ceremony in a restaurant in 1998. They were advised by the imam they needed a civil ceremony for the marriage to be legally recognised, but they failed to do so. The wife stated this was because her husband refused to arrange it. The husband disputed this. They had four children. In 2016 the wife petitioned for divorce, but the husband disputed they were married in the eyes of the law.

It was accepted the marriage was not a valid marriage because the parties had knowingly failed to comply with the formalities. But the issue was whether the marriage was a void marriage or a non-qualifying ceremony. That was important because financial orders

---

[85] See the discussion in Probert (2002b).

[86] *A-M v A-M (Divorce: Jurisdiction: Validity of Marriage)* [2001] 2 FLR 6; *El Gamal v Al Maktoum* [2011] EWHC B27 (Fam).

[87] *Gandhi v Patel* [2002] 1 FLR 603. See also *B v B* [2012] EWHC 2219 (Fam).

[88] [2009] 3 FCR 401.

[89] [2012] EWHC 60 (Fam), discussed in Herring (2012i). See also *Sharbatly v Shagroon* [2012] EWCA Civ 1507.

[90] [2016] EWHC 3380 (Fam).

[91] [2012] EWHC 60 (Fam), discussed in Herring (2012i). See also *Sharbatly v Shagroon* [2012] EWCA Civ 1507.

under the Matrimonial Causes Act 1973 could be made when declaring a marriage void, but not in the case of a non-qualifying ceremony.

Williams J, at first instance, found the marriage was a void marriage, emphasising the importance of the right to respect for family life and the right to marry under Articles 8 and 12 of the ECHR, which he thought meant the court needed to take a flexible approach and give the ceremony some legal significance. He found the couple had intended to include a civil legal ceremony; had held a ceremony in public, involving witnesses and promises; and that the ceremony had been officiated by an imam. This was sufficiently close to a marriage to be seen as a void marriage, rather than a non-qualifying ceremony. He also thought the interests of the children was a 'primary consideration' and it was in their interests that financial orders could be made. That also was a factor in favour of finding a void marriage.

The Court of Appeal allowed the appeal. It found that there was no 'marriage ceremony' which could be held to be void. The Court of Appeal described the ceremony as a 'non-qualifying ceremony' (NQC) (preferring that language to the term 'non-marriage'). NQCs do not create even a void marriage and so no financial orders under the Matrimonial Causes Act were available. The ceremony was an NQC because the couple were not marrying 'under the provisions' of the Marriage Act 1949. The building was not registered; no certificates of marriage were issued; and no authorised person was present at the ceremony (the imam had not been registered to conduct marriages under the 1949 Act). The parties were fully aware the ceremony was to have no legal effect. Evidence about what they intended to do after the ceremony (e.g. enter a civil marriage) did not change the nature of the ceremony itself. Otherwise a couple who changed their mind and decided not to have a civil ceremony would have their intentions defeated because they would be treated as being married.

The Court of Appeal rejected the arguments based on the ECHR. There was no interference with the right to marry as the couple had not married. There was an engagement with Article 8 rights but the failure to give legal effect to a Nikah marriage did not breach those rights.

The Court of Appeal rejected the argument of Williams J relying on the rights of children, because the decision was not 'an action concerning children'. In any event, it would be wrong to allow the interests of children to transform a ceremony into a valid or void marriage.

The Court of Appeal in reaching this conclusion clearly wanted to maintain a clear line between ceremonies which had legal effect and ones which did not. Had Williams J's judgment stood, it would have been very difficult to tell which ceremonies were void marriages and which were NQCs. The Court of Appeal rejected an argument that all religious ceremonies of marriage should be treated as void marriages, seeing there being no reason why the religious element should transform an ineffective ceremony into a void marriage. Allowing any ceremony that described itself as a marriage to be at least a void marriage would, in effect, deregulate marriage. The Court of Appeal explained:

> to prevent the regulatory system being fundamentally undermined and in a manner which would be contrary to the need for certainty in the interests of the parties and in the public interest, we would have decided that there are some ceremonies of marriage which do not create even void marriages.

The Court of Appeal said of Williams J's judgment: 'with respect to the judge, who was clearly seeking a route which he understandably believed would lead to a fair outcome for the petitioner, that is to say the ability to make an application for financial remedies for herself, we do not consider that his approach can withstand analysis'. That is a polite way of saying the judge decided what the fair outcome was and then found some arguments to justify it. That might be a little harsh and there are certainly two issues raised by Williams J that may require further thought.

The first is that the current law is discriminatory. In short, if you are an adherent of the Church of England and go through a religious ceremony in your church it will be treated as a legally valid marriage. However, if you are a Muslim and go through a religious ceremony in your Mosque, it may very well not be treated as having any legal significance. That seems clearly wrong: why should your religion affect the legal significance of your ceremony? Indeed, it is an even worse situation for humanists who are not able to conduct legally valid marriage, whatever paperwork is completed. In *R (Harrison)* v *Secretary of State for Justice*[92] it was accepted that was discriminatory under the Human Rights Act 1998. However, maybe, the answer to that issue is better dealt with by legislation than trying to develop the law on void marriages. Indeed, the Law Commission have announced they will be reviewing the law on marriage formalities.

The second issue involves the interests of children. Williams J saw the interests of children as significant in deciding the ceremony should be seen as a void marriage. There is a clear disadvantage to children if financial remedies are not available to their parents under the Matrimonial Causes Act (MCA) on divorce. Normally the courts will make orders which promote children's welfare. The Court of Appeal downplayed this point by noting that children of unmarried parents can receive child support under Children Act 1989, Sched. 1, so they can be in the same position as if orders were made under the MCA (see Chapter 6). This is true, but it does not account for the disadvantage of children living with, for example, a mother who is in poverty as she cannot claim under the MCA. That will be a tangible and emotional disadvantage to children. However, the problem with the argument of Williams J is that it would be odd if the status of a couple's relationship depended on whether they had children or not. Again, the answer to the disadvantage of children born to unmarried couples may also better be dealt with by legislation addressing that issue than the law of nullity.

The approach of the Court of Appeal prioritised the importance of certainty. But, as Cummings[93] has argued, this comes at a cost:

> in the Court of Appeal's decision we see the resolution of a tension between competing moral and legal imperatives: a preference for form and abstract autonomy over context and lived reality and the championing of certainty over the value of individualisation and flexibility . . . The result is that women will still fall through the cracks . . . Women are faced with a decision between their religion and their rights; their family and their autonomy.

There seems to be a common difficulty relating to Muslim couples who undertake their religious (Nikah) marriage in circumstances which mean it is legally a non-marriage.[94] One study found '60% (of the 901 respondents) did not have a civil marriage, meaning they were not legally married and instead had only conducted a nikah marriage. Within this group, a minority (28%) were unaware of their lack of status.'[95] Eighty-six per cent of respondents wanted their marriage to be legally recognised. The difficulty with such cases is that the couple may regard themselves as validly married, and be treated by their families and community as married. Yet in the event of a legal issue arising there is no formal legal marriage or recourse to legal remedies based on marriage. This is particularly an issue where women seek financial

[92] [2020] EWHC 2096 (Admin).
[93] Cummings (2020).
[94] Fisher, Saleem, and Vora (2018); Akhtar (2016).
[95] Vora (2020).

orders following the breakdown of their 'marriage'. The problem according to Vishal Vora[96] is that many Muslim couples regard the religious ceremony as the important one and civil registration as irrelevant, or even worse a state intrusion into a religious event. In half the cases in her sample the Nikah was performed at home and so was not valid and the couple assumed the imam would ensure any formalities were met. She reports particular concerns that women are far more likely than men to be mistaken as to the legal significance of the ceremony.

In 2018 the Home Office produced an independent report into the formalities around marriage.[97] The question is whether it is preferable to amend the law so that Nikahs and other religious marriages can count as legally valid marriages or to maintain the current approach that they are not formally recognised, but through the concept of void marriage can be given equivalent legal effect. It is a difficult question because treating all religious marriages as legal marriage may seem to interfere with freedom of religion, but not treating them as legally valid may leave people without the legal protections of marriage. Religious groups may object to what might be seen as secular regulation of religious sacraments.

The Government report suggests that sections 75 to 77 of the Marriage Act 1949 be amended to make it clear that the celebrant of certain marriages, including Islamic marriage, would face penalties should they fail to ensure that the marriage is also civilly registered. That would seek to persuade imams to register all Muslim marriages. However, it must be questioned whether we really want to see imams being arrested for these new criminal offences. Rebecca Probert also queries the weight in the review placed on registration. She notes:

> First, and most obviously, registration – in the sense of the act of recording the marriage in writing – is not essential to the validity of a marriage. Secondly, it misses the opportunity to remind individuals and institutions of the processes that are essential for a marriage. Thirdly, it gives the misleading impression that an informal ceremony of marriage can be validated by simply registering it after it has taken place, when of course what would be necessary is for the parties to comply with the formalities that the law requires for a valid marriage, including the giving of notice before the marriage.[98]

A better response might be to consider whether the law on formalities can be amended so no religious ceremonies of marriage have legal effect. That is the position in most countries and it might make it easier for the Government to send a clear message that to be legally married you need a certificate of marriage from the registrar. The most radical option, and one we will consider later, is to decide marriage should no longer have any legal consequence at all and we treat all cohabitants in the same way, whether they have undertaken a ceremony or not.[99]

C The difference between a void and a voidable marriage

A void marriage is one that in the eyes of the law has never existed. A voidable marriage exists until it has been annulled by the courts and, if it is never annulled by a court order, it will be treated as valid. This distinction has a number of significant consequences:

1. Technically, a void marriage is void even if it has never been declared to be so by a court, whereas a voidable marriage is valid from the date of the marriage until the court makes an order. That said, a party who believes his or her marriage to be void would normally seek a

---

[96] Vora (2016).
[97] Home Office (2018).
[98] Probert (2018b).
[99] For further discussion of this issue see O'Sullivan and Jackson (2017).

court order to confirm this to be so. This avoids any doubts over the validity of the marriage and also permits the parties to apply for court orders relating to their financial affairs.[100]

2. A child born to parties of a void marriage would be technically 'illegitimate', unless at the time of the conception either parent reasonably believed that they were validly married to the other parent.[101] The concept of illegitimacy is now not part of the law, but still there are a very few consequences that depend on whether a child's parents are married or unmarried.[102]

3. The distinction between a void and a voidable marriage may also be important in determining one person's rights to the other's pension.[103]

4. Any person may seek a declaration that the marriage is void,[104] but only the parties to the marriage can apply to annul a voidable marriage. This reflects a fundamental distinction in the grounds on which marriage can be declared void or voidable. The grounds on which a marriage may be declared void are those circumstances in which there is an element of public policy against the marriage, hence, any interested person can seek a declaration of nullity. The grounds on which a marriage may be voidable do not indicate that there is a public policy objection to the marriage, but rather that there is a problem in the marriage which is so significant that, if one of the parties wishes, the marriage can be annulled.

Having discussed these distinctions, it is now necessary to consider the grounds on which a marriage may be void or voidable.

D The grounds on which a marriage is void

Learning objective 7

Explain the grounds on which a marriage is void

As already noted, the grounds[105] on which a marriage is void are those which reflect a public policy objection to the marriage. The grounds[106] are set out in the Matrimonial Causes Act 1973, s. 11:

LEGISLATIVE PROVISION

Matrimonial Causes Act 1973, section 11

(a) that it is not a valid marriage under the provisions of the Marriage Acts 1949 to 1986 (that is to say where–

 (i) the parties are within the prohibited degrees of relationship;
 (ii) either party is under the age of sixteen; or
 (iii) the parties have intermarried in disregard of certain requirements as to the formation of marriage);

(b) that at the time of the marriage either party was already lawfully married;

(c) in the case of a polygamous marriage entered into outside England and Wales, that either party was at the time of the marriage domiciled in England and Wales.

---

[100] *Whiston v Whiston* [1995] 2 FLR 268, [1995] 2 FCR 496.
[101] Legitimacy Act 1976, s. 1(1).
[102] See Chapter 8.
[103] See *Ward v Secretary of State for Social Services* [1990] 1 FLR 119, [1990] FCR 361.
[104] Matrimonial Causes Act 1973 (hereafter MCA 1973), s. 16. This section applies to decrees after 31 July 1971.
[105] *Re Roberts (dec'd)* [1978] 1 WLR 653 at p. 656, per Walton J.
[106] Walton J suggested that the set of grounds set out in MCA 1973 is exhaustive and so there is no jurisdiction for the courts to create new grounds: *Re Roberts (dec'd)* [1978] 1 WLR 653 at p. 658.

These grounds will now be considered separately.

(i) Prohibited degrees

The marriage between two people who are related to each other in certain ways is prohibited. It is interesting that nearly all societies across the world have bars on marriages between people who are related. In Britain the restrictions are based on two groups of relations: those based on blood relationships (consanguinity) and those based on marriage (affinity). The details of the law are set out in the Marriage (Prohibited Degrees of Relationship) Act 1986, s. 6(2).

1. The prohibited consanguinity restrictions mean that marriage between the following is not permitted: parent–child; grandparent–grandchild; brother–sister; uncle–niece; aunt–nephew. These include relations of the half-blood as well as those relationships based on the whole blood. It will be noted that cousins may marry under English law.[107]

2. The affinity restrictions are traditionally based on the 'unity of husband and wife'. This is the notion that, on marriage, a husband and wife become one. These prohibited degrees based on marriage are controversial because some believe that the doctrine of unity upon which they are based is outdated. Only one remains: marrying a stepchild. A step-parent can marry the child of a former spouse if: (i) both parties are aged 21 or over; and (ii) the younger party has not been a child of the family in relation to the other while under the age of 18. The effect of the law is that if a step-parent acts in a parental role towards a step-child, the two can never marry. The bar on parents-in-law and children-in-law that used to exist was abolished by the Marriage Act 1949 (Remedial) Order 2007 No. 438.[108]

3. Even though adoption normally ends the relationship between the adopted child and his or her birth family, the restrictions on marriage between an adopted child and members of his or her birth family apply as above. An adoptive child and adoptive parent are also within the prohibited degrees of relationship.[109] However, an adopted child can marry other relations that arise from the adoption. So, a man could marry the daughter of his adopted parents.[110]

The restrictions based on these relationships are justified by three arguments. The first is the fear of genetic dangers involved in permitting procreation between close blood relations. This would not justify bars based on affinity and with the availability of genetic screening may be harder to support. A second argument in favour of these bars is that permitting marriage between close relations may undermine the security of the family. The argument is that children should be brought up without the possibility of approved sexual relations later in life with members of their family. A third argument can be based on the widespread instinctive moral reaction against such relationships. Whether this 'yuck factor' is sufficient to justify preventing two people in love from marrying may be debated. A challenge to the German law prohibiting sexual relations between related people was upheld in *Stübing v Germany*,[111] where the aims of protection of the family, self-determination and public health were said to be reasonable grounds for the prohibition.

---

[107] For a discussion of whether cousin marriage should be permitted, see Deech (2010c) and Taylor (2008) who both express concerns about the potential genetic harm to children of such marriages.

[108] This follows the decision in *B v UK* [2005] 3 FCR 353.

[109] This is a permanent bar and applies even if the child is adopted for a second time.

[110] Assuming the daughter is not his half-sister.

[111] [2013] 1 FCR 107.

It should be recalled that although these restrictions prevent, say, a father marrying his daughter, there would be nothing to prevent them cohabiting, although any sexual relations would constitute the crime of incest.

(ii) Age

There are two requirements that relate to the age of the parties:

1. A marriage will be void if either party to the marriage is under 16.[112] All western societies have some kind of age restrictions on who may marry and a minimum age for legal sexual relations, although exactly what that age is varies from state to state and generation to generation.[113] The choice of the age 16 in England and Wales reflects the policy of the criminal law that it is unlawful for a man to have sexual intercourse with a girl under 16. It also reflects the concern of society about any children that may be born of such a union: the parents may be too young to care for the children and the burden could then fall on the state. There is also the argument that, below that age, the parties may not fully understand the consequences of marriage.

2. The second requirement is that if either party is between the age of 16 and 18 then it is necessary to have the written consent of each parent with parental responsibility.[114] It is possible for the teenager to apply to the court to have the parental consent requirement revoked. However, if the marriage goes ahead without that consent (or on the basis of a forged consent), it would still be valid. The significance of this requirement, then, is that it permits a registrar to refuse to carry out a wedding without this consent. Rebecca Probert has questioned whether requiring parental consent to marry is appropriate in this day and age.[115]

(iii) Formalities

There are complex rules governing the legal formalities required for a marriage.[116] The exact requirements depend on whether the marriage was performed within the rites of the Church of England or outside. The detailed provisions will not be discussed here.

The purposes of having formalities can be said to be as follows:

1. The formality requirements help to draw a clear line between a marriage, an engagement, and an agreement to cohabit.

2. The formality requirements ensure that the parties do not enter into marriage in an ill-considered or frivolous way. To fulfil the requirements takes some time and effort. Further, they ensure that the moment of marriage is a solemn event. This reinforces the seriousness of marriage to the parties and those present.

---

[112] Marriage Act 1949, s. 2. On the issue of under-age marriage see Gangoli, McCarry and Razak (2009).

[113] Indeed, until 1929 in England a girl could marry from the age of 12.

[114] Unless there is a residence order, in which case only the parents with parental responsibility and residence order need consent: Marriage Act 1949, s. 3, as amended. A guardian or local authority can also provide consent in certain circumstances.

[115] Probert (2009b).

[116] The Registration of Marriage Bill 2018 will, if passed, reform the law on registration formalities. Most significantly it will lead to there being an electronic register of marriages and the occupation of the spouses' mothers being listed (as well as those of their fathers).

3. The existence of the formalities helps to ensure that there is a formal record of marriages.[117]

4. The formalities also ensure that anyone who wishes to object to the marriage can do so.[118]

There are, however, dangers that formalities can be too strict. There are two particular concerns. The first is that couples may be discouraged from marrying if the formalities are too onerous. This concern led to the passing of the Marriage Act 1995, which has greatly increased the number of places where a marriage can take place.[119] Secondly, if the law were interpreted too strictly, a minor breach of the rules could invalidate what might appear to be a valid marriage. The law has dealt with this concern under ss. 25 and 49 of the Marriage Act 1995, which state that a marriage is void for breaching the formalities only if the parties marry knowingly and wilfully in breach of the requirement.[120] As we have seen a major departure from the formality requirements is likely to mean the event is a non-qualifying ceremony and not even a void marriage.

One further issue is whether the parties should be required to undergo biological tests, in order to see if either party is suffering from an infectious illness. There have been calls for genetic testing to be carried out on the parties before marriage.[121] At present no biological tests are required in England and Wales. The reason may be that a requirement of tests would discourage marriage.

There have also been some calls that couples be required to attend marriage counselling sessions before marriage. The closest the Government has come was a proposal in the 1990s that a 'clear and simple guide' detailing the rights and responsibilities of marriage should be made available to all couples planning to marry.[122] This seems very sensible given the lack of understanding over the legal consequences of marriage.[123] In the US a computer questionnaire has become a popular way for a couple to check compatibility before marriage. Apparently, having taken the test and considered the results, 10 per cent of couples decided not to marry.[124]

(iv) Bigamy

If at the time of the ceremony either party is already married to someone else, the 'marriage' will be void. The marriage will remain void even if the first spouse dies during the second 'marriage'.[125] So, if a person is married and wishes to marry someone else, he or she must obtain a decree of divorce or wait until the death of his or her spouse. If the first marriage is void, it is technically not necessary to obtain a court order to that effect before marrying again, but that is normally sought to avoid any uncertainty. In cases of bigamy, as well as the purported marriage being void, the parties may have committed the crime of bigamy.[126] Chris Barton[127] has argued that there is little justification for making bigamy a crime and instead more could be done at the time of marriage to check whether parties are free to marry.

---

[117] Although see the remarkable case of *Islam v Islam* [2003] FL 815 where, although the evidence showed that the woman had been married, she was not able to show that she had married the man she claimed to be her husband. The judge asked the papers to be sent to the Crown Prosecution Service so that it could consider possible criminal proceedings against the wife.

[118] *MA v JA* [2012] EWHC 2219 (Fam).

[119] See Eekelaar (2013b) for an argument that there should be no restrictions on where a marriage can take place.

[120] See *Chief Adjudication Officer v Bath* [2000] 1 FCR 419, [2000] 1 FLR 8 for an example of a case where the parties were unaware of the non-compliance with the formalities.

[121] Discussed in Deech (2010d).

[122] Home Office (1998: 4.15).

[123] Hibbs, Barton and Beswick (2001).

[124] Hibbs, Barton and Beswick (2001).

[125] *Dredge v Dredge* [1947] 1 All ER 29.

[126] In *Khan v UK* (1986) 48 DR 253 the European Court of Human Rights rejected an argument that the bar on polygamous marriage infringed the parties' rights under Article 12 of the European Convention

[127] Barton (2004).

Many cultures do permit polygamous marriages, although in British society monogamous marriages are the accepted norm, which is rarely challenged.[128] There are concrete objections to polygamous marriages. Some argue that polygamy may create divisions within the family, with one husband or wife vying for dominance over the others, and particularly that divisions may arise between the children of different parents.[129] Supporters of polygamous marriage argue that polygamy leads to less divorce and provides a wider family support network in which to raise children. Polygamy could also be regarded as a form of sex discrimination unless both men and women were permitted to take more than one spouse. There have also been suggestions that permitting polygamous marriages involves an insult to the religious sensitivities of the majority.

A more fundamental challenge to marriage as traditionally understood comes from those who promote polyamory, defined as 'consensual openly-conducted, multi-partner relationships in which both men and women have negotiated access to additional partners outside of the traditional committed couple'.[130] Note this is different from polygamy in that it starts with the notion of a core couple, but they agree that either party might engage in sexual relationships outside the core relationship. Ronald Den Otter argues that polyamorous relationships carry the advantages of more sex, more care, more love, less jealousy and greater honesty.[131] It might be argued that 'affairs' within marriage have a long pedigree and that in that sense polyamory is not particularly revolutionary. All it is doing is being more honest about human nature. Indeed, Den Otter suggests acceptance of polyamory might strengthen marriage by making couples honest about the issues. It is not clear that acceptance of polyamory would require a change in the law as such. There is nothing in the current law which would mean a polyamorous couple could not be married. So, perhaps, this does not pose a particular challenge to the law of marriage, even if it does to the concept of marriage.

(v) Public policy

In *City of Westminster* v *C*[132] the Court of Appeal held a marriage between a man with severe intellectual impairment and a woman in Bangladesh performed over the telephone void. He lacked capacity to have any understanding of the nature of marriage and would be unable to consent to sexual relations. The marriage was described as exploitative of the woman and of the man. Although normally lack of capacity would render a marriage voidable rather than void, public policy justified this marriage being declared void. This case highlights the way the law sees sexual relations as at the heart of marriage. While a sexual relationship may not have been appropriate in this case, a relationship of care might have been. The court would have done better to focus on the issue of capacity to consent to enter a close relationship, rather than the sexual one. The decision was followed in *X County Council* v *AA*[133] where the inherent jurisdiction was used to declare invalid a marriage involving a woman with significant learning difficulties. Again, the emphasis was on the sexual issues with it being emphasised that she did not understand the differences between men and women or pregnancy. A stronger justification could be found in the fact there was no evidence that she consented to be in the relationship and that she was at risk from it.

---

[128] Shah (2003) discusses the extent of unofficial polygamy in the UK and highlights the problems in regulating against it.

[129] See Bala and Jaremko Bromwich (2002: 166–9) for a discussion of the arguments against polygamy. See Kaganas and Murray (2001) and Emens (2004) for a more supportive approach.

[130] Sheff (2013: 1).

[131] Den Otter (2018); Brunning (2018).

[132] [2008] 2 FCR 146, see Probert (2008a) for a discussion of this case.

[133] [2012] EWHC 2183 (Fam).

(vi) Marriages entered into abroad

Complex issues of private international law arise over the recognition of marriages conducted abroad, and these are not discussed in this text.[134]

LEGISLATIVE PROVISION

Matrimonial Causes Act 1973, section 12

(a) that the marriage has not been consummated owing to the incapacity of either party to consummate it;

(b) that the marriage has not been consummated owing to the wilful refusal of the respondent to consummate it;

(c) that either party to the marriage did not validly consent to it, whether in consequence of duress, mistake, unsoundness of mind or otherwise;

(d) that at the time of the marriage either party, though capable of giving a valid consent, was suffering (whether continuously or intermittently) from mental disorder within the meaning of the Mental Health Act 1983 of such a kind or to such an extent as to be unfitted for marriage;

(e) that at the time of the marriage the respondent was suffering from venereal disease in a communicable form;

(f) that at the time of the marriage the respondent was pregnant by some person other than the petitioner;

(g) that an interim gender recognition certificate under the Gender Recognition Act 2004 has, after the time of the marriage, been issued to either party to the marriage;

(h) that the respondent is a person whose gender at the time of the marriage had become the acquired gender under the Gender Recognition Act 2004.

E The grounds on which a marriage is voidable

Learning objective 8

Explain the grounds on which a marriage is voidable

The grounds on which a marriage is voidable are set out in the Matrimonial Causes Act 1973, s. 12.

These grounds will now be considered separately.

(i) Inability or wilful refusal to consummate

The consummation grounds only apply to marriages involving couples of the opposite sex. The importance of consummation was originally based on the theological ground that the act of sexual intercourse united the two spouses in a spiritual union and was therefore necessary to complete the sacrament of marriage. The requirement of consummation can also be explained in non-religious terms in that it is the act of sexual intercourse that most clearly distinguishes marriage from a close relationship between two platonic friends. However, given the increase in sexual relations outside of marriage it is harder to argue that sexual intercourse has a unique place in marriage.[135]

---

[134] See, e.g., Murphy (2005).
[135] Herring (2016a).

In order for a marriage to be consummated, there need only be one act of consummation; but the act must take place after the solemnisation of the marriage.[136] So in *P v P*,[137] where a husband only had sexual relations eight times in 18 years, the marriage was not voidable and divorce was the only way to end the marriage. There are two grounds of voidability connected to consummation. The first ground is a wilful refusal by a spouse to consummate the marriage, and the second is the incapacity of either party to consummate the marriage. The applicant for the nullity application can rely on his or her own inability to consummate but not on his or her own wilful refusal. This is because a party should not be able to rely on his or her own decision not to consummate in order to annul a marriage. It is useful to have the two alternative grounds as it may be difficult in a particular case to discover whether the non-consummation was due to inability or wilful refusal.

What is meant by consummation? 'Consummation' is defined as an act of sexual intercourse. Consummation can only be carried out by the penetration of the vagina by the penis. No other form of sexual activity will amount to consummation. Intercourse needs to be 'ordinary and complete, and not partial and imperfect'.[138] There needs to be full penetration, but there is no need for an ejaculation or orgasm.[139] In *Baxter v Baxter*[140] the House of Lords held that consummation took place even though the man was wearing a condom.[141] There have even been cases where a pregnancy resulted from a sexual act but the court decided there was no consummation because there was no penetration.[142] This reveals that the consummation requirement is not explained by the state's interest in the potential production of children.

'Inability to consummate' means that the inability cannot be cured by surgery[143] and is permanent. Inability can be either physiological or psychological. Inability also includes 'invincible repugnance', where one party is unable to have sexual intercourse due to 'paralysis of the will',[144] but this must be more than lack of attraction or a dislike of the other partner.[145]

There has been much debate over whether the incapacity to consummate marriage has to exist at the time of the marriage. What would happen if the husband was rendered impotent as a result of a fight he had with the bride's father during the reception? Under Canon law impotence could be relied upon only if the impotence existed at the time of marriage. This reflected the crucial distinction between nullity and marriage: nullity applies when defects exist at the time of marriage, while divorce is used when defects occur after the time of the marriage itself. However, the Matrimonial Causes Act makes no reference to the inability existing 'at the time of the marriage', whereas it makes explicit reference to 'at the time of the marriage' in relation to other grounds of voidability. It is therefore submitted that there is a strong case that the inability can occur at any time before or during the marriage as long as the union has not yet been consummated.

---

[136] *Dredge v Dredge* [1947] 1 All ER 29.
[137] [1964] 3 All ER 919.
[138] *D-E v A-G* (1845) 1 Rob Eccl 279 at p. 298.
[139] *R v R* [1952] 1 All ER 1194.
[140] [1948] AC 274.
[141] There is some doubt about *coitus interruptus* (where the man withdraws before ejaculation): *Cackett v Cackett* [1950] P 253; *White v White* [1948] P 330; *Grimes v Grimes* [1948] 2 All ER 147. The issue was left open in *Baxter v Baxter* [1948] AC 274.
[142] *Clarke v Clarke* [1943] 2 All ER 540. The marriage here had lasted 15 years.
[143] If the inability to consummate can only be cured by potentially dangerous surgery, the inability will be treated as permanent: *S v S* [1955] P 1.
[144] *G v G* [1924] AC 349.
[145] *Singh v Singh* [1971] P 226.

'Wilful refusal to consummate' requires a 'settled and definite decision not to consummate without wilful excuse'.[146] If there has been no opportunity to consummate the marriage,[147] it will be hard to show that there has been a wilful refusal unless one party has shown 'unswerving determination' not to consummate the marriage.[148] 'Wilful refusal' may also occur where the parties have agreed only to have intercourse under certain circumstances (e.g. after a religious ceremony[149]). In such a case, then, a refusal by one party to abide by the condition may constitute 'wilful refusal'.[150] The marriage will not be annulled on the ground of wilful refusal if the lack of consummation is due to a just excuse, although the case law reveals very little on the exact meaning of this.[151]

It is worth emphasising that a non-consummated marriage is a valid one until it is voided. In *Re X (A Child: Foreign Surrogacy)*[152] a married couple had never had sex and had no intention of doing so. Sir James Munby was very clear that their marriage was a perfectly valid one. He was clear a marriage could be happy, fulfilling and lawful, even with no sexual element.

(ii) Lack of consent

The Matrimonial Causes Act recognises four circumstances which may cause a person to be unable to give consent so as to render a marriage voidable. These are 'duress, mistake, unsoundness of mind or otherwise'.[153] The law seeks to resolve a tension here. On the one hand, there is the view that it should not be too easy to have a marriage annulled. On the other hand, at least in the West, consent is regarded as a highly important factor in marriage. At one time the law required that the lack of consent was apparent at the time of the ceremony.[154] Although the appearance of consent may be important as a matter of evidence, it is now clear that it is not a formal requirement.

It should be noted that lack of consent renders a marriage voidable rather than void. This means that if a party does not consent to the marriage but later changes his or her mind and is happy with the marriage, the marriage will be valid and there is no need to remarry. The separate ways in which a lack of consent may be demonstrated will now be discussed.

(a) Duress

If it could be shown that someone was compelled to enter a marriage as a result of fear or threats, the marriage may be voidable due to duress. The following issues have been discussed in the case law:

1. **What must the threat or fear be of?** At one time it was thought that it was only possible for duress to render a marriage voidable if there was a threat to 'life, limb or liberty'.[155] The Court of Appeal in *Hirani v Hirani*[156] suggested that the test for duress should focus on the effect of the threat rather than the nature of the threat. In other words, the threats can be of any kind, but it must be shown that 'the threats, pressure or whatever it is, is such as to

---

[146] *Horton v Horton* [1972] 2 All ER 871.
[147] Perhaps because the parties are living in different places (e.g. the husband is in prison).
[148] *Ford v Ford* [1987] Fam Law 232.
[149] *Kaur v Singh* [1972] 1 All ER 292.
[150] *A v J* [1989] 1 FLR 110.
[151] *Horton v Horton* [1972] 2 All ER 871.
[152] [2018] EWFC 15.
[153] Article 16(2) of the Universal Declaration of Human Rights 1948 states that: 'Marriage shall be entered into only with the free and full consent of the intending spouses.'
[154] *Cooper v Crane* [1891] P 369.
[155] *Szechter v Szechter* [1971] P 286; *Singh v Singh* [1971] P 226.
[156] (1982) 4 FLR 232.

destroy the reality of the consent and overbear the will of the individual'.[157] In the case of *Hirani v Hirani*[158] the court accepted that social pressure could overbear the consent. The woman was threatened with ostracism by her community and her family if she did not go through with the marriage, and the fear of complete social isolation was such that there was no true consent. In *P v R (Forced Marriage: Annulment: Procedure)*[159] Colderidge J followed *Hirani* and held that severe emotional pressure could be such as to mean that there was no genuine consent to marry. However, in *Singh v Singh*,[160] it was held that marrying out of a sense of duty or respect to parents could not negate consent. The effect of the *Hirani* decision is that those who have undergone an arranged marriage in the face of considerable pressure have the choice of either accepting their culture and the validity of the marriage or accepting the dominant culture's view that marriage should be made voidable.[161] This could be regarded as an appropriate compromise between respecting the cultural practice of arranged marriages and respecting people's right to choose whom to marry.[162]

2. The Law Commission has suggested that really what is at issue is the legitimacy of the threat rather than the lack of consent. After all, many people feel a pressure from family or society to get married.[163] This approach is reflected in other areas of law where duress is an issue, for example contract law, where reference to the 'overborne will' has largely been abandoned in favour of asking whether the threat is illegitimate.[164] When someone is acting under duress it is not that they do not make a choice but rather that the choice is made in circumstances in which it should not lead to legal effect. This then requires the court to make a judgment on whether the horrors of the alternative meant that the choice should not be given effect, rather than considering whether there was true consent. It may be that when the issue next comes before the Court of Appeal it will focus on the legitimacy of the threat as well as the impact of the threat on the victim. Authority for such an approach could be found in *Buckland v Buckland*[165] which focused on asking whether the threat was a reasonable or unjust one to make.

3. *Must the fear be reasonably held?* What if a threat was made, but a reasonable person would not have taken it seriously? In *Szechter* it was suggested that duress could not be relied upon unless the fear was reasonably held.[166] Against this is *Scott v Selbright*,[167] in which it was suggested that as long as the beliefs of threats were honestly held, duress could be relied upon. The *Scott v Selbright* view seems preferable because it would be undesirable to punish a person for their careless mistake by denying them an annulment.

4. *By whom must the threat be made?* The threat can emanate from a third party; it need not emanate from the spouse.[168]

---

[157] *Hirani v Hirani* (1982) 4 FLR 232 at p. 234.
[158] (1982) 4 FLR 232.
[159] [2003] 1 FLR 661. See also *NS v MI* [2006] EWHC 1646 (Fam) where the *Hirani* approach was adopted.
[160] [1971] P 226.
[161] See also *Re KR (Abduction: Forcible Removal by Parents)* [1999] 2 FLR 542, where the court was willing to use wardship to protect a 17-year-old from being taken abroad for an arranged marriage.
[162] In *NS v MI* [2006] EWHC 1646 (Fam) Munby J emphasised that the court must beware of stereotyping.
[163] Diduck and Kaganas (2006: 42).
[164] *Lynch v DPP* [1980] AC 614; *Universal Tankships Inc. v ITWF* [1983] AC 366.
[165] [1968] P 296.
[166] [1971] P 286. See also *Buckland v Buckland* [1968] P 296 at p. 301 (per Scarman J); *H v H* [1954] P 258 at p. 269 (per Karminski J).
[167] (1886) 12 PD 21 at p. 24.
[168] *H v H* [1954] P 258; *NS v MI* [2006] EWHC 1646 (Fam).

(b) Mistake

A mistake can also negate consent. So far, the law has only allowed two kinds of mistake to negate consent. The first is a mistake as to the other party's identity. It must be a mistake as to identity rather than a mistake as to attribute.[169] So, for example, a marriage would not be voidable if one party wrongly thought the other was rich,[170] or had pleasant smelling feet.[171] But a marriage would be voidable if a party to the marriage thought the person they were marrying was someone else (e.g. if there was a case of impersonation). The second kind of mistake that will make a marriage voidable is when there is a mistake as to the nature of the ceremony. So, if one party believes the ceremony is one of engagement, say, then this can invalidate the marriage.[172] However, a mistake as to the legal effects of marriage is insufficient.[173]

It is arguable that in the light of *Hirani* this area of the law is open to reconsideration; that the law should focus not on the kind of mistake, but the effect of the mistake on a person's consent. So, for example, if it was crucial to a wife that her husband belonged to a particular religion then a mistake as to his religion could invalidate her consent. Only future cases will tell whether such a liberal approach can be taken.

(c) Unsoundness of mind

If a person lacks the capacity to marry, no one else can consent on their behalf. Unsoundness will only lead to a marriage being voidable if it exists at the time of the marriage. So, a marriage will not be void if someone loses mental capacity after the marriage. There is a presumption that people are of sound mind,[174] and so the burden of proof lies on the person seeking to have the marriage annulled.

The courts have developed the test for capacity to marry in a series of cases and currently there are five things a person needs to have the capacity to marry:

(i) To understand the nature, duties and responsibility of marriage.[175] At one time this was thought to include the idea that spouses were to live together and love each other and share a common house.[176] However, Mostyn J in *Mundell v Name 1*[177] disputed this, saying there were plenty of marriages where the couple did not live together, nor were they in love.[178] Unfortunately, he does not give any guidance on what understanding the nature of marriage means exactly.

(ii) To appreciate that 'mutuality, reciprocity and the capacity for compromise are indivisible components of marriage.' In *Re RS (Capacity to Consent to Sexual Intercourse and Marriage)*[179] a man who had emotional and social disorders making it difficult for him to relate to others was found to lack capacity to marry.

---

[169] *Moss v Moss* [1897] P 263.
[170] *Ewing v Wheatly* (1814) 2 Hagg Cas 175.
[171] See *C v C* [1942] NZLR 356 for a New Zealand case where a woman who married a man she believed (incorrectly) to be a famous boxer failed in her attempt to have the marriage annulled.
[172] *Valier v Valier* (1925) 133 LT 830.
[173] *Messina v Smith* [1971] P 322.
[174] Mental Capacity Act 2005, s. 1(2).
[175] *Sheffield City Council v E and S* [2004] EWHC 2808 (Fam), discussed in Gaffney-Rhys (2006).
[176] *Sheffield City Council v E and S* [2004] EWHC 2808 (Fam).
[177] [2019] EWCOP 50.
[178] He had in mind platonic relationships, such as *Re X (A Child)* [2018] EWFC 15.
[179] [2015] EWHC 3534 (Fam).

(iii) To have the capacity to consent to sexual intercourse.[180] This means they would need to understand the character and nature of sexual intercourse and the reasonably foreseeable consequences of it. They would also need the capacity to be able to choose whether or not to engage in it. This requirement demonstrates the way the law regards sexual intercourse as an essential element of marriage.[181] Given the fact that much sexual intercourse takes place outside marriage, it may be questioned whether sexual relations should be seen as central to the notion of marriage.[182] Also the law is clear there can be a valid marriage even if the relationship does not have a sexual element.[183] Maybe, a better interpretation of the law is that if the marriage is going to lead to the parties undertaking a sexual relationship, there must be capacity to consent to sex.

(iv) The effect of a marriage on a will.[184] The person need only understand that marriage revokes an existing will and that gifts made under that will are ineffective.

(v) To understand that divorce may lead to a financial claim.[185] There is, however, no need to understand any details about the law on financial relief, something Mostyn J describe as 'a mystery to even the most sophisticated and well educated'![186]

The courts have deliberately set the test for capacity to marry at a low level. In *Sheffield City Council v E and S*[187] Munby J emphasised that:

> There are many people in our society who may be of limited or borderline capacity but whose lives are immensely enriched by marriage. We must be careful not to set the test of capacity to marry too high, lest it operate as an unfair, unnecessary and indeed discriminatory bar against the mentally disabled.

However, in *Re RS (Capacity to Consent to Sexual Intercourse and Marriage)*[188] Hayden J emphasised that for a person lacking capacity to be in a marriage they did not understand would undermine their right to dignity.

In *Sheffield City Council v E and S*[189] Munby explained that if a person's competence was challenged in court the judge must focus on whether the person had capacity to marry, not on whether it was wise for them to marry. Controversially, he held that it was not necessary to show that the person understood the character of the person they were marrying. In this case there were serious concerns that the man was a violent and abusive man, and that the woman, who suffered various learning difficulties, did not appreciate that. It might be thought the character of one's partner is central to marriage. A violent abusive marriage is a very different thing from a loving one. However, that approach was rejected. S did understand marriage in general and so had capacity to marry, even though she did not understand what her marriage, in all likelihood, was going to be like.

---

[180] *X City Council v MB* [2007] 3 FCR 371.
[181] This approach was confirmed in *Re RS (Capacity to Consent to Sexual Intercourse and Marriage)* [2015] EWHC 3534 (Fam).
[182] Some religions teach that sexual intercourse should only take place in marriage. This has been the traditional Christian view and may explain why sexual relations are regarded as central to marriage.
[183] *Re X (A Child)* [2018] EWFC 15.
[184] *Re DMM (Alzheimer's: power of attorney)* [2017] EWCOP 32 and 33.
[185] *Mundell v Name 1* [2019] EWCOP 50.
[186] *Mundell v Name 1* [2019] EWCOP 50.
[187] [2004] EWHC 2808 (Fam), discussed in Gaffney-Rhys (2006).
[188] [2015] EWHC 3534 (Fam).
[189] [2004] EWHC 2808 (Fam), discussed in Gaffney-Rhys (2006).

(d) Otherwise

The statute refers to a lack of consent through factors other than duress or mistake. These include the following:

1. *Drunkenness.* There is no clear authority on whether the marriage is voidable where one party was drunk and so did not consent to the marriage. There are two views here. One is that drunkenness should be seen as analogous to being of unsound mind and so would make a marriage voidable. Another view is that a party should not be able to rely on a lack of consent that arises due to their own fault, and so voluntary intoxication should not render a marriage voidable. In *Sullivan v Sullivan*[190] it was suggested that the groom was so drunk that he was unable to understand the nature of the ceremony and so the marriage was voidable.

2. *Fraud and misrepresentation.* Neither fraud nor innocent misrepresentation will on its own affect the validity of the marriage.[191] However, if the fraud or misrepresentation leads to a mistake as to the identity of the other party or the nature of the ceremony then, as discussed above, the marriage will be voidable.

(iii) Mental disorder

A marriage is also voidable if either party is suffering from a mental disorder[192] at the time of the marriage to such an extent that they are unfit for marriage: that is, 'incapable of carrying out the ordinary duties and obligations of marriage'.[193] It is necessary to distinguish this from the lack of consent through unsoundness of mind. The mental disorder ground covers those who are able to understand the nature of a marriage but are unable to perform the duties of marriage due to a mental illness.

It should be stressed that both of the grounds relating to mental illness only make the marriage voidable and not void, so there is nothing to stop those with mental illnesses, even extreme ones, from marrying, the one exception being where the court finds a public policy objection to the marriage.[194]

(iv) Venereal disease and pregnancy

A marriage is voidable if the respondent is suffering from venereal disease[195] at the time of the ceremony or if the respondent was pregnant by someone other than the petitioner. It should be noted that a wife cannot seek nullity on the ground that the husband has fathered a child through another woman prior to the marriage. It may be thought that venereal disease and pregnancy should no longer be regarded as sufficient grounds to annul a marriage, although, as we shall see, a petitioner will not be able to use these grounds if they were aware of the disease or the pregnancy at the time of the marriage. The continued use of the term 'venereal disease' is a little unfortunate because it is one that is no longer used in medical circles. 'Sexually transmitted disease' is the preferred phrase.[196]

---

[190] (1812) 2 Hag Con 238 at p. 246.
[191] *Swift v Kelly* (1835) 3 Knapp 257 at p. 293; *Moss v Moss* [1897] P 263.
[192] As defined by the Mental Health Act 1983.
[193] *Bennett v Bennett* [1969] 1 All ER 539.
[194] *City of Westminster v C* [2008] 2 FCR 146, see Probert (2008a) for a discussion of this case.
[195] The term is not defined in the Act.
[196] It is not clear whether the courts would be willing to stretch the meaning of venereal disease to include HIV.

(v) Gender recognition certificate

We will be discussing the position of trans people later in this chapter. There it will be explained that the Gender Recognition Act 2004 allows trans people to obtain a certificate to recognise their 'acquired gender'. If a married person obtains a certificate then this will make their marriage voidable. Notice this means that if the other party to the marriage is happy for the marriage to continue then it can. However, it allows a spouse who is unhappy with the marriage, given their spouse's 'acquired gender', to have the marriage annulled. If one person marries someone who has had a gender recognition certificate, but was unaware of that, they can have their marriage annulled. Of course, if they knew about the certificate their marriage is as valid as anyone else's. This requirement has been strongly objected to by some on the basis that it gives legal support to the view that the basis of a marriage is undermined by someone transitioning.

(vi) Sham marriages

What is the position of a couple who go through a marriage purely for the purpose of pretending to be married, even though they never intend to live together as husband or wife? This is most likely to arise in a case involving immigration.[197] The House of Lords in **Vervaeke v Smith**[198] suggested that such marriages are valid, even though in that case the parties only saw each other on a few occasions after the marriage and the aim of the marriage was to enable the wife to obtain British citizenship and so avoid deportation.[199] Although such a marriage was valid, it may not be sufficient for the purposes of immigration rules. So, a person entering a sham marriage in order to enter the UK might find themselves unable come to Britain, but married to someone they do not know. It seems the use of marriage purely for immigration purposes is not uncommon.[200]

F Bars to relief in voidable marriages

There are no bars to a marriage being void, although there are some circumstances which prevent the petitioner from seeking to annul a voidable marriage. These bars are found in s. 13(1) of the Matrimonial Causes Act 1973. If the bar is established, the court may not annul the marriage. The burden is on the respondent to raise the bar as a defence. If the respondent does not mention the bar, the court cannot raise it on his or her behalf. If no statutory bar is established, the court cannot bar the annulment on the basis of public policy.[201] This indicates that the bars exist not for public policy reasons but for the protection of the petitioner. We will now consider the different bars.

---

[197] Wray (2016).
[198] [1983] 1 AC 145.
[199] Divorce may well be possible, of course: e.g. **Silver v Silver** [1955] 1 WLR 728.
[200] BBC News Online (2009a).
[201] **D v D (Nullity)** [1979] Fam 70.

(i) Approbation

Section 13(1) of the Matrimonial Causes Act 1973 states:

LEGISLATIVE PROVISION

Matrimonial Causes Act 1973, section 13(1)

The court shall not . . . grant a decree of nullity on the ground that a marriage is voidable if the respondent satisfies the court—

(a) that the petitioner, with knowledge that it was open to him to have the marriage avoided, so conducted himself in relation to the respondent as to lead the respondent reasonably to believe that he would not seek to do so; and

(b) that it would be unjust to the respondent to grant the decree.

It is essential that both paragraphs (a) and (b) be proved to the court's satisfaction. The basis of this bar is that it is seen as contrary to public policy and unjust to allow a person to seek to annul the marriage after leading the other party to believe he or she would not challenge the marriage. For example, in *D v D (Nullity)*[202] the husband relied on his wife's refusal to consummate the marriage in a nullity petition. However, he had previously agreed to the adoption of a child. It was held that his action indicated to the wife that he intended to treat the marriage as valid. Similarly, a man marrying a woman who he knows suffers from a mental disorder or is pregnant would be barred from seeking to annul the marriage on these grounds.[203] It may be that if the marriage has lasted some time the court might imply from the delay in bringing the petition that the petitioner had consented to the marriage.

In order to establish the bar, it must be shown that to annul the marriage would be unjust. For example, in *D v D* it might have been unjust to leave the wife caring for the children on her own. However, in that case the wife consented to the nullity decree and so it was thought not to be unjust to her to grant the decree. In considering justice under (b) the court is likely to consider factors such as the length of the marriage, financial implications of the nullity, and social implications of granting a decree.

(ii) Time

A decree of nullity will normally not succeed unless brought within three years of the date of the marriage,[204] the exception being a petition based on impotence. The policy behind this is clear: parties need a degree of security in their marriage – if three years have passed, then to claim that the marriage is fundamentally flawed seems unrealistic. In *B v I (Forced Marriage)*[205] a 16-year-old girl was forced into a marriage in Bangladesh and was only able

---

[202] [1979] Fam 70.
[203] See, e.g., *Morgan v Morgan* [1959] P 92.
[204] MCA 1973, s. 13(2). There is an exception if the petitioner suffered from some kind of mental disorder.
[205] [2010] 1 FLR 1721.

to alert someone over three years later. The court was unable to declare the marriage a nullity, but could declare it to be a marriage which was incapable of recognition within the UK. It was significant in that case that the woman would have faced significant stigma within her community if she had relied on divorce. Otherwise the obvious solution to her situation would have been to seek a divorce.

(iii) Estoppel

Can a party ever be prevented from obtaining a nullity decree on the basis of estoppel? There are two kinds of estoppel that might be relevant. The first is estoppel by conduct where one party so conducts himself or herself that it would be unjust for him or her to deny the facts that he or she has led the other to believe are true. *Miles v Chilton*[206] provides an example of the kind of situation under discussion. A husband sought annulment on the ground that his wife was already married at the time of the marriage. The wife argued that the husband had deceived her into believing that her 'first' husband had divorced her. The court held that this was no answer to the husband's petition, because otherwise the court would be prevented from discovering the true state of affairs.[207] So estoppel by conduct was not found relevant in this case.

The other kind of estoppel is *estoppel per rem judicatam*, meaning that a party cannot seek to overturn a court's decision. A decree of nullity is what is known as a judgment *in rem*: proceedings cannot be started which seek to undermine such a judgment. However, if the nullity petition is dismissed this affects only the parties themselves. So, if a man is granted a nullity petition on the ground that the wife is married to another man, no one can seek to undermine the basis of the annulment by suggesting in a court that the first marriage was invalid. However, if the petition had been dismissed on the ground that the first marriage was invalid, this does not bar anyone except the parties themselves from seeking to show that the first marriage was in fact valid.

G Effects of a decree of nullity

Section 16 of the Matrimonial Causes Act 1973 states:

LEGISLATIVE PROVISION

Matrimonial Causes Act 1973, section 16

A decree of nullity granted after 31st July 1971 in respect of a voidable marriage shall operate to annul the marriage only as respects any time after the decree has been made absolute, and the marriage shall, notwithstanding the decree, be treated as if it had existed up to that time.

A child of a void marriage is treated as legitimate due to s. 1(1) of the Legitimacy Act 1976, as long as at the time of the marriage either (or both) parties reasonably believed that the marriage was valid.[208] *Re Spence*[209] has clarified the law and said that if the marriage was annulled after the birth then the child was legitimate.

---

[206] (1849) 1 Rob Eccl 684.
[207] There are contrary dicta in *Bullock v Bullock* [1960] 2 All ER 307 at p. 309.
[208] Under the Family Law Act 1986, s. 56 a declaration of legitimacy can be made if there is any doubt.
[209] [1990] 2 FLR 278, [1990] FCR 983.

Due to ss. 23 and 24 of the Matrimonial Causes Act 1973 on granting a decree of nullity, the court has the power to make ancillary relief orders to the same extent as if a divorce order was being made. However, following *Whiston v Whiston*,[210] as interpreted in *Rampal v Rampal (No. 2)*,[211] if the marriage is void on the ground of bigamy then the court might decide that the applicant's conduct was such that the court should not award her any ancillary relief.

In *J v S-T*[212] the applicant was born a woman, underwent a partial sex-change operation, lived as a man, and then married a woman. After 17 years of marriage the wife[213] petitioned for a declaration that the marriage was void on the ground that the parties were not respectively male and female. The husband applied for ancillary relief. The court held that there was a discretion in the court to award ancillary relief. However, in exercising its discretion the court decided not to make any award bearing in mind his deception as to his sex.[214] By contrast, in *Ben Hashem v Al Shayif*[215] as both the husband and wife had been fully aware of the bigamous nature of their marriage, the bigamy had no impact on the amount awarded.

H Reform of nullity

There were 345 petitions for annulments in 2011, of which 206 were granted.[216] The tiny numbers involved raise the question of whether we need all the complex law on nullity that we have. Indeed, the Office for National Statistics no longer reports the number of nullity applications as they are so few. The concept of a void marriage is necessary if there are to be limits on who may marry and to whom. However, there has been some debate over whether the concept of voidable marriage should be abolished. The Law Commission[217] supported the retention of voidable marriage by arguing that to some couples it is particularly important that annulment rather than divorce ends their marriage. This tends to be for religious reasons. Cretney has argued that the law on voidable marriage could be abolished, leaving questions of annulment to the church or other religious bodies.[218] There is much to be said for this approach, given that the vast majority of annulment petitions are brought for religious reasons.[219]

I Forced marriages

Forced marriage is a major invasion of human rights. Article 12 of the European Convention on Human Rights (ECHR) protects the right to marry. This includes the right not to be forced into a marriage against your will. It will also often involve a torture or inhuman or degrading

---

[210] [1995] 2 FLR 268, [1995] 2 FCR 496.
[211] [2001] 2 FCR 552.
[212] [1997] 1 FLR 402, [1997] 1 FCR 349.
[213] It took the wife 17 years to find out that her husband had not been born a man. The facts of the case reveal the dangers of looking in a man's sock drawer.
[214] As a result of ss. 1(1)(a) and 25(4) of the Inheritance (Provision for Family and Dependants) Act 1975, a person who in good faith has entered into a void marriage may apply to the court for reasonable provision out of the estate.
[215] [2009] 1 FLR 115.
[216] Ministry of Justice (2012b).
[217] Law Commission Report 33 (1970).
[218] Probert (2005).
[219] Herring (2016b).

treatment and hence breach Article 3. McFarlane P explained in *Re K (Forced Marriage: Passport Order)*:[220]

> The abusive nature of a forced marriage does not begin and end on the day of the marriage ceremony. Rather, the marriage forms the start of a potentially unending period in the victim's life where much of her daily experience will occur without their consent and against their will, or will otherwise be abusive. In particular, the consummation of the marriage, rather than being the positive experience, will be, by definition, a rape. Life for an unwilling participant in a forced marriage is likely to be characterised by serial rape, deprivation of liberty and physical abuse experienced over an extended period. It may also lead to forced pregnancy and childbearing. The fate of some victims of forced marriage is even worse and may include murder, other 'honour' crime or suicide.

The Government's Forced Marriage Unit dealt with 1,355 cases of alleged forced marriage in 2019.[221] There has been a steady increase in the numbers year on year since the Unit was created. Of these cases:

- 363 cases (27%) involved victims below 18 years of age.
- 485 cases (36%) involved victims aged 18–25.
- 137 cases (10%) involved victims with a learning disability.
- 1,080 cases (80%) involved female victims, and 262 cases (19%) involved male victims. Gender in the remaining 13 cases was unknown.[222]

It should be noted from these statistics that the issue is not restricted to children or women, although women are involved in the large majority of cases.

The problem of 'forced marriages' is one which the courts have had to deal with increasingly often.[223] We have already seen that if a party is forced into a marriage as a result of threats or pressures then the marriage can be annulled on the basis of no consent. Here we will consider how the court will deal with a case where there are concerns that a forced marriage is about to take place.[224]

It should be emphasised that there are no legal objections to an arranged marriage, where the parents determine who their adult child should marry. Parents may encourage or persuade their child to marry the person they propose. There are many communities where this is common practice and the courts will not invalidate a marriage or seek to prevent the parents urging their child to marry, unless the pressure used becomes illegitimate. In *A Local Authority v N*[225] Munby J warned that courts must be sensitive to cultural, social and religious circumstances and the courts should not assume that an arranged marriage is a forced one. The Government is aware that it is necessary to draw a clear distinction between a forced marriage and an arranged marriage:

> There is a clear distinction between a forced marriage and an arranged marriage. In arranged marriages, the families of both spouses take a leading role in arranging the marriage but the choice whether or not to accept the arrangement remains with the prospective spouses. In forced marriage, one or both spouses do not (or, in the case of some adults with disabilities, cannot) consent to the marriage and duress is involved. Duress can include physical, psychological, sexual, financial and emotional pressure.[226]

---

[220] [2020] EWCA Civ 190, para 24.
[221] Forced Marriage Unit (2020).
[222] Forced Marriage Unit (2020).
[223] See Dauvergne and Millbank (2010) for a discussion of the international dimension.
[224] Pepper (2019).
[225] [2005] EWHC 2956.
[226] HM Government (2009: 10).

It is easy to be over-simplistic in an understanding of forced marriages. In fact, they involve a complex interplay of gender and age discrimination.[227] They should not be seen simply as the product of a minority cultural practice, as economic difficulties, attitudes towards gender and disability and immigration policies also play an important role.[228] Nor should it be assumed that only young women are affected – men can be,[229] as can older women.[230] It should be remembered, too, that it is not just the entry into forced marriages that needs tackling, but women need to be enabled to leave such marriages.[231]

The courts have shown an increased willingness to make orders to protect someone from a forced marriage.[232] There are three jurisdictions the courts can use: Forced Marriage (Civil Protection) Act 2007; the Mental Capacity Act 2005; and the inherent jurisdiction. Where the only issue of concern is the forced marriage, then the 2007 Act should be used. Where, however, there are a range of issues over which the court needs to make orders, the Mental Capacity Act 2005 should be used if the person lacks mental capacity; or the inherent jurisdiction order if the person does not.

(i) Forced Marriage (Civil Protection) Act 2007

The 2007 Act was passed to provide specific protection to people at risk of being forced into a marriage. The Act does not deal with the validity of forced marriages, those are dealt with by the law on voidability. The Act enables the court to make 'forced marriage protection orders'. In 2017, 247 such orders were made.[233] A forced marriage is defined as one where one person forces another to enter into a marriage without their 'full and free consent'.[234] Force here includes physical and psychological threats; and includes threats, whoever they are directed towards.[235] In *West Sussex County Council and Another v F*[236] Williams J declined to make a forced marriage protection order because there was a only a 'loose commitment' between the families that a 13-year-old girl would marry her cousin and he believed that the family accepted that when she was older she would be free to depart from the agreement if she wished.

The Act gives the court a broad discretion to make whatever order is necessary to protect the individual at risk: it can order 'such prohibitions, restrictions or requirements . . . and . . . other terms . . . as the court considers appropriate for the purposes of the order'.[237] This could include surrendering a passport, or prohibiting a party from contacting another. In deciding whether to make an order the court must have regard to 'all the circumstances including the need to secure the health, safety and well-being of the person to be protected'. Notably the Act states that in ascertaining that person's well-being, the court is to have regard to his or her wishes and feelings (so far as reasonably ascertainable) and giving them 'such weight as the court considers appropriate given his or her age and

---

[227] Mody (2016).
[228] Gill and Anitha (2009); Chantler, Gangoli and Hester (2009).
[229] Samad (2010).
[230] Gangoli and Chantler (2009).
[231] Chantler, Gangoli and Hester (2009).
[232] See Gill and Anitha (2011) for an excellent analysis of the issues.
[233] Ministry of Justice (2018b).
[234] Family Law Act 1996 (FLA), s. 63A(4).
[235] FLA, s. 63A(4). Note there does not need to be a threat of violence: *A v SM and HB (Forced Marriage Protection Orders)* [2012] EWHC 435 (Fam).
[236] [2018] EWHC 1702 (Fam).
[237] FLA, s. 63B.

understanding'.[238] So the wishes are not relevant in themselves, but only in so far as they reveal what is in a person's best interests.[239] The legislation is clear that an order can be made even if the person it is protecting does not want the order to be made. In *Bedfordshire Police Constabulary* v *RU*[240] a forced marriage protection order was made to protect a young woman aged 16. She later applied to dispense with it. The court determined she had been pressurised into making the application and so kept the order in force.

In *West Sussex County Council and Another* v *F*[241] Williams J drew a distinction between protective orders which were designed to prevent an act which would facilitate a forced marriage and mandatory orders which required people to act in a particular way (e.g. return children to the jurisdiction). Protective orders 'could not seriously be objected to' as, in effect, they were prohibiting people from doing illegal acts. Mandatory orders, however, could interfere with human rights and so it would be necessary to show they were justified and proportionate. However, if orders are necessary to protect someone from a forced marriage (which would be a breach of Article 3 of the ECHR) these must be made, regardless of other human rights. In *Re K (Forced Marriage: Passport Order)*[242] McFarlane P emphasised:

> Where the evidence establishes a reasonable possibility that conduct sufficient to breach Article 3 may occur, the court must at least do what is necessary to protect any potential victim from such a risk. The need to do so cannot be reduced below that necessary minimum even where the factors relating to the qualified rights protected by Article 8 are particularly weighty.

Applications can be brought by a local authority.[243] The Act can be used in a case where a person has been forced into an invalid marriage abroad and then brought to England.[244] In one dramatic case when a 20-year-old became aware that her parents intended to marry her and her five siblings (aged between 18 and 6), forced marriage protection orders were made against all of the parents' children.[245] According to practitioners working in the field, the courts are becoming sensitive to the way that concepts of 'shame' and 'honour' can be manipulated to force people into marriage.[246] However, they argue these same concepts mean that many victims are very reluctant to come forward to seek help. This can be a problem particularly because if an order is breached the police have no standing to seek committal of those who breach the order. Only the victim can do that and she may be very reluctant to seek orders which may result in the imprisonment of her family.[247] In *Bedfordshire Police Constabulary* v *RU*[248] a teenager who had been subject to a marriage protection order, but was forced into a religious marriage, was not willing to bring committal proceedings. Holman J stated:

> Forced marriages are a scourge, which degrade the victim and can create untold human misery. It is vital that FMPOs have real teeth and that people bound by them . . . appreciate that they are capable of being enforced and will be enforced even though the young person may not seek enforcement himself or herself. The scope for psychological or other pressures in this field is obvious and enormous.

---

[238] FLA, s. 63A
[239] *Re K (Forced Marriage: Passport Order)* [2020] EWCA Civ 190.
[240] [2013] EWHC 2350 (Fam).
[241] [2018] EWHC 1702 (Fam).
[242] [2020] EWCA Civ 190.
[243] Family Law Act 1996 (Forced Marriage) (Relevant Third Party) Order 2009.
[244] *Re P (Forced Marriage)* [2010] EWHC 3467 (Fam).
[245] *A v SM and HB (Forced Marriage Protection Orders)* [2012] EWHC 435 (Fam).
[246] Chokowry and Skinner (2011).
[247] *Bedfordshire Police Constabulary* v *RU* [2013] EWHC 2350 (Fam).
[248] [2013] EWHC 2350 (Fam).

Perhaps recognising this difficulty, the Government has made forced marriage a criminal offence. In s. 121 of the Anti-Social Behaviour, Crime and Policing Act 2014 it states that a person will commit an offence if he or she uses violence, threats or any other form of coercion for the purpose of causing another person to enter into a marriage, and believes, or ought reasonably to believe, that the conduct may cause the other person to enter into the marriage without free and full consent. Section 120 of the same Act makes it an offence to breach a forced marriage protection order. While these offences will provide a solution in cases like *Bedfordshire Police Constabulary v RU*,[249] where the victim is reluctant to enforce the order, they are controversial. Some fear that victims will be reluctant to inform the police or seek help if doing so puts their parents at risk of a criminal conviction. Also, there are fears that parents will take children abroad to force their marriages, in an attempt to avoid prosecution.[250] One year since the implementation of the legislation there has been one conviction, a serious case involving rape and kidnapping.[251]

(ii) Mental Capacity Act 2005

The Mental Capacity Act 2005 enables courts to make orders to promote the best interests of mentally incompetent people.[252] The Act can only be used in relation to issues over which a person lacks capacity. An order could be made under the Act protecting a person lacking capacity from entering a marriage or even entering a relationship. The courts have been willing, for example, to find that a person lacks the capacity to consent to sex, thereby requiring the local authority to ensure that such a person is protected from entering a sexual relationship.[253] Of course, that is likely to lead to a significant restriction on their liberty. That has led the courts to be reluctant to find that someone lacks the capacity to enter a sexual relationship.[254]

In *PC v City of York*[255] a vulnerable woman had married a man who was in prison. He was due to be released and the local authority were concerned that he posed a risk to her. He had a history of violence against his partners, but the woman refused to accept that. The Court of Appeal found that although her capacity to make the decision was impaired (she did not understand the nature of the risks of living with him) this was not due to a mental disorder and so she fell outside the Mental Capacity Act 2005. The court said it had to allow her to cohabit with him and hope that it all turned out well in the end.[256] By contrast in *YLA v PM*[257] a woman who had severe learning difficulties and was timid had married a man and given birth to their child. However, it was found in the Court of Protection that she lacked the capacity to engage in sexual relations; consent to marry; or decide where to live. It was ordered she was removed from her husband to protect her from being the victim of sexual offences.

---

[249] [2013] EWHC 2350 (Fam).
[250] See the discussion in Proudman (2012) and Gaffney-Rhys (2015).
[251] Gaffney-Rhys (2015).
[252] See the discussion in *Re SK* [2008] EWHC 636 (Fam).
[253] *A Local Authority v H* [2012] EWHC 49 (COP), discussed in Herring (2012j).
[254] *IM v LM* [2014] EWCA Civ 37, discussed in Herring and Wall (2014b).
[255] [2013] EWCA Civ 478, discussed in Herring and Wall (2013 and 2014a).
[256] For an argument that this failed to protect her human rights see Herring and Wall (2013).
[257] [2013] EWHC 4020 (COP).

(iii) The inherent jurisdiction

Recently, the courts have also shown a willingness to use the inherent jurisdiction to protect individuals who are at risk of being forced into a marriage. It has even been used in respect of British nationals living overseas.[258] The jurisdiction can be exercised over vulnerable adults. These are people who might have capacity to make the decision on whether or not to marry, but are for some other reason vulnerable. This may be because they have some disability or because someone is exercising undue influence over them.[259]

7 Equal marriage

A The debates over equal marriage

It is possible to identify a journey which several countries, including England and Wales, have taken in response to same-sex couples.[260] First, the law removes criminal offences outlawing same-sex activity. Secondly, the law grants same-sex couples an increasing set of rights. Thirdly, a status equivalent to marriage, but different from it, is granted to same-sex couples. Finally, same-sex couples are allowed to marry. This final step occurred in England and Wales with the passing of the Marriage (Same Sex Couples) Act 2013, which allows couples of the same sex to marry.

In *Home Affairs v Fourie*,[261] a South African case, Justice Albie Sachs has made a powerful case in favour of allowing same-sex marriage:

> The exclusion of same sex couples from the benefits and responsibilities of marriage, accordingly, is not a small and tangential inconvenience resulting from a few surviving relics of societal prejudice destined to evaporate like the morning dew. It represents a harsh if oblique statement by the law that same sex couples are outsiders, and that their need for affirmation and protection of their intimate relations as human beings is somehow less than that of heterosexual couples. It reinforces the wounding notion that they are to be treated as biological oddities, as failed or lapsed human beings who do not fit into normal society, and, as such, do not qualify for the full moral concern and respect that our Constitution seeks to secure for everyone. It signifies that their capacity for love, commitment and accepting responsibility is by definition less worthy of regard than that of heterosexual couples.

Indeed, there is evidence that married same-sex couples feel legitimacy and security in their relationships.[262]

There are, of course, voices against same-sex marriage. Many of these are based on religious beliefs,[263] arguing that marriage is a religious concept and that allowing same-sex marriage infringes the religious concepts of marriage. However, there is no need for the legal concept of marriage to match religious ones; indeed, it does not, at present, for many religions. The law reflects very few traditional religious views about marriage, why should it do so about the sex of the parties?[264] Even if it was thought that the law should match religious views of

---

[258] *Re B; RB v FB and MA (Forced Marriage: Wardship: Jurisdiction)* [2008] 2 FLR 1624.
[259] *Re SK (An Adult) (Forced Marriage: Appropriate Relief)* [2005] 2 FCR 459; *M v B* [2005] EWHC 1681 (Fam).
[260] Glennon (2005); Eekelaar (2013a).
[261] [2005] ZACC 19, para 71.
[262] Kennedy and Dalla (2020).
[263] Carey (2013). But see White (2010) for a discussion of economic arguments against same-sex marriage.
[264] Herring (2016a).

marriage, then which religious view should be followed? There are plenty of religious groups who support same-sex marriage. More importantly, the offence caused to those who have religious objections to same-sex marriage must be weighed against the harm caused to those same-sex couples who wish to marry, some of whom will themselves be religious. In weighing these it may be thought that harm to the same-sex couple would be far greater and more personal than that to those with religious objections.[265]

A non-religious objection to marriage has been voiced by Patrick Parkinson, a leading Australian academic:

> A consequence of extending marriage to same-sex relationships is that there will be almost nothing left of the legal definition of marriage as a union of a man and a woman for life to the exclusion of all others. Robbed of its distinctiveness, and detached from its cultural and religious roots, marriage as an institution is unlikely to retain its cultural importance and vitality. We simply won't know what marriage is any more.[266]

This view suggests that there is something unique about relationships between people of the opposite sex, although it is unclear what that is. Lynn Wardle, seeking to present a non-religious argument against same-sex marriage, argues:

> The union of two persons of different genders creates a union of unique potential strengths and inimitable potential value to society. It is the *integration* of the universe of gender differences – profound and subtle, biological and cultural, psychological and genetic – associated with sexual identity that constitutes the core and essence of marriage. Just as men and women are different, so a union of two men or of two women is not the same as the union of a man and a woman.[267]

Notice that this view is based on a strong belief in the differences between the genders. Indeed, a strong case can be made for saying that the opposition to same-sex marriage inevitably reflects a desire to maintain a difference between sexual roles.[268] Even if you agreed with Wardle that there is a benefit in integrating the universes of two different people, does that only occur when they are of different sex? Others argue that same-sex relationships are less desirable than opposite-sex ones in other ways: they are less stable, less likely to raise children, or less effective in raising children.[269] The argument that appears to carry the most merit is that a same-sex couple will not be able to produce a child together, without medical intervention.[270] But we allow opposite-sex couples who are infertile, or who have no intention of having children, to marry.[271]

Not all members of the gay and lesbian community are supporters of 'gay marriage'. The main concern is that by adopting marriage gay relationships may start to mimic heterosexual ones.[272] Lesbians and gay men should be seeking to develop their own kinds and forms of relationship, rather than adopting heterosexual models.[273] However, even those who adopt

---

[265] In *Islington LBC v Ladele* [2009] EWCA Civ 1357 a registrar who was sacked after refusing to conduct a civil partnership because of her religious beliefs was found to have been justifiably dismissed.

[266] Parkinson, P. (2012).

[267] Wardle (2006: 53 and 2016). See also Stewart (2004), Pontifical Council for the Family (2000), Duckworth (2002b) outlining some of the non-religious arguments against permitting same-sex marriage. Bamforth (2001) and Woelke (2002) respond to some of these arguments.

[268] Case (2010).

[269] Duckworth (2002a: 91); Gallagher (2001). See Eskridge and Spedale (2006) for evidence rejecting such claims.

[270] It is developed in Deech (2010e).

[271] Cretney (2006a: 14–15).

[272] Jowett and Peel (2019).

[273] Weeks (2004: 35); Boyd and Young (2003).

this view are likely to accept that the law should give same-sex couples the option of marriage, even if they think that same-sex couples should not take up that right.[274] There is also a concern among some that although civil partnerships will offer recognition and protection for 'orthodox' same-sex couples, those gay men and lesbians who do not match the marriage model (e.g. they have more than one regular partner) will be further ostracised.[275]

A rather different concern has been voiced by Rosemary Auchmuty.[276] That is, that calls for same-sex marriage might be seen as suggesting that marriage is something good that should be encouraged and is an ideal to aspire to. However, she sees marriage as being an institution which has and still does oppress women. She is not opposed to gay marriage, but believes it should not be seen as the most important issue for those promoting the interests of the gay community. She explains:

> [W]hether you see marriage as an oppressive bastion of male power, as the second-wave feminists did, or simply as outmoded and irrelevant, as many contemporaries do, the goal should surely be to get rid of it, or at least to let it die out of its own accord – not to try to share in its privileges, leaving the ineligible out in the cold.

Although it was suggested earlier that in time civil partnerships will be regarded as a stepping stone on the way to recognising same-sex marriage, that is not the only possible consequence of official recognition of same-sex relationships. Will it (further) challenge the traditional gender roles within marriage and heterosexual relationships? Will it open up the possibility of a child having two fathers or two mothers?[277] Will it further challenge the legal distinction between male and female?[278]

B Marriage (Same Sex Couples) Act 2013

Under the Marriage (Same Sex Couples) Act 2013 couples of the same sex can now marry.[279] The first same-sex marriages took place on 29 March 2014. While it was widely regarded as inevitable that same-sex marriage would become part of the law at some point, it all happened earlier than many commentators predicted. The pressure to change the law did not come from Europe. The European Court of Human Rights has so far refused to require states to allow same-sex couples the right to marry, as long as they have access to the same rights and protections as married couples.[280] Although, it may well be that in the future the Court will recognise there is a sufficient consensus across Europe for the right of same-sex couples to marry to be recognised.[281]

The legislation was passed with relatively little opposition. The most vocal groups were religious, but they struggled to explain why their particular understanding of marriage should be accepted by the law. It also became clear that even among religious groups there was a range of views on same-sex marriage.

Section 1 of the Marriage (Same Sex Couple) Act 2013 was refreshingly simple:

> Marriage of same-sex couples is lawful.

---

[274] Glennon (2006); Auchmuty (2004); Toner (2004).
[275] See the discussion in Barker (2004) and Leckey (2014).
[276] Auchmuty (2008: 485).
[277] Kelly (2004).
[278] Chau and Herring (2004).
[279] See Gilbert (2014) for an interesting discussion of some of the politics around the legislation.
[280] *Vallianatos v Greece* (App. nos. 29381/09 and 32684/09); *Schalk and Kopf v Austria* (App. no. 30141/04) [2011] 2 FCR 650; *Hamalainen v Finland* [2015] 1 FCR 379; *Oliari and others v Italy* (App. nos. 18766/11 and 36030/11), 21 July 2015. See Van der Sloot (2015) for a detailed discussion.
[281] Johnson (2015).

However, the legislation then requires some 64 pages and seven schedules to work through the consequences of that statement. Couples who have civil partnership are permitted to convert their relationships to marriage.[282]

One might expect that no differences would exist between marriages between people of the same sex and the opposite sex, but that has not occurred. These primarily involve sexual matters:

- Paragraph 4 of Sched. 4 states that same-sex couples will not be able to rely on the consummation grounds for having a marriage annulled.

- Paragraph 3(2) of Sched. 4 states that in respect of the law of divorce: 'Only conduct between the respondent and a person of the opposite sex may constitute adultery for the purposes of this section.'[283] Since the Divorce, Dissolution and Separation Act 2020, abolishing the adultery fact for divorce, this is no longer of legal significance.

- The common law presumption that a mother's spouse is the father does not apply in same-sex marriages.[284]

Hence same-sex marriage is 'de-sexed'.[285] The courts need not examine marital same-sex sexual behaviour to ensure that there is consummation; nor non-marital same-sex activity to see if it ensures adultery. They can coyly avert their gaze. To some commentators this is justified given the difficulty in defining what amounted to consummation within the context of a same-sex couple. There would, of course, have been no technical difficulty in doing so. The Sexual Offences Act 2003 contains descriptions of a wide range of sexual acts which could have been drawn on. A more obvious solution would have been to remove the adultery and consummation provisions from all marriages. They are both outdated and hard to justify.

The religious opposition to same-sex marriage was dealt with by inserting into the Act provisions designed to protect religious groups or ministers from being sued for failing to marry same-sex couples on the basis of discrimination. These are extensive and are known as the 'quadruple lock'. It is noticeable that in just the second section of the Act it is made clear that no religious group or minister is required to celebrate same-sex marriages. A religious denomination (although bizarrely not the Church of England) can choose to 'opt in' to allow same-sex marriages.[286] Although the 'quadruple lock' provisions ensure there is a solid protection for those taking a traditional approach to marriage, they also make it particularly burdensome for religious groups which would like to conduct same-sex marriages.

This whole debate raises the issue of whether it would be more appropriate to separate legal and religious marriages. This would free religious groups to develop their own understandings and teaching of a religious marriage and leave legal marriage as a secular institution. This is common in many countries in Europe.

As there are still some differences between marriages between couples of the same sex and those of the opposite sex, we still need to consider how the law defines who is a man and who is a woman.

---

[282] Section 9.
[283] It does this by amending the Matrimonial Causes Act 1973.
[284] Marriage (Same Sex Couples) Act 2013, Sched. 4, para 2.
[285] Crompton (2013a).
[286] Marriage (Same Sex Couples) Act 2013, ss. 4 and 5. Several groups have, including the Quakers and the United Reformed Church.

8 Marriage and the definition of sex

A Trans people

The question of deciding how to define sex has arisen in particular because of the law's treatment of trans people.[287] These are people who are at birth assigned a particular sex as a result of some biological characteristics, but identify as belonging to the other sex.[288] Some, but not all, trans people undergo 'gender realignment surgery', which is available on the National Health Service[289] and in private hospitals.

The law relating to trans people is now dominated by the Gender Recognition Act 2004. Before that legislation the leading case on trans people and marriage was *Corbett v Corbett*,[290] a decision of Ormrod J. He argued that for the purpose of the law an individual's sex is fixed at birth: 'The law should adopt in the first place the first three of the doctor's criteria, i.e., the chromosomal, gonadal and genital tests, and if all three are congruent, determine the sex for the purpose of marriage accordingly, and ignore any operative intervention.'[291] So, in the case before him, April Ashley, born as a man but having undergone a 'sex change operation' and living as a woman, was a man and could not enter into a marriage with a man.[292] The law based on that case was found incompatible with the European Convention on Human Rights (ECHR) in *Goodwin v UK*[293] and *I v UK*.[294] Following *Goodwin,* the case of *Bellinger v Bellinger*[295] issued a declaration that the definition of sex in s. 11(c) of the Matrimonial Causes Act 1973 which prohibited a trans person marrying in her declared sex was incompatible with Articles 8 and 12 of the ECHR.

The Government responded by producing the Gender Recognition Act 2004. Under the Act a person can apply for a Gender Recognition Certificate. Section 9(1) explains:

LEGISLATIVE PROVISION

Gender Recognition Act 2004, section 9(1)

Where a full gender recognition certificate is issued to a person, the person's gender becomes for all purposes the acquired gender (so that, if the acquired gender is the male gender, the person's sex becomes that of a man and, if it is the female gender, the person's sex becomes that of a woman).

---

[287] Sharpe (2002); Whittle (2002).
[288] There is no definitive data on the number of trans people, but estimates vary between 65,000 and 300,000: Equality and Human Rights Commission (2009).
[289] Although there is no right to such treatment: *R v North West Lancashire HA, ex p A* [2000] 2 FCR 525.
[290] [1971] P 83. For a fascinating discussion of the history surrounding this case, see Gilmore (2011b), including the fact that in 2005 April Ashley was given a Gender Recognition Certificate and could at last legally be a woman.
[291] At p. 106.
[292] Sharpe (2002) and Whittle (2002: ch. 7) provide a detailed analysis and criticism of his decision. See also Chau and Herring (2002: 347–51).
[293] [2002] 2 FCR 577.
[294] [2002] 2 FCR 613.
[295] [2003] UKHL 21, [2003] 2 FCR 1. See Gilmore (2003b) for a powerful critique of the decision.

There are two alternative grounds on which a person may apply to the Gender Recognition Panel for a certificate.[296] First that they have 'changed their gender'[297] under the law of another country. Secondly, they are living in the gender which is not that on their birth certificate. To issue a certificate on the second ground the panel must be persuaded that the applicant meets the conditions set out in s. 2(1):

LEGISLATIVE PROVISION

Gender Recognition Act 2004, section 2(1)

    (a)   has or has had gender dysphoria,

    (b)   has lived in the acquired gender throughout the period of two years ending with the date on which the application is made,

    (c)   intends to continue to live in the acquired gender until death.[298]

The applicant is required to produce reports from experts in the field to establish these facts.[299] The panel requests further evidence if needed.[300] In *Carpenter v Secretary of State for Justice*[301] Thirlwall J rejected an argument that the requirement in s. 3(3) of the Gender Recognition Act that details of surgery had to be provided breached her rights to respect for private life under Article 8 of the ECHR. It was held it was a justifiable provision as it enabled the committee to have all the relevant information before it. However, as an individual does not need to have had surgery before obtaining a certificate it is hard to see why the committee needs to know the details of the surgery, if that has taken place. Indeed, in *Jay v Secretary of State for Justice*[302] the panel was found to have attached too much weight to the failure of the applicant to provide all of the evidence required by the regulation. The panel should have focused on the statutory criteria: was there gender dysphoria, rather than getting too tied up in the details of forms of evidence. In part that decision may have been influenced by the fact the applicant did not have legal representation and was struggling to understand what the panel needed. The case also highlights the sensitivity of the issues raised, with the applicant attempting surgery on herself after the panel's refusal.

Once a certificate is issued, the individual's gender is changed for all purposes. In *R (AB) v Secretary of State for Justice*[303] AB had been issued with a certificate meaning she was a woman and it was therefore held to be unlawful to place her in a man's prison.

As already stated, the full certificate changes the legal categorisation of the person's sex, but it does 'not affect the status of the person as the father or mother of a child'.[304] In *R (JK) v Registrar General for England and Wales*[305] a trans woman who was registered as the father of

---

[296] www.gov.uk/apply-gender-recognition-certificate.

[297] This phrase is given in quotation marks because many trans people do not regard themselves as having changed sex, but as having their body altered to align to their true sex.

[298] Gender Recognition Act 2004 (GRA 2004), s. 2(1).

[299] GRA 2004, s. 3.

[300] *Carpenter v Secretary of State for Justice* [2012] EWHC 4421 (Fam).

[301] [2015] EWHC 464 (Admin).

[302] [2018] EWHC 2620 (Fam).

[303] [2009] EWHC 2220 (Admin).

[304] GRA 2004, s. 12.

[305] [2015] EWHC 990 (Admin).

a child, could not on having obtained a gender recognition certificate amend the certificate to name her as mother. This means that a person could be the mother of one child and the father of another.[306] It should also be noted that those trans people who do not apply for a certificate have their sex determined by the *Corbett* test set out above.[307] In 2019–20, 403 applications were dealt with, with 364 receiving full Gender Recognition Certificates and 11 Interim Certificates. Only 14 applications were refused.[308]

Generally, the Act has been welcomed. At last trans individuals can be recognised in law as having the sex with which they identify. Yet there are some who raise concerns about the legislation. Alison Diduck[309] has expressed concern that the legislation appears to regard 'gender dysphoria' as an abnormal dysfunction that needs special medical and legal treatment. It is almost as if it is some highly contagious condition which needs careful control and monitoring. Certainly, the wait for two years is a long time. While a wait before undergoing surgery may be sensible given it is so hard to reverse, is there a need for a wait before obtaining a certificate? John Eekelaar objects to the fact that on the issue of a gender recognition certificate a new birth certificate is issued. He argues doing so feeds the climate of discrimination and harassment that the legislation is designed to combat. If society approves of gender reassignment surgery it should 'shout about it from the rooftops'.[310] However, trans people claim that the surgery is bringing their body in line with their true sex. So, reissuing the birth certificate is correcting an erroneous document. Indeed, the Act does nothing to challenge the *Corbett* test for sex, with its focus on genital factors, which remains the starting point for the law's approach and takes no account of the sex with which a person identifies.

Another issue is that, as mentioned earlier, a person who does not disclose their gender past can render their marriage voidable. Alex Sharpe argues that the fact the Act makes a failure to disclose gender a ground of annulment of a marriage reveals the suspicion the law retains about trans people.[311] When marrying someone one is not required to disclose any other information. Is one's gender history any more significant than other important information about oneself, such as one's criminal record?[312]

Others have complained that the legislation does nothing for trans or intersex people who wish to be regarded as neither male nor female. Indeed, the legislation can be said to reflect the law's obsession with categorising people into being either male or female.[313] Some commentators have argued that far from there being two boxes for biological male and female, there is rather a scale of maleness and femaleness,[314] while it is often said this is too radical a suggestion given the extent to which gender roles are rigidly defined in our society. However, notably in a 2015 poll, 49 per cent of those aged 18–24 said they were not strongly heterosexual.[315]

---

[306] Gilmore (2003b). Where a woman gives birth to a child, is later given a gender recognition certificate and thereafter, with his new female partner, receives fertility treatment at a licensed clinic and a child is born as a result.
[307] *Re P (Transgender Applicant for Declaration of Valid Marriage)* [2019] EWHC 3105 (Fam).
[308] Office for National Statistics (2020f).
[309] Diduck (2003: ch. 1).
[310] Eekelaar (2006b: 76).
[311] Sharpe (2007).
[312] Sharpe (2012).
[313] Chau and Herring (2004: 201); Sandland (2005).
[314] Chau and Herring (2004).
[315] YouGov (2015).

In its review of the current law the House of Commons Women and Equalities Committee[316] concluded:

> The Gender Recognition Act 2004 was pioneering but is now dated. Its medicalised approach pathologises trans identities and runs contrary to the dignity and personal autonomy of applicants. The Government must update the Act, in line with the principle of gender self-declaration.

It looks forward to a day when a person can legally be the sex they want to be. There is increased acceptance of those who reject the male–female distinction and identify as queer, non-binary, gender fluid or intersex, for example. Increasingly, bathrooms and other facilities are being offered as gender-neutral spaces to recognise the complexity of the gender binary. It may be that we are gradually moving to a society and law which reject sex as a fundamental category. An even bolder one is a day when we are all people and sex is legally irrelevant.[317]

B People with intersex bodies

Trans people must be clearly differentiated from intersex people who are born with sexual or reproductive organs of both sexes. As the biological sex of an intersex person is ambiguous at birth, the doctors, in consultation with the family, will select a sex for the child.[318] It can later become clear that the doctors made the wrong choice and the child's body develops in a way clearly in line with the opposite sex. In such cases it is possible to amend the birth certificate to reflect the fact that an error was made in determining the sex at birth and the child will be regarded as having the later sex.[319]

The leading case in this area is now *W v W (Nullity)*,[320] where Charles J held that if a person was born with ambiguous genitalia, the individual's sex was to be determined by considering: (i) chromosomal factors; (ii) gonadal factors; (iii) genital factors; (iv) psychological factors; (v) hormonal factors; and (vi) secondary sexual characteristics (such as distribution of hair, breast development, etc.). Notably, Charles J accepted that a decision as to someone's sex could be made at the time of the marriage, taking these factors into account.

In *R (Elan-Cane) v Secretary of State for Home Department*[321] a non-binary person sought to challenge the refusal to allow them to have their passport list them as being neither male nor female but rather X. The case failed as there was no European Consensus on the right to have a non-binary sex category on passports. However, the Court of Appeal indicated some sympathy for the claimant:

> There can be little more central to a citizen's private life than gender, whatever that gender may or may not be. No-one has suggested (nor could they) that the appellant has no right to live as a non-binary, or more particularly as a non-gendered, person. Indeed, a gender identity chosen as it has been here, achieved or realised through successive episodes of major surgery and lived through decades of scepticism, indifference and sometimes hostility must be taken to be absolutely central to the person's private life. It is the distinguishing feature of this appellant's private life.

---

[316] House of Commons Women and Equalities Committee (2016).
[317] Herring (2017).
[318] For a detailed discussion of the medical and legal issues surrounding intersexual people, see Chau and Herring (2002 and 2004).
[319] See House of Commons Women and Equalities Committee (2016) for calls for the law to take account of intersex people.
[320] [2000] 3 FCR 748; discussed in Herring and Chau (2001). See also *B v B* [1954] 2 All ER 598.
[321] [2020] EWCA Civ 363.

They went on to indicate that in the years ahead a different outcome may prevail:

> . . . there is a respectable argument that we are approaching a time when the consensus within the Council of Europe's Member States will be such that there will be a positive obligation on the State to recognise the position of non-binary including intersex individuals . . . the State will then have to take steps towards implementing that obligation.

As we have seen, some commentators take the view that the position of intersex people reveals that there is no hard and fast division between male and female, but rather there is a scale between maleness and femaleness and people are placed at various points on that scale.[322] To them we should simply treat everyone as a person and not classify people as male or female. That would mean, in this context, that any two people should be allowed to marry. Objectors to this view might reply that it overlooks the reality that the vast majority of people clearly do strongly regard themselves as either male or female. It is highly artificial to refer to a scale when virtually everyone is at either end of it. Although in reply it might be said that until society opens up the possibility of people being on a scale of sexual identity, we cannot know how people will respond.[323]

9 Civil partnerships

Learning objective 9

Explain and evaluate the law relating to civil partnerships

This status was created by the Civil Partnership Act 2004 (CPA 2004).[324] There were 956 civil partnerships formed in England and Wales in 2018, a notable drop from 1,683 in 2014 and a significant decrease from the figure of 16,106 in 2006.[325] That is not so surprising, because 2006 was the first full year during which civil partnerships were available and no doubt many couples had been waiting for some time. Further, now same-sex couples have the alternative of marriage and many prefer that. Notably, the average age of entering a civil partnership in 2018 was 50.5 for men and 51.6 for women. Further, in 2018 65 per cent of couples entering civil partnerships were both male. This might indicate that younger same-sex couples are preferring marriage and that civil partnerships are primarily used by older gay men.

In 2014 following the Marriage (Same Sex Couples) Act 2013 civil partners could convert their civil partnerships into marriages. However, as John Haskey notes:

> Couples may have seen no need to hurry, if at all, to avail themselves of same-sex marriage (especially if they had already formed a civil partnership). Support for this interpretation might be borne out by the fact that, roughly, only about one in eight civil partnership couples has so far converted their civil partnership into a marriage.[326]

It might be thought that these statistics indicate that civil partnership is a dying institution since equal marriage was introduced.

---

[322] The argument is developed in Chau and Herring (2002) and Grenfell (2003).
[323] For further discussion see Mitchell and Travis (2018) and Gössl and Völzmann (2019).
[324] Mallender and Rayson (2006). For critical discussion of the Act, see Barker (2006 and 2012).
[325] Office for National Statistics (2018c).
[326] Haskey (2016).

A Who can enter a civil partnership?

Originally civil partnerships could only be entered into by same-sex couples.[327] However, the Civil Partnership (Opposite-sex Couples) Regulations 2019 now allow opposite-sex couples to enter civil partnerships. A civil partnership is created when the parties sign a civil partnership document 'at the invitation of, and in the presence of, a civil partnership registrar' and 'in the presence of each other and two witnesses'.[328] There are restrictions on who can enter a civil partnership: the parties must not be married or already a civil partner; they must both be over the age of 16[329] and they must not be within the prohibited degrees of relationship.[330] These restrictions are the equivalent of the ones found in marriage.

The 2019 regulations, allowing opposite-sex couples to enter civil partnerships, followed prolonged debates on the future of civil partnerships. Some argued for their abolition as a legal status; others that they should be opened up to opposite-sex couples; and others that they should remain as an option for same-sex couples only. The Government consultation[331] listed these reasons for not extending civil partnership to opposite-sex couples in the report as follows:

- Civil marriage entirely free from any religious element was already available to opposite-sex couples.
- There was no need for opposite-sex couples to have an alternative to marriage.
- Only very few opposite-sex couples would want a civil partnership.
- Marriage is felt to be the appropriate relationship for an opposite-sex couple.
- Civil partnership was a relationship created specifically for same-sex couples.
- It would create a two-tier system based on the assumption that civil partnership entails a lesser degree of commitment and is less stable than marriage.
- It would entail significant costs.

The arguments for the minority view that opposite-sex couples should be permitted to enter civil partnerships were given as follows:

- This is needed for fairness and equality and to eliminate discrimination between opposite-sex and same-sex couples. All couples should have the same options for formalising their relationship in law.
- Civil partnership would enable opposite-sex couples to enter a legal relationship that was a secular alternative to marriage without its traditional associations.
- Couples may prefer civil partnership to marriage; they should be able to make this personal choice.

The Government decided not to make any changes to the law as a result of the consultation. However, in the following case the law prohibiting opposite-sex couples from accessing civil partnership was found to be inconsistent with the Human Rights Act 1998.

---

[327] Civil Partnership Act 2004 (CPA 2004), s. 1(1).
[328] CPA 2004, s. 2(1).
[329] Where a person is under 18, parental consent is required: s. 4.
[330] CPA 2004, s. 3.
[331] Department for Culture, Media and Sport (2014).

> **KEY CASE:** *R (on the application of Steinfeld and Keidan) v Secretary of State for International Development* [2018] UKSC 32
>
> Rebecca Steinfeld and Charles Keidan had brought the case arguing the fact that they could not enter a civil partnership was a breach of their Article 8 rights to respect for their private and family life, together with Article 14, the right to freedom of discrimination. The Supreme Court accepted this argument. It held the wording of the Civil Partnership Act 2004 was clear that civil partnership was only for couples of the same sex and it was not possible to read the statute in a way compatible with the Convention. They therefore issued a declaration of incompatibility.
>
> The Government's central argument was that when the Marriage (Same Sex Couples) Act was passed it was not clear whether civil partnership would be used. They wanted to wait to see if it was still used before deciding whether to abolish it or to open it up to all couples. Lord Kerr did not find that a convincing argument: 'taking time to evaluate whether to abolish or extend could never amount to a legitimate aim for the continuance of the discrimination.'[332]

Following this decision, the Civil Partnership (Opposite-sex Couples) Regulations 2019 were enacted to allow opposite-sex couple to enter civil partnerships.[333] While heralded as a dramatic development in the law, in fact it is unlikely to make significant changes. Many people who currently cohabit do so because they do not want a formal status for their relationship and cannot be bothered to go through the hassle of a formal ceremony. They are unlikely to be attracted by civil partnership.[334] For those with more principled objections to marriage, it is likely the same arguments will apply to civil partnership. Civil partnership still involves having the state involved in your relationship; is modelled on marriage; and only in a limited way allows you to determine the legal consequences of your relationship. Some see civil partnership as more 'equal' but as Miles and Probert[335] write:

> It is therefore important to ask whether the source of the problem [of inequality within marriage] really is the institution of marriage or rather the characteristics of the people involved, and – more particularly – the wider societal structures that create and sustain the gender inequalities that play out in the conduct of many relationships. Whatever the best, equality-minded intentions of the parties might be, those wider structures may inevitably constrain their choices.

DEBATE

Should civil partnership be retained?

Supporters of retention of civil partnership suggest that marriage is imbued with its heterosexual and religious nature and it is important to offer civil partnership as a secular and non-hetero-normative alternative to marriage.[336] Hayward and Fenwick refer to:

---

[332] At para 50.
[333] Bowcott and Carroll (2018).
[334] Miles and Probert (2019)
[335] Miles and Probert (2019).
[336] Fenton-Glynn (2018).

The worth of civil partnerships as a particular, more neutral, less gendered, 'blank canvas' conception of the public expression of a relationship, untainted or less tainted by patriarchal or religious associations.[337]

As they note, care must be taken with this argument. It is important to remember that it is perfectly possible to have a non-religious marriage ceremony and indeed most marriages are not conducted in religious ceremony. So, there is no reason why a marriage need have any religious element at all. Further, few same-sex marriages today can hardly be described as heteronormative. Indeed, they often celebrate the queer. So, the argument in favour of retention of civil partnerships may be a combination of two points. The first is that despite what has just been said that for centuries marriage was a deeply religious and heteronormative institution, try as might modern marriage cannot really shake off its history and we need civil partnership as an alternative. The second is that if for a particular couple marriage has negative connotations, we should allow them to choose an alternative status, even if we disagree with them about the nature of marriage.

The problem is, supporters of 'modern marriage' might say, that retaining civil partnership re-enforces the traditional image of marriage being religious and heteronormative, the very thing modern marriage is trying to shake off. Indeed, they might point out that the very argument that civil partnership should be extended to opposite-sex couples shows that a legal status can develop and change (from an alternative to marriage for same-sex couples to a secular alternative to marriage). If civil partnership can be seen to undertake such a change, why cannot marriage change from its traditional form to its modern form?

The argument based on choice is also complex. It is claimed, whether you think modern marriage is or is not secular or heteronormative, should we not give people the choice to decide the name of their relationship? It may even be seen as a human right to determine the nature of their relationship.[338] A modern marriage supporter might think the views of a person who wants civil partnership are mistaken and based on a misunderstanding of marriage, but they should allow them the choice. A modern marriage supporter, however, is likely to further add that by allowing the choice, the state is seen to give legitimacy to the view that marriage is still in its traditional form. Indeed, Lucinda Ferguson[339] argues:

The *Steinfeld* couple's own argument that they should be 'entitled' to choose the form of legal recognition by which they acquire legal rights and responsibilities assumes the state interest either is irrelevant or, to the extent it is relevant, supports or is neutral toward their claim.

She then claims that 'the extension of civil partnership to opposite-sex couples seems capable only of undermining marriage'. That is because marriage would cease to be seen as having in itself a particular meaning (there would be alternative ways of getting the same legal position). If the law were to offer marriage or civil partnership to all couples, that might be seen to reinforce the view that marriage is heteronormative and religious. A further point is that if the issue is simply seen as a matter of personal choice, we would have to allow couples a far wider range of choices than marriage, civil partnership or cohabitation. It would lead to a collapse of status regulation of adult relationships into simply contract law if respecting people's choice became the only principle in deciding what statuses to offer.

---

[337] Hayward and Fenwick (2018).
[338] Draghici (2017).
[339] Ferguson (2016).

> ## Questions
>
> 1. *Do you think that marriage is inherently religious and/or patriarchal?*
> 2. *If we give people the choice of marriage or civil partnership, should we allow them a far wider range of choices over how they regulate their relationship?*
>
> ### Further reading
> Read **Ferguson** (2016) and **Hayward and Fenwick** (2018) for further discussion of the points outlined above.

Another issue is whether civil partnership should be open to relatives.[340] The issue arose in **Burden v UK**[341] where two unmarried sisters had lived together for many years. They were concerned that if either of them died the other would be liable to pay inheritance tax. They complained to the European Court of Human Rights (ECtHR) that they were denied the exemption from inheritance tax that was available to married couples and civil partners. The Grand Chamber of the ECtHR rejected their complaint, stating that a relationship between siblings is 'qualitatively of a different nature to that between married couples and [civil partners] . . . The very essence of the connection between siblings is consanguinity, whereas one of the defining characteristics of a marriage or [Civil Partnership Act union] is that it is forbidden to close family members.' They went on to explain that what is special about a civil partnership is the existence of the public undertaking and the rights and obligations that go with that, which makes civil partnership (and marriage) different from cohabitation. This seems the correct response to this case. What the sisters really wanted was to be exempt from inheritance tax, rather than become civil partners.[342] The strength of their case indicates a need to reform inheritance tax, rather than extend the law on civil partnerships. As Clare Fenton-Glynn[343] points out:

> The purpose of civil partnerships is not to provide financial benefits, but to provide a public acknowledgement of an intimate partner relationship, the commitment two people have made to each other. They are about identity, and equality between loving couples . . . This can be contrasted with siblings entering into a civil partnership, where the financial benefits would be the whole point – their relationship is otherwise already recognised.

B How do you form a civil partnership?

In many ways the creation of a civil partnership is much like a civil wedding. There are two important differences, however. First, in a civil wedding it is the exchange of vows, rather than the signing of the register, which creates the marriage.[344] Secondly, no religious services can be used while a civil partnership registrar is officiating at the signing of the register.[345] Of course, there is nothing to stop the couple from having a religious service after they have

---

[340] Fenton-Glynn (2018).
[341] [2008] ECHR 357, [2008] 2 FCR 244.
[342] Auchmuty (2009).
[343] Fenton-Glynn (2018).
[344] Cretney (2006a: 23).
[345] CPA 2004, s. 2(5).

become civil partners. However, the Equality Act 2010[346] allows for religious groups to have a civil partnership as part of a religious service. This recognises the fact that some religious groups are supportive of same-sex relationships.

C Annulling a civil partnership

A civil partnership can be void or voidable. It will be void if:[347]

- either of the parties is currently a civil partner or married;
- either of them is under the age of 16;
- the parties are within the prohibited degrees of relationship; or
- they both know that certain key formality requirements had not been complied with.[348]

A civil partnership will be voidable on the following grounds:[349]

LEGISLATIVE PROVISION

Civil Partnership Act 2004, section 50

(a) either of them did not validly consent to its formation (whether as a result of duress, mistake, unsoundness of mind or otherwise);

(b) at the time of its formation either of them, though capable of giving a valid consent, was suffering (whether continuously or intermittently) from a mental disorder of such a kind or to such an extent as to be unfitted for civil partnership;

(c) at the time of its formation, the respondent was pregnant by some person other than the applicant;

(d) an interim gender recognition certificate under the Gender Recognition Act 2004 has, after the time of its formation, been issued to either civil partner;

(e) the respondent is a person whose gender at the time of its formation had become the acquired gender under the 2004 Act.

These match the void and voidable grounds for marriage, with two notable exceptions: the non-consummation grounds are not included, nor is the venereal disease ground. We will look at the reasons for this later. The Act also contains bars to relying on annulment and these match those discussed above for marriage.[350]

D The end of the civil partnership

Civil partnerships will end on the death of the party or on an order for dissolution (the equivalent of divorce). The law on dissolution of a civil partnership is very similar to the law on divorce (see Chapter 4).

---

[346] Equality Act 2010, s. 202.
[347] CPA 2004, s. 49.
[348] CPA 2004, s. 49.
[349] CPA 2004, s. 50.
[350] CPA 2004, s. 51.

E The effect of a civil partnership

Baroness Hale in *Secretary of State for Work and Pension* v *M*[351] explained that civil partnerships have 'virtually identical legal consequences to marriage'. We shall be looking at the consequences of marriage and civil partnerships later in this section. Jill Manthorpe and Elizabeth Price have argued that although civil partnership has enabled same-sex couples to have the relationship between themselves formally recognised, their relationship with their partner's children or wider family is not recognised in law or socially to the same extent as occurs in marriage.[352] In particular, a civil partner of a woman may not be in as strong a position as a husband in relation to their children. This is explored further in Chapter 10.

F The differences between civil partnership and marriage

As has been repeated several times, there are very few differences between spouses and civil partners. As Stephen Cretney explains, the care taken by Parliament to ensure that marriage and civil partnerships were treated in the same way is revealed by the fact that the CPA 2004 amends legislation as diverse as the Explosive Substances Act 1883 and the Law of Property Act 1925.[353] The most important differences between marriage and civil partnership are the following:

1. The formalities at the start of the relationship: in a civil partnership it is the signing of the register, rather than the exchange of vows, which creates the legal relationship. Further, unlike a marriage, a civil partnership ceremony cannot contain a religious service.[354] However, s. 202 of the Equality Act 2010 allows for regulations to be passed which will permit religious groups to have civil partnership ceremonies in the context of a religious service.

2. The non-consummation grounds and venereal disease ground are not present as a ground of voidability in civil partnerships, while they are in marriage.

3. It used to be that adultery was not a fact establishing the ground for dissolution of a civil partnership, although it is for divorce. However, the law on divorce and dissolution has been recently reformed and now there is no difference (see Chapter 4).

4. If a woman receives assisted reproductive services, her husband will be regarded as the father of the child. Her civil partner would not be regarded as a parent of the child.[355]

What are we to make of these differences? One response is to suggest that they are so minor as to be of negligible practical significance. The exact moment when the status is created is of no practical relevance; nullity is very rarely used and is mainly of significance for those with strong conservative religious beliefs; and in a case of adultery a civil partner can rely on a behaviour ground for dissolution.[356] Another response is to be more cynical. The lack of reference to adultery and non-consummation demonstrates the law's failure to recognise that gay sex is real sex. Baroness Scotland, a Government minister at the time of the passing of the CPA, explained: 'There is no provision for consummation in the Civil Partnership Bill. We do not look at the nature of the sexual relationship, it is totally different in nature.' The coyness

---

[351] [2006] 1 FCR 497 at para 99.
[352] Manthorpe and Price (2005).
[353] Cretney (2006a: 29).
[354] Interestingly, a survey of same-sex couples found that a significant minority wanted a religious element in the civil partnership celebration: Readhead (2006).
[355] The Court of Appeal recognised this in *Re G (Children)(Residence: Same-Sex Partner)* [2006] 1 FCR 681.
[356] Spon-Smith (2005: 271).

apparent in the Government's explanation that it was not possible to produce a same-sex equivalent to consummation and adultery may indicate a reluctance to accept same-sex relationships at full value. Is the law suggesting that same-sex sexual behaviour is something that should not be talked about?

In the first in-depth study of same-sex couples who had entered civil partnerships a number of interesting points emerged.[357] Among civil partners it was common to refer to themselves as 'married' and few had faced negative reactions to their status. Many couples noted that they had been accepted as sons-in-law or daughters-in-law and as full members of their partner's family.[358] Interestingly, while 80 per cent of the members of the gay and lesbian community welcomed the Act, only 50 per cent wanted marriage to be extended to include same-sex couples. Another study found ambivalence towards civil partnership in the gay and lesbian community, with some describing it as 'pretend marriage' or 'second class'. Others were, however, wary of marriage, seeing it as a 'church thing' and not a label they would feel comfortable with.[359] Some civil partners work hard to ensure their relationship does not follow the traditional pattern of gendered roles within marriage.[360]

10 Unmarried cohabiting couples

Learning objective 10

Explain how the law has defined cohabitation

There is enormous difficulty in discussing unmarried couples because there are so many forms of cohabitation.[361] The term 'cohabiting couple' can range from a group of students living together in a flat-share, to a boyfriend and girlfriend living together while contemplating marriage, to a couple who have deliberately decided to avoid marriage but wish to live together in a permanent stable relationship. Lord Hoffmann in *Re G*[362] stated: 'Statistics show that married couples, who have accepted a legal commitment to each other, tend to have more stable relationships than unmarried couples, whose relationships may vary from quasi-marital to ephemeral.' Baroness Hale in the same case stated:

> Some unmarried relationships are much more stable than some marriages, and vice versa. The law cannot force any couple, married or unmarried, to stay together. But being married does at least indicate an initial intention to stay together for life. More important, it makes a great legal difference to their relationship. Marriage brings with it legal rights and obligations between the couple which unmarried couples do not have.[363]

One set of researchers[364] suggested that there are essentially four categories of cohabitants:

- the Ideologues: those in long-term relationships, but with an ideological objection to marriage;
- the Romantics: those who expect to get married eventually and see cohabitation as a step towards marriage, which they saw as a serious commitment;

---

[357] Smart, Masson and Shipman (2006).
[358] See Browne (2011) for an interesting discussion of how class can affect acceptance of civil partnership.
[359] Clark, Burgoyne and Burns (2006).
[360] Rolfe and Peel (2011).
[361] Probert (2012b) provides an outstanding history of the legal interaction with cohabitation.
[362] *Re G (Adoption: Unmarried Couple)* [2009] AC 173.
[363] *Re G (Adoption: Unmarried Couple)* [2009] AC 173.
[364] Barlow, Burgoyne and Smithson (2008).

- the Pragmatists: who decided whether or not to get married on legal or financial grounds;
- the Uneven Couples: where one partner wanted to marry and the other did not.

The law has not yet provided a coherent approach to cohabitation, but in several statutes married and unmarried couples have been treated in the same way. Apart from these special provisions, the law treats unmarried couples as two separate individuals, without regard to their relationship. If there is no specific statutory provision, the law treats an unmarried couple in the same way as it would two strangers.[365]

Tyrer J in **Kimber v Kimber**[366] suggested the following factors be considered in deciding whether there is cohabitation:

- whether the parties were living together under the same roof;
- whether they shared in the tasks and duties of daily life (e.g. cooking, cleaning);
- whether the relationship had stability and permanence;
- how the parties arranged their finances;
- whether the parties had an ongoing sexual relationship;
- whether the parties had any children and how the parties acted towards each other's children; and the opinion of the reasonable person with normal perceptions looking at the couple's life together.

There are some statutory attempts at defining cohabitation. Section 144 (4)(b) of the Adoption and Children Act 2002 states that 'two people (whether of different sexes or the same sex) living as partners in an enduring family relationship' can adopt. A more common form of definition of cohabitation is found in the Family Law Act 1996: 'two persons who, although not married to each other, are living together as husband and wife or (if of the same sex) in an equivalent relationship'.[367]

Same-sex couples who have not entered into a civil partnership can claim the rights that are available to opposite-sex unmarried couples.[368] In 1999 the House of Lords in **Fitzpatrick v Sterling Housing Association Ltd**[369] accepted that a gay person was a member of his partner's family. Lord Nicholls in **Secretary of State v M**[370] has stated that 'under the law of this country as it has now developed a same sex couple are as much capable of constituting a "family" as a heterosexual couple'. Little could Sister Sledge have foreseen that the theme from their song 'We are family' would be repeated by a Law Lord, albeit in a slightly more erudite way. In **Ghaidan v Godin-Mendoza**[371] the House of Lords accepted that the phrase 'a person who was living with the original tenant as his or her wife or husband' could include a same-sex couple.[372] These decisions were influenced in part by the fact that it is unlawful under the European Convention to discriminate upon the grounds of sexual orientation.[373]

---

[365] See Smart and Stevens (2000) for a discussion of the wide range of cohabiting relationships.

[366] [2000] 1 FLR 232. See also **Re J (Income Support Cohabitation)** [1995] 1 FLR 660 and **Kotke v Saffarini** [2005] EWCA Civ 221 for other discussion of what cohabitation means.

[367] FLA, s. 62(1)(a) (as amended by the Domestic Violence, Crime and Victims Act 2004).

[368] CPA 2004, Sched. 24 amends statutes to ensure that same-sex and opposite-sex cohabitees are treated in the same way.

[369] [2000] 1 FCR 21. The case is discussed in Glennon (2000) and Diduck (2001a).

[370] [2006] 1 FCR 497 at para 506.

[371] [2004] 2 AC 557.

[372] In **Nutting v Southern Housing Group** [2004] EWHC 2982 (Ch) it was emphasised that to be living as a spouse one had to have a life-long commitment.

[373] **JM v United Kingdom** [2010] ECHR 1361; **EB v France** [2008] 1 FCR 236; **Da Silva Mouta v Portugal** [2001] 1 FCR 653, discussed in Herring (2002b).

More and more couples are choosing to cohabit. In 1971, 8.4 per cent of births in England and Wales were outside marriage or civil partnership; by 2018 this had increased to 48.4 per cent. There are 3.4 million cohabiting families, compared with 12.8 million married or civil partnership families and 2.9 million lone parent families.[374]

The evidence suggests that some cohabitants are living together, but planning to marry; while others see cohabitation as an alternative to marriage. Certainly, cohabitation before marriage has become the norm, although there is no longer an assumption that if you have children you must marry.

11 Comparisons between the legal position of spouses or civil partners and unmarried couples

Learning objective 11

Compare and contrast the legal position of spouses and civil partners with unmarried couples

It is surprisingly difficult to compile a complete list of the differences between the legal positions of spouses or civil partners and unmarried couples, primarily because the law does not provide a clear statement of the rights and responsibilities of marriage. Some of the main differences in the legal treatment of married and unmarried couples will now be discussed.[375]

A Formalities at the beginning and end of a relationship

The law closely regulates the beginning and end of a marriage or civil partnership. It sets out certain formalities that must be complied with in order for a legal marriage or civil partnership to start, and it only ends when the court grants a decree absolute of divorce, or a dissolution. An unmarried cohabiting relationship can, by contrast, begin or end without any notification to any public body. While every marriage and civil partnership is centrally registered, there is no such record of cohabitation. One consequence of these formalities is that, although the law can restrict who can enter marriage or civil partnership, there is obviously no restriction as to who may cohabit – there is nothing to stop any number of men or women, unmarried or married, from cohabiting.

It is easy to overestimate the practical importance to the parties of the legal formalities at the beginning and end of a relationship. The legal requirements of marriage or civil partnership are not particularly difficult to comply with, and the legal formalities take up little time when compared with the non-legal trappings that often accompany marriage or civil partnership, which take up much more of the money and attention of the parties. Similarly, in relation to separation, although divorce or dissolution does include legal formalities, when compared with the paperwork and practical arrangements of the ending of a long-term relationship the legal formalities of divorce or dissolution can be of minor importance. The paperwork concerned over, for example, separating joint bank accounts, resolving the occupation of the home, dealing with the mortgage or tenancy, changing arrangements over electricity, gas bills, etc. can make the formalities connected to the divorce or dissolution itself seem small.

---

[374] Office for National Statistics (2018c).
[375] See also Barlow *et al.* (2005: 7–11).

B Financial support

During the marriage or civil partnership itself each party can seek a court order requiring one to pay maintenance to the other,[376] but one unmarried cohabitant cannot seek maintenance from another. In fact, it is very rare for one spouse to seek maintenance from the other except in the context of divorce. Where it is sought, the amounts awarded tend to be low and difficult to collect.[377]

Of far more significance is the fact that on divorce or dissolution the court has the power to redistribute property owned by either party. However, on the ending of an unmarried relationship the court only has the power to declare who owns what and has no power to require one party to transfer property to the other or to pay maintenance. Although this is a crucial distinction between spouses or civil partners and unmarried couples, three important factors need to be stressed. The first is that for many couples the Child Support Act 1991 and Children Act 1989 cover the maintenance for children. These Acts apply equally to married and unmarried couples. Secondly, once the child support has been resolved, there is often not enough spare money to consider spousal or partner support. In fact, in fewer than half of all divorces do the courts make any order dealing with the parties' financial resources.[378] The third distinction is that, as we shall see later, in resolving disputes between unmarried cohabitants over property the courts have utilised various equitable doctrines (for example, constructive trusts) which have in effect given the courts wide discretion in deciding the appropriate share of the equitable interest. Indeed, in some cases involving unmarried couples the results using the equitable doctrines are those which would be expected if the couple were married and the court were hearing the case under the Matrimonial Causes Act 1973.

Cohabiting couples, unlike spouses or civil partners, can enter binding cohabitation contracts which will determine what will happen to their property on separation.[379] However, care must be taken in the wording of such contracts. In *Sutton v Mischon de Reya*[380] the claimant asked a firm of solicitors to draft a cohabitation contract. Sutton and a Swedish businessman, Mr Stahl, wished to conduct a 'master–slave' relationship. They asked that the contract back this up by confirming that Sutton was to have absolute power over Stahl, to obey him in everything he said on pain of punishment and to hand over to Sutton all his property. Charles J held that such a contract amounted to, in effect, a contract for sexual services. He saw a key distinction between a contract for sexual relations outside marriage which was not enforceable and a contract between people who are cohabiting in a relationship which involves sexual relations. Charles J, in a surprising turn of phrase, stated that 'even a moron in a hurry'[381] could tell that the contract in this case fell into the former category and so was not enforceable.

C Children

There used to be a crucial distinction drawn between 'legitimate' and 'illegitimate' children. This affected the status of children and the nature of parental rights over children. The label of illegitimacy has now been abolished by the Family Law Reform Act 1987 and only minor

---

[376] See Chapter 6.
[377] The common law duty on a husband to maintain a wife was abolished in s. 198 of the Equality Act 2010.
[378] Barton and Bissett-Johnson (2000).
[379] They cannot contract out of child support obligations, however: *Morgan v Hill* [2006] 3 FCR 620.
[380] [2004] 3 FCR 142; [2004] 1 FLR 837.
[381] At para 23.

differences exist in the legal position of 'legitimate' and 'illegitimate' children.[382] However, there are still important differences between the legal position of married and unmarried fathers. As we shall see, one of the key concepts of the law relating to parenthood is parental responsibility. Every mother of a child automatically acquires parental responsibility for her child, but the father of the child will automatically acquire parental responsibility only if he is married to the mother. An unmarried father may acquire parental responsibility by being registered as the father on the child's birth certificate, lodging at the court a parental responsibility agreement, or the father may apply to the court for a parental responsibility order. This is a significant difference between married and unmarried fathers, but is of less importance than it might at first appear, for two reasons. First, the courts have been very willing to award parental responsibility to a father who applies for it. The second is that in day-to-day issues parental responsibility is of limited importance. Many unmarried fathers carry out their parental role unaware that they do not have parental responsibility. Whether or not a father has parental responsibility is only really of significance when major decisions have to be made in respect of the child, such as whether a child should have a medical operation.

D Inheritance and succession

Where a person dies without having made a will, the person is intestate. In such a case the deceased's spouse or civil partner will be entitled to some or all of the estate, depending on the application of various rules which will be discussed in Chapter 12. However, an unmarried partner of the deceased is not automatically entitled to an intestate estate. All an unmarried partner can do is to apply under the Inheritance (Provision for Family and Dependants) Act 1975 for an order that in effect alters the intestacy rules and awards them a portion of the estate. So, a bereaved unmarried partner must apply to the court in order to be put in the same position as the bereaved spouse if his or her partner is intestate.

E Criminal law

There used to be important distinctions between married and unmarried couples in criminal law, but many of these have been removed.

1. *Rape.* It used to be a common law rule that a husband could not be guilty of raping his wife.[383] This was justified in two ways. First, there was an emphasis on the concept of the unity of husbands and wives – as a husband and wife are one in the eyes of the law, sexual intercourse between them could be no crime.[384] Secondly, it was argued that on marriage the wife impliedly consents to intercourse at any time during that marriage and that such consent was irrevocable. Eventually, the House of Lords in *R v R (Rape: Marital Exemption)*[385] abolished the marital exception for rape and this was confirmed by Parliament in the Criminal Justice and Public Order Act 1994. Lord Keith explained that marriage 'is in modern times regarded as a partnership of equals and no longer one in which the wife must be the subservient chattel of the husband'.[386] So now the substantive law on rape is the same whether the defendant be the victim's husband or not.[387]

---

[382] See Chapter 8.

[383] Although he could be guilty of other criminal offences against his wife.

[384] This was never a very convincing explanation, because a husband could be convicted of assaulting his wife.

[385] [1991] 4 All ER 481, [1992] 1 FLR 217. See now Sexual Offences Act 2003, s. 1.

[386] [1991] 4 All ER 481 at p. 484.

[387] Although it appears that marital rapists still receive lower sentences than non-marital rapists (Warner (2000)).

2. ***Actual bodily harm and grievous bodily harm.*** There is some confusion in the criminal law over the circumstances in which one person may injure another with their consent. In *R v Brown*[388] the House of Lords confirmed the conviction of some sadomasochists who were convicted of assaulting each other even though their 'victims' had consented to the infliction of the pain. In *R v Wilson*[389] a husband was convicted of assault occasioning actual bodily harm for branding his initials on his wife's buttocks in spite of her consent. The Court of Appeal overturned the conviction. There is some dispute over how to reconcile these two cases. One argument is that the courts distinguished between injuries caused within marriage and injuries caused by gay couples.[390]

3. ***Theft.*** Under s. 30 of the Theft Act 1968 a person can only be prosecuted for theft against his or her spouse if the Director of Public Prosecutions has given consent.

4. ***Conspiracy.*** A person cannot be guilty of conspiring with his or her spouse or civil partner, unless it is alleged that they conspired with other people.[391]

5. The Anti-social Behaviour, Crime and Policing Act 2014, s. 177, abolished the special defence of coercion which used to be available to a wife who committed an offence as a result of her husband's pressure.

F Contract

It was only after the Law Reform (Married Women and Tortfeasors) Act 1935 that wives were able themselves to enter contracts that were legally effective. Husbands and wives can enter into contracts with each other, but will have to show that there is intent to create legal relations.[392] The position for unmarried couples is similar. A crucial difference is that a married couple or civil partners cannot enter into a binding contract which governs what would happen to their property in the event of their divorce or dissolution. Following *Radmacher v Granatino*[393] a court may give effect to such a contract, but not if the court thinks it would be unfair to do so. An unmarried couple can sign a contract which will determine what happens to their property when the relationship ends and the court will give effect to it as long as it is a valid contract.

G Tort

The rule that a spouse could not sue his or her spouse in tort was revoked by the Law Reform (Husband and Wife) Act 1962 and the rule that a husband had to be joined in any tortious action brought by or against a wife was abolished by statute in 1935.[394] In relation to tort, married and unmarried couples are therefore now treated in the same way. The most remarkable case of partners suing in tort is *P v B (Paternity; Damages for Deceit)*[395] where a man sued

---

[388] [1993] 1 AC 212.

[389] [1996] 3 WLR 125.

[390] Although in *Emmett*, unreported, 15.10.99 a man's conviction following injuries caused to his partner during an (alleged) sadomasochistic incident with his fiancée was upheld. For an alternative explanation and discussion see Herring (2009c: ch. 6).

[391] Criminal Law Act 1977, s. 2(2)(a).

[392] *Balfour v Balfour* [1919] 2 KB 571.

[393] [2010] UKSC 42.

[394] Married Women's Property Act 1882 and Law Reform (Married Women and Tortfeasors) Act 1935.

[395] [2001] 1 FLR 1041.

in deceit after his partner had falsely told him he was the father of her child, as a result of which he claimed he paid her £90,000 to support the child. His action was held not to be barred on the grounds of public policy.[396]

H Evidence

There are two issues here: can a spouse give evidence against the other spouse (is he or she competent), and can a spouse be forced to give evidence against the other spouse (is he or she compellable)? At one time spouses were not compellable[397] witnesses in civil or criminal proceedings against their spouses, the idea being that a spouse should not be forced into the appalling dilemma of either committing perjury or giving evidence which would harm his or her spouse in the proceedings. The spouse was considered an incompetent witness in criminal proceedings because the evidence would be so tainted that a jury would not be able to treat it fairly. These positions have been changed by statute.

The present law is now that in civil proceedings a spouse or civil partner is both a compellable and a competent witness. In criminal proceedings, generally, the spouse or civil partner is competent but not compellable.[398] In other words, if a spouse or civil partner is willing to give evidence against his or her spouse or partner he or she may do so, but will not be forced to. The exceptions are that if the husband and wife or civil partners are jointly charged for an offence, then neither is competent to give evidence for the prosecution (unless the charges against them are dropped or they plead guilty). Under s. 80 of the Police and Criminal Evidence Act 1984 there is a shortlist of offences for which the spouse or civil partner is compellable. These are offences which involve an assault or injury or threat of injury to the spouse or any person under the age of 16, or a sexual offence against a person under 16.[399] There are no special rules relating to the evidence of cohabitants.[400]

I Matrimonial property

The Family Law Act 1996 provides married couples and civil partners with home rights which provide a right to occupy the matrimonial home.[401] There are also special provisions relating to family property during bankruptcy, and pension rights, which we will discuss later. These provisions do not apply to cohabitants, who are given no particular protection on bankruptcy.

J Marital confidences

Communication between spouses used to be subject to special protection so that a spouse who disclosed confidential information about the other could be found in breach of confidence. However, the law on confidential information has now developed so that it covers

---

[396] A spouse will not be permitted to sue a former spouse in tort if this is regarded as an attempt to unsettle the financial orders reached on divorce: *Ganesmoorthy* v *Ganesmoorthy* [2003] 3 FCR 167.

[397] By saying a witness is compellable it is meant that a witness can be forced to give evidence.

[398] In *R (On the Application of the Crown Prosecution Service)* v *Registrar General of Births, Deaths and Marriages* [2003] 1 FCR 110 a defendant to a charge of murder married the chief prosecution witness to take advantage of this rule. The Crown Prosecution Service in that case unsuccessfully applied to prevent that marriage.

[399] This includes attempting, conspiring, aiding, abetting, counselling, procuring or inciting their commission.

[400] This was confirmed by the Court of Appeal in *R* v *Pearce* [2001] EWCA Crim 2834, [2002] 3 FCR 75. It rejected an argument that, following the Human Rights Act 1998, cohabitants should not be compellable witnesses.

[401] See Chapter 5.

cohabitants.[402] It has even been found that there could be confidential relations between a husband and the person he was having an adulterous relationship with.[403]

K Taxation and benefits

There are special exemptions from tax that apply to married couples and civil partners but not unmarried couples. The most important are in respect of inheritance tax and capital gains tax allowance. The Labour Government removed the married couples' tax allowance, which was an allowance against income tax available to married couples but not to unmarried couples. It is significant that the Labour Government replaced the married couples' tax allowance with a tax credit for those who care for children. In relation to state benefits, unmarried couples and married couples are generally treated in the same way. It has been alleged that now some married couples are disadvantaged as compared to lone parents in the tax and benefits systems.[404] The Coalition Government announced that it will give a tax credit to married couples where both are in employment and neither is a higher-rate taxpayer.[405]

L Citizenship

Anyone who is not a citizen of the UK and colonies does not become a citizen by marrying someone who is. She or he may obtain nationality by naturalisation or by one of the other methods. The spouse's requirements for naturalisation are less strict than for others. If a person is settled in the UK, the spouse will be given entry clearance as long as he or she can show the marriage is not a sham and that the couple are able to accommodate and maintain themselves. There is a similar power for engaged couples, but not unmarried cohabitants.[406] Following the Civil Partnership Act spouses and civil partners are treated in the same way for immigration purposes.

M Statutory succession to tenancies

Statute has provided rights to a tenant's family to succeed to the tenancy on the death of a tenant. The phrase 'family' has been interpreted to include opposite-sex or same-sex cohabitants.[407] The phrase 'as husband and wife' includes opposite-sex or same-sex couples.[408]

N Domestic violence

Married couples, civil partners and cohabitants are associated persons and so can apply for non-molestation injunctions. Cohabitants can also apply for occupation orders, although if the applicant does not have property rights in the property, she will be treated less favourably than she would have been had she been married or a civil partner.[409]

---

[402] *Stephens v Avery* [1988] 1 Ch 449; *A v B (a company)* [2002] 1 FCR 369.
[403] *CC v AB* [2008] 2 FCR 505. See also *John Terry (previously 'LNS') v Persons Unknown* [2010] EWHC 119 (QB).
[404] BBC News Online (2007a).
[405] Probert (2013a).
[406] Cretney, Masson and Bailey-Harris (2002: 92–3) for the detail of the law.
[407] *Fitzpatrick v Sterling Housing Association Ltd* [2000] 1 FCR 21.
[408] *Ghaidan v Godin-Mendoza* [2004] 2 FCR 481.
[409] See Chapter 7.

O Fatal Accident Act 1976

The Fatal Accident Act 1976 permits a spouse or civil partner of a deceased killed in an accident to claim damages under certain circumstances. Under this Act a cohabitant is able to have a claim in the same way as a spouse or civil partner if he or she had been living with the deceased for at least two years immediately before the date of death.[410]

The next two issues are differences of a theoretical rather than practical nature.

P The doctrine of unity

The principal effect of marriage at common law is that the husband and wife become one. The doctrine of unity finds its basis in Christian theology.[411] Blackstone[412] wrote:

> By marriage, the husband and wife are one person in law; that is, the very being or legal existence of the woman is suspended during the marriage, or at least is incorporated and consolidated into that of the husband . . . Upon this principle of a union of person in husband and wife, depend almost all the legal rights, duties, and disabilities, that either of them acquire by the marriage.

The effects of this doctrine were never fully explained in the law and today the doctrine is regarded with cynicism. Lord Denning MR in *Midland Bank Trust Co. Ltd v Green (No. 3)*[413] explained that the position used to be that '. . . the law regarded the husband and wife as one and the husband as that one'. However, he made it clear that the doctrine of unity is now of very limited application.[414]

Q Consortium

The concept of consortium is not clear but has been defined by Munby J in *Sheffield CC v E and S*[415] as 'the sharing of a common home and a common domestic life, and the right to enjoy each other's society, comfort and assistance'. At one time there was an obligation on the wife to provide her husband with 'society and services', although a husband did not owe the wife a corresponding duty. However, Munby J emphasised that nowadays spouses are 'joint co-equal heads of the family' and any rights of consortium are equal and reciprocal. However, the concept of consortium is rarely enforced in law. In *R v Reid*[416] it was confirmed that a husband could be guilty of kidnapping his wife and that the right of consortium did not provide a defence to such a charge.

---

[410] It does not cover those who were 'going out' together but not cohabiting: *Kotke v Saffarini* [2005] 1 FCR 642. In *Swift v Secretary of State for Justice* [2012] EWHC 2000 (QB) and *Smith v Lancashire Teaching Hospitals NHS Trust* [2016] EWHC 2208 (QB) claims that the difference in treatment between married and cohabiting couples breached human rights failed.

[411] The Bible, Genesis 2: 24; Genesis 3: 16.

[412] Blackstone (1770: 442).

[413] [1982] Ch 529 at p 538.

[414] In *Ünal Tekeli v Turkey* [2005] 1 FCR 663 it was said to be contrary to the ECHR to require a married couple to both take the husband's surname; that was sex discrimination and could not be justified in the name of promoting marital unity. The Court left open the question of whether it would be permissible to require the couple to share a surname.

[415] [2004] EWHC 2808 (Fam) at paras 130–1. The case is discussed in Gaffney-Rhys (2006).

[416] [1973] QB 299.

12 Engagements

Before marriage it is common for couples to enter into an engagement, when the parties agree to marry one another.[417] In the past, under common law, such agreements were seen as enforceable contracts, and so if either party, without lawful justification, broke the engagement then it would be open for the other to sue for breach of promise and to obtain damages. Such an action was abolished by the Law Reform (Miscellaneous Provisions) Act 1970, s. 1, which stated that no agreement to marry is enforceable as a contract. The abolition was justified on the basis that it was contrary to public policy for people to feel forced into marriages through fear of being sued.

In general, engaged couples are treated in the same way as unmarried couples, though engagement and agreement to enter a civil partnership still has legal significance in a number of ways:

1. *Property of engaged couples.* When resolving property disputes between an engaged couple s. 37 of the Matrimonial Proceedings and Property Act 1970 applies.[418] In brief, it states that if someone improves a house, he or she thereby acquires an interest in it (see Chapter 5 for more details). Apart from this provision, the property of an engaged couple is treated in the same way as that of an unmarried couple.[419]

2. *Gifts between engaged couples.* The Law Reform (Miscellaneous Provisions) Act 1970, s. 3(1) states that: 'A party to an agreement to marry who makes a gift of property to the other party to the agreement on the condition (express or implied) that it shall be returned if the agreement is terminated shall not be prevented from recovering the property by reason only of his having terminated the agreement.' So, each case will turn on its own facts and depend on whether the gift was subject to an implied condition that the gift should be returned if the marriage did not take place. For example, furniture bought for the intended matrimonial home may be thought to be conditional upon marriage and therefore should be returned if the engagement is broken. A Christmas gift would probably be regarded as unconditional.

3. The gift of an engagement ring is presumed to be an absolute gift and therefore can be kept by the recipient, but this presumption can be rebutted if it can be shown there was a condition that the ring be returned in the event of the marriage not taking place.[420] For example, if the ring had belonged to the man's grandmother and was intended to be passed down within her family, it may be presumed that the ring should be returned if the engagement is broken.

4. *Domestic violence.* Engaged couples are 'associated' people for the provisions of Part IV of the Family Law Act 1996 and so can automatically apply for a non-molestation order against one another. However, the Act requires the engagement be proved in one of a number of distinct ways (see Chapter 7).

---

[417] It is possible for a party to be engaged even though he or she is married to someone else: *Shaw v Fitzgerald* [1992] 1 FLR 357, [1992] FCR 162.

[418] *Mossop v Mossop* [1988] 2 FLR 173 CA, because of s. 2(1) of the Law Reform (Miscellaneous Provisions) Act 1970. See also *Dibble v Pfluger* [2010] EWCA Civ 1005.

[419] See Chapter 6.

[420] Law Reform (Miscellaneous Provisions) Act 1970, s. 3(2). See *Cox v Jones* [2004] 3 CR 693 for a case where the man was not able to show that the ring was not intended as a gift.

13 Should the law treat cohabitation and marriage or civil partnership in the same way?

It should be noted that many European countries have legislated to treat married and unmarried couples in the same way.[421] There are various ways of considering this question.

A Does the state benefit from cohabitation to the same extent as from marriage or civil partnership?

The state has traditionally favoured marriage and sought to encourage people to marry, most explicitly by providing tax advantages to married couples which are not available to unmarried people. However, marriage is not only encouraged through such explicit means. As Katherine O'Donovan explains: 'Marriage endures as symbol . . . it may be presented as private but it is reinforced everywhere in public and in political discourse.'[422] As late as 1989 a sizeable majority – 70 per cent – of respondents to the British Social Attitudes Survey took the view that 'people who want children ought to get married'. By contrast, in a recent survey 77 per cent of people believed that single parents can be a proper family; and 59 per cent believed that same-sex couples can be a family. Only 36 per cent of those questioned believed that a couple with children had to be married to be a proper family.[423] Although it seems that people accept that parents can be just as good whether they are married or not, this does not mean marriage is not valued. A 2010 poll found surprisingly traditional attitudes on the issue: 57 per cent believed the law should promote marriage in preference to other kinds of family structure; 58 per cent thought giving cohabitants similar legal rights as the married would undermine marriage and make people less likely to wed; and 85 per cent supported a tax break to promote marriage.[424] Another poll found that 70 per cent of those aged between 20 and 35 wanted to marry, including 79 per cent of those currently cohabiting.[425] But why is it that the Government, through public statements and policies, seeks to encourage marriage and civil partnership?

There are five particular advantages to the state which are often cited:

1. Sir George Baker, a former President of the Family Division, has argued that marriage provides the 'building blocks' of society and is 'essential to the well-being of our society, as we understand it'.[426] Lord Hoffmann has declared: 'The state is entitled to take the view that marriage is a very important institution and that in general it is better for children to be brought up by parents who are married to each other than by those who are not.'[427] This view, although a popular notion among politicians, lacks precision. What does it mean that marriage is a building block or the foundation of society? It could be argued that a married couple may feel they have a greater stake in society than two single people, and so may be more willing to contribute to it. This is certainly open to debate as, for example, single people may well be

---

[421] Thorpe LJ (2002: 893).
[422] O'Donovan (1993: 57).
[423] Centre for the Modern Family (2011).
[424] Fairburn (2010).
[425] de Waal (2008).
[426] *Campbell v Campbell* [1977] 1 All ER 1 at p. 6.
[427] *Re G (Adoption: Unmarried Couple)* [2009] AC 173.

more likely to use public transport and perhaps even be more vulnerable to crime. It has been suggested that marriage makes a couple wealthier, happier and healthier.[428] These arguments are all hard to prove either way. We have not tried a society without marriage, and so do not know whether society would be different without marriage.

2. It may be that the state wishes to support marriage and civil partnership in order to promote the production of and caring for children. Ruth Deech argues:

> Children deserve natural parents who are prepared to make the act of commitment and aspiration found only in marriage, in order to demonstrate to those children that they intend to be there for them, without question, as they grow up. Thus it is with marriage and its promises in a formal ceremony complete with special clothes, rituals, and insignia It is the strongest bond ever invented to link two people and two families, for now and for posterity – intimately, legally, politically, religiously, civilly, and publicly.[429]

The Conservative Party's Centre for Social Justice has also voiced its support for the institution of marriage.[430] It emphasises: 'By the time they turn five, 53% of children of cohabiting parents will have experienced their parents' separation; among five-year-olds with married parents, this is 15%.'[431] It also claims that those children not in two-parent families are:[432]

- 75 per cent more likely to fail at school;
- 70 per cent more likely to be a drug addict;
- 50 per cent more likely to have an alcohol problem;
- 40 per cent more likely to have serious debt problems;
- 35 per cent more likely to experience unemployment/welfare dependency.

They claimed that married relationships were more stable than unmarried relationships[433] and so it was in society's interests to promote marriage. This claim is controversial and we shall return to it shortly.

3. A third alleged benefit to the state is that by managing the start of a relationship the state is able to regulate the relationship if it breaks down. The state may wish to ensure that at the end of a relationship the arrangements for children will promote the child's welfare, and that the spouse's or civil partner's property is divided between them in a way that is just. If a marriage or civil partnership breaks down, the couple must turn to the courts for a divorce or dissolution so that the marriage or civil partnership can be officially terminated; however, if an unmarried couple separate, the court may well not be involved at the end of the relationship. The strength of this view is weakened in the light of the present law. First, the law, in both financial and child-related matters, essentially allows the parties themselves to resolve these matters and intervenes only if there is a dispute. Secondly, this view does not explain why the law does not try to provide the same intervention for unmarried couples.

4. A fourth benefit is economic. If a person falls ill, or becomes unemployed, and so no longer has an income, then the financial responsibility is likely to fall on the state if that person is single, whereas spouses or civil partners would depend on each other. A further economic

---

[428] Waite and Gallagher (2001).
[429] Deech (2012).
[430] Centre for Social Justice (2009).
[431] Centre for Social Justice (2020).
[432] Centre for Social Justice (2010).
[433] The Labour Government claimed this too: HM Government (2010a).

benefit is the straightforward fact that a couple sharing accommodation require less housing than two single people.

5. Marriage and civil partnership can be used as an effective evidential and bureaucratic tool. If the law were to abolish the legal significance of marriage then it would be necessary to create some kind of alternative in order legally to regulate family life. Perhaps cohabitation would provide that alternative. The difficulty is that a couple might be sharing a house, but not necessarily sharing their lives. The definition of cohabitation and the investigation that would be necessary to decide whether or not a couple were sharing their lives would be far more complex and expensive than deciding whether a person is married. The couples who marry or enter civil partnerships therefore save the state's and courts' time, money and effort in formally establishing the nature of their relationship.

Many of these benefits of marriage or civil partnership are also provided by cohabiting relationships. Further, it is unclear whether all or even most married couples or civil partners provide these benefits.[434] For example, in 2019, only 39 per cent of married couple families had dependent children.[435] However, the core question is whether unmarried cohabiting couples are as stable as married or civilly partnered ones. This is especially important when considering their role in raising children. It is very difficult to obtain statistics on cohabiting relationships because there are no formalities marking their beginning and end. The evidence available suggests that unmarried cohabiting relationships are shorter lived.[436] One study found that around 27 per cent of couples that were cohabiting when their child was born have separated by the time the child is aged five, compared with 9 per cent of couples that were married when their child was born.[437] Further, while cohabiting couples make up only around 19 per cent of parents, they accounted for 48 per cent of family breakdown cases.[438]

Sir Paul Coleridge is convinced marriage offers benefits for children and the couple:[439]

> Unmarried parents are nearly 3 times more likely to break up before their first child's seventh birthday. And the chances of a 15 year old still living with both his parents, if they are unmarried, is very small indeed. About 7% of unmarried parents are still together by the time their children reach 15 whereas 93% are married.

The problem with such arguments is even if we accept these statistics, we cannot conclude that it is marriage which causes the stability of relationships. It is also clear that unmarried cohabitants tend to be economically less well off, and it may be their economic position rather than their marital status that truly affects the stability of their relationship.[440] In other words, even if the cohabiting couple had married, their relationship would not have lasted any longer.

After an extensive review of the literature Alissa Goodman and Ellen Greaves conclude:[441]

> Our findings suggest that while it is true that cohabiting parents are more likely to split up than married ones, there is very little evidence to suggest that this is due to a causal effect of marriage.

---

[434] Huston and Melz (2004) argue that although there are benefits in some couples marrying, that is not true for all couples.

[435] Office for National Statistics (2020a). This statistic looks surprising but remember many older married couples' children may no longer be dependent.

[436] Haskey (2001); Kiernan (2001).

[437] Benson (2009). See also Kiernan and Mensah (2010).

[438] Marriage Foundation (2014c).

[439] Coleridge (2014).

[440] Goodman and Greaves (2010b).

[441] Goodman and Greaves (2010b).

Instead, it seems simply that different sorts of people choose to get married and have children, rather than to have children as a cohabiting couple, and that those relationships with the best prospects of lasting are the ones that are most likely to lead to marriage.

Similarly, Miles, Pleasence and Balmer found that, once age and socio-economic factors were taken into account, 'there was little difference in breakdown rates between married and cohabiting respondents'.[442]

Goodman and Greaves make similar findings in relation to child welfare,[443] concluding that encouraging parents to marry is unlikely to lead to significant improvements in young children's outcomes. They found that there are differences in development between children born to married and cohabiting couples but this reflects differences in the sort of parents who decide to get married rather than to cohabit. For example, compared to parents who are cohabiting when their child is born, married parents are more educated, have a higher household income and a higher occupational status, and experience a higher relationship quality early in the child's life. It is these and other similar factors that seem to lead to better outcomes for their children. Having taken account of these (largely pre-existing) characteristics, the parents' marital status appears to have little or no additional impact on the child's development. Similarly, Claire Crawford and colleagues[444] found that while at ages three and five children born to married parents have a higher cognitive and socio-emotional development, as compared to children of parents who are not married, marriage plays a relatively small, if any, role in causing this.

We might ask if there are any rational reasons why married relationships or civil partnerships might be stronger than unmarried ones. The Centre for Social Justice argues:[445]

> Marriage provides clarity for the future of a relationship, removing ambiguity by sending a clear signal to each partner of mutual commitment for life. The public declaration of commitment makes it difficult for asymmetrically committed relationships – where one partner has a higher commitment than the other – to survive, thereby filtering out less viable relationships. Cohabiting couples are less likely to have the specific moment of articulated commitment in marriage that forces ambiguity into the open. Cohabitation increases the constraints which tie a couple together, such as shared property or finances, thereby providing a correlative increased commitment. Marriage has a powerful social meaning that conditions the behaviour of its participants. It will never be possible to fully isolate the selection effect, not least because of the ethics around conducting such an experiment. When we consider whether marriage produces stability or if stability produces marriage there are reasons to think that there is a causal element – in the public and intentional commitment of a marriage – in addition to a selection effect. It is as much a mistake to rule out the likelihood of cause as it would be to assume that it's there.

These kinds of arguments in favour of marriage can be broken down into four reasons. The first is that marriage or civil partnership may indicate a deeper commitment to the relationship.[446] This may be true for many couples but is clearly not true for all. The current divorce rate demonstrates that marriage is not a guarantee of lifelong commitment. Indeed, in Eekelaar and Maclean's research[447] no difference in the level of commitment to the relationship was found between married and unmarried couples. There is, however, one sense in

---

[442] Miles, Pleasence and Balmer (2009: 54).
[443] Goodman and Greaves (2010a).
[444] Crawford *et al.* (2012).
[445] Centre for Social Justice (2009).
[446] Morgan (2000); Gallagher and Waite (2001).
[447] Eekelaar and Maclean (2004).

which it might be argued that a spouse or civil partner has a greater commitment to the relationship and that is in terms of the legal responsibilities undertaken. The potential financial liability of a spouse or civil partner is certainly greater than that undertaken by a cohabitee.[448] In financial and legal terms, at least, a child is likely to be better off if his or her parents are married than if they are unmarried.[449] Anita Bernstein sees one of the strongest arguments in favour of marriage being that 'as a form of enforced commitment, state-sponsored marriage facilitates investment – that is, the sacrifice of short-term gain for the prospect of returns in the long term'.[450] This may well be true but, as Maclean and Eekelaar[451] point out, 'marriage is neither a necessary nor sufficient condition for the acceptance of personal obligation'. They argue:

> It becomes increasingly difficult to identify being married in itself as necessarily, or even characteristically, constituting a significant source of personal obligations in the eyes of the participants in such relationships.[452]

They suggest it is the obligations negotiated by the parties which are the source of the obligation for all couples, be they married or cohabiting. As John Eekelaar[453] has argued:

> Marriage clearly therefore has great social value, but much of the nature of its value is conferred upon it by those who enter it, and it is unlikely that its value can primarily be defined by law.

The second reason why one might believe that marriages or civil partnerships are more enduring than cohabitation is that the social pressure against ending a marriage or civil partnership may be greater than the pressure against ending an unmarried relationship. Again, this may be true, depending on the attitude and culture of the parties, their families and communities.

Thirdly, the legal barriers to divorce or dissolution may slow down the marital breakdown process, which might increase the chance of reconciliation. The strength of these arguments is very much open to debate. Even if it could be shown that marriage itself makes couples more stable, it could still be argued that the state should do more to encourage and support unmarried relationships rather than privileging married relationships. Fourthly, it can be suggested that the characteristics or values of cohabiting couples differ from married ones and these make them more likely to separate.[454]

An argument that is sometimes made in this debate is that treating unmarried couples in the same way as married couples will discourage marriage or civil partnership, thereby harming society.[455] The Conservative Party's Centre for Social Justice[456] commissioned research which suggested that 58 per cent of those questioned thought giving cohabitants the same rights as married couples would undermine marriage. This argument is weak. Kiernan, Barlow and Merlo[457] have analysed marriage rates in Australia and Europe and have found 'little evidence of a relationship between the introduction of legislation giving rights to cohabiting couples with subsequent changes in the propensity to marry'. Kathy Griffiths,[458] also exploring the

---

[448] Cleary (2004).
[449] Lewis (2006) rejects the arguments that attitudes of married and unmarried couples towards their relationship are identical, especially in cases of recoupling.
[450] Bernstein (2003: 203).
[451] Maclean and Eekelaar (2005b).
[452] Eekelaar (2004: 536).
[453] Eekelaar (2010).
[454] See, e.g., Lye and Waldron (1997).
[455] Morgan (2000).
[456] Centre for Social Justice (2009).
[457] Kiernan, Barlow and Merlo (2007: 72).
[458] See also Griffiths (2019).

Australian experience, explained that couples still seek the bureaucratic convenience and the symbolic value of marriage. As has already been mentioned, it is very unlikely that people decide not to marry because of the legal consequences. Simply put, few people know the law in this area.[459] Even those who do are more likely to base their decision to marry on religious and social views, or to be influenced by their families, friends and culture.

B Choice

An alternative approach is to focus on 'choice'.[460] Ruth Deech[461] has argued that if a couple choose not to marry it is wrong for the law to treat them as if they were married as this would negate their choice and show a lack of respect for their decision.[462] She argues:

> My preference is for the rights of the individual, or human rights, in this instance autonomy, privacy, a sphere of thought and action that should be free from public and legal interference, namely the right to live together without having a legal structure imposed on one without consent or contract to that effect. It is better not to have legal interference in cohabitation and leave it to be dealt with by the ordinary law of the land, of agreements, wills, property and so on.[463]

There are perhaps three difficulties with this view, despite its persuasive power.[464] The first is that it is doubtful to what extent many couples *choose* not to marry, at least to what extent they choose not to take on the legal consequences of marriage. In reality few couples decide positively not to get married because of the legal differences in treatment and, indeed, few marry because of the legal benefits.[465] The 2019 British Social Attitudes Survey[466] found that 46 per cent of people in cohabiting relationships believed cohabitants were treated as 'common law' married and had the same legal status as marriage. There have been Government information campaigns and much media coverage trying to debunk this 'common law marriage myth', but the percentage of people who believe in it has only decreased by one percentage point since 2005. A second problem is that some couples disagree over whether or not to marry. It may be, for example, that the woman wants to get married but the man does not. It seems a little harsh to say she has chosen not to marry. Deech, rather bluntly, replies that such a person should either leave her partner or accept the unmarried status. A third argument is that some of the legal consequences of marriage do not reflect the couple's decision but rather the justice of the situation or the protection of a state interest (for example, protecting the interests of children).[467] One might take the view that it should not be possible to choose not to have justice or not to protect a state interest. Alternatively, it could be said that although cohabiting couples might not want all of the consequences of marriage, this does not mean they do not want the law to intervene at all at the end of their relationship.[468] In spite of these responses, where both members of a couple have decided firmly to reject the legal consequences of marriage, to deny respect to that choice seems unduly interventionist.

---

[459] Smart and Stevens (2000).
[460] Deech (2012); Dnes (2002). See Glennon (2010) for a very helpful discussion of choice in this context.
[461] Deech (2012 and 2010d). See also Garrison (2004) who takes a similar line.
[462] Chan (2012).
[463] Deech (2010d).
[464] Leckey (2018).
[465] Hibbs, Barton and Beswick (2001).
[466] National Centre for Social Research (2019).
[467] Herring (2005a).
[468] Haskey (2001: 53).

It may be that Deech's argument is more persuasive when seen as a call for marriage to be treated in the same way as cohabitation. In other words, regardless of whether the couple are married or not, the law's response should focus on their commitment to each other, rather than having the consequences of the status of marriage 'imposed upon them'.

C Discrimination

It might be argued that to treat married and unmarried people's family rights and responsibilities differently amounts to discrimination of their rights under Article 8 of the European Convention on Human Rights in a way prohibited by Article 14. The European Court has not yet specifically stated that discrimination on the grounds of marital status is covered by Article 14, but it has been implied in several cases. In *Re P*[469] the House of Lords held that for the purposes of the Human Rights Act 1998 treating cohabitants differently from married couples did amount to discrimination, although that could be justified in some cases. However, the European Court has not taken such a clear line. In *Gomez v Spain*[470] a woman who separated from her cohabitant of 18 years complained that her inability to make the financial claims that a wife could make against her husband on divorce infringed her Convention rights. The Commission held that any difference in treatment was justifiable by the need to protect the traditional family. She had chosen not to take up the advantages of marriage and therefore the discrimination was proportionate. Similarly, in *Van der Heijden v Netherlands*[471] differences in the law of evidence as it related to married and cohabiting couples were justified as marriage conferred a 'special status' and gave rise to 'social, personal and legal consequences' that meant differences in treatment could be justified. The implication of this might be that some differences in treatment between married and unmarried couples will be unlawful discrimination under the ECHR and others will not. It may be, for example, that parental rights should not differ as between married and unmarried parents, but the rights they have between themselves can.[472]

The discrimination argument was considered in the following case:

CASE: *Re Siobhan McLaughlin (Northern Ireland)* [2018] UKSC 48

Ms McLaughlin's partner of 23 years died. They were not married, but had four children together. Had she been married to him she would have been entitled to widowed parent's allowance under the Northern Ireland benefits scheme. However, as she was not married, she could not. She claimed that this discriminated against her and the children on the basis of marital or birth status contrary to Article 14 of the European Convention on Human Rights in respect of their right to family life under Article 8 and the protection of property rights in Article 1 of the First Protocol.

The Supreme Court, by a majority of 4 to 1 agreed there was discrimination and issued a declaration of incompatibility. They focused on what was the basis for the payment of this benefit. They determined it was not the fact of public commitment, but rather the co-raising of children. They attached weight to the fact that the benefit was justified in

---

[469] [2008] UKHL 38, discussed in Herring (2009a).

[470] App. No. 37784/97 (19 January 1998).

[471] [2013] 1 FCR 123.

[472] Although see *B v UK* [2000] 1 FCR 289 where the ECtHR upheld differences in relation to parental responsibility between married and unmarried fathers.

large part to protect the interests of the children of the deceased parent. The majority held the discrimination between married and unmarried parents could not be justified. They accepted that in other contexts the promotion of marriage and civil partnership was a legitimate aim for discriminating, but was not reasonable in this context.

D Should marriage be discouraged?

There are, of course, arguments that the state should not encourage marriage and we should be working therefore to remove any special legal status of marriage.[473] Some feel that marriage is an institution which has helped perpetuate disadvantage against women.[474] Katherine O'Donovan has sought 'to break free from marriage as a timeless unwritten institution whose terms are unequal and unjust'.[475] The argument is that marriage ensures the maintenance of patriarchal power, through the power given to husbands as 'head of the household'.[476] Martha Fineman[477] has argued that 'Marriage allows us to ignore dependency in our policy and politics' and that means care-givers (normally women) bear the burden of caring with no social reward. Clare Chambers writes:

> The white wedding is replete with sexist imagery: the father 'giving away' the bride; the white dress symbolising the bride's virginity (and emphasising the importance of her appearance); the vows to obey the husband; the minister telling the husband 'you may now kiss the bride' (rather than the bride herself giving permission, or indeed initiating or at least equally participating in the act of kissing); the reception at which, traditionally, all the speeches are given by men; the wife surrendering her own name and taking her husband's.[478]

And this continues into married life. As Auchmuty[479] argues when she writes of the practical disadvantages:

> When children arrive, or when one person's career progression requires the subordination of the other's, they almost always have to choose which party will be the principal breadwinner and which the principal homemaker. These roles are routinely mapped onto sex . . . earning less than men and cheaper than paid-for childcare, they end up forced into economic dependence on a husband even when that was never the couple's intention . . .

Auchmuty makes a powerful point, but it must be asked whether this is true of all heterosexual relationships, rather than marriage in particular. And some would argue she is using an outdated understanding of marriage. Marsha Garrison argues that few people now understand marriage in terms of fixed gender roles and instead marriage is based on companionship or personal fulfilment.[480]

Other criticisms have been similar to those launched against the family, namely that marriage can be self-centred, with the couple focusing on preparing their home rather than working in the community around them. From an opposite perspective, marriage can be seen as anti-individualist. O'Donovan summarises Weitzman's view of marriage:

---

[473] See Chapter 1.
[474] Slaughter (2002).
[475] O'Donovan (1993).
[476] Auchmuty (2019).
[477] Fineman (2006: 63).
[478] Chambers (2013).
[479] Auchmuty (2020).
[480] Garrison (2014).

[T]his unwritten contract, to be found in legislation and case-law, is tyrannical. It is an unconstitutional invasion of marital privacy, it is sexist in that it imposes different rights and obligations on the husband and wife, and it flies in the face of pluralism by denying heterogeneity and diversity and imposing a single model of marriage on everyone.[481]

However, these criticisms may be said to be overcome by a modern understanding of marriage which is based on a partnership of equals, sharing the burdens of homemaking, child-caring and wealth creation,[482] although the extent to which such marriages occur in reality, rather than as an aspiration, is a matter of debate.

E Protection

Baroness Hale, writing extra-judicially, has argued that the law needs to protect cohabitants from inequality. She writes:

> Intimate domestic relationships frequently bring with them inequalities, especially if there are children. They compromise the parties' respective economic positions, often irreparably. This inequality is sometimes compounded by domestic ill-treatment. These detriments cannot be predicted in advance, so there should be remedies that cater for the needs of the situation when it arises. They arise from the very nature of intimate relationships, so it is the relationship rather than the status that should matter.[483]

Notably, this argument does not necessarily require that cohabitation be treated identically to marriage, but it does call for protection from inequality that flows from cohabitation – particularly the unfairness that women face as a result of undertaking the child-caring role in the relationship.

The Centre for Social Justice note: 'Marriage has become a middle-class secret. Among high income couples (the top quintile) 83% have tied the knot; among low-income parents (bottom quintile) only 55% are married.' This could be significant on relationships breakdown, particularly for those caring for children, typically women. Cohabitants will have no financial orders available and will be left in poverty, while married ones can receive some share of the family assets, as we shall see in Chapter 6.

Rosemary Auchmuty is wary of this protection argument. As she points out:

> Divorce law does not, as is often claimed, protect *couples* or *partners*; it protects only the financially vulnerable party to the marriage, and only to the extent that his or her ex-spouse can afford to pay. It follows that the assets of the party in a stronger financial position will *not* be protected; rather, their assets may be taken away.
>
> . . .
>
> Conservative forces in society do not really want women to be independent; they want to see them tied to men as breadwinners and providers, holding the family together. For women to be demonstrably able to cope on their own would render marriage, and even men (they fear), superfluous.[484]

This argument, however, overlooks the point that at the start of a relationship a couple do not know what the future will hold. Divorce (or dissolution) offers them the assurance that if needed the court will ensure a fair distribution of assets, which can be an advantage to both parties.

---

[481] O'Donovan (1984: 114).
[482] Schwartz (2000) describes such marriages as 'peer' marriages.
[483] Hale (2004a).
[484] Auchmuty (2016).

14 The Law Commission's proposed reforms

Learning objective 12

Appreciate potential reform options for marriage

The Law Commission's Consultation Report 2007, *Cohabitation: The Financial Consequences of Relationship Breakdown*, proposes reform to the law. (This is discussed in Chapter 5.) Their proposal will give cohabitants some financial remedies on separation, but these will be less extensive than available to married couples.[485] The Government in 2011 said it had no plans to implement the proposals within the current Parliament. In 2014 a private member's Bill (the Cohabitation Rights Bill 2014) was presented to Parliament to give effect to these proposals, but it was not passed.

15 What if the state were to abolish legal marriage?

One point of view is that marriage should cease to have any legal significance, although most holders of this view would be happy for marriage to continue to have religious and social significance.[486] Supporters of this view argue it is not the job of the state to promote a particular kind of relationship, especially one as undesirable as marriage. As Chambers[487] argues:

> Marriage is fundamentally a gendered institution. It has been the main mechanism for maintaining the gendered division of labour, for regulating men's access to women's bodies, and for giving men ownership and control of children. Marriage provides a structure within which men and women are represented as opposites: complementary but stratified, roles separate and ranked. He works, she cooks and cleans; his work is paid, hers is not; his work is borne of power and entitlement, hers of love and duty. The state recognition of marriage has been the state recognition of this gendered arrangement: a celebration of separation simultaneous to unification. Two become one: one household, one legal entity, husband and wife separable only by the public/private divide. Or death.

If the state seeks to be neutral between relationships, this would mean that any legal regulation of relationships would not depend on whether couples are married or not, but rather on different criteria: for example, whether a couple have children, or the length of time a cohabitation has existed. So, for example, if the Government wishes to give benefits to stable couples who care for children, these could be directed towards couples with children who have stayed together for five years, rather than giving the benefit to all married couples, which would be over-inclusive.[488]

One option would be to replace marriage with a contractual model so that each couple can set out for themselves the terms of their relationship. This would avoid the one size fits all model of the current marriage law. Chambers writes:

> Marriage presents and represents a particular symbolic meaning that transcends individuals' subjective self-understandings and experiences. Instead, it appeals to supposedly shared social understandings of value, understandings that can fail to respect minority and historically-oppressed groups. In particular, marriage reinforces the idea that the monogamous heterosexual union is the (only) sacred form of relationship.[489]

---

[485] Hale (2009b).
[486] See Bernstein (2006) for a useful set of essays discussing this.
[487] Chambers (2017: 201).
[488] Such a proposal is developed in Law Commission of Canada (2002).
[489] Chambers (2013).

While this argument might be slightly mitigated by the legalisation of equal marriage, it still highlights the problem that a particular set of rights and duties are seen as met within a particular kind of relationship, such as marriage. Those whose relationships do not fit within that standard framework are disadvantaged, but the primary model for relationship regulation, namely marriage, is not avoidable for them. Chambers prefers 'piecemeal regulation':

> Piecemeal regulation involves the state regulating the different functions or parts of a relationship separately. There would be no assumption that, in any particular case, all the functions coincided in one relationship. Thus there would be separate regulations for property, child custody, immigration and so on. Each of these regulations would stand separately, and individuals could form relationships with different people for different functions.[490]

DEBATE

After marriage?

If the law does not rely on marriage, how might the law distinguish two strangers from two people in a close relationship, assuming it wishes to?[491] The following are some possibilities:

1. *The law could rely on cohabitation.* This proposal could be that if a couple have cohabited for two years and/or have a child then they are given the rights married couples and civil partners currently have.[492] In effect, this would create a system where you must 'opt out' of marriage. A couple not wishing to be treated as being married would need to lodge a form with a government agency. Most proponents of such a scheme would accept that people could marry in the 'normal' way too. The difficulty is in defining cohabitation. Does it require staying overnight: how many nights a week are necessary?[493] Proof of cohabitation (or non-cohabitation) may also prove difficult.

2. Some commentators have promoted an approach that seeks to promote relationships of care.[494] As I have written:

   > A sexual relationship between two parties may be fun for the parties involved, but is not itself producing any great social benefit. Care does. If the Government announced a no sex week and the citizens complied no great loss would arise. If the Government announced no care week and the citizens complied, significant harm would result.

   Elizabeth Brake[495] has argued in favour of 'minimal marriage' which she sees as designed to promote caring, reciprocal relationships. She rejects the view that only romantic, two-persons relationships should be covered, as that too narrowly restricts the kind of marriages which should be promoted. These caring relationships are 'primary goods' whose value nearly everyone will agree on and therefore make them a less controversial goal than traditional marriage.

   A major difficulty with this approach is that it is difficult to know what counts as care in this context. Would a person who helps a neighbour now and then be in a caring

---

[490] Chambers (2013).
[491] For a discussion of whether family law could be reduced to a network of personal rights and obligations, without obligations emanating from 'the family', see Eekelaar (2000a).
[492] See Baker (2009b) for a discussion of Australian law which has taken an approach similar to this.
[493] Cf. *Santos v Santos* [1972] Fam 247.
[494] Fineman (2004); Herring (2013a).
[495] Brake (2012).

relationship?[496] If so, what kind of legal rights and remedies would follow?[497] Supporters would argue that these problems should not deter a promotion of care.

3. Craig Lind takes these arguments further and argues that the primary focus should be on friendship, not just cohabitation. He argues:

> Voluntarily assumed responsibility creates vulnerabilities and (inter)dependencies. These benefit our society while the relationships in which they are discovered continue. When those relationships end, the law's tendency to refuse recognition to those responsibilities – its refusal to acknowledge the vulnerabilities and dependencies that are their result – places the law on the side of the powerful, pitted against the powerless. And that is a role the law should be loathe to play.[498]

4. Another approach is to focus on the agreement between the parties.[499] This could require or encourage the parties to prepare and sign a legal agreement.[500] This is only satisfactory where the parties are aware of the benefits of doing so. It is notoriously difficult to persuade people to make wills. It is doubtful we will be more successful in persuading people to make cohabitation contracts. (We will return to this issue in Chapter 6.)

5. It would be possible for the state to create an alternative to marriage, for example registered partnerships.[501] However, it is unlikely that people who do not wish to marry would choose to register their partnerships. Partnerships would be useful, however, for those who are legally barred from marriage (e.g. sisters).

Questions

1. *If two friends came to see you asking your advice as a lawyer as to whether they should enter a civil partnership or whether they should cohabit, what would you recommend and why?*

2. *Would it really make any difference to the law if it was decided that marriage was of no legal significance?*

3. *It has been claimed that we have been witness to a steep rise in the number of 'death bed' marriages, with cohabiting couples formalising their relationship at the last minute to claim the tax and other advantages of the inheritance law.[502] If that is correct, does it indicate that the law on cohabitation should be reformed or is it an argument against doing so?*

Further reading

Read **Deech** (2010d) for a passionate argument against treating unmarried couples in the same way as married ones. Read **Auchmuty** (2008) for an argument that marriage is outdated and is on its way out.

---

[496] Rainey (2017) suggests that marriage is open to those in caring relationships who wish to enter marriage. This would keep the standard model for 'getting married' but mean many caring relationships would fall outside its scope.

[497] Cave (2018).

[498] Lind (2011).

[499] For a useful discussion, see Lewis (2001b).

[500] Todd (2006). Mills and Reeve (2017) found that only 10 per cent of cohabitants questioned had signed a cohabitation agreement.

[501] Bradley (2001). See Francoz-Terminal (2009) for a discussion of the French approach.

[502] Bowcott (2018).

16 Conclusion

This chapter has considered the nature of marriage, civil partnership and cohabitation. Increasing numbers of people are deciding to live together outside marriage and, in response, the legal distinctions between married and unmarried couples are lessening. Most significantly, the tax advantages awarded to married couples and civil partners have been replaced by a tax credit to those caring for children (whether married or not). This reflects a suggestion that it is parenthood rather than marriage or civil partnership that is at the heart of family law. This is not to say there are no legal differences between married and unmarried couples, but those differences that remain are controversial and many argue that the distinctions should be removed.

Governments still seem to promote marriage as a way of encouraging commitment, stability and personal responsibility within relationships. The difficulty is that such values may not resonate with everyone.[503] Some couples may place greater weight on financial stability and/or personal freedom within their relationships.

Rosemary Auchmuty has suggested that marriage has lost so much social and legal significance that it should now be regarded as simply as a 'life-style choice'. Certainly, as the legal consequences of marriage lessen, it is harder to justify the restrictions on who can marry whom. Further, if marriage or civil partnership is not to be the touchstone for deciding who are a legally recognised couple, what should replace it? There are great difficulties in finding an alternative: cohabitation or the intentions of the parties, for example, are not susceptible to ready proof, particularly when compared to examining the marriage register to see if a couple are married. The truth is that the term 'cohabitants' can cover a vast range of different kinds of relationship. The bureaucratic difficulties caused by defining cohabitation[504] might lead, ultimately, to the law deciding that intimate relationships between adults give rise to no legal obligations whatsoever and that obligations should flow instead from parenthood.[505]

Further reading

Acker, A. van (2016) 'Disconnected relationship values and marriage policies in England', *Journal of Social Welfare and Family Law* 38: 36.

Auchmuty, R. (2012) 'Law and the power of feminism: how marriage lost its power to oppress women', *Feminist Legal Studies* 20: 71.

Auchmuty, R. (2016) 'The limits of marriage protection: in defence of property law', *Oñati Socio-Legal Series* 6: 1196.

[503] Acker (2016).

[504] See Garrison (2007) who regards this as one of the great benefits of marriage. *Kotke v Saffarini* [2005] EWCA Civ 221 shows the difficulties the courts can face in defining cohabitation.

[505] See Bernstein (2006) for a useful collection of essays on the legal regulation of family life without reference to marriage.

Auchmuty, R. (2020) 'Feminist Responses to Same Sex Relationship Recognition' in C. Ashford and A. Maine (eds) *Research Handbook on Gender, Sexuality and the Law,* Cheltenham: Edward Elgar.

Barker, N. (2012) *Not the Marrying Kind: A Feminist Critique of Same-Sex Marriage,* London: Macmillan.

Barker, N. and Monk, D. (eds) (2015) *From Civil Partnership to Same-sex Marriage. Interdisciplinary Reflections,* Abingdon: Routledge.

Bernstein, A. (ed.) (2006) *Marriage Proposals: Questioning a Legal Status,* New York: New York University Press.

Brake, E. (2012) *Minimising Marriage,* Oxford: OUP.

Cave, E. (2018) 'Liberalism, civil marriage, and amorous caregiving dyads', *Journal of Applied Philosophy.*

Centre for Social Justice (2020) *Family Structure Still Matters,* London: CSJ.

Chambers, C. (2013) 'The marriage-free state', *Proceedings of the Aristotelian Society* 1.

Chambers, C. (2017) *Against Marriage,* Oxford: Oxford University Press.

Chau, P.-L. and Herring, J. (2004) 'Men, women and people: the definition of sex', in B. Brooks-Gordon, L. Goldsthorpe, M. Johnson and A. Bainham (eds) *Sexuality Repositioned,* Oxford: Hart.

Cummings, T. (2020) 'Gendered dimensions and missed opportunities in *Akhter* v *Khan (Attorney-General and others intervening)', Child and Family Law Quarterly* 239.

Deech, R. (2010d) 'Cohabitation', *Family Law* 40: 39.

Den Otter, R. (2018) 'A perfectionist argument for legal recognition of polyamorous relationships', in E. Brake and L. Ferguson (eds) *Philosophical Foundations of Children's and Family Law,* Oxford: OUP.

Douglas, G. (2016) 'Towards an understanding of the basis of obligation and commitment in family law', *Legal Studies* 36: 1.

Eekelaar, J. (2010) 'Evaluating legal regulation of family behaviour', *International Journal of Jurisprudence of the Family* 1: 17.

Eekelaar, J. (2014) 'Perceptions of equality: the road to same-sex marriage in England and Wales', *International Journal of Law, Policy and the Family* 28: 1.

Eekelaar, J. and Maclean, M. (2004) 'Marriage and the moral bases of personal relationships', *Journal of Law and Society* 4: 510.

Equality and Human Rights Commission (2009) *Trans Research Review,* London: Equality and Human Rights Commission.

Ferguson, L. (2016) 'The curious case of civil partnership: the extension of marriage to same-sex couples and the status-altering consequences of a wait-and-see approach', *Child and Family Law Quarterly* 347.

Gilbert, A. (2014) 'From "pretended family relationship" to "ultimate affirmation": British conservatism and the legal recognition of same-sex relationships', *Child and Family Law Quarterly* 26: 463.

Gill, A. and Anitha, S. (eds) (2011) *Forced Marriage,* London: Zed Books.

Girgis, S., George, R. and Anderson, T. (2010) 'What is Marriage?' *Harvard Journal of Law and Public Policy* 34: 245.

Gössl, S. and Völzmann, B. (2019) 'Legal Gender Beyond the Binary', *International Journal of Law Policy and the Family* 33: 403.

Griffiths, K. (2019) 'From "form" to function and back again: a new conceptual basis for developing frameworks for the legal recognition of adult relationships', *Child and Family Law Quarterly* 27: 227.

Hayward, A. and Fenwick, H. (2018) 'From same-sex marriage to equal civil partnerships: on a path towards "perfecting" equality?' *Child and Family Law Quarterly* 30: 97.

Hayward, J. (2019) 'The Steinfeld effect: equal civil partnerships and the construction of the cohabitant', *Child and Family Law Quarterly* 31: 283.

Herring, J. (2017b) 'Is law too sexy?' *Modern Believing* 58: 361.

Johnson, P. (2015) 'Marriage, heteronormativity, and the European Court of Human Rights: a re-appraisal', *International Journal of Law, Policy and the Family* 29: 56.

Kennedy, H. and Dalla, R. (2020) '"It may be legal, but it is not treated equally": marriage equality and well-being implications for same-sex couples', *Journal of Gay & Lesbian Social Services* 32: 67.

Law Commission Consultation Paper 179 (2006) *Cohabitation: The Financial Consequences of Relationship Breakdown,* London: TSO.

Leckey, R. (2018a) 'Cohabitants, choice, and the public interest', in E. Brake and L. Ferguson (eds) *Philosophical Foundations of Children's and Family Law,* Oxford: OUP.

Leckey, R. (2018b) 'Judging in marriage's shadow', *Feminist Legal Studies* 26: 25.

Lyndon Shanley, M. (2004) 'Just marriage', in M. Lyndon Shanley (ed.) *Just Marriage,* Oxford: OUP.

Miles, J., Mody, P. and Probert, R. (eds) (2016) *Marriage Rites and Rights,* Oxford: Hart.

Miles, J. and Probert, R. (2019) 'Civil partnership: ties that (also) bind?' *Child and Family Law Quarterly* 31: 303.

Mitchell, F. and Travis, M. (2018) 'Legislating intersex equality: building the resilience of intersex people through law', *Legal Studies* 38: 587.

O'Sullivan, K. and Jackson, L. (2017) 'Muslim marriage (non) recognition: implications and possible solutions', *Journal of Social Welfare and Family Law* 39: 22.

Rainey, S. (2017) 'In Sickness and in health: cripping and queering marriage equality', *Hypatia* 32: 230.

Scherpe, J. and Hayward, A. (2018) *The future of registered partnerships: family recognition beyond marriage?* Cambridge: Intersentia.

Sharpe, A. (2007) 'Endless sex: the Gender Recognition Act 2004 and the persistence of a legal category', *Feminist Legal Studies* 15: 57.

Vora, V. (2020) 'The Continuing Muslim Marriage Conundrum: The Law of England and Wales on Religious Marriage and Non-Marriage in the United Kingdom', *Journal of Muslim Minority Affairs* 40: 148.

Waal, de, A. (ed) (2013) *The Meaning of Matrimony,* London: Civitas.

Visit **go.pearson.com/uk/he/resources** to access **resources** specifically written to complement this text.

4 Divorce

Learning objectives

When you finish reading this chapter you will be able to:

1. Discuss the statistics on divorce
2. Explain the theories around the causes of divorce
3. Set out the current law on divorce
4. Analyse the criticisms of the old law on divorce
5. Examine the law on dissolution of civil partnerships

1 Statistics on divorce and dissolution

KEY STATISTICS

- Between 1961 and 1991 there was a fivefold rise in the divorce rate. Currently, however, we are seeing a rapidly declining number of divorces.[1]

- In 2018 there were 90,871 divorces of opposite-sex couples, down from the 2013 figure of 114,720 divorces; and notably lower than the figure of 153,282 in 2004. The 2018 figure is the lowest annual number since 1971.

- The divorce rate (the number of divorces per 1,000 marriages per year) rose from 4.7 in 1970 to 13.7 in 1999. However, since then it has fallen and by 2018 it was 7.5.

- There were 428 divorces of same-sex couples in 2018, with three-quarters of those being between female couples.

- For those married in 1968, 20% of marriages had ended in divorce by the fifteenth wedding anniversary whereas for those married in 1998, almost a third of marriages (32%) had ended by this time. However, it seems the chances of divorce are decreasing. For those who married in 2013, only 6% of marriages had ended by their fifth anniversary and 19% of those who had married in 2008 had divorced by their tenth anniversary. Couples who have been married for 26 years have a 1% risk of divorce.[2]

[1] All the statistics in this box come from Office for National Statistics (2020d).
[2] Office for National Statistics (2020d).

- In 2018 the median duration of a marriage was 12.5 years. This is an increase from 1993–96 when it hovered between 9.8 and 9.9 years. This shows that the popular perception that marriages are ending more quickly is not true. The median rate of marriages today now matches that of 1972.

- Unreasonable behaviour was the most common reason for opposite-sex couples divorcing, with 51.9% of wives and 36.8% of husbands petitioning on these grounds in 2018.

- There were 927 civil partnership dissolutions granted in the United Kingdom in 2018 and 956 new civil partnerships.

Learning objective 1

Discuss the statistics on divorce

These statistics surprise many. It is commonly assumed that divorce rates are ever-rising, but in fact they have been consistently falling for quite some time. However, it may be that the fall in the number of divorces is largely caused by the fact that fewer people are marrying. That said, those who do marry do seem to have marriages that last for longer than in recent decades.

All that said, the seeming picture of gloom painted by these figures could be misleading. Some 45 per cent of divorces involved couples at least one of whom had been divorced previously.[3] What this reveals is that the divorce rate figures are somewhat skewed by the number of people marrying, divorcing, remarrying and divorcing again. Further, if we look at marriages which have survived the first 10 years, there is little difference in the divorce risk for couples in the 1960s, 70s, 80s or 90s.[4] Even if we take the estimate that of those marrying today 39 per cent will divorce,[5] it should not be forgotten that the clear majority of marriages last for life.

A final word on the gloom that can surround the divorce statistics. Although a divorce is normally marked by emotional turmoil, it can provide a release for the parties from an unhappy relationship and a new beginning. A divorce may be a tragedy, but less of a tragedy than being stuck in a deeply unhappy relationship.

2 Causes of divorce

Learning objective 2

Explain the theories around the causes of divorce

Here we will consider the factors that are statistically linked to divorce. It must be stressed that these are only statistical links, so it does not mean that because one of these factors is present the couple will divorce; it is simply more likely that they might. The factors predictive of divorce are being married as a teenager; being previously married; having a lower level of education; having children from a previous relationship; having one's parents separate; and having lived together before marriage.[6] One study suggests that a relationship becomes unhappy and then a trigger event such as violence and adultery causes the official break up.[7] The study notes that while adultery and violence used to predominate among the reasons given for separation, other explanations such as 'growing apart' have become increasingly common, and now make up about half of cases. Around a fifth of couples mentioned behaviour relating to money.

---

[3] Office for National Statistics (2020d).
[4] Benson (2013).
[5] Benson (2013).
[6] Amato (2010); Hayward and Brandon (2011). Although see Bridges and Disney (2012) and Pleasence and Balmer (2012) who argue the link between poverty and relationship breakdown is complex.
[7] Lampard (2014).

To these must be added important social changes, including assumptions about what we can expect from marriage. Anthony Giddens has maintained that in modern times people stay in intimate relationships only for as long as the relationships meet their own goals of personal autonomy and fulfilment.[8] Shelley Day Sclater summarises his view: 'we no longer look for Mr or Mrs Right, but rather we search for the perfect relationship; when one fails to satisfy, the individual in late modernity increasingly feels free to move on to try another'.[9] Further increased access to the labour market for women makes divorce an economically viable alternative when it was not in the past.

3 The new law: Divorce, Dissolution and Separation Act 2020

Learning objective 3

Set out the current law on divorce

The law on divorce is now governed by the Divorce, Dissolution and Separation Act 2020 (DDSA) which significantly amends the Matrimonial Causes Act 1973 (MCA). This section will set out the new law. We will then look at the old law and why the law was reformed.

Section 1(1) of the MCA, as amended by the DDSA, now reads:

1. Subject to section 3, either or both parties to a marriage may apply to the court for an order (a "divorce order") which dissolves the marriage on the ground that the marriage has broken down irretrievably.

2. An application under subsection (1) must be accompanied by a statement by the applicant or applicants that the marriage has broken down irretrievably.

3. The court dealing with an application under subsection (1) must—

    (a) take the statement to be conclusive evidence that the marriage has broken down irretrievably, and

    (b) make a divorce order.

    . . .

In simple terms this means that the court will make a divorce order following an application by one party, stating that the marriage has broken down irretrievably. In effect this is divorce on demand. It you want a divorce and apply for it with the correct form you will get it.

Pedantically it may be said this is not 'divorce on demand' because s. 1(1) states the divorce is granted by the court not because one party wants it but because the marriage has broken down irretrievably. Perhaps that is not such a pedantic point. The new Act could simply have said the divorce will be issued following an application, but it does not. It makes it clear it is irretrievable breakdown which is the justification for the divorce. This sends a powerful message that the law is still committed to the idea that divorce is not just an individual choice. Rather, marriages end when the law determines they have broken down irretrievably. The problem is that the message is somewhat blunted by s. 1(3)(a) which states that the statement of one party is conclusive evidence that the marriage has broken down. However, that is the only way of retaining the irretrievable breakdown ground without requiring the parties to prove it, which would be to reintroduce the idea that one party must blame the other for the divorce. And, as we shall see, one of the primary reasons for the new law was to move away from a fault-based system for divorce.

---

[8] Giddens (1992).
[9] Day Sclater (2000: 68).

The DDSA sets out the procedure. Twenty weeks after the receipt of the application, if the party (or parties) seeking the order wish the application to continue, the court makes a conditional divorce order.[10] Six weeks later it can make a final divorce order. It is possible for the court to shorten these time periods. This is only likely to occur where there are strong reasons for doing so. One could imagine a court doing this to allow a terminally ill person to remarry, for example. This new terminology of conditional divorce and final divorce orders replaces the outdated language of a decree nisi and decree absolute used under the old law. The time periods here are present to ensure the parties have time to reflect on their decision.[11] You do not want 'deliveroo divorce' at the click of a button!

The system for dissolution of a civil partnership is identical to that for a divorce. The only difference is in the terminology: conditional dissolution and final dissolution orders. As we shall see, under the old law there were differences in the facts that could be used for a divorce and a dissolution. There is none under the new law.

Section 17 MCA, as amended by the DDSA, allows parties to gain a judicial separation. This is very rarely used. Under such an order the parties remain married but there is a formal acknowledgement they live separately. It is most commonly used by couples who have religious objections to divorce, but wish a formal acknowledgement they are no longer living together.

The significance of this new law on divorce can be appreciated better when you have an outline knowledge of the old law.

4 The old law

A The requirements for divorce under the old law

Prior to 1857 the ecclesiastical (church) courts determined the law on divorce.[12] This meant that although nullity decrees could be made, divorce was not available through the courts. The only form of divorce was by an Act of Parliament, a hugely expensive procedure that was open only to a few people. Gradually the law was liberalised and the Matrimonial Causes Act 1973 covered the law until it was amended in 2020.

Divorce under the Matrimonial Causes Act 1973 was granted on the basis of a petition where one party (the petitioner) presented an application for divorce which the other party (the respondent) may choose either to defend or not. It was not possible to petition for divorce until the couple had been married for one year. The sole ground for divorce was set out in s. 1(1) of the Matrimonial Causes Act 1973: that the marriage has irretrievably broken down. But the only way of establishing irretrievable breakdown was by proving one of the five facts listed in s. 1(2). If none of the five facts was proved, a divorce could not be granted, even if the court was convinced that the marriage had irretrievably broken down.[13] About three-quarters of petitions were based on either adultery or unreasonable behaviour as these grounds did not involve delay.[14] The five facts were as follows.

---

[10] MCA s. 1(4), (5)
[11] Interestingly, section 1(6) provides the Lord Chancellor can shorten, but not lengthen, these time periods.
[12] For a discussion of the history of divorce law, see Cretney (2003a).
[13] *Buffery v Buffery* [1988] 2 FLR 365, [1988] FCR 465.
[14] Office for National Statistics (2020d).

(i) The respondent's adultery

LEGISLATIVE PROVISION

Matrimonial Causes Act 1973, section 1(2)(a)

. . . that the respondent has committed adultery and the petitioner finds it intolerable to live with the respondent.

[A]Section 1(6) of the Matrimonial Causes Act 1973 further adds:

Only conduct between the respondent and a person of the opposite sex may constitute adultery for the purposes of this section.

It should be noted that it was not enough just to show that the respondent had committed adultery – it was also necessary to demonstrate that the petitioner found it intolerable to live with the respondent.[15] It is remarkable that adultery was restricted to voluntary sexual intercourse between people of the opposite sex. This is hard to justify, but mattered little in practice because other sexual unfaithfulness can fall under the unreasonable behaviour fact.

(ii) The respondent's behaviour

LEGISLATIVE PROVISION

Matrimonial Causes Act 1973, section 1(2)(b)

. . . that the respondent has behaved in such a way that the petitioner cannot reasonably be expected to live with the respondent.

It was not enough just to prove that the respondent had engaged in unreasonable behaviour. It had to be behaviour that a right-thinking person would think was such that this petitioner could not reasonably be expected to live with the respondent.[16] So, the court should take into account the personality of the parties in deciding whether the conduct was sufficient to prove the ground.[17] It was possible to rely on a series of incidents which, although minor in themselves, cumulatively established that the petitioner could not live with the respondent. There are probably few marriages where a party would not be able to recall a few incidents of unreasonable behaviour by his or her spouse! The Law Commission acknowledged that 'virtually any spouse can assemble a list of events which, taken out of context, can be presented as unreasonable behaviour sufficient to found a divorce petition'.[18] The cases reveal a wide range of conduct constituting unreasonable behaviour, ranging from a DIY enthusiast husband who removed the door of the toilet and took eight months to replace it,[19] to a husband who required his wife to tickle his feet for hours every evening, leaving his wife with uncontrollable movements in her hands.[20]

---

[15] Although it did not need to be shown that it was the adultery that made the living together intolerable.
[16] *Birch v Birch* [1992] 1 FLR 564, [1992] 2 FCR 564.
[17] *Birch v Birch* [1992] 1 FLR 564, [1992] 2 FCR 564.
[18] Law Commission Report 192 (1990).
[19] *O'Neill v O'Neill* [1975] 3 All ER 289.
[20] *Lines v Lines* (1963) *The Times*, 16 July. See also *Le Brocq v Le Brocq* [1964] 3 All ER 464 where the wife claimed that her husband's submissive character and refusal to argue infuriated her.

(iii) The respondent's desertion

> **LEGISLATIVE PROVISION**
>
> ## Matrimonial Causes Act 1973, section 1(2)(c)
>
> . . . that the respondent has deserted the petitioner for a continuous period of at least two years immediately preceding the presentation of the petition.

If the petitioner could show that the respondent had deserted the petitioner for a continuous period of two years preceding the petition, this could form the basis of the divorce application. Desertion was defined as an unjustifiable withdrawal from cohabitation, without the consent of the remaining spouse and with the intent of being separated permanently.

(iv) Two years' separation with the respondent's consent to the divorce

> **LEGISLATIVE PROVISION**
>
> ## Matrimonial Causes Act 1973, section 1(2)(d)
>
> . . . that the parties to the marriage have lived apart for a continuous period of at least two years immediately preceding the presentation of the petition . . . and the respondent consents to a decree being granted.

If the petitioner could establish that there had been two years' separation immediately before the presentation of the petition and that the respondent consented to the petition, a divorce could be granted. This ground was significant because the law accepted that divorce could be obtained by consent without proof of wrongdoing. The intention was that this would be the most commonly used fact, but actually it was never more popular than behaviour.[21]

(v) Five years' separation

> **LEGISLATIVE PROVISION**
>
> ## Matrimonial Causes Act 1973, section 1(2)(e)
>
> . . . that the parties to the marriage have lived apart for a continuous period of at least five years immediately preceding the presentation of the petition . . .

The petitioner could rely on the fact that the parties had separated for five years prior to the date of the petition. This was the most controversial ground because it permitted divorce to be ordered against a spouse without their consent and without any proof of wrongdoing. Opponents called the section a 'Casanova's charter', although with a five-year wait between marriages, a Casanova would require patience!

---

[21] Office for National Statistics (2020d).

Section 5 of the Matrimonial Causes Act 1973 provided a defence to a respondent facing a petition based on this ground. That could be used where the divorce would result in grave financial or other hardship to the respondent and it would be wrong in all the circumstances to dissolve the marriage. This was very rarely used.

B The special procedure under the old law

To understand how the Matrimonial Causes Act 1973 worked in practice it is crucial to appreciate the court procedures that were in place to deal with petitions for divorce.[22] Prior to 1973 each divorce required a hearing where the petitioner in open court would have to present evidence to support the grounds set out in the petition, by introducing witnesses if necessary. This was expensive, embarrassing and stressful for the parties and it involved the judiciary in lengthy hearings. A special procedure was introduced that, by 1977, covered all grounds for divorce where the petition was undefended.[23] Under the special procedure the petitioner simply needed to lodge at the court the petition outlining the grounds for the divorce; a statement concerning the arrangements for the children; and an affidavit confirming the truth of these documents.[24] Originally a district court judge would read through the documents and, if satisfied that the petitioner had proved his or her case, pronounce a decree nisi. However, recently there have been trials where this is done by a court administrator, rather than a judge. So, although there is some limited scrutiny to ensure that the formal paperwork is present, there is no attempt to ensure that what is stated on the petition is true. Indeed, the petition may be entirely false; there is no need to prove the veracity of what is stated, unless the respondent defends the divorce. The law works on the assumption that if the respondent does not attempt to defend the petition then it can be assumed to be true. This assumption is in fact unreliable. If a respondent receives a petition based on falsehoods, he or she must decide whether or not to defend the petition. The expense involved in defending the petition (there is no community legal services funding available and it is likely to cost around £6,000)[25] and the reluctance of lawyers to become involved in defended divorces[26] meant that very few petitions (around 0.015 per cent)[27] were defended. Even in the few cases when a divorce was defended it was rarely on the basis that there should not be a divorce, but rather on what grounds the divorce should be granted.[28]

5 Problems with the old law

Learning objective 4

Analyse the criticisms of the old law on divorce

The MCA 1973 had been subject to mounting criticism and it became inevitable that the law would be reformed at some point. Before looking at some of the specific complaints about the old law, we will look at two cases which exemplify the problems with it.

---

[22] The law on recognition of overseas divorces is not covered here: Family Law Act 1986 and Council Regulation (EC) 2201/2003 deal with the issue.

[23] The procedural change was reinforced by the withdrawal of legal aid for divorce.

[24] It is also necessary to provide other documents in some cases.

[25] Trinder (2018a).

[26] They are widely regarded by lawyers as a waste of time. If one party is determined to obtain a divorce, is there any practical benefit in preventing them?

[27] Trinder (2018a).

[28] *Owens v Owens* [2018] UKSC 41.

KEY CASE: *VW v BH (Contested Divorce)* [2018] EWFC B68

The couple had been married for 35 years. The wife petitioned for divorce after discovering the husband had been committing adultery with her best friend for 25 years. The husband cross-petitioned for divorce on the basis of the wife's behaviour. Although the couple agreed the marriage had broken down irretrievably, they could not agree on which facts should be used as the basis of the petition. A lengthy, extremely expensive, three-day hearing took place, covering everything from the details of the husband's adultery to a consideration of the hygiene of the family dogs. Finally, the decree nisi was pronounced on the basis of the wife's petition and the husband's was dismissed. It is hard to see how this case was of any benefit to anyone, except the lawyers involved!

KEY CASE: *Owens v Owens* [2018] UKSC 41

Mr and Mrs Owens married in 1978 and had two small children. In 2015 Mrs Owens left their home and applied for a divorce based on the unreasonable behaviour fact. The content of that petition referred to the fact the husband had prioritised his work over the marriage; that his treatment of the wife lacked love and affection, involving disparaging comments and arguments; and that the wife felt upset, unappreciated and unhappy. The husband defended the suit on the basis that the marriage had been largely successful. HHJ Tolson QC described the petition as 'anodyne', 'flimsy', insufficient to show a 'persistent course of conduct', and 'scarcely' meriting criticism of Mr Owens. He accepted that the marriage had broken down but held that the unreasonable behaviour fact had not been made out and so the divorce could not be granted. The Court of Appeal dismissed Mrs Owens's appeal, as did the Supreme Court.

There is a distinct sense of discomfort in the Supreme Court judgment. Their Lordships clearly felt unhappy about ruling that although the marriage has irretrievably broken down, the divorce could not be granted because none of the facts had been made out. They felt compelled by the clear meaning of the words in MCA 1973 s. 1 to reach this conclusion.

The Supreme Court acknowledged that the current system was problematic. If there is no defence, it is 'almost certain' that a divorce will be granted. If the divorce is defended then Lord Wilson said:

> The degree of conflict between the parties which is evident in a fully defended suit will of itself suggest to the Family Court that in all likelihood their marriage has broken down.[29]

Looking at the key legal issue, their Lordships explained that the behaviour fact requires the court to look at the allegations in the petition and assess the impact of the respondent's behaviour on the particular petitioner; then to evaluate whether as a result of the behaviour and its effect on the petitioner, it would be unreasonable to expect the petitioner to live with the respondent. This was in line with the earlier case law and was the approach taken by HHJ Tolson QC.

---

[29] At para 15.

Lord Wilson emphasised that the question was whether as a result of Mr Owens's behaviour Mrs Owens could not reasonably be expected to live with him. It was not whether Mrs Owens believed she could not reasonably be expected to live with her husband. That then is an objective question (the judge decides if the wife can reasonably be expected to live with the husband), but it does take into account the effect of the husband's behaviour on the wife. He also helpfully clarified that: 'The subsection requires not that the behaviour should have been unreasonable but that the expectation of continued life together should be unreasonable.'[30]

The primary argument for Mrs Owens was that the law had to take into account changing social attitudes. However, the Supreme Court held that although changing social attitudes might affect the application of the test (particularly whether or not it was reasonable to expect the petitioner to live with the respondent), they could not change the essence of the test itself. Their Lordships noted that now marriage is recognised as a 'partnership of equals' and reflecting equality between the sexes and that might impact on whether a wife could be reasonably expected to live with the husband. But it did not change the fact that it is for the court, not the spouse, to make that determination.

The majority did invite Parliament to consider reform of the law. Lady Hale gave a concurring speech, which agreed with the dismissal of the appeal but expressed misgivings about the approach taken by the judge. The claim that the husband was authoritarian was best considered by looking at a large number of incidents which appeared minor in themselves, but taken together generated a picture of control. Yet the judge had focused on just a small number of key incidents. Lady Hale explained that these misgivings led her to consider sending the case back to be reheard. However, that was not the outcome Mrs Owens sought. Lord Mance gave a separate speech approving of the way the judge had dealt with the issues raised.

These cases highlighted the problems with the MCA. In both, the marriages had clearly broken down. It is hard to see what anyone had to gain from keeping the marriage going. The cases created extraordinary expense, wasted court time, and generated publicity around matters probably best kept private. Under the DDSA, both cases would have been quickly dealt with in an efficient, cheap and private way.

Here are some of the more specific problems with the old law:

A It was confusing and misleading

The confusion is said to flow from the fact that although irretrievable breakdown was stated to be the ground for all divorces, it was in fact insufficient simply to show that the marriage was irretrievably broken down: one of the five facts also had to be proved. *Owens* is a fine example of where that occurred. It is hard to explain to a layperson why a petitioner who has proved the ground for divorce, but not by using the right 'facts', was denied a divorce. Mears,[31] however, claims that the law is not misleading because lawyers can always explain the true

---

[30] At para 37.
[31] Mears (1991).

position of the law to their clients. This is not, it must be said, a very satisfactory excuse for having a confusing law. Further it does not deal with those who are unable to get advice. Trinder's report claims:

> In general, the public are not aware that the 'behaviour' fact does not actually require serious allegations in practice. Those who can afford lawyers, or get good free advice, will be 'let into the secret'. Otherwise, unrepresented parties may end up having to wait out long separation periods because they do not have access to insider information about how the law works in practice. That is patently unfair.[32]

A linked complaint is that the law requires the parties to cite a fact as the cause of the marital breakdown, a fact that might not actually be the real cause of the marital breakdown.[33] Indeed, Liz Trinder's research shows that it is common for petitions not to reflect the real cause of the breakdown.[34] Forty-three per cent of people who had been identified as being at fault by their spouse disagreed with the reasons cited for the marriage breakdown. In only 29 per cent of cases was the petition said to match the real cause of the breakdown. Trinder quotes one lawyer who explained 'you cobble up some words which will . . . do the business'. A different survey found 27 per cent of respondents accepted that the facts listed in the petition were not true.[35]

The law was also misleading as it implied the courts carefully checked that the facts were made out. However, the special procedure meant the courts were in effect rubber stamping petitions. In **Baron v Baron**[36] Munby J had to deal with three cases where the court official had not spotted that it was not yet a year after the marriage and so a decree nisi should not have been granted. The judge was critical of the 'slapdash' way the petitions were granted, but perhaps that demonstrates the way divorce had become a somewhat mechanical procedure. Trinder's study of nearly 600 non-contested divorce files found none where the court queried the factual basis of the petition.[37]

B It distorted the parties' bargaining positions

The argument here concerns the situation where one spouse was desperate for the divorce to go through as quickly as possible (e.g. because they wanted to remarry) but the other spouse was happy for there to be a delay in the divorce. As the party who was desperate for a divorce was dependent on the other party's consent (if it was a two-year petition) or willingness not to defend the petition, either way, this gave the non-consenting spouse a weapon that can be used to advantage in the bargaining process. For example, one spouse could threaten to delay the divorce unless the other party agreed to a more generous financial settlement.

C It provoked unnecessary hostility and bitterness

The old law encouraged the parties to use the fault-based facts because they were so much quicker to use.[38] This produced distress, bitterness and embarrassment in the making of that allegation, particularly because such allegations are made in public documents. The legal

---

[32] Trinder (2017).
[33] Haskey (2018).
[34] Trinder (2017).
[35] Roiser (2015).
[36] [2019] EWFC 26.
[37] Trinder (2017) also backs this perception up.
[38] A divorce based on the fault-based grounds can often take between four and six months to complete.

process required the parties to look to the past and focus on the bad aspects of their marriage. This destroyed any last hope of reconciliation. If a wife visited her solicitor and said that she wanted to divorce her husband then the first thing the solicitor would do[39] would be to ask the wife to recount all the very worst things that her husband had done during the marriage. These would be typed up into a draft petition and sent to the husband. It would be hard to imagine a procedure better designed to increase the parties' ill feelings towards each other.

In Trinder's study[40] 62 per cent of petitioners and 78 per cent of respondents said that in their experience of the law, using fault had made the process more bitter. Not only that but of respondents in cases where a fault fact had been used in the petition, 21 per cent said fault had made it harder to sort out arrangements for children, and 31 per cent said it made sorting out finances harder. Respondents to her survey indicated cases where there were threats to show children the divorce petition to show how the other spouse had behaved.

6 Theoretical issues on the law on divorce

Learning objective 5

Describe proposals to reform the law on divorce

A Individualisation of divorce

Should divorce be seen as simply a private matter for individuals or is there a public interest in regulating divorce? The history of the law on divorce might suggest we have seen a shift from the state being the regulator of divorce, only permitting when satisfied there were good reasons for it; to divorce being at the will of one of the parties, and the law playing essentially a record-keeping role.

We might, therefore, see divorce as a private matter, left to the autonomous choice of the parties. But that would be too quick. In the United States in particular there have been moves towards offering people a range of marriages from which they can choose the model which suits them best.[41] For example, a couple could choose a marriage that could end in divorce whenever either party chooses, in other words divorce on demand. However, if they wished, the parties could select a divorce clause stating that the marriage could only come to an end if adultery was proved, or maybe even that the marriage could never be ended.[42] These are sometimes known as 'covenant marriages'. The main argument in favour of this approach is that it provides freedom of choice, that parties should be able to choose to limit their freedom to divorce in order to give deeper commitment to the marriage. The argument can be made that in some marriages sacrifices need to be made early on in the marriage, for the long-term benefits of a committed relationship. For a party to leave after the other party has made sacrifices and before the benefits arrive is unjust. For example, a wife may decide to give up work, and concentrate on caring for the children and making the home. From her perspective, entering into a marriage where her husband is bound to stay with her for at least 10 years may be a more attractive option than a marriage where he could leave at any time. Opponents of this approach argue that it would be very difficult to enforce. In the above example, preventing the husband from divorcing for 10 years will not keep him from simply leaving his wife. Alternatively, the proposed clause could be redefined so that

---

[39] After discussing fees.
[40] Trinder (2017).
[41] Shaw Spaht (2002). The take-up rate for the 'covenant marriage' (with fault-based divorce) has been low (Ellman (2000b)).
[42] See discussion in Brinig (2000).

if either party ceases to cohabit with the other there would be a financial penalty. This could create problems of its own; in particular, there are concerns that it could lead to domestic violence. Further, the financial penalty might work against the interests of a poorer spouse who would be unable to make the payments necessary if she or he wished to separate. This discussion shows that the argument that divorce should be left as a private choice of the parties is not straightforward, if the parties decide they want a marriage with no divorce permitted, or only divorce on proof of serious harm. If that concerns you, it might suggest you think there is a state interest in divorce, which is that couples should be allowed to leave an unhappy marriage, whatever arrangements they privately made.

Reece[43] sees a post-liberal approach to divorce in the unsuccessful proposals in the Family Law Act 1996 to reform the law: that divorce should be an exercise of choice, but that this choice should be a carefully thought out and considered one. She explains: 'For the post-liberal, it is no longer sufficient to establish whether the subject wants to divorce: instead, we need to discover whether divorce would help him or her to realise himself or herself, or whether remaining married would more authentically reflect him or her.' The 1996 Act had proposed creating periods of reflection and consideration and information meetings to ensure that the decision to divorce was thought through. However, the pilot studies of these reforms were unsuccessful, in part because they were seen as infantilising and failing to acknowledge the particular situation individuals found themselves in.

To some commentators there is an important state interest in divorce law and that is that it should seek to support the institution of marriage.[44] Divorce is not only a tragedy for the couple; it also involves expense to the state. It has been suggested that the annual cost of family breakdown on the state is £50 billion.[45] Divorce may also be said to shake social stability by challenging the image of the family as comforting, secure and enduring.[46] However, these arguments assume that there is a link between divorce law and the rate of divorce. Colin Hart, Chairman of Coalition for Marriage (C4M), said of the new Act: 'Far from helping families to stick together, making separating easier and quicker will lead to more divorces, more broken families and makes a mockery of the Government's claims to be pro-family.'[47]

In this way, he argues, the changes in divorce law have led to an increase in the divorce rate. Liz Trinder disagrees and in her survey of the international picture concludes:

> Looking at the research as a whole then there is little consensus that no-fault or unilateral divorce have had any clear impact at all on the propensity to divorce, though it is common to find short-term blips in response to policy changes.

John Haskey,[48] an acknowledged expert on family law statistics, believes the DDSA is likely to see an initial increase in numbers of divorces but that 'after the surge there will probably be a fall back in numbers so that, overall, the total number of divorces over several years would not necessarily be larger than had the new legislation not been enacted.'

The debate over the statistics will rumble on in the years ahead.[49] What is far from clear is *how* changes in the divorce law *could* cause marital breakdown.[50] Clearly the rate of divorce

---

[43] Reece (2003: 18).
[44] Family Law Act 1996 (hereafter FLA 1996), s. 1(1)(a).
[45] The Marriage Foundation (2020a).
[46] Day Sclater (1999: 4).
[47] Christian Institute (2020). See also Deech (1994: 121).
[48] Haskey (2019).
[49] Reinhold, Kneip and Bauer (2013).
[50] Richards (1996b).

and law on divorce are linked. We could have no legal divorce at all, and so a divorce rate of nil! That would not mean, of course, that all the couples who would have divorced would still be living together. No doubt, they would simply separate. We, therefore, would have a large number of 'empty shell' marriages. So, the real question is whether the divorce law affects the marital *breakdown* rate. If the divorce procedure is perceived to be difficult, spouses may be reluctant to seek the advice of a solicitor until they think that they would be entitled to a divorce.[51] Delaying the visit to the solicitor and the institution of legal proceedings may possibly help reduce breakdown rates. So, it is possible that the *perception* of the divorce law might affect the breakdown rate. However, it should be stressed that there is a whole range of factors that might affect marital breakdown.

If the Government did wish to discourage divorce, it might do so more effectively by making marriage – rather than divorce – harder. Increasing the age at which one could marry might well reduce the divorce rate, as might requiring the parties to have a year of reflection and consideration before being permitted to marry. However, both of these proposals might lead to a reduction of the marriage rate,[52] as well as the divorce rate.

B No-fault versus fault-based divorce

There has been much debate over whether there should be a fault- or no-fault-based divorce system. In fact, this rather simplifies the options available to the law. The forms of divorce law most discussed have been the following:

1. *A pure fault-based system.* This system allows divorce only if one party proves that the other party has wronged them in a particular way. The most common faults cited are that one party has committed adultery, or otherwise behaved in an unacceptable way.

2. *Requiring proof of irretrievable breakdown.* Here divorce would be granted if there is proof that the marriage has broken down and cannot be saved.

3. *Divorce over a period of time.* Divorce would be available after the spouses had waited a period of time following an indication that they wished to separate.

4. *Divorce by agreement.* If both parties agreed to a divorce, that would be available without proof of any fault on either side.

5. *Divorce on demand.* In this form divorce is granted at the request of one of the parties. There is no need to prove fault or irretrievable breakdown.

In modern times models 1 and 2 have few supporters, mostly on the basis that it is impossible for a court to ascertain whether there is irretrievable breakdown or who was at fault in causing the end of the marriage.[53] Around the world, legal systems have been moving towards a no-fault divorce procedure.

---

[51] See Fahey (2012) who argues from the experience of Ireland that a liberalisation of the divorce law had only a limited impact on divorce or separation behaviour.
[52] Which may or may not be objectionable.
[53] Bainham (2001a) discusses the role fault plays in family law generally.

DEBATE

Should divorce or dissolution be fault based?

Arguments in favour of fault-based divorce

(a) Psychology

Richards argues that although the law may seek to discourage parties from asking who is to blame for the ending of the marriage, this is unrealistic:

> The coming of legal 'no fault' divorce has perhaps allowed us to believe that couples separate with a similar detached view of divorce. They don't. Blame, accusation, and strong feelings of injustice are the norm at divorce and they get in the way of couples making reasonable arrangements about children and money. Neither legal fiction of the lack of fault or imposed orders do anything to relieve the situation, rather the reverse.[54]

A no-fault system can therefore be criticised on the basis that it does not deal with the issues which really concern the parties. Indeed, in one study of divorcing couples' attitudes to divorce the law's failure to address who was at fault in causing the breakdown of the marriage was cited as a major flaw.[55] To some divorcing spouses justice is served only if the court declares that the other party was the cause of the marriage breakdown.[56] Psychologists argue that blame is a psychologically crucial part of the divorce process,[57] and that making allegations of fault can even be cathartic.[58] As one experienced mediator put it, for most of his clients: 'their marriage has not died, it has been killed'.[59] It has been suggested that ignoring fault in the divorce petition means that proceedings over divorce or money become more acrimonious.[60]

While these arguments reveal the importance to divorcing parties of finding fault, some argue that it is not the place of the courtroom to explore these issues, especially at the taxpayer's expense.[61] Perhaps one benefit of mediation is that it can do something to deal with the parties' allegations of fault in a private setting, although most mediators try to persuade clients to focus on the future rather than the past.

(b) Justice

Linked to the argument above is a further point that it is not only the parties' psychological needs that are relevant here, but that it is the law's responsibility to uphold society's values and to discourage conduct which damages society. Where one spouse is to blame for ending the marriage and thereby harming the children, the law should declare the wrongdoing and, if appropriate, punish it.[62] However, others reply that the law cannot prevent marital misconduct or even be responsible for deciding who has caused the end of a relationship.[63] For example, Bainham[64] has argued that the party who commits adultery may not be the one who is at

---

[54] Richards (1994: 249).

[55] Smart *et al.* (2005) emphasises how important fault is to those actually divorcing.

[56] Davis, Cretney and Collins (1994).

[57] Day Sclater and Piper (1999).

[58] Hood (2009).

[59] Richards (2001).

[60] Deech (2009b).

[61] Rasmusen (2002) surveys the range of legal remedies there may be to penalise adultery, apart from denying divorce.

[62] Trinder's study of public opinion found some support for the view that if a party is responsible for ending the marriage, that should be publicly acknowledged. But that was a minority view.

[63] O'Donovan (1993).

[64] Bainham (1995b).

fault, because they may have been driven to do so as a result of the coldness of their spouse. This is controversial but demonstrates that it is far from easy to determine who is at fault.

(c) Marriage

It can be argued that having no-fault divorce undermines marriage: no-fault divorce permits a spouse to end a marriage whenever she or he wishes and this undermines the ideal of marriage being a life-long obligation. As Baroness Young has argued:

> The message of no fault is clear. It is that breaking marriage vows, breaking a civil contract, does not matter. It undermines individual responsibility. It is an attack upon decent behaviour and fidelity. It violates common sense and creates injustice for anyone who believes in guilt and innocence.[65]

Sir Paul Coleridge, a Family Division judge, has complained that divorce is easier to get than a driving licence.[66] The Coalition for Marriage[67] argues that making divorce easier makes marriage less secure and attractive. Others reply that if a couple are staying together only because of what the law says, their marriage is worth little; what makes marriages strong or weak is the love and commitment of the spouses, and not the legal regulation. As already noted, there is much debate over whether the law on divorce can in fact affect the rate of marital breakdown.[68] A survey of public opinion in 2018 found that 72 per cent of those questioned believed no-fault divorce could make couples more blasé about a divorce, although 89 per cent supported moving to such a system.[69]

Some economists have entered the debate to argue in favour of using divorce to maintain the stability of marriage. Rowthorn[70] argues that a no-fault divorce system undermines the notion of commitment that is key to the nature of marriage. It provides men, in particular, the opportunity to leave the marriage when it is opportune for them, leaving women severely disadvantaged. Cohen puts the argument this way:

> At the time of formation, the marriage contract promises gains to both parties. Yet the period of time over which these gains are realized is not symmetrical. As a rule, men obtaining early in the relationship, and women late. This follows from women's relative loss in value. Young women are valued as mates by both old and young men. When they choose to marry a particular man they give up all their other alternatives . . . The creation of this long-term imbalance provides the opportunity for strategic behaviour whereby one of the parties, generally the man, will perform his obligations under the marriage contract only so long as he is receiving a net positive marginal benefit and will breach the contract unless otherwise constrained once the marginal benefit falls below his opportunity cost.[71]

Scott is sympathetic to the aims of those who seek a fault-based system of divorce. She argues that the law should impose restrictions on exiting marriage as these will 'discourage each spouse from pursuing transitory preferences that are inconsistent with the couple's self-defined long-term interest' and therefore 'each spouse, knowing the other's commitment is enforceable, receives assurance that his or her investment in the relationship will be protected'.[72] However, Scott argues that fault is not the most effective way of doing this and

[65] Baroness Young, Hansard (HL) Vol. 569, col. 1638.
[66] Quoted Whitehead (2011).
[67] Coalition for Marriage (2018).
[68] Ellman (2000b).
[69] Slater and Gordon (2018).
[70] Rowthorn (1999).
[71] Cohen (2002: 25).
[72] Scott (2003: 162).

instead suggests three other ways of providing a disincentive to divorce:[73] mandatory waiting periods before divorce; mandatory marital counselling before a divorce petition can be presented; and that on divorce most marital property be held on trust to provide for the children. Reece considers a similar argument from a different perspective. She suggests that it could be argued that no-fault divorce denies the parties the opportunity of engaging in a long-term committed project, fully immersing themselves in the marriage, confident that the other party cannot (without good reason) withdraw from the marriage.[74]

Arguments in favour of no-fault systems

(a) 'Empty shell'

It has been maintained that if one spouse wishes to divorce there is little value in forcing the couple to stay married. There is no point in keeping 'empty shell' marriages alive. Making divorce available only on proof of fault does not lead to happier marriages, but to parties separating, although legally married, or to cantankerous divorce. After all 'no statute, no matter how carefully and cleverly drafted, can make two people love each other.'[75] A recent poll suggested that only 17 per cent of the public thought a couple should stay together 'for the sake of the children'.[76] Evidence from psychologists suggests children living in unhappy homes do worse on a number of levels than children in separated homes.[77]

(b) The 'right to divorce'

Some argue that it is now a human right to divorce.[78] Forcing someone to remain married against their wishes is an infringement of their right to marry or right to family life. Generally, that claim is taken to be that there is a duty on the state to provide an effective law on divorce, rather than the other spouse has a duty to permit a divorce. However, the European Court of Human Rights has made it clear that the European Convention does not include a right to divorce.[79]

(c) Bitterness

A common complaint is that a fault-based system promotes bitterness. By focusing the spouses' minds on the past and the unhappiness of the marriage and making these public, it is argued that fault-based systems exacerbate the anger and frustration they feel towards each other.

(d) The impossibility of allocating blame

We have already referred to this argument – that the law cannot really determine who was truly to blame for the break-up. There are practical difficulties in discovering the facts of the case, particularly as the husband and wife are often the only two witnesses. But even if all the facts were known, the court may still not be in a position to allocate blame. Bainham suggests that many people would take the view that for 'a very large number of people, the obligation of lifelong fidelity to one partner was at best an impossible dream'.[80]

---

[73] Ellman (2000b) argues that such waiting periods do more harm than good.
[74] Reece (2003: 121).
[75] Lord Chancellor's Department (1995: para 3).
[76] Resolution (2010).
[77] See Chapter 10 for further discussion.
[78] Rivlini (2013).
[79] *Johnston v Ireland* (1986) 9 EHRR 203. Although *Babiarz v Poland* (App. No. 1955/10) indicates a blanket ban on divorce would infringe the Convention.
[80] Bainham (2002c: 177).

Questions

1. If there is a psychological imperative for spouses to blame each other on divorce, what is the best way to channel those feelings?

2. What would be wrong with having a system where simply filling in a form led to a divorce? Is that, in fact, much different from what we have at the moment?

3. Is there a good reason for treating marriages differently from other contracts, where we do seek to establish fault?

4. Do you agree that divorce is a disaster for society and the individuals? What can be done about it?

Further reading

Read **Eekelaar** (1999) for a discussion of the attempts to control people during the divorce process. Read **Reece** (2003) for a consideration of the Family Law Act 1996 reforms.

C Administrative or judicial procedure

Another area of dispute is the extent to which divorce should be a legal, judicial process or simply an administrative process. For example, if a child is born, their birth must be registered. This does not require any involvement of a court; it is an administrative procedure. Traditionally divorce has been seen as different from birth registration and requires a court order. However, under the DDSA it is becoming closer to an administrative system, although the courts are still involved. It will appear all the more so as petitions for divorce can now be made online. This will save judicial time (it has been suggested that perhaps 10,000 judicial hours will be saved[81]) and potentially costs for the parties. The Family Review explains:

> There is scope to increase the use of administrators in the courts to reduce burdens on judges and create a more streamlined process in the 98% of cases where divorce is uncontested. The current process requires judges to spend time in effect to do no more than check that forms have been filled in correctly, with accurate names and dates. This is a waste. To change it would not make any difference to the ease or difficulty of obtaining a divorce. It would just make more judge time available for more important things.[82]

Liz Trinder[83] argues that a computer-based system 'has the potential to provide a fast, reassuring and accessible process for individuals going through a highly stressful life event, particularly litigants in person unable to access the advice and support of a family lawyer.'

The evidence to date is that the online system is very popular, with 13 people issuing divorce proceedings on Christmas Day 2018! Significantly, only 1 per cent of forms needed to be returned, compared with a 40 per cent return rate with paper forms.[84] This is largely as the online system will alert the user of questions that are unanswered or incomplete or that an obvious error (e.g. over a date) is made. The problem with improper forms is not just delays in them being returned but the genuine problems that can arise if a divorce is granted on the basis of what turns out to be an erroneous form, especially if the parties go on to remarry.[85]

---

[81] Family Justice Review Final Report (2011).
[82] Family Justice Review Final Report (2011).
[83] Trinder (2017a).
[84] Aggarwal (2019).
[85] *M v P (The Queen's Proctor Intervening)* [2019] EWFC 14.

Moving to an online system may cause concern for some.[86] Divorce law is dealing with people who are often feeling chaotic emotions and powerful passions. We should acknowledge the feelings of 'damage, death, failure, guilt' and anger that divorce typically creates.[87] Does the completion of an internet form assessed by an administrator demonstrate the solemnity that should mark the end of a marriage? Is divorce to be achieved with a form which will presumably be slightly shorter than that required for a credit card somehow undignified? Does it fail to encourage the parties to take the decision to divorce seriously or fail to show this is an act which is significant for the state?[88] Perhaps this is all rather old-fashioned. The internet is used for all kinds of important transactions and requiring paper forms is outdated. Further, even accepting solemnity should mark a divorce, need this be done in expensive courtrooms or by judges? Maybe religious or secular services could mark the passing of the marriage if that is what people need.

D Reconciliation and divorce

The history of divorce law is replete with examples of attempts to use the divorce law to encourage reconciliation. Notably, this seems absent from the DDSA. Attempting to save a marriage once one of the parties has taken the drastic step of seeking a divorce appears to be far too late.

One of the main aims of the proposed Family Law Act 1996 reforms was to persuade couples to become reconciled.[89] At the information meeting, couples were to be encouraged to consider saving their marriage, and counsellors were available to assist those who wished to pursue this option. Further, the Act required a three-month gap between the information meeting and the making of the statement of marital breakdown.[90] The aim of this gap was to provide a 'cooling off' period, a time for the parties to consider reconciliation and the offer of marriage guidance facilities. These facilities were to be available free of charge throughout the period of 'reflection and consideration'.

Initial research from the pilot studies indicated that this aim was not being achieved. In fact, there was some evidence that the information meetings inclined those who were uncertain about their marriage towards divorce. Further, the information meetings were usually attended by only one of the parties (the one seeking the divorce), in which case talking about reconciliation was of little effect.[91] Indeed, in Trinder's thorough review of the evidence she concluded that it indicated that decisions to end a marriage were not taken lightly and that by the time divorce proceedings had started it was unrealistic to think anything could be done to try to save the marriage.

It may be a better aim to help the parties to have as good a post-divorce relationship as possible. If there is to be a divorce, the law should not exacerbate the bitterness between the parties.[92] Sir Paul McCartney described his divorce from Heather Mills as 'going through hell'[93] and many who have experienced divorce will empathise with that. To expect a legal system to

---

[86] Herring (2012a).
[87] Ibid, p. 154.
[88] Deech (2009b).
[89] Mackay (2000).
[90] FLA 1996, s. 8(2). There were exceptional circumstances where this requirement could be waived.
[91] Walker (2001a).
[92] FLA 1996, s. 1(1)(c)(i).
[93] BBC News Online (2007c).

enable the parties to separate happily and then have a good post-divorce relationship is pure idealism. This is why it is better to say that the law should *not exacerbate* the bitterness, rather than *remove* it. As Beck and Beck-Gernsheim explain:

> Only someone equating marriage with sex, loving and living together can make the mistake that divorce means the end of marriage. If one concentrates on problems of material support, on the children and on a long common biography, divorce is quite obviously not even the legal end of marriage but transforms itself into a new phase of post-marital 'separation marriage'.[94]

E Religion and divorce

Problems can arise when the requirements for divorce in a religion do not match the legal requirements. For example, under Jewish religious law unless the former husband provides what is known as a *get*, the wife is not permitted to remarry.[95] She can remarry under secular law, but not under religious law.[96] At first sight this appears to be solely a religious matter and it would be inappropriate for the law to intervene. But Hamilton has suggested four reasons why the state might want to intervene in these types of situations:[97]

1. To promote remarriage. Marriage and family are seen as the framework of society, and the state should have the power to intervene to permit remarriage and to require a religion to recognise the marriage.

2. The right to marry under the European Convention[98] could be said to justify intervention by the law to recognise remarriage.

3. General perceptions of fairness and equality require that the courts and legislature intervene where a religious divorce is unjustly withheld.

4. An unscrupulous husband may use his control of the religious divorce to get a more favourable settlement.

However, there are serious problems for legal intervention in this area. The main one is that under Jewish law the *get* must be provided voluntarily, and so a court order to provide a *get* might be counterproductive. So far, the courts have been very unwilling to intervene where a *get* has not been provided.[99]

The Divorce (Religious Marriages) Act 2002 enables the courts to refuse to make a final divorce order unless a declaration has been made by both parties that they have taken such steps as are required to dissolve the marriage in religious terms. This does not resolve all the problems because it does not help in situations where the wife seeks a divorce but the husband refuses to grant it, or in cases where the couple have already divorced. Their one option may be to require a husband to pay a further lump sum if he fails to comply with the religious aspects of the divorce.[100]

---

[94] Beck and Beck-Gernsheim (1995: 147).
[95] She will then be an *agunah* (a 'chained wife').
[96] There can be similar problems under Islamic law.
[97] Hamilton (1995: ch 3).
[98] Article 12.
[99] *Brett v Brett* [1969] 1 All ER 1007.
[100] *A v T (Ancillary Relief: Cultural Factors)* [2004] 1 FLR 977.

7 Death and marriage

The most common reason a marriage comes to an end is that one of the parties dies. Usually there will be no doubt that a person has died.[101] However, there can be situations where, although it is suspected that someone has died, it cannot be proved: for example, if a husband fails to return home from work and his car is found abandoned near a cliff but his body is never found. This kind of situation puts the wife in a difficult position. Is she free to remarry or is she prevented from remarrying until she can prove that her husband has died?

Under the Presumption of Death Act 2013 anyone[102] can apply for a declaration that the absent party is presumed to be dead. An order can be made if the court is persuaded that either:

(a) the person has died, or

(b) the person has not been known to be alive for at least seven years.

Under the first ground there is no need to wait for seven years since the disappearance but there needs to be evidence that the person has died. In *Re CD*[103] a man was kidnapped in Yemen in 2009. The next year the Foreign Office announced it was satisfied he must have died. The court was willing to declare that he had died, even though his body had never been found. Under the second ground all that needs to be shown is that nothing has been heard of the person for the last seven years. There are regulations about advertisements that need to be made and notifications issues if this ground is to be used.

8 Conclusion

There are few family lawyers who have not welcomed the new law on divorce. There is nothing the law can do to make divorce enjoyable, but the old law seemed to do much to exacerbate its unpleasantness. The law here is how to channel the strong feelings often produced during divorce through a legal system traditionally designed to be governed by rational thought rather than wild emotion. As Eekelaar suggests:

> We may, however, become uncomfortable when the government intervenes at these points in the institutional processes of marriage and divorce and attempts to impose its own vision of how people should be behaving at these times. At best it risks being made to appear foolish and ineffectual. Worse it can appear heavy-handed, domineering and insensitive . . . [104]

It is not that the state has no interests in divorce or that divorce should be seen as just a private matter. It is rather that there is not much the law can do other than make the legal formalities as painless as possible.

The days when divorce was seen as shameful are largely passed. Divorce is generally seen as sad, but not necessarily indicating a moral failure. Divorce and relationship breakdown may cause harms, but whether they are any worse than unhappy couples staying together is clearly debatable. For some, divorce is a tragedy, but for others it can be the start of a happy new future.

---

[101] Normally, death and marriage are clearly evidenced by the registers of death and marriage.
[102] If the applicant is not the spouse, civil partner, parent, child or sibling the court must be persuaded they have sufficient interest to bring the application
[103] [2019] EWHC 2785 (Ch).
[104] Eekelaar (1999).

Further reading

Auchmuty, R. (2016) 'The experience of civil partnership dissolution: not "just like divorce"', *Journal of Social Welfare and Family Law* 38: 152.

Day Sclater, S. and Piper, C. (1999) *Undercurrents of Divorce,* Aldershot: Ashgate.

Deech, R. (2009b) 'Divorce – a disaster?' *Family Law* 39: 1048.

Eekelaar, J. (1991a) *Regulating Divorce,* Oxford: Clarendon Press.

Eekelaar, J. (1999) 'Family law: keeping us "on message"', *Child and Family Law Quarterly* 11: 387.

Haskey, J. (2019) 'Some scenarios on the numerical implications of the proposed new divorce reform legislation for England and Wales', *Family Law* 49: 1040.

Hasson, E. (2003) 'Divorce law and the Family Law Act 1996', *International Journal of Law, Policy and the Family* 17: 338.

Herring, J. (2012a) 'Divorce, internet hubs and Stephen Cretney', in R. Probert and C. Barton (eds) *Fifty Years in Family Law,* London: Intersentia.

Reece, H. (2003) *Divorcing Responsibly,* Oxford: Hart.

Rivlini, R. (2013) 'The right to divorce: its direction and why it matters', *International Journal of Jurisprudence of the Family* 4: 133.

Trinder, L. (2017) *Finding Fault? Divorce Law and Practice in England and Wales,* London: Nuffield Foundation.

Visit **go.pearson.com/uk/he/resources** to access **resources** specifically written to complement this text.

5 Family property

Learning objectives

When you finish reading this chapter you will be able to:
1. Explain who owns personal property in the family setting
2. Examine the law on maintenance during marriage
3. Evaluate the law on resulting and constructive trusts of family homes
4. Summarise the law on proprietary estoppel
5. Debate the arguments over the law on family property

1 Introduction

In this chapter we will consider partners' financial position during their relationship, whether they are spouses, civil partners or unmarried couples. In Chapter 6 we will consider the power of the courts to redistribute the property of spouses and civil partners on divorce. One of the key themes in this area is whether it is appropriate to use normal rules of property law to deal with family property. Traditionally, property law has been based on the assumption that parties to a property dispute are strangers and it emphasises the rights of individuals to control their property and to protect their rights from interference from others. However, family property is used by people in a relationship. Many couples regard their property as communal, for the use of the family as a group. This has led to a tension in using the more individualistic property rules in a family setting. Lorna Fox has warned that there are dangers in seeing property as owned by the family as a unit, because that would weaken the interests of each individual member of the family.[1] On the other hand, emphasising the formal property rights of individuals can mean that technicalities of property law dominate, which may not reflect the real intentions of the parties or produce fairness.

---

[1] Fox (2005).

2 The reality of family finances

As shall be seen, the law does not normally intervene in the way in which the family distributes its money among its members. It is therefore important to understand how families deal with their money and property in the absence of formal legal regulation.

One notable feature of the latter half of the twentieth century was the increasing number of women in paid employment. Now, 75 per cent of working-age mothers are in employment.[2] However, it is important to look behind that headline figure. While among employed men many more were employed full time than part time, among employed women a smaller majority were working full time. So, although rates of employment are equalising, women are often being employed in part-time work. For children aged 0–2 in only 48 per cent of cases was the mother working full time, and for children aged 5–10 that percentage only rose to 49 per cent. Even when the child was 16–18 in only 61 per cent of cases was the mother working full time. We are certainly moving away from the traditional image of the 'wife who stays at home' and 'the husband who goes out to work'. Indeed, it has been argued that the lifestyle of many families can only be maintained by having two wage earners. This has led Patricia Morgan to maintain that some couples cannot afford a 'traditional marriage' and married couples relying on one income cannot afford to have children.[3]

Despite the widespread existence of families with dual earners, there is still a common presumption that men are the main breadwinners, and this presumption has a powerful effect. For example, even if both people are working, research indicates that if the child falls ill it is far more often the mother rather than the father who takes time off work to care for the child.[4]

Many more women than men fall into the category of homemakers. Homemakers are largely unpaid and have no access to unemployment or sickness benefits.[5] Further, in social terms the work is undervalued and lacks prestige.

3 The ownership of family property: general theory

Who owns the family's property?[6] Of course, most of the time there is no need for members of a family to know who in law owns a particular piece of family property. In most families 'Who owns the television?' is not a question that is usually asked. (Ownership of the remote control is, of course, another question!) There are, however, a number of reasons why it can be important to know who owns a certain piece of property:

1. If the couple are unmarried, it is crucial to know who owns what because there is no power in the court to redistribute property if the relationship breaks down. Therefore, when the couple separate, each person is entitled to take whatever property is theirs.

2. If someone becomes bankrupt, all of their property falls into the hands of the trustee in bankruptcy. The property of the bankrupt's spouse or partner does not. It is therefore necessary to know whether certain property belongs to the bankrupt person or their partner.

---

[2] Office for National Statistics (2020a).
[3] Morgan (1999b: 82).
[4] Harkness (2005).
[5] Employment Rights Act 1996, s. 161.
[6] Under s. 17 of the Married Women's Property Act 1882 an application can be made to a court for a declaration of ownership if the couple are married.

3. If a third party wishes to purchase property, it may be important to know who is the owner. Particularly when a house is to be sold, it is necessary to know who the owner of the house is so that he or she can sign the appropriate paperwork. There have been cases where husbands have sold the family home behind their wives' backs. In such cases it is important to know whether the wife had an interest in the property and, if so, whether the purchaser is bound by her interest.

4. On the death of a family member, it is important to know who owns what. So, if a wife left all her books to her brother in her will, it would be important to know which books were hers and which books belonged to her husband.

5. Ownership of family property has important symbolic power. At one time the husband owned all of his wife's property. This reflected the fact that he was regarded as in control of all of the family's affairs. It is arguable that if the law were to state that family property is jointly owned, this would reflect a principle of equality between spouses in marriage.

Law in this area should seek to pursue three particular aims. First, the law should produce as high a degree of certainty as possible. Secondly, the law should reflect the wishes and expectations of most couples. Thirdly, the law should be practical and easy to apply. Some of the approaches the law could take are as follows:

1. **Sole ownership.** The law could decide that one spouse owns all the family's property. Historically, a woman could not own property in her own right[7] and so the husband owned all the family's property. This approach might have the benefit of certainty, but it would not reflect the expectations of many couples nowadays and would be unacceptable in a society committed to equality between men and women.

2. **Community of property.** The law could state that on marriage (or cohabitation) all property becomes jointly owned.[8] This may be thought to reflect the expectations of most couples, but does it? On marriage would the husband expect a half interest in his wife's collection of shoes? The law could deal with such concerns by producing exceptions to the rule, but these might create uncertainty.[9] Many European regimes have some form of community of property regime.[10]

3. **Community of gains.** The law could be that each party owns the property he or she owned before the marriage (or cohabitation), but all property acquired during the relationship will be jointly owned. Many countries that have adopted this approach have created exceptions for special gifts or inheritance received during the relationship.

4. **Community of common property.** The law could take the approach that all items intended for joint use would be jointly owned.[11] So the car, television, cooker, etc. would be jointly owned but the wife's golf clubs would not. This approach could be criticised on the basis that in some cases there might be doubt whether a particular item was for common use, and this could cause uncertainty over ownership.

---

[7] The Married Women's Property Act 1882 has removed the incapacity of the wife to own property.
[8] Barlow, Callus and Cooke (2004). Some countries have 'deferred community of property', which only comes into play on separation, e.g., Family Law (Scotland) Act 1985.
[9] Law Commission Report 175 (1988: para 3.2).
[10] Barlow, Callus and Cooke (2004).
[11] Basically, the approach proposed by Law Commission Report 175 (1988).

5. *Purchaser-based ownership.* Another option is simply to use the normal rules of property and not create any particular regime for couples. In effect, this would mean that the person who buys a piece of property owns it. The objection to this is that it may be a matter of chance whose money happened to be used to buy a piece of property.

6. *Intention-based ownership.* The law could decide that ownership would be determined by the intentions of the parties. There would have to be rules that would apply if it were not possible to discover the parties' intentions. This approach would have the disadvantage of making it particularly difficult for third parties to ascertain the ownership of a piece of property.

As we shall see, the law of England and Wales does not plump for one or other of these approaches but instead is based on a rather arbitrary set of rules, which have developed over the years.

Before setting out the law, it is necessary to distinguish between real property and personal property. Basically, real property is land and buildings, personal property is all other kinds of property (e.g. books, cars, furniture).

4 The ownership of personal property

Learning objective 1

Explain who owns personal property in the family setting

So, how do the courts decide who owns what? The law can be summarised with the following statements:

1. Income belongs to the person who earns it.[12]

2. Personal property *prima facie* belongs to the person whose money was used to buy the property.[13] This is a presumption which can be rebutted.[14] For example, if a husband bought his wife perfume it may well be that the court would find the presumption rebutted and that the perfume belonged to the wife, not the husband.

3. Ownership of property can be transferred from one person to another if there is effective delivery of the property[15] with evidence that it is intended as a gift. So, if a wife hands a piece of property to her husband saying that it is a present for him, this would be an effective transfer of ownership from her to him.

4. The act of marriage, engagement or cohabitation itself does not change ownership of property.

There are a number of scenarios where the law is a little more complicated, and these will now be discussed in detail.

A Jointly used bank accounts

Where the parties pool their incomes into a common account, it seems that normally they both have a joint interest in the whole fund.[16] The crucial question is: what is the purpose for which the fund is held? The leading case is *Jones v Maynard*.[17] The husband authorised his wife to draw from his bank account. Although the husband's contribution to the account was

---

[12] *Heseltine v Heseltine* [1971] 1 All ER 952.
[13] *The Up-Yaws* [2007] EWHC 210 (Admlty).
[14] *Re Whittaker* (1882) 21 Ch D 657.
[15] *Re Cole* [1904] Ch 175.
[16] This is so regardless of in whose name the account stands.
[17] [1951] Ch 572.

greater than the wife's, they treated the account as a joint account. When the marriage was dissolved the ownership of the account became an issue. Vaisey J argued:

> In my view a husband's earnings or salary, when the spouses have a common purse and pool their resources, are earnings made on behalf of both; and the idea that years afterwards the contents of the pool can be dissected by taking an elaborate account as to how much was paid in by the husband or the wife is quite inconsistent with the original fundamental idea of a joint purpose or common pool. In my view the money which goes into the pool becomes joint property.

So, the court should focus on the intentions of the parties. Was the account intended to be a 'common purse'? If the account was in both names, then it is very likely it will be regarded as joint. This is true whether the couple are spouses, civil partners or cohabitants. Even if it was in only one person's name, the court will examine whether in fact the fund was used jointly.

Where property is bought using a joint bank account, the key issue will be the intentions of the parties.[18] If the purchased item was for joint use, it is likely to be jointly owned. However, if the property was bought for the use of one of the parties then it seems likely that it will be regarded as belonging to that party. So, if a woman bought a rare stamp for her stamp collection using money from a joint bank account, the stamp is likely to be seen as hers, but if she bought a sofa, it will probably be seen as for joint use and therefore jointly owned.[19] In *Re Bishop*[20] investments were purchased from the common fund. Some were purchased in joint names, others in the name of the husband and one in the wife's name. It was held that the fact that the investments were put in specified names indicated they were owned by the named parties.

B Housekeeping and maintenance allowance

According to s. 1 of the Married Women's Property Act 1964:

LEGISLATIVE PROVISION

Married Women's Property Act 1964, section 1

If any question arises as to the right of a husband or wife to money derived from any allowance made by [either of them] for the expenses of the matrimonial home or for similar purposes, or to any property acquired out of such money, the money or property shall, in the absence of any agreement between them to the contrary, be treated as belonging to the husband and the wife in equal shares.

The provision was amended in the Equality Act 2010[21] so that it applies to husbands and wives in the same way.[22] The Act only applies to spouses or civil partners. It does not apply to cohabitants, nor engaged couples. However, for engaged couples and cohabitants the courts may still decide that the parties intended to share such property. Little use seems to be made of the Act, perhaps because it is based on a rather outdated scenario of family finances.

---

[18] See *Re Northall* [2010] EWHC 1448.
[19] A specific agreement could rebut these presumptions.
[20] [1965] Ch 450.
[21] Section 200.
[22] Section 70A of the Civil Partnership Act 2004 has a similar provision for civil partners.

C Gifts from one partner to the other

Where it is clear that one party intended to make a gift and transferred possession of the property to the other party, then ownership will have passed from one to the other. So, if a wife purchased a book using money from her own bank account, the law will presume it belongs to her. However, if she wrapped it up and presented it to her husband on his birthday, ownership will have passed to him.[23]

D Gifts to partners from third parties

Where a third party makes a gift to a couple, ownership of the gift depends on the donor's intention. This intention can be inferred from the surrounding circumstances. For example, it is reasonable to assume that a wedding gift was intended for joint ownership unless there is evidence to the contrary.[24] By contrast, a birthday present given to the husband will be presumed to belong to him alone.

E Improvements to personal property

If a spouse, civil partner or fiancé(e) (but not a cohabitant) does work that improves a piece of property, then he or she can rely on s. 37 of the Matrimonial Proceedings and Property Act 1970 to establish an interest in the property. We will discuss this provision later when real property is considered.[25]

F Express declarations of trust

An owner of a piece of personal property can declare him or herself trustee of it. The declaration can be oral and does not require the use of formal language. For example, in *Rowe* v *Prance*[26] a man bought a boat and wrote to his lover referring to what he would like to do with her on 'our boat'. This was held by the court to be sufficient evidence of an express declaration of trust and he therefore shared equitable ownership with his lover.

G Criticisms of the present law

The present law has been widely criticised.[27] The Law Commission has characterised the existing rules as arbitrary, uncertain and unfair.[28] There is too much emphasis placed on who purchased a piece of property, while this is often a matter of chance. Some of the presumptions seem out of date and based on sexist presumptions no longer appropriate for our law. Further, there is also much uncertainty over when an express trust can be found. The case of *Rowe* v *Prance*, which we have just discussed, demonstrates that even casual comments can have legal significance attached to them, perhaps out of all proportion to their intended effect. By contrast, there may be couples whose general lifestyle demonstrates that they wish to share

---

[23] The presumption of advancement (that a husband intended to give his wife a gift when transferring property to her) was abolished by the Equality Act 2010, s. 199.
[24] *Midland Bank v Cooke* [1995] 4 All ER 562, [1995] 2 FLR 915.
[25] See 'Improvements to the home' later in this chapter.
[26] [1999] 2 FLR 787.
[27] See, e.g., Tee (2001).
[28] Law Commission Report 175 (1988: para 1.4).

everything, but if there are no statements which reflect this, they may have difficulty in proving co-ownership. An unmarried couple who go to court for an order deciding who owns their collection of CDs could find themselves in for a protracted court case.

5 Maintenance during marriage

Learning objective 2

Examine the law on maintenance during marriage

The law on the payment of maintenance on divorce will be discussed in Chapter 6. This section will consider maintenance payments during marriage and cohabitation.

A Unmarried cohabitants

There is no obligation on one unmarried partner to support the other. However, there is an obligation on a parent to provide for children whether the parents are married or not (see Chapter 6). Income could result, however, from an order under s. 40 of the Family Law Act 1996, requiring a party to make payments of maintenance for the dwelling house, or rent or mortgage, in connection with an occupation order.[29]

B Married couples

There are two potential sources of maintenance liability for spouses while the couple are married: from statutes and from separation agreements reached between themselves. We will discuss the liability to maintain spouses on divorce in Chapter 6. The common law duty on a husband to maintain a wife was abolished by the Equality Act 2010.[30]

(i) Statutory obligations to maintain

Research suggests that although there are statutory means of enforcing an obligation to pay maintenance during the marriage, in practice very small sums are involved and they are rarely collected.[31] No doubt many spouses who have separated rely on benefits or earnings while pursuing divorce proceedings. The liability to support a child under the Child Support Act 1991 dominates the financial relationship between parties prior to divorce.

There are four statutory provisions that are relevant for spousal maintenance during marriage:

1. Under s. 2 of the Domestic Proceedings and Magistrates' Courts Act 1978, periodical payment orders and lump sum orders for less than £1,000[32] can be made. Section 1 sets out the criteria. In calculating the level of spousal maintenance, the first consideration is the welfare of any minors and there is a list of factors to consider, virtually identical to those in s. 25 of the Matrimonial Causes Act 1973.[33] Sums that are awarded are usually small. In *E v C (Child Maintenance)*[34] it was held to be inappropriate to order a man on income support to pay

---

[29] Discussed in Chapter 7, although it seems orders under this section are very rarely made in practice.
[30] Section 198.
[31] Cretney, Masson and Bailey-Harris (2002: 78).
[32] There is no such limitation if there is a consent order.
[33] Discussed in Chapter 6.
[34] [1995] 1 FLR 472, [1996] 1 FCR 612.

£5 per week. In fact, if someone is on income support, it would only be appropriate to order a nominal sum. Applications under this statute are made to the magistrates' court. This is a cheaper procedure than the other three provisions and is therefore the most popular.

LEGISLATIVE PROVISION

Domestic Proceedings and Magistrates' Courts Act 1978, section 1

Either party to a marriage may apply to a magistrates' court for an order under section 2 of this Act on the ground that the other party to the marriage—

(a) has failed to provide reasonable maintenance for the applicant; or

(b) has failed to provide, or to make a proper contribution towards, reasonable maintenance for any child of the family; or

(c) has behaved in such a way that the applicant cannot reasonably be expected to live with the respondent; or

(d) has deserted the applicant.

---

2. Under s. 27 of the Matrimonial Causes Act 1973 periodic payment and lump sum orders can be made without limit. It is necessary to show that the respondent has failed to provide reasonably for the spouse or for a child of the family. The provision is only available for married couples.

3. Prior to divorce and nullity or judicial separation it is possible to apply for maintenance pending suit.[35] Interim lump sum orders can now be made.[36]

4. Section 40 of the Family Law Act 1996 can require the payment of rent, mortgage, and outgoings in respect of a property when an occupation order is made.[37]

(ii) Separation agreements

Especially before divorce became more readily available, private agreements were a popular option for couples who could not divorce (or did not want to divorce) but intended to separate. Nowadays separation agreements are often used by couples to deal with the parties' financial affairs while waiting for the final financial orders to be made. An agreement is only binding if the normal requirements of contract law are in place. In particular, there must be an intention to create legal relations.[38] There is a presumption that agreements between married couples are not intended to be legally binding.[39] The law's approach to such agreements is that they can be legally enforced, but are open to alteration by the courts. The broader issue of pre-marital agreements is considered further in Chapter 6.

---

[35] Matrimonial Causes Act 1973, s. 22; see *G v G (Maintenance Pending Suit: Costs)* [2003] Family Law 393.

[36] Matrimonial Causes Act 1973, s. 22A(4).

[37] See Chapter 7.

[38] *Soulsbury v Soulsbury* [2007] 3 FCR 811.

[39] *Balfour v Balfour* [1919] 2 KB 571.

6 Ownership of real property: the family home: legal ownership

The home is one of the most valuable assets that many people own.[40] This is true not just in monetary terms but in emotional terms: to many people the home is of great psychological importance. A dispute over ownership of the home can therefore be particularly heated. We will first consider how the law determines who owns a house.[41] This is particularly important for unmarried couples because at the end of their relationship the court has no jurisdiction to require one party to transfer their share of the home to the other and can only declare who at the moment owns the house.

English and Welsh law has not developed a special regime for dealing with family homes. So, the law governing the family home is the same as that concerning any two people who happen to share a house, whether they be business partners or lovers.[42] As a result of the way in which the law has evolved, it is necessary to distinguish ownership of property at law (common law) and at equity. In this section we will focus on ownership at common law.

Determining ownership of land[43] is not difficult. If the land is registered, which nearly all land is now,[44] the legal owner can be determined by discovering who is registered as the owner of the land. When a couple buy a house together it is common for the house to be put into joint names, so both will share legal ownership. If the land is not registered, it is necessary to discover into whose name the lease or property was conveyed. Section 52(1) of the Law of Property Act 1925 makes clear that legal title can only be conveyed by deed.[45] So words alone cannot transfer legal ownership.

Just because someone owns the property at common law, it does not mean they are the absolute owner, because the legal owner may hold the property on trust for someone else. It is therefore necessary to consider who owns the property in equity.

7 Ownership of real property: the family home: equitable ownership

Learning objective 3

Evaluate the law on resulting and constructive trusts of family homes

In the eyes of equity, it matters not in whose name the property is registered, nor into whose name the property was conveyed. In equity the legal owner of the property may be found to hold the property on trust for someone else who will then have an equitable interest in the property. A trust may be express or implied.

---

[40] Pensions can be worth significantly more.
[41] Although references will be made to a house, the law is essentially the same over flats.
[42] *Pettitt v Pettitt* [1970] AC 777; *Gissing v Gissing* [1971] 1 AC 886.
[43] Land here includes ownership of the house on the land.
[44] Eventually the Land Registration Act 2002 will end unregistered title.
[45] Law of Property (Miscellaneous Provisions) Act 1989, s. 2.

A Express trusts

The leading statutory provision is s. 53(1)(b) of the Law of Property Act 1925, which states that a declaration of trust in respect of land must be manifested and proved in writing. So, an oral statement from the owner that they wish to hold the land on trust for someone else would not be sufficient for an express trust.[46] It may be that there is a trust deed that sets out the shares of the parties in equity. The deed may be part of the conveyance (for example, the conveyance may specifically state that the property is transferred 'to A to hold on trust for A and B in shares of 60 per cent and 40 per cent respectively') or there may be a separate document signed by the owner setting out the terms of the trust. In these cases, unless there is any fraud or mistake, this document will identify the shares and there will be no need for the court to consider the ownership question further.[47] This was made clear in *Goodman v Gallant*.[48] It is therefore highly advisable, and very common, for a couple purchasing a house to make it quite clear the shares they are to own in equity.[49]

However, all too often there is no written declaration of interests. Typically, this arises where one person buys a house and later on his or her partner moves in. The parties do not think about seeing a lawyer to produce a written document. In such cases s. 53(2) of the Law of Property Act 1925 is crucial, because it states that s. 53(1) does not affect the creation of implied, resulting and constructive trusts. So, in the absence of a formal document it is necessary to turn to the law of implied trusts.[50] There are three of these, which will be considered next: resulting trusts, constructive trusts and proprietary estoppel. As we shall see, the role now played by resulting trusts in relation to the family home is small.[51] It is now generally accepted that in the family home context special rules have developed concerning constructive trusts which may not apply to constructive trusts generally.[52]

B Resulting trusts

The presumption of a resulting trust is that if A and B both contribute to the purchase price of a house and the property is put into B's name then, although B will be owner at common law, she will hold it on trust (a resulting trust) for herself and A.[53] Similarly, if A transfers property into B's name, without B providing any consideration,[54] then B will hold the property on trust solely for A. Both of these resulting trusts are presumptions, based on the belief that people do not give money or property expecting nothing in return. The presumption can be rebutted if it can be shown that the contribution to the purchase price was given as a gift or a loan.[55] For example, if an aunt helps provide the purchase price for her nephew's first house it may readily be shown that she intended this money to be a gift and did not intend him to hold it on trust for her. Today resulting trusts are primarily used in cases where the parties are not in a close relationship.[56]

---

[46] Although such a statement may well form the basis of an implied trust.
[47] *Clarke v Harlowe* [2006] Fam Law 846.
[48] [1986] 1 FLR 513.
[49] *Springette v Defoe* [1992] 2 FLR 388 at p. 390, per Dillon LJ.
[50] *Gissing v Gissing* [1971] 1 AC 886.
[51] *Fowler v Barron* [2008] EWCA Civ 377.
[52] *Crossco No. 4 Unlimited v Jolan Ltd* [2011] EWCA Civ 1619.
[53] See *Huntingford v Hobbs* [1993] 1 FLR 736 for a discussion of the position where a mortgage is used.
[54] E.g. a payment.
[55] *Sekhon v Alissa* [1989] 2 FLR 94.
[56] *Wodzicki v Wodzicki* [2017] EWCA Civ 95.

C Constructive trusts

The law on constructive trusts is now governed by the decisions of the House of Lords in three key cases: *Lloyds Bank v Rosset;*[57] *Stack v Dowden*[58] and *Jones v Kernott.*[59]

The current law on constructive trusts draws a sharp distinction between two questions: first, whether a constructive trust exists and second, if it does, what shares a party has under a constructive trust. First, we will consider how the court decides whether the trust exists.

Lord Bridge in *Rosset* stated that a constructive trust could be found only if: (1) there is a common intention to share ownership; and (2) the party seeking to establish the constructive trust has relied on the common intention to his or her detriment. These two requirements need to be considered in further detail.

(i) Common intent

There are three well-established ways of establishing common intent:

(i)   If the property is registered in the joint names of both parties.

(ii) 'Any agreement, arrangement or understanding reached between them that the property is to be shared beneficially.'[60]

(iii) A common intent can be inferred from a direct contribution to the purchase price or mortgage instalment. It seems that the courts may be willing to find evidence of a common intention, even if none of these is established, but only in exceptional circumstances.[61]

The three accepted ways of establishing a common intention will now be considered separately.

(a) Registration in joint names

Where the property has been registered in joint names, that is taken as clear evidence that the parties intended to share ownership. This is hardly surprising, especially as it is very likely they will have received legal advice and therefore be aware of the significance of doing so. That principle was established by the House of Lords in *Stack v Dowden.*[62]

(b) An agreement to share ownership

This requires evidence of an actual conversation between the parties in which it was agreed that the parties would share ownership. It is not enough that there is a mutual, but uncommunicated, belief.[63] There must be proof that a conversation took place.[64] Where there is a written record, that will be powerful evidence of what is agreed;[65] otherwise the court will hear the parties' accounts of what happened and look at their conduct. The cultural context of the relationship may be a relevant factor, but the court will not automatically assume the couple intended to share or not share because that was common within a particular cultural group.[66] It should be

---

[57] [1991] 1 AC 107. For a useful discussion of the law on constructive trusts, see Sawyer (2004).
[58] [2007] UKHL 17.
[59] [2011] UKSC 53.
[60] *Lloyds Bank v Rosset* [1991] 1 AC 107.
[61] *Pillmore v Miah* [2019] EWHC 3696 (Ch).
[62] *Stack v Dowden* [2007] UKHL 17.
[63] *Fowler v Barron* [2008] EWCA Civ 377, discussed in Hayward (2009).
[64] Although the Court of Appeal has suggested it might be willing to infer from the surrounding circumstances that there was a conversation agreeing to share the property: *Springette v Defoe* [1992] 2 FLR 388 at p. 395; *Hyett v Stanley* [2003] 3 FCR 253.
[65] *Ely v Robson* [2016] EWCA Civ 774.
[66] *Arif v Anwar and Rehan* [2015] EWHC 124 (Fam).

stressed that the agreement must be to share ownership, not just to share occupation.[67] A man who lets his sister use his spare room while she is looking for somewhere to live will be agreeing to share accommodation, but not necessarily agreeing to share ownership. Similarly, an agreement to run a business together in a property is not the same thing as agreeing to share ownership of the property.[68] Also an agreement by a father to transfer ownership to a daughter 'when he thought she was ready'[69] was not an agreement to share ownership. It seems an agreement that a party might have a share of the ownership in certain circumstances in the future would be sufficient if those circumstances indeed materialised.[70] The statement to share must be made by the owners of the property. In *Smith v Bottomley*[71] a promise by a man to his partner that a property in the name of a company would be shared with her could not create a constructive trust of the company's property. Also, the agreement must relate to an agreement to share now, not a promise that a party might get property in the future.[72]

Lord Bridge accepted that it is not easy to prove an oral agreement, but that evidence of agreements can be introduced 'however imperfectly remembered and however imprecise their terms must have been'.[73] The difficulties with this have been recognised in *Hammond v Mitchell* by Waite J who noted that:

[T]he tenderest exchanges of a common law courtship may assume an unforeseen significance many years later when they are brought under equity's microscope and subjected to an analysis under which many thousands of pounds of value may be liable to turn on this fine question as to whether the relevant words were spoken in earnest or in dalliance and with or without representational intent.[74]

Cases following *Rosset* have been very willing to find evidence of common intention. The following comments have been evidence of an agreement: 'Don't worry about the future because when we are married [the house] will be half yours anyway and I'll always look after you and [our child]';[75] 'You will always have a home';[76] and 'You need a secure home.'[77] These examples are controversial because the promises appear to relate to rights in the future, rather than being agreements to share in the present, which is what Lord Bridge required. It may be that the judgments after *Rosset* are trying to loosen the strictness of the approach taken by Lord Bridge, although it should not be thought that any old statement will be sufficient. In a more recent decision, the comment concerning improvements to a property 'this will benefit us both' and an assurance to his partner that if he were to die 'you will be well provided for' were insufficient to found a claim for a constructive trust.[78] The comments did not clearly indicate an intention to share ownership.

Lord Bridge stated there were two 'outstanding examples' of the kind of agreements revealing common intention that he had in mind. Both cases involved property which was in the man's name and he gave an excuse to his partner for not putting the property into

---

[67] *Lloyds Bank v Rosset* [1990] 1 All ER 1111 at p. 1115; *G v G (Matrimonial Property: Rights of Extended Family)* [2005] EWHC 1560 (Admin).
[68] *Geary v Rankine* [2012] EWCA Civ 555.
[69] *Wodzicki v Wodzicki* [2017] EWCA Civ 95.
[70] *Ledger-Beadell v Peach and Ledger-Beadell* [2006] EWHC 2940 (Ch).
[71] [2013] EWCA Civ 953.
[72] *Curran v Collins* [2015] EWCA Civ 404.
[73] In *Lightfoot v Lightfoot-Brown* [2005] EWCA Civ 201, para 23.
[74] *Hammond v Mitchell* [1992] 2 All ER 109 at p. 121. See also *Buggs v Buggs* [2003] EWHC 1538 (Fam).
[75] *Hammond v Mitchell* [1992] 2 All ER 109, [1992] 1 FLR 229.
[76] *Southwell v Blackburn* [2014] EWCA Civ 1347.
[77] *Savil v Goodall* [1993] 1 FLR 755, [1994] 1 FCR 325.
[78] *James v Thomas* [2007] 3 FCR 696; discussed in Piska (2009).

their joint names.[79] In *Eves v Eves*[80] the man (untruthfully) stated that his partner was too young to be put on the title deed. In *Grant v Edwards*[81] the man involved (again untruthfully) said he would not put the property into their joint names because it would prejudice a dispute between her and her husband (whom she was divorcing). Some commentators[82] have pointed out that these cases, far from showing a common intention that the property was to be shared, in fact indicate that the men did not intend that their partners should have a share. Others have supported these cases on the basis that in each instance the men, having led the women to believe it was their intent that the property should be in their joint names, cannot deny there was a common intention to share ownership.[83] In *Curran v Collins*[84] the Court of Appeal was adamant that there was not a rule that a spurious reason for not putting a partner on the title was automatically evidence of an intention to share ownership. All of the evidence had to be looked at in the round.

(c) Inferring an agreement to share

If it is not possible to find evidence of an express agreement to share, it will be necessary to infer an agreement to share, from the surrounding evidence. The only circumstance in which Lord Bridge in *Rosset* was willing to accept that such an inference could be made was where there was a direct contribution to the purchase price or at least one of the mortgage instalments. However, in more recent cases (*Stack v Dowden;*[85] *Abbott v Abbott*[86]) the courts have been open to inferring a common intention to share ownership from other kinds of evidence.

The whole course of conduct of the parties can be examined in order to consider whether the parties intended to share the property. In *Geary v Rankine*[87] the Court of Appeal emphasised that an actual intention to share had to be found and could not be created simply to achieve a fair result.[88] However, they referred to 'inferring' the common intention from the parties' conduct, without restricting the kind of conduct that is to be taken into account. This was confirmed in *Thompson v Hurst*[89] where it was confirmed that the court must find 'evidence of the parties' actual intentions, express or inferred, objectively ascertained'. In *Capehorn v Harris*[90] the Court of Appeal said that an agreement could be inferred 'from conduct'. This suggests that there must be some objective evidence from which the courts deduce the intention of the parties, rather than it being simply guesswork. They were very clear that the court could not create an intention to share in order to achieve a fair result.[91] In *Pillmore v Miah*[92] Kramer J held that 'taking part in the business of the spouse or, for instance, carrying out works on the property' would not be sufficient to infer the agreement, presumably because such conduct could be explained by the fact they were married, rather than necessarily indicating

---

[79] See, for a more recent example, *Van Laethem v Brooker* [2006] 1 FCR 697.
[80] [1975] 3 All ER 768.
[81] [1987] 1 FLR 87.
[82] Gardner (1993).
[83] Mee (1999).
[84] [2015] EWCA Civ 404.
[85] [2007] UKHL 17.
[86] [2007] UKPC 53.
[87] [2012] EWCA Civ 555.
[88] A point reinforced in *Capehorn v Harris* [2015] EWCA Civ 955.
[89] [2012] EWCA Civ 1752.
[90] [2015] EWCA Civ 955.
[91] See also *Gallarotti v Sebastianelli* [2012] EWCA Civ 865.
[92] [2019] EWHC 3696 (Ch).

an agreement to share ownership. He was also clear that it was not permissible to infer an agreement to share simply from the fact the couple had been married a long time (28 years). He noted: 'What a long marriage shows generally is that there is an affection and parties are content to remain together, it says nothing about how they own their assets.' Similarly, the fact the property was purchased as a family home did not of itself indicate anything about the ownership of the property.

It should be emphasised that while the court will focus on the intention of the parties at the time of purchase of the property they may be persuaded that this intention changed over time.[93] So, even though it was the intention of the parties at the time of purchase for just one to own the property, the court may be persuaded by clear evidence that subsequently they formed the intention to share ownership and therefore a constructive trust can be found.[94] In *Aspden v Elvy*[95] it was found that when a man transferred a barn to his former cohabitant he intended it to be a complete gift. However, he later spent much money and work converting the barn and the court held that at that point there must have been a common intention that he had a share in it.

(ii) Detrimental reliance

According to *Rossett* a common intent to share is not in and of itself sufficient for a constructive trust. There must also be acts showing that a party has relied on that common intention to his or her detriment.[96] However, considerable uncertainty surrounds this requirement. First, it is far from clear what constitutes detrimental reliance. Second, there are some doubts over whether the requirement exists at all.

The approach with the most authority is that detrimental reliance requires conduct upon which the claimant 'could not reasonably have been expected to embark unless she was to have an interest in the house'.[97] In *Eves v Eves*[98] the act of reliance was the woman's manual work on the property, including breaking up concrete, demolishing and rebuilding a shed, and renovating the house. This conduct was held to be detrimental reliance because it was not the kind of conduct one would expect from a 'normal' female cohabitant. It could be inferred, therefore, that she must have acted in this way because she believed she had an interest in the property. By contrast, in *Thomas v Fuller-Brown*[99] a man who moved in with a woman and carried out various pieces of DIY around the house did not thereby acquire an interest in it. This was partly because the acts of DIY were the kind of things a man living in the house could be expected to have done, and so was not the type of conduct he would only have performed had he believed he had an interest in the property. In *Rosset* the wife's conduct in supervising the builders because her husband was abroad was insufficient to amount to detrimental reliance as 'it would seem the most natural thing in the world for any wife, in the absence of her husband abroad, to spend all the time she could'[100] working on the house, and therefore did not reveal that she believed that she had an interest in the house. Several of these examples

---

[93] *Geary v Rankine* [2012] EWCA Civ 555.
[94] *Aspden v Elvy* [2012] EWHC 1387 (Ch).
[95] [2012] EWHC 1387 (Ch).
[96] *Chan Pui Chun v Leung Kam Ho* [2003] 1 FCR 520 CA See also *Churchill v Roach* [2004] 3 FCR 744 where, although detrimental acts were found before the agreement to share ownership, none were found after and so there could be no constructive trust.
[97] Nourse LJ in *Grant v Edwards* [1986] Ch 638, [1987] 1 FLR 87.
[98] [1975] 3 All ER 768.
[99] [1988] 1 FLR 237.
[100] [1990] 1 All ER 1111 at p. 1117.

demonstrate the danger that gender stereotyping can determine whether a party is able to establish detrimental reliance or not.

There is some authority for alternative approaches. Sir Nicholas Browne-Wilkinson V-C (as he then was) suggested that detrimental reliance requires any conduct of the kind that relates to a couple's 'joint lives' together.[101] This is a very liberal interpretation of the requirement; it simply stipulates that there were detrimental acts that related to the couple's joint lives. This might include caring for the couple's children or a substantial amount of housework. If a couple were living together it would almost be inevitable that there would be acts that were referable to their joint lives together. Whichever approach is taken, a direct contribution to the purchase price or mortgage instalments can constitute detrimental reliance. This means that such payments will be evidence from which both a common intention can be inferred and detrimental reliance shown and therefore in and of themselves establish a constructive trust. Notably, *Stack v Dowden*[102], *Abbott v Abbott*[103] and *Jones v Kernott*[104] do not mention the requirement of reliance, causing one leading commentator to refer to 'the demise' of the reliance requirement.[105] In *de Bruyne v de Bruyne*[106] it was held that a constructive trust could be imposed even in the absence of detrimental reliance, as long as there were other circumstances which meant that it would be unconscionable for the owner to hold the property absolutely.[107] However, recently the Court of Appeal in *Smith v Bottomley*[108] held that detrimental reliance was: 'a critical element of [the] claim to a beneficial interest in the properties in question . . . by way of constructive trust'. Perhaps the best view is that proof of detrimental reliance is still required to establish a constructive trust, but in an exceptional case a court may well be willing to overlook its absence. To add to the confusion in *Archibald v Alexander*[109] Fancourt J suggested that there were two kinds of constructive trusts: a common intention constructive trust (of the kind in *Stack v Dowden*) which did require detrimental reliance, and a constructive trust designed to prevent unconscionable behaviour (of the kind in *de Bruyne v de Bruyne*) which did not require unconscionable behaviour. If that view is correct then it seems you either need detrimental reliance or some other reason to make it unconscionable to deny the applicant a property interest. Without doubt the issue needs a clear resolution by the Court of Appeal.

(iii) Calculating what share a party is entitled to under a constructive trust

The shares the parties are entitled to under a constructive trust are determined by the parties' intentions.[110] In some cases that will be simple. If the parties have set out clearly what percentage share they are to have, the court will simply follow that.[111] Similarly, if the court finds there was an express agreement over what share to own, that will be followed. In *Agarwala v Agarwala*[112] the court accepted evidence that there was a clear agreement that an investment

---

[101] *Grant v Edwards* [1986] Ch 638 at p. 657.

[102] [2007] UKHL 17.

[103] [2007] UKPC 53.

[104] [2011] UKSC 53.

[105] Gardner (2008).

[106] [2010] 2 FCR 251.

[107] Sloan (2013) finds it hard to imagine a claim being justifiable in the absence of detrimental reliance.

[108] [2013] EWCA Civ 953.

[109] [2020] EWHC 1621 (Ch).

[110] *Crossley v Crossley* [2006] 1 FCR 655. There it was emphasised that if it is clear what the parties' intentions were there is no need to consider what a 'fair share' of the equitable interest would be.

[111] *Fowler v Barron* [2008] 2 FCR 1; *Pankhania v Chandegra* [2012] EWCA Civ 1438. The only exception being where there is a fraud: *Bhura v Bhura and Others (No 2)* [2014] EWHC 727.

[112] [2013] EWCA Civ 1763.

property bought in the name of the sister-in-law would be owned solely by the brother-in-law. The sister-in-law's name was only used to help get credit for the purchase. The court held the sister-in-law held the property entirely on trust for the brother-in-law.

Where there is no clear evidence as to what the parties agree the court will seek to determine what the intentions of the parties were. If the property is put in joint names but with no indication of how to share the beneficial interest it will be presumed the parties intended to share the property equally, even though they may have contributed unequally. Lady Hale in *Stack v Dowden*[113] said 'cases in which the joint legal owners are to be taken to have intended that their beneficial interests should be different from their legal interests will be very unusual'. However, where there is evidence that a sharing of beneficial interest was not intended then the constructive trust will reflect the intention. The presumption of shared beneficial interest in cases of joint name purchases applies equally to homes a couple buy to live in and to investment property if that is 'an enterprise reflecting their joint commercial as well as their personal commitment'.[114] In fact it nowadays will rarely be necessary to rely on this joint names presumption because in 1998 the Land Registry introduced a new form (TR1) which contains an express declaration of trust sharing the beneficial interest in cases of property bought in joint names.

It gets more complicated in cases where the parties have not put the property in joint names. If the couple talked generally about sharing, but did not make it clear what percentage each were to have, in such a case the basic principle is that the court must attempt to infer their intention by referring to all the evidence in the case. This was the approach as stated by the House of Lords in *Stack v Dowden*.[115] They rejected an approach of asking: 'What would be a fair share for each party having regard to the whole course of dealing between them in relation to the property?'[116] The focus must be on the intentions of the parties, rather than fairness. That was re-emphasised in the following decision:[117]

CASE: *Jones v Kernott* [2011] UKSC 53

Ms Jones and Mr Kernott bought a property in joint names in 1985. They later separated and for 12 years Ms Jones lived in the property and paid for its maintenance and mortgage, while the man made no contribution at all. The trial judge declared a constructive trust under which Ms Jones had a 90 per cent and Mr Kernott a 10 per cent share. The Court of Appeal allowed an appeal and declared equal ownership. The Supreme Court reinstated the 90/10 per cent division of the trial judge.

The central question is how to determine the beneficial interests of a house bought in joint names by an unmarried couple. The Supreme Court, following *Stack v Dowden* [2007] UKHL 17, [2007] 2 All ER 929, set out the key principles. Where a couple buy a house in joint names, but there is no express declaration of beneficial interest, then there is a rebuttable presumption of equal sharing of the beneficial interest. The Supreme Court

---

[113] *Stack v Dowden* [2007] 2 AC 432.
[114] Where a property is bought simply for a commercial endeavour and not as an aspect of a relationship the court is likely to assume the beneficial shares reflect the shares of the money the parties contributed to the purchase: *Marr v Collie* [2018] AC 631.
[115] [2007] UKHL 17; followed in *Qayyum v Hameed* [2009] 2 FLR 962.
[116] As proposed in *Oxley v Hiscock* [2004] 2 FCR 295 at para 69.
[117] For discussion on *Kernott* see Newnham (2013) and Sloan (2013).

thought that it would be 'very unusual' (at [68]) for the equal share presumption to be rebutted. The fact the parties had contributed to the purchase of the house in unequal shares was not in itself normally sufficient to rebut the presumption. However, a court could, after looking at their whole course of conduct to ascertain their common intentions, decide that the presumption of equal sharing of the beneficial interest was rebutted.

The key issue before the Supreme Court was whether the focus should be on the parties' actual intentions and the extent to which these needed to be expressed, or could be inferred or imputed from their conduct. Lord Walker and Lady Hale held that the search is 'primarily to ascertain the parties' actual shared intentions' (at [31]). These could be expressed or inferred from their conduct. However, they did allow that in cases where it is not possible to ascertain the proportions of sharing, then the court 'is driven to impute an intention to the parties which they may never have had' (at [31]). Lord Kerr and Lord Wilson in their judgments seem far more ready to employ the term 'impute'.

What is perhaps more important than whether the word 'impute' is used or not, is what is meant by that term. Is it that in cases where we do not have evidence of what their intention is, we can make an educated guess about their intention or is it that in cases where we do not know their intentions, we impute the intention they ought to have? Lord Walker and Lady Hale, supported by Lord Collins appear to take the former view emphasising 'the primary search must always be for what the parties actually intended, to be deduced objectively from their words and their actions'. Relying on an assessment of what is fair is a last resort. Lord Kerr appears to take the latter view (at [75]):

> As soon as it is clear that inferring an intention is not possible, the focus of the court's attention should be squarely on what is fair and, as I have said, that is an obviously different examination than is involved in deciding what the parties actually intended.

Lord Kerr appears to be supported in his approach by Lord Wilson.

In cases where the couple have registered the property in joint names but not declared the percentage shares they will have, there is a strong presumption that they intend to share the property equally.[118] However, the presumption can be rebutted if there is clear evidence as to the parties' intentions.[119] What is unclear after **Stack v Dowden** is how strong the evidence has to be to rebut the presumption.[120] In **Jones v Kernott**[121] it was said to be 'very unusual' for property bought in joint names not to be shared equally, although on the facts of that case (see below) the presumption was rebutted. The fact the parties had contributed to the purchase of the house in unequal shares was not in itself normally sufficient to rebut the presumption. However, a court could, after looking at their whole course of conduct to ascertain their common intentions, decide that the presumption of equal sharing of the beneficial interest was rebutted by clear evidence of an intention to share in unequal shares.[122]

---

[118] The presumption could not be relied upon if the parties planned to put the property in joint names, but were dissuaded from doing so: *Thompson v Hurst* [2012] EWCA Civ 1752.

[119] *Stack v Dowden* [2007] UKHL 17.

[120] Probert (2007a) suggests that there was little exceptional about the facts in the case itself, where the presumption was rebutted.

[121] [2011] UKSC 53.

[122] *Barnes v Phillips* [2015] EWCA Civ 1056.

If the property is not in joint names then all the evidence must be considered to ascertain the common intention of the parties.[123] Baroness Hale held that financial contributions would be an important factor to take into account; so, too, would the following:

> any advice or discussions at the time of the transfer which cast light upon their intentions then . . . the purposes for which the home was acquired; the nature of the parties' relationship; whether they had children for whom they both had responsibility to provide a home; how the purchase was financed, both initially and subsequently; how the parties arranged their finances, whether separately or together or a bit of both; how they discharged the outgoings on the property and their other household expenses.[124]

She explained that although how much each contributed financially was relevant, it would be quite possible to conclude that 'they intended that each should contribute as much to the household as they reasonably could and that they would share the eventual benefit or burden equally'.[125] In such a case an applicant may be entitled to a 50 per cent share even though she had contributed to less than 50 per cent of the purchase price. In **Stack v Dowden**[126] the parties kept their financial affairs 'rigidly separate' and took careful notice of who paid for what. In that case it was found that the financial contributions should be particularly significant in ascertaining their share, because the parties attached great significance to that.[127] Similarly, where the property purchased is an investment property held in joint names, with no declaration of beneficial interest, the court will generally focus only on the financial contributions of the parties because it is assumed the parties were looking at this as simply a financial issue.[128]

Generally, the court will be willing to look at all of the circumstances of the case to ascertain the parties' intentions as to shares.[129] In **Barnes v Phillips**[130] the Court of Appeal took into account the failure of the man to pay child support as evidence that they intended his partner to have a greater than half share in their former home. The court in saying that were adamant they were not using the forbidden line of reasoning: 'he has not paid child support and so it would be fair to give his partner a greater share in the house'. They were using the permitted reasoning: 'he has not paid child support and so the parties must have intended that she have a greater share in the home to make up for that.'

If looking at all of the evidence it is not possible to determine what share the parties intended each other to have, the Court of Appeal in **Thompson v Hurst**[131] confirmed that it is then permitted to consider what is fair and 'impute' that intention to the parties. As the division of opinion in **Kernott** indicates it is a little unclear whether what the courts are doing is using fairness as evidence of intention or 'imposing' fairness on the parties.

It may be that, in practice, there is little difference between these two approaches because in the absence of other evidence we might guess that most people would want there to be a fair share between them and their partner. Indeed, on the facts of **Kernott** Lord Walker,

---

[123] *Fowler v Barron* [2008] EWCA Civ 377.
[124] Paragraph 69.
[125] Paragraph 69. See Burgoyne *et al.* (2006) for a sociological discussion of how unmarried couples understand their finances.
[126] [2007] UKHL 17.
[127] See also *Fowler v Barron* [2008] 2 FCR 1.
[128] *Laskar v Laskar* [2008] EWCA Civ 347; *Geary v Rankine* [2012] EWCA Civ 555. Similarly, where the parties are not in a close relationship it is not normally appropriate to impute intention: *Wodzicki v Wodzicki* [2017] EWCA Civ 95.
[129] *O'Kelly v Davies* [2014] EWCA Civ 1606.
[130] [2015] EWCA Civ 1056.
[131] [2012] EWCA Civ 1752.

Lady Hale and Lord Collins thought the 90/10 split could be inferred from the evidence as the intentions of the parties, while Lords Kerr and Wilson decided intention could not be inferred, but a 90/10 split should be imputed.[132]

But, what does fairness means in this context? In *Graham-York v York*[133] the Court of Appeal considered a case where a woman had survived a lengthy abusive relationship with her partner. The court accepted there was an intention to share the property, but no overt evidence as to what those shares would be. The court went on to consider what percentage share would be 'fair'. However, they emphasised that the court in considering fairness should focus on their relationship in relation to the property:

> Thus it is irrelevant that it may be thought a 'fair' outcome for a woman who has endured years of abusive conduct by her partner to be allotted a substantial interest in his property on his death. The plight of Miss Graham-York attracts sympathy, but it does not enable the court to redistribute property interests in a manner which right-minded people might think amounts to appropriate compensation. Miss Graham-York is 'entitled to that share which the court considers fair having regard to the whole course of dealing between them in relation to the property'.

They upheld a 25 per cent share in the property, making it clear in a sole name case there was no presumption in favour of an equal sharing being the fair outcome. This restriction to considering fairness in relation to the property is controversial. It does not sit easily with *Barnes v Phillips*[134] where the failure to pay child support was taken into account. It is notable that *Jones v Kernott* did not seem to limit fairness in a particular way. It is submitted it is better to leave fairness as an unfettered concept.

D Proprietary estoppel

Learning objective 4

Summarise the law on proprietary estoppel

For *A* to establish a proprietary estoppel claim over *B*'s property, it is necessary to show:[135]

1. *A* reasonably believes she has or is going to be given an interest over *B*'s property as a result of something *B* (or someone acting on *B*'s behalf) has said or done;[136]

2. *A* must act reasonably in reliance on this belief;[137] and

3. it must be conscionable (fair) in all the circumstances to give *A* a remedy.

However, Lewison LJ in *Davies v Davies*[138] emphasised that: 'no claim based on proprietary estoppel can be divided into watertight compartments. The quality of the relevant assurances may influence the issue of reliance; reliance and detriment are often intertwined.' In other words, it seems that if a case is rather weak on the first requirement (the reasonable belief), that may be made up by a significant amount of reliance.

The law has been examined by the House of Lords.

---

[132] See George (2012a) for a helpful discussion.
[133] [2015] EWCA Civ 72.
[134] [2015] EWCA Civ 1056.
[135] *Re Basham (Deceased)* [1987] 1 All ER 405; *Gillet v Holt* [2000] FCR 705.
[136] *Habberfield v Habberfield* [2018] EWHC 317 (Ch).
[137] *Liden v Burton* [2016] EWCA Civ 275 stated this needed to be detrimental reliance, but that does not seem to have been regarded as an essential requirement in the recent cases.
[138] [2016] EWCA Civ 463.

CASE: *Thorner v Major* [2009] 1 WLR 776

Thorner had worked on his cousin's farm for 29 years without pay. The cousin was said by the court to be a man of few words. However, some statements were made which led Thorner to believe he would leave him the farm in his will. For example, he gave some life insurance policy documents to Thorner, saying they were for his 'death duties'. The cousin did make a will leaving the farm to Thorner, but then revoked the will, having fallen out with another legatee. He made no other will. Under the rules of intestacy, the farm passed to the cousin's siblings. Thorner argued that the farm was his. At first instance it was found that the vague comments were sufficient for a proprietary estoppel. However, the Court of Appeal allowed an appeal, principally on the basis that the statements were not promises and had not been relied upon by Thorner.

The House of Lords held that to establish a propriety estoppel the assurance had to be 'clear enough'. Whether the assurance was clear enough depended on the context of the words or actions. Insisting that statements had to be 'clear and unambiguous' would be too strict a test and would be unrealistic. Normally, it would be sufficient if the claimant could show that he or she reasonably understood the words or conduct to be an assurance on which he could rely. In this case, given that the cousin was 'taciturn and undemonstrative', the judge was entitled to accept the words and conduct as amounting to an estoppel. What the cousin actually intended was not really relevant, because the focus was on Thorner's reasonable interpretation of what was said. Nor was it relevant to consider whether a reasonable person would have relied on what the cousin said: the question was whether it was reasonable for Thorner to rely on it. Only in exceptional cases might a person seek to defend a propriety estoppel on the basis that they did not intend to convey the promise as it was reasonably understood by the claimant. Their Lordships also confirmed that a proprietary estoppel claim had to relate to an identified property. In this case it was clear what property was being talked about.

As a result of this decision, the key question in estoppel is whether it was reasonable for the claimant to believe an assurance[139] or promise was made and reasonable to rely on it.[140] In deciding that, the court will look at statements throughout the relationship and in the context of how couples live their lives.[141] The courts appreciate that couples in love are unlikely to use legally precise terminology. The courts will look at all the comments taken together and in context.[142] A series of somewhat ambiguous statements could, taken together and in context, create a sufficiently clear representation.[143] Where, however, there is a written document, that is likely to be taken as evidence of the intentions of the parties.[144] The court will also take into account the personality of the parties. In *Gee v Gee*[145] the father was 'a man of his word, not given to idle discussions' and that meant it was reasonable for the son to rely on his occasional assurances.

---

[139] See Samet (2015) for a discussion of when this might be found from silence.
[140] *Suggitt v Suggitt* [2011] EWHC 903 (Ch).
[141] *Southwell v Blackburn* [2014] EWCA Civ 1347. See Hayward (2015) for a helpful discussion of this case.
[142] *Wills and Wills v Sowray* [2020] EWHC (Ch) 939.
[143] *Habberfield v Habberfield* [2018] EWHC 317 (Ch).
[144] *Horsford v Horsford* [2020] EWHC 584 (Ch).
[145] [2018] EWHC 1393 (Ch).

Their Lordships approved *Gillet v Holt* which had stressed that the crucial principle under-lying proprietary estoppel is conscionability.[146] As it was put in *Davies v Davies*[147] by the Court of Appeal: 'the essence of the doctrine of proprietary estoppel is to do what is necessary to avoid an unconscionable result.' Conscionability in essence means fairness.[148] However, that does not mean there are limits on when a proprietary estoppel can be found. Even substantial detriment will not found a claim for a proprietary estoppel without some representation.[149] The assurance need not be to a specific property right, but must refer to a piece of property.[150] So, the statement to a girlfriend that she 'would not want for anything' could not form the basis of an estoppel claim.[151] Nor was an assurance that a woman would have a roof over her head.[152] Similarly, statements which the parties expressly agreed were not intended to be binding or have any legal effect could not form the basis of a proprietary estoppel.[153] There does not need to be financial reliance on the statement,[154] but where there is detrimental reliance on the statement that will help show it would be conscionable to provide a remedy.[155] In *Horsford v Horsford*[156] a son relied on some equivocal promises he would be left his parents' farm. The court noted that in fact he had through his work on the farm become wealthy and received a good salary. It could not be said there was detrimental reliance and the claim failed.

Having established a proprietary estoppel claim, the next question is: What interest in the property should thereby be acquired by the plaintiff?[157] The simple answer is that the remedy given is that which would 'satisfy the equity'; in other words, that remedy which would be just. In *Moore v Moore*[158] the Court of Appeal stated that the court should award the minimum necessary to satisfy justice, although it is possible to find cases where the courts have not always taken that line. The courts have been willing to grant a wide range of remedies including a fee simple[159] or a sum of money.[160] There has been academic debate over whether the courts place most weight on the nature of the interest that was promised or assured by the owner or whether the amount of detriment suffered by the claimant is key.[161] In *Guest v Guest*[162] the Court of Appeal refused to resolve that debate, saying the appropriate remedy is a matter for the court's discretion, focusing on avoiding an unconscionable outcome. In some cases it seems what was promised is the key factor determining the remedy;[163] in others the remedy is proportionate to the financial value of the detriment.[164] In *Liden v Burton*[165] the Court of Appeal upheld a

---

[146] *Gillet v Holt* [2000] FCR 705.
[147] [2016] EWCA Civ 463.
[148] For a detailed discussion, see Dixon (2010), who offers a much narrower definition of unconscionability in the context of proprietary estoppel.
[149] *Walsh v Singh* [2010] 1 FLR 1658.
[150] See for further discussion McFarlane and Robertson (2009), Mee (2009) and Dixon (2010).
[151] *Lissimore v Downing* [2003] 2 FLR 308.
[152] *Negus v Bahouse* [2008] 1 FCR 768.
[153] *Shield v Shield* [2014] EWHC 23 (Fam).
[154] *Davies v Davies* [2016] EWCA Civ 463.
[155] *Southwell v Blackburn* [2014] EWCA Civ 1347.
[156] [2020] EWHC 584 (Ch).
[157] Gardner (2006).
[158] [2018] EWCA Civ 2669.
[159] *Pascoe v Turner* [1979] 1 WLR 431; *Q v Q* [2009] 1 FLR 935. A fee simple is absolute ownership.
[160] *Southwell v Blackburn* [2014] EWCA Civ 1347.
[161] *Jennings v Rice* [2003] 1 FCR 501.
[162] [2020] EWCA Civ 837.
[163] *Wills and Wills v Sowray* [2020] EWHC (Ch) 939.
[164] *Jennings v Rice* [2003] 1 FCR 501. The question of whether a proprietary estoppel creates an interest in land and, if so, when is discussed in Bright and McFarlane (2005).
[165] [2016] EWCA Civ 275.

first instance judgment which had taken a strict mathematical approach in calculating the award: by returning to the claimant the financial contributions she had made towards the house, with 3 per cent interest. The court found this was at least the minimum which justice could require and so the judgment could not be overturned. In *Habberfield v Habberfield*[166] the claimant had worked for many years fulfilling 'her side of the bargain' and so it was right to award her what had been promised. The closest the courts have come to offering clear guidance was *Davies v Davies*[167] where it was held there should be 'a sliding scale by which the clearer the expectation, the greater the detriment and the longer the passage of time during which the expectation was reasonably held, the greater would be the weight that should be given to the expectation.' However, it is clear much will depend on the facts of the case. In *Moore v Moore*[168] both parties were alive, but had fallen out. The parties could not be expected to live together. This meant an order dividing the property and so achieving a clean break was more appropriate than expecting both parties to live in the property.[169]

E The interrelation of constructive trusts and proprietary estoppel

It will have been noticed that the requirements of a constructive trust and proprietary estoppel are very similar. Indeed, some commentators take the view that proprietary estoppel and constructive trusts should be amalgamated.[170] Certainly the courts have not taken great efforts to distinguish the two. Lord Bridge, for example, said that where a person has acted to his or her detriment on reliance of an agreement to share property, this will 'give rise to a constructive trust or proprietary estoppel'. The Court of Appeal has accepted that the requirements for the two are very similar.[171] However, the current view of the courts is that, although at some point the doctrines might be merged, they are not yet assimilated.[172] For example, in *Southwell v Blackburn*[173] although the claim of a constructive trust failed, the claim for a proprietary estoppel was successful. Carnwath LJ will have expressed the views of many experienced practitioners on the history of the case law in this area when saying:

> To the detached observer, the result may seem like a witch's brew, into which various esoteric ingredients have been stirred over the years, and in which different ideas bubble to the surface at different times. They include implied trust, constructive trust, resulting trust, presumption of advancement, proprietary estoppel, unjust enrichment, and so on. These ideas are likely to mean nothing to laymen, and often little more to the lawyers who use them.[174]

---

[166] [2018] EWHC 317 (Ch).
[167] [2016] EWCA Civ 275; approved in *Guest v Guest* [2020] EWCA Civ 837.
[168] [2018] EWCA Civ 2669.
[169] *Moore v Moore* [2018] EWCA Civ 2669.
[170] See Nield (2003).
[171] *Yaxley v Gotts* [2000] Ch 162, [1999] 2 FLR 941.
[172] *Stokes v Anderson* [1991] 1 FLR 391. See also *Churchill v Roach* [2004] 3 FCR 744 at p. 759 where Judge Norris QC suggested that while constructive trusts focus on the intention of the parties at the time of purchase, proprietary estoppel focuses on the time when a party seeks to go back on an assurance or promise.
[173] [2014] EWCA Civ 1347.
[174] *Stack v Dowden* [2005] 2 FCR 739, at para 75.

8 Improvements to the home

Section 37 of the Matrimonial Proceedings and Property Act 1970 states that if a spouse, civil partner or fiancé(e) (but not an unmarried cohabitant) makes a substantial contribution to the improvement of property[175] in which the other spouse, civil partner or fiancé(e) has an interest, the improvement will create an interest in the property. However, the section states that this rule is subject to any agreement that the parties reach. A number of requirements need to be satisfied if the section is to apply:

1. The improvement must be of monetary value. Section 37 applies whether the contribution is in real money or money's worth. The improvement may be made by the claimant him- or herself or by someone employed by the claimant.[176] So if an incompetent husband carries out DIY work on the house, which in fact decreases the value of the house, he will be unable to invoke this section, as no improvement of monetary value has been made.

2. The contribution must be identifiable with the improvement in question. So, if it could be shown that a wife pays the household expenses thereby enabling the husband to pay for the improvements to a piece of property, s. 37 could be relied upon by the wife.[177]

3. The contribution must be of a substantial nature. *Re Nicholson (Deceased)*[178] provides a good example of this: installing central heating worth £189 in a house worth £6,000 was substantial, but spending £23 on a gas fire was not.

4. The contribution must constitute an improvement to the property and not merely maintenance of it.[179]

The share acquired will be that which reflects any agreement of the parties, and if there is not one, then what the court regards as just. Normally, the party will receive a share in the property reflecting the increase in the value of the property that the improvements caused.

There is some debate over the policy behind this section. It could be regarded as putting into legal effect the presumed intentions of the parties: that is, what the parties themselves would have expected to happen as a result of their actions to improve the property had they thought about it. Alternatively, s. 37 could be seen as a way of achieving a just result in recognition of a party's contribution to improving the house, regardless of the parties' intentions. The fact that the parties can reach an agreement which negates the effect of the section would suggest that the statute is primarily seeking to reflect the parties' intentions.[180] The section is rarely relied upon because works carried out on the house will often form the basis of a proprietary estoppel or constructive trust claim.

---

[175] The section applies to real and personal property.
[176] *Griffiths v Griffiths* [1979] 1 WLR 1350.
[177] *Harnett v Harnett* [1973] 2 All ER 593 at p. 603.
[178] [1974] 1 WLR 476.
[179] *Re Nicholson (Deceased)* [1974] 1 WLR 476.
[180] It is therefore analogous to the working of resulting trusts.

9 Criticism of the present law

Learning objective 5

Debate the arguments over the law on family property

The law on ownership of the family home has been heavily criticised.[181] The potential harshness of the law was well revealed in the recent case of *Geary v Rankine*[182] where the primary asset of an unmarried couple was a business property in the man's name. There was no evidence of an agreement to share ownership and so the Court of Appeal declined to find a constructive trust. Although their relationship had lasted 19 years and the woman had done much work for the business, she left the relationship with no share of the fruits of their labours.[183]

The Law Commission has stated that: 'Current property law rules are generally agreed to be highly complicated and uncertain. In addition to the technical difficulties they present, the nature of the evidence required to prove the elements of a claim makes it difficult in practice to predict the likely outcome of cases. Most significantly, the rules lead to outcomes which many people would consider to be unfair.'[184]

There is much academic support for the need to change the law.[185] The following are some of the main criticisms:

1. The emphasis in the case law on an oral agreement between the parties or a direct financial contribution in order to establish a constructive trust has been heavily criticised. It is unrealistic to expect all couples to discuss the legal ownership of their property. You cannot expect lovers to talk to each other in the way people do when negotiating a business deal.[186] The cases demonstrate that the courts have had to pick up on casual comments made during the relationship. In a recent case much time was spent discussing what was or was not said over a dinner at a Thai restaurant some five years previously.[187]

2. The emphasis on spoken promises in both constructive trusts and proprietary estoppel works against the less articulate or assertive partner, who may not seek an unequivocal promise from the owner.[188] Ruth Deech says that she warned her male students to conduct their love affairs in silence to ensure they would not unintentionally create a constructive trust![189] Even worse, in *Graham-York v York*[190] the fact the male legal owner was abusive and controlling was taken as evidence that it was unlikely he intended his partner to have an equal share in the property.

3. It has been argued that the law reveals gender bias. In the absence of a conversation, common intention can only be established through a direct contribution to the purchase price or mortgage instalments. It is far more likely that men will be able to contribute in these ways than women, given the greater rates of paid employment among men and of care work among women.[191] Further, the law devalues non-financial contributions to the

---

[181] See Douglas, Pearce and Woodward (2007) and Gardner (2008).
[182] [2012] EWCA Civ 555.
[183] For other examples, see Douglas, Pearce and Woodward (2007: chs 4 and 5).
[184] Law Commission Consultation Paper (Overview) (2006: 15).
[185] See Gardner (1993); Law Commission Report 278 (2002).
[186] See Hayward (2012).
[187] *Ashby v Kilduff* [2010] EWHC 2034 (Ch).
[188] Gardner (1993).
[189] Deech (2010d).
[190] [2015] EWCA Civ 72.
[191] Leckey (2019); Wong (2005) suggests this leaves the law open to challenge under the Human Rights Act 1998.

household by treating them as insufficient to establish a constructive trust. Notably, in relation to the redistribution of property of married couples on divorce, the House of Lords has held that there should be no discrimination between the money-earner and the homemaker or child-carer.[192] This principle is not reflected in the law governing cohabitants.

4. The emphasis placed on whether the property is in joint names has also been challenged. It has been argued that whether the property is in joint names is often a matter of chance and often does not reflect a careful consideration by the parties as to ownership of the property.[193] Indeed, it has been claimed by psychological economists that financial payments are a very unreliable guide to intentions.[194]

5. We have already noted that the results of these cases can be particularly unpredictable. This produces uncertainty and causes particular difficulties for negotiations between the parties before the case reaches the court. Simon Gardner[195] argues that is not necessarily a problem because cohabiting couples will not live their lives based on what they reasonably believe the legal position to be. This makes them different from, say, commercial contractors who may rely on the contract being enforceable.

10 Reform of the law

The Law Commission, after many years' work, produced a report proposing reform of the law relating to the ownership of property of unmarried couples.[196] The Law Commission proposed allowing cohabiting couples to make some financial claims against each other, but these would normally be at a lower level than would be available if they were married. It also proposed that a claim can be made if the couple meet the 'eligibility criteria': these should be either that the couple have a child or that they have lived together for a certain period of time.[197] By cohabitation the Law Commission means that a couple are living as a couple in a joint household.[198] A couple would be free to opt out of the scheme if they wished.[199] However, the court could set aside an opt-out if following it would cause manifest unfairness. An applicant would need to prove that:

- the respondent has a retained benefit; or

- the applicant has an economic disadvantage as a result of qualifying contributions the applicant has made.[200]

A qualifying contribution is 'any contribution arising from the cohabiting relationship which is made to the parties' shared lives or to the welfare of the members of their families'.[201]

---

[192] *White v White* [2001] AC 596; see Chapter 6.
[193] Douglas, Pearce and Woodward (2009a).
[194] Burgoyne and Sonnenberg (2009).
[195] Gardner (2013).
[196] Law Commission Report 307 (2007). The proposals and surrounding issues are discussed in Bridge (2007a, b and c) and Wong (2006).
[197] The Law Commission suggested that a figure between two and five years might be appropriate.
[198] Couples who were closely related or one or both of whom were under age 16 would be excluded.
[199] Any opt-out would need to be in writing and signed by both parties.
[200] Law Commission Report 307 (2007: para 4.33).
[201] Law Commission Report 307 (2007: para 4.33).

Contributions can include financial, non-financial and future contributions, but they must have an enduring consequence for the couple at the time of the separation. An economic disadvantage could, therefore, include loss of earning potential as a result of caring for children during the relationship and afterwards. A retained benefit could be capital acquired during the relationship or enhanced earning capacity created during the relationship. The court would make an order ensuring a fair sharing of the gains and losses resulting from the relationship. This might require a party who had made a benefit from the relationship to share that, or require a party who had suffered a disadvantage to be compensated. However, the court would take into account, as first consideration, the welfare of any child of both parties. The court could make lump sum orders, property transfers and pension sharing orders. However, it could not make ongoing periodic payment orders.[202]

The Law Commission rejects an argument that once a couple satisfy the 'eligibility criteria' they should be treated in the same way as a married couple for financial relief purposes. It argues that the notion of 'equal partnership' which applies to marriage cannot necessarily be said to apply to cohabitants.

> Where parties are married, the formal commitment that they have entered into may be taken as good evidence that they have assumed mutual responsibilities to support each other in case of need . . . Cohabitants currently have no legal obligation of mutual support either during or after their relationship. Even in long relationships, there may be no clear basis for concluding that the parties have assumed that sort of responsibility towards each other.[203]

Whether treating couples in the same way as a married couple would undermine marriage is a matter for debate. One study of what has happened in Australia where those living together for two years or more are treated in the same way as a married couple, suggests that reform had no effect on marriage rates.[204]

The Government at first announced that it would delay responding to the Law Commission proposals until it has seen the impact of similar proposals which have been enacted in Scotland. The Government has particular concerns over the costs to the state of enacting such a scheme.[205] In 2011 it was announced that reform would not be introduced during the current term of government. This, somewhat unusually, received critical comment from the judiciary, with Lady Hale stating:

> As Professor Cooke also pointed out, the 'existing law is uncertain and expensive to apply and, because it was not designed for cohabitants, often gives rise to results that are unjust'. The reality is that the 'sufficient basis for changing the law' had already been amply provided by the long-standing judicial calls for reform (dating back at least as far as *Burns* v *Burns* [1984] Ch 317, at 332); by the Law Commission's analysis of the deficiencies in the present law and the injustices which can result; by the demographic trends towards cohabitation and births to cohabiting couples, which are even more marked south of the border than they are in the north; and by the widespread belief that cohabiting couples are already protected by something called 'common law marriage' which has never existed in the south. There was no need to wait for experience north of the border to make the case for reform.[206]

---

[202] See Douglas, Pearce and Woodward (2008) for a survey of cohabitants' opinions of how the Law Commission proposals would work.
[203] Law Commission Consultation Paper 179 (2006: 3.36).
[204] Kiernan, Barlow and Merlo (2006).
[205] Miles, Wasoff and Mordaunt (2011) found research into the Scottish scheme did not suggest there would be significant increased costs.
[206] *Gow* v *Grant* [2012] UKSC 29, para 50.

Here is a summary of some of the other approaches which could be used to reform the law in this area:[207]

1. The law could give the courts the power to redistribute the property of cohabitants in the same way as they can redistribute the property of married couples.[208] (This proposal was discussed in Chapter 3.) It should be noted that such a proposal would leave those people sharing homes who are not in a marriage-like relationship (e.g. three friends sharing a house or an older person and their carer) with the current legal regulation.

2. The law could focus on the intentions of the parties. This approach might encourage unmarried cohabitants to draw up cohabitation contracts, but, if they did not, the courts would seek to ascertain the parties' intentions from what was said and done during the relationship. The benefit of this approach is that it would promote the parties' autonomy – the law would be seeking to enforce their intentions, rather than telling them what to do. The disadvantages are shown by the law on constructive trusts. Snippets of vaguely recalled conversations may have far more emphasis placed upon them than was intended. Further, in many of these cases the intention of the owner of the property may be quite different from the intention of the cohabitee, and so seeking any kind of *common* intention could be a futile task.

3. The law could focus on the reasonable expectations of the party who is seeking an interest in the property. The difficulty with this approach is revealed by the following scenario. An owner tells the claimant that she can live with him but she will never acquire an interest in his house. If the claimant were then to move in and spend an enormous amount of effort in maintaining and improving the property, she could not reasonably expect the owner to intend that she thereby acquires an interest in the house, even though justice may call out for her to be awarded an interest. The approach also suffers from the difficulty that establishing that the claimant's belief that she had an interest in the property was reasonable is likely to require proof of conversations of the kind which bedevil the present law.

4. These concerns have produced an interesting variant of the reasonable expectation approach and this is to focus on what share the claimant might reasonably believe he or she *ought* to have.[209] In the scenario discussed in the previous paragraph, although the owner made it clear that the claimant was not to acquire an interest in the property and so she cannot reasonably believe that she was to acquire an interest, she might nevertheless reasonably expect that she ought to. The problem of this variant centres on the concept of reasonableness. Our society does not have a fixed set of views on when people should be entitled to a share in houses, so it is hard to say what is reasonable or not. In effect, this model is similar to option 1 above – it is simply a question of judicial discretion. So, it may be more desirable to give the judiciary such discretion explicitly.

5. The courts could focus on the actions performed on the property by the party who has no legal interest in the property. The law should then seek to value the work they have performed. This approach could be based on a form of unjust enrichment. This means that if the owner has received a benefit of the other party's work, the owner would be unjustly enriched by retaining the benefits of the work unless the other party acquires an interest in the property.[210] The benefit of this approach is that by focusing on what was done (rather than said, foreseen or intended), a more concrete concept is used. It is certainly easier to prove.

---

[207] Miles (2003) and Probert (2003) provide excellent discussions on this.
[208] Discussed in Wong (2009).
[209] Eekelaar (1994b).
[210] See, e.g., Dickson J in *Pettkus v Becker* (1980) 117 DLR (3d) 257 at p. 274.

The difficulty with this approach is twofold. The first is valuation of the benefit. This is a particular problem where the benefit is in the form of work which is not usually valued in economic terms, such as housework, and which at the time the parties themselves may not have regarded as of economic value.[211] Joanna Miles suggests that it should be recognised that the 'entitlement to a share in the property derives not from any presumed economic value of the contributions, but from an acknowledgement of their unique, socially valuable contribution to the joint enterprise entailed in the parties' relationship'.[212] Secondly, there is difficulty with the unjustness element. Could the owner argue that in return for housework he permitted the claimant to stay in the house, or provided for her financially in other ways and it is therefore not unjust to deny her an interest in the property?

6. The court could focus on the nature of the parties' relationship. Gardner[213] has argued that the court should consider whether the relationship of the parties has reached the stage of 'communality'. He criticises the present approach for being individualistic: dealing with disputes using the values of commercial law. It would be better to use values which governed the parties' relationship to resolve their dispute. Gardner suggests that the values promoted by a loving relationship are sharing and communality: 'that the parties have committed themselves to sharing the incidents of the relationship between them – good and bad; wealth and costs; work and enjoyment'.[214] The example he gives, however, demonstrates the great difficulties with his approach. He considers a situation where one person invites another to a meal, but the other is unable at the last minute to turn up. He suggests that if they were not yet a couple there would be no expectation to pay for their share of the food, but if they had reached communality, the one unable to attend would expect to pay for his or her share of the meal. Whether most couples would regard there to be an obligation to pay in such cases is very much open to question. Therein lies the problem: it is extremely difficult for someone from the outside to judge the nature of a relationship. Take sexual relations. For some couples the onset of sexual relations may indicate that the relationship has become a deeply committed one; for other couples, sexual relations may not indicate this at all. These concerns are greater if one considers that judges may not be best placed to assess the nature of younger people's relationships. The communality approach might also require deeply personal details of a relationship to be aired before the court. A further difficulty is that one party may regard the relationship to have reached communality and the other party not. These arguments suggest that although this approach might be the most attractive in theory, there are grave practical problems with it.

7. Another option is to rely on the law of unjust enrichment.[215] The benefit of this approach is that it shifts the focus from why the applicant should be entitled to have a share, to asking whether the defendant should be entitled to keep all the ownership of the property. There may be political benefits too as the argument is no longer attempting to put a cohabitant in the position of a married person, but is seeking to prevent a cohabitant from engaging in fraud-like behaviour.

---

[211] Gupta *et al.* (2010).
[212] Miles (2003: 641).
[213] Gardner (1993). See also Gardner (2004 and 2013).
[214] Gardner (1993).
[215] Douglas, Pearce and Woodward (2009b).

11 Rights to occupy the home

A person has the right to occupy the house if they have an interest in the property under an express trust, resulting trust, constructive trust or a proprietary estoppel. Even if the claimant is unable to establish such an interest, he or she may be able to establish a constructive trust, or a spouse may have a right to occupy the property under a contractual licence or a home right.

A Contractual licences

A contractual licence is a contract under which the owner permits the licensee to occupy the property.[216] The claimant needs to show all the requirements of an ordinary contract. There can be particular difficulties for family members in demonstrating that the owner intended to create legal relations.[217] The holder of the contractual licence might be able to obtain damages if the owner excludes him or her, but the contractual licence will not bind third parties.[218]

B Home rights

(i) When are home rights conferred?

Section 30(1) of the Family Law Act 1996[219] explains when a home right is bestowed. Home rights are conferred in respect of a dwelling-house,[220] which has been or was intended to be the home of the spouses where:

LEGISLATIVE PROVISION

Family Law Act 1996, section 30(1)

(a) one spouse or civil partner ('A') is entitled to occupy a dwelling-house by virtue of—

    (i)   a beneficial estate or interest or contract; or

    (ii) any enactment giving A the right to remain in occupation; and

(b) the other spouse or civil partner ('B') is not so entitled.

The right is also awarded to spouses or civil partners who have an equitable interest in the home.[221] The home right ceases on divorce, dissolution or death of either spouse or civil partner,[222] unless a court orders otherwise.[223]

---

[216] *Tanner v Tanner* [1975] 3 All ER 776.
[217] *Horrocks v Forray* [1976] 1 All ER 737.
[218] *Tanner v Tanner* [1975] 3 All ER 776.
[219] As amended by Civil Partnership Act 2004, Sch 9.
[220] Defined widely in Family Law Act 1996 (hereafter FLA 1996), s. 63 to include, e.g., a caravan
[221] FLA 1996, s. 30(9).
[222] FLA 1996, s. 30(8).
[223] FLA 1996, s. 33(5).

(ii) What do home rights consist of?

A home right consists of:

LEGISLATIVE PROVISION

Family Law Act 1996, section 30(2)

(a) if in occupation, a right not to be evicted or excluded from the dwelling-house or any part of it by the other spouse except with the leave of the court given by an order under section 33;

(b) if not in occupation, a right with leave of the court so given to enter into and occupy the dwelling-house.[224]

The real significance of the right is that, otherwise, the spouse or civil partner without it could be evicted by the other.

Section 30(3) of the 1996 Act states that payments made by the person with the home right in respect of rent or mortgage should be treated by the recipient as if made by the owner or tenant of the property. So, if a husband stops paying rent on a house taken in his name, the wife can pay the rent and the landlord would have to accept the payment as if made by the husband, and so cannot evict her for non-payment of rent.

(iii) Protection of home rights against third parties

The home rights should be protected by a notice on the land register if the land is registered under the Land Registration Act 2002, or as a class F Land Charge if the land is unregistered.[225] The significance of this is that if the owner sells the house to a third party and the home right is registered then the third party must permit the home rights holder to occupy the property.

---

12 The sale of a family home: enforcing trusts

If a cohabiting couple split up, there are two questions for the court. The first is: who owns or has the right to occupy the property? That is the question we have just discussed. The second is whether the property should or may be sold. This is the question which will now be addressed.

If two unmarried cohabitants[226] co-own a property (for example, under a constructive trust), there may then be a dispute over whether or not the property should be sold. The Trusts of Land and Appointment of Trustees Act 1996 governs the present law. Land that is co-owned is now held under a trust of land. The trustees have a power to sell and also a power to postpone sale. Section 14(1) permits any trustee or beneficiary under a trust to apply to the court for an order. The court then has the power to make any order relating to the exercise of the trustees' functions as it sees fit.[227] Most significantly, the court can order the trustees to sell the property and pay

---

[224] FLA 1996, s. 30(2).

[225] The home right is not an overriding interest, even if the holder is in occupation: FLA 1996, s. 31(10)(b).

[226] Disputes between married couples over whether a house should be sold should normally be resolved under the Matrimonial Causes Act 1973, although see *Miller Smith v Miller Smith* [2010] 1 FLR 1402 where the wife was obstructing the divorce and the court was willing to make an order under the Trusts of Land and Appointment of Trustees Act 1996.

[227] According to *Lawrence v Bertram* [2004] FL 323 one party can be ordered to buy out the other party.

the beneficiaries their cash share of the property.[228] The court could also refuse to order sale but require the party remaining in occupation of the home to pay the other 'rent'.[229]

There is a set of guidelines to be considered by the court when deciding whether to exercise its powers.[230] The guidelines are set out in s. 15 of the Trusts of Land and Appointment of Trustees Act 1996. These do not rob the courts of a wide discretion, but rather give them some factors to take into account.[231]

Different guidelines apply to a trustee in bankruptcy.

LEGISLATIVE PROVISION

Trusts of Land and Appointment of Trustees Act 1996, section 15

(a) the intentions of the person or persons (if any) who created the trust,

(b) the purpose for which the property subject to the trust is held,

(c) the welfare of any minor who occupies or might reasonably be expected to occupy any land subject to the trust as his home, and

(d) the interests of any secured creditor of any beneficiary.[232]

The general attitude of the courts has been that a house is bought by the couple as a home, but if they split up then the purpose of the trust has failed (factor (b) above) and a sale can be ordered.[233] If there are children living in the house, the interests of the children will often be an important consideration, particularly if ordering the sale of the property will disrupt their education.[234] The aim of the Act is to give the courts wide discretion, and so each case will be decided on its own special facts.[235] Notably, this is one of those areas of the law where the interests of children are not made paramount.[236]

There have been some attempts to use s. 14 where the parties are divorcing or have divorced. The courts have adopted a strict approach: couples who are divorcing or have divorced must apply for orders under the Matrimonial Causes Act 1973 and may not use the Trusts of Land and Appointment of Trustees Act 1996.[237]

---

13 Conclusion

This chapter has revealed that the law has failed to find a consistent approach to family property. The law in this area is interesting in its treatment of the ownership of the family home. As there is no discretion in the court to redistribute the property of unmarried couples on

---

[228] Trusts of Land and Appointment of Trustees Act 1996, s. 15.

[229] Trusts of Land and Appointment of Trustees Act 1996, s. 13.

[230] See Dixon (2011) for a detailed discussion.

[231] *TSB v Marshall and Rodgers* [1998] 2 FLR 769; *The Mortgage Corp v Shaire* [2000] 1 FLR 973.

[232] Under s. 15(3) the wishes of the majority of the beneficiaries should be taken into account.

[233] *Jones v Challenger* [1961] 1 QB 176 CA. But see *Holman v Howes* [2005] 3 FCR 474 where the woman was promised on purchase that she could stay in the house as long as she needed, and so no sale was ordered.

[234] *Bernard v Joseph* [1982] Ch 391; *Edwards v Lloyds TSB Bank* [2005] 1 FCR 139.

[235] *The Mortgage Corp v Shaire* [2000] 1 FLR 973. See Pawlowski and Brown (2012) for a helpful discussion. The court can order that the property be sold to one of the beneficiaries: *Bagum v Hafiz and Hai* [2015] EWCA Civ 801.

[236] Warren (2002) discusses the impact of bankruptcy on children.

[237] *Laird v Laird* [1999] 1 FLR 791; *Tee v Tee and Hamilton* [1999] 2 FLR 613.

the breakdown of their relationship, the law on who owns the family home is particularly important for them. This has led the court to develop (manipulate, some would say) land law to enable a cohabitant to establish an interest in a home even if the normal formality requirements that attach to the transfer of interests in land have not been complied with. The current law is widely seen as unsatisfactory. In particular it appears to give exaggerated emphasis to conversations between the parties and inadequate weight to how they live their relationships and what disadvantages they suffer or gains they make from living together. The Law Commission proposals which seek to ensure a fair distribution of the economic gains and disadvantages from the relationship have much to commend them.

Further reading

Chan, W. (2013) 'Cohabitation, civil partnership, marriage and the equal sharing principle', *Legal Studies* 33: 1.

Dixon, M. (2010) 'Confining and defining proprietary estoppel: the role of unconscionability', *Legal Studies* 30: 408.

Dixon, M. (2011) 'To sell or not to sell: that is the question of the irony of the Trusts of Land and Appointment of Trustees Act 1996', *Cambridge Law Journal* 70: 579.

Fox, L. (2006) *Conceptualising Home: Theories, Law and Policies*, Oxford: Hart.

Galloway, K. (2019) 'The role of Pateman's Sexual Contract in beneficial interests in property', *Feminist Legal Studies* 27: 263.

Gardner, S. (1993) 'Rethinking family property', *Law Quarterly Review* 109: 263.

Gardner, S. (2013) 'Problems in family property', *Cambridge Law Journal* 72: 301.

Hayward, A. (2012) '"Family property" and the process of "familialisation" of property law', *Child and Family Law Quarterly* 18: 284.

Law Commission Report 278 (2002) *Sharing Homes*, London: The Stationery Office.

Leckey, R. (2019) 'Cohabitation, female sacrifice, and judge-made law', *Journal of Social Welfare and Family Law* 41: 72.

Miles, J. and Probert, R. (eds) (2009a) *Sharing Lives, Dividing Assets*, Oxford: Hart.

Pahl, J. (2005) 'Individualisation in couples' finances', *Social Policy and Society* 4: 4.

Sloan, B. (2015a) 'Keeping up with the *Jones* case: establishing constructive trusts in "sole legal owner" scenarios', *Legal Studies* 35: 226.

Wong, S. (2009) 'Caring and sharing: interdependency as a basis for property redistribution', in A. Bottomley and S. Wong (eds) *Changing Contours of Domestic Life, Family and Law*, Oxford: Hart.

Visit **go.pearson.com/uk/he/resources** to access **resources** specifically written to complement this text.

6 Property on separation

Learning objectives

When you finish reading this chapter you will be able to:

1. Discuss the theoretical issues around child support
2. Examine the law on child support
3. Summarise the powers available to the court in financial disputes
4. Debate the issues around spousal support
5. Describe how the relevant provisions of the Matrimonial Causes Act 1973 relate to financial disputes
6. Evaluate the principles developed by the courts in financial cases
7. Assess the law on pre-nuptial agreements

1 Introduction

In 2009 a man who was divorcing his wife sought the return of his kidney that he donated to her when she needed a transplant.[1] He failed, of course, but it's a powerful metaphor for the difficulties that can arise in seeking to divide a couple's property on divorce or dissolution. There is a widespread perception that divorce causes financial ruin for a wealthy spouse, although, as we shall see, it is women who generally do particularly badly out of divorce. The process can certainly be profitable for lawyers. In 2018 a couple spent over a million pounds in costs and were left with no liquid assets, only debts.[2]

It is notable that while a couple are married or civil partners the law does little to interfere in the property interests of the parties. By contrast, on separation the law is willing to intervene to ensure that the spouse's or civil partner's financial interests are adequately protected. The law distinguishes financial support for children from financial support for partners. In relation to child support, the law is now governed by the Child Maintenance and Other Payments Act 2008 and, to a lesser extent, the Children Act 1989. The 2008 Act replaces the previous child support scheme in the Child Support Act 1991. The child support legislation applies equally to parents who are married, civil partners and those who are unmarried. However, in

[1] BBC News Online (2009d).
[2] *Daga v Bangur* [2018] EWFC 91

relation to financial support for partners an important distinction is drawn between spouses or civil partners and unmarried couples. For married couples and civil partners, the courts have the power to redistribute the family's property between the parties as they consider just, taking into account all the circumstances of the case. For unmarried couples the courts can simply declare who owns what, and have no power to require one party to transfer property to another, except as a means of providing child support. (We discussed the law on property ownership in Chapter 5.) This chapter will not explore the enforcement of financial orders, which raises complex issues.

2 Child support: theoretical issues

Learning objective 1

Discuss the theoretical issues around child support

There is grave concern over the economic circumstances in which many children are brought up in the United Kingdom. There were 4.2 million children living in poverty in the United Kingdom in 2019. That is 30 per cent of all children.[3] The Child Poverty Act 2010 places a statutory duty on the Secretary of State to eradicate child poverty by 2020.[4] However, child poverty increased by 600,000 between 2011/12 and 2018/19. Current projections are that child poverty will increase to 5.2 million by 2022.[5] So, sadly, since the 2010 Act, far from eradicating child poverty, the problem has worsened. The issue has a major race dimension with 46 per cent of BAME children now in poverty, compared with 26 per cent of children in White British families. There are particular concerns about children of lone parents. Almost half of all lone parent households are in poverty.[6]

As this discussion demonstrates, the question of financial support is crucial if children's interests are to be adequately protected. The issue raises some important questions of theory, which will now be discussed.

A Does the obligation to support children fall on the state or on the parents?

A key issue concerning child support is: on whom does the burden of support for children primarily fall?[7] Ultimately, is the state responsible for the financial support of children (although the state can recoup the money from parents) or are the parents responsible (although the state can step in to support children if the parents fail)? In other words, is it the state's primary role to enforce parental responsibility to pay child support, or to provide guaranteed support itself for the child? Krause suggests that the obligation is shared between society and the parents: 'children have a right to a decent start in life. This right is the obligation of the father and equally of the mother, and in recognition of a primary and direct responsibility, equally the obligation of society.'[8]

Looking at this issue from another angle, it is possible to regard the question as one of children's rights. If it is accepted that children should have rights, it seems inevitable that

---

[3] Child Poverty Action Group (2020). Poverty here is defined as below 60 per cent of contemporary median net disposable household income after housing costs.
[4] Although see Palmer (2010) for a sceptical consideration of the statute.
[5] Penington (2020).
[6] Child Poverty Action Group (2020).
[7] See the excellent discussion in Ferguson (2008).
[8] Krause (1994: 232).

children have a right to the financial support necessary so that they can, at least, be fed and clothed.[9] Article 27(4) of the United Nations Convention on the Rights of the Child declares: 'State parties shall take all appropriate measures to secure the recovery of maintenance for the child from the parents or other persons having financial responsibility for the child, both within the State Party and from abroad . . . ' Given that the state is a more reliable supporter than the parent, it is in the child's interests that the state should have the primary obligation to ensure children receive sufficient support, but how the state's obligation is performed may vary from family to family.

We shall be discussing the legislation shortly but the Child Support Act 1991 regarded the burden of child support as clearly on the parents, and sees the Government's role as 'helping' parents to meet their responsibility.[10] Such an approach can also be seen in the Child Maintenance and Other Payments Act 2008 which emphasises the importance of parents negotiating with each other the appropriate level of child support, with even less direct assistance from the state. The Child Poverty Act 2010, however, recognises that the state has obligations too. The question is made even more complex in that the state's approach to child support may seek to pursue a variety of aims. As well as ensuring that the child is adequately provided for, a scheme may also endeavour to discourage births out of marriage; to punish unmarried fathers; or to decrease the legal aid costs associated with relationship breakdown.[11]

There are three main aspects of the state's response to poverty among children. First, there is a complex system of benefits and tax credits for low-income and unemployed parents. The state does recognise some obligation to *all* children by providing child benefit payments to all parents regardless of wealth,[12] although since 2010 child benefit is not paid to higher rate taxpayers. Second, there are the incentives on all parents to seek employment, especially on those currently claiming benefits.[13] The current Government's policies on child poverty are primarily directed towards encouraging parents to work (e.g. by increasing the provision of childcare), rather than by giving increased benefits to non-working parents.[14] Fortin is critical of such an approach. She claims that:

> [D]espite the Government's assertions that 'Work is good for you' work clearly does not increase the income of all families and may not benefit all children . . . The confident claims that work produces good outcomes for children are also surprising given the lack of agreement over the potential impact on young children of long-term nursery care, rather than full-time maternal care at home.[15]

Third, there is the child support legislation that seeks to find an effective way to ensure money for child support is paid by non-residential parents (those parents who no longer live with the child). A Government document on child support states:

> Parents, whether they live together or not, have a clear moral as well as legal responsibility to maintain their children. Relationships end. Responsibilities do not. Government and society as a whole have a clear interest in making sure these responsibilities are honoured.[16]

Sally Sheldon, by contrast, is not convinced that the present law adequately protects the interests of children. She argues: 'Leaving children dependent on the economic means of their

---

[9] Wikeley (2006c).
[10] Department of Social Security (2000: 1).
[11] Krause (1994).
[12] See Ferguson (2008) for further discussion of the state's responsibility to children
[13] A useful summary is Douglas (2000a).
[14] Daly and Scheiwe (2010).
[15] Fortin (2009b: 340–1).
[16] Department for Work and Pensions (2006c: 1).

parents has contributed significantly to the widespread poverty of women and children and, in countries where the wealth to rectify this situation exists, this should be cause for national shame.'[17] She therefore argues that the state should be regarded as primarily responsible for the financial support of children.

B Are the parents' obligations independent or joint?

Accepting that parents are obliged to support their children, the question is then whether parents are separately responsible for the support of the child or whether they share this burden, in that each parent should only be expected to pay their own half of the child support. If, for example, a mother who is receiving income support is raising the child, should a non-residential employed father be required to pay all the expenses of the child or only 'his half' of them?[18] Or is a non-resident father expected to pay child support if the mother is earning significantly more than he is? It is arguable that the residential parent provides her 'share' of the child support through the time and effort she puts in day to day for the child, and that therefore the full financial burden should fall on the non-residential parent.[19]

C Biological or social parents?

If children should be supported jointly by their parents, the next question is: What is meant by parents in this context? Specifically, where a parent has both stepchildren and biological children, how should his or her resources be shared between them? Imagine A and B have a child, Y. A moves out and later lives with C, who has a child, X, by a previous relationship. Should A support Y or X? Or should he try to support both? Prior to the Child Support Act 1991, the practice in many cases was that if a man left his first family and later moved in with a second family, he would provide for the second family and the state would support the first family through benefits. The Child Support Act 1991 and Child Maintenance and Other Payments Act 2008 attach liability to biological parenthood. So, in our example, A is liable in law to support Y and not X.[20] Interestingly, one study suggests that this is in line with the views of children whose parents have separated.[21] Gillian Douglas[22] makes the case for why this should be so:

> The act of knowingly engaging in behaviour that runs the risk that a child will be created who will be vulnerable and dependent is a valid moral basis for imposing the prior obligation to support that child. Causation both reflects the current legal rationale for the duty to maintain the child and provides a valid and sufficient moral basis for it, which caters for the situation where the parent is not committed to the child.

There are a number of issues here:

1. *Should financial responsibility be linked with parental responsibility?* Is it fair that under English and Welsh law an unmarried father is automatically required to support the child financially, but is not automatically granted parental responsibility? It can be argued that as it is inevitably in the child's interests to receive financial support from his or her father, but not inevitably in the child's interest for his or her father to have parental responsibility,

---

[17] Sheldon (2003: 193).
[18] Young and Wikeley (2015).
[19] Eekelaar (1991a: 111).
[20] See Chapter 8 for a general discussion on the differences between biological and social parenthood.
[21] Peacey and Rainford (2004) found that 81 per cent of respondents agreed that non-resident parents had an obligation to support their child.
[22] Douglas (2016).

the position can be justified. For example, if the father does not know the child at all, it may be in the child's interests to require him to pay but not to permit him to make decisions on the child's behalf. However, from a father's perspective the position appears most unjust.[23] Indeed, there is some evidence that both mothers and fathers in their minds link the payment of child support and contact.[24]

2. *Should financial responsibility be coupled with social parenting?* It could be argued that the law should match fiscal legal liability with the feelings of social or moral obligation that parents have. This, it has been maintained, would make the law more effective and acceptable. Eekelaar and Maclean found in their survey that fathers thought financial obligations should be tied to the social role played by fathers, but mothers thought the obligations should follow the blood tie.[25] The study demonstrated that there was a strong link between payment of financial support and contact with the child. Where the father had contact with the child, he was more likely to support the child than where he did not. Eekelaar and Maclean argued:

> A support obligation which accompanies or arises from social parenthood is embedded in that social parenthood; thus the payment of support can be seen as part of the relationship maintained by continued contact. But an obligation based on natural parenthood rests on the policy of instilling a sense of responsibility for individual action and equity between fathers who do and fathers who do not exercise social parenthood.[26]

The workings of the child support legislation in practice has revealed that where there is an ongoing level of contact between the non-resident parent and the child there is more likely to be payment of child support and that such payments are perceived to be fair.[27]

3. *Should it matter whether the pregnancy was planned or not?* Hale J in *J v C (Child: Financial Provision)*[28] confirmed that liability under the Children Act 1989 and the Child Support Act 1991 did not depend on whether the pregnancy was planned or not. Although it may be understandable that, from a parent's perspective, whether the pregnancy was planned or not should be relevant in determining liability, from the child's viewpoint he or she should not be prejudiced because of his or her parents' attitudes at the time of the conception.[29] That said, some commentators have argued that the man should be liable only if he has intentionally impregnated the mother and thereby can be said to have consented to taking on the financial liability.[30] As Kapp has argued:

> To saddle a man with at least eighteen years of expensive, exhausting child support liability on the basis of a haphazard vicissitude of life seems to shock the conscience and be arbitrary, capricious, and unreasonable, where childbirth results from the mother's free choice . . . a man no longer has any control over the course of a pregnancy he has biologically brought about [and] it is unjust to impose responsibility where there is no ability to exercise control.[31]

---

[23] By contrast, in *P v B (Paternity; Damages for Deceit)* [2001] 1 FLR 1041 a father sued in deceit his cohabitant whom he claimed had falsely told him her child was his, leading to him paying £90,000 by way of child support.

[24] Herring (2003a).

[25] Eekelaar and Maclean (1997). These might not reflect the views of the public at large: Herring (1998b: 214).

[26] Eekelaar and Maclean (1997: 150).

[27] Davis and Wikeley (2002).

[28] [1999] 1 FLR 152, [1998] 3 FCR 79.

[29] Spon-Smith (2002: 29) notes a case in which a man who was deceived into thinking that he was the father of a child was refunded by the CSA £30,000 that he had paid by way of child support when it turned out he was not the father.

[30] Brake (2005).

[31] Kapp (1982: 376–7).

Others argue that, at least, a father should not be liable if he has been misled by the mother into believing that she is using contraception or is infertile.[32] There is, perhaps, here a clash between what may be fair to the father and what is in the interests of the child. Nick Wikeley[33] has written:

> There is an unspoken value judgment that child support is not a right of the child but an imposition on the father which must be construed as restrictively as possible . . . such a perspective is based upon the Lockean philosophical tradition which emphasizes property rights and individual autonomy and views child support as a taking which demands a justification. The result is that the rights of the parent and the children inevitably come a poor second to those of the non-resident parent.

D What level should the support be?

There are many options for setting the correct level of child support. Some of the options are:

1. *Subsistence costs*. This would be the amount of money that would be necessary to support the child at a minimally decent level. It could be assumed to be the amount of the welfare payment from the state that would be paid in respect of the child.

2. *Acceptable costs*. This would be the estimated level of support required to keep a child at a reasonably acceptable standard of living. It might be suitable to look at the level of payments made by local authorities to foster parents as a guide for the appropriate figure.

3. *Expected lifestyle costs*. This would be the amount needed to keep the child at the lifestyle level which would have been expected had the parents not separated. The argument would be the child should not suffer a change in lifestyle because of a decision of their parents.

4. *Actual expenditure*. The law could focus on the amount actually spent by the residential parent, in so far as it was reasonable, and require the non-residential parent to share these costs. The difficulty with this approach would be the ambiguity which surrounds the term 'reasonableness'. The average cost of raising a child until the age of 21 has recently been calculated at £227,226.[34]

5. *Cost-effective level*. The amount of support should be fixed at a level which can be regularly paid. That might be a fixed percentage of the non-residential parent's income. This approach is highly pragmatic. It focuses not on the child but on the expense to the state of enforcing and collecting the payments. It argues that, whatever the ideal, if the level is fixed at too high a rate and seen as unfair, then the money will not be paid. It is therefore better to set a lower rate which is more likely to be paid and thereby avoid the costs of enforcement.

6. *Equality of households*. This approach would seek to achieve an equal standard of living between the father's and mother's households. This would not necessarily mean fixing equal income, because the cost of caring for the child would involve the residential parent in greater expense. This method requires integration of the maintenance of the parent with support for the child.

---

[32] See further the discussion in Sheldon (2001a).
[33] Wikeley (2005: 98).
[34] Osborne (2014).

E Paternity fraud

There have been cases where a man has paid child support after being falsely told that he was the father of a child. In *A v B (Damages: Paternity)*[35] a man obtained damages against a former partner for deceit in relation to a paternity issue. He was awarded damages to compensate him for sums paid for the benefit of the child, but he could not recover the sums spent on his partner. In *FRB v DCA*[36] a husband found out on divorce that the child he and his wife had raised was not, as he believed, his. He sued in the tort of deceit for damages, but it was held the issue was better dealt with under the Matrimonial Causes Act 1973, rather than a tort claim. That was not an option in *A v B (Damages: Paternity)*, as there the couple were unmarried.

F Lone-parent poverty

It is difficult to separate the question of child support from concerns over the position of lone parents. There has been a substantial increase in the number of lone-parent households. In 2019 in England and Wales there were 2.9 million lone parent households; a lone parent headed 14.9 per cent of families. In 1971 the figure was 8 per cent.[37] The reaction to the increase in lone parenthood has been varied.[38] Some see lone parents as an alarming sign of social disintegration, while others view lone parenthood as a crucial aspect of the liberation of women from the traditional family.[39] As discussed (in Chapter 3), while there is general agreement that children in lone parents families do less well than children raised in two parent households, there is much debate as to why this is so. Some argue that the root cause of the disadvantage faced by children of lone parents is the poverty associated with lone parenthood, while others cite the lack of a father figure or stable family background as the primary cause. In political terms, these arguments lead to debates over whether state benefits to lone parents encourage lone parenthood and so should be restricted or whether such benefits help alleviate the disadvantages attached to lone parenthood and should be increased.

Although it is common to refer to 'the problem of lone mothers', it might be more appropriate to refer to 'the problem of non-residential fathers'. Lady Thatcher, who as Prime Minister had steered the Child Support Act 1991 through Parliament, notably recalled in her memoirs that she was 'appalled by the way in which men fathered a child and then absconded, leaving the single mother – and the taxpayer – to foot the bill for their irresponsibility and condemning the child to a lower standard of living'.[40] Similar attitudes were expressed when it was disclosed that a 21-year-old man had just fathered his seventh child.[41] But a better way to express this concern may be not shocked by the 'immorality' of the father, but concerned at the poverty of the children. Some 4.5 million children are eligible to receive payments from non-resident parents, but fewer than a third actually receive anything at all. Many others receive only a small portion of the sum due to them.[42] Currently under the Child Support Act 1991 system, which only deals with some cases, just under £4 billion of child support is due

---

[35] [2007] 3 FCR 861, discussed in Wikeley and Young (2008). See also *P v B (Paternity: Damages for Deceit)* [2001] 1 FLR 1041.
[36] [2019] EWHC 2816 (Fam).
[37] Office for National Statistics (2020a).
[38] Fox Harding (1996).
[39] Morgan (2007).
[40] Thatcher (1995: 630).
[41] BBC News Online (2006h).
[42] Bryson *et al.* (2013).

but has not been paid. Government benefits do not make up the shortfall. The children of lone parents suffer considerable poverty levels, with the legal regime doing little to protect them.

G Child support and parental support

If a parent is obliged to support a child, should he or she necessarily be required to provide for the residential parent?[43] There is no point in supplying a child with food and clothing if there is no one to feed or clothe the child. So, a strong case can be made that if a child is to be cared for by a residential parent, then the non-residential parent should be liable to support the residential parent at some level. Another key question is how to balance the claims of children and spouses on divorce. A straightforward approach could be that first the courts should resolve the issues related to the child's support, and then turn to spousal support. In truth, for most couples nowadays, child support takes up such a large part of income that very limited resources are available for spousal support.

H Should child support be a private issue?

Should the level of child support be fixed by the Government or is it a private matter to be left to negotiation between the parties? In considering this issue it is useful to distinguish cases where the child and resident parent are receiving state benefits and cases where they are not. Where they are, the state has a clear interest in ensuring that the non-resident parent recompenses the state for the amount paid out in benefits, if he or she can afford to do so. But if neither party is in receipt of benefits, does the state have an interest, justifying intervention, in how the parties decide to arrange child support? For example, if a couple decide that the best way to arrange their post-separation finances is that the wife and children will receive the former matrimonial home, but to compensate the husband for his loss in the share of the house he will have to pay less by way of financial support than he would have done, is it proper for the state to intervene to require the husband to pay a certain minimum amount? Or should this be regarded as a private matter which should be left to the decision of the couple themselves? It could be argued that the issue of child poverty is an important one for the state, and parents should not be permitted to enter an agreement which leaves the child only barely provided for.[44] However, the Child Maintenance and Other Payments Act 2008 is based on the principle that individuals should negotiate for themselves child payments, and the primary role of the state is to assist in these negotiations and give effect to them.

3 Financial support of children

A Financial support of children living with both parents

A crucial point about the present law is that generally it does not intervene in the financial affairs of a family who are living together. As long as the child is provided for at a basic level and the child is not suffering significant harm, the state will not interfere. Indeed, many fathers have complained that they are required to pay more for their child after the separation than they did when living with the child. It is on parental separation that the law intervenes and can require a parent not just to provide for the basic needs of the child, but also to apply a fair

[43] See the discussion on Children Act 1989, Sched. 1 below.
[44] Wikeley (2006c).

level of support. This non-intervention in family life except upon the separation of parents is one aspect of the weight the law places on the protection of the private life of the family.[45] In fact, a child who wishes to complain that he or she is not being given enough pocket money could seek an order under s. 8 of the Children Act 1989, but it is hard to imagine a court being willing to hear such a case!

B The Child Maintenance and Other Payments Act 2008

Learning objective 2

Examine the law on child support

Frankly, the current law is in a mess. The Child Maintenance and Other Payments Act 2008 now governs the law on child support.[46] It was intended to replace the Child Support Act 1991 and the work of the Child Support Agency. The old system was widely regarded as a failure, as the following statistics demonstrate.

KEY STATISTICS

- By March 2016 the accumulated debt under the Child Support Act 1991 owed by non-resident parents since 1993 stood at over £3.9 billion. A report in 2019 concluded that £3.7 billion of unpaid arrears would have to be written off.[47] Of that sum £2.5 billion would have gone to children, many of whom were living in poverty.

- 30% of non-resident parents who had been assessed did not pay.

- Under the Child Support Act 1991 it cost around 60 pence in administration costs to get each £1 of maintenance to a child.

- Only one-half of lone parents had a maintenance order or agreement in their favour. Where they did, only 64% received anything.[48] Of all parents with care on benefits, only 25% were actually receiving any money from the Agency.[49] As the legislation was especially designed to help this group, this is particularly disappointing.

These figures represent but the tip of the iceberg of a range of problems for the old system. There was widespread miscalculation of the sums due; those seeking to contact the Agency found it almost impossible to get through on the telephone;[50] morale among staff at the Agency was generally seen as appallingly low; and there was little use of the Agency's enforcement powers.[51] The Government announced that the Child Support Agency (CSA) would be abandoned and replaced under the Child Maintenance and Other Payments Act 2008. However, the implementation of that legislation has been a long and tortuous process. Currently there are a few cases still being dealt with under the 1991 Act scheme, but most under the 2008 Act. So, for now we will focus on the 2008 Act scheme as that is the one predominantly in use.

The key principles are as follows. A parent, either a mother or father, who is not living with their child is liable to pay child support for that child. The definition of the parent is that as

---

[45] See Chapter 1.
[46] As amended by the Welfare Reform Act 2012.
[47] Jarrett (2019).
[48] Willitts et al. (2005).
[49] Wikeley (2006b).
[50] House of Commons Work and Pensions Committee (2005).
[51] Wikeley (2006b).

defined in law.[52] It does not apply to parents living outside the United Kingdom.[53] A child is a person under 16 or a person under 20 who is in full-time education.[54] The Act only applies to separated parents. The 'parent with care' does not need to provide child support, but the other does. The term parent with care refers to the parent providing day-to-day hands-on care.[55] Where care is shared an assessment is made as to who is the resident and who is the non-resident parent, based on the amount of care provided.[56]

When a couple separate, they have two choices in relation to child support:

1. They can reach their own agreement. That is known as a 'family-based agreement' and it is clear this is the option which is most strongly encouraged. If that happens there is no official involvement in the agreement. It does not need to be approved by a court. A government agency, Child Maintenance Options, can provide information to facilitate an agreement.

2. A party can apply to the Child Maintenance Service (CMS), although only after contact has been made with Child Maintenance Options who can advise on and encourage a 'family-based agreement'. The CMS explain they can assist with matters such as the following:

   - try to find the other parent if you don't know where they live, to sort out child maintenance
   - sort out disagreements about parentage
   - work out how much child maintenance should be paid
   - arrange for the 'paying' parent to pay child maintenance – the parent who doesn't have main day-to-day care of the child
   - pass payments on to the 'receiving' parent – the parent who has main day-to-day care of the child
   - look at the payments again when changes in parents' circumstances are reported
   - review the payment amount every year
   - take action if payments aren't made.[57]

To apply to use one of these services there is a £20 fee, although that is not payable for victims of domestic violence or those under 19. There are also charges if the CMS has to take enforcement measures. For example, there is a £300 fee if they seek a liability order.

If the CMS is asked to work out how much maintenance is to be paid it undertakes a 'maintenance calculation'. In most cases this is worked out using the 'basic rate'. For those whose income is between £200 and £800 per week, the figures are as follows:

- 12 per cent of gross income for one child;
- 16 per cent of gross income for two children;
- 19 per cent of gross income for three or more children.

---

[52] Child Support Act 1991, s. 54. See Chapter 8.
[53] Although there are exceptions for those employed in the civil service, the armed forces or UK companies. In *Ipekci v McConnell* [2019] EWFC 19 Mostyn J made a financial order under the MCA, which was made on the basis a wife would not claim in the CSA and said an indemnity would be paid if she did.
[54] Not including higher education
[55] *GR v CMEC* [2011] UKUT 101 (AAC).
[56] *MR v Secretary of State for Work & Pensions* [2018] UKUT 340 (AAC).
[57] HM Government (2016a).

It seems once you have three children, you can have as many as you like at no extra cost! For those with gross weekly income above £800 the percentages are:

- 9 per cent of gross income for one child;
- 12 per cent of gross income for two children;
- 15 per cent of gross income for three or more children.

These percentages do not apply to income over £3,000 per week, which is, in effect, ignored in any calculation.

These percentages can be amended in the following cases:

1. Where a non-resident parent has other 'qualifying children'[58] in which case there will be an 11 per cent reduction for one other child; 14 per cent reduction for two; and 16 per cent for three or more.

2. If the non-resident parent's gross weekly income is between £100 and £200, they pay a reduced rate, but that may not be less than £7.

3. If the non-resident parent's gross weekly income is £100 or less then a flat rate £7 per week is payable.

4. If the non-resident parent's income is below £7 then they need pay nothing.

5. If the non-resident parent has other children who are being maintained under a mainte-nance order or agreement, there is an apportionment between the maintained children. Similarly, if a parent is due to pay for children living in different households an apportion-ment operates to ensure each child receives a reasonable sum.

6. If the non-resident parent has the child to stay overnight then the following reductions apply depending on how many nights a year the child spends:

    - for 52–103 nights: a one-seventh reduction;
    - for 104–155 nights: a two-sevenths reduction;
    - for 156–174 nights: a three-sevenths reduction;
    - for more than 175: a half reduction.

    This can be understood as a way to encourage the non-resident parent to have the child to stay and keep up contact. Indeed, for the price of a burger and a DVD it might seem a good economic bargain. It might be thought unfair to parents who incur expenses in looking after the children during the day. It might be thought unfair also to the resident parent who has a nearly equal split of care for the child but still needs to pay half the maintenance.

7. In exceptional cases a variation from the calculation can be made under s. 28F of the 2008 Act if the Child Maintenance Services believes it would be equitable to do so.[59] The kind of cases envisaged are where there are exceptional costs in travelling to work or maintaining contact with the child.

If the Child Maintenance Service has made an assessment it has a wide range of enforcement powers set out in s. 31 of the 1991 Act. This includes ordering an employer to deduct child support from earnings or applying to the court for an order that goods can be sold and even for an order disqualifying the non-payer from having a driving licence.

---

[58] These may be children living with him. They are children for whom he or his non-resident partner is receiving child benefit.

[59] Detailed regulations are found in Sched. 4B of the 2008 Act.

A major problem with the scheme is that it is a little crude. In *EG v CA*[60] the father had assets worth over £5 million, but he had arranged his wealth so that he was only paying the minimum £7 per week child support. The court were critical of the fact that there was no process under the child support system for assessing him on the basis of his apparent (rather than paper) wealth. Mostyn J called on the Government to urgently consider reform. The charity Gingerbread's report, *Children Deserve More*[61] claimed that parents were discouraged from using the Child Maintenance Options gateway through charging a £20 fee and increased costs where the administration manages payments: the recipient suffers a 4 per cent deduction in the amount received and the payer must pay 20 per cent more. The latest statistics suggest that at the end of March 2020, 737,600 arrangements were managed by CMS.[62] Of these, 471,700 were using the direct payment scheme, 111,700 were paying nothing at all, and 149,400 were paying something; CMS said there was a 68 per cent compliance rate, although 'compliance' including making some, but not all payments. More revealing is the fact that £354 million of child support was recorded as unpaid by CMS in 2019/20. It has been claimed that fewer than half of lone parents receive the support they are entitled to.[63] The situation will worsen with COVID as the DWP has decided to allow payers to CMS to stop payment if they are having difficulties in payment. This will deprive children of income, with no replacement.[64]

C The encouragement to agree

Although we have just looked at how CMS will calculate payment, it is clearly the Government's hope that most couples will reach agreement themselves and they will not need to rely on the Government to help them. As already mentioned, Child Maintenance Options[65] will offer advice and will facilitate people to reach their own agreement. Their website[66] provides suggestions on how an appropriate figure might be agreed. It explains:

> The quickest and easiest way to arrange child maintenance is for you and the other parent to set up an arrangement between yourselves. More than half a million children in the United Kingdom now benefit from this kind of family-based arrangement.
>
> You and the other parent can work together to make an arrangement between yourselves that suits your own circumstances. You can agree on the amount and how often payments are paid or received, and you can choose to include other kinds of support, for example, providing school uniforms.

Whether relying on couples to reach their own agreement is a realistic goal or not remains to be seen. If the Government found it impossible to produce a formula under the old law which was regarded as fair or to enforce effectively child support payments, is there any reason to suspect parents will be any more effective at doing so? Indeed, it is worth remembering that the whole reason the CSA was created was due to the problems lone parents faced in seeking to collect child maintenance.

There is much to be concerned about in leaving the issue of child support to parental agreement. Baroness Hollis noted that non-resident fathers were likely to welcome the reforms:

[60] [2017] EWFC 52 and [2017] EWFC 24.
[61] Gingerbread (2018).
[62] CMS (2020).
[63] Gingerbread (2020).
[64] Gingerbread (2020).
[65] Originally, the Child Maintenance and Enforcement Commission (CMEC) was to have this role, but it was abolished before it really got going.
[66] https://www.gov.uk/making-child-maintenance-arrangement.

They think that they will get a better deal; they think that they will pay less money; they think that there will be less pressure on them to pay; and they think that they will be able to hug knowledge and information that she – the parent with care – will not have and which will allow them, to a degree, to control what they pay.[67]

As Nick Wikeley puts it: 'There is a clear risk, in the absence of adequate advice and support services, that any existing power imbalances between parents will simply be reinforced, to the detriment of children's interests.'[68]

A survey found that 24 per cent of those on benefits said that if left to their own devices they would agree that the non-resident parent would not have to pay child support.[69] Another survey found that under the old scheme, when the Child Support Agency was involved, six out of 10 mothers received the child support due, but where the Agency was not involved and the parties dealt with the issue themselves, only four out of 10 mothers did.[70] Of schemes under the CMS, the Government states that 77 per cent are working 'effectively'.[71] If that reflects what happens when the Act is in operation it will mean that children will lose out significantly under the new legislation. Not surprisingly, surveys suggest that the new regime is welcomed by twice as many non-resident parents as resident parents.[72]

In *Supporting Separated Families; Securing Children's Futures*, the Government set out its thinking behind the new scheme.[73] It notes the current system is not efficient:

> We believe that the current child maintenance system places too much emphasis on the state determining financial support and not enough on supporting separated and separating families to reach their own arrangements. Research shows that only an estimated one in five parents makes their own child maintenance arrangements. Despite the Government spending almost half a billion pounds per annum on the child maintenance system, only half of children in separated families benefit from effective maintenance arrangements.

While these are genuine problems it is far from clear that encouraging family-based agreements or the work of the CMS is going to produce better results. The statistics cited indicate there are still very high sums of unpaid maintenance.

One way in which couples are encouraged to reach their own agreement is through the fees that are chargeable to those using the CMS. Critics will argue that given the levels of poverty among children and that child support should be seen as a right of the child, charging is inappropriate. There will be an upfront assessment fee of £20.[74] There will also be fees for collecting sums due. As Gillian Douglas notes:

> The paying parent is required to pay 20% on top of the calculated amount, and 4% is deducted from the amount paid to the recipient. If a parent is sufficiently determined, deluded or desperate to overcome these hurdles [to using the CMS], she will then find that, should the Service fail to collect the payments due, she has no standing to seek to recover the money herself.[75]

Another concern is that the new scheme does not do enough for victims of domestic violence. Encouraging them to negotiate child maintenance payments themselves may be dangerous.

---

[67] Quoted in Wikeley (2008a: 1027).
[68] Wikeley (2008a: 1027).
[69] Wikeley *et al.* (2008).
[70] Bryson *et al.* (2013).
[71] O'Reilly (2019).
[72] Wikeley *et al.* (2008).
[73] Department for Work and Pensions (2012).
[74] This will not be applied if the applicant has declared that they are a victim of domestic violence, or if they are aged 18 or under.
[75] Douglas (2016).

Further, they are required to disclose financial information which can be available to the other party and might disclose their current whereabouts.[76] Kristin Natalier[77] claims that former partners can withhold child support as a means of continuing to control and abuse their partners.

In very limited circumstances the court can make a top up order. The ground most likely to be used is that the gross income of the non-resident parent exceeds £3,000 gross per week. The problem is that with very wealthy parents who might have income of this kind, they are likely to be able to disguise their income and an application cannot be made based on their wealth in terms of capital assets.[78]

So, in a sense, under the new scheme we are seeing a return to the position before the 1991 Child Support Act where the responsibility of collection of child support is put into the hands of the resident parent. Given the importance of child support in relieving poverty it is striking that rather than seeking to make the Child Support Agency more effective, the state's responsibility is being reduced. If the resident parent is in desperate need of money and the non-resident parent is reluctant to pay this hardly puts them in an equal bargaining position when deciding how much the non-resident parent should pay. It is hard to believe the new scheme will produce higher levels of child support being paid.

D The Children Act 1989 and child support

The Children Act 1989 can require parents to support children, regardless of whether the parents are married or unmarried. This is an important part of ensuring that the law governing the financial support of children does not depend on whether the parents were married or not. However, in practice the Children Act 1989 has been very little used, in part because so few separating cohabitants seek advice from solicitors.[79]

(i) Who can apply under the Children Act 1989?

The following people can apply for a financial order under s. 15 of the Children Act 1989 in respect of a child:

1. A parent. This includes adoptive parents as well as natural parents. It also includes 'any party to a marriage (whether or not subsisting) in relation to whom the child . . . is a child of the family'.[80] A step-parent would be covered by the definition.

2. A guardian.

3. Any person who has a residence order in force in respect of a child.

4. An adult student, or trainee, or other person who can show special circumstances can apply for an order against his or her parents.[81] This order cannot be made if both parents are living together in the same household. So, for example, if the child's parents are still happily married or cohabiting the law will not intervene to force them to provide for the student's upkeep.[82]

---

[76] Stone (2016).
[77] Natalier (2018).
[78] O'Reilly (2019).
[79] Maclean *et al.* (2002).
[80] See Chapter 8 for further discussion of this term.
[81] E.g. *C* v *F (Disabled Child: Maintenance Orders)* [1999] 1 FCR 39, [1998] 2 FLR 1.
[82] The only orders these applicants can claim are periodical payments or lump sum orders.

The court in its own discretion can make an order under the section, even if there has been no application. For example, if the child has been made a ward of court, the court might make an award under the Act.

(ii) Who is liable to pay?

1. *Parents.* This includes biological parents and adoptive parents. A parent is liable to pay even if he or she does not have parental responsibility or never sees the child. A person who has played the role of a parent, but is not a parent in the eyes of the law, cannot be made liable.[83] In theory a resident parent could be ordered to pay to a non-resident parent but that would require most unusual circumstances.[84]

2. *Those who have treated the child as a child of the family.* This can only apply to spouses or civil partners. An unmarried cohabitant of the mother, who is not the father of the child, will not be liable.[85]

(iii) Orders which can be made

Under the Children Act 1989 periodical payments and lump sum orders can be made.[86] A periodic payment order cannot be made, unless the court is varying a consent order for periodic payments.[87] In such a case the court should 'almost invariably' make an order which would match the formula that the child support legislation would use.[88] The court cannot get around this restriction on period payments by using a lump sum order as a way of providing income.[89] A party can also be required to make a transfer of property. This is most likely to be used in relation to the family home and may, for example, direct that a child and the residential parent stay in a property until the child ceases education. There is also the power to transfer a secure tenancy to the other parent for the child's benefit.[90]

(iv) Factors that the court will consider

The courts will take into account the following factors in deciding whether to make an order:

LEGISLATIVE PROVISION

Children Act 1989, Schedule 1, para 4(1)

    (a)   the income, earning capacity, property and other financial resources which [the applicant, parents and the person in whose favour the order would be made] has or is likely to have in the foreseeable future;

---

[83] *T v B* [2010] EWHC 1444 (Fam).
[84] *N v C (Financial Provision: Schedule I Claims Dismissed)* [2013] EWHC Fam 399.
[85] *J v J (A Minor: Property Transfer)* [1993] 1 FCR 471, [1993] 2 FLR 56; *T v B* [2010] EWHC 1444 (Fam).
[86] This can include a lump sum to meet expenses incurred before the court hearing, including expenses connected to the birth of a child (Children Act 1989, Sched. 1, para 5(1)).
[87] *N v C (Financial Provision: Schedule I Claims Dismissed)* [2013] EWHC Fam 399.
[88] *Re TW and TM (Minors)* [2015] EWHC 3054 (Fam).
[89] *Dickson v Rennie* [2014] EWHC 4306 (Fam).
[90] *K v K (Minors: Property Transfer)* [1992] 2 FCR 253, [1992] 2 FLR 220; although the courts have indicated that they will be cautious in exercising this power: *J v J (A Minor: Property Transfer)* [1993] 1 FCR 471, [1993] 2 FLR 56.

(b) the financial needs, obligations and responsibilities which [each of those persons] has or is likely to have in the foreseeable future;

(c) the financial needs of the child;

(d) the income, earning capacity (if any), property and other financial resources of the child;

(e) any physical or mental disability of the child;

(f) the manner in which the child was being, or was expected to be, educated or trained.

Where the liability of a person who is not the child's legal parent is taken into account, the court should also consider:

LEGISLATIVE PROVISION

Children Act 1989, Schedule 1, para 4(2)

(a) whether that person had assumed responsibility for the maintenance of the child and, if so, the extent to which and basis on which he assumed that responsibility and the length of the period during which he met that responsibility;

(b) whether he did so knowing that the child was not his child;

(c) the liability of any other person to maintain the child.

The welfare of the child is not the paramount consideration because, as is made clear by s. 105(1), property orders are not deemed concerned with the upbringing of the child and so fall outside the scope of s. 1(1) of the Children Act 1989.[91] However, the child's welfare will be an important consideration.[92] The following points will influence the court in deciding the appropriate level of the award:

1. The level of the award should not depend on whether the child's parents were married or not.[93]

2. The child should be brought up in a manner which is in some way commensurate with the non-residential parent's lifestyle.[94] In *J v C (Child: Financial Provision)*[95] the child's non-residential father became a millionaire and it was held that the child should be brought up in a way appropriate for a millionaire's daughter, including living in a four-bedroomed house and being driven around in a Ford Mondeo(!).[96]But there are limits: a mother in *GN v MA (Child Maintenance: Children Act Sch. 1)*[97] sought unsuccessfully for a box

---

[91] *J v C (Child: Financial Provision)* [1999] 1 FLR 152; *Re P (A Child) (Financial Provision)* [2003] 2 FCR 481.

[92] *Re P (A Child: Financial Provision)* [2003] EWCA Civ 837; *FG v MBW (Financial Remedy for Child)* [2011] EWHC 1729 (Fam).

[93] In *A v A (A Minor: Financial Provision)* [1994] 1 FLR 657 at p. 659.

[94] *Dickson v Rennie* [2014] EWHC 4306 (Fam). See Ellman *et al.* (2014) for evidence this accords with the views of the public.

[95] [1999] 1 FLR 152.

[96] Some readers may think the award of a series 1 BMW in *PG v TW (No. 2) (Child: Financial Provision)* [2012] EWHC 1892 was closer to the mark.

[97] [2015] EWHC 3939 (Fam).

at the Emirates football stadium and Ascot and membership of two golf clubs for her seven-year-old son, whose father was a member of the Saudi Royal family.

In other cases, it has been emphasised that where the child is having contact with the father the child will feel uncomfortable if his or her home circumstances are vastly different from those enjoyed by his or her father. In *Re P (A Child) (Financial Provision)*[98] the mother's claim for a top-of-the-range Range Rover from the very wealthy father was found to be excessive. However, she could expect a £20,000 car and £450,000 for a house in a 'suitable' part of London. In *F v G (Child: Financial Provision)*[99] the father was worth over £4.5 million and earned over half a million pounds a year. It was held that the level of award should enable the mother to raise the child in a manner 'not too brutally remote' from the father's lifestyle. In *T v T (Financial Provision: Private Education)*[100] a lump sum order was made under Sched. 1 to cover the children's private school fees, that being commensurate with the parents' wealth. By comparison in *Re M-M (Schedule 1 Provision)*[101] the father had modest means and it was held the child's house and income had to reflect that.

3. The court should be wary of making an award which will benefit the resident parent but not the child.[102] Of course, some provision for the child will inevitably also benefit the resident parent and other children living with them (e.g. a house) and there can be no objection to this.[103] Payment for nanny care could be expected, even if the mother was not working.[104] In *Re P (A Child: Financial Provision)*[105] it was held that the mother was entitled to an allowance in her capacity as the child's carer, even though she could not make any claim in her own right. In *DN v UD*[106] £200,000 per annum was awarded for carer's allowance, although it is interesting that the judge noted this was a lower sum than would have been awarded to the mother for maintenance had she been married to the father. In *Re S (Child: Financial Provision)*[107] where the Court of Appeal said that the phrase 'for the benefit of the child' in para 1(2) of Sched. 1 would be interpreted widely, it therefore could include awarding the mother money so that she could travel to see the child, who had been abducted to Sudan.[108] In deciding the appropriate sum for the carer, account can be taken of the mother's income and earning capacity.[109] Occasionally the courts have allowed lump sum payments to cover litigation costs over child support.[110]

4. It is not possible to use a Sched. 1 award for 'day to day' living expenses.[111] It can be used for particular capital expenditure for the child. This often includes a house or a car. It has also been used to pay for a school trip.[112]

---

[98] [2003] 2 FCR 481.
[99] [2005] 1 FLR 261.
[100] [2005] EWHC 2119 (Fam).
[101] [2014] EWCA Civ 276.
[102] *Re P (A Child) (Financial Provision)* [2003] 2 FCR 481. See the useful commentary in Gilmore (2004d).
[103] *J v C (Child: Financial Provision)* [1998] 3 FCR 79.
[104] *Re P (A Child) (Financial Provision)* [2003] 2 FCR 481.
[105] [2003] 2 FCR 481.
[106] [2020] EWHC 627 (Fam). Contrast *Re M-M (Schedule 1 Provision)* [2014] EWCA Civ 276, where questions were raised over a carer's allowance for parents.
[107] [2004] EWCA Civ 1685.
[108] Followed in *CF v KM* [2010] EWHC 1754 (Fam); *R v F (Child Maintenance: Costs of Contact Proceedings)* [2011] 2 FLR 991; *FG v MBW (Financial Remedy for Child)* [2011] EWHC 1729 (Fam).
[109] *FG v MBW (Financial Remedy for Child)* [2011] EWHC 1729 (Fam).
[110] *Dickson v Rennie* [2014] EWHC 4306 (Fam).
[111] *Green v Adams* [2017] EWFC 24.
[112] *Green v Adams* [2017] EWFC 24.

5. A parent is liable to support a child only during the child's minority.[113] So, if a large sum is provided for accommodation for the child, the sum will normally be held on trust to revert to the paying parent on the child reaching the age of 18 or finishing his or her education.[114] This means that, when the child reaches 18, if a house was provided it may be sold and the sum returned to the paying parent.[115] Similarly, funds to support the child will cease on majority, unless there are exceptional circumstances such as disability of the child.[116] A striking example is *DN v UD*[117] where adult children of a violent father were vulnerable to financial pressure from him and payments beyond the age of 18 were thought necessary to protect them from manipulation.

6. If the court is considering the liability of a step-parent, it will take into account their liability to support any biological child of theirs.

7. Where the applicant is a disabled adult, they can claim against their parents. Although the expenses are restricted to expenses that directly relate to the disability while under the jurisdiction of the Child Support Act, under the Children Act other expenses can be considered.[118]

8. It is not possible for the parents to enter a contract which prevents them applying for an order under Sched. 1.[119] This can be particularly important in a case where the parties have signed a 'pre-nup'. Even if it is given effect (see below), it will not prevent a claim under Sched. 1.[120]

4 Matrimonial Causes Act 1973 and children

A Powers of the court on divorce or dissolution

Learning objective 3

Summarise the powers available to the court in financial disputes

On divorce or dissolution, the court has wide powers to redistribute the parties' property. This includes the power to make orders especially designed to benefit children. For example, an order could demand regular payment of money to the child or, more commonly, a payment to the resident parent for the benefit of the child.

B 'Child of the family'

Many of the court's powers to redistribute in divorce proceedings apply in respect of 'a child of the family'. The meaning of this phrase will be discussed in Chapter 8. The definition most notably includes a stepchild. Such a child can be treated under the child support legislation as the biological parents' responsibility, but under the Matrimonial Causes Act 1973 (hereafter MCA 1973) as the step-parents' responsibility.

---

113 *Re N (A child) (Payments for Benefit of Child)* [2009] 1 FCR 606.
114 *H v P (Illegitimate Child: Capital Provision)* [1993] Fam Law 515; *T v S (Financial Provision for Children)* [1994] 1 FCR 743, [1994] 2 FLR 883.
115 Although the order may provide for the residential parent to have an option to purchase the house.
116 *Re N (A Child) (Payments for Benefit of Child)* [2009] 1 FCR 606.
117 [2020] EWHC 627 (Fam).
118 *C v F (Disabled Child: Maintenance Orders)* [1999] 1 FCR 39, [1998] 2 FLR 1.
119 *Morgan v Hill* [2006] 3 FCR 620.
120 *DB v PB (Pre-nuptial Agreement: Jurisdiction)* [2016] EWHC 3431 (Fam).

The MCA 1973 does list special considerations that apply where a step-parent is being asked to pay. The following factors must be taken into account:

LEGISLATIVE PROVISION

Matrimonial Cause Act 1973, section 25(4)

(a) to whether that party assumed any responsibility for the child's maintenance, and, if so, the extent to which, and the basis upon which, that party assumed such responsibility and the length of time for which that party discharged such responsibility;

(b) to whether in assuming and discharging such responsibility that party did so knowing that the child was not his or her own;

(c) to the liability of any other person to maintain the child.[121]

C Applications by children

A child who is over the age of 18 can apply for a financial or property order if his or her parents are divorcing, or apply for a variation of an order made earlier.[122] Although normally orders will cease once the child reaches the age of 18, the court can order that periodical payments extend beyond the 18th birthday if the child is or will be receiving instruction at an educational establishment or undergoing training and there are special circumstances which justify the order.[123]

D Factors to be taken into account

The factors to be considered in deciding the appropriate level of an award under the MCA 1973 will be discussed in detail shortly. It should be noted that the welfare of any child is to be regarded as the first consideration[124] and the courts regard ensuring the children are adequately housed as especially important.[125] The courts have indicated that the amount that would be awarded under the child support legislation will be a starting point.[126] However, in wealthy cases, substantial sums of maintenance can be ordered and can include private school fees, university tuition fees, funding for gap years and private medical insurance.[127]

---

5 Theoretical issues concerning financial support on divorce or dissolution

Learning objective 4

Debate the issues around spousal support

For ease of expression we will discuss how the courts deal with financial issues on the breakdown of a marriage. The Court of Appeal in *Lawrence v Gallagher*[128] held that exactly the same principles that apply to financial orders on divorce apply to the

---

[121] Matrimonial Causes Act 1973 (hereafter MCA 1973), s. 25(4).
[122] See *Downing v Downing* [1976] Fam 288.
[123] MCA 1973, s. 29.
[124] MCA 1973, s. 25.
[125] *M v B (Ancillary Proceedings: Lump Sum)* [1998] 1 FLR 53, [1998] 1 FCR 213.
[126] *GW v RW* [2003] Fam Law 386.
[127] *H v H (Financial Relief)* [2010] 1 FLR 1864.
[128] [2012] EWCA Civ 394, discussed in Herring (2012b).

dissolution of a civil partnership.[129] Presumably the courts will draw no distinction between opposite-sex and same-sex marriages when determining financial issues, although Bendall and Harding have argued that same-sex couples place high importance on financial independence and so the approaches used for opposite-sex couples may not be appropriate.[130]

Proceedings for financial orders on divorce is a controversial issue.[131] There is a wide range of competing policies that the law seeks to hold together. There is a desire to ensure that on divorce a fair redistribution of the property takes place so that one party is not unduly disadvantaged by the divorce. On the other hand, there is the desire to enable the parties to achieve truly independent lives after the divorce. As the Law Commission put it:

> The reality of divorce means that former spouses should not be tied to each other for life; the law gives them freedom to re-marry and take on new responsibilities, and this is hampered if the financial commitment of a former relationship is unnecessarily prolonged. For the economically weaker party, dependence means vulnerability to another's employment, health and willingness to pay.[132]

But to achieve independence and fairness is often impossible. The truth is that for many couples suitable financial orders cannot be made. Neither party will be able to live at a standard of living they regard as acceptable. Both will feel they have been hard done by. There is simply not enough money for most married couples to support two individuals in separate households after divorce, certainly not at the level to which they had become accustomed.[133]

One of the difficulties in dealing with this area of the law is that most of the cases in the law reports involve extremely wealthy clients. It means the principles that have been developed in the courts are often of little relevance to ordinary couples.[134] The fact that the judge could comment of one case, 'The assets in the case are by no means large, in the region of a little more than a total of £4 million',[135] shows how easy it is when looking at the case law to lose touch with reality.

To understand how 'everyday' cases are dealt with, one is better off looking at empirical studies, rather than the case reports.[136] The picture from these is that in around two thirds of cases no financial order is made at all, presumably because the parties have so few assets (or primarily debts) and there is nothing to argue over. Of those cases where an order is made, the vast majority are consent orders, rather than a judge deciding what financial order to make.

A The economic realities of divorce

There is convincing evidence that following divorce women who are caring for children suffer a detrimental downturn in their finances, while their ex-husbands do not.[137] The conclusions of a study of the impact of divorce on women was blunt:

---

[129] *Lawrence v Gallagher* [2012] EWCA Civ 394. See Bendall and Harding (2018), Chan (2013), Wilson (2007) and Allen and Williams (2009) for a discussion of whether there are any arguments that civil partnerships will be treated any differently from marriages in this area

[130] Bendall and Harding (2018).

[131] The Family Procedure Rules 2010 introduced the terminology 'proceedings for financial orders'. Previously the terminology 'ancillary relief orders' had been popular.

[132] Law Commission Consultation Paper 208, *Matrimonial Property, Needs and Agreements* (2012).

[133] Barton and Bissett-Johnson (2000) noted that in the majority of cases no financial orders are made by the court. In some cases this will reflect the fact that there are simply no assets to redistribute.

[134] *Jones v Jones* [2011] EWCA Civ 41.

[135] *R v R (Financial Remedies: Needs and Practicalities)* [2011] EWHC 3093 (Fam), Colderidge J.

[136] Woodward (2015).

[137] Sigle-Rushton, W. (2009); Perry *et al.* (2000).

> The stark conclusion is that men's household income increases by about 23 per cent on divorce once we control for household size, whereas women's household income falls by about 31 per cent. There is partial recovery for women, but this recovery is driven by repartnering: the average effect of repartnering is to restore income to pre-divorce levels after nine years. [For] those who do not repartner . . . the long term economic consequences of divorce are serious.[138]

The extent of disadvantage for women on divorce is closely related to their employment history during marriage. There is convincing evidence that following divorce those who have undertaken primary care of the child (normally the wife) suffer significantly.[139] Childcare responsibilities mean that women are far more likely to have given up employment than men; where they are employed, mothers are more often in part-time, low status, poorly paid jobs.[140] Even where they have returned to full-time employment, the time taken out to care for children will have set back their earning potential.[141] In part, ex-wives' financial hardships also reflect the wage differences which exist generally between men and women: average earnings of women are 17.3 per cent lower than men.[142] Women face discrimination in finding employment, both on the basis of their sex and on the basis that they are caring for children and therefore in a weaker position to advance their careers.[143] It is not just childcare that can restrict a woman's ability to advance her career. Women still carry the primary duty of housework.[144] One study found women did 28 per cent more housework and 31 per cent more childcare than men.[145] Interestingly, 28 per cent of women thought their male partners did not do their fair share of work around the house, but only 7 per cent of men agreed.[146] Another found that women did on average 16.6 hours of housework per week, whereas men did 6.6 hours, although it also found an interesting difference among different ethnic groups with Black Caribbean men doing 7.12 hours per week, compared with 6.05 for White British men.[147] In one survey 48 per cent of men did no or a little housework.[148] The impact of this becomes especially apparent on retirement where women suffer particular poverty as compared with men because they have not been able to build up pension provision.[149]

B Why should there be any redistribution?

To assist in the discussion of this question, it will be assumed that the husband is in the stronger position economically, and that the wife is seeking a court order. Similar arguments can, of course, be made if it is the wife who is the higher earner; or in the case of a same-sex couple.[150]

(i) Spousal support and the care of children

Supporting the child should inevitably require providing benefits to the residential parent. So, if it is decided that the child should live in a luxury-level house, this will benefit both the child and the parent with whom they are living. Further, included in the support required

---

[138] Fisher and Low (2009: 254). See also Fisher and Low (2018).
[139] Dex, Ward and Joshi (2006).
[140] Lyonette (2015); Scott and Dex (2009); Fawcett Society (2010).
[141] Scott and Dex (2009).
[142] Office for National Statistics (2020k).
[143] Herring (2013a).
[144] Trew and Drobnic (2010); Crompton and Lyonette (2008); Sayer (2010).
[145] Oxfam (2016).
[146] Oxfam (2016).
[147] Kan and Laurie (2016).
[148] Mintel (2004). Geist (2010) notes that in surveys men tend to exaggerate the amount of housework they do.
[149] See Chapter 12.
[150] See Fehlberg (2004) for a useful discussion of some of the theories discussed here.

for the child must be an element to provide personal care for the child. So, one ground for spousal support is that the spouse be maintained at the level required to ensure adequate care of the child. Eekelaar and Maclean have supported the 'equalisation of the standard of living of the two households, and thus of the children within them'.[151] They argue that this equalisation is not due to any kind of implied undertaking between the parents (as some of the models below emphasise), but due to the moral claim of the child; that is, the child's household should not be disadvantaged to the benefit of the non-residential parent's household.

(ii) Contract

It could be argued that it is a part of the marriage contract that, on breach of the contract, one party will pay the other 'damages'; that on marriage the spouses promise to support each other for the rest of their lives. If a husband decides to divorce his wife, he must pay her damages so that she is in the economic position she would have been in had he not broken the contract. This would mean that the husband would have to pay the wife financial support so that she could enjoy the level of wealth she experienced during the marriage.[152] Nowadays this theory does not really explain the English law: first, because it might be questioned whether marriage does (or should) include a promise to remain with the other spouse forever, given the ready availability of divorce; secondly, because the law has abandoned trying to work out which party breached the contract, that is, who it is that has caused the marriage breakdown. It may be for these reasons that Milton Regan puts the argument more in terms of an assumed obligation, than a contract, arguing that marriage is:

> a distinctive open-ended relationship of mutuality, interdependence, and care, in which responsibilities may arise without express consent and impacts may linger after divorce . . . Financial obligation at divorce . . . rests not on the duty of charity to a dependant, but on the responsibility for economic justice toward a spouse.[153]

(iii) Partnership

The view here is that marriage should be regarded as analogous to a partnership.[154] The husband and wife cooperate together as a couple as part of a joint economic enterprise.[155] It may be that one spouse is employed and the other works at home, but they work together for common benefits. Therefore, on divorce each spouse should be entitled to their share, normally argued to be half each. Lord Nicholls in *Miller v Miller*[156] accepted the validity of what he called the 'equal sharing' principle. He put the argument this way:

> [in marriage] the parties commit themselves to sharing their lives. They live and work together. When their partnership ends each is entitled to an equal share of the assets of the partnership, unless there is a good reason to the contrary. Fairness requires no less.

The partnership model does not necessarily lead to an equal division. John Eekelaar suggests:

> [A]t the end of the relationship, the investment which each party has put into the marriage is assessed on one side of the balance sheet and set against the value of the assets which each is

---

[151] Eekelaar and Maclean (1997: 197).
[152] This would justify the minimal loss theory behind the Matrimonial Proceedings and Property Act 1970.
[153] Regan (1999: 188).
[154] See the approach of the Canadian Supreme Court in *Moge v Moge* (1993) 99 DLR (4th) 456, discussed in Diduck and Orton (1994).
[155] Fehlberg (2005).
[156] [2006] 2 FCR 213 at para 16.

taking out of it and also the earning power which each has at that time. If there is a disparity between the parties with regard to what was put in and what is being taken out, an adjustment will be made to equalize the position between them. Marriage is a joint enterprise in a capitalist society demanding, at least *prima facie,* equal rewards for effort.[157]

This kind of approach has been described as 'merger over time' by the Law Commission, and is captured by this quote:

> [An approach to spousal support] is to see the spouses as merging into each other over time. In this model, the longer they are married, the more their human capital should be seen as intertwined rather than affixed to the individual spouse in whose body it resides . . . After a while, one can less and less distinguish what was brought into the marriage and what was produced by the marriage.[158]

This argument might need some modification to take account of the fact that nowadays people have typically lived together for quite some time before marriage. Marriage is rarely the start of an intertwining of lives, but the expression of a complete interconnection. It is for this reason, as we shall see, that the courts tend to take account of the length of the relationship, rather than the length of the marriage.

The partnership model might appear to suggest that we should redistribute assets that have accumulated during the marriage, but would not apply to assets owned by the parties before entering the marriage or assets acquired after the marriage breakdown. However, the approach can be developed to extend to future assets. It is possible to argue that the partnership assets are not limited to tangible assets, but extend to the earning capacity of the parties.[159] So, if the wife had supported the husband at home while he developed his career, she could argue that he has only been able to reach the position where he is able to earn as much money as he does because of the help she provided. This argument would entitle the wife to a share in his future earnings, reflecting the increase in his earning potential acquired during the marriage. If you wanted to say it applied to assets generated before the marriage you could argue that on marriage the parties will bring to the relationship a variety of different assets, skills, personalities, interests, etc. Throughout the marriage each party will enjoy and share their personalities, interests and skills. If the relationship involves the mutual sharing of all aspects of their lives, this should include their material assets.

The partnership approach is one of the most popular ways of justifying the powers of redistribution on divorce but there are difficulties with it:

1. Some argue that the partnership approach is inappropriate in the absence of an express agreement to share the family assets. It could be replied that the partnership concept is part of the marriage package, and is an obligation which the parties accept by marrying. Another response is that the partnership approach is not necessarily designed to reflect the intentions of the parties, but rather what is conscionable or fair; that, as the spouses worked together on a common enterprise, they should share the fruits, even if they had not explicitly agreed to do so. Seen in this way the partnership approach is closer to unjust enrichment than contract law.[160]

---

[157] Eekelaar (2007: 431).
[158] Sugarman (1990: 159).
[159] This argument is developed in Frantz and Dagan (2002 and 2004). It was rejected in *Q v Q* [2005] EWHC 402 (Fam) by Bennett J.
[160] Regan (1999: 188).

2. Where the argument extends to future earnings, the partnership approach requires the court to calculate what share of the husband's earning capacity is a result of the marriage. This is difficult to ascertain.[161] Also, if the husband could show that, had he not married, he would have done just as well in his career, he could argue that no proportion of his earning capacity could be said to result from the partnership. Finally, if one friend helps another to advance in her career, we do not normally think this creates a financial obligation, even if the friend has been instrumental in obtaining the break.[162] Why should it be different in marriage?

3. It can be argued that the approach takes insufficient account of the needs of the parties. Particularly where one spouse is raising the child, a one-half share may not adequately meet his or her needs. In other words, dividing the assets equally might leave the spouse with the child effectively in a worse-off financial position (because of the extra expenses of childcare) and not receiving a 'fair' share of the economic benefits of the joint enterprise.

Despite these objections, the partnership approach certainly provides a sound basis for financial support. It is important to appreciate that the approach is not arguing that one spouse should transfer money to the other, but rather that the family assets should be regarded as jointly owned. So, a home-working mother is not asking for some of her husband's money on divorce; she is seeking her share of their assets.

(iv) Equality

Some argue that on the breakdown of the marriage the parties should be treated equally as a basic aspect of justice.[163] As Eekelaar has pointed out, this could mean two things: first, equality of outcome; and, secondly, equality of opportunity.[164] Equality of outcome requires that at the point of divorce each spouse has the same total value of assets. Equality of opportunity is that 'each former spouse should be in an equal position to take advantage of the opportunities to enhance her or his economic position in the labour market'.[165] Neither in its most simple form is satisfactory. The difficulty with equality of outcome is that as the needs of the parties (particularly in relation to children) are different, giving the parties equal assets will not truly produce an equal standard of living. The problem with the equality of opportunity approach is that the prevailing social structures (such as discrimination against women in the employment market) are such that perfect equality of economic opportunity would be impossible to achieve.

A more sophisticated version of equality of income for both households post-divorce would have to take carefully into account the costs of raising children. This might involve ensuring that each household has the same amount of spare cash after the payment of essential expenses. That would normally involve giving more money to the household that has children living in it.

(v) Compensation

Here the argument is that on divorce the non-earning spouse should be compensated for the disadvantages she has suffered as a result of the marriage.[166] This was accepted as a principle in *Miller v Miller*,[167] where Lord Nicholls explained:

---

[161] See further Ellman (2005); and the American Law Institute proposals discussed by Ellman (2005) and Eekelaar (2006b: 51–2).
[162] Eekelaar (2006b: 48).
[163] Parkinson (2005).
[164] Eekelaar (1988).
[165] Eekelaar (1988: 192).
[166] In *VB v JP* [2008] 2 FCR 682 the wife refused to take up a promotion because the husband did not want to move. This was regarded as an economic disadvantage due to the marriage.
[167] [2006] 2 FCR 213 at para 13. See the discussion in Ellman (2007).

[Compensation] is aimed at redressing any significant prospective economic disparity between the parties arising from the way they conducted their marriage. For instance, the parties may have arranged their affairs in a way which has greatly advantaged the husband in terms of his earning capacity but left the wife severely handicapped so far as her own earning capacity is concerned. Then the wife suffers a double loss: a diminution in her earning capacity and the loss of a share in her husband's enhanced income.

Baroness Hale referred to the need to compensate for 'relationship-generated disadvantage'. The compensation argument can take two forms (assuming the wife to be the non-earning spouse):

1. The non-earning spouse should be compensated for loss of the earnings which she would have gained had she not been at home caring for the children or the home.

2. The non-earning spouse should in retrospect be paid an appropriate wage for her work by the husband. A court could assess how much the house-cleaning and child-caring would have cost the husband had he employed people to do it. Some who adopt this approach accept that, as the non-earning spouse herself benefits from the housework, the cost should be shared and so the husband should only pay for half of this work.

There are difficulties with the compensation approach. As one group of solicitors argue:

Seeking to 'compensate' a party who has prioritised family over career is also demeaning to homemakers because it implies that h/she is a victim . . . There is, after all, no way of compensating the breadwinner for having missed his or her children growing up. The proposal elevates money over emotional advantages. It seems fairer and less artificial to regard the two parties as having voluntarily assumed varying levels of responsibility for different aspects of their lives, and in some circumstances these responsibilities continue after divorce.[168]

Whether the authors are correct in implying there is a fair division of gains and losses in relationships is open to dispute. Saying the breadwinner misses out on their children growing up is debatable. Most workers get to see their children at evening and weekends. It might be said they get the fun part of parenting, rather than the daily grind of getting the children ready for school and their homework done. Further, this argument, however, overlooks the fact that the choice of bearing and raising children is one that is essential to society's well-being. It is therefore a choice which society must seek to encourage and support. Others argue that the costs that women who care for children suffer are due to the inequalities of society, rather than being married. It is the state's failure to provide adequate childcare facilities and employment protection for mothers that is the root cause of the disadvantages suffered. The losses women suffer should be compensated for by the state rather than by husbands.[169] However, in the absence of state support, it is surely unfair for mothers alone to have to carry the burden of financial sacrifice for the raising of children.

Eekelaar sees a different objection to the compensation approach, arguing that even if the wife had not married her husband she would have married someone else, and so it is not realistic to claim that the lack of development in her career is this man's fault.[170] It can be argued that if, say, the wife gives up her career to care for the children then the resulting loss of income is a loss for both parties because they would have shared her income. The wife cannot therefore claim compensation for it, because the couple would have already equally shared

---

[168] Marshall *et al.* (2014).
[169] Ferguson (2008).
[170] Eekelaar (1988).

the loss of the income. Carbone and Brinig[171] refute these kinds of arguments by suggesting that, as the husband himself has benefited from his wife's sacrifices (by having the pleasure of fatherhood and a pleasant home life), it can be seen as reasonable to require him to compensate the wife for her loss of earnings. A difficulty then arises in calculating what the wife would have earned had she not given up her career in order to undertake family responsibilities.[172] A final argument against compensation is that it can act as a deterrent against a wife who undertakes paid work during the marriage. She may find herself on divorce no better off, or even worse off, than a wife who gives up her career early in the marriage.[173]

(vi) The state's interests

The arguments so far have assumed that the issue is about achieving fairness between the parties themselves.[174] Indeed, in *DL v SL*[175] Mostyn J stated that 'Ancillary relief (or financial remedy) proceedings are quintessentially private business'.

However, it is arguable that financial orders on divorce can be justified by interests of the state, regardless of what would be fair or just between the parties.[176] As Alison Diduck has put it:

> It seems to me, however, that how the law distributes a family's wealth and financial responsibilities at the end of their relationship says as much about the way society and the state organize their economic, reproductive, and caring responsibilities as it does about the way family members do (and should do).[177]

So what state interests are there here? The following are suggested:[178]

1. *Saving public money.* Orders should be made to avoid costs to the state of the children or either spouse becoming dependent on welfare payments now or in the future.

2. *Childcare issues.* The state might take the view that each member of society should be as economically productive as possible, and so it would want to discourage a spouse giving up employment to take up childcare, in which case the state might want to limit financial awards on divorce. If there were no financial orders on divorce, this would discourage a spouse from thinking of giving up employment to care for children; instead they would be likely to rely on day care. However, the state might believe that children's interests are promoted if one spouse gives up work to care for the children, in which case some form of protection from financial disadvantage would be necessary. Hale J in the Court of Appeal in *SRJ v DWJ (Financial Provision)*[179] has stated:

> It is not only in [the child's] interests but in the community's interests that parents, whether mothers or fathers, and spouses, whether husbands or wives, should have a real choice between concentrating on breadwinning and concentrating on home-making and child-rearing, and do not feel forced, for fear of what might happen should their marriage break down much later in life, to abandon looking after the home and the family to other people for the sake of maintaining a career.

---

[171] Carbone and Brinig (1991).
[172] Mee (2004: 437).
[173] Davis (2008).
[174] Many commentators make the assumption that redistribution of property on divorce is a private matter: see, e.g., Cretney (2003b).
[175] [2015] EWHC 2621 (Fam).
[176] Herring (2005b).
[177] Diduck (2011). See also Miles (2011c); Diduck (2018).
[178] Herring (2005b).
[179] [1999] 2 FLR 176 at p. 182.

3. *The symbolic valuing of childcare.* The state should place a far higher value on the unpaid work of raising children than is done at present.[180] Financial orders on divorce are one way of demonstrating that the state treasures childcare as an important social activity.[181] Merle Weiner[182] puts this in terms of compensation for the spouse who is not undertaking their due care of the child (be that during or after the marriage):

> [P]arents should have a legal obligation to share fairly the caregiving responsibility for their children . . . Every parent should be obligated 'to give care or share', i.e., to pay compensation to the other parent for any disproportionate and unfair caregiving that occurs.

4. *The interests of children.* The level of support for the spouse with primary care of the child will have a significant impact on the welfare of the child. It will affect whether the primary carer will need to undertake work to earn money; their state of emotional and their material well-being; and their sense of self-respect. All of these will have an impact on the well-being of the child.

5. *Stability of marriage.* Some economists have argued that the level of maintenance can act as a deterrent against divorce.[183] Whether this is correct and whether we wish to pressure people into remaining in a marriage which they wish to leave is a matter for debate.

6. *Post-divorce life.* The level of financial support after divorce will affect the behaviour of the spouses after divorce. Do we want ex-wives to find employment and seek to become financially self-sufficient or is it proper to recognise that the duties owed to a spouse continue after divorce because the disadvantages flowing from the marriage do?[184] Whatever one's view on such questions the kind of orders made on divorce will affect the spouse's behaviour.

7. *Sex discrimination.* The state is entitled to seek to promote equality between men and women. As already mentioned, divorce plays a significant role in leading to inequality among women. The state can legitimately seek to combat discrimination through state orders.

Not everyone, by any means, will agree that all of these state interests are weighty. But they do demonstrate that the issue of financial orders on divorce is not just of significance to the parties themselves, but can have effects on the wider society. Lucinda Ferguson argues that the state has over-extended the appropriate interpersonal obligations owed between spouses and by parents to children in order to deal with poverty which should be resolved by state support:

> The notion of interpersonal obligation has been distorted in both contexts in an attempt to respond to social inequality. More concerning than this distortion, however, is the fact that neither of these support obligations manages to successfully respond to social inequality anyway. Separated and divorced women and children raised in single-parent families represent a disproportionate percentage of those Canadians[185] living below the low income cut-off. Focus on expanding and strengthening these interpersonal obligations has distracted us from the urgent need to address the root causes of the inequality that these obligations have been adapted to address.[186]

---

[180] Herring (2013a).
[181] Orders on divorce are not a very effective way of getting this message across. Unmarried parents are not rewarded and the level of the award does not reflect the amount or quality of the work done.
[182] Weiner (2015: 136).
[183] See the discussion in Cohen (2002: 24–5).
[184] See Regan (1993a).
[185] The point could equally well be made about this in England.
[186] Ferguson (2008: 75). See also Case (2011).

Many of the difficulties that this section deals with are caused by the unequal sharing of childcare. Although there is evidence of fathers seeking to play an increased role in childcare[187] the vast majority is still undertaken by women.[188] Some commentators take the view that the Government should attempt to encourage a more equal division of childcaring roles. However, the trend is for those working to be working for longer and longer hours, making it harder for couples to share childcare and work.[189] The alternative is to encourage both parties to work and for even greater use to be made of day care. However, this raises the debate over whether day care or care at home is preferable for children. This is a heated debate. Although the evidence suggests that there are some advantages and disadvantages to both, there is controversy as to whether overall one is preferable.[190]

Having spent all this time considering the academic justifications for financial orders on divorce, it is regrettable to note that they have not impressed the judiciary. Thorpe LJ has stated:

> [I]n this jurisdiction we should not flirt with, still less embrace, any of the categorisations of the defining purposes of periodical payments advanced by academic authors. The judges must remain focused on the statutory language, albeit recognising the need for evolutionary construction to reflect social and economic change . . . [T]o adopt one model or another or a combination of more than one is to don a straitjacket and to deflect concentration from the statutory language.[191]

C The case for the abolition of maintenance

There is a case for the abolition of maintenance. The argument is that the existence of maintenance perpetuates the fact that women are dependent upon men.[192] A vicious circle exists in that, because the law tells wives that they will be entitled to financial support if their relationship ends, they are willing to take lower-paid jobs and they thereby do become dependent upon their husbands.[193] If maintenance were abolished and financial independence encouraged, women would have to find jobs that paid adequately.[194] Although there may be a short period during which women would suffer from the lack of maintenance, over time the market would have to provide adequately paid jobs for women, or provide economic rewards for homemaking and child-rearing activities. O'Donovan,[195] although sympathetic to this argument, has suggested that the abolition of maintenance can only fairly be accomplished when there:

- is equality of division of labour during marriage, including financial equality;
- is equal participation in wage-earning;
- are wages geared to people as individuals and not as heads of families;
- is treatment of people as individuals (rather than family units) by the state in taxation and benefit provision.

---

[187] Maushart (2001: 129–34) and see Chapter 1.
[188] E.g. Eekelaar and Maclean (1997: 137).
[189] Moen (2003).
[190] Ermisch and Francesconi (2001; 2003) argue that children whose parents both work suffer in a variety of ways.
[191] Thorpe LJ in *Parlour v Parlour* [2004] EWCA Civ 872 at para 106. See Miles (2005) for an insightful discussion of his statement and Gilmore (2012) for a more general discussion of the relationship between academic writing and family law.
[192] In practice, it is far more common for a wife to be awarded maintenance than a husband.
[193] Deech (2009a).
[194] Although the levels of maintenance are low, and it is unlikely that women would choose not to work in the hope of getting maintenance should they divorce. Perhaps more convincing is the argument that maintenance is symbolic of the culture of dependency.
[195] O'Donovan (1982).

A second objection to maintenance has already been mentioned: that the economic disadvantages that women suffer are due to inequalities within society, such as the lack of provision of childcare services and family-friendly working practices, etc. Therefore, the state, and not husbands, should recompense wives on the breakdown of their marriage for the losses that society has caused.

D Certainty or discretion?

As we shall see, the current law is based around fairness. Although there are some factors and principles a judge can refer to, the outcome is largely in the discretion of the judge. The task of the family judge has been likened to:

> . . . a bus driver who is given a large number of instructions about how to drive the bus and the authority to do various actions such as turning left or right. There is also the occasional advice or correction offered by three senior drivers. The one piece of information which he or she is not given is where to take the bus. All he or she is told is that the driver is required to drive to a reasonable destination.[196]

But Holman J[197] has recently sought to suggest that judges' decisions in these cases are entirely arbitrary:

> I have reached this decision in the exercise of the judicial discretion which Parliament has imposed upon, and entrusted to, the courts. Of course, on one level the decision is arbitrary. I could have awarded more, or less, and two judges might (and probably would) have reached conclusions which differed to some degree . . . I, personally, consider that there is nevertheless a distinction between an award which is arbitrary in the true sense, and one which is the product of judicial discretion. An arbitrary result would be one yielded by sticking in a pin, or tossing a coin, or drawing a lot. Judicial discretion is the product of a weighing of all relevant factors and wise, considered and informed decision making by an experienced adjudicator after hearing argument. My decision is a discretionary one, but it is not an arbitrary one.

DEBATE

Certainty or discretion?

A major issue in the area of spousal financial support is whether the financial support for spouses should be based on some formula to ensure certainty of result and consistency or whether the case should be resolved in reliance upon discretion. As we shall see, spousal financial support is at present based on a very broad discretion, considering a list of factors. This can be contrasted with the law on child support, where the level of the award was based upon a mathematical calculation, with only a limited discretion to depart from the calculation.
    The Court of Appeal in **Work v Gray**[198] stated that:

> [T]he bespoke approach to the determination of financial claims . . . requires the court to consider what weight to give to each of the s. 25 factors and all the other relevant circumstances in the individual case. The tension that this creates, between the need for a sufficient degree of certainty in the exercise by the courts of their discretionary powers and the need for sufficient flexibility to meet the justice of the individual case, has been the subject of debate over the

---

[196] Patrick Parkinson, quoted with approval by the Law Commission (2014).
[197] *Robertson v Robertson* [2016] EWHC 613 [68].
[198] [2017] EWCA Civ 270.

years. Consistency in the exercise of discretion . . . not only assists judges when determining financial claims but also, importantly, facilitates agreement between parties to a marriage seeking to resolve the consequences of their separation and divorce. This has become particularly important with the withdrawal of legal aid and the increase in unrepresented litigants.

Some of the arguments for and against discretion will now be considered:

1. *Enforcement.* One of the arguments against discretion is that enforcement is easier if the system is seen to be fair and consistent. One common reason for non-payment of maintenance is that the amount payable is seen to be unfair. Having a clearly applied formula, which the parties could be made aware of before marriage, might improve enforcement levels.

2. *Certainty.* Another argument against discretion is that the parties in negotiations are assisted by having clear guidance on what amount the law regards as fair in a particular case. The problem with the present law is that it can be very difficult for solicitors to predict how much a court will award a client. Not only does a discretion-based system make negotiations harder, it also increases the powers of solicitors. As Jackson *et al.* argue:

> [A]long with discretion goes uncertainty; the elevation of professional judgement (because only lawyers, who deal with these matters all the time, have the necessary knowledge and skill to weigh up the competing factors); an almost limitless need for information about family finances (because discretion, if it is to [be] justified at all, has to be based on a minute examination of differing circumstances) and the demand for large amounts of professional time (because discretion, if it is not to be exercised arbitrarily, takes time).[199]

Dewar, however, argues that there is no evidence that less discretion means it will be easier for the parties to reach an agreement, because the parties can disagree how even a rigid formula should apply.[200] Lord Nicholls in **Miller; McFarlane** accepted there was a difficulty for the courts here. On the one hand ensuring fairness between the parties meant that the court needed flexibility, but that created unpredictability and that conflicted with another aspect of fairness: that like cases should be treated alike.[201] Practitioners claim that if you 'know your District Judge' (i.e. the arguments that that judge is usually persuaded by) this can be an advantage for your client.[202] This is in part due to the discretionary nature of the system.[203]

3. *Flexibility.* A benefit of the discretion-based system is that it can apply unique solutions that may better fit the circumstances of individual parties. A blanket rule cannot consider the particular events during the relationship which justify a particular award. Perhaps the core question is: to what extent are we willing to put up with injustices in a few cases to enable speedy and efficient responses for the majority? As Miles[204] notes:

> Rules help us to decide large numbers of cases in an efficient, consistent, and so predictable manner. They give us more or less rough justice, providing pretty decent answers for the bulk of cases. To the extent that the answer is sometimes imperfect, that may be tolerable where the issues at stake are relatively minor (in dollar amounts or qualitatively) and/or where the transaction costs of fixing on a more 'accurate' answer, customised to each case's more detailed facts, would be disproportionate for the system and the parties.

---

[199] Jackson, Wasoff, Maclean and Dobash (1993: 256).
[200] Dewar (1997).
[201] [2006] 1 FCR 213 at para 6.
[202] Watson-Lee (2004: 349).
[203] Although similar claims are made about district judges in areas of the law where there is much less discretion.
[204] Miles (2019: 266).

Questions

1. *Do you think there would be disputes even if the law were crystal clear?*

2. *Should a judge use his or her own moral values when exercising discretion? Or the values of society at large? Or the values of the couple?*

Further reading

Read **Cooke** (2007) and **Harris** (2012) for a helpful discussion of the nature of uncertainty in this area of the law.

E The importance of discovery

Crucial to the success of the parties' negotiations and any court hearing is having full disclosure of each party's assets, income and liabilities. There is a duty on both clients and lawyers to make a full, frank and clear disclosure of the parties' present assets (*Sharland v Sharland;*[205] *Bokor-Ingram v Bokor-Ingram*[206]). Each party must file at court a form, which sets out income and assets. However, it is 'all too common'[207] for people to try to hide their assets. Indeed, for lawyers in practice, far more time is often spent ascertaining the other party's true wealth than in deciding what would be a fair division of the property. The problem can be a simple deliberate failure to disclose, but in more sophisticated forms can involve hiding income and property behind companies or trusts controlled by the parties.[208] Although the courts have powers for ordering discovery of relevant documents, too often it is impossible to be sure that all the relevant material has been provided. The court has two further tools at its disposal if it cannot ascertain a party's true financial position. First, the court can order that the non-disclosing party be punished by being ordered to pay all or some of the legal costs incurred in the attempt to ascertain his or her wealth.[209] Second, the court can, if it is convinced that it does not have the full picture, presume that a party has a certain level of wealth.[210] This could be done where the court decides that a person's lifestyle is not commensurate with their claimed income.[211] If a non-disclosure only comes to light after an order has been made, the court can give leave to appeal out of time, even if that is years later.[212]

The difficulty in ascertaining the wealth of the parties is likely to work in favour of the richer party. It is far harder to hide the income of a part-time worker than to hide the true income of a managing director of a company whose salary may be but a small portion of his or her true income.[213] At the other end of the spectrum, the courts have complained of solicitors seeking too much information from the other side in the hope of uncovering assets which may be available to their clients. Intensive financial questioning can lead to enormous solicitors' costs.

---

[205] [2015] UKSC 60.

[206] [2009] 2 FLR 922.

[207] Thorpe LJ in *Purba v Purba* [2000] 1 FLR 444.

[208] *ND v SD* [2017] EWHC 1507 (Fam).

[209] *W v W (Ancillary Relief: Non-Disclosure)* [2003] 3 FCR 385. In *Young v Young* [2012] EWHC 138 (Fam) the husband's passport was detained until he made disclosure.

[210] *Gulobovich v Gulobovich* [2011] EWCA Civ 479; *Hutchings-Whelan v Hutchings* [2012] EWCA Civ 38; although see *US v UR* [2014] EWHC 175 (Fam), where there was no evidence other assets existed.

[211] *Moher v Moher* [2019] EWCA Civ 1482; *Thomas v Thomas* [1996] 2 FLR 544, [1996] FCR 668; *Al Khatib v Masry* [2002] 2 FCR 539; *Minwalla v Minwalla* [2005] 1 FLR 771.

[212] *Sharland v Sharland* [2015] UKSC 60.

[213] *Young v Young* [2014] 2 FCR 495. See also *Velupillai v Velupillai* [2015] EWHC 3095 (Fam).

The Family Proceedings Rules 2010 are designed to prevent unnecessary investigation, but the practitioner is in a difficult position. There is a danger that if he or she does not follow up a lead in disclosure, they may be sued in negligence, but if the practitioner does, they may be penalised in costs for unnecessary work.

An issue of considerable importance in practice arose in *Tchenguiz v Imerman*.[214] The wife had obtained information about her husband's assets from a computer, which she was not authorised to access. This amounted to a breach of his rights of confidentiality, the court held, and so she was not permitted to use the information in the court hearing. Although it was accepted there was a real problem with spouses not disclosing their assets, that did not justify a party breaking the law in order to discover the truth. The difficulty is that if it is discovered that a spouse has misled the court, the intrusion into privacy seems justified. A party should not be able to rely on claims of privacy in relation to material they should have disclosed to the court. However, if they have made proper disclosure and the breach of confidentiality was a mere 'fishing expedition' then the rights to confidentiality seem to be infringed. One argument the court, perhaps surprisingly, did not find convincing was that in marriage a spouse loses the right of confidentiality in relation to the other. Perhaps the better argument in this context is that on divorce the couple's assets become available for redistribution and cease to be regarded as his or her assets. The conclusion in this case that information obtained without consent of the other spouse sometimes cannot be used in evidence is likely to make disclosure of the truth of the parties' positions even harder and lead to an increase in the number of orders made on the basis of false facts. Rich spouses will be delighted.

6 Orders that the court can make

In 2019 there were 43,515 financial orders made. But of these 4,516 were contested, indicating that most financial disputes are negotiated, rather than fought out in courts. Note too, that given there were 116,889 divorces initiated in 2019 that indicates for around two-thirds of couples no financial orders are made at all.[215] The court has a range of orders that it can make. It is useful to divide these up into those orders that relate to income, and those that relate to capital and property.

A Income orders

The main income order is the periodical payments order (PPO) under s. 23 of the MCA 1973.[216] These payments can be weekly, monthly or annual. For example, a husband could be ordered to pay his ex-wife £400 per month. The order can be secured or unsecured. If it is a secured PPO and the payments are not made, then the property providing the security can be sold to enable payment. The security could be, for example, shares or the matrimonial home. This is an attractive option for the recipient, as she will not have to worry about non-payment, and also secured periodical payments can continue after the death of the payer. However, if there are sufficient assets to provide security for periodical payments, then it might be better

---

[214] [2010] EWCA Civ 908.

[215] Ministry of Justice (2020a).

[216] MCA 1973, s. 22 allows for 'maintenance pending suit' which allows for payments prior to the litigation being completed. Its primary use today is to enable a party to pay their solicitors: *Moses-Taiga v Taiga* [2008] 1 FCR 696.

simply to transfer those assets over to the wife as a lump sum instead of requiring regular payments. It is, therefore, not surprising that Thorpe LJ has suggested that secured PPOs 'have [been] virtually relegated to the legal history books'.[217]

A payments order will cease on any of the following events:

1. The death of either party.[218] However, if the order is a secured periodical order, the order need not cease on the death of the payer.[219]

2. The remarriage of the recipient.[220] The explanation is that on remarriage the new spouse would be financially responsible for the recipient. While that might have some validity if the payments are in the nature of support, that argument does not apply where the maintenance payments represent a share in the assets the couple have built up together during the marriage.

3. The court order may specify a date on which the payments will end. For example, the order may state that there are to be periodical payments for the next three years only.[221]

Maintenance orders can be made against either parent for the benefit of a child. If the child is over 18 years of age then PPOs can be made only if the child is in full-time education or under specific circumstances, such as disability.

B Property orders

There are three main types of property order:

1. *Lump sum orders.* A lump sum order (LSO) requires a lump sum of money to be handed over by one spouse to the other. The LSO may be made to a parent for the benefit of a child. It is possible to order that the LSO be paid in instalments. The LSO is often used when considering housing issues: assuming one party is to stay in the matrimonial home, the other will need some money to use as a deposit to rent or buy a home.

2. *Transfer of property orders.* The most common transfer of property order is an order that one party transfers a share in the matrimonial home to the other. A transfer of property order could also be used to transfer ownership of other property, such as a car or piece of furniture. The court can make an order to transfer property to the other spouse or to an adult for the benefit of a child under a trust.

3. *Power to order sale.* Under s. 24A of the MCA 1973 the court can order the sale of property which either spouse owns outright or which the spouses own jointly. The order is effectively ancillary to an LSO. The owner is normally required to sell the item and then the proceeds are divided between the spouses by means of an LSO.[222]

---

[217] *AMS v Child Support Officer* [1998] 1 FLR 955 at p. 964.
[218] MCA 1973, s. 28(1)(a).
[219] MCA 1973, s. 28(1)(b).
[220] MCA 1973, s. 28(1)(a). Remarriage will not prevent a court making a lump sum order, if the application for such an order was made before the remarriage: *Re G (Financial Provision: Liberty to Restore Application for Lump Sum)* [2004] 2 FCR 184.
[221] The recipient could apply to vary the order so as to extend that period unless the order contains a direction under s. 28(1A) or the date on which the payments are due to cease has passed, in which case it is not possible to apply for variation.
[222] MCA 1973, s. 24A(6): if a third party has an interest in the property this does not mean that there cannot be an order for sale, but that third party's interests must be taken into account. Under the Family Law Act 1996, Sched. 7 there is a power to transfer tenancies.

C Clean break orders

(i) What is a clean break order?

When considering what financial order to make, the court must consider whether to make a clean break order. If a clean break order is not made, the parties can potentially have further financial obligations placed upon them after divorce for the rest of their lives. For example, if on divorce the husband is required to pay the wife £100 per month, and two years after the divorce the husband wins the National Lottery, the wife could apply to the court for a significant increase in the amount she should receive. Similarly, if she won the National Lottery, the husband could apply to have the payments ended. By contrast, if a clean break order is made, it ends any continuing obligation between the spouses. So the court may make a lump sum or property adjustment order, and neither party would be able to make any further applications to the court.[223] The financial responsibilities to each other in relation to the divorce are at an end.[224] However, it should be stressed that the clean break cannot end the possibility that a spouse may be liable under the Child Support Act 1991. It is only spousal support that can be cleanly broken; child support cannot.

A delayed clean break order is also possible.[225] This is where the periodical payments order is set for a certain period, say two years, and after that period the payments will end, with no option for the spouse receiving the payments to apply to extend that period.

(ii) The statutory provisions

In every divorce case there is an obligation on the court to consider whether to make a clean break order. Under s. 25A(1) of the MCA 1973 there is a duty on the court in all cases to consider 'whether it would be appropriate so to exercise [its] powers that the financial obligations of each party towards the other will be terminated as soon after the grant of the decree as the court considers just and reasonable'.[226] In *Quan v Bray*[227] Mostyn J stated:

> the court's goal should be wherever possible to achieve, if not immediately, then at a defined date in the future, a complete economic separation between the parties.[228]

If the court is making a periodic payments order, it should consider whether to limit the length of time over which payments will be made, and whether a delayed clean break order would be appropriate.[229] A clean break should not be regarded as something to be achieved at all costs. Certainly, it would be wrong to make an order which produced an unfair or unjust division in the name of achieving a clean break order.[230] Emma Hitchings and Jo Miles[231] found in their sample only 16 per cent of cases had an ongoing maintenance obligation.

---

[223] Although it would be possible to appeal against the making of the order, discussed below.
[224] A clean break order should also contain a term making it impossible to apply under the Inheritance (Provision for Family and Dependants) Act 1975 should the paying spouse die: *Cameron v Treasury Solicitor* [1996] 2 FLR 716 CA
[225] MCA 1973, s. 28(1A).
[226] MCA 1973, s. 25(1)(a), (2).
[227] [2018] EWHC 3558 (Fam).
[228] Para 48.
[229] MCA 1973, s. 25A(2).
[230] *F v F (Clean Break: Balance of Fairness)* [2003] 1 FLR 847.
[231] Hitchings and Miles (2018).

(iii) The benefits and disadvantages of a clean break order

The benefits of a clean break order include:

1. The parties are each free to pursue their own careers or start new careers without fear that their actions will lead to applications to vary maintenance payments. If the husband is paying maintenance, he may be reluctant to increase his income for fear that such an increase would simply result in his ex-wife seeking a larger maintenance payment. The wife might be deterred from seeking a new job for fear that if she had more income her husband would seek to have the maintenance payments reduced.

2. There may be emotional reasons for having a clean break: the parties may not feel that they are completely released from the marriage until all financial issues are resolved;[232] although if there are children the parties will be encouraged to keep in contact,[233] and so the strength of this benefit may be questioned.[234]

3. If the recipient intends to remarry, she may prefer a lump sum clean break arrangement as this will free her to remarry without the risk of losing her maintenance.

4. It avoids the future problems in the payment and collection of periodic payments. As Baroness Hale put it in *Miller; McFarlane*:[235] 'Periodical payments are a continuing source of stress for both parties. They are also insecure. With the best will in the world the paying party may fall on hard times and be unable to keep them up. Nor is the best will in the world always evident between formerly married people.'

The main disadvantage of the clean break order is that it fails to account for the fact that the disadvantages that flow from undertaking childcare continue well beyond the end of the relationship. The idea the parties can, after divorce, 'return to their normal lives' may be possible for a spouse who continued their career during the marriage, but is not for the spouse whose career was interrupted with childcare responsibilities, which will be ongoing. As Gordon-Bouvier argues:

> Although, it is frequently proclaimed that the greater certainty offered by the prenup and clean break is of universal benefit, the expectation on the caregiver to self-right and become economically self-sufficient is often an unrealistic one. Unlike the imagined autonomous subject, she cannot merely leave the past behind, as her future continues to be defined by previous time out of economic work, as well as the perceived risk that her caregiving obligations will constitute a risk to an employer. The clear linear path to progress envisaged by the autonomy-centred temporality does not account for this. Self-righting is presented as a possibility for all, meaning that a failure to do so (or to do so outside of the acceptable temporal boundaries) is labelled as a personal refusal to move on, rather than as a symptom of a broader societal issue that needs to be addressed.[236]

A further disadvantage of the clean break is that the court ties its hands and, whatever tragedy befalls the parties, the courts cannot reopen the court order. For example, if the court assumes that the wife will be able to support herself with the income from a new job and therefore makes a clean break order, nothing can be done if, a few months later, she is made redundant.

---

[232] Lord Scarman in *Minton v Minton* [1979] AC 593 at p. 608.
[233] And financial liability may continue under the Child Support Act 1991.
[234] See Hale J in *SRJ v DWJ (Financial Provision)* [1999] 2 FLR 176.
[235] [2006] 2 FCR 213 at para 133.
[236] Gordon-Bouvier (2020).

The following case is a dramatic example of what might happen if a clean break order is not made:

CASE: *Vince v Wyatt* [2015] UKSC 14

The couple married in 1981 and lived a 'new age or traveller creed and lifestyle', largely living on benefits. They lived together until around 1984, but did not divorce until 1992. At that time, they had few assets and so they did not seek any orders dealing with their finances. At the time of the Supreme Court hearing their son lived with Mr Vince and a girl they had raised together lived with Ms Wyatt. Ms Wyatt was in poor health and on benefits or in low-paid jobs. However, since the divorce Mr Vince had become extremely wealthy through a green energy company and by 2015 had wealth of at least £57 million. He had remarried and had a young wife. Ms Wyatt applied for financial orders on divorce in 2011, nearly 20 years since her divorce. The Court of Appeal found there was no chance of her application succeeding and so it could be dismissed without a full hearing. The Supreme Court disagreed. The Supreme Court accepted that had the couple sought a financial order on divorce it was likely that the court would have made a clean break order, with no payments of significance. However, because financial orders had not been made at divorce, Ms Wyatt was still entitled to make an application, at least in theory. The issue was what order was appropriate. Lord Wilson thought the award of £1.9 million sought by Ms Wyatt was 'out of the question', given the short duration of their marital cohabitation; the length of time since the relationship had broken down, the low standard of living during the marriage; and the fact she could not be said to have contributed to Mr Vince's wealth. Nevertheless, he believed she did have a claim based on her contribution to the family, including looking after the children, which had continued after the breakdown of the relationship. The Supreme Court left it for the parties (or future litigation) to resolve the precise amount to reflect this. [Subsequently[237] a consent order was made granting the wife a £300,000 lump sum.]

Supporters of clean break might be horrified by this case.[238] Why should a wife be able to claim against a husband some 20 years after the marriage finished, to claim a share in money he generated after the marriage was over? Supporters of the decision will claim that Ms Wyatt was entitled to an award to recognise her contribution to the family, especially the care of the children. Although his poverty at the time of divorce meant that an adequate award could not be made, why should she not be compensated when her husband came into wealth and was in a position to recognise financially her contribution? In *A v B (No. 2)*,[239] *Vince* was not applied because the couple following their separation had informally agreed a comprehensive financial settlement; they had shared the childcare equally between them; and the wife (who was wealthier) had generously supported the husband for the years he was involved in childcare.

---

[237] *Wyatt v Vince* [2016] EWHC 1368 (Fam).
[238] See Sloan (2015b) for a discussion
[239] [2018] EWFC 45.

(iv) When a clean break order is appropriate

The court must consider in each case whether or not to make a clean break order.[240] There is no presumption in favour of making the order,[241] but in *Matthews v Matthews*[242] it was held there was a legislative 'steer' in favour of a clean break and such an order should be made whenever possible. Baroness Hale referred to the benefits of a clean break as producing 'independent finances and self-sufficiency'.[243] Clean break orders have been considered appropriate in the following circumstances:

1. *When continuing support offers no benefit to the wife.* In *Ashley v Blackman*[244] the wife was unemployed. The husband was of limited means. The court accepted that the wife would see a very limited benefit if the husband were ordered to pay maintenance because any small amounts of money transferred to her would lead to a corresponding reduction in her state benefits.[245] The court therefore made a clean break order.[246]

2. *Short, childless marriages.* If the marriage was short and childless, and the parties are easily able to return to the position they were in before they married, a clean break order may be appropriate.[247] Even if the marriage is short, if there is a child the court may well decide that the future for mother and child is too uncertain to make a clean break order.[248]

3. *The very wealthy.* With wealthy people it is often particularly appropriate to require one spouse to pay the other a substantial lump sum as part of a clean break order.[249] The lump sum can meet any future needs the wife might have.

4. *Both spouses have well-established careers.* In *Burgess v Burgess*[250] the wife was a doctor in general practice and the husband was a partner in a firm of solicitors. Both were well established in their careers and their children were students at university. It was held that dividing all the family assets equally and making a clean break order was the most appropriate course, given that they were both clearly able to support themselves from their careers.

5. *Where there is antagonism between the spouses.* A clean break between spouses is appropriate where the relationship has broken down. In such a case continuing financial responsibility may only increase the bitterness affecting the relationship. However, even if the relationship is an unhappy one it might still be impossible to make a clean break order which achieves fairness.[251]

6. *Non-disclosure.* In *Quan v Bray*[252] the husband had been guilty of 'brazen' non-disclosure and it was best not to make a clean break so the court could respond if future assets emerged.

---

[240] MCA 1973, s. 25A(1).
[241] *Fisher v Fisher* [1989] 1 FLR 423, [1989] FCR 308.
[242] [2013] EWCA Civ 1874.
[243] *Miller v McFarlane* [2006] 2 AC 618.
[244] [1988] FCR 699, [1988] 2 FLR 278.
[245] *Seaton v Seaton* [1986] 2 FLR 398.
[246] See also *Matthews v Matthews* [2013] EWCA Civ 1874.
[247] E.g. *Hobhouse v Hobhouse* [1999] 1 FLR 961.
[248] *B v B (Mesher Order)* [2003] Fam Law 462.
[249] For a rare case where despite the parties' wealth a clean break order was not appropriate, see *F v F (Clean Break: Balance of Fairness)* [2003] 1 FLR 847.
[250] [1996] 2 FLR 34, [1997] 1 FLR 89.
[251] *Parra v Parra* [2002] 3 FCR 513, although the judgment was overturned on the facts by the Court of Appeal ([2003] 1 FCR 97).
[252] [2018] EWHC 3558 (Fam).

(v) When a clean break order is inappropriate

1. *Where there are still young children.* In **Suter v Suter and Jones**[253] there were children, but very limited capital assets. It was held that it was not appropriate to make a clean break order and that the husband should be required to pay a nominal sum of £1 a year. The court stressed that simply because there were dependent children did not mean that there was no possibility of making a clean break order. However, in this case it was necessary to provide a 'backstop' in case there were future unforeseen events which might lead the court to want to make financial provision orders. In **Murphy v Murphy**[254] the wife had stopped work to care for twins, who were aged three at the time of divorce. Her position was described as precarious and a clean break order inappropriate as it was not possible to tell what the future might bring. There are signs of a changing attitude. The Court of Appeal in **Wright v Wright**[255] dealt with a case where the district judge specifically stated in her judgment that 'there is a general expectation in these courts that once a child is in year 2, most mothers can consider part time work consistent with their obligation to their children.' She therefore only needed financial support for two years. She went on: '. . . vast numbers of women with children just get on with it, and Mrs X should have done as well.' Notably, however, even with those points in mind a clean break order was not made and so if the wife could not find a job, she could apply to extend the period of financial support (although her chances of success might be low). The order was upheld as permissible by the Court of Appeal, although they did not specifically approve the comments made.

2. *Where there is too much uncertainty over the recipient's financial future.* In **Whiting v Whiting**[256] the wife had, at the time of the divorce, started a job. The husband, who had been well paid, had recently been made redundant, but had become self-employed, earning at that time £4,500. The trial judge decided that the husband should be ordered to pay a nominal sum and declined to make a clean break order. This was because, although it appeared that the wife was in a position where she would be able to become financially independent, it was not possible to predict her future.[257] The majority of the Court of Appeal decided that the judge's decision could not be said to be entirely wrong, even though they would have made a clean break order. Balcombe LJ, in the minority, thought the trial judge's ruling was fundamentally wrong and should be overturned. Less controversial was **M v M (Financial Provision)**,[258] where a woman, aged 47, had a limited earning capacity. Here the court declined to make a clean break order as she had not worked for the last 20 years and there was no certainty that she would be able to become self-sufficient in the future. In **D v D**[259] the uncertainty of the value of the husband's private company was said to justify not making a clean break.[260]

3. *Where there is a lengthy marriage.* In **SRJ v DWJ (Financial Provision)**[261] the couple had been married for 27 years, during which the wife had spent most of her time caring for the

---

[253] [1987] 2 FLR 232, [1987] FCR 52.
[254] [2014] EWHC 2263 (Fam).
[255] [2015] EWCA Civ 201.
[256] [1988] 2 FLR 189, [1988] FCR 569.
[257] See also *H v H (Financial Provision)* [2009] 2 FLR 795.
[258] [1987] 2 FLR 1.
[259] [2007] 1 FCR 603.
[260] See also *P v P* [2010] 1 FLR 1126.
[261] [1999] 2 FLR 176.

children and the house. The Court of Appeal felt that this strongly militated against a clean break order.

4. *To achieve fairness.* Where one spouse has undertaken childcare responsibilities during the marriage, while the other has pursued his or her career and this causes economic disparity after the marriage which cannot be rectified by provision of a lump sum then ongoing periodic payments may be required to achieve fairness.[262] In such a case to make a clean break order would not be fair.[263]

(vi) Deferred clean break orders

If the court decides that a clean break order is not appropriate, then the next question is whether a delayed clean break order can be made. A delayed clean break order is useful where a party could adjust, without undue hardship, to the termination of financial provision orders in the foreseeable future.

In *Flavell v Flavell*[264] Ward LJ was concerned that the lower courts were too ready to make these delayed clean break orders. He stated:

> There is in my judgment, often a tendency for these orders to be made more in hope than in serious expectation. Especially in judging in the case of ladies in their middle years, the judicial looking into a crystal ball very rarely finds enough of substance to justify a finding that adjustment can be made without undue hardship. All too often these orders are made without evidence to support them.

As Ward LJ put it in *C v C (Financial Provision: Short Marriage)*,[265] 'Hope, without pious exhortations to end dependency, is not enough.' The court therefore must have clear evidence that the recipient will certainly be financially independent come the end of the period of maintenance payments if a delayed clean break order is to be appropriate. Such comments may be welcomed by those who believe that the courts have too readily decided that a wife who has been out of the job market for a long time can easily find employment, particularly women from minority cultural groups.[266]

D Interim orders

Given the length of time that litigation and negotiations can take, it is understandable that a divorcing spouse might need financial support before the making of a final court order. Hence the MCA 1973 permits the court to order interim support under s. 22. There are no formal guidelines, but the courts will take into account all the circumstances of the case. In fact, it seems that interim awards are 'almost unknown', according to Thorpe J in *F v F (Ancillary Relief: Substantial Assets)*.[267] This is because the courts do not want to tie their hands before they have heard all the facts in a full hearing. They have been used to assist a party to pay for their lawyers' fees, although only in cases of very wealthy couples.[268]

---

[262] *Miller; McFarlane* [2006] 2 FCR 213 at para 39.
[263] Ouazzani (2009).
[264] [1997] 1 FLR 353, [1997] 1 FCR 332.
[265] [1997] 2 FLR 26, [1997] 3 FCR 360.
[266] S. Edwards (2004: 811).
[267] [1995] 2 FLR 45.
[268] *F v F (Ancillary Relief: Substantial Assets)* [1995] 2 FLR 45.

7 Statutory factors to be taken into account when making orders

Learning objective 5

Describe how the relevant provisions of the Matrimonial Causes Act 1973 relate to financial disputes

In deciding what order to make the courts must consider the statutory factors listed in s. 25 of the MCA 1973 and the principles developed by the courts. There is not a clear distinction between these because, arguably, the principles developed by the courts can be seen as interpretations of the s. 25 factors. Nevertheless, it is easier to understand if they are considered separately. We will start by looking at the statutory factors and then turn to the general principles. But before doing that, it is important to highlight two key points.

First, the courts have consistently emphasised that there is one overarching principle governing this area of the law and that is fairness. This was first highlighted in *White v White*[269] where it was said that fairness is the overriding purpose of financial orders. That said, the concept of fairness is not particularly useful. Lord Nicholls accepted that this guidance was not of enormous assistance: as he put it, 'fairness, like beauty, lies in the eye of the beholder'.[270] In *Miller; McFarlane* he said: 'Fairness is an illusive concept. It is an instinctive response to a given set of facts. Ultimately, it is grounded in social and moral values. These values, or attitudes, can be stated. But they cannot be justified, or refuted, by any objective process of logical reasoning.'[271] Wilson LJ said in *Jones v Jones*:[272] 'Application of the sharing principle is inherently arbitrary.' That appeared to say it was subject to the whim of the judge. Interestingly, Moylan J in *Goddard-Watts v Goddard-Watts*[273] suggested that Wilson LJ meant to suggest the principle was discretionary, rather than arbitrary.

Baroness Hale was perhaps more helpful in suggesting an overarching objective for the law, namely that: 'The ultimate objective is to give each party an equal start on the road to independent living.'[274] But, she was clear that that was only one aspect of fairness.

Second, key to understanding the way judges decide what financial orders to make under the MCA 1973 is to appreciate that they are given wide discretion.

The House of Lords has accepted that different judges may quite properly reach different conclusions as to what the most appropriate order is in a particular case.[275] In *Robson v Robson*[276] the Court of Appeal stated:

The statute does not list those factors in any hierarchical order or in order of importance. The weight to be given to each factor depends on the particular facts and circumstances of each case, but where it is relevant that factor (or circumstance of the case) must be placed in the scales and given its due weight.

Further, it is permissible for the court to take into account factors not listed in s. 25, if it believes them to be relevant.[277] Less charitably, Peter Harris suggests that the s. 25 factors are 'little more than a rag-bag of Parliamentary anxieties and statements of the obvious'.[278]

It is time to look at the statutory factors which are listed in s. 25 of the MCA 1973.

---

[269] [2000] 2 FLR 981, [2000] 3 FCR 555.
[270] *White v White* [2000] 3 FCR 555 at para 1.
[271] [2006] 2 FCR 213 at para 4.
[272] [2011] EWCA Civ 41, para 35.
[273] [2016] EWHC 3000 (Fam).
[274] Paragraph 144.
[275] *Piglowska v Piglowski* [1999] 2 FLR 763. See also Herring (2012b).
[276] [2010] EWCA Civ 1171, para 48.
[277] *Co v Co* [2004] EWHC 287 (Fam).
[278] Harris (2008).

A The welfare of children

The court must take into account all the factors listed in s. 25. However, it is required 'to have regard to all the circumstances of the case, first consideration being given to the welfare while a minor of any child of the family who has not attained the age of eighteen'.[279] It was made clear in **Suter v Suter and Jones**[280] that although the child's welfare is the first consideration, that does not mean that it is the overriding consideration; that is to say, it is the most important factor, but not the only factor. The Court of Appeal explained that, as well as protecting the child's interests, it is necessary to reach 'a financial result, which is just as between husband and wife'.

The criteria to be taken into account when considering awards to spouses with children are set out in s. 25(3):

LEGISLATIVE PROVISION

Matrimonial Causes Act, section 25(3)

(a)   the financial needs of the child;

(b)   the income, earning capacity (if any), property and other financial resources of the child;

(c)   any physical or mental disability of the child;

(d)   the manner in which he was being and in which the parties to the marriage expected him to be educated or trained;

(e)   the considerations mentioned in relation to the parties to the marriage in paragraphs (a), (b), (c) and (e) of [s. 25(2) of the MCA 1973].

The child's interests are obviously significant when considering the appropriate level of child support but are also very relevant when deciding the financial support for spouses. The child's interests can be pertinent in a number of ways:

1. It has been held that it would be contrary to the child's interests if either of his or her parents had to live in straitened circumstances, as this would cause the child distress[281] and affect the parents' ability to care for him or her. Baroness Hale in **Miller; McFarlane** explained that part of promoting the child's welfare was to ensure that the primary carer is 'properly provided for, because it is well known that the security and stability of children depends in large part upon the security and stability of their primary carers'.[282] In **RK v RK**[283] the court went further and suggested it was not in a child's interests for there to be a marked disparity in the standard of living of the mother and father.

2. The child's interests can also be important in deciding what should happen to the matrimonial home. It may well be thought that it is in the child's best interests if he or she and the parent who is caring for him or her remain in the matrimonial home. In **B v B (Financial**

---

[279] MCA 1973, s. 25(1). 'Child' here includes any child of the family of the couple (see Chapter 8 for further discussion of this term).
[280] [1987] 2 FLR 232, [1987] FCR 52.
[281] **E v E (Financial Provision)** [1990] 2 FLR 233 at p. 249.
[282] [2006] 2 FCR 213 at para 128.
[283] [2012] 3 FCR 44.

Provision: Welfare of Child and Conduct)[284] the need to ensure that the child (who had had a disturbed background) had a secure and satisfactory home meant that there was no money to enable the husband to purchase a house. This was justified by Connell J on the basis that the child's welfare was to be the first consideration.

3. The child's interests are also relevant in deciding whether or not the court should expect the residential parent to go out to work to support him- or herself, or order the other spouse to pay maintenance support.[285] The courts generally accept that a parent caring for young children should not be expected to seek employment.[286]

The court will take into account the future interests of children, even beyond their minority, as well as the interests of children already over the age of minority, even though the interests of such children are not the first consideration.[287]

B Financial resources

LEGISLATIVE PROVISION

Matrimonial Causes Act 1973, section 25(2)(a)

The income, earning capacity, property and other financial resources which each of the parties to the marriage has or is likely to have in the foreseeable future, including in the case of earning capacity any increase in that capacity which it would in the opinion of the court be reasonable to expect a party to the marriage to take steps to acquire.

Clearly, the financial resources of the parties are a key element, although the truth is that the courts are often dealing with the debts, rather than the assets, of the parties.[288] All of the assets of a party will be considered, even those they owned before the marriage. A number of controversial issues have been discussed by the courts in regard to financial resources:

1. The court cannot take into account the resources of a third party.[289] So, if the wife now has a rich boyfriend, his income cannot be taken into account. However, the court may assume that a spouse's new partner might be in a position to contribute to her household expenses, thereby reducing her needs.[290] In *TL v ML*[291] it was held that it might be appropriate to make an award on the assumption that a third party (such as a parent or trustee) would meet the award, but only if that would be fair to do so, for example where the third party has indicated they are willing to provide the funds to meet any court order.[292] However, it would be wrong of the court to make an order that put undue pressure on a third party to make a payment.[293]

---

[284] [2002] 1 FLR 555.
[285] *Waterman v Waterman* [1989] 1 FLR 380, [1989] FCR 267.
[286] *Leadbeater v Leadbeater* [1985] 1 FLR 789.
[287] *Young v Young* [2013] EWHC 3637 (Fam).
[288] Eekelaar and Maclean (1986).
[289] *Wodehouse v Wodehouse* [2018] EWCA Civ 309.
[290] *Atkinson v Atkinson (No. 2)* [1996] 1 FLR 51, [1995] 3 FCR 788 CA
[291] [2006] 1 FCR 465.
[292] Although in *Re C (Divorce: Ancillary Relief)* [2007] EWHC 1911 (Fam) Baron J was more willing to assume that a wife who was a beneficiary under a discretionary trust could expect to receive money from the trust. See also *A v A and St George Trustees Ltd* [2007] EWHC 99 (Fam) and *Whaley v Whaley* [2011] EWCA Civ 617.
[293] *M v W (Ancillary Relief)* [2010] EWHC 1155 (Fam).

2. With rich individuals, often their assets are hidden within a company that he or she controls. Can the property of the company be used to pay the wife financial payments on divorce?

CASE: *Prest v Petrodel Resources Ltd and Others* [2013] UKSC 34

The parties had been married for nearly 20 years, having four children and an affluent lifestyle. The husband was a prominent oil trader who owned the Petrodel Group of companies. The companies owned seven residential properties. The question arose whether the property of the companies, especially the residential properties, was to be available for redistribution on divorce.

The Supreme Court held that in cases where it was alleged that property owned by a company was in practice owned by the company, in very exceptional cases the courts would be willing to 'pierce the corporate veil' in a divorce case. This was limited to cases where a person was deliberately evading a legal obligation to provide financially on divorce. That did not apply in this case as there was no suggestion these companies had been created to avoid having to meet financial orders on divorce. An argument that s. 24 of the MCA 1973 gave a broad power to look behind company ownership was rejected. Nevertheless, it was open to the wife to argue that although the company was the legal owner the properties were held on trust for the husband. As he owned the equitable interest in the properties these could be taken into account in the making of financial orders. The husband and the company had refused to provide paperwork in connection with the purchase of the properties and the court was entitled to conclude that they revealed that the husband intended to keep an equitable interest in them.

Although Mrs Prest won the case it should not be thought that this means that generally spouses whose wealth is hidden within corporate entities will be required to use those assets to pay financial orders. Indeed, the Supreme Court upheld the general principle that companies have their own legal personhoods and that corporate property is owned by the company, not the directors or shareholders. Only where a company has been created specifically to try and avoid having to make payments on divorce will the court look behind the corporate veil. Mrs Prest won her case on the details concerning the purchase of the property, relying on the principles of resulting trust (see Chapter 5), meaning the parties were presumed to have created a trust when the property was bought, with the company being the trustee and the husband the beneficiary. In other similar cases it may well not be possible to find the parties intended to create a trust. The wife was helped in this case by the husband's refusal to provide evidence, leaving the court with the option of making presumptions of fact against him. Critics will complain that this case makes it very easy for husbands to severely limit the amounts they may need to pay out on divorce.[294]

3. 'Other resources' include income from discretionary trusts;[295] personal injury damages;[296] and even inheritance received after the divorce.[297] Property inherited during the marriage

---

[294] *RK v RK* [2012] 3 FCR 44.
[295] *RK v RK* [2012] 3 FCR 44.
[296] *Mansfield v Mansfield* [2011] EWCA Civ 1056; *C v C (Financial Provision: Personal Damages)* [1995] 2 FLR 171, [1996] 1 FCR 283. But the court will not assume an outcome in proceedings which are yet to be concluded: *George v George* [2003] 3 FCR 380.
[297] *Schuller v Schuller* [1990] 2 FLR 193, [1990] FCR 626.

can be divided on divorce, although the fact that it was inherited by one spouse should be taken into account in determining whether it would be fair to distribute it.[298] In *B v B (Ancillary Relief)*[299] it was held to be unfair to divide assets equally on divorce after a 12-year marriage where all of the available capital had been brought into the marriage by the wife from an inheritance. Only very rarely will the court assume that one spouse will receive money under someone's will at some point in the future.[300]

4. The court will consider not only the spouse's present income, but also the extra earnings that could be gained by receiving bonuses,[301] working overtime[302] or taking out loans.[303] If a person is unemployed, he or she may be expected to find work. If a spouse has reduced their income just prior to separation, they may be expected to return to their normal levels of income.[304] In *Roxar v Jaledoust*[305] the husband's income had dropped after the divorce and he explained 'it is totally right to say that I've taken my foot off the throttle. I don't see why I should pay my ex-wife what I do'. The judge treated him as having the income he had received during the marriage.

One difficult issue involves the earning capacity of spouses, normally wives, who have dedicated their lives to childcare. The courts will not generally expect a middle-aged spouse who has been out of the job market to find employment.[306] Hence, in *A v A (Financial Provision)*[307] it was held not to be reasonable to expect a woman of 45 to seek full-time employment or set up her own business, even though she had an engineering degree. Had she been much younger, or had there been no children, the court might have reacted differently.[308] In *AB v FC*[309] it was said a mother with a pre-school child and no established career had to be treated as having 'virtually no earning capacity'.

C The needs, obligations and responsibilities of the parties

> ### LEGISLATIVE PROVISION
>
> ### Matrimonial Causes Act 1973, section 25(2)(b)
>
> The financial needs, obligations and responsibilities which each of the parties to the marriage has or is likely to have in the foreseeable future.

Having looked at the plus side (the resources of the parties), the court will then turn to the minus side (the needs, obligations and responsibilities of the parties). Needs here are not

---

[298] *White v White* [2000] 2 FLR 981, [2000] 3 FCR 555.
[299] [2008] 1 FCR 613.
[300] *HRH Tessy Princess of Luxembourg v HRH Louis Prince of Luxembourg* [2018] EWFC 77. In *Alireza v Radwan* [2017] EWCA Civ 1545 the relative lived in a jurisdiction which required 'forced heirship' and so there was no uncertainty that the spouse would inherit. In such a case it can be taken into account.
[301] *P v P* [2013] EWHC 4105 (Fam).
[302] *J-PC v J-AF* [1955] P 215.
[303] *Newton v Newton* [1990] 1 FLR 33, [1989] FCR 521.
[304] *Tattersall v Tattersall* [2013] EWCA Civ 774.
[305] [2017] EWHC 977 (Fam).
[306] *Barrett v Barrett* [1988] 2 FLR 516, [1988] FCR 707.
[307] [1998] 2 FLR 180, [1998] 3 FCR 421.
[308] See *N v N (Consent Order: Variation)* [1993] 2 FLR 868, [1994] 2 FCR 275.
[309] [2016] EWHC 3285 (Fam).

restricted to those that arise directly from the marriage.[310] The concept of 'needs' is inevitably subjective. Do you *need* a sofa? If so, should it be from Argos, John Lewis or Harrods? The courts have interpreted 'needs' loosely. Needs will be understood in the context of the kind of lifestyle the couple enjoyed during their marriage.[311] This has, in fact, caused the courts some embarrassment, in that saying a spouse *needs* three houses[312] sounds peculiar, and so the courts have suggested that, at least in the context of the rich, 'reasonable requirements' of the spouses should be referred to, rather than their 'needs'. In *FF v KF*[313] Mostyn J was surprisingly open, commenting on the cases involving needs:

> Like equity in the old days, the result seems to depend on the length of the judge's foot. It is worth recalling that Heather Mills-McCartney was awarded over £25m to meet her 'needs' (*McCartney v McCartney* [2008] EWHC 401 (Fam), [2008] 1 FLR 1508). Mrs Juffali was awarded £62m to meet her 'needs' (*Juffali v Juffali* [2016] EWHC 1684 (Fam), [2017] 1 FLR 729). In the very recent case of *AAZ v BBZ* [2016] EWHC 3234 (Fam) the court assessed the applicant-wife's 'needs' in the remarkable sum of £224m. Plainly 'needs' does not mean needs. It is a term of art. Obviously, no-one actually *needs* £25m, or £62m, or £224m for accommodation and sustenance. The main drivers in the discretionary exercise are the scale of the payer's wealth, the length of the marriage, the applicant's age and health, and the standard of living, although the latter factor cannot be allowed to dominate the exercise.

Reasonable requirements are not limited to essentials, and so, for example, in **Robson v Robson**[314] the wife was a keen and successful equestrian and it was said her needs included being able to continue to ride horses. In *AR v AR (Treatment of Inherited Wealth)*[315] financial security was seen as a need. The court might also consider the needs of the parties for a pension or income during retirement.[316] Although when a court had to deal with a husband who claimed he could not live a reasonable lifestyle with an income of £130,000 Holman J was unimpressed, noting that was in excess of the salary of the Master of the Rolls.[317]

Are the courts only to take into account needs that arise as a result of the marriage? In *Miller* Baroness Hale said that in relation to wealthy couples needs had to be interpreted 'generously',[318] although slightly earlier in her judgment she referred to needs 'generated by the relationship'.[319] It would be surprising if the need of a spouse not generated by the marriage (e.g. a disability) did not count as a need for the purposes of the legislation. Indeed, Lord Nicholls made it clear that needs based on disability was included. Maybe Baroness Hale was simply emphasising that special weight would attach to needs which were caused by the marriage.[320] Mostyn J in *SS v NS (Spousal Maintenance)*[321] suggested that periodic payments should be based solely on the needs of the parties save in exceptional cases.[322] He explained:

> I find it difficult to see why it is just and reasonable that an ex-husband should have to pay spousal maintenance or enhanced spousal maintenance by reference to factors which are not

---

[310] *Miller; McFarlane* [2006] 2 FCR 213 at para 11.
[311] *RK v RK* [2012] 3 FCR 44. *AB v FC* [2016] EWHC 3285 (Fam) indicates that in shorter marriages the lifestyle during the marriage may play less of a role in determining needs.
[312] *F v F (Ancillary Relief: Substantial Assets)* [1995] 2 FLR 45.
[313] [2017] EWHC 1093 (Fam).
[314] [2010] EWCA Civ 1171.
[315] [2011] EWHC 2717 (Fam).
[316] *Fields v Fields* [2015] EWHC 1670 (Fam).
[317] *Daga v Bangur* [2018] EWFC 91.
[318] *Miller; McFarlane* [2006] 2 FCR 213, para 142.
[319] Emphasised in *R v R* [2009] EWHC 1267 (Fam).
[320] See Hale (2009b).
[321] [2014] EWHC 4183 (Fam).
[322] *B v S (Financial Remedy: Marital Property Regime)* [2012] EWHC 265.

causally connected to the marriage, unless one is looking at the issue in a macro-economic utilitarian way and deciding that in such circumstances it is better that the ex-husband picks up the cost of the ex-wife's support rather than the hard-pressed taxpayer. This, again, is a matter of social policy. But I would suggest that in such a case spousal maintenance payments should only be awarded to alleviate significant hardship.

His views[323] were described by the Court of Appeal in **Aburn v Aburn**[324] as 'interesting', but they declined to confirm whether it represented the law. In **HC v FW**[325] a wife was awarded £15 million, largely to cover medical and care expenses connected with a brain tumour which developed towards the end of the marriage and meant she needed significant long-term care. The expenses generated by the tumour were not 'relationship generated' but nevertheless the husband could be expected to cover them. In **FF v KF**[326] Mostyn J suggested that only in cases of real hardship would needs that were not generated by the marriage be considered. So maybe the current position is that the court will definitely want to meet the needs generated by the relationship, but will only make an order to meet other needs where it would be fair to do so.[327]

In many cases the first need the court will consider is housing.[328] As Thorpe LJ put it in **Cordle v Cordle**: 'nothing is more awful than homelessness'.[329] The court will therefore always seek to ensure that the children and their carer are housed. Where there is sufficient money it is likely that the housing for the children will be at a similar level to that enjoyed during the marriage.[330] However, the court will not do that if doing so means that the non-resident parent will not be able to have adequate housing.

It should be stressed that the courts are concerned with what a spouse needs, not with what he or she might actually spend the money on. The court's responsibility is to ensure that there is enough money, as far as possible, to meet the spouse's needs, and it is the spouse's responsibility to spend it appropriately.[331] A spouse cannot refuse to pay maintenance on the basis that the recipient would spend it in an inappropriate manner.[332]

As well as needs, the court must consider legal obligations a party has, such as debts. Occasionally, the courts will consider a moral obligation (e.g. to support an elderly parent), but that will rarely play a significant role.[333] The court will not normally take into account obligations which are voluntarily assumed. If a spouse has increased expenditure because he or she insists on living in an unduly large house,[334] or lives a long way from work and so has high travel expenses,[335] then the court may regard these as voluntarily assumed obligations and therefore will not include them when considering the appropriate award. But the court may be willing to take into account the costs of a new family and the needs of a new spouse.[336]

---

[323] *B v S (Financial Remedy: Marital Property Regime)* [2012] EWHC 265.
[324] [2016] EWCA Civ 72.
[325] [2017] EWHC 3162 (Fam).
[326] [2017] EWHC 1093 (Fam).
[327] Heenan (2018).
[328] *AB v FC* [2016] EWHC 3285 (Fam).
[329] [2002] 1 FCR 97 at para 33.
[330] *J v J* [2011] EWHC 1010 (Fam).
[331] *Duxbury v Duxbury* [1987] 1 FLR 7.
[332] *Duxbury v Duxbury* [1987] 1 FLR 7.
[333] *Judge v Judge* [2009] 1 FLR 1287.
[334] *Slater v Slater* (1982) 3 FLR 364 CA
[335] *Campbell v Campbell* [1998] 1 FLR 828, [1998] 3 FCR 63.
[336] *Barnes v Barnes* [1972] 3 All ER 872.

D 'The standard of living enjoyed by the family before the breakdown of the marriage'

This factor[337] tends to be relevant to rich couples in particular.[338] For wealthy couples, a spouse's reasonable requirements are calculated by considering the expenditure during the marriage.[339] So, if the wife during the marriage normally spent £50,000 per annum on clothes then, when calculating her reasonable needs, it will be assumed that that figure represents her reasonable requirements for clothing. In *S v S*[340] the couple had both been heavily involved in horses during the marriage. It was held that after the divorce the wife should be given enough money so that she could continue her love of horses. As the court emphasised, that was only appropriate because the husband was a wealthy man. An exception to this approach was highlighted in *A v A (Financial Provision)*,[341] where the spouse lived a frugal life despite being extremely wealthy.[342] In such a case the court suggested that the wife's reasonable needs could be calculated by asking what standard of life she might have expected to enjoy being married to a man of that wealth.

The factor was also mentioned in *Vince v Wyatt*[343] where the couple had lived in poverty during their marriage. Although the husband later became very wealthy the standard of living during the marriage was a reason against the wife being given a huge award.

E 'The age of each party to the marriage and the duration of the marriage'

The shorter the marriage, the less likely the court will make a substantial award.[344] In *Attar v Attar*,[345] where the couple had lived together as a married couple only for six months, it was suggested that the sum awarded should reflect the amount necessary to return the parties to the position they were in before they were married.[346] That is a common approach to take to short marriages. However, just because a marriage is short does not mean that an order will not be made. This was clearly revealed in *C v C (Financial Provision: Short Marriage)*,[347] where the marriage had lasted only nine months. However, a child had been born during the marriage. As the wife could not be expected to enter employment[348] and the child's health was uncertain, there was no likelihood that the wife would be able to become independent. Therefore, a substantial lump sum order and periodical payments order were made.

Such a decision could be supported by the approach recommended by Lisa Glennon who argues that the courts should focus on the length of caregiving undertaken as a result of the relationship, rather than its length.[349] In *FF v KF*[350] after a four-and-a-half-year relationship

---

[337] MCA 1973, s. 25(2)(c).
[338] *Leadbeater v Leadbeater* [1985] 1 FLR 789.
[339] *Dart v Dart* [1996] 2 FLR 286, [1997] 1 FCR 21.
[340] [2008] 2 FLR 113.
[341] [1998] 2 FLR 180, [1998] 3 FCR 421.
[342] Singer J suggested that their frugality was revealed by the fact their sofa was purchased at Ikea rather than Harrods.
[343] [2015] UKSC 14.
[344] MCA 1973, s. 25(2)(d). See the discussion in Eekelaar (2003c).
[345] [1985] FLR 649.
[346] See also *Hobhouse v Hobhouse* [1999] 1 FLR 961.
[347] [1997] 2 FLR 26, [1997] 3 FCR 360 CA
[348] The wife had worked as a prostitute (her husband had met her in her 'professional capacity') but the husband could not expect her to return to her former 'occupation'.
[349] Glennon (2008).
[350] [2017] EWHC 1093 (Fam).

to a wealthy man a wife was awarded £4.24 million. Weight was placed on the fact she was in a 'position of great damage and vulnerability' as a result of the marriage. It seems in that case the judge felt it necessary to explain why such a relatively short marriage should lead to such a large sum and emphasised the losses caused by the marriage to the wife.

In *Miller v Miller*[351] a wife was awarded £5 million after a marriage of under three years. The House of Lords explained that such a large sum could be justified because during the course of the short marriage the husband had made a significant amount of money. The wife was entitled to her share of the money generated during the marriage, even in the case of a short marriage.

In considering the length of the marriage, the court will also take into account the total length of the relationship. In *Krystman v Krystman*[352] a couple were married for 26 years but they had actually lived together for only two weeks and so no order was made. Where the couple have cohabited before the marriage, the court will take into account the total length of the relationship. Ewbank J in *W v W (Judicial Separation: Ancillary Relief)*[353] and Mostyn QC in *GW v RW*[354] drew no distinction between the period of cohabitation and the period of marriage.[355] This factor is increasingly important given it is now common for couples to spend time cohabiting before marriage. In short, the courts look at the length of the relationship when it shows 'sufficient mutuality of commitment to equate to marriage'[356] rather than the technical length of the marriage.

F 'Any physical or mental disability of either of the parties to the marriage'

In reality, this factor is subsumed under the needs heading.[357] The most notable case is *C v C (Financial Provision: Personal Damages)*[358] where a husband who was badly disabled was held entitled to £5 million, even though the wife was to be left on social security benefits. The husband's disabilities meant he required constant care and complex equipment, and this meant that he had to have all the assets.

G Contributions to the welfare of the family

> **LEGISLATIVE PROVISION**
>
> **Matrimonial Causes Act 1973, section 25(2)(f)**
>
> The contributions which each of the parties has made or is likely in the foreseeable future to make to the welfare of the family, including any contribution by looking after the home or caring for the family.

---

[351] [2006] 2 FCR 213 at para 55. See further Cooke (2007).
[352] [1973] 3 All ER 247.
[353] [1995] 2 FLR 259.
[354] [2003] EWHC 611, [2003] 2 FCR 289.
[355] See Gilmore (2004a) for criticism of this, arguing that it will penalise those who do not cohabit prior to marriage and undermines personal choice as to when the obligations of marriage begin.
[356] *MB v EB* [2019] EWHC 1649 (Fam); *IX v IY* [2018] EWHC 3053 (Fam).
[357] MCA 1973, s. 25(2)(e).
[358] [1995] 2 FLR 171, [1996] 1 FCR 283.

Under this heading the courts have discussed the position of the spouse (normally wife) who has not been earning, but who has worked as a homemaker and child carer. The courts have recognised this to be an important contribution to the welfare of the family. Indeed, as we shall see, the courts have emphasised it should be seen as an equal contribution to that from a 'money maker'.

Note that the contribution to the family through childcare is not restricted to the care during the marriage, but can include a consideration of the care of a wife to the children in the years after the marriage has broken down (*Vince v Wyatt*[359]).

H Conduct

> **LEGISLATIVE PROVISION**
>
> ### Matrimonial Causes Act 1973, section 25(2)(g)
>
> The conduct of each of the parties if that conduct is such that it would in the opinion of the court be inequitable to disregard it.

At one time conduct was considered very important. A wife who was regarded as guilty of marital misconduct could expect a low award.[360] However, in line with the trend generally in family law, it is now rare for conduct to be taken into account.[361] As the statute states, the conduct must be 'such that it would . . . be inequitable to disregard'. The cases suggest that the conduct must be of an extreme kind in order to be relevant. It is well established that adultery will not be sufficient to take into account, not even where the husband has used his wife's money as gifts to his partner.[362]

Sir George Baker P suggested that conduct should be 'of the kind that would cause the ordinary mortal to throw up his hands and say, "surely that woman is not going to be given any money" or "is not going to get a full award"'.[363] Burton J[364] suggested that to be taken into account the conduct had to be such that to ignore it would produce a 'gasp'. Conduct which only led to a 'gulp' would be insufficient. For example, in *K v K (Financial Provision: Conduct)*[365] the wife helped her depressed husband's suicide attempt as she wished to acquire his estate and to set up a new life with her lover. Her conduct was such that it should be taken into account and her award was reduced from the £14,000 she would have received but for her misconduct to £5,000.[366] Notably, conduct, even in these extreme cases, does not lead to the award being reduced to nil. In *H v H (Financial Relief: Attempted Murder as Conduct)*[367] the husband attacked the wife with knives in front of the children. He was sentenced to 12 years' imprisonment for attempted murder. It will not surprise the reader to learn that this was

---

[359] [2015] UKSC 14.
[360] *Wachtel v Wachtel* [1973] Fam 72 marked the change in the courts' attitude.
[361] Eekelaar (1991a).
[362] *JS v RS* [2015] EWHC 2921 (Fam), although in that case the husband voluntarily returned the money.
[363] *W v W* [1976] Fam 107 at 110.
[364] In *S v S (Non-Matrimonial Property: Conduct)* [2006] EWHC 2793 (Fam).
[365] [1990] 2 FLR 225, [1990] FCR 372.
[366] *HM Customs and Excise and another v A* [2002] 3 FCR 481 held that the fact that the husband was a convicted drug dealer was conduct which it was inequitable to ignore.
[367] [2006] Fam Law 264.

regarded as conduct which it was inequitable to disregard. In *K v L*[368] the husband sexually abused the wife's grandchildren. The Court of Appeal agreed that this entitled the judge to award the husband nothing, even though the wife owned property valued at over £4 million. It was explained that his conduct was so appalling and its 'legacy of misery' so profound that a nil award was appropriate. Surprisingly in *FZ v SZ*[369] it was held that a false allegation of domestic violence by the wife was sufficient to conduct which should affect the level of the award. That is surprising because in other cases actual domestic violence has not been regarded as relevant unless it is especially serious.

So, rarely will misbehaviour be taken into account. However, where the conduct in question is financial misconduct (e.g. one of the spouses has spent money just to make sure the other party does not get any or engaged in unnecessary litigation[370]), the court will be particularly willing to take it into account. Normally, this is done by 're-attributing' the wasted money to the spouse who spent it.[371] This means they will be treated as still having the money they wasted, although in *MAP v MFP (Financial Remedies: Add-Back)*[372] Moor J suggested that this was appropriate in cases where a spouse has deliberately spent money to avoid the other spouse getting it ('wanton dissipation of the assets'). In this case the husband had spent a quarter of a million pounds on prostitutes and cocaine. This was seen as a result of the husband's personality and a spouse had to take their partner 'as they found them'. He explained:

> A spouse must take his or her partner as he or she finds them. Many very successful people are flawed . . . it would be wrong to allow the wife to take advantage of H's great abilities that enabled him to make such a success of the company, while not taking the financial hit from his personality flaw that led to his cocaine addiction and his inability to rid himself of the habit.

Whether the use of prostitutes and cocaine demonstrates a character flaw or a decision to waste assets could be hotly debated!

In *FRB v DCA*[373] the fact the wife had untruthfully told her husband he was the father of her child was said to be potential conduct that could be taken into account. The case arose as a claim in the tort of deceit, but the court made no award, suggesting the issue was better addressed when financial orders under the MCA were made, with the deceit being a potential conduct factor. If it were to be considered under the MCA there might be complex questions about whether the joys he had received from the relationship with the child outweighed the economic expense. One might also query why this deceit is seen as sufficiently serious to be taken into account when domestic abuse is not.

Where a court decides that conduct is sufficiently serious to be taken into account, the judge must explain how it affects the level of the award. In *Clark v Clark*[374] the Court of Appeal held that the wife's misconduct was so bad 'it would be hard to conceive graver misconduct'.[375] The Court of Appeal criticised the lower court judge, who accepted that the conduct was bad but had decided that it should not affect the level of the award. The Court of Appeal felt that serious misconduct should be taken into account in deciding the appropriate order, although

---

[368] [2010] EWCA Civ 125.
[369] [2010] EWHC 1630 (Fam).
[370] *R v B* [2017] EWFC 33; *Bloom v Bloom (Financial Remedies)* [2017] EWFC B109.
[371] *Vaughan v Vaughan* [2007] 3 FCR 532.
[372] [2015] EWHC 627 (Fam).
[373] [2019] EWHC 2816 (Fam).
[374] [1999] 2 FLR 498.
[375] [1999] 2 FLR 498 at p. 509. The wife (described by the judge as a woman of considerable charm and physical attraction) was in her early 40s and the husband nearly 80. She oppressed the husband, refused to consummate the marriage and virtually imprisoned the husband in a caravan in the garden of his house.

it was open to a court to decide that no deduction would be made. In *H v H (Financial Relief: Attempted Murder as Conduct)*[376] Coleridge J held that in assessing the significance of conduct the court should not be punitive, but rather it should lead the court to place greater emphasis on the needs of the 'victim' and less on the blameworthy party. Notably in *AF v SF (Dynastic Trust: Needs-Based Award)*[377] Moor J justified not taking the husband's conduct into account as it had not been shown to affect the wife's needs. This seems to conflate the conduct element into the needs element.

The court will consider not only the bad conduct, but also the good conduct of the spouses. In *A v A (Financial Provision: Conduct)*[378] the husband gave up his job and made no effort to work, while the wife undertook a degree course and started a new career. The court thought that the contrast between what they regarded as the good conduct of the wife and the bad conduct of the husband should be taken into account in calculating the correct award.

Whether conduct should or should not be relevant has given rise to some debate.[379] There are some who argue that if the court is to achieve justice, it must ensure that grossly wrong conduct is taken into account. Shazia Choudhry and I have criticised the failure of the courts to attach weight to domestic violence in financial cases.[380] Others argue that, with the increasing acceptance of no-fault divorce, it is harder to justify the relevance of fault here, except in the most extreme cases. That said, as Lord Nicholls in *Miller; McFarlane* acknowledged, there is a widespread feeling among the public that conduct is relevant. He suggested that the average person would think: 'If a wife walks out on her wealthy husband after a short marriage it is not "fair" this should be ignored. Similarly, if a rich husband leaves his wife for a younger woman.' However, Lord Nicholls said that it would be impossible for a judge to 'unravel mutual recriminations about happenings within the marriage'.[381]

I Loss of benefits

LEGISLATIVE PROVISION

Matrimonial Causes Act 1973, section 25(2)(h)

The value to each of the parties to the marriage of any benefit (for example, a pension) which, by reason of the dissolution or annulment of the marriage, that party will lose the chance of acquiring.

The most obvious issue here is the pension rights that a spouse may lose the right of acquiring, although rights under an inheritance might be relevant. The law on pensions will be discussed shortly.

---

[376] [2006] Fam Law 264.
[377] [2019] EWHC 1224 (Fam).
[378] [1995] 1 FLR 345.
[379] Carbone and Brinig (1991).
[380] Choudhry and Herring (2010: ch 10). See further Easteal, Young, and Carline (2018) and Crisp and Hunter (2019).
[381] [2006] 2 FCR 213 at para 60.

J Other factors

In this section we have focused on the factors listed in s. 25, but there is nothing to stop a court considering factors not listed. In *Thiry v Thiry*[382] during the marriage the husband had acted in a 'financially predatory fashion' by gradually transferring many of the wife's substantial assets through a range of clever devices so they were under his own control. The approach of the court was dominated by restoring to the wife the assets that had been taken from her during the marriage.

8 Principles developed by the courts

Learning objective 6

Evaluate the principles developed by the courts in financial cases

We have just been considering the factors listed in s. 25 of the MCA. However, the courts, particularly in the past few years, have been producing further guidelines and principles to govern the courts' discretion. In most cases the decision of the court will be dominated by the needs of the parties. The judge will be trying to do his or her best to meet as many of the parties' needs, and especially those of the children, with the limited resources. It is only in cases involving wealthier couples that the principles we will now consider come into play. Following from *Miller v Miller; McFarlane v McFarlane*,[383] and *Radmacher v Granatino*[384] we can see four key principles that assist the court:

- needs;
- equal sharing;
- compensation;
- autonomy.

Before setting these principles out it should be noted that an applicant can seek to rely on all of them or indeed none of them in their arguments. It may well be, as we shall see, that the sums awarded will vary depending on which principle is used. In such a case the courts will award the applicant on the basis of the principle that produces the higher sum.[385] For example, Moylan LJ in *Hart v Hart*,[386] considering cases where the needs principle might produce a different total from the equal sharing principle stated that it was 'well-established . . . that the court's award is the higher of that reached by the application of the sharing principle and that reached by application of the need principle'.

A The principle of meeting needs

We have discussed the idea of meeting needs already. This has become the primary principle. The court will only turn to the other principles once it is sure that the basic needs of the parties have been met.[387] For most people, the idea of needs will be limited to ensuring the

---

[382] [2014] EWHC 4046 (Fam).
[383] [2006] 1 FCR 213.
[384] [2010] UKSC 42.
[385] *AF v SF (Dynastic Trust: Needs-Based Award)* [2019] EWHC 1224 (Fam).
[386] [2017] EWCA Civ 1306, para 60.
[387] *Charman v Charman* [2007] EWCA Civ 503.

parties have the basics: a roof over their heads, and enough money for food and clothing. With a couple with significant assets, with a long marriage, the court is likely to try to enable both parties to continue with the kind of lifestyle they enjoyed during the marriage. In *AB v FC*[388] after a marriage of nineteen months it was held not to be appropriate to considering sharing, but the fact the wife had a very young child to look after meant that provision for her and the child was required under the needs heading.

B The principle of equal sharing

The principle of equal sharing was introduced by the decision of the House of Lords in *White v White.*

CASE: *White v White* [2000] 3 FCR 555

The Whites had assets of roughly £4.5 million when their marriage ended after 33 years together. The trial judge awarded the wife £800,000 which he assessed as meeting the wife's reasonable needs for the rest of her life. The judgment was appealed to the Court of Appeal and then to the House of Lords. In a major reconsideration of the exercise of discretion, the House of Lords suggested that equality of division of the family assets should be seen as a 'yardstick'. Lord Nicholls explains:

> As a general guide equality should only be departed from if, and to the extent that, there is good reason for doing so. The need to consider and articulate reasons for departing from equality would help the parties and the court to focus on the need to ensure the absence of discrimination. This is not to introduce a presumption of equal division under another guise.[389]

The justification for this principle was that contributions to a marriage through childcare should be seen as equal to a contribution through money making:

> [W]hatever the division of labour chosen by the husband and wife, or forced upon them by circumstances, fairness requires that this should not prejudice or advantage either party when considering [MCA 1973, s. 25(2)(f)] . . . If in their different spheres, each contributed equally to the family, then in principle it matters not which of them earned the money and built up the assets. There should be no bias in favour of the money earner and against the home-maker and the child-carer.[390]

As their contribution were equal, it would be fair to divide the assets equally.

The importance of not discriminating between the contributions of the money-earner and the homemaker or child carer was repeated by the House of Lords in *Miller; McFarlane*.[391] Coleridge J in *RP v RP* put it this way:

> At the end [of the marriage] both are entitled to a full share of the fruits of their combined and equal contribution; she to ensure that she has a secure future both with and later without

---

[388] [2016] EWHC 3285 (Fam).
[389] *White v White* [2000] 3 FCR 555 at para 24. Singer HHJ (2001) provides a useful discussion of discrimination in this context.
[390] This was repeated in *Miller; McFarlane* [2006] 2 FCR 213, para 1 and said to be true for all marriages.
[391] [2006] UKHL 24. See also *Gray v Work* [2017] EWCA Civ 270.

the children, and the husband so that he can re-establish himself. She has earned it . . . and so has he. This is not largesse by the husband, it is her entitlement deriving from her valuable contribution.[392]

Lord Nicholls, however, makes it clear, then, that the equal sharing principle is not to be regarded as a presumption, but rather a yardstick. In *Lambert* Thorpe LJ described the yardstick of equality as a 'cross check'.[393] Both of these approaches suggest a judge should look at the statutory factors and determine a provisional order. The judge should then check whether the order departed from equality and if so whether there was a good reason for departing from equality. In most of the reported cases equality has been departed from. In *White* itself, for example, the wife ended up with less than half because the husband's family had made a significant financial contribution to the family business.

In more recent cases there are signs of a slightly different approach being used. In *Charman v Charman*[394] it was suggested that the principle of equal sharing is the starting point, rather than a 'cross check' to be used at the end of the process. Under the 'starting point' approach the judge will start with an assumption of equal sharing, unless the parties can provide a good reason for departing from it. It may be that whether one starts with the principle of equal sharing or whether one uses it at the end of the process as a 'cross check' will not affect the ultimate outcome. However, the approach of starting with an assumption of equal division makes it clear that the principle is a central one in this area of the law.[395]

The principle of equal sharing is far less straightforward than might at first appear and raises a number of questions:

(i) Which assets are to be shared equally?

Is the property to be divided equally under the *White* yardstick all the property that the couple possess or only those assets generated during the marriage? This question has proved one of the most controversial in the current law.[396] It is clear that all the assets a couple have are available for redistribution, especially where the needs of the parties require it.[397] However, in cases of wealthy couples where there is more than enough money to meet their needs, the courts will normally only divide marital assets (assets generated during the marriage) and exclude from the division non-marital assets (e.g. property owned by one party before the marriage started).[398] It has also been suggested that the longer the marriage, the less weight will attach to the fact some property was non-marital and the more likely the courts will divide all the assets a couple have.[399]

The relevance of whether an asset is marital or not has been explained differently in different cases. Sometimes it is said that the fact some property is non-marital provides a reason

---

[392] [2008] 2 FCR 613, para 63.
[393] [2002] 3 FCR 673 at para 38.
[394] [2006] EWHC 1879 (Fam); [2007] EWCA Civ 503.
[395] *Gray v Work* [2017] EWCA Civ 270.
[396] Mostyn J in *JL v SL (No. 2) (Financial Remedies: Rehearing: Non-Matrimonial Property)* [2015] EWHC 360 (Fam).
[397] *Charman v Charman* [2007] EWCA Civ 503; *J v J* [2009] EWHC 2654 (Fam), discussed in Herring (2010d); *H v H (Financial Provision)* [2009] 2 FLR 795; *R v R* [2009] EWHC 1267 (Fam).
[398] *Miller; McFarlane* [2006] 2 FCR 213; *SK v WL* [2010] EWHC 3768 (Fam); *Lawrence v Gallagher* [2012] EWCA Civ 394.
[399] *N v F (Financial Orders: Pre-Acquired Wealth)* [2011] EWHC 586 (Fam).

for departing from equality.[400] In other cases it is said that the equal sharing principle only applies to marital property.[401]

There is no uniformity of approach.

In *Jones v Jones*[402] the Court of Appeal started with the assumption all property could be shared, but suggested that the fact an asset was non-marital could provide a sufficient reason for departure from equality. By contrast, Lord Wilson in a Privy Council case, *Scatliffe v Scatliffe*,[403] supported the approach that the equal sharing principle primarily applied to marital assets:

> [I]n an ordinary case the proper approach is to apply the sharing principle to the matrimonial property and then to ask whether, in the light of all the matters specified in s. 26(1) and of its concluding words, the result of so doing represents an appropriate overall disposal. In particular it should ask whether the principles of need and/or of compensation, best explained in the speech of Lady Hale in *Miller; McFarlane* at paras [137] to [144], require additional adjustment in the form of transfer to one party of further property, even of non-matrimonial property, held by the other.[404]

The difference in approach has resulted in a series of conflicting decisions involving Mostyn J, who supported the *Scatliffe* approach and Moylan J who supported the *Jones* approach.[405] The Court of Appeal has sought to resolve the debate, with Moylan J being the winner, at this stage.

CASE: *Hart v Hart* [2017] EWCA Civ 1306

The couple had total assets of £9.4 million. The wife was awarded £3.5 million on divorce. The husband was 20 years older than the wife and when they had met the husband was a 'man of substance', while the wife had no significant assets. The judge determined that these factors justified an unequal division of assets.

The Court of Appeal emphasised that it was not always possible to draw a sharp distinction between matrimonial and non-matrimonial assets. An asset can be a combination of both marital endeavour and a non-marital endeavour. It is not necessary to prove the existence of pre-marital assets by clear documentary evidence. The court may be unable to make a specific factual demarcation but can use a broad-brush approach.

The Court of Appeal noted the long-standing disagreement between Moylan LJ and Mostyn J over how to handle non-marital property. Mostyn J had adopted a more 'formulaic approach' which requires the exclusion of non-marital assets from the pot, which is then divided equally. Moylan LJ has supported a more broad-brush approach with all assets being open to division and the emphasis on overall fairness. Moylan LJ's approach has the advantage that costs can be saved because less turns on an accurate assessment of whether an asset is matrimonial or non-matrimonial. Mostyn J's approach may be seen as ensuring there is consistency and predictability. The Court of Appeal (perhaps not surprisingly given that Moylan LJ was one of those sitting!) determined Moylan LJ's approach was correct.

---

[400] *N v F (Financial Orders: Pre-Acquired Wealth)* [2011] EWHC 586 (Fam).
[401] *B v PS* [2015] EWHC 2797 (Fam).
[402] [2011] EWCA Civ 41. The Court of Appeal in *Jones* said they were not setting down an approach that was to be followed in every case. However, later cases such as *N v F (Financial Orders: Pre-Acquired Wealth)* [2011] EWHC 586 (Fam) have followed it.
[403] [2016] UKPC 36.
[404] Lord Wilson (2017).
[405] *FF v KF* [2017] EWHC 1093 (Fam); *AAZ v BBZ* [2016] EWHC 3234.

It may be that whether one sees the marital/non-marital property distinction as dictating which property is divided or a reason for departing from an equal division of all property does not matter all that much in practice. However, it becomes relevant in a case where it is ambiguous whether property is marital or not.[406] Then, it may be divided equally under the *Jones* approach as it has not been established as non-marital and a reason for departing from equality; but under the *Scatliffe* approach it would not be divided equally as it has not been shown that it is marital property which should be divided. Whatever approach is taken the Court of Appeal has emphasised there should be fairness.[407]

A good example of where it was key whether the assets were marital or not is *Miller* (heard alongside the case of *McFarlane* by the House of Lords):

CASE: *Miller; McFarlane* [2006] UKHL 24

The House of Lords heard two cases together. In *Miller* the marriage had lasted a little under three years. The husband, at the time of divorce, owned assets in excess of £17 million. The trial judge, approved by the Court of Appeal, granted the wife £5 million. The Court of Appeal, in justifying such a sum, emphasised the fact that the husband had caused the breakdown of the marriage (by 'running off' with another woman) and that he had caused the wife reasonably to expect a generous provision in the event of a divorce. The House of Lords rejected both these arguments as irrelevant. However, it held that even though it was a short marriage she was entitled to an equal share in the assets acquired during the marriage. The husband's wealth had increased significantly during their short marriage and the £5 million could be said to be a fair share of that money.

In *Miller v Miller*[408] Lord Nicholls held that in a short marriage it may be fair only to divide marital property, that is, the property acquired during the marriage. In *Miller* this meant the wife was awarded £5 million after a marriage of under three years: the couple had generated about £15 million during the short marriage and she was entitled to a fair share of that.[409]

Perhaps the best we can say as a general summary is that the court will take into account the distinction between marital and non-marital assets in deciding what is a fair result, but there is no hard and fast rule on how to do that. Certainly, in the recent cases involving wealthy couples the distinction between marital and non-marital has become key and often justifies a departure from equal sharing, especially in shorter marriages.

(ii) What are non-marital assets?

The leading definition has been provided in *Hart v Hart*:[410]

Non-matrimonial property can, therefore, be broadly defined in the negative, namely as being assets (or that part of the value of an asset) which are not the financial product of or generated by the parties' endeavours during the marriage. Examples usually given are assets owned by one

---

[406] E.g. *IX v IY* [2018] EWHC 5053 (Fam).

[407] See also *Martin v Martin* [2018] EWCA 2866

[408] [2006] 2 FCR 213, para 19.

[409] In *Kingdon v Kingdon* [2010] EWCA Civ 1251 a suggestion that something might be partially a matrimonial asset was rejected by Wilson LJ.

[410] [2017] EWCA Civ 1306, para 2.

spouse before the marriage and assets which have been inherited or otherwise given to a spouse from, typically, a relative of theirs during the marriage.

So, we can start with some easy examples. Non-marital assets include:

- Assets a spouse owned before the relationship started.
- Assets a spouse has inherited, at any point in time.[411]
- Gifts to a spouse from friends and family.
- Money earned after a relationship is over[412] unless it can be referred back to work done during the marriage.[413] So, if a wife wrote a novel during the marriage, but the royalties started being paid after the separation, those royalties could be regarded as marital.
- Maybe money earned during the marriage unrelated to their relationship. We will discuss this further shortly.

Marital assets will include:

- Assets earned by the parties in their careers during the marriage. The starting point is that money generated during the marriage is the 'product of the relationship'.[414]
- The home the couple lived in during their marriage will always be a marital asset, even if one of the parties owned it before the relationship started.[415]

The significance of the meaning of marital assets in the case of a short marriage was central to one of the most notorious divorce cases in recent years:

CASE: *McCartney v Mills-McCartney* [2008] 1 FCR 707

The husband, Paul McCartney, a famous musician and composer, had been married to Heather Mills for four years. At the time of divorce, the wife claimed that the husband was worth £400 million. Bennett J held that it was important to note that the vast bulk of the husband's fortune was made before the marriage and indeed before the couple met. The amount of money generated during the marriage was very small. There was no evidence that Heather Mills had suffered a financial loss as a result of the marriage. In the light of these facts, the primary focus of the courts would be to ensure that the wife and child's reasonable needs (interpreted in a generous way) were met. Focusing on those, he was ordered to pay her £16.5 million, meaning she would leave the marriage worth £24.3 million. Maintenance for the child was set at £35,000 per annum and the nanny's salary at £30,000.

---

[411] *BD v FD (Financial Remedies: Needs)* [2016] EWHC 594 (Fam); *JL v SL (No. 2) (Financial Remedies: Rehearing: Non-Matrimonial Property)* [2015] EWHC 360 (Fam).

[412] *SK v WL (Ancillary Relief: Post-Separation Accrual)* [2011] 1 FLR 1471. But note that if the increase in value of an asset after the marriage breaks down is simply a 'latent accrual' it will be treated as a marital asset: *R v R (Financial Orders: Contributions)* [2012] EWHC 2390 (Fam); *Evans v Evans* [2013] EWHC 506 (Fam).

[413] *Evans v Evans* [2013] EWHC 506 (Fam).

[414] *J v J* [2009] EWHC 2654 (Fam), para 304.

[415] Applied in *Lawrence v Gallagher* [2012] EWCA Civ 394. Although only part of a home bought by the husband's father three years before the divorce was found to be a matrimonial asset in *AD v BD* [2020] EWHC 857 (Fam).

Those are relatively straightforward examples and we must now move on to the harder cases.

The first issue is whether assets created during the marriage might sometimes be non-marital. There was a difference of opinion in the House of Lords in *Miller*. Lord Nicholls understood marital property[416] to be all assets acquired by either party during the marriage, save those acquired by gift or inheritance. Baroness Hale, by contrast, used a narrower understanding of 'marital assets', preferring the phrase 'family assets'. These were restricted to assets generated by the family: it could include the family home,[417] family savings, income generated by a business organised by both parties. It would not include assets which were produced by the efforts of one party alone. She explained that in relation to non-family assets 'it simply cannot be demonstrated that the domestic contribution, important though it has been to the welfare of the family as a whole, has contributed to their acquisition'.[418]

The difference between the views would be revealed in a case involving a business project in which the wife was not involved in any way (perhaps she did not even know about it). This could be a marital asset for Lord Nicholls because it was an asset acquired during the course of the marriage. But it would not be a family asset under Baroness Hale's test if the wife could not in any way be said to have contributed to its acquisition. In the House of Lords, Lord Hoffmann agreed with Baroness Hale, and Lord Hope (diplomatically, but unhelpfully) agreed with both. Lord Mance did not express a clear view, but he did advocate flexibility.[419]

In *S v S (Non-Matrimonial Property: Conduct)*,[420] following Baroness Hale's approach, it was held that commercial properties owned by a husband before the marriage and which he did not deal with during the marriage were non-marital property. The wife could not claim a share of an increase in their value during the marriage. By contrast, a share portfolio he brought into the marriage, but which he had spent much time dealing with during it, could be marital property.[421] The wife could claim a share in the increase in their value during the marriage. Another good example of Baroness Hale's approach could be *S v AG and another (Financial Remedy: Lottery Prize)*,[422] which involved a win on the National Lottery. Mostyn J said the key question was whether the purchase of the ticket was a 'joint enterprise' between the spouses, in which case it would be marital property, or whether it was a lone enterprise, in which case it would be non-marital property. In deciding which it was, the court would consider any agreement or understanding between the parties and whose money had been used. In this case the wife had bought the ticket without her husband's knowledge and with money from her own account (not the joint account). This indicated it was non-marital.

The most recent cases, however, seem to have sought a middle route between the two and acknowledge that in many cases a distinction between business assets which are the contribution of one spouse and those that are the result of the joint endeavour. In *Hart v Hart*,[423] *N v N*,[424] and *Charman (No. 4)*[425] it was emphasised that the courts should not undertake

---

[416] He used the phrase 'matrimonial property', but later cases have preferred the terminology 'marital property'.
[417] Although see *B v PS* [2015] EWHC 2797 (Fam) for a rare case of where the family home was not seen as a marital asset.
[418] [2006] 2 FCR 213 at para 151.
[419] At para 160.
[420] [2006] EWHC 2793 (Fam). In *Charman v Charman* [2007] EWCA Civ 503 it was said that Baroness Hale's approach was the correct one.
[421] *AC v DC* [2012] EWHC 2420 (Fam).
[422] [2011] EWHC 2637 (Fam).
[423] [2017] EWCA Civ 1306.
[424] [2010] EWHC 717 (Fam).
[425] [2007] EWCA Civ 503.

lengthy and time-consuming investigations as to which assets are or are not marital assets. Fairness may mean that a detailed analysis of the origins of assets is not normally necessary.[426] In *Davies* v *Davies*[427] the main asset of the couple was a hotel the husband brought into the marriage. The Court of Appeal sought to make an order that acknowledged the fact the husband had brought the asset into the marriage, while also acknowledging the fact the wife had done much to help the hotel to flourish as a business. It was not necessary to precisely work out in terms of percentages the amount the wife could be said to have contributed towards. A broad-brush approach based on fairness would be appropriate.

In recent cases there has also been weight attached to the autonomy principle (see below) which seeks to respect the way the parties arranged their finances. It may well be that this will become the focus as the courts develop. Where the parties kept their finances separate, and were careful not to intermingle their assets, the courts will pay more attention to whether assets were created by one spouse's efforts.[428] But where the parties generally intermingle their assets the court will find all the assets to be family assets. But, at the end of the day it should be remembered that the courts will never be prevented from making a fair order because property is labelled marital or non-marital.[429]

A second tricky issue over the definition of marital assets is whether assets generated post-separation will be treated as non-marital assets. In *JL* v *SL* (No. 2) (Financial Remedies: Rehearing: Non-Matrimonial Property)[430] a distinction was drawn between income produced post-separation, but from a marital asset (which would also be a marital asset), and income which is 'a truly new venture which has no connection to the marital partnership or to the assets of the partnership'. So, if a spouse wrote a novel during the marriage, but it was published after the divorce and made much money, even though the income arose after the divorce, it would be seen as a marital asset, because it was generated by work during the marriage. However, if a spouse wrote a novel after the breakdown, that would be clearly income from post-separation work and would not be seen as a marital asset.[431]

A third, linked and important debate, surrounds whether or not a spouse's earning capacity can be seen as a marital asset. Imagine a case where a wife claims to have enabled a husband to make remarkable progress in his career – can she claim that his future income is relatable to her endeavours during the marriage? She might claim that he was only in his high-earning job because of her efforts and so his post-divorce income results from her marital work. In *Jones* v *Jones*[432] Wilson LJ rejected the argument. Although earning capacity was relevant in relation to future needs, it should not be regarded as a marital asset. The same line was taken in *Waggott* v *Waggott*.[433] The justification was that otherwise the policy of promoting a clear break where possible would be undermined.[434]

It seems the issue is settled at Court of Appeal level. However, it is hoped that the Supreme Court will consider this issue. A genuine assessment of the benefits created through a marriage should acknowledge career progression during a marriage creates gains not only during

---

[426] *H* v *H* [2008] 2 FLR 2092.

[427] [2012] EWCA Civ 1641.

[428] This will be particularly so where the marriage was short and childless: *XW* v *XH (Financial Remedies: Business Assets)* [2019] EWCA Civ 2262.

[429] *Christoforou* v *Christoforou* [2016] EWHC 2988 (Fam).

[430] [2015] EWHC 360 (Fam).

[431] *C* v *C (Post-Separation Accrual)* [2018] EWHC 3186 (Fam).

[432] [2011] EWCA Civ 41.

[433] [2018] EWCA Civ 727.

[434] See also *JS* v *RS* [2015] EWHC 2921 (Fam) and *C* v *C (Post-Separation Accrual)* [2018] EWHC 3186 (Fam); *O'Dwyer* v *O'Dwyer* [2019] EWHC 1838 (Fam).

a marriage but very significant sums after it. Acceptance of the argument does not need to undermine policies for a clean break because a lump sum could assess the future income likely to accrue from the benefits of the marriage. Not taking earning capacity into account allows a party to benefit from a product of the marriage, without sharing it.

(iii) When should the principle of equal sharing be departed from?

As we have noted already, the courts have accepted that there will often be good reasons to depart from equal sharing. The following are some of the circumstances in which it may be appropriate to depart from equality:

(a) *The needs of the parties.* In most cases the needs of the children and resident parent will require a departure from equality.[435] Couples may lack sufficient assets to meet the most basic needs of the children and primary carer. In such a case an equal distribution will be unacceptable;[436] indeed, the children and carer may well need all of the assets and, in addition, ongoing maintenance payments.[437] Only where the couple are very rich will there be sufficient assets to meet the basic needs of the parties and equal division can be considered as a possibility. This will be true for many couples. In *Arbili v Arbili*[438] the couple had £1,066,000; the Court of Appeal described it as not a 'big money case' and a departure from equality was required to meet the needs of the parties. Even more surprisingly, in *Rapp v Sarre*,[439] where there were £13.5 million in assets, the case was dealt with on a needs basis, with the wife receiving nearly 55 per cent of the assets.

In *S v S*[440] the husband was living with a woman and her children. It was held he therefore had greater needs than the wife who was living alone. This justified giving him slightly more than half the assets. However, subsequently *H-J v H-J (Financial Provision: Departing from Equality)*[441] and *Norris v Norris*[442] have suggested that it is wrong in principle for a wife to get less than she would otherwise have been awarded because her husband has left her for another woman and has had children with her.

(b) *Exceptional/special contribution.* In *Lambert v Lambert*[443] Thorpe LJ made it clear that in exceptional cases the contribution to the marriage of one of the parties be regarded as a good reason for departing from equality.[444] So far this has been restricted to exceptional businesspeople who have made extraordinary sums of money in their careers.[445] The courts have interpreted this very narrowly. In *Sorrell v Sorrell*[446] the husband was 'regarded within his field and the wider business community as one of the most exceptional and

---

[435] *J v J* [2009] EWHC 2654 (Fam); *Ipekci v McConnell* [2019] EWFC 19. In *Miller; McFarlane* [2006] 1 FCR 213 at para 13, Lord Nicholls said that most cases begin and end with a consideration of needs.

[436] *Tattersall v Tattersall* [2013] EWCA Civ 774.

[437] Although the judge must take into account the needs of all the parties; *A v L (Departure from Equality: Needs)* [2011] EWHC 3150 (Fam).

[438] [2015] EWCA Civ 542.

[439] [2016] EWCA Civ 93. The case is perhaps best explained on the basis the husband had refused to be involved in the litigation and the judge wanted to ensure an order was made which she could enforce.

[440] [2001] 3 FCR 316.

[441] [2002] 1 FLR 415.

[442] [2003] 2 FCR 245.

[443] [2002] 3 FCR 673.

[444] This was approved by Lord Nicholls in *Miller; McFarlane* [2006] 2 FCR 213 at para 68. See *Norris v Norris* [2003] 2 FCR 245 where the wife's contribution to the marriage was 'as full as it could have been', but not exceptional.

[445] *Cowan v Cowan* [2001] 2 FCR 332.

[446] [2006] 1 FCR 62.

most talented businessmen'; his 'spark of genius' had created the family fortune; and he should be given 60 per cent of the family assets to recognise his outstanding contribution. In *Charman* v *Charman*,[447] where the husband was an extraordinarily successful businessman, creating £131 million, it was accepted that his contribution was such that it would be inequitable not to have regard to it. In *Cooper-Hohn* v *Hohn*[448] the husband was described as a 'financial genius' who had made £869 million during the marriage. This was an exceptional contribution and justified a departure from equality. However, these cases are rare. Indeed, the latter three mentioned in this paragraph are the only reported cases of exceptional contributions to date.

A spouse claiming to have made an exceptional contribution will need to do more than show they have made a large sum of money. In *Chai* v *Tan*[449] a husband who had, as boss of Laura Ashley, generated wealth of over £200 million was found not to have made an exceptional contribution. At one time it was suggested there had to be a 'genius element' to make the contribution special.[450] This is interesting because it suggests that a windfall, not reflecting genius (e.g. a win on the National Lottery), will not constitute a special contribution. In *Gray* v *Work*[451] Holman J doubted the helpfulness of the terminology 'genius', which he thought was 'properly reserved for Leonardo Da Vinci, Mozart, Einstein, and others like them'. His preference was for some 'exceptional and individual quality which deserves special treatment.' The Court of Appeal in *Gray* v *Work*[452] upheld his judgment. In that case the husband had made £144 million in a private equity firm. The wife was awarded half, the court rejecting the argument that the husband had made an exceptional contribution with the remark that it had not been shown that a similar person in his position would not have performed as well.[453] The wife argued they should abolish the concept of special contributions, but the court refused to do that. The Court of Appeal rejected the argument that it was discriminatory as all the cases where it succeeded had involved remarkable business people and remarkable child carers were, in effect, unable to make the argument. The response of the Court of Appeal was that the exception could hardly be discriminatory as there were so few cases in which it applied. That is a slightly odd argument. The fact that discrimination is rare does not mean it is not discriminatory. The Court of Appeal also rejected an argument that moneymaking alone could not as a matter of principle constitute a special contribution.

The discrimination against child carers argument is in the forefront of the court's mind. Indeed it was alluded to by Baroness Hale in *Miller; McFarlane*, who stated: 'only if there is such a disparity in their respective contributions to the welfare of the family that it would be inequitable to disregard should this be taken into account in determining their shares.'[454] The obstacle is, of course, that it is extremely difficult to calculate how good someone is at being a child carer or homemaker.[455] The courts do not want to get into the

---

[447] For a helpful discussion, see Miles (2008).
[448] [2014] EWHC 4122 (Fam).
[449] [2017] EWHC 792 (Fam).
[450] In the absence of an exceptional contribution, the courts will not consider whether there was a difference in the contributions of the parties to the marriage: *AR* v *AR (Treatment of Inherited Wealth)* [2011] EWHC 2717 (Fam).
[451] [2015] EWHC 834 (Fam); upheld in [2017] EWCA Civ 270.
[452] [2017] EWCA Civ 270.
[453] *Robertson* v *Robertson* [2016] EWHC 613 (Fam).
[454] [2006] 2 FCR 213 at para 146. Applied in *Evans* v *Evans* [2013] EWHC 506 (Fam) and *Gray* v *Work* [2017] EWCA Civ 270.
[455] *Miller; McFarlane* [2006] 2 FCR 213 at para 27.

position where they are deciding whether the wife was a domestic goddess or not.[456] In *AAZ* v *BBZ*[457] it was accepted the husband had worked extremely hard to generate great wealth but his contribution was not 'unmatched' as the wife had been working very hard 'keeping the home fires burning . . . running the home and caring for the [children]'. In *Chai* v *Tan*[458] the husband's considerable financial success was matched by the wife's raising of five children over a 42-year marriage. In *X* v *X (Application for a Financial Remedies Order)*[459] it was accepted the contributions of the husband and wife were unequal, but not so unequal as to justify a departure from equality. In *XW* v *XH (Financial Remedies: Business Assets)*[460] the Court of Appeal allowed an appeal against a decision of Baker J at first instance that the husband was held to have made an exceptional contribution through his company, because he had failed to weigh this up against the contribution of the wife, including as a mother. Only where there was such a disparity that 'it would be inequitable to disregard' should it be a factor. This seems to open the door to an analysis of a spouse's childcare and housekeeping role. But the Court of Appeal offered no guidance as to how the different contributions are to be weighed. In *WM* v *HM*[461] Mostyn J stated: 'The problem with the whole concept of special contribution is that it gives rise to the Orwellian oxymoron that "all contributions are equal but some are more equal than others"'. Indeed, he said 'it should be confined to cases which are as rare as a white leopard.'[462]

The Court of Appeal in *Charman* v *Charman*[463] refused to set a figure at which it would be said that the contribution was special, but did state that where the contribution did justify a departure the maximum departure would be to a 66/33 division and the minimum 55/45. In the case before the court, the husband's contribution in generating the enormous wealth of the couple was 'special' and so a departure from equality was appropriate. The district judge's granting of 36.5 per cent of the assets to the wife was upheld. Roberts J in *Cooper-Hohn* v *Hohn*[464] awarded the wife some 36 per cent of the husband's £330 million fortune. The departure from equality was appropriate to acknowledge his exceptional contribution and the fact some of his wealth had been created after the marriage.

(c) *Non-marital property.* As already discussed, the fact that one or other of the couple own non-marital property (such as an inheritance or a gift) can be a reason for departing from an equal sharing. For example, in *White* and *Dharamshi* v *Dharamshi*[465] the fact that the family business had been started by money from the father's parents was a reason for giving him slightly more than half the family assets. However, it seems the longer the marriage the less likely it is that the court will justify a departure from equality based on this distinction.[466] In *Chai* v *Tan*[467] where a couple had been married for over 40 years and amassed a fortune of over £200 million, this was divided equally with no account being paid to the fact the husband had brought some wealth into the marriage. That was, in part, due to the fact that so much time had passed it had become difficult to identify the pre-marital assets.

---

[456] Baroness Hale, in *Miller; McFarlane* [2006] 2 FCR 213 at para 146.
[457] [2016] EWHC 3234 (Fam).
[458] [2017] EWHC 792 (Fam).
[459] [2016] EWHC 1995 (Fam).
[460] [2019] EWCA Civ 2262.
[461] [2017] EWFC 25. The case was heard on appeal ([2018] EWCA 2866).
[462] At para 28.
[463] For a helpful discussion, see Miles (2008).
[464] [2014] EWHC 4122 (Fam).
[465] [2001] 1 FCR 492.
[466] *Miller* [2006] 2 FCR 213.
[467] [2017] EWHC 792 (Fam).

(d) *Assets of sentimental value.* An asset which has a special emotional attachment to one spouse, may well be seen as unsuitable for equal sharing. Ward LJ in **Robson v Robson**[468] explained 'the ancestral castle may (note I say "may" not "must") deserve different treatment from a farm inherited from the party's father who acquired it in his lifetime, just as a valuable heirloom intended to be retained *in specie* is of a different character from an inherited portfolio of stocks and shares. The nature and source of the asset may well be a good reason for departing from equality within the sharing principle.'

(e) *Obvious and gross misconduct.* As discussed above, in extreme cases the conduct of a party may be relevant and that might justify a departure from equality.

(f) *Difficulties in liquidation.* If it is not possible to liquidate assets (e.g. they are tied up in a business in a way which makes their extraction impossible), this will be a reason to depart from equality.[469]

(g) *To achieve a clean break.* A court may be persuaded that in order to achieve a clean break a departure from equality may be required.[470] For example, if the wife is not to have periodic payments, she may need a lump sum to replace them and, therefore, may get over 50 per cent of the assets.[471]

(h) *To ensure there was adequate compensation for losses caused during a relationship to a spouse.* We shall return to this later, but the courts will try to ensure there is compensation for a spouse who suffers a loss as a result of the marriage. Most obviously, this would arise if one spouse gave up a career to care for children, during the marriage. In such a case the court will consider whether an equal division of the property will ensure there is adequate compensation. If not then periodic payments or a share greater than 50 per cent may need to be given to her.[472]

(i) *The way the parties organised their finances.* In **J v J**[473] Charles J suggested the court would take account of the way the couple arranged their finances and treated their property. He did not expand on this but it may be that if a couple have throughout their marriage kept their financial arrangements separate, this may mean it would be unfair to divide their property equally. In **Lawrence v Gallagher**[474] the Court of Appeal emphasised that the couple's finances were intermingled and they therefore rejected an argument that each should keep the money they had earned. This emphasis on the way the parties organised their finances reflects the principle of autonomy we shall discuss later. (We will explore this further under 'The principle of autonomy'.)

C The principle of compensation

If one spouse is a substantial wage earner and the other is not, then equal division of assets on divorce will mean equality at that point in time, but a few years down the line there is likely to be a sharp inequality.[475] Baroness Hale in **Miller v Miller**[476] explained that the court

---

[468] [2010] EWCA Civ 1171 at para 7.
[469] *N v N (Financial Provision: Sale of Company)* [2001] 2 FLR 69; *A v A* [2004] EWHC 2818 (Fam).
[470] But not if doing so results in unfairness: *D v D* [2010] EWHC 138 (Fam).
[471] *Vaughan v Vaughan* [2007] 3 FCR 532.
[472] *McFarlane* [2006] UKHL 24.
[473] [2009] EWHC 2654 (Fam).
[474] [2012] EWCA Civ 394.
[475] But see the warning of Thorpe LJ in *Parra v Parra* [2003] 1 FCR 97 at para 27 of relying on speculation as to what the parties' financial position might be in the future.
[476] [2006] 2 FCR 213 at para 129.

is concerned with fairness not just at the time of divorce but also with the 'foreseeable (and on occasions more distant) future'. The unfairness of future inequality is particularly acute when one spouse has given up a career to pursue childcare, leaving the other to generate substantial earning potential.[477] The leading case is *McFarlane*.

CASE: *McFarlane* [2006] UKHL 24

At the time of the marriage, both parties had been in successful careers. However, the wife gave up her career to care for the children and family. The marriage ended after 16 years. The couple had assets of around £3 million which they agreed to share; they could not agree on the periodic payments. The House of Lords ordered payments of £250,000 per year (the husband earned about £1 million per annum): these would ensure that the wife was compensated fairly for the losses created during the marriage, particularly to her earning potential. Unlike the Court of Appeal, the House of Lords refused to make a s. 28(1A) order that the length of time for the payments could not be extended.

This point in *McFarlane*[478] was that equal division would not have produced fairness. The couple had assets worth around £3 million; the husband was earning about £1 million a year. If the £3 million were divided equally (£1.5 million each), within a few years the husband would be many times wealthier than the wife. The wife had lost significant earning potential as a result of the marriage. The periodic payments were necessary to compensate her for this.

Mrs McFarlane returned to the courts several years later (*McFarlane v McFarlane*).[479] She applied for an increase in maintenance payments for herself and the children. Charles J agreed, although he ordered that the payments would stop in 2015, that being the date when the husband was due to retire. Interestingly, the order was made in terms of a percentage of the husband's earnings, rather than a specific sum. That meant that the parties would not need to return to court if the husband's income fluctuated.

In *VB v JP*[480] Sir Mark Potter suggested that compensation was just one of the strands of fairness and it would not necessarily be appropriate to try to calculate a precise figure as to the loss of earnings caused by the marriage. In a big money case, he suggested that normally an equal division of the assets would compensate the wife for her lost career prospects, although it was always a question of what would be fair. Indeed, it seems that generally compensation is the most rarely used of the four principles. In part this is because it can be difficult to calculate what income a wife has lost as a result of the marriage, especially if she was not in a clearly established career path at the time she stopped employment. One of the few recent cases relying on the compensation principle is *H v H (Periodical Payments: Variation: Clean Break)*[481] where the wife was given a substantial capital sum on the husband's retirement following a 22-year marriage. In part this was to compensate her for her lost earnings and ability to develop a pension during the marriage.

However, in the following case Mostyn J launched a fierce attack on the notion of compensation.

---

[477] See also *Murphy v Murphy* [2009] EWCA Civ 1258.
[478] [2006] 2 FCR 213.
[479] [2009] 2 FLR 1322.
[480] [2008] 2 FCR 682.
[481] [2014] EWHC 760 (Fam).

CASE: *SA v PA (Pre-Marital Agreement: Compensation)* [2014] EWHC 392 (Fam)

The case involved a couple who had been married for 18 years. They were both solicitors at the start of the marriage, but the wife had ceased work to care for the children, while the husband's career had flourished with him now earning in excess of half a million pounds a year. She claimed for a financial order on divorce which reflected compensation for her lost earnings.

Mostyn J stated that he found the compensation principle 'extremely problematic and challenging both conceptually and legally'. He gave five reasons. First, the idea of compensation normally reflected the fact that someone had been wronged by someone else, and did not apply in a case where the victim was 'not an active enthusiastic voluntary participant in the events that give rise to the claim'. Second, that any award was based on speculation as to what would have happened if the wife had not married the husband. Third, he thought it could result in arbitrary awards in giving larger awards to a wife who gave up a lucrative career as compared with one who gave up a low-paid career, if the courts are saying that the contribution through childcare is equal. Fourth, calculating how the wife's career would have progressed and what her income would be could not be computed rationally or predictably. Finally, he thought that the decision in *McFarlane* could be reached without reference to compensation. Despite these concerns Mostyn J accepted compensation was part of the law, but he suggested it would only be invoked in a 'rare and exceptional case'.

Mostyn J's statement highlights the difficulty in calculating an award which reflects the loss of income and earning potential in compensation cases. However, the Court of Appeal does not appear to agree with him. In *H v H*[482] it upheld an order of Coleridge J containing a compensation element for a wife who left a well-paid job to undertake care of the couple's children. Indeed, the Court of Appeal were concerned that Coleridge J had not awarded a sufficient sum for compensation.

The leading authority is now the following case. The wife in this case put her argument in the alternative: either she was entitled to a share in her husband's future income as his earning capacity was a marital asset, or she was entitled to a share as compensation for her lost earning capacity.

CASE: *Waggott v Waggott* [2018] EWCA Civ 727

The couple had been living together for over 20 years and married for 12. They had one child. Very early into the marriage the husband took up a new job and the family moved home, with the wife having to leave her job and not then returning to work. By the time of separation, the couple had capital assets of £14.4 million and the husband had an income of £3.7 million per year while the wife had no income. The wife was awarded £3.25 million as her housing needs and annual income of £175,000. On appeal the wife claimed the judge had failed to give due weight to her claim for a share in her husband's future earnings, claiming his earning capacity was a product of joint marital endeavour.

---

[482] [2014] EWCA Civ 1523.

The Court of Appeal were clear that earning capacity could not be regarded as a matrimonial asset. To include future earnings in the equal sharing principle would undermine the ability of the court to effect a clean break. The wife's argument also contradicted the clear approach of the courts that the marital relationship could not be kept alive for future sharing, unless that was required by need or compensation.

The wife also relied on a claim for compensation for lost earnings. The entitlement to compensation claim, the court emphasised, focused on the lost earnings of the applicant, not the gain to the other spouse. The court was a little more sympathetic to this argument and held it had to be asked whether on the balance of probabilities the applicant's career would have resulted in the applicant having greater resources than she currently had and that the sum that would compensate her would exceed that awarded under the needs or equal sharing principle. The judge in this case ruled that a term order under s. 28(1A), to end in 2021, was appropriate. That would recognise her lost income for a few years after the marriage, but gave her time to re-enter the employment market and re-establish her career.

So, it seems the compensation principle is alive and well, but there may be few cases where there will be sufficient evidence of what income was lost for it to be a decisive principle. Critics argue that the failure to acknowledge compensation (or acknowledge it sufficiently) ignores the serious impact of career breaks to undertake care work.[483] Schumm and Abbotts argue that childcare is still undertaken primarily by women and they suffer significant losses, even if they return to the labour market when the child is old enough. They refer to research which shows that:

> In Sweden 90% of men take some shared parental leave, in the UK uptake is only 5% . . . 427,000 of UK female workers are currently estimated to be on a career break. Of these, three in five are likely to enter lower skilled, lower paid roles on return to work. There are another 29,000 women returning to part-time work who would prefer to work longer hours, but cannot due to a lack of flexible roles.[484]

The courts do not seem currently to acknowledge the depth of impact on careers that undertaking care can cause.

D The principle of autonomy

In the past few years, a fourth principle has been developed by the courts: the principle of autonomy.[485] The most obvious way that autonomy works is in the rare cases where the parties have signed a pre-nuptial agreement. The Supreme Court in *Radmacher v Granatino*[486] amended the law so that now significant weight is attached to a pre-nuptial agreement (a pre-nup). More on that later. For now, it is worth noticing the reason why they think to do that is appropriate:

> The reason why the court should give weight to a nuptial agreement is that there should be respect for individual autonomy. The court should accord respect to the decision of a married

---

[483] Schumm and Abbotts (2017).
[484] Schumm and Abbotts (2017).
[485] *V v V (Prenuptial Agreement)* [2011] EWHC 3230 (Fam).
[486] [2010] UKSC 42.

couple as to the manner in which their financial affairs should be regulated. It would be paternalistic and patronising to override their agreement simply on the basis that the court knows best. This is particularly true where the parties' agreement addresses existing circumstances and not merely the contingencies of an uncertain future.[487]

This autonomy principle is of far wider significance than pre-nup cases.

The courts have in several recent cases paid especial attention to how a couple organised their finances. Where they have kept their finances completely separate it is more likely the court will not divide the assets equally and simply allow the couple to retain what they have earned, particularly in dual career families with no children.[488] Although in *XW v XH (Financial Remedies: Business Assets)*,[489] the Court of Appeal thought the way the couple arranged their finances was a more powerful factor in short marriages than it would be in long marriages.

A striking case is *K v L (Non-Matrimonial Property: Special Contribution)*[490] where a wife brought into the marriage shares which were valued at £59 million at the time of the divorce. However, the wife had kept the shares separate from the family assets and had not touched them during the marriage. Indeed, the couple lived very modestly during the 21-year marriage. The husband was awarded £5 million, a small percentage, but appropriate the court thought, given the non-marital asset had never been mingled with the family assets. Contrast *Robson v Robson*[491] where the couple's 10-year marriage involved an extravagant lifestyle as they lived off a substantial inheritance from the husband's father. They lived their 10-year marriage in a somewhat profligate, equestrian country lifestyle using up much of the £20 million inherited by the husband from his father. The court noted: 'They have by their mutually extravagant lifestyle killed the goose that was capable of laying the golden eggs had they fed her properly.' Here the court placed some weight on the fact this was inheritance, but noted the couple had treated the inheritance as for their joint use. Less than half the inheritance was ring-fenced and not shared equally. The following case is a further striking example of the relevance of autonomy.

KEY CASE: *Sharp v Sharp* [2017] EWCA Civ 408

The couple had been together for six years, had no children, and were in their early forties. At the start of the relationship both had been earning around £100,000 but as the marriage continued the wife earned more than the husband, receiving bonuses over £10.5 million. A year before the end of the relationship the husband took early retirement. Their total assets were £6.9 million.

The key issue on appeal was whether this should be regarded as a *Miller* type case with a straightforward division of the assets generated through the marriage. The wife argued against that approach, claiming that this was a 'genuine dual career family' who did not pool their finances.

---

[487] Paragraph 78.
[488] *Christoforou v Christoforou* [2016] EWHC 2988 (Fam).
[489] [2019] EWCA Civ 2262.
[490] [2011] EWCA Civ 550.
[491] [2010] EWCA Civ 1171.

The wife's argument met with some success in the Court of Appeal. McFarlane LJ emphasised that the 'nature of the relationship' could be a reason for departing from the equal sharing principle, especially where there was no financial dependence between the parties. He further emphasised that in this case there were no children; no 'double shift' of work in employment and at home; and no career sacrifices. He also attached significance to the fact the finances were kept separate, to the extent that they, for example, split restaurant bills. He also noted the wife had bought three Aston Martin cars and given them as a gift to the husband, which showed they did not regard their money as joint. He rejected an argument that only in pre-nuptial cases could the intentions of the parties be used to justify a departure from equal sharing. The court therefore awarded the husband half the value of the matrimonial homes (around £1.3 million) and £700,000 as a limited share in the assets of the wife, to acknowledge his needs, bearing in mind the standard of living during the marriage.

9 Particular issues relating to redistribution of property on divorce

A The poor

The case law has established that a spouse cannot expect the state to meet his or her liability towards the other spouse. It is very unusual for a party on benefits to be ordered to make payments.[492] More commonly, a nominal order is made that could be varied if the person ever got a job. The courts have also made it clear that a payer in employment should not be made to pay so much that he or she is left with only the same income he or she would have if receiving benefits, because that would rob him or her of the incentive to be employed. In *Ashley v Blackman*[493] the wife was a 48-year-old schizophrenic woman on state benefits and the husband was a 55-year-old on an income of £7,000 per annum. The judge thought it important to allow the husband to see the 'light at the end of the tunnel' and be spared paying the few pounds that separated him from penury as there was no corresponding benefit to the wife. In *Delaney v Delaney*[494] the husband was left with insufficient income to pay his mortgage and support his new cohabitant. The Court of Appeal balanced the availability of state benefits and the husband's need to support his new cohabitant. A nominal payments order in favour of the children was all the court was willing to make.[495] The court thought it important to be aware that there was 'life after divorce'. However, it must be appreciated that the law on child support means that any attempt by the courts to make a clean break order is impossible in regard to children.

It is easy to overlook the fact that the kind of cases which have troubled the Supreme Court and Court of Appeal in recent years have been 'big money cases'. Although the principles articulated in those cases are relevant for the few who have great wealth and can afford to finance litigation, the principles are of limited relevance to the 'everyday case'. In a study of practitioners

---

[492] *Billington v Billington* [1974] Fam 24 at p. 29.
[493] [1988] FCR 699, [1988] 2 FLR 278.
[494] [1990] 2 FLR 457, [1991] FCR 161.
[495] See also to similar effect, *Matthews v Matthews* [2013] EWCA Civ 1874.

by Emma Hitchings[496] it was found that for most high-street practitioners these cases are of little relevance. The everyday case is met with trying to meet the basic needs of the parties.[497]

B Pensions

For most couples the home and pension are the two most valuable family assets.[498] The difficulty arises where one spouse, normally the husband, has substantial pension provision, but the other, normally the wife, has wholly inadequate provision. As Lord Nicholls in **Brooks v Brooks**[499] explained, the 'major responsibility for family care and home-making still remains with women' and 'the consequent limitations on their earning power prevents them from building up pension entitlements comparable with those of men'. Twice as many women as men (two-thirds of the female population) have an income below poverty level on their retirement. If the couple remain married, the wife will be able to share in her husband's pension and, if her husband dies while he is receiving a pension, his widow will be entitled to payments. However, if they divorce, the wife's financial position will be much weaker than had she remained married.[500] A different view is expressed by Deech, who suggests that it is arguable that wives who do not ensure that they have adequate pension provision in their own name are negligent.[501]

There is now a duty on the court to consider the pension position of the parties on divorce under the MCA 1973, s. 25B.[502] Under s. 25B(1) of the Act the courts are under a duty to consider the parties' pension entitlements:

LEGISLATIVE PROVISION

Matrimonial Causes Act 1973, section 25B(1)

(a) . . . any benefits under a pension scheme which a party to the marriage has or is likely to have, and

(b) . . . any benefits under a pension scheme which, by reason of the dissolution or annulment of the marriage, a party will lose the chance of acquiring.

Singer J, in **T v T (Financial Relief: Pensions)**,[503] has made it clear that this provision does not require the courts to compensate a party for loss of a share in a pension, but it does mean that the courts have to consider any loss of pension rights. The court, in deciding what (if any) order to make, has the following options. In explaining these options, it will be assumed that it is the husband who has substantial pension provision and the wife whose pension position is inadequate.

1. *'Set off'*. The husband could be ordered to pay the wife money in order to ensure she has adequate provision.[504] So a husband might be ordered to pay his wife a lump sum which the wife should invest so that it will provide for her retirement. The difficulty is that there

---

[496] Hitchings (2008).
[497] Hitchings (2010 and 2017).
[498] See Salter (2000); for relevant discussions of the pension issue.
[499] [1995] 2 FLR 13 at p. 15.
[500] Price (2009).
[501] Deech (1996).
[502] Pensions Act 1995, s. 166.
[503] [1998] 1 FLR 1072, [1998] 2 FCR 364.
[504] *MD v D* [2009] 1 FCR 731; *Richardson v Richardson* [1978] 9 Fam Law 86. See Taylor (2015) for a detailed discussion.

are few couples who have sufficient funds to provide an adequate sum for a pension. But where there are sufficient funds, that is the preferred option.[505]

2. *'Earmarking' part of pension.* This is a delayed LSO or PPO. The court has power to order the trustees or managers to make payments (including lump sums) for the benefit of a pensioner's spouse when sums become payable to the pensioner under the terms of the pension.[506] From 1 December 2000, earmarking orders must be expressed in percentage terms.

3. *Delay.* The court may prefer to delay deciding what should happen to the pension until the husband retires.[507] On divorce, the court will therefore make a PPO and not dismiss the application for an LSO. The issue will therefore be delayed until the husband retires and at that point the wife should apply for an LSO and/or a variation of the PPO.

4. *Commutation of pension.*[508] The court can order the pension to be commuted:[509] that is, that the pension fund be turned into a lump sum, which can then be divided by means of an LSO. Normally, to commute a pension is financially disadvantageous and is therefore rarely ordered.[510]

5. *Undertakings.* If the court lacks the jurisdiction to order a particular kind of provision, it may still be able to accept an undertaking. For example, a court cannot order a husband to take out a policy of insurance on his own life for his wife's benefit, but the court may be willing to accept an undertaking from a husband that he will do so.[511]

6. *Pension sharing.* Since December 2000, the court has been able to split the husband's pension into two portions on the spouses' divorce.[512] The husband will thus have his share and the wife will have her share and each will be responsible for paying into their pensions as appropriate. The two pensions will then operate independently.[513] This order is available only as a result of the Welfare Reform and Pensions Act 1999.[514] The wife will be entitled to keep her share of the pension with the provider of her husband's pension scheme or transfer her share to a different company. The Government has stressed that there is no presumption that there should be a 50:50 split or indeed any form of order at all.[515] It may be that *White v White* implies that an equal split of the pension should be ordered in a case of a long marriage unless there is a good reason not to.[516] However, in shorter marriages account should be taken of what proportion of the pension is referable to the marriage and what proportion relates to payments made before the marriage. In *Martin-Dye v Martin-Dye*[517] the Court of Appeal suggested that, as it had been decided that the other assets would be allocated 57 per cent to the wife and 43 per cent to the husband, the pensions should be divided in the same

---

[505] *JS v RS* [2015] EWHC 2921 (Fam).
[506] MCA 1973, s. 25B(4).
[507] *Burrow v Burrow* [1999] 1 FLR 508.
[508] MCA 1973, s. 25B(7).
[509] Since 1 December 2000, the court can require a portion of the pension to be commuted (MCA 1973, s. 25B(7)).
[510] *Field v Field* [2003] 1 FLR 376.
[511] *W v W (Periodical Payments: Pensions)* [1996] 2 FLR 480.
[512] See also The Divorce and Dissolution etc. (Pension Protection Fund) Regulations 2011 (SI 2011/780), the Pension Protection Fund (Pension Compensation Sharing and Attachment on Divorce etc.) Regulations 2011 (SI 2011/731) ('the Main Regulations 2011') and the Pension Protection Fund (Pensions on Divorce etc.: Charges) Regulations 2011 (SI 2011/726).
[513] *R (on the application of Smith) v Secretary of State for Defence* [2004] EWHC 1797 (Admin), confirmed in *R (Thomas) v Ministry of Defence* [2008] 2 FLR 1385.
[514] In the unusual facts of *Brooks v Brooks* [1995] 2 FLR 13, [1995] 3 FCR 214 the House of Lords was willing to split a one-person pension scheme under the MCA 1973, treating it as a prenuptial contract.
[515] Baroness Hollis, Official Report (HL) 6 July 1999, col. 776.
[516] *SRJ v DWJ (Financial Provision)* [1999] 2 FLR 176.
[517] [2006] 2 FCR 325.

proportions. The Court of Appeal in that case warned of the danger of treating a pension valued at a certain sum as equivalent to cash of that value. That would be wrong.[518]

The pension sharing option is certainly the most desirable option for many wives.[519] As mentioned already, a set-off is available only for the richest of couples. The difficulty with earmarking and delay (options 2 and 3 above) is that, if the wife remarries, this will end her PPO. A further difficulty with earmarking is that the husband may be deterred from paying into the pension scheme after the order is made and may prefer to set up a separate pension scheme.[520] There is also a concern that the parties may not want to have their relationship reawakened maybe 20 years after the divorce when the husband retires. It is not surprising to learn that the number of earmarking orders has been small.[521] With option 3 there is the difficulty that, by the time the husband retires, he may have several ex-wives who seek to claim a portion of the pension. We will now look in further detail at pension sharing, which will be the most appropriate option for most couples with a substantial pension. A study in 2019 found of a sample of court files 80 per cent had a relevant pension, but in only 14 per cent was a pension sharing order made.[522]

(i) What pensions can be split?

Pension sharing is available 'in relation to a person's shareable rights under any pension arrangement other than an excepted public service pension scheme'.[523] The basic state pension cannot be split, although the State Earnings Related Pension Scheme (SERPS) can be.

(ii) What is a pension sharing order?

A pension sharing order is defined in s. 21A(1) of the MCA 1973 as:

LEGISLATIVE PROVISION

Matrimonial Causes Act 1973, section 21A(1)

. . . an order which—

   (a) provides that one party's—

      (i)   shareable rights under a specified pension arrangement, or
      (ii) shareable state scheme rights,
      be subject to pension sharing for the benefit of the other party, and

   (b) specifies the percentage value to be transferred.[524]

---

[518] See Salter (2008) and Rosettenstein (2005) for a discussion of the problems in valuing pensions and other financial products.

[519] Ginn and Price (2002).

[520] There are also difficulties where the husband dies before the pension is payable.

[521] Bird (2000).

[522] Langdon-Down (2019).

[523] MCA 1973, s. 27(1) explains that a person's shareable rights under a pension arrangement are 'any rights of his under the arrangement' other than rights of a description specified by regulations made by the Secretary of State for Social Security (MCA 1973, s. 27(3)). See also Pension Sharing (Valuation) Regulations 2000 (SI 2000/1052), reg. 2.

[524] A pension sharing order can be made only in respect of petitions filed after 1 December 2000 (Welfare Reform and Pensions Act 1999, s. 85(2)(a)). If the petition is filed before that date there is conflicting case law on whether a decree nisi can be rescinded in order to permit the petitioner to re-petition and be able to take advantage of the new provisions (*S v S (Rescission of Decree Nisi: Pension Sharing Provision)* [2002] FL 171; *H v H (Pension Sharing: Rescission of Decree Nisi)* [2002] 2 FLR 116; but see *Rye v Rye* [2002] FL 736).

The essence of the order is therefore that a portion of one party's shareable rights is transferred to the other party.[525] The order transfers rights to the other party and it must specify the percentage value to be transferred.[526]

(iii) The effects of pension sharing

The effects of pension sharing are defined in s. 29 of the Welfare Reform and Pensions Act 1999:

LEGISLATIVE PROVISION

Welfare Reform and Pensions Act 1999, section 29

    (a)   the transferor's shareable rights under the relevant arrangement become subject to a debit of the appropriate amount, and

    (b)   the transferee becomes entitled to a credit of that amount as against the person responsible for that arrangement.

The transferor therefore loses the percentage required to be transferred, so that his pension fund is reduced in value, and the transferee acquires the right to require the pension scheme trustee or manager to credit her with that amount so that she gains a pension fund of that value. The transferee in effect has a pension of her own.[527]

(iv) Factors to be taken into account

Under s. 25(2) of the MCA 1973 the court is to have regard to all the circumstances of the case and include 'any benefits under a pension arrangement which a party to the marriage has or is likely to have' and 'any benefits under a pension arrangement which . . . a party to the marriage will lose the chance of acquiring'.

The court cannot make a pension sharing order if there is in force an earmarking order in respect of that pension.[528] Similarly, an earmarking order cannot be made if a pension sharing order is in force.

A study into the use of pensions on divorce[529] found that pensions are made use of in only 1 in 12 divorces. In a study of selected files of divorce cases it was found that in 82.5 per cent of cases although there were pensions that could be shared there was no pension sharing order.[530] Pension sharing orders were most commonly made with wealthy couples who had been married a long time. It seems pension attachment orders are very rarely made.[531] The study found that practitioners found pension sharing complex and hard to understand. One explained:

> Pensions are very scary, they're difficult; people don't understand them. Judges don't understand them often. And so we do shy away from the whole pension issue . . . [532]

---

[525] It is not possible to obtain an order against an off-shore pension fund: *Goyal v Goyal* [2016] EWCA Civ 792.
[526] The order must rely on percentages rather than a cash sum. See further *H v H* [2009] EWHC 3739 (Fam).
[527] *Slattery v Cabinet Office* (Civil Service Pensions) [2009] 1 FLR 1365.
[528] MCA 1973, s. 24B(5).
[529] Woodward and Sefton (2014).
[530] Pension Advisory Group (2018).
[531] Woodward (2015).
[532] Woodward (2015).

C Housing

In many cases the matrimonial home is the most valuable asset that the parties have. There is real difficulty in balancing the interests of the husband, the wife and the children in deciding who should occupy the family home. *M v B (Ancillary Proceedings: Lump Sum)*[533] provides some indication of how these interests are to be ranked:

> In all these cases it is one of the paramount considerations, in applying the s. 25 criteria, to endeavour to stretch what is available to cover the need of each for a home, particularly where there are young children involved. Obviously the primary carer needs whatever is available to make the main home for the children, but it is of importance, albeit it is of lesser importance, that the other parent should have a home of his own where the children can enjoy their contact time with him. Of course there are cases where there is not enough to provide a home for either. Of course there are cases where there is only enough to provide for one. But in any case where there is, by stretch and a degree of risk-taking, the possibility of a division to enable both to rehouse themselves, that is an exceptionally important consideration and one which will inevitably have a decisive impact on the outcome.[534]

These dicta were approved by the House of Lords in *Piglowska v Piglowski*.[535] So the first aim is to house the children and then, if possible, to enable both spouses to be housed.[536] There are three good reasons for permitting the children to remain in the matrimonial home if at all possible. First, the children will benefit from the security of staying in the house they have been brought up in, given the other huge changes that are going on around them. Secondly, there are educational reasons for keeping the children in their present home, as they can continue to attend their present school. Thirdly, it may be important for the children's psychological welfare that they keep up their friendships with other children who live nearby.

Clearly, whether the parties have alternative accommodation is an important consideration. So, in *Hanlon v Hanlon*,[537] where the husband had a flat that came with his job, the court readily required him to transfer to his wife his interest in the matrimonial home. By contrast, if a spouse has special needs then this is an important factor. In *Smith v Smith*[538] the wife was awarded the house as she suffered from a kidney complaint. In *Lawrence v Gallagher*[539] one civil partner was left with a valuable flat in London and the other a less valuable cottage in the country. These were treated as equivalent because despite the difference in their value they were equally desirable places to life and met the different needs of the parties.

The harsh truth is that if the house were to be sold and the equity divided[540] then it may be that neither spouse would have sufficient cash to purchase another house of the same size. On the other hand, not selling the house and permitting the children and the residential parent to remain in the house may seem harsh on the non-residential spouse. So, the courts have sought ways of enabling one spouse to stay in the house with the children while seeking to protect the

---

[533] [1998] 1 FLR 53 at p. 60.
[534] Approved in *Piglowska v Piglowski* [1999] 2 FLR 763.
[535] [1999] 2 FLR 763.
[536] See *Walker v Walker* [2013] EWHC 3973 (Fam), where the importance of ensuring both spouses could find accommodation was emphasised.
[537] [1978] 2 All ER 889.
[538] [1975] 2 All ER 19n.
[539] [2012] EWCA Civ 394.
[540] Under MCA 1973, s. 24A

other spouse's financial interest in the property.[541] If the couple own a house, then on divorce the court can consider the following options:

1. The court might order one spouse to pay money in exchange for the other's share in the property. This is likely to be an option only for reasonably well-off couples.

2. The court could order that the house be sold under s. 24A of the MCA 1973 and the proceeds be divided between the parties in such proportion as the court orders. This might be particularly appropriate if there are no children and the sale would provide enough money to enable both parties to buy their own homes.

3. The court can postpone the sale of the property until a specified event has occurred. There are two main kinds of orders that can been used:

   (i) A *Mesher* order.[542] The parties will hold the property as equitable tenants in common and the sale will be deferred until the children reach the age of 17; or complete their full-time education; or the wife dies or remarries; or until further order. If one of these events occurs, the house will be sold and the equity divided as decided by the court. The option 'or until further order' enables the court to preserve a discretion in cases where an unforeseen event occurs. Until the sale, the wife (or residential parent) will be permitted to occupy the property with the children. Until recently it had been thought that the *Mesher* order had fallen out of favour. There are a number of disadvantages with it:

      (a) The wife and husband will have to communicate and discuss the sale many years after the divorce. It thereby keeps a certain tie between the couple years after the marriage has formally ended.

      (b) When the children have finished their education they may still be reliant on the mother for accommodation, and the sale of the house could cause them harm.

      (c) The time when the mother is forced to leave her home is at a time in her life when she is most vulnerable. She may be middle-aged, with limited earning capacity and in no position to find appropriate alternative housing.

   However, in *Elliott v Elliott*[543] the Court of Appeal supported the making of a *Mesher* order on the basis of *White v White.* It was held that to avoid gender discrimination and to promote equality the husband was *prima facie* entitled to half the value of the family home. Although the needs of the children justified delaying the husband's access to his share, once the children no longer needed the home the husband should be entitled to his share. A *Mesher* order enabled that to occur. *White,* therefore, might lead to an increase in the number of *Mesher* orders.[544] However, in *Tattersall v Tattersall*[545] a *Mesher* order was said to be inappropriate in a case where there were young children and so the husband was not likely to see his share for 20 years and the divorce was acrimonious and the order could lead to ongoing tensions.

   An interesting twist on the *Mesher* order was provided by *Sawden v Sawden*[546] where the Court of Appeal made an order with the triggering event not being that the children had finished their full-time education but rather that the children had left the home

---

[541] *Fisher-Aziz v Aziz* [2010] EWCA Civ 673.
[542] *Mesher v Mesher* [1980] 1 All ER 126.
[543] [2001] 1 FCR 477.
[544] Fisher (2002: 111). Although see *B v B (Mesher Order)* [2003] Fam Law 462 for an expression of judicial concern about *Mesher* orders. See *Mansfield v Mansfield* [2011] EWCA Civ 1056 where it was used.
[545] [2013] EWCA Civ 774.
[546] [2004] 1 FCR 776.

and were living independently of the mother. This recognises the reality that children nowadays often remain living with their parents, not just during education but for some time afterwards.

(ii) A *Martin* order.[547] The *Martin* order is similar to a *Mesher* order in that the property is jointly owned, but the wife (or residential parent) can stay in the home for as long as she wishes. A common form of the order is that she can stay in the house until she dies or remarries. In *Clutton v Clutton*[548] the Court of Appeal approved a *Martin* order where the sale was to take place on the death, remarriage or cohabitation of the wife. There is concern over this kind of 'cohabitation clause', as it might lead to spying by the husband and involve an invasion of the wife's privacy.[549] The Court of Appeal in *Clutton* suggested that this concern was outweighed by the bitterness the husband would otherwise feel if the wife were to cohabit in 'his' house with another man.

4. The court can give a spouse occupation rights. If, say, a husband was the beneficial owner of the property, it would be possible to give the wife a right to occupy without giving her ownership of the property. There is no provision for such an order under the MCA 1973, but it can be achieved through an order under s. 30 of the Family Law Act 1996 that a wife's home rights continue after divorce.

5. The court could order a transfer of the house from one spouse to the other, subject to a charge in the transferor's favour. For example, a husband could be ordered to transfer to his wife his share in the house, subject to a charge in his favour. So, he would not own the house, but when the house is sold he would be entitled to a share in the proceeds.[550] The benefit of this order is that, as the wife would be the owner, she would decide when the house should be sold, but the husband does not completely lose his financial interest in the property.

6. The court could order that the house be held on trust for the child. In *Tavoulareas v Tavoulareas*[551] the husband was ordered to purchase a house to provide accommodation for his wife and child during the child's dependency. The house was to be held on trust for the husband with the fund reverting to the child rather than to the husband. Once the child reached majority he could, in theory, remove his mother from the home.

D Pre-marriage or prenuptial contracts

Learning objective 7

Assess the law on pre-nuptial agreements

The traditional position in English and Welsh law is that pre-marriage contracts carry little weight in a court's consideration of an application under the MCA 1973.[552] However, as we shall see shortly, that view has recently been rejected by the Supreme Court. The reasoning behind the traditional approach is that Parliament has given the courts the job of determining how property should be distributed on divorce, and the parties

---

[547] *Martin BH v Martin BH* [1978] Fam 12.
[548] [1991] 1 FLR 242, [1991] FCR 265.
[549] For an example of such spying, see *B v B* (Mesher Order) [2003] Fam Law 462.
[550] It is not normally appropriate to phrase the order in terms of a sum of money but rather a percentage, as a specific sum would be ravaged by inflation: *S v S* [1976] Fam 18.
[551] [1998] 2 FLR 418, [1999] 1 FCR 133.
[552] Scherpe (2012) provides a comparative overview of the treatment of marital agreements.

cannot rob the court of its jurisdiction.[553] It used to be said that pre-marriage contracts were contrary to public policy in that they require people to enter marriage while contemplating its breakdown. However, the courts do not seem to find this a convincing argument given the high rates of divorce.[554]

The current approach of the courts is governed by the following decision:

CASE: *Radmacher v Granatino* [2010] UKSC 42

A German wife and French husband had signed a pre-nuptial agreement in Germany which stated that neither would have a financial claim on the other in the event of a divorce. Baron J, the judge at first instance, placed negligible weight on the agreement and granted the husband (the less wealthy of the two spouses) over £5 million. The Court of Appeal held that Baron J had erred. The law on pre-marriage contracts was moving on and there was a clear trend to give greater weight than previously to pre-marriage contracts. The agreement should have carried due weight. In some cases the agreements should have 'decisive weight' and even be of 'magnetic importance'. The husband appealed to the Supreme Court.

The Supreme Court divided 8:1. The majority summarised their views by saying:

> The court should give effect to a nuptial agreement that is freely entered into by each party with a full appreciation of its implications unless in the circumstances prevailing it would not be fair to hold the parties to their agreement.[555]

The agreement could only carry weight if the spouses 'enter into it of their own free will, without undue influence or pressure, and informed of its implications'.[556] If there was a material non-disclosure by one of the parties to the agreement, that could render it of no or little effect. Normally, each party would need legal advice,[557] but not if each understood the implications of the agreement. Similarly, any 'unworthy conduct, such as exploitation of a dominant position to secure an unfair advantage' could mean that little or no weight would attach to the agreement. The parties' emotional state would be considered when deciding whether the agreement had been entered into freely. Their Lordships felt that in this case the husband was an experienced businessman and, although not legally advised, he did understand the nature of the agreement.

The agreement would carry weight only if it was fair. An agreement which failed to take into account the needs of the children would lack fairness. Similarly, an agreement which failed to meet the needs of either spouse, or failed to compensate them for losses caused by the marriage, would not be covered. As the majority explained:

> The parties are unlikely to have intended that their ante-nuptial agreement should result, in the event of the marriage breaking up, in one partner being left in a predicament of real need, while the other enjoys a sufficiency or more, and such a result is likely to render it

---

[553] Hence, contracts between a spouse and a parent-in-law providing for what should happen in the event of a divorce are similarly not enforceable: **Uddin v Ahmed** [2001] 3 FCR 300.

[554] Connell J in **M v M (Prenuptial Agreement)** [2002] Fam Law 177.

[555] Para 75.

[556] Para 68.

[557] See **Gray v Work** [2015] EWHC 834 (Fam) for a case where a pre-nup was given no effect as the wife had not received any legal advice on the impact of the agreement outside the jurisdiction of Texas and had not understood its terms.

unfair to hold the parties to their agreement. Equally if the devotion of one partner to looking after the family and the home has left the other free to accumulate wealth, it is likely to be unfair to hold the parties to an agreement that entitles the latter to retain all that he or she has earned.[558]

A contract may also lack fairness if there had been an unforeseen event after the making of the contract during the marriage. As their Lordships pointed out, this is particularly likely to have occurred in the case of longer marriages.[559] However, an agreement which tried to ensure that the other party did not claim on existing property (i.e. property acquired before the marriage) would be likely to be seen as fair.

If the court concluded that the contract had been properly entered into and was not unfair, the court would give effect to it when making an order for financial provision. *Obiter* the majority held that a pre-marriage agreement could be regarded as a contract and could be enforced as such, although that would be subject to any application to the court under the MCA 1973.

At the heart of the approach of the majority was an appeal to autonomy, mentioned earlier. The law should respect the decision the couple have made about how they wish their property to be divided. It is 'paternalistic and patronising' to assume the court knows better than the couple themselves about what is fair.[560]

The decision has proved controversial. Before looking at the debate surrounding it, we will explore the current law further. ***Radmacher v Granatino***[561] marks a 'seismic shift' in the law relating to marital agreements.[562] In a case where there is a pre-nuptial contract the court will make an order giving effect to the agreement unless either of these two can be shown:

- the parties did not freely and fully agree to the contract;
- it would not be fair to hold the parties to the agreement given the circumstances at the time of the court hearing.

It seems that the burden of proof for showing that it would not be fair to hold the parties to the agreement is on the person claiming that it would be unfair to do so. It is worth considering these two factors in more detail.[563]

(i) Did the parties freely and fully agree to enter the contract?

In answering this question, the court will consider a range of factors. Undue influence; a lack of understanding of the implications of the agreement; a failure to make appropriate disclosure of the parties' assets; the absence of suitable legal advice; uncertainty whether the agreement was meant to be binding;[564] and 'unworthy conduct, such as exploitation of a dominant position

---

[558] Para 81.

[559] In *Gray v Work* [2015] EWHC 834 (Fam) the pre-nup was given no effect, in part because it had been signed 14 years prior to the divorce and there had been significant changes in the parties' financial positions.

[560] Para 78.

[561] [2010] UKSC 42.

[562] *Z v Z (No. 2)* [2011] EWHC 2878.

[563] See Clark (2011); Thompson (2011).

[564] In *Gray v Work* [2015] EWHC 834 (Fam) the agreement was seen as primarily entered into for tax reasons, rather than being intended to settle financial claims and so was not a binding pre-nup.

to secure an unfair advantage' could all mean the agreement will not be given effect. Each case will be considered on its own facts and the courts have avoided creating any mandatory procedural requirements for a pre-nup to be valid. The following issues may be particularly relevant:

(a) Undue influence

The issue of undue influence was discussed in **Thorne v Kennedy**[565] where the Australian High Court were willing to explore the emotional context within which the agreement was signed. The court, they suggested, should consider whether there was an explicit or implicit threat to end an engagement if a pre-nup was not signed.

The closest English authority on this question is **KA v MA**[566] where the husband had always made it clear he did not want to marry. He eventually agreed as long as the wife signed the pre-nup. The court accepted she felt pressurised because she feared what might happen if she objected or sought alternative terms. However, it noted both spouses were mature, had married previously and the wife was financially independent at the time. The husband's stance was described as principled and could not constitute duress. Interestingly, the fact that the wife took independent legal advice, but decided to reject it was seen as evidence she had free will, although that could have been seen as evidence of the opposite.

Undue influence was also at issue in **Hopkins v Hopkins**[567] where the husband had a history of bullying the wife. However, she received very extensive legal advice and the court was persuaded that the agreement was entered into freely. This is a little surprising. While legal advice might reassure us that concerns about a party's ignorance are allayed, it is not clear why legal advice necessarily allays fears of undue influence.[568]

(b) Legal advice

Lack of legal advice has become a key issue. A straightforward case is **AB v BD**[569] where a husband presented his wife with a pre-nup the day before a wedding with no chance for her to get legal advice on it. It was held to be of no legal effect. In **Radmacher** itself the husband did not receive legal advice, but he was an experienced businessman and fully understood the terms of the agreement and so that did not invalidate the agreement.[570] More surprisingly, in **V v V**[571] an agreement signed by a pregnant 24-year-old woman at the request of her husband to be, a man 10 years her senior, was upheld. Although she did not receive legal advice, the agreement was readily understood by an intelligent reader and the court was persuaded that she would have signed the agreement even if she had received independent legal advice. Similarly, in **Hart v Hart**[572] Lewison LJ suggested the court should consider whether the advice would have made any difference to the decision of the party.

Whether the parties are familiar with pre-nups will be a factor. In **Versteegh v Versteegh**[573] the agreement was signed in Sweden, a country in which pre-nups are common, and the agreement was in a standard form. Even though there was no legal advice the parties could be taken

---

[565] [2017] HCA 49 (HC (Aus)).

[566] [2018] EWHC 499 (Fam).

[567] [2015] EWHC 812 (Fam).

[568] Indeed, for evidence it does not, see Thompson (2015).

[569] [2020] EWHC 857 (Fam).

[570] For a similar finding, see *Z v Z (No. 2)* [2011] EWHC 2878. This reasoning is criticised in Harris, George and Herring (2011) because legal advice ensures not just that a party understands the agreement, but provides a check that they are entering it freely.

[571] *V v V* [2011] EWHC 3230.

[572] [2017] EWCA Civ 1306.

[573] [2018] EWCA Civ 1050.

to be familiar with the standard Swedish pre-nups. By contrast in *D v D (Financial Remedies: Pre-Marital Agreement and Unequal Shares)*[574] the wife had no knowledge of pre-nups and did not know anyone who had one, so the lack of independent legal advice meant the agreement could not be seen as valid.

Similarly, in *Kremen v Agrest (No. 11) (Financial Remedy: Non-disclosure: Post-Nuptial Agreement)*[575] there was no proper legal advice or disclosure and the wife did not really understand what she was signing. Mostyn J referred to the agreement as a 'parlour game' because it seemed the parties did not even mean it to be taken seriously at the time it was signed. He had no difficulty in concluding that no weight should be attached to the agreement. He then made comments suggesting a stricter approach to the legal advice issue than some of the earlier cases:

> It seems to me that it will only be in an unusual case where it can be said that absent independent legal advice and full disclosure, a party can be taken to have freely entered into a marital agreement with a full appreciation of its implications . . . It would surely have to be shown that the spouse, like Mr Granatino, had a high degree of financial and legal sophistication in order to have a full appreciation of what legal rights he or she is signing away.

So, it seems the position is that it must be shown that either the spouse received independent[576] legal advice or they had sufficient understanding of the pre-nup that the advice was not needed.

(c) Disclosure

In *BN v MA (Maintenance Pending Suit: Prenuptial Agreement)*[577] the court expressly denied that there was a requirement of full disclosure before a pre-nup could be given effect. In that case there was sufficient disclosure for the spouse to understand the general financial situation and that was enough to uphold the pre-nup. In *V v V*[578] the court were also unconcerned by the lack of disclosure as the wife was uninterested in the precise wealth of her husband and disclosure would not have affected whether she would have entered the agreement. So, it seems that only significant non-disclosures, which would have affected the spouse's decision to sign will render the agreement unfair.[579]

(d) Interpretation

As well as looking at the circumstances of the formation of the agreement, the court will consider whether the pre-nup was intended to apply in other jurisdictions. In *XW v XH*[580] Baker J was satisfied the agreement was only intended to have effect under Italian law, which had a very different system of marital property to that in the UK.

Even if a pre-nup is found to be ineffective due to flaws in the way it was entered into, it might still carry some weight.[581] It might provide some indication of how the parties understood their financial position, even though its precise terms will not be given effect. That might be taken into account by the court determining what a fair order would be under the MCA 1973.[582]

---

[574] [2020] EWHC 857 (Fam).

[575] [2012] EWHC 45.

[576] In *Ipekci v McConnell* [2019] EWFC 19 the husband (the less well-off spouse) had received legal advice, but from a lawyer who had previously worked for the wife and so it was not seen as *independent* advice.

[577] [2013] EWHC 4250 (Fam).

[578] *V v V* [2011] EWHC 3230.

[579] Unsurprisingly you cannot rely on your own non-disclosure to invalidate an agreement! *WW v HW (Pre-Nuptial Agreement: Needs: Conduct)* [2015] EWHC 1844 (Fam).

[580] [2017] EWFC 76.

[581] *H v PH (Scandinavian Marriage Settlement)* [2013] EWHC 3873 (Fam).

[582] *DB v PB (Pre-nuptial Agreement: Jurisdiction)* [2016] EWHC 3431 (Fam).

(ii) Would it not be fair to hold the parties to the agreement given the circumstances at the time of the court hearing?

There are four primary examples of where an agreement would not be fair at the time of the hearing:

- where the needs of the children were not met;
- where a spouse was left in real need;
- where there was inadequate compensation for losses caused by the marriage;
- where events had occurred which had not been foreseen by the parties when signing the pre-nup.

A good example of an agreement being unfair because it left a spouse in real need is *Luckwell v Limata*[583] where had the pre-nup been complied with the husband would have been left with no home, no income, no capital, no borrowing capacity and considerable debts. It was also noted that it would harm the children if the husband lived in dire poverty, while the wife lived in splendour. However, even there, although the court did not follow the pre-nup, it only made a relatively modest award (less than he would have received had there been no pre-nup) to meet his basic needs under the MCA.

Mostyn J in *Kremen v Agrest (Financial Remedy: Non-Disclosure: Post-Nuptial Agreement)*[584] suggested that when in *Radmacher* the Supreme Court referred to a case where a pre-nup would be invalid if it failed to meet 'real need' it had in mind a case where a spouse was left destitute. That interpretation was rejected in *WW v HW (Pre-Nuptial Agreement: Needs: Conduct)*[585] where it was held that whether there was real need or not depended on the circumstances of the case, and presumably a consideration of the lifestyle of the couple during the relationship. A spouse left with a very significantly depreciated standard of living may be in 'real need' even if not absolutely destitute.

At one time it seemed the courts were taking a strict line and would only depart from a validly created pre-nup when there were compelling reasons.

In *BN v MA (Maintenance Pending Suit: Prenuptial Agreement)*[586] Mostyn J held that the 'principle of party autonomy' was extremely important. In a case where intelligent and sophisticated people with excellent legal advice had entered agreement it would be very unusual for a court to declare a pre-nup unfair. In particular, an agreement will not be unfair just because the agreement did not provide for sharing of the couple's assets.[587]

However, more recent cases seem to have indicated greater willingness to set aside a valid pre-nup on the grounds that its effect would be unfair. The Court of Appeal in *Brack v Brack*[588] held in deciding whether to give effect to a pre-nup a court could consider the principles of sharing, compensation and needs. It would be wrong to say only needs were relevant in deciding whether the agreement was fair. The Court of Appeal explained:

> in the ordinary course of events, where there is a valid prenuptial agreement, the terms of which amount to the wife having contracted out of a division of the assets based on sharing, a court is likely to regard fairness as demanding that she receives a settlement that is limited to that which provides for her needs. But whilst such an outcome may be considered to be more likely than

---

[583] [2014] EWHC 502.
[584] [2012] EWHC 45 (Fam).
[585] [2015] EWHC 1844 (Fam).
[586] [2013] EWHC 4250 (Fam).
[587] *Z v Z (No. 2)* [2011] EWHC 2878.
[588] [2018] EWCA 2862.

not, that does not prescribe the outcome in every case. Even where there is an effective prenuptial agreement, the court remains under an obligation to take into account all the factors found in s 25(2) in of the Matrimonial Causes Act 1973, together with a proper consideration of all the circumstances, the first consideration being the welfare of any children. Such an approach may, albeit unusually, lead the court in its search for a fair outcome, to make an order which, contrary to the terms of an agreement, provides a settlement for the wife in excess of her needs.[589]

The court were clearly not saying that in order to be fair an agreement had to abide by the equality principle, but, at the same time, they made it clear that just because an agreement met the needs of the parties did not mean it was necessarily fair.

One factor the court will consider is whether there is a sound principle behind the pre-nup. In *WW v HW (Pre-Nuptial Agreement: Needs: Conduct)*[590] a very wealthy wife wanted to protect her substantial inherited family wealth from a sharing claim from her husband to be, although the agreement made appropriate provision for the children. This was described to be an 'entirely sensible ambition' and the court gave effect to the agreement, even though the husband received under the agreement significantly less than he might have done had the court made an order without considering the agreement. In *MB v EB*[591] Cohen J, in applying *Radmacher* to a separation agreement, had little truck with the husband's argument that the effect of the agreement was unfair given that it had been drafted by his lawyers in line with his instructions.

Another basis on which an agreement might be found to be unfair is if an unforeseen event occurred during the marriage. In *Z v Z (No. 2)*[592] Moor J rejected an argument that the wife having a child and giving up work and following her husband to England could be regarded as events that undermined the fairness of the agreement. Interestingly, he focused on the fact that the disadvantages she had suffered as a result of the marriage were provided for by the needs-based provision in the contract. This suggests that if there are unexpected events, but they did not lead to an unfairness in the result, the agreement will still be upheld. Moor J's approach may be questioned here. The wife may have agreed to needs-only provision on the basis that her career would continue during the marriage. She may not have thought it fair to have needs-only provision if she had known she was going to have to give up her job. The concerns over unforeseen events mean that pre-nups will be under great scrutiny if they were signed many years ago at the start of a long marriage.[593]

As already mentioned, if the pre-nup is found to be unfair the court will consider the factors under the MCA to determine the appropriate order. In *SA v PA (Pre-Marital Agreement: Compensation)*[594] the pre-nup set out what should happen to the capital assets on divorce and that was given effect to by the court. However, the pre-nup did not address the question of ongoing periodic payments and so the court fixed these at a level to meet the wife's needs. This shows that a court will be willing to supplement a pre-nup if there are gaps or issues which the pre-nup does not address.

One issue which the court will need to address in due course is whether a pre-nuptial agreement can be varied by an oral agreement between the parties. The issue was raised in *Z v Z (No. 2)*[595] where Moor J suggested there needed to be 'clear and compelling' evidence

---

[589] Para 103.
[590] [2015] EWHC 1844 (Fam).
[591] [2019] EWHC 1649 (Fam).
[592] [2011] EWHC 2878.
[593] *BN v MA (Maintenance Pending Suit: Prenuptial Agreement)* [2013] EWHC 4250 (Fam).
[594] [2014] EWHC 392 (Fam).
[595] [2011] EWHC 2878.

of any variation, but left open the question of whether an oral variation was possible. An emotional letter from the husband, written without legal advice, was insufficient to vary the agreement. By contrast the fact that the parties in *Luckwell v Limata*[596] has signed several documents reconfirming the pre-nup during the marriage was held to be a significant factor in favour of giving as much weight to the contract as possible.

The Law Commission has issued a consultation paper on marital agreements.[597] It proposes that Qualifying Nuptial Agreements (QNA) can be given effect if contractually valid, made in writing and signed by the parties, following full and frank material disclosure of the parties' financial situation and legal advice. It asks for views on whether there should be a limit on what property is covered by the agreement, in particular, whether agreements should be prevented from applying to marital property. The key question is the extent to which a court should be able to override a QNA. They see the minimum is that the law must ensure that children are provided for sufficiently and that neither party should be avoidably left dependent on benefits. Other options include setting the agreement aside:

- on the occurrence of specified events; or
- if the agreement would produce significant injustice;
- to the extent that the agreement failed to cover two of the *Miller; McFarlane* principles: needs and compensation for relationship-generated disadvantage (note that the equal sharing principle would remain excluded); or
- if the agreement failed to meet the parties' needs, narrowly defined.

The decision in *Radmacher* and the issues raised by the Law Commission are controversial. The benefits of pre-nups appear exaggerated. It is far from obvious that they will make the law more certain. Assuming there is to be some limit on pre-nups, for example that they must not be unfair, we need to have a yardstick against which to measure fairness.[598] A solicitor advising a client with a pre-nup will need to assess what the court would do without the pre-nup and then compare that with how the court will interpret the pre-nup. There may be extensive disputes over the correct interpretation of the pre-nup.[599] That is not making the solicitor's job easier, quicker or cheaper.

It will be extremely difficult for lawyers to draft a pre-nup.[600] As Rix LJ stated in *Radmacher*: 'Over the potential many decades of a marriage it is impossible to cater for the myriad different circumstances which may await its parties.'[601] To cover all eventualities in a fair way will require an extensive document. And where there are extensive documents there are substantial bills!

Any attempt to set down in advance the responsibilities of parties could work against the interests of a party who had to undertake unexpected care work. That is likely to be a woman. As I have written:

> Relationships are unpredictable and messy. The sacrifices called for can be unpredictable and obligations without limit. Ask any partner caring for their demented loved one. To seek to tie these down at the start of the relationship in some form of 'once and for all' summation of their claims against each other, ignores the realities of intimate relationships.[602]

---

[596] [2014] EWHC 502.
[597] For discussion see Parker (2015). Baroness Deech's Divorce (Financial Provision) Bill would have given effect to pre-nups entered into under certain circumstances, but the Bill failed to become law.
[598] George, Harris and Herring (2009).
[599] *Gray v Work* [2015] EWHC 834 (Fam).
[600] Scherpe (2010).
[601] Paragraph 73.
[602] Herring (2010b: 270). See also Reece (2016).

Nor is it certain either that pre-nups will reduce litigation. There is ample room to challenge them. A person unhappy with the pre-nup could claim there was inadequate disclosure at the time of the agreement; they were not given adequate advice at the time of entering the agreement; there was undue influence or misrepresentation; the contract has been frustrated by later unforeseen events; that the contract is manifestly unfair. Further, there might be all kinds of disputes over the correct interpretation of the wording of the pre-nup. Even if all of that were clear, many of the problems which beset the current law would still be there: non-disclosure of assets; attempts to dispose of assets; excessive expenditure. Indeed, whole new areas of dispute could arise if ownership of assets had to be determined for the purposes of the contract.[603] At least under the current law the court does not normally have to determine issues of ownership on a divorce or dissolution. Jurisdictions which have enforced pre-nups have faced substantial levels of litigation challenging them.[604] So a hefty lawyer's bill to get the pre-nup arranged in the first place and a hefty lawyer's bill to undo it when you divorce. No wonder pre-nups are so popular among the lawyers![605] And perhaps no wonder so few people choose to enter them.[606]

Perhaps the most significant argument against pre-nups is that financial orders on divorce should not reflect simply the interests of the two parties, as supporters of pre-nups seem to assume; they should also protect the interests of the state.[607] For example, much of the case law from *White* onwards has aimed to ensure women are not discriminated against. That work will be undone if parties are able to contract in a discriminatory way. It was left to Baroness Hale to bravely point out the gendered dimensions of the case (and, even more bravely, of the make-up of the Supreme Court):

> Would any self-respecting young woman sign up to an agreement which assumed that she would be the only one who might otherwise have a claim, thus placing no limit on the claims that might be made against her, and then limited her claim to a pre-determined sum for each year of marriage regardless of the circumstances, as if her wifely services were being bought by the year? Yet that is what these precedents do. In short, there is a gender dimension to the issue which some may think ill-suited to decision by a court consisting of eight men and one woman.[608]

It should not be forgotten that the vast majority of pre-nups involve very wealthy men seeking to prevent their wives obtaining what the law regards as a fair share of assets on divorce.[609] In *Gray v Work*[610] a husband worth over £155 million sought to rely on a pre-nup to restrict his wife to £71,000, to be paid over five years.

We do not give effect to employment contracts which allow an employer to discriminate against an employee or pay them below the minimum wage. Similarly, we should not give effect to pre-nups which allow a money maker to discriminate against a child carer.

Despite these points, the arguments relied upon by the House of Lords based on autonomy do chime with other moves in family law, which attach greater weight to autonomy.[611] The move to no-fault divorce and increased use of mediation encourage parties to decide for themselves the nature of their legal relationship.[612] Of course, many people will not be interested in pursuing pre-marriage contracts. Even the Beckhams, apparently, decided against having a

---

[603] *F v F (Pre-Nuptial Agreement)* [2010] 1 FLR 1743.
[604] Fehlberg and Smyth (2002).
[605] George, Harris and Herring (2009).
[606] Hitchings (2009a).
[607] Herring (2005a).
[608] Paragraph 137.
[609] Ouazzani (2013).
[610] [2015] EWHC 834 (Fam).
[611] Centre for Social Justice (2010).
[612] Franck (2009).

pre-nup on the basis that it is 'unromantic'.[613] After all, you only want a pre-nup signed if you want to prevent a judge giving a fair share of the family property to your spouse in the event of a divorce. Why would you want to do that?

The position on pre-marriage contracts should be contrasted with unmarried couples where cohabitation contracts are enforceable.[614] The difference is that cohabitation contracts cannot be seen as robbing the courts of any jurisdiction to redistribute property. Such contracts are rarely made, although they are increasing in popularity.[615]

E Periodic payments

As explained earlier, courts try to make clean break orders where possible. However, sometimes there is simply insufficient capital to ensure that future needs are met or adequate compensation for losses caused by the marriage is provided. In such a case the judge will seek to award monthly payments by way of a periodic payments order to meet the needs of the spouse. One difficult issue is to set the length of time for these orders. In the following case the key principles were helpfully summarised.[616]

KEY CASE: *SS v NS (Spousal Maintenance)* [2014] EWHC 4183 (Fam)

Mostyn J summarised the key principles governing spousal maintenance as follows:

(i)   A spousal maintenance award is properly made where the evidence shows that choices made during the marriage have generated hard future needs on the part of the claimant. Here the duration of the marriage and the presence of children are pivotal factors.

(ii) An award should only be made by reference to needs, save in a most exceptional case where it can be said that the sharing or compensation principle applies.

(iii) Where the needs in question are not causally connected to the marriage the award should generally be aimed at alleviating significant hardship.

(iv) In every case the court must consider a termination of spousal maintenance with a transition to independence as soon as it is just and reasonable. A term should be considered unless the payee would be unable to adjust without undue hardship to the ending of payments. A degree of (not undue) hardship in making the transition to independence is acceptable.

(v)   If the choice between an extendable term and a joint lives order is finely balanced the statutory steer should militate in favour of the former.

(vi) The marital standard of living is relevant to the quantum of spousal maintenance but is not decisive. That standard should be carefully weighed against the desired objective of eventual independence.

(vii) The essential task of the judge is not merely to examine the individual items in the claimant's income budget but also to stand back and to look at the global total and to ask if it represents a fair proportion of the respondent's available income that should go to the support of the claimant.

---

[613] Barton (2008a). But see Barlow and Smithson (2012) for evidence that attitudes may be changing.
[614] *Sutton v Mischon de Reya* [2003] EWHC 3166 (Ch), discussed in Probert (2004b).
[615] Barlow, Burgoyne, Clery and Smithson (2008).
[616] See also *G v G* [2012] EWHC 167.

(viii) Where the respondent's income comprises a base salary and a discretionary bonus the claimant's award may be equivalently partitioned, with needs of strict necessity being met from the base salary and additional, discretionary, items being met from the bonus on a capped percentage basis.

(ix) There is no criterion of exceptionality on an application to extend a term order. On such an application an examination should be made of whether the implicit premise of the original order of the ability of the payee to achieve independence had been impossible to achieve and, if so, why.

(x) On an application to discharge a joint lives order an examination should be made of the original assumption that it was just too difficult to predict eventual independence.

(xi) If the choice between an extendable and a non-extendable term is finely balanced the decision should normally be in favour of the economically weaker party.

10 A discussion of the approach taken to financial orders by the courts

Before discussing the approach taken by the courts, it is worth recapping the central principles:

1. In all cases the overarching objective of the courts is to reach a fair result.

2. The courts will consider all of the factors listed in s. 25 of the Matrimonial Causes Act 1973.

3. The court will be guided by the four principles of: meeting needs; equal sharing; compensation; and respecting autonomy. In most cases the principle of needs will determine the result.

4. Where there are more assets than needs, the courts will use equal division of all the couple's assets as a starting point. However, there may be a good reason why it is necessary to depart from equality in order to achieve a fair result. Good reasons might include the fact there are non-marital assets or the parties have made it clear they did not intend to share their assets.

There has been much debate over the rulings in *White v White* and *Miller; McFarlane*.[617] Perhaps it is still too early to assess properly the impact of those decisions because its ramifications are still being worked out by the Court of Appeal. Even the argument that in all but exceptional cases the contributions of the money-earner and the child carer/homemaker should be regarded as equal is controversial. Stephen Cretney asks:

> [I]s it far-fetched to suggest that there is something rather simplistic about the notion that home-making contributions are to be equated in terms of economic value with commercially motivated money-making activity? And even if right-thinking people now want to make such an equation, is this not essentially a matter of social judgment for decision by Parliament rather than the courts?[618]

Cretney's point about whether the approach in *White* was a matter for Parliament rather than the courts is a matter for debate. If the House of Lords felt that the lower courts' interpretation of the word 'contribution' in s. 25 was effecting gender discrimination and was misconceived,

---

[617] See Duckworth and Hodson (2001); Eekelaar (2001a).
[618] Cretney (2001: 3).

was it not right to set out what the word should mean?[619] That is a normal aspect of the House of Lords' role in statutory interpretation.

Francis has also challenged the assumption of equal contribution: 'If . . . a lazy spouse with round-the-clock support staff, who spends his or her life lunching and playing tennis is to receive half, how is the hard-working spouse who has assisted the other in running the (family) business, looked after the children and run the home to be rewarded?'[620] However, it is interesting that the principle of equality appears to accord with the general public's views on what is appropriate on the breakdown of a relationship. One study found that equal division was felt by many people to be a fair way of dividing matrimonial assets on divorce, although (*inter alia*) where one party had given up earning prospects to look after a child or there was fault in the ending of relationships many felt there should be a departure from equality.[621] Perhaps the response to Francis is that non-monetary contributions to marriage are so varied and valued by spouses in different ways that we cannot in each case calibrate the contribution. What the courts are saying is that we assume in marriages that both parties are giving something, and that they are different, but of equal value.

An aspect of **White** which has been less discussed by the courts and commentators is Lord Nicholls's argument that focusing on the needs of the party would mean that an older wife after a long marriage would receive less than a younger wife with a shorter marriage. Focusing on contributions rather than needs avoided this. Eekelaar has suggested that the shift in the approach of the courts indicated a shift from a welfare-based approach (meeting the needs of the parties) to an entitlement-based approach (what the spouse has 'earned' through the marriage).[622] In other words, it is no longer a case of the money-earner having to give the child carer/homemaker some of 'his' money; rather it is the court dividing the couple's joint assets. Opponents of this suggestion might argue that English and Welsh law clearly does not recognise community of property (i.e. that on marriage the couple's property becomes jointly owned).[623]

11 Consent orders

Increasingly, parties are being encouraged to resolve their financial disputes on divorce without going to court, either through negotiation between their lawyers, or more rarely through mediation. Further impetus is given by the Family Proceedings Rules 1999,[624] which have as their aim the enabling of parties to reach agreement. If the parties do reach an agreement, it is normally incorporated into the form of a draft court order which is presented to court for formal approval. The court retains the power to examine the contents of the agreement and consider the factors in s. 25 of the MCA 1973 (*Sharland v Sharland*[625]). Ward LJ in *Harris v Manahan*[626] described the role of the court in these cases: 'the court is no rubber stamp nor is it some kind of forensic ferret'. In other words, the court will not blindly accept the parties' proposed orders, nor will it spend enormous effort considering the proposal with a high level

---

[619] See the discussion in Hale (2009b).
[620] Francis (2006: 105).
[621] Lewis, Arthur, Fitzgerald and Maclean (2000).
[622] Eekelaar (2001a).
[623] *Miller; McFarlane* [2006] 2 FCR 213 at para 123. Eekelaar (2003c). Cretney's (2003c) suggestion that the recent case law had created a community of property regime was rejected in *Sorrell v Sorrell* [2006] 1 FCR 62 at para 96.
[624] SI 1999/3491.
[625] [2015] UKSC 60.
[626] [1997] 1 FLR 205, [1997] 2 FCR 607.

of scrutiny.[627] The court will assume that if the parties were advised independently then the terms are reasonable and will make an order on the terms agreed by the parties.[628] Once the consent order has been made, it has the same legal effect as if it had been made by the court after a contested hearing.

A The status of agreement before a court order has been made

What if the parties have reached an agreement, but before the agreement is turned into a consent order by the court one of the parties seeks to resile from it?

The position is that the court must then hold a contested hearing, but, following *Macleod* v *Macleod*,[629] then providing the agreement is in writing it will bind the parties, subject to three important caveats.[630] First, the agreement could be challenged because of the circumstances of the agreement. For example, if the parties were not adequately advised or if there was a misrepresentation, non-disclosure or undue pressure.[631] Second, it may be varied under s. 35 of the MCA 1973 if there has been a change of circumstance which would make the arrangement 'manifestly unjust'[632] or where the agreement fails to make adequate provision for the child. Third, the court would not enforce the agreement if it was an improper attempt to 'cast a public obligation on the public purse'. That would occur if the parties arranged the agreement on the basis that one spouse would claim benefits, even though the other spouse could easily afford to pay them maintenance.

It should be remembered that there is nothing to stop spouses entering into a contract as long as the contract does not prohibit either party from seeking financial provision orders. In *Soulsbury* v *Soulsbury*[633] the husband promised to pay his wife a lump sum in his will if she did not enforce her claim for maintenance. As the agreement did not prevent the wife from seeking enforcement of the court order, it was a valid agreement.

12 Variation of, appeals against, and setting aside court orders

It may be that some time after the order has been made, one of the parties believes that the order is no longer appropriate.[634] It may be that, since the making of the order, the needs of one of the parties has increased (for example, he or she suffers a serious injury following a car crash) or that one of the parties has greater resources (for example, he or she has won the National Lottery).[635] The courts have found these cases difficult because as Black LJ explained in *Critchell* v *Critchell*:[636]

> [I]t involved a conflict between two important legal principles and a decision as to which should prevail. One principle was that cases should be decided, so far as practicable, on the true facts and the other was that it was in the public interest that there should be finality in litigation.

---

[627] Davis, Pearce, Bird *et al.* (2000) in empirical research found that there was rarely sufficient information before a judge properly to evaluate the proposed order.

[628] *Xydhias* v *Xydhias* [1999] 1 FLR 683, [1999] 1 FCR 289.

[629] [2008] UKPC 64.

[630] The court developed the law from *Edgar* v *Edgar* [1980] 2 FLR 19.

[631] *Briers* v *Briers* [2017] EWCA Civ 15.

[632] Paragraph 41.

[633] [2007] 3 FCR 811.

[634] See Chandler (2020) for a discussion of whether the coronavirus is a reason to have an order set aside or varied.

[635] For the law on variation of undertakings see *Birch* v *Birch* [2017] UKSC 53.

[636] [2015] EWCA Civ 436, para 22.

One of the most dramatic examples of events after the making of an order which justified amending the order is *Barder* v *Barder (Caluori Intervening)*,[637] where following a divorce the wife killed the family's two children and committed suicide. In her will she left the property to her mother.[638]

It is important to distinguish three ways of challenging an order.

1. The applicant could apply to vary or discharge orders. The amount payable under a periodical payments order may be increased or decreased, or the order discharged and brought to an end.[639] An application to vary an order is based on an argument that, although the order was correct at the time when it was made, subsequent events mean that the order should be varied to reflect the new positions of the parties. It is not possible to apply to vary a lump sum order.[640]

2. The applicant could appeal against an order. Here the claim is that there was a fundamental flaw in the judge's reasoning, and the order should not have been made.

3. The applicant could apply to have the order set aside. This is normally done on the grounds of fraud or non-disclosure of property,[641] although not every non-disclosure will justify setting an order aside.[642] The approach is similar to an appeal but the crucial difference is that the application to set aside accepts that the correct decision was made by the judge on the facts as presented, but maintains that the other party misled the court into making the wrong order.

A Variation

The power of the courts to vary the order is highly controversial (unlike the power to vary or set aside the order which exists for all court orders). If the couple have divorced and an appropriate order is made by the court, why should the fact that, say, the husband wins the National Lottery justify the wife in being entitled to more money? Looking back at the justifications discussed earlier in this section, apart from the contract approach the others would not seem to justify a claim to the lottery winnings. However, a case can be made to justify variation. This is that on divorce all too often there are not sufficient assets to make the order that the court may believe just, bearing in mind all the circumstances. For example, even though the marriage may be a long one and the wife may have contributed significantly to it through care of the children and the home, the husband may have disposed of his assets and so there are not enough to give her the level of income she deserves. In such a case, if the husband subsequently does receive a lottery win and the court can now make the order which would be just and appropriate, should it not do so? Against this is the argument that court orders should represent finality, so that the parties can plan for the future. Further, there is a fear that the power to vary court orders may discourage the parties from seeking to improve their financial position. Payers may fear that if they increase their income the payee will apply to increase the level of payments; similarly, payees may be concerned that any improvement in their standard of living will lead to an application to reduce the level of payments.

---

[637] [1987] 2 FLR 480.
[638] See also *WA* v *The Estate of HA (Deceased and Others)* [2015] EWHC 2233 (Fam).
[639] MCA 1973, s. 31.
[640] Unless it is a lump sum order in instalments.
[641] *Bokor-Ingram* v *Bokor-Ingram* [2009] 2 FLR 922.
[642] *I* v *I (Ancillary Relief: Disclosure)* [2008] EWHC 1167 (Fam).

(i) Which orders can be varied?

An application can be made to vary a periodical payments order.[643] The court could increase, decrease or terminate the payments, or could vary for how long the payments are to be made. It can also terminate a periodical payments order and replace it with a lump sum order. Any application for variation must be made before the order expires.[644] In other words, if the order states that periodical payments are to be made to the wife until 1 January 2013, the wife can only apply to extend the period of payments if she applies to do so before 1 January 2013. If a court wants to make an order for periodical payments which cannot be extended, an order under s. 28(1A) of the MCA 1973 must be made.[645] On hearing an application for variation, the court could decide to terminate payments altogether.[646] The court can also vary a PPO by making an LSO in its place.[647] So if a husband had been paying a wife £1,000 per year maintenance and he acquired some capital, the court might decide to order him to make a lump sum payment of, say, £25,000 and then end his PPO. When making orders of this kind the court should use the lump sum as payment in place of the ongoing periodical payments order. It should not reopen arguments about how the couple's assets should be distributed.[648]

As property adjustment orders (PAOs) and lump sum orders are designed to produce finality, the general principle is that they cannot usually be varied.[649]

(ii) Factors to be taken into account

In considering variation of a PPO, the court will have regard to all the circumstances of the case, the first consideration being the welfare of the child. This includes any change in matters to which the court had regard when first making the order. Under s. 31(7) of the MCA 1973, in considering variation the court is also to consider:

LEGISLATIVE PROVISION

Matrimonial Causes Act 1973, section 31(7)

(a) . . . whether in all the circumstances and after having regard to any such change it would be appropriate to vary the order so that payments under the order are required to be made or secured only for such further period as will in the opinion of the court be sufficient to enable the party in whose favour the order was made to adjust without undue hardship to the termination of those payments;

(b) in a case where the party against whom the order was made has died, the circumstances of the case shall also include the changed circumstances resulting from his or her death.

---

[643] A lump sum order cannot be varied, unless it is a lump sum order payable in instalments (*Hamilton* v *Hamilton* [2013] EWCA Civ 13), discussed in detail in Horton (2013).

[644] *Jones* v *Jones* [2000] 2 FCR 201.

[645] *Mutch* v *Mutch* [2016] EWCA Civ 370; *L* v *L (Financial Remedies: Deferred Clean Break)* [2011] EWHC 2207 (Fam); *Richardson* v *Richardson (No. 2)* [1997] 2 FLR 617, [1997] 2 FCR 453.

[646] *Penrose* v *Penrose* [1994] 2 FLR 621.

[647] MCA 1973, s. 31(7B), as inserted by the Family Law Act 1996. See *Harris* v *Harris* [2001] 1 FCR 68 and *Tattersall* v *Tattersall* [2018] EWCA Civ 1978.

[648] *Pearce* v *Pearce* [2003] 3 FCR 178.

[649] Although the time of payment can sometimes be changed: *Omelian* v *Omelian* [1996] 2 FLR 306, [1996] 3 FCR 329 CA

Section 31(7)(a) therefore specifically requires the court to consider the possibility of ending the payments altogether to enable the parties to become financially independent. Most cases for variation will involve a fundamental change in circumstances since the order was made,[650] although this is not essential according to the Court of Appeal in *Flavell v Flavell*.[651] In *North v North*[652] the husband had been paying the wife nominal periodical payment orders. Some 20 years after the divorce she had gone to Australia, lived a lavish lifestyle and used up her money. On her return to the United Kingdom, she sought an increase in the level of payments. The Court of Appeal held that the husband was an 'insurer against all hazards'. Here the wife had created her needs from her own extravagance or irresponsibility. The periodical payments should not be increased. In *Vince v Wyatt*[653] it was held that 'in order to sustain a case of need, at any rate if made after many years of separation, a wife must show not only that the need exists but that it has been generated by her relationship with her husband.' In that case the Supreme Court thought an application based on an award to acknowledge her contribution (through care of the children) was more likely to succeed than one based on needs. In *Hvorostovsky v Hvorostovsky*[654] the husband's income had increased substantially after the divorce (he was an international singer) and this justified an increase in the level of maintenance paid to the wife. The Court of Appeal emphasised that in such a case an ex-wife could not claim more than her reasonable needs.

On a hearing to vary a periodical payments order, the court should not reopen the division of capital. In *Lauder v Lauder*[655] the husband became very wealthy in the years following the divorce. However, that did not justify the court varying the PPO to give the wife a share of his wealth. The court would only consider whether in the light of her current needs and the economic disadvantages caused to her by the marriage, there was a justification for increasing the order. As the current order met her needs, there was not.

CASE: *Mills v Mills* [2018] UKSC 38

The Supreme Court identified the central question in this case in this way:

> In circumstances in which at the time of a divorce a spouse, say a wife, is awarded capital which enables her to purchase a home but later she exhausts the capital by entry into a series of unwise transactions and so develops a need to pay rent, is the court entitled to decline to increase the order for the husband to make periodical payments to her so as to fund payment of all (or perhaps even any) of her rent even if he could afford to do so?

The answer to that question was yes, the court was entitled to do that, but did not have to. That said, the Supreme Court added:

> [A] court would need to give very good reasons for requiring a spouse to fund payment of the other spouse's rent in the circumstances identified by the question. A spouse may well have an obligation to make provision for the other; but an obligation to duplicate it in such circumstances is most improbable.

---

[650] A party will be prevented from seeking to vary an order if they have led the other party to act to his or her detriment on an assumption that they will not apply for variation.
[651] [1997] 1 FLR 353, [1997] 1 FCR 332.
[652] [2007] 2 FCR 601.
[653] [2015] UKSC 14.
[654] [2009] 2 FLR 1574.
[655] [2008] 3 FCR 468.

The Supreme Court in *Mills* wanted to make it clear that a spouse would not be entitled to spend money provided as financial settlement and then return to the court to ask for more, without a good reason. Fatal to the wife's case in *Mills* itself seemed to be her inability to explain how she had spent her award and ended up in such dire need.

There is a strict rule that if the spouse who is in receipt of periodical payments remarries then the payments will automatically come to an end.[656] But what if she or he cohabits rather than remarries? In *Atkinson v Atkinson (No. 2)*[657] the Court of Appeal rejected an argument that, as the wife was now cohabiting, the periodical payments should come to an end. However, the Court of Appeal accepted that the ex-wife's needs were less on the basis that her cohabitant could be expected to contribute to her household expenses and so the level of maintenance should be reduced. On the husband's behalf it was argued that an ex-wife who remarries should not be disadvantaged compared to an ex-wife who cohabits and that therefore cohabitation and marriage should automatically end the payments. The court rejected this argument, stating that if the court did end the wife's payments on cohabitation this would pressurise her into marrying her new cohabitant to ensure she had financial security. The court stated that it would be wrong for the law to place such pressure on her. This approach was recently approved by the Court of Appeal in *Fleming v Fleming*,[658] where an argument that changing social attitudes meant that marriage and cohabitation should be treated in the same way in this context was rejected.[659] However, in *K v K (Periodic Payment: Cohabitation)*[660] Coleridge J thought that a cohabiting couple should strive towards financial independence from a husband.[661] He thought the law had to acknowledge that a 'social revolution' had taken place in connection with cohabitation. Nothing in the earlier case law stopped a judge from deciding that in the light of the cohabitation periodical payments should cease. However, in *Grey v Grey*[662] the Court of Appeal approved the approach in *Fleming*. So, a judge should now consider what financial contribution the new cohabitant was making, or could make, to the spouse's household and take that into account in assessing the level of periodic payments.[663]

To deal with the problem with the spouse receiving payments while living with someone else, it is possible to draft the PPO or PAO to cease if there is cohabitation. For example, a typical order relating to the home is 'the wife to have occupation of the former matrimonial home, sale of the property to be postponed until such time as she remarry or cohabit with another man'; a typical PPO is that 'the order for periodical payments shall terminate in the event of the wife's cohabitation with another man'. There are difficulties with such orders. The first is the complexity of cohabitation. If the wife has a partner who visits her regularly, when does this amount to cohabitation?[664] Further, such clauses can even lead to spying by the paying spouse to try to discover whether there is cohabitation.

---

[656] Although this will not necessarily defeat a claim for a lump sum or for child maintenance: *Re G (Financial Provision: Liberty to Restore Application for Lump Sum)* [2004] Fam Law 332.

[657] *Atkinson v Atkinson* [1995] 2 FLR 356, [1995] 2 FCR 353; *Atkinson v Atkinson (No. 2)* [1996] 1 FLR 51, [1995] 3 FCR 788.

[658] [2003] EWCA Civ 1841.

[659] Although the court decided that given the wife's cohabitation and current financial position there was no reason to extend the period of her periodic payments.

[660] [2005] EWHC 2886 (Fam).

[661] The husband had argued in that case that it was inconsistent that cohabitation prior to marriage could be taken into account when assessing the length of a marriage (*Co v Co* [2004] 1 FLR 1095), but was not relevant when considering termination of spousal maintenance.

[662] [2010] 1 FCR 394.

[663] *Grey v Grey* [2010] 1 FCR 394.

[664] See *X v Y (Maintenance Arrears: Cohabitation)* [2012] EWCC 1 (Fam); *Kimber v Kimber* [2000] 1 FLR 383 and the discussion in Mahmood (2013).

In *Vaughan* v *Vaughan*[665] an ex-wife sought to increase her period payments or to have them capitalised. The primary issue was that her husband had remarried. He argued that if he paid his ex-wife a capital sum that would leave his present wife in a vulnerable position if ever they were to split up. The Court of Appeal disagreed. Although it was proper for the court to take account of the husband's obligation to support his current wife, they should not consider the hypothetical possibility of him divorcing his current wife.[666] Notably, the court thought it important that the ex-wife receive a level of maintenance that was adequate compensation for her loss of earning potential caused by the marriage.[667]

B Setting aside a consent order

Once a consent order has been made by the court, the court will be very reluctant to permit any challenges to the order. The following are examples of the circumstances upon which an application can be made to set aside a consent order:

1. *Non-disclosure.* The court, in deciding whether to set aside a consent order on the basis of non-disclosure, will consider whether the non-disclosure was fundamental enough to merit setting the order aside.[668] In *Livesey* v *Jenkins*[669] the House of Lords thought the failure by the wife to reveal that she was engaged to remarry was of sufficient importance that the order should be set aside. The test, their Lordships suggested, was that had the court been aware of the information that had not been disclosed it would have made a substantially different order. This test strikes the balance between, on the one hand, ensuring fairness between the parties and discouraging non-disclosure, and, on the other hand, preventing a large number of appeals on the basis of the tiniest non-disclosures. A mistake as to value will not be sufficient to justify setting aside a court order.[670] A particularly controversial issue has arisen in the following case:

CASE: *Sharland v Sharland* [2015] UKSC 60

The Supreme Court were asked what approach should be taken if it transpired that a consent order was obtained following a fraud. In negotiations the husband said he had no plans to sell his private company for at least seven years. However, it transpired that at the time of the negotiations he was planning to sell the company for hundreds of millions of dollars (although in fact that sale never went through). The Supreme Court placed much weight on the fact that in a normal contract law case if a person used fraud to persuade another person to enter into a contract, that contract would be set aside. They thought the same should be true if fraud was used to persuade a victim to agree to a financial agreement on divorce. They quoted Briggs LJ in the Court of Appeal who had said 'fraud unravels all'. The general principle was that a consent order procured by fraud should be

---

[665] [2010] 2 FCR 509.
[666] In *Fields v Fields* [2015] EWHC 1670 (Fam) it was said to be 'totally impermissible and impossible' for the court to assess a wife's prospects of remarriage.
[667] See also *McFarlane (No. 2)* [2009] EWHC 891 (Fam).
[668] *Kingdon v Kingdon* [2010] EWCA Civ 1251.
[669] [1985] FLR 813.
[670] *Judge v Judge* [2008] EWCA Civ 1458, [2009] 2 FCR 158.

set aside. The one exception was if the court was persuaded that even if the other party had known the truth of the fraud, they would have entered into the agreement anyway, or that had the court known of the fraud it would have made a significantly different order. The perpetrator of the fraud had to persuade the court the exception applied. Applying that to the case at hand it was clear that had the wife known of the fraud she would not have agreed to the proposal, nor would the court have approved of the consent order. The consent order could, therefore, be set aside. The wife was entitled to reopen negotiations or, if they failed, seek a new court order.

It is important to remember that this case was one involving deliberate fraud.[671] In *Neill v Neill*[672] Moor J defined fraud as 'the intentional use of false or misleading information in an attempt illegally to deprive another person of money, property or legal rights'. Moor J also confirmed that if it was shown the victim of fraud would still have agreed to the order had they known the truth, the order will not be set aside. Although that would be rare.

The courts are faced with a difficult dilemma. They want to avoid being too ready to permit attempts to set aside consent orders. Court orders are intended to be final and allow the parties to move ahead. On the other hand, there is much merit in the Supreme Court view that a fraudster should not be permitted to gain by misleading the other party or the court.

2. *Bad legal advice.* In *B v B (Consent Order: Variation)*[673] it was accepted that 'manifestly bad advice' could be a ground for setting aside a consent order. In *Harris v Manahan*[674] the Court of Appeal seemed to restrict this to cases where there was an exceptional case of the 'cruellest injustice'. It might be more profitable in such cases for a person to bring negligence proceedings against his or her solicitors.

C Appeal

It is possible to appeal against a court order. However, there are time restrictions on when an application can be made. A crucial issue is when it is possible to appeal against an order out of time. This is particularly relevant in relation to clean break orders when variation cannot be relied upon. There is a balance to be drawn between on the one hand ensuring there is finality of litigation, so that the parties are not constantly challenging the orders made in the court, while, on the other hand, it could be seen to be contrary to justice to uphold a judgment known to be based on a falsehood. The leading case is *Barder v Barder (Caluori Intervening)*,[675] which suggested that an application to appeal out of time will occur only if the following conditions are shown:

1. The basis of the order, or a fundamental assumption underlining the order, has been falsified by a change of circumstances since the making of an order. Perhaps the most common example of this is where a valuation relied upon by the court of, for example, a business

---

[671] Diduck (2016).
[672] [2019] EWFC 3330.
[673] [1995] 1 FLR 9, [1995] 2 FCR 62.
[674] [1997] 1 FLR 205, [1997] 2 FCR 607.
[675] [1988] AC 20.

or a house, has proved inaccurate,[676] although it should be stressed that an application for leave can only rely on an unsound valuation as the basis of appeal if they have sought leave as quickly as possible and are not at fault for the misvaluation.[677] Even then the courts take the view that valuations are an 'inexact science' and so only if they are very badly wrong will they form the basis of a successful appeal.[678] Where the value of the property has fallen as a result of fluctuation in the property market, that will not be a *Barder* event.[679] Similarly, a mistake as to the value of an item by the parties will not be a *Barder* event.[680] In *Williams v Lindley*[681] an order was made which included a lump sum to meet the wife's housing needs. A few weeks after the order was made the wife became engaged and subsequently married a very wealthy man. The Court of Appeal by a majority found that this destroyed the foundation of the order which was to meet her housing needs. However, the wife's death six weeks after the order in *Richardson v Richardson*[682] did not undermine the order as the basis of it was not to meet the needs of the wife, but to award her her share of the marital property.

In *Maskell v Maskell*[683] it was held that the husband's redundancy could not be regarded as a supervening event. It was not an unpredicted event, but part of life's normal difficulties. In *Critchell v Critchell*[684] a month after the order the husband of a not well-off couple unexpectedly obtained an inheritance. That was a *Barder* event as the order was premised on the need to enable the husband to pay off loans.

2. Such change is within a relatively short time of the order, usually two years at most.[685] However, the court may be sympathetic if the applicant has applied as quickly as could reasonably be expected once he or she knew of the change of circumstances, especially in cases of fraud.[686]

3. The applicant must show that had the true situation been known or event foreseen the court would have made a materially different order.[687]

4. The application for leave must have been made reasonably promptly once the change of circumstances was known about.

5. The granting of leave should not prejudice unfairly third parties who have acquired interests for value in the property affected.

6. Only in an 'exceptionally small number of cases' will these factors justify the overruling of a decision in a family law case.[688]

---

[676] E.g. *Kean v Kean* [2002] 2 FLR 28.

[677] *Kean v Kean* [2002] 2 FLR 28.

[678] *B v B* [2007] EWHC 2472 (Fam).

[679] *Horne v Horne* [2009] 2 FLR 1031.

[680] *Walkden v Walkden* [2009] 3 FCR 25.

[681] [2005] 1 FCR 813.

[682] [2011] EWCA Civ 79.

[683] [2001] 3 FCR 296.

[684] [2015] EWCA Civ 436.

[685] *Worlock v Worlock* [1994] 2 FLR 689 (four years after application and two years after change then 'far too late').

[686] Although see *Burns v Burns* [2004] 3 FCR 263 where the applicant was so slow in bringing the matter to court that leave was not granted. However, note *Den Heyer v Newby* [2005] EWCA Civ 1311 where it was said that, if such a delay in bringing the matter to court was caused by the respondent's failure to make proper disclosure, the respondent could not complain.

[687] *S v S (No. 2) (Ancillary Relief: Application to Set Aside Order)* [2010] 1 FLR 993.

[688] *Shaw v Shaw* [2002] 3 FCR 298 at para 44.

The Court of Appeal has said that *Barder* events are 'extremely rare'.[689] In *Myerson v Myerson (No. 2)*[690] there was a huge drop in the value of the husband's assets soon after the making of an order. The value of his assets was now 14 per cent of what they had been valued to be at the time of the order. However, this was held not to be a *Barder* event. It represented the normal process of price fluctuation. When he had agreed to the order, the husband had realised that his assets were volatile and could increase or decrease in value. In *Dixon v Marchant*[691] a husband claimed that his wife's remarriage just seven months after the making of a clean break order amounted to a *Barder* event. The majority of the Court of Appeal disagreed. The husband realised that a clean break order carried the risk the wife might remarry soon after it was made and so he would end up paying more than he would have done had he been paying periodical payments (which would stop on remarriage). Importantly, the court found that there was no evidence that the wife had deceived her husband during the negotiations leading up to the clean break order. The case can be contrasted with *Williams v Lindley*[692] where the wife's remarriage shortly after the making of a consent order did justify variation. In that case it seems that the wife's need for housing had dominated the negotiations prior to the order. As her housing needs were met on the unforeseen marriage so soon after the making of the order, this was held to be a *Barder* event.[693]

13 Reform of the law on financial support for spouses

There has been much criticism of the current state of the law. Coleridge J in *RP v RP*[694] stated that:

> After three decades of silence (1970–2000) when the House of Lords declined to give any guidance, there have now been two momentous decisions in six years. They run to hundreds of paragraphs. In addition they have been subjected to further interpretation in cases in the Court of Appeal and/or below. A new statute could not have had more far reaching social or forensic consequences. At present, on the ground, considerable confusion abounds.

He called for a plea for 'reflective tranquillity', concluding: 'Section 25 says it all, thereafter perhaps for the moment, the least said the better.'[695]

Despite Coleridge J's wise words, the discussion has continued.[696] The Law Commission has undertaken a consideration of the issue.[697] Mary Welstead[698] has written:

> The law relating to ancillary relief oscillates in a schizophrenic manner as attempts are made by the judiciary to find overriding principles, such as the tripartite ones put forward in *Miller v MacFarlane,* to guide them through the discretionary morass of s. 25 of the Matrimonial Causes Act 1973. No sooner than new principles are articulated, they are followed by decisions which erode them or expand them depending on the viewpoint of the judiciary.

---

[689] *Richardson v Richardson* [2011] EWCA Civ 79.
[690] [2009] 2 FLR 147.
[691] [2008] 1 FCR 209.
[692] [2005] 1 FCR 269.
[693] See Saunders (2011) for further discussion.
[694] [2008] 2 FCR 613, para 77.
[695] This, notably, is at para 78 of his judgment.
[696] Harris (2008).
[697] Law Commission Consultation Paper 208 (2012).
[698] Welstead (2012).

The complaints about the current law are often exaggerated. The complexity of the issues raised by big money financial provision questions should not be underestimated. Any attempt to produce a clear formula to deal with these cases is unlikely to be sufficiently nuanced to provide the certainty so many crave. At least it would do so only at the cost of unfairness in individual cases. In fact, Emma Hitchings,[699] in her study of 'everyday' cases, found little uncertainty in the law. She writes:

> I would suggest that the findings in this study do not support the argument that the law of ancillary relief is uncertain and chaotic. At the everyday level at least, there does not appear to be a pressing need for additional principle to increase certainty of outcome. In the everyday case where needs dominate, the findings demonstrate that the advice given to clients is pretty consistent, subject to local court culture and the practicalities of the individual case.

It is suggested that the complexity that has been introduced has largely resulted from a reluctance to accept the principle of equality that was at the heart of the decision of the House of Lords in *White v White*. Indeed, much of the subsequent case law, and resulting complexity, can be seen as an attempt to diminish the significance of that decision. The concepts of marital and non-marital property, extra-ordinary contributions and pre-nups have been developed by the lower courts to mean that the significance of the principle of equality is diminished. Nearly always the post-*White* developments mean that the money-earner gets to keep much more than half of the assets, to the disadvantage of the homemaker and the child carer.[700] In *AAZ v BBZ*[701] it was accepted the wife was 'in principle' entitled to half the assets but as she had only claimed for much less, she would be limited to that.

In recent years there has been some discussion about whether the law needs to be reformed to give it a clearer structure.[702] Although there have been many voices calling for change, there is little agreement over what system would be better.[703] There are a number of options that have been mooted, including the following:

1. The Law Commission Report[704] deals with three issues at the heart of the disputes over reform of the law: financial needs; marital agreements; and the concept of non-matrimonial property. In relation to needs the report is clear that a couple have financial responsibilities which continue after divorce. The report considered the current law in relation to needs and determined no reform is necessary. The law seeks to balance the need to meet the core requirements of the parties, with the need to encourage the parties to be financially independent, a process which in some cases can take several years. This, the Commission believes, is the correct approach.

   In relation to pre-nups the Law Commission has proposed that legislation is needed to clarify the law. It recommends the notion of 'qualifying nuptial agreements' (QNA) which would be enforceable contracts and not subject to the scrutiny of the courts. These QNAs could determine the financial consequences of divorce or dissolution. Before an agreement could be a QNA certain procedural requirements would have to be satisfied (such as the

---

[699] Hitchings (2009b: 204).
[700] Murray (2013).
[701] [2016] EWHC 3234 (Fam).
[702] Barlow (2009b); Bailey-Harris (2005); Miles (2005); Bird (2002).
[703] Maclean and Eekelaar (2009).
[704] Law Commission Report 343 (2014).

need for legal advice and disclosure) and they would have to meet the financial needs of both parties. These are summarised as follows:

(a) The agreement must be contractually valid (and able to withstand challenge on the basis of undue influence or misrepresentation, for example).

(b) The agreement must have been made by deed and must contain a statement signed by both parties that he or she understands that the agreement is a qualifying nuptial agreement that will partially remove the court's discretion to make financial orders.

(c) The agreement must not have been made within the 28 days immediately before the wedding or the celebration of civil partnership.

(d) Both parties to the agreement must have received, at the time of the making of the agreement, disclosure of material information about the other party's financial situation.

(e) Both parties must have received legal advice at the time that the agreement was formed. It is recommended that it should not be possible for a party to waive their rights to disclosure and legal advice.

On the final issue of non-matrimonial property, the Law Commission felt that the current practice of the courts that non-matrimonial property (property acquired before the marriage or received during the marriage as a gift or inheritance) is not to be subject to the sharing principle.[705]

2. *Pre-marriage contracts.* We discussed arguments about these above. It might be possible to require people to make pre-marriage agreements as a pre-condition to marriage.

3. *Equal distribution.* Some have proposed that there should be a presumption of equality in distribution of assets. The Conservative Party's Centre for Social Justice[706] argues:

> Our proposal on financial provision is that all assets of the couple on divorce should be categorised into marital assets and non-marital assets and divided differently. Marital assets should be divided equally subject to overriding calls on those assets, and non-marital assets should stay with the relevant spouse again subject to overriding calls on those assets and unless there is any good reason to make any distributive orders. Non-marital assets would be pre-marital assets, inheritances or gifts and certain post-separation assets with provision that some non-marital assets would become marital assets in particular circumstances and over time. The court would have power to make different orders if there was significant injustice but otherwise the present very wide discretion would be fettered.

That is close to the current law as it applies to big money cases, but it appears that they want it to apply to all cases. Their proposals should be understood bearing in mind they also would like to see pre-marriage contracts enforced unless they would cause significant injustice. The major concern with their equal division proposal is that in many cases there is an unequal division in order to meet the basic needs of the children and their carer. A strong equality approach would be likely to work against the interests of children and their carers.[707] As Baroness Hale has acknowledged: 'Too strict an adherence to equal sharing and the clean break can lead to a rapid decrease in the primary carer's standard of living and a rapid increase in the breadwinner's.'[708]

---

[705] See also Scherpe (2013).
[706] Centre for Social Justice (2009), discussed in Hodson (2009).
[707] Wilson J (1999).
[708] *McFarlane,* para 142. See also Hale (2011a).

4. *Unequal distribution.* In **Wachtel v Wachtel**[709] Denning LJ suggested that the wife should be entitled to one-third of the family's assets. He explained that the husband would have to find 'some woman to look after his house', while it would be unlikely a woman would need to. This view has few supporters nowadays. It is clearly based on traditional gender roles and, even from its own sexist perspectives, overlooks the need of the wife to employ a handyman to help with house repairs!

5. *Formula.* John Eekelaar[710] has suggested an approach which attaches greater significance to the length of time the parties have lived together than the current law.[711] He explains that 'duration of marriage is an excellent proxy for measuring a number of factors which are important in achieving a "fair" outcome. They include: the degree of commitment to a relationship; the value of contributions made to it, which is not susceptible of straightforward economic measurement; and the extent of disadvantage undergone on separation.'[712] By contrast, Thorpe LJ has stated: 'What a party has given to a marriage and what a party has lost on its failure cannot be measured by simply counting the days of its duration.'[713] John Eekelaar accepts that in a lengthy marriage equality is appropriate, but where one party brings to the marriage substantial assets the poorer party should be regarded as gradually earning an increasing share in the other's assets. He suggests 2.5 per cent per annum, leading to an equal share after 20 years. Similarly, in relation to maintenance he suggests that the person who has taken on the majority of childcare receive an award of 30 per cent of the income at the time of separation after a 20-year marriage, scaled down if the marriage is shorter. Payments should last for 60 per cent of the duration of the marriage.[714]

Eekelaar's argument is strongest when considering an extreme case: if, for example, a woman marries a multi-millionaire but the marriage lasts only a few weeks she should not be entitled to half the fortune. But if the marriage has lasted 30 years, she has a strong claim for an equal share of the fortune. Against his argument is the view that it does not accord with how most couples understand their marriage and finances. The notion of the child carer/homemaker day by day earning a little more in his or her spouse's assets is not one with which many couples would feel an affinity. Rebecca Bailey-Harris[715] also argues that it is discriminatory that domestic contributions earn equal value only over time, whereas financial ones do not. Eekelaar responds to this comment by suggesting that unlike financial contributions homemaking is linked to duration. His point is that one day's housework cannot be worth more or less than one day's housework; however, the money-earner's value depends on the amount brought home. So, homemaking can be valued only by time, but money-earning need not be.[716] 'Homemaking for one day, however brilliantly done, is in itself of relatively little value,' he says. This, at least if it includes childcare (as it appears to), is debatable. Would that be true of the day of birth? Or the day the child finally was helped by the parent to understand multiplication? Or the day the teenager was given comfort for their first broken heart?

---

[709] [1973] Fam 72. See Douglas (2011c) for a discussion of the significance of this case.
[710] Eekelaar (2001a; 2003c).
[711] See also Ellman (2005).
[712] Eekelaar (2006a: 756).
[713] *Miller* [2005] EWCA Civ 984, para 34.
[714] Eekelaar (2006a: 758).
[715] Bailey-Harris (2003a).
[716] The argument is less convincing if one includes as a contribution to the marriage not only money-earning, childcare and household tasks, but also emotional support, love, etc.

6. *The 'Deech proposals'.* Baroness Deech proposed a Divorce (Financial Provision) Bill in 2017. This was based on three core components which would make up all financial orders on divorce:

- There is to be equal division of matrimonial assets.[717]
- Periodic payments could only last to a maximum of five years, save in cases of serious financial provision.
- Pre-nuptial agreement would be dividing.

There is a sense in which it might be thought that this is not particularly radical and largely reflects the current law in many cases. However, its main significance would be to prevent the courts from departing from these principles in the name of fairness. For example, a pre-nuptial agreement would be enforceable however unfair the court might believe it to be. One difficulty with the Bill is that it would end up producing results which were 'unfair' but these would need to be set alongside the alleged benefits of certainty the Bill promises. The problem is the certainty is questionable. As we have seen the distinction between marital and non-marital property is very uncertain. That does not matter much in a system where there is no mathematical formula and the courts are seeking fairness. It is problematic in a system where there is a rule which depends on the solidity of the marital/non-marital property distinction. The reform would be likely to impact on women, who still suffer significantly after divorce. This would be particularly true with the restriction of maintenance to five years. Ruth Deech justified this by saying the 'divorcing wives of oligarchs' are being awarded '£83,000 per annum [for] cocktail dresses – a sum that would provide 19.7 million water purification tablets for Africa'.[718] That argument seems based on the unlikely premise that if the oligarchs did not pay their money to their former wives they would be spending it on overseas aid.[719]

7. *Societal changes.* Others argue that if there is to be financial fairness between spouses on divorce, some fundamental change in society is required. Diduck and Orton look forward to a better future:

> Along with true equality in employment and pay and affordable good quality child care, an adequate valuation of domestic work would mean it would not be necessary that each partner play exactly the same role in wage earning . . . Roles in marriage could be adopted based on the partners' actual interests and skills. Maintenance on divorce would still sometimes be necessary, then, but it would no longer overwhelmingly be women who require it and it would no longer result in economic disadvantage for the recipient. Maintenance would be seen as a right, expected and earned, rather than as a gift, act of benevolence or based on a notion of women's dependency on men.[720]

As it is, many of the problems with finding a fair law of financial provision are due to the fact that we live in a flawed society with gendered inequalities in term of wages, childcare, housework and discrimination, a society which does not recognise caring for others in financial terms. Given such a background, the law on financial provision is bound to fail. Much of the approach of the current law is based on trying to enable a woman to enter the

---

[717] And only matrimonial assets, defined in the Bill broadly in the terms understood by the courts.
[718] Hansard, HL Deb vol. 778, col. 946, 27 January 2017.
[719] Hitchings and Miles (2018).
[720] Diduck and Orton (1994: 686–7).

job market or to compensate her for 'missing out' on employment. The assumption is that care work is not valuable and that the ideal wives should be striving for is to match the 'male' ideal of employment. An alternative would be to recognise the value of care work not just for the couple themselves, but for society in general.[721]

14 Conclusion

Ruth Deech opens her discussion of financial orders on separation by asking her readers to consider three sisters:

> One is very pretty and marries a national footballer; they have no children and it is a short marriage before she leaves him for an international celebrity. The second sister marries a clergyman and has several children; the marriage ends after 30 years as he is moving into retirement. The third sister never marries; she stays at home and nurses first their mother, who has a disability, and then their father, who has Alzheimer's, and dies without making a will. Which of the three sisters will get the windfall: an amount sufficient to keep her in luxury for the rest of her days, when her relationship with a man comes to an end? And which one most needs and deserves financial support, even of the bare minimum? The message is that getting married to a well-off man is an alternative career to one in the workforce.[722]

Her implied message is that the current law on financial orders on separation has gone badly wrong. The undeserving footballer's wife ends up with millions, the carer of the father with Alzheimer's ends up with nothing. She is right that this seems unfair. But, of course, it does not follow that the problem is the award to the footballer's wife. It may be the real issue is the lack of provision for carers, rather than excessive awards to wives. And the way resources are distributed in the world is generally unfair.

This chapter has focused on the financial position of partners on the breakdown of their relationship. For many couples it is the financial support for children which is the key issue, with limited resources available for spousal support. For both married and unmarried couples, child support is calculated by means of a rigid formula, set out in the Child Support Act 1991. This is by contrast with the wide discretion the courts have to determine spousal support under the Matrimonial Causes Act 1973. The two systems reveal the contrasting benefits and disadvantages of rule-based and discretion-based systems. The section also reveals the different bases upon which financial support obligations are based. In *White* v *White* the House of Lords has stressed the importance of fairness between spouses, although in many ordinary cases it is enough of a struggle meeting the basic needs of the parties and the children, let alone considering broader theoretical concepts. Running through this chapter is the requirement for the law to be realistic. Imposing obligations which cannot be enforced, or requiring people to support those to whom they feel no particular moral obligation, is unlikely to result in an effective law. That said, finding a law on financial support for family members which is regarded as fair, reflects the social obligations which people feel, and is practicably enforceable, might be an impossible task.

---

[721] Glennon (2010).
[722] Deech (2009a).

Further reading

Altman, S. (2003) 'A theory of child support', *International Journal of Law, Policy and the Family* 17: 173.

Barton, C. (2018) 'Financial remedies today: "tools", "rules", "guidelines", "benchmarks", "yardsticks", "ordinary consequences" and "departure points"', *Family Law* 558.

Bendall, C. and Harding, R. (2018) 'Heteronormativity in dissolution proceedings', in E. Brake and L. Ferguson (eds) *Philosophical Foundations of Children's and Family Law*, Oxford: OUP.

Cooke, E. (2007) 'Miller/McFarlane: law in search of a definition', *Child and Family Law Quarterly* 19: 98.

Crisp, J. and Hunter, R. (2019) 'Domestic abuse in financial remedy applications', *Family Law* 1440.

Eekelaar, J. (2006a) 'Property and financial settlement on divorce – sharing and compensating', *Family Law* 36: 754.

Ellman, I. (2005) 'Do Americans play football?' *International Journal of Law, Policy and the Family* 19: 257.

Ferguson, L. (2015b) '*Wyatt* v *Vince*: the reality of individualised justice – financial orders, forensic delay, and access to justice', *Child and Family Law Quarterly* 195.

Fisher, H. and Low, H. (2016) 'Recovery from divorce: comparing high and low income couples', *International Journal of Law, Policy and the Family* 30: 338.

George, R.H., Harris, P. and Herring, J. (2009) 'Pre-nuptial agreements: for better or for worse?' *Family Law* 39: 934.

Glennon, L. (2010) 'The limitations of equality discourses on the contours of intimate obligations', in J. Wallbank, S. Choudhry and J. Herring (eds) *Rights, Gender and Family Law*, Abingdon: Routledge.

Gordon-Bouvier, E. (2020) 'The open future: analysing the temporality of autonomy in family law', *Child and Family Law Quarterly* 32(1): 75.

Hale, Baroness (2011a) 'Equality and autonomy in family law', *Journal of Social Welfare and Family Law* 33: 3.

Heenan, A. (2018) 'Causal and temporal connections in financial remedy cases: the meaning of marriage', *Child and Family Law Quarterly* 30: 75.

Herring, J. (2005a) 'Why financial orders on divorce should be unfair', *International Journal of Law, Policy and the Family* 19: 218.

Hitchings, E. (2017) 'Official, operative and outsider justice: the ties that (may not) bind in family financial disputes', *Child and Family Law Quarterly* 359.

Law Commission Report 343 (2014) *Matrimonial Property, Needs and Agreements: the future of financial orders on divorce and dissolution*, London: The Stationery Office.

Miles, J. (2005) 'Principle or pragmatism in ancillary relief: the virtues of flirting with academic theories and other jurisdictions', *International Journal of Law, Policy and the Family* 19: 242.

Miles, J. (2011c) 'Responsibility in family finance and property law', in J. Bridgeman, H. Keating and C. Lind (2011) *Regulating Family Responsibilities*, Aldershot: Ashgate.

Miles, J. (2019) 'Should the regime be discretionary or rules-based?' in J. Palmer *et al.* (eds) *Law and Policy in Modern Family Finance*, Cambridge: Intersentia.

Murray, A. (2013) 'Are our higher courts prejudiced against the role of the married woman? The need for reform', *Family Law* 43: 66.

Natalia, K. (2018) 'State facilitated economic abuse: a structural analysis of men deliberately withholding child support', *Feminist Legal Studies* 26: 121.

Ouazzani, S. (2013) 'Prenuptial agreements: The implications of gender', *Family Law* 43: 421.

Pension Advisory Group (2019) *A Guide to the Treatment of Pensions on Divorce,* Cardiff: University of Cardiff.

Scherpe, J. (2012) *Marital Agreements and Private Autonomy,* Oxford: Hart.

Thompson, S. (2015) *Prenuptial Agreements and the Presumption of Free Choice: Issues of Power in Theory and Practice,* Oxford: Hart.

Weiner, M. (2015) 'Caregiver payments and the obligation to give care or share', *Villanova Law Review* 59: 135.

Wikeley, N. (2009) 'Financial support for children after parental separation: parental responsibility and responsible parenting', in R. Probert, S. Gilmore and J. Herring (eds) *Responsible Parents and Parental Responsibility,* Oxford: Hart.

Woodward, H. (2015) '"Everyday" financial remedy orders: do they achieve fair pension provision on divorce?' *Child and Family Law Quarterly* 151.

Visit **go.pearson.com/uk/he/resources** to access **resources** specifically written to complement this text.

7 Domestic abuse

Learning objectives

When you finish reading this chapter you will be able to:

1. Explain and evaluate the definitions of domestic abuse
2. Discuss the orders available under the Family Law Act
3. Analyse the response of the criminal law to domestic abuse
4. Summarise the issues around parental abuse
5. Debate the theoretical issues around the response of the law to domestic abuse

1 Introduction

For some people the home is a place of rest, relaxation and relief from the stresses of the outside world. For others, the home is a place of torture, terror and tears. Intimate relationships, which should be used to build people up and help them to thrive, are used in domestic abuse to knock them down and destroy their sense of self-worth.

Traditionally, domestic abuse was seen as a private matter, best left for the parties to resolve. Today it is recognised as a major interference of human rights.[1] The state has responsibilities to take positive action to prevent domestic abuse. But that is much easier said than done. As we shall see in this chapter, the causes and nature of domestic abuse are complex and there is no easy solution to the issue.

2 Definition of domestic abuse

Learning objective 1

Explain and evaluate the definitions of domestic abuse

There is no agreement over the correct terminology to be used to describe violence that takes place between adults in a close relationship. At one time it was common to talk about domestic violence or 'battered wives', but now the violence between those in close emotional relationships is seen as a wider problem, being restricted not just to wives

---

[1] Herring (2020).

nor even to domestic situations.[2] Further, the forms of mistreatment extend beyond what has traditionally been understood as violence. Hence, nowadays it is more common to find talk of domestic abuse or intimate abuse.

For a long time, there was no clear legal definition of domestic abuse. Now we have one!

A The Domestic Abuse Bill 2020

The Domestic Abuse Bill 2020 introduces a new definition of domestic abuse, to be used throughout the law. Clause 1(2) states:

(2) Behaviour of a person ("A") towards another person ("B") is "domestic abuse" if—

    (a) A and B are each aged 16 or over and are personally connected to each other, and

    (b) the behaviour is abusive.

(3) Behaviour is "abusive" if it consists of any of the following—

    (a) physical or sexual abuse;

    (b) violent or threatening behaviour;

    (c) controlling or coercive behaviour;

    (d) economic abuse (see subsection (4));

    (e) psychological, emotional or other abuse;

and it does not matter whether the behaviour consists of a single incident or a course of conduct.

The term 'economic abuse is explained in clause 1(4):

"Economic abuse" means any behaviour that has a substantial adverse effect on B's ability to—

    (a) acquire, use or maintain money or other property, or

    (b) obtain goods or services.

Several points are worth highlighting about this definition. First, it clearly sees domestic abuse as broader than physical attacks and includes, for example, coercive control and emotional abuse. We will explore the concept of coercive control further, shortly. Second, the definition strikes new ground in including economic abuse within domestic abuse. Economic abuse had not been included in previous governmental definitions. Third, it should be noted that clause 1(5) makes it clear that the behaviour can be treated as 'towards B' even if it is directed at another person, such as B's child. So, the law can recognise how an abuser might use the victim's child as a tool in abuse. Fourth, the definition only applies to someone 'personally connected' to the victim. Clause 2 defines that as being if the relationship falls into any of these categories:

    (a) they are, or have been, married to each other;

    (b) they are, or have been, civil partners of each other;

    (c) they have agreed to marry one another (whether or not the agreement has been terminated);

    (d) they have entered into a civil partnership agreement (whether or not the agreement has been terminated);

    (e) they are, or have been, in an intimate personal relationship with each other;

---

[2] See Kaganas (2007a) for a refutation of claims that women are often violent to men

(f) they each have, or there has been a time when they each have had, a parental relationship in relation to the same child (see subsection (2));[3]

(g) they are relatives.[4]

That means that people who have only met a few times or 'friends of friends' cannot fall within the law of domestic abuse. There is other legislation (such as the Protection from Harassment Act 1997) which can be used. We will discuss further which relationships should be included within domestic abuse shortly.

Fifth, the definition is not gendered. It is clearly designed to cover cases where a man is the victim of the abuse and/or where the perpetrator is a woman. As we shall see later, this is a controversial issue.

Sixth, it is notable that the definition covers only abuse on those over the age of 16. This is controversial because teenagers can experience domestic abuse within dating relationships. However, the Government[5] explained: 'We do not want to risk blurring the lines between domestic abuse and child abuse.' As we shall see later, there are some who argue that in fact these concepts should be seen as closely linked.

B Other definitions in the literature

Ward LJ has stated: 'Domestic violence, of course, is a term that covers a multitude of sins. Some of it is hideous, some of it is less serious.'[6] This is captured by many of the definitions of domestic abuse found in the academic literature, which have sought to move away from a single definition, but acknowledge there can be different forms and aspects of domestic abuse.

Michael Johnson has suggested we can separate three forms of domestic violence:[7]

1. 'Intimate terrorism' (IT) – When one intimate partner uses a variety of tactics to exert power and control over another;

2. 'Situational couple violence' (SCV) – When an argument between partners gets 'ugly' and escalates out of control; and

3. 'Violent resistance' (VR) – When a victim, usually a female, uses violence to retaliate against being abused.

Not everyone would agree that the third category should be regarded as domestic violence at all. Nevertheless, this categorisation is helpful in bringing out the different contexts in which domestic violence can occur. Under his model it is 'intimate terrorism' which is the most serious form of domestic violence.

Michelle Madden Dempsey[8] has suggested that we need to draw a distinction between domestic violence in the 'strong sense' and domestic violence in the 'weak sense'. Domestic violence in a 'strong sense' requires the intersection of three elements – illegitimate violence, domesticity and structural inequality in the relationship – while domestic violence in its 'weak sense' only requires domesticity and structural inequality. Adopting this approach, it is possible to recognise that violence is especially serious, while still retaining the label of domestic

---

[3] Defined as being a parent of a child or having parental responsibility for the child.
[4] As defined in Family Law Act 1996, s. 63(1).
[5] HM Government (2020).
[6] *Re P (Children)* [2009] 1 FLR 1056, para 12.
[7] Johnson *et al.* (2010: 2).
[8] Madden Dempsey (2006).

violence for not physical but abusive behaviour.[9] And this distinction between domestic violence in its strong sense and in its weak sense is, Madden Dempsey suggests, helpful if there are limited resources at the hands of prosecutors. They should focus on prosecuting domestic violence in the strong sense, although she is certainly not opposed to prosecution of cases involving domestic violence in the weak sense.

C Coercive control

An extremely important aspect of the new definition in the 2020 Bill is that it recognises that domestic violence is best understood as a pattern of behaviour, rather than a single incident. It is the definition of a kind of relationship, rather than an act of a particular kind. Evan Stark, a leading commentator on coercive control, defines it as:

> a course of calculated, malevolent conduct deployed almost exclusively by men to dominate individual women by interweaving repeated physical abuse with three equally important tactics: intimidation, isolation and control.[10]

At the heart of domestic abuse is a relationship where a person is coercing and controlling another person through a range of behaviours, including, but not limited to, physical attacks. As Stark explains:

> [M]ost abused women have been subjected to a pattern of sexual mastery that includes tactics to isolate, degrade, exploit, and control them as well as to frighten them or hurt them physically . . . These tactics include forms of constraint and the monitoring and/or regulation of commonplace activities of daily living, particularly those associated with women's default roles as mothers, homemakers, and sexual partners, and run the gamut from their access to money, food, and transport to how they dress, clean, cook, or perform sexually.[11]

Adrianne Barnett has highlighted that the form of conduct used to coercively control is 'insidiously calibrated to the specificity of the particular woman herself, that women find most devastating'.[12] It can involve a combination of violence, intimidation, isolation and control. Tactics can involve surveillance in an attempt to find out and control everything the victim is doing. Barnett adds: 'Abusers may degrade, humiliate and shame women to establish their moral superiority, by, for example, swearing at them, ordering them around, putting them down, enforcing rules and activities which humiliate or dehumanise the victim, or through visible marking. Coercively controlling men can also make women "question their own reality" by thinking they are "going mad".'

It is not possible to understand domestic abuse by just considering isolated incidents. Psychologist Mary Ann Dutton explains:

> Abusive behaviour does not occur as a series of discrete events. Although a set of discrete abusive incidents can typically be identified within an abusive relationship, an understanding of the dynamic of power and control within an intimate relationship goes beyond these discrete incidents. To negate the impact of the time period between discrete episodes of serious violence – a

---

[9] In a later work she has replaced 'structural inequality' in the relationship with 'domesticity': Madden Dempsey (2009: ch. 6).
[10] Stark (2007: 5).
[11] Stark (2012).
[12] Barnett (2017).

time period during which the woman may never know when the next incident will occur, and may continue to live with on-going psychological abuse – is to fail to recognize what some battered woman experience as a continuing 'state of siege.'[13]

The aim of the coercive control is to dominate the victim and diminish her self-worth, through tactics designed to isolate, degrade and exploit the victim. Samantha Jeffries[14] explains that:

> The tactics or behaviours exhibited by perpetrators of coercive control may include: emotional abuse (e.g., victim blaming; undermining the victim's self-esteem and self-worth); verbal abuse (e.g., swearing, humiliation and degradation); social abuse (e.g., systematic social isolation); economic abuse (e.g., controlling all money); psychological abuse (e.g., threats and intimidation); spiritual abuse (e.g., misusing religious or spiritual traditions to justify abuse); physical abuse (e.g., direct assaults on the body, food and sleep deprivation); sexual abuse (e.g., pressured/unwanted sex or sexual degradation).

Not everyone approves of focusing on coercive control as being at the heart of domestic abuse. Brendon O'Neill[15] complains: 'the everyday emotional ups and downs of living together, of commitment itself, are now treated by officialdom as terrible instances of "abuse" which might require the intervention of the state.'

Coercive control can be difficult to prove in court, particularly as practitioners are encouraged to focus on five key incidents to ensure trials do not get too long.[16] It is very easy for a coercive control case to appear to be simply a case where a couple keep having arguments over money or household arrangements. To appreciate fully the nature of the relationship is time consuming and expensive. Sadly, too often the courts fail to see the severity of violence. In *R v Widdows*[17] a couple had lived together for nearly two years during which time the man raped the woman and subjected her to a series of violent assaults. The Court of Appeal nevertheless felt it appropriate to describe the relationship as 'predominantly affectionate'.

D The need for an intimate relationship

Traditionally domestic violence has been understood as involving violence between couples who are married or living together. Otherwise Reece argues domestic abuse loses its special character and 'if domestic violence occurs everywhere then domestic violence occurs nowhere'.[18] However, the definition in the 2020 Bill covers couples who are not living together but includes, for example, relatives. Other commentators have gone further and argued that what is key is whether there is a close relationship between the parties; and that the location of the abuse does not matter.[19] On such a wider definition there could be domestic abuse between an older person and their carer, for example, even though they would not be in a family-type relationship. The point may be taken even further and it might be asked if we should see all examples of where a relationship is used as a tool of abuse as falling under the same umbrella. This might bring bullying, cyber-abuse, elder abuse, child abuse and domestic abuse all within the same concept.

---

[13] Dutton (2003: 1204).
[14] Jeffries (2016).
[15] O'Neill (2013).
[16] Ciborowska (2019).
[17] [2011] EWCA Crim 1500.
[18] Reece (2006: 791).
[19] Herring (2011).

E Gender and domestic abuse

There is a lively debate over whether or not domestic abuse should be seen as a gendered activity, with it being predominantly men engaging in violence against their female partners. The argument against a gender-specific definition is that the statistics do show that women can engage in domestic abuse against men; and that it can occur in same-sex relationships. If we describe domestic abuse as simply male violence against women this will mean victims of domestic abuse who fall outside that model will not have their abuse recognised and will not receive the services they need. The Government[20] in drafting the 2020 Bill was aware of the dispute over gender but justified the gender neutral terminology on the grounds that 'we want to ensure that all victims and all types of domestic abuse are sufficiently captured, and no victim is excluded from protection or access to services.' As Goldscheid writes:[21]

> Heterosexual, gay, trans men and trans women are subjected to sexual assault as well as intimate partner violence at rates that are difficult to quantify, though no doubt are higher than commonly recognized. The woman-specific frame erases the experiences of these survivors and excludes them from services as well as from legal and other forms of redress.

The argument in favour of having a gender-based definition has several elements. First, it accepted that domestic abuse can occur outside the male on female paradigm but it is important to acknowledge in the definition that the vast majority of serious domestic abuse is male on female and that reality is ignored if we use a gender-neutral term. The vast majority of domestic violence takes place against women.[22] This is not to say that men are never the subject of domestic violence. However, most violence by women against men is quite different from violence by men against their female partners because women's violence is often in self-defence or an isolated incident.[23] It is very rare for women's violence against men to be part of an ongoing oppressive relationship.[24] Also, where men are the victims the injuries involved tend to be less serious.[25] Despite this a study by Hester found that where women are assessed by the police to be the perpetrator of domestic violence they are three times more likely to be arrested than men.[26] She suggests that in many of the cases of arrest the women were in fact using force in self-defence:

> [M]ale domestic violence suspects were able to influence decisions made by officers at the scene of the crime, minimising their own role as primary aggressors and making women who were the victims appear as perpetrators.[27]

The statistical likelihood of domestic abuse impacts on all women. As Debbie Cameron explains:

> All women—including those who will never experience an actual assault—have to live with the fear of being assaulted by men, and with the restrictions that fear imposes on their freedom of movement, action and speech. Violence perpetrated by women against men, however heinous and individually deserving of punishment it may be, does not have the same political function. All men's lives are not circumscribed by their fear of being attacked by women.[28]

---

[20] HM Government (2020).
[21] Goldscheid (2014).
[22] Hester (2013).
[23] Hester (2012).
[24] Dobash and Dobash (2004: 343).
[25] Buzawa and Buzawa (2003: 13).
[26] Hester (2012).
[27] Hester (2013).
[28] D. Cameron (2016) 'The Amazing Disappearing "Women"', Language: A Feminist Guide, 12 September 2016. Available at: https://debuk.wordpress.com/2016/09/12/the-amazing-disappearing-women/ (accessed 30.4.20).

Second, some have argued that domestic violence should be seen as but part of the spectrum of violence faced by women.[29] The lines between domestic violence and stalking, sexual harassment, violence by children against parents, elder abuse, 'honour violence' and 'date rape' are not easy to draw.[30]

Third, and most significantly, it is argued that domestic abuse when it is male on female reflects and is reinforced by sexist structures within society.[31] Madden Dempsey explains:

> [T]he patriarchal character of individual relationships cannot subsist without those relationships being situated within a broader patriarchal social structure. Patriarchy is, by its nature, a social structure – and thus any particular instance of patriarchy takes its substance and meaning from that social context. If patriarchy were entirely eliminated from society, then patriarchy would not exist in domestic arrangements and thus domestic violence in its strong sense would not exist . . . Moreover, if patriarchy were lessened in society generally then *ceteris paribus* patriarchy would be lessened in domestic relationships as well, thereby directly contributing to the project of ending domestic violence in its strong sense.[32]

Catherine MacKinnon explains: '[w]omen are sexually assaulted because they are women: not individually or at random, but on the basis of sex, because of their membership in a group defined by gender.' Domestic abuse in this way reinforces other social structures that inhibits women's access to places of power. It typically reinforces messages that women's roles are to provide food, comfort and sex for men. Accounts of domestic abuse commonly involve behaviour which is designed not just to humiliate a partner, but to reinforce a particular role for women (e.g. as homemaker) and a particular status (e.g. as lesser than men).[33] Further, it replicates the disadvantages in the outside world within the domestic. For example, the attempts by the male perpetrators of abuse to prevent their female partners entering the workplace or public arena are but imitations of broader attempts to restrict women's access to the workplace.

Not only does domestic abuse draw strength from patriarchal forces, but patriarchy supports and enables domestic abuse. As Ruth Gavison[34] explains:

> When women are battered at home, it is not because each particular victim has triggered an unfortunate 'individual' tragedy. . . Social structures are involved, social structures which are not simply 'natural'. They are person-made, and they benefit males.

The patriarchal family structure with the husband/father as the dominant figure in the family normalises violence within the family by reinforcing the subordination of women and treating 'rule making' as a natural part of being the 'leader' of the family.[35] As I have written:

> For a man to be the victim of abuse will not tune in with other societal messages about his masculinity. Indeed, they will be inconsistent with it. He will feel 'less of man'. By contrast the abuse for a woman confirms the many patriarchal messages that she is meant to be less than a man. Being the victim of domestic abuse is where she is meant to be, or where she deserves to be if she does not comply with the expectations about how women are meant to behave.[36]

Even those sympathetic with these points might have concerns about a gender-specific definition of domestic abuse. First, as already mentioned, it seems to posit a very heterosexist vision

---

[29] Kelly and Lovett (2005); Herring (2018b).
[30] Idriss (2017); Stewart *et al.* (2006).
[31] Carline and Easteal (2016).
[32] Madden Dempsey (2007).
[33] Stark (2007).
[34] Gavison (1992).
[35] Namy, Carlson and O'Hara (2017).
[36] Herring (2020).

of domestic abuse. However, supporters of a gendered approach are not claiming that violence outside the context of patriarchal abuse is not serious. It is just in a significantly different sense from patriarchal domestic abuse. The 'woman-specific frame' does not erase the experience of other victims any more than targeting child abuse erases the experiences of adult victims of abuse. It simply identifies a particular wrong which is not present in non-patriarchal domestic abuse. An alternative response may be to say that some same-sex and female on male violence could reflect and reinforce patriarchal attitudes. Part of patriarchy is the promotion of heteronormativity and that can certainly play a role in same-sex violence.[37] And even among same-sex couples we can see a difference between gay and lesbian couples, indicating that gender norms may be playing a role.[38] Certainly, as Michelle Madden Dempsey notes, 'in at least some cases of same-sex battering, salient features can be illuminated within an account of domestic violence which takes male violence against women as its paradigm.'[39]

A second problem is that seeing domestic abuse as male violence against women ignores the ways in which race, class, disability and sexuality can interact, so that the experience of domestic violence of a disabled black woman may be different from that of an affluent white woman.[40] This intersectional analysis would argue that we should not group all women together under one label, and instead focus on the different impacts of different groups of women in particular contexts.[41] This is a difficult issue. We need to recognise that individuals do not fit into single identity groups but are made from intersections of identities and forces. In the past the voice of powerful women was seen to represent women and non-mainstream women were silenced.[42] Yet, there is a danger too of losing sight of the importance of gender. Few feminist commentators would suggest that gender is the only social influence in town. The real challenge of the intersectionality claim is whether the consideration of these other factors is such that to talk of 'women' loses all meaning. Part of the value of humanity is identifying with others in communal endeavours, rather than seeking always to emphasise what separates us. We can surely do both to recognise common groupings of humanity, while at the same time accepting there are differences too. It is, therefore, preferable not to ditch the concepts of race or sex, but rather make them more tentative.[43] There are important unifying characteristics of those identified as being a woman and also important differences. Even more to the point, even if our actual identities are important combinations of intersections, patriarchy treats women as a homogenous group.

A third problem is that the gendered model reinforces the view of the male/female binary, rather than acknowledging a complex, fluid range of genders. Of course, some people will believe that the binary should be maintained. Others might accept that although we cannot be readily broken down into male and female biologically, society still does so. People are categorised, designed, coerced to being male or female by society and that is a reality that we need to challenge.[44] The gendered model of domestic abuse can acknowledge that we are looking at violence against *those categorised and treated as women* and who suffer disadvantages as they are so labelled without having to accept that these labels are correctly given.[45]

---

[37] Madden Dempsey (2009).
[38] Donovon and Hester (2006).
[39] Madden Dempsey (2009).
[40] Nixon and Humphreys (2010). And see further for ethnicity, Thiara and Gill (2010); same-sex relationships, Donovan (2016), Kaganas (2007a) and Donovan and Hester (2011); disabilities, Hague, Thiara and Mullender (2010).
[41] E.g. Goodmark (2009).
[42] Choudhry (2016).
[43] Conaghan (2009).
[44] McNeilly (2014).
[45] Otto (2013).

F Domestic abuse and children

An issue of particular recent concern is the impact of domestic violence on children.[46] There is widespread acceptance that children raised in a household where there is domestic violence suffer in many ways, as compared to households where there is not.[47] This includes psychological disturbance and often a feeling that they are to blame for the violence.[48] The impact of the domestic violence on the mother may itself harm the child. Indeed, one study of children who had suffered abuse showed that 39 per cent of them had come from families in which there was domestic violence.[49] Marianne Hester found that children were present in 55 per cent of cases of domestic violence.[50] Ten per cent of children who witnessed domestic violence witnessed their mother being sexually assaulted.[51]

G The wrongs of domestic abuse

This discussion on the nature of domestic abuse helps identify the key wrongs it involves. These clarify why domestic abuse should be taken seriously and what its wrongs are.

- *Domestic abuse and loss of freedom.* Domestic abuse involves a loss of freedom. As we have seen, the coercive control model explains domestic abuse as coercive control and one where every aspect of a person's life is controlled.[52] This is not just a temporary interference, but it controls a person's choices over time.[53] A typical crime such as an assault may momentarily impeded the victim and may have impacts on the body of the victim for some time afterwards, but these are limited and not the complete control and taking over of the victim which takes place in the case of domestic abuse. This is why kidnapping and torture are used as the closest analogies from traditional crimes.[54]

- *Domestic abuse as a breach of trust.* Intimate relationship abuse involves a serious breach of trust. Trust is essential for intimacy and love. It is in being able to be completely honest and vulnerable with a partner that relationships can deepen, an understanding of self can grow and sense can be made of life. But all of that depends on trust. In a case of domestic violence, the abuse has misused the intimate sphere as a tool against the victim.

- *Domestic abuse and the attack on the self.* The abuse of trust within an intimate relationship causes an especial harm. Intimate relationships are central to our identity and sense of self.[55] Within our intimate relationships we can be truly ourselves, free of pretence. Through them, we can there explore and discover ourselves. Domestic abuse strikes at the very conception of the self for the victim. As it is through our relationships we form our identifies

---

[46] Hester (2009).

[47] Kitzmann *et al.* (2003); Mullender *et al.* (2002); Humphreys (2001).

[48] Barnardo's (2004).

[49] Farmer and Pollock (1998).

[50] Hester (2009). According to a study by the charity Barnardo's (2004), in nine out of 10 cases of domestic violence children are in the room of, or in the room next door to, the violence.

[51] Mullender (2005).

[52] A Burke, 'Domestic violence as a crime of pattern and intent: an alternative reconceptualization' (2007) *George Washington Law Review* 552.

[53] V. Bettinson and C. Bishop, 'Is the creation of a discrete offence of coercive control necessary to combat domestic violence?' (2015) 66 *Northern Ireland Law Quarterly* 179.

[54] C. Wright, 'Torture at home: borrowing from the torture convention to define domestic violence' (2013) *Hastings Women's Law Journal* 457.

[55] O. Rachmilovitz, 'Bringing down the bedroom walls: emphasizing substance over form in personalized abuse' (2007) 14 *William and Mary Journal of Women and the Law* 495.

as to who we are and try to make sense of the world, domestic abuse turns what should be a tool for self-affirmation and self-identification into a tool for alienation and self-betrayal. The victim almost becomes used as a tool against herself.[56]

● *Domestic abuse and the impact on children.* Children living with domestic abuse suffer a wide range of long-term harms. These can include affecting their own personal relationships as adults.

● *Domestic Abuse and public harms.* As we have just seen, domestic abuse sustains patriarchy. Domestic abuse and the fear of domestic abuse plays an important role in restricting women's access to goods and to restrict them to a subservient role. The harm is not just to the individual victims but to women generally and to our society more broadly.

3 The incidence of domestic violence

The occurrence of domestic violence is often underestimated in the public consciousness. Giddens has written: 'The home is, in fact, the most dangerous place in modern society. In statistical terms, a person of any age or of either sex is far more likely to be subject to physical attack in the home than on the street at night.'[57] It is not easy to gather comprehensive statistical information on domestic violence, given that so little of it is reported.[58] However, the following shocking array of statistics demonstrates the prevalence of domestic violence:

KEY STATISTICS

● Domestic violence is the largest cause of morbidity worldwide in women aged 19–44, greater than war, cancer or motor vehicle accidents.[59]

● Just over one-third (35%) of women worldwide have experienced either physical and/or sexual intimate partner violence or non-partner sexual violence in their lifetime.[60]

● In England and Wales, it is estimated that 28.4% of women and 13.6% of men have experienced some form of domestic abuse since the age of 16.[61] In the year up to March 2019, 7.5% of women and 3.8% of men reported suffering domestic abuse in the previous year.

● An incident of killing, stabbing or beating takes place on average every six minutes in a home in Britain.[62]

● In the year ending March 2019, an estimated 2.4 million adults aged 16 to 74 years experienced domestic abuse in the last year (1.6 million women and 786,000 men).[63]

● Police recorded 1,316,800 domestic abuse incidents in the year ending March 2019.[64]

---

[56] L Arnault, 'Cruelty, horror, and the will to redemption' (2003) 18 *Hypatia* 155.
[57] Giddens (1989).
[58] Home Affairs Select Committee (2008).
[59] Home Affairs Select Committee (2008: 1).
[60] World Health Organization (2017).
[61] Office for National Statistics (2019).
[62] Ibid.
[63] Ibid.
[64] Ibid.

- 113 women were killed by men in England, Wales and Northern Ireland in 2016. Nine in ten women killed that year were killed by someone they knew; 78 women were killed by their current or former intimate partner and 65 of those were killed in their own home or the home they shared with the perpetrator.[65]

- A survey of disadvantaged youth found over half of girls reported being the victim of physical violence in the partner relationship.[66] Another survey of teenage girls found that 31% thought it acceptable for a boy to be 'aggressive' to his girlfriend if he thought she had been unfaithful to him.[67]

- There are significant financial costs which fall on the state as a result of domestic violence. Domestic violence is estimated to have cost England £5.5 billion in 2011.[68]

- Of women who had been the subject of domestic violence who left home, 76% suffered continued violence.[69]

- 30% of cases of domestic violence start during the victim's pregnancy.[70]

- On average, women are attacked 35 times before seeking assistance.[71] One study looking at only the very worst cases of domestic violence found that only 23% were reported to the police.[72]

- Around 50% of women in contact with mental health services have experienced child sexual abuse; a significant number have also suffered abuse as adults. The majority of women in prison have a background of child abuse or domestic violence.[73]

- In the United Kingdom, one in four young people aged 10–24 reported that they experienced domestic violence and abuse during their childhood.[74]

- In a 2019 survey 53% of people reported experiencing bullying or controlling behaviour by their partner.[75]

4 Causes of domestic violence

The explanations of the causes of domestic violence fall into three categories:[76]

1. *Psychopathological explanations.* These tend to see the problem of domestic violence as flowing from the psychological make-up of the abuser. It is said that domestic violence is caused by the abuser having an underdeveloped personality, including an inability to control his anger or deal with conflict. There is also a strong link between alcohol and abuse, although the alcohol may just exacerbate other factors.[77] Some even argue that male violence is

---

[65] Women's Aid (2017).
[66] Wood, Barter and Berridge (2011).
[67] BBC News Online (2005b).
[68] Trust for London (2011).
[69] Humphreys and Thiara (2002).
[70] Home Office (2003a: 20). See also Burch and Gallup (2004).
[71] Falconer (2004).
[72] Walby and Allen (2004).
[73] Home Office (2009).
[74] HMIC (2014).
[75] Ryan (2019).
[76] A useful discussion on the causes of domestic violence is found in Miles (2001: 80–7).
[77] See Home Office (2004) on the links between alcohol and domestic violence.

natural, pointing to the fact that male animals are more violent than female animals. The psychopathological approach is criticised by others on the ground that pathology cannot be the only explanation for domestic violence, as abusers are able to control their tempers outside the home, when dealing with people at work, for example. The Government has sought opinions on whether there should be a register of domestic violence abusers.[78]

2. *Theories about the position of women in society.* These theories focus on patriarchy and the domination of women by men throughout society.[79] One argument is that the attitude of the law and state authorities perpetuates abuse. Society, through the multifarious ways that men are permitted to exercise power over women, makes domestic abuse appear acceptable to the abuser. This can be supported by evidence which shows that violence often occurs when women do not fulfil their traditional roles and men use violent means to reassert their authority.[80] Further, the lack of an effective response by the law means that women are unable to find suitable ways to escape from abuse.[81] Elizabeth Schneider states:

> [H]eterosexual intimate violence is part of a larger system of coercive control and subordination; this system is based on structural gender inequality and has political roots . . . In the context of intimate violence, the impulse behind feminist legal arguments [is] to redefine the relationship between the personal and the political, to definitively link violence and gender.[82]

3. *The family relationship.* Some argue that the failure of family relationships leads to domestic violence. Poor communication skills or volatile partnerships are to blame as the causes of violence. This is a controversial approach, because it suggests that it is the fault of both the abuser and the victim that the violence has occurred. It also fails to explain why it is the man rather than the woman who is usually violent.

The truth, no doubt, is that domestic violence occurs as a result of the complex interaction between these and many other factors.

5 Human rights and domestic abuse

The Human Rights Act 1998 may be relevant to domestic violence in the following ways:[83]

1. Article 3 requires the state to protect citizens from torture or inhuman or degrading treatment from other people.[84] Article 2 requires the state to protect citizens from a risk of death at the hands of others.[85] A state will infringe an individual's right under Articles 2 or 3 if it is aware that she or he is suffering the necessary degree of abuse at the hands of another and fails to take reasonable[86] or adequate[87] or effective[88] steps to protect that individual.[89]

---

[78] Home Office (2003a: 36).
[79] See, for example, Hanmer (2000).
[80] Herring (2011b).
[81] Hester and Westmarland (2005).
[82] Schneider (2000a: 5–6).
[83] Herring (2020); Choudhry and Herring (2010: ch. 9); Burton (2010).
[84] *A v UK (Human Rights: Punishment of Child)* [1998] 2 FLR 959, [1998] 3 FCR 597; *E v UK* [2002] 3 FCR 700.
[85] *Opuz v Turkey* (App. No. 33401/02); *A v Croatia* [2010] ECHR 1506; *Van Colle v CC of Hertfordshire* [2008] UKHL 50.
[86] *Z v UK* [2001] 2 FCR 246.
[87] *A v UK* [1998] 3 FCR 597, para 24.
[88] *Z v UK* [2001] 2 FCR 246, para 73.
[89] *E v UK* [2002] 3 FCR 700; *Van Colle v CC of Hertfordshire* [2008] UKHL 50.

The phrase 'inhuman treatment' in Article 3 includes actual bodily harm or intense physical or mental suffering.[90] 'Degrading treatment' includes conduct which humiliates or debases an individual; or shows a lack of respect for, or diminishes, human dignity. It also includes conduct which arouses feelings of fear, anguish or inferiority capable of breaking an individual's moral and physical resistance.[91] It is clear, then, that the more serious forms of domestic violence that involve physical abuse are likely to fall within Article 3. If the police, prosecuting authority or courts fail to take positive steps to provide an effective remedy for someone suffering torture or inhuman or degrading treatment, they will be in breach of Article 3.[92]

2. Article 8 protects an individual's right to respect for their private and family life. The right to private life includes the right to personal integrity, both physical and psychological.[93] Domestic violence which imposes physical or psychological harm could therefore infringe this. If the violence interfered in the way that a mother was able to care for her children, this could amount to an interference in her right to respect for her family life. As with Article 3, the state has a positive obligation to ensure that one individual does not interfere with another individual's Article 8 right.[94] The obligation can arise where it would be reasonable for the state to intervene to protect someone's rights and there is an 'element' of culpability in the state's failure to intervene.[95]

    An order requiring someone to leave their home would appear clearly to breach the right under Article 8 of the Convention to respect for private and family life.[96] However, the making of orders could readily be justifiable under para 2 of Article 8 on the grounds of public safety; prevention of disorder or crime; protection of health or morals; or protection of rights and freedoms of others. In particular, an occupation order could be justified in order to protect the rights of the applicant or the child. It might even be argued that an abuser loses his rights in his home by using his home as a place in which to be violent to others.[97] A more interesting question is whether the high hurdles placed in the way of obtaining occupation orders adequately protect the right to respect for the private and family life of the applicant and child.

3. Article 6 is relevant in requiring a public hearing. As will be discussed later, it is arguable that an *ex parte* occupation order infringes a party's rights under Article 6. Of potentially more significance is a suggestion that an occupation order could be regarded as punishment following a criminal charge and so the requirements of Article 6 must be complied with, the argument being that removal from one's home is equivalent to a criminal punishment.[98]

4. Article 14 prohibits discrimination. A failure by a state to properly respond to domestic violence has been held to be sex discrimination.[99] Domestic violence far more commonly affects women than men and therefore an inadequate legal response disproportionately

---

[90] *Ireland v United Kingdom* (1978) 2 EHRR 25.

[91] See, *Price v United Kingdom* (App. No. 33394/96), (1988) 55 D & R 198, paras 24–30; and *Valašinas v Lithuania* [2001] ECHR 479.

[92] *MC v Bulgaria* (2005) 40 EHRR 20; *ES v Slovakia* (App. No. 8227/04).

[93] *Anufrijeva v Southwark LBC* [2003] 3 FCR 673; *Pretty v UK* (2002) 12 BHRC 149, para 61.

[94] *Hadjuova v Slovakia* (App. No. 2660/03).

[95] *Anufrijeva v Southwark LBC* [2003] 3 FCR 673.

[96] See *McCann v The United Kingdom* [2008] 2 FLR 899.

[97] Choudhry and Herring (2006b).

[98] *Öztürk v Germany* (1984) 6 EHRR 409.

[99] *Opuz v Turkey* (App. No. 33401/02).

impacts women. It might also be argued that the law on occupation orders discriminates against unmarried couples. If an applicant is able to show that because she was not in a married relationship or a civil partnership, she was not able to get an order under the Family Law Act, she could argue that this amounts to discrimination contrary to Article 14.

The *Council of Europe Convention on Preventing and Combating Violence Against Women and Domestic Violence* (the Istanbul Convention) has provided an important alternative analysis of the response to domestic abuse.[100] Notably this Convention is explicitly directed at violence against women. The Convention in its preamble explains:

> recognising that violence against women is a manifestation of historically unequal power relations between women and men, which have led to domination over, and discrimination against, women by men and to the prevention of the full advancement of women;
>
> Recognising the structural nature of violence against women as gender-based violence, and that violence against women is one of the crucial social mechanisms by which women are forced into a subordinate position compared with men;
>
> Recognising that women and girls are exposed to a higher risk of gender-based violence than men;
>
> Recognising that domestic violence affects women disproportionately, and that men may also be victims of domestic violence;
>
> Recognising that children are victims of domestic violence, including as witnesses of violence in the family;
>
> Aspiring to create a Europe free from violence against women and domestic violence . . .

Several things are striking about this preamble.[101] First, the convention starts with the social reality from which rights are granted, rather than rights emerging from a hypothetical abstracted person. It is the reality of violence against women and their disadvantage in the world that generates these rights. Second, these are notably gendered comments. Third, it notes that violence against women affects a number of rights, not just rights to protection from violence, but also economic, social and housing rights.

The Convention gives rights to protection: Article 4, paragraph 1 states:

> Parties shall take the necessary legislative and other measures to promote and protect the right for everyone, particularly women, to live free from violence in both the public and the private sphere.

It goes on to require states to, among other things, ensure there is effective prosecution of domestic abuse offences; ensure there are adequate refuges; and provide education to combat sexist attitudes. Although the UK has signed the Istanbul Convention, it is yet to fully ratify it.

6 Orders under the Domestic Abuse Bill

The new Domestic Abuse Bill introduces two new important orders to cover domestic abuse. We will explore these, before looking at the orders available under the current law. You should note the Bill will not replace the existing orders, but supplement them.

---

[100] For a detailed discussion see Herring (2020b).
[101] Herring (2020b).

A Domestic abuse protection notice

Clause 20 of the 2020 Bill allows a senior police office to give a person [P] a domestic abuse protection notice (DAPN) if they have reasonable grounds to suspect two things:

1. P has been abusive towards a person aged 16 or over to whom P is personally connected.
2. It is necessary to give the notice to protect that person from domestic abuse, or the risk of domestic abuse, carried out by P.

The notice can only be given to a person who is 18 or older.[102] The notice can provide that P may not contact the person for whose protection the notice is given, or come within a specified distance of a house.[103] This can include removing a person from a house. The notice is designed for use as a short-term measure until an order from the court can be sought. For example, if the police are called to a domestic abuse incident, a DAPN may be appropriate, ordering the abuser to leave the home and not to contact the victim; while preparations are made to bring other proceedings.

Before issuing the notice the senior police office must consider the welfare of any child the officer considers relevant in relation to the notice and the opinion of the person protected by the notice.[104] This last ground may mean that if a police officer is called to an incident of domestic abuse and is minded to give a DAPN, but the victim says she has forgiven the abuser, this is a factor that can lead to a DAPN not being issued. But the legislation is clear that the views of the victim are only to be taken into account and so the officer may decide to make the order nonetheless, particularly where the interests of children would support issuing one. Indeed, clause 22(4) make this explicit: 'It is not necessary for the person for whose protection a domestic abuse protection notice is given to consent to the giving of the notice.'

The grounds for making a DAPN are relatively easy to satisfy. Someone loudly swearing at their partner could be said to be 'abusing' them and, if there is a risk of further abuse, a DAPN could be issued. However, it should be noted this is a short-term order: there must be a hearing within 48 hours. So, any interference in P's rights will be limited.

B Domestic abuse protection order

A domestic abuse protection order (DAPO) is intended to become the primary civil remedy in cases of domestic abuse. The Government[105] states that:

> Our policy intention in creating new DAPNs and DAPOs is to bring together the strongest elements of existing protective orders into a single comprehensive, flexible order which will provide more effective and longer-term protection to victims of domestic abuse and their children.
> It is our intention that DAPOs will become the 'go to' protective order in cases of domestic abuse.

Orders under the FLA (e.g. non-molestation orders and occupation orders) are still available but it is envisaged they will be left for cases where there is no domestic abuse (e.g. where the two people are not personally connected; or where they are connected but have simply fallen out).

---

[102] Cl 20(6).
[103] Cl 21.
[104] Cl 22.
[105] HM Government (2020a).

(i) Who can apply for a DAPO?

The following can apply for a DAPO:

(a) the person for whose protection the order is sought;

(b) the appropriate chief officer of police (see subsection (4));

(c) a person specified in regulations made by the Secretary of State;

(d) any other person with the leave of the court to which the application is to be made.[106]

At the time of writing, we do not have any regulations to indicate who will be included within (c). It is interesting that any person can apply with the leave of the court. You might imagine a case where someone's parent or friend wishes to apply for an order to protect them from abuse. Indeed, this means an order could be made even though it was against the wishes of the victim.

(ii) What needs to be shown before an order can be made?

Two conditions must be satisfied on the balance of probabilities before the court may make an order:

● P has been abusive towards a person [V] aged 16 or over to whom P is personally connected.

● The order is necessary and proportionate to protect [V] from domestic abuse, or the risk of domestic abuse, carried out by P.[107]

It should be noted that Clause 30 states that if these two conditions are met the court *may* make an order. So, even if the conditions are met a court is entitled to decide not to make an order.

Before deciding to make an order, the following factors should be taken into account:

(a) the welfare of any person under the age of 18 whose interests the court considers relevant to the making of the order (whether or not that person and P are personally connected);

(b) any opinion of the person for whose protection the order would be made—

(i) which relates to the making of the order, and

(ii) of which the court is made aware;

(c) in a case where the order includes provision relating to premises lived in by the person for whose protection the order would be made, any opinion of a relevant occupant—

(i) which relates to the making of the order, and

(ii) of which the court is made aware.

. . .

(3) It is not necessary for the person for whose protection a domestic abuse protection order is made to consent to the making of the order.[108]

Clause 32 allows the orders to be made without notice to P, where it is just and convenient to do so. In deciding whether to make such an order without notice the court should take into account the following factors:

(3) (a) any risk that, if the order is not made immediately, P will cause significant harm to the person for whose protection the order would be made,

---

[106] Cl 26.
[107] Cl 30.
[108] Cl 31.

(b) in a case where an application for the order has been made, whether it is likely that the person making the application will be deterred or prevented from pursuing the application if an order is not made immediately, and

(c) whether there is reason to believe that—

   (i) P is aware of the proceedings but is deliberately evading service, and

   (ii) the delay involved in effecting substituted service will cause serious prejudice to the person for whose protection the order would be made.

It should be noted that a without notice order carries a danger of unfairness to P because it means an order will be made based solely on the basis of the evidence of the victim. However, the court under clause 32(4) must give P the chance to make representations about the order 'as soon as just and convenient'. Without allowing for these without notice orders P could go into hiding and terrorise V from a hidden location and V could not get an order for protection until she located P and served him with the documents. These without notice orders are therefore important for the protection of V.

It is difficult to assess whether these orders will make it easier or harder for victims to get a protective order as compared to the current law. There are five points particularly to note. The first is that with DAPOs there is no difference to draw between couples who are married or unmarried, unlike the current law under the Family Law Act 1996 (FLA) (to be discussed shortly). Second, DAPOs do not distinguish between cases where the applicant has a property interest and those who do not, again unlike the current law under the FLA. Third, under the FLA, if the balance of harm test is satisfied (see below), the court *must* make an order, but there are no circumstances under the Bill where a DAPO must be made. This might be seen as weakening the protection for victims of domestic abuse, but much depends on how the courts interpret the 2020 Bill. Fourth, and following on from that last point, as we shall see under the FLA the courts have seen an order removing someone from their home as 'Draconian' because it interferes with a person's property rights. It will be interesting to see if the same language is used when the courts consider orders for DAPOs. Fifth, it is notable that a DAPO can be applied for by someone other than the victim, and this could be done without the victim's consent. Courts will have to decide what weight, if any, attaches to the wishes of victims in such a case (see below).[109]

(iii) What can be contained within the order?

Under clause 33 a court can impose 'any requirements that the court considers necessary to protect the person for whose protection the order is made from domestic abuse or the risk of domestic abuse.' In considering what conditions to apply clause 33(2) requires the court to consider the different kinds of abuse. So, for example, requirements protecting from economic abuse may be necessary as well as orders to protect from physical abuse. Clause 33 gives examples of the kinds of requirements that may be included:

- that P not contact V;
- that P not come within a specified distance of a home;
- that P be required to leave a home;
- that P be prevented from evicting V from a home;
- that P be subject to electronic monitoring.

---

[109] Bates and Hester (2020).

The requirements can include positive steps and so could include that a person seek medical help.[110] Clause 34 states that the requirements should avoid so far as practical 'conflict with a person's religious beliefs' or interfere with their work or education. It should be noted that the Bill does not prevent a court to make such an order.

Breach of a DAPO is a criminal offence and carries a five-year imprisonment. The fact that breach is a criminal offence is significant because it means that the police are in charge of bringing the charge. That may mean that even though the victim is willing to forgive the defendant for the breach and not want legal involvement, the police may still decide to bring the case. To some people this is welcome because it means the victim will not have the stress of bringing any case and will not face threats or pressure from the abuser seeking to stop them bringing the proceedings. To others, this robs the victim of their autonomy and means it lies in the hands of the police whether any breach is penalised.

7 Injunctions and orders under the Family Law Act 1996

Learning objective 2

Discuss the orders available under the Family Law Act

There are essentially two kinds of order available under the Family Law Act 1996. The victim of domestic violence (the applicant) can seek a court order that the abuser (the respondent), first, does not molest her and, secondly, that he leaves and stays away from the family home. These are known as non-molestation orders and occupation orders respectively. Both are primarily designed to deter the respondent from abusing the applicant in the future. If he does so in breach of a non-molestation or occupation order, he could face imprisonment.

A The non-molestation order

The non-molestation order is an order that one party does not molest the other.[111] Molestation is not defined in the Act but includes conduct that harasses or threatens the applicant. Such an order is less intrusive than an order forcing someone to leave his or her home and so is more readily and widely available than an occupation order. Indeed, many acts that would constitute molestation are crimes (especially after the Protection from Harassment Act 1997). So viewed, the non-molestation order can be regarded as odd – an order that someone not commit a crime against another. Cynics argue that the use of non-molestation orders is merely a means of delaying treating domestic abuse as a crime.

(i) Who can apply for a non-molestation order?

There was much debate over who should be able to apply for non-molestation injunctions under the Act. Under the Act only associated persons can apply for a non-molestation order. 'Associated persons' are defined in s. 62(3). Before listing those who come under this heading, it is important to note that Wall J in *G v F (Non-Molestation Order: Jurisdiction)*[112] suggested that if it is unclear whether the relationship between two people falls within one of these definitions, it should be treated as if it does.

---

[110] Clause 34(2) states: A domestic abuse protection order that imposes a requirement to do something on a person ("P") must specify the person who is to be responsible for supervising compliance with that requirement.

[111] Family Law Act 1996 (hereafter FLA 1996), s. 42.

[112] [2000] 2 FCR 638.

Indeed, he thought that unless it was clear that the couple were not associated, it should be presumed that they were. A person is associated with another person if:

1. They are or have been either civil partners or married to each other.

2. They are cohabitants or former cohabitants. Under s. 62(1)(a) 'cohabitants' are defined as 'two persons who are neither married to each other nor civil partners of each other but are living together as husband and wife or as if they were civil partners'. In *G v F (Non-Molestation Order: Jurisdiction)*[113] the respondent stayed with the applicant a few nights a week in her home and she visited him for two nights a week at his home. Wall J held that this should be regarded as cohabitation. Particular weight was placed on the fact that they had had a sexual relationship, had lived in the same household, and had had a joint account.[114]

3. They have or have had an intimate personal relationship with each other which is or was of a significant duration. This category was added in by the Domestic Violence, Crime and Victims Act 2004. Before then couples who were going out together but not actually cohabitants or were not engaged could not apply for non-molestation orders as they were not associated people. Now they are. We will look forward to the courts' attempts to define an 'intimate personal relationship' and 'significant duration'. Given the approach in *G v F (Non-Molestation Order: Jurisdiction)*,[115] it may well be that borderline cases will be included in the definition.

4. They live or have lived in the same household, otherwise than merely by reason of one of them being the other's employee, tenant, lodger or boarder. This category includes many people living together and would cover, for example, students living together in a student house; or two elderly people sharing accommodation companionably. A sexual relationship is not required. Under this heading a child may claim to be associated with a parent and therefore be entitled to apply for a non-molestation order against a parent.[116]

5. They are relatives. This is given a very wide definition in s. 63(1):

LEGISLATIVE PROVISION

Family Law Act 1996, section 63(1)

(a) the father, mother, stepfather, stepmother, son, daughter, stepson, stepdaughter, grandmother, grandfather, grandson, or granddaughter of that person or of that person's spouse or former spouse; or

(b) the brother, sister, uncle, aunt, niece, nephew or cousin (whether of the full blood or of the half blood or by affinity) of that person or of that person's spouse or former spouse; and includes, in relation to a person who is cohabiting or has cohabited with another person as husband and wife, any person who would fall within paragraph (a) or (b) if the parties were married to each other.

---

[113] [2000] 2 FCR 638.
[114] See *Clibbery v Allan* [2002] 1 FLR 565 where the couple were not found to be cohabiting.
[115] [2000] 2 FCR 638.
[116] *Re Alwyn (Non-Molestation Proceedings by a Child)* [2010] 1 FLR 1363.

This is a wide definition and is rather arbitrary. It includes, for example, a former cohabitant's half-niece, although it does not include cousins.

6. They have agreed to marry one another or enter a civil partnership (whether or not that agreement has been terminated). It should be stressed that this is not as broad a category as it may at first appear. This is because there are limited ways one can prove that there is an agreement to marry.[117]

7. In relation to any child, a parent of a child or someone who has parental responsibility for the child. In relation to any child who has been adopted, the natural parent of the child; a parent of the natural parent; or a person with whom a child has been placed for adoption.

8. They are parties to the same family proceedings (other than proceedings under Part IV of the 1996 Act). Family proceedings are defined in s. 63. The list includes, for example, parties to a contact application.

If the applicant is associated with the respondent, she can apply for a non-molestation injunction against him, even if the dispute between them is not a family dispute.[118]

The court can make a non-molestation order on its own motion.[119] This might be appropriate where the court decides that a party or a child needs the protection of the order but is for some reason (maybe fear) unwilling to apply for the order.[120]

A child can apply for an order with the leave of the court if he or she is under the age of 16 but the 'court may grant leave for the purposes of subsection (1) only if it is satisfied that the child has sufficient understanding to make the proposed application for the occupation order or non-molestation order'.[121] In making its decision the court is likely to consider the kinds of factors that are relevant when a child applies for an order under the Children Act 1989.[122]

(ii) On what grounds can the order be granted?

Under s. 42(5) of the Family Law Act 1996:

LEGISLATIVE PROVISION

Family Law Act 1996, section 42(5)

In deciding whether to exercise its powers under this section and, if so, in what manner, the court shall have regard to all the circumstances including the need to secure the health, safety and well-being—

(a) of the applicant or, in a case falling within subsection (2)(b), the person for whose benefit the order would be made; and

(b) of any relevant child.

---

[117] FLA 1996, s. 44. See Civil Partnership Act 2004, s. 73 for the definition of a 'civil partnership agreement'.
[118] *Chechi v Bashier* [1999] 2 FLR 489.
[119] But only to protect parties to the proceedings before it.
[120] FLA 1996, s. 42(2).
[121] FLA 1996, s. 43.
[122] See Chapter 9.

This is clearly a very widely drawn test, permitting the court to take into account any circumstances it believes relevant. The aim of the test is to focus on the need for protection in the future rather than requiring proof of the fact or threat of violence in the past.[123] So the order can be made even if there has not been any contact in the past, but it is feared there may be in the future.[124] 'Health' is defined to include 'physical or mental health' and so it is not necessary to show that there is even a threat of physical violence. One factor the court will consider is whether the order may be misused. If the court fears that the order will simply be used as a weapon in the party's disagreements, rather than to provide protection, the court may decline to make the order.[125]

(iii) What can the order contain?

A non-molestation order will prohibit one person from molesting another. Molestation is not defined in the statute. That is a deliberate omission and was recommended by the Law Commission, which argued that there should not be a definition for fear that it might provide loopholes that a respondent could exploit.[126] In *Re T (A Child) (Non-Molestation Order)*[127] the Court of Appeal thought judges should use 'common sense in judgment' in deciding what amounted to molestation, and should be wary of providing a precise definition. The Law Commission stated that molestation could encompass 'any form of serious pestering or harassment and applies to any conduct which could properly be regarded as such a degree of harassment as to call for the intervention of the court'.[128] In *C v C (Non-Molestation Order: Jurisdiction)*[129] the Court of Appeal stated that a husband could not obtain a non-molestation order to prevent his former wife making revelations in newspapers about their relationship. It was explained that molestation does not involve simply a breach of privacy but 'some quite deliberate conduct which is aimed at a high degree of harassment of the other party'. Here it was felt that the husband was seeking protection of his reputation rather than protection from molestation. This case might be contrasted with *Johnson v Walton*,[130] where a man sent semi-naked photographs of his former girlfriend to the press. It was held that this could constitute molestation. A distinction between these cases may be made on the basis that the press involvement was directly aimed at humiliating the woman in *Johnson v Walton*, whereas in *C v C (Non-Molestation Order: Jurisdiction)*[131] the wife's conduct was intended to explain her version of events rather than disgracing her husband.[132]

Under s. 42(6) the order can refer to specific acts of molestation. This might be appropriate where the applicant wishes to prevent a particular kind of conduct which the respondent (or the police) might not appreciate would constitute molestation. Persistent telephone calls might be an example. In *R v R (Family Court: Procedural Fairness)*[133] it was said that orders restricting people from an area or prohibiting any kind of contact were serious interferences in the respondent's rights and so should be used sparingly.

---

[123] Law Commission Report 192 (1990: 3.6).
[124] *Re T (A Child) (Non-Molestation Order)* [2017] EWCA Civ 1889.
[125] *Chechi v Bashier* [1999] 2 FLR 489.
[126] Law Commission Report 207 (1992: 3.1).
[127] [2017] EWCA 1889.
[128] Law Commission Report 207 (1992: 3.1).
[129] [1998] 1 FLR 554, [1998] 1 FCR 11.
[130] [1990] 1 FLR 350, [1990] FCR 568.
[131] [1998] 1 FLR 554, [1998] 1 FCR 11.
[132] The court in *C v C (Non-Molestation Order: Jurisdiction)* [1998] 1 FLR 554, [1998] 1 FCR 11 also took into account the importance of freedom of the press.
[133] [2014] EWFC 48.

A non-molestation order could not be used to remove someone from a house because that would require an occupation order. There is no limit to the duration of a non-molestation order. It can be stated to last until a further order is made.[134]

(iv) Can the order be made against someone who is unable to control his or her actions?

Prior to the Family Law Act 1996, case law suggested that only deliberate acts could constitute molestation.[135] This is probably no longer correct. In **Banks v Banks**[136] it was seen as inappropriate to make a non-molestation injunction against a woman who was suffering from a manic-depressive disorder and therefore unable to control her behaviour. The reasoning was that it would be wrong if she were to be guilty of contempt of court through conduct that was beyond her control. This was only a decision of a county court and so is not a strong precedent. The concern is that a similar argument could be used to prevent an injunction being made against an alcoholic abuser. It is arguable that in this area the law should focus on protection of the victim rather than fairness to the perpetrator of the violence. In the light of these arguments and the decision of the Court of Appeal in **G v G (Occupation Order: Conduct)**[137] that an occupation order could be made after unintentional conduct,[138] it is submitted that a non-molestation injunction should be able to be made even following unintentional conduct. However, it should be borne in mind that a person can only be guilty of contempt if he or she has sufficient mental capacity to understand that a court order has been made forbidding certain conduct, under threat of punishment.[139]

(v) Enforcement of the orders

Section 42A of the Family Law Act (inserted by the Domestic Violence, Crime and Victims Act 2004) states that it is a criminal offence for a person to do something he is prohibited from doing by a non-molestation order without reasonable excuse.[140] A person can only be guilty of the offence if when they engaged in the conduct they were aware[141] of the existence of the order.[142] The prosecution has the burden of proof of showing that the defendant did not have a reasonable excuse.[143] Prior to the insertion of s. 42A, a breach of a non-molestation order would be dealt with by the victim applying to court for an order of contempt of court. The significance of this change in the law is that if there is a breach it no longer lies in the hands of the victim to decide whether or not to bring contempt proceedings; it is the decision of the police. Before the Act, following a breach, if the victim decided not to instigate contempt proceedings nothing further would happen. Now, even if the victim objects, the police may

---

[134] *Re B-J (A Child) (Non-Molestation Order: Power of Arrest)* [2000] 2 FCR 599.

[135] *Johnson v Walton* [1990] 1 FLR 350, [1990] FCR 568, but contrast *Wooton v Wooton* [1984] FLR 871.

[136] [1999] 1 FLR 726.

[137] [2000] 2 FLR 36.

[138] *G v G (Occupation Order: Conduct)* [2000] 2 FLR 36.

[139] *P v P (Contempt of Court: Mental Capacity)* [1999] 2 FLR 897.

[140] See Platt (2008) for a useful discussion of the practical significance of this section.

[141] Normally, this will be because he has formally been served with the order, but it need not be.

[142] FLA 1996, s. 42A(2). As well as committing the s. 42A offence the person will be guilty of a contempt of court. They cannot be convicted in respect of both (s. 42A(4)).

[143] *R v Richards* [2010] EWCA Crim 835.

decide to bring proceedings for the offence under s. 42A.[144] This has led to complaints by some that this provision disempowers the victim in taking away the choice of whether or not to bring proceedings if an order is breached.[145] Supporters claim that police prosecution protects victims from being pressurised into not commencing enforcement proceedings, and demonstrates how seriously society regards such breaches. However, there is evidence that the police are using cautions or informal warnings, rather than prosecuting for this offence.[146] If this happens, victims may be worse off than they would have been in the past. Another concern is the delay in police procedures, and particularly those of the Crown Prosecution Service, before a decision over prosecution is taken. This can mean it might be weeks before the offender is brought to court, while under the previous system a respondent who was arrested under a power of arrest for a breach of a non-molestation order could be brought before the court to be sentenced the next day.[147]

B Occupation orders

An occupation order can remove an abuser from the home and can give a right to the victim to enter or remain in the home. Although the occupation order is most commonly used in cases of domestic violence, it can be applied for if there is no violence, but simply a dispute over who should occupy the property. Where the order is that someone be removed from their home, this is a severe infringement of the rights of the person who is removed from their home. However, the order may be the only way possible to provide effective protection for the victim(s). In the very worst cases it might be crucial that the abuser does not know where the victim is, in which case alternative accommodation will be essential. Given the greater infringement of the rights of the respondent, access to occupation orders is far more restricted than to non-molestation orders. There are five different sections, which apply to different groups of applicants, and each section has slightly different requirements, some being harder to satisfy than others.

An applicant can only obtain an occupation order against a respondent to whom she is associated. If the applicant is married to the respondent or is entitled to occupy the property, she should use s. 33.[148] However, if the applicant is not entitled to occupy the property, the key question is whether the applicant is the ex-spouse of the respondent or is the cohabitant or former cohabitant of the respondent. If she is the ex-spouse, s. 35 is appropriate; if she is the cohabitant or ex-cohabitant then an application should be made under s. 36. In the very unlikely event that neither the applicant nor the respondent is entitled to occupy the dwelling-house, s. 37 or s. 38 should be used. It seems unlikely that a child could seek an occupation order against a parent as they would not fall within any of these categories.[149] This section will now consider these different sections in further detail.

---

[144] The court can no longer attach a power of arrest to a non-molestation order (para 38 of Sched. 10 to the Domestic Violence, Crime and Victims Act 2004).

[145] Hitchings (2005).

[146] Home Affairs Select Committee (2008); Platt (2008).

[147] Hester, Westmarland, Pearce and Williamson (2008).

[148] Except in the very unusual situation where neither spouse is entitled to occupy their home (e.g. if they are squatters).

[149] *Re Alwyn (Non-Molestation Proceedings by a Child)* [2010] 1 FLR 1363.

(i) Section 33: married and entitled applicants

(a) Who can apply?

'Entitled' applicants can use s. 33. An entitled person is a person who:

LEGISLATIVE PROVISION

Family Law Act 1996, section 33

(a) is entitled to occupy a dwelling-house by virtue of a beneficial estate or interest or contract or by virtue of any enactment giving him the right to remain in occupation, or

(b) has home rights in relation to a dwelling-house.

Nearly all spouses or civil partners, therefore, are 'entitled' because they will have home rights.[150] Also, anyone who has a right to occupy a dwelling-house is entitled. This includes those who own the house (for example, those who are registered owners) and those who, although not registered owners, have a beneficial interest in the property by virtue of a resulting trust, a constructive trust, a proprietary estoppel or an interest under a trust for land. The question of whether a person has a right to reside in the property under a proprietary estoppel or trust can be highly complex. Cases deciding such issues have been known to go on for weeks.[151] It might seem odd that an applicant seeking urgent protection from violence could need to introduce evidence of promises made often years earlier in order to determine which section of the Act should be used.[152]

(b) In respect of what property can the order be sought?

There are two requirements here. The first is that the property is a dwelling-house. So, if a couple ran a business together it would not be possible to get an order in respect of the business premises. The second is that the home must be or was intended to be the home of the applicant and a person to whom she is associated. So, if a flat was bought with the sole intention of it being the wife's pied-à-terre while she worked in London, an occupation order could not be obtained concerning the flat as it was never meant to be the home of the couple together. Similarly, if the applicant left the marital home and moved in with her mother, she could not get an occupation order requiring the respondent to stay away from her mother's home.[153] Whether a holiday cottage would be defined as a home is open for debate.

(c) Against whom can the order be made?

The order can be sought by the applicant against any person with whom she is associated and with whom she shared or intended to share a home.

---

[150] The exception being where neither is entitled to occupy the house, in which case either s. 37 or s. 38 applies.
[151] *Hammond v Mitchell* [1992] 1 FLR 229, [1991] FCR 938.
[152] In *S v F (Occupation Order)* [2000] 1 FLR 255 Judge Cryan found that there was not enough time at the hearing to hear all the evidence necessary to decide whether the applicant had an interest and so treated the application as if made under s. 35.
[153] Although a non-molestation order may offer some protection here.

(d) What factors will the court take into account?
The 'significant harm test'
The starting point for the court's deliberations is the significant harm test set out in s. 33(7):

LEGISLATIVE PROVISION

Family Law Act 1993, section 33(7)

If it appears to the court that the applicant or any relevant child is likely to suffer significant harm attributable to conduct of the respondent if an order under this section containing one or more of the provisions mentioned in subsection (3) is not made, the court shall make the order unless it appears to it that—

(a) the respondent or any relevant child is likely to suffer significant harm if the order is made; and

(b) the harm likely to be suffered by the respondent or child in that event is as great as, or greater than, the harm attributable to conduct of the respondent which is likely to be suffered by the applicant or child if the order is not made.

The court must first ask itself what will happen if the court makes no order: is it likely that the applicant or relevant child will suffer significant harm attributable to the conduct of the respondent? If the answer is 'no' then the significant harm test is not satisfied. If the answer is 'yes', the court must consider what will happen if the court does make an order: will the respondent or any relevant child suffer significant harm? If the answer to that question is 'no', the court *must* make an occupation order. If the answer is 'yes', then the question is whose risk of harm is greater. If the harm the applicant or child will suffer is greater than that which the respondent and any relevant child will suffer, an order *must* be made. Otherwise, the significant harm test is not satisfied.

B v B[154] shows how the subsection operates.

CASE: *B v B* [1999] 1 FLR 715, [1999] 2 FCR 251

The case concerned a married couple who had two children living with them: the husband's son from his previous relationship and a baby of their own. The husband was extremely violent and so the wife and baby moved out to temporary accommodation, leaving the husband and his son in the flat. The court considered the significant harm test. They were satisfied that if they made no order the mother and baby who were living in unsatisfactory temporary accommodation would continue to suffer significant harm and that this was attributable to the husband's violence. However, the court also accepted that if the husband and his son were ordered from the flat, they would suffer significant harm too. In particular, the local authority would not be under any obligation to house them and so the son's education and general welfare would suffer. The court decided that the harm, especially to the son, if the order was made would be greater than the harm that the mother and baby would suffer if the order was not made, and so the significant harm test was not satisfied.

---

[154] [1999] 1 FLR 715, [1999] 2 FCR 251.

A few points on the wording of the test will now be considered:

1. *Who is a 'relevant child'?* A relevant child here is broadly defined to include 'any child whose interests the court considers relevant'.[155] The child does not need to be the biological child of either the applicant or the respondent. In most cases, the child will be living with the applicant and respondent, but conceivably the interests of a child not living with them will also be relevant, for example if the making or not making of an occupation order prevents the child having contact with the parties.

2. *What is harm?* Harm is defined as including 'ill-treatment and the impairment of health' (which includes emotional health).[156] For a child, harm also involves impairment of development. Ill-treatment 'includes forms of ill-treatment which are not physical and, in relation to a child, includes sexual abuse'.[157]

3. *What is significant harm?* There is no definition of significant harm in the Family Law Act 1996, although in a similar context Booth J suggested it was harm that was 'considerable, noteworthy or important'.[158] In *Chalmers v Johns*[159] the Court of Appeal rejected an argument that a one-and-a-half mile walk to school for the mother and child was 'significant harm'. The court stressed that in order to be 'significant harm' some kind of exceptional harm needed to be shown. In *PF v CF*[160] Baker J held that emotional harm was harm for the purposes of s. 33. The husband was controlling and intimidating and that was sufficient to create significant harm.

4. *What does 'attributable' mean?* One point of particular importance on the wording of the test is that when considering whether the applicant or relevant child will suffer significant harm it must be shown that the significant harm will be attributable to the conduct of the respondent. In *B v B*, the facts of which are explained above, the mother was able to show that it was her husband's extreme violence which had forced her from the house and so the significant harm was attributable to her husband's conduct. If there had been no violence and she had moved out simply because she did not like her husband any more, she would have had grave difficulty in showing that the significant harm was attributable to the husband's conduct. However, notably, when considering the risk of significant harm to the respondent there is no need to show that it is attributable to the conduct of the applicant. So, in *B v B* it was irrelevant that the significant harm that the son and husband would suffer if the order was made would not be due to the wife's conduct. *G v G (Occupation Order: Conduct)*[161] makes it clear that conduct is attributable to the respondent even if it is unintentional conduct: the court's focus is on the effect of the respondent's conduct, not his or her intention. In *Dolan v Corby*[162] the woman suffered from psychological problems. Although she was suffering significant harm and her condition would be improved if the man left, Black LJ said it could not be found that her significant harm was attributable to the conduct of the man. Nevertheless, an occupation order was made based on the general factors, to be considered shortly.

---

[155] FLA 1996, s. 62(2).
[156] FLA 1996, s. 63(1).
[157] FLA 1996, s. 63(1).
[158] *Humberside CC v B* [1993] 1 FLR 257 at p. 263.
[159] [1999] 1 FLR 392.
[160] [2016] EWHC 3117 (Fam).
[161] [2000] 2 FLR 36.
[162] [2011] EWCA Civ 1664.

5. *What does 'likely' mean?* It is not clear what 'likely' means here. The word 'likely' in s. 31 of the Children Act 1989 has been defined by the House of Lords to signify 'a real possibility'.[163] It is suggested that a similar interpretation is given to the term here.

6. *What if the risks of significant harm are equal?* It should be noted that if the harm likely to be suffered by the applicant is equal to the harm that may be suffered by the respondent then an order does not have to be made.

The significant harm test sets out the circumstances in which the court *must* make an order. It is important to appreciate that simply because the significant harm test is not satisfied does not mean that an order cannot be made.[164]

(e) General factors

If the significant harm test is satisfied then the court must make an order. If, however, it is not, the court must then consider the general factors.[165] These are set out in s. 33(6)(a–d):

LEGISLATIVE PROVISION

Family Law Act 1996, section 33(6)(a–d)

(a) the housing needs and housing resources of each of the parties and of any relevant child;

(b) the financial resources of each of the parties;

(c) the likely effect of any order, or of any decision by the court not to exercise its powers . . . on the health, safety or well-being of the parties and of any relevant child; and

(d) the conduct of the parties in relation to each other and otherwise.

The courts have in fact been reluctant to grant occupation orders. Thorpe LJ in *Chalmers v Johns*[166] held that when considering the general factors a judge should bear in mind that an occupation order 'overrides proprietary rights and . . . is only justified in exceptional circumstances'.[167] Occupation orders should be seen as 'draconian'.[168] In *G v G (Occupation Order: Conduct)* it was stressed that to succeed, an applicant must show that more tensions exist than normally surround a family during a divorce.[169] In *Re Y (Children) (Occupation Order)*[170] Sedley LJ suggested occupation orders should be seen 'as a last resort in an intolerable situation'.[171] More recently in *Dolan v Corby*[172] Black LJ stated: 'it must be recognised that an order requiring a respondent to vacate the family home and overriding his property rights is a grave or draconian order and one which would only be justified in exceptional circumstances.'[173] These decisions of the Court of Appeal emphasise that occupation orders should be made only

---

[163] See Chapter 10.
[164] *Chalmers v Johns* [1999] 1 FLR 392.
[165] *Dolan v Corby* [2011] EWCA Civ 1664.
[166] [1999] 1 FLR 392 CA
[167] [1999] 1 FLR 392 at p. 397; see also *Re Y (Children) (Occupation Order)* [2000] 2 FCR 470 at p. 477.
[168] See also *G v G (Occupation Order: Conduct)* [2000] 2 FLR 36.
[169] [2000] 2 FLR 36.
[170] [2000] 2 FCR 470.
[171] [2000] 2 FCR 470 at p. 480.
[172] [2011] EWCA Civ 1664.
[173] In *L v L* [2012] EWCA Civ 721, Aikens LJ also used the terminology 'draconian'.

in exceptional cases. Critics would argue that these statements are excessively restrictive. Had Parliament intended that occupation orders should only be available in exceptional cases, it would have said so.

That said, it would be wrong to state that an occupation order is only available when there is serious violence.[174] In *S v F (Occupation Order)*[175] the children were residing with the mother, who had decided to leave London to live in the country. One son wished to remain in London, especially because he was soon going to be taking examinations at school. The court was willing to make an occupation order granting the father the right to live in the matrimonial home in London so that he could provide a house for his son for the completion of the schooling, while the mother moved to the country.

A court can even make an occupation order in a case where the person being removed has not behaved in a particularly blameworthy way.[176] In *Grubb v Grubb*[177] the couple accepted their relationship had broken down and they could not live together. The husband was ordered to leave the home ('his ancestral home') because he was well off and would have no difficulty in finding alternative accommodation, while the wife had few resources of her own and the husband had refused to provide her money for accommodation.

(f) What orders can be made?

These will be divided into three categories:

1. *Declaratory orders under s. 33(4) and (5).* These orders simply enable the court to declare that a party has a right to remain in the property. This may forestall any attempt by the respondent to bring court proceedings to evict the applicant.

2. *Orders under s. 33(3):*

LEGISLATIVE PROVISION

Family Law Act 1996, section 33(3)

An order under this section may—

(a) enforce the applicant's entitlement to remain in occupation as against the other person ('the respondent'); .

(b) require the respondent to permit the applicant to enter and remain in the dwelling-house or part of the dwelling-house;

(c) regulate the occupation of the dwelling-house by either or both parties;

(d) if the respondent is entitled as mentioned in subsection (1)(a)(i), prohibit, suspend or restrict the exercise by him of his right to occupy the dwelling-house;

(e) if the respondent has matrimonial home rights in relation to the dwelling-house and the applicant is the other spouse, restrict or terminate those rights;

(f) require the respondent to leave the dwelling-house or part of the dwelling-house; or

(g) exclude the respondent from a defined area in which the dwelling-house is included.

---

[174] *Dolan v Corby* [2011] EWCA Civ 1664; *L v L* [2012] EWCA Civ 721; *PF v CF* [2016] EWHC 3117 (Fam).
[175] [2000] 1 FLR 255.
[176] *L v L* [2012] EWCA Civ 721.
[177] [2009] EWCA Civ 976.

These orders can be divided into three categories: first, there are those which enforce the applicant's existing rights ((a) and (b)); secondly, orders used to regulate the rights of both parties ((c)); thirdly, those that prevent the respondent from enforcing his rights ((d), (e), (f) and (g)). The strongest order that the court could make would require the respondent to leave the dwelling-house;[178] remove his rights to re-enter;[179] and exclude him from the area surrounding the house.[180] Subsection (c) gives the court great flexibility and permits the court to make all kinds of arrangements for the occupation of the home. It might decide that the applicant can live there during the weekdays and the respondent at the weekends, or that the respondent live on the top floor and the applicant on the ground floor. In *PF v CF*[181] Baker J held that an order removing the respondent from the property should only be considered if an order allowing both to live in the property was not possible.

3. *Section 40 orders.* There would be little point in removing the respondent from the house if the applicant was unable to pay for the rent for the house or meet the mortgage payments and so could be removed by the landlord or mortgagee. Therefore, under s. 40 supplemental orders can be made to ensure the party remaining can meet the expenses connected with living in the property. When considering an application under s. 40, the court should consider all the circumstances, including the parties' financial needs, obligations and resources.[182] Unfortunately, because statute does not provide for any method of enforcing orders requiring payment under s. 40, the Court of Appeal in *Nwogbe v Nwogbe*[183] has recommended that financial orders are not made under s. 40 until Parliament has rectified this error.[184]

(g) Duration

An order under s. 33 can be of fixed or unlimited length, until the court next hears the matter.[185] The length of the order does not seem to be limited by the extent of the property right or the duration of the marriage.

(ii) Section 35: one ex-spouse or ex-civil partner with no existing right to occupy

(a) Who can apply?

This section applies only to situations where the applicant has no right to occupy the property but the respondent (the applicant's ex-spouse or civil partner) does. If the couple are still married or civil partners and the applicant is entitled to occupy the property, s. 33 should be used.

(b) In respect of what property?

An order under s. 35 is available only in respect of a dwelling house which was the actual or intended home of the applicant and the respondent.

---

[178] FLA 1996, s. 33(3)(f).
[179] FLA 1996, s. 33(3)(d).
[180] FLA 1996, s. 33(3)(g). There is some debate over what exactly an 'area' is in this context. Would it be possible to exclude someone from the village in which the home is situated?
[181] [2016] EWHC 3117 (Fam).
[182] FLA 1996, s. 40(2).
[183] [2000] 2 FLR 744, [2000] 3 FCR 345.
[184] Parliament's response is still awaited.
[185] FLA 1996, s. 33(10).

(c) What orders are available?

The list of orders is similar to those in s. 33(3). However, there is an important difference in that if the court is going to make any order under s. 35 then the applicant must be given the right to enter or remain in the property, and the respondent must be prohibited from evicting the applicant. These orders are known as mandatory orders. The thinking behind these provisions is that it would be quite wrong to evict the respondent but not give the applicant the right to enter or remain in the property. Otherwise, it would be possible to end up with a situation where neither party would have the right to live in the property. In addition to mandatory orders, the court can make a discretionary order. Those are any of the other orders available under s. 33(3): for example, an order excluding the respondent from a defined area around the dwelling house.

(d) What factors are to be taken into account?

When considering a mandatory order, the general factors as listed in s. 33(6)[186] apply, although there are some extra factors which are to be taken into account for the ex-spouse, and these are (s. 35(6)):

LEGISLATIVE PROVISION

Family Law Act 1996, section 35(6)

(a) the length of time that has elapsed since the parties ceased to live together;

(b) the length of time that has elapsed since the marriage was dissolved or annulled; and

(c) the existence of any pending proceedings between the parties—

    (i) for an order under section 23A or 24 of the Matrimonial Causes Act 1973 (property adjustment orders in connection with divorce proceedings, etc.);

    (ii) for a property adjustment order under Part 2 of Schedule 5 to the Civil Partnership Act 2004; or

    (iii) for an order under paragraph 1(2)(d) or (e) of Schedule 1 to the Children Act 1989 (orders for financial relief against parents); or

    (iv) relating to the legal or beneficial ownership of the dwelling-house.

These three factors are to turn the court's mind to the nature of the parties' marriage or civil partnership. The shorter the marriage or civil partnership and the longer the time since the separation, the harder it will be for the applicant to succeed.

If the court decides not to make a mandatory order, it should then consider making a discretionary order. When considering whether to make a discretionary order, the court must first consider the significant harm test which operates in exactly the same way as described above in relation to s. 33. If the test does not require the court to make an order, the court will then consider the general factors listed in ss. 33(6) and 35(6)(e). This is rather odd because it means that a more wide-ranging investigation is made when the court considers making the discretionary order than when it makes a mandatory order, even though the mandatory orders involve a greater invasion of the respondent's property rights. The explanation may be that having found that the applicant deserves to have a right to occupy the property (in deciding whether to make a mandatory order), the case then involves two people who both should be

---

[186] See above, 'General factors'.

entitled to occupy the dwelling house and so the case is similar to a case involving an entitled applicant under s. 33 and the criteria for further orders should then be the same.[187]

(e) Duration

The duration of an order under s. 35 is more limited than a s. 33 order. The order cannot exceed six months, although at the end of the six months the applicant can reapply for further extensions not exceeding six months each.[188]

(iii) Section 36: one cohabitant or former cohabitant with no existing right to occupy

This section applies to an applicant who is not entitled to occupy the property and who is the cohabitant[189] or former cohabitant of the respondent. The orders are available only in respect of a property that was or was intended to be the home of the applicant and the respondent.

The orders available are exactly the same as under s. 35.

When considering whether to make a mandatory order, the court must consider the general factors listed in s. 33(6)[190] and, in addition, the following extra criteria:

LEGISLATIVE PROVISION

Family Law Act 1996, section 36(6)(e–i)

(e) the nature of the parties' relationship and in particular the level of commitment involved in it;

(f) the length of time during which they have cohabited;

(g) whether there are or have been any children who are children of both parties or for whom both parties have or have had parental responsibility;

(h) the length of time that has elapsed since the parties ceased to live together; and

(i) the existence of any pending proceedings between the parties—

    (i) for an order under paragraph 1(2)(d) or (e) of Schedule 1 to the Children Act 1989 (orders for financial relief against parents); or

    (ii) relating to the legal or beneficial ownership of the dwelling-house.

When considering whether to make a discretionary order, the court begins by asking the 'significant harm' questions. These are:

LEGISLATIVE PROVISION

Family Law Act 1996, section 33(7)

(a) whether the applicant or any relevant child is likely to suffer significant harm attributable to conduct of the respondent if [a discretionary order is not made]; and

(b) whether the harm likely to be suffered by the respondent or child if [the discretionary order is made] is as great as or greater than the harm attributable to conduct of the respondent which is likely to be suffered by the applicant or child if the provision is not included.

---

[187] Although that would not explain why (e) is taken into account when considering the discretionary stage.
[188] FLA 1996, s. 35(10).
[189] As defined in FLA 1996, s. 62(3).
[190] See above, 'General factors'.

This is very similar to the significant harm test, but it does not compel the court to make an order if the applicant's significant harm is greater than the respondent's harm would be. The significant harm that the parties are at risk of suffering are simply factors to be considered, along with the general factors in s. 33(6). Given the argument earlier that once a mandatory order is made an applicant should be viewed in the same light as an entitled applicant under s. 33(6), it is hard to justify using the significant harm questions rather than the significant harm test.[191]

An order under s. 36 cannot exceed six months in duration and can be extended on one occasion for a period of six months. This is similar to s. 35, with the important limitation that under s. 36 only one extension can be applied for, but there is no limit on the number of extensions under s. 35.

(iv) Section 37: neither spouse nor civil partner entitled to occupy

This section applies to spouses or former spouses, or civil partners or former civil partners, where neither party is entitled to occupy the property. In fact, it would be very unusual for neither party to be entitled to occupy the matrimonial home. If the spouses were squatters, then this may be so.[192] There will be very few applications under this section.

(v) Section 38: neither cohabitant nor former cohabitant entitled to occupy

This section applies to a cohabitant or former cohabitant where neither the applicant nor the respondent is entitled to occupy the property. Again, it will be very rare for applications to fall within this section.

(vi) Some core issues in occupation orders

(a) Conduct

The original Law Commission proposals did not refer to the conduct of the parties.[193] Orders, it was suggested, should be granted solely by considering the parties' needs, resources and obligations – in effect a 'no-fault' scheme to resolve disputes over the occupation of the home. It is understandable that Parliament was reluctant to follow these proposals. It would have meant that if there was a case where the violent party was less well-off and not in a position to find alternative accommodation then the victim of domestic violence could be the one ordered out of the house for her own protection. This would be unacceptable to the majority of people. That said, the parts of the Family Law Act 1996 relating to domestic violence do not sit easily with the parts intended to deal with divorce, which stress the importance of 'no-fault' divorce and discourage the parties from making allegations of misconduct against one another.

(b) Property interests

When considering occupation orders, property rights are of significant importance. Cohabitants and former spouses with property interests are treated differently from those without property interests. The importance of property interests is also revealed by the fact that

---

[191] The significant harm questions are one of the provisions inserted late in the legislative process to distinguish the treatment of married and unmarried couples.

[192] Or if they were bare licensees (e.g. if a friend had invited the couple to stay).

[193] Nor in the significant harm test (s. 33(7)) did the applicant's significant harm have to be attributable to the respondent's conduct.

cohabitants with property interests are treated in the same way as married couples with property interests. A critic would argue that considering the property interests of the parties is inappropriate when deciding how to protect an applicant from violence: are not people more important than property rights?[194]

(c) Children's interests

It is notable that the interests of children are not paramount, as they are in other issues involving children. The Law Commission was concerned that placing children's interests as paramount 'might lead to more specious applications by fathers for custody, and encourage more mothers to use "I've got the kids so kick him out" arguments'.[195] The concern is understandable, but a similar argument could be used in many circumstances where the welfare test applies. The failure to prioritise the needs of the child in the Family Law Act 1996, Part IV does not fit comfortably with the weight placed on children's interests under the Children Act 1989, Adoption and Children Act 2002 and Human Rights Act 1998.[196]

(d) The distinction between married and unmarried couples

The Family Law Act 1996 does distinguish between unmarried and married couples or civil partners, but only where the applicant has no interest in the property. If the applicant does have an interest in the property there is no difference in the law that applies. It is hard to see how any of these differences could be thought to uphold marriage, and some commentators have suggested that in this context no distinction should be drawn between married and unmarried couples.

C The reduction in the use of civil remedies

In the past few years there has been a noticeable reduction in the use of civil remedies in domestic violence cases. In 2003, 36,590 occupation and non-molestation orders were made, while this had fallen to 29,878 in 2019.[197] There has been a particularly marked drop in the number of occupation orders from 10,897 in 2003 to 5,445 in 2019.[198]

There are a number of possible explanations for this. One is that s. 42A of the Family Law Act 1996, introduced in 2004, with the creation of an offence of breaching a non-molestation order, has deterred applicants.[199] However, the percentage drop in the number of occupation orders has been higher than in relation to non-molestation orders and so that cannot be a major cause. A more plausible explanation may be that the police are now taking domestic violence more seriously and are prosecuting domestic violence cases with greater vigour. That might mean that fewer people are seeing the need to rely on domestic violence remedies.

Another explanation is that there has been a decrease in the number of public funding (legal aid) applications for domestic violence proceedings.[200] It is difficult to know whether that is because fewer clients are seeking such orders or whether it is becoming harder to get public funding to seek them. What certainly seems to be true is that there are a decreasing number of solicitors' firms doing publicly funded work. It may be that the difficulty in accessing legal

---

[194] Law Commission Report 207 (1992).
[195] Law Commission Report 207 (1992).
[196] Choudhry and Herring (2006a). See also Stanley *et al.* (2010b); Westendorp and Wolleswinkel (2005).
[197] Ministry of Justice (2020).
[198] Ministry of Justice (2020).
[199] Platt (2008).
[200] See Chapter 2.

advice is causing a decrease in the numbers.[201] On the other hand, the increase in applications for non-molestation orders, from 16,288 in 2012–13 to 22,443 in 2019, might suggest some people are applying for the order primarily as a passport to legal aid.[202]

8 Domestic violence protection notices and orders

The police have power to issue a domestic violence prevention notice (DVPN) and apply for domestic violence prevention orders (DVOs) from the court. These were introduced under ss. 24–33 of the Crime and Security Act 2010. Pilot studies were conducted in local areas and they came into force nationally in 2014. They are designed to deal with the problem that an abuser might be arrested by police and charged and then is normally released. There were cases where the abuser then returned to the victim and assaulted them, although in theory a victim could seek an emergency occupation order that would require her to be very familiar with the law and to act quickly. DVPNs can give the victims 'breathing space' and 'temporary respite' from the abusers.[203] They will be replaced by DAPNs under the Domestic Abuse Bill 2020 and so will not be discussed further.

9 Injunctions under the Protection from Harassment Act 1997 and Stalking Protection Act 2019

The orders mentioned in this section are useful in cases where the two people are not personally connected. This might include co-workers or people who have just met briefly at a club.

A Protection from Harassment Act 1997

The Protection from Harassment Act 1997 in effect creates a new tort of harassment. It is possible to obtain an injunction if there is an actual or anticipated breach of s. 1.[204] Under s. 1:

LEGISLATIVE PROVISION

Protection from Harassment Act 1997, section 1

1. A person must not pursue a course of conduct—

    (a) which amounts to harassment of another, and

    (b) which he knows or ought to know amounts to harassment of the other.

2. For the purposes of this section, the person whose course of conduct is in question ought to know that it amounts to harassment of another if a reasonable person in possession of the same information would think the course of conduct amounted to harassment of the other.

---

[201] Burton (2009a).
[202] Ministry of Justice (2020).
[203] Home Office (2015a).
[204] Protection from Harassment Act 1997, s. 3.

3. Subsection (1) does not apply to a course of conduct if the person who pursued it shows–

   (a) that it was pursued for the purpose of preventing or detecting crime,

   (b) that it was pursued under any enactment or rule of law or to comply with any condition or requirement imposed by any person under any enactment, or

   (c) that in the particular circumstances the pursuit of the course of conduct was reasonable.

This section requires proof of three elements:

1. First, it must be proved that the defendant harassed the victim. The Act does not define harassment and so the word is to be given its normal meaning. However, the Act makes it clear that 'references to harassing a person include alarming the person or causing the person distress'.[205] The most useful definition, produced by the Supreme Court in *Hayes* v *Willoughby*,[206] stated that 'harassment is a persistent and deliberate course of unreasonable and oppressive conduct, targeted at another person, which is calculated to and does cause that person alarm, fear or distress'.

2. The offence can be committed only where there is a course of conduct, which must involve conduct on at least two occasions.[207] So a single incident, however terrifying, cannot amount to an offence under the Act. Two incidents separated by four months were found not to be a 'course' of conduct in *Lau* v *DPP*.[208] However, it all depends on the nature of the conduct. If there was a threat to do an act and a year later the threat was carried out, this linked form of conduct could constitute a course of conduct.[209] What is required is some kind of nexus or theme which connects the behaviour into a course of conduct.[210] In *R* v *Widdows*[211] it was held that the offence is not appropriate for 'criminalising conduct, not charged as violence, during incidents in a long and predominantly affectionate relationship in which both parties persisted and wanted to continue'. That said, the 1997 Act has been used for a wide variety of cases beyond the traditional stalking cases, ranging from animal rights protesters to neighbours falling out with each other, and it is hard to see why cohabitants should be seen as outside the Act's scope.

3. It is enough if it is shown that the defendant *ought* to have been aware that his or her conduct was harassing. It is therefore no defence for defendants to claim that they were unaware that their behaviour was harassing. In *R* v *Colohan*[212] the schizophrenic defendant argued that the jury should consider whether a reasonable schizophrenic person would be aware that his or her conduct was harassing. The argument was rejected: the jury or magistrates should simply consider what an ordinary reasonable person would have known.

There are various defences available, listed in s. 3(3). The one most likely to be relied upon is the defence that the course of conduct was reasonable. A defendant's mental illness will not render his or her conduct reasonable.[213] Once s. 1 is established, an injunction can be

---

[205] Section 7(2).

[206] [2013] UKSC 17.

[207] Protection from Harassment Act 1997, s. 7(3): conduct includes speech.

[208] [2000] 1 FLR 799.

[209] *Lau v DPP* [2000] 1 FLR 799.

[210] *R v Patel* [2004] EWCA Crim 3284.

[211] [2011] EWCA Crim 1500. See also *R v Hills* [2001] 1 FCR 569.

[212] [2001] 3 FCR 409.

[213] *R v Colohan* [2001] 3 FCR 409.

made. In addition, s. 3(2) states that damages can be awarded for anxiety and any financial loss.[214]

It should be stressed that this Act does not require there to be any kind of relationship between the parties. It is therefore potentially very wide. Interestingly, the first reported case under the section involved animal rights protesters picketing an animal laboratory.[215] This was not the kind of case the Government had in mind in passing the legislation, but demonstrates the potential width of the statute.

B Stalking Protection Act 2019

The Stalking Protection Act 2019 allows courts to make a stalking protection order. It can be applied for by a chief officer of police. Section 2 states:

1. A magistrates' court may make a stalking protection order on an application under s 1(1) if satisfied that –
   (a) the defendant has carried out acts associated with stalking,
   (b) the defendant poses a risk associated with stalking to another person, and
   (c) the proposed order is necessary to protect another person from such a risk (whether or not the other person was the victim of the acts mentioned in paragraph (a)).

2. A magistrates' court may include a prohibition or requirement in a stalking protection order only if satisfied that the prohibition or requirement is necessary to protect the other person from a risk associated with stalking.

Notably under section 1(2) a defendant can be ordered not to act in a particular way or be ordered to engage in positive help, for example they could be required to seek professional help. Any breach of the order without a reasonable excuse is a criminal offence.[216]

Surprisingly the legislation does not define stalking but it does refer to examples 'associated with stalking:

- following a person;
- contacting, or attempting to contact a person by any means;
- publishing any statement or other material which relates or purports to relate to a person or purports to originate from a person;
- monitoring a person's internet, email or other forms of electronic communication;
- loitering in any place;
- interfering with a person's property;
- watching or spying on a person.[217]

---

[214] In *Singh v Bhakar* [2006] FL 1026, £35,000 was awarded to a wife harassed by her mother-in-law.
[215] *Huntingdon Life Services Ltd v Curtis* (1997) *The Times,* 11 December.
[216] Stalking Protection Act 2019, s. 8.
[217] Taken from Protection from Harassment Act 1997, s. 2A(3).

10 Protection under the Mental Capacity Act and inherent jurisdiction

If a person lacks mental capacity an order can be made protecting them under the Mental Capacity Act 2005. In **Tower Hamlets London Borough Council v TB**[218] a woman with a severe learning disability was found to have married her cousin and had four children with him. There had been a series of incidents of domestic violence. It was held she lacked capacity to consent to sex with her husband and to be married to him. It was held to be in her best interests to be separated from him.

In **A Local Authority v DL**[219] the Court of Appeal confirmed that a local authority can seek an order under the inherent jurisdiction to protect victims of domestic violence. It will be interesting to see if this power is used extensively by local authorities concerned about victims of domestic violence who do not take steps to protect themselves and where there is insufficient evidence for a criminal prosecution.

CASE: *A Local authority* v *DL* [2012] EWCA Civ 253

DL, a middle-aged man, lived with his parents (Mr and Mrs L). Mrs L was seriously disabled. There were concerns that DL was violent towards his parents and sought to control their lives. Mrs L opposed any legal action for fear she would lose contact with DL and that he might commit suicide. Had Mr and Mrs L lacked mental capacity then proceedings under the Mental Capacity Act 2005 could have been brought. However, they had capacity to decide where to live. The local authority sought to use the inherent jurisdiction to protect vulnerable adults. The Court of Appeal accepted that in a case like this the inherent jurisdiction could be used. Even though the couple had capacity, they were vulnerable, given DL's influence over them. The court would make an order which promoted their welfare. MacFarlane LJ explained that overruling the wishes of Mrs L in this case was not necessarily restricting autonomy: '. . . The jurisdiction . . . is in part aimed at *enhancing or liberating* the autonomy of a vulnerable adult whose autonomy has been compromised by a reason other than mental incapacity . . .'[220] In other words, removing the source of influence would mean they could genuinely exercise their choice.

Surprisingly, the inherent jurisdiction was not used in the case of *PC v York*.[221] Here a young woman with intellectual impairment had fallen in love with a man in prison. Although he had a history of violence against former partners, she refused to believe he was guilty or posed a risk to her. She married him while he was in prison. Shortly before he was due to be released the local authority sought an order preventing her from living with him. The Court of Appeal found that she had capacity to make the decision as defined under the Mental Capacity Act

---

[218] [2014] EWCOP 53.
[219] [2012] EWCA 253. For another example see *Al-Jeffery v Al-Jeffery (Vulnerable Adult: British Citizen)* [2016] EWHC 2151 (Fam).
[220] Paragraph 54.
[221] [2013] EWCA 478.

2005 and so the court should not intervene. The possibility of using the inherent jurisdiction was not referred to. This was surprising given the court had determined her failure to understand the risk he posed meant that she did not understand the key facts in deciding whether to live with him, but she did not fall under the 2005 Act because it had not been shown that her mental disorder had caused that lack of knowledge.[222] Critics complain the case left her in a relationship, which experts strongly predicted would be violent, on the basis of a decision she made based on a serious misapprehension about her partner.[223]

11 The Children Act 1989 and domestic violence

It is not possible to obtain a prohibited steps order or specific issue order under s. 8 of the Children Act 1989, which has the same effect as an occupation or non-molestation order.[224] There are two reasons for this. The first is that the basis of making an order under the Children Act 1989 is the welfare principle, whereas Parliament has set out different criteria in the Family Law Act 1996 for occupation and non-molestation orders. To allow someone to be able to get an occupation order under the Children Act 1989 would be to bypass the criteria in the Family Law Act 1996. The second is that an order under s. 8 of the Children Act 1989 can be made only in respect of an issue which relates to an exercise of parental responsibility. An order that one partner does not molest the other would not relate to an exercise of parental responsibility and so could not be made under s. 8 of the Children Act 1989.

12 Domestic violence and the criminal law

Learning objective 3

Analyse the response of the criminal law to domestic abuse

The fact that a violent incident occurred in a home does not affect its position in the criminal law.[225] An assault in a home is as much an assault as if it took place in a pub; at least, that is the theory. However, the history of the criminal law in this area shows that the police and courts have often regarded domestic violence as a less serious offence than other crimes. In recent years Parliament, the courts and police have shown an increasing awareness of the problems of molestation, domestic violence and stalking, but there is still much dissatisfaction with the operation of the criminal law.

A The substantive law

As already stated, the fact that an offence takes place in a home makes no difference to the substantive law. It is nowadays uncontroversial to say that a domestic assault is as serious as any other. However, some commentators have gone further and argued that in fact domestic assaults should be regarded as aggravated assaults.[226] There could be special offences connected with domestic violence in the same way as there are offences dealing with racist assaults. There used to be a common law rule that a husband could not be guilty of raping his wife. The reasoning behind this rule was that, on marriage, a wife gave her irrevocable consent to sexual

---

[222] Presumably it was her love that blinded her to the dangers.
[223] See Herring and Wall (2013) for further discussion.
[224] *Re H (A Minors) (Prohibited Steps Order)* [1995] 1 FLR 638, [1995] 2 FCR 547.
[225] Cowan and Hodgson (2007).
[226] Herring (2020).

relations throughout marriage. In *R v R (Rape: Marital Exemption)*[227] the House of Lords stated that the traditional view that a husband could not be guilty of raping his wife was now unacceptable and the common law rule was abolished. Now, a husband can be guilty of raping his wife. The fact that the law did not change until 1992 reveals the reluctance of Parliament and the courts to deal with domestic violence.[228]

Criminal courts, on conviction or acquittal of a defendant for any criminal charge, can now impose a restraining order for the purpose of protecting someone from conduct that amounts to harassment by the defendant.[229] The idea behind this is that if there is a criminal trial and it is clear that a person needs protection from domestic violence or harassment, the court will be able to offer the protection immediately, rather than the victim having to make an application of their own. In *AJR v R*[230] the court emphasised the need to show that the precise terms of the order were all necessary to protect the victim.

There have been cases where a victim of domestic violence has killed her abuser and been charged with murder. The courts have been willing to develop the law on the defence of loss of control and diminished responsibility to deal with such cases.[231] However, there are still grave concerns over whether the current defences work effectively in these cases.[232]

Section 5 of the Domestic Violence, Crime and Victims Act 2004 creates an offence of failing to protect a child who was at risk of death or serious physical harm.[233] While this has been welcomed by some as an important aspect of protecting children from violence, others have expressed concern that the offence has to date been used against mothers who were themselves the victims of domestic violence from the person who killed the child.[234] It is suggested that the state would do better offering effective protection to victims of domestic violence, rather than prosecuting them for failing to protect their children, when the state itself has so manifestly failed to protect them.[235]

B The coercive control offence

Section 76 of the Serious Crime Act 2015 creates a new offence of controlling or coercive behaviour in an intimate family relationship. It is designed specifically to deal with cases where there is domestic abuse but there has been no physical violence.

LEGISLATIVE PROVISION

Serious Crime Act 2015, section 76

1. A person (A) commits an offence if—

   (a) A repeatedly or continuously engages in behaviour towards another person (B) that is controlling or coercive,

   (b) at the time of the behaviour, A and B are personally connected,

---

[227] [1992] 1 AC 599. The decision was put into statutory form in Criminal Justice and Public Order Act 1994, s. 142 and see now Sexual Offences Act 2003.
[228] Herring (2011a) argues the law still fails to deal adequately with marital rape.
[229] Protection from Harassment Act 1997, s. 5A
[230] [2013] EWCA Crim 591.
[231] See Herring (2012c) for a detailed discussion of the law.
[232] Kaganas (2002).
[233] Domestic Violence, Crime and Victims (Amendment) Act 2012 extended the offence to cover physical harm.
[234] Herring (2007a).
[235] Herring (2008b).

(c) the behaviour has a serious effect on B, and

(d) A knows or ought to know that the behaviour will have a serious effect on B.

2. A and B are 'personally connected' if—

(a) A is in an intimate personal relationship with B, or

(b) A and B live together and—

(i) they are members of the same family, or

(ii) they have previously been in an intimate personal relationship with each other.

3. But A does not commit an offence under this section if at the time of the behaviour in question—

(a) A has responsibility for B, for the purposes of Part 1 of the Children and Young Persons Act 1933 (see section 17 of that Act), and

(b) B is under 16.

4. A's behaviour has a 'serious effect' on B if—

(a) it causes B to fear, on at least two occasions, that violence will be used against B, or

(b) it causes B serious alarm or distress which has a substantial adverse effect on B's usual day-to-day activities.

5. For the purposes of subsection (1)(d) A 'ought to know' that which a reasonable person in possession of the same information would know.

6. For the purposes of subsection (2)(b)(i) A and B are members of the same family if—

(a) they are, or have been, married to each other;

(b) they are, or have been, civil partners of each other;

(c) they are relatives;

(d) they have agreed to marry one another (whether or not the agreement has been terminated);

(e) they have entered into a civil partnership agreement (whether or not the agreement has been terminated);

(f) they are both parents of the same child;

(g) they have, or have had, parental responsibility for the same child.

7. In subsection (6)—

'civil partnership agreement' has the meaning given by section 73 of the Civil Partnership Act 2004;

'child' means a person under the age of 18 years;

'parental responsibility' has the same meaning as in the Children Act 1989;

'relative' has the meaning given by section 63(1) of the Family Law Act 1996.

8. In proceedings for an offence under this section it is a defence for A to show that—

(a) in engaging in the behaviour in question, A believed that he or she was acting in B's best interests, and

(b) the behaviour was in all the circumstances reasonable.

9. A is to be taken to have shown the facts mentioned in subsection (8) if—

    (a) sufficient evidence of the facts is adduced to raise an issue with respect to them, and

    (b) the contrary is not proved beyond reasonable doubt.

10. The defence in subsection (8) is not available to A in relation to behaviour that causes B to fear that violence will be used against B.

11. A person guilty of an offence under this section is liable—

    (a) on conviction on indictment, to imprisonment for a term not exceeding five years, or a fine, or both;

    (b) on summary conviction, to imprisonment for a term not exceeding 12 months, or a fine, or both.

Home Office guidance[236] gives some examples of the kinds of behaviour that might fall within this offence:

- isolating a person from their friends and family;
- depriving them of their basic needs;
- monitoring their time;
- monitoring a person via online communication tools or using spyware;
- taking control over aspects of their everyday life, such as where they can go, who they can see, what to wear and when they can sleep;
- depriving them of access to support services, such as specialist support or medical services;
- repeatedly putting them down such as telling them they are worthless;
- enforcing rules and activities which humiliate, degrade or dehumanise the victim.

This offence is a welcome addition to the range of offences the police can use in prosecuting perpetrators of domestic violence. It will be interesting to see how often it is used. There are a number of features to highlight. First, the offence is only committed if the couple are 'personally connected', meaning they are relatives or have had an intimate relationship. So, it does not cover a case where a stalker is following someone they do not know. Second, the offence applies even if there has been no physical violence. It covers cases where the defendant is 'coercive and controlling'. However, it needs to be shown that this has a serious effect on the victim, as defined in subsection (4) to include fear of violence or alarm or distress which has a substantial adverse effect on B's usual day-to-day activities. This might, in some cases, be difficult to prove. Third, it is noticeable that the defendant is guilty if he 'know or ought to know' that his behaviour will have a serious effect on the victim. A defendant who claims that he did not realise his conduct was bothering the victim could still be convicted if he ought to have realised the impact on the victim.

    A very surprising aspect of the offence is that a person with parental responsibility cannot be convicted of it in relation to their child under the age of 18. Why should a parent who is exercising coercive control over their child so as to have a serious effect on them not be guilty of a crime? Presumably Parliament feared that it might be seen as punishing strict parents and so be unacceptable to the general public. Another controversial aspect is the defence in

---

[236] Home Office (2015b).

subsection (9), which imagines a case where the coercive and controlling behaviour is reasonable. Perhaps such a case might be where a spouse has dementia and their partner needs to restrict their freedom of movement to keep them safe.[237] Although in such a case it might be thought the jury would readily conclude the behaviour was not coercive and controlling.

C The criminal law in practice

There has been a history of the criminal law not, in practice, taking domestic violence seriously. A 2014 report by Her Majesty's Inspectorate of Constabulary (HMIC) admitted:

> The overall police response to victims of domestic abuse is not good enough. This is despite considerable improvements in the service over the last decade, and the commitment and dedication of many able police officers and police staff. In too many forces there are weaknesses in the service provided to victims; some of these are serious and this means that victims are put at unnecessary risk. Many forces need to take action now.
>
> Domestic abuse is a priority on paper but, in the majority of forces, not in practice. Factors that contribute to this in many forces are:
>
> - a lack of visible leadership and clear direction set by senior officers;
> - alarming and unacceptable weaknesses in some core policing activity, in particular the collection of evidence by officers at the scene of domestic abuse incidents;
> - poor management and supervision that fails to reinforce the right behaviours, attitudes and actions of officers;
> - failure to prioritise action that will tackle domestic abuse when setting the priorities for the day-to-day activity of frontline officers and assigning their work;
> - officers lacking the skills and knowledge necessary to engage confidently and competently with victims of domestic abuse; and
> - extremely limited systematic feedback from victims about their experience of the police response.[238]

In a survey conducted for the report a third of victims felt no safer as a result of the police intervention.

In a file review of 600 domestic abuse cases of actual bodily harm (where the victim will have a visible injury), HMIC found that photographs of the injury were taken in only half of the cases, and in three cases out of 10 the officer's statement lacked important details such as a description of the scene or the injuries of the victims. There are also striking variations in practices around charging perpetrators of domestic abuse with criminal offences. In some forces, there are high levels of cautioning. In addition, in some forces there appear to be comparatively fewer charges for domestic abuse-related crimes compared with other offences. HMIC is concerned that these data further underline that some forces are not prioritising the issue of domestic abuse. In 2019 an updated report[239] found some improvement, but more work needed to be done, particularly to educate police in understanding coercive control and in response times. Two-thirds of domestic violence practitioners felt the police response had improved from 2014. Although given the grim picture in 2014, it might be hoped that a higher percentage would perceive improvements.

---

[237] Home Office (2015a).
[238] HMIC (2014).
[239] HMIC (2019).

As the HMIC report indicates, although at present much work is being done to change attitudes, for too long the approach of the police was that 'domestics' were not proper crimes which warranted a thorough investigation.[240] Further, the prosecution authorities were reluctant to take such cases to court unless there was a very high chance of success. The Government has declared it as an aim of its domestic violence policy to increase arrest and prosecution rates.[241] This seems to have succeeded. The number of domestic abuse-related convictions rose to 70,583 in 2016–17, an increase of 61 per cent from 2007–08.[242] These are welcome figures, but are still a small percentage of domestic violence incidents. The Director of Public Prosecutions, however, has admitted that more work needs to be done on combatting domestic violence among minority ethnic groups.[243] Similarly, more work is needed in ensuring that gay and lesbian victims of domestic violence do not see contacting the police as 'seeking help from the enemy'.[244]

There are basically three stages at which an incident of domestic violence may fail to lead to a successful prosecution: the arrest; the decision to prosecute; and the trial.

(i) Arrest policies

Criminologists have written much on the importance of police culture and have argued that in police culture domestic violence is often not taken seriously enough. At present in England and Wales there is a wide range of practice in cases where the police respond to a domestic violence incident. In Northamptonshire just over 40 per cent of cases lead to an arrest, while in Cleveland well over 90 per cent do.[245] The official policy on arrest is set out in the HMIC report:

> [W]here there are *'grounds for arrest in the context of domestic abuse, it will normally be necessary for the officer to exercise that power'*. The decision to arrest lies with the arresting officer at the scene, based on the circumstances of the offence, and their professional judgment about whether this power should be exercised. This is not a mandatory arrest policy, but a policy with a strong expectation that where arrest is justified it will be carried out, and if the arrest is not made it needs to be justified and reasons recorded. Where the decision is made not to arrest, there are still likely to be other actions that the officer needs to take in order to meet the requirements of a positive action policy. These will include actions to ensure the safety of the victims and of any children.

There are three main problems which limit the likelihood of arrest. First, for various reasons, the victim may fail to contact the police after an assault. For example, the victim may feel that what happened was not a crime, or she may feel that she would not be taken seriously. Secondly, the police may not make an arrest because they themselves do not regard domestic violence as a 'proper crime', or because they find it impossible to discover what actually happened. The police arrive at scenes which are often emotionally charged and not easy to deal with. Certainly, a domestic violence incident is not as clear-cut an issue as dealing with a fight outside a pub. Thirdly, the victim, even though she may have contacted the police, may not

---

[240] See also Hester and Westmarland (2005).

[241] Home Office (2006a).

[242] HM Government (2018).

[243] Starmer (2012); Thiara and Gill (2010).

[244] Donovan and Hester (2011). Andrews and Johnston Miller (2013) suggest the increasing number of women police officers has helped improve attitudes towards domestic abuse.

[245] HMIC (2014).

actually want an arrest, but just want the man to be removed. This decision might be encouraged explicitly or implicitly by the police's reaction to the situation.

(ii) 'Down-criming' and decisions not to prosecute

Some people have alleged that although there has been an increase in the number of arrests for domestic violence following changes made in police practice, the number of convictions has not changed, because of the attitude of the Crown Prosecution Service (CPS).[246] It is the job of the CPS to decide either to prosecute the offence; to 'down-crime' (that is, to charge a lesser offence than the one the victim alleges); or not to pursue the case to a court hearing.[247] The decision not to prosecute, or to 'down-crime', may be caused by difficulties of proof, especially as often the only witnesses to the incident are the victim and the defendant. It may be that the victim is unwilling to pursue the prosecution because of her fear of reprisals or because she believes that it will be of no tangible benefit to her. Indeed, the imprisonment of the abuser might cause the victim financial and emotional harm. In cases where a victim withdraws her testimony, the CPS has been instructed to investigate to ensure that her decision truly reflects her wishes.[248] The CPS may prosecute even if the victim does not wish to give evidence.[249] However, in practice it is rare for there to be a prosecution if the victim is unwilling to cooperate.

(iii) The trial

Even if the case reaches trial, a conviction is, of course, not guaranteed. There are particular problems if the victim does not want to give evidence.[250] Under s. 23 of the Criminal Justice Act 1988 a written statement of the victim of an assault may[251] be admissible as evidence.[252] So in suitable cases there may be no need for the victim to give evidence in court. Nevertheless, live evidence is likely to be more persuasive to a jury. It would be possible to compel the victim to give oral evidence, by threatening them with contempt of court if they fail to testify in person.[253] In one case a victim refused to give evidence and this led to the case being dropped against her attacker, but as a result the judge decided to sentence the victim to prison for contempt of court.[254]

D Reforming the criminal procedure

A more radical approach could be taken by the criminal law in dealing with domestic violence. Some of the options are as follows.

(i) Pro-arrest guidelines or pro-prosecution

Some jurisdictions have adopted 'pro-arrest' policies or even 'mandatory arrest' policies.

---

[246] See Crown Prosecution Service (2009) for their current policy.
[247] 'Down-criming' occurs in all offences.
[248] Home Office (2000c: 2b:ii.4).
[249] Crown Prosecution Service (2009).
[250] Home Office (2000b: ch. 2) sets out guidance for courts in order to make the experience of giving evidence as untraumatic as possible.
[251] The court has a discretion to decide whether to admit the statement, and in particular to rule whether the evidence can be subject to the scrutiny of cross-examination.
[252] Although only if the witness was able to give that evidence 'live'.
[253] Police and Criminal Evidence Act 1984, s. 80.
[254] *R v Renshaw* [1989] Crim LR 811.

TOPICAL ISSUE

Pro-arrest policies

With pro-arrest policies the police are required or strongly encouraged to arrest an abuser if the victim of domestic violence makes a complaint.[255] Even if the victim subsequently withdraws her consent, the prosecution should still continue. In the United Kingdom the closest statement to a mandatory arrest policy is the most recent guidance of the Home Office, suggesting that, unless there are good reasons not to, an arrest should be carried out in cases of domestic violence.[256] Further, there could be a strong presumption in favour of prosecuting domestic violence cases, even where the victim opposes this.

One argument in favour of a mandatory arrest and prosecution policy is that a potential abuser, aware of the high likelihood of being arrested, may be deterred from violence. Others suggest that it is unlikely that batterers would be aware of the policy, and, even if they were, it would not operate as a deterrent in the 'heat of the moment'. A further justification of a pro-arrest or mandatory arrest policy is that the batterer will automatically be publicly labelled as an abuser. The publicity that would surround such a policy might make a powerful statement to society in general that domestic violence is unacceptable.[257] The policy would also lead to less pressure being put on victims, who would not have to decide whether or not to seek arrest or prosecution, and because of this might also be more willing to assist police officers.[258] This, supporters claim, will disempower batterers, by removing their ability to thwart criminal procedures by terrifying the victim into withdrawing her complaint.[259] Critics could reply that such policies in fact disempower the victim by assuming that society knows what is best for her, rather than letting her decide whether to pursue her complaint.[260] Such policies, some claim, work against the interests of women and racial minorities.[261]

One well-known example of a mandatory arrest policy in practice was the Minneapolis Experiment in the United States. Although this policy led to a reduction in the rate of reported domestic violence, it was unclear whether this was because victims were not reporting violence because of the policy or whether the policy did indeed reduce the level of violence.[262] Further replica studies in Omaha, Nebraska and Charlotte, North Carolina failed to replicate the Minneapolis results.[263] There is therefore no conclusive evidence that such a policy would lead to a reduction in the level of violence. The argument that such a policy would send out a clear message of society's disapproval of domestic violence still stands.

Carolyn Hoyle and Andrew Saunders have argued:

> The pro-arrest approach assumes a position opposite to that of the victim choice model approach: that victims have little agency and that the police and policy makers know what is best for them. It seems presumptuous that policy makers or the feminist advocates who have influenced them

---

[255] Ellison (2002a).
[256] Home Office (2000c: ch. 2).
[257] Madden Dempsey (2007 and 2009) describes how effective prosecution of domestic violence can exhibit the characteristics of a feminist state.
[258] Ellison (2002a).
[259] Schneider (2000b: 488).
[260] Dayton (2003); Miccio (2005).
[261] Gruber (2007).
[262] Buzawa and Buzawa (2003).
[263] A further difficulty with the approach is that it might lead to both parties being arrested, if both have been violent. It might be possible to require arrest of the primary aggressor, but this would not be an easy policy to implement on the ground.

can easily determine what is best for, or in the interests of, a diverse group of battered women. It is as much a conceit as the theory of deterrence in this area, which assumed that violent men are a homogeneous group.[264]

This, however, assumes that it is straightforward to ascertain what a victim wants. Even in cases where the victim is saying that she does not want a prosecution, this may not represent her true wishes. She may be acting out of fear of reprisal or she may have contradictory wishes: I do not want the violence to continue, but I do not want a prosecution. In such a case, ascertaining her wishes is not straightforward.

A pro-arrest policy could also be supported on human rights grounds.[265] As explained earlier in this section, the state has an obligation to take reasonable steps to protect citizens from inhuman and degrading treatment.[266] A failure to arrest or prosecute a perpetrator of domestic violence could infringe the victim's rights under Articles 2, 3 or 8 of the ECHR.[267] This could lead to a claim for damages under ss. 7 and 8 of the Human Rights Act 1998.

(ii) 'Rehabilitative psychological sentences'

An alternative approach would be for the criminal law to focus on the rehabilitation of domestic violence offenders rather than on punishment. In other jurisdictions those arrested for domestic violence offences can be sent on 'batterers' programmes'.[268] Linda Mills has argued for a model 'therapeutically fostering reconciliation' loosely modelled after the Truth and Reconciliation Commission in South Africa.[269] Other models focus on the apparent psychological inadequacies of the aggressor: they can teach the aggressor acceptable ways of expressing anger; challenge the abuser's general attitude towards women; or treat both the abuser and the victim together by finding ways to improve their communication.[270] Supporters of such programmes suggest that in this way the law can actually prevent future violence, but opponents argue that the method fails to take violence seriously enough and treats it as an illness rather than as criminal behaviour. Further, there is little evidence yet that they are effective.[271] Mullender and Burton found that a large majority of victims did not want prosecutions of the alleged abuser, some because they did not want to break up their relationships.[272] For such cases the psychological course may find favour with victims. There is, however, much debate over the effectiveness of such programmes.[273] Interestingly the HMIC report takes a very negative line towards them: 'The police should not use restorative justice in intimate partner domestic abuse cases and should do so with extreme caution in other forms of domestic abuse.'[274] One journalist has rather scathingly written the message sent by such programmes is 'Violent men beware! Beat up your wife and go on a course'.[275]

---

[264] Hoyle and Sanders (2000: 19).
[265] Choudhry and Herring (2010: ch. 9); Choudhry (2010).
[266] *Opuz v Turkey* (App. No. 33401/02).
[267] Burton (2010).
[268] In the UK there are a few programmes for those who have engaged in domestic abuse (see CAFCASS (2018)).
[269] Mills (2003) and Stark (2005) are strongly critical of approaches of this kind.
[270] Dobash and Dobash (2000) and Bowen, Brown and Gilchrist (2002) describe such programmes.
[271] Mullender and Burton (2000).
[272] Mullender and Burton (2000). Some victims are concerned that informing public authorities about violence will lead to investigation by social workers into the welfare of their children: McGee (2000).
[273] Bullock *et al.* (2010).
[274] HMIC (2014).
[275] Bindel (2015).

(iii) Not using the criminal law at all

It could be argued that the criminal law is inappropriate in cases of domestic violence. Given that there are such difficulties in proof and in finding punishments that meet the victims' needs, rather than developing criminal law and policing, the law should focus on attempting to find alternative housing for abused women. Some say that imprisoning the abuser can only worsen the position of the victim.[276] However, this approach fails to recognise the interest that society has in preventing domestic violence and in expressing its condemnation of such acts through the criminal law. Offering alternative accommodation can be used in conjunction with the criminal law, but should not be a replacement for it.

Another line of approach is to help people avoid entering abusive relationships. Education at schools may assist here. In 2014 the domestic violence disclosure scheme came into effect. This allows someone to ask the police whether their partner has a violent past and so might pose a risk of violence.[277] A recent review of the scheme found it had some success, although its take-up was lower than expected.[278] There is a concern that it puts the obligation of protection on a would-be victim to check out their future partner. However, as long as it is seen as only one part of a major raft of measures to counter domestic abuse this concern need not be realised.

13 Children abusing their parents

Learning objective 4

Summarise the issues around parental abuse

One problem that is only recently receiving the attention it deserves is that of teenagers abusing their parents. In her overview of the research Amanda Holt[279] found its prevalence varies from 7–29 per cent of parents. Mothers bore the vast brunt of the violence. However, the Parentline survey found both boys and girls were roughly equally likely to be aggressive, although physical violence was much more common among boys. In another survey of parents receiving violence, 35 per cent had not sought help because they did not know where to go to find that help, and a further 11 per cent did not seek help because of the stigma.[280]

The causes of parental abuse are complex. It should not be assumed that the issue can be directly analogised to domestic violence,[281] although there are clear similarities. Parents suffering parental abuse often report feelings of guilt and shame: they see the violence as reflecting badly on their parenting.[282] They also report confusion as the child appears loving and kind one moment and aggressive the next. The legal solution is not straightforward. Understandably, parents are reluctant to voice their concerns about such a problem. Few parents would want to see their children prosecuted or removed from them. Indeed, in many cases parents will feel that they are to blame, due to their failure to parent their children effectively.

The issue does not neatly fall into the categories of family law. Is it best regarded as an issue of domestic violence or child protection? Does the fact that a child is being violent indicate

---

[276] Hoyle and Sanders (2000: 19).
[277] Gay (2014).
[278] Duggan and Grace (2018).
[279] Holt (2012).
[280] Family Lives (2012).
[281] Baker (2012).
[282] Holt (2011).

that they need to be taken into care or receive punishment? It may be that there are elements of both issues in some of these cases.[283]

14 Why the law finds domestic violence difficult

Learning objective 5

Debate the theoretical issues around the response of the law to domestic abuse

Around the world, legal systems struggle to find the correct response to domestic violence. There are a number of reasons for the difficulties.

A The traditional image of the family

Domestic violence challenges the traditional images within family law of the family as a place of safety, a haven in a harsh world.[284] The presumption of non-intervention in family life is based on this peaceful view of families, although, as we saw when considering the statistical information on domestic violence, abuse is common in the home. The strength of the image of the family may explain why some victims refuse to regard themselves as the victims of crime, even regarding violence as an aspect of 'normal life'.[285]

B Privacy

At the start of this text the importance of the concept of privacy in family law was stressed.[286] O'Donovan[287] suggests: 'Home is thought to be a private place, a refuge from society, where relationships can flourish uninterrupted by public interference.' So not only is the home regarded as a refuge; some consider it essential that the law should 'stay out of the home'. Catharine Mackinnon characterised the ideology of privacy as 'a right of men "to be let alone" to oppress women one at a time'.[288] However, despite the strength that has traditionally been attached to the privacy argument, there are good reasons in favour of state intervention in cases of domestic violence.

1. Battering can be seen as causing public harm: it can cause increased costs to the NHS; extensive loss to the economy of police time, victims having to take time off work, etc. It has been estimated that domestic violence alone costs the economy £5.8 billion per year, once the costs to the National Health Service, police and lost work have been taken into account.[289] Notably, half of women seeking help for mental health problems have been the victim of domestic violence.[290]

2. It could be said that domestic violence is caused by and reinforced by patriarchy. As the state upholds and maintains patriarchy, it has responsibility for it and so is under a duty to mitigate its effects.

3. Intervention in domestic violence could be required in order to uphold the equal rights of men and women. If there is to be equality between the sexes in the home, there must be effective remedies for domestic violence.

---

[283] See Herring (2015) for further discussion.
[284] Lasch (1977). See Suk (2009) who argues this image has now disappeared.
[285] Kaganas and Piper (1994).
[286] Schneider (1994).
[287] O'Donovan (1993: 107).
[288] Mackinnon (1987: 32).
[289] Walby (2004).
[290] Home Office (2003a: 10); Walby (2004).

It has been argued that if society focuses on the victim's privacy rather than the privacy of the 'home', intervention is justified. Schneider[291] maintains that the state needs to promote 'a more affirmative concept of privacy, one that encompasses liberty, equality, freedom of bodily integrity, autonomy and self-determination, which is important to women who have been battered'. Intervention in domestic violence can therefore be justified in order to promote the privacy of the victim. However, Jeannie Suk is concerned that arguments such as these mean that the notion of intimate space has been lost. She is not convinced that this is necessarily good for women. 'The abuser is out, and the state is in',[292] she explains, expressing her concern that women who were controlled by abusers might now be controlled by the state. This may be exaggerating what is happening. The state in removing the abuser is not remaining in the home in a controlling way.

C Difficulties of proof

One of the difficulties of domestic violence is that often the only witnesses to the violence are the two parties themselves. In many cases it is one person's word against another's. This requires the courts to make orders that may infringe important rights of either party on the basis of meagre evidence. If the court makes the wrong decision, an innocent person may be removed from his or her home, or a victim may be denied protection from further violence. An obvious objection to mandatory prosecution is that without the evidence of the victim it is going to be extremely difficult to obtain a conviction. The incident is often only witnessed by the victim: so, in a practical sense, is it possible to prosecute where the victim opposes the prosecution? Those who wish to see more extensive prosecution in this area might suggest two solutions. One would be to compel victims of domestic violence to testify under pain of imprisonment for contempt of court. This has few supporters. As the primary justification offered for intervention is the protection of the rights of the victim and any children, to imprison the victim would undermine that aim. The second alternative has more support. This involves a prosecution without the involvement of the victim. At present it is very rare for this to happen.[293] Louise Ellison[294] has argued that 'victimless prosecution' is the way forward.[295] She argues that, although it is often assumed that without victim involvement a prosecution is not possible, more imaginative policing and prosecution techniques would make it feasible. She discusses, for example, the use of cameras as soon as the police arrive on the scene, to capture objective evidence of injuries.[296] She recommends that police procedure in domestic violence cases should be premised on the assumption that there will be a 'victimless prosecution'.[297] There may also need to be changes to the law of evidence – and in particular the hearsay rule and the admissibility of previous convictions – to assist in victimless prosecution. The advantages of victimless prosecution are clear: it involves less invasion of the victim's autonomy if the victim is opposed to it; the victim can avoid the pressures associated with giving evidence in these kinds of cases; and it can prevent threats or other pressures being used to dissuade victims from participating in litigation. Of course, none of this should be seen as

---

[291] Schneider (1994: 37).
[292] Suk (2009: 34).
[293] Edwards (2000).
[294] Ellison (2002a and b).
[295] See also Edwards (2000) arguing for a greater willingness to use victims' written statements in cases where victims are unwilling to give evidence in court.
[296] HMIC/CPSI (2004: 10) contains useful discussions of some of the practical steps that can be taken.
[297] Ellison (2002b) and Crown Prosecution Service (2009).

seeking not to prosecute with the victim's consent; much more should be done to enable and encourage the victim to support the litigation. The use of specialist domestic violence police, advisers,[298] prosecutors and courts might assist in these procedures.[299] The pilot studies to date indicate that in specialist domestic violence courts victimless prosecutions have been successfully brought.[300] In the 2019 HMIC report[301] a review was undertaken of 554 cases where the victim did not support prosecution. It was found that in 215 it would have been appropriate to continue the prosecution without the victim's involvement and in 71 per cent of those cases the prosecution had indeed continued.

D Occupation or protection

There are two kinds of cases in which someone may apply for an order relating to the occupation of a home: the first type involves domestic violence, where the applicant is seeking protection; the second kind involves no violence and the dispute concerns who should occupy the home until a final resolution is reached regarding the financial affairs of the couple (this being more in the nature of a property dispute). Although these are quite different kinds of cases, the Family Law Act 1996 deals with them both under ss. 33, 35 and 36.

E Victim autonomy

DEBATE

What weight should be attached to the wishes of the victim?

There can be real difficulties in finding a correct solution to a situation once domestic violence is proved. In some cases, the ideal solution from the victim's point of view is that her partner returns to the home but ceases to be violent. The victim may be emotionally and financially dependent on the abuser and to imprison him might cause her further harm.[302] It can be argued that a victim who wishes to remain in a violent relationship is not expressing her genuine wishes, and that, rather than respect what the victim says she wants, we should seek to put the victim where the victim, free from violence, can make genuine choices.[303] As one victim is reported as saying: 'He basically reprogrammed me to make me think that I was just worthless and absolutely nothing.'[304]

Another argument is that the common attitudes of victims to domestic violence – 'I want the relationship to continue, but the violence to stop' – represent incompatible wishes. The law is not able to respect both of these desires of the victim. The law could take the view that the desire for the violence to stop is the more important aspect of the wishes of the victim.

There may also be a conflict here between the interests of the state and the victim. The state may wish to express its abhorrence of domestic violence by a severe punishment, whereas the

---

[298] Howarth *et al.* (2009).
[299] Lewis (2004). Crown Prosecution Service and Department of Constitutional Affairs (2004) reports particularly favourably on developing a multi-agency framework to provide improved support to victims.
[300] Burton (2006).
[301] HMIC (2019).
[302] In certain cultures, there may be severe social disadvantages following public intervention in domestic violence.
[303] The argument is discussed in Miles (2001: 101).
[304] Quotes Casciani (2014).

victim may not seek such stern treatment. This tension is revealed in civil law in that s. 60 of the Family Law Act 1996 permits third parties to bring proceedings on a victim's behalf, but the courts may make orders on their own motion under s. 42 of the Family Law Act 1996. Both sections suggest that it may be proper to provide a victim with protection which she does not want. In criminal law, encouraging arrest and pressurising a victim into providing evidence demonstrates the tension between protecting the victim's right to choose what should happen and voicing society's opposition to domestic violence. A leading body representing family lawyers has urged that protection rather than punishment should be at the heart of law on domestic violence.[305] At the extreme it might even be alleged that a victim's autonomy is threatened, on the one hand, by her abusive partner and, on the other, by state agencies acting to 'protect her' contrary to her wishes.[306] However, whether an abused woman is in a position to exercise autonomy following what might be years of abuse is also open to question.[307] Further, it could be argued that the interests of potential future victims of domestic violence justify a tough approach against current incidents of violence.[308] The reasons for this reluctance on the part of the victim may include: a fear of retaliation if they are seen to cooperate in legal proceedings; a desire that the relationship with the abuser continue; concerns about the welfare of children; difficulties in obtaining legal aid for civil proceedings;[309] a failure on the part of the police and others in supporting victims; and a sense that none of the 'remedies' on offer by the law is helpful.

Questions

1. Is it demeaning to treat victims of domestic violence as 'vulnerable adults' who do not deserve the full protection of autonomy?

2. Do you think that domestic violence crimes are not really 'crimes against the state' and therefore can be treated differently from assaults in public places?

Further reading

Read **Hoyle and Sanders** (2000) and **Choudhry and Herring** (2006a) for contrasting views on the correct response to whether mandatory arrest and prosecution would be a good idea.

F Integrated approaches

One of the difficulties that the law has faced in this area has been integration of the work of the civil courts and criminal courts. An incident of domestic violence can lead to both a criminal prosecution and a civil application by the victim. We have not had room to cover housing law, but that is another area where domestic violence can be very relevant. If the courts which hear the different applications are not coordinated, there is a danger of conflicting remedies being provided.

One solution is the creation of specialist domestic violence courts which hear all kinds of cases of domestic violence.[310] The other benefit of this is that the courts become expert in the law and issues surrounding domestic violence. A further example of integrating civil and criminal remedies is s. 5A of the Protection from Harassment Act 1997: a court which acquits a defendant on a charge under the Act may nevertheless make a restraining order protecting

---

[305] Solicitors Family Law Association (2003).
[306] Mills (2003).
[307] Hoyle and Sanders (2000).
[308] Ellison (2002b).
[309] Rights of Women (2004: 5).
[310] Crown Prosecution Service and Department of Constitutional Affairs (2004). See Burton (2006) for an excellent discussion of the work of these courts.

the alleged victim. This might be appropriate in a case where, although it has not been proved that the defendant committed an offence, there is enough evidence to demonstrate that the 'victim' requires protection. Certainly, it must not be forgotten that the making of a court order is only the start of the process of responding to domestic violence. There are often long-term issues arising from it which require extensive involvement from a range of agencies.[311]

A different issue of integration is the need to achieve cooperation between the different groups who work with victims of domestic violence: battered women's refuges, the police, local authority housing departments and benefits agencies might all need to work together to provide effective protection for victims of domestic violence. The Government has been seeking to improve communication between the different groups.[312] Ninety per cent of police forces have now appointed domestic violence officers who will coordinate the responses to domestic violence cases.[313]

G The law is not appropriate

Some feminists argue that the law's treatment of domestic violence is doomed to fail, given the patriarchal domination of the language, procedures and personnel of the legal process.[314] They maintain that domestic violence can only be combatted if the domination of women by men throughout society is brought to an end. Until then the law can only tinker at the edges of the problem. Indeed, it is worth noting the depressing statistic that in one survey over 90 per cent of abused women continued to face abuse even after they had separated from the abuser.[315]

The Domestic Abuse Bill 2020 will create the Commissioner for Domestic Abuse. Clause 7(1) states that the Commissioner must encourage good practice in the following areas:

(a) the prevention of domestic abuse;

(b) the prevention, detection, investigation and prosecution of offences involving domestic abuse;

(c) the identification of—

  (i) people who carry out domestic abuse;

  (ii) victims of domestic abuse;

  (iii) children affected by domestic abuse;

(d) the provision of protection and support to people affected by domestic abuse.

15 Conclusion

This chapter has considered the law on domestic violence. This is an area where the notion of privacy has been particularly influential: that behaviour between partners in their home is their own business and the state should not interfere. In recent years the extent of domestic violence has become more widely acknowledged, both in terms of the severity of the violence and the number of people involved. However, acknowledgement of the problem is but a small step towards providing a solution. The Family Law Act 1996 and the judicial interpretation of that statute reveal that ousting abusive partners runs counter to the protection of property rights and (now) the right to respect for family and private life under the Human Rights Act 1998.

---

[311] Abrahams (2010).
[312] Home Office (2006a).
[313] HMIC/CPSI (2004: 3.26).
[314] Smart (1984).
[315] Kelly, Sharp and Klein (2013).

So, even if ousting an abusive partner will provide the most effective protection to a victim of domestic violence, the courts will require convincing evidence before being willing to do so. It will be interesting to see if a new attitude develops as the courts interpret the 2020 Bill. A further difficult issue is to what extent the law should respect the right of autonomy of the victim of domestic violence and therefore rely on her to pursue the remedy she wishes; and to what extent the state should seek to protect the victim (regardless of whether she wants the intervention). This is an area where, perhaps, the solution lies not so much in the hands of the law, but in a wholesale change in attitudes towards violence in the home.[316]

There is little doubt that in the past few decades there has been real progress in the legal response to domestic violence. It is taken more seriously in the criminal justice system and there is a greater awareness of the issue among the judiciary. However, as Marianne Hester[317] argues, there is a problem with what she calls the 'three planets' of domestic violence law, the law on contact disputes and child protection issues.[318] While in straightforward applications for domestic violence orders the law's response is generally reasonable, when the issue arises outside that context, in a child contact case, for example, it is sidelined. Sensitivity to domestic violence issues should not be restricted to 'domestic violence cases'.

Further reading

Barnes, R. and Donovan, C. (2019) 'Domestic violence in lesbian, gay, bisexual and/or transgender relationships', *Sexualities* 22: 741.

Barnett, A. (2017b) '"Greater than the mere sum of its parts": coercive control and the question of proof', *Child and Family Law Quarterly* 379.

Bates, L. and Hester, M. (2020) 'No longer a civil matter? The design and use of protection orders for domestic violence in England and Wales', *Journal of Social Welfare and Family Law* 42: 133.

Burton, M. (2015) 'Emergency barring orders in domestic violence cases: what can England and Wales learn from other European countries?' *Child and Family Law Quarterly* 25.

CAFCASS (2018) *Domestic Abuse Perpetrator Programme*, London: CAFCASS.

Carline, A. and Easteal, P. (2016) *Shades of Grey – Domestic and Sexual Violence Against Women*, Abingdon: Routledge.

Choudhry, S. (2010) 'Mandatory prosecution and arrest as a form of compliance with due diligence duties in domestic violence – the gender implications', in J. Wallbank, S. Choudhry and J. Herring (eds) *Rights, Gender and Family Law*, Abingdon: Routledge.

Choudhry, S. (2016) 'Towards a transformative conceptualisation of violence against women – a critical frame analysis of Council of Europe discourse on violence against women', *Modern Law Review* 79: 406.

---

[316] Home Office (2000d and 2000e) discusses how the Government intends to change attitudes towards domestic violence.

[317] Hester (2011).

[318] Financial orders on separation should be added to make four planets.

Choudhry, S. and Herring, J. (2006a) 'Righting domestic violence', *International Journal of Law, Policy and the Family* 20: 95.

Donovan, C. and Hester, M. (2011) 'Seeking help from the enemy: help-seeking strategies of those in same-sex relationships who have experienced domestic abuse', *Child and Family Law Quarterly* 23: 26.

Herring, J. (2007b) 'Familial homicide, failure to protect and domestic violence: who's the victim?' *Criminal Law Review* 923.

Herring, J. (2011b) 'The meaning of domestic violence', *Journal of Social Welfare and Family Law* 33: 297.

Herring, J. (2018) 'The Istanbul Convention: Is domestic abuse violence against women?' in G. Douglas, M. Murch and V. Stephens (eds) *International and National Perspectives on Child and Family Law,* London: Intersentia.

Herring, J. (2020) *Domestic Abuse and Human Rights,* London: Intersentia.

Hester, M. (2011) 'The three planet model: towards an understanding of contradictions in approaches to women and children's safety in contexts of domestic violence', *British Journal of Social Work* 41: 837.

Hester, M. (2013) 'Who does what to whom? Gender and domestic violence perpetrators in English police records', *European Journal of Criminology* 10: 623.

HMIC (2014) *Everyone's Business: Improving the Police Response to Domestic Abuse,* London: HMIC.

Holt, A. (2012) *Adolescent-to-Parent Abuse,* Bristol: Policy Press.

Hunter, R. (2014c) 'Domestic violence: a UK perspective', in J. Eekelaar and R. George (eds) *Routledge Handbook of Family Law and Policy,* Abingdon: Routledge.

Idriss, M. (2017) 'Not domestic violence or cultural tradition: is honour-based violence distinct from domestic violence?' *Journal of Social Welfare and Family Law* 39: 3.

Kelly, L. and Westmarland, N. (2016) 'Naming and Defining "Domestic Violence": Lessons from Research with Violent Men', *Feminist Review* 113.

Lombard, N. and Whiting, N. (2017) 'What's in a Name? The Scottish Government, Feminism and the Gendered Framing of Domestic Abuse', in N. Lombard (ed) *Routledge Handbook of Gender and Violence,* Abingdon: Routledge.

Madden Dempsey, M. (2009) *Prosecuting Domestic Violence,* Oxford: OUP.

Reece, H. (2006a) 'The end of domestic violence', *Modern Law Review* 69: 770.

Reece, H. (2009a) 'Feminist anti-violence discourse as regulation', in E. Jackson *et al.* (eds) *Regulating Autonomy: Sex, Reproduction and Families,* Oxford: Hart.

Stark, E. (2007) *Coercive Control: How Men Entrap Women in Personal Life,* Oxford: OUP.

Thiara, R. and Gill, A. (2010) *Violence against Women in South Asian Communities: Issues for Policy and Practice,* London: Jessica Kingsley Publishers.

Visit **go.pearson.com/uk/he/resources** to access **resources** specifically written to complement this text.

8 Who is a parent?

Learning objectives

When you finish reading this chapter you will be able to:

1. Explain and evaluate the different theories about the definition of parenthood
2. Define who is a mother according to law
3. State who is a legal father
4. Summarise how the status of parenthood can be lost
5. Discuss the position of the social parent
6. Explain who has parental responsibility
7. Debate who should get parental responsibility
8. Critically examine how parenthood issues are dealt with in cases involving same-sex couples

1 Introduction

It may seem rather odd to ask, 'Who is a parent?'[1] But the concept of parenthood is far from straightforward. It is often assumed that the parents of a child are the woman whose egg and the man whose sperm together ultimately produce the child. In the past, although there may have been practical problems in proving who was the biological father, that definition of parenthood was generally agreed. In recent times this definition has become problematic.[2] Four developments in particular have caused a re-examination of the concept of parenthood. The first is new reproductive technologies.[3] Now the woman who carries the child need not be genetically related to the child; a man may donate sperm to a hospital without ever intending to play a parental role; a whole range of options have been opened up for same-sex couples wishing to produce a child. Technologies continue to evolve and in 2008 it was announced that a man had been

---

[1] The United Nations Convention on the Rights of the Child does not include a definition of a parent. For a general discussion on defining parenthood, see Bainham (1999) and Steinbock (2005).
[2] Jones (2007).
[3] Sheldon (2005).

enabled to become pregnant.[4] In 2014 technology was approved which would enable a child to be born genetically related to three or more people.[5] It is now plausible to talk of a right to procreate because methods are available to help anyone to be involved in the creation of a child.[6] Secondly, with increased rates of divorce and breakdown of relationships it is now common for a child to be cared for by someone who is not necessarily a genetic parent but, for example, a step-parent. Indeed, a child may have a series of adults who carry out the social role of being a parent. For such children there has been a separation between who is the person caring for them day to day and who is their genetic parent. Thirdly, there has been an increased interest in child psychology among lawyers, and an acceptance that children may have a 'psychological parent' who is not genetically their parent, but is regarded by the children as their parent.[7] Fourthly, what it means to be a mother or father in our society is undergoing complex and interesting changes. Men are sometimes seen as dispensable in the reproductive process; men are mere 'mobile sperm banks' it is said.[8] Yet many men greatly value the paternal role.[9] Sally Sheldon and Richard Collier have written of the 'fragmentation' of fatherhood, with it appearing to involve a number of disparate and sometimes conflicting roles.[10]

Shortly, the law on parenthood will be considered, but it will be useful to consider briefly the understanding of parenthood from three other disciplines.

2 Psychological, sociological and biological notions of parenthood

Learning objective 1

Explain and evaluate the different theories about the definition of parenthood

It is interesting to examine how different academic disciplines understand the notion of parenthood. Here are some examples.

A Child psychologists

One influential group of child psychologists has argued that, from a child's perspective, 'psychological parenthood' is of greater significance than biological parenthood.[11] Goldstein *et al.* write:

> Whether any adult becomes the psychological parent of a child is based on day-to-day interaction, companionship and shared experiences. The role can be fulfilled either by a biological parent or by an adoptive parent or by any other caring adult – but never by an absent, inactive adult, whatever his biological or legal relationship to the child may be.[12]

They explain that children's and adults' perceptions of parenthood may differ:

> Unlike adults, children have no psychological conception of blood tie relationship until quite late in their development. For the biological parents, the experience of conceiving, carrying and giving birth prepares them to feel close to and responsible for their child. These considerations carry no

---

[4] BBC News Online (2008c).

[5] Chau and Herring (2015).

[6] Eijkholt (2010).

[7] See ***Re CC (Adoption Application: Separated Applicants)*** [2013] EWHC 4815 (Fam) for judicial use of the terminology 'psychological parents'.

[8] Deech (2000).

[9] See Collier (2009a) and Daniels (2006) for the tensions between reproduction and notions of masculinity.

[10] Collier and Sheldon (2008).

[11] For discussion of the psychological importance to a child of 'attaching' to a parent-figure, see Aldgate and Jones (2006).

[12] Goldstein *et al.* (1996: 19).

weight with children who are emotionally unaware of the events leading to their existence. What matters to them is the pattern of day-to-day interchanges with adults who take care of them and who, on the strength of such interactions, become the parent figures to whom they are attached.[13]

B Sociologists

Some sociologists have argued that parenthood is a socially constructed term, meaning that the rules on who is a parent reflect common norms within society, rather than reflecting an inevitable truth. Indeed, anthropologists looking at different societies in different parts of the world and at different times have found a wide variety of understandings of parenthood. For example, Goody has noted the following different aspects of parenthood: bearing and begetting children; endowment with civil and kinship status; nurturance; and training and sponsorship into adulthood.[14] Different people in different cultures may carry out these roles. Callus[15] has argued that parenthood is important in giving a child a place and identity in society:

> As an institution, parenthood is at the core of society in providing each individual with a recognised identity . . . there is a parenthood morality in having a coherent structure for recognising a child's parents, both for the resulting children and as a reflection of a partnership between generations. This partnership provides a recognised and recognisable social space in which we interact with others.

C Biological perceptions

Johnson has usefully distinguished four kinds of parenthood in a biological sense.[16] First, there is genetic parentage. At present, there is a need for sperm from the man and an egg from the woman to produce a conceptus which will ultimately develop into a person. Secondly, there is coital parentage, which involves the meeting or joining of the sperm and egg.[17] Thirdly, there is a gestational or uterine component of parentage, involving the rearing and support of the foetus, which in humans is undertaken by the mother in pregnancy. Finally, there is the post-natal component: the raising of the child after birth.

It is obvious from this very brief outline that the definition of a parent is unclear and the term 'parent' can cover a wide range of ideas. The traditional image of one mother and one father for each child is under strain, yet so far the law has struggled with the idea a child might have more than one mother or one father.[18]

3 The different meanings of being a parent in law

It is not surprising that the law has a variety of understandings on being a parent. Baroness Hale in *Re G (Children) (Residence: Same-Sex Partner)*[19] has looked at different aspects of parenthood and has usefully suggested that it is necessary to distinguish three key elements: legal, genetic and social parenthood.[20]

---

[13] Goldstein *et al.* (1996: 9).
[14] Goody (1982).
[15] Callus (2019).
[16] Johnson (1999). See also Rothstein *et al.* (2006).
[17] For the majority of human parents this will be through sexual intercourse.
[18] Harder and Thomarat (2012).
[19] [2006] 1 FCR 436 at paras 32–5. See the excellent discussion in Diduck (2007).
[20] A similar distinction had been earlier drawn by Eekelaar (1991c) and Bainham (1999). See further Callus (2008) and Masson (2006c) who also discuss ways of breaking down aspects of being a parent.

1. Legal parenthood is concerned with who is deemed in the eyes of the law to be the parent.

2. Genetic parenthood relates to whose sperm or eggs led to the creation of the child.

3. The social parent is the person who carries out the day-to-day nurturing role of a parent.

These roles are often acted out by the same person, but can be carried out by different people. For example, a step-parent may be the social parent of a child without being the biological or legal parent. Bainham has usefully explained that the law distinguishes between parentage, parenthood and parental responsibility.[21] Some legal consequences flow from the mere genetic link between an adult and a child (parentage); some flow from the legal status of being a parent (parenthood); and some flow from having parental responsibility (the rights and duties of being a parent).

The benefit to the law in having these different understandings of 'parent' is that it increases flexibility. The law can decide that some people will have parenthood but not parental responsibility, or indeed that some people will be regarded as having parental responsibility but not parenthood. For some children it is possible that different people will have parentage, parenthood and parental responsibility under the present law. For example, imagine a woman who gives birth following assisted reproductive services provided to her and her unmarried partner but using the sperm of a sperm donor. After the birth she leaves her partner and marries another man, who is awarded a residence order in respect of the child. In such a case the sperm donor would have parentage; the partner parenthood; and the husband parental responsibility.

Bainham argues that having different ways of being a parent assists in the debate over whether social or biological parenthood should be regarded by the law as the crucial element of parenthood: 'Increasingly the question will not be whether to prefer the genetic or social parent but how to accommodate both on the assumption that they both have distinctive contributions to make to the life of the child.'[22]

However, Bainham's enthusiasm for accepting a wide range of different kinds of parent is controversial. It is important to note that the 'problem' in defining parenthood is largely one of defining fathers. There is relatively little difficulty in defining motherhood. In the vast majority of cases, there is no separation between parentage, parenthood and parental responsibility for mothers, as they relate to the same person. Increasing the number of people who can be regarded as parents is in reality increasing the number of people who can be regarded as fathers.[23] From the mother's viewpoint, the greater the recognition given to different kinds of fathers, the weaker the mother's position may become.[24] For example, a requirement that mothers should consult with a child's father(s) over important issues is a more onerous requirement if several men are regarded as father, rather than just one. Indeed, some commentators argue that the only kind of parenthood the law should be interested in is the 'doing' of parenting: the person who undertakes the day-to-day care of the child. A person whose only link to the child is one of blood has no link which deserves any recognition. But that goes against the very strong feelings about blood ties which many people have.

These debates can be put in broader social context. The financial and emotional burdens of the gestation, rearing and caring for children fall disproportionately on women. Shari Motro[25] claims there is a 'fundamental gender imbalance' in the responsibilities that flow from

[21] Bainham (1999).
[22] Bainham (1999: 27).
[23] Masson (2006c: 135).
[24] See further Herring (2001: 137).
[25] Motro (2010).

sex. Indeed, she argues that women should be able to sue their partners for damages for the costs flowing from a pregnancy and child-raising. That may be going too far for many, but it suggests that in determining the rights and responsibilities of parents, the gendered nature of division of responsibilities in practice is important.

We will now consider the legal definitions of who is the mother and who is the father of a child.[26]

4 Who is the child's mother?

Learning objective 2

Define who is a mother according to law

For legal purposes, the mother of a child is the woman who gives birth to the child.[27] This is so even where there is assisted reproduction and the woman who carries and gives birth to the child is not genetically related to the child. Section 33(1) of the Human Fertilisation and Embryology Act 2008 (hereafter HFEA 2008) states:

LEGISLATIVE PROVISION

Human Fertilisation and Embryology Act 2008, section 33(1)

The woman who is carrying or has carried a child as a result of the placing in her of an embryo or of sperm and eggs, and no other woman, is to be treated as the mother of the child.

This indicates that, in relation to motherhood, it is the gestational rather than the genetic link which is crucial. In fact, the genetic link is irrelevant in establishing legal motherhood.[28] This could be explained in any one of three ways. The most convincing argument is that the care, pain and effort of pregnancy and childbirth and the closeness of the bond which develops through pregnancy and birth justifies the status of motherhood.[29] The gestational mother has given more of herself to the child than the genetic mother. In other words, the law emphasises the caring aspect of parenting over the genetic link. Secondly, the law could be justified on the basis of certainty. It is far easier to discover who gave birth to the child than to ascertain who (if anyone) donated the egg.[30] Thirdly, the law might be seen as a way of encouraging egg donation. Egg donors may be deterred from donating if they were to be regarded as the parents of the child. Baroness Hale in *Re G (Children) (Residence: Same-Sex Partner)*[31] explained the law in this way:

> While this may be partly for reasons of certainty and convenience, it also recognises a deeper truth: that the process of carrying a child and giving him birth (which may well be followed by breast-feeding for some months) brings with it, in the vast majority of cases, a very special relationship between mother and child, a relationship which is different from any other.

---

[26] For a discussion of the medical law issues surrounding reproduction, see Herring (2018a: ch 7).
[27] *Ampthill Peerage Case* [1977] AC 547 at p. 577.
[28] Contrast *Johnson v Calvert* [1993] 851 P 2d 774. See also *Moschetta v Moschetta* (1994) 25 Cal App 4th 1218.
[29] Herring (2013a).
[30] This argument was stressed by the Warnock Report (1984: 6.6–6.8).
[31] [2006] 1 FCR 436, para 34.

A woman can also become a child's mother through the making of an adoption order or a parental order.[32] It should be noted that, unlike the position in France, a woman who gives birth does not have the option to disclaim motherhood.[33] However, if the child is adopted, the birth mother will cease to be the legal mother.

While the law on motherhood might suggest that the law's focus is on the social role, rather than the genetic link, it is the social role *in gestation* which seems to matter. In ***Removal of Person Identified as Mother from Birth Certificate (No.1)***[34] Williams J in a surrogacy recognised that the applicant was the 'the person who [the child] has known as her mother since her birth', but she had not given birth to the child and so was not the mother. The point was made even more dramatically in the following case:

KEY CASE: *R (McConnell and YY)* v *Registrar General* [2020] EWCA 559

Alfred McConnell, a trans man, applied to be registered as the father (or failing that parent or gestational parent). He held a gender recognition certificate and was a man for legal purposes. The Registrar General ruled that as he had given birth to YY he should be registered as the mother, even though at the time of the birth he was legally a man. Mr McConnell sought a judicial review of that decision. The Court of Appeal, agreeing with McFarlane P at first instance, refused to grant the review.

The court focused on s. 12 of the Gender Recognition Act 2004, which states that: 'The fact that a person's gender has become the acquired gender under this Act does not affect the status of the person as the father or mother of a child.' This meant the gender recognition certificate could alter McConnell's status as a mother, achieved by the fact he had given birth. McFarlane P held that the word mother was a non-gender specific term and so there was no difficulty in holding that a mother is a man. The Court of Appeal did not emphasise that particular point.

The Court of Appeal accepted that there was a 'significant' interference in Mr McConnell's Article 8 rights in that when YY's birth certificate was viewed by schools or other public authorities his gender history would become apparent. However, this interference was justified in the name of children's rights to know who had given birth to them and the public interest in a 'clear and coherent scheme of registrations of births'. Changing the rules for the definition of motherhood and fatherhood was complex ('mother' is used 45 times in the Children Act 1989 alone, it was noted) and if change was required the issue was best left to Parliament to determine, rather than the courts. There were important social issues as well. The court explained, for example, they had no idea whether generally trans men in the situation of Mr McConnell objected to being labelled a mother or not; or what the views of the public were on the issue. All of this indicated that it was best for Parliament and not the courts to change the law.

The Court of Appeal also rejected an argument that Mr McConnell should be seen as the father, based on the best interests of children:

> The view that Parliament has taken is that every child should have a mother and should be able to discover who their mother was, because that is in the child's best interests. Others may take a different view and in time may be able to persuade Parliament to take a different view. What cannot be doubted is that Parliament has taken into account the best interests of children as a primary consideration.

---

[32] These will be discussed shortly.
[33] See the discussion in Simmonds (2013) and Marshall (2008).
[34] [2018] EWHC 3360 (Fam) and *(No.2)* [2018] EWHC 3361 (Fam)

The outcome of the Court of Appeal case was a major interference in Mr McConnell's human rights, as the Court acknowledged:

> . . . a significant interference with a person's sense of their own identity, which is an integral aspect of the right to respect for private life in Art 8. It is also an interference with the right to respect for family life of both Mr McConnell and his son because the state describes their relationship on the long form of YY's birth certificate as being that of mother and son; whereas, as a matter of social life, their relationship is that of father and son.

At a deeper level too, the decision seems to challenge acceptance of trans identity. As Margaria[35] puts it, as a result of this decision:

> the trans man who gives birth is depicted as 'not a real man' even if his legal gender indicates so, not a man deserving and capable to become a father . . . The Court seems to suggest that, in order to be legally registered as a father, a person needs to be assigned male gender at birth or otherwise participate in the procreation experience as a 'male'. By giving priority to birth assigned gender when determining parenthood, the law reconstitutes the biological link between semen and man/father, thereby privileging a cisgender reality. Moreover, fatherhood continues – indirectly – to be constructed as in need of a (female) connector to be legally relevant.

The justification for this breach seemed to be twofold. The first is that every child must have a mother. McFarlane P made the point that if McConnell's argument was accepted, YY 'will not have, and will never have had, a "mother" as a matter of law, he will only have a father'. But we might ask what is wrong with that. As we shall see, not all children are born with a father (e.g. where donated sperm is used for assisted reproduction with a single woman); so why must all children have a mother? Does this reflect some deep-seated, unarticulated, perhaps sexist, assumption that fathers are disposable but mothers are core to a child's identity?

The second is that the court emphasises that a child has a right to know who their mother is. We will explore the 'right to know one's genetic origins' below. How weighty that claim is may be a matter for debate, and certainly whether it is sufficient to justify the breach of McConnell's rights. But, perhaps more importantly, even if you think there is a right to know who was your gestational parent, it is not clear this needs to be on a birth certificate which is commonly used for identity purposes.

That last point highlights perhaps a core issues in this case: what are birth certificates for? In England and Wales, they are commonly used as forms of identity document. But for those purposes the outcome in this case would mean the document would be misleading in that it would record McConnell as the mother when his current identity (vis-à-vis YY) would be as father. Maybe it would be better, if this decision is to stand, to have a record of the birth, but a separate form of identity document to be used to record who is a person's parent.

The definition of mother may also be challenged by female same sex couples seeking assisted reproductive treatment together or making private arrangements for one of them to become pregnant.[36] They may argue that they wish to raise the child as a couple together and so both should be recognised as parents. The current law is clear: only the woman who gives birth is the mother. If the mother and her partner have entered a civil partnership or marriage then under s. 42(1) of the HFEA 2008, the partner will be treated as a parent (but not a mother), unless it can be shown she did not consent to the placing of the sperm or eggs into the mother.[37] If the mother

---

[35] Margaria (2020). See also Baars (2020).
[36] Sifris (2009). See also Almack (2006).
[37] It will be presumed that there is consent unless there is evidence to the contrary: *Re G (Human Fertilisation and Embryology Act 2008)* [2016] EWHC 729 (Fam).

(W) and other woman (P) are not in a civil partnership or marriage, the partner can become a parent if she meets the 'agreed female parenthood provisions':

LEGISLATIVE PROVISION

Human Fertilisation and Embryology Act 2008, section 44(1)

(1) The agreed female parenthood conditions referred to in section 43(b) are met in relation to another woman ('P') in relation to treatment provided to W under a licence if, but only if,—

    (a) P has given the person responsible a notice stating that P consents to P being treated as a parent of any child resulting from treatment provided to W under the licence,

    (b) W has given the person responsible a notice stating that W agrees to P being so treated,

    (c) neither W nor P has, since giving notice under paragraph (a) or (b), given the person responsible notice of the withdrawal of P's or W's consent to P being so treated,

    (d) W has not, since the giving of the notice under paragraph (b), given the person responsible—

        (i) a further notice under that paragraph stating that W consents to a woman other than P being treated as a parent of any resulting child, or

        (ii) a notice under section 37(1)(b) stating that W consents to a man being treated as the father of any resulting child, and

    (e) W and P are not within prohibited degrees of relationship in relation to each other.

(2) A notice under subsection (1)(a), (b) or (c) must be in writing and must be signed by the person giving it.

(3) A notice under subsection (1)(a), (b) or (c) by a person ('S') who is unable to sign because of illness, injury or physical disability is to be taken to comply with the requirement of sub-section (2) as to signature if it is signed at the direction of S, in the presence of S and in the presence of at least one witness who attests the signature.

It is worth noting that it is not actually necessary for the mother and partner to be in a sexual relationship. Although the clinic is unlikely to agree to treat a couple if it is felt they do not have a close relationship of some kind.

The fact that the partner of the mother can be recognised as a 'second parent', but not mother, is odd. There is no legal significance in the difference in name; she is fully a parent in the eyes of the law. The fact that the female partner is not described as a mother is also odd, especially given that the male partner of the mother (as we shall see shortly) in equivalent circumstances is treated as a father.[38] One possible explanation is that the law is wedded to the idea that a child can have only one mother and one father. Indeed, the HFEA 2008 seems to go to considerable lengths to ensure that a child does not have two of one kind of parent. Critics will see this as the law not being able to break free from a hetero-normative understanding of the family.

In 2015 Parliament passed the Human Fertilisation and Embryology (Mitochondrial Donation) Regulations 2015.[39] These permit and regulate Mitochondrial Replacement Therapy (MRT), which is designed to help mothers who have or carry mitochondrial DNA diseases. A donated egg is used and the nuclear genetic material is removed and replaced with the

---

[38] L. Smith (2007). See also Wallbank (2004a).
[39] See Chau and Herring (2015).

nucleus of the egg of the intended mother. This can then be fertilised with sperm and placed in the mother. Technically a child born through such a process will be genetically related to three people. However, the donor is, effectively, donating only the mitochondrial DNA. Although there is some dispute over this, it is generally thought that that plays a relatively small part in the person's genetic make-up. The regulations make it clear that the donor of the egg is not a parent of the child and even states that unlike the position with sperm donors the child cannot discover the identity of the egg donor. This has been criticised by Thana C. de Campos and Caterina Milo[40] who argue: 'By negating the legal right of the conceived children to know and trace their genetic origins, the regulations not only discriminate against children born as a result of mitochondrial donation but also violate their natural and basic human right.'

5 Who is the child's father?

Learning objective 3

State who is a legal father

The law on fatherhood is even more complex than the law on motherhood! A man[41] who wishes to prove that he is the father of a child must show:

- that he is genetically the father of the child;[42] or
- that one of the legal presumptions of paternity applies and has not been rebutted; or
- that he is a father by virtue of one of the statutory provisions governing assisted reproduction; or
- that an adoption order or parental order has been made in his favour.

The core notion of paternity has traditionally been seen as a biological or genetic concept. A man is the father of a child genetically related to him.[43] Until recently it was difficult to prove whether a father was genetically related to a child and so the law had to rely on certain presumptions. Now DNA testing can prove conclusively whether a man is the father of a child. However, the legal presumptions are still of importance because they explain who the father of a child is if no tests have been carried out.[44]

A Legal presumptions of paternity

These are the circumstances in which fatherhood is presumed:

1. If a married woman gives birth, it is presumed that her husband is the father of the child.[45] This presumption is sometimes known as *pater est quem nuptiae demonstrant* (or *pater est* for short). It does not apply to unmarried cohabitants nor in a case of same-sex marriage.[46] If the birth takes place during the marriage but conception took place before the marriage, the *pater est*

---

[40] De Campos and Milo (2018).
[41] Only a man can be a father: *X, Y, Z v UK* [1997] 2 FLR 892, [1997] 3 FCR 341 ECtHR This was confirmed in *J v C* [2006] EWCA Civ 551.
[42] A sperm donor to a licensed clinic cannot rely on this ground (HFEA 1990, s. 28(6)).
[43] This was confirmed in **Leeds Teaching Hospital NHS Trust v A** [2003] EWHC 259, [2003] 1 FCR 599.
[44] See Freeman and Richards (2006) for a fascinating study of the legal and social ramifications of DNA testing.
[45] *Banbury Peerage Case* (1811) 1 Sim & St 153 HL
[46] Although it does to parties in a void marriage: Legitimacy Act 1976, s. 1.

presumption still applies. The presumption also applies if it is clear[47] that the conception took place during a marriage, even if death or divorce has ended that marriage by the time the birth occurs.[48] There will be conflicting presumptions, therefore, if the child could have been conceived during a first marriage but is born during the course of the wife's second marriage. It is not clear who the law would regard as the father in such a situation. It is suggested that the second husband should be regarded as the father, it being more likely that he is the genetic father. He is also the man who would act in the parental role during the child's upbringing. Against this view is the argument that it would be wrong to presume that the wife committed adultery.

The *pater est* presumption is controversial, although no doubt statistically it is more likely than not that a husband is the father of his wife's child. It is also possible to see the presumption as being based on the policy of seeking to avoid a child not having a father. Thorpe LJ in *Re H and A (Children)*[49] has doubted the relevance of the presumption. He explained, 'as science has hastened on and as more and more children are born out of marriage it seems to me that the paternity of any child is to be established by science and not by legal presumption of inference'.[50] Without the presumption, however, children will have no legal father until tests are carried out. There is some doubt over the extent to which children of married couples are the children of the husband. It has been claimed that around 15 per cent of children born to married couples are in fact not the children of the husband.[51] A more reliable estimate puts the figure at 4 per cent.[52]

2. The law presumes that if a man's name appears on the birth certificate of a child, he is the child's father.[53] If the couple is married, there is a statutory obligation on both parties to register the birth within 42 days. If the mother is unmarried, the obligation rests on her, but the couple can jointly register.

   Section 56 and Sched. 6 of the Welfare Reform Act 2009 required a mother registering the birth to name the father. However, the Government has announced it will not be bringing those provisions into force.[54] While the Welfare Reform Act 2009 was designed to compel the mother to name the father, there was an extensive list of exceptions. If a mother wished to conceal the identity of the father, she could simply tell the register she does not know his identity ('I think he was called Tom and he had ginger hair, but it was after a great party and it's all a bit of a blur') and there is not much the registrar can do but leave the name of the father blank.[55] It seems the Government was persuaded not to bring in the provisions as there were concerns that mothers may have good reasons for not naming the father, such as fear of violence.

3. It is not clear whether the making of a parental responsibility agreement will be regarded as *prima facie* evidence of paternity, although the Lord Chancellor's Consultation Paper[56] believes it does. *R v Secretary of State for Social Security, ex p West*[57] suggests that a parental responsibility order by consent can be regarded as evidence of paternity by the Child Support Agency.

---

[47] The court will refer to the normal gestation period.

[48] A cynic might regard this presumption as unrealistic in some cases. If a child is conceived and shortly afterwards there is a divorce, that may well suggest that a third party is the father.

[49] [2002] 2 FCR 469.

[50] At p. 479.

[51] Sterling (2009). This figure was based on the percentage of Child Support Agency paternity tests undertaken when a man denies he is the father which revealed the assumed father was not the father. But that is hardly a representative sample of the population.

[52] King and Jobling (2009).

[53] Births and Deaths Registration Act 1953, s. 34(2); *Brierley v Brierley* [1918] P 257.

[54] Clifton (2014).

[55] Although it is an offence under s. 4 of the Perjury Act 1991 to provide incorrect information at birth registration.

[56] Lord Chancellor's Department (1998).

[57] [1999] 1 FLR 1233.

4. The court may also infer paternity simply from the facts of the case. For example, if it were shown that the mother and the man spent the night together at the time the conception is said to have taken place, this would be evidence of the man's paternity.

B Birth registration

We have just mentioned the disputes over the abandoned Welfare Reform Act 2009 reforms and as those indicate, the issue of birth registration has proved a highly controversial one. Andrew Bainham argues there are four interests at stake in the process: the state, the child, the mother and the father.[58]

1. *The state.* Bainham argues that the state has an interest because the state has an interest in ensuring the 'orderly assumption of responsibility by parents from the moment of the child's birth'.[59] This is true, but it is debatable whether registration has much to do with ensuring that parents look after their children. One area where the state might have an interest is in relation to enforcement of child support. Child support rests in biological parentage (as seen in Chapter 6) but it is not always clear who is a child's father and in such a case child support may not be collectable. If all fathers were registered, this difficulty could be overcome. Less important interests of the state may include the collection of demographic data and the creation of identity confirming documentation.

2. *The child.* Bainham claims that a child has a right to be registered at birth.[60] This right is included in the United Nations Convention on the Rights of the Child.[61] It can be seen as a way of protecting the right of the child to know their genetic origins, which is protected in Article 8 of the European Convention on Human Rights (ECHR). We will be discussing this alleged right later in this section. Jane Fortin[62] notes that the child also has interests to ensure that the mother is not caused emotional harm or put in physical danger as a result of the registration process.

3. *The mother.* Bainham[63] sees the interest of the mother as being part of her right to respect for private life under Article 8. By being registered as the mother she can establish herself as having the legal rights and responsibilities of parenthood. He notes that she has an interest in the naming of the father under the current law, in that the registered father will thereby acquire parental responsibility. Another interest (not emphasised by Bainham) is that the mother may wish to keep the identity of the father hidden, either to protect her private life or to protect herself or the child from violence.

4. *The father.* As Bainham argues, the father has a particular interest in registration because although birth is a readily observable event establishing maternity, the birth registration document is the most obvious way a father can establish paternity. It enables the possibility of establishing a relationship with the child at some point. If his name is not on the birth certificate and the mother does not want the father to see the child, there is little likelihood of the child and father having a relationship at any point.

Bainham's conclusion in weighing up these interests is that the fundamental rights of the child should be central. As he emphasises, these rights are not based in welfare, but autonomy.

[58] Bainham (2008c).
[59] Bainham (2008c: 450).
[60] Bainham (2008c).
[61] Article 7.
[62] Fortin (2009a).
[63] Bainham (2008c).

The significance being, he argues, that simply showing that the registration will cause harm to the child will not necessarily be sufficient to defeat a claim based on autonomy. In putting the argument this way he does not support the approach of the Government which puts the case for joint birth registration on the basis that it is beneficial for the child to know who the father is.[64] Bainham argues there should be a clear legal duty on mothers to identify the father wherever possible. Except in a case of rape he does not think that mothers have a good reason not to name the father. As Jane Fortin[65] notes, it is hard to see why only rape counts as an exception. If the father has been abusive to the mother in the past, he may well pose a serious risk to the mother and child in the future. However, as she points out, Article 8 is not an absolute right and needs to be balanced against the interests of others. Bainham's assumption that the right to know one's genetic origins necessarily trumps the interests of the mother is not made out in the ECHR case law. Nor does Bainham seem to recognise that if the right is an autonomy right the child should have the right *not* to know who their parents are, but if this is on a birth certificate, which they need to use for identification purposes, they will not be able to make that choice.

It is interesting that Bainham does not go so far as to suggest there should be a DNA test of all children and their alleged parents, 'something which would be a move too far for almost everyone'.[66] It is not clear why he thinks this is 'too far'. If we think registration of genetic parentage is a fundamental right the minor inconvenience for adults of the test or the expense involved does not seem a good enough reason not to do this. Perhaps the fact that DNA tests of all do not seem plausible, and few suggest it, indicates that in fact even supporters of the importance of genetic parentage, like Bainham, accept it is not that fundamental a right.

The resolution of these debates turns on two questions. First, how important is the right to know one's genetic origins? This is an issue we shall look at later in this chapter. Second, how much weight do we attach to a woman's choice not to register the father? Do we respect her assessment of what is best for the child, bearing in mind the socio-economic circumstances of the couples in question, or is it necessary to override her concerns in order to protect the child and the father's rights?

C Rebutting legal presumptions of paternity

Section 26 of the Family Law Reform Act 1969 states that the legal presumptions of paternity can be rebutted on the balance of probabilities.[67] In *S v S, W v Official Solicitor (or W)*[68] Lord Reid thought that the presumptions should be regarded as weak, and could be rebutted with only a little evidence.[69] There are two main ways whereby a man presumed to be the father could rebut the presumption. The first and most reliable is to seek a court order for genetic tests (normally through comparing DNA samples). There is power to order such tests under s. 20 of the Family Law Reform Act 1969, although, as will be noted later, the court in some cases will refuse to order tests to be performed. If a man is shown to be the father of the child through genetic tests, then he is legally the father of the child, and if another man was presumed to be the father, he is no longer so regarded. In *F v CSA*[70] it was unclear whether the

---

[64] Department for Children, Schools and Families (2009).

[65] Fortin (2009a).

[66] Bainham (2008c: 459).

[67] *MS v RS and BT (Paternity)* [2020] EWFC 30.

[68] [1972] AC 24.

[69] In *Re Moynihan* [2000] 1 FLR 113 a higher standard of proof was suggested, but the Court of Appeal in *Re H and A (Children)* [2002] 2 FCR 469 preferred *S v S.*

[70] [1999] 2 FLR 244.

father of the child was the mother's husband or her lover. The lover was assessed by the Child Support Agency. He refused to undergo blood tests: this refusal led to a presumption that he was the father.[71] This presumption was held to be stronger than the presumption of legitimacy. The second way that a man could seek to rebut a presumption that he was the father would be to introduce evidence to undermine the logical basis of the presumption. So, a husband could rebut the presumption that he was the father of his wife's child by introducing evidence that he was abroad at the time of the alleged conception, or that he was impotent.

D Fathers and assisted reproduction

There are various forms of assisted reproduction:

1. *Assisted insemination.* This refers to the placing of sperm into the mother (other than by sexual intercourse) leading to fertilisation. It is common to distinguish artificial insemination using the husband's sperm (AIH) and artificial insemination using a donor's sperm (AID).

2. *In vitro fertilisation (IVF).* This technique involves mixing in a dish an egg and sperm. The fertilised egg is then placed in the woman's uterus. The sperm and/or egg may come from the couple themselves or donors.

3. *Gamete intrafallopian transfers (GIFT).* Here a donated egg is placed with the sperm (either of the husband or a sperm donor) in the womb.

4. *Intra-cytoplasmic sperm injection (ICSI).* This involves the injection of a sperm into an egg with a very fine needle. The resulting embryo is placed in the woman.

The law governing assisted reproduction is found in the Human Fertilisation and Embryology Acts 1990 and 2008. The starting point in ascertaining parenthood in cases of assisted reproduction is that the same rules that govern fatherhood in other cases apply. The genetic father, or a man presumed to be the father by virtue of one of the presumptions above, will be the father in a case of assisted reproduction unless he can find a statutory provision that states otherwise. In other words, the 'default' position, in the absence of any provision to the contrary, is that the genetic father is the legal father. Any man who is a father as a result of provisions in the Act is a father in the full sense of the law and cannot, for example, seek to escape liability under the child support legislation on the basis that he is not the biological father.[72]

The Human Fertilisation and Embryology Acts provides for the following exceptions to the basic rule that the genetic father is the child's father:

1. Section 41 of the HFEA 2008 makes clear that a man who donates sperm to a licensed clinic is not the father of any child born using that sperm as long as his sperm is used in accordance with his consent under Sched. 3 of the 1990 Act. The protection does not cover the donor who consents to sperm for use with his wife, but it is used for another woman.[73] He will be regarded as the father of any child born. The donor must trust the clinic not to use his sperm outside the terms of his consent. The sperm donor's identity can be revealed to a child who seeks to discover the donor's identity if the sperm was donated after April 2005.[74]

---

[71] See also *Re P (Identity of Mother)* [2011] EWCA Civ 795.

[72] *Re CH (Contact Parentage)* [1996] 1 FLR 569, [1996] FCR 768; *Leeds Teaching Hospital NHS Trust v A* [2003] EWHC 259 (Fam), [2003] 1 FCR 599.

[73] *Leeds Teaching Hospital NHS Trust v A* [2003] EWHC 259 (Fam).

[74] Human Fertilisation and Embryology Authority (Disclosure of Donor Information) Regulations 2004.

2. A man who has died before his sperm is used in procedures leading to pregnancy is not the father of any child born using that sperm.[75] A dead man's sperm can only be used where he has consented to its use.[76] In *Y v A Healthcare NHS Trust*[77] the sperm was taken from a man in a coma, something that was lawful under the Mental Capacity Act 2005 because it was said to be in his best interests.[78] A man can be a father and registered on the birth certificate if the child is conceived after his death using sperm where he had given permission, or if donor sperm is used before his death.[79]

The HFEA 2008 also provides that a man not genetically related to a child is the legal father in the following circumstances:

1. Under s. 35 the husband of a woman who gives birth as a result of a licensed clinic's assisted reproductive treatment is presumed to be the child's father unless he shows that he did not consent *and* that he is not the child's genetic father.[80] The lack of consent will be assessed subjectively and does not need to be communicated to the sperm donor for it to operate.[81] It should be noted that a clinic is very unlikely to provide services to a married woman without her husband's consent[82] and so it should be rare that the question of consent will be raised. In *Leeds Teaching Hospital NHS Trust v A*[83] a wife's egg was mixed by mistake with the sperm of Mr B, rather than that of her husband (Mr A). It was held that Mr A had not consented to the treatment of his wife *with that sperm* and therefore he was not the father under s. 28 of the 1990 Act (which is in similar terms to s. 35 of the 2008 Act). As Mr B's sperm had been used without his consent, s. 28(6) (the equivalent to s. 41, discussed above) did not apply and so he was the father. Sally Sheldon[84] makes the interesting point that had it been the eggs that had been mixed the position would have been different. Mrs A would be the mother because she gave birth. Why should it matter whether it was the sperm or the eggs that were muddled up?

2. Under s. 37 a man will be treated as the father of a child born to a woman[85] as long as the 'agreed fatherhood conditions' are satisfied. These are as follows:

LEGISLATIVE PROVISION

Human Fertilisation and Embryology Act 2008, section 37(1)

1. The agreed fatherhood conditions referred to in section 36(b) are met in relation to a man ('M') in relation to treatment provided to W under a licence if, but only if,—

    (a) M has given the person responsible a notice stating that he consents to being treated as the father of any child resulting from treatment provided to W under the licence,

    (b) W has given the person responsible a notice stating that she consents to M being so treated,

---

[75] HFEA 2008, s. 42(1).
[76] In *Centre for Reproductive Medicine v U* [2002] FL 267, Butler-Sloss P rejected an argument that the husband's withdrawal of his consent before his death was the result of undue influence.
[77] [2018] EWCOP 18.
[78] He had previously indicated he would want to proceed with fertility treatment even if he were to die.
[79] HFEA 2008, ss. 39, 40.
[80] HFEA 1990, s. 28(2).
[81] *M v F and another (declaration of parentage: circumstances of conception)* [2014] 1 FCR 456.
[82] The Human Fertilisation and Embryology Authority Code of Practice, para 5.7 makes this clear.
[83] [2003] 1 FCR 599, discussed in Ford and Morgan (2003).
[84] Sheldon (2005).
[85] The provision does not apply to married women receiving treatment with their husbands (s. 28(2) is the relevant provision for them): *Leeds Teaching Hospital NHS Trust v A* [2003] EWHC 259 (Fam), [2003]1 FCR 599.

> (c) neither M nor W has, since giving notice under paragraph (a) or (b), given the person responsible notice of the withdrawal of M's or W's consent to M being so treated,
>
> (d) W has not, since the giving of the notice under paragraph (b), given the person responsible—
>
> > (i) a further notice under that paragraph stating that she consents to another man being treated as the father of any resulting child, or
> >
> > (ii) a notice under section 44(1)(b) stating that she consents to a woman being treated as a parent of any resulting child, and
>
> (e) W and M are not within prohibited degrees of relationship in relation to each other.

Notice that for this provision to apply there is no need to show that the man and woman are in a sexual relationship or even living together. However, a clinic is only likely to provide treatment to a couple in a close relationship. To rely on s. 37, the treatment must take place in a licensed clinic,[86] registered by the British Human Fertilisation and Embryology Authority.[87] Cases of so-called DIY treatment will be discussed next.

Unfortunately, there have been a series of cases where clinics have made mistakes with the paperwork, which has been lost or incorrectly completed.[88] This seems to have happened in a surprising number of cases. A strict reading of the 2008 Act indicates that without completion of the appropriate paperwork the partner of the mother cannot be the father. Later cases, however, (*PG v RS*;[89] *Re Human Fertilisation and Embryology Act 2008 (Cases A, B, C, D, E, F, G and H)*[90] and *X and Y v St Bartholomew's Hospital Centre for Reproductive Medicine (CRM)*[91]) have been more flexible. The focus will be at the intentions of the parties when their received treatment. So, if they intended to be parents when they received treatment any faulty documentation will, where possible, be rectified or interpreted to ensure that happens. The fact the couple later separate will not impact on the assessment of intention at the time the paperwork is completed.[92] The courts seem more keen on ensuring there is effective consent evidenced, rather than whether all the correct forms are fully signed.[93] However, in *AB v CD and the Z Fertility Clinic*[94] Cobb J held that approach could not be used where the clinic had failed to seek the consent of the partner and no paperwork ever existed. In such a case there is no paperwork that can be interpreted or rectified to be in line with the parties' intentions.

E DIY assisted reproduction

Section 35 of the HFEA 2008 suggests that if the mother is married then her husband (and not the sperm donor) is the father, unless it can be shown that the husband did not consent to the use of the sperm, even in cases of unlicensed treatment.[95] There is a similar provision making

---

[86] *U v W (Attorney-General Intervening)* [1997] 2 FLR 282, [1998] 1 FCR 526.
[87] Human Fertilisation and Embryology Authority (2010).
[88] Mistakes over the forms have arisen in a surprising number of cases; e.g. *Re I (Human Fertilisation and Embryology Act 2008)* [2016] EWHC 791 (Fam); *Jefferies v BMI Healthcare Ltd (Human Fertilisation and Embryology)* [2016] EWHC 2493 (Fam).
[89] [2019] EWFC 65.
[90] [2015] EWHC 2602 (Fam).
[91] [2015] EWFC 13 (Fam).
[92] PG v RS [2019] EWFC 65.
[93] See also *Re AD (Human Fertilisation and Embryology Act 2008)* [2017] EWHC 1026 (Fam).
[94] [2013] EWHC 1418 (Fam).
[95] According to BBC News Online (2009g) there is an 'underground world' of sperm donation through the Internet.

the mother's civil partner or spouse a parent. In all other cases, the sperm donor in a DIY case will be the father and can thereby become liable to pay child support for the child.[96] Mind you, there were news reports of two men making £250,000 from selling sperm via the Internet.[97]

TOPICAL ISSUE

Why not DIY?

In a case of do-it-yourself insemination, where, for example, a woman obtains sperm via the Internet[98] or from a friend and uses a syringe to impregnate herself, it used to be thought that the normal rules apply. The donor of the sperm will be treated as the father, and the woman who gives birth as the mother. However, the issue has been thrown into doubt by *M v F and another (declaration of parentage: circumstances of conception).*[99] There the husband had had a vasectomy and decided to use assisted reproduction to produce a child. The wife made contact with a sperm donor (F) on the Internet and met with him several times, against her husband's wishes, and became pregnant following sexual intercourse. Peter Jackson J found that F was the biological and legal father. The case fell outside the scheme of the Human Fertilisation and Embryology Act 1990 (HFEA 1990) because it involved sexual intercourse. The general common law therefore applied and so the genetic father was the legal father. Intriguingly Peter Jackson J did suggest that the Act could apply to cases outside the context of licensed sperm donation if there was no sexual intercourse, but did not develop his reasoning on that. He did suggest that given the prevalence of people engaging in DIY insemination it might be a good idea to have new regulations governing it. He noted the benefit of regulation under the HFEA 1990: 'regulation is broadly successful in protecting participants from exploitation and from health risks, while providing some certainty about legal relationships'.

F An analysis of the allocation of parenthood in the HFE Acts

There are several notable features of the law on allocation of parenthood following the HFEA 2008. One is that in cases of assisted reproduction the father's status is secured through the mother.[100] He acquires parental status through being her husband or as a result of her consenting to him being recognised as the father in order to satisfy the agreed parenthood conditions. That might reflect a lingering suspicion that a non-genetic father is not a real father and that there is a need for the mother to vet and approve him as a suitable man.

As a result of the provisions in the Human Fertilisation and Embryology Acts 1990 and 2008, some children can be deemed fatherless. This might arise where a single woman (or a married woman acting without her husband's consent) becomes pregnant as a result of artificial insemination by donor (AID) provided by a licensed clinic. The donor could not be the father due to s. 41, and the legislation does not provide for anyone else to be the father.

---

[96] [2014] 1 FCR 456.
[97] An unmarried couple cannot rely on s. 28(3) because that applies only where the couple receive treatment in a licensed clinic.
[98] BBC News Online (2007h).
[99] BBC News Online (2010e).
[100] Lind and Hewitt (2009).

A similar situation arises if a man's sperm is used after his death. Some have criticised the fact that the law allows a child to be fatherless; but, without breaching the principle that sperm donors should not be fathers, it is hard to see how the law can avoid this. However, it fits uneasily with the approach taken elsewhere in the law that assumes it is important for a child to have a link with a father.[101]

One interesting observation on these legally fatherless children is that the law here, for the first time, is moving away from the view that a child must have one father and one mother.[102] Hale LJ has stated that it is clearly in the child's interests to have a father, if possible.[103] However, she went on to accept that that was not always possible. One prominent theme within the present law is that a child, as far as possible, should have one father and one mother, and can never have more than one mother or one father. Richards has complained of the 'very persistent prejudice that children should never have more than two parents and when a new one arrives, an old one has to go'.[104] The assumption that there can be only one mother and one father is, presumably, tied to genetic parentage. However, technological advances mean that it would now be possible for a child to be born genetically related to two women. Techniques involving artificial sperm are progressing quickly.[105] If biology no longer necessitates the two-parent rule, maybe it is time to abandon it.[106] Also it restricts the law and means that the law cannot recognise that there may be a number of men or women playing a parental role in the child's life.[107]

These points may reflect a broader point that the law seems fixated on the traditional family form of a mother and father for each child.[108] This explains why the law is reluctant to accept a child having two mothers, which produces such a strange set of provisions dealing with same-sex parents.[109]

From a different perspective, there have been complaints that the HFEA 2008 departs too much from the principle that parentage should match genetics. However, not everyone is happy about the extension to the notion of parenthood provided for in the 2008 Act reforms. Thérèse Callus[110] objects that the reforms confuse parental role and parental status. She thinks the parental role is very important, but carrying out a parental role is different from having a parental status. Andrew Bainham argues:

> The fact that someone is doing some of the things which parents do does not make that person the parent. The true claim which same-sex partners and other social parents have is that they should be given the legal powers which are necessary to enable them to look after a child properly and it is the status of possessing parental responsibility which is best designed to achieve this.[111]

Such arguments lead some to the conclusion that parentage should follow genetics and that we should use parental responsibility to recognise the role played by the partners of women receiving assisted reproduction using donated sperm.[112]

---

[101] Smith (2010).
[102] Lind and Hewitt (2009).
[103] *Re R (A Child)* [2003] 1 FCR 481, para 27.
[104] Richards (1995a: 21).
[105] BBC News Online (2009b).
[106] Wallbank (2004a).
[107] Lind and Hewitt (2009).
[108] Lind and Hewitt (2009); McCandless and Sheldon (2010a).
[109] Diduck (2007).
[110] Callus (2008).
[111] Bainham (2008a: 348).
[112] See the discussion in Bainham (2008a).

G Surrogacy

Surrogacy involves an agreement whereby the 'gestational mother'[113] (sometimes called the 'surrogate mother') agrees to bear a child for someone else ('the intended or commissioning parent or parents'). The Surrogacy Arrangements Act 1985 defines a surrogacy arrangement as one made before the woman began to carry the child 'with a view to any child carried in pursuance of it being handed over to, and parental responsibility being met (so far as practicable) by another person or persons'.[114] The aim is that the gestational mother will hand over the baby after birth to the intended parent and that the gestational mother will not exercise parental responsibility. Surrogacy can cover a wide range of different forms. The genetic link between the intended parents can vary: the gestational mother could be impregnated with the sperm and/or the egg of the intended parents; and/or the child could be born using donated gametes.

Whatever the form of the surrogacy, the legal attribution of parenthood is straightforward. It is clear that the gestational mother is the mother and the genetic father is the legal father unless he is a sperm donor providing sperm to a licensed clinic. Although if the gestational mother is married her husband will be presumed to be the father, until DNA tests are performed. However, that default position can be changed by subsequent events. We will first consider what happens if the child is handed over and the intended parents want to become recognised as parents in the law. Later we will look at what happens if the gestational mother does not want to hand over the child.

(i) Parental orders

If the surrogacy arrangement goes to plan and the gestational mother hands over the child, the intended parents can apply to a court for a parenting order, the effect of which is that they will be treated as the parents of the child. On the making of the order, the child will be treated as the child of the applicants and the gestational mother will no longer be a parent.[115] The order is 'declaratory' and so it can be made even though one of the applicants has died between the birth and court hearing.[116] The order will vest parental responsibility exclusively in the applicants, and the parental status and parental responsibility of anyone else (and specifically the gestational mother) will be thereby extinguished.[117] The order will be registered in the Parental Order Register.[118] Section 54 of the HFEA 2008 lists a number of factors which need to be shown before an order can be made:

1. Either the sperm, or eggs, or both, came from the commissioning husband or wife.

2. The applicants are married, civil partners or in 'an enduring family relationship and are not within prohibited degrees of relationship in relation to each other'.[119] The couple need not be living together, but must be in a committed relationship.[120]

3. The applicants must both be over 18.

---

[113] Cook, Day Sclater and Kaganas (2003) provides useful discussions of surrogacy.
[114] Section 1(2) (as amended by Children Act 1989, Sched. 13, para 56).
[115] Although the child will still be within the prohibited degrees of the birth family for marriage purposes and the law of incest.
[116] *A v P (Surrogacy: Parental Order: Death of Applicant)* [2011] EWHC 1738 (Fam).
[117] HFEA 2008, s. 54.
[118] When someone is 18, he or she can be supplied with a copy of his or her birth certificate (which will reveal the identity of the birth family), and counselling facilities will be available: Adoption Act 1976, s. 51, applied by Parental Orders (Human Fertilisation and Embryology) Regulations 1994.
[119] This does not need to be shown at the time of the hearing, as long as there was an enduring family relationship at the time of the application, or perhaps earlier: *K v L* [2019] EWFC 21.
[120] *DM and Another v SJ and Others (Surrogacy: Parental Order)* [2016] EWHC 270 (Fam).

4. At least one of the applicants must be domiciled in the United Kingdom.[121]

5. The child must, at the time of the order, live with the applicants.[122]

6. The order must be made within six months of the child's birth.[123]

7. The father must give full and unconditional consent[124] to the making of the order.[125]

8. The gestational mother must give her full and unconditional consent to the making of the order, at least six weeks after the birth.[126]

9. The husband of the woman who gave birth to the child must give his full and unconditional consent.[127]

10. Money or other benefits have not been given to the surrogate mother, unless they are reasonable expenses or the court has retrospectively authorised the payments.

11. The pregnancy was not the result of sexual intercourse between the surrogate mother and male applicant.

12. The court must decide to make the order with the child's welfare being the paramount consideration and the checklist of factors in s. 1 of the Adoption and Children Act 2002 being applied.[128]

This appears to be a highly restrictive list of requirements. They have caused the courts real difficulties. The problems arise particularly in cases involving a surrogacy arrangement entered into abroad and the couple then bringing the child to England. The couple then seek a parental order, but one of the requirements is not met. In such a case it is often seen to be in the child's best interests that a parental order is made; otherwise the child will be without a legal parent. In a series of cases the courts have determined that the s. 54 requirements are not 'essential' and the court will make a parental order even though they are not all met. A good example is the following:

CASE: *Re X (A Child) (Surrogacy: Time Limit)* [2014] EWHC 3135 (Fam)

The commissioning couple entered a surrogacy arrangement with a woman in India who carried the child using donated eggs and the commissioning father's sperm. The child was born in December 2011 and entered the United Kingdom in 2013. The couple did not realise they needed to apply for a parental order until 2014. The central issue for Sir James Munby was whether a parental order could be made even though s. 54(3) of the HFEA 2008 provides that 'the applicants must apply for the order during the period of six months beginning with the day on which the child is born', when the applicants were

---

[121] See *Z and B v C (Parental Order: Domicile)* [2011] EWHC 3181 (Fam) for a detailed discussion of this requirement.

[122] HFEA 2008, s. 54(4).

[123] HFEA 2008, s. 54(3).

[124] The consents mentioned are unnecessary if the person cannot be found or is incapable of giving agreement.

[125] This requirement is of consent to the order, not just consent to the application: HFEA 2008, s. 54.

[126] If the mother cannot be found despite all reasonable efforts her consent can be dispensed with: *Re D and L (Minors) (Surrogacy)* [2012] EWHC 2631 (Fam).

[127] *Re X and another (foreign surrogacy)* [2009] 2 FCR 312.

[128] Human Fertilisation and Embryology (Parental Orders) Regulations 2010 (SI 2010/985), Sched. 1. A consideration of welfare will not be restricted to the child's childhood, but their whole life: *Re X and Y (Parental Order: Retrospective Authorisation of Payments)* [2011] EWHC 3147 (Fam); *D and L (Surrogacy)* [2012] EWHC 2631 (Fam).

> applying two years and two months after the birth. He held the order could be made. He emphasised the importance of looking at the purpose of the statute. He could not believe that Parliament intended a court could be barred from making an order if it were just one day after the six-month limit. Given the importance to the child of the security provided by a parental order and the child's human rights the court should not interpret the time limit as a strict one. Further, although the commissioning couple were not living together (a requirement under s. 54(4)(a)) that too was not an absolute requirement and in this case the child shared time with each parent and so it was in line with the child's human rights and welfare that the order be made.

Taking a similar line the courts have been willing to make a parental order even though the couple have separated;[129] the application was brought three years after the birth, rather than the required six months;[130] the intended father died before the birth of the child;[131] or the surrogate could not be found and so her consent could not be provided.[132] The current position is well summarised by Russell J:

> [W]hen a child's welfare demands that a parental order is made it can only be refused in the *'clearest case of the abuse of public policy'*.[133]

So far there have only been two reported cases where the courts have declined to make an order on the basis that the s. 54 requirements be fulfilled. The first was *Re Z (A Child: HFEA: Parental Order)*[134] where a single man had arrangements for an overseas surrogate to carry a child for him and he wanted a parental order to be made in favour of him alone. The requirement in s. 54 for there to be two applicants was seen as indispensable as it was a 'fundamental feature' of the legislation. No real explanation was offered by Munby P for why this requirement was fundamental and the others were not. In subsequent litigation (*Re Z (A Child) (No. 2)*[135]) the government conceded that s. 54(1) and (2) of the HFEA 2008 are incompatible with the rights of the father and child under Article 14 in conjunction with Article 8, in so far as they prevent the father from obtaining a parental order on the sole ground of his status as a single person, as opposed to being part of a couple.[136]

The second case was *AB v CD*[137] where a couple came to court to seek a parental order in relation to two girls. The woman and her ex-husband used a surrogate in India and brought the children to the UK. They never applied for a parental order. They had separated and the mother started a relationship with a new partner when the children were around four. The children were now about eight and the couple realised they had no formal legal connection to the children. Keehan J stated that in fact the legal position was that the surrogate mother in India and her husband were the parents of the children. He could not make an order in favour

---

[129] *K v L* [2019] EWFC 21; *A and B (No. 2) (Parental Order)* [2015] EWHC 2080 (Fam).

[130] *AB and CD v CT (Parental Order: Consent of Surrogate Mother)* [2015] EWFC 12 (Fam).

[131] *Re X (Parental Order: Death of Intended Parent Prior to Birth)* [2020] EWFC 39 (Fam): the order was made in favour of both the mother and the father.

[132] *X v Z* [2018] EWFC 86.

[133] *Re A and B (Children) (Surrogacy: Parental Orders: Time Limits)* [2015] EWHC 911 (Fam).

[134] [2015] EWFC 73.

[135] [2016] EWHC 1191 (Fam).

[136] See Fenton-Glynn (2015) for a helpful review of the literature.

[137] [2018] EWFC 1590.

of the woman as she was a single person. Even if he did make a parental order in her favour her partner, who played a full role in the children's life, could not be given parental responsibility. Keehan J found the position absurd, but ended up making the children wards of court, a child arrangement order in favour of the couple, and an order that the surrogate and her husband could not exercise parental responsibility. He noted the real losers were the children for whom the court could not make sensible orders in relation to parenthood.

A further oddness in the current system was exposed in *R(H) v Secretary of State for Health and Social Care*[138] where a surrogate received licenced treatment using the sperm of the intended father. The relationship between the surrogate and the intended father broke down. The court ordered after birth that the children should live with the man and his male partner. The issue in the case concerned the birth certificate. The mother registered her husband as the father of the child. Section 35 of the HFEA 2008 provided that where a birth mother was married to a man who was not the genetic father, the husband was to be treated as the father unless he had not consented to the pregnancy. Section 38 provided that no other person was to be treated as the father in those circumstances. Applying those provisions in this case meant that the surrogate's husband was the father, even though the applicant was the intended and social father.

What are we to make of the 'generous' approach of the judiciary towards the s. 54 requirements and the outcome in these cases? Perhaps the obvious lesson is the law is in need of reform, and we shall look shortly at the Law Commission proposals. Another point is that the cases highlight how family judges will always want to put the interests of the child first. If an order will promote the welfare of a child a judge will strain every rule of statutory interpretation to be able to make the order.

The generous approach to interpreting s. 54 can be criticised. Where applicants cannot obtain a parental order there is nothing to stop them applying to adopt the child. On this view, denying a parental order is hardly leaving the child in limbo[139] or being cruel to intending parents, it is rather requiring them to arrange an adoption. That argument, however, might be rejected by intending parents who prefer a parental order that declares they *are* the parents of the child, rather than adoption whereby they *become* the parents. Such an argument might be seen to imply adoptive parents are somehow second-rate parents of a child and the law might not want to support that view. However, Theis J in *AB v CD (Surrogacy: Time Limit and Consent)*[140] agreed with the arguments of the parents that an adoption order was not an adequate alternative:

> I agree a parental order and the consequences that flow from it are, from a welfare perspective, far more suited to surrogacy situations. They were specifically created to deal with these situations. Put simply, they are a more honest order which reflects the reality of what was intended, the lineage connection that already exists and more accurately reflects the child's identity. An adoption order in these situations leaves open the risk of a fiction regarding identity that may need to be resolved by the child later in life.

Not everyone will be convinced by the argument. It is not quite clear why the parental order is more 'honest' than an adoption order: it may be less 'honest' about who the mother is (in cases where at least one of the commissioning couple is a woman). What may be more relevant is that if adoption is used the commissioning couple will need to be approved by an adoption agency and they may find that oppressive. But, is it a bad thing to have commissioning couples checked by an agency before they become parents?

---

[138] [2019] EWHC 2095 (Admin).
[139] If a child born following surrogacy was left with no legal parents, that might interfere with the child's human rights: *Mennesson and Labasee v France* [2014] ECHR 664.
[140] [2015] EWFC 12.

There have been cases where the child has been handed over to the commissioning parents who have taken no legal steps to formalise the situation. In legal terms the gestational mother would be the mother and the genetic father the father. The commissioning parents (without a court order) would not have parental responsibility and so would be bringing up the child without formal legal authority. If the child's status ever did come to court, the judge may have little choice but to affirm the status quo and grant a residence order to the commissioning parents. This is demonstrated by *Re H (A Minor) (S. 37 Direction)*,[141] where a mother gave birth, but did not want to care for the child. She handed the baby over to two friends, a lesbian couple. One had a history of mental illness and the other had a criminal conviction. Nine months after the birth, the matter was brought to the court's attention. By now the child had bonded with the couple and the court accepted that unless there was danger of significant harm to the child, it would have to affirm the present arrangements. Had the matter come to court shortly after the birth, with the couple applying for a residence order, it would have been highly unlikely that the court would have made the order. This case demonstrates the difficulties of legal intervention in this area. A surrogacy arrangement may not come to the court's attention until so much time has passed that the court has little option other than to affirm the transaction.

(ii) Commercial surrogacy

Section 2(1) of the Surrogacy Arrangements Act 1985 states:

LEGISLATIVE PROVISION

Surrogacy Arrangements Act 1985, section 2(1)

No person shall on a commercial basis do any of the following acts in the United Kingdom, that is—

(a) initiate or take part in any negotiations with a view to the making of a surrogacy arrangement,

(b) offer or agree to negotiate the making of a surrogacy arrangement, or

(c) compile any information with a view to its use in making, or negotiating the making of surrogacy arrangements;

and no person shall in the United Kingdom knowingly cause another to do any of those acts on a commercial basis.[142]

To constitute an offence the arrangement needs to be made before the gestational mother becomes pregnant. It should be stressed that the gestational mother and the commissioning mother are not liable for the offence; only third parties who make the arrangements can be guilty of the offence. The United Kingdom, therefore, will never allow the situation which arises in the United States, where companies will advertise mothers at varying rates depending on their age, intelligence and health.[143]

---

[141] [1993] 2 FLR 541, [1993] 2 FCR 277.

[142] Section 3 outlaws advertising in relation to surrogacy.

[143] In *JP v LP and Others (Surrogacy Arrangement: Wardship)* [2014] EWHC 595 (Fam) it was noted that unintentionally a firm of solicitors who had been paid a fee for drawing up a surrogacy agreement had breached this law.

It is also an offence to pay money that constitutes a reward or profit to the gestational mother under a surrogacy arrangement, but payment can cover expenses.[144] A recent report found that 27.1 per cent of respondent surrogates received less than £10,000 and the mean amount was £10,859,[145] suggesting that we are not yet in the situation where commercial surrogacy is the norm. Any payments can be authorised under s. 30(7) of the Human Fertilisation and Embryology Act 1990, thereby allowing the court to make a parental order.

There has been extensive litigation over what expenses the court will authorise.[146] In *Re C (Parental Order)*[147] payments of $51,200 to the American surrogate couple and $15,000 to the agency were authorised even though they exceeded the expenses. The payments were said by Theis J to be not disproportionate to the expenses; the payments did not overbear the will of the surrogate; and the commissioning couple had acted in good faith and had complied with the authorities. She was therefore willing to authorise them. Generally, courts have been willing to approve sums.[148] Unless the sum appears to be completely in excess of expenses incurred and be a blatant case of 'baby selling' then it is unlikely a court will not approve the payments.[149]

Emily Jackson concludes:

> The UK's prohibition on commercial surrogacy is, therefore, completely ineffective. If the people applying for a parental order are decent, or even adequate parents, it is unlikely that the fact that they had paid the surrogate mother would prevent them from being granted a parental order.[150]

Further strains on the law's approach to commercial surrogacy are clear in this case:

CASE: *XX v Whittington Hospital NHS Trust* [2020] UKSC 14

Through a series of errors, a hospital failed to detect Ms X's cervical cancer. As a result of the delay the only suitable treatment she could be given removed her fertility. She desperately wished to be a biological mother and was able to have some eggs harvested prior to her cancer treatment. She sought damages from the hospital to fund use of commercial surrogacy in California, using her eggs and her partner's sperm. In California surrogacy is well established, lawful and surrogacy contracts are enforced. She therefore preferred to use treatment there, rather than in England where commercial surrogacy was not possible and surrogacy contracts could not be enforced. The hospital conceded they were negligent but disputed the level of damages. The trial judge found that commercial surrogacy was contrary to public policy, but damages to cover the costs of surrogacy that was permitted in England would be possible. The Supreme Court, by a majority, held that damages could be to cover the cost of surrogacy in California. The law prohibiting commercial surrogacy related to acts in the UK; there was nothing unlawful about using surrogacy in other jurisdictions. She was entitled to be put in as close a position as possible to where she would have been had she not been wronged. The Californian surrogacy offered the best way of doing this. Lord Carnworth and Lord Reed dissented, arguing there was no legal coherence in an English court ordering damages to do something overseas that would be illegal in England.

---

[144] *Re Adoption Application AA 212/86 (Adoption Payment)* [1987] 2 FLR 291. In *Re C (Application by Mr and Mrs X)* [2002] Fam Law 351, £12,000 was accepted as a payment covering expenses.

[145] Horsey (2015).

[146] Payment for compensation for pain was not a payment for expenses: *Re L (Commercial Surrogacy)* [2010] EWHC 3146 (Fam).

[147] [2013] EWHC 2408 (Fam).

[148] For other examples see *AB v DE* [2013] EWHC 2413 (Fam); *J v G* [2013] EWHC 1432.

[149] *Re P-M* [2013] EWHC 2328.

[150] Jackson (2014).

(iii) What happens when surrogacy arrangements break down?

So far, we have been thinking of cases where the gestational mother hands over the child on birth, in line with the agreement. However, there have been cases where the gestational mother refuses to give the child to the commissioning couple. What happens in such a case?

The starting point is that a surrogacy agreement is not a binding contract. Section 1A of the Surrogacy Arrangements Act 1985 states: 'No surrogacy arrangement is enforceable by or against any of the persons making it.' So, the commissioning couple could not bring an action for breach of contract. The most likely course of action is that they will apply for a child arrangement order that the child live with them.[151] Leave to make the application will be required unless the commissioning husband is the genetic father of the child. In considering the application, the court's paramount consideration will be the welfare of the child, and the court will not in any sense feel bound by the terms of the surrogacy agreement. However, if the gestational mother does not oppose the application it is likely to be granted.[152] Normally, if the child has bonded with the surrogate mother, the court will be reluctant to order the child be handed over to the father. An exceptional case is *Re P (Surrogacy: Residence)*[153] where the surrogate mother lied to the father and told him that she had miscarried.[154] He later found out the truth and with his wife applied for a residence order. Although the child was now 18 months old and had spent all its life with the mother, it was held to be in the child's best long-term interests that the child be raised by the father and his wife. Evidence of the mother's psychological state indicated she would not be able to parent a child in the long term.[155]

By contrast, in *Re Z (A Child)*[156] it was the commissioning couple who were found to have deceived the surrogate mother and shown a lack of concern and respect towards her. Their conduct was taken into account in deciding the child should live with the surrogate mother.

The kind of problems which can arise on the breakdown of a surrogacy are well illustrated by this case:

CASE: *RE TT* [2011] EWHC 33 (Fam)

Mr and Mrs W were unable to have a child and used the Internet to find a surrogate. The initial contact from the mother (M), aged 25, is revealing:

> hello sweetie my name is [name given] and I am a surrogate mother in the UK . . . I read our [sic] ad on yedda [the surrogacy website] and I am truly interested in helping you to make your family complete. I hope you contact me back and I can tell you all about me. (para 10)

From this, negotiations by text and the Internet followed, under which it was agreed that Mr W's sperm would be used to impregnate the mother. The agreement was that the mother would receive several thousand pounds and that the child would be handed over to Mr and Mrs W on birth. After several unsuccessful attempts pregnancy was achieved

---

[151] *JP v LP* [2014] EWHC 595 (Fam); *Re C (A Minor) (Wardship: Surrogacy)* [1985] FLR 846; *Re P (Minor) (Wardship: Surrogacy)* [1987] 2 FLR 421, [1988] FCR 140.
[152] E.g. *Re C (A Minor) (Wardship: Surrogacy)* [1985] FLR 846.
[153] [2008] Fam Law 18.
[154] There was evidence she had done this to several men.
[155] See also *H v S (Disputed Surrogacy Agreement)* [2015] EWFC 36.
[156] [2016] EWFC 34.

and in July 2010 a baby girl (T) was born. The mother refused to hand the child over. The matter was brought to court.

Baker J noted that the legal position was that in this case M was the mother and Mr W was the father. In deciding with whom the child should live, the key question was the welfare of the child. Baker J decided the child should stay with the mother. He attached little weight to the fact that M had agreed to hand over the baby:

> . . . in my judgment, the court should not attach undue weight to the fact that the mother originally promised to give up the baby. In some cases, such a promise may indicate a lack of commitment to the child so as to call into question the mother's capacity to care for her. In my judgment, the situation in the present case is very different. I am satisfied that the mother has genuinely changed her mind (para 63).

He emphasised the child had formed an attachment with M, and that through breast-feeding the mother was able to meet the child's physical and emotional needs. Breaking these bonds would 'undoubtedly create a risk of emotional harm' (para 61).

(iv) Reform?

As will have been clear from this discussion the current law is uncertain and widely seen as unsatisfactory. However, there is little agreement over the direction of reform. A fundamental issue is whether surrogacy is something that should be encouraged and enabled, or whether it is something to be discouraged. If it is to be encouraged, how are the interests of the gestational and intended parents to be balanced.

The Law Commission in 2019 produced a consultation document on reform of the law. It intends to produce a final report and draft Bill in 2022. This timescale indicates the complexity of the law.

The consultation proposals are to create a new 'Pathway to Surrogacy'. It imagines the new pathway will be through licensed clinics who will be responsible for ensuring compliance with the regulations. To enter on the new pathway, intending parents would need to meet certain eligibility and safeguarding requirements. These include:

- All stages of the process have taken place in the UK. The proposals do not cover international surrogacy arrangements.
- It covers cases: 'For medical (whether physical or mental) or biological reasons, the single intended parent is, or both intended parents are, unable to gestate a foetus to term, or deliver a healthy baby'. That is designed to exclude cases where a woman does not want to carry a child purely for social reasons (e.g. she does not like the appearance of being pregnant). There is no need for there to be a genetic link between the child and the intended couple.
- The surrogate and intended parents must sign a written document setting out their surrogacy arrangement which would record:
  - the details of the surrogate, the intended parents, any gamete donors, and the clinic or regulated surrogacy organisation which has overseen the arrangement;
  - the genetic material used for conception;
  - that the biological and gestational parenthood of the child will be entered in a national register of surrogacy;

- that all parties to the agreement had complied with the eligibility and screening requirements and the proposed safeguards (see below);

- that all parties had undergone an assessment of the welfare of the child whom they wish to conceive;

- that all parties understood that the intended parents will become the legal parents of the child at birth with parental responsibility, or parental responsibilities and rights, and that they consent to such a change of status, subject to the surrogate's right to object during the defined time period.

- The surrogate and the intended parents would obtain independent legal advice.

- The surrogate and her spouse or civil partner and the intended parents would seek independent counselling on the implications of a surrogate birth.

- The surrogate and her spouse or civil partner and the intended parents would be medically screened.

- Criminal record checks would be made on the surrogate and her spouse or civil partner, and the intended parents.

If these were met then, on birth, the intended parents would become the legal parents of the child, with parental responsibility. This would, therefore, be in marked contrast to the current law where, on birth, the gestational mother is the mother and a parental order is required to make the intended parents legal parents. However, in an important safeguard the gestational mother has the right to object in writing to parental status (for around 35 days after the birth). If such an objection is made then the traditional rules apply and the motherhood would revert to the surrogate and the intended parents would need to apply for a parental order. The court would then need to decide what should happen to the child based on the welfare principle.

The proposal seems to have been broadly welcomed, but there are some controversial issues:

1. The gestational mother's right to objection deprives the intended parents of the certainty they may hope for from any reform. They cannot rely on or be completely secure they will be the parents of the child until the time for objections has run its course. The advantage is that it means there is still recognition of the work the surrogate has done through the pregnancy and birth; and the bond she may have with the child. It means the court will decide based on the welfare principle who is best to care for the child. If we did not have this right of objection, we may have a child raised in circumstances which a court would, if they were asked, think was not the best for the child.

2. The surrogate's spouse or civil partner would not be party to the agreement, but they would need to fulfil the safeguarding requirements. It seems that the Law Commission did not want to send a message that the surrogate needed her husband or partner's permission to be a surrogate, but did want to make sure he posed no risk to the child.

3. Some surrogate mothers have supported the proposals because it strengthens their position if the intended parents change their mind during pregnancy or following birth, or indeed if they die. Under the new scheme the intended parents are the parents and so unless the surrogate wishes to take care of the child, by objecting, the intending parents would need to make the arrangements with the local authority for adoption.

4. The Law Commission did not produce clear guidance on payments for surrogates. It accepted there was a need for payment for costs relating to the pregnancy and in connection with the

making of the surrogacy payments. This might also include a loss of earnings and compensation for pain and inconvenience. The consultation paper suggested that there could be set categories for compensation and that guidelines or limits could be set by the regulator. On the key issue of whether a fee could be paid to the surrogate the Law Commission did not express a concluded view but did go so far as to say if a fee was permitted it could only be acceptable as a payment for the work of gestation rather than a payment for the child.

5. Critics might suggest the review has not sufficiently drawn a line between adoption (where any parents have to be approved by the adoption agency) and surrogacy (where, apart from basic safeguarding checks, there is no assessment of the parents). If there is no genetic link between the intended parents and the child, why should they be treated any differently from adopters?[157]

DEBATE

Arguments over surrogacy

Arguments against surrogacy

1. It has been argued that surrogacy arrangements are contrary to the best interests of children. Bainham has suggested that: 'It is difficult to see how it could be argued that surrogacy is designed *primarily* for the benefit of the child.'[158] However, he adds that talking of the benefits for the child is a little odd in this context. Would it be in a child's interests not to be born? Perhaps the strongest way the argument can be put is that it is not desirable for a child to be born in circumstances that are so likely to result in a dispute between adults, which may well harm the child. Some argue that children born as a result of surrogacy will be confused as to their identity.

2. Surrogacy can be seen as demeaning to women – they are being used as little more than 'walking incubators'. There are some areas of life, it is argued, that are too intimate to be the subject of a contract. Alternatively, it may be argued that the decision to give up a child is such a complex one that it cannot validly be made until after the birth.[159] There are particular concerns where women are forced through poverty to offer themselves as surrogate mothers.[160]

3. Surrogacy does not challenge the attitude of society towards infertility and means that resources are not directed towards discovering the causes of infertility.

4. The Roman Catholic Church has argued that surrogacy is analogous to adultery, in that it brings a third party into the marriage.

5. There are concerns expressed by some that the child after birth might be rejected by both the gestational mother and the commissioning parents, particularly if the child is born disabled. Even if this does not happen, there are concerns that children will be confused over their biological origins or that the child will be harmed by being denied contact with his or her birth mother.[161] Whether these concerns are such that it would be better for the child not to be born is hotly debated.

---

[157] See the discussions in Welstead (2019); Bracken (2020).
[158] Bainham (1998a: 209).
[159] See the discussion in Lane (2003).
[160] Rao (2003).
[161] Lane (2003: 131).

6. Commercial surrogacy arrangements commodify children and treat them as chattels to be bought and sold. Of course, this argument is only really of weight when considering commercial surrogacy.

Arguments in favour of surrogacy

1. A woman should be allowed to do with her body as she wishes. If she wishes to enter into a surrogacy arrangement and use her body in that way, she should be allowed to. Surrogacy can also be argued as an aspect of procreative freedom. Indeed, it is possible to regard surrogacy as a 'gift' to be encouraged.[162]

2. Some people believe that surrogacy is a more appropriate solution for infertile couples than artificial insemination by donor (AID) or other forms of treatment. However, as Bainham notes, 'surrogacy will be triggered by a man's desire to have his own *genetic* child where his wife or partner is unable to conceive or bear a child'.[163]

3. Surrogacy is inevitable, and therefore best regulated by the law. Its history goes back to biblical times, and, were it to be outlawed, this would simply lead to a black market in the practice.

4. It has been argued that surrogacy encourages and enables a variety of family forms. For example, a gay couple would be able to have a child through a surrogate. In early 2000 the media paid much attention to a gay couple who travelled over to the United States and produced a child, using a surrogacy arrangement, and then returned to Britain with the child.[164] In a different case a couple sought unsuccessfully to use a surrogate mother and the sperm of their dead son so that they could have a grandchild.[165] Some will see these examples as a welcome break from the traditional nuclear family form; but others will see them as a misuse of technology.

Questions

1. *Should a surrogacy contract be enforced? If so, how?*

2. *Should surrogacy be regulated in the same way as adoption? Specifically, should surrogate parents require approval from the local authority?*

Further reading

Read **Horsey and Biggs** (2007) for a useful collection of essays on surrogacy.

6 Adoption

Adoption will be discussed in detail in Chapter 11. There are two points to be stressed here. The first is that before adoption takes place, prospective adoptive parents must undergo close scrutiny through the adoption panel of the local authority. The court will further consider whether the adoption is in the child's best interests. The court can make the order only if the

---

[162] See the discussion of the use of gift in this context: Ragoné (2003).
[163] Bainham (1998b: 202) (italics changed from the original).
[164] *Independent on Sunday* (2000).
[165] Laurance (2000).

parents consent or, *inter alia*, the court decides that it would be in the child's welfare for the parents' consent to be dispensed with. Secondly, once the adoption order is made, the adoptive couple acquire the full status of parenthood. They do not merely obtain parental responsibility but are considered by the law to be the child's parents.

7 Losing parenthood

Learning objective 4

Summarise how the status of parenthood can be lost

Legal parenthood will only come to an end if an adoption order is made or a parental order under s. 54 of the Human Fertilisation and Embryology Act 2008 is awarded. In either of these cases the original parents (the parents at birth) cease to be the legal parents and the applicants take over as parents.

8 Social parents

Learning objective 5

Discuss the position of the social parent

Under this heading we will discuss the various ways the law treats those who are caring for the child in a parental way, even though they may not actually be the parents. There are several categories: guardianship; foster parents; special guardians; treating a child as a child of the family; step-parents; and others caring for children.

A Guardianship

The law is naturally concerned about children whose parents die. In part this is dealt with by enabling parents with parental responsibility to appoint someone to be a guardian of their children in the event of their death. The courts can also appoint a guardian. There is no restriction over who can be appointed as a guardian[166] and more than one guardian can be appointed.[167] The parents may appoint anyone they choose, although step-parents are common choices. Surprisingly, one study found that children are rarely consulted when parents select guardians.[168] A local authority cannot be appointed as a guardian.[169]

(i) The appointment of guardians by parents

Parents with parental responsibility can appoint guardians,[170] as can people who are guardians themselves. But a father without parental responsibility cannot appoint a guardian; nor can a non-parent with parental responsibility. The appointment of a guardian must be written, dated, and signed.[171] Usually the appointment is made as a term in a will, although this is not necessary.

---

[166] It seems even a child can be a guardian of a child, but this would be highly unusual.
[167] Children Act 1989 (hereafter CA 1989), s. 6.
[168] Hazan (2013).
[169] Nor can the director of social services be appointed in order to circumvent this restriction (*Re SH (Care Order: Orphan)* [1995] 1 FLR 746 at p. 749).
[170] Although a guardian can only be appointed by a person over the age of 18.
[171] CA 1989, s. 5(5).

At what point does the guardianship come into effect? This depends upon whether or not one of the parents has a residence order at the time when a parent dies:

1. Where a residence order has been made in favour of one of the parents, the guardianship will take effect on the death of the parent with the residence order, even if the other parent is still alive and has parental responsibility. In such a case the child will have both a parent and a guardian.

2. Where there is no residence order in place, the guardianship only comes into effect once the last remaining parent with parental responsibility dies.[172] So, if a couple are married and the mother appoints a guardian and then dies, the appointed guardian will not actually become a guardian until the father also dies. By contrast, if a father is unmarried and without parental responsibility, the mother can appoint a guardian who will take office immediately on her death.

The person appointed to be guardian does not need to have been approved by the court or the local authority. It is notable that there is a very limited control on the making of an appointment; the absence of control over such appointments is in marked contrast to adoption or fostering. However, there is power in the court to revoke a guardianship and this power could be used if the guardian was unsuitable. It is still arguable that a power to revoke guardianship once it has become apparent the guardian is unsuitable is not as effective protection for a child as requiring a would-be guardian to undergo some kind of vetting process.

(ii) The appointment of guardians by courts

The court may consider appointing a guardian where the parents have both died without either of them appointing anyone as guardian of their children.[173] The court can also appoint a guardian even though the parents have appointed other guardians. This might occur if the person appointed by the parents as guardian is unable or unwilling to carry out the role. The court only has the power to appoint a guardian if there is no parent with parental responsibility who is alive, or if the parent with the residence order has died.[174] Usually this will follow an application to the court by the proposed guardian, although the court can act on its own motion. In deciding who to appoint, the child's welfare is to be the paramount consideration.[175] Clearly the court is likely to want to appoint someone who knows the child well.[176]

(iii) The legal effects of guardianship

The effects of guardianship are as follows:

1. The guardian acquires parental responsibility.

2. The guardian can object to adoption.

3. The guardian can appoint a guardian to replace them on their death.

4. A guardian is not liable to provide financially for a child under the Children Act 1989 or child support legislation, nor under social security legislation.[177]

---

[172] CA 1989, s. 5(7), (8). The surviving parent can apply for the appointment to be ended if he or she wishes.
[173] Or having appointed an unsuitable or unwilling guardian
[174] Although there is no requirement to consult the checklist in s. 1(3) of CA 1989.
[175] Although there is no requirement to consult the checklist in s. 1(3) of CA 1989.
[176] *Re C (Minors) (Adoption by Relatives)* [1989] 1 FLR 222, [1989] FCR 744.
[177] Social Security Administration Act 1992, s. 78. It should be noted that guardians might be liable to support the child on their divorce under the Matrimonial Causes Act 1973 if the child were regarded as a 'child of the family'.

5. There are no succession rights on the intestate death of the guardian.[178]

6. No citizenship rights pass through a guardian.

It should be noted that guardians are given more 'rights' than a non-parent with parental responsibility (e.g. the rights on adoption), although they are not given all of the rights and responsibilities of a parent with parental responsibility. Although guardians are not liable for assessment under the child support legislation, guardians are under a legal duty to maintain the children and provide education, adequate food, clothing, medical aid and lodging. The explanation is that there was a fear that guardians would be deterred from accepting guardianship if they could become financially responsible for the child under the child support legislation.

(iv) Revoking an appointment

Section 6 of the Children Act 1989 deals with revocation of a guardianship appointment. The guardianship can be revoked in the following ways:

1. The parent who made the appointment makes a subsequent appointment. This will revoke the first appointment unless it is clear the parent was seeking to appoint a second guardian.[179]

2. The parent who made the appointment can revoke it by a signed and dated document.[180]

3. If the appointment is made in a will it is revoked if the will or codicil is revoked.[181]

4. If the appointment is made by a document, the destruction of the document will end the appointment.[182]

5. If a spouse is appointed as guardian,[183] this will be revoked by a subsequent divorce.[184]

(v) Disclaimer

A guardian can disclaim the appointment within a reasonable length of time.[185] The disclaimer must be in writing. Once someone disclaims guardianship, he or she ceases to have the rights and responsibilities of guardianship. There is no need for a person to consent to becoming a guardian, so the burden rests on the guardian to make the non-acceptance of the appointment clear as soon as possible.

(vi) Termination

A court order can terminate guardianship. Anyone with parental responsibility, or the child him- or herself, can apply for a revocation, as can the court on its own motion.[186] The welfare principle governs the issue. The court may also decide to appoint a replacement guardian. The kind of circumstances in which the court may terminate a guardianship are where the guardian is failing properly to care for the child or where there is a dispute between, say, an unmarried father and the guardian which cannot be resolved, and the court decides the child's long-term future is with the father.

---

[178] Nor can the guardian claim in the event of the child's death
[179] CA 1989, s. 6(1).
[180] CA 1989, s. 6(2).
[181] CA 1989, s. 6(4).
[182] CA 1989, s. 6(3).
[183] For example, if a step-parent is appointed as guardian
[184] CA 1989, s. 6(3A).
[185] CA 1989, s. 6(5).
[186] CA 1989, s. 6(7).

Termination of guardianship will occur on the death of the child, the death of the guardian, or on the child reaching majority. It may well be that the guardian's powers will terminate on the minor's marriage, but there is no clear provision to this effect.

B Foster parents

(i) The nature of foster parenthood

Foster parents[187] are people who look after children on a long-term basis, but are not related to them. The term therefore covers a wide variety of arrangements: from a friend asked by a mother to care for her child while the mother has a lengthy time in hospital, to a family approved by a local authority to look after children who have been taken into local authority care. The law draws an important distinction between those placements which are private (arranged by parents) and those which are public (arranged by the local authority).

(ii) Private foster parents

The Children Act 1989 defines a 'privately fostered child'[188] as a child under 16 years of age cared for by someone who:

- is not a parent;
- does not have parental responsibility for the child;
- is not a relative; and
- has accommodated the child for at least 28 days.

The requirement that a foster parent must accommodate a child for at least 28 days means that babysitters, day-care centres, playgroups and nurseries are not classified as foster parents.

There is, in practice, limited regulation of private foster parents.[189] There is no need for a court or local authority to approve a private fostering arrangement, although the local authority should be notified by the foster parents of the fact they are fostering or intend to foster.[190]

The local authority, in theory, can inspect the house where the child is living to check that it is suitable for fostering and may even supervise the fostering. In practice, many private fostering arrangements go unreported to any organ of the state. Even where the local authority is notified of the arrangement, it is unlikely to intervene unless there is evidence that the child is being harmed.

Foster parents do not automatically acquire parental responsibility.[191] They are normally in the same position as anyone else who happens to be caring for a child at a particular time. They can rely on s. 3(5) of the Children Act 1989:

---

[187] Although the statute refers to 'foster parents', local authorities prefer to refer to 'foster carers'.
[188] CA 1989, s. 66. See Laming (2003) for a call that the Governments reconsider the law on private foster arrangements.
[189] It is now possible for a person who is thought by a local authority to be unsuitable to be a foster parent to be disqualified.
[190] Children (Private Arrangements for Fostering) Regulations 1991 (SI 1991/2050), r 4.
[191] In *Re M (A Child)* [2002] 1 FCR 88 the child was found to have family life with the foster carers for the purposes of Article 8 of the European Convention on Human Rights.

LEGISLATIVE PROVISION

Children Act 1989, section 3(5)

A person who—

    (a)   does not have parental responsibility for a particular child; but

    (b)   has care of the child

may (subject to the provisions of this Act) do what is reasonable in all the circumstances of the case for the purpose of safe-guarding or promoting the child's welfare.

(iii) Local authority foster parents

Local authority foster parents (or foster carers as they tend to be called) have a very special position in the Children Act 1989 and the details of their position will be discussed in Chapter 11. However, the law seeks to hold together two policies. On the one hand, there is the realisation that foster carers and children can form a close relationship which should be recognised and protected.[192] On the other hand, local authority foster carers are not normally intended to be permanent carers and it is necessary to ensure that local authorities can remove the child (perhaps with a view to placing the child with prospective adopters) when necessary. The balance is struck by restricting the foster carer's ability to apply for a residence order until they have cared for the child for three years.

C Special guardians

The Adoption and Children Act 2002 created the status of special guardianship. This is intended to cover those who are full-time carers of children but are not going to take on the full status of parenthood. (This is discussed further in Chapter 11.)

D Those who treat a child as a child of the family

Even if an adult is not a child's genetic parent, legal consequences will follow if he or she treats a child as 'a child of the family'.

(i) What does 'a child of the family' mean?

The phrase 'child of the family' means any child of a married couple and any child treated by a married couple as a child of their family.[193] The definition therefore covers both genetic children of the marriage and a child to whom the spouses are not genetically related, but whom they have brought up as their child.[194] It covers stepchildren who are treated by step-parents as their own child. The phrase does not cover children brought up by unmarried couples.[195]

---

[192] Foster carers and their children can have family life together for the purposes of Article 8: *Kopf and Liberda v Austria* (App. No. 1598/06).

[193] CA 1989, s. 105(1).

[194] Foster children placed by a local authority or voluntary agency are excluded from the definition.

[195] *J v J (A Minor: Property Transfer)* [1993] 2 FLR 56, [1993] 1 FCR 471.

To decide whether a child is a child of the family, the Court of Appeal has proposed the test: 'the independent outside observer has to look at the situation and say: "Does the evidence show that the child was treated as a member of the family?"'[196] Therefore, the test focuses on the conduct of the adult rather than their beliefs.[197] The child must be treated as a child of *a family*. There must be a family – spouses living together.[198] The child cannot be treated as a child of a family due to actions before he or she was born.[199]

(ii) The consequences of treating a child as a child of the family

1. On divorce, a spouse is liable to provide financial support for any child he or she treated as a child of the family under s. 52 of the Matrimonial Causes Act 1973.[200]

2. A person who has treated a child as a child of the family may be liable to provide financial support under Sched. 1 to the Children Act 1989.[201]

3. A person who has treated a child as a child of the family may be liable to provide financial support under the Domestic Proceedings and Magistrates' Courts Act 1978, s. 38.

4. A person who has treated a child as a child of the family can apply as of right for a residence or contact order without needing to apply to the court for leave.[202]

5. A child may be able to claim against the estate of a deceased adult who has treated them as a child of the family under the Inheritance (Provision for Family and Dependants) Act 1975.[203]

By using the concept of a child of the family, the law gives some recognition to social parenthood, although it is restricted to those who are married. The emphasis is on the imposition of responsibilities rather than granting rights. The person treating the child as if the child is his or hers acquires responsibilities towards the child as listed above, although he or she does not thereby acquire parental responsibility. The biological parents will still be liable to support the child under the Child Support, Pensions and Social Security Act 2000, the Children Act 1989 or the Matrimonial Causes Act 1973; and the social parent may also be liable to support the child under the concept of a child of the family. From the child's viewpoint, this greatly increases the chances that someone will support the child financially.

E Step-parents

(i) The legal position of step-parents

A step-parent is a person who marries the mother or father of a child.[204] Inaccurately, but commonly, the term is also used for an unmarried cohabitant who moves in with a child's parent.[205] Step-parents, and particularly stepmothers, have often been stigmatised in fairy tales as terrifying figures for children. Of course, the quality of relationship between stepchildren

---

[196] *D v D (Child of the Family)* (1981) 2 FLR 93 at p. 97, *per* Ormrod LJ. See *Re A (Child of the Family)* [1998] 1 FLR 347 for an application of the test.

[197] *Carron v Carron* [1984] FLR 805.

[198] Cohabiting for a fortnight was sufficient in *W v W* [1984] FLR 796.

[199] *A v A (Family: Unborn Child)* [1974] Fam 6.

[200] See Chapter 6.

[201] See Chapter 6.

[202] CA 1989, s. 10(5)(a).

[203] Inheritance (Provision for Family and Dependants) Act 1975, s. 1(1)(d). (See Chapter 12.)

[204] The social and legal position of step-parents is discussed in M. Smith (2003). Ribbens McCarthy *et al.* (2003) found that many stepfamilies reject the 'step-' terminology and regard themselves simply as families.

[205] Barton (2009).

and step-parents varies enormously, as indeed does the relationship between genetic parents and their children.[206] A study found that many stepfamilies did not describe themselves using the label 'step-' but simply as families.[207] However, the research suggested that, in times of family stress, the stepfamily emphasised the genetic relationships, rather than the step-relationships.[208]

The law's treatment of step-parents is ambiguous. Even though a step-parent in practice often acts towards the child as a parent and indeed may be treated by the child as if they were their biological parent, the step-parent does not automatically acquire parental responsibility on marrying the parent.[209] However, if the step-parent reaches an agreement with the child's parents with parental responsibility, he or she can thereby gain parental responsibility.[210] It should be noted that a step-parent will need the consent of the non-resident parent (if he or she has parental responsibility) for this to happen. The alternative for a step-parent is to apply to the court for a parental responsibility order. This will be used, no doubt, mainly where the non-resident parent is refusing to consent to the sharing of the parental responsibility. The step-parent who acquires parental responsibility in either of these two ways will not lose it if their marriage to the parent comes to an end. However, they can have that parental responsibility brought to an end by a court order.[211] These provisions apply only to a person who marries a parent; they do not apply to a cohabitant of a parent. Another option for a step-parent is to adopt the child.[212] The step-parent is not under a legal obligation to support stepchildren, although if he or she treats a child as a child of the family he or she may be liable on divorce or separation to support the child, under the Matrimonial Causes Act 1973. On divorce, a court may award a step-parent a contact order, but there is no presumption in favour of such an order.[213]

F Others caring for the child

A family friend or relative may care for a child on a day-to-day basis without having an official role. Such a person does not acquire parental responsibility simply because he or she is caring for a child. However, the law does provide some ways in which day-to-day carers are regulated by the law:

1. It is possible to delegate parental responsibility. Under s. 2(9) of the Children Act 1989 a person with parental responsibility may 'arrange for some or all of it to be met by one or more persons acting on his behalf'.[214] Hence, a parent may delegate responsibility to a babysitter or childminder.[215] There is no need to obtain court approval of the delegation. However, delegation does not absolve someone with parental responsibility from any legal liability. For example, a parent may be guilty of a criminal offence involving neglect of children, even though they have delegated parental responsibility to someone else, as s. 2(11) makes clear.

---

[206] Ribbens McCarthy *et al.* (2003).
[207] Ribbens McCarthy *et al.* (2003).
[208] Ribbens McCarthy *et al.* (2003).
[209] See Bainham (2006a: 61) for an argument for not treating a step-parent the same as a natural parent.
[210] CA 1989, s. 4A This section was added by the Adoption and Children Act 2002.
[211] The application to do so can be brought by a person with parental responsibility for the child.
[212] See, further, Chapter 11.
[213] A contact order is available but there is no presumption of contact between a child and a step-parent, as was made clear in *Re H (A Minor) (Contact)* [1994] 2 FLR 776, [1994] FCR 419.
[214] CA 1989, s. 2(9).
[215] Department for Children, Schools and Families (2008a: para 2.18).

2. Under s. 3(5) of the Children Act 1989 if an adult is caring for a child, he or she 'may . . . do what is reasonable in all the circumstances of the case for the purpose of safeguarding or promoting the child's welfare'. The exact scope of this power and to what extent such a carer must consult with the parent is unclear.[216] It is generally accepted that a person relying on s. 3(5) cannot overrule a decision of a person with parental responsibility, but there is no provision explicitly to this effect.

3. A social parent with leave could apply to the court for a s. 8 order.[217] If the child is living with that adult, then he or she could acquire parental responsibility by virtue of a residence order.

4. A carer could seek to use wardship. The best-known circumstances are *Re D (A Minor) (Wardship: Sterilisation)*,[218] in which there were plans to sterilise an 11-year-old girl. Her parents did not object, but an educational psychologist who had been seeing the girl was concerned and used wardship to bring the issue to the court. However, wardship is available only in extreme cases. Following the Children Act 1989, in most cases an application for such a s. 8 order will be most appropriate.

5. People caring for children have responsibilities. They commit criminal offences if they assault, ill-treat, neglect, abandon or expose a child in a way likely to cause unnecessary suffering or injury. Also, a child can be taken into care on the basis of the lack of care provided by a carer.[219]

9 Relatives

Here we will consider the position of those who are a child's relatives.[220] First, we will look at the rights of family members under the Children Act 1989. It will also be necessary to examine the right to respect for family life protected under the Human Rights Act 1998. The Children Act defines relatives as including 'a grandparent, brother, sister, uncle, or aunt (whether of the full blood or half blood or by affinity) or step-parent'.[221] In the Children Act there is no clear legal status which flows from being a relation. There are some who argue for a more formalised position for relatives, giving them a clear set of rights.[222] The arguments are made especially in respect of grandparents.[223] Sociological studies demonstrate that most children hold their grandparents in special affection[224] and indeed grandparents often play a major role in child-care arrangements.[225] Over one-half of women in paid work with a child under five left the child with the child's grandparents.[226] Where a child is disabled, the role played by grandparents can be particularly significant.[227] There are dangers in talking about grandparents as a general

---

[216] In *B v B (A Minor) (Residence Order)* [1992] 2 FLR 327, [1993] 1 FCR 211 a grandmother without parental responsibility caring for a child had difficulty in dealing with doctors and the educational authority in cases relating to children.

[217] CA 1989, s. 10.

[218] [1976] Fam 185.

[219] *Lancashire CC v B* [2000] 1 FLR 583, [2000] 1 FCR 509.

[220] For a useful discussion of the psychological role that relatives can play, see Pryor (2003).

[221] CA 1989, s. 105. The Family Law Act 1996 gives a much longer list of relatives (discussed in Chapter 7).

[222] Family Matters Institute (2009); see Masson and Lindley (2006) for an argument that relatives caring for children lack adequate support from the state.

[223] See Herring (2008c: ch. 7) for a detailed discussion on the law and social practice of grandparenting.

[224] Step-grandparents can play a significant role too.

[225] Douglas and Murch (2002a). For a discussion of the support siblings can offer each other, see Monk and Macvarish (2019).

[226] Social and Community Planning Research (2000).

[227] *Re J (Leave to Issue Application for Residence Order)* [2003] 1 FLR 114.

group. One study suggested that grandmothers tended to play a more significant role in children's lives than grandfathers, and maternal grandparents than paternal grandparents.[228] In a recent study it was found that, on parental divorce, paternal grandparents often lost contact with their grandchildren and that grandparents suffered depression as a result.[229] This has led some to call for the law to grant grandparents a special legal status with attendant rights.

Opponents of such suggestions reply that giving wider family members rights will impinge on the rights of parents to raise their children as they think fit;[230] further, that to give grandparents and others rights would be to give them rights without having responsibilities for the child.[231] Douglas and Ferguson,[232] arguing against giving grandparents special legal rights, maintain that this would work against the norms that generally govern relations between grandparents, their children and grandchildren. They argue that these relationships are governed by 'the norm of non-interference': that is, that grandparents seek to support but not interfere in the role carried out by parents. Further, they argue that the sacrifices that grandparents make for their grandchildren are not seen as part of a reciprocal relationship (i.e. grandparents do not expect anything back from their labours of love for their grandchildren).[233]

This is a complex issue, partly because the nature of the relationships varies so much.[234] For example, some children never see their aunts and to others an aunt may be a 'second mother'. It is therefore perhaps not surprising that the law is reluctant to set out specified rights and obligations flowing from a particular blood relationship. One danger in this area is that, by giving relatives parental responsibility, the child might become confused. An aunt is an aunt, not a parent. That said, parental responsibility is a legal term of art and a phrase unlikely to be used in everyday family life. If parental responsibility gives the carer of the child the legal rights they need to look after the child, perhaps we should not get too worried about the device used to achieve this.

Under the Children Act 1989 there are various consequences of being a relative:

1. A relative can apply for a residence order or contact order without leave of the court where the child has lived with the relation for one year (or with the consent of the parents). Even if the child has lived with the relatives less than one year, the relative can still apply for a s. 8 order, but leave of the court will be required.[235] A relative is unlikely to be successful in applying for a residence order against the wishes of the parents unless it is shown that the parents are clearly unsuitable or the relative has formed a very close attachment to the child. (We will discuss this further in Chapter 10.) More commonly, a relative may apply for a contact order. In *Re A (Section 8 Order: Grandparent Application)*[236] the grandmother wanted contact with her young grandchildren after a bitter divorce. The Court of Appeal stated that, although there was a presumption in favour of contact between a parent and a child, there was no such presumption of contact between a grandparent and a child, nor between any other relative and a child. It is clear that in each case the court will need to be persuaded that the relationship between the grandparent and the child is a close one and that contact will benefit the child.[237] The courts have acknowledged that to force a parent to permit contact between a child and a grandparent may be counter-productive if, for example,

---

[228] Douglas and Ferguson (2003); Hunt (2006b).
[229] Merrick (2000).
[230] See Crook (2001).
[231] Kaganas (2007b); Kaganas and Piper (2001: 268).
[232] Douglas and Ferguson (2003).
[233] Ferguson (2004).
[234] Taylor (2019).
[235] CA 1989, s. 10(5B).
[236] [1995] 2 FLR 153, [1996] 1 FCR 467.
[237] *Re M (Care: Contact: Grandmother's Application for Leave)* [1995] 2 FLR 86, [1995] 3 FCR 550.

the parents regard the grandmother as interfering.[238] Siblings have a strong right to contact, but more distant relatives have been less successful than grandparents in contact cases.[239]

2. A grandparent and other relatives will have a strong case for contact with a child who is in care. If a local authority is 'looking after a child' then it is under a duty to promote contact between the child and the wider family.[240] The cases certainly suggest that contact between a grandparent and a child in care will normally be granted.[241]

3. Where the parents of a child have died without appointing a guardian, the courts are likely to consider appointing a relative as guardian.

4. The local authority is under an obligation to consider placing a child with relatives before taking a child into care.[242] Further, a local authority which is considering putting a child up for adoption should consider the possibility of placing a child with a relative before considering adoption by a stranger.[243] (We will discuss this later in Chapter 11.)

5. Domestic violence injunctions. Under the Family Law Act 1996 non-molestation injunctions are available between 'associated persons', which includes relatives.[244]

6. Relatives may treat a child as a child of their family and this will trigger a series of rights and responsibilities.[245]

7. In certain circumstances a relative may be in a position to invoke wardship.[246]

10 The Human Rights Act 1998 and the right to respect for family life

Under Article 8 of the ECHR:

LEGISLATIVE PROVISION

European Convention on Human Rights, Article 8

1. Everyone has the right to respect for his private and family life, his home and his correspondence.

2. There shall be no interference by a public authority with the exercise of this right except such as is in accordance with the law and is necessary in a democratic society in the interests of national security, public safety or the economic well-being of the country, for the prevention of disorder or crime, for the protection of health or morals, or for the protection of the rights and freedoms of others.[247]

---

[238] *Re F and R (Section 8 Order: Grandparent's Application)* [1995] 1 FLR 524. See also *Re S (Contact: Grandparents)* [1996] 1 FLR 158, [1996] 3 FCR 30.
[239] *G v Kirklees MBC* [1993] 1 FLR 805, [1993] 1 FCR 357 and *Re A (A Minor) (Residence Order: Leave to Apply)* [1993] 1 FLR 425, [1993] 1 FCR 870.
[240] See Chapter 11.
[241] *Re M (Care: Contact: Grandmother's Application for Leave)* [1995] 3 FCR 550.
[242] Adoption and Children Act 2002, s. 1(4)(f) requires the court to consider the child's relationship with her relatives before making an adoption order.
[243] *Re R (A Child) (Adoption: Disclosure)* [2001] 1 FCR 238.
[244] See Chapter 7.
[245] See above, 'An analysis of the allocation of parenthood in the HFE Acts'.
[246] See *Re H (A Minor) (Custody: Interim Care and Control)* [1991] 2 FLR 109, [1991] FCR 985.
[247] Article 8 of the European Convention.

This is a clear recognition that family members other than parents can be protected through the law. The relevance of this article will be discussed throughout the text, but here a few general points will be made.[248]

A What is family life?

In defining family life it is clear that the paradigm of family life for the European Court of Human Rights (ECtHR) has been a husband and wife and children.[249] However, the European Court has not restricted family life to married couples and relationships through blood.[250] In **Kearns v France**[251] it was held that it covered a mother and child in a case where the mother had given her child up for adoption shortly after birth. Article 8 has been found to cover unmarried couples;[252] siblings;[253] uncle/nephew;[254] grandparents/grandchild;[255] same-sex couples[256] and foster parents/foster child.[257] However, it appears that the further the relationship departs from the paradigm (i.e. the more remote the blood relationship), the more evidence is needed to show that there was a close social relationship between the parties. For example, in **Boyle v UK**[258] it was accepted that the uncle and nephew had 'family life' because the uncle proved he was a father figure to the boy. Had he actually been the boy's father, the court would readily have accepted that their relationship constituted family life and there would have been no need to show that their relationship was especially close. The English courts have been more willing to assume family life exists with wider relatives. In **Re R (A Child) (Adoption: Disclosure)**[259] Holman J was willing to hold that a newborn baby had family life with her wider family, including uncles and aunts. If the relationship does not fall within family life, it may still be protected by Article 8 as an aspect of the parties' private life. In **Znamenskaya v Russia**[260] it was held that 'close relationships short of "family life" would generally fall within the scope of 'private life"'. In **Bogonosovy v Russia**:[261]

> The right to respect for family life of grandparents in relation to their grandchildren primarily entails the right to maintain a normal grandparent-grandchild relationship through contact between them, even though that contact normally takes place with the agreement of the person who has parental responsibility

Perhaps the most controversy surrounds fathers and children. Although mothers inevitably have family life with their children,[262] this is not true of fathers. As the European Court in

---

[248] See Choudhry and Herring (2010) for a detailed discussion.
[249] Choudhry and Herring (2010). In *Ahmut v The Netherlands* (1997) 24 EHRR 62 it was stated that once two people have family life, only in exceptional circumstances will that be lost.
[250] *X, Y, Z v UK* [1997] 2 FLR 892, [1997] 3 FCR 341.
[251] [2008] 2 FCR 1.
[252] *X, Y, Z v UK* [1997] 2 FLR 892, [1997] 3 FCR 341. A suggestion that, on divorce, a couple ceases to have family life was made by the court in *L v Finland* [2000] 2 FLR 118 at p. 148; but this seems inconsistent with the general approach in the previous cases: e.g. *Keegan v Ireland* (1994) 18 EHRR 342.
[253] *Moustaquim v Belgium* (1991) 13 EHRR 802 and *Senthuran v Secretary of State for the Home Department* [2004] 3FCR 273.
[254] *Boyle v UK* (1994) 19 EHRR 179.
[255] *L v Finland* [2000] 2 FLR 118; *Adam v Germany* [2009] 1 FLR 560.
[256] *Schalk v Austria* [2011] 2 FCR 650.
[257] *X v Switzerland* (1978) 13 DR 248.
[258] (1994) 19 EHRR 179. See also *Jucius and Juciuviene v Lithuania* [2009] 1 FLR 403.
[259] [2001] 1 FCR 238.
[260] [2005] 2 FCR 406 at para 27.
[261] Case 38201/16.
[262] *Re B (Adoption by One Natural Parent to Exclusion of Other)* [2001] 1 FLR 589, per Hale LJ.

Lebbink v *Netherlands*[263] stated: 'The court does not agree with the applicant that a mere biological kinship, without any further legal or factual elements indicating the existence of a close personal relationship, should be regarded as sufficient to attract the protection of Art. 8.' It explained that in considering a claim of a father the court would consider 'the nature of the relationship between the natural parents and the demonstrable interest in and commitment by the father to the child both before and after its birth'.[264] It appears that fathers can acquire family life with their children in two ways:

1. By actually caring for the child in a practical way and thereby demonstrating his interest in and commitment to the child.[265] This does not require the father to live with the child,[266] but must involve some kind of contact.[267]

2. If the conception of the child takes place in the context of a committed relationship. Therefore, if the father was married, engaged or in a permanent cohabiting relationship at the time of the conception he will have family life with the resulting child.[268]

This means that if the conception is part of a casual relationship and the man does not undertake a significant role in the care of a child, he will not be regarded as having family life with a child. In *G* v *The Netherlands*[269] a man donated sperm to a lesbian couple. After the child's birth he sought to have regular contact with the child. The European Court held that he did not have family life with the child.[270] In *Görgülü* v *Germany*,[271] where a mother gave up a child for adoption shortly after birth, the court was willing to find that the father had 'family life' with the child. He did not have an actual relationship with the child, but that was because he was prevented from doing so. The court did add, however, that due to his limited involvement in the child's life, it might be easier to justify an interference in his family life rights than it would have been if he had spent many years caring for the child. Recently in *Ahrens* v *Germany*[272] the man had a brief relationship with a woman, before she settled down with another man and had a child. The woman and the new partner raised the child as their own. It was held the man did not have family life with the child. It seems the settled family life the child was in played a role in determining that there was no family life with the man. However, arguably, that should have been seen as a factor justifying interference in the man's rights, rather than denying he had family life with the child.

In *Re CD (A Child)*[273] Bellamy J said that to establish family life a father needed to show evidence of a close personal relationship, demonstrable interest in, and commitment to, the child. In ruling that the father in that case did not have an Article 8 right in relation to the child it was found the father was a 'peripheral character' in the child's life.

---

[263] [2004] 3 FCR 59 at para 37.
[264] At para 36.
[265] *Lebbink* v *Netherlands* [2004] 3 FCR 59.
[266] *Lebbink* v *Netherlands* [2004] 3 FCR 59.
[267] *Söderbck* v *Sweden* [1999] 1 FLR 250.
[268] *Keegan* v *Ireland* [1994] 3 FCR 165 although subsequently the European Commission on Human Rights in *M* v *The Netherlands* (1993) 74 D&R 120 stated that there had to be some close personal ties to establish family life.
[269] (1990) 16 EHRR 38.
[270] See also *Mikulic* v *Croatia* [2002] 1 FCR 720 and *Haas* v *The Netherlands* [2004] 1 FCR 147.
[271] [2004] 1 FCR 410.
[272] App. No. 45071/09.
[273] [2017] EWFC 34.

To some these cases constitute gender discrimination and there is no justification for assuming that a mother, but not a father, deserves family life with the child.[274] To others the courts are recognising that through pregnancy and birth all mothers have demonstrated a relationship which deserves protection under the European Convention on Human Rights, while fathers' relationships with their children can be so minimal that they do not automatically justify protection.

B What is respect?

The European Court has made it clear that the requirement of respect for family life places both positive and negative obligations on the state. Article 8 may not only require the state not to interfere in family life but it may on occasions require the state to act positively to promote family life. For example, in *Hokkanen v Finland* the European Court held that the failure of the state to provide an effective mechanism for enforcing a contact order between a father and his child was an infringement of the right to respect for family life.[275] In *Stubbings v UK*[276] it was explained:

> [A]lthough the object of Article 8 is essentially that of protecting the individual against arbitrary interference by the public authorities, it does not merely compel the state to abstain from such interference: there may, in addition to this primary negative undertaking, be positive obligations inherent in an effective respect for private or family life. These obligations may involve the adoption of measures designed to secure respect for private life even in the sphere of the relations of individuals between themselves.

Thus, the court has reasoned that some positive acts may be a necessary part of respect for family or private life and so a failure to provide these can be an interference with respect for family life. This is certainly so where the state has intervened in family life (e.g. by taking a child into care) in which case a duty arises requiring steps to be taken to reunite the child and family.[277] It also means the state must take steps to enable family ties to be established. For example, *Rasmussen v Denmark*[278] suggests that respect for family life may involve providing an effective and accessible remedy so that a man can establish that he is the father of a child.

The word respect does not necessarily involve approval. One might respect a person's religious beliefs, without agreeing with them. All that would be needed for respect would be an acknowledgement that the thing to be respected has some value. This suggests that the ECHR requires the state to value all forms of family life which have value, even if the Government believes they are below the ideal forms of family life. More controversially, it might be suggested that some forms of family life are so devoid of value that they do not deserve respect. That might be so where the relationship is characterised by abuse.[279]

---

[274] Bainham (2005: 216) argues the approach is inconsistent with Article 7 of the United Nations Convention on the Rights of the Child (UNCRC) which recognises the right of the child to know both parents from birth.
[275] [1996] 1 FLR 289, [1995] 2 FCR 320 ECtHR
[276] (1997) 1 BHRC 316.
[277] See Chapter 11.
[278] (1985) 7 EHRR 371. See also *Paulik v Slovakia* [2006] 3 FCR 323.
[279] These arguments are developed in Herring (2008c).

C When can infringement be justified?

Paragraph 2 of Article 8 sets out the circumstances in which an infringement of the right to respect for family life is justified. To justify the interference in the right it must be shown that:

1. The interference was in accordance with the law.

2. The interference was in pursuance of one of the listed aims (e.g. national security).

3. The interference must be necessary. It is not enough to show that the interference was reasonable or desirable; it must be shown that there was a pressing need for the interference.[280] Further, it must be shown that the extent of the intervention was proportionate; in other words, there was not a less interventionist measure which would have adequately protected national security (or whichever of the listed aims was being pursued).

It is submitted that the nature of the quality of relationship between the parties is relevant, not only in deciding whether there is family life, but also in deciding whether the interference is justified under para 2. The weaker the relationship between adult and child, the more likely it is that state action will not be regarded as interference in the relationship; or if it is interference that it will be seen as justifiable.

11 Who has parental responsibility?

Learning objective 6

Explain who has parental responsibility

In many ways this is a more important question than 'who is a parent?' but, as we shall see, 'who is a parent?' and 'who has parental responsibility?' are actually linked questions. It is necessary to distinguish the way mothers, fathers, non-parents and local authorities may obtain parental responsibility. First, the law will be set out in broad outline and then more detailed points will be discussed.

A Outline of the law

(i) Mothers

All mothers[281] automatically have parental responsibility.

(ii) Fathers

A father[282] will have parental responsibility in any of the following circumstances:

- he is married to the mother;[283] or

- he is registered as the father of the child on the birth certificate;[284] or

- he enters into a parental responsibility agreement with the mother; or

- he obtains a parental responsibility order from the court;[285] or

---

[280] *Dudgeon v UK* (1982) 4 EHRR 149.
[281] That is, the woman regarded as the mother in the eyes of the law.
[282] That is, a man who is regarded as a father under the legal definition.
[283] The phrase 'married to the mother' has a wide definition. This includes a child born as a result of assisted reproduction (CA 1989, s. 2).
[284] CA 1989, s. 4, as amended by the Adoption and Children Act 2002.
[285] CA 1989, s. 4.

- he has been granted a residence order;[286] or
- he has been appointed to be a guardian;[287] or
- he has adopted the child.

(iii) Non-parents

Someone who is not a parent can obtain parental responsibility in the following ways:

1. He or she will acquire parental responsibility if appointed as a guardian.[288]

2. A person who is not a parent or a guardian will acquire parental responsibility when he or she obtains a residence order.

3. A person who is granted an emergency protection order thereby acquires parental responsibility.

It should be noted that, in these circumstances, although the non-parent will have parental responsibility, he or she will not obtain the rights that flow from being a parent.

(iv) Local authorities

Local authorities can acquire parental responsibility as follows:

1. When a local authority obtains a care order it acquires parental responsibility.[289]

2. When a local authority obtains an emergency protection order it acquires parental responsibility.

B Consideration of the law in more detail

It is necessary to discuss some specific aspects of some of the points above.

(i) Mothers

The rule that all mothers automatically have parental responsibility for their children can be explained on the basis that the mother throughout the pregnancy has sustained the child and has undergone great sacrifices for her child. As she has demonstrated her commitment to the child through pregnancy and has accepted that she will be involved in the care for the child after the birth, it is in the child's interests that she obtains parental responsibility.

(ii) Fathers

There is much debate over whether all fathers should automatically obtain parental responsibility. The present law restricts which fathers might obtain parental responsibility. For a father there are two sources of parental responsibility: first, the mother (if she has married him or has permitted him to be registered as the father on the birth certificate or has entered a parental responsibility agreement with him); and secondly, the court (if the unmarried father is granted one of the orders mentioned above). The law appears to take the view that a father needs to be vetted and approved before he can acquire parental responsibility. But it should also be

[286] CA 1989, s. 12(2).
[287] CA 1989, s. 5(6).
[288] CA 1989, s. 5(6).
[289] CA 1989, s. 44(4)(c).

noted that a father (unlike the mother) has a choice: if a man wishes to father a child without having parental responsibility he may do so. There is no way that a mother can force the unmarried father of her child to have parental responsibility against his wishes.[290] The mother does not have the option of giving birth to a child but not taking parental responsibility. This may well indicate cultural assumptions that it is 'natural' for mothers to care for children, but this is not necessarily expected of fathers.

We shall consider in further detail the different ways in which an unmarried father can acquire parental responsibility.

(a) The registered father

The Adoption and Children Act 2002 amended s. 4 of the Children Act 1989 to provide that fathers who are registered as the father of the child on the birth certificate will automatically acquire parental responsibility.[291] This significant change in the law will greatly increase the number of unmarried fathers who have parental responsibility. Around 80 per cent of births to unmarried couples were registered by both mother and father. There have been concerns that the new law will in fact deter fathers from being registered because they falsely believe that if they are given parental responsibility they will become financially liable for the child.[292] Eekelaar voices a different concern, that mothers may be deterred[293] from registering the father's name for fear that doing so would give him rights he could use to interfere with her upbringing of the child.[294] If either of these concerns materialised, this would work against the policy of enabling children readily to discover the identity of their birth parents, discussed below. Another concern is that a mother may not appreciate the significance of registering the child's father.[295]

(b) Parental responsibility agreements

A father and a mother can enter a parental responsibility agreement under s. 4(1)(b) of the Children Act 1989. The agreement must be in the prescribed form and recorded.[296] It must be signed by both parties and taken to a court where the certificate will be witnessed and signed. Critics of the procedure argue that the technicalities that surround it deter fathers from using it. Indeed, the number of parental responsibility agreements has not been high. The reason, no doubt, is that if the parents are happy together, they do not see the need for a formal agreement, but if they are in dispute then there will be no agreement. On the other hand, there are those who suggest that the procedure is too easy. There is no effective check to ensure that the applicant is the father of the child; that the mother's consent is freely given; or that the man is suitable to have parental responsibility.

In *Re X (Parental Responsibility Agreement)*[297] the Court of Appeal regarded the right of a mother and father to enter into a parental responsibility agreement 'free from state intervention'[298] as an important aspect of the right of respect for family life under Article 8. The right to enter into the parental responsibility agreement exists even though the child has been taken into care.[299]

---

[290] She cannot register him on the birth certificate without his consent.

[291] Of course, a father who misleads a registrar into putting his name on the certificate cannot thereby acquire parental responsibility: *A v H (Registrar General for England and Wales and another intervening)* [2009] 3 FCR 95.

[292] In fact, fathers are liable under the Child Support Act 1991 whether or not they have parental responsibility.

[293] In fact, he suggests they would be 'well advised' not to (Eekelaar (2001d: 430)).

[294] Although he points out that having the father registered may make it easier to claim child support against him.

[295] Diduck and Kaganas (2006: 229).

[296] An oral agreement could amount to a delegation of parental responsibility under CA 1989, s. 2(9).

[297] [2000] 1 FLR 517.

[298] This is perhaps a little misleading, as the agreement does have to be lodged at the court and so the state is involved.

[299] In *Re X (Parental Responsibility Agreement)* [2000] 1 FLR 517.

(c) Section 4 applications

If the father is not registered on the birth certificate and is unable to obtain the mother's consent, he can apply under s. 4 of the Children Act 1989 for a parental responsibility order. Only genetic fathers can apply under s. 4, and if there is any doubt whether the applicant is the father, DNA evidence will be required. Orders are available only in respect of a child under 18.[300]

In deciding whether to grant parental responsibility, s. 1(1) of the Children Act 1989 applies,[301] and therefore the welfare of the child is to be the paramount consideration.[302] Although the Court of Appeal in *Re H (Parental Responsibility)*[303] has stated that it is wrong to suggest that there is a presumption in favour of awarding parental responsibility, we shall see that the cases demonstrate that only in unusual circumstances will parental responsibility not be granted. In 2011 there were 5,586 court hearings involving parental responsibility orders and in only 45 cases was the order refused.[304] Given that we are dealing with cases where the mother believed the father should not have parental responsibility, it is a tiny number of refusals.

Most of the cases considering applications under s. 4 use as a starting point *Re H (Minors) (Local Authority: Parental Responsibility) (No. 3)*,[305] where it was stated that these factors should be taken into account:

1. the degree of commitment which the father has shown towards the child;

2. the degree of attachment which exists between the father and the child; and

3. the reasons of the father applying for the order.

A little more focus to the test was set out in the question posed by Mustill LJ in *Re C (Minors)*:

> . . . was the association between the parties sufficiently enduring; and has the father by his conduct during and since the application shown sufficient commitment to the child to justify giving the father a legal status equivalent to that which he would have enjoyed if the parties had married?[306]

The fact that the applicant has applied for an order shows commitment in itself,[307] but the Court of Appeal has stressed that even if there is attachment and commitment the court still might not award parental responsibility if other factors indicate that it would be contrary to the child's interests.[308] Each case depends very much on its own facts, but the following points have arisen in previous cases and will be considered:[309]

1. *Contact with the child.* Where there is regular contact and financial support the court will readily find there is sufficient commitment between the father and the child for a parental responsibility order to be appropriate.[310] However, just because there has never been contact between the father and the child, it does not necessarily mean that parental responsibility will not be granted, especially if the father can demonstrate that the lack of contact

---

[300] There is no need to demonstrate that the circumstances are exceptional: cf. CA 1989, s. 9(6).
[301] The presumption of parental responsibility (discussed in Chapter 9) applies. As does CA 1989, s. 1(5): *Re P (Parental Responsibility)* [1998] 2 FLR 96, [1998] 3 FCR 98, although see Gilmore (2003a).
[302] *Re H (Parental Responsibility)* [1998] 1 FLR 855.
[303] [1998] 1 FLR 855.
[304] Six per cent of the applications were refused and in 4 per cent of cases no order was made.
[305] [1991] 1 FLR 214, [1991] FCR 361.
[306] *Re C (Minors) (Parental Rights)* [1992] 2 All ER 86 at p. 93.
[307] *Re S (A Minor) (Parental Responsibility)* [1995] 2 FLR 648 at p. 659.
[308] *Re P (Parental Responsibility)* [1998] 2 FLR 96, [1998] 3 FCR 98.
[309] Gilmore (2003a) provides a very useful discussion of the case law.
[310] *Re S (A Minor) (Parental Responsibility)* [1995] 2 FLR 648.

was due to the mother's actions. That said, as yet there is no case where a father has never seen the child but was awarded parental responsibility. Indeed, in *Re J (Parental Responsibility)*[311] parental responsibility was refused on the basis that the child never knew her father, he was 'almost a stranger'.

2. *Status.* In *Re S (A Minor) (Parental Responsibility)*[312] the Court of Appeal emphasised that parental responsibility gave an unmarried father the status 'for which nature had already ordained that he must bear responsibility'. This judgment suggests that the parental responsibility order merely confirms what the father's status is according 'to nature'. The parental responsibility order was referred to as a 'stamp of approval'. In this case, even though the father had been convicted of possessing paedophilic literature, he was still awarded parental responsibility. More recent cases appear to have rejected an argument that simply the status of the father is enough to generate a grant of parental responsibility. In *Re D (Withdrawal of Parental Responsibility)*[313] Ryder LJ held that parenthood and having parental responsibility had to be kept separate. Simply because someone was a parent did not give them the right to have parental responsibility. Parental responsibility was given based on the child's welfare. A good example of applying this approach is *Re B (A Child) (No. 2) (Welfare: Child Arrangement Order)*[314] where the mother's former partner was given parental responsibility due to 'the significant parental role that the applicant played in B's life. It is a role that B recalls and which formed part of the foundation of her infancy and will have positively affected her sense of identity when she was very small and growing up'. This case involved someone who had no genetic link to the child being given parental responsibility to acknowledge the significant role they played in the child's life.

The following is now the leading case and it emphasises that the focus must be on what is in the child's welfare.

CASE: *Re M (Parental Responsibility Order)* [2013] EWCA Civ 969

The father of a boy, aged 11, M, was not married to the mother. He did not have parental responsibility. He separated from the mother, but had significant levels of contact with M. One night he disappeared with the boy and evaded the police who were seeking to locate him. Following that, contact ceased and a residence order in favour of the mother was granted. The father sought a parental responsibility order. The mother and boy opposed the application because the boy did not want his father knowing about his education. The father had developed entrenched views about the case and was convinced he was the victim of a corrupt legal system, and there were concerns the father might use the boy in his campaigns. The trial judge refused to grant him parental responsibility.

On appeal the Court of Appeal upheld the refusal. M was of sufficient age and understanding to have his views respected. Having regard to his wishes, the mother's vulnerability and the father's past behaviour it was right not to grant him parental

---

[311] [1999] 1 FLR 784.
[312] [1995] 2 FLR 648.
[313] [2014] EWCA Civ 315.
[314] [2017] EWHC 488 (Fam).

responsibility. There was cogent evidence that the parental responsibility might be misused. The argument that parental responsibility was a 'status' recognising his parental role was not a 'stand alone' factor. Ryder LJ went on to explain 'while there is no presumption, a parental responsibility order should normally be made on a father's application and it will be a rare case where it is not' (para 18). The court should focus on the welfare of the child. In this case the welfare balance came down against granting parental responsibility.

3. *Child's reaction to failed application*. In *C and v (Minors) (Parental Responsibility and Contact)*[315] Ward LJ stated that it was good for a child's sense of self-esteem that the child thought positively about an absent parent and so 'wherever possible the law should confer on a concerned father that stamp of approval because he has shown himself willing and anxious to pick up the responsibility of fatherhood and not to deny or avoid it'.[316] Similarly, in *Re S (A Minor) (Parental Responsibility)*[317] it was stated that:

> . . . the law confers upon a committed father that stamp of approval, lest the child grow up with some belief that he is in some way disqualified from fulfilling his role and that the reason for the disqualification is something inherent which will be inherited by the child, making her struggle to find her own identity all the more fraught.[318]

4. *The child's view*. If the child is sufficiently mature, the child's views on whether the application should succeed can be taken into account.[319] In *Re G (A Child) (Domestic Violence: Direct Contact)*[320] the fact that a child (aged nearly four) did not want to have any contact with the father and was fearful when he was mentioned led Butler-Sloss P to hold that it was inappropriate to grant him parental responsibility.

5. *Misuse*. A father should not be denied a parental responsibility order simply because there are fears that the father may misuse the order.[321] If necessary, the court can make orders restricting the father's use of parental responsibility or requiring him to obtain the leave of the court before bringing any proceedings.[322] It is even possible to remove parental responsibility from a father.[323] In *Re S (A Minor) (Parental Responsibility)*[324] the mother's argument that the father might misuse the order on the basis that he had been unreliable about providing financial support for the child and had been convicted of possessing paedophilic literature failed. It was stated that it was wrong to focus on the potential misuse of the order and, instead, a father wishing to undertake the responsibilities

---

[315] [1998] 1 FLR 392, [1998] 1 FCR 57; see Eekelaar (1996).
[316] See also *Re M (Parental Responsibility Order)* [2013] EWCA Civ 969.
[317] [1995] 2 FLR 648.
[318] At p. 657. A cynic might doubt whether the child will appreciate the significance of parental responsibility if he or she does not see his or her father. The order is more likely to affect the father's image of himself than his child's.
[319] *Re M (Parental Responsibility Order)* [2013] EWCA Civ 969. *Re J (Parental Responsibility)* [1999] 1 FLR 784.
[320] [2001] 2 FCR 134.
[321] *Re W (Parental Responsibility Order: Inter-Relationship with Direct Contact)* [2013] EWCA Civ 335.
[322] CA 1989, s. 91(14).
[323] CA 1989, s. 4(3).
[324] [1995] 2 FLR 648.

associated with parenthood should be entitled to do so. By contrast, in *Re H (Parental Responsibility)*[325] the father had injured the son deliberately and there was even some suggestion that sadism was involved, and therefore the court did not grant parental responsibility as there was a future risk. Similarly, in *Re T (Minor) (Parental Responsibility)*[326] the application was denied because the father had shown no understanding of the child's welfare and had treated the mother with violence and hatred.[327] The court can grant a father parental responsibility and at the same time make an order that he must not exercise his parental responsibility in a particular way.

6. *Parental responsibility and other orders.* A parental responsibility order can be made even though a child arrangements order is inappropriate.[328] In other words, it is not necessary to show that the father will ever practically be able to exercise parental responsibility in order for him to be awarded it. So, parental responsibility can be ordered even though the child is about to be adopted.[329] A good example of this point is *Re C and v (Minors) (Parental Responsibility and Contact)*,[330] where a father had a close relationship with a child. Unfortunately, the child had severe medical problems and needed constant medical attention. The mother had learned the skills necessary to care for the child, but the father had not. It was therefore felt inappropriate to allow the child to visit the father, but still he was granted parental responsibility as a mark of his commitment to the child. Indeed, MacFarlane LJ went further in *Re W (Parental Responsibility Order: Inter-Relationship with Direct Contact)*[331] and suggested a refusal to order direct contact could strengthen the case for making a parental responsibility order, because the father would need it to confirm his status as a father.

By contrast, in *R v E and F (Female Parents: Known Father)*[332] a father was to have contact with the child, but was not granted parental responsibility. It was held that s. 3(5) of the Children Act 1989 enabled him to make decisions about the child during the contact sessions and so he did not need parental responsibility.

7. *Mother's possible reaction to the granting of the order.* The fact that the mother might bitterly oppose the order and there is hostility is not a reason for refusing the order,[333] although if the child's mother will be so upset that this may affect her parenting ability and cause the child to suffer, then parental responsibility may be denied.[334] In *Re R (Parental Responsibility)*[335] parental responsibility was not given to a man who was the psychological, but not biological, father of the child. Although deeply committed to the child, giving him parental responsibility would create tension and instability, given the breakdown.

8. *Mother's death.* In some cases the argument had been accepted that parental responsibility should be granted to a father so that he can take over care of the child if anything happens that might prevent the mother from caring for the child: for example, if she dies.[336]

---

[325] [1998] 1 FLR 855.

[326] [1993] 2 FLR 450, [1993] 1 FCR 973.

[327] See also *Re G (A Child) (Domestic Violence: Direct Contact)* [2001] 2 FCR 134.

[328] *Re P (A Minor) (Parental Responsibility Order)* [1994] 1 FLR 578.

[329] *Re H (Minors) (Local Authority: Parental Responsibility) (No. 3)* [1991] 1 FLR 214, [1991] FCR 361.

[330] [1998] 1 FLR 392, [1998] 1 FCR 57, confirmed in *Re M (Parental Responsibility Order)* [2013] EWCA Civ 969.

[331] [2013] EWCA Civ 335.

[332] [2010] EWHC 417 (Fam).

[333] *D v S* [1995] 3 FLR 783; *Re P (A Minor) (Parental Responsibility Order)* [1994] 1 FLR 578.

[334] *Re K* [1998] Fam Law 567.

[335] [2011] EWHC 1535 (Fam).

[336] *Re E (Parental Responsibility: Blood Test)* [1995] 1 FLR 392, [1994] 2 FCR 709; *Re H (A Minor) (Parental Responsibility)* [1993] 1 FLR 484, [1993] 1 FCR 85.

9. *The father's ability to exercise parental responsibility.* In *M v M (Parental Responsibility)*[337] the father suffered from a learning disability and head injuries and Wilson J argued that therefore he was incapable of exercising the rights and responsibilities of parental responsibility and so should not be given it.

10. *Encouraging commitment.* In **Re B and C (Change of Names: Parental Responsibility: Evidence)**[338] Cobb J held that 'The parental responsibility which attaches to parenthood may bring added commitment to the child which would be likely to be to the child's benefit'. It seems surprising that a court order will make a father more committed to his child than he would be otherwise, but that seems the approach this judge took.

As the above discussion demonstrates, the cases do not always reveal a consistent approach, but it appears that if a father has shown sufficient commitment to the child then a parental responsibility order will be made unless there are serious concerns that he may harm the child. This has led one leading family lawyer to complain of the 'degradation of parental responsibility'.[339] Indeed, it is striking that we needed a decision of the Court of Appeal (in **Re H (Parental Responsibility)**[340]) to tell us that a father who had sadistically injured his child should not have parental responsibility.

In 2019, there were 1,240 applications for a parental responsibility order, with only a tiny number being refused.[341] The readiness of the courts to award parental responsibility is controversial. In discussing these cases it is crucial to remember that they all involve families where the mother is opposing the grant of parental responsibility. If she was in accord, the couple would lodge a parental responsibility agreement.

What from one perspective appears to be the court encouraging the father to play his role in the child's life might appear to the mother to be a licence to the man who may have abused her child to interfere in every aspect of the child's life. The real difficulty here is that perhaps the notion of parental responsibility is not sufficiently fine-tuned. Returning to *Re S (A Minor) (Parental Responsibility)*,[342] discussed above, to give a father who had a conviction for possession of paedophilic literature the right to clothe, feed and bathe a child might seem inappropriate, even if there is an argument that he should have a say in fundamental issues, such as where the child should be educated. Subsequent cases have been more open to the argument that a parent might get parental responsibility but limit the kind of rights this gives them, as in **Re B (A Child) (No. 2) (Welfare: Child Arrangement Order)**[343] where the applicant was given parental responsibility but not given access to medical or educational records of the child.

(iii) Non-parents

It is sensible that if a non-parent is given an order that the child live with them, parental responsibility will also be granted because this will reflect the fact that he or she will be carrying out the parental roles. At present only parents or those with residence orders can be granted parental responsibility. There is an argument that the court should have a wider power to make parental responsibility orders. A good example of the problems of the present

[337] [1999] 2 FLR 737.
[338] [2017] EWHC 3250 (Fam).
[339] Reece (2009b).
[340] [1998] 1 FLR 855.
[341] Ministry of Justice (2020).
[342] [1995] 2 FLR 648.
[343] [2017] EWHC 488 (Fam).

law is *Re A (A Child) (Joint Residence: Parental Responsibility)*[344] where a child was raised by a man (A) and a woman. A believed himself to be a father and played a full role in raising the child. However, it was found after the child's second birthday that in fact A was not the father. The Court of Appeal approved the making of a shared residence order in order to recognise the role that he played as the child's social and psychological parent and to ensure he had parental responsibility. The making of the joint residence order was the only way of granting him parental responsibility. The order was made even though in reality the child was to live with the mother, and A was to have regular contact with the child.

(iv) Local authorities

This will be discussed in Chapter 11.

12 Who should get parental responsibility?

A Unmarried fathers

Learning objective 7

Debate who should get parental responsibility

As we have explained, unmarried fathers[345] in English law do not obtain parental responsibility automatically. An unmarried father may acquire parental responsibility in three ways. The first is by agreement with the mother and being registered as the father on the birth certificate or registering a parental responsibility agreement with the court. The second is by marrying the child's mother.[346] The third is by persuading the court to make a parental responsibility order. Whether this law is satisfactory is hotly disputed and there is much debate over whether unmarried fathers should get parental responsibility automatically.[347]

The difficulty is that the term 'unmarried father' covers a wide range of relationships. The European Court of Human Rights in *B v UK*[348] has explained the dilemma: 'The relationship between unmarried fathers and their children varies from ignorance and indifference to a close stable relationship indistinguishable from the conventional family-based unit.' As 82 per cent of births to unmarried parents are joint registrations the large majority of unmarried fathers will have parental responsibility.[349] However, fathers who are not on the birth certificate may not realise they may lack parental responsibility. Research by Pickford[350] found that although four-fifths of fathers were aware that they were financially liable to support their children, only one-quarter of all fathers were aware that there was a difference in the legal rights of married and unmarried fathers. Similarly, Elmalik and Wheeler[351] found that more than 80 per cent of couples incorrectly believed a father cohabiting with his child had parental responsibility, even if unmarried. Indeed, they found doctors' ignorance of law led them to operate on

---

[344] [2008] 3 FCR 107. See also *Re H (Shared Residence: Parental Responsibility)* [1996] 3 FCR 321; and *Re WB (Residence Order)* [1995] 2 FLR 1023, discussed in Wallbank (2007).

[345] The widely used term unmarried father is not ideal; he may well be married – to someone other than the mother.

[346] Only the father of a child obtains parental responsibility of the child by marrying the mother. A step-parent does not thereby acquire parental responsibility.

[347] Sheldon (2001b); Bainham (1989).

[348] [2000] 1 FLR 1 at p. 5.

[349] National Statistics (2005: table 3.2).

[350] Pickford (1999).

[351] Elmalik and Wheeler (2007).

children on the basis of consent from an unmarried father and thereby, technically, acting without lawful authorisation. So, ignorance of the law is not just found among the parents, but those professionals dealing with them.

Very broadly, five approaches could be taken to unmarried fathers and parental responsibility:

1. All unmarried fathers could be given parental responsibility automatically.
2. All unmarried fathers could be given parental responsibility, but this could be removed on application to the court.[352]
3. A group of unmarried fathers could be given parental responsibility. There could be removal or addition to this group on application to the court.
4. No unmarried fathers could be automatically given parental responsibility, but a procedure could exist whereby they could acquire parental responsibility (or to remove parental responsibility). This is the position in England and Wales at present.
5. No unmarried father is given parental responsibility.

The essential question is, where should the burden lie? Should it be on the mother or the state to establish that the father is unsuitable, or on the father to show that he is suitable? At the heart of this issue is what parental responsibility means. The stronger the 'rights' that parental responsibility provides, the more reluctant the law will be in granting it to a wide group of people. However, the more limited the rights, the more willing a legal system may be to grant all fathers parental responsibility. The meaning of parental responsibility is discussed later in the text (Chapter 9). There is also a dispute over the role of the law here. On the one hand, there are those who emphasise the 'message' that the law gives. They often argue that fathers should be encouraged and expected to fulfil their role as parents and this should be emphasised by giving as many unmarried fathers as possible parental responsibility. Others emphasise the practical effect of giving unmarried fathers parental responsibility and are concerned by the fact that parental responsibility could be misused.

Some of the key issues that have been raised in the debate are as follows:

DEBATE

Should all fathers automatically get parental responsibility?

1. *The balance of power between mothers and fathers.* The case for awarding parental responsibility to only a selection of unmarried fathers runs as follows. Why does the father need parental responsibility? He can carry out all the duties and joys of parenthood (feeding, clothing, playing with the child) without parental responsibility. He only needs parental responsibility when he is dealing with third parties such as doctors and schools. At such times the mother can provide the necessary consent. He would only need parental responsibility if he were wishing to exercise it in a way contrary to the mother's wishes.[353] An unmarried father who has been fully involved in the raising of the child might be thought validly to have an important say in the raising of children. But an unmarried father who had

---

[352] Parental responsibility for mothers cannot be revoked, except when following the making of an adoption order or a parental order.
[353] Eekelaar (1996).

limited or no contact with the child should surely not be able to override the mother's wishes. Ruth Deech has argued that parental responsibilities:

> . . . include feeding, washing and clothing the child, putting her to bed, housing her, educating and stimulating her, taking responsibility for arranging babysitting and day-care, keeping the child in touch with the wider family circle, checking her medical condition, arranging schooling and transport to school, holidays and recreation, encouraging social and possibly religious or moral development. Fatherhood that does not encompass a fair share of these tasks is an empty and egotistical concept and has the consequence that the man does not know the child sufficiently well to be able sensibly to take decisions about education, religion, discipline, medical treatment, change of abode, adoption, marriage and property.[354]

Julie Wallbank[355] has argued that because women assume the primary responsibility for the child their views should be given priority in decisions about whether the father should acquire parental responsibility. She suggests that those who support giving all fathers parental responsibility rely on the 'ethic of justice' (which emphasises the importance of formal equality and general rules), rather than 'the ethic of care' (which emphasises the importance of responsibilities and relationships).[356] She supports privileging the position of mothers who undertake the bulk of the day-to-day work with the child.[357] Opponents of such views will claim that it is wrong to presume that unmarried fathers do not take part in the 'work' of parenting or do not have relationships with their children that are of equal worth to those that mothers have.

2. *Fears of misuse.* There is a concern that the non-residential father may misuse parental responsibility. He may see it as a justification for 'snooping' on the mother and continuing to exercise power over her, although it may be said that if a man is of the kind who will pester the mother with legal actions and 'snooping' to check she is being a good mother, he will do so whether or not he has parental responsibility.

3. *Parental responsibility should reflect the social reality.* The argument here is that if a father is carrying out a parental role, he should receive parental responsibility. This would mean that the legal position of the father and his social position would match. The parental responsibility could then be seen as the law's stamp of approval for the task he is carrying out.[358]

4. *Rights of the child.* The issue could be examined from the perspective of the rights of the child. It could be argued that a child has a right to have the responsibilities of parenthood imposed on both his or her mother and father. Deech strongly opposes such an argument: 'The basic rights of the child are not furthered by delivering more choice to the unmarried father. Legal rights which he may acquire are choices for him; that is, he may or may not choose to exercise them. Such choice is a limitation on the rights of the child.'[359]

---

[354] Deech (1993: 30).

[355] Wallbank (2002a).

[356] See further Smart and Neale (1999b).

[357] Sheldon (2001b: 105) argues there is not yet sufficient evidence to demonstrate that unmarried fathers undertake sufficient childcare to be in a position to make important decisions for children. There is sufficient evidence in relation to mothers to make this assumption.

[358] Eekelaar (1996).

[359] Deech (1993: 30).

5. *The rights of the father.* Some claim that the English law, in failing to provide an unmarried father with parental responsibility, breaches the Human Rights Act 1998.[360] There are ways that such a claim may be made:

    (a) *Discrimination on the grounds of sex.* Article 14 states: 'The enjoyment of the rights and freedoms set forth in this convention shall be decreed without discrimination on any ground such as sex, race, colour, language, religion, political or other opinion, natural or social origin in association with a natural minority, property, birth or other status.' It might be argued that, by giving mothers but not fathers automatic parental responsibility, this is discrimination on the ground of sex. However, this was rejected in *McMichael v UK*[361] and *B v UK*.[362] This, it is argued, is correct because of the greatly differing roles that men and women play during pregnancy.

    (b) *Discrimination on the grounds of marital status.* Again, referring to Article 14, it could be said that the list of prohibited grounds of discrimination is not closed (the article says 'such as', indicating that there could be other grounds apart from the ones mentioned in the article). It could be argued, therefore, that marital status could be added as another prohibited ground and that denying automatic parental responsibility to unmarried fathers is therefore prohibited. *B v UK*[363] and *Sporer v Austria*[364] have accepted that it is permissible under the European Convention on Human Rights for a state to treat married and unmarried couples in different ways, if a sound reason for doing so exists.[365] It was suggested that, given the wide varieties of unmarried fathers, it was legitimate for the state to restrict which could receive parental responsibility.[366]

    (c) *Breach of right to respect for family life.* Article 8 of the European Convention on Human Rights states that: 'Everyone has the right to respect for his private and family life, his home and his correspondence.' This article certainly protects unmarried fathers[367] but this does not require automatic legal status. The approach taken by the European Court seems to be that, as long as there is a route available by which a father can establish that he should be given parental responsibility, there is no breach of the Convention.

6. *Wrong to impose responsibilities but no rights.* An unmarried father is liable to pay child support under the Child Support Act 1991 but is not automatically awarded parental responsibility. Is it fair that he should suffer the burdens but not gain the benefits that flow from parental responsibility? Deech has argued the opposite: if the father is not willing to show the commitment to the mother and the child by marriage, he should not receive parental responsibility, but should bear financial responsibility.[368] Indeed, it could be argued that although it always promotes a child's welfare to have both parents under a duty to support him or her financially, it is not true that it is necessarily in a child's interests to have both

---

[360] Booth (2004: 355).

[361] (1995) 20 EHRR 205.

[362] [2000] 1 FLR 1, [2000] 1 FCR 289.

[363] [2000] 1 FLR 1, [2000] 1 FCR 289.

[364] App. No. 35637/03, ECHR

[365] Hofferth and Anderson (2003) argue that the sociological data (at least from the US) indicates that a marriage to the mother is a better indication of parental commitment than a genetic tie.

[366] Although in *Sporer v Austria* (App. No. 35637/03) because an unmarried father could not put himself in the position of a married father there was discrimination.

[367] E.g. *Johnston v Ireland* (1986) 9 EHRR 203.

[368] Deech (1993).

parents having the power to make decisions over his or her upbringing. This is true especially if a parent with that power does not know the child.

7. *The rapist father.* The argument that carried much weight in the parliamentary discussion of the issue was that a man who fathered a child through rape should not obtain parental responsibility. To require a victim of rape to persuade a court that the rapist father should have his parental responsibility removed was clearly inappropriate and it was therefore better not to give the unmarried father automatic parental responsibility.[369] This argument is perhaps not as strong as might at first sight appear. It would be possible to have a specific statutory provision excluding convicted rapists[370] (although this would deal only with those rapists who were convicted). In any event there is a danger in relying on a rare situation to establish a general rule.

8. *Uncertainty.* This is one of the strongest arguments in favour of the present law. One benefit of the present law is that it is relatively easy to know whether a man has parental responsibility for a child. He will need to produce his certificate of marriage with the mother, the child's birth certificate, a parental responsibility order or copy of a parental responsibility agreement. If the law were to state that all unmarried fathers automatically obtained parental responsibility then, unless biological tests were done, it would be impossible to know whether a man claiming to have parental responsibility was or was not the father of the child. As the most common situation where it really matters whether a man has parental responsibility or not is when a child needs medical treatment, it is important that doctors can readily discover whether a father has parental responsibility. Bainham's response to such a point is to suggest that from birth a father should be recognised as having 'inchoate' rights which are 'perfected and converted into recognisable' legal rights when paternity is established in the legal process.[371] If this suggests that a father's rights will be enforceable only when his paternity is recognised in law, then few unmarried fathers will be able to rely on these rights because few of them will have their paternity established at law, except those named on the birth certificate, who have parental responsibility under the current law.

9. *Efficiency and public resources.* The present law seems to suggest that it is not at all difficult for an unmarried father to obtain parental responsibility (although it does involve expense and time) and, if so, it may be asked whether there is any point in having these administrative hoops, with the public costs they involve.[372] On the other hand, it may be that increasing the number of people with parental responsibility will merely increase the scope for bringing disputes to court.

10. *Marriage promotion.* It might be argued that the distinction between married and unmarried fathers is important as part of the promotion of marriage. The belief of the majority of people that marriage does not affect parental rights undermines this argument to a large extent.[373]

---

[369] The argument overlooks the fact that a husband who rapes his wife gets parental responsibility under the law.
[370] Bainham (1989: 231).
[371] Bainham (2006b: 163).
[372] In terms of judicial resources and legal aid.
[373] Pickford (1999).

Questions

1. Which is worse: that a deserving father is not given parental responsibility or that an unde-serving father is given parental responsibility?

2. Are there good reasons for treating mothers and fathers differently in the allocation of paren-tal responsibility?

3. Is the concept of parental responsibility trying to do too many things?

Further reading

Read **Gilmore** (2003) for a discussion of the arguments around the allocation of parental responsibility. Consider the arguments in **Masson** (2006c) over whether parental responsibility should be about a blood tie or caring.

The arguments over who should get parental responsibility are well balanced.[374] The diffi-culty is that the cases where parental responsibility matters the least (where the mother and father are jointly raising the child together) are the cases where there are the strongest argu-ments for awarding both parents parental responsibility, and the cases where parental respon-sibility matters the most (the parents have separated and are in dispute over the raising of the child) are the cases where there is the strongest case for putting special weight on the wishes of the parent who carries out the bulk of the day-to-day caring for the child. The truth is that the law is requiring too much of responsibility. A single concept cannot do the job of an acknowledgement of a parent's commitment; be a stamp of approval for their parenting role; provide a parent with all the rights and responsibilities of parenthood; and decide who can make important decisions in relation to children. At a risk of further complicating the law, it is suggested that the law should develop two categories of parental responsibility: that which acknowledges that the father has shown commitment to the child and that which reflects the reality that he is sharing in the day-to-day upbringing of the child.

13 Losing parental responsibility

A person with parental responsibility cannot give up parental responsibility just because he or she does not want it any more. Even if the child has to be taken into care because of the parent's abuse, parental responsibility does not come to an end.[375] In *Re M (A Minor) (Care Order: Threshold Conditions)*[376] the father had killed the mother in front of the children and was sentenced to a lengthy term of imprisonment. He still retained parental responsibility. How-ever, parental responsibility can be extinguished in a few ways:

1. Anyone with parental responsibility will lose it when an adoption order is made. Once an adoption order is made, only the adoptive parents will have parental responsibility.

---

[374] Although most of the academic writing supports a change in the law to permit all fathers to acquire parental responsibility automatically (see Gilmore (2003a); Clifton (2014)).

[375] See Chapter 11.

[376] [1994] 2 FLR 577, [1994] 2 FCR 871.

2. A child's birth mother and her husband will lose parental responsibility when a parental order under s. 30 of the Human Fertilisation and Embryology Act 1990 is made.[377]

3. Once a child reaches 18, all parental responsibility for the child comes to an end.[378] In *Re D (Parental Responsibility: Consent to 16-Year-old Child's Deprivation of Liberty)*[379] the Court of Appeal held that 'the exercise of parental responsibility comes to an end not on the attaining of some fixed age but on attaining "*Gillick* capacity"'.[380]

4. If a father has parental responsibility through a parental responsibility order or birth registration, this can be brought to an end if the court so orders under s. 4(2A) of the Children Act 1989.[381] However, the court may not end a parental responsibility order if there is a residence order still in force in favour of the father. Nor is it possible to end parental responsibility of a father who has acquired it by marriage.[382] An application to do so can be brought by someone with parental responsibility (including the father applying himself) or the child.[383] The welfare principle governs the issue.[384] In *Re P (Terminating Parental Responsibility)*,[385] although the parents had made a parental responsibility agreement under s. 4, it became clear that the father had caused the baby severe injuries, causing permanent disability. It was held that by his conduct he had forfeited his entitlement to parental responsibility and it was removed.[386] Similarly, in *C v D*[387] a father derided his son's autism, rejected him, and sought to use his parental responsibility to interfere in his son's care. It was held his parental responsibility should be terminated. It will require extreme conduct of this kind if the court is to remove parental responsibility under s. 4(3).[388]

CASE: *Re D (Withdrawal of Parental Responsibility)* [2014] EWCA Civ 315

The father was convicted of sexual offences against the mother's two daughters when child D was five years old. He was sentenced to four years in prison. On his release the mother sought to have his parental responsibility terminated. The Court of Appeal confirmed that the child's welfare was the paramount consideration on such an application. The judge's decision to remove parental responsibility was upheld. The father had inflicted devastating emotional harm on the whole family, including child D. He continued to deny what he had done and was not in a position to exercise his rights and duties in a responsible way. Any interference in the father's human rights was justified by the welfare of the child.

---

[377] See above, 'Parental orders'.

[378] CA 1989, s. 91(7), (8).

[379] [2017] EWCA Civ 1695.

[380] See Chapter 9 for a definition and discussion of 'Gillick-competence': *Gillick v W Norfolk and Wisbech AHA* [1986] 1 FLR 229, [1986] AC 112.

[381] Another option is to limit the extent to which a parent can exercise parental responsibility: *H v A (No. 1)* [2015] EWFC 58.

[382] *Re B and C (Change of Names: Parental Responsibility: Evidence)* [2017] EWHC 3250 (Fam).

[383] With leave of the court (see Chapter 10).

[384] *Re D (Withdrawal of Parental Responsibility)* [2014] EWCA Civ 315.

[385] [1995] 1 FLR 1048, [1995] 3 FCR 753.

[386] For another example, see *Re D (Withdrawal of Parental Responsibility)* [2014] EWCA Civ 315.

[387] [2018] EWHC 3312 (Fam).

[388] *Re A (Termination of Parental Responsibility)* [2013] EWHC 2963 (Fam); *PM v CF (Section 91(14) Order: Risk to Mother and Children)* [2018] EWHC 2658 (Fam).

That decision has been criticised by Stephen Gilmore[389] in part because he believes it overlooked earlier authority but also because it does not appreciate the draconian nature of the order. As he notes, even a care order which requires proof that the child is suffering significant harm as a result of the parent's actions does not end parental responsibility. However, a care order is typically about removing a child from a parent with whom they are living and is a major interference in a parent's right to family life. Here the father was having little to do with his daughter and so the removal of parental responsibility was of little practical significance to him. With that in mind the straightforward welfare test seems appropriate.

5. If a person has parental responsibility by virtue of being granted a residence order, then when the residence order comes to an end so does the connected parental responsibility. However, a father who has been awarded a residence order (and therefore parental responsibility) will retain parental responsibility even if the residence order is ended.

6. Wardship and the inherent jurisdiction can be used to greatly restrict the effect of parental responsibility. In *T v S (Wardship)*[390] the couple disagreed vehemently on just about every issue concerning the child. The child was made a ward of court so that the court could determine disputed issues. While not terminating parental responsibility, in effect, it was the court, rather than the parents, who determined issues around the child's upbringing.

7. Parental responsibility will, of course, end on the death of the child, although there may be separate rights in respect of burial of the child's body.[391]

In cases where parental responsibility cannot be terminated, the court may still restrict parental responsibility. In *Re B and C (Change of Names: Parental Responsibility: Evidence)*[392] a father was seen to pose a serious threat to the children and so the court approved them being given new identities and the father was prohibited from exercising any aspect of his parental responsibility. Cobb J emphasised that such a course of action was rare.

14 Wider issues over parenthood

Having looked through the law regulating parents, we can now look at some of the key issues of debate in this area.

A What is the basis for granting parenthood?

There has been much discussion on what is at the heart of the concept of parenthood. Four main views will be considered: first, that genetic parenthood is the core idea in the law; secondly, that the law focuses on intent to be a parent; thirdly, that parenthood is earned by commitment to and care of the child; and fourthly, that social parenthood (the day-to-day caring of the child) is the most important part of parenthood. Before considering the

---

[389] Gilmore (2015).
[390] [2011] EWHC 1608 (Fam).
[391] *R v Gwynedd, ex p B* [1992] 3 All ER 317.
[392] [2017] EWHC 3250 (Fam).

arguments in favour of these approaches, it should be noted that they are not necessarily incompatible. All four could be persuasive. Therese Callus[393] suggests that the genetic link plus the intent to produce a child should be used to allocate parenthood. Further, as Bainham has argued,[394] by using a variety of understandings of 'parent' the law can recognise different aspects of parenthood. For example, it is then possible for the law to acknowledge that both genetic parent *and* social parent have a role to play in a child's life. Putting it another way, it may be that the law is expecting too much of the single term 'parent'.[395]

(i) Genetic parentage

It could be claimed that the core notion of parenthood is genetic parenthood. It is clear that there is not an exact correlation between genetic parentage and legal parenthood. The circumstances where a man who is not biologically the father of the child can still be recognised as the father were discussed above. The circumstances where the legal father will not be the genetic father are as follows:

1. A husband may be presumed to be the father of his wife's child, but in fact not be the genetic father. If the genetic father does not seek to challenge the presumption, the husband will be treated as the father.

2. In cases of AID treatment where either the husband is the father under s. 28(2), or the partner is the father under s. 28(3) of the Human Fertilisation and Embryology Act 1990, the child's father will not be the genetic father.

3. An adopted father will be a father in the eyes of the law, even if he is not the genetic father.

4. Where a father has the benefit of a parental order, he will be the legal father but may not be the genetic father.

However, these circumstances are all rare. The vast majority of genetic parents are parents in law, although not all genetic fathers are awarded parental responsibility, as we have seen. That said, if genetic parentage is at the heart of legal parenthood, it is surprising that the law does not take stronger steps to determine genetic parenthood. It would be possible for our legal system to require genetic testing of every child born to ensure that paternity is known, but it does not.[396] Instead, we are happy to rely on the presumptions of law. One journalist[397] has suggested that 30 per cent of husbands are unaware that they are not the father of their wife's children. If this figure is anything like accurate, then it must bring into question whether genetic parentage is in reality of significance for parenthood, because these husbands will be presumed to be the father in the law's eyes without being genetically the father. Further, there are claims which emphasise that genetic parentage can be unfair in cases of 'sperm bandits' (where men claimed that women obtained their sperm either by lying about whether they were using contraception or when the men were asleep or unconscious).[398] Another example was the following case:

---

[393] Callus (2012).
[394] Bainham (1999).
[395] Callus (2012).
[396] Eekelaar (2006b: 75) argues that to do so would be too great an intrusion into a private area of life.
[397] Illman (1996).
[398] Sheldon (2001a).

> ### KEY CASE: *ARB* v *IVF Hammersmith* [2018] EWCA Civ 2803
>
> ARB and his partner stored embryos during fertility treatment. The couple separated. She then forged his signature on a form consenting to the thawing and use of the embryos. A child was born and ARB claimed a breach of contract. He sought damages for the cost of raising the child.
>
> His claim failed. The arguments in *Rees* v *Darlington*[399] dealing with similar claims in the law of tort following a negligently performed sterilisation applied here. It was contrary to public policy to receive damages for expenses connected to the birth of a healthy child.

Similarly, the court in *FRB* v *DCA*[400] was not sympathetic to a husband whose wife lied to him about being the father of her child. He sued in the tort of deceit for the money he had spent on the child. The claim failed. It was impossible to weigh up the pleasure of the relationship he gained from being with the child.

But why should genetic links be regarded as important at all? There are two main arguments that have been relied upon in favour of biology:

1. *Genetic identity.* It is argued that our genetic parents play a crucial role in our self-identity. The strongest evidence for this is in relation to adopted children, who often seek to find information about their genetic parents. To recognise genetic parenthood acknowledges the importance to the child of the genetic link. It also recognises the importance many parents place on the genetic link to their children. This argument may, however, merge the questions of knowing your genetic origins and the allocation of parenthood. The law could give a child the right to know their genetic origins, without giving parenthood to the biological father.

2. *Genetic contribution.* Some argue that the genetic link is important because the child has been born out of the genetic contribution of the parents. As the child's being results from the contribution of the two genetic parents, that contribution must be recognised. Parenthood should not be based on a whim or current emotion, but on the permanence of the genetic link.[401]

Baroness Hale in *Re G (Children) (Residence: Same-Sex Partner)*[402] explained the significance of genetic parentage in this way:

> For the parent, perhaps particularly for a father, the knowledge that this is 'his' child can bring a very special sense of love for and commitment to that child which will be of great benefit to the child (see, for example, the psychiatric evidence in *Re C (MA) (An Infant)* [1966] 1 WLR 646). For the child, he reaps the benefit not only of that love and commitment, but also of knowing his own origins and lineage, which is an important component in finding an individual sense of self as one grows up. The knowledge of that genetic link may also be an important (although certainly not an essential) component in the love and commitment felt by the wider family, perhaps especially grandparents, from which the child has so much to gain.

---

[399] [2003] UKHL 52.
[400] [2019] EWHC 2816 (Fam).
[401] Callus (2012).
[402] [2006] 1WLR 2305. See L. Smith (2007) for further discussion.

Some writers have argued that it is deeply embedded in nature that a child should be raised by his or her biological parents. Margaret Somerville argues:

> ... that the most fundamental human right of all is a child's right to be born from natural human biological origins ... Children also have a right to be reared within their biological families and to have a mother and a father, unless an exception can be justified as being in the 'best interests' of a particular child.[403]

However, evidence suggests that children who live with their non-biological parents (e.g. adopted children) or same-sex parents do not suffer any hardship and, if anything, do slightly better than other children.

(ii) Intent

Some have argued that the law should now place less emphasis on genetic parentage and that, instead, intent to be a parent is of far more importance.[404] A parent is a parent only if he or she intends to be a parent. Or as Katharine Baker[405] prefers, a man is the father if he has struck a bargain to take on that role with the gestational mother. There is no doubt that there are some situations where intent to be a parent can be seen as crucial:

1. In assisted reproduction a man jointly receiving treatment with a woman can be treated as the father, even though he has no genetic link. Here his intention to be a parent is respected.

2. A sperm donor can waive his parental status. Here the law respects an intention not to be a parent.

3. Guardianship seems based on intention, but in a negative way in that, unless the guardian expressly disclaims the guardianship, they will be a guardian.[406]

4. Adoption is intent based. An adoption order is made only after a person volunteers to be an adoptive parent.

As Kirsty Horsey[407] puts it:

> ... because the intended parents initiate, plan and prepare for the birth of the child, they should be legally recognised as the parents of that child that, but for them, would not exist. It is they who choose to use assisted conception, thus choosing whether to use a donor of genetic material or a surrogate. They are the 'first cause' of the child and as such are of prima facie importance in the procreational relationship.

However, there are problems in emphasising intent when considering the most common origin of parenthood, where normal sexual intercourse is involved. It could be argued that to have sexual intercourse reveals an intent to be a parent.[408] At first this seems an implausible argument, given the rate of unintended pregnancies. However, it is possible to argue that, given the availability of contraception and abortion, where the couple decide to go ahead with a pregnancy they manifest their intent to be parents. But there are difficulties with this. First, a father will have a limited role in law in the decision whether or not the

---

[403] Somerville (2010).
[404] Vonk (2007).
[405] Baker (2004).
[406] It does reflect the intention of the parent of who should carry on the parenting role.
[407] Horsey (2010).
[408] Callus (2012). She argues that even where contraception is used you can at least detect an assumption of the risk of becoming a parent.

mother has an abortion.[409] Secondly, the decision not to abort may be due to religious or moral beliefs and not necessarily indicate an intention to become a parent. It could be argued that each time a couple engage in sexual intercourse they willingly accept the risk of becoming parents, and this is sufficient intent to be a parent. However, where contraception is used but fails, such a presumption would appear to fly in the face of the facts.

Further, it seems a very odd test for parenthood. If Y notices that a neighbour is pregnant and would like to act as a father of the child, Y cannot claim he has an intent to be the child's parent, which should be recognised by law. There is also a concern that such an approach would lead to uncertainty. For example, how does one prove one's intent? What exactly is an intent to be a parent? There are also fears that, under the guise of using intent to be a parent, different policies could be used. Could it be said, for example, that a drug addict could have no intent to be a parent because he or she would not be capable of being an effective parent?[410] There are also concerns that focusing on intent might lead to the burdens of parenthood falling on more women than men because it is more likely that a man than a woman will successfully be able to argue that he did not intend to be a parent.[411]

There might, however, be an argument that the intent to be a parent is useful where there are competing claims based on biology. For example, in **Johnson v Calvert**,[412] a Californian case, the mother gave birth following a surrogacy arrangement, the commissioning mother having provided the egg. Here both could be said to be the biological parent (the commissioning mother by providing the egg, the gestational mother through the care provided during the pregnancy). The court said that intent could be used to resolve the dispute. The court argued that 'but for' the intent of the commissioning parents, the child would not have been born and so they should therefore be regarded as the parents. It was held by Panelli J that it was the commissioning mother 'who intended to procreate the child – that is, she who intended to bring about the birth of a child that she intended to raise as her own – is the natural mother under Californian law'. The argument is not straightforward, as it could equally be suggested that if the gestational mother had not been involved, the child would not have been born. A similar claim could be made for the medical team involved in the assisted reproduction.[413]

It is certainly true that intent-based parenthood would help avoid gender stereotypes or overemphasis of traditional family structures. Recognising intent rather than the stereotypical male and female roles would acknowledge a variety of parenting forms. It would permit more than two people to be parents of a child, and parents would not need to be of the opposite sex. This could be seen as a great benefit of the approach or a great disadvantage, depending on one's view on the traditional family form.[414]

(iii) Earned parenthood

It can be argued that parenthood must be earned: the mother, through pregnancy, has demonstrated her commitment to the child and has formed a bond with the child. If the father has married the mother and, therefore, can be presumed to have offered the mother support

---

[409] A father cannot stop a mother having an abortion: C v S [1987] 2 FLR 505 CA. For a critique of such arguments see Sheldon (2003).

[410] Douglas (1991: ch 9).

[411] See the interesting discussion in Sheldon (2001a).

[412] [1993] 851 P 2d 774.

[413] See Probert (2004a) who suggests a definition of parent based on who was the legal cause of the child coming into existence.

[414] See Chapter 1.

through the pregnancy, this also indicates a commitment to the child. But the unmarried father has not earned the parenthood, as he has not shown the commitment to the mother and child by marrying the mother.

(iv) Social parenthood

At the start of this section it was noted that psychologists have stressed the importance of psychological parents. This has led some to argue that the law should recognise the day-to-day work of parenting, rather than the more abstract notions of intended parenthood or genetic parenthood.[415] As noted earlier, psychological evidence suggests that, for children, it is the person who provides their constant care and with whom they have an emotional relationship who is most important. The emphasis on social parenthood would also appeal to those who would argue that the law should emphasise and value caring interdependent relationships between parties.[416] I have argued:

> Parental status should be earned by the care and dedication to the child, something not shown simply by a biological link. It is the changing of the nappy; the wiping of the tear; and the working out of maths together that makes a parent, not the provision of an egg or sperm.[417]

Such an approach may recognise that a range of adults have the authority to make decisions over a child's life.

(v) Child welfare

James Dwyer[418] claims that the welfare of the child should be key to the allocation of parent.[419] We should not, therefore, 'thrust a parent–child relationship on a child where the adult is presumptively unfit to parent'.[420] This leads him controversially to suggest that where a biological parent is too young;[421] has committed serious crimes; has an IQ less than 70;[422] or is drug dependent, she or he should not be treated as a parent, unless they can show they are competent. He complains that the current law pays inadequate attention to the character or capacity of those it creates as parents.[423] Critics may reply that this is entering dangerous territory. Once we start trying to predict who may be a good or bad parent, we are slipping into 'social engineering'. It is simply impossible to predict who will or will not be a good parent.

B Is there a right to know one's genetic parentage?

(i) What could such a right entail?

The question: 'Does a child have a right to know genetic parentage?' is often asked, but is ambiguous. It is necessary to be quite clear about what such a right would entail. The following could be included:

---

[415] Herring (2013a).
[416] Herring (2013a).
[417] Herring (2013a).
[418] Dwyer (2006).
[419] See Masson (2006c) who also suggests that the welfare of children should determine the allocation of parenthood, but with very different results from Dwyer.
[420] Dwyer (2006: 35).
[421] He suggests under the age of 18.
[422] Dwyer (2006: 260).
[423] Dwyer (2006: 255).

- a right to know some non-identifying information about genetic parents;
- a right to be told the names of genetic parents;
- a right to meet one's genetic parents.

These rights might arise from as early an age as possible, or only once the child has reached the age of majority. It should be borne in mind that children have a right *not* to know their genetic parentage.[424] This was recently recognised in *MS v RS and BT (Paternity)*[425] where McFarlane P emphasised that children had a right to decide if and when they were told about paternity and explicitly recognised that children had a right not to know their genetic origins. In *AB v CD*[426] a distinction was drawn between being told that a presumed father was not a father and being told who was the 'real' father. In that case a wife disclosed to the husband (AB) some years after the child's birth[427] that the child was in fact another man's (X's). It was decided that although the child should be told AB was not his father, he should only be told of X's identity when he wanted to be told.[428]

Even if we recognise the child's rights, it is necessary to appreciate that as well as these rights there are rights of parents that might also be relevant. There may be a right for a genetic parent to be acknowledged as the parent of a child. There may also be said to be a right of privacy: the right *not* to be acknowledged as the parent. There may also be rights of the social parent – that unwanted revelation of genetic parentage may amount to interference with their family life. Some countries in Europe offer a mother the opportunity to renounce her status of motherhood: the state will arrange alternative carers for the child and there will be no link between the mother and child.[429] Such laws are said to encourage women not to abandon their babies or to abort unwanted children. There are no equivalent laws in England and Wales.[430]

(ii) Does the law recognise the right to know one's genetic parentage?

In *Re A (Paternity: DNA Testing: Appeal)*[431] Black LJ, obiter, referred to the fact that 'The importance of and the right of children to know the identity of their biological father has long been recognised.' However, it is clear that the law does not recognise this right as a general one. We do not test every child at birth to determine genetic parentage. That said, with the Child Support Act 1991 and the expense that can fall on a non-residential father, it is likely that more fathers will seek to deny parentage and require tests which will establish the genetic truth. There are certain specific circumstances where the right to know one's genetic parentage arises.

(a) Children born as a result of sexual intercourse

A child can discover from his or her birth certificate who are registered as his or her parents. Once a child is 18, he or she can obtain a copy of the birth certificate, although the name of the father might have been left blank on the certificate. Even if it was filled in, there is no guarantee that the named man is the true father. A child might also discover his or her genetic

---

[424] Herring and Foster (2011).
[425] [2020] EWFC 30.
[426] [2019[EWHC a (Fam).
[427] The judgment does not disclose the age of the child.
[428] [2019] EWHC 2244 (Fam).
[429] See the discussion in O'Donovan (2000).
[430] Although a mother can shortly after birth place her child with the local authority and ask for an adoption to be arranged.
[431] [2015] EWCA Civ 133.

parenthood if his or her mother is assessed by the Child Support Agency. However, the child has no right to be told who his or her father is by the Child Support Agency[432] and after the Child Maintenance and Other Payments Act 2008 there is no obligation on a mother receiving benefits to name a father.

An adult may seek to rebut one of the presumptions of parentage. However, it is not possible to make a free-standing application for a declaration of parenthood.[433] In other words, a man cannot seek a declaration that he is or is not the father simply out of curiosity. Instead, there must be some other application to which parenthood is relevant; for example, if a man is seeking to have contact with the child or if there is a dispute over whether a man should be financially responsible for a child. Even then the court may decide that the application can be decided without recourse to tests. For example, in *O v L (Blood Tests)*[434] the mother argued that her husband was not the father of the child three years after their separation when the husband sought contact. During the marriage the husband had assumed that he was the father of the child and the court held that, given the close relationship between the husband and the child, contact would be ordered regardless of what the blood tests showed. There was therefore no need to pursue the tests.[435]

When should tests be ordered?

In deciding whether to order tests, the child's welfare is not the paramount consideration. This is because the child's upbringing is not in question and so s. 1 of the Children Act 1989 does not apply. Instead, the test is as set out in *S v S, W v Official Solicitor (or W)*,[436] a decision of the House of Lords: 'the court ought to permit a blood test of a young child to be taken unless satisfied that that would be against the child's interests'.[437] The case law on whether tests should be ordered reveals that the courts are pulled by two countervailing arguments. On the one hand, the courts have placed importance on the child's right to know their genetic origins; on the other hand, the courts have placed weight on the concern that if it is found that the child's father is not the mother's husband or present partner, the child's family unit will be disrupted and this will harm the child. The cases show that it can be hard to predict which argument will carry the day.

The leading case emphasising the importance of the child knowing the truth is the Court of Appeal decision in *Re H (A Minor) (Blood Tests: Parental Rights)*.[438] The mother and her husband cared for three children. It was alleged that the youngest of the children was the result of an affair the mother had had. All three children and the husband had a good relationship. Ward LJ argued that 'every child has a right to know the truth unless his welfare clearly justifies the cover-up'.[439] He claimed that such a right was apparent in Article 7 of the UN Convention on the Rights of the Child: 'The child should be registered immediately after birth and shall have the right from birth to a name, the right to acquire a nationality and, as far as possible, the right to know and to be cared for by his or her parents.'[440]

---

[432] *Re C (A Minor) (Child Support Agency: Disclosure)* [1995] 1 FLR 201.
[433] *Re E (Parental Responsibility: Blood Test)* [1995] 1 FLR 392.
[434] [1995] 2 FLR 930, [1996] 2 FCR 649.
[435] See also *K v M (Paternity: Contact)* [1996] 1 FLR 312, [1996] 3 FCR 517.
[436] [1972] AC 24.
[437] As summarised in *Re F (A Minor) (Blood Test: Parental Rights)* [1993] Fam 314 at p. 318. Tests can be carried out on an adult lacking capacity: *LG v DK* [2011] EWHC 2453 (COP), discussed in Herring (2011c).
[438] [1996] 2 FLR 65, [1996] 3 FCR 201.
[439] *Re H (A Minor) (Blood Tests: Parental Rights)* [1996] 2 FLR 65 at p. 80.
[440] The importance of ascertaining the truth was emphasised by the Court of Appeal in *Re H and A (Children)* [2002] 2 FCR 469, [2002] 1 FLR 1145.

Ward LJ did add that it was important here that the child's relationship with the husband was not likely to be harmed by finding out the truth about his biological paternity and that the child was likely to find out in any event, as the older brothers were aware of the doubt over the child's paternity. It was better to have the issue resolved now than for the child to find out later.[441]

The arguments in favour of ordering tests have been strengthened after the Human Rights Act 1998.[442] In *Mikulic v Croatia*[443] the European Court of Human Rights held that a child had a right to know her biological parenthood as part of her right to respect for private life under Article 8. The state was required to put in place procedures which would protect that right.[444] Notably, the court did not claim that a father has the right to establish his paternity under Article 8.[445] Indeed, in *Yousef v The Netherlands*[446] the European Court held that even though a father had family life with his child it was not in the child's interests to declare formally that he was the father. However, *Yousef* could be criticised on the basis that it failed to consider the child's right to have his paternity declared. In *Ahrens v Germany*[447] the importance of reinforcing the child's life with the mother and her partner justified not ordering tests to establish whether a former boyfriend was the father. This last, most recent, case shows that although the right to establish genetic truth is protected under the ECHR, it can be interfered with if necessary to promote the welfare of the child.

The leading case in favour of not ordering tests is *Re F (A Minor) (Blood Test: Parental Rights)*:[448]

CASE: *RE F (A Minor) (Blood Test: Parental Rights)* [1993] Fam 314

A wife became pregnant at a time when she was having sexual relations with both her husband and another man. After the affair she was reconciled with her husband and they raised the child together. There had been no contact between the alleged father and the child. The lover applied for parental responsibility. It was claimed that the blood tests would not benefit the child. Indeed, there was evidence that the mother's marriage would be harmed and the security of the child's upbringing would be diminished if the blood tests showed the lover to be the father. The Court of Appeal stressed that the welfare of the child depended upon the stability of the family unit, which included the mother's husband. The advantages to the child of the blood tests were, the court thought, minimal, when compared with the benefits of a secure family upbringing.[449]

---

[441] This case has been followed in several other cases: e.g. *Re G (Parentage: Blood Sample)* [1997] 1 FLR 360, [1997] 2 FCR 325.
[442] See Beesson (2007) for a discussion of the ECHR case law.
[443] [2002] 1 FCR 720. See also *Novotný v Czech Republic* (Application No 16314/13).
[444] *Roman v Finland* [2013] 1 FCR 309; *Capin v Turkey* (Application No 44690/09) (where notably the applicant, seeking to establish who his father was, was 45 years old).
[445] *Re T (A Child) (DNA Tests: Paternity)* [2001] 3 FCR 577. But see *Rozanski v Poland* [2006] 2 FCR 178 where a father who had helped raise a child did have a right to be recognised legally as the father.
[446] [2002] 3 FCR 577.
[447] (App. No. 45071/09). See also *Kautzor v Germany* (App. No. 23338/09); *Shofman v Russia* [2002] 3 FCR 577, [2006] 1 FLR 680.
[448] [1993] Fam 314.
[449] A similar attitude was taken in *Re CB (Unmarried Mother) (Blood Test)* [1994] 2 FLR 762, [1994] 2 FCR 925.

In *Re K (Specific Issue Order)*[450] Hyam J stated that the child's right to know the identity of his father could be outweighed by the child's welfare.[451] There the mother had an obsessive hatred of the biological father, and if the child was told about the father's identity the child would suffer due to the mother's emotional turmoil. He therefore refused to require the mother to inform the child who her father was.

The most recent cases have favoured ordering tests: *Re H (A Minor) (Blood Tests: Parental Rights)*;[452] *Re T (A Child) (DNA Tests: Paternity)*;[453] and *Re H and A (Children)*.[454] This suggests that only in cases where there is overwhelming evidence that children will suffer grave harm if tests are ordered are the courts likely to decline to order tests. However, it is clear that the courts still will, on occasion, refuse to order tests:

CASE: J v C [2006] EWHC 2837 (Fam)

A man sought tests to establish paternity and contact in respect of his child in 2004. The hearing was adjourned and there were further delays in the litigation. By the time of the hearing in October 2006 the father had disappeared and it became clear that the child, now aged 10, believed that the mother's current partner was his father. As the man was no longer pursuing the litigation, the court considered whether the court on its own motion should order that the child be told the truth. A psychiatric report before the court advised against this, stating that the mother was vulnerable and to tell the child the truth would have been detrimental to her health. A CAFCASS[455] report also agreed that telling the truth would harm the mother and child. Sumner J started by confirming that a court was entitled to make orders on its own motion, if necessary, to protect the welfare of the child. He emphasised that the mother agreed that the child should be told the truth when he reached 16, but not at the moment. Sumner J held that in this case the harm to the child and his family of knowing the truth outweighed the benefits.

CASE: Re D (Paternity) [2006] EWHC 3545 (Fam), [2007] 2 FLR 26

A man claimed to be the father of a child (D) aged 11. D had been raised by a woman he believed to be his paternal grandmother. D's only stability in his troubled life had been living with this woman. The man (not the person assumed by the boy to be his father) sought blood tests to establish that he was the father and then contact to be ordered. He and D's mother had a relationship at the time D was conceived. D, described by the judge as a troubled and angry person, strongly objected to the applications. Hedley J accepted that there was a serious possibility that the man was the father. He also confirmed that, as established in the earlier case law (e.g. *Re H and A (Children)*[456]), the general approach

---

[450] [1999] 2 FLR 280.
[451] *Re A (Paternity: DNA Testing: Appeal)* [2015] EWCA Civ 133.
[452] [1996] 3 FCR 201.
[453] [2001] 3 FCR 577, [2001] 2 FLR 1190.
[454] [2002] 2 FCR 469, [2002] 1 FLR 1145.
[455] Children and Family Court Advisory and Support Service.
[456] [2002] 2 FCR 469.

was that in a case of disputed paternity the truth should be known and tests performed. He referred to 'the general proposition that truth, at the end of the day, is easier to handle than fiction', and explained that the courts' approach 'is designed to avoid information coming to a young person's attention in a haphazard, unorganised and indeed sometimes malicious context and a court should not depart from that approach unless the best interests of the child compel it so to do'.[457]

However, he held that this principle could be departed from where the best interests of the child compelled the court to decide otherwise. In this case the strong objections of the child played an important role in the decision making. Even though the child may not have been *Gillick* competent,[458] Hedley J found that he understood the issues and had a strong view. At this stage of his life it was best not to press the issue. Interestingly, the court ordered that the man supply samples and these be stored so that if the child later wanted tests to be done, they could be performed quickly.

These two cases demonstrate that there can be circumstances in which the child's welfare will outweigh any 'right to know'.[459] Two particular points of interest are, first, that the courts have seen these cases as a matter of welfare and made no reference to the now extensive jurisprudence of the European Court of Human Rights on rights to know (e.g. *Mikulic v Croatia*).[460] Second, the weight placed on the child's views in *Re D* is notable, especially given that he was found not to be *Gillick* competent. Analysed in terms of rights, it raises the issue of the extent to which a child has the right *not* to know their genetic origins. That is a question yet to receive sufficient judicial or academic attention.[461] It is interesting to note that in *Re A (Paternity: DNA Testing: Appeal)*[462] where the child was seeking to find out their parentage the court seemed very supportive of the right to know. Third, the cases were, in part, driven by a reluctance to force a mother to disclose information she so clearly did not want to disclose. In *Re F (Children) (Paternity: Jurisdiction)*[463] the court showed a more robust approach with a mother being ordered through a specific issue order to inform the children of their father's identity.[464]

Tests and consent

Section 21 of the Family Law Reform Act 1969 states that the court can direct biological tests but not force adults to take blood tests.[465] A child can be tested if the person with 'care and control' of the child consents, or if they do not then the court can order that the tests be carried out if that would not be contrary to the best interests of the child.[466] In *L v P (Paternity Test: Child's Objection)*[467] tests were not ordered against the wishes of a mature and rational child.

---

[457] *Re D (Paternity)* [2006] EWHC 3545 (Fam), [2007] 2 FLR 26 at para 22.

[458] See Chapter 9.

[459] See also *Re L (Identity of Birth Father)* [2009] 1 FLR 1152.

[460] [2002] 1 FCR 720.

[461] See Herring and Foster (2011).

[462] [2015] EWCA Civ 133.

[463] [2008] 1 FCR 382.

[464] In *Re F (Paternity: Registration)* [2011] EWCA Civ 1765 an order that children be told of their paternity within four years of the order was said to be plainly wrong. Four months would have been at the limit of the courts' discretion.

[465] Section 21(1).

[466] Section 21(3)(b), inserted by Child Support, Pensions and Social Security Act 2000. Blood Tests (Evidence of Paternity) (Amendment) Regulations 2001 (SI 2001/773).

[467] [2011] EWHC 3399 (Fam).

In *Re P (Identity of Mother)*[468] the Court of Appeal said that a child aged 15 who refused to be tested should not be tested against her will, even if a parent had consented.

The issue arose in a different context in *Re C (A Child)*.[469] A mother gave birth when she was 13 years old. The father was aged 15. The baby was placed with foster carers at birth with a view for adoption in line with the mother' view. The mother suffered anxiety and self-harm. She had high intelligence and was planning to go to university. She did not want the father to be told; as he lived nearby, she feared he would be violent towards her (he had convictions for assault) and her privacy would be breached. The local authority sought court advice on whether the father should be informed of the birth and the fact he was a father. The court determined the father should not be informed. The impact on the mother of making the disclosure would be profound in social and emotional terms; she had genuine fears about her safety; and there was no realistic option that the father or his family could offer the child a home. The local authority was directed not to tell the father. This was, no doubt, the correct outcome, although it is interesting that the child's right to know their paternity did not feature in the judicial analysis.

Adverse inferences and refusals to be tested

Section 23(1) of the Family Law Reform Act 1969 states that if a person fails to take a biological test then the court will draw inferences.[470] If a man is seeking to show that he is the father of a child but refuses to undergo blood tests, it will be presumed that he is not the father.[471] Similarly, if a man is seeking to show he is not the father but refuses to undergo blood tests, it will be presumed that he is the father.[472] If a mother refuses to allow a child to be tested when a man claims he is the father, it will be presumed that the man is the father. If a mother refuses to consent to the child being tested when her husband claims he is not the father, then it will be presumed that the husband is not the father. In effect, the law is saying that if a person refuses to undergo blood tests, which will establish the truth, then it must be that he or she knows the test will show his or her claim to be false. The position is summarised by Ward LJ in *Re G (Parentage: Blood Sample)*:[473] 'the forensic process is advanced by presenting the truth to the court. He who obstructs the truth will have the inference drawn against him.' The inferences are also a way of encouraging the parties to undergo tests. However, in *MS v RS and BT (Paternity)*[474] McFarlane P expressed considerable reservations about relying on presumptions because they failed to give the child a conclusive determination of the issue and a later test could undermine the court order. In that case both the children (who were teenagers) and the father were refusing to participate in DNA tests. Rather than make a presumption he ordered the father and mother to provide samples and that the children should do so, when they were ready. It seems these orders were not intended to enforce but to pressurise the parties into giving samples.

An adverse inference will not be drawn if there is a reason for refusing a biological test which is fair, just and reasonable,[475] rational, logical and consistent.[476] For example, if it

---

[468] [2011] EWCA Civ 795.
[469] [2020] EWCA 987
[470] *Re A (A Minor) (Paternity: Refusal of Blood Tests)* [1994] 2 FLR 463.
[471] *Re G (Parentage: Blood Sample)* [1997] 1 FLR 360, [1997] 2 FCR 325.
[472] *Re A (A Minor) (Paternity: Refusal of Blood Tests)* [1994] 2 FLR 463.
[473] [1997] 1 FLR 360, [1997] 2 FCR 325.
[474] [2020] EWFC 30.
[475] *Re A (A Minor) (Paternity: Refusal of Blood Tests)* [1994] 2 FLR 463.
[476] *Re G (Parentage: Blood Sample)* [1997] 1 FLR 360, [1997] 2 FCR 325.

was contrary to someone's religious beliefs to give a sample for testing then this might be accepted as a valid reason. These examples may reflect a more general principle that although generally if a man refuses to undergo a DNA test that will be because he believes it will show he is the father, there are some cases where that assumption will not follow. In *Re M and N (Twins: Relinquished Babies: Parentage)*[477] a man accepted he was the father of the twins and was happy to consent to their adoption. However, he refused to undergo DNA tests. The court declined to make a declaration that he was the father. Although the court were not explicit about this, it may be that he was refusing to undergo tests for fear they would show he was not the father and another man's consent might be required. So, on the facts of that case the man's refusal might have been driven by a fear it would be shown he was *not* the father.

(b) Children born as a result of assisted reproduction

Following the Human Fertilisation and Embryology Authority (Disclosure of Donor Informa-tion) Regulations 2004[478] all children born as a result of donated gametes can discover the donor's name; the donor's date of birth and town of birth; the appearance of the donor; and (if provided) a short statement made by the donor. This applies to all children born from donations provided after 1 April 2005. Before that date a child could discover only certain information necessary for medical purposes and whether they were related to a person they wished to marry.[479] The change in the law was promoted as an important part of ensuring that a child has a right to know their genetic origins.[480] The Human Fertilisation and Embryology Act 2008 requires the Human Fertilisation and Embryology Authority to keep a register of gamete donors. Once an individual has reached the age of 16, he or she can request informa-tion about those whose gametes were used to produce them, subject to regulations which will be produced later. This can include information about genetic siblings. A gamete donor can also find out limited information about the number and sex of children born using their gametes. Interestingly, the debate tends to surround sperm donors; there seems to be little consideration of egg donors.[481]

However, all those sources of information presume that a child knows that he or she has been born as the result of assisted reproductive technology. There is no requirement that a child's birth certificate indicate that a child was born as a result of donated sperm or eggs and there is no legal obligation on parents to tell their children of the circumstances of their con-ception.[482] There is evidence that over 70 per cent of parents who use reproductive techniques do not tell children of their genetic origins,[483] although the Human Fertilisation and Embry-ology Authority encourages parents to tell their children.[484] Without a legal requirement that children born of donated sperm be told of their origins, the law's protection of their right to

---

[477] [2017] EWFC 31.

[478] SI 2004/1511.

[479] HFEA 1990, s. 31(4)(b). Marrying your half-sibling may seem fanciful, but in cities where there is a severe shortage of sperm donors (such as Glasgow apparently) this is not so far-fetched.

[480] In *Rose v Secretary of State for Health* [2002] 2 FLR 962 it was accepted that children had a right to know the identity of their sperm donor fathers as part of their right to respect for their private and family life. However, the court left open the question of whether respect for the sperm donor's rights justified an interference in the child's rights.

[481] Jones (2010).

[482] See M. Roberts (2000) and Blyth *et al.* (2009) for further discussion.

[483] Maclean and Maclean (1996). See also the studies by Cook (2002) and Golombok *et al.* (2002) also finding widespread secrecy surrounding assisted reproduction.

[484] See Grace and Daniels (2007) for an interesting discussion of what causes parents to either disclose or not disclose their child's genetic origins.

know their genetic origins is rather half-hearted.[485] Bainham[486] and others[487] strongly assert that since children have a right to know the truth about their biological parentage, the law should oblige parents to tell their children that they are donor-conceived.[488]

The change in the law has had predictable results. There has been a dramatic drop in the number of men donating sperm and there is evidence of infertile couples seeking treatment abroad in order to avoid the sperm donor father's identity ever being discovered.[489] A BBC report claims that 70 per cent of clinics are unable to access donor sperm, or find it extremely difficult. It may also be that the reforms have made it even less likely that a couple will inform their child that he or she has been born as a result of assisted reproduction.[490] Turkmendag, Dingwall and Murphy express their objections strongly:

> The removal of anonymity has had identifiable detrimental effects: donors are reluctant to donate, UK clinics cannot meet the demand for gametes, there are long waiting lists for patients who wish to get treatment, and increasing use of international travel to avoid the law. None of these consequences were unforeseen or unpredictable: worries about donor shortage were voiced by major stakeholders (e.g. clinics, BFS, Royal College of Obstetricians and Gynaecologists, and British Medical Association) before the new law was introduced.[491]

(c) Adopted children

This is discussed in Chapter 11.

(iii) Should there be a right to know one's parentage?

DEBATE

Should there be a right to know one's parentage?

The main arguments in favour of recognising a right to know one's parentage include the following:[492]

1. Eekelaar argues that there is a right to be informed of one's parentage.[493] He asks whether anyone would choose to live their life on the basis that they had been deliberately deceived about their genetic origin.[494] On that basis he suggests we should recognise the right to know one's parentage.

2. There are claims that knowing parentage produces psychological benefits. There is evidence that some adopted children feel that unless they find out about their genetic origins they

---

[485] In *J v C* [2006] EWCA Civ 551 at para 13. Wall LJ had grave doubts whether a specific issue order could be made to require a parent to tell their child of the circumstances of their birth.

[486] Bainham (2008c).

[487] E.g. Cowden (2012).

[488] See Millbank (2015) who calls for greater use of voluntary registers to enable people to link up with those to whom they are genetically related.

[489] Turkmendag *et al.* (2008: 293).

[490] Blyth and Frith (2009); Nordqvist (2014).

[491] Turkmendag *et al.* (2008: 293).

[492] Richards (2003) provides a useful summary of the arguments in favour of the right to know in the context of children born as a result of assisted reproduction.

[493] Eekelaar (1994a). See also Wallbank (2004b).

[494] Eekelaar (1994a).

suffer psychologically. Barbara Almond seeks to explain the importance of knowing one's genetic origins:

> Without this, [the children] are born as exiles from the kinship network and are orphans in a sense previously unknown to human beings. They may in fact have unknown half-siblings, cousins, aunts, grandparents, but they will never meet them. Of course, there is every chance that they will be provided by an alternative family network that will provide love and security, but the subtle similarities of genetic relationships may come to haunt them in the future, particularly when they have children of their own and start to look for such things as shared resemblances, attitudes, interests, tendencies, qualities of character and physical features in their own offspring.[495]

3. There is no evidence that children of assisted reproduction are harmed on discovering their origins.[496] Freeman notes that Sweden, Germany, Austria and Switzerland do permit disclosure, without there being disadvantageous consequences.[497]

4. O'Donovan[498] notes that there are medical reasons why one needs to know one's parentage. For example, if a child is aware that he or she is genetically predisposed to a particular illness, it might be possible to receive preventive treatment.

The main arguments against the right to know one's parentage are:

1. Some argue that social parents have an interest in not having their family life disrupted by information being given to the child they are caring for about his or her genetic origins.[499] Values of caring and relationship are valid and can be undermined by emphasis on genetic truth.[500] Carol Smart argues 'secrets may be felt to be necessary for the preservation of relationships, and the "truth" may be taken to be less important than stabilising fictions.'[501]

2. The genetic parents may have a right to privacy, which would be infringed by informing the child of their existence. There is evidence that parents who have used assisted reproductive services would suffer grave emotional harm if they were forced to disclose to their child that they were born as a result of assisted reproductive services.

3. The child may have the right not to know his or her genetic parentage. This argument would be that the law should wait until the child is old enough to be able to decide for him- or herself. The fact that some adopted children choose not to discover their genetic parentage suggests that they would rather not know the information.

4. In the context of assisted reproduction there are concerns that giving children the right to discover their parentage may discourage donation. Many donors are not particularly interested in contact. This will depend on the motivation behind the donation of the sperm or egg. Empirical evidence suggests that the typical sperm donor is a student donating for beer money;[502] although, now that anonymity of sperm donors has changed, the kind of men who will donate sperm may well change.[503] Egg donors seem to be motivated more

---

[495] Almond (2006: 116). See also Somerville (2010).
[496] Smart (2010).
[497] Freeman (1996).
[498] O'Donovan (1988).
[499] Discussed in Maclean and Maclean (1996).
[500] Smart (2009 and 2010).
[501] Smart (2009: 558).
[502] At £15 a go (Horsey (2006)), it won't buy many rounds! An HFEA (2006) review suggested £250 plus expenses for a 'course' of sperm donation. It is not quite clear what a 'course' would be.
[503] Turkmendag et al. (2008).

strongly by altruism; indeed, egg donation (unlike sperm donation) is not paid. This is partly because egg donation involves a higher degree of risk and injury than sperm donation. More controversially, the technology exists to extract eggs from foetuses. The benefit of this might be thought to be that there would be no possible genetic mother who could seek to play a role in the resulting child's life.

5. Genetic origins are not very important. We each share 99.9 per cent of our genes with each other. Indeed, you share 50 per cent of your genes with a banana according to Professor John Harris![504] So, perhaps the importance given to our unique genetic inheritance is overemphasised.[505] Many millions of people over the centuries have been brought up deceived as to their genetic origins; they don't seem to have suffered too much. It is only because we have the technology to do tests that this right has arisen.

6. Claims that a child has a right to know can easily be misused by adults to pursue their own agendas. Jane Fortin argues:[506]

> The DNA testing applications brought by putative fathers are not brought to provide the child with information alone, they are the initial stages of attempts to establish a social relationship between father and child based on assumptions about biological connectedness. The putative fathers' assumption that once the biological ties between father and child have been clearly identified, they should be fulfilled by a social relationship, produces an elision of the right to know the parent's identity, with the right to know and have a relationship with that parent. Whether or not claims can be justified by reference to the child's own rights, such an elision concentrates the court's attention on the putative father's position and his own interests – countered by those of the mother. Such an approach thereby produces considerable tensions, not least those arising from the false assumption that the biological link between child and parent can magically transform a previously non-existent relationship into a fruitful one for both parties.

Questions

1. *Is a child who does not know their genetic origins harmed?*
2. *Are the issues of a right to know genetic origins and the definition of parenthood linked?*
3. *Why do some people seem to value the blood tie so much and others not?*

Further reading

Compare **Bainham** (2008c) and **Fortin** (2009a) on the importance of the blood tie and the right to know one's genetic origins.

C Is there a right to be a parent?

(i) What might the 'right to procreate' mean?

It is hard to claim a positive right to procreate, not least because natural procreation requires two people. Few people would seriously suggest that the state should be obliged to provide partners for anyone who wishes to produce a child! A more realistic right to procreate might be understood in two ways. First, it can be said there is a right not to have one's natural ability

---

[504] Harris (2003).
[505] Richards (2006: 61) questions whether one's genetic origins are central to one's sense of identity given that twins can have identical DNA, but clearly separate identities.
[506] Fortin (2009a).

to procreate removed by the state.[507] The notion of compulsory sterilisation, or having to be approved as a suitable parent before engaging in sexual intercourse, would not be acceptable in most democracies.[508] The second sense in which one might claim a right to procreate is to argue that one should not be denied fertility treatment without good reason.[509]

Article 12 of the European Convention states that 'men and women of marriageable age have the right to marry and according to national laws governing the exercise of this right found a family'. Although this might suggest a positive right to procreate on a literal reading, this notion has been rejected in *Paton v UK*.[510] In *R v Secretary of State for the Home Office, ex p Mellor*[511] the Court of Appeal held that a married prisoner had no right under Article 12 to have access to artificial insemination services to enable his wife to have a child. Such services were a privilege or benefit and no one could claim them as of right.[512] However, the Court of Appeal went on to suggest that there might be exceptional circumstances in which it would be a disproportionate interference in a prisoner's Article 8 rights to deny access to assisted reproduction.[513]

The issue of a 'right to be a parent' came to the fore in *Evans v Amicus Healthcare Ltd and others*.[514]

CASE: *Evans v Amicus Healthcare Ltd and others* [2004] 3 All Er 1025

In October 2001 Natalie Evans and Howard Johnston, who were engaged, underwent IVF treatment. It was discovered that Natalie Evans had tumours on her ovaries. Her ovaries had to be removed as soon as possible and she was required quickly to make a decision on whether she wanted any ova removed and frozen. There were three main options: either that she freeze her ova; or her eggs be fertilised with donated sperm and frozen; or that her ova be fertilised with Mr Johnston's sperm and then frozen. She chose the last option, a decision she would subsequently deeply regret. There were two main reasons for it. The first was that frozen ova do not freeze well and many do not survive. The second was that Mr Johnston assured her that he wanted to be the father of her children; that they were not going to split up; and that she should not be negative. Six eggs were harvested, fertilised and frozen. Later that month her ovaries were removed. In May 2002 the couple separated and Mr Johnston wrote to the clinic asking them to destroy the embryos. Ms Evans sought an order preventing the destruction of the embryos.

The Court of Appeal found the case straightforward in legal terms and decided against Ms Evans and authorised the destruction of the embryos. The decision was reached primarily on the basis of the interpretation of the Human Fertilisation and Embryology

---

[507] Although not expressed in such terms, *R v Human Fertilisation and Embryology Authority, ex p Blood* [1999] Fam 151, [1997] 2 FCR 501 and *Warren v Care Fertility* [2014] EWHC 602 (Fam) could be regarded as accepting a right to procreate.

[508] *Re B (A Minor) (Wardship: Sterilisation)* [1988] AC 199; *Re F (Mental Patient: Sterilisation)* [1990] 2 AC 1; *Re D (A Minor) (Wardship: Sterilisation)* [1976] Fam 185.

[509] For further discussion, see Sutherland (2003). A lack of state resources is a common and lawful reason to deny access to NHS fertility treatments; *R (Rose) v Thanet Clinical Commissioning Group* [2014] EWHC 1182 (Admin).

[510] (1981) 3 EHRR 408 ECtHR

[511] [2000] 3 FCR 148.

[512] For an interesting discussion of this case, see Williams (2002).

[513] [2003] 3 FCR 148, at para 45. See further *Dickson v UK* (App. No. 44362/04), discussed in Jackson (2007b); *SH v Austria* (2011) 52 EHRR; and *Nedescu v Romania* (App. No. 70035/10).

[514] [2004] 3 All ER 1025.

Act 1990 (HFEA 1990). That Act makes it clear that a licensed clinic is only permitted to store an embryo which has been brought about *in vitro* if there is effective consent by each person whose gametes were used to bring about the creation of the embryo (HFEA 1990, Sched. 3, paras 6(3), 8(2)). Although Mr Johnston had consented to the original storage of the sperm and its use in fertilising the egg, he had now withdrawn his consent and so the clinic was no longer permitted to store it. It was not just the wording of the statutory provisions which convinced the Court of Appeal that this was the correct interpretation of the Act; they emphasised that there were two principles underlying the Act:

(i) The welfare of any child born by treatment was to be of fundamental importance.

(ii) The requirement of informed consent, capable of being withdrawn at any point prior to the transfer of the embryos to the woman receiving treatment.

Both of these principles supported the conclusion that the embryos should be destroyed. As to the first, it was not in the child's interests to be born to a father who did not want the child to be born. As to the second, it clearly required the destruction of the embryo.

The Court of Appeal also considered whether the Human Rights Act 1998 required the Court to reinterpret the HFEA 1990 in a way which was consistent with the parties' rights under the European Convention on Human Rights. The court quickly concluded that the embryo had no rights under the Convention.[515] As to the rights to respect for private and family life, it was noted that Ms Evans's right to reproduce had to be balanced against Mr Johnston's right not to reproduce. This was problematic because it involved 'a balance to be struck between two entirely incommensurable things'.[516] In essence, the Court of Appeal felt that the HFEA 1990 had taken a reasonable approach between balancing these rights and so it could not be said to be incompatible with the Convention; although, had the Act permitted Ms Evans to implant the embryo, this too might have been a reasonable balance.

The case went to the European Court of Human Rights.[517] The European Court of Human Rights (Grand Chamber) held that English law in the HFEA 1990 did not improperly interfere with the parties' rights under the ECHR; although their judgment implies that a statute which would have decided that she could have used the embryos would also have been compliant with the ECHR. In other words, this was an area where states within their margin of appreciation could legislate as they felt appropriate. The European Court of Human Rights held that the case involved a complex clash of Article 8 rights: in essence, the right to be a parent (of Ms Evans) and the right not to be a parent (of Mr Johnston). It also involved some broader social issues, such as the principle of primacy of consent and the need for certainty. The UK law which favoured the right not to be a parent could not be said to be improper. It could not be said that the state had a positive obligation to ensure that a woman should be permitted to implant her embryo notwithstanding the withdrawal of consent by the gamete provider. She had not been prevented from becoming a mother in a social, legal or physical sense because she could adopt a child or use donated gametes.

---

[515] This was confirmed in *Vo v France* [2004] 2 FCR 577.

[516] [2004] 3 All ER 1025 at para 66.

[517] *Evans v UK* [2006] 1 FCR 585 and [2007] 2 FCR 5. See Wright (2008) and Morris (2007) for interesting discussions of the issues.

The case as an interpretation of the HFEA 1990 was relatively uncontroversial.[518] However, dealing with the human rights issues was less straightforward.[519] The Court of Appeal concluded that the Article 8 rights of Ms Evans and Mr Johnston were equal and this was seen as acceptable by the ECtHR. However, the claimed right to implant the embryo and thereby become a mother and the claimed right to destroy the embryo and thereby avoid becoming a father both fall within the right to respect for private and family life under Article 8; this does not mean that the rights are equal. Many people will agree with Thorpe LJ that these rights are incommensurate. Only the most hard-hearted can fail to find sympathy with Ms Evans being denied the only chance she had to have a child of her own. But many will also sympathise with Mr Johnston's principled objection to becoming a father against his wishes. One could go back to what is at the heart of the rights claimed here. In essence, this is the right of autonomy: the right to live your life as you wish. It is common to talk in terms of encouraging people to find and live out their version of the 'good life' free from interference from the state. This provides us some benchmark against which to measure these competing rights. Would it be a greater setback to their version of living their 'good life' for Ms Evans to be denied having the child she so desperately wanted or for Mr Johnston to have to live his life knowing there was a child of his whom he did not know and in whose life he was not able to play an effective role?[520]

D 'Illegitimacy'

Historically, in England and Wales a lesser status has been accorded to children whose parents are not married. At common law an illegitimate child was referred to as a *filius nullius* and had no legal relationship with his or her father, nor even, at one time, with his or her mother. There has been a gradual shifting of the position by permitting a child to be legitimated by the parents' subsequent marriage,[521] and there has been a gradual removal of the legal disadvantages of children born outside of marriage. Now, as we shall see, very few consequences flow from illegitimacy. The key argument behind the reforms is that a child's legal position should not be affected by the parents' decision whether or not to marry. This is reflected in Article 2(1) of the UN Convention on the Rights of the Child and in the European Convention on the Legal Status of Children Born out of Wedlock, which both state that a child's status should not depend on whether his or her parents were married. Some jurisdictions have removed the status of the illegitimate child altogether.[522] As confirmed by the European Court of Human Rights in *Sahin* v *Germany*,[523] the Human Rights Act 1998 means that any distinction between legitimate and illegitimate children may infringe Article 8 in conjunction with Article 14, unless that distinction can be justified as necessary under para 2 of Article 8.[524]

The Family Law Reform Acts of 1969 and 1987 have done much to limit the distinction made between legitimate and illegitimate children. Now children whose parents are not married have nearly the same rights as children whose parents are married. Section 1(1) of the

---

[518] Department of Health (2005b) recommends improvements be made in explaining to couples the paperwork they sign when agreeing to treatment at a licensed clinic.

[519] An excellent discussion of the Court of Appeal case is Sheldon (2004).

[520] See Wright (2008). See *Warren* v *Care Fertility Ltd* [2014] EWHC 602 (Fam) where a woman's Article 8 right was relied upon to permit her to use her deceased husband's sperm. And see *R (IM and MM)* v *Human Fertilisation and Embryology Authority* [2016] EWCA Civ 611, where parents of a deceased woman successfully challenged the HFEA's refusal that they be allowed to use their daughter's eggs to create a child.

[521] Legitimacy Act 1976.

[522] E.g. New Zealand.

[523] [2003] 2 FCR 619. See also *Sporer* v *Austria* (App. No. 35637/03).

[524] *Camp and Bourimi* v *The Netherlands* [2000] 3 FCR 307. *Genovese* v *Malta* (App. No. 53124/09).

Family Law Reform Act 1987 states that for all future legislation any reference to a parent would (unless there was contrary indication) cover both married and unmarried parents.

However, there are a few distinctions between children whose parents were married and those whose parents were unmarried, in the areas of citizenship, titles of honour[525] and maintenance.[526] There is also a distinction drawn in the father's legal position because an unmarried father, unlike a married father, does not acquire parental responsibility. It is also notable that the judiciary still in judgments refer to 'illegitimate' children, even in the House of Lords.[527] Indeed, we still have a Legitimacy Act 1976 on the statute books and it is technically possible to apply for a declaration of legitimacy.[528] So despite the formal removal of legitimacy from family law, it still lingers around.[529]

E Same-sex couples and parenthood

Learning objective 8

Critically examine how parenthood issues are dealt with in cases involving same-sex couples

The legal response to same-sex couples who wish to produce and raise a child together reveals clearly the difficulties the law is facing in using the traditional concept of a child with one mother and one father. The law is looking increasingly outdated as it struggles to apply the traditional heterosexual family model to same-sex couples.[530]

As already noted under the HFEA 2008, if a same-sex couple seek treatment at a licensed clinic, the woman who gives birth as a result is the mother, but her partner will be described as the 'other parent'. The law's reluctance to see a child having two mothers is manifest. It was also demonstrated by Baroness Hale in *Re G (Children) (Residence: Same-Sex Partner)*,[531] dealing with a residence dispute between a lesbian couple. She placed weight on the fact that one woman was the genetic and gestational mother, while her partner was not, and that led to the residence order being made in the genetic mother's favour. This judgment might give the impression that lesbian parents can never be fully equal in the eyes of the law because the genetic and/or gestational parent will have a legal advantage.[532] While a heterosexual couple are therefore able to be equally the parents of the child, the law prevents a same-sex couple being equal parents.

The difficulties are also shown in a number of cases where a lesbian couple have asked a man to provide sperm which they have used to impregnate one of them.[533] The understanding is typically that the man should play only a limited role in the child's life. Problems then arise where the man subsequently seeks to become more involved in the child's life. The courts' response to these cases is revealing about the assumptions on parenthood and shows the difficulties the courts face in using traditional concepts of parenthood in modern family life.

---

[525] Family Law Reform Act 1987, s. 19(14).
[526] See Chapter 6.
[527] *Dawson v Wearmouth* [1999] 1 FLR 1167; for criticism of them doing so, see Bainham (2000b: 482 and 2009c). Hale LJ in *Re R (A Child)* [2001] EWCA Civ 1344 was critical of case reporters who had used the word 'illegitimate' in the title of a case.
[528] Family Law Act 1986, s. 56.
[529] Bainham (2009c).
[530] Wallbank (2010); McCandless (2012).
[531] [2006] UKHL 43 at para 33. See L. Smith (2007) for further discussion.
[532] That may be a slightly unfair reading of the case because Lady Hale only mentioned the genetics and gestational link because in relation to all the other relevant factors the parents were equal.
[533] Bremner (2017).

The courts have not developed a clear response to such cases. In *Re D (Contact and Parental Responsibility: Lesbian Mothers and Known Father)*[534] Black J gave parental responsibility to a man who had been selected by a lesbian couple to impregnate one of them so that the couple could raise a child together. Justifying his decision, he said that 'perhaps most importantly of all' is the reality that the man *was* the child's father. This suggests that biological parenthood itself is a good reason for granting parental responsibility to an informal sperm donor. Later cases seem to have required something more to justify granting a sperm donor parental responsibility. In *R v E and F (Female Parents: Known Father)*[535] a father who donated sperm to a lesbian couple was not granted parental responsibility on the basis that there was no doubt he was the father and did not need parental responsibility to reinforce that. In *JB v KS and E (A Child Acting by his Children's Guardian)*[536] the father was again granted parental responsibility. However, Hayden J went to lengths to emphasise that the sperm donor had developed and maintained a close relationship with the couple and that it had always been agreed he would have a role in the child's life, even if not a parental one. He already had regular contact with the child and had shown himself to be responsible. The judgment in that case seems to indicate that some good reasons are needed to justify granting parental responsibility. In *Re X*[537] Theis J believed the welfare of the child was tied up with ensuring the lesbian couple had a secure relationship. Allowing the sperm donor indirect contact (through letters) meant he could retain a link with the child without disrupting the mothers' relationship.

The solution adopted in some cases has been to grant the father parental responsibility, but then restrict the kind of issues about which he can exercise parental responsibility. Another response, used in *Re R (Parental Responsibility)*,[538] is not to grant the father parental responsibility, but to make a specific issue order requiring him to be kept up to date with important issues in the child's life.

The following is the leading case:

CASE: A v B and C (Lesbian Co-Parents: Role of Father) [2012] EWCA Civ 285

B and C were a lesbian couple who asked A (a man who was in a relationship with another man) to help produce a child. A married B, in order to avoid the religious concerns of B's family. A's sperm was used to make B pregnant. The intention was that the child would be raised by B and C and that A play a secondary role. The relationship broke down and A sought a contact order.

As the Court of Appeal acknowledged, as A was the biological father of the child and married to B it was clear he was the child's father and had parental responsibility for the child. The dispute focused especially on the extent of contact as it was agreed that a joint residence order for B and C was appropriate. The Court of Appeal rejected any suggestion of a general rule to such cases and emphasised that each case must depend on its fact

---

[534] [2006] 1 FCR 556.
[535] [2010] EWHC 417 (Fam).
[536] [2015] EWHC 180 (Fam).
[537] [2015] EWFC 83.
[538] [2011] EWHC 1535 (Fam).

and on an assessment of the welfare of the child. It was wrong in this case to assume that because a child benefited from having two parents that the addition of a third would be disadvantageous. Thorpe LJ went further:

> [The mother and her partner] may have had the desire to create a two parent lesbian nuclear family completely intact and free from the fracture resulting from contact with the third parent. But such desires may be essentially selfish and may later insufficiently weigh the welfare and developing rights of the child that they have created.

Thorpe LJ explained that the role of the court was not to give effect to the intentions of the parties, but rather to promote the welfare of the child.

The Court of Appeal also rejected an approach which had been developed by Hedley J which in similar cases had described the lesbian couple as the primary parents and the sperm donor as secondary.[539] Thorpe LJ explained:

> I would not endorse the concept of principal and secondary parents. It has the danger of demeaning the known donor and in some cases he may have an important role. In the present case some would say that the primary carer is the full-time nanny. However, let me rank the three parents in the context of care. Clearly [mother and her partner] are primary carers. Clearly [father] is only presently on the threshold of providing secondary care. Whether or not he should cross that threshold is the question that is likely to be decided by a judge in the future. But I would certainly not categorise him as a secondary parent.

Black LJ acknowledged that the courts had struggled to develop a principled approach to these cases. However, the court should not develop rules and allow each case to be determined by the welfare principle. She stated that 'The adults' pre-conception intentions were relevant factors in this case but they neither could nor should be determinative.'

The case was returned to the Family Division with a direction that the judge focus on the welfare of the child and find a solution that enabled the relationship between the child and A to thrive and develop, but in a flexible way taking account of accumulating evidence as the child grew up.

It seems that the approach the courts are taking in these cases is twofold. First, they are keen to solidify the parental role of the same-sex couple in relation to the child. This is typically done by making a shared residence order in their favour, which grants both women parental responsibility (*T v T (Shared and Joint Residence Orders)*).[540] Second, they are seeking to maintain the parental role of the father, by acknowledging he is the father and ensuring this is a meaningful role by ensuring he has contact with the child.

The problem is that these two goals are to some extent in conflict. The lesbian couple may feel their role as parents is undermined by the fact that (as they may see it) a third party is given a role to interfere in the way they wish to raise the child. A contrast might be made with surrogacy, where if the surrogate mother hands over the child a parental order can be made and she has no link with the child.[541]

---

[539] See e.g. *MA v RS (Contact: Parenting Roles)* [2011] EWHC 2455 (Fam) and *Re P and L (Contact)* [2011] EWHC 3431 (Fam).

[540] [2010] EWCA Civ 1366.

[541] L. Smith (2011).

It might have been thought that the HFEA 2008 would change the courts' approach in that it recognised that two women could be recognised as parents. In *Re G; Re Z (Children: Sperm Donors: Leave to Apply for Children Act Orders)*[542] two cases were heard together. They both involved lesbian couples who had produced a child using assisted reproduction and the sperm of a male friend. Following the birth, the male friend wanted to take on a significant role in the life of the child and applied for leave to bring an application for a contact order. The couple objected. The mothers relied on s. 48 of the 2008 Act that sperm donors are 'to be treated in law as not being a parent of the child for any purpose'. However, Baker J accepted the argument that had Parliament intended men in the donor's position never to have contact it would have barred them from seeking leave to apply for contact. He went further: 'the potential importance of genetic and psychological parenthood is not automatically extinguished by the removal of the status of legal parenthood, and that social and psychological relationships amounting to parenthood can and often do co-exist with legal parenthood'.[543] Notably he, somewhat controversially, described the men as 'fathers who have been deprived of the status of legal parent by the HFEA 2008 Act', rather than referring to them as sperm donors.[544] Baker J also placed weight on the fact the mothers had chosen to use a known donor and hence acknowledged the men would play some role in the child's life. It will be interesting to see if subsequent cases follow this line.

In *Re B (A Child) (No. 2) (Welfare: Child Arrangement Order)*[545] Cobb J reviewed these cases on same-sex parents and emphasised that there should be no departure from the key principle that the welfare of the child was the paramount consideration. The courts should not develop special rules for these cases but simply determine what orders, given the particular facts of each case, would best promote the welfare of the child.

If the law is going to continue on its current path, it needs to be made clearer why it is important that the father is given the role the Court of Appeal seem to want him to have. The two reasons commonly given are unconvincing. The claim a child needs a 'male parental influence' seems unsupported by evidence showing that children raised by lesbian parents do just as well, if not better, than comparable children raised by opposite-sex parents.[546] The claim that the child needs to know their genetic origins can be met without the father being given any particular role. The argument must be that getting to know one's genetic parents is a benefit, but evidence would be needed to show why that is so. Many adopted children do not know their genetic parents, and do not want to. They do not appear to suffer as a result.[547] Given the weakness of the arguments for giving the sperm donors in these cases parental status or parental responsibility it might be better to recognise the social reality that for these children it is the lesbian couple who are the child's parents. After all, that is how the child will understand the situation. Mary Welstead[548] has promoted a different view:

> To deprive a child of a biological father who wishes to be part of his child's life cannot be said to be in the child's best interests without further compelling evidence that such a relationship would be damaging to the child. Parental intention prior to conception, or the seemingly selfish desires of mothers, whether heterosexual or lesbian, to be sole carers, should rarely be an important factor in determining a child's future. The paramountcy principle must remain the sole basis for determining relationships between biological fathers and their children and would-be-parents should be aware of it before they embark on their journey to procreation.

[542] [2013] EWHC 134 (Fam).
[543] Para 116.
[544] Para 115.
[545] [2017] EWHC 488 (Fam).
[546] Leckey (2012); Golombok (2015).
[547] Everett and Yeatman (2010). See Callus (2012) for an argument seeking to attach weight to the genetic role.
[548] Welstead (2016).

She clearly places weight on the importance of the biological link, but would we say the same to a sperm donor who has donated sperm through a licensed clinic to a heterosexual couple?

What we are seeing in these cases is the courts struggling to fit lesbian couples and sperm donors into the case law. Black LJ said in one case:

> I had to adjudicate upon the issue of parental responsibility for the biological father equipped only with concepts and language which were not designed to cater for the situation I had before me.[549]

Leanne Smith identifies a paradox in the current debates:

> Excluding known donors from legal recognition through a system which recognises only two parents validates and protects lesbian families but also reinforces the dyadic parenting norm based on heterosexual reproduction. Conversely, giving legal recognition to multiple parents undermines the dyadic norm but reasserts heteronormativity by elevating the importance of genetic parentage and fathers.[550]

A further important point is that in many of these cases the lesbian couple have asked a gay friend to be the sperm donor. That can make the parenting enterprise 'a political and social endeavour for lesbians and gay men to challenge the patriarchal nuclear family'. Wallbank and Dietz[551] argue that the validity of this challenge should be acknowledged as an aspect of the child's welfare. However, currently the courts in cases such as *DB v AB*[552] have taken a straightforward understanding of welfare and seen it as beneficial for a child to retain links with their biological father. Although in that case it is, perhaps, notable that the court emphasised that it had been found that the lesbian couple and man had agreed that the man was to play some role in the child's life.

A more radical solution may be to break down the sharp distinctions that are drawn between parents and non-parents and to recognise the broad range of adults that play an important role in the life of a child.[553] Any adult with a close beneficial relationship in relation to a child should have legal rights and responsibilities to the child. We might recognise how different adults in a child's life are especially well placed to make particular decisions about a child. In short, we abolish the concepts of parents in the eyes of the law. Such an approach would open up our thinking about adult–child relationships, but it seems the law is a long way from departing from the paradigm of parenthood. Those who want to retain parenthood may refer to the writing of Brighouse and Swift[554] who argue in favour of the notion of a parent:

> In order to develop into flourishing adults, and to enjoy the goods intrinsic to childhood, children need to have a particular kind of relationship with one or more, but not many more, adults . . . When we say that children need parents – indeed that they have a right to a parent – we are saying . . . that there is an essential core to what they need that is best delivered by particular people who interact with them continuously during the core of their development . . . Continuity and combination are implied by the idea that what children need is a particular kind of relationship.

15 Conclusion

It was not long ago when to ask, 'What is a parent?' would have appeared to be asking the obvious, but now the question is the subject of lengthy books. The complex sets of relationships within which children are raised require the law to recognise that a variety of people may

---

[549] *A v B and C* [2012] EWCA Civ 285.
[550] L. Smith (2013), at p. 378.
[551] Wallbank and Dietz (2013).
[552] [2014] EWHC 384 (Fam).
[553] Herring (2013a: ch. 6).
[554] Brighouse and Swift (2014: 85).

act towards the child in a parental or quasi-parental way and those who are the child's genetic parents may play little part in the child's life. One major debate in this area concerns whether greater legal recognition should be given to those who are the genetic parents of the child or to those who act socially as the parents of the child.[555] The law is developing ways of recognising both these understandings of parenthood, but the 'balance of power' between the adults involved is controversial. This part of the text has also considered other complex issues which have been created by the advent of assisted reproduction: Is there a right to be a parent? Does a child have a right to know his or her genetic origins? The future development of reproductive technologies will, no doubt, create many more legal problems.

Further reading

Alghrani, A. (2018) *Regulating Assisted Reproductive Technologies: New Horizons*, Cambridge: Cambridge University Press.

Baars, G. (2019) 'Queer Cases Unmake Gendered Law, Or, Fucking Law's Gendering Function', *Australian Feminist Law Journal* 45: 43.

Bainham, A. (2008a) 'Arguments about parentage', *Cambridge Law Journal* 67: 322.

Bainham, A. (2008c) 'What is the point of birth registration?' *Child and Family Law Quarterly* 20: 449.

Callus, T. (2012) 'A new parenthood paradigm for twenty-first century family law in England and Wales', *Legal Studies* 32: 347.

Callus, T. (2019) 'What's the point of parenthood? The agreed parenthood provisions under the HFE Act 2008 and inconsistency with intention', *Journal of Social Welfare and Family Law* 41: 389.

Clifton, J. (2014) 'The long road to universal parental responsibility: some implications from research into marginal fathers', *Family Law* 44: 859.

Crawshaw, M. and Wallbank, J. (2014) 'Is the birth registration system fit for purpose? The rights of donor conceived adults', *Family Law* 44: 1154.

Diduck, A. (2007) 'If only we can find the appropriate terms to use the issue will be solved: law, identity and parenthood', *Child and Family Law Quarterly* 19: 458.

Eekelaar, J. (1991c) 'Parental responsibility: state of nature or nature of the state?' *Journal of Social Welfare and Family Law* 13: 37.

Fenton-Glynn, C. (2015) 'The regulation and recognition of surrogacy under English law: an overview of the case-law', *Child and Family Law Quarterly* 83.

Fortin, J. (2009a) 'Children's right to know their origins – too far, too fast?' *Child and Family Law Quarterly* 21: 336.

Gilmore, S. (2003a) 'Parental responsibility and the unmarried father – a new dimension to the debate', *Child and Family Law Quarterly* 15: 21.

Gilmore, S. (2015) 'Withdrawal of parental responsibility: lost authority and a lost opportunity', *Modern Law Review* 78: 1042.

---

[555] Millbank (2008a).

Hale, B. (2014) 'New families and the welfare of children', *Journal of Social Welfare and Family Law* 36: 26.

Harding, R. (2014) 'Re(inscribing) the heteronormative family', in R. Leckey (ed.) *After Legal Equality*, Abingdon: Routledge.

Horsey, K. (2010) 'Challenging presumptions: legal parenthood and surrogacy arrangements', *Child and Family Law Quarterly* 22: 439.

Horsey, K. (2015) *Surrogacy in the UK: myth busting and reform,* Surrogacy UK.

Lind, C. and Hewitt, T. (2009) 'Law and the complexities of parenting: parental status and parental function', *Journal of Social Welfare and Family Law* 31: 391.

Margaria, A. (2020) 'Trans men giving birth and reflections on fatherhood: What to expect', *International Journal of Law, Policy and the Family* forthcoming.

Masson, J. (2006c) 'Parenting by being; parenting by doing – in search of principles for founding families', in J. Spencer and A. du Bois-Pedain (eds) *Freedom and Responsibility in Reproductive Choice,* Oxford: Hart.

McCandless, J. (2012) 'The role of sexual partnership in UK family law: the case of legal parenthood', in D. Cutas and S. Chan (eds) *Families: Beyond the Nuclear Ideal,* London: Bloomsbury.

McCandless, J. and Sheldon, S. (2010a) 'The Human Fertilisation and Embryology Act 2008 and the tenacity of the sexual family form', *Modern Law Review* 73: 175.

Millbank, J. (2008a) 'Unlikely fissures and uneasy resonances: lesbian co-mothers, surrogate parenthood and fathers' rights', *Feminist Legal Studies* 16: 141.

Nordqvist, P. (2014) 'The drive for openness in donor conception: disclosure and the trouble with real life', *International Journal of Law Policy and the Family* 28: 321.

Smart, C. (2010) 'Law and the regulation of family secrets', *International Journal of Law, Policy and the Family* 24: 397.

Smith, L. (2010) 'Clashing symbols? Reconciling support for fathers and fatherless families after the Human Fertilisation and Embryology Act 2008', *Child and Family Law Quarterly* 22: 46.

Smith, L. (2013) 'Tangling the web of legal parenthood: legal responses to the use of known donors in lesbian parenting arrangements', *Legal Studies* 33: 355.

Somerville, M. (2010) 'Children's human rights to natural biological origins and family structure', *International Journal of Jurisprudence of Family Law* 35: 35.

Taylor, R. (2019) 'Grandparents and grandchildren: relatedness, relationships and responsibility', in B. Clough and J. Herring (eds) *Ageing, Gender and Family Law,* London: Routledge.

Turkmendag, I., Dingwall, R. and Murphy, T. (2008) 'The removal of donor anonymity in the UK: the silencing of claims by would-be parents', *International Journal of Law, Policy and the Family* 22: 283.

Wallbank, J. (2010) 'Channelling the messiness of diverse family lives: resisting the calls to order and de-centring the hetero-normative family', *Journal of Social Welfare and Family Law* 32: 353.

Wallbank, J. and Dietz, C. (2014) 'Lesbian mothers, fathers and other animals: is the political personal in multiple parent families?' *Child and Family Law Quarterly* 25: 452.

Visit **go.pearson.com/uk/he/resources** to access **resources** specifically written to complement this text.

9

Parents' and children's rights

Learning objectives

When you finish reading this chapter you will be able to:

1. Explain when childhood begins and ends
2. Discuss the nature of parental rights
3. Explain and evaluate the concept of parental responsibility
4. Analyse the welfare principle
5. Describe how the Human Rights Act 1998 interacts with the welfare principle
6. Consider the issues around children's rights

---

1 Introduction

This chapter will consider the legal position of parents and children.[1] What rights do parents and children have? How can the law balance the interests of parents and children? Chapter 10 will look at how the courts resolve disputes between children and parents. Here we are concerned with the legal position if no court order has been made. The chapter will start by considering when childhood begins or ends. It will then examine the position of parents: what obligations and rights does the law impose upon parents? The chapter will then turn to the legal position of children: how does the law protect the interests of children? Do children have any rights? The complex questions of how to deal with clashes between the interests of children and parents and also between different children will be examined. The chapter will conclude by looking at particular issues to see how, in practice, the interests of children and parents are balanced.

---

[1] See Fortin (2009b) for an excellent discussion of the themes of this section.

2 When does childhood begin?

Learning objective 1

Explain when childhood begins and ends

English law takes the position that a person's life begins at birth.[2] Before birth the foetus is not a person. But this does not mean that the unborn child is a 'nothing'. In the eyes of the law the foetus is a 'unique organism'[3] which is protected by the law in a variety of ways.[4] For example, it is an offence to procure a miscarriage unless the procedure is permitted under the Abortion Act 1967. However, the law is unwilling to protect the foetus at the expense of the rights of the mother to bodily integrity and self-determination. For example, in *Re F (In Utero)*[5] the social services were concerned about the well-being of the unborn child and wanted to make it a ward of court. The court stated that the foetus could not be made a ward of court, as it was not a child; although once the child was born there was nothing to stop the court warding him or her.[6] It was held that to enable a foetus to be warded would give the court inappropriate control over the mother's life.[7]

Fathers have no rights in relation to foetuses and, therefore, are not able to prevent an abortion.[8] The only possible route for a father seeking to prevent an abortion is to argue that the proposed abortion is illegal. However, in *C v S*[9] it was suggested that the Director of Public Prosecutions is the person who should be bringing any such proceedings, rather than the father.[10]

3 When does childhood end?

Childhood is a concept in flux. Societies at different times and in different places have had a variety of ideas about when childhood ends. In 1969 the legal age at which a child ceased to be a minor in England and Wales was reduced from 21 to 18.[11] The Children Act 1989 confirms this by defining a child as 'a person under the age of eighteen'.[12] However, there is not a straightforward transformation in the status of the child at age 18. For example, 16 is the age at which a child is entitled to perform some activities[13] and there are still some legal limitations that apply until the person is 21.[14] By contrast a child can be convicted of a criminal offence from the age of 10.[15] Further, in *Gillick v W Norfolk and Wisbech AHA*[16] the House of Lords accepted that the law must recognise that children develop and mature at different rates and a child under 16 who is sufficiently mature should be recognised as competent to make some

---

[2] For a detailed discussion see Herring (2016b).

[3] *Attorney-General's Reference (No. 3 of 1994)* [1998] AC 245 at p. 256.

[4] *St George's Healthcare NHS Trust v S* [1998] 2 FLR 728. *Vo v France* [2004] 2 FCR 577 made it clear that the foetus has no rights under the ECHR, although it is open to signatory states to pass legislation to protect foetuses if they wish.

[5] [1988] Fam 122.

[6] See Chapter 11 for further discussion of when a care order can be obtained in such cases.

[7] For a general discussion of the law, see Seymour (2000); Herring (2000a).

[8] *C v S* [1987] 2 FLR 505; *Paton v BPAST* [1979] QB 276. Approved by the European Convention on Human Rights: *Paton v UK* (1981) 3 EHRR 408.

[9] [1987] 2 FLR 505.

[10] Infant Life (Preservation) Act 1929, s. 1.

[11] Family Law Reform Act 1969, s. 1. Eighteen is the age used by the UN Convention on the Rights of the Child, Article 1.

[12] Children Act 1989, s. 105(1); subject to exemptions relating to financial support.

[13] A child can marry at age 16.

[14] For example, applicants for adoption need to have reached the age of 21.

[15] For discussion see Keating (2015).

[16] [1986] 1 FLR 229, [1986] AC 112.

decisions for him- or herself. We shall discuss the notion of '*Gillick*-competence' and when under 16-year-olds can make decisions for themselves in further detail shortly.

Although childhood legally ends at age 18, the parental role does not necessarily end then. Many over-18-year-olds continue to live with parents, who will continue to provide them with practical, financial and emotional support. Indeed, under certain circumstances parents can be legally obliged to support children financially beyond the age of 18.[17]

4 The nature of childhood

As we have seen already, there is no hard and fast line between childhood and adulthood. This has led some to claim that childhood is a social construction. In other words, that there is not an objectively true definition of childhood, rather the concept is created by societies. Certainly, the notion of childhood is a powerful one in our society and the media are constantly concerned by the position of children. To some we are living in times when childhood is disappearing, with children becoming exposed to adult life at an earlier and earlier stage. In particular, there are concerns about the sexualisation and commercialisation of children.[18] These are rushing children through what should be an innocent and stress-free time of life.[19] However, others claim that the lines between childhood and adulthood are being reinforced more than ever. Children are being excluded from public places either because their parents fear for their safety or because of concerns about their behaviour.[20] Children's play is nowadays made up of commercialised leisure activities, usually overseen by adults.[21] Much government legislation has been directed towards tackling truants and children with anti-social behaviour. Children have been regarded as a resource the state needs to invest in.[22] It may, in fact, be that both these perspectives have an element of truth:[23] that children are simultaneously being treated as dangerous young people in need of control in some areas of life, but also as vulnerable minors needing protection and/or restraint. Are children sometimes seen as little angels and sometimes little devils?[24]

Many commentators have argued that children's vulnerability is the primary justification for controlling children and ignoring their rights.[25] They argue we need to recognise that children are far more competent than they are given credit for and should be entitled to many of the rights adults have. Taking a rather different tack, I have argued:

> . . . the law is right to regard children as vulnerable, where it is at fault is in failing to recognise the vulnerability of adults. Children are vulnerable, as is everyone. In children we adults see our own vulnerability and flee from it.[26]

So, rather than treating children more like adults, I argue we need to be treating adults more like children. Many will regard that as a dangerous argument that allows people's human rights to be easily undervalued.

---

[17] For example, *B v B (Adult Student: Liability to Support)* [1998] 1 FLR 373 (and see Chapter 6).
[18] Although children's materialism simply reflects society's.
[19] Mayall (2002: 3).
[20] Valentine (2004).
[21] Mayhew *et al.* (2005).
[22] Piper (2009).
[23] Smart, Neale and Wade (2001) suggest that in the media children are often represented as either little angels or little devils.
[24] Valentine (2004: 1).
[25] See the analysis of vulnerability in Fineman (2011).
[26] Herring (2012e).

There has been a growth of philosophical interest in the nature of childhood too. One particular theme is whether the status of childhood is a good one or not. In her article entitled 'Why Childhood is Bad for Children' Sarah Hannan[27] argues that childhood leads to 'impaired capacity for practical reasoning, lack of an established practical identity, a need to be dominated, and profound and asymmetric vulnerability'. Not everyone agrees. Macleod[28] suggests that 'as innocents children are untroubled by disturbing and troubling dimensions of the adult world' and that makes childhood good. Harry Brighouse and Adam Swift[29] controversially suggest 'innocence about sexuality . . . is a good in childhood'. They also suggest that the ability of children to live and trust without reservation is a good. Hannan rejects these suggestions, as 'the existence of sexual exploitation, sexual violence, and even unrequited sexual desire' in children's lives means these alleged goods are not present. This debate, and clearly there is much more that could be discussed, is relevant for lawyers as it helps determine whether we should preserve childhood as a 'special time' and the law should allow children to enjoy that time of innocence, or whether the law (and broader society) should be hastening children on to adulthood as quickly as possible. On the other hand, it might be suggested that it is not helpful to think of childhood as something that is good or bad, but rather that it is 'an ethically necessary step on the way to adulthood'.[30] However, that might be seen as limiting the goods of childhood to simply a means to the end of adulthood. Is not childhood of value in and of itself?

TOPICAL ISSUE

Childhood in crisis?

Regularly in the media there are concerns that childhood is in crisis. Whether it is levels of mental ill-heath; obesity; insomnia; addiction to mobile phones; or access to pornography, rarely a week passes without a new story raising concerns about children. Interestingly sometimes it is the fact that children are growing up too fast which is the subject of concern, and sometimes that they are 'snowflakes', over-protected from the realities of life. Clearly there are real challenges facing young people. For example, around one in ten children have a diagnosable mental health disorder.[31] But the causes of that are complex. One book expressed grave concern that society was creating a 'toxic childhood' with worrying levels of stress, obesity and pornography among children.[32] One might think that the same could be said about adults too!

5 Parents' rights, responsibilities and discretion

Learning objective 2

Discuss the nature of parental rights

Parental responsibility is the key legal concept which describes the legal duties and rights that can flow from being a child's parent. It is significant that the Children Act 1989 talks of 'parental responsibility' rather than 'parental rights', because this stresses

---

[27] Hannan (2018).
[28] Macleod (2010).
[29] Brighouse and Swift (2014).
[30] Weinstock (2018).
[31] Young Minds (2016).
[32] Palmer (2015).

that children are not possessions to be controlled by parents, but instead children are persons to be cared for. Parents should have their responsibilities, rather than their rights, in the forefront of their minds. However, when the Children Act comes to define parental responsibility in s. 3, it states:

LEGISLATIVE PROVISION

Children Act 1989, section 3

In this Act 'parental responsibility' means all the rights, duties, powers, responsibilities and authority which by law a parent of a child has in relation to the child and his property.

It will be noted that the first word used to describe parental responsibility is 'rights'. This demonstrates that it would be quite wrong to say that parents do not have rights.[33] But we have already identified a key issue on the law on parenthood: how to balance and understand the notions of responsibilities and rights in parenthood. Before exploring that a little more it is important to be clear what we mean by parental rights.

A Parental rights

When we consider parental rights, it is important to distinguish between:

1. The rights a parent may have as a human being. These will be called a parent's human rights and would include, for example, the right to life, free speech, etc.
2. The rights that a parent may have because he or she is a parent. These will be called a parent's parental rights and would include the right to decide where the child will live.

Most people will accept the first set of rights. You do not lose your basic human rights by becoming a parent! The notion of parental rights is, however, more controversial.

When talking about a parent's parental rights it is important to be clear what might be meant by such a right. Take, for example, the parent's right to feed the child. By this could be meant one (or more) of three things:

1. Third parties or the state cannot prevent the parent carrying out this particular activity. So, no one is entitled to prevent a parent feeding the child what food the parent believes appropriate. This is often called a 'liberty'.
2. The acts of the parents are lawful. This means that although it may be unlawful for a stranger to feed a child,[34] the parental right means it is not unlawful for a parent to feed a child. This can be regarded as a 'legal authority'.
3. The state must enable the parent to perform this activity. For example, in relation to the right to feed, the state is obliged to ensure that parents have sufficient money so that they can supply the food the child needs. This can be regarded as a 'claim right'.

---

[33] See Scherpe (2009) for a comparative analysis of the notion of parental rights.
[34] It is far from clear whether this would be a criminal offence (assuming the substance is not harmful), although it could be a battery.

In English law, it is rare to find parents having a claim right, but there are plenty of examples of liberties and legal authorities. A good example of the latter is that it is generally unlawful to deprive someone of their liberty (e.g. in a secure hospital) without a court order, but a parent with parental responsibility can provide legal authorisation in relation to a child.[35]

Having made these distinctions, we can explore further the nature of the legal consequences of parenthood.[36]

B Are parents' rights and responsibilities linked?

In the House of Lords decision in *Gillick,* Lord Scarman argued that parents' rights exist only for the purpose of discharging their duties to children: 'Parental rights are derived from parental duty and exist only so long as they are needed for the protection of the person and property of the child.'[37] Lord Scarman is talking here about a parent's parental rights and is making the important point that any parental rights a parent has exist for the purpose of promoting children's interests. Andrew Bainham, however, suggests that the position is not that straightforward. He has suggested that parents have rights *because* they have responsibilities and they have responsibilities *because* they have rights.[38] By contrast, Michael Freeman puts the issue in terms of children's rights: children have a right to have responsible parents.[39]

Disagreeing with Lord Scarman, Alexander McCall Smith[40] has argued that not all parental rights exist for the benefit of children. He suggests that parents have two kinds of parental rights: parent-centred and child-centred rights. Child-centred rights are rights given to parents to enable them to carry out their duties. So, the parent has the right to clothe the child as an essential part of enabling the parent to fulfil his or her duty of ensuring the health of the child. By contrast, parent-centred rights exist for the benefit of the parent. One example McCall Smith gives is that of the parental right to determine the religious upbringing of children. He argues that this right is given to enable parents to bring up children as they think is most appropriate. Parent-centred rights, he explains, are justified not because they positively promote the welfare of the child, but because they cannot be shown to harm the child, but can benefit the parent. Such an approach has been supported by Andrew Bainham. He argues: 'It is simply not reasonable to take the position that those who bear the legal and moral burdens which society expects of a parent should be denied all recognition of their independent claims or interests.'[41]

The distinction between child-centred and parent-centred rights is an important one, but there are difficulties with McCall Smith's approach. It can be difficult to decide whether a right is a parent-centred or child-centred right. Is the right to feed the child parent- or child-centred? Such a right is essential for the health of the child and so appears to be child-centred. But what kind of food is provided (for example, whether the parents choose to feed their children only vegetarian food) appears to be a parent-centred right. Further, it could be argued that parental rights do promote a child's welfare and do not exist solely for the benefit of parents. This is because many believe that living in a society where people like different kinds of food, have different religious beliefs, and different senses of humour is part of what makes life enjoyable. If so, it could be said to be in a child's interests to be brought up in a diverse society.

---

[35] *Re D (A Child) (Deprivation of Liberty)* [2015] EWHC 922 (Fam).
[36] See Archard (2003: ch. 2) for a useful discussion of parents' rights.
[37] *Gillick v W Norfolk and Wisbech AHA* [1986] AC 112 at p. 184, *per* Lord Scarman.
[38] Bainham (1998a).
[39] Freeman (2008).
[40] McCall Smith (1990), discussed in Bainham (1994b).
[41] Bainham (2009d).

What is most useful about McCall Smith's distinction is that it stresses that there are certain areas of parenting over which parents do not have a discretion: they may not starve their child; the child must be adequately fed. There are, however, other areas of parenting where there is no state-approved standard of parenting (for example, what kind of clothes the child should wear; whether children should be allowed to drink small amounts of alcohol)[42] and so the issue is left to the discretion of each individual parent. So, while it is clear that if an issue relating to a child's upbringing comes before the court it will give 'respect' to the wishes of a responsible parent, at the end of the day it is for the court to decide what is in the best interests of the child.[43] However, if the court finds that it is unclear what is in the best interests of the child, it will permit the resident parent to make the decision. The court may take the view that it cannot in practical terms force a parent to treat a child in a particular way and so to make an order would be pointless.[44] This can mean that it is difficult for a non-resident parent to obtain a court order seeking to change the way the resident parent raises the child. So in *Re W (Residence Order)*[45] a non-resident parent who objected to the naturism of the resident parent and her new partner failed in their application to stop naturism in front of their children. Families have different attitudes about nudity and it was not appropriate for the court to intervene. Nonetheless, the Court of Appeal in *Re B (Child Immunisation)*[46] was willing to permit the vaccination of a child with the MMR vaccine, against the wishes of the resident parent, following an application for such an order by the non-resident parent. This may be explained on the basis that the order did not involve an invasion of the resident parent's rights on how to live her day-to-day life. It would, no doubt, have been quite different if the non-resident parent had sought an order that the resident parent feed the child at least five portions of fresh fruit or vegetables a day. It is unlikely that a court would make such a court order, despite the clear scientific evidence of the benefits of such a diet.[47]

Baroness Hale, in *R (On the Application of Williamson) v Secretary of State for Education and Employment*,[48] stated:

> Children have the right to be properly cared for and brought up so that they can fulfil their potential and play their part in society. Their parents have both the primary responsibility and the primary right to do this. The state steps in to regulate the exercise of that responsibility in the interests of children and society as a whole. But 'the child is not the child of the state' and it is important in a free society that parents should be allowed a large measure of autonomy in the way in which they discharge their parental responsibilities. A free society is premised on the fact that people are different from one another. A free society respects individual differences.

Baroness Hale returned to this theme in *The Christian Institute v The Lord Advocate*,[49] seeing allowing children to be raised by their parents being key to a democratic state. She noted:

> The first thing that a totalitarian regime tries to do is to get at the children, to distance them from the subversive, varied influences of their families, and indoctrinate them in their rulers' view of the world.

---

[42] BBC News Online (2007d).
[43] *Re A (Conjoined Twins: Medical Treatment)* [2000] 3 FCR 577.
[44] *Re C (A Child) (HIV Test)* [1999] 2 FLR 1004, although see Strong (2000) for criticism of the argument on the facts of that case.
[45] [1999] 1 FLR 869.
[46] [2003] 3 FCR 156, discussed in O'Donnell (2004).
[47] See Probert, Gilmore and Herring (2009) for a detailed discussion of parental discretion.
[48] [2005] 1 FCR 498 at para 72.
[49] [2016] UKSC 51.

This is a remarkably different approach to parents' rights to that taken by Lord Scarman, mentioned above. In light of the points made by McCall Smith, it is respectfully suggested that it is also a more accurate one.

Jo Bridgeman has argued that any understanding of parental responsibilities should not be regarded as a set of abstract principles, but to flow from the parent–child relationship. She writes:

> In any relationship, responsibilities are partly determined by social expectation, in part individually interpreted, and depend upon current needs . . . In contrast to traditional philosophy, which insists that what the individual ought to do should be determined according to abstract principles, it is argued that a moral concept of responsibility should be informed by practices of caring responsibility. That is, that what parents ought to do with regard to the care of their children's health should be informed by guidelines developed through consideration of what parents do in caring for their children's health.[50]

This approach warns against trying to set out an abstract set of rights or responsibilities for parents, but rather suggests we look at the appropriate set of rights and responsibilities for the particular child–parent relationship at hand.

This debate over the nature of parents' rights and responsibilities has taken on an interesting dimension, with parents being held to account for their children. Parents are responsible for ensuring their children do not commit crimes, are not obese, and attend school. Helen Reece has suggested that: 'In the case of parents, in recent years their responsibility *for* their children has been undermined by their responsibility *to* external agencies.'[51] Indeed, she sees a move towards parental accountability:

> The shift in the meaning of parental responsibility enables the law to be uniquely intrusive and judgmental, because every parent, on being held up to scrutiny, is found lacking. Accordingly the blurry spectrum of facilitation and support that has recently replaced clear-cut punishment and enforcement can be explained by its much better fit with parental responsibility as accountability.

The difficulty with this emphasis on the responsibility of parents to raise 'good citizens' is that it can become excessively burdensome for parents. It might even feed into 'hyper-parenting' where parents seek to take complete control of their children's lives to ensure their children become champion sports people; wonderful musicians; or brilliant scientists depending on the whim of the parents. I have argued against this phenomenon, suggesting:

> Hyper-parenting and competitive parenting reflect the desire of parents to produce the ideal child. Government rhetoric, backed up by legal sanctions, reinforces this by emphasising that parents are responsible for their children in ways that are increasingly onerous and unrealistic. [I argue for] a different vision for parenthood. Parenthood is not a job for which parents need equipment and special training to ensure they produce the ideal product. It is a relationship where the parent learns from the child, is cared for by the child and is nourished by the child, as much as the parent does these things for the child. In short, parenthood should be framed not as a job, but as a relationship.[52]

This discussion feeds into a bigger debate over the extent to which the state should be interfering in family life, to protect children from being improperly influenced by parents or whether the kind of spontaneous loving family life that Brighouse and Swift talk about is only possible

---

[50] Bridgeman (2007: 36).
[51] Reece (2009d).
[52] Herring (2017).

if there is no regulation. Even taking their approach this does not seem to lead to a conclusion that no interference should take place. Regulation on the wearing of seatbelts does interfere in family life, but not so as to undermine Brighouse and Swift's vision of it.[53] Even regulations such as prohibition of corporal punishment or requiring parents to ensure children receive appropriate education do not. So, this would seem only an argument against the harshest of regulations.

C Why do parents have rights and responsibilities?

It may seem self-evident that on the birth of a child the mother and father are under legal and moral obligations concerning the child and have the right to care for the child. But this need not be so. We could have a society where the state takes care of every child at birth in giant children's homes and the parents have no legal standing in relation to the child; or where on birth the child is handed over to the person who has scored highest in a parenting examination organised by the state. Most people would regard these alternatives with horror, but why is it that it seems so 'natural' that parents should be responsible for and should have rights over 'their' children?

Closely linked to this issue is whether it can be right for a parent to seek to instil values into a child or affect the child's personality. Is there anything wrong in raising the child to be, like their parents, devoted fans of Fulham Football Club? Or enthusiastic members of the Methodist Church? Or devout atheists? Or people who think that giving money to charity is a good thing to do? Such questions raise lively debates and there is a temptation to believe it is appropriate for parents to influence children 'for the good', but 'not the bad'. But the problem is that virtually all parents think they are influencing children for the good.

Philosophers and lawyers have struggled with this question and in truth there is no entirely satisfactory answer, but some of the suggestions are as follows:

(i) Children as property

Children can be seen as the fruit of the parent's labour through procreation and therefore as the property of the parent. This could be seen as the basis of parental rights. Indeed, Arden LJ[54] has stated that the common law 'effectively treats the child as the property of the parent'.[55] At first sight, this is a rather unpleasant way of seeing children and such a theory has great difficulties.[56] We do not normally regard people as pieces of property which can be owned, and to describe parents' legal relationship with their children in the same terms used to describe their relationship with their cars seems clearly inappropriate.[57]

That said, our society is based on a strong belief that parents should normally be allowed to bring up 'their' children, and children can only be removed from parents if there is sufficient justification. Jean Kazez[58] thinks there is a profound claim to a child being 'of my flesh', which she claims is quite not the same as a property claim, but seeks to describe the closeness of a parent–child relationship. However, despite some similarities there are many other ways in which children are treated quite differently from property. One can legally destroy one's computer but not one's child, for example.

---

[53] Altman (2018).
[54] *R (On the Application of Williamson) v Secretary of State for Education and Employment* [2003] 1 FLR 726, 793.
[55] See Reece (2005) for an argument that no one has ever taken seriously the claim that children are property.
[56] Archard (2004b).
[57] Not least because once a child reaches majority parental rights cease.
[58] Kazez (2018).

(ii) Children on trust

This theory is that children have rights as people. As the child is unable to exercise these rights, the parents exercise these rights on the child's behalf. This version of explaining parents' rights is more popular than the property formulation.[59] It can take three forms:

1. The parents hold the rights of the child on trust for the child until he or she is old enough to claim these rights for him- or herself.

2. The parents hold the rights of the child on trust for the state. The parents care for the child until the child is able to become a citizen and a member of the state him- or herself.

3. The parents hold the rights of the child on a purpose trust – the purpose being the promotion of the welfare of the child.

The exact formulation matters little in practice, but the alternative approaches indicate important theoretical differences. The crucial difference is to whom the parent is responsible for the exercise of their rights: under 1 the parent is responsible to the child, whereas under 2 the parent is responsible to the state, while 3 leaves it unclear who has responsibility for enforcing the trust. The point to stress in all of these formulations is that the rights that parents exercise are not theirs, but those of the child and so should not be exercised for the benefit of the parent, but of the child.

There are three particular benefits of the trust analysis.[60] First, the law on trustees (fiduciaries) has been specifically developed to deal with fears that the trustee will misuse his or her powers as a trustee for his or her own benefit, rather than for the benefit of the subject of the trust. Such rules may be used by the law in ensuring that parents do not misuse their parental rights. Secondly, the law on trusts has developed realistic standards in policing the fiduciary's behaviour. The trustee cannot be expected always to make perfect choices, and is allowed a degree of discretion, but this does not permit the trustee to make manifestly bad decisions. These rules may also be useful in the parenting context. Thirdly, the trust approach means that the law would not need to see parents' interests and children's interests as in conflict.

There are, however, difficulties with the trust approach. There are some uncertainties of a technical nature: precisely what is the subject of the trust? (the rights of the child is the most common answer); who created the trust? Other problems are more practical. It may be justifiable to place on fiduciaries heavy obligations never to consider their own interests when dealing with the trust property, but for parents the obligation to care for children is a 24-hour-a-day obligation, involving decisions which profoundly affect their own private lives. To require the same standards of a trustee (and never to consider their own interests) may seem therefore overly onerous.[61] Further, although the law can readily establish a widely accepted standard on, for example, the duty of investment upon a trustee, finding community standards as to what is reasonable parenting would be well-nigh impossible on many issues.[62] Also, the trust model does not readily capture the notion that children may have the right to make decisions for themselves. This could be dealt with by stating that the number of rights which are the subject of the trust lessen as the child becomes older and the child is able to exercise these for him- or herself. Finally, it has been claimed that the trust model fails to capture the sense of interconnection between parent and child.[63]

---

[59] See Holgate (2005).
[60] O'Donovan (1993).
[61] Schneider (1995).
[62] Schneider (1995).
[63] Reshef (2013).

(iii) Imposition by society

The flip side of the question of why parents should have rights is to ask: 'Why should parents be under a duty to care for children?' Eekelaar argues that there are two aspects of a parent's obligations to care for a child.[64] First, he suggests that every person owes a basic duty to other people to promote human flourishing. Secondly, on top of that basic duty there are special duties that society chooses to impose on particular people in particular circumstances. Our society chooses to impose special duties on parents to care for children. This is because children are vulnerable and need to be cared for by someone if society is to grow. Parents are best placed to provide the required care and that is widely accepted within our society. In other words, parents are only obliged especially to care for children because that is the choice of our society, not because of some underlying moral principle. Barton and Douglas[65] are unhappy with this approach because it suggests that there would be nothing morally objectionable for a state to require all children at birth to be removed from their parents and raised by state-approved agencies. They argue that most people would find such a system objectionable, even if it could be shown not to be particularly harmful to children, which is why they think that parents have something akin to an ownership right in respect of the child.

(iv) Voluntary assumption by parents

Barton and Douglas[66] argue that the key element behind imposing the responsibilities of parenthood is that parents have voluntarily accepted the obligation. A parent who does not want to care for the child is not necessarily obliged to. For example, they argue that if a mother gives birth to a child following a rape, she is not obliged to raise the child, although she is under a duty to ensure the child receives some care, as would someone who came across an abandoned baby. However, any parent who chooses to undertake the parental role is under a duty to carry out the role reasonably well. There is much to be said for this theory, but it cannot completely explain why parents are under parental obligations.[67] If X notices that her neighbour has just had a baby and X steals her and undertakes to care for her, this does not give X the rights and duties of parenthood, despite her intent to be a parent. So, as Barton and Douglas[68] suggest, an element of the property argument or Eekelaar's argument needs to be relied upon in addition to the argument based on voluntary assumption of obligation if this theory is to explain the law's attitude towards parents.

A stronger version of this argument is that parents' rights emerge through their investment of 'parental work'.[69] By investing time, money and effort into the child's life they have a legitimate say in the child's life. Certainly, a stronger say than others who will not have made the same investment. Interestingly such a model places no particular weight on the concept that giving parents rights benefits children, but is a just reward for parents' endeavours. It is, perhaps, at its strongest when there is an issue over which there is no single 'right answer' and we are trying to decide who is to be given the choice to select between a reasonable range of options. But if that is its scope, it is limited. And that leads us on to the view that parents should not have particular rights.

---

[64] Eekelaar (1991b).
[65] Barton and Douglas (1995).
[66] Barton and Douglas (1995).
[67] See Chapter 6 for further discussion of such arguments in the context of child support.
[68] Barton and Douglas (1995).
[69] Millum (2018).

(v) Best interests of the child

This approach argues that the parents of the child should be those who are best placed to make decisions on the child's behalf. This may be those who are in a close caring relationship with the child.[70] One problem with this view is it does not explain why parents have a claim over a child at birth. It also might not explain the extent to which parents have discretion over how to raise the child. Further, it may be thought to give too much scope for the state to remove children from parents who are not acting in an ideal way. These are not necessarily overwhelming problems. We might say that it will cause a child trauma to be removed from parents unless they are causing a serious harm. That protects children from being too readily removed from their parents.

(vi) The good of family life

Harry Brighouse and Adam Swift argue that an essential good of family life is 'family relationship goods': that children and parents share a common life, marked by 'a spontaneous, loving, intimate sharing of lives'.[71] They explain:

> The spontaneous sharing with their children of at least some of who parents really are is crucial to healthy family life: that sharing is bound to result in some shaping of values . . . The idea that parents should constantly monitor themselves in their relations with their children in order to screen out anything that might have any influence on their children's emerging values is ludicrous.[72]

It would be a very odd family if the parents went off to watch their favourite football team, but left the children at home for fear that otherwise they would indoctrinate their child in favour of that team. And some people would say this is the same even if we are talking about religious or political groups meeting. However, it might be possible to distinguish different activities. For example, Matthew Clayton suggests parents should not instil values with which reasonable parents would dispute.[73] That might explain that few would object to parents being encouraged to promote generosity in their children, but most would object to inculcating racist beliefs with their children. However there seem so many issues on which there is controversy that it is hardly a helpful guide. An alternative might be to distinguish beliefs where a child has little choice but to accept the belief. Norvin Richards[74] has helpfully suggested that there is a difference where parents engage in productions which are 'joint endeavours' and those where parents seek to mould children in a particular way. So, to use the examples above, we might wonder how the parents would respond if the child suddenly became a fan of West Ham's women's football team or became fascinated by Buddhism. Would the family continue to act only in line with the parents' interests or would the family find a way of appreciating all the interests of the members?

(vii) Arguments against parental rights

Anca Gheaus[75] argues that children's vulnerability is such that there should not be a monopoly of care over them. By ensuring a range of adults are involved in children's care we might lessen the risk of abuse. It is not clear this follows. One might argue that the larger the number of

---

[70] Herring (2013a: ch. 6); Boyd (2016).
[71] Brighouse and Swift (2014).
[72] Brighouse and Swift (2014).
[73] Clayton (2006).
[74] Richards (2018).
[75] Gheaus (2018).

adults involved in a child's life the greater the risk one will be an abuser. Her second argument against giving parents exclusive rights is that one of the great goods of childhood is it gives children a chance to discover, create and experiment with the self. As she notes, by adulthood most people become pretty 'set in their ways' and we should celebrate childhood as a time of self-discovery and exploration. That, she argues, is likely to occur if there are a range of adults assisting in this enterprise.[76] She may have an overly negative view of adulthood in this description. Further, some lifestyle choices may require emersion into a culture or community (cultural and religious groups in particular) and are simply not compatible with a child being raised by multiple adults.

To conclude, it is surprisingly difficult to find a single theory that adequately explains why parents should be responsible for their children. Perhaps the answer lies in the strength of a combination of these views.

D The vulnerability of parents

Normally when thinking about parents, commentators emphasise the power and rights of parents. But, in fact, parenthood can be exhausting hard work. While parents are held responsible, both in law and socially, for the behaviour of their children, their ability to control their children may be limited. We assume that parents are the ones with the capacity, resources and power; and children are vulnerable, dependent and powerless. However, parenthood can create considerable vulnerability for parents.[77]

So far, we have been looking at parents' rights and responsibility from a theoretical perspective. What is the law itself?

6 Parental responsibility

Learning objective 3

Explain and evaluate the concept of parental responsibility

The law on the duties and rights of parenthood is covered by the notion of parental responsibility.

A What is parental responsibility?

Given that parental responsibility is one of the key concepts in family law, one might have thought it would be easy to define it, but it is not.[78] The root cause of the uncertainty is that the notion of parental responsibility is required to fulfil a wide variety of functions. Eekelaar has suggested that there are two aspects of parental responsibility:[79]

1. *What that responsibility means.* It encapsulates the legal duties and powers that enable a parent to care for a child or act on the child's behalf. Parents must exercise their rights 'dutifully' towards their children.

---

[76] Gheaus (2018).
[77] Herring (2020d).
[78] See Probert, Gilmore and Herring (2009) for a useful set of essays on the topic.
[79] See Eekelaar (1991c).

2. *Who has the responsibility?* It explains that the law permits the person with parental responsibility rather than anyone else to have parental responsibility. It determines who has the authority to make a decision relating to a child. As MacFarlane LJ has put it:

> The Children Act 1989 does not place the primary responsibility of bringing up children upon judges, magistrates, CAFCASS officers or courts; the responsibility is placed upon the child's parents . . . [80]

In an attempt to explain further what parental responsibility means, we need to look at the legislative and judicial understanding of parental responsibility:

(i) The Children Act

The starting point is s. 3 of the Children Act 1989:

LEGISLATIVE PROVISION

Children Act 1989, section 3

In this Act 'parental responsibility' means all the rights, duties, powers, responsibilities and authority which by law a parent of a child has in relation to the child and his property.

This leaves unanswered as many questions as it answers, because it fails to explain what those rights etc. are. The Law Commission decided against a statutory definition of the responsibilities of parents because they change from case to case and depend on the age and maturity of the child. For example, parental responsibility in relation to a disabled child might be thought to impose different obligations on a parent than if the child were not disabled.[81] In any event, it would not be possible to list all the responsibilities that attend parental responsibility. Rob George[82] suggested the following:

- naming the child;
- providing a home for the child;
- bringing up the child;
- having contact with the child;
- protecting and maintaining the child;
- administering the child's property;
- consenting to the taking of blood for testing;
- allowing the child to be interviewed;
- taking the child outside the jurisdiction of the United Kingdom and consenting to emigration;
- agreeing to or vetoing the issue of the child's passport;

---

[80] *Re W (Children)* [2012] EWCA 999.
[81] See Corker and Davis (2000) for a discussion of the legal treatment of disabled children.
[82] George (2012b: 131); building on Lowe and Douglas (2007: 377).

- agreeing to the child's adoption;
- agreeing to the child's change of surname;
- consenting to the child's medical treatment;
- arranging the child's education;
- determining the child's religious upbringing;
- disciplining the child and sometimes take responsibility for harm caused by the child;
- consenting to the child's marriage;
- representing the child in legal proceedings;
- appointing a guardian for the child;
- disposing of the child's corpse.

No doubt this is not a complete list, but it gives an indication of the range of issues for which parents may be responsible.

Rather than trying to list the issues over which parents can make decisions about a child, it may be more profitable to consider what limitations there are on the parental power to decide how to raise a child. The parent can make decisions about all areas of the child's life, subject to the following:

1. *The criminal law.* For example, it is a criminal offence to assault a child, which restricts the power[83] of parents to administer corporal punishment.

2. *Any requirement to consult or obtain the consent of anyone else with parental responsibility.* For example, s. 13 of the Children Act 1989 requires a parent wishing to change a child's surname to obtain the consent of anyone else with parental responsibility before doing so.

3. *The power of the local authority to take a child into care.* If a child is taken into care by a local authority, this effectively restricts the powers of parents to make decisions about their child's upbringing.[84]

4. *Any orders of the court.* There may be a court order in force which deals with a specific aspect of a child's upbringing, in which case a parent may not act in a way contrary to the court order.[85]

5. The ability of children who are sufficiently mature (*Gillick*-competent) to make decisions for themselves. This will be discussed shortly.

6. *The human rights of the child.* Many interferences in the human rights of the child will also be a crime, but not all. In **RK v BCC**[86] it was held that although a parent could restrict the liberty of a child (for example, confining them to their bedroom), doing so to a significant extent might infringe their right to liberty under Article 5 of the European Convention on Human Rights (ECHR), particularly if they are a teenager.

(ii) Judicial understanding of parental responsibility

Unfortunately, the courts have not been consistent in their understanding of parental responsibility. In some cases it is seen as being largely of symbolic value (indicating a parent is

---

[83] Offences Against the Person Act 1861, s. 47.
[84] See Chapter 11.
[85] Children Act 1989, s. 2(8).
[86] [2011] EWCA 1305.

committed to a child),[87] while in others it is seen as about allocating real decision-making power.[88] There have been several cases where a father has been granted parental responsibility, but is not permitted to contact the child. In such cases parental responsibility appears to be little more than a pat on the back and an official confirmation that the father is a committed father.[89] Helen Reece looking at this case law has suggested that parental responsibility is being used as a form of therapy.[90] It is designed to make the father feel good about himself and his relationship with the child, even if, in reality, the relationship has little substance. By contrast other cases have seen parental responsibility as about real rights and about the exercise of parental responsibility. For example, in *M v M (Parental Responsibility)*,[91] despite obvious love and commitment to his child, the father was denied parental responsibility because he lacked the mental capacities to make decisions on behalf of the child. Given the somewhat contradictory case law, it is perhaps reassuring to read Black J's statement: 'parental responsibility can be an inaccessible concept at the best of times, not infrequently difficult for lawyers to grasp and often very challenging for those who are not lawyers'.[92]

B Parental responsibility in practice

A person who does not have parental responsibility, of course, can act as a parent towards a child in a variety of ways. They can feed, clothe, educate and play with the child. There are many people carrying out the tasks of parenthood, without parental responsibility. Indeed, no doubt, some people without parental responsibility act more like a parent towards a child than other people with parental responsibility. So, when does it actually matter whether a person has parental responsibility? The following are rights and responsibilities that a person with parental responsibility has, which a person without parental responsibility does not have.

1. They can withhold consent to adoption and freeing for adoption.[93]

2. They can object to the child being accommodated in local authority accommodation[94] and remove the child from local authority accommodation.[95]

3. They can appoint a guardian.[96]

4. They can give legal authorisation for medical treatment.[97]

5. They have a right of access to the child's health records.

---

[87] For example, *Re S (A Minor) (Parental Responsibility)* [1995] 2 FLR 648, [1995] 3 FCR 225; *Re C and V (Minors) (Parental Responsibility and Contact)* [1998] 1 FCR 57.

[88] *M v M (Parental Responsibility)* [1999] 2 FLR 737.

[89] See also the odd use of a joint residence order in *W v A* [2004] EWCA Civ 1587 even though the mother was to take the child to South Africa The joint residence order, Wall LJ explained, would emphasise that both parents shared parental responsibility.

[90] Reece (2009c).

[91] [1999] 2 FLR 737.

[92] *Re D (Contact and Parental Responsibility: Lesbian Mothers and Known Father)* [2006] 1 FCR 556.

[93] Adoption Act 1976, s. 72.

[94] Children Act 1989, s. 20(7).

[95] Children Act 1989, s. 20(8).

[96] Children Act 1989, s. 5.

[97] Eekelaar (2001d: 429) argues that a father without parental responsibility can give effective consent to medical treatment because he has a duty to promote the health of his children and that duty can only realistically be imposed if he has the right to provide the consent necessary for that treatment. See Probert, Gilmore and Herring (2009) for a questioning of this view.

6. They can withdraw a child from sex education and religious education classes and make representations to schools concerning the child's education.[98]

7. Their consent is required if the child's parent seeks to remove the child from the jurisdiction.[99]

8. They can sign a child's passport application and object to the granting of a passport.

9. They have sufficient rights in relation to a child to invoke the international child abduction rules.[100]

10. They can consent to the marriage of a child aged 16 or 17.[101]

11. They will automatically be a party to care proceedings.[102]

12. They can authorise a deprivation of liberty of the child (e.g. in a secure hospital).[103]

Although this is a lengthy list, in fact, these rights do not arise very often in practice. The most common situations are where a third party wishes to treat a child in a particular way which would be a crime or tort without the consent of someone who has parental responsibility:[104] for example, a doctor wishes to provide medical treatment for a child.[105] Ros Pickford[106] found that over 75 per cent of fathers without parental responsibility were unaware that they lacked it. Many of these fathers were fathers of teenagers. This indicates that it is quite possible to carry out a full parental role without having to rely on parental responsibility. Notably, even of those fathers who were aware they lacked parental responsibility few went on to seek it. Again, this suggests that it is of little relevance in day-to-day life.

If parental responsibility is of limited practical significance, then why is it so important? John Eekelaar sums up the position well: 'parental responsibility can best be understood as legal recognition of the exercise of social parenthood. It thus comprises a factual (recognition of a state of affairs) and a normative (giving the state of affairs the "stamp of approval") element'.[107] As this implies, parental responsibility is more about confirming an existing situation or sending a message of approval to the parent, rather than actually creating rights. However, as most unmarried fathers are unaware of whether they have parental responsibility or not,[108] the effectiveness of such a stamp of approval may be questioned.

C The rights of a parent without responsibility

Although parental responsibility is the primary source of parental rights, there are rights and responsibilities that flow simply from being a parent. These are the benefits and responsibilities that follow from parenthood in and of itself. Notice two things about this list. First, these

---

[98] Education Act 1996. Eekelaar (2001d) argues that a father without parental responsibility can make decisions in relation to the child's education.

[99] Children Act 1989, s. 13.

[100] See Chapter 10.

[101] Marriage Act 1949, s. 3.

[102] A father without parental responsibility can also be a party in certain limited circumstances: Children Act 1989, Appendix 3.

[103] *Re D (A Child) (Deprivation of Liberty)* [2015] EWHC 922 (Fam).

[104] Or the consent of the court.

[105] *B v B (Grandparent: Residence Order)* [1992] 2 FLR 327, [1993] 1 FCR 211.

[106] Pickford (1999).

[107] Eekelaar (2001d: 428).

[108] Pickford (1999).

rights apply to a parent, whether or not they have parental responsibility. Second, most of these do not apply to a person who has parental responsibility but is not a parent.

1. A parent has a right to apply without leave for a section 8 order.[109]

2. A parent has rights of succession to the estate of the child.[110]

3. There is a presumption that a child in local authority care should have reasonable contact with each parent.[111]

4. On application for an emergency protection order, there is a duty to inform the child's parents.[112]

5. A parent can apply to discharge an emergency protection order.[113]

6. Rights of citizenship pass primarily through parentage.

7. Parents are liable persons under social security legislation.

8. A parent cannot marry his or her child.[114]

9. The criminal law on incest forbids sexual relations between parents and children.

10. A parent who is not living with his or her child will be liable to make payments under the child support legislation.

As can be seen from this list, the parent without parental responsibility has some rights, but they do not directly relate to the child's day-to-day upbringing. As Baroness Hale, in *Re G (Residence: Same-Sex Partner)*,[115] puts it:

> To be the legal parent of a child gives a person legal standing to bring and defend proceedings about the child and makes the child a member of that person's family, but it does not necessarily tell us much about the importance of that person to the child's welfare.

D The extent of parental responsibility

Once a parent has parental responsibility, this cannot be removed, except in a few special cases.[116] Even if the parent has behaved in such a way that the child has to be taken into care, he or she will not lose parental responsibility.[117] However, in *A Local Authority v D*[118] the parents had caused serious emotional abuse to their son. He was taken into care. Although the parents still retained parental responsibility the abuse was such that Munby J held they were not in a position to consent to the child's deprivation of liberty. The statutory basis for this finding is unclear, nor is it clear whether it can apply to other kinds of cases. Notably Munby J was not saying their bad conduct had led to the removal of their parental responsibility. It had just, somehow, limited its effectiveness.

---

[109] Children Act 1989, s. 10(4).
[110] See Chapter 12.
[111] Children Act 1989, s. 34.
[112] Children Act 1989, s. 44(13).
[113] Children Act 1989, s. 45(8).
[114] Marriage Act 1949, s. 1.
[115] [2006] 1 FCR 681 at para 32.
[116] If a non-parent has parental responsibility through a residence order, then when the order comes to an end the parental responsibility ceases. In *Re F (Indirect Contact)* [2006] EWCA Civ 1426 a father's parental responsibility (given to him under a parental responsibility order) was revoked after a sustained campaign of violence and harassment against the mother and child.
[117] See Chapter 11.
[118] [2015] EWHC 3125 (Fam).

Parental responsibility comes to an end when a child reaches the age of 18. There is some ambiguity over whether it ceases when a child has *Gillick* capacity (i.e. has sufficient under-standing and maturity to make the decision). Several recent cases have suggested it does.[119] And that seemed to be the line taken by Lady Hale in *Re D (A Child)*[120] when she stated: 'as a general rule, parental responsibility extends to making decisions on behalf of a child of any age who lacks the capacity to make them for himself.'

Although a parent cannot surrender parental responsibility, it is possible to delegate it.[121] The fact that a new person acquires parental responsibility does not mean that anyone else loses it.[122] As shall be seen later, the nature of parental responsibility may change with the age and development of the child.

7 Sharing parental responsibility

It is clear from the scheme of the Children Act 1989 that there will be many situations where several people have parental responsibility. Although a child can have only two parents, any number of people can have parental responsibility. The question therefore arises whether each person with parental responsibility can exercise his or her parental responsibility alone or whether it is necessary to have the agreement of all those with parental responsibility in respect of each decision concerning the upbringing of the child.[123]

Although there are a few exceptions, s. 2(7) appears to give a clear answer:

LEGISLATIVE PROVISION

Children Act 1989, section 2(7)

Where more than one person has parental responsibility for a child, each of them may act alone and without the other (or others) in meeting that responsibility; but nothing in this Part shall be taken to affect the operation of any enactment which requires the consent of more than one person in a matter affecting the child.

There are two crucial points that appear clear from this subsection. The first is that, except where the statute provides otherwise, each person with parental responsibility can exercise parental responsibility alone without obtaining the consent of the others with parental respon-sibility or even consulting them. It has been suggested that in this way the Act promotes 'inde-pendent' rather than 'cooperative' parenting.[124]

The second is that there is no hierarchy among those with parental responsibility. So, in the Children Act 1989 there is no preference given to mothers over fathers, or between those with whom the child lives and those with whom the child does not live. If a child who normally

---

[119] See below, 'Under 16-year-olds'.
[120] [2019] UKSC 52.
[121] Children Act 1989, s. 2(9).
[122] Children Act 1989, s. 2(6), although an adoption order will end any existing parental responsibility.
[123] See the discussion in Maidment (2001b).
[124] Bainham (1990).

lives with her mother is visiting her father (with parental responsibility), he can take her to a church service, arrange for her to have an unusual haircut, or feed her meat – even if the mother strongly opposes these activities. The mother could apply for a prohibited steps order[125] to prevent the father doing this, but in the absence of such an order he is free to do this.[126] Similarly, when the child lives with the mother, she can bring up the child as she believes best.[127]

There are a number of exceptions to the rule that there is no need to consult, although in all of these situations if the consent is not provided then the court may be able to dispense with the consent and authorise the act:

1. Adoption and freeing for adoption can take place only if *all* parents[128] with parental responsibility consent.[129]

2. If the child aged 16 or 17 wishes to marry, then *all* parents with parental responsibility and any guardians must consent.[130]

3. If the child is to be accommodated by the local authority, then *none* of those with parental responsibility must have objected.[131]

4. Section 13 of the Children Act 1989 states that if a residence order has been made and one party wishes to change the surname of the child then the consent of all those with parental responsibility is required.[132] In *Re PC (Change of Surname)*[133] it was suggested that even if there was not a residence order in force then it was necessary to have the consent of all those with parental responsibility.[134]

5. Section 13 of the Children Act 1989 states that if there is a residence order it is not possible to remove a child from the United Kingdom without the consent of all those with parental responsibility.[135] It is arguable, by analogy with the decisions relating to surnames, that in order to remove a child from the United Kingdom the consent of all those with parental responsibility is required.

6. There are cases which suggest that the consent of all those with parental responsibility is required for any decision which is of fundamental importance to the child and is irreversible.[136] Which decisions are of fundamental importance? This will, it seems, be decided on a case-by-case basis. We know the following are issues of fundamental importance:

   - *Education. In **Re G (A Minor) (Parental Responsibility: Education)***[137] it was suggested that there is a duty to consult over long-term decisions relating to education. Here the question was whether the child should be moved from one school to another.

---

[125] Under Children Act 1989, s. 8.
[126] A local authority has a duty to consult parents and people with parental responsibility about all decisions unless this is not reasonably practicable.
[127] There is no question of the parties being bound by pre-birth agreements: *Re W (A Minor) (Residence Order)* [1992] 2 FLR 332.
[128] And guardians.
[129] But not others with parental responsibility: Adoption Act 1976, s. 16; Children Act 1989, ss. 12(3), 33(6).
[130] Marriage Act 1949, s. 3(1A).
[131] See Chapter 11.
[132] Children Act 1989, s. 13.
[133] [1997] 2 FLR 730.
[134] Indeed (as we shall see in Chapter 10), it may be necessary to obtain the consent of every parent.
[135] Children Act 1989, s. 13.
[136] Eekelaar (1998).
[137] [1994] 2 FLR 964, [1995] 2 FCR 53.

- *Circumcision.* In *Re J (Specific Issue Orders)*[138] the Court of Appeal held that if a male child[139] is to undergo a circumcision all of those with parental responsibility should be consulted.

- *Changing the child's surname.* Consultation with all those with parental responsibility is required before a child's surname can be changed.[140]

- *The MMR vaccine.* If the resident parent decides not to give her child the MMR vaccine, she should consult with the non-resident parent if he has parental responsibility.[141]

It is arguable that these decisions fly in the face of s. 2(7) of the Children Act 1989,[142] which makes it clear that, in the absence of statutory provisions to the contrary, a parent can exercise parental responsibility alone. However, MacFarlane LJ has recently emphasised that respecting the rights of the other parent is part of parental responsibility: 'where two parents share parental responsibility, it will be the duty of one parent to ensure that the rights of the other parent are respected, and vice versa, for the benefit of the child'.[143]

It appears from the case law that the duty on the resident parent is to consult, rather than obtain, the non-resident parent's consent. The significance of this consultation requirement is therefore that it gives the non-resident parent the opportunity to bring legal proceedings to prevent the resident parent from acting in the proposed way. However, it is far from clear what the court will do if the resident parent fails to consult. For example, if the mother arranges for the circumcision without consultation with the father, there is not much the law can do. The requirement to consult appears unenforceable in many cases. If a parent arranges circumcision without consultation, it will be too late for the court to intervene.

A Are all parental responsibilities equal?

It seems clear from s. 2(7) of the Children Act 1989 that each parent with parental responsibility is equal. However, in *Re P (A Minor) (Parental Responsibility Order)*[144] the courts have suggested that the parent with whom the child lives is to have the power to decide 'day-to-day' issues relating to the child. So the non-residential parent cannot use his or her parental responsibility to upset the day-to-day parenting of the residential parent.[145] In *Re C (Welfare of Child: Immunisation)*, Sumner J stated: 'Where parents do not live together, the court recognises the importance of the particular bond which exists in most cases between a child and the parent with the principal care of the child . . . It does not give that parent greater rights. It does mean that the court will take care to safeguard and preserve that bond in the best interests of the child.'[146] In *A v A (Children) (Shared Residence Order)*[147] it was suggested that a resident parent should not interfere in day-to-day issues in the way the non-resident parent treats the child during contact sessions.

---

[138] [2000] 1 FLR 517, [2000] 1 FCR 307.
[139] Female genital mutilation (previously known as 'female circumcision') is forbidden under the Female Genital Mutilation Act 2003.
[140] *Re PC (Change of Surname)* [1997] 2 FLR 730.
[141] *Re B (A Child) (Immunisation)* [2003] 3 FCR 156.
[142] Eekelaar (2001d).
[143] *Re W (Children)* [2012] EWCA 999.
[144] [1994] 1 FLR 578.
[145] For example, *Re J (Specific Issue Orders)* [2000] 1 FLR 517, [2000] 1 FCR 307.
[146] [2003] 2 FLR 1054 at para 305.
[147] [2004] 1 FCR 201 at para 118.

An interesting issue arose in *Re Jake (Withholding Medical Treatment)*:[148] do parents who lack mental capacity lose parental responsibility? That case involved medical treatment and the court was deciding whether treatment was in a child's best interests. They held that despite the difficulties the parents had, their views and wishes had to be taken into account by the court, just as the court would take any parents' views into account. They did not express a view on the harder question of whether a third party, such as a doctor, could rely on the consent of a parent with parental responsibility to give legal justification for treatment, or whether if there was a dispute between a parent with capacity and one without, the views of the one with capacity would carry greater weight.

B Is the law in a sound state?

If a residential parent (the parent with whom the child lives) exercises parental responsibility in a way objected to by the non-residential parent, the latter could bring the matter before the court by way of a specific issue order or prohibited steps order. There is, therefore, a sense that it matters little whether there is a formal duty to consult because, whether or not there is a requirement to consult, if those with parental responsibility disagree, the matter will be brought before a court. There are, however, three points of practical significance in whether or not there is a duty to consult. The first is that it determines whose responsibility it is to bring the matter before the court. For example, if the law is that one parent cannot change the name of the child without the other's consent then the parent seeking to change the name will have the burden of bringing the matter before the court. However, if the law was that a parent could independently change a name, then it would be the responsibility of the person objecting to the change to bring the matter before the court. Secondly, the issue of who should be liable to pay the legal costs of both parties if the matter is brought before the court may depend on whether there was a duty to consult, with which a parent did not comply. Thirdly, there is the 'message' that the law wishes to send out. Does the law wish to encourage cooperative or independent parenting?

The following are some of the approaches that the law could take regarding those who share parental responsibility:

1. All those with parental responsibility must agree on every issue relating to the child.

2. The residential parent can make all decisions relating to the child, and the non-residential parent has rights only to bring a matter to court.

3. The residential parent should make all important decisions, although the non-residential parent can make day-to-day decisions when the child is spending time with them.

4. The parents must consult on all important issues; otherwise each parent can take day-to-day decisions when the child is spending time with them.

5. Each parent with parental responsibility can exercise parental responsibility independently and does not need to consult with the other over any issue.

It should be clear that approach 1 is impractical. It would not be realistic to expect a parent to contact and discuss with the other parent the contents of every meal, for example.

---

[148] [2015] EWHC 2442 (Fam).

Approach 2 is likewise impractical, at least if the non-residential parent is to have contact with the child. The choice is therefore between the last three options. The issues seem to be as follows:

DEBATE

Should parenting be cooperative?

1. *Fears of misuse.* There are fears that giving the non-residential parent a say in how the child is brought up by the residential parent could constitute a major infringement of the rights of private life of the residential parent. For example, if the non-residential parent could compel the vegetarian parent to prepare meat for the child to eat, this may be seen as an infringement of the residential parent's rights. There are particular concerns in cases where there has been domestic violence, where there is evidence that abusers continue to exercise control over their victims through whatever route is available.[149] Giving powers to the non-residential parent to direct how the residential parent brings up the child is therefore open to abuse.

2. *Involvement of the non-residential parent.* There are concerns that the non-residential parent will be excluded from the child's life. If there is no duty to consult, the non-residential parent may not even be aware that there is a crucial issue to be decided in respect of the child and will not be able to carry out an effective parenting role.

3. *Lack of knowledge of non-residential parent.* Some claim that non-residential parents do not know the child well enough to make important decisions in relation to the child. Of course, this is a generalisation, but the law in this area must rest on generalisations and it may well be argued that, as a general rule, the residential parent will be better poised to make a decision in respect of a child than a non-residential parent.

4. *Onerous obligation on residential parent.* Some are concerned that an obligation to obtain consent could be unduly time-consuming, stressful and burdensome for the residential parent, especially where the other parent may be difficult to contact.[150]

5. *Disruption for child.* There is a concern that permitting each parent to exercise parental responsibility will lead to disruption for the child by constantly changing lifestyles.

   For example, in **Re PC (Change of Surname)**[151] it was argued that if each parent with parental responsibility could change the child's surname, this would lead to the child's name constantly being changed, first by one parent and then by the other. Similarly, a child receiving religious instruction from one parent and conflicting religious instruction from another could feel confused and pressurised.

6. *Law should stress 'doing'.* Smart and Neale[152] criticise the law for failing to place sufficient emphasis on the 'doing' aspects of caring. They argue it is wrong to stress 'caring about' children above 'caring for' children. They see a danger in giving non-residential parents' rights, without having to perform the day-to-day care for children. Indeed, the burden of

---

[149] See Chapter 7.
[150] Law Commission Report 175 (1988: para 2.10).
[151] [1997] 2 FLR 730, [1997] 3 FCR 544.
[152] Smart and Neale (1999a).

ensuring there is cooperation seems to fall on the resident parent. It is she who must find and discuss the issue with the non-resident parent.

7. *Ignorance of the law.* Given the ignorance of the requirements of family law, it seems wrong to impose an obligation to consult, as it is likely to be unknown by most people. It would therefore be honoured more in the breach than the observance and would, as suggested above, effectively be unenforceable.

8. *Reality.* It could be argued that there is little the law can do here. Whether there will be cooperative or independent parenting will depend on the relationship and personality of the parties, rather than the requirements of the law. Compelling consultation or cooperation is unlikely to be productive.

Questions

1. *Can the law do anything to encourage cooperative parenting?*

2. *If one parent spends more time with the child than the other should they have a greater say in disputes over the child's upbringing?*

Further reading

Read **Bainham** (2009d) for a discussion of whether parents have rights.

As can be seen from the above, there are strong arguments on both sides. Whatever the law is, there will be some cases where a consultation requirement will be beneficial and others where it is open to abuse. This key issue is whether it is worth running the risks of misuse in the name of sending a message encouraging cooperation. Further, although we may generally want parents to consult over important issues concerning their children's upbringing, that does not mean that we should turn that into a legal obligation. Also, it is arguable that if there is to be a duty to consult, we need to be a little more careful in deciding who should have parental responsibility.[153] Should the father in *Re S (A Minor) (Parental Responsibility)*,[154] who was known to be a possessor of paedophilic literature, be consulted about his daughter's medical treatment? Even if he has not seen her for years? Should a mother be required to consult a father if he has been violent towards her in the past?

8 The welfare principle

Learning objective 4

Analyse the welfare principle

At the heart of the law relating to children is the principle that whenever the court considers a question relating to the upbringing of children the paramount consideration should be the welfare of the children. In Chapter 10 we will explore the application of the welfare principle in particular contexts. For this chapter we will explore the concept as a general principle.

---

[153] Eekelaar (2001d).
[154] [1995] 2 FLR 648, [1995] 3 FCR 225.

Section 1(1) of the Children Act 1989 clearly states the central principle of child law:

LEGISLATIVE PROVISION

Children Act 1989, section 1(1)

When a court determines any question with respect to—

(a)   the upbringing of a child; or

(b)   the administration of a child's property or the application of any income arising from it, the child's welfare shall be the court's paramount consideration.

This apparently simple principle is, in fact, complex. Several issues require explanation.

A   What does 'welfare' mean?

The Children Act has attempted to add some flesh to the concept of a child's welfare.[155] There is no definition of 'welfare' in the Children Act 1989, although there is a list of factors which a judge should consider when deciding what is in the child's welfare. These are listed in s. 1(3):

LEGISLATIVE PROVISION

Children Act 1989, section 1(3)

(a)   the ascertainable wishes and feelings of the child concerned (considered in the light of his age and understanding);

(b)   his physical, emotional and educational needs;

(c)   the likely effect on him of any change in his circumstances;

(d)   his age, sex, background and any characteristics of his which the court considers relevant;

(e)   any harm which he has suffered or is at risk of suffering;

(f)   how capable each of his parents, and any other person in relation to whom the court considers the question to be relevant, is of meeting his needs;

(g)   the range of powers available to the court under this Act in the proceedings in question.

(The interpretation of these factors is discussed in detail in Chapter 10.)

---

[155] For an interesting discussion that it would be preferable to talk in terms of well-being rather than welfare, see Eekelaar (2002a: 243).

B What does 'paramount' mean?

The courts' interpretation of the word 'paramount' is based on the decision of the House of Lords in *J v C*,[156] which considered the meaning of the words 'first and paramount' in the Guardianship of Infants Act 1925. Lord McDermott explained that the phrase means:

> . . . more than the child's welfare is to be treated as the top item in a list of items relevant to the matter in question. [The words] connote a process whereby, when all the relevant facts, relationships, claims and wishes of parents, risks, choices and other circumstances are taken into account and weighed, the course to be followed will be that which is most in the interests of the child.[157]

This clearly expresses the view that the welfare of the child is the sole consideration.[158] As was stated by the Court of Appeal in *Re P (Contact: Supervision)*,[159] 'the court is concerned with the interests of the mother and the father only in so far as they bear on the welfare of the child'. Baroness Hale in *Re G (Children) (Residence: Same-sex Partner)*,[160] following *J v C*, explained that section one means that the welfare of the child 'determines the course to be followed.' *J v C*[161] itself was especially significant because the House of Lords made it quite clear that the interests of the children outweigh the interests of even 'unimpeachable' (perfect) parents.[162] So whether an order is 'fair' or infringes the rights of parents is not relevant; all that matters is whether the order promotes the interests of children. Notice this does not mean that parents are irrelevant to the welfare principle because if a parent is harmed this may mean they will be a less effective parent and that will harm the child. So, the parent's interests can be taken into account, but only if they directly impact on the child. A good example of this point is *Re C (A Child)*[163] where a father had been imprisoned after abusing his child (C). The first instance judge had ordered that he could not have contact with C, but that he should be sent a passport size photograph of C every year. The Court of Appeal overturned the order. Although the photograph would provide comfort to C, in no way did it promote C's welfare. The order could not be justified based on the benefit to the father.

The interpretation adopted by the courts is surprising because, had Parliament intended welfare to be the only consideration, it could have said so. There was no need to interpret the word 'paramount' to mean sole. It is interesting to note that the UN Convention on the Rights of Children, in Article 3, states that the child's welfare should be the primary consideration. This appears to place slightly less weight on children's interests than s. 1 of the Children Act 1989.

Of course, when the courts are told they are to promote the child's welfare, they are not fairies with a magic wand and must deal with the situation in which the child finds themselves. In *M v H (A Child) (Educational Welfare)*[164] Charles J suggested that often all the courts were able to do was to find the 'least bad solution' for the child. The ideal solution may be for the parents to live together happily and raise the child together. That may not be possible and the court would have to select from the available options the one that caused least harm.

---

[156] [1970] AC 668. The background to the decision is helpfully discussed in Lowe (2011).
[157] At pp. 710–11.
[158] See, for example, Lord Hobhouse in *Dawson v Wearmouth* [1999] 1 FLR 1167.
[159] [1996] 2 FLR 314 at p. 328.
[160] [2006] 1 WLR 2305.
[161] [1970] AC 668.
[162] Quoted with approval in *Re W (A Child) (Adoption: Delay)* [2017] EWHC 829 (Fam).
[163] [2012] EWCA 918.
[164] [2008] 2 FCR 280.

C The nature of welfare

Two recent leading cases have helped clarify the nature of welfare:

CASE: *Re G (Education: Religious Upbringing)* [2012] EWCA Civ 1233

The parents had raised their five children aged between 3 and 11 within the Chassidic (or Chareidi) community of ultra-Orthodox Jews. The marriage broke down and the children lived with the mother, although they had extensive contact with the father. The mother left the Chareidi community, although she considered herself an Orthodox Jew. The children attended a single-sex ultra-orthodox school attended by other Chareidi community children. The parents disagreed over where the children should attend school and with whom the children should live.

Munby LJ in deciding the children should live with the mother, with contact with the father, made some wide-ranging comments on the nature of the welfare of children. This summary will focus on those particular comments.

He emphasised that welfare in s. 1 of the Children Act 1989 should be understood broadly to cover the child's well-being:

> Evaluating a child's best interests involves a welfare appraisal in the widest sense, taking into account, where appropriate, a wide range of ethical, social, moral, religious, cultural, emotional and welfare considerations. Everything that conduces to a child's welfare and happiness or relates to the child's development and present and future life as a human being, including the child's familial, educational and social environment, and the child's social, cultural, ethnic and religious community, is potentially relevant and has, where appropriate, to be taken into account. The judge must adopt a holistic approach (para 27).

Somewhat controversially he made it clear this is not simply a matter of happiness:

> I have referred to the child's happiness. Very recently, Herring and Foster[165] . . . have argued persuasively that behind a judicial determination of welfare there lies an essentially Aristotelian notion of the 'good life'. What then constitutes a 'good life'? There is no need to pursue here that age-old question. I merely emphasise that happiness, in the sense in which I have used the word, is not pure hedonism. It can include such things as the cultivation of virtues and the achievement of worthwhile goals, and all the other aims which parents routinely seek to inculcate in their children (para 29).

Further that the child's welfare has to be considered in their relational context:

> The well-being of a child cannot be assessed in isolation. Human beings live within a network of relationships. Men and women are sociable beings. As John Donne famously remarked, 'No man is an Island . . . ' Blackstone observed that 'Man was formed for society'. And long ago Aristotle said that 'He who is unable to live in society, or who has no need because he is sufficient for himself, must be either a beast or a god'. As Herring and Foster comment, relationships are central to our sense and understanding of ourselves. Our characters and understandings of ourselves from the earliest days are charted by reference to our relationships with others. It is only by considering the child's network of relationships that their well-being can be properly considered. So a child's relationships, both within and without the family, are always relevant to the child's interests; often they will be determinative (para 30).

---

[165] Herring and Foster (2012).

The judge, when deciding about a child's welfare had to act as a 'judicial reasonable parent' and have regard to the general standards in 2012 and the 'ever-changing nature of the world'. He expounded three aspects of this:

First, we must recognise that equality of opportunity is a fundamental value of our society: equality as between different communities, social groupings and creeds, and equality as between men and women, boys and girls. Second, we foster, encourage and facilitate aspiration: both aspiration as a virtue in itself and, to the extent that it is practical and reasonable, the child's own aspirations. Far too many lives in our community are blighted, even today, by lack of aspiration. Third, our objective must be to bring the child to adulthood in such a way that the child is best equipped both to decide what kind of life they want to lead – what kind of person they want to be – and to give effect so far as practicable to their aspirations. Put shortly, our objective must be to maximise the child's opportunities in every sphere of life as they enter adulthood. And the corollary of this, where the decision has been devolved to a 'judicial parent', is that the judge must be cautious about approving a regime which may have the effect of foreclosing or unduly limiting the child's ability to make such decisions in future (para 80).

Applying these principles to the case, the children should not be brought up in the Chareidi school which discouraged children pursing further education and limited the opportunities later in life, especially for girls. In saying that, he emphasised that the courts were neutral as between religions.

CASE: Re M (Children) (Ultra-Orthodox Judaism: Transgender Parent) [2017] EWCA Civ 2164

A couple separated and the 'father' transitioned and lived as a woman. The children had been raised with the Chareidi Jewish community. The father left the community on his transition. He sought contact with the children, but the mother claimed that she and the children would be marginalised and excluded from their community if contact took place, due to the opposition to trans people. Peter Jackson J at first instance accepted evidence that this would occur and, emphasising the importance of making the order which would best promote the children's welfare, ordered that there be indirect contact four times a year. While accepting this may be unfair on the 'father' and even discriminatory, he focused on determining what was best for the children and concluded:

So, weighing up the profound consequences for the children's welfare of ordering or not ordering direct contact with their father, I have reached the unwelcome conclusion that the likelihood of the children and their mother being marginalised or excluded by the ultra-Orthodox community is so real, and the consequences so great, that this one factor, despite its many disadvantages, must prevail over the many advantages of contact.

The Court of Appeal allowed the appeal and ordered the case to be reheard.

The Court of Appeal emphasised that in determining welfare the court had to operate as the 'judicial reasonable parent', based on the standards of reasonable men and women today. They determined this included that the reasonable person is broadminded, tolerant and slow to condemn. This meant that discriminatory attitudes could not dictate the outcome in this case. The human rights issues were important and should be discussed. In particular if, as the 'mother' claimed the school would ostracise her children if they had contact with the 'father', that would be unlawful discrimination and such unlawful conduct could not justify a denial of contact.

They also noted that contact should only be stopped as a last resort and it is clear that ongoing attempts at contact will not benefit the children. [Sadly, it later transpired that attempts at contact were unsuccessful and were only causing distress to the children. The court agreed that there should not be further attempts to achieve contact.]

There are a number of issues which are raised by these cases:

1. It is notable that in both, the court sees the application of the welfare principle not being what the judge thinks is in the best interests of the child, but what 'reasonable men and women today' think. Munby P in *Re M (Children) (Ultra-Orthodox Judaism: Transgender Parent)*[166] explained:

> The first is the core principle that the function of the judge in a case like this is to act as the 'judicial reasonable parent,' judging the child's welfare by the standards of reasonable men and women today, 2017, having regard to the ever changing nature of our world including, crucially for present purposes, *changes in social attitudes*, and always remembering that the reasonable man or woman is receptive to change, broadminded, tolerant, easy-going and slow to condemn. We live, or strive to live, in a tolerant society. We live in a democratic society subject to the rule of law. We live in a society whose law requires people to be treated equally and where their human rights are respected. We live in a plural society, in which the family takes many forms, some of which would have been thought inconceivable well within living memory.

> Seeing the welfare principle as an application of contemporary parenting standards may be designed to protect judges from suggestions that they are imposing their own view on families. However, it may be seen as a challenge for religious groups and other communities which do not take the same view about children's welfare. Traditionally, the law seemed to acknowledge diverse ways of raising children which are all acceptable, save when the child suffers significant harm. This case could be seen as a challenge to that view. For example, it is interesting to contrast the approach of the Court of Appeal in these cases to that in *Re T (Minors) (Custody: Religious Upbringing)*,[167] a case concerning Jehovah's Witnesses, where Scarman LJ said:

> It is not for this court, in society as at present constituted, to pass any judgment on the beliefs of the mother or on the beliefs of the father. It is sufficient for this court that it should recognise that each is entitled to his or her own beliefs and way of life, and that the two opposing ways of life considered in this case are both socially acceptable and certainly consistent with a decent and respectable life . . . It does not follow . . . that it is wrong, or contrary to the welfare of children, that life should be in a narrower sphere, subject to a stricter religious discipline.[168]

---

[166] [2017] EWCA Civ 2164.
[167] [1981] 2 FLR 239, 245.
[168] See Dwyer (2018) for an interesting discussion of these issues.

In effect, the two recent judgments indicate that members of religious groups that treat girls in a disadvantageous way as compared with boys or have highly traditional views on sexuality and sex will find it difficult to win arguments over upbringing if the other parent does not subscribe to such a religion.

2. It is a little surprising that the Court of Appeal in neither case paid much attention to the views of the children. In *Re M (Children) (Ultra-Orthodox Judaism: Transgender Parent)*[169] at first instance Peter Jackson J had met with the older child and his judgment contained a careful assessment of the child's views. It may be that the Court of Appeal were acting on the, unspoken, assumption that the children's views were not really their own.

3. There seems to be an assumption in Peter Jackson J's judgment in *Re M (Children) (Ultra-Orthodox Judaism: Transgender Parent)*[170] that the children will be cis and heterosexual. No attention was paid to the fact that if the children did not conform to the traditional sexual ethics of the community there would be considerable benefits in having a relationship with the father.[171]

4. The Court of Appeal in *Re G (Education: Religious Upbringing)*[172] emphasised that the network of the relationships was central to a child's well-being. One of the issues in relation to education which could have been made is that had the father won the argument over education, the children would be raised in a school which would have been critical of the way of life they had with the mother. As Tamara Tolley[173] suggests, had the children lived with the mother and it was she who wanted the children to go to the ultra-orthodox school, the dispute over education might have been decided differently. Interestingly the importance of relational values seemed to fall out of the picture in *Re M (Children) (Ultra-Orthodox Judaism: Transgender Parent)*.[174]

5. A controversial aspect of the decision in *Re M (Children) (Ultra-Orthodox Judaism: Transgender Parent)*[175] was where Munby P in saying that the court should not be bound by the discriminatory attitudes of the 'mother' and 'the community' then added:

> Should I not directly and explicitly challenge the parents and the community with the possibility that, absent a real change of attitude on their part, the court may have to consider drastic steps such as removing the children from the mother's care, making the children wards of court or even removing the children into public care?

This might be read as an implied threat to have the children put into care due to the discriminatory attitudes of parents. That seems surprising given that normally the law does permit parents with offensive attitudes to raise children. If only those with 'good attitudes' were allowed to raise children we are in danger of creating social engineering. That said, it may be this is somewhat unfair on Munby P. His point may have been more rhetorical than intending to indicate that it was a real possibility. Indeed, he earlier made the point that:

> It is important at the outset to be clear as to why the court – the State – is involved in the present case. It is because the parents have been unable to resolve their family difficulties themselves, whether with or without the assistance, formal or informal, of the community,

---

[169] [2017] EWCA Civ 2164.
[170] [2017] EWCA Civ 2164.
[171] Herring (2017c).
[172] [2012] EWCA Civ 1233.
[173] Tolley (2014).
[174] [2017] EWCA Civ 2164.
[175] [2017] EWCA Civ 2164.

and because one of the parents, in this case the father, has sought the assistance of the court. The court cannot decline jurisdiction.

The clear implication from this is that, save the fact the couple were in disagreement, there would be no question of the law being involved.

6. There may be some concern at the harsh language used about the Chareidi community, particularly in *Re M (Children) (Ultra-Orthodox Judaism: Transgender Parent)*.[176] Munby P stated:

> The careful reader of Peter Jackson J's judgment might be forgiven for identifying the implication as being that the more enmeshed a child is in a narrow and constricting way of life, and the more intransigent the adults are in seeking to protect the child from what the adults see as the undesirable aspects of any other way of life, the more hamstrung the court will be, the less it will feel able to intervene to further what would otherwise be seen as plainly required in the child's best interests.

The reference to living in the community as a 'narrow and constricting way of life' should (if accepted) be put alongside the benefits of being raised in such a close-knit supportive community.

7. Finally, it might be claimed that the latter case lost sight of determining what was best for these particular children. There is much in the decision about the importance of non-discrimination, tolerance and open-mindedness, but did that distract from an assessment of the welfare of the child? John Eekelaar, for example, insists that Peter Jackson J in *Re M (Children) (Ultra-Orthodox Judaism: Transgender Parent)*[177] was not discriminating against the father, but simply comparing the alternative options based on what was best for the child.[178] Some would say not, because raising a child to have the values of tolerance and openness promotes the child's welfare.[179] Others would say we cannot decide which virtues make up well-being and we would be better off focusing on what will make the child happy and content. Arguably the decision of the Court of Appeal will not do that.

D When does the welfare principle apply?

The welfare principle applies when the court is asked to determine any question that concerns a child's upbringing or the administration of their property. Bracewell J in *Re X (A Child) (Injunctions Restraining Publication)*[180] stated that upbringing means 'the bringing up, care for, treatment, education, and instruction of the child by its parents or by those who are substitute parents'. It is of wide application and not restricted to the Children Act 1989. For example, s. 1(1) applies where the court considers making an order under s. 8 of the Children Act 1989; where the High Court is exercising the inherent jurisdiction;[181] and when the court considers public law orders such as care orders.[182] Rather than listing all the orders when the welfare principle applies, it is in fact easier to consider the issue from the opposite perspective and ask when the welfare principle does not apply.

---

[176] [2017] EWCA Civ 2164.
[177] [2017] EWCA Civ 2164.
[178] Eekelaar (2018b).
[179] See Zanghellini (2018) and Foster and Herring (2012) for discussions of competing theories of well-being.
[180] [2001] 1 FCR 541 at 546f.
[181] *Re T (A Minor) (Wardship: Medical Treatment)* [1997] 1 FLR 502, [1997] 2 FCR 363.
[182] *Humberside CC v B* [1993] 1 FLR 257, [1993] 1 FCR 613, *per* Booth J; applied in *F v Leeds City Council* [1994] 2 FLR 60, [1994] 2 FCR 428.

E When does the welfare principle not apply?

The welfare principle does not apply in the following cases:

1. *If the issue does not relate to the child's upbringing.* It is clear from the wording of s. 1 of the Children Act 1989 that the welfare principle applies only if the issues involve the upbringing of the child. Even if the issue does not involve the upbringing of the child, the court may still pay special attention to the welfare of the child, although the welfare of the child will not be paramount.[183] It is not always easy, however, to know whether an issue relates to the upbringing of the child, as is clear from some of the following examples:

   (a) In *Re A (Minors) (Residence Orders: Leave to Apply)*[184] the Court of Appeal held that deciding whether or not to grant leave to an adult to apply for an order under s. 8 of the Children Act 1989 was not an issue that involved the upbringing of a child and so the child's welfare was not paramount. However, the welfare principle does apply where a child is seeking leave to bring a s. 8 application.[185]

   (b) In considering whether to order blood tests to determine who is the father of a child, the welfare principle does not apply, as the taking of blood does not relate to the child's upbringing.[186]

   (c) It is held that the welfare principle does not apply when a court is deciding whether a parent should be committed to prison for breach of a court order concerning a child.[187]

   (d) In *Re Z (A Minor) (Identity: Restrictions on Publication)*[188] the Court of Appeal held that the decision whether a television company be allowed to film a programme about a child's education related to her upbringing and so the welfare principle applied. However, if the television programme relates not to the child's upbringing, but rather to publicity about the child's parent, then the child's welfare is not paramount, although it may be a factor to be taken into account.[189]

2. *Part III of the Children Act.* The welfare principle does not apply to Part III of the Children Act 1989, which sets out the various duties that a local authority owes to children in its area (see Chapter 11).

3. *Express statutory provision.* The welfare principle does not apply if a statute expressly states it should not. A notable example is in relation to redistribution of property and financial issues on divorce: the child's interests are said to be 'first', but not paramount.[190] Perhaps most significantly, in deciding whether or not to grant a divorce to a child's parents, the child's welfare is not paramount; indeed, the courts are not even required to consider the child's welfare.

4. *Outside the context of litigation.* It is arguable that the welfare principle does not apply to parents with respect to their day-to-day decisions relating to the child, for example where

---

[183] *S v S, W v Official Solicitor (or W)* [1972] AC 24; *Richards v Richards* [1984] AC 174.
[184] [1992] 2 FCR 174, [1992] 2 FLR 154.
[185] *Re SC (A Minor) (Leave to Seek Section 8 Orders)* [1994] 1 FCR 837, [1994] 1 FLR 96; *Re C (Residence: Child's Application for Leave)* [1995] 1 FLR 927, [1996] 1 FCR 461.
[186] *Re H (A Minor) (Blood Tests: Parental Rights)* [1996] 2 FLR 65, [1996] 3 FCR 201.
[187] *A v N (Committal: Refusal of Contact)* [1997] 2 FCR 475, [1997] 1 FLR 533.
[188] [1997] Fam 1.
[189] *Re LM (A Child) (Reporting Restrictions: Coroner's Inquest)* [2007] 3 FCR 44.
[190] Matrimonial Causes Act 1973, s. 25(1).

to live or what jobs to do. However, there are some dicta which have suggested that the welfare principle does affect a parent's day-to-day life. Ward LJ suggested:

> [A] parent may choose to conduct himself in a way which has insufficient regard to his responsibilities to his children. If a person has no parental responsibilities, he is at liberty to conduct himself as he chooses . . . if he has parental responsibilities, those responsibilities may restrict his freedom of action. He is required, where his children's upbringing is involved, to have regard also to the welfare of his children.[191]

It is far from clear how to interpret these dicta. Perhaps the best way to understand the law is that there is a duty on parents to avoid causing the child harm, but not a duty positively to promote the child's welfare.

In the Supreme Court in *ZH (Tanzania) v Secretary of State for the Home Department*[192] Baroness Hale explained that even where the welfare principle does not apply, other provisions or international obligations may require children's interests to be prioritised. She explained, discussing an immigration case:

> For our purposes the most relevant national and international obligation of the United Kingdom is contained in Art. 3(1) of the UNCRC: 'In all actions concerning children, whether undertaken by public or private social welfare institutions, courts of law, administrative authorities or legislative bodies, the best interests of the child shall be a primary consideration.' This is a binding obligation in international law, and the spirit, if not the precise language, has also been translated into our national law. Section 11 of the Children Act 2004 places a duty upon a wide range of public bodies to carry out their functions having regard to the need to safeguard and promote the welfare of children.[193]

The United Kingdom has signed the United Nations Convention on the Rights of the Child (UNCRC), but has not taken any steps to make it directly enforceable in the courts.[194] Nevertheless, the courts do refer to it, particularly in cases where the welfare principle does not apply.[195] Notice that the obligation under the UNCRC is that the interests of children should be primary, which is different from the paramountcy requirement.[196] The children's interests must be identified first, Baroness Hale explained, and are particularly important, but are not the only consideration. Hence, in *HH v Italy*[197] the Supreme Court upheld the extradition of two people who had been arrested overseas on suspicion of drug trafficking, but had fled with their children to the United Kingdom and settled here. While it was accepted it was not in the best interests of the children for the parents to be extradited, doing so was justified by the overwhelming public good in taking this action. As this case shows, allowing children's interests to predominate in every decision would mean parents could escape the administration of justice and ride roughshod over the interests of the other. That would lead to a society of a kind which would not promote children's welfare.[198]

---

[191] *Re W (Wardship: Discharge: Publicity)* [1995] 2 FLR 466 at p. 477.
[192] [2011] UKSC 4.
[193] At para 23.
[194] See Alderson (2015) for a helpful discussion.
[195] See Gilmore (2017) for a detailed analysis. He found 170 cases in the Family Law Reports up until 2017.
[196] Eekelaar (2015a).
[197] [2012] UKSC 25.
[198] See for further discussion Fortin (2014).

In *R (on the application of SG) v Secretary of State for Work and Pensions (Child Poverty Action Group)*[199] Lord Hughes helpfully summarised how the UNCRC could be used in English cases:

> First, if the construction (i.e. meaning) of UK legislation is in doubt, the court may conclude that it should be construed, if otherwise possible, on the footing that this country meant to honour its international obligations. Second, international treaty obligations may guide the development of the common law . . . Thirdly . . . the UNCRC may be relevant in English law to the extent that it falls to the court to apply the European Convention on Human Rights . . . via the Human Rights Act 1998. The European Court of Human Rights has sometimes accepted that the Convention should be interpreted, in appropriate cases, in the light of generally accepted international law in the same field, including multi-lateral treaties such as the UNCRC.

Stephen Gilmore's analysis of the use of the UNCRC in English law confirms it is primarily used where the domestic law is seen to be ambiguous.[200]

R (on the application of SG) v Secretary of State for Work and Pensions (Child Poverty Action Group)[201] is a good illustration of how the courts deal with cases involving children when the welfare principle does not apply.

KEY CASE: *R (on the application of SG) v Secretary of State for Work and Pensions (Child Poverty Action Group)* [2015] UKSC 16

As part of its 'austerity' programme the Government introduced a cap on welfare payments which set a maximum on the amount of benefits (including child tax credit and child benefit) that could be paid to any one household. The regulations introducing these reforms were challenged under the Human Rights Act 1998. Various arguments were used, but the one of most interest to family lawyers is that the scheme was most likely to impact on single parents with several children and was, therefore, indirectly discriminatory against women and children. The appellants referred to Article 3(1) of the UNCRC which said that 'the best interests of the child' should be a primary consideration. The majority of the Supreme Court (Lords Reed, Hughes and Carnwath) held the cap was not unlawfully discriminatory. They held that although women were more likely to be impacted than men, the difference in treatment had an objective and reasonable justification (securing the economic well-being of the country) and was a proportionate means of reaching that end (given that many children in non-welfare payment households had to live in households with less income). Lord Reed for the majority thought the interests of children were not relevant to the argument as they were impacted similarly whether with father or mothers. Lord Carnwath, however, also in the majority, accepted the cap did deprive children of money for reasons that were not connected to their needs and that was not compatible with the UNCRC. However, it was for Parliament and not the courts to deal with that clash. Baroness Hale, dissenting, held there was a breach of the UNCRC obligations: 'Claimants affected by the cap will, by definition, not receive the sums of money

---

[199] [2015] UKSC 16; see below.
[200] Gilmore (2017).
[201] [2015] UKSC 16.

which the state deems necessary for them adequately to house, feed, clothe, and warm themselves and their children. Furthermore, the greater the need, the greater the adverse effect. The more children there are in the family, the less each of them will have to live on.' Depriving children of the basic necessities of life could not be in their best interests. She concluded that the benefit cap could not, therefore, be said to be a proportionate means of achieving a legitimate end. Lord Kerr agreed with her analysis. Indeed, he went further and considered 'that the time has come for the exception to the dualist theory in human rights conventions'.

The issue of the benefits cap returned to the courts in **R (DA) v Secretary of State for Work and Pensions**.[202] While the majority accepted that the way the cap operated caused disadvantage to single parents and their children, and thereby engaged their Article 8 rights, any breach was justified in terms of the overall goals of the policy (e.g. not to discourage people from seeking work by having high levels of benefit payments). It could not be said that the interference was 'manifestly without reasonable foundation'. Lord Wilson was particularly wary of the court using rights of children to override what was a political question, once it had been shown the Government had considered the position of children and:

> This court must impose on itself the discipline not, from its limited perspective, to address whether the government's evaluation of its impact was questionable; nor whether its assessment of the best interests of young children was unbalanced in favour of perceived long-term advantages for them at the expense of obvious short-term privation.[203]

Lord Kerr, dissenting, disagreed:

> UNCRC contains a number of enjoinders to those countries which subscribe to it. Some of these are expressed in imperative terms. The duty of the state is to keep faith with the spirit of the Convention. Whether it has discharged that duty is not to be answered solely on whether it can be said to be in technical breach of its terms. The proportionality of a government measure which has an impact on the best interests of children is not to be judged by a mechanistic approach to the question whether there has been technical compliance with article 3. It must be assessed on the basis of whether, given the injunctions in UNCRC, the government's decision, taking into account where the best interests of children lie, represents a balanced reaction to those interests and the aims which a particular measure seeks to achieve.

It is interesting to note that in such non-family law cases, the interests of children still play a central role.[204]

F What if the case involves two children – whose interests are paramount?

There is a real difficulty in using the welfare principle in cases where two or more children are concerned and their interests are in conflict.

---

[202] [2019] UKSC 21.
[203] Para 87.
[204] Taylor (2016).

(i) The basic rule: 'who is the subject of the application?'

Birmingham City Council v H (A Minor)[205] involved a mother who was herself a minor, being under 16, and her baby. The mother and baby had been taken into care, but had been separated. The mother applied for contact with the baby. It was felt that it was in the minor mother's interest that contact take place but that contact was not necessarily in the baby's interests. It was therefore crucial for the court to determine whose interest was paramount: the mother's or the baby's. The House of Lords took the view, relying on the wording of s. 1(1) of the Children Act 1989, that it was the child who was the subject of the proceedings whose welfare was paramount. It was held that because the mother was applying for contact with the baby, the baby was the 'subject of the proceedings' and so it was the baby's interests which were paramount and therefore contact was not ordered.[206]

This is not a very satisfactory approach because it may be a matter of chance what form the application takes and which child happens to be the subject of the application. Although the approach of the House of Lords was correct as a matter of statutory interpretation, the House of Lords could have approached the issues on a more theoretical level: either by saying that in such cases the interests of the two children had to be balanced with each other; or that a minor mother's interests were always lower than her baby's. However, the House of Lords rejected these alternatives.

(ii) Where there are two or more children who are the subject of an application under the Children Act 1989

What if an application[207] were made in respect of two children and it was in the interests of one child that the order be made, but not in the interests of the other? Wilson J in *Re T and E*[208] explained that in such a case both children's welfare had to be taken into account and balanced against each other. So, if the order would greatly benefit one child and slightly disadvantage the other, the order should be made. This approach was applied in *Re A (Conjoined Twins: Medical Treatment)*,[209] where there were two conjoined twins, J and M. If no medical treatment was provided, then both would die. It was, however, possible to separate the twins with the result that J would live, but M would die. The operation would therefore be in J's interests, but not in M's (she would die sooner if the operation were performed than if it were not). The Court of Appeal was willing to balance the interests of the children. The interests of J were held to be more weighty than the interest of M and so the operation was authorised.

The most recent discussion was in *Re S (Children)*[210] which involved two boys, B (aged 16 and a half) and C (aged 12), whose parents had separated. They lived with their mother but had regular contact with their father. The father wished to move to Canada to live and take the boys with him. It was found that the proposed move would be in the interests of B, but not C. The first instance judge approved the move, but the Court of Appeal overturned his judgment on the basis he had treated the two boys as a unit and failed to consider C's welfare in his own right. The judge should have considered each boy separately and decided what was in their best interests. In this case it meant that B should remain in Canada and C should remain in England.

---

[205] [1994] 2 AC 212.
[206] Applied in *Re S (Contact: Application by Sibling)* [1998] 2 FLR 897 and *Re F (Contact: Child in Care)* [1995] 1 FLR 510.
[207] Or two applications are heard together.
[208] [1995] 1 FLR 581, [1995] 3 FCR 260.
[209] [2001] 1 FLR 1, [2000] 3 FCR 577.
[210] [2011] EWCA Civ 454.

G Conflict of interests between parents and children

One might expect that, given the welfare principle, if there is a clash between the interests of the children and parents, the interests of the child would be preferred.[211] As already mentioned, the welfare principle means that the court is only interested in the welfare of the child.[212] So, however great the sacrifice demanded of parents, if there is overall a marginal increase in the child's welfare, the order should be made.

In fact, despite the existence of the welfare principle, the English courts have been able to protect the interests of parents.[213] Four of the ways that have been used to do this will now be briefly examined, although there are more:

1. The law makes no attempt to ensure that everything that adults do in relation to children day to day promotes their welfare. There is no direct supervision of the way parents treat their children, unlike the close direct regulation of day-care centres or childminders.[214] Although there are regular inspections and assessments of day-care centres, there are no equivalent investigations into the way parents raise children. If the parents bring up the child in a way that harms the child then, unless one of the parents, the local authority or the child brings the matter before a court, there is unlikely to be any formal legal intervention.

2. As already noted, there are various issues to which the welfare principle does not apply, even though the interests of the child may still be an important consideration. Such circumstances include the granting of a divorce; domestic violence; financial redistribution of property on divorce; and enforcement of court orders.[215] It may be noted that these are hardly topics where children's interests are insignificant, but rather cases where parents' interests are particularly weighty. A cynic may suggest that the law is only willing to promote a child's welfare where that does not greatly inconvenience adults.

3. A third way that the courts have protected the rights of parents is through closely identifying the interests of children and parents. Perhaps the best recent example to illustrate this is *Re T (A Minor) (Wardship: Medical Treatment)*.[216] This case concerned a dispute over whether life-saving medical treatment should be given to a child. The unanimous medical opinion was in favour, but the parents opposed it. The court decided that it would not be in the child's best interests for the treatment to go ahead, bearing in mind the pressure that this would put on the parents. Butler-Sloss LJ reasoned: 'the mother and this child are one for the purpose of this unusual case and the decision of the court to consent to the operation jointly affects the mother and son and so also affects the father. The welfare of the child depends upon his mother.'[217]

   By suggesting that the interests of the parent and the child were 'one', the Court of Appeal was able to take account of the parents' interests under the umbrella of the child's welfare. It can be argued that this case failed to consider fully the possibility of the child being cared for by alternative carers if the parents felt unable to cope, and, further, that the court placed excessive weight on the parents' views and insufficient weight on the child's right to life. By seeing the mother and child as one, the child's independent interests were hidden.

---

[211] See Henricson and Bainham (2005) on, generally, tensions in the law and policy in balancing the interests of children and parents.
[212] *Re P (Contact: Supervision)* [1996] 2 FLR 314 at p. 328.
[213] Herring (1999a).
[214] Children Act 1989, Part X, Sched. 9.
[215] *Re F (Contact: Enforcement: Representation of Child)* [1998] 1 FLR 691, [1998] 3 FCR 216.
[216] [1997] 1 FLR 502.
[217] [1997] 1 FLR 502 at p. 510.

4. The courts have sometimes protected parents' interests by explicitly limiting their jurisdiction. So, for example, in **Re E (Residence: Imposition of Conditions)**[218] the court refused to make it a condition of a mother's residence order that she remain in London because that would be to intervene in the mother's right to choose where to live.[219] There is nothing in the Children Act 1989 that limits the courts' jurisdiction in such a way, but decisions of this kind enable the court to protect the interests of parents.[220]

These indicate that, in fact, the courts are able to give effect to the interests of the parents despite purporting to uphold the welfare principle as a principle requiring the interests of parents to be subservient to the interests of children. In the light of the Human Rights Act 1998, the court will have to acknowledge explicitly that parents have human rights which cannot be automatically overridden simply by reference to the welfare principle.[221] So how should the law deal with clashes between the rights and interests of parents and children?

Here are some of the possibilities that could be adopted:

DEBATE

How should the interests of parents and children be balanced?

1. *The standard welfare principle approach.* It could be argued that, despite the acknowledgement of parents' rights in the Human Rights Act 1998, the court should continue to assert that the interests of children are the sole consideration.

2. *Primary and secondary interests (Bainham).* One of the most developed considerations of how to balance the conflicting rights and interests of family members is the analysis made by Bainham. He suggests that the answer is to categorise parents' and children's interests as either primary or secondary interests.[222] A child's secondary interests would have to give way to a parent's primary interests and similarly a parent's secondary interests must give way to a child's primary interests. In addition, the court should consider the 'collective family interest'.[223] This, he argues, should also be taken into account in the balancing exercise, so that the interests of one family member may have to be weighed against the good of the family as a unit.

3. *Relationship-based welfare (Herring).* This theory[224] argues that children should be brought up in relationships which overall promote their welfare.[225] It argues that families, and society in general, are based on mutual cooperation and support.[226] It is beneficial for a child to be brought up in a family that is based on relationships which are fair and just. A relationship based on unacceptable demands on a parent is not furthering a child's welfare. Indeed, it is impossible to construct an approach to looking at a child's welfare which ignores the web of relationships within which the child is brought up. Supporting the child means supporting

---

[218] [1997] 2 FLR 638. Contrast *Re S (A Child: Residence Order: Condition) (No. 2)* [2003] 1 FCR 138.
[219] See Chapter 10 for further discussion.
[220] See also *D v N (Contact Order: Conditions)* [1997] 2 FLR 797, [1997] 3 FCR 721.
[221] Choudhry and Fenwick (2005); Bonner, Fenwick and Harris-Short (2003); Herring (1999b).
[222] Bainham (1998c).
[223] Bainham (1998c). See also Henricson and Bainham (2005: 11) where it is argued that the family 'as a group' have interests that deserve protection.
[224] Herring (1999b); see also Bridgeman (2010).
[225] Sevenhuijsen (2002).
[226] See Butler, Robinson and Scanlan (2005) for evidence that families are increasingly based on a democratic model with children being involved in decision-making within families.

the caregiver and supporting the caregiver means supporting the child.[227] So a court can legitimately make an order which benefits a parent, but not a child, if that can be regarded as appropriate in the context of their past and ongoing relationship.[228]

4. *Virtue as part of welfare (Foster and Herring)*. Charles Foster and I have argued that the notion of welfare should not be restricted to happiness.[229] A good life is one where a person develops virtues and has good relationships. A person who is happy, but is utterly selfish or has no friends, has not had a good life. So too with the welfare of children. Promoting the well-being of children means raising them to display virtues of altruism and experience fair relationships. So, an order may be made which will not make them happy, but will mean they develop virtue.

5. *Modified least detrimental alternative (Eekelaar)*. Eekelaar summarises his theory in this way:

> The best solution is surely to adopt the course that avoids inflicting the most damage on the well-being of any interested individual . . . [I]f the choice was between a solution that advanced a child's well-being a great deal, but also damaged the interests of one parent a great deal, and a different solution under which the child's well-being was diminished, but damaged the parent to a far lesser degree, one should choose the second option, even though it was not the least detrimental alternative for the child.[230]

However, he adds an important qualification to this test and that is that 'no solution should be adopted where the detriments outweigh the benefits for the child, unless that would be the result of *any* available solution, so that is unavoidable.'[231] He also adds that there may be a degree of detriment to which a child should never be subjected, if that is avoidable.[232] He is concerned about cases where, for example, a disabled spouse would greatly suffer if on divorce the child were to live with the other parent.

6. *Balancing all interests.* This perspective[233] simply requires the courts to weigh up the interests of each party. There would be no particular preference for the interests of each of the parties. This approach would suggest that the court should make the order which would produce the most benefit and least detriment for the parties.

The difference between these approaches can be clarified by looking at the benefit or disadvantage of the proposed orders on a scale of +50 (the most beneficial) to −50 (the least beneficial). Consider these four possible orders (F being the father, M the mother and C the child):

Solution 1: C (−30); F (+30); M (+30)

Solution 2: C (−5); F (−5); M (+35)

Solution 3: C (+10); F (−30); M (−40)

Solution 4: C (+5); F (−5); M (−5)

The balancing all the interests approach would support solution 1 because this is the one that produces the greatest total benefit adding together all the disadvantages and benefits for each party and treating them equally. Solution 1 would be unacceptable to the welfare principle because it harms the child. It would be unacceptable to Bainham because it involves

---

[227] Kavanagh (2004).
[228] See Bonthuys (2006) who complains that seeing parents' interests just through the prism of welfare fails to place sufficient weight on parents' interests.
[229] Herring and Foster (2012).
[230] Eekelaar (2002a: 243–4).
[231] Eekelaar (2002a: 243).
[232] Eekelaar (2002a: 245).
[233] This appears to be supported by Reece (1996).

the infringement of a primary interest of the child. It would also be unacceptable to Eekelaar because he refuses to accept making an order which causes a detriment to a child unless any order the court would make would cause a detriment to a child.

The welfare principle approach would promote solution 3. Despite the fact this may harm (quite seriously) the father and mother, under the welfare principle the harms caused to the parents are irrelevant and this is the solution that would best promote the child's welfare. Eekelaar would prefer solution 4. Although solution 3 promotes the child's welfare to the greatest extent, it does so by causing the parents significant harm. Solution 4 manages still to promote the child's welfare (albeit to a lesser extent than solution 3) and it does so causing less harm to the parents. Bainham might also approve of solutions 2 or 4 because they do not involve the infringement of anyone's primary or secondary interests.

The Herring–Foster approach would consider what will promote virtue and an appreciation for relational values for a child. Perhaps options 2 or 4 could be justified as they are ones a virtuous person may take; neither claims a benefit for themselves at too great a cost to others.

Herring's relational welfare approach is less straightforward because it requires an understanding of the nature of the relationship in the past, and the foreseeable future. If, for example, in the past the mother and father have had to make unusual and extreme sacrifices for the benefit of the child, solution 2 or even 1 may be acceptable.[234]

Questions

1. *Are there any circumstances in which it is appropriate for a court to make a decision which will harm a child?*

2. *Should parents be taken to accept that by choosing to become parents their interests will count for less than their children's?*

3. *How would these different approaches deal with a case where a child's sibling needed an organ donation and the child was seen as the best possible donor?[235] What about a case where parents wanted a child to enrol as a participant in medical research?[236] Is there a danger in the Foster/Herring proposal leading to a slippery slope of children being used for the benefit of others?[237]*

Further reading

Compare **Eekelaar** (2002a) and **Herring** (1999b) for contrasting answers to this issue.

9 The Human Rights Act 1998 and children's welfare and rights

Learning objective 5

Describe how the Human Rights Act 1998 interacts with the welfare principle

It is generally accepted that the European Convention on Human Rights (ECHR) does not provide adequately for the rights of children.[238] The Convention was clearly drawn up with adults (rather than children) as the focus of attention.

---

[234] This perhaps indicates a concern with this approach. Most parents make enormous sacrifices for their children and so the approach might too easily lead to an argument that it is justifiable to promote parents' interests over those of children.

[235] Contrast Cherkassky (2015) and Taylor-Sands (2013) on this.

[236] Dar (2013).

[237] Ferguson (2015c).

[238] Choudhry and Herring (2010); Harris-Short (2005); Fortin (1999a); Herring (1999b).

Indeed, there are no articles in the Convention explicitly dealing with children.[239] However, that is not to say that children receive no protection under the Convention.[240] Children are entitled to the same rights under the Convention as adults. Article 1 states: 'The High Contracting Parties shall secure to everyone within their jurisdiction the rights and freedoms in this Convention.'[241] The European Court has accepted that 'everyone' in Article 1 includes children.[242] To give two examples: children have been able to bring applications before the European Court of Human Rights (ECtHR) claiming that they are entitled to state protection under Article 3 (to protect them from corporal punishment which constitutes torture or inhuman or degrading treatment)[243] and Article 5 (to complain of being wrongfully detained in a hospital).[244] Children's interests can also sometimes be protected when an adult enforces his or her own rights. So, the enforcement of a parent's rights of contact with his or her child inevitably leads to an enforcement of the right of the child to contact with his or her parent.[245]

The relevance of particular rights of children under the Convention will be discussed where appropriate throughout the text; but now the way the Convention deals with clashes between the interests of adults and children will be considered.

A Balancing the rights of parents and children under the Convention

The Convention, rather surprisingly, includes no explicit reference to ensure that the enforcement of adult rights does not harm a child's welfare. However, the European Court has been able to give weight to the interests of the child by considering the wording in the articles which restrict rights. For example, the most quoted article in cases concerning children is Article 8:

LEGISLATIVE PROVISION

European Convention on Human Rights, Article 8

1. Everyone has the right to respect for his private and family life, his home and his correspondence.

2. There shall be no interference by a public authority with the exercise of this right except such as is in accordance with the law and is necessary in a democratic society in the interests of national security, public safety or the economic well-being of the country, for the prevention of disorder or crime, for the protection of health or morals, or for the protection of the rights and freedoms of others.

---

[239] Fortin (2002 and 2006a).
[240] For a thorough discussion of the rights of children under the European Convention, see Kilkelly (2000).
[241] Article 14 states that the rights must be granted without discrimination 'on any ground such as sex, race, colour . . .' Although age is not specifically mentioned, the use of the words 'such as' indicates that the list is not intended to be exhaustive and so it could be argued that age should be included as a prohibited ground of discrimination.
[242] *Nielsen v Denmark* (1989) 11 EHRR 175.
[243] *A v UK (Human Rights: Punishment of Child)* [1998] 2 FLR 959.
[244] *Nielsen v Denmark* (1988) 11 EHRR 175.
[245] For example, *Eriksson v Sweden* (1989) 12 EHRR 183.

So, a permitted interference of the right must be in accordance with the law;[246] it must pursue a legitimate aim; it must be proportionate[247] and necessary.[248] It is clearly established that a 'legitimate aim' includes preserving the rights and welfare of children.[249] In other words, an infringement of an adult's right to respect for private and family life can be justified if necessary to protect the children's interests.

The correct approach, then, where there may be a clash between the rights of children and adults (or between any two parties) is to start by looking at the rights that each individual has and consider whether the issue engages a right under the ECHR. If it does then the court will need to consider whether an infringement of that right is justified. So, a parent may have a right under Article 8(1) to have contact with a child, but under Article 8(2) it may be permissible to interfere with that right if necessary in the interests of the child or the resident parent. It would be necessary then to consider the right of each party involved (each parent and the child) and consider in each case where the rights and interests of others are sufficiently strong to justify an interference with that right. The difficulty with this approach is that you may end up with a clash between two rights under the ECHR.[250]

There are a number of solutions to a case where there is a clash between the rights of the parties. According to the European Court of Human Rights when considering the competing rights of adults and children in this case, the rights of children should be regarded as being of crucial importance (see below). Shazia Choudhry and Helen Fenwick[251] have suggested that the rights of children should be 'privileged'. However, Jane Fortin[252] complains that this is too vague and, while she is generally supportive of this kind of approach, feels that how the interests of children are privileged needs to be explained. Is it claimed that if there is a clash of rights the rights of children always win out? If not, when will children's rights lose out to an adult's right?[253]

Rachel Taylor and I have suggested that in a case of clashing rights the court should look at the values underpinning the right.[254] In the case of Article 8, which is the most common right used in family cases, the underlying value might be that of autonomy: the right to pursue one's vision of the 'good life'; or the right to have a flourishing family life. We could then consider the extent to which the proposed order would constitute a blight on each of the party's opportunities to pursue these values. The court should make the order which causes the least blight.

The European Court of Human Rights has not yet given much guidance on the issue. It is clear that in cases involving families, the interests of children must be considered. In *Hendriks* **v** *Netherlands*[255] it was stated: 'the Commission has consistently held that, in assessing the question of whether or not the refusal of the right of access to the non-custodial parent was in conformity with Article 8 of the Convention, the interests of the child would predominate'. This was accepted as an accurate statement of the approach of the Convention by the Court of

---

[246] The procedure must be accessible, foreseeable and reasonably quick: *W* v *UK* (1988) 10 EHRR 29.

[247] *Price* v *UK* (1988) 55 D&R 1988.

[248] States have a margin of appreciation in deciding whether the intrusion is necessary.

[249] For example, *R* v *UK* [1988] 2 FLR 445.

[250] Choudhry and Herring (2010); Choudhry and Fenwick (2005); Taylor (2006); Harris-Short (2005).

[251] Choudhry and Fenwick (2005).

[252] Fortin (2006a).

[253] Fortin (2006a) suggests that only if the rights are 'equal' should the child's win out; although it is not quite clear what 'equal' means here.

[254] Herring and Taylor (2006). This seeks to develop Choudhry and Fenwick (2005) and the dicta of Lord Steyn in *Re S (A Child) (Identification: Restrictions on Publication)* [2005] 1 AC 593 at para 17 which refer to the need to consider the values underlying the right when considering cases of clashing rights.

[255] (1982) 5 D&R 225.

Appeal in *Re L (A Child) (Contact: Domestic Violence)*.[256] The European Court of Human Rights in *Scott v UK*[257] has stated that the interests of the child are 'of crucial importance' in cases involving the interests of parents and child. In *Hoppe v Germany*[258] it was said that the interests of children were of 'particular importance'.[259] In *Yousef v The Netherlands*[260] it was held that, under the European Convention, where the rights of children and parents conflict, the rights of children will be the 'paramount consideration'. In *Neulinger and Shuruk v Switzerland* it was said: 'The Court notes that there is currently a broad consensus – including in international law – in support of the idea that in all decisions concerning children, their best interests must be paramount.'[261] This is very close to the interpretation by the English and Welsh courts of the welfare principle;[262] however, a close reading of the judgments suggests that in these cases the ECtHR was not intending paramount to mean that the welfare of the child is the sole consideration.[263] Most subsequent cases[264] have not used the term 'paramount' and preferred to say children's interests are particularly important[265] or crucial.[266] It seems then that in cases involving clashes between the rights of adults and children, while under the Children Act 1989, only the interests of children should be considered, under the ECHR the interests of children and adults should be considered, but the interests of children will be regarded as having significant weight.[267]

Despite these rulings, there are concerns that the Human Rights Act 1998, by explicitly giving parents rights, will weaken the interests of children. As Fortin[268] argues:

> It is of fundamental importance that the judiciary shows a willingness to interpret the European Convention in a child-centred way, as far as its narrow scope allows. It would be unfortunate in the extreme, if such a change heralded in an increased willingness to allow parents to pursue their own rights under the Convention at the expense of those of their children.

B Is there any practical difference between the approaches of the European Convention and the Children Act 1989?

It has been seen that the European Convention, based upon rights, can take into account the welfare of children and that the Children Act 1989, based upon the welfare principle, has taken into account the rights of parents. It is therefore inevitable that the question be asked: is there any practical difference between the two approaches?[269]

---

[256] [2000] 2 FCR 404.
[257] [2000] 2 FCR 560 at p. 572.
[258] [2003] 1 FCR 176 at para 49.
[259] See also *Sahin v Germany* [2003] 2 FCR 619 and *Haase v Germany* [2004] 2 FCR 1.
[260] [2000] 2 FLR 118 at para 118.
[261] (Application 41615/07), para 135. See also *YC v United Kingdom* [2012] ECHR 433.
[262] In *Re S (A Child) (Contact)* [2004] 1 FCR 439 at para 15 Butler-Sloss cited *Yousef* as showing that the ECHR had recognised the principle of the paramountcy of the child's welfare.
[263] Simmonds (2012).
[264] Harris Short (2005: 357) describes *Yousef* as an isolated decision. Although, see *Maire v Portugal* [2004] 2 FLR 653 at para 77, which followed *Yousef* in using the 'paramount' terminology. In *Kearns v France* [2008] 2 FCR 1, at para 79 the child's interests were said to be paramount, but that statement appears to relate to the particular context of the case.
[265] For example, *Haase v Germany* [2004] 2 FCR 1 at para 93; *Suss v Germany* [2005] 3 FCR 666 at para 88; *Hunt v Ukraine* [2006] 3 FCR 756; *Chepelev v Russia* [2007] 2 FCR 649, para 27.
[266] *Nanning v Germany* [2007] 2 FCR 543, para 63. See also, *C v Finland* [2006] 2 FCR 195 and *Buchleither v Germany* (App. No. 20106/13) which use both the crucial and particular terminology.
[267] Choudhry and Herring (2010: chs. 2 and 3).
[268] Fortin (2006a and 2009b).
[269] See Herring (1999b); Choudhry (2003).

The UK courts have consistently taken the approach that there is no difference in outcome, whether the welfare principle is applied or an analysis based on human rights used.[270] This was recently confirmed by Ryder LJ in *Re Y (Children: Removal from Jurisdiction: Failure to Consider Family Segmentation)*:[271]

> There is no suggestion that the [Children Act] 1989 . . . and in particular sections 1 and 8 and the principles extracted from them, are inconsistent with the Convention. Far from it. There is ample jurisprudence to support the proposition that domestic law . . . is Article 8 compliant.

It is respectfully suggested that this statement is not entirely accurate and that there are important differences between the approach of the Children Act 1989 and the European Convention on Human Rights.[272] Imagine a case concerning contact between a child and a non-residential parent. Under the European Convention, the starting point is the parent's right to respect for family life which will be infringed if contact is denied. In order to justify the breach, there must be clear and convincing evidence that the contact would infringe the rights and interests of the child or resident parent to such an extent that the infringement was necessary and proportionate. However, under the Children Act there is a factual assumption that contact will promote the child's welfare, although this could be rebutted by evidence that contact would not promote the child's welfare in this particular case.

The difference between the two approaches is twofold. First, less evidence would be required under the Children Act to show the assumption that contact promotes a child's welfare than would be required under the Convention to show that infringement of the parent's rights is necessary and proportionate. Secondly, the nature of the question is different. Under the Children Act the question is a factual one – will contact promote the child's welfare? Whereas under the European Convention approach it is a question of legal judgment – whether the harm to the child is sufficient to make the breach 'necessary' as understood by the law.

A further difference between the approach of the welfare principle and the Convention is that the Convention is in this area essentially restrictive – it tells governments and courts what they may not do;[273] while the welfare principle requires the court to act positively to promote the child's welfare.[274] A good example is Article 2 of the first Protocol: 'no person shall be denied the right to education'. It should be noted that this does not give a positive right to education, just a right not to be denied any education offered by the state. Similarly, Article 8 requires that the state should not interfere with respect for family life, but the wording does not appear to require the state to promote family life. That said, as seen earlier (Chapter 7), Article 8 has been interpreted to require the state in some circumstances to act positively to promote the child's welfare.

---

[270] *Re KD (A Minor) (Ward: Termination of Access)* [1988] FCR 657. *Re B (Adoption by One Natural Parent to Exclusion of Other)* [2002] 1 FLR 196.

[271] [2014] EWCA Civ 1287.

[272] This view has been taken by many commentators: Fortin (2006a); Harris-Short (2005); Choudhry and Fenwick (2005); Herring and Taylor (2006). Indeed, the writer knows of no academic commentator who agrees that the welfare principle as interpreted by the courts and an approach based on the ECHR are the same.

[273] Hale (2006) sees this as a weakness of the ECHR from a child's point of view.

[274] Although note s. 1(5) of the Children Act 1989.

10 Criticisms of the welfare principle

The welfare principle seeks to ensure that children are not exploited for the interests of adults.[275] At least, judicial decisions concerning children's upbringing must be phrased in terms of benefit for children. This can be justified on the basis that children are likely to be the least responsible for the difficulties that have led to the court case. They are also the least likely to be able to escape from the family difficulties and are least equipped to respond positively to the effect of any order which is against their interests.

Despite its predominance in the law relating to children, the welfare principle has been criticised.[276] Some of the main objections will now be outlined.

1. *The law has a narrow perception of welfare.* King and Piper have argued that 'the broad range of factors – genetic, financial, educational, environmental and relational – which science would recognise as capable of affecting the welfare of a child are narrowed by law to a small range of issues which fall directly under the influence of the judge, the social workers or the adult parties to the litigation process'.[277] As Jo Bridgeman writes:

   > [U]nless consideration is given to the individual child, to the person they are, their personality, character, feelings of pleasure and pain, and relational interests (relationships with those upon whom they depend), determinations about the best interests of the child are reached according to current ideas about the child and according to adult memories of childhood.[278]

   Further, the court's focus on child welfare tends not to consider issues such as pollution, the quality of public housing and wider political questions which can have a powerful effect on the interests of children.[279]

2. *Uncertainty.* Mnookin[280] argues that the welfare principle gives rise to inconsistency and unpredictability.[281] Guggenheim[282] writes:

   > However alluring and child-friendly the 'best interests' test appears, in truth it is a formula for unleashing state power, without any meaningful reassurance of advancing children's interests.

   The uncertainty arises from the great many unknowns concerning welfare. The facts are not known because often there is only the conflicting evidence of the father and mother as to the history of the parents' relationship. Even if the facts are established, it is impossible to predict how well the parties will be able to care for children. Even if the court could predict how the parents will act, it may be hard to choose who is the better parent, given the lack of agreed values over what makes an ideal parent. These uncertainties in effect give a judge a wide discretion in deciding what is in a child's welfare.[283] Some have even suggested it enables a judge to give free reign to his or her prejudices.[284] The uncertainty also creates problems for parents in negotiating. As it is hard to anticipate how a judge might decide a

---

[275] Eekelaar (2002a).
[276] See, for example, Reece (1996). For support of the principle in the face of these criticisms see Herring (2005b).
[277] King and Piper (1995: 50). This is based on autopoietic theory (see Chapter 1).
[278] Bridgeman (2007: 9).
[279] Henaghan (2015).
[280] Mnookin (1975).
[281] For a good discussion of inconsistencies among Court of Appeal decisions in applying the welfare principle, see Gilmore (2004c).
[282] Guggenheim (2006: 41).
[283] Elster (1987).
[284] Reece (1996).

case, the parties may well prefer chancing a judicial hearing, rather than reaching a negotiated settlement. By contrast, if it was predictable how a judge would resolve a dispute between the parties then there would be little point in incurring the expenses involved in taking the matter to court.

3. *Smokescreen.* There is a concern that, given the uncertainty surrounding the welfare principle, the real basis for the decision will be hidden.[285] In particular, the prejudices of the professionals involved (the judiciary, the expert witnesses and the lawyers) provide the true reason behind the decision. For example, an individual's ideology of what makes a good mother or father can be extremely significant.[286] This then can lead to the welfare presumption being used in a way which works against the interests of women.[287]

4. *Increased costs.* It can be argued that the welfare principle simply increases the costs for the parties. Its unpredictability means that it is harder to negotiate a settlement and the complexity of the test means that court hearings take longer and require more substantial preparation.

5. *Unfairness.* The welfare principle can be attacked for failing to give adequate (or indeed any) weight to the interests of adults.[288] Eekelaar explains: 'the very ease of the welfare test encourages a laziness and unwillingness to pay proper attention to all the interests that are at stake in these decisions and, possibly, also a tendency to abdicate responsibility for decision making to welfare professionals'.[289] Those who see the force of such an approach would prefer the courts paid greater attention to the impact of the Human Rights Act 1998, which they say requires the court to pay attention to the rights of adults and children. The benefit of such an approach has been summarised by Sonia Harris-Short in this way:

> Rights-based reasoning has the potential to introduce much greater intellectual rigour and discipline to judicial reasoning in the family law context, ensuring the needs and interests of all family members are clearly articulated and considered in the decision-making process and preventing untested assumptions and prejudices, currently obscured behind the vagaries of the welfare principle, from determining the outcome of common family disputes.[290]

6. *Unrealistic.* If there is a dispute over the medical treatment for a child and the matter is brought before the court, a judge considering what is best for the child may decide that the child should be flown to the top medical hospital in America to be treated by the world's leading expert in the field, with no expense spared.[291] Of course, a court could not make such an order. As this indicates, it is often for practical reasons impossible to make the order that would best promote the child's welfare.

7. *Children's rights.* As we will discuss later, those who advocate children's rights and in particular those who support the idea that children should be allowed to make decisions for themselves, even if that slightly harms them, would not support the welfare principle.

---

[285] Reece (1996: 296–7).
[286] Boyd (1996).
[287] Fineman (1988).
[288] Reece (1996: 303).
[289] Eekelaar (2002a: 248).
[290] Harris-Short (2005: 359).
[291] Archard (2003: 41).

8. *Too narrow*. There is a real danger with the best interests test in that it assumes that adults know best for children and should control them. I have argued that seeing parenting as about the imposing of decisions on a child is misguided. The arguments for paternalism:

> . . . fall away once a parent relinquishes claims to control. This is particularly apparent for those of us whose children do not fall into the conventional sense of 'normal'. The notion of parental control and responsibility for what a child is seems absurd in this context. The rule books are long since discarded and it is a matter of finding day-by-day what works or, more often, what does not work. Parents of disabled children come to know that the greatest success for the child will be a failure by the objective standards of any Government league table or examination board. But such social standards fail to capture a key aspect of parenting – children can cause parents to be open to something more wonderful, particularly when they are more markedly different from a supposed social norm.[292]

In the face of such powerful criticisms, is there anything that can be said in favour of the welfare principle?[293] As to indeterminacy, Gillian Douglas[294] has written that the 'uncertainty and inconsistency may be both the greatest strength and greatest weakness of the "welfare principle"'. The benefit of the uncertainty surrounding the welfare principle is that it enables courts to produce results which are flexible and responsive to the individual needs of each child. Further, the welfare principle sends an important symbolic message.[295] It recognises the value, the importance and the vulnerability of children. Quite simply, if a court order causes a loss or hurt, children have fewer resources open to them than adults do. Children lack the material, psychological and relational resources that parents have. Another point is that without the welfare principle it would be easy in court proceedings for the interests of the children to be lost, especially because rarely in disputes over children is there an independent advocate for the child or is the child heard herself. Finally, the message sent to separating parents by the welfare principle is one they desperately need to hear: forget about your own rights; put the interests of your children first. Black LJ in *T v T*[296] put the point well:

> [The parents] must put aside their differences . . . if the adults do not manage to resolve things by communicating with each other, the children inevitably suffer and the adults may also pay the price when the children are old enough to be aware of what has been going on . . . It is a tremendous privilege to be involved in bringing up a child. Childhood is over all too quickly and, whilst I appreciate that both sides think that they are motivated only by concern for the children, it is still very sad to see it being allowed to slip away whilst energy is devoted to adult wrangles and to litigation. What is particularly unfair is that the legacy of a childhood tainted in that way is likely to remain with the children into their own adult lives.

11 Alternatives to the welfare principle

If the law were to abandon the welfare principle, what alternatives could be used?

1. *Presumptions*. The law could seek to rely on presumptions. These could be, for example, that children should live with their mothers and the view of the mother should be

---

[292] Herring (2019b).
[293] Herring (2005b) seeks to defend the welfare principle.
[294] Douglas (2016: 173).
[295] More cynically, see Van Krieken (2005) who sees the welfare principle being used as a way of 'civilising parents'.
[296] [2010] EWCA Civ 1366.

preferred over the view of the father in any issue of dispute or that on separation a child should spend an equal amount of time with each parent. We shall discuss such presumptions further later in the text (see Chapter 10). A major difficulty is that they are based on generalisations. Opponents argue that courts should deal with the particular children and family before them, and not rely on assumptions about what is often good for families in general. What is good for the majority of children is of limited use in determining what is good for the particular child before the court.[297] For example, research from Australia which has developed a strong presumption in favour of shared residence shows that it has worked against the interests of children in many families where the model is inappropriate.[298]

2. *Letting the child decide.* There is much evidence that although children wish to be listened to when their parents separate, most do not want to be forced to decide between their parents. It is therefore unlikely that this would be appropriate except for mature teenagers who have strong views. There are further dangers that the approach might encourage parents to manipulate the child's views. In other cases the child will be too young to express a view.

3. *Tossing a coin.* Elster suggests that disputes over children could be resolved by tossing a coin.[299] In part this approach is a counsel of despair: the courts are not able to predict what will promote the welfare of the child and so they may as well toss a coin. The approach is cheap and treats each side equally. However, the approach cannot really be acceptable, because it abdicates responsibility for children. It is true there are some cases where it is impossible to know what is in a child's interest, but there are many others where the court can ascertain what is in a child's interests or at least what is not in a child's interests. Not to protect the child in such a case would appear irresponsible.

4. *Non-legal solutions.* It is perhaps too readily assumed that disputes between family members should be resolved by a court hearing. It is certainly arguable that social work to assist the family may be more effective than legal intervention. Thorpe LJ in *Re L (A Child) (Contact: Domestic Violence)*, also talking about disputes over contact, has suggested:

> The disputes are particularly prevalent and intractable. They consume a disproportionate quantity of private law judicial time. The disputes are often driven by personality disorders, unresolved adult conflicts or egocentricity. These originating or contributing factors would generally be better treated therapeutically, where at least there would be some prospect of beneficial change, rather than given vent in the family justice system.[300]

Such thinking has been influential in the Children and Adoption Act 2006 which provides extra-legal methods of seeking to encourage parties to resolve their differences over contact. Whether such an approach could be justified in the light of the Human Rights Act 1998, and the requirement that the state protects the rights of parents and children, is open to debate. This gives rise to some of the debates over mediation which were considered in Chapter 2.

Of all of the alternatives to the welfare principle, it is an approach based on children's rights which has been most influential and so we will consider that next.

---

[297] Herring (2014b).
[298] Rhoades (2010a). (See Chapter 10 for further discussion.)
[299] Elster (1987).
[300] [2000] 2 FCR 404 at p. 439.

12 Children's rights

Learning objective 6

Consider the issues around children's rights

So far, we have looked at the law's attempts to promote the welfare of the child. However, in the last few decades there have been calls that, rather than adults attempting to promote the child's welfare, the law should recognise that children have rights of their own.[301] After all, it is hard to resist the argument 'children have human rights, because children are human'.[302] Michael Freeman has argued:

> Rights are important because they recognise the respect their bearers are entitled to. To accord rights is to respect dignity: to deny rights is to cast doubt on humanity and on integrity. Rights are an affirmation of the Kantian basic principle that we are ends in ourselves, and not means to the ends of others.[303]

Colin Macleod[304] has summarised the key arguments for using the language of rights when talking about children. First there is a 'signalling function' indicating that individuals and the state should be particularly attentive to the claims protected by a right. So, if person A has a right to X, others may have a moral responsibility to ensure, in so far as is possible, A has access to X. Second, that rights have a normative weight so that ensuring rights are protected is more important than other claims. Normally only the rights of another person will be a good enough reason to deny a person their rights. Third, rights have an enforcement dimension, so that generally there should be a method of a person bringing legal or other actions to give effect to their right. Macleod argues that seen in this way it is important children are given rights as they reflect significant interests that they have.

Indeed, children's rights are protected by a variety of international instruments,[305] including most notably the United Nations Convention on the Rights of the Child (UNCRC).[306] Although the UNCRC has been signed by Britain, it has not been made officially part of English law. That said, as we have already seen, the courts are increasingly turning to some of its principles in interpreting the law, particularly in areas such as immigration and planning.[307]

Katherine Federle[308] explains the significance of seeing that children have rights, rather than just being people who should be looked after:

> Rights have a transformative aspect because they have the potential to reduce victimization and dependence by changing the rights holder into a powerful individual who commands the respect of those in the legal system . . . rights create mutual zones of respect, challenging those who want to act in the best interests of children to promote the empowerment of children instead.

---

[301] For a consideration of children's rights from a broad perspective, see John (2003), Freeman (2004b), Archard and Macleod (2002), Willems (2007) and Woodhouse (2000 and 2008).
[302] Herring (2003b: 146).
[303] Freeman (2007: 7 and 2010).
[304] Macleod (2018).
[305] Alderson (2017). See also Stalford (2012) on children's rights in EU law.
[306] MacDonald (2009a). The Government had been criticised for failing fully to implement the Convention by the Committee on the Rights of the Child (2016).
[307] Fortin (2014).
[308] Federle (2009).

There is relatively little dispute that children should have some of the basic rights, such as right to life, rights to education, or rights to protection from serious harm;[309] and so we will focus on whether children have rights in terms of two key questions:

1. Should children have all the rights that adults have or should we limit the rights available to children?

2. Should children be given extra rights over and above those given to adults?[310]

A Should children have all the rights adults have?

A simple approach is that children are people and so should have all the rights that adults have.[311] These will include the right to vote,[312] work, travel, use drugs and to engage in sexual relations.[313] Such an approach is taken by a group of thinkers known as child liberationists or colloquially as 'kiddy libbers'.[314] For example, Holt[315] has written that the law supports the view of a child 'being wholly subservient and dependent . . . being seen by older people as a mixture of expensive nuisance, slave and super-pet'. He argues that childhood is used by adults to interfere in children's rights in a way that would be unacceptable for adults. For example, he claims that requiring children to attend schools 'for about 6 hours a day, 180 days a year, for about 10 years . . . is such a gross violation of civil liberties that few adults would stand for it'.[316]

Initially, the argument children should have the same rights as adults seems unacceptable: surely, we cannot accept a society where children have the same rights to sexual freedom, to marry, or to drive cars as adults?[317] Farson replies to such arguments in this way:

> [A]sking what is good for children is beside the point. We will grant children rights for the same reason we grant rights to adults, not because we are sure that children will then become better people, but more for ideological reasons, because we believe that expanding freedom as a way of life is worthwhile in itself. And freedom, we have found, is a difficult burden for adults as well as for children.[318]

In other words, he accepts that giving children rights might lead to them being harmed, but the same thing happens to adults when we give them rights.

The child liberationist position is often criticised for failing to appreciate the physical and mental differences between children and adults.[319] But this is not quite what most child liberationists nowadays claim; they argue that the same laws should apply to adults and children. It is quite permissible to ban from driving those incapable of driving competently, but the state should not ban people from driving on the grounds of age. So, children should not be barred from driving simply on the basis of their age, but can be on the basis of their inability at

---

[309] Alderson (2015).

[310] See Herring (2003b) for more detailed discussion. See also Ferguson (2018).

[311] Although still today some academic commentators take the view that it is appropriate to call a child 'it'.

[312] For a contemporary argument that children should have the right to vote, see Olsson (2008).

[313] Holt (1975: 18). See Waites (2005) for a wide-ranging discussion on the age of consent to sexual relations.

[314] Children's liberationists include Foster and Freund (1972) and Holt (1975). For a sympathetic reading see Byrne (2016).

[315] Holt (1975).

[316] Holt (1975: 163).

[317] Archard (2003: 9) suggests that some writers are 'rhetorical child liberationists' in that they do not really mean that children should have all the rights of adults, but that to make such a claim is eye-catching and therefore politically a useful way of increasing the number of rights children have.

[318] Farson (1978: 31).

[319] Fortin (2009a: 5).

driving. Similarly, in sexual matters, if the child is not competent to consent then it would be unlawful for someone to have sexual relations with him or her.[320] But that would be true for all who have sexual relations with those who do not consent. Another way of putting this argument is that children should not be discriminated against on the grounds of their age.[321] It must be admitted that the present law on at what age young people are able to do something is illogical. To give one example: a 16-year-old is deemed old enough to consent to sexual relations with her or his MP, but not to vote for her or him!

This more moderate liberationist approach is harder to rebut. It is necessary to show some morally relevant distinction between children and adults in order to justify rejection of the liberationist position. One argument may be based on bureaucratic difficulties in assessing competence. To expect a bartender to interview every person who orders a drink to ascertain whether they have sufficient understanding of the potential harms of alcohol to make a reasoned decision to purchase it would be unworkable.[322] A slightly different point is that using age provides a clear impersonal requirement, because the assessment of each individual's capacity can involve 'contested norms'.[323] To start to test everyone (children or adults) to assess capacity to make decisions would be hugely controversial. Age provides a predictable criterion which enables adults to plan their lives, without fearing that they will be found incompetent.

As can be seen already, much of the discussion about children's rights centres on the right to autonomy. The right to autonomy is essentially the right to decide how you wish to live your life. John Eekelaar has called autonomy 'the most dangerous but precious of rights: the right to make their own mistakes'.[324] Most people accept that if an adult wishes to spend all his or her free time playing computer games or watching television or writing a law textbook he or she can, providing these activities do not harm anyone else. Sometimes writers talk about each person being permitted to pursue their own vision of the 'good life'. This is generally regarded as not only good for each individual but also good for society. Our society would be a less culturally rich society if everyone were to spend all their free time jogging, for example. It is good for society that there is diversity in the kinds of hobbies people enjoy. The difficulty is in applying this approach to children. Specifically, children do not have the capacity to develop their own version of their 'good life', at least in the sense of defining long-term goals. The essential problem is this: the way a child lives his or her childhood affects the range of choices and options available later on in life.[325] A simple example is that allowing a child to pursue their vision of a good life and allowing them not to go to school may mean that they will be prevented from pursuing what they regard as the good life once they reach majority because they will not have the education needed to pursue their goals. It, therefore, may be justifiable to infringe a child's autonomy during minority in order to maximise their autonomy later on in life. This, then, could explain why children cannot be treated as adults and why the state may be entitled to restrict autonomy rights in the name of promoting the child's welfare and ultimately their autonomy. John Eekelaar has developed a well-respected version of

---

[320] The Sexual Offences Act 2003 contains a range of sexual offences that can be committed against children under the age of 16; s. 5 makes it an offence for a man to have sex with a girl under the age of 13, whether or not she consents. See further *R v G* [2008] UKHL 37, confirming it was no defence if the man believed the victim to be over the age of 13 and consenting. See Keating (2012) for a critique of the law.

[321] Herring (2003b).

[322] How many adults would pass the test?

[323] Haldane (1994).

[324] Eekelaar (1986: 161).

[325] Eekelaar (1994b).

children's rights.[326] He started with Joseph Raz's definition of a right that: 'a law creates a right if it is based on and expresses the view that someone has an interest which is sufficient ground for holding another to be subject to a duty'.[327] Eekelaar suggests that three kinds of interest are relevant for children:

1. *Basic interests.* These are the essential requirements of living – physical, emotional and intellectual interests. They would include the interest in being provided with food and clothing and in developing emotionally and intellectually. Eekelaar argues that the duty to promote these basic needs lies on parents, but there is also a duty on the state to provide these where parents fail to do so.

2. *Developmental interests.* Eekelaar describes these as 'all children should have an equal opportunity to maximise the resources available to them during their childhood (including their own inherent abilities) so as to minimise the degree to which they enter adult life affected by avoidable prejudices incurred during childhood'.[328] Eekelaar accepts that, apart from education, these would be hard to enforce as legal rights.

3. *Autonomy interest.* This is the freedom for the child to make his or her own decisions about their life.

Of these three interests, Eekelaar would rank the autonomy interest as subordinate to the developmental and basic interests.[329] So children would not be able to claim autonomy interests in a way that would prejudice their basic or developmental interests. He would therefore allow children to make decisions for themselves, even if those were bad mistakes, unless the decision involved infringing one of the basic or developmental interests. This would mean that a child's decision not to go to school would be overridden, because this would be infringing their developmental interests. But their decision to wear jeans should not be overridden as it would not infringe their interests.[330] Of course, there may be borderline cases (would nose piercing be permitted?) but such borderline cases are present in every theory. Eekelaar's approach has the benefit of providing an explanation of why children do not have all the rights of adults – so that they can have greater autonomy as adults – and provides a sensible practical model enabling children to make some decisions for themselves, but not so as to cause themselves serious harm.[331]

Eekelaar has developed his thinking by suggesting that the law should promote a child's welfare by encouraging dynamic self-determinism.[332] He explains that:

> The process is dynamic because it appreciates that the optimal course for a child cannot always be mapped out at the time of decision, and may need to be revised as the child grows up. It involves self-determinism because the child itself is given scope to influence the outcome.[333]

The aim of this approach is:

> To bring a child to the threshold of adulthood with the maximum opportunities to form and pursue life-goals which reflect as closely as possible an autonomous choice.[334]

---

[326] Eekelaar (1994b and 2006b: ch. 6).
[327] Raz (1994).
[328] Eekelaar (1994b).
[329] Eekelaar (1994b). Freeman (1997a) proposes a similar theory and agrees with the subordination of autonomy to other basic needs of the child.
[330] Unless he or she were not allowed to attend school while wearing jeans.
[331] Giddens (1998: 191–2) argues for the democratisation of family life, with children being treated as equal citizens in the family.
[332] Eekelaar (1994a).
[333] Eekelaar (1994a: 48).
[334] Eekelaar (1994a: 156).

This means that:

> . . . in making decisions about children's upbringing, care should be taken to avoid imposing inflexible outcomes at an early stage in a child's development which unduly limit the child's capacity to fashion his/her own identity, and the context in which it flourishes best.[335]

This approach then would give children an increasing role in making decisions for themselves as they grow up.

One way to test Eekelaar's theory would be to ask (as Eekelaar has) how as adults looking back on our childhood we would have wished to have been raised. The answer is probably that we would not have wanted every desire we had as children to be granted. It may well be that we would come up with a set of guidelines similar to Eekelaar's. Interestingly, a survey of children's views found a general agreement that although children should be able to make some decisions, parents should make important ones.[336] Surely listening to children to find out what rights they think they ought to have is a productive way of considering the issue.

A dramatic example of the exercise of children's rights concerned a 14-year-old Dutch sailor who wished (with her parents' consent) to sail around the world. The Dutch authorities were concerned about her welfare and she was put into care by the Dutch authorities. She managed to escape and start her voyage. She was later given permission by the courts to undertake her expedition.[337]

However, Eekelaar's approach is problematic. David Archard[338] considers parents who face a choice of encouraging a child to play sport or music. If we ask what as an adult the child would want, this is problematic because what the child would think when he or she grows up will depend on the choice. If the parents choose music and the child grows up a talented musician, he or she will approve of his or her parents' decisions. However, if the parents choose sport and the child becomes a successful sportsperson, the child will approve of that decision.[339] There are also problems because the hypothetical adult will decide using adult eyes. Would the adult let the child go to an expensive Santa's grotto at Christmas, or would the hypothetical adult regard that as a waste of money? There is a real danger that children are regarded only as 'adults in the making' and childhood is not appreciated in its own right.[340] Lucinda Ferguson has strongly criticised much writing on children's rights for failing to take a child-centred version of children's rights, giving children the rights adults think they should have, rather than looking at the issue from children's perspective.[341] Indeed, there is a danger of assuming that adulthood is better than childhood. Certainly, one study of children found they thought adults did not have much fun or time to play.[342] As we saw earlier in this chapter there is a lively debate among philosophers over whether childhood is a good.[343]

There are also difficulties with applying Eekelaar's theory practically in modern society. Imagine a child who is a highly gifted artist. What are the parents to do? Should the parents permit or

---

[335] Eekelaar (2004: 186).
[336] Cherney (2010).
[337] BBC News Online (2010d).
[338] Archard (2003: 51).
[339] A similar issue arises in raising a child with a particular religious belief, or ethnic identity. Eekelaar (2004) sees advantages in raising children with a variety of identities to choose from, although he sees nothing wrong with raising a child with a clear single sense of a single identity.
[340] Cassidy (2009 and 2012).
[341] Ferguson (2013b). She does not, unfortunately, suggest what a child-centred version of children's rights would look like.
[342] Cassidy *et al.* (2017).
[343] See above, 'The nature of childhood'.

encourage the child to devote most of her life to developing this talent? If the parents do, is it not arguable that that will limit the child's range of lifestyles in adulthood: she will be aged 18, a gifted artist, but with a limited range of alternatives in life. If, however, the parents seek to encourage her to develop a wide range of interests and hobbies and not dedicate a large portion of her life to art, it is unlikely that she will be sufficiently skilled to become a professional artist. With increased specialisation (especially in artistic, academic and sporting activities), dedication in childhood is essential in order to live out some life goals. A more common example is of children whose parents have undergone a bitter divorce. The court may have to decide whether the child will live with the mother or the father, knowing that contact with the other parent is unlikely to be effective. In such a case the court cannot keep the options open for the child to decide when they are an adult; the court must decide on some basis which is best for the child. Indeed, a parent who tried to ensure that a child had a maximum range of options available at adulthood would soon collapse with exhaustion! Perhaps it is more realistic to say that a child must be left with a realistic set of options.[344] But even that may be difficult if the child is a prodigy.

A second problem with Eekelaar's approach is that it is not clear why it is restricted to childhood. The university student who fails to work towards their degree and ends up failing their examinations could be said to have lessened their ability to choose their life choices. Is there a good reason for not permitting a child to limit their life choices but allowing university students to do so?!

A third objection is that Eekelaar's approach may lead to an open-ended solution. Leaving the question so that the child can make decisions when they are old enough may leave issues connected with the child's upbringing unresolved and open-ended. For example, in relation to a dispute over religious upbringing, Eekelaar's approach may suggest that a child be brought up within both religions so that they can decide their religion for themselves later on in life. However, this may leave the child confused and unsettled.[345] Despite these difficulties, it is submitted that Eekelaar's approach provides the best approach to examining children's rights.

It should not be thought that all supporters of children's rights are happy to give children the leeway to make decisions that even Eekelaar's model gives. Dwyer[346] is adamant that any rights that children have must protect their best interests; they have a right to have their welfare promoted.[347] Therefore, children should not be permitted to make decisions which will harm them. We will return to this issue later when we consider whether there is a difference between a rights-based approach and a welfare-based approach. There is, of course, a range of mid-way responses which suggest that children should be consulted over decisions concerning their upbringing, but their views will not be determinative.[348]

The Equality Act 2010 provides protection from discrimination on a broad range of characteristics, including age. However, it does not apply to children. The Government explained:[349]

> Age discrimination provisions do not extend to the under 18s because it is almost always appropriate to treat children of different ages in a way which is appropriate to their particular stage of development, abilities, capabilities and level of responsibility.

---

[344] Altman (2018).
[345] Although see Eekelaar's (2004) reply to points of this kind. He rejects an argument that the child would find being raised with a variety of religions confusing.
[346] Dwyer (2006: 11).
[347] Dwyer (2006: 132). See also Fortin (2006a) who rejects suggestions that rights can ever be used in a way which fundamentally harms a child.
[348] Archard and Skivenes (2009).
[349] HM Government (2010b: 11).

However, the fact that discrimination against children may often be justified does not mean that children should not be protected from it when it is not justified. Having recognised in the Equality Act that unjustified age discrimination is a degrading treatment which needs to be challenged, it is hard to justify why that should be only true in the case of adults. The fact children are excluded from protection from age discrimination is a striking example of the failure to accord full weight to children's rights. The Government justified the exclusion by saying:

> It was decided that age discrimination legislation is not an appropriate way to ensure that children's needs are met. It is almost always right to treat children of different ages in a way which is appropriate to their particular stage of development. Any such legislation would require a large number of exceptions.[350]

The Equality Act 2010 makes it clear that discrimination can be justified if there are sufficiently good reasons for it. So, it is not quite correct to say the legislation would require exceptions; it would be more accurate to say there may be a larger number of cases (as compared to, say, race discrimination) where there would be discrimination, but it would be justifiable under the Equality Act 2010. However, even that may be questioned. Flacks claims it is now well established that 'adults consistently underestimate children's capacities' and that research shows 'most 14 year olds have equivalent competence to adults'. Even if that is disputed[351] the UN Committee on the Rights of the Child emphasises that state parties 'cannot begin with the presumption that a child is incapable of expressing his or her own views. On the contrary, State parties should presume a child has the capacity to form her or his own views . . .'[352] (paragraph 20). So, maybe the question is not whether the majority of 14-year-olds are as competent at making decisions as adults are, but rather whether it is right to presume all 14-year-olds lack decision making ability, just because some, maybe many, do.[353]

B The argument against rights for children

DEBATE

Is there a case for children not having rights?

Here are some of the arguments that have been put forward against children having rights:

1. There are two main theories of rights: the will theory and the interest theory.[354] The will theory argues that rights can only exist where the right-holder can have choice in deciding whether or not to enforce the rights. This would mean that children (especially if very young) could not have rights.[355] MacCormick and other supporters of children's rights argue that this would be unacceptable and hence he rejects the will theory of rights in favour of the interest theory, which protects the interests of the right-holder and is not dependent on the

---

[350] Quoted in Flacks (2014).
[351] Herring (2012e).
[352] Flacks (2014).
[353] Watkins (2016).
[354] MacCormick (1976).
[355] It could be argued by supporters of the will theory who wish to support children's rights that if children are not competent to choose whether or not to enforce their rights, parents are entitled to enforce those rights on children's behalf. See the discussion in Archard (2003: 7).

ability to make a choice.[356] The arguments for and against these theories are discussed in detail in books on jurisprudence.[357]

2. A second objection would be that focusing on rights does not provide adequate protection for children.[358] Children are vulnerable and need protection from adults who can seek to take advantage of them and from children's own foolish decisions. Lucinda Ferguson[359] claims that children's rights can only be justified if they lead to better outcomes for children and so she could not support a version of children's rights that harms children.

A moderate version of children's rights, such as Eekelaar's, might diffuse such fears. However, there are still concerns that too much weight may be placed on children's wishes. Sir Thomas Bingham MR in *Re S (A Minor) (Independent Representation)*[360] has explained:

> First is the principle, to be honoured and respected, that children are human beings in their own right with individual minds and wills, views and emotions, which should command serious attention. A child's wishes are not to be discounted or dismissed simply because he is a child. He should be free to express them and decision-makers should listen. Second is the fact that a child is after all a child. The reason why the law is particularly solicitous in protecting the interests of children is that they are liable to be vulnerable and impressionable, lacking the maturity to weigh the longer term against the shorter, lacking the insight to know how they will react and the imagination to know how others will react in certain situations, lacking the experience to match the probable against the possible . . .

3. A further difficulty with rights for children is that an enforcement of a right of autonomy for a child will mean in many cases an infringement of a parent's or other carer's rights. Children live much of their childhood dependent on adults, and their relationship with adults is crucial.[361] That argument will be of less concern if we accept that there needs to be a fair balancing between the rights of children and parents.

4. It is arguable that the language of rights is quite inappropriate in intimate family relationships, where sacrifice and mutual support are the overriding values of the family unit, rather than the individual market-place philosophy where rights might make more sense.[362] It may be possible to produce a vision of rights that promotes individual autonomy *and* interpersonal connection, but these would not be identical to rights as they are commonly understood.[363]

Much work among feminist writers sympathetic to such arguments has been in developing an 'ethic of care'.[364] Sevenhuijsen explains that the ethic of care: 'is encapsulated in the idea that individuals can exist only because they are members of various networks of care and responsibility, for good or bad. The self can exist only through and with others and vice versa . . .'[365] Such a model would seem to emphasise the values of

---

[356] The benefits and disadvantages of these approaches are beyond the scope of this text.
[357] See, for example, Tobin (2013 and 2015); Eekelaar (2011c); Griffin (2008); MacCormick (1976); Archard (2003: ch 1); Federle (2009).
[358] Purdy (1994).
[359] Ferguson (2013b).
[360] [1993] 2 FLR 437, [1993] 2 FCR 1.
[361] Guggenheim (2006).
[362] Regan (1993a).
[363] Herring (1999a).
[364] See, for example, Sevenhuijsen (2000); Noddings (2003).
[365] Sevenhuijsen (2002: 131). See also Herring (2007a).

interdependence and relationships, rather than individualistic versions of rights. Smart has explained that the ethic of care:

> . . . need not be carried forward on the basis of individual rights in which the child is construed as an autonomous individual consumer of oppositional rule-based entitlements, but more where the child is construed as part of a web of relationships in which outcomes need to be negotiated (not demanded) and where responsibilities are seen to be reciprocal.[366]

Fiona Kelly has argued that children must be seen as relational beings. An ethic of care approach can do this, but neither a welfare (protectionist) approach, nor a rights-based approach does this:

> While protectionism and children's rights go some way towards understanding children as relational beings, both are fundamentally incompatible with such a construction. The protectionist model does acknowledge the parent/child relationship, but the relationship it protects is inherently unequal. It is premised on children's incapacity and the right of adults to speak on behalf of children. Similarly, while there is some acknowledgement under the children's rights model of the importance of connection in children's lives – for example, the Convention on the Rights of the Child gives the child a right to maintain relationships with caregivers if it is in his or her best interests – because the rights model is focused on producing a rational and autonomous adult, connection is treated as a stage in the maturity process which will ultimately be supplanted by detached individualism. In addition, the relationships a children's rights model envisages protecting arise out of the enforcement of rights, rather than the acknowledgement or valorisation of connection; caregiver relationships are protected because the child has a 'right' to maintain them.[367]

I have made a wider point, that the law in its emphasis on individualised rights can fail to attach sufficient significance to relationships of care:

> We are not self-sufficient but interdependent; not isolated individuals but people in relationships; not people with rights clashing with those who care for us and for whom we care, but people who live with entwined obligations and interests with those we love. We are not easily divided up into carers and cared for. We are in mutually supportive relationships. We need then a legal and ethical approach that promotes just caring: respects it; rewards it; and protects those rendered vulnerable by the caring role – an approach which has relationships at its heart.[368]

It may be possible, however, to deal with these concerns within a human rights framework, by developing an approach to rights which attaches appropriate weight to relational values.[369]

5. O'Neill[370] has suggested that it would be more profitable to focus on the notion of duties that adults owe towards children, than to stress the rights of children.[371] She is particularly concerned with impressive-sounding rights when it is unclear who has the duty to provide the child with the benefit. She warns:

> [M]any of the rights promulgated in international documents are not perhaps spurious, but they are patently no more than 'manifesto' rights . . . that cannot be claimed unless or until practices and institutions are established that determine against whom claims on behalf of

---

[366] Smart (2003: 239).
[367] Kelly (2005: 385).
[368] Herring (2007a). See also Rhoades (2010b).
[369] See Rhoades (2010b); Choudhry and Herring (2010: ch 3); Wallbank *et al.* (2009).
[370] O'Neill (1992).
[371] See also Ferguson (2015c). For a discussion over whether too much is expected of children's rights, see Freeman (2000c).

a particular child may be lodged. Mere insistence that certain ideals or goals are rights cannot make them into rights . . .[372]

O'Neill therefore argues that there are obligations owed to children, which cannot be recognised as rights, but that should still be recognised as obligations. This might be particularly desirable in cases where children lack maturity to be able to enforce rights themselves.[373] The main remedy she suggests to deal with children's powerlessness is to grow up. Her approach can be used to support the view that we should focus on dealing with the wrongs done to children, rather than giving them rights;[374] although rights supporters would argue that giving children rights is the best way of protecting them from wrongs. They might also agree with O'Neill that imposing obligations on adults is important, but this can be done in addition to giving children rights.

6. Are the models of rights used based on a particular western conception of human rights? Faulkner and Nyamutata argue:

> We need to continue to reflect critically on whether the imposition of rules on non-Western states through the UNCRC (for example, under the guise of the 'best interests principle') perpetuates particular Westernised ideals which are ill-fitted (and perhaps even damaging) for children in other contexts. The colonial legacy present within the discourse of children's rights needs to be challenged; from the development and implementation of the international legal framework, to the teaching of children's rights, to removing barriers to scholars from the Global South to participating within the discourse.[375]

7. A further argument is that even if in theory children's rights are beneficial, in practice children's rights can be used to the disadvantage of women and children.[376] The fear is that rights are of use to those who have strength within society and, in particular, rights are of use to men to be used as tools of oppression. For example, children's rights could be used to investigate and control the intimate lives of women.

8. There are also concerns that children's rights reflect the norms within society, which may be discriminatory. Frances Olsen asks why getting children to help mother bake cookies at home is not a form of child labour.[377] This question, although a little tongue in cheek, does lead us to enquire how many of what we regard as human rights are in fact just a reflection of the cultural values of our society.

9. There is a concern over the enforcement of children's rights. If children's rights can only realistically be enforced by adults, it may be that such rights will be used only for the benefit of adults.[378] For example, the courts have held that a child has a right to know his or her genetic origins, but in practice this only occurs when a father seeks to have biological tests carried out to determine whether or not he is the father. This example may lead one to conclude that in reality this is a right for fathers to establish paternity, rather than for children to know their genetic identity. In *R (On the Application of Williamson) v Secretary of State for Education and Employment*[379] Baroness Hale memorably opened her speech: 'My lords, this is, and has always been, a case about children, their rights and the rights of their parents and teachers. Yet there has been no one here or in the courts below to speak on

---

[372] Discussed further in Freeman (1997a).
[373] Federle (2009: 343).
[374] Simon (2000).
[375] Faulkner and Nyamutata (2020).
[376] Olsen (1992).
[377] Olsen (1992).
[378] Guggenheim (2006).
[379] [2005] 1 FCR 498 at para 71.

behalf of the children . . . The battle has been fought on ground selected by the adults.' She returned to the theme in *R (On the Application of Kehoe)* v *Secretary of State for Work and Pensions*:[380] 'My lords, this is another case which has been presented to us largely as a case about adults' rights when in reality it is a case about children's rights.'

A slightly different point is about the problems the adult world may have in listening to children: children in our society are not used to being listened to. In schools and homes children become accustomed to not being expected to make decisions for themselves. Lowe and Murch also raise the issue of difficulties over communication between children and adults:

> [C]hildren, in certain respects, inhabit different cultural worlds from adults. Moreover, they can be baffled by the language of adults, especially by professional jargon. Equally, adults are often unfamiliar with children's language codes which, in any event, can differ from age group to age group.[381]

The ease of misconception is demonstrated by the finding of one study which suggested that children associated courts with criminal wrongdoing, even if in fact the court is a family one.[382]

10. Some commentators have argued that the most important right children have is 'the right to be a child'.[383]

This argument emphasises that children should not be expected to bear the responsibilities of adulthood. There is, for example, evidence from psychologists interviewing children whose parents are divorcing which suggests that, although children do wish to be listened to by their parents and the courts, they do not wish to be required to choose between their parents.[384] Neale found that children wanted to be involved in decision making, but to reach decisions with adults and not to be expected to reach decisions on their own.[385] Critics suggest that such arguments are based on an idealised childhood – a time of innocence, free from the concerns and responsibility of the adult world – that is a far cry from the poverty, bullying and abuse which is the lot of all too many children.[386]

11. Some commentators from a more traditionalist perspective have been concerned about the way children's rights could be used to interfere in the privacy rights accorded to the family. Lynette Burrows writes:

> State intervention into family life is feared and loathed by most children more than anything. They are more troubled by the state interfering than they are reassured by the protection offered. Children do not want rights, they want love and protection and the majority of them do not want social workers or anyone else coming into their families and telling their parents they are not behaving properly.[387]

However, you might wonder whether what she is saying is true for children who are being abused by their parents.

---

[380] [2005] 2 FCR 683 at para 49.
[381] Lowe and Murch (2001: 145).
[382] Lowe and Murch (2001: 152).
[383] Campbell (1992).
[384] Tisdall *et al.* (2004).
[385] Neale (2004). See also Smart (2002).
[386] See Phillips (2003) who discusses the pervasive violence faced by many children in their everyday lives.
[387] Burrows (1998: 54).

Questions

1. *Should children who are as competent as adults be treated exactly the same as an adult?*

2. *Do rights work in the context of intimate relationships?*

3. *Do children want rights?*

Further reading

Read **Archard and Skivenes** (2009) for a discussion of how to balance attaching weight to the wishes of children and to their protection.

C Extra rights for children

So far, we have focused on whether children are entitled to all the rights that adults have. But can children claim rights which adults do not have? It certainly seems so.[388] Children may be thought to have rights to education, protection from abuse[389] and financial support to a greater extent than might be claimed by adults. These would reflect the developmental interests expounded in Eekelaar's approach. A clear example is that a parent is liable to support a child financially until (normally) the child reaches the age of 18.[390] These rights, then, are the rights of the child to enable him or her to become an adult and take on the full mantle of rights an adult has.

D Children's rights for adults

Most of the discussion on children's rights has centred on the debate whether children are as competent as adults. Although difficult to gauge, probably most commentators appear to accept that the vulnerability of children and their dependency on their parents means that children cannot be granted the same rights as adults. However, it is interesting to ask the question the other way around: are adults as vulnerable and dependent as children? Although the law tends to assume that adults are self-sufficient, fully competent adults, this is an ideal which is unrealistic for many adults.[391] Maybe the fact we are uncomfortable with children having the rights adults have tells us that our model of rights for adults is faulty. It can be argued that 'once cooperative, care-giving relationships among vulnerable people (rather than autonomous individuals) are seen as the basis around which rights work, the difficulties with children having the same rights to a large extent fall away'.[392]

E Children's rights in practice

As we have seen, most of the academic discussion on children's rights has centred on children's rights of autonomy. However, this discussion of children's rights is skewed from a western perspective. Notably, looking at the main English and Welsh textbooks on family law it is

---

[388] Ferguson (2013b).
[389] For example, Children Act 1989, Part IV.
[390] See Chapter 6.
[391] Lim and Roche (2000).
[392] Herring (2003b: 172).

easier to find a discussion on whether children should be allowed to pierce their noses than on children's right to clean water. We tend to take for granted that the basic needs of children are met. However, Britain need not be complacent:[393]

KEY STATISTICS

- 4.2 million children live in poverty in the United Kingdom according to the figures for 2020.[394]

- UNICEF in 2020 looked at child well-being in the 41 wealthiest countries. The UK ranked 29th for mental well-being, 19th for physical health and 26th for skills. Overall, it was ranked 27th. The report found 36% of 15-year-olds rated their mental well-being as poor; 37% of children lacked basic literacy and numeracy skills and 31% of children in the UK are obese or overweight.

- One in eight children have a diagnosable mental health condition. But fewer than 1 in 3 children and young people with a diagnosable mental health condition get access to NHS care and treatment.[395]

- One in seven children arrive at school hungry.[396]

- 22% of 10-year-olds report being bullied, with disabled children and children from ethnic minorities most at risk of bullying.[397]

- 8% of children consumed five or more portions of fruit and vegetables a day in 2018.[398]

- In 2019/20, 9.7% of children in Reception were classified as obese and 20.2% of children in Year 6.[399]

- In 2017, suicide was the most common cause of death for both boys (16.2% of all deaths) and girls (13.3%) aged between 5 and 19.[400]

- A survey found that children and young people reported spending on average 2.5 hours a day on a computer or tablet; three hours a day on a phone; and two hours watching television. UK children watch an average of more than two hours of television and spend over three hours online each day.[401]

- A major survey by Girlguiding in 2013 found that: 'Sexual harassment is commonplace, girls' appearance is intensively scrutinised and their abilities are undermined.' Three-quarters of 11–17-year-old girls said that sexism affected most areas of their lives. Another Girlguiding report in 2019 found 22% saying they had their hair or clothes pulled or skirt lifted up; 93% reported witnessing bullying on the grounds of a person's sexuality.[402]

- The former president of the Family Division once pointed out that Britons give far more money by way of charitable giving to donkey sanctuaries than to children in need.[403]

---

[393] See Committee on the Rights of the Child (2016) for a discussion of the position of children in the UK
[394] Child Poverty Action Group (2020).
[395] Young Minds (2020).
[396] Kelloggs (2020).
[397] Long, Roberts and Loft (2020).
[398] NHS (2020a).
[399] NHS (2020b).
[400] Young Minds (2020).
[401] Royal College of Pediatrics and Child Health (2019).
[402] Girlguiding (2013 and 2019).
[403] Butler-Sloss (2003).

Indeed, the United Nations Committee on the Rights of the Child had no difficulty in providing extensive criticism of the position of children within the United Kingdom.[404] To those reports must be added this shocking case.

KEY CASE: *Re X (A Child) (No. 3)* [2017] EWHC 2036 (Fam); *Re X (A Child) (No. 4)* [2017] EWHC 2084 (Fam)

X was a few days short of her 17th birthday and was being detained under a sentence imposed by a Youth Court in a secure unit (ZX). The hearing started in June and X was due to be released in mid-August. What raised concerns was that X had made determined attempts to commit suicide.

At the first hearing Munby P said:

> If there is no effective, realistic and above all *safe* plan in place for X when she is released from ZX, the consequences, given her suicidal ideation, do not bear thinking about . . . The court has expressed the need for the local authority to make urgent enquiries in relation to potential placements for X forthwith. It has been clear that there must be no delay in instigating these enquiries; the local authority will make such enquiries forthwith.

The case returned a couple of weeks later. Munby P was unimpressed by the progress made:

> For all that has actually been achieved in the last few weeks, however, despite unrelenting efforts both by the local authority and by other agencies, I might as well have been talking to myself in the middle of the Sahara.

He emphasised that X had an overwhelming need for a suitable secure clinical setting. He was told there was 'no such placement' available anywhere in the country. Munby P was left saying that releasing her without protection was a 'suicide mission to a catastrophic level'. Even her current conditions were 'shocking', the judge concluded, asking 'how is this treatment compatible with her humanity, her dignity, let alone with her welfare?' He doubted her treatment was consistent with Articles 3 and 8 of the Convention and the duty of the State to preserve life under Article 2. In a judgment of considerable rhetorical power that went on 'shocking . . . disgraceful . . . utterly shaming', he concluded:

> In modern times the principle has expanded, so that, as is often said, 'One of the measures of a civilised society is how well it looks after the most vulnerable members of its society.' If this is the best we can do for X, and others in similar crisis, what right do we, what right do the system, our society and indeed the State itself, have to call ourselves civilised? The honest answer to this question should make us all feel ashamed. For my own part, acutely conscious of my powerlessness – of my inability to do more for X – I feel shame and embarrassment; shame, as a human being, as a citizen and as an agent of the State; embarrassment as President of the Family Division, and, as such, Head of Family Justice, that I can do no more for X.
> . . . If, when in eleven days' time she is released from ZX, we, the system, society, the State, are unable to provide X with the supportive and safe placement she so desperately needs, and if, in consequence, she is enabled to make another attempt on her life, then I can only say, with bleak emphasis: we will have blood on our hands.

---

[404] Committee on the Rights of the Child (2016); Children's Rights Alliance for England (2020).

> The judgment had its intended effect and by 4 August the NHS had found a bed in a 'safe and appropriate care setting'. This did little to appease Munby P's righteous anger, who pointed out that X was fortunate her case came before a senior judge and that there were far too many young women in similar predicaments.

F Is there a difference between a welfare-based approach and a rights-based approach?

Does it really make any difference whether the law talks in terms of children's rights or their welfare?[405] Traditionally there has been seen to be a clash between those who are paternalists and those who are supporters of children's rights. Paternalism takes as its starting point that children are vulnerable and in need of protection from the dangers posed by adults, other children and themselves. Children lack the knowledge, experience or strength to care for themselves, and therefore society must do all it can to promote the child's welfare.[406] Within paternalism there is some dispute over who should decide what is in the child's best interests: the child's parents or the state, taking the advice of expert psychologists.

After all, the rights of children to clothing, food, education, etc. could all equally be supported in terms of a child's right to their basic needs and as necessary in order to promote a child's welfare. Indeed, as Eekelaar has pointed out, 'if people have rights to anything, it must include the right that their well-being be respected'.[407] In fact, in the vast majority of situations there would be no difference in result whether a rights-based approach or a welfare-based approach was taken. But, in practical terms, when would it matter which approach is taken? Looking at Eekelaar's approach, the welfare approach would justify promoting a child's basic or developmental interests. The difference between the approaches is revealed when considering autonomy. The rights-based approach would permit children to make decisions for themselves as long as there is no infringement of the developmental or basic interests. A welfare approach would also permit children to make some decisions for themselves. This is because it could be said to be in a child's interests to learn from their own mistakes. Alternatively, it could be argued that refusing to follow the child's wishes would cause the child emotional distress. The difference between a welfare approach and Eekelaar's rights-based approach would be over a small band of cases where allowing a child to decide for him- or herself would not infringe their basic or developmental interests, but would cause enough harm for a welfare approach to decide that more harm would be caused by allowing them to make the decision than not.

A child welfarist can, therefore, readily accept that children should be able to make decisions for themselves, and a children's rights proponent can readily accept that children's choices should be restricted in order to promote their welfare. Indeed, it would be quite possible for a children's rights advocate to be less willing than a child welfarist to allow children to make decisions for themselves. This would be so where a children's rights advocate emphasised children's rights to protection from harm, the right to a safe environment or the right to discipline and/or where a child welfarist placed much weight on the benefit to children

---

[405] See the very useful discussion in Bainham (2002a) and Moylan (2010).
[406] Fox Harding (1996).
[407] Eekelaar (2002a: 243).

of developing their own personalities through making decisions for themselves and learning from their mistakes.

It could be said that children have a right to have their welfare promoted.[408] However, Eekelaar[409] has rejected any suggestion of such a right:

> A claim simply that some should act to further my welfare as they define it is in reality to make no claim at all. Running behind these explicit propositions lies the suggestion that to treat someone fully as an individual of moral worth implies recognizing that that person makes claims and exercises choices: that is, is a potential right-holder.

Even if in practical terms there are few cases when the approaches would produce different results, there are important conceptual differences between the two approaches. The first is that although both rights and welfare models can be explained on the basis that they protect the child's interest, in the welfare model the courts or parents determine what children's interests are, whereas the rights-based model seeks to promote the interests as the child sees them to be, or would see them were they capable. A second important difference is that the existence of rights implies that there are duties: that is, that the child (or those acting on behalf of the child) can make claims against the court or parents. However, a welfare approach imposes no obligation on the parents or courts, unless we merge the two approaches and give the children a right to have their welfare promoted by the courts and their parents.[410] A third difference is that there may be rights which a child has, which cannot necessarily be demonstrated to promote his or her welfare. For example, it is increasingly recognised that a child has a right to know his or her genetic origins, even though it might not be possible to demonstrate that this knowledge promotes a child's welfare.

There is also an important difference between the two approaches in the form of reasoning used. Under the welfare approach the focus of the court is solely on what is best for the child, while under a rights-based approach all of the interests of the parties are considered. Supporters of a rights-based approach argue that that improves the quality of the reasoning and means that each party can leave court feeling that the case has been looked at from their perspective and that they had their rights considered.[411] Opponents might respond that as soon as the focus of the court's attention is diverted from considering the position of the child, the results are likely to harm children.

To see how the theoretical discussion operates in practice, this chapter will now briefly discuss cases where the interests of children, parents and the state have had to be balanced. The area that reveals the issues better than any other is medical law.

13 Children and medical law

Many of the cases involving disputes between children and adults have concerned medical treatment.[412] The cases are useful beyond the medical arena because they give some general guidance on how disputes between children and adults should generally be resolved.

---

[408] See Fortin (2006a) who is critical of those who see rights and welfare as incompatible.
[409] Eekelaar (1992: 221).
[410] Eekelaar (1994d).
[411] Choudhry and Herring (2010: ch. 3).
[412] But see *Re Roddy (A Child) (Identification: Restriction on Publication)* [2004] 1 FCR 481 for an example of the use of children's rights in the area of freedom of expression.

However, it should not be assumed that the approach taken in the medical context will necessarily be applied in other situations.[413] Indeed, given that the consequence of respecting a child's refusal of medical treatment is likely to be a very serious harm, even death, it might not be surprising if less weight were attached to children's refusal in the medical arena than other areas of the law.

The law on when a doctor can treat a child can be summarised as follows.[414] Unless there has been a court order forbidding the carrying out of the treatment, a doctor can provide treatment to a child which he or she believes to be in the child's best interests if, and only if:

- the child is competent and consents to the treatment; or
- those with parental responsibility consent; or
- the court declares the treatment lawful; or
- the defence of necessity applies.

The court cannot force a doctor to provide treatment which the doctor does not wish to provide. An understanding of the law must start with the fact that a doctor who touches a patient commits a battery, which is a criminal offence, unless he or she has a defence. A defence is provided in any one of the four circumstances listed above. These will now be considered in further detail.

A 16- and 17-year-olds

Section 8(1) of the Family Law Reform Act 1969 states:

LEGISLATIVE PROVISION

Family Law Reform Act 1969, section 8(1)

The consent of a minor who has attained the age of sixteen years to any surgical, medical or dental treatment . . . shall be as effective as it would be if he were of full age; and where a minor has by virtue of this section given an effective consent to any treatment it shall not be necessary to obtain any consent for it from his parent or guardian.

This indicates clearly that a child aged 16 or 17 can give legal effect to treatment, unless they are shown to be incompetent, using the same rules as for an adult. This might arise if they suffered from a mental disability.

What if a child aged 16 or 17 refused to consent but their parents did consent to the treatment? Following *Re W (A Minor) (Medical Treatment: Court's Jurisdiction)*,[415] a doctor can rely on the consent of the parents of a 16- or 17-year-old, despite the opposition of the child. However, this decision is subject to an important caveat. The doctor can only treat a patient if he or she believes the treatment is in the best interests of the patient. It would be most unusual for a doctor to decide that it would be in the interests of a 16- or 17-year-old to receive medical

---

[413] Lady Hale was explicit about this in *Re D (A Child)* [2019] UKSC 42, para 24.
[414] Freeman (2005) provides a useful summary and discussion of the current law.
[415] [1993] 1 FLR 1, [1992] 2 FCR 785.

treatment against their wishes. Balcombe LJ stated in *Re W (A Minor) (Medical Treatment: Court's Jurisdiction)*:[416]

> As children approach the age of majority they are increasingly able to take their own decisions concerning their medical treatment . . . It will normally be in the best interests of a child of sufficient age and understanding to make an informed decision that the court should respect its integrity as a human being and not lightly override its decision on such a personal matter as medical treatment. All the more so if that treatment is invasive.

Even if a doctor did wish to treat such a patient, relying on the consent of the parents, he or she may well prefer to obtain the authorisation of the court before so doing.[417] In *Re C (Detention: Medical Treatment)*[418] C, aged 16, suffered from anorexia nervosa. The court under the inherent jurisdiction directed that C should remain as a patient at a clinic until discharged by her consultant or further order of the court. This power included the use of reasonable force to detain her for the purposes of treatment. This is a highly controversial decision because it is unlikely that, had C been over 18, it would have been lawful to detain her. In *Re P (Medical Treatment: Best Interests)*[419] a blood transfusion was ordered on a young woman who was nearly 18. Johnson J emphasised his reluctance to make the order given that she was so nearly 18. However, in the life or death situation facing him he was willing to make the order authorising the transfusion if that was the only way to save her life.

B Under 16-year-olds

The leading case here is *Gillick*.[420]

> ### CASE: *Gillick v W Norfolk and Wisbech AHA* [1985] 3 All ER 402, [1986] 1 FLR 229, [1986] AC 112 HL
>
> In 1980 the Department of Health and Social Security provided a notice that in 'exceptional circumstances' a doctor could give contraceptive advice to a girl under 16 without parental consent or consultation. Victoria Gillick, a committed Roman Catholic, sought to challenge the legality of the notice after she unsuccessfully requested assurances that none of her five daughters under 16 would receive advice without her permission. She lost at first instance, but won unanimously at the Court of Appeal, but lost 3–2 in the House of Lords.[421] The fact that the majority of judges who heard the case decided in her favour, even though she lost at the end of the day, reveals the difficulty of the issues involved.
>
> The majority of the House of Lords accepted that if a doctor decided that it was in the best interests of an under 16-year-old that she be given the contraceptive advice she sought and that she was competent to understand the issues involved, then the doctor was permitted to provide the treatment without obtaining the consent of the parents first. This was a hugely important decision because it recognised that under 16-year-olds had the right to give effective legal consent to medical treatment.

---

[416] [1993] 1 FLR 1 at p. 19, [1992] 2 FCR 785 at p. 786.
[417] *Re W (A Minor) (Medical Treatment: Court's Jurisdiction)* [1992] 2 FCR 785.
[418] [1997] 2 FLR 180, [1997] 3 FCR 49.
[419] [2003] EWHC 2327 (Fam).
[420] Discussed in Fortin (2011b).
[421] The case also gave rise to some interesting issues of criminal law, which will not be discussed here.

The *Gillick* decision was reconsidered in the following case:[422]

CASE: R (On the Application of Axon) v Secretary of State for Health (Family Planning Association Intervening) [2006] 1 FCR 175

Mrs Axon applied for judicial review of Department of Health guidance which said that medical professionals could provide advice on sexual matters, including abortion, to under 16-year-olds, without their parents being notified. Silber J, following *Gillick*, ruled that there was a duty of confidence owed to young people and so advice on abortion and other matters could be given without informing the parent. He placed particular weight on evidence that if confidentiality concerning sexual matters could not be guaranteed, young people may be deterred from seeking medical advice and this would have 'undesirable and troubled consequences'.[423] He rejected a claim that parents had a right to be informed of advice or treatment given to their children under Article 8 of the ECHR, explaining that parents have no right to family life in respect of a competent child who does not want the parents to have that right.[424] Even if they did have a right to be told of treatment given to their children, this could be justifiably interfered with in the name of promoting good sexual health among young people.[425] Having said all of that, Silber J stated that he hoped most young people would want to discuss sexual health issues with their parents.

It would be wrong to see *Axon* as a case which is a total victory for adolescent autonomy. Silber J listed five criteria that a doctor would have to be satisfied had been met before giving treatment to an under 16-year-old without informing his or her parents: they must understand all aspects of the advice; the medical professional had not been able to persuade the young person to inform his or her parents; (in the case of contraception) the young person is very likely to have sexual intercourse with or without the contraception; unless the young person receives the advice or treatment his or her physical or mental health are likely to suffer; and it is in the best interests of the young person to receive the treatment on sexual matters without parental consent. Notably, then, a doctor may refuse to provide a competent minor with medical treatment where if the patient were an adult, they would be entitled to receive it as of right.

The *Gillick* decision, subsequently followed in *Axon,* left a number of issues unanswered:

(i) When is a child competent to give consent?

The Mental Capacity Act 2005 sets out the test for mental capacity in relation to adults, but it does not apply to children.[426] However, in developing the law in relation to children the courts may pay attention to the Act.

---

[422] [2006] 1 FCR 175.

[423] At para 66. In *Local Authority v M* [2018] EWHC 3939 (Fam) a child in care was entitled to confidentiality concerning treatment she was receiving at a gender identity clinic.

[424] See Douglas (2016: 273) who questions this holding. It would seem preferable to say that the parent does have a right of family life in connection with the decision, although this right can be interfered with because that is necessary in the interests of the child. After all, if the decision is not to have an abortion this will have a huge impact on the parent's life.

[425] Although see Lee (2004) for a discussion of the practical difficulties young people face in accessing abortion services.

[426] Chico and Hagger (2011). See Cave (2014b) for further discussion.

> ## KEY CASE: *Re S (Child as Parent: Adoption: Consent)* [2017] EWHC 2729 (Fam)
>
> The case turned on whether or not a girl under 16 had capacity to consent to her child being adopted. Cobb J drew on the test in the Mental Capacity Act 2005 to list the following key features of capacity:
>
> (i) Understand the nature and implications of the decision and the process of implementing that decision.
>
> (ii) Understand the implications of not pursuing the decision.
>
> (iii) Retain the information long enough for the decision-making process to take place.
>
> (iv) Weigh up the information and arrive at a decision.
>
> (v) Communicate that decision.
>
> Cobb J added that 'on an issue as significant and life-changing as adoption, there is a greater onus on ensuring that the child understands and is able to weigh the information than if the decision was of a lesser magnitude'.[427] He also emphasised that in relation to understanding, the question was whether or not there was understanding of the 'salient' information and there was no need to understand all the peripheral facts. Cobb J further stated in his summary:
>
> > When determining the competence of a child parent in these circumstances, 'all practicable steps to help' her, as the decision maker, to make the decision, must have been taken; a young person *under* the age of 16 will be treated as understanding the information relevant to a decision if she is able to understand an explanation of it given to her in a way which is appropriate to her circumstances (using simple language, visual aids or any other means).[428]
>
> On an issue as significant and life-changing as adoption, there was a greater onus on ensuring that the child understood and was able to weigh the information than if the decision was of a lesser magnitude. That approach enhanced the mother's right to exercise autonomous decision-making under Article 8 of the European Convention for the Protection of Human Rights and Fundamental Freedoms (1950).

The term '*Gillick*-competent' has been widely used to describe children who are sufficiently competent to give consent to treatment. In considering whether a child is *Gillick*-competent or not, the court will consider a number of issues:

1. *Does the child understand the nature of their medical condition and the proposed treatment?* Relevant here is not just the fact that the child understands what it is that is proposed to be done, but the possible side-effects of any treatment.[429] A fairly straightforward case was *Re JA (Medical Treatment: Child Diagnosed with HIV)*[430] where a 15-year-old boy was described as 'thoughtful, intelligent and articulate', but refused medication for HIV as he would not accept he had the condition. His failure to understand his medical state meant he lacked capacity to refuse treatment for it. There is some debate over whether the child must also

---

[427] At para 61.
[428] At para 62.
[429] *Re R (A Minor) (Wardship: Consent to Medical Treatment)* [1992] 1 FLR 190, [1992] 2 FCR 229.
[430] [2014] EWHC 1135 (Fam).

understand what will happen if the treatment is not performed.[431] Rather controversially, in *Re L (Medical Treatment: Gillick Competency)*[432] L was found not to be competent because she did not appreciate the manner of her death if the treatment was not performed. The reason why she did not was because the doctors thought it would cause her undue distress if they were to tell her. It seems highly unsatisfactory that a child can be found not competent because the doctors have failed to give her the relevant information that she needs to be competent.[433] Emma Cave has argued that medical professionals are under a duty to maximise a child's capacity.[434]

2. *Does the child understand the moral and family issues involved?* This was stressed by Lord Scarman in *Gillick*. It was also thought relevant in *Re E (A Minor) (Wardship: Medical Treatment)*,[435] where the court was concerned that the child did not appreciate how much grief his parents would suffer if he were to die.

3. *How much experience of life does the child have?* The courts have relied on this ground in particular when considering children brought up by parents of strong religious views. In *Re L (Medical Treatment: Gillick Competency)*[436] a 14-year-old had been brought up by Jehovah's Witness parents. The court felt that she had lived a sheltered life and had not been exposed to a variety of different religious views. This pointed to the fact she was not competent.[437] Similarly in *F v F*[438] it was held that a 15-year-old was too strongly influenced by her mother to have capacity to make the decision.[439]

4. *Is the child in a fluctuating mental state?* If the child is fluctuating between competence and incompetence, the court will treat the child as not competent. This was the approach taken in *Re R (A Minor) (Wardship: Consent to Medical Treatment)*.[440] The decision could be justified on the basis that, otherwise, the hospital would be in a very difficult position in having to decide each time the child was touched whether she was competent or not. Opponents of the decision would argue that inconvenience for medical professionals should not justify not taking the rights of children seriously.

5. *Is the child capable of weighing the information appropriately to be able to reach a decision?*[441] Here the court will consider not only the child's ability to understand facts, but also the ability to weigh the facts in reaching a decision. Lord Scarman noted that it is necessary to ask whether the child 'has sufficient discretion to enable him or her to make a wise choice in his or her own interest'. Michael Freeman suggests this means the child needs to have 'wisdom', which is not necessarily the same thing as knowledge.[442] He argues there needs to be 'less emphasis on what these young persons know – less talk in other words of knowledge and understanding – and more on how the decision they have reached furthers their

---

[431] Gilmore and Herring (2011a) say the child does not need to understand that and Cave and Wallbank (2012) say he must. The statements in *Gillick* on this are not crystal clear.

[432] [1998] 2 FLR 810.

[433] Indeed, since this decision the British Medical Association has suggested that doctors should not fail to give minor patients information on the basis that to do so would cause them distress.

[434] Cave (2011).

[435] [1993] 1 FLR 386.

[436] [1998] 2 FLR 810.

[437] See also *Re S (A Minor) (Medical Treatment)* [1993] 1 FLR 376. For criticism of such cases see Eekelaar (1994a: 57).

[438] [2013] EWHC 2683 (Fam).

[439] See Herring (2013b) for criticism

[440] [1992] 1 FLR 190, [1992] 2 FCR 229.

[441] *Re MB* [1997] Med LR 217.

[442] Freeman (2007).

goals and coheres with their system of values'.[443] In *F v F*[444] a 15-year-old refused to take the MMR vaccine because as a vegan she objected to the fact it contained animal products. It was said she was not competent because she was fixated on the ingredients of the vaccine and did not consider the wider picture. This decision has been criticised. Many adult vegans would have a similarly hard line against taking animal products and it is not clear why having a strong moral stance on an issue should mean you lack capacity.[445] It is also worth adding that some psychiatrists are adamant that children have the reasoning capacities of adults in exceptional cases.[446]

6. Has the child developed their own views or are they simply repeating those of their parents? In *An NHS Trust v BK*[447] an 11-year-old boy, who was seriously ill, objected to pain relief and other medication. MacDonald J held that he was not *Gillick*-competent because he drew heavily on his mother's views and lacked sufficient understanding to make his own decision.

(ii) When the doctor can rely on the parent's consent

Lord Scarman had suggested in *Gillick* that 'the parental right yields to the child's right to make his own decisions when he reaches a sufficient understanding and intelligence to be capable of making up his own mind on the matter requiring decision'. This seemed to suggest that if the child was competent and refused to give consent then this refusal could not be overridden by someone with parental responsibility. However, the Court of Appeal has made it clear in cases following *Gillick* that, even if a competent child does not consent, the doctor can still treat a child if he or she believes that to do so would promote the welfare of the child, and someone with parental responsibility for the child gives consent. In *Re W (A Minor) (Medical Treatment: Court's Jurisdiction)*[448] it was explained that a doctor who wishes to treat a patient needs a 'flak jacket' of consent that would provide protection from liability in criminal or tort law. It was stated that this flak jacket could be provided by either the competent child *or* a person with parental responsibility[449] or by the court.[450] So the fact that the child had refused to provide the flak jacket did not prevent someone with parental responsibility providing one. Indeed, in *Re K, W, and H (Minors) (Medical Treatment)*[451] it was held that, where someone with parental responsibility gives consent, it was unnecessary and inappropriate to bring the matter before the court; the doctors should simply provide the treatment. In *Re M (Medical Treatment: Consent)*[452] a 15-year-old girl refused a heart transplant, stating that she did not want to have someone else's heart. Her mother consented to the treatment. The Court of Appeal authorised the operation, stating that the preserving of the girl's life justified overriding her views. Notably here the Court of Appeal did not state whether she was or was not *Gillick*-competent. This was because it did not matter; someone with parental responsibility had provided the flak jacket and the operation was in the best interests of the girl so her views

---

[443] Freeman (2007).
[444] [2013] EWHC 2683 (Fam).
[445] Herring (2013b).
[446] Steinberg (2013); Wilhelms and Reyna (2013).
[447] [2016] EWHC 2860 (Fam).
[448] [1993] 1 FLR 1, [1992] 2 FCR 785.
[449] Only the consent of one parent with parental responsibility is required: *An NHS Trust v SR* [2012] EWHC 3842 (Fam). Although if the parents disagree it may be best to get a court order.
[450] In an emergency, where the doctor cannot obtain the consent of the parent or the court the doctors may be able to rely on the defence of necessity if they are acting in the child's best interests. However, that is available only where there is no time to go to the courts: *Glass v UK* [2004] 1 FCR 553.
[451] [1993] 1 FLR 854, [1993] 1 FCR 240.
[452] [1999] 2 FLR 1097.

were irrelevant. In *Nielsen v Denmark*[453] the European Court of Human Rights appeared to accept that the European Convention would permit treatment to be carried out on children against their wishes, relying on the consent of the parent.[454] A shadow of doubt may have been created by Silber J's judgment in *R (On the Application of Axon) v Secretary of State for Health*[455] where he stated: 'the parental right to determine whether a young person will have medical treatment terminates if and when the young person achieves a sufficient understanding and intelligence to understand fully what is proposed.'[456] This implies that if a child is competent then the parent has no right to determine what treatment a child shall receive. However, this is a single obiter statement of a first instance judge and it cannot, of course, overrule a well-established line of Court of Appeal cases.[457] More recently, in *Plymouth Hospitals NHS Trust v YZ and ZZ*[458] MacDonald J confirmed that: 'With respect to children under the age of 16, the court has the power to override the decisions of a *Gillick*-competent child where it is in the child's best interests for it to do so.'

The most explicit example of the courts using this jurisdiction is the following:

KEY CASE: *University Hospitals Plymouth NHS Trust v B (Urgent Treatment)* [2019] EWHC 1670 (Fam)

B, aged 16, was refusing treatment (insulin) for the life-threatening condition diabetic ketoacidosis ('DKA'). The young woman was found to be *Gillick*-competent, but MacFarlane P said that the case law was clear that her refusal could be overridden if it was found to be in her best interests to do so. In this case it was. While the court gave weight to her views, at the end of the day it was a best interests assessment. Interestingly, MacFarlane P noted that B had consented to admission to hospital, to a series of blood tests and to the insertion of a cannula. That suggested her views were not 'concrete' and also that she was likely to cooperate with treatment.

Stephen Gilmore and I[459] have argued that in *Re W (A Minor) (Medical Treatment: Court's Jurisdiction)*[460] the court was dealing with a child who was *Gillick*-competent to refuse a particular treatment, but was not found to be competent to refuse all treatment. The case is not, we suggest, authority for finding that where a child is competent to refuse all treatment a parent can provide an effective consent. This is a controversial interpretation of the case law[461] and it remains to be seen if it would be accepted by the courts.

---

[453] (1988) 11 EHRR 175.

[454] In an obiter comment in *Re S (A Child) (Identification: Restrictions on Publication)* [2003] 2 FCR 577 Hale LJ suggested that a child might be competent enough to consent to an interview with a newspaper and her parents would not have any power to stop her.

[455] [2006] 1 FCR 175.

[456] At para 56.

[457] See further Taylor (2007). See also *Mabon v Mabon* [2005] EWCA Civ 634, [2005] 2 FLR 1011, [2005] 2 FCR 354 where, at para 28, Thorpe LJ emphasised the importance of letting competent teenagers make decisions for themselves.

[458] [2017] EWHC 2211 (Fam).

[459] Gilmore and Herring (2011b).

[460] [1993] 1 FLR 1, [1992] 2 FCR 785.

[461] It is rejected in Cave and Wallbank (2012).

It may be that, despite the official line taken by the courts, in practice the views of children are given weight by doctors. In one much publicised case a 14-year-old, Hannah Jones, refused the heart transplant recommended by her doctors even though without it she was likely to die. The doctors decided to abide by her wishes, although she subsequently decided to accept the transplant.[462] In 2010 there were newspaper reports of a 15-year-old Jehovah's Witness, Joshua McAuley, who died after refusing a blood transfusion. In both these cases the issue was not brought to the courts.[463]

(iii) If the matter is brought before the court, how should the court resolve the issue?

Where cases involving disputes over the medical treatment of children have been brought before them, the courts have been very willing to approve the treatment proposed by the doctors, even if the treatment is opposed by the parents and the children.[464] It would be quite wrong, however, to conclude that children's or parents' wishes are largely ignored. The fact that only these rather extreme cases come before the court indicates that, normally, doctors abide by the parent's or children's wishes and, if not, try very hard to persuade the child or parent to consent to the treatment.

If the opposition is coming from the child, the court will attach weight to the views of the child even if they are not *Gillick*-competent.[465] In part that is because if a child is opposing treatment and force will need to be used to impose the treatment upon them, only in the most serious of cases will this be in their welfare. In that regard the decision in *F v F*[466] is striking in that although the court determined that it was in the welfare of the children to receive the inoculation against their wishes, they did not order the doctors to provide it.[467] However, the views of the child lacking capacity may be relevant even beyond the point about the need for force. In *Re X (A Child)*[468] a 13-year-old girl was pregnant and wanted an abortion. Although Munby P determined that she lacked the capacity to make the decision in determining what order to make based on her best interests, her views carried weight in the welfare assessment. In that case it was ordered that the termination went ahead. By contrast in *An NHS Foundation Trust v A and Others*[469] a 15-year-old girl who had anorexia nervosa refused treatment. It was held that she lacked capacity to refuse treatment and although her refusal was due respect it was overall in her best interests that she receive treatment.

In other cases, the child is too young to have a view and the primary dispute is between the parents and doctors. There have been tragically difficult cases involving children who have been born severely disabled and there is dispute over the appropriate medical treatment for the child.[470] The criminal law prohibits any acts of doctors designed to end the child's life, or acts aimed at shortening the child's life (as opposed to aimed at relieving pain).[471] What is strictly forbidden is the performing of any act designed to end the life of the child: that would be murder. However, the courts may authorise the doctors to refrain from offering treatment.

---

[462] BBC News Online (2010c).
[463] Roberts (2010).
[464] *Re E (A Minor) (Wardship: Medical Treatment)* [1993] 1 FLR 386.
[465] *Re JM (A Child) (Medical Treatment)* [2015] EWHC 2832 (Fam).
[466] [2013] EWHC 2683 (Fam).
[467] Cave (2014a).
[468] [2014] EWHC 1871 (Fam).
[469] [2014] EWHC 920 (Fam).
[470] See Nuffield Council on Bioethics (2007) and Morris (2009). If there is a dispute between the parents and doctors, such cases should be brought before the court: *R v Portsmouth NHS Trust, ex p Glass* [1999] 2 FLR 905.
[471] *Royal Wolverhampton Hospitals NHS Trust v B* [2000] 1 FLR 953 at p. 956, *per* Bodey J.

The general approach has been that, if there is medical evidence that the child's life will be painful or undignified if the child lives, the court will approve the non-treatment or withdrawal of treatment, even if the parents are in favour of providing treatment.[472] The leading cases are the following:[473]

KEY CASE: *Great Ormond Street Hospital v Yates and Others* [2017] EWHC 972 (Fam), [2017] EWHC 1909 (Fam); *Yates and Another v Great Ormond Street Hospital for Children NHS Foundation Trust and Another* [2017] EWCA Civ 410; *'In the matter of Charlie Gard, Determination of Permission to Appeal Hearing',* 8 June 2017, The Supreme Court; *Gard and Others v United Kingdom* (App. No. 39793/17)

The legal proceedings over the treatment of Charlie Gard made international headlines. He was born with a rare genetic condition that caused multiple disabilities, including very severe brain damage. The doctors at Great Ormond Street Hospital (GOSH) decided it would be best to withdraw ventilation and enable him to die peacefully. His parents disagreed. They wanted him to be transported to the United States and receive nucleoside bypass therapy. In the proceedings it was clear that the use of this therapy had never been used for humans with Charlie's condition and not even reached the experimental stage on mice. An American doctor, nevertheless, was willing to attempt the treatment and money had been crowdfunded to pay the £1.3 million costs.

In many ways the legal issue at the heart of the case was straightforward. The court had to determine what was in Charlie's best interests. Francis J determined that the therapy had no realistic chance of success. As Francis J put it: 'The prospect of the nucleoside treatment having any benefit is as close to zero as makes no difference.' In this way, the harm would be in sustaining 'existence which is offering the child no benefit' – the continued pain of intensive care, ventilator support, and invasive treatments to keep him alive; and the transport to America could also cause harm, so Francis J made a declaration ordering the withdrawal of treatment. This was upheld by the Court of Appeal and leave to the Supreme Court was refused. Lady Hale stated that 'parents are not entitled to insist upon treatment by anyone which is not in their child's best interests'. The case went to the European Court of Human Rights where the parents' case again was rejected. It finally returned to Francis J who again approved the withdrawal. By now even the American doctor was of the view that the treatment would not help Charlie. Francis J stated:

> The parents have had to face the reality, almost impossible to contemplate that Charlie is beyond any help even from experimental treatment and that it is in his best interests for him to be allowed to die. Given the consensus that now exists between parents, the treating doctors and even Dr Hirano [from the USA] it is my very sad duty to confirm the declarations that I made in April this year, and I now formally do so. I do not make a mandatory order.

At the heart of the parents' case was the claim that parents should make decisions about children and only where their decisions are going to cause the child significant harm

---

[472] *King's College Hospital NHS Foundation Trust v T, V and ZT* [2014] EWHC 3315 (Fam); *Central Manchester University Hospitals NHS Foundation Trust v A* [2015] EWHC 2828 (Fam).
[473] See Goold, Herring and Auckland (2020) for a helpful collection of essays on the issues raised by these cases.

should the state intervene. An analogy was drawn to s. 31 of the Children Act which sets out the significant harm threshold for determining when a local authority can obtain a care order. This argument was rejected by the Court of Appeal on the basis that the courts make orders in these cases based on the welfare of the child. The views of the parents would be taken into account but it was for the court, not the parents, to make this assessment. The European Court of Human Rights declined to express a view on the issue as it accepted the English courts' finding that the proposed therapy and the transport to get there would cause significant harm. McFarlane LJ stated in his judgment that the court should not engage in any evaluation of the reasonableness of the parents' case nor 'any other factor or filter before it embarks upon deciding what is in the best interests of the child'.

CASE: *Alder Hey Children's NHS Foundation Trust* v *Evans and Another* [2018] EWHC 308 (Fam), [2018] EWHC 953 (Fam)

Alfie Evans was on a ventilator system and the Trust sought a declaration that the support was not in his best interest and that it was in his best interests to stop such treatment. His parents had found a doctor overseas who was willing to attempt a treatment. Hayden J granted the declaration. All the medical evidence was that there was no prospect of treatment anywhere in the world for Alfie's condition. If he was to be flown to another country he may die in transit. It was in his best interests to have good-quality palliative care and to give him peace, quiet and privacy to conclude his life with dignity.

It is worth quoting from the judge's assessment of Alfie's condition:

> But I came, on the consensus of every doctor from every country who had ever evaluated Alfie's condition, to the inevitable conclusion (following 7 days of evidence) that Alfie's brain had been so corroded by his Neurodegenerative Brain Disorder that there was simply no prospect of recovery. By the time I requested the updated MRI scan in February, the signal intensity was so bright that it revealed a brain that had been almost entirely wiped out. In simple terms the brain consisted only of water and CSF.[474]

An innovation in his Lordship's judgment was his extensive quotation, with approval, of Pope Francis' open letter to the President of the Pontifical Academy for Life in November 2017:

> *It thus makes possible a decision that is morally qualified as withdrawal of 'overzealous treatment'. Such a decision responsibly acknowledges the limitations of our mortality, once it becomes clear that opposition to it is futile. 'Here one does not will to cause death; one's inability to impede it is merely accepted' (Catechism of the Catholic Church, No. 2278). This difference of perspective restores humanity to the accompaniment of the dying, while not attempting to justify the suppression of the living. It is clear that not adopting, or else suspending, disproportionate measures, means avoiding overzealous treatment; from an ethical standpoint, it is completely different from euthanasia, which is always wrong, in that the intent of euthanasia is to end life and cause death.*

---

[474] [2018] EWHC 953 (Fam) at para 3.

In refusing leave to appeal to the Supreme Court, Lady Hale said:

On the first occasion that an application came before us, we held that Alfie's best interests were the 'gold standard' against which decisions about him had to be made. It had been decided, after careful examination of the evidence, that it was not in his best interests for the treatment which sustained his life to be continued or for him to be taken by air ambulance to another country for this purpose.

It is worth noting that these cases were different from other cases where the parents were simply disagreeing with the treatment offered by the doctors. The parents in both cases sought to present the case as involving a dispute between two sets of medical opinion. In both cases the court determined it needed to decide what was in the best interests of the child and the views of the UK doctors were clearly preferred. The courts in reaching that conclusion determined the simple best interest test should be applied. They explicitly rejected an argument that only if the views of the parents caused significant harm should the views of parents be overridden. Imogen Goold and Cressida Auckland have argued in favour of the significant harm test:

Re-framing the analysis to include a presumption of parental authority unless rebutted by serious harm would also result in the parent's authority being subjected to direct evaluation by the court, which would be called upon to scrutinise their reasoning before overtly overriding it, if it is not accepted. This would arguably challenge the authority of the parents more directly than under the 'best interests' approach, where although parents' views are given considerable weight, they remain just one of many important factors that must be taken into account when determining a child's interests.[475]

In favour of the courts' approach it might be argued that while in many areas of life (religion, diet, hobbies) we are happy to leave issues to parents unless their decision is going to cause significant harm (see Chapter 11), that is because in those issues there is no expert who could legitimately say that they know better than a parent about issues around religion or hobbies. If, for example, the Archbishop of Canterbury would be to claim he knew better than parents how to raise their children in religious matters, he would quite rightly be laughed out of court. However, medical matters are different because there we do have societal consensus that doctors know better than parents about what medicines are better. Further, while we might think it good that children are raised with different religions and hobbies, we do not think it good that children have different levels of health. This argument would suggest that the significant harm test is suitable for many issues where there is no societal consensus, but on medical matters we do have recognised experts and the issues are highly significant to the child, and so the best interests test is sufficient. While this is a powerful argument, it might still be questioned whether the manner of a child's death is a matter of medical expertise.[476]

---

[475] Auckland and Goold (2018). See also Taylor (2020).
[476] Herring (2020b).

This last point arose in the following case:

> **CASE:** *Re M (Declaration of Death of Child)* [2020] EWCA Civ 164
>
> M was a very sick baby which at birth was placed on a ventilator. The doctors, applying the standard brain stem death criteria, determined that M was dead and applied to withdraw the ventilator. The parents objected believing the child to still be alive as, although the brain stem was dead, the body was still warm and appearing to breathe. They referred to alternative definitions of death in the ethical literature under which it might be said M was alive. The court authorised the removal of the ventilation and declared that M was dead.

While this might be seen as a straightforward case of preferring the views of doctors over parents, it is not clear why it would harm M to be kept on the ventilator or why it was in M's best interests to be removed. Perhaps an argument can be made in terms of it being undignified to be kept on a ventilator when one is dead. Or maybe, and the court would not want to say this, it was a waste of NHS resources to use an expensive ventilator on a child deemed dead by the mainstream medicine.

There have been two notable cases where the court sided with the parents, rather than the medical establishment. The first is *Re T (A Minor) (Wardship: Medical Treatment)*.[477] Here a baby, C, had a life-threatening liver complaint. There was a unanimous prognosis from the medical experts that, without a liver transplant, C would not live beyond two-and-a-half years of age. However, if a transplant could be found the prognosis was very good. The parents refused to consent to the transplant. This time the courts sided with the parents and refused to authorise the transplant without the consent of the parents. The decision seemed to place much weight on the intrusion that ordering the treatment would make in the lives of the parents: they would need to return from their new country and would be required to provide extensive care for the child. Arguably, these concerns were misplaced because, even if the parents were unwilling to make these sacrifices, they could hand the child over to be cared for by a local authority. In fact, despite the Court of Appeal's ruling, the parents did return to the United Kingdom and the child received treatment.

The second case where the parents 'won' is the following:

> **CASE:** *Raqeeb v Barts NHS Foundations Trust* [2019] EWHC 2531 (Admin), [2019] EWHC 2530 (Fam)
>
> Tafida, aged five at the time of the hearing, was well until she suffered from a bleed on the brain caused by a rare condition. She was kept alive on artificial ventilation. The Trust decided it was best for her to receive palliative care and the ventilation to be withdrawn, even though that would lead to her death. Tafida's parents, who were committed Muslims, believed she did have some awareness of her family and was making some progress. They objected to the withdrawal of life-sustaining treatment and instead sought to remove her to Gaslini Hospital in Italy where a group of doctors were willing to treat her. The Trust believed the move to Italy was not in her best interests.

---

477 [1997] 1 FLR 502, [1997] 2 FCR 363; discussed in Bainham (1997).

The case arose by virtue of two proceedings: an application by the parents for judicial review of the decisions of the Trust and an application by the Trust for a specific issue order or order under the inherent jurisdiction to authorise the withdrawal of the treatment. MacDonald J refused to grant relief on the judicial review but dismissed the Trust's application for the orders.

On the judicial review issue, the Trust had failed to take into account Tafida's right to receive services under EU law and so the decision was unlawful. However, had the Trust taken those rights into account it would have reached the decision that the interference was justified and so there was no purpose in ordering the Trust to remake the decision.

On the Trust's application it was decided it was not in her best interests to withdraw the treatment. It was emphasised that Tafida was not in pain and the treatment she was receiving was not burdensome. The Italian doctors were a respected body of medical opinion which believed that a care plan was feasible. There was no evidence the travelling to Italy would cause her harm. Being kept alive was consistent with her family's religious beliefs and the sanctity of life. MacDonald J explained:

> I am satisfied that if Tafida was asked she would not reject out of hand a situation in which she continued to live, albeit in a moribund and at best minimally conscious state, without pain and in the loving care of her dedicated family, consistent with her formative appreciation that life is precious, a wish to follow a parent's religious practice and a non-judgmental attitude to disability.

There seem to be four features of this case which were key and explain how it was different from *Yates* and *Evans*:

1. There was a highly respectable body of medical opinion (the Italian doctors) that supported not withdrawing the treatment and an alternative package.

2. There was no evidence that Tafida would suffer travelling to Italy.

3. There was no evidence Tafida's current state was painful to her, even though it appeared to offer few positive experiences.

4. Tafida had been alive and well for the first part of life and had enjoyed her family's religious activities. That meant that, while she could not be said to have adopted the beliefs as her own, it could be assumed she would want to be part of her family's religious community. This was important when considering her best interests *from her perspective*.

It would be quite wrong to read this case as a victory for parents' rights.[478] MacDonald J noted:

> The views and opinions of both the doctors and the parents must be considered. The views of the parents may have particular value in circumstances where they know well their own child. However, the court must also be mindful that the views of the parents may, understandably, be coloured by emotion or sentiment.

Rather, it is better seen as a case where the judge focused on the best interests of this particular child. 'The court must ask itself what the child's attitude to treatment is or would be likely to

---

[478] Taylor (2020).

be,' MacDonald J emphasised. This is not saying that the views of the child dominate, but that an assessment of best interests must focus on the particular child in issue.

It was reported in early 2020 that Tafida was in Italy and was now out of intensive care, although she still suffers profound disabilities.[479]

(iv) Can a doctor be forced to treat a child?

The issue here relates to the situation where the doctor refuses to treat a child. This may be because the doctor believes that the treatment is not appropriate, or may be because of health-care rationing (for example, that the treatment is too expensive). It is clear that if a doctor declines to offer treatment, the court cannot force him or her to perform the operation.[480] However, a court might indicate that it believed a procedure would benefit a patient, in the hope that this might influence the judgement of the medical professionals.[481] One option in such a case is for a patient to apply for judicial review, although such an option is unlikely to succeed unless there is strong evidence that the decision is unreasonable.[482] In any event, even if judicial review is successful, the NHS trust would be required only to reconsider the decision and would not necessarily be required to perform the operation. If a doctor is unsure about the propriety of treatment (for example, because it is a risky, untried procedure), the matter could be brought before a court for guidance.[483]

(v) Can the parents be criminally liable for failing to arrange suitable medical care for a child?

It is an offence when anyone over 16 with responsibility for a child 'wilfully assaults, ill-treats, neglects, abandons, or exposes him . . . in a manner likely to cause him unnecessary suffering or injury to health'.[484] This means that a parent who wilfully fails to ensure that the child receives adequate medical treatment commits an offence. It should be stressed that it must be shown that the failure to arrange treatment is wilful. Therefore, as *R v Sheppard*[485] suggests, if parents do not provide treatment due to their low intelligence they will not be punished.[486] If the child dies after his or her parents fail to organise suitable medical treatment, there is even the possibility of a manslaughter or murder conviction.[487]

(vi) Are there some kinds of treatment which cannot be carried out on children?

Is there a limit to what the doctors, with the parents' consent, can do to a child? The dispute here surrounds non-therapeutic treatment, that is, treatment which has no direct medical benefit to the child. It seems that some non-therapeutic treatment can be carried out, but only if it can be shown that the treatment benefits the child in the wider sense. So, for example, the

---

[479] BBC News Online (2020).

[480] *An NHS Trust v S* [2017] EWHC 3619 (Fam).

[481] *An NHS Trust v S* [2017] EWHC 3619 (Fam).

[482] *R v Cambridge District Health Authority, ex p B* [1995] 1 FLR 1055.

[483] E.g. *Simms v Simms* [2003] 1 FCR 361; *An NHS Foundation Trust v AB, CD and EF (By his Children's Guardian)* [2014] EWHC 1031 (Fam).

[484] Children and Young Persons Act 1933, s. 1(1).

[485] [1981] AC 394.

[486] It is no defence to show that even had one attempted to obtain medical assistance there would have been none available.

[487] *R v Senior* [1899] 1 QB 283, where for religious reasons a parent refused to obtain medical treatment. See also the offence of causing or allowing the death of a child or vulnerable adult under s. 5 of the Domestic Violence, Crime and Victims Act 2004.

parent can consent to a blood test to determine a child's paternity. Although such a blood test does not provide medical benefits, it is thought to be in a child's interests as it enables his or her paternity to be ascertained. However, problems may arise where the child is asked to donate bone marrow or organs for the treatment of someone else. If the bone marrow or organ is to a close relative, it may be possible to find a benefit to the child. For example, if a child is donating an organ to their sister and without the treatment the sister will die, the benefit to the child of maintaining the relationship with the sister may be sufficient to make the donation to the child's benefit.[488]

A procedure that is clearly to the detriment of a child may not be lawful. For example, it may be that a parent could not effectively consent to multiple body piercing of a child.[489] One particularly controversial issue is circumcision. Female genital mutilation (FGM) is unlawful, unless necessary for medical reasons.[490] But the position as regards male circumcision seems to be that it is lawful. There are those who claim that this is an irreversible operation, which is an attack on the child's physical integrity, and unless there are medical benefits to the child it should be unlawful.[491] There are others who argue that a child has a right to a religious or cultural heritage and, at least where circumcision is an aspect of religious background, it should be permissible.[492] Where a child's liberty is being infringed in a way which breaches Article 5, parental responsibility cannot authorise this.[493]

In *LA v SB*[494] parents refused to agree to the treatment recommended by the hospital in response to life-threatening seizures a child was having. The local authority and doctors decided to withdraw from legal proceedings they had initially instigated. Unsurprisingly, Wall P concluded that he could not compel the local authority to continue litigation. More surprisingly, he concluded that the court should not intervene on its own motion. As this indicates, the court may be more willing to intervene where a parent wants to do something harmful to a child than where a parent is failing to improve a child's situation. In *BC v EF*[495] the judge declined to enforce an order that the children receive vaccinations. When the order was made it was imagined the father, who supported vaccinations, would take the children for them. However, now both parents opposed them and Rogers J thought it unrealistic and undesirable that a stranger would take the children to be vaccinated.

C Comments on the law

(i) The case law and children's rights

Some have argued that the present law is illogical, by arguing as follows: the law permits a competent minor to consent to treatment, but not to refuse it. This is shown in *Plymouth*

---

[488] By analogy with the reasoning in *Re Y (Mental Incapacity: Bone Marrow Transplant)* [1996] 2 FLR 787.

[489] Similarly, sterilisation may be permitted if the child suffers from mental handicap, if that sterilisation can be said to be in the best interests of the child, and the court has given its approval: *J v C* [1990] 2 FLR 527, [1990] FCR 716; *Practice Note (Official Solicitor: Sterilisation)* [1993] 2 FLR 222; and *Practice Note (Official Solicitor: Sterilisation)* [1996] 2 FLR 111.

[490] Female Genital Mutilation Act 2003. The Serious Crimes Act 2015 introduced Female Genital Mutilation Protection Orders, which are designed to prevent FGM. For an example of their use see *Re E (Children) (Female Genital Mutilation Protection Orders)* [2015] EWHC 2275 (Fam) and *Re A (A Child: Female Genital Mutilation)* [2019] EWHC 2475 (Fam).

[491] Fox and Thomson (2005 and 2012).

[492] Circumcision of boys is regarded by many Jews and Muslims as an important aspect of their religious practice.

[493] *Re D (A Child)* [2019] UKSC 52.

[494] [2010] EWHC 1744 (Fam).

[495] [2017] EWFC 49.

Hospitals NHS Trust v *YZ and ZZ*.[496] MacDonald J found in that case it was unclear whether the child was *Gillick*-competent, but he did not need to decide the issue because her views could be set aside as it was in her interests to receive treatment. The problem is that if the child is competent to decide the question, it seems a bit odd to say to him or her: 'You can decide this issue but only if you decide to answer "yes". If you decide "no" we may override your wishes.' It is especially odd because it is a far greater infringement of a child's rights to operate on him or her without their consent than to deny them treatment that they would like to have. If anything, the law would be more logical if it said that the doctor cannot operate on the child if he or she refuses but has a discretion if he or she consents.[497] Such arguments have led Fortin to suggest that the present law may be open to challenge under the Human Rights Act in that forcing treatment on young people breaches their rights to protection from inhuman and degrading treatment and right to liberty and security of the person.[498]

There are two ways that current law could be justified. One approach focuses on capacity. In a controversial argument Stephen Gilmore and I have argued that a child may have capacity to consent to treatment, but lack the capacity to refuse treatment.[499] Further, a child may have the capacity to refuse a particular treatment, but not refuse all treatment. Examples will clarify our argument. Imagine a child has grazed her knee and a teacher offers a plaster. Most children will know what it is like to have a plaster and be able to understand the process sufficiently to consent. They may not, however, understand the consequences of refusing to accept the plaster (the risks of septicaemia) and so lack the capacity to refuse. Similarly, in a more complex case, a child may be offered a range of treatments for their condition and have the capacity to refuse one (maybe one they have tried before), but not have sufficient capacity to refuse to consent to other more complex treatments. The child needs to understand the details about what they are consenting to or what they are refusing in order to have capacity to do so. It is, therefore, quite plausible that a child has the capacity to consent, but not refuse.[500] This argument has been objected to by those who argue that in order to have capacity to make a decision about a medical treatment the child must understand what both receiving and refusing a treatment involves.

An alternative justification is to argue that the law is perfectly logical once it is recalled that the basis of the law relating to children is set out in s. 1 of the Children Act 1989 – the welfare principle.[501] The law is based on the view that, if the doctor wants to perform treatment, this is in the best interests of the child because it is the view of the medical expert. The law is then engineered to make it as easy as possible to enable the doctor to go ahead. The doctor can operate if the mature minor consents, or the parents consent, or the courts give approval. The law could hardly do more to enable the doctor to treat, once he or she has decided that the treatment is in the best interests of the child. Put this way, the law is a clear example of ensuring that the child's best interests are promoted.

(ii) The importance of doctors

There is some concern that the law places too much weight on the opinions of doctors. It has just been argued that the law relating to children is best understood on the basis that the doctor is presumed to make decisions that are in the child's interests. In effect, if the parent consents

---

[496] [2017] EWHC 2211 (Fam).
[497] The law become particularly illogical when the parent is under 16 (see Fovargue (2013)) where a child can have a greater say over her child's body than her own.
[498] Fortin (2003: 129).
[499] Gilmore and Herring (2011a and b; 2012).
[500] The detail of the argument is set out in Gilmore and Herring (2011a).
[501] See Gilmore (2009) for further discussion of this.

and the child does not, it is the doctor who has the final say unless the child decides to bring the matter before the court. Of course, generally, doctors will be best placed to decide whether a medical treatment is in a patient's best interests. However, where the issue involves moral as well as medical issues (abortion, for example), giving so much power to doctors may be controversial.[502] Also, in many areas of medicine there is more than one point of view as to the best kind of medical treatment. The present law favours the views of the particular doctor dealing with the patient, on what might be the reasonable objections of the patient.

(iii) Misuses of capacity

It has been argued that the test for capacity for children is too strict. Certainly, the test of capacity for children is stiffer than that for adults. Further, there is a danger that the child will be found incompetent if the doctor or court believes the child's decision to be wrong, but the child will be found competent if the decision is one which is thought to promote his or her best interests.[503] However, arguments over the appropriate test for competence are complex. If the law was that a competent child's decision could not be vetoed by the courts or the parents, the law would wish to have a very strict test of competence. A further complaint about the law on competence for children is that it is wrong for the law to categorise children as either competent or not and, instead, decisions should be made with children, enabling them to participate in the decision-making process to as great an extent as possible.[504]

(iv) Is the law not adequately protecting children?

As mentioned above, if the parents oppose a form of treatment, the doctors will seek to find alternative forms of treatment or persuade the parents to change their minds. It is only where this fails that the doctors are likely to turn to the courts for authorisation to treat the child contrary to the parents' wishes. For example, where a child's parents are Jehovah's Witnesses, who oppose blood transfusions, doctors may try to use non-blood substitutes before eventually seeking court intervention.[505] Caroline Bridge[506] has argued that this delay in providing the ideal treatment could be seen as protecting the parents' rather than the child's interests.

14 Children's rights in other cases

The reasoning in *Gillick* has been applied outside the context of medical cases. In *Re Roddy (A Child) (Identification: Restriction on Publication)*[507] a 16-year-old girl wanted to tell her story to the media. She had become pregnant at age 12. Munby J memorably stated:

> We no longer treat our 17-year-old daughters as our Victorian ancestors did, and if we try to do so it is at our – and their – peril. Angela, in my judgment, is of an age, and has sufficient understanding and maturity, to decide for herself whether that which is private, personal and intimate should remain private or whether it should be shared with the whole world.[508]

---

[502] Herring (1997).
[503] Freeman (2005); Shaw (2002).
[504] Herring (1997).
[505] *A Hospital NHS Trust v LP and TP* [2019] EWHC 2989 (Fam).
[506] Bridge (2009).
[507] [2004] 1 FCR 481.
[508] At para 56.

He concluded that the court had to respect the right of free speech of a child who has sufficient understanding to make an informed decision. It was part of her dignity and integrity as a human being.[509] The implication from the case is that *Gillick* will be of general application and that a *Gillick*-competent child can give effective consent to what would otherwise be a legal wrong, unless there is a specific statutory provision saying otherwise.[510]

The following case is a striking application of the *Gillick* approach.

KEY CASE: *PD v SD and Others* [2015] EWHC 4103 (Fam)

A boy when aged 14 told his adoptive parents that he wished to be recognised as male, rather than female. He was receiving expert help, but his parents struggled to understand his position and continued to call him by his female name. This caused the boy considerable distress and he decided he did not want to live with them and did not want them to receive any information about his treatment or life generally. He sought a court order confirming this. Keehen J granted the order. He was sufficiently mature to make decisions about his life and this included disengaging with his parents and deciding what information, if any, they should receive. His rights to respect his private and family life under Article 8 of the ECHR and his welfare required the order to be made. Keehen J rejected the argument that parents had rights under Article 8, saying:

> It is not clear why the parent should have an Article 8 right . . . where the offspring is almost 16 years of age and does not wish it . . . where the parent no longer has a right to control the child . . . and where the young person, in Lord Scarman's words [see *Gillick*] 'has sufficient understanding of what is involved to give a consent valid in law'.

A notable case where the rights of children played an important role was *R (On the Application of Begum)* v *Headteacher and Governors of Denbigh High School*.[511] The House of Lords considered a school dress code that prevented Shabina Begum from wearing the *jilbab* (a long coat-like garment) which she believed she was required to wear by her religion. Their Lordships accepted that children had a right to manifest their religion under Article 9 of the ECHR, just as adults did. The majority held that there was no interference in her right to manifest her religious belief because she was free to go to another school where she could wear the *jilbab*. Unanimously their Lordships agreed that, in any event, even if there was a breach it could be justified in the name of protecting the freedoms of other pupils at the school (particularly girls) who might otherwise feel pressurised into wearing the *jilbab* against their wishes.[512]

The issue has returned to the courts. In *R (Playfoot)* v *Governing Body of Millais School*[513] Lydia Playfoot sought to wear a purity ring to school. The ring was said to symbolise her promise to God to abstain from sexual intercourse until marriage. She was told by the school that the ring infringed the school policy of 'no jewellery'. She claimed the school policy improperly infringed her right to manifest her religious beliefs, as protected under Article 9 of the ECHR. This argument was rejected primarily on the basis that the wearing of the ring was not a manifestation of her religious belief. Her beliefs did not require her to wear the ring. While the case

---

[509] At para 57.
[510] As there is, for example, in relation to sexual activity: Sexual Offences Act 2003.
[511] [2006] 1 FCR 613, discussed in Edwards (2007).
[512] The banning of headscarves in French schools was held not to infringe the ECHR in *Aktas v France* (App. No. 43563/08). See also *Lautsi v Italy* (App. No. 30814/06) on state sponsorship of religion in schools.
[513] [2007] 3 FCR 754.

is primarily about the interpretation of manifestation of religious belief, it is remarkable that the court placed little right on the child's right to respect for her private life, which included wearing the clothing or jewellery she had wanted. The case should be contrasted with *R (Watkins-Singh) v Governing Body of Aberdare Girls' High School*[514] where a Sikh girl was prohibited from wearing a *kara* (a religious steel band of about one-fifth of an inch wide). There it was found that the wearing of the *kara* was central to her religious beliefs, and barring it was indirect religious discrimination and hence unlawful.[515] Important in that case was the fact that there was no evidence that the wearing of the *kara* would impact on other pupils.

A fascinating line of cases has developed in relation to children with challenging behaviours, who need to be looked after by local authorities in an environment which restricts their freedom of movement. Where this is done through a secure accommodation order under s. 25 of the Children Act 1989, that is relatively unproblematic. The difficulty arises because Secure Accommodation Orders are only available where the accommodation in question is approved accommodation. This is in very scarce supply and so many local authorities seek to place children in accommodation which has not been approved and seek to protect them and others by restricting their movements. The courts have held that doing this can amount to an interference in the liberty of the child and so infringe their rights under Article 5 of the ECHR. That interference can be justified (to protect the child or others) but only if it is approved by the court. The route to obtain this approval has so far been by using the inherent jurisdiction to authorise the interference in rights.

The court have found it difficult in some cases to determine when there is a deprivation of liberty so that Article 5 is engaged. The general law on deprivation of liberty in relation to adults is that it involves:

(a) an objective component of confinement in a particular restricted place for a not negligible length of time;

(b) a subjective component of lack of valid consent; and

(c) an attribution of responsibility to the state.[516]

The first of these means that simply because a person feels constrained does not mean they are, if in fact they are free to leave whenever they want. In the case of children, the court will consider the restrictions that are normally placed on a child of that age. In *Hertfordshire CC v NK*[517] it was held that a 16-year-old living in a residential unit was not having his liberty deprived. Although there were regulations, the doors were not locked, he was allowed unsupervised contact with his mother, had unlimited access to his phone and internet and he was not regularly searched. He had a planned daily schedule, but this did not amount to continuous supervision and control.

The second element means that if there is consent to the deprivation then there is no interference in the right, and the third requires the breach to be attributable to the state, which will be straightforward in cases where the child is being looked after by the state. However, the courts have acknowledged that when considering children, the normal approach to adults must be modified. That is because it is normal for children to be restrained. Few parents allow their children complete freedom to come and go as they please, at least until their teenage years.

---

[514] [2008] 2 FCR 203.

[515] Under s. 1(1a) of the Race Relations Act 1976 and s. 45(3) of the Equality Act 2006.

[516] *Storck v Germany* (App. No. 61603/00) (2006) 43 EHRR 6 and *Cheshire West and Chester Council v P* [2014] UKSC 19.

[517] [2020] EWHC 139 (Fam).

The leading case is the following:

> ### KEY CASE: *Re D (A Child)* [2019] UKSC 42
>
> The case concerned a young man who had a range of conditions, including Asperger's syndrome and Tourette's syndrome. Since the age of 14 he had lived in a specialist mental health unit at a hospital and his freedom of movement was restricted. When 16 he was discharged from hospital to a residential placement where he was under constant supervision. Before the age of 16 it had been accepted that the consent of his parents meant there was no interference with his rights to liberty under Article 5 of the ECHR. However, it was not clear whether now he was 16 the consent of the parents still meant there was no deprivation of liberty.
>
> The Supreme Court held that D had been subject to a level of control that was not normal for a child of his age and so was deprived of his liberty for the purposes of Article 5 of the ECHR. To decide if there was a deprivation a comparison should be made with a child of a similar age but without disabilities. The deprivation needed to be justified under Article 5 in a court hearing. The authorisation by the Court of Protection, acting in the best interests of D was sufficient to do this.
>
> In the case of a 16- or 17-year-old, parental responsibility could not justify the deprivation of liberty. While in this case there was no question of people not having D's interests at heart, in other cases that would be an issue and court proceedings were necessary to ensure that parental responsibility was exercised in a way which was in D's best interests. This reflected the idea that the parental power of physical control was a dwindling right as the child became competent to make their own decisions. Lady Black was explicit that as a matter of common law parental responsibility did not include authorising the confinement of a child aged 16 or 17. Lady Hale did not express a concluded view on that, but preferred to view the issue in terms of the ECHR, that parental responsibility even if it did apply to deprivation of liberty, was insufficient to deal with the need under Article 5 for a court hearing.
>
> Lord Carnwath gave a dissenting judgment, agreeing with the Court of Appeal that parental responsibility could authorise a deprivation of liberty for those aged 16 or 17.

This fascinating case raises a number of issues. First, the discussion of deprivation of liberty is interesting. Lady Hale clearly wants to ensure that mentally disabled children do not have fewer rights than other children. She stated 'a mentally disabled child who is subject to a level of control beyond that which is normal for a [non-disabled] child of his age has been confined within the meaning of Article 5'. She backs up her conclusion by referring to Article 2 of the UNCRC, which requires children's rights to be protected without discrimination.

Second, the limitations of parental responsibility are notable. In particular, Lady Hale rejects the idea of parents giving 'substituted consent' for a child who cannot make a decision. She thought it a 'startling proposition that it lies within the scope of parental responsibility for a parent to license the state to violate the most fundamental human rights of a child'.

Third, the practical significance of this decision for local authorities is considerable. If they have a 16- or 17-year-old in their care who is not agreeing to restrictions on their liberty then court approval will be required. Rather surprisingly, the Supreme Court do not go into detail as to what legal form the authorisation will take. Presumably it will be an application to the Court of Protection for a declaration under the inherent jurisdiction or (if the child has a mental disorder leading to a lack of mental capacity) under the process using the Liberty Protection Safeguards in the Mental Capacity Act 2005 (MCA). For local authorities with very limited cash budgets that might be a considerable expense. Some might question the wisdom of the decision if in nearly all cases the court simply approves the arrangements for the child. The potential expense increases if local authorities need to check whether even 16- or 17-year-olds in their area cared for by their parents are having their Article 5 rights infringed.

Fourth, the case leaves plenty of questions unanswered. Clearly the case applies where a local authority is accommodating a child in a way which deprives their liberty. But what about when a child is living at home and has their liberty restricted? Lady Hale seems to imply that Article 5 still applies as the state has an obligation to protect people's rights, whether the interference is by the state or another private person. As already indicated, that will increase the costs for a local authority, and also may be seen as an interference in privacy of family carers.

It also leaves unanswered questions about other parental rights that might be exercised over 16- and 17-year-olds, particularly in relation to medical treatment. The majority were clear they were not addressing that issue. The logic of the approach is that in relation to children aged 16 or 17 who lack *Gillick*-competence, parents do not have the authority to consent to treatment and that the MCA applies, allowing a doctor to provide treatment if it is in the best interests of the patient lacking capacity. Future cases will determine if that is correct.

More importantly it is unclear how the judgment affects children under the age of 16. Lady Hale accepted that 'logically' her reasoning would apply to a child under the age of 16 whose liberty was restricted more than is normal for a child of that age. However, she and Lady Black were clear they were leaving the question open. Indeed, Lord Carnwath expressed concern at Lady Hale's view. If the decision does apply to under 16-year-olds it would mean that parents of a child with mental capacity or health issues who restricted the liberty of their children more than normal for a child of that age would need court authorisation to do so. That could be extremely burdensome for parents of disabled children who are facing enough challenges, especially economic and bureaucratic ones, as it is.

There were arguments before the Supreme Court over whether a 16- or 17-year-old is dealt with by the Mental Capacity Act 2005 alone or whether *Gillick*-competence had any role to play. Lady Black (at para 71) did not accept that the MCA had replaced issues of *Gillick*-competence for that age group but other members of the Supreme Court did not express a view.

Children's rights can be relevant in a wide range of other contexts, including immigration law, education law and criminal law. There is not space in this text to explore all of these.[518]

15 Children in court

Children's rights would mean little without an effective mode of enforcement. It is therefore crucial that children have access to courts.[519] It is also important that the decisions of courts are communicated and explained to children.[520] The fact that children should be heard in proceedings does not require that their views will necessarily determine the question. The right of a child to be heard is therefore less contentious than a right to autonomy. However, there is a delicate balance to be drawn between listening to children and not placing them in the position where

---

[518] See Bainham and Gilmore (2016).
[519] UN Convention on the Rights of the Child, Article 12. See also the European Convention on the Exercise of Children's Rights, not yet signed by the UK See Lowe and Murch (2001) for an excellent discussion.
[520] Wilson, J. (2007).

they have to decide between their parents.[521] Many commentators have been persuaded by the view that if children have autonomy rights then they must have a means to bring applications to enforce those rights. However, there are also serious concerns about involving children in litigation.[522] There is considerable evidence that requiring a child to choose whether they live with their father or mother causes the child much harm. There is also a concern that children's rights to bring matters before a court are open to misuse, either from parents seeking to manipulate the children[523] or even from solicitors keen to promote their professional standing.

There are three ways in which a child may be directly involved in family proceedings:

1. The child may bring proceedings through a solicitor in their own right.

2. The child's 'next friend' (normally one of their parents) can bring proceedings on the child's behalf.

3. The child's interests can be represented in the case between adults by a guardian *ad litem*.[524]

A Children bringing proceedings in their own right

Under rule 9.2A of the Family Proceedings Rules 1999 (SI 1999/3491), a minor can bring (or defend) proceedings under the Children Act 1989 or involving the inherent jurisdiction either:

- if the court gives leave; or
- where a solicitor, acting for the child, considers that the child is able to give instructions in relation to the proceedings.[525]

However, the most likely proceedings that a child will want to bring is for an order under s. 8 of the Children Act 1989 and, for such an application, the court must give leave, even if the child's solicitor is satisfied that the child is competent.[526]

There was a fear when the Children Act 1989 was first introduced that the courts would be swamped with applications from children seeking to 'divorce' their parents (although this has proved to be unfounded). Before granting leave, the court must be satisfied 'that [the child] has sufficient understanding to make the proposed application'.[527] There has been some dispute over whether the welfare of the child is relevant when considering whether or not to grant leave. Following *Re H (Residence Order: Child's Application for Leave)*,[528] it now seems to be accepted that the welfare of the child is not the paramount consideration. This was significant in that case because H was 15, and since the age of six he had come under the influence of a Mr R, who had been arrested for committing offences against children. As H was a mature and intelligent young man, it was held that he should have separate representation, even though there were grave concerns surrounding his desire to have unrestricted contact with Mr R. In considering whether to grant leave, the court will consider the following factors:

---

[521] King (2007: 190).

[522] This was recognised by Thorpe LJ in *Re HB (Abduction: Children's Objections)* [1998] 1 FLR 422.

[523] In *Re K (Replacement of Guardian ad Litem)* [2001] 1 FLR 663 the court decided that the child had been pressurised by his father into applying to dispense with the services of his guardian.

[524] See Doughty (2008b) for a history of the role played by court welfare officers.

[525] *Re H (A Minor) (Role of the Official Solicitor)* [1993] 2 FLR 552. Even if the solicitor decides that the child is competent, it is open to the court to stop the proceedings if the court is not satisfied that the child is competent: *Re CT (A Minor) (Child Representation)* [1993] 2 FLR 278, [1993] 2 FCR 445.

[526] *Practice Direction* [1993] 1 FLR 668; *Re N (Contact: Minor Seeking Leave to Defend and Removal of Guardian)* [2003] Fam Law 154.

[527] Section 10(8).

[528] [2000] 1 FLR 780.

1. *Is the matter serious enough to justify a court hearing?* In *Re C (A Minor) (Leave to Seek Section 8 Order)*[529] a 14-year-old wanted to go on holiday with her friend's family to Bulgaria. Her parents opposed this and she applied for a specific issue order that she be permitted to go on the holiday. Johnson J refused to grant leave, claiming that the issue was too trivial to be suitable for resolution by the courts. If this issue is too trivial, it is likely that many other issues which children may want to raise before a court (e.g. what time they go to bed) will also be too trivial. Freeman has forcefully argued that, where the child has instituted proceedings, this is an indication that, to the child, it is an important issue and there is therefore a need for some kind of intervention for the child's benefit.[530] This is correct, but whether the intervention need be in the form of a court hearing or some kind of informal social work is a matter for debate. It should be recalled that issues that may appear trivial to adults, may appear hugely important from a child's perspective.

2. *Should the family resolve the issue themselves?* Johnson J in *Re C (A Minor) (Leave to Seek Section 8 Order)*[531] also considered the girl's application that she be allowed to move in with her friend's family. He also refused to grant leave for that application on the basis that he thought the issue should be left to the family to sort out between themselves, rather than involving the courts. The court feared that giving the child leave might give her an advantage in her dispute with her parents, although it might be thought that denying her leave gave her parents an advantage point.

3. *How mature is the child?* In *Re S (A Minor) (Independent Representation)*[532] it was stressed that the real issue is not the child's age but her understanding.[533] The very fact that the child had applied to the court would indicate maturity.[534] In *Re H (A Minor) (Role of the Official Solicitor)*[535] it was stressed that what had to be considered was whether the child would be able to give instructions in the light of the evidence that would be produced to the court. Where the evidence might be complex there may be difficulty in demonstrating this. The court may also take the view that the emotional turmoil that would be caused to the child by becoming involved in the litigation would be contrary to his or her welfare.[536]

4. *What is the likelihood of the success of the application?*[537] In *SC (A Minor) (Leave to Seek Section 8 Orders)*[538] it was confirmed that the fact that the application was not a hopeless application would be a factor in favour of granting leave.

5. *Would the child suffer from being involved in a protracted dispute between the parents?* In *Re S (A Minor) (Independent Representation)*[539] an 11-year-old boy wanted to replace his guardian *ad litem*. In the Court of Appeal, Bingham MR said that it was necessary to respect the child's wishes but at the same time protect the child from danger. It was held here that the effect of being closely involved with a bitter dispute between parents could harm a child and it was better for the boy to have the 'buffer' of a guardian *ad litem*. In *Re C (Residence: Child's*

---

[529] [1994] 1 FLR 26.
[530] Freeman (1997a: 168; 2000c).
[531] [1994] 1 FLR 26.
[532] [1993] 2 FLR 437, [1993] 2 FCR 1.
[533] In *Re S (Contact: Application by Sibling)* [1999] Fam 283, a nine-year-old was found to have sufficient understanding to apply for leave for a contact order with her half-brother.
[534] *Re C (A Minor) (Leave to Seek Section 8 Order)* [1995] 1 FLR 927, [1996] 1 FCR 461.
[535] [1993] 2 FLR 552.
[536] *Re N (Contact: Minor Seeking Leave to Defend and Removal of Guardian)* [2003] Fam Law 154.
[537] *Re C (A Minor) (Leave to Seek Section 8 Order)* [1995] 1 FLR 927, [1996] 1 FCR 461.
[538] [1994] 1 FLR 96, [1994] 1 FCR 837.
[539] [1993] 2 FLR 437, [1993] 2 FCR 1.

Application for Leave)[540] it was thought not to be to the child's benefit to hear the evidence of his warring parents. Fortin has argued that, rather than using this as a reason for denying access to the courts, consideration should be given as to how court procedures can be altered to protect child litigants' psychological welfare.[541] Further, it should not be forgotten that children are likely to have heard far worse arguments between their parents at home than they might witness in a court setting.[542]

6. *Will all the arguments that a child wishes to raise be presented to the court?* In **Re H (Residence Order: Child's Application for Leave)**[543] a 12-year-old boy sought to apply to the court for a residence order in his father's favour on his parents' divorce. Although he was mature enough to make the application, Johnson J held that the child would not bring before the court any argument that the father would not be making in his application for a residence order. There was therefore nothing to gain from granting leave. This argument fails to appreciate the importance to the child of feeling that he or she is being listened to.

7. *The impact of the Human Rights Act 1998.* A child may have a right to be represented and heard in proceedings with which they are involved.[544] *Re A (Contact: Separate Representation)*[545] accepted that a boy who wished to alert the judge to the dangers he believed his father posed to his young half-sister should have leave to do so.

In the light of this list of reasons for not permitting access, it is not surprising that it is rare for children successfully to bring applications before the court. It has been argued that the leave requirement improperly infringes a child's right to a fair hearing under Article 6 of the European Convention, in a way which improperly discriminates on the basis of age, contrary to Article 14.[546] In reply it could be said that children may need protection from the rigours of the court procedures such as cross-examination and this justifies the imposition of the leave requirement.[547] The ability of children to represent themselves would mean that the court could hear the child's views in his or her own words, rather than mediated through the reports of welfare officers. Notably, Dame Margaret Booth has argued that children should not be required to seek leave from the High Court before applying for a section 8 order.[548]

If leave is granted, the full application will be heard. The welfare principle will govern the issue. (The law governing the case is as discussed in Chapter 10.)

B Representation

In 2001 the Government created the Children and Family Court Advisory and Support Service (CAFCASS).[549] This agency was created to provide courts with services in cases involving children.[550] It is in charge of ensuring that children's interests are properly represented in court cases.[551] It is necessary to distinguish public and private law cases.

---

[540] [1995] 1 FLR 927, [1996] 1 FCR 461.
[541] Fortin (2009a).
[542] Wilson, J. (2007).
[543] [2000] 1 FLR 780, discussed in Sawyer (2001).
[544] Lyon (2007).
[545] [2001] 1 FLR 715.
[546] Lyon (2000).
[547] Lowe and Murch (2001).
[548] Her views are noted and discussed in Children Act Sub-Committee (2002a: para 12.6).
[549] Criminal Justice and Court Service Act 2000, s. 11.
[550] Murch (2003) provides an excellent discussion of the issues.
[551] See Wall LJ (2006) and MacDonald (2008) for a discussion of the failures in child representation in court hearings.

(i) Public law cases

In public law cases (e.g. where a child is being taken into care) the child's interests will be protected by a guardian.[552] The guardian will appoint a solicitor whose job it will be to represent the child's interests in any court hearing. The guardian and solicitor will work together to ascertain the wishes of the child and present these to the court. Courts can allow children who are the subject of public law proceedings to attend their hearing, although research indicates that at present many children who wish to attend the court are not allowed to do so.[553] Fortin[554] suggests that the awareness of children's rights under Articles 6 and 8 might lead to a change in practice. Although the representation of children in public cases is generally well thought of, it is under huge threat from cutbacks in legal aid in public law cases.[555]

(ii) Private law cases

The representation of children's interests in private law cases is less effective.[556] In a private case any of the following could occur:

1. The case proceeds without the court ever hearing of the child's views.

2. The court requests a child and family reporter[557] to prepare a report on the child, which will include a summary of the child's views.

3. The child could have party status (i.e. be treated as a party to the proceedings) and his or her interests be represented by his or her own lawyer.

4. The child may be able to litigate and bring applications on his or her own behalf with the leave of the court.[558]

Many commentators have expressed concern that all too often point 1 is what happens and that children's wishes and interests are not specifically addressed in a court proceeding. The United Nations Committee on the Rights of Children has expressed concern about the lack of representation of children's wishes in private cases.[559] Fortin has gone so far as to complain that 'The most serious procedural weakness undermining the Children Act's direction to the courts to consider the child's wishes and feelings is that there is no guarantee that the court will receive any evidence indicating what those wishes are.'[560] In part the reluctance to call for reports can be explained by the delays that can result while a report is being prepared.[561] Further, courts are aware that CAFCASS is understaffed and underfunded. Judges are therefore, understandably, reluctant to ask for reports unless absolutely necessary. The situation has been worsened by the fact that the Government has asked CAFCASS officers to concentrate on assisting parents to reach agreements and thereby avoid a costly hearing. Ironically this means it is even less likely that the voices of children will be heard and CAFCASS officers, rather than

---

[552] Bainham (2017).

[553] Fortin (2009b).

[554] Fortin (2009b: ch. 7).

[555] Blacklaws and Dowding (2006).

[556] James, James and McNamee (2003).

[557] A specialist social worker attached to CAFCASS.

[558] It is very difficult for children to get leave in such cases: see *Re H (A Minor) (Care Proceedings: Child's Wishes)* [1993] 1 FLR 440 and *Re C (Secure Accommodation Order: Representation)* [1993] 1 FLR 440.

[559] Committee on the Rights of the Child (2016).

[560] Fortin (2009b: 256).

[561] In *M v A (Contact: Domestic Violence)* [2002] 2 FLR 921 there was a seven-month delay in the preparation of a report.

listening to children and reporting their concerns, will be talking to parents and attempting to persuade them to reach an agreement, regardless of the views of the children.[562] It has been reported that guardians will only be appointed to assist in private children's cases in the most urgent of cases.[563]

In the past few years there has been an increasing acknowledgement of the need to ensure that children are heard in disputes over their upbringing.[564] Even if children's wishes are not to determine the case, they should at least be heard and have their views taken seriously.[565] The case for child representation can be made on two bases.[566] First, it can be promoted as a way of advancing children's welfare. There is much evidence that children who are the subject of litigation can be confused and anxious.[567] They report feeling ignored; not surprisingly, when it is claimed that in only 2 per cent of cases are children listened to and given a response.[568] It is well established that the existence of conflict between parents can be more harmful for the child than the ending of the relationship.[569] Having children's representation can be seen as necessary to promote children's welfare. Secondly, it can be seen as part of the rights of a child, protected by the United Nations Convention on the Rights of the Child, Article 12.[570]

The judiciary itself now recognises the importance of listening to the views of children.[571] This is even true (perhaps particularly true) where the parents appear to agree over what is best for the child. Indeed, arguably a child has a right under Article 6 of the European Convention on Human Rights to have her or his views given due consideration.[572] This may require, as well as a report, separate representation of the child's interests.[573] The leading case is *Mabon v Mabon*.[574]

CASE: *Mabon v Mabon* [2005] 2 FCR 354

The Court of Appeal overturned a judge's decision that three 'educated, articulate and reasonably mature' boys aged 17, 15 and 13 should not be separately represented in a bitterly contested application over residence and contact.[575] Thorpe LJ was blunt: 'It was simply unthinkable to exclude young men from knowledge of and participation in legal

---

[562] Fortin (2006b).

[563] Walsh (2010).

[564] Ruegger (2001); Murch (2003). Thomas (2001) emphasises that listening to children is also more likely to produce good decisions.

[565] Archard (2003: 54) emphasises that children have a right not just to be listened to, but also to be heard.

[566] Harold and Murch (2005).

[567] Douglas *et al.* (2006); Cashmore (2003).

[568] Harold and Murch (2005).

[569] Harold and Murch (2005).

[570] James, James and McNamee (2004); Davey (2010).

[571] *Re A (Contact: Separate Representation)* [2001] 1 FLR 715.

[572] Fortin (2009b: ch 10).

[573] Adoption and Children Act 2002, s. 122 means that applications under CA 1989, s. 8 are now 'specified proceedings' for the purpose of CA 1989, s. 41 and so separate representation can be ordered. *Re A (Contact: Separate Representation)* [2001] 1 FLR 715 CA But *CAFCASS Practice Note (Officers of Legal Services and Special Casework: Appointment in Family Proceedings)* [2001] 2 FLR 151 suggests that separate representation is appropriate only in special cases.

[574] [2005] 2 FCR 354. See also *Cambra v Jones* [2014] EWHC 913 (Fam).

[575] Though see *Re N (Contact: Minor Seeking Leave to Defend and Removal of Guardian)* [2003] 1 FLR 652 where the 11-year-old boy lacked the maturity to be able to give instructions.

proceedings that affected them so fundamentally . . . I am in no doubt that the judge was plainly wrong.'[576] Indeed, he thought that even if participation would be contrary to the welfare of the child that would not necessarily mean that it should not be permitted: 'the right of freedom of expression and participation outweighs the paternalistic judgement of welfare'.[577] However, he could imagine very limited circumstances in which it would not be appropriate to permit a competent child participation:

> If direct participation would pose an obvious risk of harm to the child arising out of the nature of the continuing proceedings and, if the child is incapable of comprehending that risk, then the judge is entitled to find that sufficient understanding has not been demonstrated. But judges have to be equally alive to the risk of emotional harm that might arise from denying the child knowledge of and participation in the continuing proceedings.[578]

This approach, Thorpe LJ held, was required in order to protect children's rights to autonomy under Article 8 and also the right in Article 12 of the UN Convention on the Rights of the Child for children to express their views.

The Family Proceedings Rules 2010, r. 16 now covers the representation of children. In Practice Direction 16A of the Rules it is made clear that the child as a party to the proceedings is a step that will be taken only in cases which involve an issue of significant difficulty and consequently will occur in only a minority of cases. The court must determine whether it is in the welfare of the child to be represented, taking account of the fact that representation can cause delay.[579] In *CS v SBH*[580] a child who was nearly 13 was permitted her own solicitor to make an appeal against an order, but was to be represented by a guardian as well.

Mabon must now be read in the light of *Re P-S*[581] where a 15-year-old wanted to be heard in care proceedings. The Court of Appeal, referring to both Article 6 of the ECHR and the UNCRC, confirmed that children had a right to be heard in proceedings concerning them, but that did not mean children had the right to give evidence. Part of a fair trial was that the wishes and feelings of the child be known to the judge and indeed that was part of the welfare assessment under the Children Act 1989. In this case the welfare reports had made clear the children's wishes. Seeing them in the court would add nothing. In *Cambra v Jones*[582] a 16-year-old child was joined as a party. She was profoundly affected by the proceedings (about which country she should live in); very much wanted to participate; and she would add evidence insights that would not otherwise be available to the court.[583]

---

[576] [2005] 2 FCR 354. At paras 23–24.
[577] At para 29.
[578] At para 29.
[579] *Re W (A Child)* [2016] EWCA Civ 1051.
[580] [2019] EHWC 634 (Fam).
[581] [2013] EWCA Civ 223.
[582] [2014] EWHC 913 (Fam).
[583] Surprisingly in *Re H (Children)(Care Orders)* [2015] EWCA Civ 115 a 14- and 12-year-old were said to lack the maturity to appreciate the significance and importance of their own needs and so did not need separate representation in care proceedings.

Despite the fine rhetoric in *Mabon,* the reality is that there is neither the funding nor the staff at CAFCASS to provide the representation for children that Thorpe LJ would evidently like to see.[584] In fact, research suggests that representation is used as a 'last resort' where there are complex disputes.[585]

Even if not represented, a child may well be permitted to attend the hearing. In *A CC v T*[586] Peter Jackson J said that it could no longer be assumed that a child's attendance in court proceedings was likely to be harmful. Children do not need to prove that their attendance will promote their welfare. The court should focus on the following factors in deciding whether the child could attend:

- the child's age and level of understanding;
- the nature and strength of the child's wishes;
- the child's emotional and psychological state;
- the effect of influence from others;
- the matters to be discussed;
- the evidence to be given;
- the child's behaviour.

Despite the acknowledgement that listening to and appreciating children's wishes is important, there are still grave concerns over the way in which reports concerning children are prepared and the length of time taken to prepare them. The problem that many commentators recount is that it is difficult for social workers to ascertain and report the wishes of children accurately. Children may feel intimidated and unable to say what they wish. Further, the questions asked of them by the Family Court Advisor may not reflect the way the problem is perceived by the child.[587] The reporter therefore (unintentionally) deprives children of the ability to express their views in their own terms.[588] James *et al.*[589] argue that their research indicates that the reporters have a particular image of childhood (e.g. that children become competent at particular ages) and this prevents an effective evaluation of every child. Indeed the very concept of 'listening' to children may too easily slip into taking a paternalistic approach to them.[590] A survey of cases by May and Smart[591] found that in only one-quarter of cases was there any kind of record on the paperwork of cases as to the wishes of the child; however, this could be largely explained by the age of the child or the fact that the parents were in agreement. They found that where children's wishes did not coincide with the welfare officer's view it was rare for the children's views to prevail. It is not surprising that there has, therefore, been encouragement for judges meeting with children directly, not least from Baroness Hale and Justice Munby.[592]

---

[584] *R v CAFCASS* [2011] EWHC 1774 (Admin). See *Re C (Children) (Appointment of Guardian)* [2008] 1 FCR 359 where the National Youth Advisory Service was asked to represent and assist the children.
[585] Douglas *et al.* (2006). Bellamy and Lord (2003) found that rule 9.5 was used in 7.3 per cent of contested cases.
[586] [2011] 2 FLR 803.
[587] Mayall (2002: 166).
[588] Buchanan *et al.* (2001).
[589] Murch (2003). James, James and McNamee (2003). See also HM Inspectorate of Court Administration (2005).
[590] Clucas (2005: 291).
[591] May and Smart (2004).
[592] Hale (2016); Cobb (2015). See also King (2017).

As well as preparing the reports, the child and family reporter can be responsible for communicating with the child after the order has been made. This is also important because part of taking a child's views seriously is reporting back to the child the court's decision and discussing it with him or her.[593]

16 The Children's Commissioner

The Children Act 2004 created the post Children's Commissioner for England. There are separate ones for Wales, Scotland and Northern Ireland. As at 2021 Anne Longfield is the Children's Commissioner for England and Sally Holland for Wales.

The primary role of the English Commissioner is set out in s. 2(1) of the Children Act 2004: 'promoting and protecting the rights of children in England'.[594] Further detail is provided in the statute:

LEGISLATIVE PROVISION

Children Act 2004, section 2

1. The primary function includes promoting awareness of the views and interests of children in England.

2. In the discharge of the primary function the Children's Commissioner may, in particular—

    (a) advise persons exercising functions or engaged in activities affecting children on how to act compatibly with the rights of children;

    (b) encourage such persons to take account of the views and interests of children;

    (c) advise the Secretary of State on the rights, views and interests of children;

    (d) consider the potential effect on the rights of children of government policy proposals and government proposals for legislation;

    (e) bring any matter to the attention of either House of Parliament;

    (f) investigate the availability and effectiveness of complaints procedures so far as relating to children;

    (g) investigate the availability and effectiveness of advocacy services for children;

    (h) investigate any other matter relating to the rights or interests of children;

    (i) monitor the implementation in England of the United Nations Convention on the Rights of the Child;

    (j) publish a report on any matter considered or investigated under this section.

3. In the discharge of the primary function, the Children's Commissioner must have particular regard to the rights of children who are within section 8A (children living away from home or receiving social care) and other groups of children who the Commissioner considers to be at particular risk of having their rights infringed.

4. The Children's Commissioner may not conduct an investigation of the case of an individual child in the discharge of the primary function.

---

[593] Buchanan *et al.* (2001: 93).
[594] The role of the Commissioner was redefined in the Children and Families Act 2014.

United Nations Convention on the Rights of the Child

1. The Children's Commissioner must, in particular, have regard to the United Nations Convention on the Rights of the Child in considering for the purposes of the primary function what constitute the rights and interests of children (generally or so far as relating to a particular matter).

The Secretary of State can ask the Children's Commissioner to hold an inquiry into a case of an individual child if that would raise wider issues relevant for children.[595] Under s. 2D of the Children Act 2004 the Commissioner can give advice and assistance to children who are living away from home or receiving social care. The Commissioner produces a wide range of reports and guidance for children and public bodies who deal with children. Recent projects have involved work on sexual exploitation, online safety, and how children can complain about schools.[596]

The Children's Commissioner for Wales[597] has as his or her principal aim to safeguard and promote the rights and welfare of children.[598] He or she should have regard to the United Nations Convention on the Rights of the Child when exercising his or her functions.[599]

17 Corporal punishment

Corporal punishment has been defined as 'the use of physical force with the intention of causing a child to experience pain but not injury for the purposes of correction or control of the child's behaviour'.[600] Corporal punishment is one of the most controversial topics surrounding parenting.[601] Although nearly everyone agrees that children require some form of discipline,[602] there is much dispute about what form that discipline should take. For some, the issue is straightforward: 'Hitting people is wrong – and children are people too.'[603] Indeed, it can be regarded as a basic human right not to be hit.[604] The impact on children can be underestimated. One child respondent to a Government survey stated 'the memory of how it made me feel inside was so much stronger than how it felt on my skin – that was over in a few seconds'.[605] Others argue that corporal punishment is an important part of bringing children up well and even cite some biblical support.[606] A third group (perhaps the majority of parents) do not think that corporal punishment is necessarily a positive good but admit that, when at

---

[595] Children Act 2004, s. 4.
[596] Visit www.childrenscommissioner.gov.uk/ or www.childcom.org.uk for current projects.
[597] Children's Commissioner for Wales Act 2001 and Part V of Care Standards Act 2000.
[598] Care Standards Act 2000, s. 72A
[599] Children's Commissioner for Wales Regulations 2001, SI 2001/2787 (W237), reg. 22. See Thomas *et al.* (2010) for a discussion of the work of the Commissioner.
[600] Strauss and Donnolly (1993: 420).
[601] For useful discussions of the use of force against children in a variety of contexts, see Saunders and Goddard (2010), Barton (2008c), Keating (2006) and Booth (2005).
[602] Rhona Smith (2004) suggests a child has a right to discipline.
[603] Newell (1989).
[604] United Nations Committee on the Rights of the Child (2008) called on the UK to remove the defence of 'reasonable chastisement'.
[605] Barton (2008c: 65).
[606] Proverbs 13: 24; see *R (On the Application of Williamson) v Secretary of State* [2005] 1 FCR 498.

the end of their tether, they use corporal punishment. A survey revealed that corporal punishment is widespread: 81 per cent of interviewees supported corporal punishment by parents of their own children; 45 per cent by carers or nannies; 67 per cent by teachers; 71 per cent by head teachers; and (remarkably) 70 per cent by courts.[607] Another survey found that 88 per cent of parents stated that they felt it sometimes necessary to hit their children.[608] However, it may be that attitudes are changing, with the most recent survey finding only 59 per cent of those questioned believing that parents should be allowed to smack their children.[609] Corporal punishment starts surprisingly young: three-quarters of one-year-olds have been smacked and among four-year-olds 48 per cent were hit once a week.[610]

The present law is that corporal punishment is *prima facie* an assault. It could be a battery, an assault occasioning actual bodily harm,[611] or wounding or inflicting or causing grievous bodily harm,[612] depending on the severity of the punishment. However, under common law there is a defence to these offences if the conduct constitutes 'lawful chastisement'. Precisely what 'lawful chastisement' is not clear. Section 58 of the Children Act 2004 makes it clear that 'reasonable chastisement' cannot provide a defence to a charge of assault occasioning actual bodily harm or the offences involving grievous bodily harm. In other words, to rely on the defence of reasonable chastisement the level of harm used must cause less than actual bodily harm. As actual bodily harm includes a bruise, only 'mild corporal punishment' is permitted. The Crown Prosecution Service guidelines state:

> ... for minor assaults committed by an adult upon a child that result in injuries such as grazes, scratches, abrasions, minor bruising, swelling, superficial cuts or a black eye, the appropriate charge will normally be ABH[613] for which the defence of 'reasonable chastisement' is no longer available.
>
> However, if the injury amounts to no more than reddening of the skin, and the injury is transient and trifling, a charge of common assault may be laid against the defendant for whom the reasonable chastisement defence remains available to parents or adults acting *in loco parentis*.[614]

The Government Review of the current law decided no change was necessary. Section 58 of the Children Act 2004 had improved the protection for children while not producing significant practical problems.[615] While the Government 'does not condone smacking and believes that other methods of managing children are more effective',[616] it 'does not believe the state should intervene in family life unnecessarily'. Therefore, the current law remains, and as the *Daily Telegraph* put it: 'Parents can smack – if they're gentle.'[617]

As well as involving potential criminal charges, corporal punishment might also lead to investigation by a local authority.[618] Corporal punishment is now forbidden in state and

---

[607] ICM poll (*The Guardian*, 7 November 1996).

[608] Sawyer (2000).

[609] Department for Education and Skills (2008: para 31).

[610] Phillips and Alderson (2003).

[611] Contrary to Offences Against the Person Act 1861, s. 47.

[612] Contrary to Offences Against the Person Act 1861, s. 18 or s. 10.

[613] Actual bodily harm.

[614] Crown Prosecution Service (2007: 1).

[615] See Choudhry (2009) for an excellent discussion of the current law.

[616] Department for Education and Skills (2008: para 55).

[617] Quoted Barton (2008c: 68).

[618] *Re F (Children) (Interim Care Order)* [2007] 2 FCR 639 where a single act of excessive force in punishment was found on the facts to be insufficient to justify an interim care order.

independent schools[619] and in residential care homes.[620] The European Court and Commission have had to address the issue of corporal punishment on a number of occasions.[621] *A v UK (Human Rights: Punishment of Child)*[622] has had the biggest impact. A cane was used on more than one occasion by a mother's partner on her child. The European Court of Human Rights did not make a general statement on chastisement but did state that Article 3 was breached. The defence of 'reasonable chastisement' was too vague and inadequately protected the child from inhuman and degrading treatment.[623] The European Court of Human Rights took the view that corporal punishment breached Article 19 of the UN Convention, which requires the state to protect children from all forms of violence.[624]

In *R (On the Application of Williamson) v Secretary of State for Education and Employment* the House of Lords had to consider whether parents or teachers could claim a right to administer corporal punishment.

> ### CASE: *R (On the Application of Williamson)* v *Secretary of State for Education and Employment* [2005] 1 FCR 498
>
> The House of Lords rejected a claim by parents that the prohibition of corporal punishment in private schools (in Education Act 1996, s. 548) infringed their right to respect for family life. They had sent their children to a private Christian school and the parents and teachers wanted the teachers to be able to use corporal punishment in the school. Their Lordships accepted that the Act did interfere with the right to religious freedom in Article 9 of the ECHR, but held that the interference could be justified. Lord Nicholls explained: 'Corporal punishment involves deliberately inflicting physical violence. The legislation is intended to protect children against the distress, pain and other harmful effects infliction of physical violence may cause.' But it would be quite wrong to think that this case indicates that children have the right never to suffer corporal punishment. Lord Nicholls makes it clear he does not think that corporal punishment necessarily infringes a child's rights under Article 3 or Article 8. Baroness Hale is less clear. She states at one point: 'If a child has a right to be brought up without institutional violence, as he does, that right should be respected whether or not his parents and teachers believe otherwise.'[625] However, she earlier states that in a free society parents should have a 'large measure of autonomy' in deciding how to raise children.[626]

Despite the changes to the law in the Children Act 2004, there are many who argue that the law should never permit corporal punishment.[627]

---

[619] Education Act 1996, s. 548(1) as amended by the Schools Standards and Framework Act 1998, s. 131 abolished corporal punishment in independent schools. A challenge that this provision infringed parents' rights under the European Convention on Human Rights failed in *R (On the Application of Williamson) v Secretary of State for Education and Employment* [2005] 1 FCR 498.

[620] Day Care and Child Minding (National Standards: England) Regulations 2003 (SI 2003/1996), reg. 5 prohibits childminders and day-care workers from 'smacking' children.

[621] Including *Tyrer v UK* (1978) 2 EHRR 1; *Campbell and Cosans v UK* (1982) 4 EHRR 293; *Warwick v UK* (1986) 60 DR 5; *Y v UK* (1992) 17 EHRR 238; *Costello-Roberts v UK* (1995) EHRR 112; *A v UK (Human Rights: Punishment of Child)* [1998] 2 FLR 959, [1998] 3 FCR 597.

[622] [1998] 2 FLR 959, [1998] 3 FCR 597.

[623] The court left open a possible claim under Article 8.

[624] United Nations Human Rights Committee (2008).

[625] At para 84.

[626] At para 72.

[627] E.g. Fenton-Glynn (2018b); Keating (2006); United Nations Committee on the Rights of the Child (2016).

18 Children's duties

Although much has been written on children's rights, there is very little said about children's duties.[628] Indeed, children appear to be under few duties under the law. By far the most significant is the duty to obey the criminal law, at least once they have reached the age of 10.[629] However, there is not even an obligation upon children to attend school.[630]

At a theoretical level, as children's rights are increasingly recognised, it is arguable that greater emphasis should be placed on children's responsibilities. If children are thought to have sufficient capacity to be able to make decisions for themselves, then it is arguable that they have sufficient capacity to have responsibilities. As Sir John Laws has written:

> A society whose values are defined by reference to individual rights is by that very fact already impoverished. Its existence says nothing about individual duty, nothing about virtue, self-discipline, self-restraint, to say nothing of self-sacrifice.[631]

However, the difficulty arises in enforcing any duties imposed upon children. Even though children are subject to the criminal law, the punishments imposed on children are not the same as those placed on adults. Certainly, where a child is exercising a right, like others she must ensure she respects the rights of others. In *Re Roddy (A Child) (Identification: Restriction on Publication)*[632] a 16-year-old was permitted to tell the media her story of how she became pregnant at age 12. However, she was not permitted, in doing so, to reveal the identity of her child nor of the father of the child, both of whom were under the age of 18. In *Re M (A Child) (Care Proceedings: Witness Summons)*[633] a child was forced to give evidence against her will in child abuse proceedings. The importance of discovering the truth about the alleged abuse in that case justified overruling her wishes.

19 Conclusion

This chapter has considered the ways in which the law looks at children. Two particular approaches have been contrasted: that in which the law seeks to promote the child's welfare; and that in which the law protects the rights of the child. In respect of many issues, despite their important theoretical differences, these approaches would adopt the same solution. The issue of most disagreement is over whether a child should be able to make decisions for him- or herself. The leading cases in this area have focused on the medical arena. In the rather extreme circumstances of those cases, the courts have not been willing to permit children to make decisions which have the effect of ending their lives. These cases might give the impression that children's wishes will be readily overridden by the courts, whereas in fact forcing any form of action on an unwilling teenager is rare, although this may be as much because of the practical problems in compelling a person to do something against their will as any theoretical principle. In *Mabon v Mabon*, Thorpe LJ indicated that in the twenty-first century there was a keener awareness of children's autonomy rights.[634] We will wait and see if this leads to changes

---

[628] Bainham (1998c).
[629] Notably, a young offender can be subject to a curfew order. Such orders cannot be made against adults.
[630] The obligation to ensure attendance at school is placed upon the parents, rather than the child.
[631] Laws (1998: 255).
[632] [2004] 1 FCR 481.
[633] [2007] 1 FCR 253.
[634] [2005] 2 FCR 354 at para 26.

in the approaches of the courts. The chapter has also considered the ways in which the law must balance the interests of parents and children. The issue is often not made explicit in the case law. The simple approach that the interests of children are paramount and always trump those of the parent has been shown not to represent the law and not to be appropriate in theory.[635] The Human Rights Act 1998 will no doubt lead to many more cases where the court will be required to balance the interests of parents, children and the state; and, hopefully, more well-thought-out principles will be developed.[636]

Further reading

Altman, S. (2018) 'Reinterpreting the right to an open future: from autonomy to authenticity', *Law and Philosophy* 37: 415.

Archard, D. (2004b) *Children: Rights and Childhood,* London: Routledge.

Auckland, C. and Goold, I. (2019) 'Parental rights, best interests and significant harms: Who should have the final say over a child's medical care', *Cambridge Law Journal* 78: 287.

Bainham, A. (2009d) 'Is anything now left of parental rights?' in R. Probert, S. Gilmore and J. Herring (eds) *Responsible Parents and Parental Responsibility,* Oxford: Hart.

Bainham, A. and Gilmore, S. (2016) *Children: The Modern Law,* Bristol: Jordans.

Bridgeman, J. (2007) *Parental Responsibility, Young Children and Healthcare Law,* Cambridge: CUP.

Bridgeman, J. (2015) 'The right to responsible parents?' in A. Diduck, N. Peleg and H. Reece (eds) *Law in Society,* Leiden: Brill.

Brighouse, H. and Swift, A. (2014) *Family Values: The Ethics of Parent-Child Relationships,* Oxford: Princeton University Press.

Byrne, B. (2016) 'Do Children still need to escape childhood?' *International Journal of Children's Rights* 24: 113.

Cassidy, C. (2012) 'Children's status, children's rights and "dealing with" children', *International Journal of Children's Rights* 20: 57.

Cave, E. (2014b) 'Goodbye *Gillick*? Identifying and resolving problems with the concept of child competence', *Legal Studies* 34: 103.

Cave, E. and Wallbank, J. (2012) 'Minors' capacity to refuse treatment: a reply to Gilmore and Herring', *Medical Law Review* 20: 423.

Choudhry, S. and Fenwick, H. (2005) 'Taking the rights of parents and children seriously: confronting the welfare principle under the Human Rights Act', *Oxford Journal of Legal Studies* 25: 453.

Committee on the Rights of the Child (2016) *Concluding Observations on the Fifth Periodic Report of the United Kingdom of Great Britain and Northern Ireland,* Geneva: United Nations.

Daly, A. (2018) 'No weight for "due weight"? A children's autonomy principle in best interest proceedings', *International Journal of Children's Rights* 26: 61.

---

[635] Although see Dwyer (2006) for further discussion.
[636] Fortin (2011a).

Eekelaar, J. (1994a) 'The interests of the child and the child's wishes: the role of dynamic self-determinism', *International Journal of Law and the Family* 8: 42.

Eekelaar, J. (2004) 'Children between cultures', *International Journal of Law, Policy and the Family* 18: 178.

Eekelaar, J. (2015a) 'The role of the best interests principle in decisions affecting children and decisions about children', *International Journal of Children's Rights* 23: 3.

Faulkner, E. and Nyamutata, C. (2020) 'The decolonisation of children's rights and the colonial contours of the Convention on the Rights of the Child', *International Journal of Children's Rights* 28: 66.

Ferguson, L. (2013b) 'Not merely rights for children but children's rights: The theory gap and the assumption of the importance of children's rights', *International Journal of Children's Rights* 21: 177.

Ferguson, L. (2015c) 'The jurisprudence of making decisions affecting children: an argument to prefer duty to children's rights and welfare', in A. Diduck, N. Peleg and H. Reece (eds) *Law in Society,* Leiden: Brill.

Ferguson, L. (2018) 'An argument for treating children as a "special case"', in E. Brake and L. Ferguson (eds) *Philosophical Foundations of Children's and Family Law,* Oxford: OUP.

Flacks, S. (2014) 'Is childhood a 'disability'? Exploring the exclusion of children from age discrimination provisions in the Equality Act 2010', *Child and Family Law Quarterly* 421.

Fortin, J. (2009b) *Children's Rights and the Developing Law,* London: LexisNexis Butterworths.

Fortin, J. (2014) 'Children's rights – flattering to deceive?' *Child and Family Law Quarterly* 26: 51.

Freeman, M. (2010) 'The human rights of children', *Current Legal Problems* 63: 1.

Gheaus, A. (2018) 'Children's vulnerability and legitimate authority over children', *Journal of Applied Philosophy* 35: 60.

Gilmore, S. (2009) 'The limits of parental responsibility', in R. Probert, S. Gilmore and J. Herring (eds) *Responsible Parents and Parental Responsibility,* Oxford: Hart.

Gilmore, S. (2017) 'Use of the UNCRC in family law cases in England and Wales', *International Journal of Children's Rights* 25: 500.

Gilmore, S. and Herring, J. (2011a) '"No" is the hardest word: consent and children's autonomy', *Child and Family Law Quarterly* 23: 3.

Goold, I., Herring, J. and Auckland, C. (eds) (2020) *Parental Rights, Best Interests, and Significant Harm,* Oxford: Hart.

Goosey, S. (2019) 'Is age discrimination a less serious form of discrimination?' *Legal Studies* 39: 533.

Guggenheim, M. (2005) *What's Wrong with Children's Rights*? Cambridge, MA: Harvard University Press.

Harris, P. (2014) 'Article 8 of the European Convention and the welfare principle: a thesis of conflict resolution', *Family Law* 44: 331.

Herring, J. (1999b) 'The Human Rights Act and the welfare principle in family law – conflicting or complementary?' *Child and Family Law Quarterly* 11: 223.

Herring, J. (2005b) 'Farewell welfare', *Journal of Social Welfare and Family Law* 27: 159.

Herring, J. (2012d) 'Vulnerability, children and the law', in M. Freeman (ed.) *Law and Childhood Studies,* Oxford: OUP.

Herring, J. (2014b) 'The welfare principle and the Children Act: presumably it's about welfare?' *Journal of Social Welfare and Family Law* 36: 14.

Herring, J. (2017) 'Parental responsibility; hyper-parenting and the role of technology', in R. Brownsword, E. Scotford and K. Yeung (eds) *Oxford Handbook on Law and Regulation of Technology*, Oxford: OUP.

Herring, J. (2019b) 'Maternalism and making decisions for children', in H. Willekens, K. Scheiwe, T. Richarz and E. Schumann (eds) *Motherhood and the Law*, University of Gottingen.

Herring, J. and Foster, C. (2012) 'Welfare means relationality, virtue and altruism', *Legal Studies* 32: 480.

Kazez, J. (2017) *The Philosophical Parent: Asking the Hard Questions About Having and Raising Children,* Oxford: OUP.

King, E. (2017) 'Giving children a voice in litigation: are we there yet?' *Family Law* 289.

Lyons, B. (2010) 'Dying to be responsible: adolescence, autonomy and responsibility', *Legal Studies* 30: 257.

Macleod, A. (2018) 'Are children's rights important?' in E. Brake and L. Ferguson (eds) *Philosophical Foundations of Children's and Family Law*, Oxford: OUP.

Millum, J. (2018) *The Moral Foundations of Parenthood,* Oxford: OUP.

Nolan, A. (2011) *Children's Socio-Economic Rights,* Oxford: Hart.

Parkinson, P. and Cashmore, J. (2010) *The Voice of a Child in Family Law Disputes,* Oxford: OUP.

Peleg, N. (2009) *The Child's Right to Development*, Cambridge: CUP.

Probert, R., Gilmore, S. and Herring, J. (eds) (2009) *Responsible Parents and Parental Responsibility,* Oxford: Hart.

Reshef, Y. (2013) 'Rethinking the value of families', *Critical Review of International Social and Political Philosophy* 16:1.

Stalford, H. (2012) *Children and the European Union,* Oxford: Hart.

Stalford, H., Hollingsworth, K. and Gilmore, S. (eds) (2017) *Rewriting Children's Rights Judgments,* London: Bloomsbury.

Taylor, R. (2016) 'Putting children first? Children's interests as a primary consideration in public law', *Child and Family Law Quarterly* 45.

Taylor, R. (2020) 'Parental decisions and court jurisdiction: best interests or significant harm?' *Child and Family Law Quarterly* 141

Tobin, J. (2013) 'Justifying Children's Rights', *International Journal of Children's Rights* 22: 295.

Trotter, S. (2018) 'The child in European human rights law', *Modern Law Review* 81: 412.

Watkins, D. (2016) 'Where do I stand? Assessing children's capabilities under English law', *Child and Family Law Quarterly* 25.

Wilhelms, E. and Reyna, V. (2013) 'Fuzzy trace theory and medical decisions by minors: Differences in reasoning between adolescents and adults', *The Journal of Medicine and Philosophy* 38: 268.

Zanghellini, A. (2018) 'Children's welfare, religious freedom, LGBTQ rights, and state neutrality: a philosophical discussion, by reference to *J v B* and *Lee v McArthur*', *Child and Family Law Quarterly* 178.

Visit **go.pearson.com/uk/he/resources** to access **resources** specifically written to complement this text.

10

Private disputes over children

Learning objectives

When you finish reading this chapter you will be able to:

1. Explain the orders available to the court in disputes over children
2. Describe who can apply for section 8 orders
3. Explain and evaluate how the court interprets the welfare principle
4. Summarise the issues around contact disputes
5. Describe how the courts use wardship and the inherent jurisdiction

1 Introduction

This chapter will consider the law in situations when there is a private dispute concerning children. Chapter 11 will examine public law cases, that is, where the local authority is seeking to protect a child whom it fears is in danger of being abused. Here we will concentrate largely on the cases which involved disputes between parents over the upbringing of children, although, as will become apparent, adults other than parents, and indeed children themselves, may seek court orders over children.

Generally, parents are left to resolve disputes themselves. You might have strong views about the decisions your neighbours are making about their child's diet, religion or clothing, but unless it could be shown that the child was suffering significant harm and the local authority were willing to become involved, you would be extremely unlikely to be able to bring your case to the courts. The law is based on the assumption that parents promote the welfare of their children, and so there is normally no need for the intervention of the court in normal family life.[1] The courts become involved only if there is a dispute between the parents over the upbringing of their child or, rarely, if the child themselves applies to the court. Of course, the vast majority of parents are able to resolve their disagreements about their children themselves. For 90 per cent of separated families there is no need for court intervention because parents are able to negotiate arrangements between themselves or with the help of mediation. (This was discussed in Chapter 2.)

[1] Probert, Gilmore and Herring (2009).

If the couple cannot reach agreement by any means, they may turn to the courts. The Children Act 1989 brought together the orders appropriate for most private disputes involving children, but sometimes the courts must use their inherent jurisdiction if it is not possible to make the order needed to protect a child under the Children Act 1989.[2] This chapter will begin by setting out the orders available under the Children Act, and then consider how the courts decide what order to make.

2 The orders available to the court

Learning objective 1

Explain the orders available to the court in disputes over children

In private cases involving children the courts may make one of the orders mentioned in s. 8 of the Children Act 1989. A section 8 order cannot be made in respect of a person over the age of 18. The different orders that can be made under s. 8 will now be considered. The law on orders relating to children has been dramatically reformed by s. 12 of the Children and Families Act 2014.[3] There are three kinds of orders that a court can make under s. 8 of the Children Act 1989: child arrangements orders; specific issue orders and prohibited steps orders.

A Child arrangements orders

> **LEGISLATIVE PROVISION**
>
> **Children Act 1989, section 8**
>
> '[A] child arrangements order' means an order regulating arrangements relating to any of the following—
>
> (a) with whom a child is to live, spend time or otherwise have contact, and
>
> (b) when a child is to live, spend time or otherwise have contact with any person;

The child arrangements order (CAO) replaces the old 'residence order' and 'contact order' which determined with whom a child should primarily live and with whom a child should have contact.[4] These have been abandoned because the Family Justice Review suggested that separating couples had come to believe that whoever obtained residence was the 'winner' and whoever just had contact was 'the loser'. This made proceedings more antagonistic than necessary. As Justice Moylan,[5] writing extra-judicially, put it:

> Words – even, or perhaps particularly, words used in a legal context – can all too easily be invested with a significance beyond that which the words themselves justify. For example, as outlined below, parents when conflicted or in dispute can attribute significance to a word because

---

[2] For an interesting discussion of the history of the making of the Children Act 1989, see Harris (2006).
[3] Practice Direction 12B – Child Arrangements Programme deals with procedural matters.
[4] Under Article 6 of the Children and Families Act (Transitional Provisions) Order 2014 all existing contact and residence orders will be transformed into child arrangements orders.
[5] Moylan (2013).

of the status which it is perceived to represent or reflect rather than to take it merely as a word which denotes the form of practical arrangements in respect of their children.

Moving away from this terminology and phrasing the order in terms of a child arrangements order it is hoped will make the issue less contentious. The difference in terminology is, therefore, largely semantic. It is not imagined that the redefinition of section 8 orders will result in a notable change in the orders made. It may not even succeed in its stated aim. The House of Commons Justice Committee stated:

> We think that it is unlikely that a change to the wording of orders from 'residence' and 'contact' to 'child arrangements order' will remove the perception of winners and losers within the family courts, although a change of terms would not, in itself, be objectionable.

There are some issues which are unclear given the definition of the child arrangements order:

(i) Who has the obligation under a child arrangements order?

Although the CAO can state who is to spend time with a child it is not entirely clear what, if anything, is required of anyone. Notably the definition of a CAO is not that a parent must ensure the other parent is able to spend time with the child. Presumably a parent who takes steps to actively prevent the other parent seeing the child under the terms of the order will be seen to be in breach of it and liable to punishment as a result. However, a parent who simply fails to facilitate contact may well not be. But quite what is required of the other parent is far from clear. The line between 'preventing' and 'not facilitating' is a blurred one.

A further issue is whether a child can be required to have contact. It is hard to imagine a court threatening a child with imprisonment if they fail to spend time with their parent as the CAO states.

(ii) Can the parent be forced to have contact with the child?

The wording of a CAO is also unclear on whether a parent can be *required* to have contact with the child. If the evidence is clear that the child would benefit from regular contact with the non-resident father, but the father does not wish to have contact, can he be compelled to see the child?[6] The definition of a CAO would not seem to include an order that binds the person named to have contact.[7] Indeed, Thorpe LJ in *Re L (A Child) (Contact: Domestic Violence)*[8] speaking of the old law explicitly denied that a parent could be ordered to spend time with a child against the parent's wishes. In any event, it would probably be counterproductive to compel a reluctant parent to see a child and so it is hard to image the court would want to make such an order.[9]

(iii) What can 'contact' involve?

The CAO allows the court to regulate contact. This will normally involve face-to-face meetings, but the CAO can also involve indirect contact, for example in the form of letters, e-mails, texting, Skyping[10] or phone calls. An indirect contact order may be appropriate if the contact parent cannot see the child: for example, if the parent is in prison;[11] or the child is strongly

---

[6] Of course, he could not physically be forced to do so, but he could be ordered to do so under threat of punishment.
[7] Although a specific issue order may have this effect.
[8] [2000] 2 FCR 404 at para 43. See also *Re S (A Child)* [2010] EWCA Civ 705.
[9] But see the discussions on the duties of contact later in this chapter.
[10] E.g. *Re A (Contact: Witness Protection Scheme)* [2005] EWHC 2189 (Fam).
[11] *A v L (Contact)* [1998] 1 FLR 361, [1998] 2 FCR 204.

opposed to face-to-face contact.[12] It may also be appropriate if the child and the contact parent do not have a relationship at present, and they need to establish or re-establish links before direct contact would be appropriate.[13] It would be most unusual for a court to decide that even indirect contact would be inappropriate.[14]

If contact is to be face to face, it can be supervised by the social services.[15] This may be particularly appropriate where there is a fear that the contact parent may endanger the child.[16] If contact is to be supervised, it will often take place at a contact centre, a place set up by the local authority to assist in meetings between contact parents and children. In *Re C (Abduction: Residence and Contact)*[17] it was held that the Human Rights Act 1998 indicated that there was a presumption in favour of normal contact and there had to be clear evidence to justify requiring contact to be supervised. If supervised contact has successfully taken place for a considerable period of time, the court may well be minded to permit unsupervised contact.[18] However, in some cases it has been accepted that contact will always need to be supervised. In *Re S (Child Arrangements Order: Effect of Long-Term Supervised Contact on Welfare)*[19] a father had a conviction for making paedophilic images and was found to be sexually attracted to girls. It was likely that supervised contact with his daughter would always be needed, at least during her minority.

(iv) Is a no contact order possible?

A 'no contact order' is an order prohibiting contact between a child and parent.[20] That is different from the lack of a contact order, which simply means the parent has no right of contact. It seems a 'no contact order' needs to be made as a CAO or as a prohibited steps order.[21]

B Specific issue orders

> **LEGISLATIVE PROVISION**
>
> **Children Act 1989, section 8**
>
> '[A] specific issue order' means an order giving directions for the purpose of determining a specific question which has arisen, or which may arise, in connection with any aspect of parental responsibility for a child.

The specific issue order (SIO) may require someone to act positively in some way or may require someone to refrain from a particular activity.[22] It is designed to deal with a particular

---

[12] *Re A and B (Contact) (No. 4)* [2015] EWHC 2839 (Fam).
[13] *Re L (Contact: Transsexual Applicant)* [1995] 2 FLR 438, [1995] 3 FCR 125.
[14] *Re P (Contact: Indirect Contact)* [1999] 2 FLR 893; *A Local Authority v A, B and E* [2011] EWHC 2062 (Fam).
[15] *Practice Direction (Access: Supervised Access)* [1980] 1 WLR 334.
[16] Although where there has been sexual abuse indirect contact is normally ordered: *Re M (Sexual Abuse Allegations: Interviewing Techniques)* [1999] 2 FLR 92.
[17] [2005] EWHC 2205 (Fam).
[18] *R v P (Contact: Abduction: Supervision)* [2008] 2 FLR 936.
[19] [2015] EWCA Civ 689.
[20] *P v D* [2014] EWHC 2355 (Fam).
[21] *Q v Q (Contact: Undertakings) (No. 3)* [2016] EWFC 5; *ME v MP* [2019] EWHC 132 (Fam).
[22] Gilmore (2004c) provides an excellent discussion of the use of specific issue orders.

one-off issue relating to the child's upbringing: for example, in *Re C (A Child) (HIV Test)*[23] an SIO was made that a baby be tested for HIV and in *M v M (Specific Issue: Choice of School)*[24] an SIO was used to decide that the child should attend a voice test for a cathedral school. Arguably its most bizarre use was in *Re JS (Disposal of Body)*[25] where it was used to authorise the mother to make arrangements to have cryonic preservation (long-term freezing) of the body of a seriously ill 14-year-old.[26] It is not designed to deal with ongoing disputes – for example, what kind of clothes the child may wear.[27]

C Prohibited steps orders

LEGISLATIVE PROVISION

Children Act 1989, section 8

'[A] prohibited steps order' means an order that no step which could be taken by a parent in meeting his parental responsibility for a child, and which is of a kind specified in the order, shall be taken by any person without the consent of the court.

The prohibited steps order (PSO) is entirely negative – it tells a parent what he or she may not do in respect of their child. The order can be used, for example, to prevent a child being known by a different name,[28] or to prevent a child being removed from the United Kingdom.

D Restrictions on the use of section 8 orders

The section 8 orders are loosely defined and so could be open to abuse were they not restricted in their scope in the following ways.

(i) The order must relate to an aspect of parental responsibility

This means that the order must relate to an issue concerning the upbringing of the child and not just concerning the relationship between the parents. So, for example, section 8 orders cannot prevent contact between adults,[29] nor require a husband to provide the wife with a *get* so that their divorce can be recognised within Jewish law.[30] By contrast, requiring a mother to inform her children that a man is the children's father does fall under the scope of parental responsibility.[31]

---

[23] [1999] 2 FLR 1004 CA
[24] [2005] EWHC 2769 (Fam).
[25] [2016] EWHC 2859 (Fam). See Conway (2018) for a broader discussion of this case.
[26] This was done in due course.
[27] Whether an SIO can state that in future a named person (e.g. the mother) can make decisions concerning a particular topic is unclear: see Gilmore (2004c: 369–71).
[28] *Dawson v Wearmouth* [1999] 1 FLR 1167, [1999] 1 FCR 625.
[29] *Croydon LB v A* [1992] 2 FLR 341, [1992] 1 FCR 522.
[30] *N v N (Jurisdiction: Pre-Nuptial Agreement)* [1999] 2 FLR 745.
[31] *Re F (Children) (Paternity: Jurisdiction)* [2008] 1 FCR 382.

(ii) There is no power to make an occupation or non-molestation order through a section 8 order

A specific issue or prohibited steps order cannot be made if the effect is the same as an occupation or non-molestation order.[32] Any such order must be sought under the Family Law Act 1996, Part IV.[33] However, if it can be shown that the order sought is not identical to an order available under the Family Law Act 1996 then the order can be made. In *Re H (Minors) (Prohibited Steps Order)*[34] a PSO preventing a stepfather visiting a child could be made because a non-molestation order would only prevent molestation and not prohibit all contact with the child. The PSO, therefore, was not identical to a non-molestation order.

(iii) There is no power to make a disguised CAO order using a PSO or SIO

Section 9(5)(a) of the Children Act 1989 states that neither a PSO nor an SIO can be made 'with a view to achieving a result which could be achieved by making a child arrangements order'.[35] The real significance of this restriction relates to local authorities: they can apply for specific issue orders or prohibited steps orders, but cannot apply for child arrangements orders.

(iv) A section 8 order cannot be made if the High Court would not be able to make the order acting under the inherent jurisdiction

The practical effect of this restriction is that a local authority is prevented from accommodating the child or obtaining the care or supervision of a child through a specific issue order.[36] If the local authority wishes to accommodate, care for or supervise a child, they must use its powers under the Children Act 1989, Part III, rather than use section 8 orders.

(v) The courts will not normally make a PSO or SIO in relation to trivial matters

In *Re C (A Minor) (Leave to Seek Section 8 Order)*[37] Johnson J refused to give leave to apply for an SIO permitting a child to go on holiday to Bulgaria with her friend's family against her parents' wishes. This was held to be too trivial an issue to be suitable for a section 8 order. If going on holiday is too trivial an issue for an SIO, many other questions that may concern a child or non-residential parent (such as whether the child has to eat green vegetables) can also be seen as too trivial.[38] However, there is nothing in the wording of the statute to suggest that section 8 orders should not deal with what might appear to be trivial matters. A court might feel it is appropriate to deal with a 'trivial issue' (for example, what hairstyle the child should have)[39] if the issue has come to dominate the parents' and child's relationship to such an extent that it is harming the child.[40] So the better view is that SIOs or PSOs can be made in relation to trivial issues, but only rarely will it be appropriate to do so.

---

[32] *Re D (Prohibited Steps Order)* [1996] 2 FLR 273, [1996] 2 FCR 496 CA; *Re D (Residence: Imposition of Conditions)* [1996] 2 FLR 281, [1996] 2 FCR 820.

[33] See Chapter 7.

[34] [1995] 1 FLR 638, [1995] 2 FCR 547.

[35] *Re B (Minors) (Residence Order)* [1992] 2 FLR 1, [1992] 1 FCR 555.

[36] See Harding and Newnham (2016) for a discussion of the use by local authorities of section 8 orders.

[37] [1994] 1 FLR 26.

[38] *Re C (A Minor) (Leave to Seek Section 8 Order)* [1994] 1 FLR 26.

[39] E.g. what time the child should go to bed: *B v B (Custody: Conditions)* [1979] 1 FLR 385.

[40] *M v M (Specific Issue: Choice of School)* [2005] EWHC 2769 (Fam).

(vi) The orders must be in precise terms

A prohibited steps or specific issue order must be in clear terms. An order prohibiting the publishing of 'any information' about two children was found to be in too general terms and restricted by the Court of Appeal to information that identified the children.[41] Similarly in *Re A and B (Prohibited Steps Order at Dispute Resolution Appointment)*[42] the father (a UKIP candidate) was prohibited in involving his children in political activities. The order was over-turned on appeal because it was too imprecise.

(vii) Only residence orders are available if the child is in care

Under s. 9(1) of the Children Act 1989 the only section 8 order that can be applied for if a child is in care is a CAO.[43] The reasoning is that the local authority, rather than the court, should make decisions relating to the upbringing of a child in care.[44] In *Re SL (Permission to Vaccinate)*[45] the court were willing to use the inherent jurisdiction[46] to authorise the vaccination of children in care, as the local authority could not use a section 8 order.

(viii) There may be restrictions on section 8 orders where the child has capacity

There is some dispute over whether a PSO can overrule the decision of a child who has capacity to make it. For example, if a mature child and doctor agree on a form of contraception, could a court make a PSO to prevent the doctor providing the contraception? One view is that the PSO can only prevent an exercise of parental responsibility. As a parent cannot overrule the consent of a competent child to such treatment, neither can a PSO.[47] The opposite view is that the PSO can overrule the wishes of a competent minor because the definition of a PSO in s. 8(1) refers to the decision that 'a' parent, rather than 'the' parent, could make. The best view of the present law is that the court is unlikely to make a section 8 order against the wishes of a competent child, but it is open to the court to do so if necessary for the child's welfare. Even if this view were not taken, it would still be open to the court to overrule the child's wishes through the use of the inherent jurisdiction.

(ix) The order must not unjustifiably interfere with a parent's rights

In *Re A and B (Prohibited Steps Order at Dispute Resolution Appointment)*[48] a PSO that stopped a UKIP candidate involving his children in political activities was said to breach the father's ECHR Article 8 rights. It was held that such an order could be made, but the court would need to explain that the harm to the children was sufficiently seriously to justify the interference in the parent's rights.

(x) Exceptionally CAO orders can be anticipatory

In rare cases it is possible to use conditions to make 'anticipatory orders'. In *L v L (Anticipatory Child Arrangements Order)*[49] an order was made setting out what would happen when a child left hospital because it was important for the family to have certainty as to the future

---

[41] *Re G (A Child) (Contempt: Committal Order)* [2003] 2 FCR 231.
[42] [2015] EWFC 816.
[43] *Re A and D (Local Authority: Religious Upbringing)* [2010] EWHC 2503 (Fam).
[44] See Chapter 11 for further discussion.
[45] [2017] EWHC 125 (Fam).
[46] See below, 'Wardship and the inherent jurisdiction'.
[47] *Gillick v W Norfolk and Wisbech AHA* [1986] 1 FLR 229, [1986] AC 112.
[48] [2015] EWFC 816.
[49] [2017] EWHC 1212 (Fam).

arrangements. Normally, however, a court will be reluctant to make orders based on hypothetical future happenings.

E Attaching conditions

When making any order under s. 8, the court can attach conditions to the order. This power enables the court to 'fine-tune' the order. The conditions can give detailed arrangements as to how the order should be carried out. For example, there may be conditions stating where the contact is to take place. A fine example is a case recorded by Annika Newnham and Maebh Harding[50] that a child be polite and not wear their headphones when having a contact session with the father. I can imagine quite a few parents being keen on such a legal obligation for their own children![51] There is a fine balance here between encouraging the parties to be flexible and resolving minor issues between themselves, and making the order sufficiently detailed that it is clear what is required. Section 11(7) provides that an order under s. 8 can:

LEGISLATIVE PROVISION

Children Act 1989, section 11(7)

(a) contain directions about how it is to be carried into effect;

(b) impose conditions which must be complied with by any person—

    (i) in whose favour the order is made;

    (ii) who is a parent of the child concerned;

    (iii) who is not a parent of his but who has parental responsibility for him; or

    (iv) with whom the child is living, and to whom the conditions are expressed to apply;

(c) be made to have effect for a specified period, or contain provisions which are to have effect for a specified period;

(d) make such incidental, supplemental or consequential provision as the court thinks fit.

The power to attach conditions is not as wide as it might at first appear, and the courts have developed a number of restrictions on the use of the power:

1. Conditions are intended to be supplemental to the section 8 order and should not be used as the primary purpose of the order.[52] Hence, a Jewish wife failed in an application for a condition to be attached to a contact order that a husband provided her with a *get* so that she could obtain a religious divorce. It was held that this condition would not be appropriate as it was not supplemental to a contact order and was raising a completely new issue.[53]

2. The condition must not be incompatible with the main order. In ***Birmingham CC v H***[54] Ward J said that a residence order could not contain a condition that the mother had to live at a specialised unit for mothers and children and comply with reasonable instructions from the staff at the unit. The court explained that the basis of a residence order is that the person

---

[50] Newnham and Harding (2016).
[51] Oddly the obligation was put on the mother to ensure that it happened.
[52] *Re D (Prohibited Steps Order)* [1996] 2 FLR 273, [1996] 2 FCR 496.
[53] *N v N (Jurisdiction: Pre-Nuptial Agreement)* [1999] 2 FLR 745.
[54] [1992] 2 FLR 323.

with the benefit of the order can choose where the child should live and how to raise the child; the condition was inconsistent with both of these.

3. The condition cannot affect the fundamental rights of a parent. In **Re D (Residence: Imposition of Conditions)**[55] children were returned to the mother under a residence order with a condition that the children should not be brought into contact with her partner and that her partner should not reside with her and the children. The Court of Appeal allowed an appeal against the imposition of the condition. Ward LJ explained that:

> ... the case concerned a mother seeking, as she was entitled to, to allow this man back into her life because that is the way she wished to live it. The court was not in a position so to override her right to live her life as she chose. What was before the court was whether, if she chose to have him back, the proper person with whom the children should reside was herself or whether it would be better for the children that they lived with their father or with the grandmother.

In other words, the court should not use conditions attached to residence orders to 'perfect' a parent. Instead, in deciding who should have a residence order, the court should choose between the parents as they are. However, in **BB v CC**[56] Moor J approved of a condition that a mother move to the South East of England so that a 'shared residency' arrangement could succeed. In **Re M (A Child)**[57] the Court of Appeal had suggested that only in exceptional cases might such a condition be appropriate.

4. The condition cannot be used as a back-door route to obtaining an order that is available under other pieces of legislation. So, in **D v N (Contact Order: Conditions)**[58] the Court of Appeal stated that it was inappropriate to use conditions to prevent the father molesting the mother, as such an order was available under the Family Law Act 1996.

5. The condition must be enforceable. In **B v B (Custody: Conditions)**[59] a condition that the child be in bed before 6.30 pm was struck out. There was no way that the court could realistically enforce such an order. For the same reason, in **Re C (A Child) (HIV Test)**[60] the Court of Appeal agreed that it would be inappropriate to order a mother not to breastfeed her child.

6. There is no power to use conditions to interfere with the local authority's exercise of its statutory or common law powers. So, a condition cannot be used to require a local authority to supervise contact[61] or to exercise its powers in a particular way.[62]

3 Who can apply for section 8 orders?

Learning objective 2

Describe who can apply for section 8 orders

When considering who can apply for section 8 orders it is necessary to distinguish two separate groups of applicants: those who have the automatic right to apply for a section 8 order, and those who have the right to apply only if the court grants leave. The detailed law will be discussed shortly but, generally, those who

---

[55] [1996] 2 FCR 820 at p. 825.
[56] [2018] EWFC B78.
[57] [2014] EWCA Civ 1755.
[58] [1997] 2 FLR 797, [1997] 3 FCR 721.
[59] [1979] 1 FLR 385.
[60] [1999] 2 FLR 1004. For criticism of this decision see Strong (2000).
[61] *Leeds CC v C* [1993] 1 FLR 269, [1993] 1 FCR 585.
[62] *D v D (County Court Jurisdiction: Injunctions)* [1993] 2 FLR 802, [1994] 3 FCR 28.

have a very close link with the child can automatically apply for a section 8 order. Anyone else must first seek the leave of the court to bring the application. Only if the court thinks there is an issue which requires a full hearing will it give leave for the application to be heard. If it thinks the application is frivolous or mischievous, the court will refuse to grant leave. The law in this area is seeking to strike a balance between making the court accessible to all those who have legitimate concerns about the upbringing of children, and protecting those who care for children from the stress of facing challenges to their parenting in the courts. The requirement for leave enables the court to filter out applications that the court thinks are inappropriate, without causing the residential parent the expense and stress of preparing a defence and attending the hearing.

A Persons who can apply without leave

Those who can apply for any section 8 order without leave of the court are:

1. Parents. This includes an unmarried father without parental responsibility. It does not include former parents, for example those whose children have been freed for adoption.

2. Anyone who has parental responsibility for the child.[63]

3. Guardians or special guardians.

4. '[A]ny person who is named, in a child arrangements order that is in force with respect to the child, and person with whom the child is to live'.

There is a special category of people who can apply without leave only for a CAO. They are:

1. Any party to a marriage[64] or civil partnership if the child has been treated by the applicant as a 'child of the family'.[65] This includes step-parents.

2. Any person with whom the child has lived for at least three years.

3. A relative or foster carer with whom the child has lived for at least one year.[66]

4. Any person who has the consent of:

    (a) each of the persons in whose favour a CAO is in force directing the child live with them; or

    (b) the local authority, if the child is subject to a care order; or

    (c) in any other case, each of the people who have parental responsibility for the child.[67]

5. Any person who has parental responsibility for a child by virtue of a CAO.

The explanation seems to be that the listed people have a sufficiently close relationship with the child to have a say in where the child should live (particularly where the parents have become incapable of caring for the child), but they do not have a right to have a say in the details of how the parent should bring up the child.

---

[63] *M v C and Calderdale MBC* [1993] 1 FLR 505, [1993] 1 FCR 431.
[64] Even if the marriage has been dissolved.
[65] CA 1989, s. 10(5)(a).
[66] CA 1989, s. 10(5B). The period need not be continuous but needs to have started more than five years before the application and be subsisting three months before the making of the application
[67] CA 1989, s. 10(5)(b).

B People who need the leave of the court

Anyone else can apply for a section 8 order once they have obtained the leave of the court. This includes the child themselves. The one exception to this is local authority foster carers, who must have the consent of the local authority to apply for a section 8 order unless they are related to the child or the child has been living with them for at least three years preceding the application.[68]

C How the court decides whether to grant leave

If it is necessary to obtain the leave of the court, the factors that the court will take into account in deciding whether to give leave depend on whether the applicant is an adult or a child.

(i) Adults seeking leave

The factors to be considered are listed in s. 10(9) of the Children Act 1989:[69]

LEGISLATIVE PROVISION

Children Act 1989, section 10(9)

(a) the nature of the proposed application for the section 8 order;

(b) the applicant's connection with the child;

(c) any risk there might be of that proposed application disrupting the child's life to such an extent that he would be harmed by it; and

(d) where the child is being looked after by a local authority—

    (i) the authority's plans for the child's future; and

    (ii) the wishes and feelings of the child's parents.

In *Re A (Minors) (Residence Orders: Leave to Apply)*[70] the Court of Appeal held that the paramountcy principle under s. 1(1) of the Children Act 1989 does not apply when considering whether to grant leave.[71] This is because the question of leave does not itself involve an issue relating to the child's upbringing. The court can consider factors that are not listed in s. 10(9), most notably the child's wishes.[72]

In deciding whether or not to grant leave, the courts must now take account of the applicant's rights under Articles 6 and 8 of the European Convention.[73] This suggests that only where the application is thought frivolous, vexatious or otherwise harmful to the child will

---

[68] CA 1989, s. 9(3).

[69] These do not apply to an application for leave following a s. 91(14) application: *Re A (Application for Leave)* [1998] 1 FLR 1, [1999] 1 FCR 127.

[70] [1992] 2 FLR 154, [1992] 2 FCR 174.

[71] Confirmed in *Re G; Re Z (Children: Sperm Donors: Leave to Apply for Children Act Orders)* [2013] EWHC 134 (Fam).

[72] *Re A (A Minor) (Residence Order: Leave To Apply)* [1993] 1 FLR 425, [1993] 1 FCR 870.

[73] *Re B (Paternal Grandfather: Joinder as Party)* [2012] EWCA Civ 737; *Re J (Leave to Issue Application for Residence Order)* [2003] 1 FLR 114.

leave not be granted.[74] There is no need to show that the applicant has 'a good arguable case' before being granted leave.[75] Special considerations apply if the application concerns a child in care (see Chapter 11).

It is clear that if leave is granted there is no presumption that the application will succeed at the full hearing.[76]

(ii) Children seeking leave

This was discussed earlier in the text (Chapter 9).

(iii) Applying for section 8 orders in favour of someone else

It is not clear whether it is possible to apply for a section 8 order on behalf of someone else, although, as there is no statutory bar, it is presumably possible. Certainly, an adult can apply for leave on behalf of a child.[77] It also seems that a child can apply for leave for a CAO in favour of someone else.[78] There is some debate over whether a local authority can apply for a CAO in favour of a third party. Such an application would fail if it were thought that a local authority was seeking to circumvent the prohibition on a local authority to apply for a residence or contact order themselves.

(iv) Court acting on its own initiative

Under s. 10(1)(b) the court can make an order in someone's favour, even though they have not applied for it. That, of course, will be rare. In **Re G (A Child)**[79] a man who had donated sperm to a same-sex couple to produce a child had sought an order for contact. This was granted, but the court also made an order in favour of the man's parents (the child's biological grandparents), even though they had not applied for such an order. That order was justified on the basis it would ensure the child had a full understanding of their background.

D Restricting section 8 applications: section 91(14)

One parent may be intent on pursuing applications against the other out of bitterness or desperation. For example, a non-residential parent may constantly apply to the court for SIOs relating to tiny aspects of the child's upbringing.[80] Repeated fruitless applications to the court could cause severe distress to the child and their carer, not least because each application must be defended in court.[81] In **Re G (Children) (Intractable dispute)**[82] in less than four years the father had made 56 'incessant' applications and there had been 30 hearings. In order to restrict such applications, the court under s. 91(14) can require a party to obtain the leave of the court before applying for any further orders.[83] This way the child and their carer will not be bothered

---

[74] *Re M (Care: Contact: Grandmother's Application for Leave)* [1995] 2 FLR 86, [1995] 3 FCR 550.
[75] *Re J (Leave to Issue Application for Residence Order)* [2003] 1 FLR 114.
[76] *Re W (Contact: Application by Grandmother)* [1997] 1 FLR 793, [1997] 2 FCR 643.
[77] There may be financial reasons for doing this, as the child may then be able to obtain legal aid: *Re HG (Specific Issue Order: Sterilisation)* [1993] 1 FLR 587, [1993] 1 FCR 553.
[78] So, a child cannot apply for a residence order that he or she live by him- or herself.
[79] [2018] EWCA Civ 305.
[80] *Re N (Section 91(14) Order)* [1996] 1 FLR 356.
[81] *C v W (Contact: Leave to Apply)* [1999] 1 FLR 916. A resident parent improperly objecting to contact can also be ordered to pay costs: *Re T (A Child) (Orders for Costs)* [2005] 1 FCR 625.
[82] [2019] EWCA 548.
[83] The order can be made even if the child is in care: *Re J (A Child) (Restrictions on Applications)* [2007] 3 FCR 123.

by having to defend an application unless the court has considered it worthy of a full hearing and granted leave. In *Re N (Section 91(14))*[84] a s. 91(14) order against both parents was said to be required because the parties had been litigating for five years, causing the child serious anxiety and stress. A court can make a s. 91(14) order whenever it disposes of an application for any order under the Children Act 1989. It is possible under the subsection to restrict only a certain kind of application: for example, applications for a residence order.[85]

A s. 91(14) order is appropriate only where there is evidence that future applications are likely to be unreasonable, vexatious, or frivolous.[86] In deciding whether or not to make an order under s. 91(14), the court should keep in mind, *inter alia*, the following factors:[87]

1. The welfare of the child is the paramount consideration.[88]

2. It is a draconian[89] order which should be used sparingly[90] and only as a last resort.[91]

3. The court should weigh up the child's interests in being protected from inappropriate applications with the fundamental right of access to the courts: *Re R (Residence: Contact: Restricting Applications)*.[92]

4. The order is appropriate if there have been repeated and unreasonable applications,[93] or there is clear evidence there will be.[94]

5. The order should be limited to last only as long as it is necessary.[95] In *Re B (A Child)*[96] the Court of Appeal suggested that to make a s. 91(14) order that would last for the whole of the child's minority was a disproportionate infringement of the father's rights, given that the father had never sought to misuse court proceedings. It was held that the order should last only two years.[97] By contrast, in *PM v CF (Section 91(14) Order: Risk to Mother and Children)*[98] an order for the whole of the child's minority was appropriate as the father posed a significant risk of harm or death to the mother and children.

If a s. 91(14) order is made against a party, they can still apply for leave to make an application. The important point is that the hearing for leave will not require the attendance of the residential parent; indeed, they need not even know of the application.[99] This protects the

---

[84] [2010] 1 FLR 1110A

[85] A s. 91(14) order cannot be made in relation to a child in care: *Re M (Education: Section 91(14) Order)* [2008] 2 FLR 404.

[86] *F v Kent CC* [1993] 1 FLR 432, [1992] 2 FCR 433.

[87] A complete list of relevant factors is listed in *Re P (Section 91(14) Guidelines) (Residence and Religious Heritage)* [1999] 2 FLR 573.

[88] *Re M (Section 91(14) Order)* [1999] 2 FLR 553.

[89] Butler-Sloss P in *Re G (A Child) (Contempt: Committal Order)* [2003] 2 FCR 231.

[90] *Re N (Children)* [2019] EWCA Civ 903.

[91] *Re C-J (Section 91(14) Order)* [2006] EWHC 1491 (Fam).

[92] [1998] 1 FLR 749.

[93] *Re M (Section 91(14) Order)* [2012] EWCA Civ 446.

[94] *Re C (Contact: No Order for Contact)* [2000] Fam Law 699, [2000] 2 FLR 723.

[95] The order infringes a party's human right of access to the courts and so must be proportionate: *Re P (Section 91(14) Guidelines) (Residence and Religious Heritage)* [1999] 2 FLR 573.

[96] [2003] EWCA Civ 1966.

[97] Although see *Re H (A Child)* [2011] EWCA Civ 1773 where in the exceptional circumstances of the case a s. 91(14) order was made without time limit.

[98] [2018] EWHC 2658 (Fam).

[99] In *Re G and M (Child Orders: Restricting Applications)* [1995] 2 FLR 416 it was expressly ordered that the mother should not be informed of applications for leave. However, if there is no such specific order the other party should be told that leave has been sought: *Re P & N (s 91(14): application for permission to apply: appeal)* [2019] EWHC 421 (Fam).

residential parent or children from the worry that such applications may cause.[100] If an application for leave is made, the test in deciding whether to grant leave is whether the application for leave demonstrates a need for renewed investigation by the court[101] and whether the application has a realistic chance of success.[102]

4 Children's welfare on divorce and relationship breakdown

We will now consider the evidence of child psychologists that children suffer on the breakdown of their parents' relationship, and how the law responds to this. It is widely accepted that, statistically, children whose parents separate are more likely to suffer in various ways than those whose parents stay together.[103] As one of the leading experts in the field, Martin Richards, has stated:[104]

> Compared with those of similar social backgrounds whose parents remain married, children whose parents divorce show consistent, but small differences in their behaviour throughout childhood and adolescence and a somewhat different life course as they move into adulthood. More specifically, the research indicates on average lower levels of academic achievement and self-esteem and a higher incidence of bad conduct and other problems of psychological adjustment during childhood. Also during childhood a somewhat earlier social maturity has been recorded. A number of transitions to adulthood are typically reached at earlier ages; these include leaving home, beginning heterosexual relationships and entering cohabitation, marriage and child bearing. In young adulthood there is a tendency toward more changes of job, lower socio-economic status, a greater propensity to divorce and there are some indications of a higher frequency of depression and lower measures of psychological well-being. The relationship (in adulthood) with parents and other kin relationships may be more distant.

It is important to appreciate what is *not* being claimed here. Clearly not all children whose parents separate suffer in these ways and some children whose parents do not separate do suffer in these ways. The point is merely that, on average, children whose parents separate are slightly more likely to suffer these harms than those whose parents have not separated. In fact, only a minority of children whose parents separate suffer in these ways,[105] although they appear to be twice as likely to do so as children whose parents stay together.[106] It should also be stressed that although children whose parents have separated can suffer in these various ways, it does not necessarily follow that this is because their parents have separated. It may not be the separation that causes these problems, but the earlier tensions in the marital relationship;[107] or poverty connected to relationship breakdown; or society's reaction to separated families, although there is some evidence that the quality of parenting declines immediately following a divorce as the parents come to terms with lone parenthood.[108] Further, the research does not support the view that parents should 'stay together for the sake of the children'. Indeed, evidence suggests that children brought up in continually warring families do even

---

[100] *Re S-B (Children)* [2015] EWCA Civ 705.
[101] *Re A (Application for Leave)* [1998] 1 FLR 1, [1999] 1 FCR 127.
[102] *Re ED (A Child) (s 91(14))* [2020] EWHC 881.
[103] Coleman and Glenn (2010b).
[104] Richards (1997: 543).
[105] Coleman and Glenn (2010b).
[106] Rogers and Pryor (1998).
[107] Kelly (2003). Notably, children who experience the death of a parent do not suffer in these ways to the same extent as children whose parents have divorced.
[108] Rogers and Pryor (1998).

less well than children whose parents separate.[109] There is also clear evidence that family breakdown affects the health of the parents.[110]

There do seem to be some factors that are particularly linked to the problems children suffer on their parents' divorce, namely: poverty before or after the separation; conflict before, during or after the separation;[111] a parent's psychological distress; multiple changes in family structures;[112] and a lack of high-quality contact with the non-residential parent.[113] Richards[114] suggests that there are steps that can be taken to lessen the harm caused to children on divorce. He argues that society should seek to encourage the maintenance of ties with both parents and kin; ensure adequacy of income for the child; reduce conflict over children involved; provide emotional support for parents; and limit the need for the child to move house or school.[115] As will be seen, these aims are pursued by the law only to a limited extent. There is also ample evidence that listening to children and keeping them informed during the separation process is important to their welfare.[116]

5 How the court obtains information on the child's welfare

Obviously, not all children are alike and the arrangements which might promote one child's welfare will not benefit another.[117] Therefore, the court needs to consider the position of each child before it as an individual. In deciding what is in the interests of the child's welfare the judge does not rely on his or her own instincts, but seeks expert advice. Although the parties themselves are free to call witnesses to support their case, the court often needs independent evidence about a child and may seek a report, known as a welfare report.[118] The report is not requested in every case, but only when there is no realistic possibility that the parties can be persuaded to mediate the dispute.

These reports are normally prepared for the court by an appointed social worker, a family court adviser or other expert.[119] The report considers issues over which there is dispute; the options that are available to the court; and, if appropriate, recommends a course of action. In preparing the report, the reporter should interview each party as well as the child. Normally, quite a number of visits will be needed. The importance placed on the report means that great care should be taken in its preparation.[120] Often the report will be highly influential on the eventual outcome of the case, although it would be wrong to think that the court must follow the welfare report.[121] If the judge is minded to depart from the report, he or she should obtain oral evidence from the reporter.[122] The welfare report often records the child's wishes. However, there is increasing recognition of the desirability to the court of hearing the child's voice directly.[123] If necessary, the judge can interview the child in private to protect them from the

---

[109] Eekelaar and Maclean (1997: 53–7).
[110] Coleman and Glenn (2010b).
[111] Wild and Richards (2003).
[112] E.g. living with a parent who has a number of partners during the child's minority.
[113] Rogers and Pryor (1998); Hawthorne *et al.* (2003).
[114] Richards (1994).
[115] See also Richards and Connell (2000); Parkinson (2011).
[116] Rogers and Pryor (1998).
[117] Smart, Neale and Wade (2001: 166).
[118] CA 1989, s. 7(1).
[119] CAFCASS (2008) discusses proposed reforms of CAFCASS.
[120] *Re P (A Minor) (Inadequate Welfare Report)* [1996] 2 FCR 285.
[121] *Re P (A Minor) (Inadequate Welfare Report)* [1996] 2 FCR 285.
[122] *Re CB (Access: Court Welfare Reports)* [1995] 1 FLR 622.
[123] Indeed, this is required under Article 12(1) of the UN Convention on the Rights of the Child. See further, e.g., in Smart and Neale (2000).

ordeal of appearing in court.[124] The judge is more likely to interview a child in order to determine what order will best promote their welfare, than to determine what happened in the past.[125] If the judge does this they must be careful not to move beyond the role of asking questions to find out the views of the child and stray into the area of trying to influence the child.[126]

There has been a growing interest in the right of children to express their views in any court case concerning their upbringing.[127] However, in *Re P-S*[128] it was held that Article 12 of the United Nations Convention on the Rights of the Child 1989 and the European Convention on Children's Rights 1996 does not give a child a right to be personally heard in a court case, as long as their views are presented.[129] In difficult cases it may be appropriate for the child to be separately represented by his or her own counsel, but rarely is there funding for that.[130] There are, however, concerns that in problematic cases there may be difficulties in listening to children. Children may not be used to being listened to by adults and find it disturbing talking to professionals.[131] One report on children's experiences of professionals depressingly concluded: 'Professionals may be perceived as inflexible, intrusive, condescending, deceitful and reinforcing in a myriad of ways their superiority to the child.'[132] Another research team found that children wanted a conversation with their parents about the separation, rather than being asked for a formal expression of their views.[133] A disturbing account of the way children's wishes were used by professionals and couples seeking to negotiate a settlement and thereby avoid a court hearing, showed that children's views were used as tools in the negotiation, rather than being the starting point of the discussion.[134]

In *F-D v CAFCASS*[135] a father sought to sue CAFCASS in tort. He claimed CAFCASS had been negligent in preparing a report in connection with a dispute over contact. He failed before Judge Bidder QC on the basis that it would not be just or reasonable to impose a duty of care on CAFCASS towards the father. In any event it was found there had been no negligence. Whether a claim brought by a child would have more success is an issue which will, no doubt, be decided another day.

6 How the court decides what is in the welfare of the child: the statutory checklist

Learning objective 3

Explain and evaluate how the court interprets the welfare principle

When considering applications under section 8, the court must take into account the checklist of factors in s. 1(3), in deciding what is in the welfare of the child.[136] The court is required to

---

[124] *Re R (A Minor) (Residence: Religion)* [1993] 2 FLR 163, [1993] 2 FCR 525.

[125] *Re A (Fact-Finding Hearing: Judge Meeting with Child)* [2012] EWCA Civ 185.

[126] *Re KP (A Child)* [2014] EWCA Civ 554.

[127] Caldwell (2011); Lowe and Murch (2003); Murch (2003).

[128] [2013] EWCA Civ 223.

[129] To which the UK is not a signatory.

[130] *Re C (Contact: Evidence)* [2011] EWCA Civ 261; *Re A (A Child) (Separate Representation in Contact Proceedings)* [2001] 2 FCR 55.

[131] Lowe and Murch (2003: 18–19).

[132] Neale and Smart (1999: 33).

[133] Smart, Neale and Wade (2001: 169).

[134] Trinder, Firth and Jenks (2010).

[135] [2014] EWHC 1619 (QB).

[136] CA 1989, s. 1(4).

consider all the different factors and weigh them in the balance, although the court can also take into account other factors not mentioned in the list.[137]

There are contrasting attitudes towards the checklist among the judiciary. Waite LJ in *Southwood LBC v B*[138] referred to the checklist as an *aide-mémoire*. To Staughton LJ in *H v H (Residence Order: Leave to Remove from the Jurisdiction)*[139] the checklist was not 'like the list of checks which an airline pilot has to make with his co-pilot, aloud one to the other before he takes off'. By contrast, *B v B (Residence Order: Reasons for Decisions)*[140] described going through the individual items on the checklist as a good discipline. Baroness Hale in *Re G (Children) (Residence: Same-Sex Partner)*[141] suggested that in difficult cases it would be helpful to consider each item on the checklist. This suggests that the exact use of the checklist differs from judge to judge. What is clear is that if it can be shown that a judge failed to take into account one of the factors on the checklist which was relevant to the case in hand, then the decision would be liable to be overturned on appeal.[142]

A The various factors

The various factors listed in s. 1(3) will now be considered.

(i) The ascertainable wishes and feelings of the child concerned (considered in the light of his age and understanding) (s. 1(3)(a) CA 1989)

The child's wishes are only one of the factors to be taken into account, but where the child is mature it is likely to be the most important factor.[143] In *Re R (A Child) (Residence Order: Treatment of Child's Wishes)*[144] the Court of Appeal criticised a judge who failed to attach sufficient weight to the views of a child aged 10. In deciding whether a child's views should be taken into account the court will consider whether the child is competent.[145] 'Full and generous' weight should be given to a mature child's wishes.[146] In *L v L (Anticipatory Child Arrangements Order)* MacDonald J explained:

> . . . the wishes and feelings of a mature child do not carry any presumption of precedence over any other factors in the welfare checklist . . . The child's preference is only one factor in the case and the court is not bound to follow it . . . on the face of it, the older the child the more influential will be his or her views in the decision-making process. However, in the end the decision is that of the court and not of the child . . . Where adherence to the wishes of an older child may seriously compromise their long-term welfare, the court may override those views.[147]

In *Re LC*,[148] a Supreme Court decision considering the habitual residence of a child, the views of 'adolescents' (a term not defined) had to be taken into account, but not, the majority held, younger children.

---

[137] Baroness Hale in *Re G (Children) (Residence: Same-Sex Partner)* [2006] UKHL 43 at para 40.
[138] [1993] 2 FLR 559 at p. 573.
[139] [1995] 1 FLR 529 at p. 532.
[140] [1997] 2 FLR 602.
[141] [2006] UKHL 43 at para 40.
[142] *Re H (Contact Order)* [2010] EWCA Civ 448.
[143] *B v B (M v M) (Transfer of Custody: Appeal)* [1987] 2 FLR 146; *Re T (Abduction: Child's Objections to Return)* [2000] 2 FLR 193. UN Convention on the Rights of the Child, Article 12, requires the court to give due weight to children's views in accordance with their age and maturity; discussed in Parkes (2009).
[144] [2009] 2 FCR 572.
[145] *Re S (Change of Surname)* [1999] 1 FLR 672.
[146] *Re H (Residence Order: Child's Application for Leave)* [2000] 1 FLR 780.
[147] [2017] EWHC 1212 (Fam) at paras 42–43.
[148] [2014] UKSC 1, discussed in Gilmore and Herring (2014).

Sturge and Glaser, two leading psychologists, suggest that the wishes of children under the age of six should be regarded as indistinguishable from the wishes of the main carer, and the wishes of children over 10 should carry considerable weight, while those between six and 10 are at an intermediate state.[149] However the courts tend to focus on the ability of the particular child rather than their age.

Baroness Hale has explained why she regards hearing the views of children as important:

> . . . there is now a growing understanding of the importance of listening to the children involved in children's cases. It is the child, more than anyone else, who will have to live with what the court decides. Those who do listen to children understand that they often have a point of view which is quite distinct from that of the person looking after them. They are quite capable of being moral actors in their own right. Just as the adults may have to do what the court decides whether they like it or not, so may the child. But that is no more a reason for failing to hear what the child has to say than it is for refusing to hear the parents' views.[150]

Even if a judge believes the child to be mistaken, it may still be appropriate to follow the child's views. There are two reasons why a judge may do this. First, there are practical considerations. If a teenager insists on not living with or visiting a particular parent, the child may simply ignore any court order awarding residence to that parent.[151] There will be little point in making an order that the child will simply disobey.[152] In *Re H (Residence)*,[153] for example, a girl who was nearly 12 threatened to take her own life if she was not permitted to live with her father. The strength of her views was such that it would be impractical to force her to live with her mother.

Secondly, it may damage a child psychologically to ignore his or her wishes. As Butler-Sloss LJ has argued:[154] 'nobody should dictate to children of this age, because one is dealing with their emotions, their lives, and they are not packages to be moved around. They are people entitled to be treated with respect.' In *Re JS (Disposal of Body)*[155] where a seriously ill 14-year-old girl wanted her body cryogenically preserved on her death, although the judge declined to express a view on such a procedure, he was persuaded to make an order authorising the mother to make the preparation to avoid distress in the days leading up to her death. That is not to say that the wishes of a mature minor can never be overridden, because the welfare principle is always the paramount criterion.[156]

When the court considers the views of the child, it will have regard to the following factors:

1. The maturity of the child. In *AS v CPW*[157] Mostyn J held that 'the wishes of a Gillick-competent child on a particular issue, where they are not objectively foolish or unreasonable, should normally be given effect.' In *Re B (Minors) (Change of Surname)*[158] it was held that it would be exceptional for a court to make orders contrary to the wishes of a teenager.[159] In *S v S (Relocation)*[160] in relation to the views of children aged 13 and 15 about wishing to move to Switzerland to live with their father, Jackson J stated:

---

[149] Sturge and Glaser (2000: 624). See also Parkinson and Cashmore (2010).
[150] *Re D (A Child) (Abduction: Rights of Custody)* [2007] 1 AC 619. See also her similar comments in *Re LC* [2014] UKSC 1.
[151] *Re G (Children: Intractable Dispute)* [2019] EWCA Civ 548.
[152] *Re H (Residence)* [2011] EWCA Civ 762.
[153] [2011] EWCA Civ 762.
[154] *Re S (Minors) (Access: Religious Upbringing)* [1992] 2 FLR 313 at p. 321.
[155] [2016] EWHC 2859 (Fam).
[156] *Re P (A Minor) (Education)* [1992] 1 FLR 316, [1992] FCR 145.
[157] [2020] EWFC 1238 (Fam).
[158] [1996] 1 FLR 791, [1996] 2 FCR 304.
[159] See also *Re M (Intractable Contact Dispute: Court's Positive Duty)* [2006] 1 FLR 627; *Re C (Older Children: Relocation)* [2015] EWCA Civ 1298.
[160] [2017] EWHC 2345 (Fam).

At their age, those wishes and feelings are a very important element in their welfare. That is so even if the wishes and feelings are unwise. There is nothing in the law that says that the wishes and feelings of older children should be wise or reasonable. They may be foolish or immature but respecting children's points of view must, in the case of older children, accept to some extent the risk of them making mistakes. Unless the consequences of mistaken choices are profoundly harmful, the court cannot protect older children from every mistake that they may make.

2. The importance of the issue is clearly relevant. The more important the issue, the more willing the court may be to overrule the wishes of a child. For example, if the child refuses to consent to medical treatment which would save his or her life, the court will readily override the child's decision.[161]

3. The courts are also concerned with the possibility that an adult may heavily influence the views of the child.[162] So before attaching weight to the child's views, the court will try to ensure that they truly are the views of the child and they are not simply repeating what they have been told by one of their parents.[163] In *Puxty v Moore*[164] Thorpe LJ, when considering the fact that a nine-and-a-half-year-old girl wanted to live with her mother, noted she was influenced by the fact her mother had bought her a pony. In *Re M (Intractable Contact Dispute: Court's Positive Duty)*[165] the opposition of a 15-year-old girl and 13-year-old boy to contact with their mother was not given great weight because 'their understanding in this case is corrupted by the malignancy of the views, with which they have been force-fed [by the father] over many years of their life, until so blinded by them that they cannot see the truth either of their mother's good qualities or of the good it will do them to have some contact with her'.

4. There is some psychological evidence that requiring children to choose between parents is very harmful.[166] The court will readily be prepared to accept that the child has no wishes in such cases. Interestingly, in one study only 55 per cent of children interviewed said they would like to have been asked whether they would prefer to live with their mother or father after the separation of their parents.[167] However, in other cases children will have views that they want to be heard.[168]

5. The court will wish to examine the basis of the child's views. In *Re M (A Minor) (Family Proceedings: Affidavits)*[169] the wishes of a 12-year-old girl to live with her father were over-ridden because her decision was based on occasional visits to her father while she lived with her grandparents. It was felt that her occasional visits did not give her a clear view of what life with her father would be like.[170] The case indicates that where a child has a strong view based on factual error, the court will readily override that view. The courts have also expressed a concern that children may put undue weight on short-term gains and not take a long-term view of their welfare.[171]

---

[161] *Re M (Medical Treatment: Consent)* [1999] 2 FLR 1097.
[162] *Re S (Transfer of Residence)* [2010] 1 FLR 1785; *EY v RZ (Family Proceedings)* [2013] EWHC 4403 (Fam); *Re N-A (Children)* [2017] EWCA Civ 230.
[163] *Re A (Letter to a Young Person)* [2017] EWFC 48.
[164] [2005] EWCA Civ 1386.
[165] [2006] 1 FLR 627 at para 26.
[166] *Re A (Specific Issue Order: Parental Dispute)* [2001] 1 FLR 121.
[167] Douglas *et al.* (2001).
[168] Holt (2018).
[169] [1995] 2 FLR 100, [1995] 2 FCR 90.
[170] In particular, she did not appreciate that she might have to do a lot of housework!
[171] *Re C (A Minor) (Care: Children's Wishes)* [1993] 1 FLR 832, [1993] 1 FCR 810.

(ii) The child's physical, emotional and educational needs (s. 1(3)(b) CA 1989)

In many cases the child's needs, together with the parents' capacity for meeting those needs, are the crucial issue. The emotional welfare of the child is particularly important.[172] The welfare report will consider the closeness of the relationship between the child and each of the parents. This might require the court to compare different styles of parenting. In *May v May*[173] the court preferred the father's parenting, partly because he stressed the importance of academic achievement, to the mother's more relaxed attitude towards school. In *NP v BR*[174] the mother denigrated the father in front of the child and discouraged contact. This was said to cause emotional harm and provide an argument that the child would be better off living with the father. In *Re G (Education: Religious Upbringing)*[175] the father proposed the children attended an ultra-Orthodox Jewish school which segregated boys and girls and from which very few children went on to universities. The Court of Appeal preferred the mother's alternative which left the children with a broader range of opportunities to choose from for their adult lives and treated boys and girls equally.

(iii) The likely effect on the child of any change in his circumstances (s. 1(3)(c) CA 1989)

The courts have stressed the importance of maintaining the status quo for children if possible.[176] Changing children's schools and housing can cause even further disturbance for children at a time when their lives are already under stress. In practice, as empirical evidence shows, the court will normally confirm the presently existing arrangements for the child.[177] In effect, then, if a child has a settled life with one parent, good reasons will be needed to justify a move to the other parent.[178] This was stressed by the Supreme Court in *Re B (A Child)*[179] where it was emphasised that a child should not be moved from an arrangement which was thriving unless there was a good reason to do so.[180]

(iv) The child's age, sex, background and any characteristics of the child which the court considers relevant (s. 1(3)(d) CA 1989)

These factors are likely to be of special relevance in choosing foster parents and potential adopters for children. The Children Act 1989 requires a local authority to take account of the child's 'religious persuasion, racial origin and cultural and linguistic background' in deciding what care arrangements are appropriate for the child. As we shall discuss shortly, there has been some debate in the case law as to whether girls are better looked after by their mothers and boys by their fathers.

(v) Any harm which the child has suffered or is at risk of suffering (s. 1(3)(e) CA 1989)

Harm is defined in s. 31(9): 'harm means ill-treatment or the impairment of health or development including, for example, impairment suffered from seeing or hearing ill-treatment of another'. The last 12 words of the subsection refer to the harm a child may suffer if aware of

---

[172] *Re J (Children) (Residence: Expert Evidence)* [2001] 2 FCR 44.
[173] [1986] 1 FLR 325.
[174] [2019] EWHC 3854 (Fam).
[175] [2012] EWCA Civ 1233.
[176] *Re H (Children) (Residence Order)* [2007] 2 FCR 621.
[177] Smart and May (2004a).
[178] *Re L (Residence: Justices' Reasons)* [1995] 2 FLR 445.
[179] [2009] UKSC 5.
[180] [1998] 1 FCR 549. A recent study suggested that in residence disputes the status quo was a significant factor: Giovannini (2011).

domestic violence in his or her household. The court, of course, would never make an order which it thought might place a child in a situation where there was a risk that the child would suffer harm. It has been made clear by the Court of Appeal in *Re M and R (Child Abuse: Evidence)*[181] that, before taking a risk into account, the court must find proved facts on the balance of probabilities which reveal that risk.[182] So the court must first consider what facts are proved. Once facts are proved, the next issue is whether those proven facts indicate a risk of harm.[183] The risk only needs to be of a real possibility of harm; it does not need to be shown that it is more likely than not that the child will be harmed.[184]

It is not always easy to tell whether an arrangement will cause harm to a child. In *Re W (Residence Order)*[185] the mother and her new partner had an uninhibited attitude towards nudity and were often nude in front of the children. The Court of Appeal thought the trial judge had been misled in assuming that this would harm the children. There was no clear evidence that the nudity would harm the children and so it should not have been taken into account. The risk need not be that the child will be directly harmed, but a risk of harm to someone close to the child (e.g. their primary carer) is often a risk that the child will thereby be harmed.[186]

(vi) How capable each of the child's parents (and any other person in relation to whom the court considers the question to be relevant) is in meeting his needs (s. 1(3)(f) CA 1989)

This factor must be read in conjunction with the needs of the child. If, for example, the child has a medical condition requiring careful management which only one parent is capable of providing, this would be a crucial consideration.[187] In *RO v A Local Authority and Others*[188] a child's mother had died and she had complex emotional needs, which it was held could be better met by her aunt than her father. In *Re M (Handicapped Child: Parental Responsibility)*[189] the father's inability to care effectively for his disabled daughter was fatal to his application for a residence order. The phrase 'other person' could include the new partner of the parent. The court may regard it as an advantage to the child to live in a two-adult household rather than a single-person one.[190]

(vii) The range of powers available to the court under the Children Act 1989 in the proceedings in question (s. 1(3)(g) CA 1989)

The court has the power to make orders other than those sought by the parties.[191] The court, in considering an application for a particular order, must decide whether the order sought would be better than any other order available under the Children Act 1989.

As well as the checklist of factors, the court must also take into account three further provisions of the Act which are relevant in deciding whether to make a section 8 order.

---

[181] [1996] 2 FLR 195, [1996] 2 FCR 617.
[182] This is explained and discussed further in Chapter 11.
[183] *Re A (Contact: Witness Protection Scheme)* [2005] EWHC 2189 (Fam).
[184] *Re A (Contact: Witness Protection Scheme)* [2005] EWHC 2189 (Fam).
[185] [1999] 1 FLR 869.
[186] *Re A (Contact: Witness Protection Scheme)* [2005] EWHC 2189 (Fam).
[187] *Re C and V (Minors) (Parental Responsibility and Contact)* [1998] 1 FLR 392, [1998] 1 FCR 57.
[188] [2013] EWHC B31 (Fam).
[189] [2001] 3 FCR 454.
[190] *Re DW (A Minor) (Custody)* [1984] 14 Fam Law 17; *M v Birmingham CC* [1994] 2 FLR 141.
[191] CA 1989, s. 10(1).

(viii) The presumption of shared involvement in the child's life

The Children and Families Act 2014 has amended the way welfare should be understood in the Children Act 1989. The provisions are complex, even tortuous. They will be set out here and then explained:

LEGISLATIVE PROVISION

Children Act 1989, section 1

(2A) . . . as respects each parent within subsection (6)(a) to presume, unless the contrary is shown, that involvement of that parent in the life of the child concerned will further the child's welfare.

(2B) In subsection (2A) 'involvement' means involvement of some kind, either direct or indirect, but not any particular division of a child's time.

(6) In subsection (2A) 'parent' means parent of the child concerned; and, for the purposes of that subsection, a parent of the child concerned—

   (a) is within this paragraph if that parent can be involved in the child's life in a way that does not put the child at risk of suffering harm; and

   (b) is to be treated as being within paragraph (a) unless there is some evidence be fore the court in the particular proceedings to suggest that involvement of that parent in the child's life would put the child at risk of suffering harm whatever the form of the involvement.

The effect of these provisions appears to be as follows. When considering an application for a section 8 order or a parental responsibility order, the court must ask the following:

1. *Does the parent fall within s. 6(b), that is to say, is there evidence to suggest that involving the parent in the child's life would involve the risk of the child suffering harm whatever the form of involvement?*

   If there is evidence that involving the parent risks the child suffering harm, whatever the form of involvement, then the court will simply proceed with the normal welfare analysis. Of course, as there is evidence that the parent's involvement will pose a risk to the child it is very unlikely the court will order that the parent will have a full role in the life of the child.

   If there is no such evidence then the parent falls within s. 6(a) and the court must consider the next question.

2. *Is there any evidence to show that involving the parent in some way in the child's life will not promote the child's welfare?*

   If there is evidence that involving the parent will not promote the child's welfare, then the court will proceed on the normal welfare analysis. However, as there is evidence that involving them in the child's life will not promote the child's welfare it is unlikely the court will order that they play a full role in the child's life.

   If there is no such evidence, then the court will presume that it is in the child's welfare that the parent be involved in their life to some extent and the court must look at all the evidence and decide what order will best promote the welfare of the child.

This might be read as saying in essence something pretty simple: unless it is shown that involving the parent in the child's life is harmful to the child, it should be presumed that it is in the welfare of the child to involve the parent in their life. That may seem to be so obvious as to hardly need saying.

Indeed, it is difficult to think of a case where these new provisions will have any impact on a case. It is interesting that in one of the leading cases on parental involvement in recent years *Re M (Children) (Ultra-Orthodox Judaism: Transgender Parent)*[192] the presumption did not get even a mention. If the court has found that involving a parent in the child's life will harm the child, then the presumption does not come into play. If the court has decided that involving the parent will benefit the child, it is bound to take it that will be in the child's welfare. So, the only kind of case where the presumption seems to have any meaningful role is where the court determines that the involvement of the parent will be neutral, in other words neither benefit nor harm the child. Then it seems that the court must now presume the involvement will be in the child's welfare. One might, however, think that cases where the involvement of a parent in a child's life will be exactly neutral will be very rare.

It is also notable that the presumption does not apply if there is evidence that the involvement of a parent would put the child at risk of suffering harm. This is a very low threshold for the presumption that involving the parent in the child's life will benefit the child not to apply. It does not need to be a high risk, nor does it need to be risk of serious harm. However, it should be noted that the question is about whether 'involvement of any kind' will harm the child. Presumably sending a birthday card is involvement in the child's life. Only in very rare cases would that be seen as posing a risk of harm. This means it will be rare for the presumption not to apply.

It is worth emphasising what this presumption is not saying. It is not saying the court should presume that the child should spend an equal amount of time with both parents. Even if the presumption applies, it only presumes that some kind of involvement in the child's life will be in their welfare. Subsection 2B explicitly accepts this could be indirect contact.

However, there is a concern that whatever its intent, an equal sharing of time will be seen as the 'new norm'. As Liz Trinder[193] has observed:

> Previously, parents seeking to establish their equal status had the prospect of a symbolic shared residence order to fight for. Under the new regime the only outlet for that desire will be in terms of an equal time split rather than a label.

In *F v H*[194] Russell J suggested the child's guardian had misinterpreted the presumption. In that case there were findings of abusive behaviour by the mother and a risk that if there was contact it would be repeated. In such a case the presumption of involvement did not arise.

The explanatory note to the legislation gives, in Chapter A, a series of examples of how the presumption will operate. Here is one:

> 738. Parent A and Parent B are married and have one child together. Parent A left the marital home and Parent B refuses to let Parent A see their child. Parent A wants to be able to see the child at the weekends. Parent A applies for a child arrangements order that sets out that the child should stay over with Parent A from Saturday evening until Sunday morning.

> 739. Each parent is treated by the court as being able to have safe involvement with the child as no concerns are raised that Parent A or Parent B pose a risk of harm to the child. The presumption therefore applies and the court has to presume that it will further the welfare of the child for Parent A to be involved in the child's life.

---

[192] [2017] EWCA Civ 2164.
[193] Trinder (2014b).
[194] [2017] EWHC 3358 (Fam).

740. The child is 15 years old and the court has before it a section 7 welfare report that sets out that the child does not want to see Parent A or have any contact with Parent A as Parent A finds it difficult to come to terms with a recent declaration from the child that the child is gay and Parent A has refused to acknowledge that the child is gay. The child has expressed a strong wish to be able to explore issues of sexuality and feels that any contact with Parent A would inhibit this. The court decides that at the moment the child's welfare will not be furthered by involvement with Parent A and the presumption is rebutted.

741. The court makes its decision, weighing this factor alongside the other considerations in section 1 of the Children Act 1989, with the child's welfare remaining at all times the court's paramount consideration.

Parliament may not have meant the provisions to have much direct impact on cases, but rather to affect the general ethos surrounding parental separation. They may be seeking to create an expectation among society at large that on separation both parents should continue to be involved in the child's life, unless there is a risk of harm. If, however, that was their intention there may have been clearer ways to communicate that message to the people of England and Wales!

Felicity Kaganas[195] argues that the significance of the reforms lies not in their legal import, but the broader message they convey:

> [T]he change will have little impact in the courts, is unlikely to serve children's best interests, is unlikely to satisfy fathers' rights groups and is unlikely to reduce conflict between parents. Rather the reforms can be seen as part of a symbolic crusade to endorse the traditional importance of the father and to restore confidence in the family justice system. The new presumption is meant to affirm the status of fathers and of the separated but continuing family. As a result, the deviant nature of failing to abide by that norm is underscored. Although largely symbolic, this scapegoating may nevertheless have the effect of changing the balance of power in out-of-court settlements and so may prove damaging for some vulnerable mothers and children.

Her subsequent study of court decisions found this to be correct, concluding that: 'The presumption has not changed the way courts decide cases.'[196] In one of the few cases to discuss the presumption Russell J in *F v L*[197] was highly critical of an assumption by the first instance judge that the 2014 Act advocated a shared care arrangement, with the child spending an equal amount of time between the two parents. She emphasised the importance of focusing on the welfare of the particular child.

If Kaganas is correct then the greatest impact of the section may not be in the courtroom but in the mediation suite, where couples will feel that agreeing to a shared care arrangement is the fairest order to make. Indeed, evidence from Australia is that in mediated settlements couples feel strong pressure to agree to shared care as the only fair kind of order even in cases where that is not appropriate.[198]

Critics are concerned that these provisions detract from the court's job of ascertaining what is best for the particular child before them.[199] The concept of shared parental involvement is somewhat vague and substantial judicial time may be taken up clarifying it, without any necessary improvement in outcomes.[200] Focusing on whether or not the involvement of the parent will cause harm will take up valuable time and distract the court from focusing on the welfare of the child.[201]

---

[195] Kaganas (2014b).
[196] Kaganas (2018).
[197] [2017] EWHC 1377 (Fam).
[198] Trinder (2014b).
[199] House of Commons Justice Committee (2012).
[200] Rhoades (2012).
[201] O'Grady (2013).

(ix) The principle of no delay

Section 1(2) states:

LEGISLATIVE PROVISION

Children Act 1989, section 1(2)

In any proceedings in which any question with respect to the upbringing of a child arises, the court shall have regard to the general principle that any delay in determining the question is likely to prejudice the welfare of the child.

The legal process is notoriously slow, but the longer the court takes in cases involving children, the greater the uncertainty for the children and the higher the levels of stress felt by the parents.[202] It is therefore not surprising that the judiciary has been particularly critical of delay in family cases.[203] Indeed, Articles 6 and 8 of the European Convention on Human Rights may require a public hearing within a reasonable timescale, and so avoiding unnecessary delay is now required by the Human Rights Act 1998.[204]

The no delay principle in s. 1(2) applies to all proceedings concerning a child's upbringing, except financial orders.[205] It should be stressed, however, that while delay is not necessarily detrimental to a child, unnecessary delay is.[206] There are occasions when delay may be beneficial. It might be important for there to be a delay in order that further crucial information can be obtained or for the parties' circumstances to settle so that the best long-term decision can be reached. But any delay should be planned and purposeful.[207]

This subsection on its own would probably do little to prevent delay. The Children Act 1989 gave more powers to the judges to speed up cases. A central theme in the Family Justice Review[208] was the speeding up of the process and there have been significant procedural reforms designed to achieve this. There is a tension here between the desire to encourage speedy litigation and the desire to persuade the parties to settle without a court hearing. Encouraging people to resolve disputes themselves and to be litigants in person if they cannot may greatly lengthen the time disputes take to settle.

(x) The no order principle

This fundamental principle is set out in s. 1(5) of the Children Act 1989.

This provision emphasises that, before making an order under the Children Act concerning the upbringing of children,[209] there should be a demonstrable benefit to the child by making the order. If no positive benefit can be obtained by making the order then no order should be made. This is sometimes referred to as the 'no order' principle.

---

[202] Lord Chancellor's Department (2002c).
[203] Ewbank J in *Stockport MBC v B; Stockport MBC v L* [1986] 2 FLR 80.
[204] *Kopf and Liberda v Austria* [2012] 1 FLR 1199.
[205] See *Re TB (Care Proceedings: Criminal Trial)* [1995] 2 FLR 810, [1996] 1 FCR 101 for a discussion of how criminal and care proceedings should be coordinated.
[206] *C v Solihull MBC* [1993] 1 FLR 290, [1992] 2 FCR 341.
[207] *C v Solihull MBC* [1993] 1 FLR 290, [1992] 2 FCR 341.
[208] Norgrave (2012).
[209] *K v H (Child Maintenance)* [1993] 2 FLR 61, [1993] 1 FCR 684 states that s. 1(5) does not apply to applications under Sched. 1 to CA 1989 for financial provision for children.

LEGISLATIVE PROVISION

Children Act 1989, section 1(5)

Where a court is considering whether or not to make one or more orders under this Act with respect to a child, it shall not make the order or any of the orders unless it considers that doing so would be better for the child than making no order at all.

Some commentators have read more into s. 1(5) and have suggested that it represents the principle of deregulation or non-intervention; that is, that the subsection reflects the presumption that the parents are the best people to care for the child and they should decide what should happen to the child. Only if there are strong reasons should the law intervene. It can be said that this is in line with Article 8 of the European Convention on Human Rights, which protects family privacy. However, the statute itself does not suggest that there is a presumption that no order is best. In *L v L (Anticipatory Child Arrangements Order)*[210] MacDonald J was clear that 's. 1(5) of the Children Act 1989 does not create a presumption one way or the other, but simply requires the court to ask itself the question, "will it be better for the child to make the order than making no order at all"'.[211] All the subsection is saying is that it is necessary to show there is a positive benefit to be gained from making an order.[212] The disagreement over the meaning of the subsection is reflected in a study which found that practitioners and district judges took a variety of approaches to the subsection.[213] The view with most support is that s. 1(5) is not creating a presumption against intervention, but requires the court to be satisfied that some good will come from making the order.[214] In *Dawson v Wearmouth*[215] Lord Mackay interpreted s. 1(5) to mean that a court should make an order only if there was some evidence that to do so would improve the child's welfare. Baroness Hale has commented: 'This means that there must be some tangible benefit to the children from making an order rather than leaving the parents to sort things out for themselves'.[216] In *Re C (Older Children: Relocation)*[217] the principle was relied on to decide not to make an order in a case involving a dispute where a 17-year-old should live. He could decide that for himself and a court order would be of no assistance. By contrast in *L v L (Anticipatory Child Arrangements Order)*[218] the fact that the order would give certainty to a troubled teenager worried about her future care was sufficient to justify making an order.

Now some of the issues which have caused the courts particular difficulty in applying the welfare principle will be considered.

---

[210] [2017] EWHC 1212 (Fam).
[211] At para 41.
[212] As argued in Bainham (1998b: 2–4).
[213] Doughty (2008a).
[214] *B v B (A Minor) (Residence Order)* [1993] 1 FCR 211; *Re S (Contact: Grandparents)* [1996] 3 FCR 30.
[215] [1999] 2 AC 308.
[216] *Holmes-Moorhouse v Richmond-Upon-Thames London Borough Council* [2009] 1 FLR 904, para 30.
[217] [2015] EWCA Civ 1298.
[218] [2017] EWHC 1212 (Fam).

7 Issues of controversy in applying the welfare principle

A The use of presumptions

In the years following the Children Act the courts developed a set of presumptions to use when interpreting the welfare principle.[219] In the context of the welfare principle the kinds of presumption being considered are rebuttable: that once a certain fact is proved then there is an assumption that making a certain order will promote the welfare of the child, unless evidence shows otherwise.

These included a presumption in favour of contact, a presumption in favour of the 'natural parent' and so forth. These issues will be examined in detail below. However, in the past few years we have seen a gradual move away from presumptions and in favour of saying that in each case the court will look at the particular child and their relationships and determine what is best for that child. Statistical surveys indicating generally what is best for children might be helpful if one had to deal with a case about a child picked at random from the population on whom you had no particular evidence. However, the children who appear in court-heard cases represent a highly unusual case, where what happens to 'normal children' is of little relevance, certainly of little relevance when the court has before it detailed information about the particular child it is considering.[220]

B Shared residence

The courts are certainly open to making orders where the child will spend an equal amount of time with both parents. At one time this was seen as an exceptional order, but the courts no longer use that terminology. Shared care orders are more likely to be made where there is a good relationship between the parties so that they can communicate over day-to-day issues, but in *L v F*[221] it was denied that there was a legal principle that shared care should not be ordered if the relationship between the parties was weak. Similarly, it made it clear there was no rule that shared care should not be ordered in relation to young children, although that would be 'unusual'.

TOPICAL ISSUE

Should there be a presumption of shared residence?

Much controversy has surrounded the question of whether or not there should be a presumption in favour of shared residence. In part the debate is muddied by the ambiguity over quite what is meant by that. What is generally meant as the starting point for the law should be that the child should spend a roughly equal amount of time with each parent. The case against the presumption includes the following arguments:

---

[219] Herring and Powell (2013).
[220] Herring (2014b).
[221] [2017] EWCA Civ 2121.

1. In many cases it is simply impractical: the parents live too far apart or do not have big enough homes for the arrangement to work.[222] In *Re M-A*[223] the couple had a child who was thought to be on the autism spectrum. They originally decided that the child would spend eight weeks with the mother in England then four weeks with the father in Canada. Perhaps unsurprisingly this proved an unworkable arrangement.

2. The evidence suggests that generally children in shared residence arrangements do less well than children with one primary residence.[224] This may be because shared residence is wrongly used in cases where the couple are highly conflicted.[225] A small-scale study by Neale, Flowerdew and Smart[226] of children living under a shared residence scheme showed a mixed picture. Some children valued the sense of fairness it created and the structure it provided for their lives. Others felt they were suffering inconvenience so that neither parent felt they had 'lost' and the structure of the order restricted their social lives. Shared residence where the needs of parents were prioritised and which were inflexible in their structures worked least well. As Hunt[227] notes, shared residence creates 'substantial practical inconveniences and challenges, adjusting to different environments, loyalty conflicts and interference with peer group activities'.

   In a thorough review of the evidence, Liz Trinder[228] accepts that shared residence can be positive if parents are able to cooperate and the arrangements are focused. However, in cases marked by high conflict and litigation, shared residence is linked with negative outcomes. This suggests that shared residence should not be regarded as the panacea response. She also helpfully makes the point that the debates over shared residence may be missing the issue:

   > [I]t is typically not the arrangements themselves that matter, whether shared or not shared, but how parents manage these relationships. Whilst courts inevitably focus on timetables it is critical that every effort is made to focus on the quality of relationships that matter to children.

   Fehlberg et al.[229] in their thorough study found 'no empirical evidence showing a clear linear relationship between the amount of shared time and improving outcomes for children'. It is the quality of contact, not the amount of time, that matters.

3. It can be argued that the case for a presumption is motivated by adults' needs to be seen to be treated equally, rather than an assessment of what is in the child's best interests.[230] In the majority of cases both during a relationship and afterwards the mother undertakes the bulk of the care of a child. To use a presumption of shared care, where this does not reflect the reality, masks the reality of the mother's care.[231] Sonia Harris-Short[232] argues, relying on a survey of the experience in Sweden, that shared care after a relationship breaks down works well only if there has been shared care before the relationship comes to an end. Therefore, if we wish to encourage more post-separation shared care, we need to encourage greater levels of shared care during the relationship. She argues:

---

[222] Hunt (2014).
[223] [2018] EWCA Civ 896.
[224] Hunt et al. (2008).
[225] Newnham (2011).
[226] Neale, Flowerdew and Smart (2003).
[227] Hunt (2014).
[228] Trinder (2010).
[229] Fehlberg et al. (2011).
[230] Daniel (2009).
[231] Barnett (2009).
[232] Harris-Short (2011).

> [E]quality cannot be conjured out of nothing at the point of separation. It must be firmly rooted in the practices of the intact family. In our eagerness to embrace the progressive promise of equality, there is a danger that the realities of family life can be forgotten. Yet it is in these realities that any decision about the future interests of the child must be firmly grounded. Within the intact family, patterns of care have been established; parental–child relationships have been defined; difficult decisions have been taken; parental sacrifices and investments have been made. Choices made within the intact family have a profound and lasting impact on all the family members, especially the child. To ignore this reality at the point of separation is deeply problematic.[233]

4. Any presumption is in danger of diluting the welfare principle. As already mentioned, this was the primary reason why the Family Justice Review rejected a suggestion that there should be presumption or statement in favour of shared residence. In Australia, where a presumption of shared residence has been enacted, mothers feel under great pressure to agree to shared care even in cases where there has been abuse.[234] There is a particular concern that in many cases the presence of domestic violence or abuse will make any kind of shared residence order undesirable and dangerous. As Fehlberg *et al.*[235] highlight, the research on shared residence suggests it works least well where mothers have ongoing safety concerns and/or there is high-level parental conflict. Indeed Brinig[236] claims that in the United States a strong presumption in favour of shared contact is linked to an increase in domestic abuse following relationship breakdown. Yet cases of hostility are precisely the attributes one finds in cases that end up in court. Indeed, in England half of all litigated child contact cases involve allegations of domestic violence.[237] This makes the argument of suggesting a presumption in favour of shared care in litigated cases very weak indeed. Crawford and Pierce note:

> In Denmark, for example, where previous legislation forced shared custody, the view is now that while the original purpose of the legislation was to ensure contact of the child with both parents, the actual effect was a cause of a heightened level of conflict between the parents and stress on the child.

The argument in favour of presumption of shared residence emphasises that it provides a powerful statement that we have moved beyond an assumption that one parent (normally the mother) is the child-carer, while the other parent (normally the father) is the provider. We need to do all we can to encourage both mothers and fathers to take their parental role seriously and acknowledge the essential contribution that mothers and fathers make to children. The presumption will diffuse the battles that too often flow from separation, with one or other parent seeking to be the 'resident parent'. We should expect each parent to care equally for their children.

While that is an ideal we should strive for, that does not mean that we should enforce it through court orders as a blanket measure in all cases. To ensure a more equal involvement of parents after the relationship breaks down, we need to do better at trying to promote equal sharing during the relationship, as the evidence shows that mothers still undertake the vast majority of childcare and domestic duties.

---

[233] Harris-Short (2010).
[234] Hunt (2014); Trinder (2010).
[235] Fehlberg *et al.* (2011).
[236] Brinig (2015).
[237] Fehlberg, Smythe and Trinder (2014).

C Is there a presumption in favour of mothers?

TOPICAL ISSUE

Are mothers preferred in residence cases?

One hotly disputed issue is whether there is or should be a presumption that children are better brought up by mothers rather than by fathers. At one time it was thought that there was a presumption that babies and girls should be brought up by mothers, and boys by fathers,[238] but that has been long rejected by the courts. Nevertheless, it is certainly true that mothers are more likely to have the child live primarily with them.[239] This is especially so in the case of younger children. In **RO v A Local Authority and Others**[240] Mr Recorder Keehan QC ordered the child, whose mother had died, to live with female relatives rather than the father for various reasons, including because she was 'desperately in need of a mother figure'.

The Court of Appeal in **Re K (Residence Order: Securing Contact)**,[241] in awarding residence of a two-year-old to a father, admitted that this was 'somewhat unusual'. However, in **Re G (Education: Religious Upbringing)**[242] Munby LJ was clear:

> [M]en and women, husbands and wives, fathers and mothers have come before the family courts, as they come today, on an exactly equal footing. The voice of the father carries no more weight because he is the father, nor does the mother's because she is the mother. The weight to be attached to their views, if opposed, is to be determined on the basis of the merits or otherwise of the views being expressed, not on the basis of the gender of the person propounding them.

The courts are wary of explicitly creating a presumption in favour of mothers, as this might constitute discrimination on the grounds of sex and so be in breach of the Human Rights Act 1998. However, there is evidence that girls are particularly vulnerable to sexual abuse following divorce. Fretwell Wilson[243] points to a study which found that 50 per cent of girls living solely with their father reported sexual abuse by someone (not necessarily their father) and argues that these concerns must be addressed when the court is making decisions over where a child shall live.

The reality is that children on separation stay primarily with their mothers in 92 per cent of cases.[244] To some that reflects deeply sexist presumptions about mothers and fathers that are perpetuated by the courts. On the other hand, the statistics reflect the reality that for couples who are together, mothers undertake the vast majority of childcare. In Scandinavian countries where care is shared more equally during the relationship, unsurprisingly it is also shared more equally if the relationship breaks down.

---

[238] See *Re W (A Minor) (Residence Order)* [1992] 2 FLR 332, [1992] 2 FCR 461.
[239] This was implicitly accepted in *Humphreys v The Commissioners for HM Revenue and Customs* [2012] UKSC 18 where the Supreme Court was willing to assume that the fact child credit was paid to the parent with whom the child lived most nights indirectly discriminated against fathers.
[240] [2013] EWHC B31 (Fam).
[241] [1999] 1 FLR 583.
[242] [2012] EWCA Civ 1233.
[243] Fretwell Wilson (2002).
[244] Crawford and Pierce (2012).

D The 'natural parent presumption'

At one time the courts promoted the natural parent presumption: '[t]he best person to bring up a child is the natural parent. It matters not whether the parent is wise or foolish, rich or poor, educated or illiterate, provided the child's moral and physical health are not endangered.'[245] However, this presumption has been reconsidered by two important recent decisions of the House of Lords and the Supreme Court.

CASE: *Re G (Children) (Residence: Same-Sex Partner)* [2006] UKHL 43

A lesbian couple decided to have a child. One of them became pregnant through assisted reproductive techniques using donated sperm. In law the woman who gave birth to the child was the child's mother, but her partner did not have any parental status. The couple raised the child together. However, the couple broke up and a dispute arose over the residence of the child and contact arrangements. Initially, residence was awarded to the mother, and the partner had regular contact. However, the mother removed the child to Cornwall in an attempt to prevent contact and in breach of court orders. The Court of Appeal held that residence should be transferred to the partner. In this case they had both raised the child together and were both the psychological parents of the child. The 'natural parent' presumption applied to them both equally, Thorpe LJ believed. However, in the House of Lords their Lordships re-emphasised the importance of the natural parenthood and Lord Nicholls stated that there needed to be cogent reasons for removing a child from a 'natural' parent, in this case the mother. He stated:

> In reaching its decision the court should always have in mind that in the ordinary way the rearing of a child by his or her biological parent can be expected to be in the child's best interests, both in the short term and also, and importantly, in the longer term. I decry any tendency to diminish the significance of this factor. A child should not be removed from the primary care of his or her biological parents without compelling reason.[246]

Baroness Hale explained that the fact that one of the parties was the natural mother was an important and significant factor to which the lower courts had failed to pay sufficient attention. However, she rejected the view that there was a formal legal presumption in favour of the 'natural parent'.

While the House of Lords in *Re G*[247] appeared to acknowledge that the biological link was an important figure, they did not use the language of a presumption. The Supreme Court returned to consider the issue again.

---

[245] *Re KD (A Minor) (Ward: Termination of Access)* [1988] 1 All ER 577 at p. 578. Supported and applied in *Re M (Child's Upbringing)* [1996] 2 FLR 441 and *Re P (A Child) (Care and Placement Proceedings)* [2008] 3 FCR 243.

[246] See also *Re D (Care: Natural Parent Presumption)* [1999] 1 FLR 134 CA

[247] [2006] UKHL 43.

CASE: *Re B (A Child)* [2009] UKSC 5

The case concerned a four-year-old boy, B, who had lived with his maternal grandparents since birth. His parents, who separated before B's birth, had not been able to care for him satisfactorily, although they were in regular contact with him. In 2009 the father married and had a child with his new wife. He sought a residence order in relation to B. A report from the social services stated that B was thriving with the grandmother, but also found that the father and his new wife could provide an adequate home for him. In March 2009 a residence order was made in favour of the grandmother, and a contact order in favour of B's parents. This order was overturned in the Family Division, in an order upheld in the Court of Appeal. However, the Supreme Court affirmed the original order of residence in favour of the grandparents.

The central issue in the case was simple: what weight should be attached to the status quo and the good care that the boy was receiving from his grandmother and what weight should be attached to the possibility of the boy living with his father? Lord Kerr held that the error in the lower courts was to talk in terms of rights:

> We consider that this statement betrays a failure on the part of the judge to concentrate on the factor of overwhelming – indeed, paramount – importance which is, of course, the welfare of the child. To talk in terms of a child's rights – as opposed to his or her best interests – diverts from the focus that the child's welfare should occupy in the minds of those called on to make decisions as to their residence.[248]

Lord Kerr held that this led to the judge making the error of deciding that if the father's care was 'good enough' he should be preferred over the grandmother, even if she could offer a higher standard of care. Lord Kerr rejected that approach: 'The court's quest is to determine what is in the *best* interests of the child, not what might constitute a second best but supposedly adequate alternative.'[249]

This did not mean that Lord Kerr thought parenthood irrelevant in residence disputes. He was willing to accept that '[i]n the ordinary way one *can* expect that children will do best with their biological parents'.[250] But, as he then astutely pointed out, many disputes about residence and contact cases do not follow the ordinary way. He summarised his views thus:

> All consideration of the importance of parenthood in private law disputes about residence must be firmly rooted in an examination of what is in the child's best interests. This is the paramount consideration. It is only as a contributor to the child's welfare that parenthood assumes any significance. In common with all other factors bearing on what is in the best interests of the child, it must be examined for its potential to fulfil that aim.[251]

Four points are particularly important about this decision. The first is that their Lordships decried the use of presumptions or rights. They preferred to look at the particular child and the particular relationships in issue, rather than rely on general assumptions or presumptions about what is good for children.[252] Second, the case emphasised that the focus of the court's attention is the child, and not the parents. However unfair the decision may appear to the father in *Re B*, the court's paramount concern was with the child. Third, it is remarkable that

---

[248] Paragraph 19.
[249] Paragraph 20.
[250] Paragraph 35.
[251] Paragraph 37.
[252] See Reece (2010) for an argument against using generalisations about children.

the Human Rights Act 1998 was not mentioned by their Lordships in *Re B* even once. This demonstrates how in section 8 cases this Act has had a fairly small impact. Finally, the decision marks the demise of the natural parent presumption. Now the best we can say is that in deciding a residence dispute between a natural parent and a third party, the biological link is but one factor to take into account in assessing the child's welfare. In *Re G*, where the other factors were finely balanced, the biological link played an important role, but in most cases other factors will be decisive. This final point was well illustrated in *Re E-R (A Child)*[253] where a child (T) was living with her terminally ill mother and cared for by her and Mr and Mrs H (friends of the mother). When the mother died, the father sought an order that the child should live with him. At first instance the application was successful, with weight being given to the natural parent presumption. However, the Court of Appeal said the court should not have placed weight on the presumption. The fact the child was happy and well-settled with the mother and her friends was an important factor. The Court ordered a rehearing with a proposal to order the child remain with the mother's friends, with contact with the father. At the rehearing (*Re E-R (Child Arrangements)*[254]) Cobb J ordered that the child remain with the friends. This was in line with the child's wishes. Further:

> It is well-known that attachment is essential to the development of well-being and resilience; resilience is the ability to withstand and recover from adversity. Attachment to a significant person is critical to a child's ability to thrive; without attachment the child may fail to relate to others. As secure attachment will sustain the child in the face of adversity. While undoubtedly the father is T's biological parent, Mr and Mrs H are, or appear to have become, her psychological parents; this attachment to them paradoxically advances her capacity to attach to her father. T therefore benefits from two of the three ways in which parental relationships are achieved (i.e. [1] genetic/biological, [2] gestational and [3] psychological).[255]

The decision has been fiercely criticised by Andrew Bainham[256] who decries the failure to recognise that parents do have rights in relation to their children, albeit rights that can be interfered with if necessary in order to protect the rights of children. He argues that our legal system does assume that a child is best cared for by a natural parent and this is shown by the fact that we do not routinely on birth check whether parents are suitable carers for a child or whether others may be better placed to care for the child.

Supporters of the decision will welcome the significance attached by the court to the strong relationship between the grandparents and the child. The quality of care provided by them and the strong emotional bond between them counted for more than the blood tie between the father and the child. The Supreme Court in *Re B* were not saying that the blood tie counted for nothing, simply that it was but one factor that needed to be taken into account alongside all of the others.

E Is there a presumption that siblings should reside together?

The evidence of psychologists stresses the importance of the sibling relationship, especially on the breakdown of the parental relationship.[257] It is, therefore, not surprising that the courts have suggested that siblings should be kept in the same household unless there are strong

---

[253] [2015] EWCA Civ 405.

[254] [2016] EWHC 805 (Fam). For further litigation on this case see *Re E-R (child arrangements) (No. 2)* [2017] EWHC 2382 (Fam).

[255] Para 51.

[256] Bainham (2010).

[257] Edwards, Hadfield and Mauthner (2005), although in the study by Douglas *et al.* (2001: 376) siblings were not found to be a significant source of emotional support on family breakdown and friends were far more important.

reasons against this.[258] The same is true of half-siblings.[259] It is clear that the relationship between two siblings will be regarded as family life and so protected under the Human Rights Act 1998.[260] However, in each case much will depend on the particular relationship between the child and sibling. The further the siblings are apart in age, the weaker the assumption that they should stay together.[261] Of course, there still will be cases where the separation of the siblings is necessary. For example, in *B v B (Residence Order: Restricting Applications)*[262] the court decided that the mother should bring up two brothers, but the older brother simply refused to stay with the mother and lived with the father. The court felt that, as the older brother was intent on staying with the father and the younger brother had a close attachment to the mother, it was necessary for the brothers to live apart.[263] If the siblings are to live in different places, there is a strong presumption that there should be contact between them.[264]

F Religion

The issue of religious parenting has become controversial.[265] It has even been suggested that where parents raise their children as members of a particular religion, this is child abuse.[266] However, a study of children raised by Christian and Muslim parents found children speaking positively about their religious upbringing.[267] In one well-known 18th-century case, the poet Shelley was denied custody of his child on the basis that he was an atheist.[268] Nowadays the court would not deny a parent a residence order on the basis of their religious beliefs. Indeed, to determine a family law case simply on the basis of the religion of the parent would be contrary to the Human Rights Act 1998 because the European Convention on Human Rights protects freedom of religion and outlaws discrimination on the grounds of religion.[269] Generally, if the child has no religious views, the present law is summed up in the dicta of Munby LJ in *Re G (Education: Religious Upbringing)*:[270]

> It is not for a judge to weigh one religion against another. The court recognises no religious distinctions and generally speaking passes no judgment on religious beliefs or on the tenets, doctrines or rules of any particular section of society. All are entitled to equal respect, so long as they are 'legally and socially acceptable' . . . and not 'immoral or socially obnoxious'.

This neutrality does not prevent the court considering whether the religion involves practices that directly harm the child. So, for example, if the religion requires lengthy periods of fasting, causing medical harm to the child, then the court would be willing to take the parent's religious practices into account. The court might be willing to consider an argument that a religion caused the child to suffer social isolation[271] or indoctrination,[272] or failed to treat boys and

---

[258] E.g. *C v C (Minors: Custody)* [1988] 2 FLR 291.

[259] *Re H (A Child) (Leave to Apply for Residence Order)* [2008] 3 FCR 391.

[260] *Moustaquim v Belgium* (1991) 13 EHRR 802 at para 36. In *Senthuran v Secretary of State for the Home Dept* [2004] 3 FCR 273 it was held that adult siblings living together were capable of having family life together.

[261] *B v B (Minors) (Custody: Care Control)* [1991] 1 FLR 402, [1991] FCR 1.

[262] [1997] 1 FLR 139, [1997] 2 FCR 518.

[263] See also *Re B (T) (A Minor) (Residence Order)* [1995] 2 FCR 240.

[264] *Re S (Minors: Access)* [1990] 2 FLR 166, [1990] 2 FCR 379.

[265] For a discussion of the issues, see Taylor (2015 and 2009); Clarke (2017); M. Freeman (2003).

[266] See the discussion in Taylor (2015 and 2009).

[267] Lees and Horwath (2009); Horwath *et al.* (2008).

[268] *Shelley v Westbrook* (1817) Jac 266n.

[269] Articles 9 and 14 respectively.

[270] [2012] EWCA Civ 1233.

[271] *Hewison v Hewison* [1977] Fam Law 207.

[272] *Wright v Wright* [1980] 2 FLR 276.

girls equally.[273] This however makes it difficult for the law to claim that it is being neutral. To say 'the law does not discriminate against you on the grounds of your religion but on the grounds of your religious practices' is to disguise the truth.[274] It may be more honest to accept that there are limits to religious freedom, and that discrimination against a religion that demonstrably harms children is permitted.[275]

The court should always bear in mind that particular issues can be dealt with by means of a specific issue order. For example, the court should not be deterred from deciding that a child should live with a Jehovah's Witness parent for fear that the parent might refuse to consent to a blood transfusion should the child require it, because if that issue arose the court could overrule the parent's decision by means of a specific issue order.[276]

A consistent theme in the approach of the courts is that although parents can involve the child in religious activities, the child should be left to decide their religion for themselves. In *Re J (Specific Issue Orders: Muslim Upbringing and Circumcision)*[277] the Court of Appeal firmly rejected the argument of the father that the child was a Muslim boy, holding that the child was not yet old enough to belong to any faith. If a child has religious beliefs[278] of his or her own, the court is likely to make an order which enables the child to continue their religious practices.[279] In *Re G (Education: Religious Upbringing)*[280] Munby LJ explained that 'the court will always pay great attention to the wishes of a child old enough to be able to express sensible views on the subject of religion, even if not old enough to take a mature decision, they will be given effect to by the court only if and so far as and in such manner as is in accordance with the child's best interests'. Although oddly in that case the views of the children seem not to have played any part in the reasoning.[281] If the child has religious views of their own, the parent with whom the child is living could be required to permit the child to exercise their religious beliefs. For example, there could be a specific issue order requiring the residential parent to permit the child to attend religious services[282] or indeed preventing the parent from involving a child in the parent's religion.[283] In *Re C (A Child)*[284] a mother sought a prohibited steps order to prevent her 10-year-old daughter being baptised, a decision supported by the father. The judge refused to make the order and was particularly influenced by the clear views of the girl that she wanted the baptism.[285] Even if the child does not have beliefs of their own as they are too young, the court may still take into account the religious heritage into which

---

[273] In *Re G (Education: Religious Upbringing)* [2012] EWCA Civ 1233.

[274] Bainham (1994c).

[275] See the general discussion in Johnson (2013).

[276] *Re S (A Minor) (Blood Transfusion: Adoption Order Conditions)* [1994] 2 FLR 416.

[277] [1999] 2 FLR 678; approved in *Re J (Specific Issue Orders)* [2000] 1 FLR 517. Contrast in *Re S (Change of Names: Cultural Factors)* [2001] 3 FCR 648.

[278] The court will focus on the religious practices of the child and will *not* automatically assume that a child acquires a religion simply through being born to parents of a particular religion: *Re J (Specific Issue Orders)* [2000] 1 FLR 517.

[279] *Re R (A Minor) (Residence: Religion)* [1993] 2 FLR 163, [1993] 2 FCR 525.

[280] [2012] EWCA Civ 1233.

[281] A point emphasised by Taylor (2013).

[282] *J v C* [1970] AC 668 HL (Protestants gave an undertaking to bring up the child as a Roman Catholic); *Re R (A Minor) (Residence: Religion)* [1993] 2 FLR 163 (where the Exclusive Brethren aunt was permitted contact on condition that she did not discuss religion).

[283] *Re S (Minors) (Access: Religious Upbringing)* [1992] 2 FLR 313.

[284] [2012] EW Misc 15(CC).

[285] See also *Re L and B (Specific Issues: Temporary Leave to Remove from the Jurisdiction: Circumcision)* [2016] EWHC 849 (Fam) where it was held best to delay a decision over whether to circumcise a boy until he was old enough to decide for himself.

they were born. So, when a child who was born to an Orthodox Jewish couple was taken into care, then the court confirmed that the local authority should try to find Jewish foster parents and adopters if possible.[286]

Where the parents of a child have different religions there might be disputes over the religious upbringing of a child. If the child is not old enough to form his or her own religious beliefs the courts are likely to allow the resident parent to determine the religious upbringing of the child. In *Re S (Change of Names: Cultural Factors)*[287] Wilson J rejected the father's argument that the child should be raised as both a Muslim and a Sikh. Instead he should be raised in the religion of the mother (Islam), although he should be made aware of his Sikh identity and encouraged to respect Sikhism. Wilson J was persuaded that, having decided that the mother should have the residence order, the child would inevitably become integrated into the Muslim community of which she was part. In other cases, where there is a greater sharing of care between the parents, the courts have allowed each parent to raise the child in accordance with their religion. In *Re S (Specific Issue Order: Religion: Circumcision)*,[288] on separation there arose a dispute between a Muslim mother and a Jain Hindu father. The Court of Appeal held that children raised with a mixed heritage should be allowed to decide for themselves what religion (if any) they wished to follow when they were older. Both parents should be allowed to teach the children about their religions.[289] In *Re N (A Child: Religion: Jehovah's Witness)*[290] it was held 'where parents follow different religions and those religions are both socially acceptable the child should have the opportunity to learn about and experience both religions.' Although the parents were allowed to take the child to their different religious services (Anglican and Jehovah's Witness), neither parent was allowed to 'teach' the child. The court appeared concerned that otherwise each parent would seek to persuade the child to adopt their own religion, causing the child distress. In the case of religions with very strict rules of observance this may be very difficult. Then the court may need to determine which religion will provide the child with the opportunity to develop their lives, as illustrated in *Re G (Education: Religious Upbringing)*[291] (see Chapter 9).

A powerful critique of the law's approach to minority religions has been presented by Suhraiya Jivraj and Didi Herman[292] who argue that unconsciously in these cases the judiciary are adopting a Christian perspective. In particular, the assumption that religion is something that is chosen by an individual rather than being membership of a community reflects a Christian perspective on the nature of religious identity. Further, that the notion of attempting to raise a child in a religiously neutral way can be questioned, given that it must be understood in a society in which Christianity has a dominant position among religions.

G Employed parents

It used to be thought that a parent who stayed at home to spend as much time as possible with a child would be favoured regarding residency over a parent who spent substantial time in employed work. Such an approach tends to favour mothers over fathers; indeed a father who gave up work to look after a child was at one time criticised by a court for 'deliberately giv[ing]

---

[286] *Re P (Section 91(14) Guidelines) (Residence and Religious Heritage)* [1999] 2 FLR 573.
[287] [2001] 3 FCR 648.
[288] [2004] EWHC 1282 (Fam).
[289] See Eekelaar (2004) for an insightful analysis of children of mixed religious backgrounds.
[290] [2011] EWHC 3737 (Fam).
[291] [2012] EWCA Civ 1233.
[292] Jivraj and Herman (2009).

up work in order to go on social security'.[293] However, it seems now that a working parent will be only slightly disadvantaged over a non-working parent.[294] In *Re Dhaliwal*, both parents originally offered full-time care of the child. However, during the hearing on residence the father explained that rather than offering the child full-time care he was about to take up a job which had hours from 9 o'clock in the morning to 6 or 7 o'clock in the evening. Thorpe LJ on appeal said: 'The whole balance inevitably tips significantly in favour of the mother's proposal once the father revealed that he would be heavily dependent on the unexplored availability of the extended family.'[295] In *Re R (A Minor) (Residence Order: Finance)*[296] the court preferred to make a shared residence order so that both parents were able to continue in employment, rather than giving sole residence to the mother, because that would mean she would have to give up her job which would cause financial disadvantage to the children and involve the Child Support Agency in the family's finances. However, in *Re B (A Child)*[297] the Court of Appeal expressed very strongly the view that it was wrong in principle to let Child Support Act consequences affect residence or contact arrangements.

The court should not place much weight on the fact that one parent can offer a higher standard of living than another.[298] This is explained on the basis that 'anyone with experience of life knows that affluence and happiness are not necessarily synonymous'.[299] Although this is true, if given a choice most children would rather their parents be rich than poor, all other factors being equal. In reality, it is easier to explain the irrelevance of wealth on the basis that it would be unjust to distinguish rich and poor parents. The significance of this factor is lessened in relation to married couples because the court has the power to redistribute the couple's property.

H Disabled parents

The courts will take into account the abilities of parents to meet the needs of a child, and any disability of a parent might in a few cases be relevant. In *M v M (Parental Responsibility)*[300] Wilson J decided that it would be inappropriate to give a father parental responsibility because he suffered from learning disabilities, aggravated by an accident, which meant that he would not be capable of exercising the rights and responsibilities of parenthood. Cases involving disabled parents must now be reconsidered in the light of the Human Rights Act 1998. Although the Human Rights Act does not explicitly prohibit discrimination on the basis of disability, it is arguable that it should be added to the list of prohibited grounds in Article 14. Before refusing residence or contact to a disabled parent the court should ensure that a disabled parent cannot be enabled by the provision of suitable equipment or assistance to meet the child's needs. In *Re P (Non-Disclosure of HIV)*[301] Bodey J made it very clear that the HIV status of the mother was irrelevant to the residence/contact dispute between the parents. The mother did not need to disclose it to the father.

---

[293] *Plant v Plant* [1983] 4 FLR 305 at p. 310. See also *B v B (Custody of Children)* [1985] FLR 166 CA; contrast *B v B (Custody of Children)* [1985] FLR 462.

[294] Although see *Re B (Minors: Residence: Working Father)* [1996] CLY 615 and *Re O (Children) (Residence)* [2004] 1 FCR 169 where the court contrasted the care of a 'full-time mother' and the father who could only offer 'support' to the children's grandparents whom he proposed undertook the primary role of childcaring.

[295] [2005] 2 FCR 398, 402.

[296] [1995] 2 FLR 612, [1995] 3 FCR 334.

[297] [2006] EWCA Civ 1574. See the discussion of this case in Gilmore (2007).

[298] *Stephenson v Stephenson* [1985] FLR 1140 at p. 1148.

[299] *Re P (Adoption: Parental Agreement)* [1985] FLR 635 at p. 637.

[300] [1999] 2 FLR 737.

[301] [2006] Fam Law 177.

I Names

(i) Registration of birth

A child must be registered within 42 days of the birth and the person registering the birth can declare 'the surname by which at the date of the registration of the birth it is intended that the child shall be known'.[302]

If a father (or mother) objects to the initial registration, he (or she) can apply for a specific issue order that the child have his (or her) surname. Once the name is registered, it cannot be changed unless there has been a clerical error.[303] Unlike other countries, there is no restriction on a choice of name.[304] Parents are free to let their imagination run riot. However, there are limits. In *Re C (Children: Power to Choose Forenames)*[305] a mother with mental health issues had had her children taken into care. She wished the girl to be known as Cyanide and the boy Preacher. The court took the view that although normally it would be inappropriate to amend a parent's choice of names, it would be if the choice would cause the child serious harm. Here the name Cyanide went beyond 'the unusual, bizarre, extreme or plain foolish' and would cause serious harm and so the foster carers could choose an alternative one.

(ii) What is a child's name?

In law a child's name is not necessarily the name which appears on the birth register. *Re T (Otherwise H) (An Infant)*[306] makes it clear that the child's surname in law is simply that by which he or she is customarily known, which does not, of course, have to be the registered name. It is possible through a deed poll to provide formal evidence of a change from the registered surname, although it is not essential.[307] If a deed poll is used to recognise the new surname of a child, it must be signed by all those with parental responsibility.[308]

(iii) Can a parent allow a child to be known by a name with which he or she was not registered?

It is clear that only a person with parental responsibility can change the name of a child. What is not clear is whether a person with parental responsibility must consult with anyone else with parental responsibility before doing so. The following situations need to be distinguished.

(a) Where a residence order is in force
Where a residence order is in force the position is governed by s. 13(1) of the Children Act 1989:

LEGISLATIVE PROVISION

Children Act 1989, section 13(1)

Where a residence order is in force with respect to a child, no person may—

(a) cause the child to be known by a new surname; or

(b) remove him from the United Kingdom

---

[302] Registration of Births and Deaths Regulations 1987 (SI 1987/2088), reg. 9(3).
[303] Births and Deaths Registration Act 1953, s. 29.
[304] See, e.g., *Guillot v France* (App. No. 22500/93) (24 October 1996).
[305] [2016] EWCA Civ 374.
[306] [1962] 3 All ER 970.
[307] The procedure for this is set out in *Practice Direction (Minor: Change of Surname: Deed Poll)* [1995] 1 All ER 832.
[308] *Practice Direction (Minor: Change of Surname: Deed Poll)* [1995] 1 All ER 832.

> without either the written consent of every person who has parental responsibility for the child or leave of the court.

So, where a residence order is in force, the name of the child cannot be changed without the consent of all those with parental responsibility or the leave of the court.[309]

The section does not state that the consent of the child is needed. It was left open in *Re PC (Change of Surname)*[310] whether the consent of a *Gillick*-competent child was necessary or sufficient to change the name. Given that the mature child can, in effect, ensure that he or she is known by friends and others by a particular name, there may be little point in ordering an older child to be known by a particular name.[311] The fact that there is a debate over whether a child can choose his or her own name shows how little respect there is for children's autonomy in English law. The decision over one's name is deeply personal, but can hardly be harmful. If children cannot make such decisions one wonders what decisions the law thinks they can make.[312]

(b) Where there is no residence order in force and both parents have parental responsibility
It was held in *Dawson v Wearmouth*[313] that if two people have parental responsibility, the child's name cannot be changed without the agreement of both.[314] If there is no agreement, the court's approval is required. They rejected an argument that s. 2(7) allowed either parent to change the name, arguing that if that was correct it could lead to a chaotic situation with the name being constantly changed and re-changed by each parent. Cobb J has recently explained in *Re B and C (Change of Names: Parental Responsibility: Evidence)*[315] why changing a name is seen as important enough to require the consent of both parents:

> A surname defines, and is defined by, familial heritage and genealogy. A person's forename invariably identifies gender, and often personifies culture, religion, ethnicity, class, social or political ideology. A forename and surname together represent a person's essential identity. From very earliest childhood, one's name is an intrinsic part of who you are and who you become. Thus, the naming of a child 'is not a trivial matter but an important matter'.

As we shall see shortly, not everyone agrees with that.

(c) Where one person has parental responsibility
Holman J in *Re PC (Change of Surname)*[316] suggested that if only one parent has parental responsibility then they could unilaterally change a child's name. An unmarried father without parental responsibility could object to this by applying for a prohibited steps order, but the mother is entitled to change the name, and the burden is on the father to bring the matter to the court if he wishes to object. However, the law is unclear. Lord Mackay in *Dawson v Wearmouth*[317] in the House of Lords stated: 'Any dispute [over the registration of a child's name] should be referred to the court for determination whether or not there is a residence order in force and whoever has

---

[309] Leave of the court should probably be obtained through a section 8 application. For a discussion, see George (2008b).
[310] [1997] 2 FLR 730, [1997] 3 FCR 544.
[311] *Re B (Change of Surname)* [1996] 1 FLR 791, [1996] 2 FCR 304.
[312] Herring (2008d).
[313] [1997] 2 FLR 629 CA; affirmed [1999] 1 FLR 1167, [1999] 1 FCR 625.
[314] Confirmed in *Re B and C (Change of Names: Parental Responsibility: Evidence)* [2017] EWHC 3250 (Fam).
[315] [2017] EWHC 3250 (Fam).
[316] [1997] 2 FLR 730, [1997] 3 FCR 544.
[317] [1999] 1 FLR 1167, [1999] 1 FCR 625.

or has not parental responsibility. No disputed registration or change should be made unilaterally.'[318] This implies that even if only the mother has parental responsibility, she will need to apply to the court for permission to change a child's name. However, in *Re R (A Child)* Hale LJ appeared to suggest that a parent without parental responsibility did not have a right to be consulted over the surname of a child, but did have the right to challenge the choice in court.[319]

(iv) Child in local authority care

Under s. 33(7), if a child is in care then a child's name can only be changed in writing if all those with parental responsibility consent or the court gives leave. It would be open for a child in care, if sufficiently competent, to apply themselves to have their name changed.[320] In *Re M, T, P, K and B (Care: Change of Name)*[321] a local authority was given leave to change the surname of children in care because they lived in fear that their parents would discover their whereabouts. This was seen as a valid reason for giving leave to change the surname.

(v) How will the court resolve a disputed case?

If a dispute over a child's name is brought before the court then the child's welfare will be the paramount consideration.[322] Their Lordships in *Dawson v Wearmouth* made it clear there was no parental right to name a child.[323] At one time it was thought that the person seeking to change the name had to provide 'good and cogent reasons' for changing the name. However, the Court of Appeal in *Re W (Change of Name)*[324] said the court should simply consider what was in a child's welfare and there was no presumption for or against a change of name. The cases indicate that a court seeking to resolve a dispute over the surname of a child will consider the following issues:[325]

1. *The child's views.* The child's views will be important, but not the sole consideration. In *Re S (Change of Surname)*[326] it was held that the views of a *Gillick*-competent child over a surname should be given careful consideration.[327] Surprisingly, Wilson J in *Re B (Change of Surname)*[328] ordered that three children (two teenagers) keep their father's surname, despite their opposition, in order to maintain the link with their father. It might be thought that little more could be done to damage the relationship between a father and teenagers than forcing them to keep his name.

2. *Embarrassment.* It seems that simply arguing that the child is going to be embarrassed by having a different name from their residential parent is not a strong enough argument to justify changing the name.[329] In fact, 'there [is] no opprobrium nowadays for a child to have a different surname from that of adults in the household'.[330]

---

[318] [1999] 1 FLR 1167 at p. 1173.
[319] [2002] 1 FCR 170 at para 9.
[320] *Re S (Change of Surname)* [1999] 1 FLR 672.
[321] [2000] 1 FLR 645.
[322] *Re W (Change of Name)* [2013] EWCA Civ 1488.
[323] But see *Znamenskaya v Russia* [2005] 2 FCR 406 where a mother was held to have a right under Article 8 to give her stillborn child the biological father's surname.
[324] [2013] EWCA Civ 1488.
[325] *Stjerna v Finland* (1994) 24 EHRR 195 ECtHR
[326] [1999] 1 FLR 672.
[327] *Re R (Residence: Shared Care: Children's Views)* [2005] EWCA Civ 542.
[328] [1996] 1 FLR 791, [1996] 2 FCR 304.
[329] *Re F (Child: Surname)* [1993] 2 FLR 827n, [1994] 1 FCR 110; *Re T (Change of Name)* [1998] 2 FLR 620, [1999] 1 FCR 476.
[330] *Re B (Change of Surname)* [1996] 1 FLR 791, [1996] 2 FCR 304 CA; *Re T (Change of Name)* [1998] 2 FLR 620, [1999] 1 FCR 476.

3. *Informal use of names.* There is a difficulty where the child's surname has informally been changed and the child has used the new name for some time before the matter is brought before the court. In such circumstances the court may easily be persuaded that it would be harmful for the child to have the name changed back to the original name. For example, in *Re C (Change of Surname)*[331] the Court of Appeal felt that, although the mother's initial decision to change the surname had been undesirable, given the length of time the children had been known by the new surname it would be inappropriate to revert to the original name. It may be that a court will accept that the formal name in official documents will be different from the informal name.

4. *Strength of the child's relationship with their parents.* Where the residential parent is seeking to change the child's surname from the surname of the non-residential parent then the strength of the relationship between the child and non-residential parent will be taken into account.[332] However, it is not easy to tell how this relationship will be taken into account. If the child sees the non-residential parent only rarely, then that is an argument *in favour* of retaining the non-residential parent's name, because the name may be the strongest link between the child and the non-residential parent. Indeed, in *R v P (No. 2)*[333] Theis J refused to allow the change in the name of a 9-year-old girl to ensure she knew of her father, but intimated that when the girl was over 16, and clearly knew of the father, the issue could be revisited. By contrast, in the B case in *Re W, Re A, Re B (Change of Name)*,[334] approval was given to a change of name from the father's after the father had been imprisoned, because there was not likely to be a meaningful relationship between the child and her father in the future. In *C v D*[335] an approval in the change of surname was approved as the father had rejected his son and derided his autism. In that case it was hard to see any benefit in maintaining the link.

5. *Cultural factors.* A court might place weight on normal rules governing surnames from the parent's cultural background.[336] In *Re S (Change of Names: Cultural Factors)*[337] Wilson J held that the child's name should be changed for day-to-day purposes from a Sikh name to a Muslim name. This was because he had ordered residence to the Muslim mother and therefore the child would inevitably become part of the Muslim community; and the child should be helped to become accepted within that community. However, for formal purposes he held that the name should remain the Sikh name to remind him of his Sikh origins.

6. *Double-barrelled names.* It might be thought that suggesting the child have a double-barrelled name, linking the child to both the mother and father, would be a suitable compromise in many cases. In *Re R (A Child)*[338] it was suggested that using a combination of both surnames was to be encouraged because it would recognise the importance of both parents to the child.

---

[331] [1998] 2 FLR 656.
[332] *Re P (Parental Responsibility: Change of Name)* [1997] 2 FLR 722, [1997] 3 FCR 739.
[333] [2019] EWHC 2175 (Fam).
[334] [1999] 2 FLR 930.
[335] [2018] EWHC 3312 (Fam).
[336] *Re A (A Child) (Change of Name)* [2003] 1 FCR 493.
[337] [2001] 3 FCR 648.
[338] [2002] 1 FCR 170. The option did not appeal to Tyrer J in *A v Y (Child's Surname)* [1999] 2 FLR 5 who thought that only the mother's half (the latter half) of the name would be used. See Herring (2008d) for support for double-barrelled names.

7. *Risk of harm.* The courts have been particularly ready to approve a change of name, where this is necessary to disguise children's identity and protect them from a risk of harm from the father.[339] In *PM v CF (Section 91(14) Order: Risk to Mother and Children)*[340] a change in the children's forenames and surnames was approved because the father posed a significant risk of harm or death to the mother and children.

(vi) First names

In *Re H (Child's Name: First Name)*[341] it was held that the rules in relation to surnames do not apply to forenames. A court will not stop the resident parent from using whatever forename he or she wishes. Foster carers and adoptive parents should not change their children's first names (even by using a shortened form of the name) without the local authority's approval. If there is no agreement, the matter should be taken to the High Court.[342] In *Re C (A Child)*[343] Rogers J was even willing to authorise the removal by deed poll of a child's middle name as its use by the father was causing the child emotional harm.

(vii) What should the law be?

There are three main issues here.[344] The first is whether the question of the surname is an important one. The House of Lords has accepted that changing the surname of the child is a 'profound issue',[345] so much so that the normal rule of independent parenting does not apply. Lord Jauncey in *Dawson v Wearmouth*[346] suggested that 'the surname is . . . a biological label which tells the world at large that the blood of the name flows in its veins'. But is it really a 'profound issue'?[347] It is arguable that although the surname may be important to the parents, it is rarely a profound issue for children, for whom first names are usually far more important. It might be thought the issue of surnames should be regarded as trivial and should not be allowed to take up court time. A simple resolution avoiding court time is available: in the case of a dispute the law could say that the child will have a double-barrelled surname, with each parent choosing one surname.[348]

The second issue is how the law should treat stepfamilies. Many of these cases involve the mother remarrying or re-partnering and wanting to take on her new partner's name. The issue then arises whether the child's name should be changed to reflect the mother's new name and so tie in the child to the new family, or whether the child should keep his or her biological father's name to retain the link with him. Hale LJ in *Re R (A Child)*[349] expressed her view forcefully:

> It is also a matter of great sadness to me that it is so often assumed, and even sometimes argued, that fathers need that outward and visible link in order to retain their relationship with, and

---

[339] *Re B and C (Change of Names: Parental Responsibility: Evidence)* [2017] EWHC 3250 (Fam); *A v D* [2013] EWHC 2963 (Fam); *AB v BB* [2013] EWHC 227 (Fam).
[340] [2018] EWHC 2658 (Fam).
[341] [2002] 1 FLR 973.
[342] *Re D, L and LA (Care: Change of Forename)* [2003] 1 FLR 339.
[343] [2017] EWFC B45.
[344] Herring (1998a); Sarajlic (2018).
[345] *Dawson v Wearmouth* [1999] 1 FLR 1167 at p. 1173, *per* Lord Mackay.
[346] [1999] 1 FLR 1167 at p. 1175.
[347] Thorpe LJ in *Re R (A Child)* [2002] 1 FCR 170 called the surname issue a 'small issue' (para 1).
[348] Herring (2009d).
[349] [2002] 1 FCR 170 at para 13.

commitment to, their child. That should not be the case. It is a poor sort of parent whose interest in and commitment to his child depends upon that child bearing his name. After all, that is a privilege which is not enjoyed by many mothers, even if they are not living with the child. They have to depend upon other more substantial things.

Third, there are those who see the norm of wives and children taking the husband's surname as a way of reinforcing patriarchy. It symbolises the 'headship' of fathers over their family.[350] However, others see the use of a common name as reflecting family unity, rather than any statement of male authority.

J Relocation

It is clear from s. 13(1)(b) of the Children Act 1989[351] that if there is a residence order in force then a child cannot be removed from the United Kingdom for longer than one month unless there is the written consent of every person with parental responsibility, or the leave of the court.[352] Section 13(2) permits a child to be removed for less than one month by the person with the residence order without the consent of others with parental responsibility.[353] If there is a dispute between the parents over removal of the child from the United Kingdom, an application for a specific issue order could be made.[354] Only exceptionally will a parent not be permitted to remove a child from the jurisdiction on a short holiday.[355]

If leave to remove the child from the jurisdiction[356] is sought, the child's welfare is the paramount consideration.[357] The court must take a long-term view in deciding whether leave to remove will promote the child's welfare.[358] The most difficult cases involve the residential parent seeking to emigrate with a child.[359] Not allowing the parent to leave might cause severe distress, which will harm the child. Refusing leave may be regarded as an infringement of the parent's right to respect for private and family life, which includes being able to choose where to live.[360] The non-residential parent may well object on the ground that permitting emigration will severely restrict the practicability of any contact with the child and infringe that parent's rights under Article 8. The approach that the courts have taken is that leave will be granted if the request to emigrate is reasonable and bona fide,[361] unless it is shown that emigration would be contrary to the welfare of the child.[362] Where the children are older, their views will be given weight.[363] Where leave is granted, this may well be on the basis that the children will return to the United Kingdom for lengthy holidays.[364]

---

[350] Herring (2012h).
[351] See the box earlier in the chapter.
[352] For a general discussion of this issue, see Pressdee (2008).
[353] See also Child Abduction Act 1984.
[354] *Re A (Prohibited Steps Order)* [2013] EWCA Civ 1115.
[355] *Re A (Removal from Jurisdiction)* [2012] EWCA Civ 1041.
[356] That is, to remove the child from the country.
[357] CA 1989, s. 1(1). See George (2008b) for a discussion of whether the welfare checklist in s. 1(3) should apply.
[358] *Re B (Children) (Removal from Jurisdiction)* [2001] 1 FCR 108.
[359] For some helpful international comparisons, see George (2011a and b); Young (2011); and Henaghan (2011).
[360] European Convention on Human Rights, Article 8; *Re G-A (A Child) (Removal from Jurisdiction: Human Rights)* [2001] 1 FCR 43.
[361] That is, it is not being made solely for the purpose of bringing the contact arrangement to an end. See, e.g., *Tyler v Tyler* [1989] 2 FLR 158, [1990] FCR 22; *Re K (Application to Remove from Jurisdiction)* [1988] 2 FLR 1006.
[362] *Re H (Application to Remove from Jurisdiction)* [1998] 1 FLR 848, [1999] 2 FCR 34.
[363] *M v M (Minors) (Jurisdiction)* [1993] 1 FCR 5.
[364] *Re B (Minors) (Removal from the Jurisdiction)* [1994] 2 FLR 309; *Re H (Application to Remove from Jurisdiction)* [1998] 1 FLR 848, [1999] 2 FCR 34.

There has been a long series of cases on this issue. At one time considerable attention was paid to the guidance in *Payne v Payne*[365] which was interpreted by some as indicating that the parent with whom the child primarily lived should be permitted to remove the child from the jurisdiction unless their proposals were unreasonable. However, more recent cases have emphasised that the law on relocation is, predictably, governed by the welfare principle. The court should simply ask itself what order would best promote the welfare of the child.[366]

KEY CASE: *Re F (International Relocation Cases)* [2015] EWCA Civ 882[367]

A father appealed a decision giving a German mother leave to take their 12-year-old daughter to Germany. The father was seeing his daughter twice a week for 2.5 hours and staying in contact one weekend in three. The key question on appeal was whether the judge had stuck too rigidly to the *Payne* guidance, rather than undertaking a straightforward welfare analysis. Ryder LJ emphasised that cases on relocation had to be resolved by determining what was in the welfare of the child. The *Payne* judgment was intended to provide questions to be asked in determining what the welfare of the child was and was not intended to provide principles or presumptions. The *Payne* questions could be considered in all cases, and were not limited to cases where there was a primary carer. However, the Court of Appeal warned that 'selective or partial' citation from *Payne* would be an error of law and wider analysis of the welfare of the child was required. The court needed to consider the pros and cons of all options and consider where the welfare of the child lay. In relocation cases this required the court to consider the proposals of both parents.

The Court of Appeal in *Re W (Relocation: Removal Outside Jurisdiction)*[368] and *K v K (Relocation: Shared Care Arrangement)*[369] reiterated that the only authentic principle from the relocation cases is that the welfare of the child is the court's paramount consideration.[370] Mostyn J in *GT v RJ*[371] said the welfare principle is 'not to be glossed, augmented or steered by any presumption in favour of the putative relocator'. In *Re K (A Child: Child Arrangements Order)*[372] Williams J promoted the use of the welfare checklist in s. 1(2) to resolve relocation disputes. In *Re M (Children: Relocation)*[373] the Court of Appeal said it would be incorrect to say the parent seeking permission had to show it was 'necessary' for them to relocate. The court should simply consider whether granting permission would be in the welfare of the child.

In deciding whether relocation will promote the welfare of the child the court is likely to take into account the following factors:

1. The reasons for the wish to relocate. Reasons for relocation which have been regarded as reasonable by the court include the pursuit of a career or educational opportunity;[374]

---

[365] [2001] 1 FCR 425. See Taylor (2011) for some helpful background.
[366] *Re M (Children: Relocation)* [2016] EWCA Civ 1059.
[367] See Devereux and George (2015) for a detailed discussion
[368] [2011] EWCA Civ 345.
[369] [2011] EWCA Civ 793.
[370] *Re Z (Relocation)* [2012] EWHC 139 (Fam).
[371] [2018] EWFC 26.
[372] [2020] EWHC 488 (Fam).
[373] [2016] EWCA Civ 1059.
[374] E.g. *W v A* [2004] EWCA Civ 1587.

the wish to return to the home country or to be close to family and friends;[375] the desire to join a new partner[376] to enable that partner to pursue career or educational opportunities;[377] and the hope of establishing a new life in a new place. Of course, if the judge decides that the reason the applicant wishes to relocate is a desire to terminate the contact between the other spouse and the children it is very unlikely that leave will be granted.[378] In *Re S and V (Children: Leave to Remove)*[379] the mother wished to relocate to pursue a relationship with a man, but the couple had never lived together and the man had no experience raising children. These factors weighed against granting leave. By contrast in *Re M (Children: Relocation)*[380] the court took the view that the mother's marriage with her new partner was stable and the nurturing of the new family unit was important. Those were factors in favour of authorising the relocation. The court will consider whether there are ways of meeting the concerns of the parent seeking relocation that do not involve leaving the country. In *AY v AS*[381] the mother sought to return to Kazakhstan with the children due to difficulties she faced in finding employment in Devon. Mostyn J authorised her moving to London where there would be better employment opportunities.

2. The strength of the relationship between child and parents.[382] Where the child has a strong relationship with both parents the courts will be reluctant to approve relocation if that will have a significantly negative impact on the relationship with one parent.[383] The court should consider the impact of the possible orders on the relationship between the child and each parent. If there are other adults in the United Kingdom who have a close relationship with the child, the impact of allowing leave on those relationships can be considered.[384]

3. The impact of the refusal on the parents and the resulting effect on the children. If the children spend most time with one parent then it is likely that any emotional harm with that parent will be more significant than emotional harm to the other parent.[385] In *Re W (Relocation: Removal Outside Jurisdiction)*[386] the Court of Appeal overruled a judge's refusal to grant leave because he had failed to place adequate weight on the impact of the refusal on the mother and thereby on the children.[387] The courts are likely to require medical evidence to strengthen a case that refusal will have severe psychological impact.[388] In *Re S and V (Children: Leave to Remove)*[389] Mostyn J said a court would treat the claim of a parent who said they would not cope if leave were not granted 'very circumspectly'. He repeated comments he had previously made in *Re AR (A Child: Relocation)*:[390]

---

[375] E.g. *Payne v Payne* [2001] 1 FLR 1052.
[376] E.g. *Re A (Leave To Remove: Cultural and Religious Considerations)* [2006] EWHC 421 (Fam).
[377] E.g. *L v L (Leave to Remove Children from Jurisdiction: Effect on Children)* [2002] EWHC 2577 (Fam); [2003] 1 FLR 900; *Re J (Children) (Residence Order: Removal Outside the Jurisdiction)* [2007] 2 FCR 149.
[378] *Re P (Children)* [2014] EWCA Civ 852.
[379] [2018] EWFC 26.
[380] [2016] EWCA Civ 1059.
[381] [2019] EWHC 3043 (Fam).
[382] The same principles will apply with a step-parent: *Re S (Relocation: Parental Responsibility)* [2013] EWHC 1295 (Fam).
[383] *Re L (Relocation: Shared Residence)* [2012] EWHC 3069 (Fam); *AY v AS* [2019] EWHC 3043 (Fam).
[384] *DL v CL* [2014] EWHC 1836 (Fam).
[385] *Re E (Location: Removal from Jurisdiction)* [2012] EWCA Civ 1893.
[386] [2011] EWCA Civ 345.
[387] *Re E (Location: Removal from Jurisdiction)* [2012] EWCA Civ 1893.
[388] *Re TG* [2009] EWHC 3122 (Fam).
[389] [2018] EWFC 26.
[390] [2010] EWHC 1346 (Fam).

The problem with the attribution of great weight to this particular factor is that, paradoxically, it appears to penalise selflessness and virtue, while rewarding selfishness and uncontrolled emotions. The core question of the putative relocator is always 'how would you react if leave were refused?' The parent who stoically accepts that she would accept the decision, make the most of it, move on and work to promote contact with the other parent is far more likely to be refused leave than the parent who states that she will collapse emotionally and psychologically.

The problem with these comments is that if the welfare of the child is to be considered, the impact on their primary carer of the order is central. Perhaps the point is that solid evidence of the impact on the resident parent is required. For example, in *J v S (Leave to Remove)*[391] expert evidence established that if leave were refused the mother would suffer long-term ill health, requiring anti-depressants and input from a clinical psychologist.

4. In some cases the wishes of the children will be weighty factors.[392] In *S v S (Relocation)*[393] (Fam) when considering the strong views of the two boys aged 13 and 15 that they wished to move to live with their father in Switzerland, it was held that at that age their views were a 'very important element' in the welfare assessment.

5. The court will also scrutinise the proposals for contact. In *W v A*[394] the Court of Appeal accepted that technology had made international communication easier with telephone, e-mail, text messages, Skype and digital photography. All of these would help a non-resident parent keep up a relationship with the child even if they were now living overseas. In *B v S*[395] Sedley LJ suggested that a father might find occasional substantial periods of residence a more effective way of maintaining a relationship than regular short times of non-residential contact. In *Re E (Location: Removal from Jurisdiction)*[396] the mother agreed to bring the child to England for three months each summer. The court in granting leave noted that the father would in fact be spending no fewer days with the children per year under the proposed arrangement than he was with the current arrangement of seeing them every other weekend.

6. In *K v K (Relocation: Shared Care Arrangement)*[397] Thorpe LJ held that the court should also consider whether the non-resident parent should move with the resident parent. If there are good reasons to allow the mother to relocate and the judge believes contact with the children should continue, the judge would be entitled to ask the father why he does not move with them. There is, however, no way a father could be forced to move against his will in such a case.

7. Where the relocation is only a temporary one (e.g. on a holiday or extended visit), it is less likely the court will not approve the removal. However, the court may still do so if there is a risk the children will not be returned, particularly if they are being taken to a country where there is no international agreement making it easier to have the children returned.[398]

---

[391] [2010] EWHC 2098 (Fam).
[392] *Re J (Leave to Remove: Urgent Case)* [2006] EWCA Civ 1897. *Re S (Relocation: Interests of Siblings)* [2011] EWCA Civ 454.
[393] [2017] EWHC 2345 (Fam).
[394] [2004] EWCA Civ 1587 at para 19.
[395] [2003] EWCA Civ 1149 at para 34.
[396] [2012] EWCA Civ 1893.
[397] [2011] EWCA Civ 793.
[398] *Re DO (Temporary Relocation to China)* [2017] EWHC 858 (Fam).

The courts' approach has been controversial. Mary Hayes[399] argues that parents should accept restrictions on their liberties as one of the burdens of bringing up children. However, it should be noted that while the resident parent needs leave to go out of the jurisdiction with the child, the non-resident parent has freedom to move wherever he wishes. So, the restrictions on liberty are not equally placed on parents. While holding that the decision in *Payne* was justifiable, Bainham is concerned that the reasoning used:

> . . . apparently attached more significance to the security and stability of the child with her mother, than it did to the preservation of the child's relationship with the father, as secondary carer, and the father's family. This, again, might be criticised as an inadequate response to the child's identity rights under the UN Convention.[400]

The approach can also be said to fail to attach sufficient weight to the rights of the child and non-resident parent as required by the Human Rights Act.[401] However, it can be argued that adopting a human rights approach would not lead to a change in the results reached because the autonomy rights of the resident parent and child would normally be more weighty than the other rights of the non-resident parent and child.[402]

K Internal relocation

Normally, the court will be reluctant to restrict a parent from moving to a different part of the country on the basis that it would harm the child. It has been said that doing so is only suitable in truly exceptional cases.[403] In *Re L (A Child) (Internal Relocation: Shared Residence Order)*[404] there was a joint residence order, but the mother found a new job and wished to move to Somerset from North London, where the father lived. The Court of Appeal held that the case should be determined simply by an application of the welfare principle. The judge held that the move should not be permitted because of the impact on the child's relationship with the father. Although the Court of Appeal questioned whether the judge had placed adequate weight on the impact of refusal on the mother, it upheld the judge's decision as within his judicial discretion. The fact that this was a joint residence case was said simply to be a factor in deciding what was in the child's welfare.[405] In *Re F (Children) (Internal Relocation)*[406] the mother wished to move from Cleveland with her four children to the Orkney Islands, after a job offer. The children had regular extensive contact with the father and he objected. The Court of Appeal upheld the judge's refusal to allow the mother to move.[407] The Court of Appeal agreed with the first instance judge who noted that the removal to the Orkneys was equivalent to a removal to another country in terms of the difficulty of enabling contact. Wilson LJ questioned whether it was right to say that internal relocation should only be restricted in exceptional cases, given the impact could be comparable to removal from the jurisdiction. While making no finding on the issue, it is likely this point will be developed in

---

[399] Hayes (2006).
[400] Bainham (2002a: 285). See Judd and George (2010) for a comparative consideration of the law.
[401] See George (2011c and 2015).
[402] Herring and Taylor (2006).
[403] *Re B (Prohibited Steps Order)* [2008] 1 FLR 613 and *Re E (Residence: Imposition of Conditions)* [1997] 2 FLR 638 (CA) at 642.
[404] [2009] 1 FCR 584.
[405] *Re S (Child)* [2012] EWCA Civ 1031.
[406] [2010] EWCA Civ 1428.
[407] The mother had applied for a specific issue order allowing her to relocate, although in fact she may not have needed to have done so. In a different case the father might have applied for a prohibited steps order to prevent her moving.

other cases. In *Re R (Children: Temporary Leave to Remove from Jurisdiction)*[408] a prohibited steps order was made preventing the mother moving to London to be with her new boyfriend. The order appears to be based on the concerns over the man. A criminal records check had not been performed on him; his immigration status was unclear; and the mother had been untruthful about him to the father. The court indicated that if these concerns were overcome the restriction would be lifted.

These cases are, however, rare. In *Re S (A Child)*[409] the Court of Appeal refused to restrict where the mother and child could live, acknowledging her argument that the father's application to restrict her movement was part of a pattern of controlling behaviour by the father. Baroness Hale in *Re G (Children) (Residence: Same-Sex Partner)*[410] confirmed that orders restricting where a parent should live are generally regarded as an unwarranted imposition on the right of the parent, although they can be justified in exceptional cases.[411] The leading recent case is the following:

KEY CASE: *Re C (Internal Relocation)* [2015] EWCA Civ 1305[412]

The child lived in London sharing her time between her mother and father, with two nights per week and every other weekend with the father. The mother wished to return to Cumbria, where she had been raised. The father sought an order preventing her from moving. The Court of Appeal declined the father's application. Black LJ accepted that relocation disputes involved an interference in the rights of parents, but said the court must focus on the welfare of the child. Black LJ had this to say:

> It is no doubt the case, as a matter of fact, that courts will be resistant to preventing a parent from exercising his or her choice as to where to live in the United Kingdom unless the child's welfare requires it, but that is not because of a rule that such a move can only be prevented in exceptional cases. It is because the welfare analysis leads to that conclusion.

Vos LJ summarised the law in this way:

> In cases concerning either external or internal relocation the only test that the court applies is the paramount principle as to the welfare of the child. The application of that test involves a holistic balancing exercise undertaken with the assistance, by analogy, of the welfare checklist, even where it is not statutorily applicable. The exercise is not a linear one. It involves balancing all the relevant factors, which may vary hugely from case to case, weighing one against the other, with the objective of determining which of the available options best meets the requirement to afford paramount consideration to the welfare of the child. It is no part of this exercise to regard a decision in favour of or against any particular available option as exceptional (para [82]).

This approach was confirmed in *Re R (Internal Relocation: Appeal)*[413] where it was emphasised that the welfare principle in its pure form applied to these cases. This case was slightly different in that the mother and child had already moved to the North East of England and

---

[408] [2014] EWHC 643 (Fam).
[409] [2012] EWCA Civ 1031.
[410] [2006] UKHL 43 at para 15.
[411] Applied in *Re M (A Child)* [2014] EWCA Civ 1755. See also Bainham (2016).
[412] Discussed in Easton and Jarmain (2016) and Worwood and Hale (2016).
[413] [2016] EWCA Civ 1016.

the father was seeking that she and the child return to Kent. The judge was entitled...
mine that requiring the child to move back to Kent would not promote the child's...
Critics of this case may complain that in many cases if a child is moved and has settled...
new part of the country it is unlikely the court will find it beneficial for the child to move...
to where they came from and this puts non-resident parents in a vulnerable position. This is
true, but at the end of the day the courts put the welfare of the child first.

L When should there be contact between a child and parent?

Learning objective 4

Summarise the issues around
contact disputes

We have left the most controversial issue to the end. Baroness
Hale has declared: 'Making contact happen and, even more
importantly, making contact work is one of the most difficult and
contentious challenges in the whole of family law.'[414] Contact
disputes can become bitterly contested and impossible to resolve satisfactorily.[415] Groups such
as Fathers for Justice have claimed that the law on contact discriminates against fathers.
In *V v V (Contact: Implacable Hostility)*[416] Bracewell J admitted:

> There is a perception among part of the media, and some members of the parents' groups, as
> well as members of the public, that the courts rubber-stamp cases awarding care of children to
> mothers almost automatically and marginalise fathers from the lives of their children. There is
> also a perception that courts allow parents with care to flout court orders for contact and permit
> parents with residence to exclude the parent from the lives of the children so that the other parent
> is worn down by years of futile litigation which achieves nothing and only ends when that parent
> gives up the struggle, or the children are old enough to make their own decisions, assuming they
> have not been brainwashed in the meantime . . .

The publicity these campaigns have generated has led Wall J to state: 'The courts are not
anti-father and pro-mother or vice versa.'[417] The fact that members of the judiciary feel it is
necessary to make such comments indicates the pressure they feel under as regards this issue.
In a careful review of the evidence Joan Hunt and Alison Macleod[418] found no evidence of
bias against the father. Indeed, they found the courts were very reluctant not to order
contact.

Before considering the approach the courts have taken, the findings of psychologists on the
benefits of contact will be considered.

(i) Psychological evidence of the benefits of contact

There is much support among child psychologists for 'attachment theory': that at an early age
a child forms a psychological attachment with a parent or parent figure. This normally takes
place within the first three months of the child's life, but may occur even up to age seven.
Removing that child from the adult to whom they have become attached can cause the child
serious harm. Of course, the quality of the attachment is of great significance, but the breaking
of any attachment can cause harm.[119] The dominant view in England and Wales is that contact

---

[414] *Re G (Children) (Residence: Same-Sex Partner)* [2006] 1 WLR 2305.
[415] Geldof (2003) is a vivid expression of the emotions that arise in disputed contact cases. See generally Bainham
et al. (2003) for a useful discussion of the issues.
[416] [2004] EWHC 1215 (Fam).
[417] *Re O (A Child) (Contact: Withdrawal of Application)* [2003] EWHC 3031 (Fam) at para 3.
[418] Hunt and Macleod (2008).
[419] See, e.g., Goldstein, Solnit and Freud (1996).

between a child and both parents is in general beneficial.[420] A number of benefits have been claimed for contact with parents:

1. It avoids the child feeling rejected by the non-residential parent.

2. It enables the parent and child to maintain a beneficial relationship.

3. Contact may dispel erroneous fantasies that the child could have about the non-residential parent.

4. Contact helps the child develop or retain a sense of identity. In particular, it may help in maintaining a sense of cultural identity.

5. Contact can help the child understand the parental separation.

6. It can ensure the child retains contact with the wider family of the non-residential parent.

7. It can help the child feel free to develop relationships with a step-parent without a sense of betrayal to his or her birth parent.

However, proof of these benefits is not established beyond doubt.[421] As Eekelaar and Maclean explain:

> What has not been established is whether a child whose separated parents behave gently and reasonably to her and to one another, but who sees the outside parent rarely or never, somehow does 'less well' than a child of similar parents who sees the outside parent often.[422]

There is good evidence that benefits do not flow from the mere existence of the contact; what matters is the frequency and quality of the contact.[423] As Pryor and Daly Peoples put it:

> Fathers who are able to have a nurturing and monitoring role have a positive impact on their children in a variety of ways . . . Those fathers whose participation is confined to outings and having fun will, then, have little influence on their children's adjustment.[424]

Stephen Gilmore, summarising his extensive studies into the benefits of contact, states:[425]

> Research suggests that it is not contact per se but the nature and quality of contact that are important to children's adjustment, and there is a range of factors which impact upon the nature and quality of contact . . . The evidence does not suggest that we can, or should, generalise about the benefits of contact.

In an important study looking at children's account of contact by Fortin, Hunt and Scanlan,[426] a central conclusion was that we should not assume there is an ideal model of contact for all children:

> . . . different children will be satisfied with different amounts of contact and that the quantity of contact is less important than the quality of the child's experience.

Even if there are benefits of contact, it must be recognised that there are also potential disadvantages:[427]

---

[420] Willbourne and Stanley (2002).
[421] As Eekelaar (2002b) points out, a number of studies cast doubt on the assumption that contact is beneficial: e.g. Poussin and Martin-LeBrun (2002).
[422] Eekelaar and Maclean (1997: 55). See further Hunt (2006a).
[423] Lewis (2005); Rogers and Pryor (1998: 40); Hetherington and Kelly (2002: 133).
[424] Pryor and Daly Peoples (2001: 199). See further Hunt (2006a).
[425] Gilmore (2008a). See also Gilmore (2006a and b and 2008b).
[426] Fortin, Hunt and Scanlan (2012).
[427] Discussed in *Re L (A Child) (Contact: Domestic Violence)* [2000] 2 FCR 404.

1. Contact often leads to bitter disputes between the resident and non-resident parent, and this atmosphere of conflict may harm the child.[428]

2. The child may feel torn between the residential and non-residential parent, a feeling which may be exacerbated by emotionally intense contact sessions. This may cause psychological disturbance.

3. The relationship between the child and the non-residential parent may be an abusive or bullying one whose continuance will harm the child.

A recent study on children in stepfamilies[429] found that contact with the non-resident parent had no discernible impact on children's welfare. Crucial to a child's welfare were the relationships in the home where the child was living. This suggests that the law should not seek to promote contact where this will cause severe disturbance in the child's home.[430]

To conclude on the current state of the evidence on the benefits of contact between a child and non-resident parent: what the evidence certainly does show is that it should not be assumed that contact is always beneficial.[431] On the other hand, there are numerous benefits that *can* flow from contact in many cases where the contact is part of a constructive relationship.[432] Certainly there is evidence that children value the contact they have with their non-resident parent and would like to have more.[433] The appropriate amount of contact depends on the particular child and relationship and it should not be assumed that one model of contact (such as spending an equal amount of time with each parent) is best in all cases. It should certainly not be assumed that the more contact a child has with both parents the better.[434] As Fortin notes:

> Regular and continuous contact was both a better predictor of a good contact experience with their non-resident parent and of a close child/parent relationship through into adulthood, than quantity of contact . . . Our statistical data suggest that the more traditional order, where a child lives with one parent and has regular contact with the other, is by no means second best so far as children are concerned.

It should not be forgotten in all the debate over whether children benefit or not from contact that contact arrangements can have significant impact on the welfare of fathers[435] and mothers.[436] Most importantly, it must not be assumed that because contact is beneficial, forcing contact through court orders will be beneficial.

(ii) The courts' approach to contact

The current approach of the courts is to accept that contact cases should be decided on the basis of what is in the welfare of the child.[437] It is true that some cases have talked of children having a right to contact.[438] For, example, Sir Stephen Brown suggested in *Re W (A Minor) (Contact)*:[439] 'It is quite clear that contact with a parent is a fundamental right of a child, save

---

[428] This was accepted by Wall J in *A v A (Children) (Shared Residence Order)* [2004] 1 FCR 201.
[429] Smith *et al.* (2001).
[430] Maclean and Mueller-Johnson (2003).
[431] Rogers and Pryor (1998); Kaganas and Piper (1999).
[432] Hetherington and Kelly (2002); Poussin and Martin-LeBrun (2002); Trinder (2003a).
[433] Dunn (2003).
[434] Fortin (2015).
[435] Simpson, Jessop and McCarthy (2003).
[436] Day Sclater and Kaganas (2003).
[437] *AB v BB* [2013] EWHC 227 (Fam).
[438] E.g. *Re S (Minors) (Access)* [1990] 2 FLR 166 at p. 170, *per* Balcombe LJ; *Re F (Contact: Restraint Order)* [1995] 1 FLR 956 at p. 963.
[439] [1994] 2 FLR 441 CA at p. 447.

in wholly exceptional circumstances.' Notably, those cases which have referred to a right to contact have stressed that contact is the right of the child and not the parent.[440] However, in more recent cases the courts have preferred not to talk of a right to contact, which is a misnomer because s. 1(1) of the Children Act 1989 applies to contact applications and so the key question is whether or not the contact will promote the child's welfare.[441] In *Re M (Contact: Welfare Test)* the Court of Appeal suggested a helpful question was:

> . . . whether the fundamental emotional need of every child to have an enduring relationship with both his parents [s. 1(3)(b)] is outweighed by the depth of harm which in the light, *inter alia*, of his wishes and feelings [s. 1(3)(a)] this child would be at risk of suffering [s. 1(3)(e)] by virtue of a contact order.[442]

This quotation has been approved in the Court of Appeal in *Re L (A Child) (Contact: Domestic Violence)*,[443] where Thorpe LJ and Butler-Sloss P explained that it was not appropriate to talk of a right to contact.[444] Thorpe LJ was not keen even on referring to a presumption in favour of contact and preferred to talk of an assumption of the benefit of contact which was 'the base of knowledge and experience from which the court embarks upon its application of the welfare principle'.[445] He suggested that the strength of the case in favour of contact depended on the quality of the relationship between the non-resident parent and the child. Where there is a high-quality existing relationship, the case for contact is at its strongest, but if the child does not know the parent, or the relationship is an abusive one, the argument for contact is much weaker.[446] Whether or not the father is married to the mother should not be a relevant factor.[447] In *VB v JD*[448] Cohen J approved what he referred to as 'identity contact' with the mother. This was contact just a couple of times a year so that the child could be reassured that her mother was well. In that case it seems the purpose of the contact was not to create a meaningful relationship, but rather to offer reassurance and the child had some idea of who the mother was.

All the different factors needed to be weighed up to determine whether contact would be in the best interests of the child.

The leading case is now *Re W (Children)*.[449] MacFarlane LJ explained:

> When a court determines any question with respect to the upbringing of a child, the child's welfare must be the court's paramount consideration (CA 1989, s. 1(1)). The paramountcy principle in CA 1989, s. 1(1), coloured as it is by the requirement of the court to have regard in particular to the aspects of welfare set out in the welfare checklist in s. 1(3), is the sole statutory mandate directing the course that a court is to take in determining issues relating to the welfare of a child. Although the case of each child before a court will be unique and will justify careful scrutiny and a bespoke conclusion tailored to meet the particular welfare requirements of that young individual, the courts have nevertheless developed general approaches which indicate the contours of the landscape within which welfare determinations are likely to be taken when there is a dispute between a child's parents.

[440] *M v M (Child: Access)* [1973] 2 All ER 81.
[441] See the discussion in Bailey-Harris (2001d).
[442] [1995] 1 FLR 274 at p. 275.
[443] [2000] 2 FLR 334, [2000] 2 FCR 404 CA
[444] Kaganas and Day Sclater (2000).
[445] *Re L (A Child) (Contact: Domestic Violence)* [2000] 2 FCR 404 at p. 437.
[446] *Re L (A Child) (Contact: Domestic Violence)* [2000] 2 FCR 404 at p. 437.
[447] *Sahin v Germany* [2003] 2 FCR 619.
[448] [2019] EWHC 612 (Fam).
[449] [2012] EWCA Civ 999.

He then approved Wall J's statement in *Re P (Contact: Supervision)*[450] as an example of the general approaches he was talking about:

1. Overriding all else, as provided by s. 1(1) of the 1989 Act, the welfare of the child is the paramount consideration, and the court is concerned with the interests of the mother and the father only in so far as they bear on the welfare of the child.

2. It is almost always in the interests of a child whose parents are separated that he or she should have contact with the parent with whom the child is not living.

3. The court has power to enforce orders for contact, which it should not hesitate to exercise where it judges that it will overall promote the welfare of the child to do so.

4. Cases do, unhappily and infrequently but occasionally, arise in which a court is compelled to conclude that in existing circumstances an order for immediate direct contact should not be ordered, because so to order would injure the welfare of the child . . .

5. In cases in which, for whatever reason, direct contact cannot for the time being be ordered, it is ordinarily highly desirable that there should be indirect contact so that the child grows up knowing of the love and interest of the absent parent with whom, in due course, direct contact should be established.

Here we see a welcome reassertion of the importance of assessing the welfare of the particular child. While contact with parents, generally speaking, is good for children, that is just one of the factors to be taken into account in deciding whether on the facts of the particular case contact will be in the welfare of the particular child.[451] This is in line with the decision of the Supreme Court in *Re B (A Child)*[452] which recommended that judges should focus on assessing the welfare of the particular child, without being sidetracked by talk of presumptions. It is also in line with the new presumption in favour of parental involvement added into the Children Act by the Children and Families Act 2014, discussed above. It is clear that there is a presumption of involvement in the life of a child, but this need not involve direct contact. Indeed, the limited nature of the statutory presumption may be taken as evidence that it would be wrong to say there is a formal presumption in favour of contact. Parliament has said the only presumption is of involvement and it would be wrong for the courts to create a stronger presumption of contact.

Subsequent cases show the courts hold in tension the assertion that the welfare principle is paramount, with the additional view that contact is generally beneficial.[453] In *Re R (No Order for Contact: Appeal)*[454] Clarke LJ stated:

[T]he court has in a series of cases stressed the importance of contact between parent and child as a fundamental element of family life, which is almost always in the interests of the child, and which is to be terminated only in exceptional circumstances, where there are cogent reasons for doing so and when there is no alternative. Contact is to be terminated only where it would be detrimental to the child's welfare. The judge has a duty to promote such contact and to grapple with all available alternatives before abandoning hope of achieving some contact. Contact should be stopped only as a last resort and once it has become clear that the child will not benefit from continuing the attempt. The court should take a medium to long term view and not accord excessive weight to what appear likely to be short term and transient problems.

---

[450] [1996] 2 FLR 314.
[451] Gilmore (2008b).
[452] [2009] UKSC 5.
[453] *Re M (Contact Refusal: Appeal)* [2013] EWCA Civ 1147.
[454] [2014] EWCA Civ 1664.

There is, then a very thin line being drawn by the courts: the welfare principle applies to all contact cases; there is no presumption that contact will promote contact; but it nearly always is in the welfare of the child that contact take place (*London Borough of Croydon v BU;*[455] *Re D (A Child);*[456] *Re A (A Child);*[457] *Re R (No Order for Contact: Appeal)*[458]).

Some of the recent case law gives a flavour of the kind of cases where contact is not ordered. In *Re K (Children: Refusal of Direct Contact)*[459] the father was a serial sex offender who had been severely restricted in having contact with any children. It was held he should not be given a contact order. In *Re T (A Child: One Parent Killed by Other Parent)*[460] HHJ Clifford Bellamy held that there was no presumption that a father who killed a mother should not have contact with his children, but on the facts of this case there should be no contact. In *PM v CF (Section 91(14) Order: Risk to Mother and Children)*[461] the mother and children were at significant risk of harm and death from the father, so much so that the police had taken the rare step of putting them on the Protected Persons Scheme, and so no contact was authorised. The fact that we need court decisions to tell us contact was not appropriate in these cases shows how extreme the circumstances must be before contact is not permitted.

Although the courts have generally been reluctant to talk of a right of contact, the European Court of Human Rights has made it quite clear that the right to respect for family and private life under Article 8 of the European Convention on Human Rights includes the right of contact between parents and children.[462] In *Elsholz v Germany*[463] it was confirmed that to deny contact between a father and a child where they had an established relationship infringed Article 8, although denial of contact could be justified under paragraph 2 if necessary in the interests of the child or resident parent.[464] When weighing up the interests of parents and child in relation to contact, the welfare of the child will be of 'crucial importance'.[465] However, it must be shown that the concerns over the welfare of the child render the infringement of the father's right necessary.[466] In other words, contact should not be denied simply because it will very slightly harm the child; a significant harm to the child is required to justify denying contact. In *Wdowiak v Poland*[467] it was emphasised that the state had an obligation to take 'all necessary steps' to enforce contact. The fact the parents are in disagreement is not alone sufficient to justify the state not interfering.

This human rights reasoning sometimes appears in the English cases. In *Re A (A Child) (Intractable Contact Dispute: Human Rights Violations)*[468] the Court of Appeal stated that not making a contact order would infringe the rights of a father. The judge would have to ensure that any interference was 'justified and proportionate'. The standard approach is that taken in *Re L (A Child) (Contact: Domestic Violence)*[469] and by Munby LJ in *Re C (A Child)*[470] where

---

[455] [2014] EWHC 823 (Fam).

[456] [2014] EWCA Civ 1057.

[457] [2013] EWCA Civ 1104.

[458] [2014] EWCA Civ 1664.

[459] [2011] EWCA Civ 1064.

[460] [2011] EWHC B4.

[461] [2018] EWHC 2658 (Fam).

[462] *Hokkanen v Finland* (1995) 19 EHRR 139 and *Ignaccolo-Zenide v Romania* (2001) 31 EHRR 7.

[463] [2000] 2 FLR 486 ECtHR

[464] *Sahin v Germany* [2003] 2 FCR 619 ECtHR Although see *Hansen v Turkey* [2004] 1 FLR 142 where the fact that the child did not want to have contact was in that case not sufficient to justify an interference in the right of the father to see the child.

[465] *Sahin v Germany* [2002] 3 FCR 321 ECtHR at para 40.

[466] *Elsholz v Germany* [2000] 2 FLR 486 ECtHR; *Suss v Germany* [2005] 3 FCR 666.

[467] [2017] ECHR 133. See also *Pisica v Moldova* (App. No. 23641/17).

[468] [2013] EWCA Civ 1104.

[469] [2000] 2 FLR 334, [2000] 2 FCR 404 CA

[470] [2011] EWCA Civ 521, para 47.

it was held that the human rights to contact were protected by the application of the welfare principle used by the English courts.[471] On that view, there is no need to discuss human rights, because the human rights issues will all be dealt with by using the welfare principle. Interestingly in their study of women opposing contact claiming their partners had been abusive, Jenny Birchall and Shazia Choudhry[472] found 50 per cent of the women said the court had discussed the man's rights and 36 per cent her rights. This suggests that rights arguments are used but more often it is the right of contact which is discussed rather than rights to protection from violence.

In summary, the present law on contact is that the courts will consider the benefits and disadvantages of contact in each particular case. There is no presumption in favour of contact, although its benefits will readily be found in an appropriate case. In each case the courts will weigh up the benefits and disadvantages of contact.[473] They should make sure that contact is only denied if that is the only option consistent with the welfare of the child. The courts have not accepted the arguments of some commentators that there should be a presumption in favour of equal parenting after divorce nor that the Human Rights Act 1998 requires a different approach.[474] However, there is a presumption, if the parent poses no risk to the child, that they will be involved to some extent in the child's life.

We will now consider certain types of contact cases which have raised particular difficulties.

(iii) The opposition of the residential parent

Over the years there have been changes in approach towards cases where the resident parent is strongly opposed to contact.[475] At one time opposition was thoroughly castigated. In *Re O (Contact: Imposition of Conditions)*[476] it was stated:

> The courts should not at all readily accept that the child's welfare will be injured by direct contact . . . Neither parent should be encouraged or permitted to think that the more intransigent, the more unreasonable, the more obdurate and the more uncooperative they are, the more likely they are to get their own way.

More recently, in *Re P (Contact Discretion)*,[477] the courts have accepted that there may be very good reasons for the residential parent to oppose contact, and it is now necessary to distinguish two types of cases.[478] First, where the opposition of the parent is justified: in such a case if the residential parent's fears are 'genuine and rationally held'[479] then the court may refuse contact.[480] For example, where the resident parent reasonably claims that there is a risk of violence to the children or abduction,[481] that would be a reasonable ground to oppose contact, unless that risk can be eliminated.[482] Secondly, those cases where the opposition is 'emotional' and

---

[471] See Choudhry and Herring (2010) for further discussion.
[472] Birchall and Choudhry (2017).
[473] For an example of where the disadvantages outweighed the advantages, see *Re F (Children) (Contact: Change of Surname)* [2007] 3 FCR 832.
[474] For arguments that the Human Rights Act 1998 does require a new approach to contact cases, see Choudhry and Fenwick (2005).
[475] Wallbank (1998) discusses these cases.
[476] [1995] 2 FLR 124 at pp. 129–30.
[477] [1998] 2 FLR 696, [1999] 1 FCR 566.
[478] See also *Re D (Contact: Reasons for Refusal)* [1997] 2 FLR 48, [1998] 1 FCR 321.
[479] *Re D (Contact: Reasons for Refusal)* [1997] 2 FLR 48 at p. 53.
[480] For a thorough discussion, see Children Act Sub-Committee (2002a) and *Re H (A Child) (Contact: Mother's Opposition)* [2001] 1 FCR 59.
[481] D. Smith (2003).
[482] *Re H (Children) (Contact Order) (No. 2)* [2001] 3 FCR 385.

there is no rational basis for it: in such a case contact will be ordered unless it can be shown that the residential parent will suffer such distress if forced to permit contact that the child will be harmed.[483] In *Re H (Children) (Contact Order) (No. 2)*[484] Wall J held that the child's need to have a competent and confident primary carer outweighed their need to have direct contact with their father in a case where there was evidence that the mother might have a nervous breakdown if contact was ordered. However, in *Re A (A Child) (Intractable Contact Dispute)*[485] it was held that only in a case where there was a serious risk of harm should the 'unreasonable' objections of a parent be a reason for denying contact. In *Re S-B (Children)*[486] it was emphasised by the Court of Appeal that the mother and children finding the contact unsettling or inconvenient would certainly not be sufficient to deny contact.

The problem with the analysis just presented is that very rarely is the resident parent simply being irrational in opposing contact. The most common scenario for these cases is that the mother has alleged domestic abuse, but that has not been found proved by the courts. Her opposition is therefore 'baseless' in the eyes of the court, but she is unlikely to be persuaded by the finding of facts by the court that her fears are misguided. Gilmore[487] suggests a distinction could be drawn between cases where an allegation is unproven and one where the courts have found it positively disproved. In the latter case the courts should be wary of allowing a belief on a disproved allegation as a reason to deny contact. We will return to this issue further when we specifically discuss domestic violence and contact.

A few recent cases have focused on the father's conduct and have accepted the argument that the father, if he wishes to have contact, must behave in a more suitable way.[488] It would be wrong to say that there is a rule that a father who has behaved badly must acknowledge his misbehaviour and apologise if he has to have contact, but not doing so will harm his case.[489] The willingness of the court to look at the father's conduct is important because the earlier case law had concentrated on the mother and regarded her opposition as the problem, rather than considering whether it was the father's behaviour which created the difficulties.[490] Some commentators have suggested that the law is predicated on an image of a 'good' or 'bad' mother or father.[491] A mother is automatically 'bad' if she denies contact to a father, even when she fears that the father may harm the child; whereas a father is 'good' if he seeks contact with the child, even though he may have shown disregard of the child's welfare during the parents' relationship.[492] In *RS v SS*[493] Harris J held:

> I found the mother to be a very angry and wilful woman. Her hatred of the father is almost pathological. In my judgment, this is likely to have its origins in the circumstances of the breakdown of their marriage: the father leaving when CD was but a few weeks' old, and her belief that the father had already begun an affair with SB.

By contrast, Harris J said of the father: 'He is totally committed to his sons.' After reading the facts not everyone will agree with Harris J's assessment. Some people will find it understandable

---

[483] *Re C (Contact: Supervision)* [1996] 2 FLR 314 suggested that it may be difficult to persuade a court of this.
[484] [2001] 3 FCR 385.
[485] [2013] EWCA Civ 1104.
[486] [2015] EWCA Civ 705.
[487] Gilmore (2020).
[488] *Re M (Minors) (Contact: Violent Parent)* [1999] 2 FCR 56; *Re O (A Child) (Contact: Withdrawal of Application)* [2004] 1 FCR 687.
[489] *Re K (Contact)* [2016] EWCA Civ 99.
[490] Smart and Neale (1999a).
[491] Wallbank (2007).
[492] Kaganas and Day Sclater (2004); Boyd (1996).
[493] [2013] EWHC B33 (Fam).

if one's partner has an affair during your pregnancy and left you after your child was born, that you would feel angry with them. Further, that such a father has not thereby shown commitment to his children. Expecting parties to demonstrate great virtue when they have been so badly treated may seem to ask too much.

Some commentators take the wider point that for contact to be productive there must be trust and cooperation between the parents.[494] Contact where the parents still fear and distrust each other (whether justifiably or not) is likely to lead to the child being used as a pawn in their dispute. Research suggests that the most common reason for resident mothers refusing contact is fear that violence or sexual abuse will be carried out against them or the child.[495] Where these fears are justified, of course, contact will not be ordered.[496] But even if they are unjustified fears, some commentators argue that contact in the context of such fear is likely to be traumatic for the child, rather than beneficial.[497] Consider, for example, the case of *Re U (Children) (Contact)*[498] where the father had, when 22, been convicted of 'a particularly unpleasant and brutal' indecent assault on a child aged 11. He was convicted to a sentence of four years' imprisonment. After his release he married, but never told his wife of his conviction. The marriage broke down with the wife alleging violence. When she discovered his previous conviction, she refused to permit contact with their two daughters. However, the Court of Appeal held that the father should have been permitted to produce evidence that he had received therapy and did not pose a threat to them. One can imagine that, whatever evidence he might introduce, the mother is unlikely to be convinced he is safe. One wonders whether in such an atmosphere contact could be beneficial.

In recent years the idea of parental alienation has become a major theme in cases where resident parents object to contact. That is tied up with the issue of the child's opposition, so we shall discuss that in the next section.

(iv) The relevance of the child's opposition

In the previous section we considered cases where the opposition to contact has come from the resident parent. What if the opposition comes from the child? As has already been discussed, in deciding what is in the welfare of a child the court will place much weight on the child's views, taking into account the age of the child, the reasons behind the child's views and the seriousness of the issues. Clearly in some cases practicalities will rule the day. If a teenager really does not want to have contact, there will be little point in a court order requiring it.[499] In *Re S (Contact: Children's Views)*[500] the strong views of 16-, 14- and 12-year-olds that they did not want to have contact with their father were followed by the court. The Court of Appeal wisely stated:

> They [the children] might obey, perhaps they will obey an order of the court, but with what result? What would be the quality of what is being asked of them by me to do if I order them to do it? . . . If young people are to be brought up to respect the law, then it seems to me that the law must respect them and their wishes, even to the extent of allowing them, as occasionally they do, to make mistakes.[501]

---

[494] Herring (2003a).
[495] Rhoades (2002b); Day Sclater and Kaganas (2003).
[496] See *Re C (A Child) (Contact Order)* [2005] 3 FCR 571.
[497] Imagine what a mother with such fears will say to her child as she sends him or her off for the contact session.
[498] [2004] 1 FCR 768.
[499] *M v M (Defined Contact Application)* [1998] 2 FLR 244.
[500] [2002] 1 FLR 1156.
[501] At p. 1169.

In *Re J (Children)*[502] the Court of Appeal made it clear that 'courts are normally, for good reason, most reluctant to make orders requiring young people who are on the cusp of adulthood to engage in contact with a parent when they do not wish to do so'. For younger children, courts may not be unduly perturbed by the apparent distress of children,[503] believing that the long-term benefits of contact normally outweigh short-term distress.[504] However, in *JA v AM*[505] attempts to enforce contact with children of a range of ages ceased with it being acknowledged that the proceedings had traumatised the children and continued efforts would have a catastrophic impact on their lives. The courts must be very wary of forcing unwanted contact on children for fear that doing so will add to the emotional harm the children will suffer.

With older children who object to contact the court will want to determine the reasons for the objection.[506] Where they are based on good reasons the court is likely to give them considerable respect. In *Re A (A Child) (Intractable Contact Dispute)*[507] the Court of Appeal was critical of lower courts accepting that M (aged 13, 'a very bright girl and mature beyond her chronological age'[508]) objected to contact, without seeking to explore why, given that the father was 'unimpeachable'.[509] However, arguably such an approach fails to attach sufficient weight to M's right to have her views respected. Forcing a 13-year-old to see someone (previously arrested for assaulting her) requires a strong justification. Adults are not forced to see people they do not want to see, however nice the other person is.

In some cases where children oppose contact, the courts have put pressure on mothers to do more to encourage children to see their fathers. In *Re H-B (Children) (Contact: Prohibitions on Further application)*[510] Munby P in the Court of Appeal put the point strongly:

> I appreciate that parenting headstrong or strong-willed teenagers can be particularly taxing, sometimes very tough and exceptionally demanding . . . But parental responsibility does not shrivel away, merely because the child is 14 or even 16, nor does the parental obligation to take all reasonable steps to ensure that a child of that age does what it ought to be doing, and does not do what it ought not to be doing. I accept . . . that a parent should not resort to brute force in exercising parental responsibility in relation to a fractious teenager. But what one can reasonably demand – not merely as a matter of law but also and much more fundamentally as a matter of natural parental obligation – is that the parent, by argument, persuasion, cajolement, blandishments, inducements, sanctions (for example, 'grounding' or the confiscation of mobile phones, computers or other electronic equipment) or threats falling short of brute force, or by a combination of them, does their level best to ensure compliance. That is what one would expect of a parent whose rebellious teenage child is foolishly refusing to do GCSEs or A-Levels or 'dropping out' into a life of drug-fuelled crime. Why should we expect any less of a parent whose rebellious teenage child is refusing to see her father?

Notably these comments were made in the context of a case where the court felt it had done all it could do to enable contact and no more orders could be made. The blame for the problem was in this quotation laid at the door of the mother. Whether this is fair is open to debate.[511]

---

[502] [2018] EWCA 115.
[503] *Re H (Minors) (Access)* [1992] 1 FLR 148, [1992] 1 FCR 70.
[504] *Re R (No Order for Contact: Appeal)* [2014] EWCA Civ 1664.
[505] [2000] EWFC 3.
[506] *Re G (Intractable Contact Dispute)* [2013] EWHC B16 (Fam).
[507] In *Re A (A Child) (Intractable Contact Dispute)* [2013] EWHC B16 (Fam).
[508] Para 7.
[509] A rather surprising description given he was arrested and prosecuted for assaulting his daughter.
[510] [2015] EWCA Civ 389, para 76.
[511] The father and new partner had behaved in some blameworthy ways: see Herring (2016b).

The father had not exactly behaved angelically. Further, a wide range of professionals had sought to encourage the girls to be positive about their father, and failed. Should a parent be expected to do what trained professionals cannot? Perhaps more importantly the case involved children aged 16 and 14. The analysis of the court seems unwilling to take seriously their own views of the matter and instead regards them as pawns in the hands of their parents. Is it not possible that these young women have formed perfectly reasonable views of their own? Why should they not be listened to and respected? Is there not something rather patronising about suggesting the views of a 16-year-old need to be changed by the mother by grounding her?

In some cases the courts may fear the child is simply repeating the objections of the parent they are living with.[512] This, in recent years, has raised the controversial issue of 'parental alienation syndrome'.[513] Many psychologists deny that the 'syndrome' is a medical condition.[514] Indeed, there are concerns that any case where a child is objecting to contact is seen as a case of parental alienation.[515] The Court of Appeal in *Re H (Parental Alienation: Cult)*[516] have indicated the courts should not get sidelined into the psychologists' debate over whether or not there is a syndrome. They prefer, therefore, to talk of cases of alienation, described as:

> When a child's resistance/hostility towards one parent is not justified and is the result of psychological manipulation by the other parent.

They explain that there is no need to show that the 'manipulation of the child' was malicious or deliberate. The Court of Appeal went on to give examples of the kind of behaviour they had in mind:

> portraying the other parent in an unduly negative light to the child, suggesting that the other parent does not love the child, providing unnecessary reassurance to the child about time with the other parent, contacting the child excessively when with the other parent, and making unfounded allegations or insinuations, particularly of sexual abuse.

In the past couple of years there seems to have been a growth in the number of cases recognising parental alienation, with the courts taking a tougher line against parents seen to be guilty of causing it.[517] In *Re M (Children) (Ultra-Orthodox Judaism: Transgender Parent)*[518] the Court of Appeal explained:

> Where an intransigent parent is fostering in their child a damaging view of the other parent, and thereby alienating the child from the other parent and denying contact between them, the court does not hesitate to invoke robust methods where that is required in the child's interests. Thus, the court may make an order transferring the living arrangements (residence) from one parent to the other, either to take immediate effect or . . . suspended so long as the defaulting parent complies with the court's order for contact. The court can make the child a ward of court. The court can make an order under section 37 of the Children Act 1989 for a report from the local authority with a view to the commencement of proceedings for taking the child into public care.

---

[512] *Re G (Intractable Contact Dispute)* [2013] EWHC B16 (Fam).

[513] Hobbs (2002a) provides a basic introduction to this alleged syndrome; Gardner *et al.* (2005) provide a book-length treatment of the subject. See also Clarkson and Clarkson (2007).

[514] Doughty, Maxwell and Slater (2020); Eaton and Jarmain (2016).

[515] Walker and Shapiro (2010).

[516] [2020] EWCA Civ 568.

[517] *Re M (Intractable Contact Dispute: Interim Care Order)* [2004] 1 FCR 687. See also *C v P* [2017] EWFC 23; *Re M (Children)* [2005] EWCA Civ 1090.

[518] [2017] EWCA 1274.

The leading case is now the following:

KEY CASE: *Re S (Parental Alienation; Cult)* [2020] EWCA Civ 568

The parents separated when their daughter was one. The child stayed with the mother, who joined a group called Universal Medicine. She adhered to their doctrine, 'The Way of Livingness'. An Australian court had found Universal Medicine to be a harmful cult and its leader a 'sexually predatory charlatan with an indecent interest in young children'. The local authority investigated but found no concerns. The father successfully applied for a shared care arrangement, with a prohibited steps order barring the mother from imposing cult doctrines on the child.

The current case involved an application by the father that the child live with him, based on his concerns about the cult and concerns the child was suffering parental alienation. A CAFCASS report found the mother was 'deeply steeped' in the teachings of the cult. At first instance the judge accepted the mother had started a process of alienation, but refused the father's application given concerns that a move to sole father care would disturb the child and the mother's undertakings to dissociate herself and the child from the cult. The father appealed.

The Court of Appeal allowed the appeal and ordered a rehearing. The judge had minimised the risk of the parental alienation and given too much weight to short-term concern of the move to the father. Similarly, insufficient weight had been given to the harms caused by the cult. The mother's undertakings were insufficient. In particular there was no identifiable strategy to address the impact of the alienation. The Court of Appeal accepted the concept of parental alienation, but noted 'there is a spectrum of severity and the remedy will depend upon an assessment of all aspects of the child's welfare, and not merely those that concern the relationship that may be under threat.' The court concluded:

> . . . in a situation of parental alienation the obligation on the court is to respond with exceptional diligence and take whatever effective measures are available. The situation calls for judicial resolve because the line of least resistance is likely to be less stressful for the child and for the court in the short term. But it does not represent a solution to the problem. Inaction will probably reinforce the position of the stronger party at the expense of the weaker party and the bar will be raised for the next attempt at intervention. Above all, the obligation on the court is to keep the child's medium to long term welfare at the forefront of its mind and wherever possible to uphold the child and parent's right to respect for family life before it is breached. In making its overall welfare decision the court must therefore be alert to early signs of alienation. What will amount to effective action will be a matter of judgement, but it is emphatically not necessary to wait for serious, worse still irreparable, harm to be done before appropriate action is taken.

At the rehearing[519] Williams J ordered that the child live with the father. There was to be no contact with the mother for a short time, but then such contact as the father thought appropriate.

---

[519] [2020] EWHC 1940 (Fam)

Other cases have taken a similarly harsh line. In *Re H (Parental Alienation)*[520] a 12-year-old boy was being turned against his father. Keehan J ordered that the child immediately move to live with the father. The case is concerning as the boy turned against the father after seeing a deeply unpleasant message the father sent the mother after a serious car accident. One might think it natural that a child turns against someone who wrote so unpleasantly against their primary carer, rather than being a sign of a 'syndrome'. Keehan J also relied on the evidence of an 'expert in parental alienation' and rejected the evidence of the other professionals involved. Most concerningly the mother was a litigant in person and so particularly disadvantaged to argue her case. Dealing with such cases by transferring residence seems problematic. As Professor Mary Welstead[521] writes of this case:

> Preventing the perceived harm to H from living with his mother by sending him to live with his father simply replaces one harm by another, albeit of a different nature. It is not too difficult to imagine the inevitable trauma H will suffer as a consequence of Keehan J's decision to remove him without warning to his father's home. Even when he recovers from that initial distress, he is likely to have very confused feelings about both his parents which may well affect his ability to form stable relationships in the future. Compromise in these problematic contact cases must be sought rather than dividing parents into heroes or villains.

In a study by Trinder *et al.*[522] only 4 per cent of the cases that came to court for enforcement could be seen as cases where the parent objecting to contact was doing so out of hostility and with no justification.[523] That suggests that even if parental alienation exists it is very rare.[524] As mentioned earlier, in many cases the opposition from the resident parent (nearly always the mother) comes from a fear of violence, but the court have not found sufficient evidence to establish the abuse occurred or might reoccur. Interestingly, although it is normally mothers who are accused to have engaged in parental alienation, evidence from Australia suggests that it is far more common for non-resident parents to seek to turn children against resident parents than vice versa.[525]

The courts are somewhat alert to the dangers in relying on parental alienation.[526] In *Re O (A Child) (Contact: Withdrawal of Application)*[527] Wall J suggested the father's allegation of the syndrome was denial of his own responsibility for the problems relating to contact.[528] In *Re B (A fourteen year old boy)*[529] Wood J rejected the father's claim the children had been the victims of parental alienation caused by the mother and had 'false memories' as a result. Rather, Wood J concluded, that the father was 'utterly obsessed with placing the blame on the mother as he is resolute that he is a wholly innocent victim'. In *Re C1 and C2 (Child Arrangements)*[530] an 'aggressive and intimidating' father blamed the mother for the children's reluctance to see him, but the court found the causes lay in his attitude and personality.

---

[520] [2019] EWHC 2723.
[521] Welstead (2020).
[522] Trinder *et al.* (2013).
[523] For similar results see Harding and Newnham (2014).
[524] Fortin, Hunt and Scanlan (2012).
[525] Rhoades (2002a).
[526] *Re P (A Child) (Expert Evidence)* [2001] 1 FCR 751; *Re S (Contact: Children's Views)* [2002] 1 FLR 1156.
[527] [2004] 1 FCR 687.
[528] See also *Re Bradford, Re O'Connell* [2006] EWCA Civ 1199; *Re G (Children: Intractable Dispute)* [2019] EWCA Civ 548.
[529] [2017] EWFC B28 (Fam).
[530] [2019] EWHC B15 (Fam)

Even if the court finds there has been parental alienation, the solution to such a case is not straightforward as the following case demonstrates:

CASE: *Re S (Transfer of Residence)* [2010] EWCA Civ 291

Between 1999 and 2010, S, aged 12 in 2010, had been the subject of disputes between his parents. Originally, he was placed with his mother, and had contact with his father. The contact broke down. The father alleged the mother had parental alienation syndrome and had turned S against him. In 2010, in an attempt to ensure contact with both parents, continued residence of S was transferred to the father. S strongly opposed the move and obtained his own solicitor. The court tipstaff was directed to implement the order and take S to the father. S resisted and the court made an interim care order and he was placed with foster care. The local authority sought to effect care with the father but S sat with his head in his lap and fingers in his ears. S said he would rather remain in care than live with his father. Concerns grew over S's mental stability. Eventually, S was returned to the mother and the father gave up on seeking contact.

Depending on your point of view, this case is either one where the intransigent mother got her way or where the court failed to treat a child who did not like his father with appropriate respect. Either way, the case was a tragedy.

It seems the lessons from that case may not have been learned. In *Re A (Children) (Parental Alienation)*[531] children were found to suffer parental alienation at the hands of their mother, who had 'demonized' the father. The judge ordered residence to the father, but the children 'ran away from their father several times, refused to eat and exhibited extreme distress.' Eventually they had to be returned to their mother. Ultimately after 36 hearings it was accepted that contact could not take place.

There are grave concerns about the increasing use of parental alienation (PA). Adrienne Barnett[532] writes that it:

> is a concept that is proving more powerful than any other in silencing the voices of women and children resisting contact with abusive men. PA is not an 'equal' counterpart to domestic abuse, it is a means of obscuring domestic abuse, and should be recognised as such.

Her point is that in many cases where mothers and children oppose contact there is a history of domestic abuse. Of course, in the cases mentioned above, these have been unproven. But it is important to recall that when a man relies on parental alienation and blames a woman for her response to domestic abuse, describes her as irrational, and seeks to use state powers to get his way, his behaviour has all the hallmarks of coercive control. It would be the worst nightmare to have been the victim of domestic abuse, have one's account disbelieved, and then be told you are abusing your children by telling them of the abuse. But there can be no doubt that has happened in some cases.[533]

The problem with the concept is that any opposition to contact can be seen as a sign of alienation, making women nervous about opposing contact. As Vivienne Elizabeth writes:

---

[531] [2019] EWFC B56.
[532] Barnett (2020).
[533] Sheehy and Boyd (2020).

Mothers in contested custody cases are subject to overt exercises of juridical power through explicit judicial instructions to undertake emotion work to demonstrate they are not alienators. Yet PA(S) as a tool of gender governance operates just as powerfully through mothers' self-policing and self-regulation. Mothers' fear of being perceived as alienators and the losses of care time that would likely follow from such a perception caused them to consent to parenting orders they disagreed with and found deeply distressing.[534]

The syndrome can also be seen as a way of silencing children. It is remarkable how readily the courts seem to accept that parents can make teenagers think in a particular way. Many parents of teenagers have tried to influence their children's behaviour, but few have success! Maybe in cases of alleged parental alienation we should be trusting the views of children (who will have witnessed family life) rather than assuming they have been manipulated.[535]

The issues just discussed are part of wider debate on how the courts should respond to cases where a contact application sought by a parent who has previously engaged in domestic violence. We will discuss those cases next.

(v) Domestic violence and contact

In recent years there has been much debate in the courts and among commentators concerning cases in which there is a dispute over contact where the parental relationship had been marked by domestic violence.[536] One study of separated parents found that 56 per cent of parents interviewed reported domestic violence and 78 per cent feared it.[537] Eighty per cent of resident parents disputing contact cited violence concerns in one study.[538] A major Ministry of Justice[539] review found allegations or findings of domestic abuse in samples of child arrangements/contact cases ranging from 49 per cent to 62 per cent. In a study by Women's Aid and CAFCASS[540] nearly two-thirds of the cases in their sample of contact disputes involved allegations of domestic abuse. Their sample contained 19 per cent of cases leading to an order for no direct contact. That is a low number given the severity of the abuse in the cases of their sample. In 39 per cent unsupervised contact was ordered.

The leading case on the law is *Re L (A Child) (Contact: Domestic Violence)*.[541] The Court of Appeal decided to hear four cases together so as to analyse the law in this area.[542] It was emphasised that the fact that there had been domestic violence is not a bar to contact. However, it is one important factor in the balancing exercise. The Court of Appeal stressed that a judge should approach such cases in two stages:

1. If domestic violence is alleged, the court has to decide whether the allegations are made out or not.[543]

2. The court should weigh up the risks involved, and the impact of contact on the child, against the positive benefits (if any) of contact. Any risk of harm to the residential parent should also be considered.

---

[534] Elizabeth (2020).

[535] *P v C (Child Arrangements Order)* [2018] 2 FLR 1139; *Re R (A Child: Appeal: Termination of Contact)* [2019] EWHC 132 (Fam) are examples where at least some respect has been paid to children's views in these cases.

[536] Choudhry (2012).

[537] Trinder (2005).

[538] Hunt and Macleod (2008).

[539] Ministry of Justice (2020).

[540] Women's Aid and CAFCASS (2017).

[541] [2000] 2 FCR 404.

[542] The Court of Appeal paid particular attention to Children Act Sub-Committee (2002a). See further Sturge and Glaser (2000).

[543] *Re K and S* [2006] 1 FCR 316.

Butler-Sloss P explained:[544]

> [A] court hearing a contact application in which allegations of domestic violence are raised, should consider the conduct of both parties towards each other and towards the children, the effect on the children and on the residential parent and the motivation of the parent seeking contact. Is it a desire to promote the best interests of the child or a means to continue violence and/or intimidation or harassment of the other parent? In cases of serious domestic violence, the ability of the offending parent to recognise his or her past conduct, to be aware of the need for change and to make genuine efforts to do so, will be likely to be an important consideration.[545]

In particular, the court should consider the following factors when considering contact where there has been domestic violence:

1. The child might be abused during contact.
2. Contact might exacerbate the bitterness between the parents, and this would be detrimental to the child.
3. A bullying or dominating relationship between the child and contact parent might be perpetuated.
4. If the child had witnessed domestic violence between their parents, contact might reawaken old fears.[546]
5. If the child opposes contact, weight should be placed on their views.[547]

When considering the benefits the court should recall in particular:

1. That seeing a father may be beneficial to the child's identity.
2. The 'male contribution to parenting'[548] that a father can offer.
3. The loss of opportunity to know the paternal grandparents if contact does not take place with the father.
4. The opportunity 'to mend the harm done' may be lost if contact is not ordered.

Even if domestic violence means that direct contact is not possible, indirect contact may be appropriate.[549]

In Practice Direction 12J to the Family Procedure Rules 2010[550] it states that when considering contact in a violence case the court must consider:

(a) the effect of the domestic violence or abuse on the child and on the arrangements for where the child is living;

(b) the effect of the domestic violence or abuse on the child and its effect on the child's relationship with the parents;

(c) whether the applicant parent is motivated by a desire to promote the best interests of the child or is using the process to continue a process of violence, abuse, intimidation or harassment or controlling or coercive behaviour against the other parent;

---

[544] See Gilmore (2008b) for criticism of the Court of Appeal's handling of the expert evidence in that case.
[545] *Re L (A Child) (Contact: Domestic Violence)* [2000] 2 FCR 404 at p. 416.
[546] This factor was relied upon when denying contact in *Re G (Domestic Violence: Direct Contact)* [2000] Fam Law 789.
[547] See *Re S (Transfer of Residence)* [2010] EWCA Civ 291.
[548] It is not clear exactly what this means.
[549] *AB v BB* [2013] EWHC 227 (Fam).
[550] As amended in 2017.

(d) the likely behaviour during contact of the parent against whom findings are made and its effect on the child; and

(e) the capacity of the parents to appreciate the effect of past violence or abuse and the potential for future violence or abuse.

It also states:

The court should make an order for contact only if it is satisfied that the physical and emotional safety of the child and the parent with whom the child is living can, as far as possible, be secured before, during and after contact, and that the parent with whom the child is living will not be subjected to further domestic abuse by the other parent.[551]

The Practice Direction makes it clear that domestic violence issues should be identified at the earliest opportunity and the court should give directions to enable the allegations to be determined. Where there is a finding of domestic violence but the court determines that contact should take place nonetheless, the court should consider whether restrictions should be imposed on the contact, for example that it be supervised.

The approach of the courts is based on the principle that the welfare of the child is the paramount consideration and domestic violence is but one factor to be taken into account. This has produced some concerning cases.

- In *Re J-S (A Child) (Contact: Parental Responsibility)*,[552] despite the fact that the father had thrown a shoe at the mother, forced his way into her home, had pushed a hot tea bag in her face, and hit her across the face chipping her tooth, he was permitted contact. It was explained that the child had established a strong attachment with the father and that to end contact with the father would therefore harm the child.[553]

- In *Re A (Suspended Residence Order)*[554] a court ordered a mother to allow her daughter to visit the father even though the father had been found to have sexually abused one of the mother's other daughters and despite the strong opposition of the daughters to contact. Such cases will be opposed by those commentators who are concerned that too great a willingness to permit contact following serious domestic violence may endanger mothers and children.[555] Indeed, one may well ask in that case how a father can claim to be committed to the child when he treats the child's primary carer or half-sisters in that way.

- In *Re M (Contact Refusal: Appeal)*[556] the mother and three children escaped to a women's refuge after prolonged violence. The elder boys had suffered physical abuse at the hands of their father and were acting out his aggressive behaviour. The Court of Appeal emphasised that domestic violence is not a bar to direct contact. They held that in this case the judge had not shown that no other orders apart from a no contact order could protect the children. What seems absent from the Court's analysis is an assessment of what ways contact with the father would benefit the boys, as required by *Re L (A Child) (Contact: Domestic Violence)*.[557] The case seemed to take the benefit for granted, even though the facts indicated that their relationship with their father to date had resulted in little but harm.

---

[551] At para 36.
[552] [2002] 3 FCR 433.
[553] See *Carp v Byron* [2006] 1 FCR 1 for a case where the violence justified an order for no contact.
[554] [2010] 1 FLR 1679.
[555] Hester (2002).
[556] [2013] EWCA Civ 1147.
[557] [2000] 2 FLR 334, [2000] 2 FCR 404 CA

● In ***Re A (Supervised Contact Order: Assessment of Impact of Domestic Violence)***[558] the Court of Appeal upheld a judgment ordering supervised contact in a case where the mother had been repeatedly raped and sexually abused by the father, causing her to suffer post-traumatic stress disorder. The judge had separated out the sexual abuse of the wife, which he characterised as serious, from the physical abuse (he had thrown a book and pen at her) which he characterised as low level. The judge took the view that the father's conduct did not pose a risk to the daughter, at least in the context of supervised conduct. That a multiple rapist should have even supervised contact with the daughter of his victim is surprising.

Adrienne Barnett's study found a reluctance in courts to find domestic violence being proved in contact cases, with one practitioner describing a finding of domestic violence like 'gold dust'.[559] As noted in Chapter 6, it is notoriously difficult to prove domestic abuse because it typically takes place in private and is rarely reported to the authorities. Even where it is proved, the cases just referred to demonstrate that the courts will strive to allow some kind of contact because it is so strongly assumed that contact is beneficial. Opponents will argue that a man who has been violent towards the mother of a child has shown such a lack of regard for the child's well-being that he should not be awarded contact, unless there are compelling reasons to do so.

Adrienne Barnett[560] found that the courts regularly downplay the relevance of domestic violence and emphasise the importance of joint parental involvement. She concludes:

> The gendered relations of power that construct, underpin and sustain the law's current construction of 'the truth' about children's welfare constantly challenge and subvert attempts to focus professionals and courts on protecting children and women in private law Children Act proceedings. These relations of power give rise to a discursive and ideological terrain that downplays, trivialises and erases women's concerns about continued contact with violent fathers and have a powerful normative influence on professional and judicial perceptions and practices. The symbolic and functional power of the presumption of parental involvement may reduce even further the ability of victims/mothers to offer any opposition to father-involvement in child arrangements proceedings by reinforcing 'the deviant nature of failing to abide by [the norm] of the separated but continuing family' . . . We have seen that the parameters of what constitutes the 'safe family man' are expanding to include increasingly abusive, 'dangerous' fathers, a process that may be exacerbated by the presumption of parental involvement.

These concerns will be exacerbated in cases of mediation.[561] The emphasis that is placed on benefits of contact raises the concern that couples will agree contact orders even where there has been domestic violence and contact will not benefit the children. As Jane Craig[562] has argued, it should not be assumed that in cases where the couple agree to contact taking place that contact is necessarily beneficial or even safe for the child. As she notes, of the 29 children killed by their fathers during contact in one study, in only three of the cases had contact been ordered by the court. In the rest the mothers had agreed to contact. Kaganas and Piper[563] fear that:

> [I]n some instances, vulnerable mothers will be persuaded by the combination of education, mediation and the new law – all probably giving the same simplified message [that parental involvement of father is always good for children] – to agree to outcomes which do not include the protection they need or which leave their children in a situation which is not in their best interests.

---

[558] [2015] EWCA Civ 486.
[559] Barnett (2014b)
[560] Barnett (2014a). See also Macdonald (2013).
[561] Trinder, Jenks and Firth (2010).
[562] Craig (2007).
[563] Kaganas and Piper (2015).

Some commentators have argued in favour of a legal presumption against contact where there has been domestic violence.[564] Those who take such an approach point to the following:[565]

1. Children who live in an atmosphere of domestic violence suffer psychological harm,[566] even if they do not actually witness the abuse.[567]

2. There is evidence that there are statistical links between child abuse and spousal abuse. Judge Wall[568] quoted research that if a man is abusing his wife there is a 40–60 per cent chance he is also abusing his child.

3. There is also a fear that a father may be able to continue to dominate and exercise power over the mother through the arrangements over contact.[569] Vivienne Elizabeth uses the term 'custody stalking':[570] 'Because children legitimate ongoing parental interactions, children are also a channel through which violent and/or coercively controlling fathers can continue to violate former partners.' Custody disputes are used to 'punish, humiliate and torment women'.[571] In its ultimate form this covers fathers killing their children. A study by Woman's Aid highlighted 29 cases where children had been killed during or in connection with contact meetings.[572]

4. One survey, which looked at cases where contact had been ordered even though there had been domestic violence, suggested that 25 per cent of children were abused[573] as a result of the contact.[574]

(vi) Step-parents and hostility

Sometimes the courts are willing to accept the opposition of a step-parent to the contact order as reason enough for denying contact. In *Re SM (A Minor) (Natural Father: Access)*[575] the fear that contact with the natural father would destabilise the relationship between the mother and the stepfather was seen as a reason for denying contact. A similar finding was made in *Re B (Contact: Stepfather's Opposition)*,[576] where the stepfather gave evidence that he would leave the mother if the father were allowed contact with the child. The Court of Appeal accepted that the stepfather was sincere[577] and noted that, had contact with the father been ordered, the contact would have been very limited. These cases are very controversial, with some arguing that a step-parent's views should not be taken into account. Both cases are from the 1990s and it may well be that a different attitude would be taken if they were heard today.

---

[564] Fineman (2002); Perry (2006).

[565] For a helpful summary, see Bell (2008).

[566] Barnett (2000).

[567] *Re L (A Child) (Contact: Domestic Violence)* [2000] 2 FCR 404. Note also the definition of harm in CA 1989, s. 31(3A) including the witnessing of ill-treatment of another.

[568] Wall (1997).

[569] E.g. Kaye, Stubbs and Tolmie (2003); Masson and Humphreys (2005); Hardesty and Chung (2006); Humphreys and Thiara (2003).

[570] Elizabeth (2018).

[571] Logan and Walker (2009).

[572] Saunders (2004). See Wall (2006) who argues that in only three cases could the court possibly have foreseen any kind of risk.

[573] A term the researchers used to include emotional harm. Ten per cent were sexually abused and 15 per cent physically abused.

[574] Hester (2002).

[575] [1996] 2 FLR 333, [1997] 2 FCR 475.

[576] [1997] 2 FLR 579, [1998] 3 FCR 289.

[577] Evidence was given that his attitude was common among the Asian community.

(vii) Indirect contact

Even if direct contact is not appropriate, the court will make an order for indirect contact in all but exceptional cases.[578] That can take the form of letters or, more likely, electronic communication.[579] If necessary a third party can be asked to pass on the communications to ensure there is no contact between the parents.[580] In *Re L (Contact: Genuine Fear)*,[581] indirect contact was ordered even though the mother suffered a 'phobia' of the father (he had been a Hell's Angel who had stabbed his ex-wife, and her solicitor and boyfriend). Although it was felt that the 'phobia'[582] meant that direct contact could not take place, this was no reason for denying indirect contact. The judge asked for professional help in ensuring the indirect contact took place because it was feared that the mother might destroy any correspondence. Only very rarely will the court not even order indirect contact. In *Re C (Contact: No Order for Contact)*[583] the child was terrified of his father and destroyed all letters sent by the father. This persuaded Connell J to make an order which prohibited indirect contact between the father and the child. Similarly, the mother and children in *PM v CF (Section 91(14) Order: Risk to Mother and Children)*[584] were at such a risk of harm or death from the father that even indirect contact was not appropriate.

There is some debate over the usefulness of indirect contact.[585] It might be argued that no meaningful relationship can develop from, for example, occasional letters. It may offer some reassurance to the child to know their parent is well. Perhaps most importantly it means that if the child does later in life decide to pursue a relationship, they have contact details.

(viii) Enforcement of child arrangements orders

There is much debate over how the court should enforce contact.[586] For example, if a mother refused to permit a father to have contact with a child, despite the existence of a contact order, what should be done? Before considering the options three points must be made. First, it is for the person seeking to enforce the order to prove that the order was breached.[587] Second, as already discussed, the definition of a CAO makes it very difficult to know what is required of any parent under the order. It was suggested above that only a parent who actively prevents contact may be in breach of it. A parent who fails to facilitate it is not. Third, there are often complex issues behind contested contact hearings. It is helpful to look at what kind of cases come to the courts for enforcement. In their study of conflicted contact cases Trinder *et al.*[588] found that conflicted contact cases fell within four categories:

1. Conflicted, where 'intense competition or chronic levels of mistrust between the parents meant that they were unable to work together to implement the court order';

2. Risk/safety, where 'one or both parents raised significant adult and/or child safeguarding issues, most commonly domestic violence, child physical abuse and neglect, alcohol and drug abuse or mental health issues';

---

[578] *Re K (Contact: Mother's Anxiety)* [1999] 2 FLR 703; *Re F (A Child) (Indirect Contact through Third Party)* [2006] 3 FCR 553.
[579] *A Local Authority v A, B and E* [2011] EWHC 2062 (Fam).
[580] *Re F (A Child) (Indirect Contact through Third Party)* [2006] 3 FCR 553.
[581] [2002] 1 FLR 621.
[582] Bruce Blair QC described her fears as 'irrational', perhaps surprisingly.
[583] [2000] Fam Law 699.
[584] [2018] EWHC 2658 (Fam).
[585] Lwekowicz and Phillimore (2019).
[586] Smart and Neale (1997).
[587] *Re H (Contact: Adverse Findings of Fact)* [2011] EWCA Civ 585.
[588] Trinder *et al.* (2013).

3. Refusing, involving 'an apparently appropriate and reasoned rejection of all or some contact by an older child (10+) The refusal appeared to reflect problematic behaviours/lack of sensitivity by the non-resident parent';

4. Implacably hostile/alienating, where there was 'sustained resistance to contact by the resident parent. The resistance appeared unreasonable and was not a response to significant safety concerns or the problematic behaviour of the other parent. In some cases the resident parent may have influenced the child so that the child refused all contact but without the well-founded reasons that characterised the refusing cases'.

Trinder *et al.* estimated that only 4 per cent fell into this last category. The vast majority of the cases fall into the first three cases.

In recent years there has been a concerted effort to improve attempts to enforce contact. Ward LJ in *Re M (Contact Dispute: Court's Positive Duty)* held:

> Where, as in this case, the court has the picture that a parent is seeking, without good reason, to eliminate the other parent from the child's, or children's, lives, the court should not stand by and take no positive action. Justice to the children and the deprived parent, in this case the mother, requires the court to leave no stone unturned that might resolve the situation and prevent long-term harm to the children.[589]

However, at the same time there is a recognition that the use of the law may not be the most effective way of enforcing contact orders. In *Re C (A Child)*[590] Munby LJ observed:

> The resumption of contact, which is so much in C's interests and which the mother so ardently desires, is more likely to be achieved by therapy than by further litigation at this stage.[591]

The greater efforts taken by the court to enforce contact are a response both to judicial acceptance that previously not enough had been done to ensure the child saw both parents[592] and also to the Human Rights Act 1998. In *Re C (A Child)*[593] Munby LJ helpfully summarised the position as it would be understood under the Human Rights Act 1998, relying on the leading cases of *Hokkanen v Finland*,[594] *Glaser v UK*,[595] and *Kosmopoulou v Greece*:[596]

- Contact between parent and child is a fundamental element of family life and is almost always in the interests of the child.

- Contact between parent and child is to be terminated only in exceptional circumstances, where there are cogent reasons for doing so and when there is no alternative. Contact is to be terminated only if it will be detrimental to the child's welfare.

- There is a positive obligation on the State, and therefore on the judge, to take measures to maintain and to reconstitute the relationship between parent and child, in short, to maintain or restore contact. The judge has a positive duty to attempt to promote contact. The judge must grapple with all the available alternatives before abandoning hope of achieving some

---

[589] [2006] 1 FLR 621, para 41.
[590] [2011] EWCA Civ 521, para 47.
[591] See also *Re R (A Child: Appeal: Termination of Contact)* [2019] EWHC 132 (Fam); *Re Q (A Child)* [2015] EWCA Civ 991.
[592] *Re D (A Child) (Intractable Contact Dispute: Publicity)* [2004] 3 FCR 234.
[593] [2011] EWCA Civ 521, para 47.
[594] [1996] 1 FLR 289, [1995] 2 FCR 320.
[595] [2000] 3 FCR 193.
[596] [2004] 1 FCR 427.

contact. He must be careful not to come to a premature decision, for contact is to be stopped only as a last resort and only once it has become clear that the child will not benefit from continuing the attempt.[597]

- The court should take a medium-term and long-term view and not accord excessive weight to what appear likely to be short-term or transient problems.
- The key question, which requires 'stricter scrutiny', is whether the judge has taken all necessary steps to facilitate contact as can reasonably be demanded in the circumstances of the particular case.
- All that said, at the end of the day the welfare of the child is paramount; 'the child's interest must have precedence over any other consideration'.

The human rights dimension was taken up in the following important decision.

CASE: *Re A (A Child)* [2013] EWCA Civ 1104

The mother and father separated when their daughter was one year old. There then followed around 100 hearings involving disputes over where the daughter should live and what contact arrangements there should be. She spent most of the time with the mother. The mother had been consistently opposed to contact and sought to prevent it. The limited contact that took place was largely positive.

When the girl reached the age of 13, she started to strongly oppose contact. Although the judge was satisfied that the father was commendable and unimpeachable, it was held that all means of enabling meaningful contact to take place had been extinguished and given the considerable weight that had to be placed on the daughter's views the court 'had to accept failure'. There would be no contact and no further applications would be permitted until the girl was 16.

The father appealed to the Court of Appeal. The court acknowledged that the case represented a failure of the family justice system. As Aitken LJ put it:

It is tragic to have to agree with the judge that the Family Justice System has failed the whole family, but particularly M, whose childhood has been irredeemably marred by years of litigation. As a result of the system's failure, she has suffered the lack of a proper relationship with her father during her childhood years. Yet he, throughout, has acted irreproachably.

The court confirmed that the child's welfare was the court's paramount consideration in all matters relating to contact. The wishes of the child were a relevant factor, to be considered. The court was concerned that in enforcing contact the view of the parent with whom the child lived should not dominate:

Where, as in the present case, there is an intractable contact dispute, the authorities indicate that the court should be very reluctant to allow the implacable hostility of one parent to deter it from making a contact order where the child's welfare otherwise requires it . . . In such a case contact should only be refused where the court is satisfied that there is a serious risk of harm if contact were to be ordered.

---

[597] The phrase 'last resort' was also used in *Re M (Children) (Ultra-Orthodox Judaism: Transgender Parent)* [2017] EWCA Civ 2164.

The Court of Appeal emphasised that judges in contact cases had to ensure that the Article 6 and Article 8 rights of the parties were respected. In this case the requirements of procedural fairness in the enforcement of orders had not been met. MacFarlane LJ explained this conclusion was not based on a particular decision in the litigation but rather an overall look at what had happened:

> The finding that I have made is based in part upon the bald facts which were recited at the beginning of this judgment: this is an unimpeachable father, who has been prevented from having effective contact with a daughter who has enjoyed seeing him, in circumstances where the child's mother and primary carer has been held to be implacably opposed to that contact. In ECHR terms, there can be no dispute that the issues in this case engaged the Art. 8 right to family life of M and each of her parents. No facts have been established to support a finding that, in terms of Art. 8(2), it was 'necessary' or proportionate to refuse contact in order to protect the 'health' or 'the rights and freedoms' of others.

He went on to explain that if an order has been breached:

> . . . the judge must, in the absence of good reason for any failure, support the order that he or she has made by considering enforcement, either under the enforcement provisions in CA 1989, ss. 11J–11N or by contempt proceedings.

In an important article responding to this case John Eekelaar[598] suggests that:

[R]ather than being an example of 'system failure' as described by the court, the case might be seen as a rare, but predictable, consequence of the normal functioning of the system, just as one might view the rare acquittal of a guilty person in a criminal justice system based on the presumption of innocence. It also expresses some doubt whether the procedures can be so readily seen as a violation of the European Convention.

As he points out these cases often involve people with challenging issues and changing circumstances. He suggests it is 'over-optimistic, and possibility undesirable' to expect the courts to resolve complex cases rapidly.

It is common and desirable to allow the courts to find ways of establishing and building up trust between the parties. Only if that happens can effective and strong contact take place. This might well involve 'trial and error' and human nature means that attempts to establish trust will fail. The fact this may involve repeated attempts over the years which are not ultimately successful does not mean that the approach of the courts was misguided.

A further important point in this case is that the court was not stopping the child and father seeing each other. There was no order prohibiting contact; simply the courts did not compel it. It was the objections of the child, rather than anything the court was doing, which prevented further contact. Eekelaar therefore questions whether the courts were interfering with the right to family life of the father. It was the daughter's decision not to see the father which meant he did not have a relationship with her, not anything the court did. This was not a case like *Kopf and Liberda v Austria*[599] where the courts would not hear applications by the foster parents for contact and in which the court held there was a breach of Article 8. Quite the opposite – the courts were constantly hearing applications on this case.

---

[598] Eekelaar (2014a).
[599] (App. No. 1598/06) [2012] 1 FLR 1199.

Despite the decision in *Re A (A Child)*[600] there will be cases where the court will decide that all reasonable options to enforce have been tried and the time has come to stop seeking to enforce contact. As the Court of Appeal in *Re W (Contact Dispute) (No. 2)*[601] put it, the court had to accept 'the facts as they were', rather than what they would like them to be. There the children had consistently refused to participate in contact, despite the intervention of different professionals. There was nothing the court could do. In *JA v AM*[602] attempts to enforce contact ceased with it being acknowledged that the proceedings had traumatised the children and continued efforts would have a catastrophic impact on their lives. This is a warning that the limits of the law must be acknowledged.

We will look at the legal options available before returning to the question of what the legal response ought to be.

(a) Imprisonment

One option is imprisonment, after all that is a typical response to breach of a court order. In *A v N (Committal: Refusal of Contact)*,[603] it was confirmed that, when considering imprisonment, the welfare of the child was a material consideration but was not the paramount consideration.[604] Holman J accepted that the daughter would suffer if the mother were imprisoned but held that this was not due to the law's approach but that 'this little child suffers because the mother chooses to make her suffer'.[605] However, in more recent cases the courts have sought to avoid such a drastic conclusion. In *Re F (Contact: Enforcement: Representation of Child)*,[606] where the baby suffered cerebral palsy, it was held that the harm to the child if the mother was imprisoned was such that it would be inappropriate to attach a penal notice to a contact order. In *Re K (Children: Committal Proceedings)*[607] the Court of Appeal emphasised that imprisonment of the resident parent would infringe the Article 8 rights of both the mother and child and therefore before committal the court should ensure that the committal is justifiable under Article 8(2).[608] The Court of Appeal in *Re M (Contact Order: Committal)*[609] stated that, before committal to prison, other remedies such as further contact orders, a fine,[610] family therapy,[611] changing residence,[612], and even care proceedings should be explored[613] In *Re A and B (Contact) (No. 1)*[614] where the children had become strongly opposed to contact with the father, as a result of the mother's attitude, imprisoning the mother was seen as counter-productive as likely to set them even more strongly against the father.

Occasionally the courts are willing to imprison a resident parent who is refusing to allow contact. In *Re S (Contact Dispute: Committal)*[615] Hedley J was willing to uphold a committal to prison for seven days after a mother failed to allow a father to see his six-year-old daughter.

---

[600] [2013] EWCA Civ 1104.
[601] [2014] EWCA Civ 401.
[602] [2000] EWFC 3
[603] [1997] 1 FLR 533, [1997] 2 FCR 475.
[604] This was approved by the Court of Appeal in *M v M (Breaches of Orders: Committal)* [2005] EWCA Civ 1722.
[605] See also *F v F (Contact: Committal)* [1998] 2 FLR 237, [1999] 2 FCR 42; *CH v CT (Committal: Appeal)* [2018] EWHC 1310 (Fam).
[606] [1998] 1 FLR 691, [1998] 3 FCR 216.
[607] [2003] 2 FCR 336.
[608] The non-resident parent's and child's rights under Article 8 must also be considered.
[609] [1999] 1 FLR 810.
[610] *Re M (Contact Order)* [2005] 2 FLR 1006.
[611] *Re S (Uncooperative Mother)* [2004] EWCA Civ 597.
[612] Baroness Hale suggested that this was more often threatened than actually done.
[613] *Re A and B (Contact) (No. 2)* [2013] EWHC 4150.
[614] [2013] EWHC 2305 (Fam).
[615] [2004] EWCA Civ 1790.

It was a last resort, he accepted, but respect for the rule of law required obedience to orders of the court, and punishment if they were not obeyed.[616] In *B v S (Contempt: Imprisonment of Mother)*[617] the Court of Appeal stated that the 'days were long gone' when a mother could assume her care of the child protected her from imprisonment following breach of an order. Nevertheless, the court emphasised that the interference in the baby's human rights caused by imprisoning the mother had to be justified. Not surprisingly, a study into methods used to enforce contact found it rare for the 'nuclear option' of imprisonment to be used.[618]

(b) Fine

Another option for a court dealing with a parent who has failed to comply with a CAO is to impose a fine. This is also rarely used.[619] Many mothers cannot afford to pay a fine.[620] Such an order is only likely to increase antagonism.

(c) Unpaid work

If the court has made a CAO and is satisfied beyond reasonable doubt[621] that a person has failed to comply with that order, the court may make an enforcement order, unless the court is satisfied that the person has a reasonable excuse for not complying with the order.[622] The resident parent, the parent who is to have contact or the child[623] can apply for the enforcement order. The enforcement order will require the person breaching the contact order to undertake unpaid work. Presumably this will be of the kind undertaken by a person convicted of a criminal offence who is required to serve a community sentence.

It should be emphasised that it must be shown beyond reasonable doubt that the contact order has been breached. This is the criminal burden of proof which is, perhaps, a recognition that the unpaid work order is a punishment. The defence of reasonable excuse will no doubt be often relied upon. Whether fear of violence, particularly if the court believes it to be genuine but unjustified, is a reasonable excuse is an interesting question.[624]

Section 11L of the Children Act 1989 opens:

LEGISLATIVE PROVISION

Children Act 1989, section 11L

1. Before making an enforcement order as regards a person in breach of a contact order, the court must be satisfied that—

    (a) making the enforcement order proposed is necessary to secure the person's compliance with the contact order or any contact order that has effect in its place;

    (b) the likely effect on the person of the enforcement order proposed to be made is proportionate to the seriousness of the breach of the contact order.

---

[616] See also *Richards v Martin* [2017] EWHC 2187 (Fam).
[617] [2009] 2 FLR 1005.
[618] Trinder *et al.* (2013).
[619] Trinder *et al.* (2013).
[620] Butler-Sloss P in *Re S (A Child) (Contact)* [2004] 1 FCR 439 at para 29.
[621] *Re R (Costs: Contact Enforcement)* [2011] EWHC 2777 (Fam).
[622] The person claiming to have a reasonable excuse has the burden of proving this on the balance of probabilities: CA 1989, s. 11J(4).
[623] The child will require leave: s. 11J(6).
[624] CA 1989, s. 11K states that an enforcement order cannot be made if the individual has not been served with the order.

The court is required specifically to consider the effect of the order on the individual; in particular, whether it will interfere with his or her religious beliefs, employment or education.[625] Most significantly, s. 11L(7) of the CA 1989 states: 'In making an enforcement order in relation to a contact order, a court must take into account the welfare of the child who is the subject of the contact order.' Notably, this does not require the court to treat the welfare of the child as the paramount consideration. The child's welfare must only be taken into account. The Government has considered, but rejected, calls for curfews, removal of passports or driving licences to be added to the list of sanctions.[626]

The three options discussed so far are essentially putative. They punish the parent obstructing contact but do not provide a positive way forward. Given the research by Trinder *et al.*[627] into the kind of cases where enforcement proceedings are brought it seems that punishment is rarely the correct response. If long-term contact is to progress well it is important to establish a degree of trust between the parents so a more positive response is required. The other orders to be considered next seek to promote contact, rather than punish.

(d) Change of residence

If a mother is refusing to comply with a CAO, the court may amend the CAO so that the child lives with the other parent, if they are willing to allow contact. Of course, that will only be an option if the making of the order is in the child's welfare. A court which believes that it is important that the child retain a relationship with both parents, may determine that the child will be better off with the father who will allow contact, than with the mother who will not.[628] However, changing residence was described by the Court of Appeal in *Re A (Residence Order)*[629] as 'a judicial weapon of last resort'[630] and in *Re B (A Child)*[631] as 'a dire sanction'. Baroness Hale stated that transferring residence is more often used as a threat, than is carried out.[632] Coleridge J described it as 'putting a gun to a parent's head to force her or him to rethink'.[633] Many resident parents who are told that if they do not allow contact the children will be removed to the other parent will be thereby persuaded to allow contact.[634] In *Re W (Residence: Leave to Appeal)*[635] the Court of Appeal warned against using a change in residence to punish the mother, and emphasised it should only be used where it would promote the welfare of the child. In that case the court, having decided that transferring residence to the father was not beneficial, ordered that the residence be transferred to the grandmother, who was willing to facilitate contact with both the mother and father.

(e) A contact activity direction

This was introduced by the Children and Adoption Act 2006 and is designed to encourage a couple to resolve their disagreements. A contact activity direction is a direction to engage in the following activities:

---

[625] CA 1989, s. 11L(4).
[626] Trinder *et al.* (2013).
[627] Trinder *et al.* (2013).
[628] *Re L* [2014] EWCA Civ 167.
[629] [2010] 1 FLR 1083.
[630] Paragraph 18.
[631] [2012] EWCA Civ 858.
[632] In *Re G (Children) (Residence: Same-Sex Partner)* [2006] UKHL 43 at para 42.
[633] *Re A (Suspended Residence Order)* [2010] 1 FLR 1679.
[634] In *Re M (Contact)* [2012] EWHC 1948 (Fam).
[635] [2010] EWCA Civ 1280.

LEGISLATIVE PROVISION

Children Act 1989, section 11A(5)

(a) programmes, classes and counselling or guidance sessions of a kind that—

    (i) may assist a person as regards establishing, maintaining or improving contact with a child;

    (ii) may, by addressing a person's violent behaviour, enable or facilitate contact with a child;

(b) sessions in which information or advice is given as regards making or operating arrangements for contact with a child, including making arrangements by means of mediation.[636]

These must not include medical or psychiatric examination, assessment or treatment, or the taking of medication.[637] Rather they will require a person to attend group sessions, lectures or individual meetings in an attempt to encourage the parties to reach an appropriate agreement over contact.[638] Domestic Violence Perpetrator Programmes and Separated Parent Information Programmes have been developed for use in contact activity directions.

The parties may both be required to attend or may attend separately. Children cannot be required to attend.[639] In deciding whether to make a contact activity direction, the welfare of the child is the paramount consideration.[640] The court might decide that compelling a party to attend will be unhelpful and instead merely encourage the party to attend.[641]

Section 11B(1) of the Children Act 1989 states: 'A court may not make a contact activity direction in any proceedings unless there is a dispute as regards the provision about contact that the court is considering whether to make in the proceedings.' Presumably, this is designed to prevent a court making a contact activity direction where the parties have come to an agreement with which the court is unhappy: for example, where the couple agree there should be only negligible contact, but the court would like to see more. However, in such a case it could be argued under s. 11B(1) that there is a dispute between the judge and the parties and so a direction can be made; that interpretation would probably be contrary to the intention of the drafters of the legislation.

Before making a contact activity direction, the court must be satisfied of three matters as set out in s. 11E:

LEGISLATIVE PROVISION

Children Act 1989, section 11E

1. The first matter is that the activity proposed to be specified is appropriate in the circumstances of the case.

2. The second matter is that the person proposed to be specified as the provider of the activity is suitable to provide the activity.

3. The third matter is that the activity proposed to be specified is provided in a place to which the individual who would be subject to the direction (or the condition) can reasonably be expected to travel.

---

[636] See Perry and Rainey (2007) for a welcome response to such orders.
[637] CA 1989, s. 11A(6).
[638] See Rhoades (2003) for the negative Australian experience of these, although P. Parkinson (2006) appears more positive about it.
[639] CA 1989, s. 11B(2), unless they are the parents of the child whose case is before the court.
[640] CA 1989, s. 11A(9).
[641] *Re CB (International Relocation: Domestic Abuse: Child Arrangements)* [2017] EWFC 3.

The court is also required to consider the likely effect of imposing the condition on the individual;[642] in particular, whether there will be a conflict with religious beliefs, employment or education.[643] A fee may be charged for the contact activities, although help may be provided to those who cannot afford it.[644]

This section is an acknowledgement by the law that formal court-based intervention may not be the most effective way of dealing with a hotly contested contact dispute. It is better to assist and inform the couple so that they can reach an agreement between themselves. It may be questioned whether or not telling parents about the importance of putting children first will be of much assistance. Generally, couples accept this; where they are in dispute is whether contact will promote the welfare of the child.[645] The studies from the pilot projects on family resolution of contact disputes are mixed. Only half of the parents completed the programme, but those who did found the group sessions useful, with a change in form of contact taking place in two-thirds of cases.[646] The researchers concluded that the programmes offered little for the really hard cases.[647] However, it seems that around 40 per cent return to court within two years because the agreement has broken down.[648]

(f) Contact activity condition

This matches the contact activity direction, but is used where the court has made a contact order.[649] The same restrictions and requirements apply to a contact activity condition that apply to a contact activity direction. The condition must specify the activity and who is to provide the activity.[650] The order can require the resident parent, the parent who will be having contact or both to attend a contact activity.

One option may be to encourage the parties to attend an education programme to inform them of the benefits of contact. In an evaluation of one such programme it was found that it led to no change in the amount of contact nor in the levels of conflict between the parents.[651] Given the complexity of the kinds of cases where the courts are asked to enforce contact, as revealed in the Trinder *et al.* study,[652] it is perhaps not surprising that they cannot be readily resolved by classes.

(g) Monitoring contact activity conditions or directions

When making a contact activity condition or direction the court can require a family proceedings officer to monitor whether the condition or direction is being complied with and to report to the court any failure to attend an activity.

(h) Monitoring contact

When the court makes or varies a contact order it can require a family proceedings officer to monitor whether the order is complied with by the resident parent or the parent who is to have contact with the child.[653] The court can require the officer to report on such non-compliance as the court requests.

---

[642] CA 1989, s. 11E(5).
[643] CA 1989, s. 11E(6).
[644] CA 1989, s. 11F.
[645] Smart (2006); Kaganas and Day Sclater (2004).
[646] Trinder *et al.* (2006).
[647] Trinder *et al.* (2006).
[648] Trinder and Kellett (2007).
[649] CA 1989, s. 11C
[650] CA 1989, s. 11C(4).
[651] Smith and Trinder (2012).
[652] Trinder *et al.* (2013).
[653] CA 1989, s. 11H.

(i) Contact warning notices

Section 11I of the Children Act 1989 states: 'Where the court makes (or varies) a contact order, it is to attach to the contact order (or the order varying the contact order) a notice warning of the consequences of failing to comply with the contact order.' No doubt this will often be backed up with an oral warning given by the judge to the parties, where appropriate.

(j) Compensation for financial loss

Section 110(2) of the Children Act 1989 states:

LEGISLATIVE PROVISION

Children Act 1989, section 110(2)

1. If the court is satisfied that—

    (a) an individual has failed to comply with the contact order, and

    (b) a person falling within subsection (6) has suffered financial loss by reason of the breach,

    it may make an order requiring the individual in breach to pay the person compensation in respect of his financial loss.

The people falling within subsection (6) are the resident parent, the parent who is to have contact with the child, or a person subject to a condition attached to a contact order or the child.[654] The individual is not required to pay if they can show that they have reasonable excuse for failing to comply with the contact order.[655] The amount payable can be any sum up to the total lost.[656] In deciding whether to make an order, the court must take into account the welfare of the child.[657] Again, note that the welfare of the child is not the paramount consideration.

This provision deals with the situation where the non-resident parent buys tickets in order to take the children on an outing during a contact session, but the resident parent then refuses to hand the children over, for no good reason. In such a case the court could now order the resident parent to compensate the non-resident parent for any financial loss. It should be emphasised that, as it is not possible to make an order requiring the non-resident parent to have contact with the child, if the non-resident parent does not turn up for a contact session, technically speaking that is not a breach of the order. It appears, therefore, that the resident parent cannot seek compensation for expenses they have incurred on the assumption that the non-resident parent will have the children for the day. Possibly the court will take a broad interpretation of the statute and award damages in such a case.

(k) Family assistance orders

The Children and Adoption Act 2006 has extended the provisions dealing with a family assistance order so that they can be useful in the context of a disputed contact case. It inserts a new

---

[654] CA 1989, s. 11O(6). The child can apply only with leave and must have sufficient understanding to bring the proceedings (s. 11O(7)).

[655] CA 1989, s. 11O(3). The individual must have been served with a copy of the order: s. 11P.

[656] CA 1989, s. 11O(9).

[657] CA 1989, s. 11O(14).

s. 16(4A) of the Children Act 1989 which means that on making a family assistance order the court officer can 'give advice and assistance as regards establishing, improving and maintaining contact to such of the persons named in the order as may be specified in the order'. It also creates s. 16(6) of the Children Act 1989 under which a court officer can be required to report to the court on matters relating to contact.

(l) Care proceedings

In **Re L-H (Children)**[658] the Court of Appeal upheld the decision to make a care order and remove the children from the mother as her hostility to the father having contact was having such a harmful effect on them that they should be removed from her. It does sound a little odd to say that because the children are being turned against one parent they should see neither parent, but the court found the dispute was causing significant harm that would only stop if the court ordered the removal of the children and their placement with foster parents.

(m) Emotional pressure

Some judges have used judgments to seek to persuade recalcitrant parents to facilitate contact. For example, in **Re Q (Implacable Contact Dispute)**[659] Sir James Munby ended his judgment with comments addressed to the mother about her child Q:

> Sooner or later, and probably sooner than she would hope, Q will discover the truth – the truth about why he is not seeing his father, the truth about the harm his mother has done to him, the truth about his father, the truth that his father is not the monster he has been brought up to believe he is, the truth about, and the dreadful details of, the litigation. When he discovers that truth, what is his mother going to be able to say to him? How is she going to begin to justify her behaviour? She needs to think very carefully about how she is going to handle that day, not if but when it comes. Whatever she may think about the father, does she really want to imperil her future relationship with her son? Run the risk of being disowned by him? Run the risk of never seeing her own grandchildren? I urge her to think, long and hard, and to act before it is too late.

Academics have hotly contested the correct way of responding to a breach of a contact order:

DEBATE

How should contact orders be enforced, if at all?

Here are some of the views that have been expressed on how (if at all) contact should be enforced:

1. Smart and Neale[660] have suggested: 'Questions must be asked about where family law is going, because in its current form the law is beginning to look like a lever for the powerful to use against the vulnerable, rather than a measure to safeguard the welfare of children.' They see these cases as too often involving strong fathers using the law on contact as a tool against mothers they have abused or terrified. Contact can then become a way of continuing to exercise power over the mothers. Bainham has maintained that such an argument is in danger of equating the interests of children with those of their mothers.[661] Helen Reece puts the argument in terms of enforcement of contact maintaining gender roles:

---

[658] [2017] EWCA Civ 2603.
[659] [2015] EWCA Civ 991.
[660] Smart and Neale (1997: 336).
[661] Bainham (1998b: 7).

These critiques point to the division of labour that still exists within the intact traditional nuclear family, characterised primarily by women taking the main responsibility for childcare, and secondarily by gendered roles in relation to shared childcare, with fathers tending to perform discrete, fun activities (such as taking children to the park) and mothers tending to remain in charge of the more repetitive, continuous and mundane day-to-day care. They argue that the strong assumption of substantial post-separation contact between fathers and children is one mechanism by which the law ensures that parental separation does not fundamentally disrupt this division of labour: instead, the nuclear family is replicated post-separation.[662]

Felicity Kaganas[663] believes that the law sees the problem in disputed contact cases being the mother opposing contact, rather than recognising that the father may be to blame.

For some years mothers who oppose contact or disobey orders have been construed as the problem. What has changed is the way in which the legislature, and the courts themselves, have decided how to approach this problem. The solution chosen is to enable family courts to act in a way analogous to problem-solving courts. What family courts are 'for', now, includes not only seeking to persuade parents (mainly mothers) to comply but also deciding to refer them to services so that they address their underlying problems. Courts have become part of a therapeutic network being deployed to change attitudes and behaviour. Conversely, helping agencies have now become part of the disciplinary framework governing families, and in particular resident mothers. These 'helping' services have in effect been incorporated into the family justice toolkit, backed up by punishment.

2. Some groups promoting the interests of fathers have claimed that the non-enforcement of contact orders means that they are not worth the paper they are written on. If court orders are not enforced the law is seen as powerless and unwilling to enforce people's rights.[664] Opponents of this view may argue that if contact has taken place only following threats of imprisonment or pressure from judges or professionals there will not be effective contact.[665]

3. Bainham suggests that there must be an attempt to enforce contact in order to send the message that contact is an important right of the child which the law will protect.[666] He writes:

Unless the courts are seen to be taking the contact issue seriously, the message of the law that contact is an important right of the child may be lost. And caution needs to be exercised in equating too readily the interests of women (usually the so-called 'primary carers') and children in this matter. Moreover . . . the ECHR requires the State to take action to enforce orders for contact.[667]

4. Even if at the end of the day contact orders are not enforced, they should be made and steps should be taken to try to enforce them, he argues. Carol Smart[668] has argued against the use of rights in this context. She argues that children see contact issues not in terms of rights, but in terms of care and love. We need a law reflecting those values, rather than emphasising rights.

---

[662] Reece (2006b: 547).
[663] Kaganas (2010b).
[664] Bainham (2003a).
[665] Herring (2003a).
[666] Bainham (2003b).
[667] Bainham (2005: 160).
[668] Smart (2004).

5. John Eekelaar has warned: 'it is important not to jump from the fact that an outcome is optimally desirable to the conclusion that it should, therefore, be legally enforceable'.[669] It certainly seems odd to enforce an order designed to further a child's welfare in a way that harms a child. However, the law might be justified by the argument that the imprisonment of the mother in the case harms the child, but this promotes the welfare of children generally by encouraging parents to obey court orders.

6. Some commentators[670] have argued that where contact orders are ignored the solution lies not in imprisonment but in the use of extra-legal facilities. In **Re H (A Child) (Contact: Mother's Opposition)**[671] the mother opposed contact. The Court of Appeal took the view that the mother's opposition was without foundation and amounted to an attempt to blackmail the court. The Court of Appeal sought the assistance of a psychiatrist who was to assist the family and advise on how contact could be progressed. This indicates a recognition that some cases of this kind involve emotional and psychological difficulties more suitable for the help of a counsellor or psychiatrist than a judge or a lawyer.

7. Many commentators take the view that there is little the law can do in these cases.[672] We have to acknowledge that family law cannot always provide an answer. A recent study[673] found that couples who rely on the law to resolve their contact disputes risk making matters worse for everyone concerned. By contrast, those parents who resolve matters without recourse to the law avoid stress and distress. The researchers argued that in dealing with contentious contact cases it would be more profitable to spend time and money on services to improve the relations between the parents and children, rather than on lawyers and the legal process.[674]

8. Several commentators[675] have noted the contrast in treatment of resident and non-resident parents. If the resident parent deprives the child of the benefit of contact, he or she risks imprisonment. However, if the non-resident parent does not want contact with the child (equally depriving the child of the benefit of contact), he or she will not face any legal sanction. Both are interfering equally in the child's right of contact with both parents, but only the resident parent is punished.

9. MacFarlane LJ in **Re W (Children)**[676] in a useful contribution to the debate has focused on parental responsibility. He argues:

> In all aspects of life, whilst some duties and responsibilities may be a pleasure to discharge, others may well be unwelcome and a burden. Whilst parenting in many respects brings joy, even in families where life is comparatively harmonious, the responsibility of being a parent can be tough. Where parents separate the burden for each and every member of the family group can be, and probably will be, heavy. It is not easy, indeed it is tough, to be a single parent with the care of a child. Equally, it is tough to be the parent of a child for whom you no longer have the day-to-day care and with whom you no longer enjoy the ordinary stuff of everyday life because you only spend limited time with your child. Where all contact between a parent and a child is prevented, the burden on that parent will be of the highest order. Equally, for the parent who has the primary care of a child, to send that child off to spend

---

[669] Eekelaar (2002b: 272).
[670] E.g. Masson (2000b).
[671] [2001] 1 FCR 59.
[672] Trinder, Beek and Connolly (2002) emphasise the harm children can suffer due to stress and dispute over contact.
[673] Trinder, Beek and Connolly (2002).
[674] See Hunter and Choudhry (2018) for some helpful examples from other jurisdictions.
[675] E.g. Smart and Neale (1997).
[676] [2012] EWCA Civ 999. See also **Re D (A Child)** [2014] EWCA Civ.

time with the other parent may, in some cases, be itself a significant burden; it may, to use modern parlance, be 'a very big ask'. Where, however, it is plainly in the best interests of a child to spend time with the other parent then, tough or not, part of the responsibility of the parent with care must be the duty and responsibility to deliver what the child needs, hard though that may be.

He is not seeking to enforce this through the law but seeking to encourage an attitude in parents disputing contact to put their responsibilities as parents to promote the welfare of the child to the fore. The difficulty is that in many cases of disputed contact the resident parent is opposing contact precisely because they fear it will harm the child. They will see themselves being responsible parents in seeking to prevent contact.

The Government rejected calls to reform of the law on enforcement by considering adding 'withholding of passports and driving licences as well as the imposition of a curfew order requiring the parent concerned to remain at a specified address between specified hours' to the penalties available. It also rejected suggestions that a parent who was preventing having contact would not be required to pay child support.[677]

Questions

1. *Is the real answer to contact disputes to rely on non-legal remedies, such as counselling and mediation? Is that appropriate in cases of domestic violence?*

2. *Normally, when a court order is deliberately breached imprisonment will follow, so why not in relation to contact orders?*

3. *Would it be better for the courts to be more reluctant to make contact orders, but then stricter in enforcing them?*

Further reading

See **Bainham et al**. (2003) for a useful set of essays on contact. See **Gilmore** (2008b) for an insightful analysis of the data on the benefits of contact.

(ix) Contact centres

There has been increased interest in and use of contact centres.[678] These provide a neutral venue in which contact can take place. Although not designed to deal with potentially violent cases,[679] they are often used by courts and solicitors in cases where the resident parent has concerns over his or her own or his or her child's safety.[680] The contact can be supervised by a social worker or untrained volunteer, who can make sure that there is no abuse of the child. Also, it would be possible for the arrangements to be such that the resident parent and contact parent do not meet.

Not everyone is convinced that the use of contact centres is the solution to the intractable problem of contact.[681] Key to the success of such studies is that they create a safe and pleasant atmosphere for contact. One study suggested that (predictably) resident parents feel that the supervision at such centres is inadequate, while non-resident parents feel that the supervision is unnecessarily invasive and humiliating.[682] The study went on to note that in a significant

---

[677] Trinder *et al*. (2013).

[678] Lord Chancellor's Department (2002a); Humphreys and Harrison (2003a). See Wall P. (2010) for guidance on when contact centres should be used.

[679] A point emphasised by Humphreys and Harrison (2003b).

[680] Humphreys and Harrison (2003a).

[681] See the concerns in Caffrey (2013) over the lack of listening to children in contact centres.

[682] Aris, Harrison and Humphreys (2002).

minority of centres the well-being of women and children was being compromised due to a lack of staff and expertise, leading to inadequate supervision.[683] Indeed, it should be appreciated that in the United Kingdom many contact centres are run in community buildings such as church halls.[684] It should also be recalled that very young children might require the resident parent to remain in sight during the contact session.[685]

(x) Other relatives

Step-parents[686] and grandparents[687] can apply for contact, but there is not the same assumption of the benefits of contact that exists in relation to parents.[688] Step-parents and grandparents must persuade the court that they have a close relationship with the child and that the child will benefit from continued contact.[689] In *Re W (Contact: Application by Grandparent)*[690] Hollis J accepted that it can be extremely beneficial for a child to have contact with her grandparents, even if that contact is opposed by the parents. However, some campaigners claim that other judges too readily deny contact to grandparents, especially if that is opposed by the child's parents. Grandparents with an established relationship with a child may be able to claim that they have rights to contact under Article 8 of the ECHR, as acknowledged in *Re H (A Child)*.[691]

(xi) Duties of contact

Although there has been much discussion of the rights of contact, there has been less about the duties of contact. Yet, as Bainham has pointed out, 'to talk of contact as a *right* of anyone is devoid of meaning unless considered alongside the *obligations* which go with that right'.[692] Bainham argues that if we acknowledge that children have a right of contact then parents have a duty to exercise it. This is controversial because it suggests that a parent who does not want to have contact with his or her child could be required by a court order (on pain of imprisonment) to have contact.[693] Bainham accepts that such a duty may be unenforceable, but this does not mean that the duty should not be recognised as a way of underlining the fact that society values relationships between parents and children. Thorpe LJ in *Re L (A Child) (Contact: Domestic Violence)* suggested that such an order cannot be made: 'The errant or selfish parent cannot be ordered to spend time with his child against his will however much the child may yearn for his company and the mother desire respite.'[694]

Bainham[695] also controversially suggests that if a parent has a right of contact with a child then the child can be said to be under a duty to permit that contact. Without such a duty, the parent's right is not meaningful. Again, he accepts there may be difficulties in forcing children to see parents they do not want to see, but he suggests attempts should be made to do so. John Eekelaar forcefully rejects the notion that children may be under a duty of contact: 'to put a child under a legal duty to submit to the care and attentions of someone who is not the

---

[683] There is grave concern over decisions like *Re P (Parental Responsibility)* [1998] 2 FLR 96 where a paedophilic father who had been 'grooming a child' was allowed contact at a contact centre.

[684] Maclean and Mueller-Johnson (2003).

[685] Aris, Harrison and Humphreys (2002) found this to be so in a significant minority of cases.

[686] *Re H (A Minor) (Contact)* [1994] 2 FLR 776, [1994] FCR 419.

[687] *Re A (Section 8 Order: Grandparent Application)* [1995] 2 FLR 153, [1996] 1 FCR 467.

[688] For a useful discussion of grandparents and contact, see Kaganas and Piper (2020).

[689] *Re G (A Child)* [2018] EWCA Civ 305.

[690] [2001] 1 FLR 263.

[691] [2014] EWCA Civ 271. See also *Adam v Germany* [2009] 1 FLR 560.

[692] Bainham (2003a: 61).

[693] See also Wallbank (2010).

[694] [2000] 4 All ER 609 at pp. 637e–f.

[695] Bainham (2003a).

daily caregiver simply because that person is the child's parent . . . is to put the child under legal constraints based not on the child's interests, but on the demands of adults, or one adult, which have arisen as a result of events in which the child had no part.'[696]

(xii) Encouraging contact

The problem of the lack of contact between children and non-resident parents is only partly due to non-resident parents wanting, but not being able to have, contact. A far more common cause of the lack of contact is that non-resident parents do not seek contact with children. It is notable that those who seek to emphasise the right of the child to contact use this right as a means of forcing resident parents (normally mothers) to have contact with the non-resident parents (normally fathers) but arguably more could be done by those wishing to promote the child's rights to contact if those fathers who do not have contact with their children were encouraged to do so.[697] The reality is that after separation many non-resident fathers find their relationship with their children strained. Further, it is often difficult to fit in contact sessions with the work life of the non-resident parent and the social life of the child.[698]

(xiii) Contact in practice

The statistics suggest that contact arrangements often break down. Eekelaar and Clive[699] found that although two-thirds of non-residential parents had contact in the first six months, by five years after the divorce only one-third did. However, other studies have shown higher rates of contact. Eekelaar and Maclean in their study found contact rates of 69 per cent where the parents had been married, but 45 per cent where unmarried.[700] Trinder et al.[701] found that for only 27 of the 61 families were contact arrangements 'working'. A study by the Office for National Statistics found that 10 per cent of children saw both parents daily.[702] Around 30 per cent of resident parents reported that the child never saw the non-resident parent. Poole et al.[703] found that 59 per cent of non-resident fathers saw their children once a week and 87 per cent said they had some kind of contact. However, all the studies show a decline in the rate of contact as the years since parental separation pass. This drop-off has been explained on three grounds: the first is that some fathers may (falsely) believe they do not have to pay (or can escape payment of) child support if they do not see the child; secondly, some find occasional contact painful;[704] thirdly, some fathers believe that the child will settle down better if contact is stopped. Another important factor is that the father may remarry or re-partner[705] and his new partner may discourage contact, especially once the new couple have children of their own. Certainly, there are higher rates of non-contact among fathers who have a 'new family'.[706] Long-term contact works best where both the resident and non-resident parent are committed to making contact succeed and are willing to work through the practical difficulties.[707]

---

[696] Eekelaar (2006b: 68).

[697] See Herring (2003a) for a discussion of how the law might do this, including a suggestion of collecting child support more effectively. Where child support is paid, there is evidence that this increases the rate of contact (see Poole et al. (2013)), although Australian research is less clear on the link: Fehlberg et al. (2013).

[698] Buchanan and Hunt (2003).

[699] Eekelaar and Clive (1977).

[700] Eekelaar and Maclean (1997).

[701] Trinder, Beek and Connolly (2002).

[702] National Statistics (2008a).

[703] Poole et al. (2013).

[704] Trinder, Beek and Connolly (2002) found that children experienced difficulty in establishing a meaningful relationship with the non-resident parent.

[705] Eekelaar and Maclean (1997) found that sometimes re-partnering encouraged contact and sometimes discouraged it.

[706] Poole et al. (2013).

[707] Trinder, Beek and Connolly (2002).

(xiv) Reform of the law

As already mentioned, contact disputes are often the most bitter cases. Many believe that too often fathers are denied contact: the courts refuse to order contact, or, where they do, the orders are not enforced. Others claim that the courts too readily order contact, placing mothers and children in danger. In fact, the evidence is that where contact is applied for it is nearly always granted. Where couples negotiate and avoid the need for a court hearing, they nearly always agree some degree of contact.[708] This shows that the argument that judges are denying fathers contact because they are anti-father is false. In fact, given that around 90 per cent of contact disputes are resolved through negotiations[709] and only the most contested reach court, the number of applications refused looks worryingly low, especially given the rates of domestic violence and child abuse. A major study of the way contact cases are dealt with found no evidence of bias against fathers. In the very few cases where contact was denied there were very good reasons for this.[710] In fact, a much stronger case can be made for saying that the legal process is more ready to grant contact than it is for refusing it.

One of the difficulties in reforming this area of the law is that most cases are resolved amicably and reasonably between the parents. Less than 10 per cent of cases reach the court.[711] As the research by Joan Hunt and Liz Trinder shows, what they call 'chronically litigated contact cases'[712] involving five or more court cases, raise a host of particularly complex issues, with the contact dispute being but one of a range of problems facing the family. Mental health issues, domestic violence, sexual abuse, personality problems, substance misuse and poverty abound. These disputes are not easy to resolve because they are genuinely complex cases.

8 Wardship and the inherent jurisdiction

Learning objective 5

Describe how the courts use wardship and the inherent jurisdiction

The inherent jurisdiction provides the court with powers which do not originate from statute but from the common law.[713] The jurisdiction flows from the ancient *parens patriae* jurisdiction which the Crown owes to those subjects who are unable to protect themselves. The classic example of such subjects are children. The basis of the jurisdiction is that if a child needs protection the courts should not be inhibited from acting merely because of 'technical' difficulties. It is readily understandable that children should not be left without the protection of the law.[714] However, there is concern that use of the inherent jurisdiction bypasses the protection of the rights of children and adults in statutes. It is notable that, following the Children Act 1989, there is a limited role for the inherent jurisdiction. In *Re NY (A Child)*[715] the Supreme Court held it would be wrong to say the inherent jurisdiction cannot be used if the order required was available under the Children Act 1989, although it indicated there should be no difference in outcome if an application was made under the inherent jurisdiction, which could have

---

[708] Hunt and Macleod (2008).
[709] Hunt and Macleod (2008).
[710] Hunt and Macleod (2008).
[711] Hunt and Trinder (2011).
[712] Hunt and Trinder (2011).
[713] See Lowe (2012) for a discussion of the modern use of wardship.
[714] In *W v J (Child: Variation of Financial Provision)* [2004] 2 FLR 300 it was said to be inappropriate to use wardship as a way of getting one parent to pay the other's legal fees because that would not be for the benefit of the child.
[715] [2019] UKSC 49.

been brought under the Children Act 1989. In practice the jurisdiction will be used where it is feared the use of section 8 orders will not be sufficient to meet the needs of the child. The following are examples of cases where wardship has proved useful:

1. Wardship might be appropriate where the parents refuse to consent to medical treatment and it is necessary to take long-term decisions about the child. In *Re C (A Baby)*[716] a child was abandoned and there was no one with parental responsibility for the child who could be found. Sir Stephen Brown suggested that wardship was useful, especially as the child was severely ill, having developed brain damage after meningitis.[717]

2. Wardship might also be useful if third parties such as the press are intruding on the child's life. A prohibited steps order or specific issue order cannot be obtained against someone who is not exercising an aspect of parental responsibility. Wardship would be able to protect the child as the court has the power under wardship to prevent publicity relating to children.

3. In *Re W (Wardship: Discharge: Publicity)*[718] a father had care and control of four sons. He permitted the children to talk to the press, which led to the publication of various articles. The father also changed the children's schooling without consulting the mother. The Court of Appeal saw the need for wardship because a specific issue order could not be made which was wide enough – it was not possible to predict how the father might act in the future. It was also thought beneficial that the Official Solicitor could remain involved in the case and act as a buffer between the parents.

4. In *Re KR (Abduction: Forcible Removal by Parents)*[719] wardship was used to protect a child who, it was feared, was about to be removed from the jurisdiction to be forced to enter an arranged marriage. However, wardship can only be used for children habitually resident in the jurisdiction.[720]

5. Wardship has been found useful in cases involving children of asylum seekers where there are concerns about their welfare.[721]

6. In *T v S (Wardship)*[722] there were incessant bitter disputes between the parents over nearly every issue to do with the child's upbringing. A wardship order was made so that the court could make decisions about the child and bring the warring to an end. The court would decide with which parent the child should live and what contact arrangements should take place.

The exercise of the inherent jurisdiction is quite different from wardship. The order will simply resolve a single issue relating to the child and have no wider effect. It does not provide ongoing supervision by the court of the child's welfare. For example, in *Re SL (Permission to Vaccinate)*[723] the court used the inherent jurisdiction to approve the vaccination of children in care. The Court of Appeal has stated that its powers under the inherent jurisdiction

---

[716] [1996] 2 FLR 43, [1996] 2 FCR 569.

[717] Although see *LA v SB, AB & MB* [2010] EWCA Civ 1744 for a case where the court refused to intervene after parents refused to consent to recommended treatment.

[718] [1995] 2 FLR 466, [1996] 1 FCR 393.

[719] [1999] 2 FLR 542.

[720] *H v H (Jurisdiction to Grant Wardship)* [2011] EWCA Civ 796. Although see also *Re L (A Child) (Custody: Habitual Residence)* [2013] UKSC 75.

[721] Welstead and Edwards (2006: 278). However, in *S v S* [2009] 1 FLR 241 it was held to be a misuse of wardship to attempt to interfere in an immigration decision.

[722] [2011] EWHC 1608 (Fam).

[723] [2017] EWHC 125 (Fam).

are unlimited.[724] Specifically, it is accepted that the court, acting under the inherent jurisdiction, has wider powers than a parent.[725] Another example is *Re K (A Child: Deceased)*[726]
where the court used the inherent jurisdiction to authorise the local authority to organise
the burial of the child. The parents would not make the arrangements and there was no
legislative basis for arranging the burial of others. The court felt it was obvious a decent
disposal of the body was required and turned to the inherent jurisdiction to fill the jurisdic-
tional gap.

Controversially, in *Re LA (Medical Treatment)*[727] the court declined to invoke the inherent
jurisdiction in a case where a six-year-old boy had a progressive brain disease. The parents
refused to cooperate in agreeing to treatment options, believing it was best to offer no treatment. The local authority initially started care proceedings, but decided to withdraw them. The
court held the matter of surgery was a matter between the parents and hospital. Neither had
sought to involve the court and the local authority had withdrawn its application. Critics might
think this was exactly the kind of case where inherent jurisdiction could be used.

There have been a series of recent cases where wardship and the inherent jurisdiction have
been used in cases where it is believed children may have been 'radicalised' (see Chapter 11).

9 Child abduction

There is a special set of rules that deals with child abduction: that is, where a child is removed
from the care of the residential parent, often to another jurisdiction. This area of law is complex, and is not covered in detail in this text.

10 Conclusion

We have considered those cases where the courts have had to resolve private disputes concerning the upbringing of children. Much of this area of the law depends on the judiciary exercising their discretion and deciding each case on its own particular facts. Indeed,
increasingly the courts are willing to accept that there is no one view which represents the
child's best interests and it is rather a case of deciding which of the parents' wishes are to
predominate. That said, there are some presumptions or assumptions (e.g. in favour of
the 'natural' parent; in favour of contact with parents) which the courts have developed to
provide a degree of predictability for some kinds of cases. However, recently the courts have
been preferring to talk of an assessment of the welfare of the particular child in question,
rather than relying on presumptions. Interestingly, some of the judiciary have begun to question whether the courtroom is the appropriate forum in which to resolve family disputes.
Whether this marks the beginning of the end for court resolution of family disagreements is
unlikely, but it may well be that the cuts in legal aid mean that courts will only be troubled
by arguments between members of richer families.

---

[724] *Re W (A Minor) (Medical Treatment: Court's Jurisdiction)* [1993] Fam 64, [1992] 2 FCR 785, [1993] 1 FLR 1.
[725] *Re R (A Minor) (Wardship: Consent to Medical Treatment)* [1992] Fam 11 at p. 25.
[726] [2017] EWHC 1083 (Fam).
[727] [2010] EWHC Fam 1744.

Further reading

Bainham, A. and Gilmore, S. (2014) 'The English Children and Families Act 2014', *Victoria University Wellington Law Review* 627.

Barnett, A. (2014a) 'Contact at all costs? Domestic violence and children's welfare', *Child and Family Law Quarterly* 439.

Barnett, A. (2020) 'A genealogy of hostility: parental alienation in England and Wales', *Journal of Social Welfare and Family Law* 42: 1.

Birchall, J. and Choudhry, S. (2018) *'What About My Right Not To Be Abused?' Domestic Abuse, Human Rights and the Family Courts*, Women's Aid, Bristol.

Bremner, P. (2017) 'Collaborative co-parenting and heteronormativity: recognising the interests of gay fathers', *Child and Family Law Quarterly* 293.

Choudhry, S. (2019) 'When women's rights are *not* human rights – the non-performativity of the human rights of victims of domestic abuse within English family law', *Modern Law Review* 82: 1072.

Collier, R. (2016) 'Men, gender and fathers' rights after legal equality', in R. Leckey (ed) *After Legal Equality,* Abingdon: Routledge.

Eekelaar, J. (2014a) 'Family Justice on trial: *Re A*', *Family Law* 44: 543.

Elizabeth, V. (2017) 'Custody stalking: a mechanism of coercively controlling mothers following separation', *Feminist Legal Studies* 25: 185.

Elizabeth, V. (2019) '"It's an invisible wound": the disenfranchised grief of post-separation mothers who lose care time', *Journal of Social Welfare and Family Law* 41: 34.

Elizabeth, V. (2020) 'The affective burden of separated mothers in PA(S)inflected custody law systems: a New Zealand case study', *Journal of Social Welfare and Family Law* 42: 118.

George, R. H. **(2013)** *Relocation Disputes: Law and Practice in England and New Zealand,* Oxford: Hart Publishing.

Gilmore, S. (2006a) 'Contact/shared residence and child well-being: research evidence and its decisions for legal decision-making', *International Journal of Law, Policy and the Family* 20: 344.

Gilmore, S. (2006b) 'Court decision-making in shared residence order cases: a critical examination', *Child and Family Law Quarterly* 18: 478.

Gilmore, S. (2008b) 'Disputing contact: challenging some assumptions', *Child and Family Law Quarterly* 20: 285.

Gilmore, S. (2016) 'Less of the "P" discipline and more of the "H" word – putting *Payne* in its place! *Re F (A Child) (International Relocation Cases)* [2015] EWCA Civ 882', *Journal of Social Welfare and Family Law* 38: 87.

Gilmore, S. (2020) 'Justice and implacable hostility to contact: parental beliefs, factual foundation and justification', *Law Quarterly Review* 136: 99.

Harris-Short, S. (2011) 'Building a house upon sand: post-separation parenting, shared residence and equality – lessons from Sweden', *Child and Family Law Quarterly* 344.

Harwood, J. (2019) '"We don't know what it is we don't know": how austerity has undermined the courts' access to information in child arrangements cases involving domestic abuse', *Child and Family Law Quarterly* 321.

Hunt, J. (2012) 'Through a glass darkly: the uncertain future of private law child contact litigation', *Journal of Social Welfare and Family Law* 33: 379.

Hunt, J. (2014) 'Shared parenting time: messages from research', *Family Law* 44: 676.

Hunt, J. and Trinder, L. (2011) *Chronically Litigated Contact Cases: How Many Are There and What Works?* London: Family Justice Council.

Hunter, R and Choudhry, S. (2018) 'Conclusion: international best practices', *Journal of Social Welfare and Family Law* 40: 548.

Jivraj, S. and Herman, D. (2009) '"It is difficult for a white judge to understand": orientalism, racialisation, and Christianity in English child welfare cases', *Child and Family Law Quarterly* 21: 283.

Kaganas, F. (2010b) 'When it comes to contact disputes, what are family courts for?' *Current Legal Problems* 63: 235.

Kaganas, F. (2014a) 'A presumption that "involvement" of both parents is best: deciphering law's messages', *Child and Family Law Quarterly* 26: 270.

Kaganas, F. (2018) 'Parental Involvement: A Discretionary Presumption', *Legal Studies* 38: 548.

Kaganas, F. and Piper, C. (2020) 'Grandparent contact: another presumption?' *Journal of Social Welfare and Family* Law 42: 176.

Ministry of Justice (2020b) *Assessing Risk of Harm to Children and Parents in Private Law Children Cases*, London: MoJ.

Parkinson, P. (2011) *Family Law and the Indissolubility of Parenthood,* New York: Cambridge University Press.

Poole, E. *et al.* (2013) *What do we know about non-resident fathers?* London: NatCen Social Research.

Reece, H. (2006b) 'UK women's groups' child contact campaign: "So long as it is safe"', *Child and Family Law Quarterly* 18: 538.

Reece, H. (2017) 'Was there, is there and should there be a presumption against deviant parents?' *Child and Family Law Quarterly* 9.

Rhoades, H. (2012) 'Legislating to promote children's welfare and the quest for certainty', *Child and Family Law Quarterly* 24: 158.

Sheehy, E. and Boyd, S. (2020) 'Penalizing women's fear: intimate partner violence and parental alienation in Canadian child custody cases', *Journal of Social Welfare and Family Law* 42: 80.

Taylor, R. (2013) 'Secular values and sacred rights: *Re G (Education: Religious Upbringing)*', *Child and Family Law Quarterly* 25: 336.

Taylor, R. (2015) 'Responsibility for the soul of the child: the role of the state and parents in determining religious upbringing and education', *International Journal of Law, Policy and the Family* 29: 15.

Trinder, L. (2010) 'Shared residence: a review of recent research evidence', *Child and Family Law Quarterly* 151.

Trinder, L. (2014b) 'Climate change? The multiple trajectories of shared care law, policy and social practices', *Child and Family Law Quarterly* 30.

Wallbank, J. (2014) 'Universal norms, individualization and the need for recognition', in J. Wallbank and J. Herring (eds) *Vulnerabilities, Care and Family Law,* London: Routledge.

Women's Aid (2012) *Picking up the pieces: domestic violence and child contact*, London: Women's Aid.

Visit **go.pearson.com/uk/he/resources** to access **resources** specifically written to complement this text.

11

Child protection

Learning objectives

When you finish reading this chapter you will be able to:

1. Explain and evaluate the significance of human rights on child protection law
2. Examine the voluntary services offered by a local authority
3. Consider the use of emergency protection orders
4. State the law surrounding secure accommodation orders
5. Discuss the protection offered to children by the criminal law
6. Summarise the differences between a care order and a supervision order
7. Analyse the threshold criteria
8. Explore the use of adoption and special guardianship
9. Summarise the circumstances in which an adoption order will be made
10. Analyse the balance of power between courts and the local authority

1 The problems of child protection

One of the greatest powers the state has is to remove a child from their parents.[1] While our society generally assumes that children are best raised by their parents, it is clear that is not true for every child. Yet for many parents, one of the worst things that could happen to them would be having their children compulsorily removed by the state. On the other hand, the appalling harm that children can suffer at the hands of their parents means that the state must intervene if children's rights are to be protected.

---

[1] For a magnificent lengthy discussion of the issues, see Hoyano and Keenan (2007).

Mostyn J in *N (A Local Authority) v A*[2] has acknowledged the severity of the orders the court can make in child protection:

> To make the order sought by the local authority, severing the bond between parent and child, is a momentous thing. It has been said that with the abolition of capital punishment it is arguably the most serious order that a judge in this country can make. The child will grow to adulthood in a completely different family to that which nature had intended. The child will grow with a completely different set of values and experiences to that originally anticipated. It is because of the momentous nature of the decision that the law, both domestic and from Strasbourg, insists that the powers cannot be exercised until there has been proved past serious harm, or the risk of future serious harm. Even then, the powers cannot be exercised in the manner claimed unless the child's welfare demands such a solution and where no other solution can be found consistent with the child's welfare.

The issue of child abuse is a major one in today's society. Between 2008 and 2018 there was an increase of well over 50 per cent in the number of applications for a care order.[3] In part this was a response to the 'Baby Peter' case where there was a huge media outcry after a child was not protected from abusive parents and died.[4] Julie Doughty suggests it also reflects the fact that there is increased understanding of how neglect, as well as active abuse, can harm children.[5] Indeed, cases of neglect now make up over half of all child protection registrations.[6]

One of the major problems in the law concerning the protection of children is that if the wrong decision is made, enormous harm can be caused. Imagine that a social worker visits a home where a child has a broken arm and bruises. The social worker suspects this may have been caused by the parents, while the parents claim that the injuries were caused by a fall down the stairs. If the parents' explanation is untrue, but the social worker decides to believe it, she would be leaving the child with abusive parents and there would be a danger that the child could suffer serious injury or even death.[7] On the other hand, if the explanation is true and the social worker decides to remove the child, then the child and parents may suffer great harm through the separation. The history of the law on child protection reveals tragedies resulting from excessive intervention in family life as well as gross failure to intervene.[8] The difficulty is that it is only with hindsight that it would be apparent that in a particular case the approach was inappropriate.

This puts social workers in an impossible position. Many are happy to rush to criticise them when they are seen to be too interventionist. Wall LJ in *EH v Greenwich London Borough Council*[9] has noted:

> What social workers do not appear to understand is that the public perception of their role in care proceedings is not a happy one. They are perceived by many as the arrogant and enthusiastic removers of children from their parents into an unsatisfactory care system, and as trampling on the rights of parents and children in the process.

Yet social workers face equal levels of blame when they fail to protect children from harm, as seen in the media outcry following the Baby Peter case.[10] The report into the case found it was

---

[2] [2020] EWFC 25.
[3] CAFCASS (2018).
[4] Doughty (2014).
[5] Doughty (2014).
[6] Davis (2015).
[7] Hedley (2014).
[8] Masson (2000b).
[9] [2010] 2 FCR 106, para 109.
[10] Laming (2009).

not so much a case of inadequate guidelines, as a failure to follow them. The frustration in Lord Laming's report into the many failings that meant there was inadequate intervention to protect the child is palpable:

> [T]his document, and its recommendations, are aimed at making sure that good practice becomes standard practice in every service. This includes recommendations on improving the inspection of safeguarding services and the quality of serious case reviews as well as recommendations on improving the help and support children receive when they are at risk of harm. The utility of the policy and legislation has been pressed on me by contributors throughout this report. In such circumstances it is hard to resist the urge to respond by saying to each of the key services, if that is so 'NOW JUST DO IT!'[11]

It is easy when looking at individual dramatic failures to obtain a false picture. Many social workers engage in hugely important work for families. The difficulties have largely arisen as a result of inadequate funding, low morale and poor management. Given the huge importance of the issues at stake, social work requires significantly greater levels of funding and support from the state.

In Julia Brophy's and Martha Cover's study of care proceedings, it was found that most involved the poorest families, who had multiple needs and problems.[12] For example, in their sample 84 per cent were dependent on income support and 45 per cent of parents had serious mental health problems. As Brophy and Cover point out, the cases involve families with complex needs that are ignored until child protection issues arise. Cutbacks in social service support are likely to see more and more troubled families arriving at the doors of courts. Indeed Featherstone et al.[13] suggest that many children taken into care would have been able to thrive with their families, had the social and economic issues the family faced been addressed.

It is also clear that there are some troubled people who appear repeatedly in child protection proceedings. One study estimated that between 2007 and 2013, a total of 7,143 mothers had different children removed in separate care proceedings.[14] These women, it was found, lived family lives which had a 'toxic trio' of mental health problems, substance misuse and domestic abuse. All of this indicates that the issues of child protection interplay in complex ways with a wide range of social problems.[15]

As this discussion suggests, many of the difficulties in this area lie not so much in the substantive law as practical issues. Nevertheless, there are important legal issues to address. Here are three major difficulties that the law faces.

1. There are evidential problems. Lord Nicholls in the House of Lords recognised the difficulties facing a judge in care cases of having to 'penetrate the fog of denials, evasions, lies and half-truths which all too often descends'.[16] In other words, social workers and the courts often simply do not know the facts and have to deal with possibilities. Even experts examining the same injuries can differ widely in their interpretation of them.[17] Indeed, as the decision in *R v Cannings*[18] revealed, there are dangers in placing excessive weight on the

---

[11] Laming (2009: 1). Capitals in the original.
[12] Brophy and Cover (2012).
[13] Featherstone *et al.* (2018).
[14] Broadhurst *et al.* (2015).
[15] Roberts (2014) highlights the concern that black and ethnic minority families are overrepresented among the families with children in care.
[16] *Lancashire CC v B* [2000] 1 FLR 583 at p. 589.
[17] *Re W (A Child) (Non-accidental Injury: Expert Evidence)* [2005] 3 FCR 513.
[18] [2004] 1 FCR 193.

opinion of experts in the field. In that case a mother's conviction of murder of her babies was quashed after it was found that the prosecution expert's evidence was flawed.[19] Similarly, there are the difficulties of predicting the future. Predicting the likelihood that a parent will abuse a child on the basis of past conduct is far from easy. Yet such predictions are essential to childcare in practice.

2. Even if the facts are known, there is much controversy over how much suffering the child should face before it is suitable for the state to intervene to protect him or her. If a local authority finds a child living in a home which is dirty and untidy, where the family's diet is unhealthy, and the children spend nearly all their time watching television, what should be done? Many would argue that this kind of situation is not sufficiently serious to justify intervention. Others would argue that the state must offer support and help to the parents to improve the family's lifestyle, for the sake of the child. The issue here is whether protection of family privacy means the state should intervene only in the most serious cases, or whether the local authority is justified in acting in order to prevent abuse.

   Fox Harding has outlined four basic approaches that the law could take in relation to suspected child abuse:[20]

   (a) *Laissez-faire and patriarchy.* Here, the core approach is that the role of the state should be kept to a minimum. The privacy of the original family should be respected. This is an 'all or nothing' approach. Family privacy should be protected unless it is absolutely necessary to remove a child. Critics argue that the approach promotes non-intervention except in the most extreme cases of violence, enabling men to exercise control over women and children within their families.

   (b) *State paternalism and child protection.* This approach favours the intervention of the state in order to protect the child. It encourages state intervention, to whatever extent is necessary, to promote the welfare of children. Opponents of this policy claim that the approach places insufficient weight on the rights of birth families. The approach, they claim, can too easily slip into 'social engineering', and presumes that the state knows what is best for the child.

   (c) *The defence of the birth family and parents' rights.* The emphasis in this approach is on the benefits of psychological and biological bonds between children and parents.[21] The birth family is seen as the 'optimal context' for bringing up children. Even where parents fail, the state should see its role as doing as much as possible to preserve the family ties. The approach is not opposed to state intervention, but argues that such intervention should be aimed at supporting the family as much as possible. Even where children do have to be removed, contact with the family should be retained and the aim should be to reunite the family if at all possible. Opponents of such an approach argue that it does not provide adequate protection for children. Given the levels of abuse within families, we cannot assume that children are always best cared for by their families.

   (d) *Children's rights and child liberation.* Here the emphasis is on the child's viewpoints, feelings and wishes. There is a range of approaches focusing on children's rights. At one extreme it could be argued that the state should intervene only if the child requests it. In areas of suspected abuse, placing weight on children's views must be treated with

---

[19] See Bettle and Herring (2011) for difficulties in proof in shaken baby cases.
[20] Fox Harding (1996).
[21] For a radical challenge to the presumption that, wherever possible, children should be brought up by their parents, see Dwyer (2006).

great caution, given the complex psychological interplay that can exist between a child and his or her abuser.

Fox Harding argues that aspects of all of these approaches can be found in the Children Act 1989. This, she suggests, is not necessarily a bad thing. In some areas the law may wish to place greater weight on the powers of parents, in other areas children's rights, and in others the protection of children.

3. Even where abuse is proved, there is much debate over the correct response to it. Of particular concern is the level of abuse of children in care, and in particular of those in children's homes. Removing a child from an abusive family only to place him or her into an abusive situation in a children's home is to heap harm upon harm.[22] As Professor Maurice Place[23] has emphasised:

> [C]hildren whose early family experiences have been abusive or neglectful are likely to do better the earlier they are removed. But removal in itself does not improve the underlying difficulties, it merely reduces the risk of further damage. To improve functioning these children need subsequently to have a persistently positive living experience and to successfully engage with any therapeutic work that is deemed necessary . . . present provision falls well short of need.

This chapter will proceed as follows. It will provide an overview of child protection law in England, before exploring specifically the range of orders available and what needs to be shown for each. We will start with voluntary services that may be appropriate for families that are facing challenges; then the powers to investigate worrying situations involving children; then the orders that may be suitable in emergencies; before finally looking at longer-term solutions for children who have been abused.

2 The Children Act 1989 and child protection

The duties and responsibilities of local authorities towards families are located in Part III of the Children Act 1989. It would be quite wrong to see the state's protection of children as limited to court intervention. Health visitors, social workers, teachers and doctors can encourage the voluntary cooperation of parents and thereby encourage them to adhere to prevailing expectations about the appropriate care of children. This has been called the 'soft' policing of families.[24]

The Children Act 1989 was produced after a major rethink over child protection policy, and two major themes emerged:

1. There should be a clear line drawn between the child being in care or not in care. A child in care is one looked after by the local authority, where the local authority effectively takes over the parental role. Under the previous legislation a child could be in an ambiguous position – formally not in care, but effectively in care. Under the Children Act a child can only officially enter care as a result of a court order and there are clear criteria which govern when a care order can be made.[25] That ideal is not reflected in practice. Around a third of

---

[22] Although Wade *et al.* (2012) found children who remained in care did better than children in care who were returned home.
[23] Place (2013).
[24] Parton (1991).
[25] Although see Bainham (2013) who argues that the line between public and private proceedings in this area is being blurred.

children who enter the care of the local authority do so as a result of a care order; the other two-thirds are looked after through an agreement between parents and the local authority.[26]

2. The Act promotes 'partnership' between parents and local authorities.[27] Parents and local authorities should work together for the good of the child. This has two aspects. The first is that the local authority should be regarded as a resource for parents to use, especially if the family is having difficulties. The aim, therefore, is that parents experiencing difficulties in parenting will regard the local authority as there to provide support and assistance, rather than as a body to be feared.

The second aspect is that, even if the child is taken into care, parents should be involved with the care for the child to the greatest extent possible.[28]

There is a fear that there cannot be a partnership, or at least anything like an equal partnership, between a parent and a local authority.[29]

The local authority has the 'sword of Damocles' of a care order hanging over the parents, and so there can be little equality in the 'partnership'. The fear is that, under the guise of 'partnership', social workers will be able to exercise even more power over parents than they would if they acknowledged the intervention was compulsory. In particular, there is concern with the increased use of informal understandings between parents and the local authority concerning the child.[30] These agreements may be entered into without the parents receiving legal advice or without the protection of legal procedural safeguards.

Not only should parents and local authorities work in partnership, so also should local authorities and all the other bodies involved in child work (for example, the NSPCC, hospitals).[31] The Children Act in various ways encourages cooperation between these different agencies. Reports into failings of the child protection system regularly cite a lack of communication between different bodies as being a cause of the absence of proper care.[32]

3 The Human Rights Act 1998 and child protection

Learning objective 1

Explain and evaluate the significance of human rights on child protection law

English and Welsh law after the Human Rights Act 1998 must now start with a strong presumption that the state must respect the right to family and private life (Article 8).[33] Any infringement of human rights must be justified.[34] However, it would be wrong to assume that the Human Rights Act supports a non-interventionist approach in child protection cases. There are three ways in which the Human Rights Act can permit or even require intervention:

1. Any removal by the state of a child from his or her parents will automatically constitute an infringement of Article 8, but this may be justified by taking into account the welfare of the

---

[26] Doughty (2014).
[27] HM Government (2013).
[28] Department for Children, Schools and Families (2008a).
[29] Kaganas (1995).
[30] The increase in court fees may well increase the use of these.
[31] See Children Act 2004, Part II which is designed for better integration of the delivery of children's services.
[32] Laming (2003).
[33] Choudhry and Herring (2010: ch 8); Kaganas (2010b).
[34] *EH v Greenwich London Borough Council* [2010] 2 FCR 106, para 63.

child.[35] Paragraph 2 of Article 8 permits an infringement of the right if it is necessary in the interests of others, and this would clearly include the interests of the child.[36] In deciding whether the infringement is necessary, the consideration of the welfare of the child is 'crucial'.[37] Just because it turns out that the removal of the child was based on a false belief does not mean there was a breach of human rights – as long as the belief was a genuine and reasonably held concern.[38]

2. Although Article 8 may readily be invoked to protect parents from state intervention, it could be argued that abused children have rights to respect for private life that can be protected only by intervention. Article 8 imposes positive obligations on the state and these will include obligations to protect a child from abuse.

3. Article 3 requires the state to protect children and adults from torture and inhuman and degrading treatment[39] and Article 2 requires the state to protect children from the risk of death.[40] This is an absolute right in the sense that a breach of it cannot be justified by reference to the interests of others.[41] Therefore, if a local authority knows or should know that a child is suffering serious abuse then it is obliged to take reasonable steps to protect the child from that harm.[42] A local authority will have infringed a child's rights under Article 3 if it has failed to take measures that could have prevented the abuse. It is not necessary to show that had the local authority acted as it should the abuse would not have occurred.[43] A child who was not protected by a local authority from abuse could sue it under s. 7 of the Human Rights Act 1998. This also means it would be wrong for a court to stop a case where there were serious injuries, which required investigation.[44] There have been some shocking cases where highly vulnerable children have been left to suffer as the local authority lacks the funds to provide the necessary care.[45]

A significant concept which was introduced by the Human Rights Act 1998 is the notion of proportionality.[46] If the state is to intervene in a child's life, it must be shown that the level of state intervention is proportionate to the risk that the child is suffering.[47] We will discuss that in more detail later in this chapter.

The Human Rights Act 1998 also has important implications in the procedures used by a local authority before taking a child into care and in the decision-making process once a child has been taken into care. Both Articles 6 (the right to a fair trial) and 8 have an

---

[35] Although see the controversial argument in Herring (2008c) that abusive forms of family life may not be entitled to respect under Article 8.

[36] *North Somerset Council v LW* [2014] EWHC 1670 (Fam).

[37] *Strand Lobben v Norway* (App. No. 37283/13); *K and T v Finland* [2000] 2 FLR 79; *L v Finland* [2000] 2 FLR 118.

[38] *R v United Kingdom* (App. No. 38000(1)/05).

[39] *M and M v Croatia* (App. No. 10161/13); *A v UK (Human Rights: Punishment of Child)* [1998] 3 FCR 597 ECtHR

[40] *R (Plymouth CC) v Devon* [2005] 2 FCR 428.

[41] *A Local Authority v M and N (Female Genital Mutilation Protection Order)* [2018] EWHC 870 (Fam).

[42] *Z v UK* [2001] 2 FCR 246 and *E v UK* [2003] 1 FLR 348.

[43] *E v UK* [2002] 3 FCR 700.

[44] *Re H-L (Children: Summary Dismissal of Care Proceedings)* [2019] EWCA Civ 704.

[45] *Re D (A Child) (Significant Harm: State Responsibility)* [2018] EWHC 2828 (Fam).

[46] *Re F (A Child) (Placement Order: Proportionality)* [2018] EWCA Civ 2761; *Re C and B (Children) (Care Order: Future Harm)* [2000] 2 FCR 614; *Re S (Children)* [2010] EWCA Civ 421.

[47] *Westminster CC v RA* [2005] EWHC 970 (Fam).

impact when deciding the extent to which parents of children should be involved in local authority decision-making processes concerning their children.[48] The key test is to be found in *W v UK*:[49]

> The decision-making process must . . . be such as to secure that [the parents'] views and interests are made known to and duly taken into account by the local authority and that they are able to exercise in due time any remedies available to them . . . what therefore has to be determined is whether, having regard to the particular circumstances of the case and notably the serious nature of the decisions to be taken, the parents have been involved in the decision-making process, seen as a whole, to a degree sufficient to provide them.

Local authorities have struggled in some cases to comply with these procedural obligations. In *Re S (Children)*[50] the Court of Appeal identified seven breaches of the mother and children's human rights. Although in *A Local Authority v F*[51] the local authority had placed too much weight on human rights concerns and involved the father fully in discussions about the future of the children, even though he had seriously abused them and they were terrified of him. The local authority was said to have been so worried about not breaching the father's Article 6 rights that they had overlooked the harm caused to the children by doing so. Felicity Kaganas also suggests that the procedural human rights obligations may have caused some local authorities to bypass court proceedings by using more informal measures of protecting children.[52]

4 Defining and explaining abuse

There are great difficulties in defining child abuse. The problem is the great stigma attached to conduct which is labelled abuse. If the definition is too wide, there is a danger that the stigma will be lessened. If the definition is too narrow, this may weaken the protection offered to children. One definition is:

> A form of maltreatment of a child. Somebody may abuse or neglect a child by inflicting harm, or by failing to act to prevent harm. Children may be abused in a family or in an institutional or community setting by those known to them or, more rarely, by others (e.g. via the internet). They may be abused by an adult or adults, or another child or children.[53]

Some would regard this as too wide a definition. Arguably, letting a child watch too much television or eat too much chocolate could fall into this definition, but most would not regard that as abuse. In *Re L (A Child)*[54] a mother who masturbated in the presence of her baby of a few months old was said to be guilty of sexual abuse. It was accepted that some may be surprised by that because the baby would not know what was happening, but the case demonstrated a lack of respect for sexual boundaries.

---

[48] *Re L (Care: Assessment: Fair Trial)* [2002] 2 FLR 730.
[49] (1988) 10 EHRR 29, at paras 63–4.
[50] [2010] EWCA Civ 421, discussed in Herring (2010f).
[51] [2018] EWHC 451 (Fam).
[52] Kaganas (2010a).
[53] HM Government (2013: 85).
[54] Case no. LV18C01617.

KEY STATISTICS

- 1.2% of people experience neglect during childhood.[55]

- 20.7% adults aged 18 to 74 years experienced at least one form of child abuse, whether emotional abuse, physical abuse, sexual abuse, or witnessing domestic violence or abuse, before the age of 16 years (8.5 million people); 7.6% of respondents had experienced physical abuse and 7.5% sexual abuse.

- Childline delivered 19,847 counselling sessions to children in the UK where abuse was the primary concern for the year ending March 2019.

- At 31 March 2019, 49,570 children in England and 4,810 children in Wales were looked after by their local authority because of experience or risk of abuse or neglect.

- 10.5% of women and 2.6% of men said they had experienced some form of sexual assault (including indecent exposure or unwanted touching) before the age of 16 at the hands of an adult.

- 3.4% of women and 0.6% of men said they had experienced sexual assault by rape or penetration (including attempts) before the age of 16 at the hand of an adult.

- There has been a 24% increase in the number of children in the child protection system in the United Kingdom in the past five years.

Not surprisingly, there is no consensus on what causes abuse. The following are some of the explanations:

1. *Psychological factors.* This explanation of the abuse lies in the psychology of the abuser. For example, there is some evidence that those who were themselves abused as children are more likely to abuse children when they become adults, although the fact that by no means all abused children then later abuse indicates that this cannot be the sole explanation.

2. *Sociological factors.* This explanation focuses on the position of children within society. For example, the sexualisation of children in advertising is pointed to as indicating the ambivalent attitude of society towards children and sexual relations.

3. *Feminist perspectives.* These focus on child sexual abuse as an example of patriarchy – the exercise of male power. It reflects the fact that male sexual desire is often linked with themes of superiority and performance. It is notable that the vast majority of sexual abuse is carried out by men.[56]

4. *Family systems.* Others point to family relationships as the key to explaining sexual abuse in the home. Some suggest that it is only if other members of the family permit the abuse to occur (whether consciously or not) that it can. Some even claim that child abuse is caused by the wife's failure to meet the husband's sexual needs. Feminists have objected to this explanation on the basis that it can be read as blaming the mother for the abuse.[57]

It is perhaps easy to label child abuse as caused by social deviants. But the disadvantages that children face are deeply socially ingrained. Abuse is the lot of far too many children in the United Kingdom and it is not just the 'sick' few who are to blame. If we are looking at the causes of child abuse, we must look at society as a whole as well as the 'abusers'.

[55] The statistics here are from Office for National Statistics (2020g) and NSPCC (2019).
[56] Smart (1989).
[57] Day Sclater (2000).

5 Voluntary services provided by local authorities

Learning objective 2

Examine the voluntary services offered by a local authority

In this section we will be looking at the services that can be offered by local authorities to children who are at risk of abuse. They are largely voluntary, in the sense the child's family can refuse to accept the services. They are primarily designed to prevent more drastic intervention having to take place.

A Voluntary accommodation

One of the most basic needs of a vulnerable child is accommodation. Not surprisingly, the Children Act 1989 sets out duties on a local authority to accommodate certain children in need.[58] The Act draws a sharp distinction between children whose parents ask the local authority to accommodate their children ('voluntary accommodation') and children who have been compulsorily removed from parents under a care order and accommodated by the local authority ('compulsory accommodation'). In this chapter voluntary accommodation will be discussed.

(i) Duty to accommodate

Section 20 of the Children Act 1989 sets out the circumstances in which a local authority *must* accommodate a child in need:

LEGISLATIVE PROVISION

Children Act 1989, section 20

Every local authority shall provide accommodation for any child in need within their area who appears to them to require accommodation as a result of:

(a) there being no person who has parental responsibility for him;

(b) his being lost or having been abandoned; or

(c) the person who has been caring for him being prevented (whether or not permanently, and for whatever reason) from providing him with suitable accommodation or care.

There are basically two categories of people whom a local authority must accommodate. First, a local authority must accommodate orphaned or abandoned children (although a local authority will often prefer to apply for a care order in respect of an orphaned child so that it acquires parental responsibility for the child). Secondly, there is a duty to accommodate those children whose carers are prevented from looking after them.[59] The accommodation is usually provided for by the local authority through foster parents or children's homes. However, s. 22C of the Children and Young Persons Act 2008 imposes a duty on the local authority to explore placement for children with friends or relatives.[60]

---

[58] CA 1989, s. 22A imposes a duty on local authorities to ensure there is sufficient accommodation for looked-after children in their area

[59] Article 27(3) of the UN Convention on the Rights of the Child requires the signatory states to provide needy children with assistance with housing.

[60] *R (On the Application of SA)* v *Kent County Council (The Secretary of State Intervening)* [2011] EWCA Civ 1303.

It should be stressed that there is no need for a court to approve the voluntary accommodation and typically the courts are not involved in such cases. But, the local authority may not accommodate the child if a parent with parental responsibility objects.[61] If a person with parental responsibility objects, then he or she must show that he or she is willing and able to provide accommodation for the child. There seems to be no requirement that the accommodation the parent offers be suitable, although a court may decide that such a requirement be read into the statute. If the local authority believes that the child will be endangered if accommodated by that person, it must apply for a care order or other protective order.

There have been some concerns about children being accommodated under s. 20 as an alternative to care proceedings.[62] In *Herefordshire Council v AB*[63] Keehan J emphasised that although s. 20 might be suitable as a short-term measure pending care proceedings, it should not be used as a long-term alternative to it.[64]

(ii) Discretion to accommodate

In addition to the duty outlined above, local authorities have a discretion to provide accommodation to a child even if the child is not in need, 'if they consider that to do so would safeguard or promote the child's welfare' under s. 20(4).[65] This discretion exists even if there is a person who has parental responsibility who can provide accommodation. However, all those with parental responsibility must consent to the local authority accommodating the child.[66]

(iii) Children requesting accommodation

If the child requests accommodation him- or herself, the position depends on whether the child is above or below the age of 16.

(a) Children over 16

The local authority must accommodate any child aged 16 or 17 'in need', whose welfare it considers 'is likely to be seriously prejudiced if they do not provide him with accommodation'.[67] There is no need for parental approval, but the child must agree.[68] If the child is not in such dire need, the local authority is required only to provide advice on accommodation or housing and is not required to accommodate the child. In a case where the child no longer wishes to live with her parents, but her parents are able to offer accommodation, the duty to accommodate does not arise.[69]

---

[61] *Re N (Adoption: Jurisdiction)* [2015] EWCA Civ 1112.
[62] Welbourne (2017).
[63] [2018] EWFC 10.
[64] *Medway Council v M, F and G* [2014] EWHC 308 (Fam); *Kent County Council v M and K (Section 20: Declaration and Damages)* [2016] EWFC 28.
[65] Any person aged 16–21 can be accommodated if a local authority believes that this would safeguard or promote the young person's welfare under the Children Act 1989 (hereafter CA 1989), s. 20(5).
[66] *Coventry City Council Applicant v C, B, CA and CH* [2012] EWHC 2190 (Fam) explains the parent must have sufficient understanding of what is proposed in order to consent.
[67] CA 1989, s. 20(3). If these requirements are met the local authority cannot seek to accommodate the child under s. 17, rather than s. 20: *R (W) v North Lincolnshire Council* [2008] 2 FLR 2150.
[68] CA 1989, s. 20(3).
[69] *R (M) v London Borough of Barnet* [2009] 2 FLR 725; *R (On the Application of FL) v Lambeth London Borough Council* [2010] 1 FCR 269.

> ## CASE: R (On the Application of G) v Southwark London Borough Council [2009] 3 ALL ER 189
>
> G was 16 when his mother excluded him from her home and he approached his local authority requesting an assessment of his needs under s. 17. He also sought accommodation under s. 20. The local authority assessment concluded that he had a need for housing, but this could be provided by the authority's homeless person's unit. He was also referred to the family resource team which could help him apply for benefits. He brought legal proceedings claiming that he had a right to be housed by the local authority under s. 20.
>
> Their Lordships were clear that where a child has been excluded from the family home and asks their local authority for accommodation it was not open to a local authority to arrange for accommodation under the homelessness provisions of the 1996 Housing Act. Having determined that he was a child who was in need and that he had no permanent accommodation the authority was liable to accommodate him. It could be said that he had a need for accommodation because his mother was prevented from offering him accommodation. Baroness Hale approved the comments of Rix LJ in the Court of Appeal:
>
> > [A] child, even one on the verge of adulthood, is considered and treated by Parliament as a vulnerable person to whom the state, in the form of a relevant local authority, owes a duty which goes wider than the mere provision of accommodation.[70]

(b) Children under 16

There is much doubt concerning the position of under-16-year-olds requesting local authority accommodation. It might be argued that, following *Gillick*,[71] a competent minor should have a decisive say as to whether they are accommodated by a local authority. Eekelaar and Dingwall have suggested that when a child is *Gillick*-competent then the parents lose the power to decide where the child is to live. Those who oppose this view note that *Gillick*-competent children do not have a power of consent where there are express statutory provisions to the contrary.[72] Here, s. 20(6) states that the court should:

> ## LEGISLATIVE PROVISION
>
> ### Children Act 1989, section 20(6)
>
> so far as is reasonably practicable and consistent with the child's welfare—
>
> (a) ascertain the child's wishes regarding the provision of accommodation; and
>
> (b) give due consideration (having regard to his age and understanding) to such wishes of the child as they have been able to ascertain.

This seems explicitly to fall short of giving the competent child the exclusive right to have themselves accommodated. Section 20(7) appears to be quite clear that a child cannot be accommodated under the Children Act 1989 against the wishes of a parent with parental

---

[70] [2009] 1 FCR 357 at [35].
[71] *Gillick v West Norfolk and Wisbech AHA* [1986] 1 FLR 229, [1986] AC 112.
[72] *Re W (A Minor) (Medical Treatment: Court's Jurisdiction)* [1993] 1 FLR 1, [1992] 2 FCR 785.

responsibility. They need to give informed consent to the accommodation.[73] Bainham there-fore argues that if a parent objects, then the competent child's wishes cannot prevail.[74] The dispute has been resolved in the following decision:

KEY CASE: *London Borough of Hackney* v *Williams* [2018] UKSC 37

Eight children (aged between 14 years old and 8 months) were removed by the police following allegations by one of the children of physical abuse and the fact the police found the children living at home in unhygienic conditions. The police used their powers under s. 46 of the Children Act 1989. The children were placed in foster care by the local author-ity, relying on powers in s. 20. The parents were subject to bail conditions not to have unsupervised contact with the children. The parents signed a 'safeguarding agreement' that the children be accommodated by the local authority, but they were not informed of their right to object. Seven days later lawyers for the couple informed the local authority that the parents no longer consented to the removal of the children. Nevertheless, the children were not returned and remained in foster care for two months.

The parents sought damages under the Human Rights Act on the basis their Article 8 rights to respect for private and family life were infringed from the time the consent to the accommodation was withdrawn. They succeeded at first instance and were awarded £10,000 each. The Court of Appeal allowed the appeal, on the basis that the parents had been prevented from providing suitable accommodation and care (due to the bail condi-tions) and so the children could be looked after without parental consent under s. 20(1).

The Supreme Court agreed that the local authority had not acted unlawfully, although for different reasons than the Court of Appeal. The Supreme Court held that the key point was that the parents had not objected to the accommodation and had not unequivo-cally requested the return of the children. Lady Hale emphasised the important difference between compulsory intervention by a local authority (such as a care and supervision order) which required the sanction of a court and the provision of accommodation under s. 20 for which no court authority was required. The local authority could provide the accommodation as a 'voluntary service' subject to two limitations. First, that under s. 20(7) a person with parental responsibility and able to provide accommodation could object to the local authority's accommodation. Second, that under s. 20(8) a parent with parental responsibility had the right to remove a child from accommodation.

Lady Hale then drew a distinction between two categories of cases. The first was where a parent delegated their parental responsibility to the local authority. In such a case the parents must delegate that authority in a real and voluntary way, best done through the parents being informed fully of their rights. The second was where a local authority 'steps into the breach' where there is no one with parental responsibility for the child or the parent is not offering to look after the child. In such a case there is no need for active informed delegation, although a parent can object at any time.

This case was more in the second category. Lady Hale explained:

> This was not a case in which a local authority used their powers under section 20 to take charge of children who were then in the care of their parents. Here, the section 20

---

[73] *Herefordshire Council* v *AB* [2018] EWFC 10.
[74] Bainham (2005: 341).

arrangements replaced the compulsory arrangements under section 46, without the children returning home in the meantime. Whereas, where children move from the care of their parents into section 20 accommodation, the focus is upon whether there has been a truly voluntary delegation of the exercise of parental responsibility, the focus in a case such as this is upon subsections (7) and (8).

The key question was, therefore, whether the parents had demonstrated an 'unequivocal request' for the child to be returned (under subsection (7)) or sought to remove the children (under subsection (8)). The letter from the solicitors was a withdrawal of consent but not a request to return the children and indeed was an attempt to negotiate a return of the children on a collaborative basis. The local authority was, therefore, acting lawfully.

(iv) Removal from accommodation

Under s. 20(8) of the Children Act 1989, anyone with parental responsibility 'may at any time remove the child from accommodation provided by or on behalf of the local authority'.[75] There is not even a requirement that parents give notice to the local authority of their intention to remove their child from voluntary accommodation.[76] It is not possible for the local authority to stop a removal by obtaining a section 8 order preventing the removal by the parent,[77] nor even to require a formal undertaking from parents not to remove their child.[78] But a parent with parental responsibility is not able to remove a child if the child was placed by another person with a residence order.

There are two main arguments in favour of the right of a parent to remove their children from accommodation. First, it is important to keep a clear distinction between voluntary and compulsory care, and the power of immediate removal maintains the clarity of this distinction. There are concerns that the protections and public scrutiny into care through a care order are being by-passed by using voluntary accommodation under s. 20.[79]

Secondly, it has been suggested that voluntary accommodation should be made as attractive an option as possible, so that parents feeling under great pressure will be willing to use the 'service'.

There have been concerns that parents may misuse their power of automatic removal and remove their children in unsuitable circumstances. For example, a parent could turn up at the foster parents' house drunk, demanding the return of his or her child. The Children Act 1989 appears to suggest that the foster parents must hand the child over to the parent, but there are four options available for a local authority in such a case:

1. It could try to rely on s. 3(5) of the Children Act 1989, which allows those with care of a child, but lacking parental responsibility, to 'do what is reasonable in all the circumstances of the case for the purpose of safeguarding or promoting the child's welfare'. However, a strong opposing argument is that s. 3(5) cannot be used to prevent the exercise of the parental right to remove the child, especially where the parental right is explicitly granted in a statute.

---

[75] This might include an unmarried father with parental responsibility.
[76] *Re N (Adoption: Jurisdiction)* [2015] EWCA Civ 1112.
[77] *Nottinghamshire County Council v J* unreported 26 November 1993.
[78] CA 1989, s. 9(5), although *Re G (Minors) (Interim Care Order)* [1993] 2 FLR 839 at p. 843 suggested it was.
[79] Lynch (2017).

2. A local authority could apply for an emergency protection order if the child is likely to suffer significant harm.

3. A foster parent from whom a child was removed could apply for a residence order or even rely on wardship[80] or the inherent jurisdiction.

4. Police protection may also be available in an extreme case.[81]

It may be that the threat of the local authority applying for a care order provides a suitable deterrent to children being inappropriately removed.

It seems that a child who is aged 16 or 17 can leave voluntary accommodation provided by the local authority at will. There is no statutory basis on which a local authority can detain a child against his or her wishes. Possibly the inherent jurisdiction could be used in a case where the child was at risk of serious harm.

B Services for children in need

Clearly, prevention of abuse is better than dealing with its consequences. Section 7 of the Children and Young Persons Act 2008 imposes a general duty on the Secretary of State to promote the well-being of children. Part III of the Children Act 1989 requires the local authority to provide certain services to those children who are 'in need'. The law governing children in need is a rather strange area because the House of Lords in *R (On the Application of G) v Barnet London Borough Council*[82] has held it appears there is no effective court enforcement of a local authority's obligations under s. 17, so the 'duties' are largely of a non-enforceable nature. However, a child whose needs are inadequately assessed could use judicial review, although that would rarely succeed.[83] The importance of the Children Act 1989 here is that it helps focus a local authority's attention towards vulnerable children.

Crucial to understanding the extent of the local authority's responsibilities under the Children Act 1989 is the concept of being 'in need'.

(i) What does 'in need' mean?

A child is 'in need' if:

LEGISLATIVE PROVISION

Children Act 1989, section 17(10)

(a) he is unlikely to achieve or maintain, or to have the opportunity of achieving or maintaining, a reasonable standard of health or development without the provision for him of services by a local authority under this part;

(b) his health or development is likely to be significantly impaired, or further impaired, without the provision for him of such services; or

(c) he is disabled.

---

[80] Although if foster parents started caring for the child as a ward of court, they may lose the financial assistance of the local authority.

[81] CA 1989, s. 46.

[82] [2003] UKHL 57, [2003] 3 FCR 419, discussed in Cowan (2004).

[83] See *Re T (Judicial Review: Local Authority Decisions Concerning Children in Need)* [2003] EWHC 2515 (Admin); *R (On the Application of AB and SB) v Nottingham CC* [2001] 3 FCR 350; *R (EW and BW) v Nottinghamshire County Council* [2009] 2 FLR 974 for successful applications for judicial review.

'Development' includes 'physical, intellectual, emotional, social or behavioural develop-ment'; health includes 'physical or mental health'.[84] A disabled child is one who is 'blind, deaf, or dumb or suffers from mental disorder of any kind or is substantially and permanently handicapped by illness, injury or congenital deformity or such other disability as may be prescribed'.[85] The law here is not concerned with the causes of the need, but rather the fact of need. The need may arise from the lack of skills of the parent, or may be due to the disabilities of the child. In *A v London Borough of Enfield*[86] an 18-year-old girl who it was feared was being radicalised and was preparing to marry a much older man was held to be 'in need'.

(ii) What services should be supplied?

Part III of the Children Act 1989 was intended to establish a single code to govern the voluntary services to children and all decisions of a local authority. The general duty to provide services is set out in s. 17(1):

LEGISLATIVE PROVISION

Children Act 1989, section 17(1)

It shall be the general duty of every local authority (in addition to the other duties imposed on them by this Part)—

(a) to safeguard and promote the welfare of children within their area who are in need; and

(b) so far as is consistent with that duty, to promote the upbringing of such children by their families by providing a range and level of services appropriate to those children's needs.

The duty is described as a general duty to indicate that an individual child cannot seek to compel a local authority to provide services by relying on this section.[87] The House of Lords in *R (On the Application of G) v Barnet LBC*[88] has held that the section does not create a right for a particular child to services, but rather describes a duty that the local authority owes to a section of the public (i.e. children in need). This is because it is for the local authority to decide how to spend its resources. The majority of their Lordships held that s. 17 did not impose a duty on a local authority even to assess the needs of a particular child. Lord Steyn, for the minority, argued:

> On the local authorities' approach, since s. 17(1) does not impose a duty in relation to an indi-vidual child, it follows that a local authority is not under a duty to assess the needs of a child in need under s. 17(1). That cannot be right. That would go far to stultify the whole purpose of Pt III of the 1989 Act.[89]

What concerned the majority appears to be an attempt by the parents in this case, who were temporarily homeless and not entitled to housing, to make a claim to be housed through their

---

[84] CA 1989, s. 17(11).
[85] CA 1989, s. 17(11).
[86] [2016] EWHC 567 (Admin).
[87] *R (On the Application of G) v Barnet London Borough Council* [2003] UKHL 57; *Re M (Secure Accommodation Order)* [1995] 1 FLR 418.
[88] [2003] UKHL 57.
[89] *R (On the Application of G) v Barnet LBC* [2004] 2 AC 208.

children. Further, the courts recognised that delicate issues such as the distribution of public housing and the support of immigrants were best left to elected local authorities, rather than the decisions of courts looking at the merits of a particular case.

Services are to be made available not only to children, but also to their parents and family members,[90] as long as the services are aimed at safeguarding the welfare of the child. 'Family' is defined to include 'any person who has parental responsibility for the child and any other person with whom he has been living'.[91] 'Services' can include the provision of assistance in kind and even cash in exceptional circumstances.[92] There is also a list of special duties in Sched. 2 to the Children Act 1989. For example, there are duties to take reasonable steps to avoid the need to bring proceedings for care or supervision orders; duties to encourage children not to commit criminal offences; and duties to publicise the services that the local authority offers.[93]

C The family assistance order

The family assistance order (FAO) is governed by s. 16 of the Children Act 1989 and is a form of voluntary assistance provided to a family by the local authority.[94] The order requires either a probation officer or an officer of the local authority ('the officer') to be made available 'to advise, assist and (where appropriate) befriend any person named in the order'. The order can benefit anyone with whom the child is living and is not restricted to parents. The order is designed to provide short-term help to a family and may be as much directed at the parents as the child.[95] It might be particularly appropriate in a case where the parent is affectionate towards the child but lacks the skills to care for the child practically.

The order can be made only in exceptional circumstances[96] and only by the court acting on its own motion. In other words, a parent cannot apply for an FAO. However, it is necessary that the person in whose favour the order is made has consented to the making of the order.[97] It seems the local authority must consent to the making of the order as well.[98]

The maximum length of the order is six months.[99] The only power of enforcement that the officer has is to refer the case to the court if he or she believes there is a need for variation. They could also report their concerns to the local authority, which may wish to intervene by applying for a care order. The FAO should not be used for purposes unrelated to its primary purpose of assisting the family.

In practice, FAOs appear to be little used.[100]

---

[90] Services can only be offered to a family member if they were looking after the child and meet the child's needs: *R (OA) v Bexley LBC* [2020] EWHC 1107 (Admin).

[91] CA 1989, s. 17(10).

[92] CA 1989, s. 17(6).

[93] A local authority is under a duty to provide day-care facilities to children in need as appropriate under CA 1989, s. 18.

[94] Thorough reviews of the use of family assistance orders are to be found in HM Inspectorate of Court Administration (2007); and Seden (2001).

[95] Department for Education (2014b).

[96] CA 1989, s. 16(3)(a).

[97] CA 1989, s. 16(3).

[98] CA 1989, s. 16(7); *Re C (Family Assistance Order)* [1996] 1 FLR 424, [1996] 3 FCR 514.

[99] CA 1989, s. 16(5).

[100] Seden (2001).

6 Investigations by local authorities

There are two provisions in the Children Act 1989 under which the local authority may be required to investigate a child's welfare. Section 47 sets out specific circumstances in which a local authority must investigate a child's well-being. Section 37 permits a court to require a local authority to investigate a child's welfare. If the court wants further investigations it may make a child assessment order.

A Section 47 investigations

Under s. 47 of the Children Act 1989 the local authority is under a duty to investigate the welfare of a child in their area when:

1. a child is subject to an emergency protection order;
2. a child is in police protection;
3. a child has contravened a curfew notice;[101] or
4. the local authority has reasonable cause to suspect that a child is suffering, or is likely to suffer, significant harm.[102]

Local authorities may obtain information about potential abuse of children from a wide variety of sources. Neighbours, teachers, doctors, even children themselves may provide information. The local authority does not need proved facts before it carries out an investigation; suspicions are sufficient.[103] This means that even if a criminal prosecution against an alleged perpetrator of sexual abuse had failed, the local authority might still be authorised to carry out a s. 47 investigation.[104] However, the local authority should not undertake a s. 47 investigation because there are vague concerns without first finding out basic information from key people in the child's life such as teachers and GPs.[105]

Under these circumstances the local authority must make 'such enquiries as they consider necessary to enable them to decide whether they should take any action to safeguard or promote the child's welfare'.[106] There is no power to enter a child's home against the parents' will. However, if parents fail to permit social workers to see a child, the local authority must apply for either an emergency protection order, a child assessment order, a supervision order or a care order unless they are satisfied that the child can be satisfactorily safeguarded in other ways.[107] If the parents have permitted the local authority to see the child, the legislation leaves the choice of what to do next to the local authority. The main options are: to do nothing; to offer the family services; or to apply to the court for a child assessment order, emergency protection order, or supervision or care order. As Eekelaar has pointed out, a local authority is not under a duty to apply for an order, even if it decides that the child would be best protected by applying for such an order. There is a duty to investigate and to decide what it *should* do, but there is no duty to do anything as a result of the investigation.[108] It may be that financial limitations would cause

---

[101] Under Ch. 1, Part 1 of the Crime and Disorder Act 1998.
[102] CA 1989, s. 47.
[103] *R (On the Application of S) v Swindon BC* [2001] EWHC 334, [2001] 3 FCR 702.
[104] *R (On the Application of S) v Swindon BC* [2001] EWHC 334, [2001] 3 FCR 702.
[105] *R (on the application of AB) v Haringey LBC* [2013] EWHC 416 (Admin).
[106] CA 1989, s. 47(1)(b).
[107] CA 1989, s. 47(6).
[108] Eekelaar (1990).

a local authority not to apply for an order which it thought desirable but not essential. In practice, few s. 47 enquiries are undertaken, due to staff shortages and lack of staff training.

A leading case is *A Local Authority v A and B*[109] where a local authority found out that parents of a severely disabled child (A) were locking him in his room at night to prevent him harming himself. The local authority made an investigation under s. 47 and brought proceedings claiming the child's human rights were being infringed. The attitude of the authority was criticised by Munby J:

> People in the situation of A . . . together with their carers, look to the State – to a local authority – for the support, the assistance and the provision of the services to which the law, giving effect to the underlying principles of the Welfare State, entitles them. They do not seek to be 'controlled' by the State or by the local authority. And it is not for the State in the guise of a local authority to seek to exercise such control. The State, the local authority, is the servant of those in need of its support and assistance, not their master.

Notably it seems that the attitude of the local authority concerned Munby J more than the fact they undertook an investigation.

A court has no jurisdiction to prevent a local authority carrying out its investigative duties.[110] If a court was convinced that the investigations by a local authority were unjustified and causing harm to a child, it could make a prohibited steps order under s. 8 of the Children Act 1989 to restrain a parent from cooperating with the investigation.[111] However, it would require a most unusual case for this to be an appropriate course of action.

B Section 37 directions

The court cannot require a local authority to apply for a care order, nor can it force a care order upon a local authority which does not apply for one.[112] What the court may do is direct a local authority to investigate a child's circumstances under s. 37 of the Children Act 1989. The court can make such a direction wherever 'a question arises with respect to the welfare of any child', and it appears to the court that 'it may be appropriate for a care or supervision order to be made with respect to him'.[113] The court must not make a s. 37 direction if the case is not one where it may be appropriate to make a care or supervision order.[114] The local authority must report back to the court within eight weeks. The court cannot seek to control the local authority's investigation.[115] If, following an investigation under s. 37, the local authority does not apply for an order, it must explain this to the court and describe what services or assistance it intends to provide.[116] If the local authority after its investigations decides not to apply for a court order, the court cannot force it to do so.[117] Indeed there is not much the court can do if the local authority fails

---

[109] [2010] EWHC 978 (Fam).
[110] *D v D (County Court Jurisdiction: Injunctions)* [1993] 2 FLR 802.
[111] *D v D (County Court Jurisdiction: Injunctions)* [1993] 2 FLR 802.
[112] *Nottingham CC v P* [1993] 2 FLR 134, [1994] 1 FCR 624.
[113] CA 1989, s. 37(1).
[114] *Re L (Section 37 Direction)* [1999] 1 FLR 984.
[115] *Re M (Official Solicitor's Role)* [1998] 3 FLR 815 suggested that it was inappropriate to use the Official Solicitor to ensure that a local authority carried out an investigation in the manner requested by the judge.
[116] CA 1989, s. 37(3).
[117] *Nottingham CC v P* [1993] 2 FLR 134, [1994] 1 FCR 624.

to undertake an investigation as requested by the court.[118] It is submitted that, following the Human Rights Act 1998, where the local authority is aware that a child is suffering serious abuse following a s. 37 or s. 47 investigation, it is under a duty to protect the child.[119]

C Child assessment orders

A child assessment order is a preliminary order that allows assessments to take place to determine whether further orders may be necessary.

(i) When is a child assessment order appropriate?

A child assessment order is appropriate where the local authority has concerns about a child but needs more information before it is able to decide what action to take. The guidance makes it clear the child assessment order is for cases 'where the child is not thought to be at immediate risk'.[120] If the grounds for an emergency protection order (EPO) are made out, s. 43(4) of the Children Act 1989 states that the court may not make a child assessment order but must make an EPO. In fact, it is difficult to envisage when a child assessment order may be appropriate.[121] If there is a serious concern that the child is being abused, and the parents refuse to have the child examined, then an EPO will normally be more appropriate; whereas if the parents are happy to agree to the examination, then there may be no need for a child assessment order at all. It is not surprising that few child assessment orders are granted.[122]

In *Re I (Child Assessment Order)*[123] the Court of Appeal set out the purposes of a CAO:

> a child assessment order allows for a brief, focused assessment of the state of a child's health or development, or the way in which he or she has been treated, where that is required to enable the local authority to determine whether or not the child is suffering, or is likely to suffer, significant harm and to establish whether there is a need and justification for any further action. The purpose of the assessment is to provide a range of information, identifying not only whether harm may exist, but also describing its nature and extent. It is part of the process of gathering information so that any child protection measures can be appropriately calibrated. It is the least interventionist of the court's child protection powers and is designed to enable information that cannot be obtained by other means to be gathered without the need to remove the child from home.

(ii) When can the child assessment order be made?

A child assessment order can only be requested by a local authority or an 'authorised person' (at present, only the NSPCC). The court can make a child assessment order under s. 43(1) where:

> **LEGISLATIVE PROVISION**
>
> **Children Act 1989, section 43(1)**
>
> (a) the applicant has reasonable cause to suspect that the child is suffering, or is likely to suffer, significant harm;

[118] *Re K (Children)* [2012] EWCA Civ 1549.
[119] Choudhry and Herring (2006b).
[120] Department for Education (2014b: 35).
[121] Parton (1991: 188–90).
[122] The numbers are so small that the Government stopped collecting statistics on child assessment orders after 1993.
[123] [2020] EWCA Civ 281, para 35.

(b) an assessment of the state of the child's health or development, or of the way in which he has been treated, is required to enable the applicant to determine whether or not the child is suffering, or is likely to suffer, significant harm; and

(c) it is unlikely that such an assessment will be made, or be satisfactory, in the absence of an order under this section.

The phrase 'significant harm' has the same meaning as in s. 31, which will be discussed later in this chapter. The focus of the test is the applicant's belief of the risk of significant harm: it must be reasonable. The hurdle is lower than that for a care order, for example, because the child assessment order is less intrusive into family life.[124] Once the court is satisfied that s. 43(1) is fulfilled, it must still be persuaded that the making of the child assessment order is in the child's welfare under s. 1(1) and satisfies 'no order principle' in s. 1(5) of the Children Act 1989.[125]

(iii) The effects of a child assessment order

There are two automatic results of a child assessment order. First, the order requires any person who is able to do so to produce the child to a person named in the order (normally a social worker). The second effect is that the order authorises the named person to carry out an assessment of the child.[126] There are likely to be specific directions in the order relating to medical or psychiatric examinations: for example, who should conduct the examinations and where they should take place.[127] The local authority does not acquire parental responsibility, which remains with the parents. It seems that a child may refuse to submit to an examination if he or she is of sufficient understanding.[128]

The maximum duration of a child assessment order is seven days from the starting date specified in the order.[129] There is no power to extend this time period. Seven days is unlikely to be long enough for some psychological examinations. The justification for the limitation is that seven days should be enough to tell the authority whether further orders are required.

7 Emergencies: criminal prosecutions and protection orders

There are a range of remedies available if children need immediate assistance.[130]

A Police protection

In cases requiring urgent action, the police have some powers to protect children. The powers enable the police to act immediately, without the delay of having to apply to a court. For example, in *Re M (A Minor) (Care Order: Threshold Conditions)*[131] the police were called to

---

[124] One important difference between the child assessment order and the EPO is that an application for the child assessment order can be applied for *ex parte*.

[125] The checklist of factors in s. 1(3) does not apply: *Re R (Recovery Orders)* [1998] 2 FLR 401.

[126] CA 1989, s. 43(7).

[127] If the child is to be removed from home, this should be set out in the order: CA 1989, s. 43(10).

[128] CA 1989, s. 43(8); but note the interpretation of *South Glamorgan County Council v W and B* [1993] 1 FLR 574, [1993] 1 FCR 626 on the similarly worded s. 44(7), that the court may override the refusal of a child.

[129] CA 1989, s. 43(5).

[130] See Masson (2005) and Masson *et al.* (2007) for excellent discussions of this topic.

[131] [1994] 2 AC 424.

a house where a husband had murdered his wife in front of the children; the police were able to take the children immediately into their care.

These powers exist under s. 46(1) of the Children Act 1989: if a police constable has reasonable cause to believe that a child would be likely to suffer significant harm then the child can be removed by the constable to 'suitable accommodation'.[132] However, this section does not give the police the power to enter and search a building. This is an important limitation and means that, if the parents refuse to cooperate with the police, and the child is in the parents' house, the police have no powers under the Children Act 1989 to protect the child.[133]

The children can be kept in police protection for up to 72 hours. Once a child is taken into police protection, a designated officer will be appointed to be in charge of the case. He or she must inform the local authority of the decision to protect the child, and must let the parents or persons with parental responsibility know of the steps taken.[134] The police do not acquire parental responsibility when a child is in police protection, but the designated officer is required to do what is reasonable in all the circumstances to promote the child's welfare.[135] They must permit reasonable contact between the child and anyone with parental responsibility, or anyone else with whom the child was living.[136] The child must be released to the parent or person with parental responsibility unless there are reasonable grounds to believe that he or she is likely to suffer significant harm if released.[137]

B The emergency protection order

Learning objective 3

Consider the use of emergency protection orders

(i) When is an emergency protection order appropriate?

Where it is clear that the child is suffering significant harm, but the local authority is not in a position to decide the long-term future of the child, then an emergency protection order (EPO) is appropriate.[138] The guidance explains that the purpose of an EPO is to enable 'the child to be removed from where he or she is, or to be kept where he or she is, if this is necessary to provide immediate short-term protection.'[139] The EPO should only be used in emergencies, as it involves the immediate removal of a child, often without notice to the parents or time to prepare the child appropriately.[140] Munby J has said that an EPO requires exceptional circumstances and there must be no less drastic alternatives available.[141]

---

[132] The constable may also take reasonable steps to remove the child to a hospital or other place.
[133] Unless the police are able to use their general powers to arrest people or search houses under the Police and Criminal Evidence Act 1984.
[134] CA 1989, s. 46(3).
[135] CA 1989, s. 46(9)(b).
[136] CA 1989, s. 46(10).
[137] CA 1989, s. 46(5).
[138] For detailed judicial guidance on the procedures and purposes of the EPO see *Re X (Emergency Protection Orders)* [2006] EWHC 510 (Fam).
[139] Department for Education (2014b: 37).
[140] *Re X (Emergency Protection Orders)* [2006] EWHC 510 (Fam). If used when there is no real emergency then there may well be an infringement of parents' human rights: *Haase v Germany* [2004] Fam Law 500.
[141] *X Council v B (Emergency Protection Orders)* [2004] EWHC 2015 (Fam). See *Haringey LBC v C* [2005] Fam Law 351 for a case where Ryder J believed an emergency protection order was unnecessary.

(ii) Who may apply?

Anyone can apply for an EPO. This is by contrast with a child assessment order, care order or supervision order. Restrictions on who can apply for the order seem inappropriate, given the kind of urgent situations in which the EPO is appropriate. The police, local authorities, teachers, doctors or close relatives are most likely to be the ones who will apply. If someone apart from the local authority is applying for the EPO, the local authority can take over the application if appropriate. As it is an emergency application, the EPO will normally be applied for *ex parte*.[142]

(iii) What are the grounds for the order?

There are three grounds for obtaining an EPO.

1. Where 'there is reasonable cause to believe that the child is likely to suffer significant harm if . . . (i) he is not removed to accommodation provided by or on behalf of the applicant'.[143] This ground could be satisfied, for example, if there is reasonable cause to believe that the child is being abused.

2. Where 'there is reasonable cause to believe that the child is likely to suffer significant harm if . . . (ii) he does not remain in the place in which he is then being accommodated'.[144] This might apply where the child is currently safe, but there is a fear that he or she will be removed to a place where they may be harmed. For example, if the child has run away to his or her grandparents, but the local authority fears that the father may be on the point of finding the child and taking him or her back to an abusive home life.

3. Under s. 44(1)(b) a local authority or the NSPCC[145] can apply for an EPO where: the applicant is making enquiries into the child's welfare; and 'those enquiries are being frustrated by access to the child being unreasonably refused to a person authorised to seek access and that the applicant has reasonable cause to believe that access to the child is required as a matter of urgency'.[146]

The NSPCC (but not local authorities) need to show also that there is reasonable cause to suspect that the child is suffering or is likely to suffer significant harm.

These grounds are all prospective; they relate to the fear of harm in the future. So, an EPO cannot be made on the basis of past harm unless the fact of past harm is evidence of a fear of future significant harm. The test attempts to strike a balance between ensuring that proceedings in these emergency situations do not get bogged down in complex questions of evidence, while at the same time ensuring that children are removed only when there is evidence to justify rapid intervention.

Even if the grounds for an EPO are satisfied, the court must still decide whether or not to make an EPO using the welfare principle. Under Article 8 of the European Convention on Human Rights the local authority will be required to consider whether there were any alternatives to removing the children under the emergency order.[147]

---

[142] Family Proceedings Court (Children Act) Rules 1991 (SI 1991/1395), r. 4(5).
[143] CA 1989, s. 44(1)(a)(i).
[144] CA 1989, s. 44(1)(a)(ii).
[145] CA 1989, s. 31(9).
[146] CA 1989, s. 44(1)(b).
[147] *KA v Finland* [2003] 1 FCR 201.

CASE: *X Council v B and Others (Emergency Protection Orders)* [2004] EWHC 2015 (Fam)

Munby J provided authoritative guidance on the use of the emergency protection order (EPO). The case concerned three children who had a variety of difficulties. The parents, not surprisingly, struggled with the care of these children and there was evidence that the children suffered and were likely to suffer harm at the hands of their parents. An EPO was applied for and obtained. The case concerned an appeal against that order.

Munby J emphasised that an EPO was a drastic order to make. His description shows why:

> An EPO, summarily removing a child from his parents, is a terrible and drastic remedy . . . After all, the child of five or ten who, as in the present case, is suddenly removed from the parents with whom he has lived all his life is exposed to something the new-born baby is mercifully spared: being suddenly wrenched away in frightening – perhaps terrifying – circumstances from everything he has known and loved and taken away by people and placed with other people who, however caring and compassionate they may be, are in all probability total strangers.[148]

Partly with these concerns in mind, Munby J listed the features of the statutory regime that he believes are not entirely satisfactory. In particular, he noted that an EPO can be made without notice and the application need only be served on the parent 48 hours after the order is made; and that there is no appeal against the making or extension of an EPO. These concerns led him to consider the impact of the Human Rights Act 1998 on the law. He emphasised that the Human Rights Act 1998 requires that an EPO is appropriate only where there is an imminent danger and the order is necessary. If a less interventionist order (e.g. a child assessment order) can adequately protect the child, then it should be used.[149] Similarly, if an EPO is to be made, it should last for as short a period as is necessary, and a child should be returned by a local authority to the parents as soon as it is safe to do so. Munby J stated:

> An EPO, summarily removing a child from his parents, is a 'draconian' and 'extremely harsh' measure, requiring 'exceptional justification' and 'extraordinarily compelling reasons'. Such an order should not be made unless the FPC [Family Proceedings Court] is satisfied that it is both necessary and proportionate and that no other less radical form of order will achieve the essential end of promoting the welfare of the child. Separation is only to be contemplated if immediate separation is essential to secure the child's safety; 'imminent danger' must be 'actually established'.[150]

Not just that, but the evidence supporting the claim must be effective:

> The evidence in support of the application for an EPO must be full, detailed, precise and compelling. Unparticularised generalities will not suffice. The sources of hearsay evidence must be identified. Expressions of opinion must be supported by detailed evidence and properly articulated reasoning.[151]

---

[148] Paragraph 34.
[149] Paragraph 49.
[150] Paragraph 57.
[151] Paragraph 58.

The judgment is likely to mean that courts will be far more wary about making EPOs. Where they are made, they will be of shorter duration and local authorities will exercise their powers under EPOs with even greater care. The significance of Munby J's judgment was shown by McFarlane J's recommendation in *Re X (Emergency Protection Orders)*[152] that it should be made available to every court which hears an application for an EPO.

(iv) The effects of an EPO

Section 44(4) of the Children Act 1989 sets out the three legal effects of an EPO. The order:

LEGISLATIVE PROVISION

Children Act 1989, section 44(4)

(a) operates as a direction to any person who is in a position to do so to comply with any request to produce the child to the applicant;

(b) authorises—

    (i) the removal of the child at any time to accommodation provided by or on behalf of the applicant and his being kept there; or

    (ii) the prevention of the child's removal from any hospital, or other place, in which he was being accommodated immediately before the making of the order; and

(c) gives the applicant parental responsibility for the child.

The EPO requires any person who can comply with the request to produce the child to do so. The order also forbids the removal of the child from the place where the applicant has accommodated the child. If necessary, the applicant can enter any premises named in the EPO to search for the child,[153] although if force is required then the police should be involved and a warrant is required.[154]

The applicant will acquire parental responsibility on the making of the EPO. This is appropriate, as the applicant will remove the child and will be responsible for the child's welfare. However, the applicant obtains only limited parental responsibility – parental responsibility should only be exercised 'as is reasonably required to safeguard or promote the welfare of the child (having regard in particular to the duration of the order)'.[155] The applicant, therefore, should not make any decisions which are major or irreversible. The child should be returned home as soon as it appears to the applicant safe to do so.[156] Section 45(1) states that eight days is the maximum length of an EPO. The local authority or NSPCC can apply for an extension to a maximum total length of 15 days.[157]

---

[152] [2006] EWHC 510 (Fam), [2007] 1 FCR 551.
[153] CA 1989, s. 48(3) and (4).
[154] CA 1989, s. 48(9).
[155] CA 1989, s. 44(5)(b).
[156] CA 1989, s. 44(10).
[157] On application by the NSPCC or local authority under CA 1989, s. 45(4).

C Secure accommodation orders

Learning objective 4

State the law surrounding secure accommodation orders

The secure accommodation order (SAO) is available only to local authorities and is used to control the aggressive behaviour of children.[158] The aim is not necessarily to provide treatment, but to ensure that problematic children are in an environment where they pose no danger to themselves or others. If the child is to be placed in secure accommodation for more than 72 hours, court approval through a secure accommodation order is required. The Government Guidance indicates it is to be used sparingly:

> Restricting the liberty of a child is a serious step that can only be taken if it is the most appropriate way of meeting the child's assessed needs. A decision to place a child in secure accommodation should never be made because no other placement is available, because of inadequacies of staffing in a child's current placement, or because the child is simply being a nuisance. Secure accommodation should never be used as a form of punishment.[159]

The grounds on which a child can be subject to a secure accommodation order are set out in s. 25(1) of the Children Act 1989:

LEGISLATIVE PROVISION

Children Act 1989, section 25(1)

(a) that—

   (i) he has a history of absconding and is likely to abscond from any other description of accommodation; and

   (ii) if he absconds, he is likely to suffer significant harm; or

(b) that if he is kept in any other description of accommodation he is likely to injure himself or other persons.

The word 'likely' in this section means a real possibility that cannot sensibly be ignored.[160] In *Re M (A Child) (Secure Accommodation)*[161] the Court of Appeal declined to define absconding, but did say it was more than trivial disobedient absence. In *Re W (A Child)*[162] a 17-year-old girl was housed by the local authority but being the victim of sexual exploitation kept staying away from her accommodation at night. A secure accommodation order could be used to protect her.

---

[158] As well as the secure accommodation order, children can be detained under the Mental Health Act 1983; s. 23 of the Children and Young Persons Act 1969; and s. 38(6) of the Police and Criminal Evidence Act 1984.
[159] Department for Education (2014a).
[160] *Re M (A Child) (Secure Accommodation)* [2018] EWCA Civ 2707.
[161] [2018] EWCA Civ 2707.
[162] [2016] EWCA Civ 804.

KEY CASE: *A Local Authority v B's Mother* [2019] EWCA Civ 2025

Baker LJ provided a very helpful summary of the key questions that need to be asked to determine whether the criteria under s. 25 for a secure accommodation order have been made out:

1. Is the child being 'looked after' by a local authority, or, alternatively, does he or she fall within one of the other categories specified in regulation 7?

2. Is the accommodation where the local authority proposes to place the child 'secure accommodation', i.e. is it designed for or have as its primary purpose the restriction of liberty?

3. Is the court satisfied (a) that (i) the child has a history of absconding and is likely to abscond from any other description of accommodation, and (ii) if he/she absconds, he/she is likely to suffer significant harm or (b) that if kept in any other description of accommodation, he/she is likely to injure himself or other persons?

4. If the local authority is proposing to place the child in a secure children's home in England, has the accommodation been approved by the Secretary of State for use as secure accommodation? If the local authority is proposing to place the child in a children's home in Scotland, is the accommodation provided by a service which has been approved by the Scottish Ministers?

5. Does the proposed order safeguard and promote the child's welfare?

6. Is the order proportionate, i.e. do the benefits of the proposed placement outweigh the infringement of rights?

The Court of Appeal allowed the appeal and made some important points about the nature of SOAs:

1. Secure accommodation is accommodation provided for the primary purpose of restricting liberty. If the primary purpose is to provide treatment then it will not amount to secure accommodation, even if it also involves a degree of restriction of liberty.

2. In deciding whether to make an order under s. 25 the welfare of the child is an important element, but it is not the paramount consideration. The protection of the public will be taken into account too.

3. When deciding whether to make a secure accommodation order the court should bear in mind that the order will breach the child's liberty and so breach Article 5 of the ECHR and interfere with the child's right to family life and so breach their Article 8 rights. This means it is important that the court determines whether the order is a proportionate interference with those rights. It needs to be used as a last resort.

4. Where the criteria for a section 25 order are made out then it would be wrong to use the inherent jurisdiction to authorise a deprivation of liberty.

As is clear from this judgment, SAOs are one of the few orders about children which are not governed by the paramountcy principle. Although the welfare of the child 'looms large',[163] protection of the public can justify an order which will not promote the welfare of the child.

---

[163] Green LJ in *A Local Authority v B's Mother* [2019] EWCA Civ 2025, para 119.

In *Re K (A Child) (Secure Accommodation Order: Right to Liberty)*[164] the Court of Appeal held that a secure accommodation order deprived a child of liberty and therefore fell within Article 5 of the European Convention on Human Rights, which makes it clear that 'nobody shall be deprived of his liberty save in the following cases and in accordance with a procedure prescribed by law'.[165] The article lists the circumstances in which a detention may be permitted. A secure accommodation order could be compliant with the article on the basis of Article 5(1)(d), which permits: 'the detention of a minor by lawful order for the purpose of educational supervision or his lawful detention for the purpose of bringing him before the competent legal authority'. Dame Elizabeth Butler-Sloss explained that education in Article 5(1)(d) included education broadly defined. However, it would not be possible to use a secure accommodation order simply to punish or detain a child if there was no educational element in what was being done.[166] In *Re T (A Child)*[167] the Court of Appeal confirmed that an SAO could be made whether the child consented to being detained or not.

The court's role is simply to test the evidence and fix the duration of the order, but not to determine what happens to the child during the accommodation.[168] So, even if an SAO is made, the local authority is not obliged to place the child in secure accommodation.[169] A local authority must review the detention one month after the making of the order and thereafter every three months. The local authority must be satisfied that the criteria are still met and that detention is necessary.[170]

D Detention of a child

There has been a series of cases recently dealing with instances where the local authority has wanted to detain a troubled teenager, but outside a secure unit. Lady Black in *Re D (A Child)*[171] stated that whether accommodation is secure accommodation depends on the kind of accommodation, rather than the regime of care. A good example is *Re M (A Child: Secure Accommodation Order)*[172] where a teenager had been in trouble with the police since the age of ten and had a series of convictions. She had been taken into care, but had assaulted professionals. It had only recently been determined that in her early years she had suffered 'profound emotional, physical and sexual abuse at the highest end of the index of gravity'. The court agreed to make an SAO on the basis she was a risk to herself, her carers, other young people and the general public. However, the local authority was unable to find a suitable unit, but was able to find non-approved accommodation that might suffice. Hayden J authorised their accommodation under the inherent jurisdiction. However, he noted this was not the first time this had happened: 'I find myself, once again, in a position of considering the needs of a vulnerable young person in the care of the State where the State itself is unable to meet the needs of a

---

[164] [2001] 1 FCR 249 CA, discussed in Masson (2002b).
[165] In *Bouamar v Belgium* (1987) 11 EHRR 1, where a person with a history of aggressive behaviour was detained, the court suggested that the detention was lawful only if the matter was brought speedily before the court.
[166] *Re M (A Child) (Secure Accommodation)* [2001] 1 FCR 692 emphasises that children have rights under Article 6 to a fair trial in applications for secure accommodation orders.
[167] [2018] EWCA Civ 2136.
[168] *Re W (A Minor) (Secure Accommodation Order)* [1993] 1 FLR 692.
[169] *Re M (A Child) (Secure Accommodation)* [2018] EWCA Civ 2707.
[170] *LM v Essex CC* [1999] 1 FLR 988. A failure to do this could lead to a successful judicial review: *S v Knowsley BC* [2004] Fam Law 653.
[171] [2019] UKSC 42.
[172] [2017] EWHC 3021 (Fam).

child which they themselves purport to parent.' He referred to 'the depressing reality that current secure accommodation resources in England and Wales are inadequate'. There seems to be little improvement in the lack of appropriate secure accommodation. In **Dorset Council v AB**,[173] heard in May 2020, it had not been possible to find secure accommodation for an adolescent 'very much at risk of killing himself, being killed or coming to serious harm'. It is very distressing that adequate resources have not been put in place to fund appropriate care for these most vulnerable of young people. The fact this has been known about for many years and nothing has been done is shocking. In **Re S (Child in Care Unregistered Placement)**[174] it was announced that a file containing a series of cases of this kind was sent to the relevant Secretary of State for Education by the family court judges

This kind of case raises troubling issues about the lack of provision of suitable facilities for vulnerable young people. It also creates a legal problem. An SAO can only be made if the young person is detained within an approved unit. Yet Article 5 of the European Convention on Human Rights protects the right to liberty, unless there is a legal process authorising the detention. Local authorities have sought to use the inherent jurisdiction as a way of getting that authorisation. The following case highlights the issue.

CASE: *Re A (A Child) (No Secure Accommodation Available: Deprivation of Liberty)* [2017] EWHC 2458 (Fam)

'A' was a boy of 13 who was in care and had troubled issues. For two years he had displayed uncontrolled behaviour which had caused damage to himself and others. The local authority wanted to place him in a secure accommodation unit, but none was available. They sought to place him in a unit which was not secure accommodation but had staff who could subject him to physical restraint if needed. To obtain the legal authorisation for this they sought to use the inherent jurisdiction to authorise a deprivation of liberty.

Holman J expressed the concern that there were safeguards in s. 25 which were not present in the procedures governing the use of the inherent jurisdiction and he was concerned the use of the inherent jurisdiction outflanked these protections. In particular, an application for an SAO required the child to be offered legal representation, whereas this was not required under the inherent jurisdiction. He joined the child as a party and directed CAFCASS to appoint a guardian. As he noted, children who were being restrained in this way were particularly vulnerable and so in need of legal protections.

(In Chapter 9 we discussed these cases further with an eye on the children's rights issues raised.)

In **A City Council v LS**[175] an important limitation on the right of the inherent jurisdiction was emphasised: it could only be used in a case where a child was currently in the care of a local authority or accommodated by them. Otherwise a child could be removed from their parents under the inherent jurisdiction by-passing the protections in Part IV of the Children Act 1989.

---

[173] [2020] EWHC 1098 (Fam).
[174] [2020] EWHC 1012 (Fam).
[175] [2019] EWHC 1384 (Fam).

E Exclusion orders

Under ss. 38A and 44A of the Children Act 1989[176] exclusion orders are available to the local authority in addition to an emergency protection order and interim care orders. The exclusion requirement may include one or more of the following (s. 38A(3)):

LEGISLATIVE PROVISION

Children Act 1989, section 38A(3)

(a) a provision requiring the relevant person to leave a dwelling-house in which he is living with the child;

(b) a provision prohibiting the relevant person from entering a dwelling-house in which the child lives; and

(c) a provision excluding the relevant person from a defined area in which a dwelling-house in which the child lives is situated.

The circumstances in which an exclusion order can be made are (s. 38A(2)):

LEGISLATIVE PROVISION

Children Act 1989, section 38A(2)

(a) that there is reasonable cause to believe that, if a person ('the relevant person') is excluded from a dwelling-house in which the child lives, the child will cease to suffer, or cease to be likely to suffer, significant harm, and

(b) that another person living in the dwelling-house (whether a parent of the child or some other person)—

    (i) is able and willing to give to the child the care which it would be reasonable to expect a parent to give him, and

    (ii) consents to the inclusion of the exclusion requirement.

There are two important limitations on the exclusion order. First, the exclusion order can only be made if the grounds for an emergency protection order or interim care order are made out. Both of these orders are short-lived, and so the exclusion requirement offers only short-term protection. The second requirement is that there must be another person in the home who is able and willing to care for the child, and who consents to the inclusion of the exclusion requirement.[177] If, for example, the mother wishes to continue her relationship with the suspected abuser, she may well refuse to consent. She may then have to choose between consenting to the removal of her partner and having her child removed under a care order. In a recent lecture McFarlane P questioned whether sufficient use was being made of these provisions, especially in the case of domestic abuse.[178]

---

[176] Inserted by Family Law Act 1996.
[177] *W v A Local Authority* [2000] 2 FCR 662.
[178] McFarlane (2018).

F Wardship and the inherent jurisdiction

A local authority could seek to invoke the court's inherent jurisdiction or wardship in cases where there were urgent concerns about a child and other orders are not adequate.[179] These have been used in a series of recent cases involving young people whom it is feared are being radicalised.[180] The President of the Family Law Division has issued detailed Guidance on how to deal with 'radicalisation cases'.[181]

In *London Borough of Tower Hamlets* v *M*[182] two children were made wards of court because they were at risk of leaving the United Kingdom and being taken to 'ISIS countries' to be involved in terrorist groups. The orders included requiring the retrieval of their passports. Wardship can be particularly helpful given it has international application and can be used in relation to children who are already overseas.[183] The courts will intervene even if there is evidence that the child has chosen to be involved in terrorist activities.[184] However, not all applications in cases of this kind have succeeded.[185] In *Re X (Children) (No. 3)*[186] it was emphasised that suspicions or speculations of radicalisation were not sufficient to justify court intervention.[187] The fact that siblings have made their way to areas of terrorist activity would be evidence that children are at risk.[188]

As a longer-term solution to cases of radicalisation, care proceedings may be brought.[189] In *London Borough of Tower Hamlets* v *B*[190] an analogy was drawn between sexual abuse which violated the body and radicalisation which violated the mind. The use of care proceedings to remove the child from her parents was justified on the basis it provided the victim with peace and safety to reassert her own independence. Although if there is intervention and the family respond positively a care order may not be appropriate.[191]

Remarkably in *A Local Authority* v *HB*[192] the court refused to make orders sought by the local authority preventing a mother removing children from the jurisdiction to be radicalised. MacDonald J thought there was no evidence that the mother sympathised with extremist views, noting that no extremist material had been found at her home or on electronic devices. The local authority had suspicions but these were inadequate to make the kind of orders sought.

In *A Local Authority* v *Y*[193] a young man whose family were heavily involved in waging war in Syria and were said to be involved in radicalist movements, had been subject to intensive local authority intervention. The concern was that he was about to turn 18 and the intervention would therefore cease. Hayden J accepted that at that point it would not be possible to coerce

---

[179] It may even be used in relation to those over 18, if they are vulnerable adults: *O* v *P* [2015] EWHC 935 (Fam).
[180] For example: *Re M (Wardship: Jurisdiction and Powers)* [2015] EWHC 1433 (Fam); *Re X (Children) and Y (Children) (No. 1)* [2015] EWHC 2265 (Fam); *Re Z* [2015] EWHC 2350; *London Borough of Tower Hamlets* v *B* [2015] EWHC 2491.
[181] *President's Guidance: Radicalisation cases in the Family Courts*, 8 October 2015.
[182] [2015] EWHC 869 (Fam)
[183] *Re X (Children) and Re Y (Children) (No. 1)* [2015] EWHC 2265 (Fam); *Re M (Wardship: Jurisdiction and Powers)* [2015] EWHC 1433 (Fam).
[184] *Re Y (Wardship) (No. 1)* [2015] EWHC 2098 (Fam).
[185] *Re X (Children) and Y (Children) (No. 1)* [2015] EWHC 2265 (Fam).
[186] [2015] EWHC 3651 (Fam).
[187] Delahunty and Barnes (2015).
[188] *Re Y (Wardship) (No. 1)* [2015] EWHC 2098 (Fam).
[189] *A City Council* v *A Mother* [2019] EWHC 3076 (Fam).
[190] [2015] EWHC 2491 (Fam).
[191] *Re M (Children) (No. 2)* [2015] EWHC 2933 (Fam); *A Local Authority* v *M* [2017] EWHC 2851 (Fam).
[192] [2017] EWHC 1437 (Fam).
[193] [2017] EWHC 968 (Fam).

Y into receiving services, unless it could be said he lacked capacity under the Mental Capacity Act 2005 or he had impaired capacity and the inherent jurisdiction could be used. Hayden J also listed a long set of means through which voluntary services could be offered.

Rachel Taylor[194] has argued:

> The more recent radicalisation cases raise troubling questions as to whether it is possible to classify beliefs and ideology as harmful in themselves. Whilst the reported cases in which the threshold has been reached have all also involved exposure to violent material or groups, the language used has suggested that ideology alone is sufficient. The extension of child protection to beliefs would be a challenge to its core principles and risk the neutrality of the courts. Without consensus and evidence as to how ideas harm children, care should be taken to avoid extending the courts' reach in this way.

Srishti Suresh[195] has also expressed concern that court are willing to make orders based on speculation when issues involve Muslim families with traditional beliefs, especially in cases involving girls, in a way they are not willing when other kinds of harms are alleged.

The inherent jurisdiction is not limited to cases of radicalisation. In ***Birmingham City Council v Riaz***[196] serious concerns were raised about a 17-year-old girl who was being sexually exploited by ten men. Although there was not sufficient evidence to bring a criminal prosecution the local authority successfully applied for an order under the inherent jurisdiction preventing them from having contact with her (or any other girl under the age of 18 not previously known to them).[197] Interestingly in ***Re A (Wardship: 17-Year-Old: Section 20 Accommodation)***[198] a 17-year-old boy whose relationship with his father (his mother was not involved in his life) had broken down sought to be made a ward of court. He had become involved in issues relating to gangs. It was helpful to have the court as decision maker and someone to whom local authorities were accountable.

G Local authorities and section 8 orders

A local authority may obtain a specific issue order or a prohibited steps order subject to the following restrictions:

1. A local authority may not apply for a specific issue order or prohibited steps order which has the same effect as a child arrangements order (CAO).[199] The policy behind this restriction is that if the child is not suffering sufficiently for a care order to be made then a local authority should not be seeking to arrange accommodation for the child against the parents' wishes.

2. If the child is in care, then no section 8 order may be made apart from a CAO. As a local authority cannot apply for it, the effect is that a local authority cannot apply for a section 8 order in respect of a child it has in its care.

So, there is limited scope for a local authority to use section 8 orders. They are appropriate, however, when a local authority might be concerned about a specific aspect of a parent's care

---

[194] Taylor (2018).
[195] Suresh (2020).
[196] [2014] EWHC 4247 (Fam). See also ***Rotherham Metropolitan Borough Council v M*** [2016] EWHC 2660 (Fam).
[197] Although see ***London Borough of Redbridge v SNA*** [2015] EWHC 2140 (Fam) where there were concerns about the breadth of the order sought and it was held that criminal prosecutions were more appropriate.
[198] [2018] EWHC 1121 (Fam).
[199] See Chapter 10.

of the child and, while not wanting to take the child into care, may wish to protect the child. For example, if parents are refusing to consent to necessary medical treatment the local authority might apply to the court for a specific issue order authorising the operation.[200] Thorpe LJ in *Langley* v *Liverpool CC*[201] stated that he had never encountered a case where a local authority had decided to use a prohibited steps order to deal with a child protection case.

In research conducted by Maebh Harding and Annika Newnham[202] it was found that although local authorities were not permitted to apply for orders connected to residence, they were encouraging relatives to apply for CAOs. While on the one hand that might simply be a convenient way of avoiding care proceedings by the family internally arranging alternative care, there may be concerns if this process is avoiding the safeguards in place for care proceedings and parents are agreeing to these orders for fear that otherwise care proceedings will be brought.

H The problem of ousting the abuser

One situation which has troubled the courts and local authorities is where a child is living with the mother and a man who is suspected of abusing the child. The ideal solution may be to remove the suspected abuser, while leaving the child with the mother. This is certainly an acceptable solution where the mother agrees that the man should be removed. However, where the mother wants the man to stay, there is a complex clash between the rights of the child and the rights of adults. For the state to force the mother to separate from her partner against her will would be a grave invasion of her rights, but that may be the only solution which protects the child. In such cases the options for the local authority are as follows:

1. The local authority will no doubt prefer to deal with the issue by informal cooperation and persuade the suspected abuser to leave the house voluntarily. The local authority may be able to offer assistance or alternative housing.[203]

2. The local authority could encourage the mother to apply for an occupation order, under the Family Law Act 1996, Part IV, to remove the man from the house.

3. The local authority could apply for a care order or a supervision order. It could then remove the child from the home under the care order. Alternatively, the child could remain with the mother under a care or supervision order and the local authority would request that the abuser leave the home, with the threat that the child would be removed from the mother immediately if the abuser returns. However, the local authority cannot be forced to apply for a care or supervision order, and the court cannot make a care or supervision order unless the local authority applies for one. This is clear from *Nottingham CC* v *P*[204] in which the Court of Appeal was deeply concerned that there was no power to compel the local authority to take steps to protect the children. A local authority may be wary of applying for a care order and permitting a child to remain in the house because of the potential liability in tort if the child were abused. Further, if either a supervision or a care order was relied upon, a local authority may have grave difficulty in ensuring that the suspected abuser did not live in the house. A local authority, for these reasons, may prefer to remove a child from the house if a care order is made, and enable substantial contact between the child and his or her mother.

---

[200] E.g. *Re R (A Minor) (Wardship: Consent to Medical Treatment)* [1992] 1 FLR 190, [1992] 2 FCR 229.
[201] [2005] 3 FCR 303 at para 77.
[202] Harding and Newnham (2017).
[203] CA 1989, Sched. 2, para 5.
[204] [1993] 2 FLR 134, [1994] 1 FCR 624.

4. The availability of section 8 orders for the local authority in this kind of case is very limited. In *Nottingham CC v P* it was stressed that it was not possible for the local authority to obtain a section 8 order to remove the suspected abuser. Removing the man from the home is in the nature of a residence or contact order and cannot be applied for by a local authority. This does not prevent a prohibited steps order being granted on the application of a local authority where a suspected abuser is living apart from the mother and children. In *Re H (Minors) (Prohibited Steps Order)*[205] Butler-Sloss LJ argued that it was permissible to use a prohibited steps order to prevent a stepfather having contact with the children with whom he was no longer living.[206]

5. Exclusion orders are available under ss. 38A and 44A of the Children Act 1989. These can only offer a short-term solution, as explained above.

6. The courts have also been willing to grant orders under the inherent jurisdiction removing a suspected abuser from the home, although the limits of this are unclear.[207] In *Devon CC v S* it was argued that where the court could not make an order which adequately protected the child then the court should rely on the inherent jurisdiction.[208] If the court is persuaded that the child needs protection, and no order could be made which would protect the child, then an order under the inherent jurisdiction can protect the child.

The ideal solution is to enable or encourage the mother to separate from the abuser. Indeed, in *EH v Greenwich London Borough Council*[209] the local authority was criticised for not seeing the mother on her own and explaining the dangers to the children of continuing the relationship. Wall LJ was shocked: 'Here was a mother who needed and was asking for help to break free from an abusive relationship. She was denied that help abruptly and without explanation. That, in my judgment, is very poor social work practice.'[210]

I Protection of children by the criminal law

Learning objective 5

Discuss the protection offered to children by the criminal law

If a child is abused, as well as the question of whether the child should be taken into care there is the issue of whether criminal proceedings should be brought against the abuser. There is no one offence of child abuse; the general criminal law protects children, and so children could be the victims of the whole range of assaults in the Offences Against the Person Act 1861. There are also special offences designed to protect children.[211] For example, s. 1 of the Children and Young Persons Act 1933 states that any wilful violent or non-violent neglect or ill-treatment which is 'likely to cause him unnecessary suffering or injury to health (including injury to or loss of sight, or hearing, or limb, or organ of the body, and any mental derangement)' is an offence.[212] The Sexual Offences Act 2003 has radically reformed the criminal law on sexual offences against children. The law on child neglect was updated in 2015 to make it clear it covered emotional as well as physical abuse.[213]

---

[205] [1995] 1 FLR 638, [1995] 2 FCR 547.
[206] See Chapter 10 for discussion of this case.
[207] *Re S (Minors) (Inherent Jurisdiction: Ouster)* [1994] 1 FLR 623; *Devon CC v S* [1994] 1 FLR 355, [1994] 2 FCR 409.
[208] [1994] 1 FLR 355, [1994] 2 FCR 409.
[209] [2010] 2 FCR 106.
[210] Paragraph 105.
[211] See, e.g., Punishment of Incest Act 1908; Sexual Offences Act 1956, ss. 10–11, 14, 25 and 28.
[212] See Taylor and Hoyano (2012) for a helpful critique of this offence.
[213] Serious Crime Act 2015, s. 66.

The arguments in favour of criminal prosecution centre on the fact that prosecution demonstrates society's condemnation of child abuse. To the child, the prosecution sends the message that the state acknowledges the abuse suffered and that harm has been done. If the perpetrator is imprisoned then, even if this does not guarantee that the abuser will not abuse again, at least it ensures that during the imprisonment he or she will commit no further abuse. On the other hand, if the prosecution fails, the abuser may feel vindicated and the child less protected. Either way the criminal trial is likely to be traumatic for the victim.

8 Compulsory orders: care orders and supervision orders

Learning objective 6

Summarise the differences between a care order and a supervision order

To provide longer-term solutions for a child who is suffering serious harm the choice is between care or supervision orders.[214] Care and supervision orders should only be applied for as a last resort, if voluntary arrangements and the provision of services cannot adequately protect a child. As Bainham has put it: 'Court orders for care and supervision are . . . very much the ambulance at the bottom of the cliff while the support services are the (however inadequate) fence at the top.'[215] Once a care order has been made the local authority can plan for adoption or other forms of long-term care.

The Children Act 1989 makes it clear that a child can only be taken into care through one route, that is s. 31.[216] This was dramatically revealed in *R (G) v Nottingham CC*[217] where a local authority removed a newborn baby from a mother. They did so without any court authorisation. The authority relied on the fact that she had not opposed the taking of the baby, but Munby J held that fell well short of the consent required. The local authority, even if acting in the best interests of the child, had failed to obtain proper legal authorisation for what they did.[218]

A Who can apply?

Section 31(1) states that only a local authority or the NSPCC can apply for a care or supervision order. There is provision for the Secretary of State to add to that list, but to date there have been no additions. Before the NSPCC brings care proceedings, it should consult the local authority in whose area the child is ordinarily resident.[219]

B Who can be the subject of care or supervision proceedings?

Care and supervision orders can only be made in respect of a child who is under 18.[220] Orders should only be made if the child is habitually resident in the United Kingdom, or currently present there.[221] A married child cannot be taken into care. The court has consistently held that the foetus is not a person and so cannot be the subject of a care order, as was established

---

[214] The effects of the orders will be discussed in detail later in this section.
[215] Bainham (2005: 325).
[216] *Re T (A Minor) (Care Order: Conditions)* [1994] 2 FLR 423, [1994] 2 FCR 721.
[217] [2008] EWHC 152 (Admin) and [2008] EWHC 400 (Admin).
[218] See Bainham (2008b).
[219] CA 1989, s. 31(6) and (7).
[220] CA 1989, s. 105.
[221] *Lewisham London Borough Council v D (Criteria for Territorial Jurisdiction in Public Law Proceedings)* [2008] 2 FLR 1449.

in *Re F (In Utero)*.[222] The local authority can only intervene to protect a foetus if the mother consents to the intervention.[223] However, harm done to the foetus might be relied upon as evidence to place a child in care shortly after birth.[224] In *A Local Authority v C*[225] there were grave concerns over a pregnant woman. An order under the inherent jurisdiction was made to protect the child, which was to come into effect on birth.

C The effect of a care order

Section 33 of the Children Act 1989 sets out the effects of a care order, which are as follows:

(i) Care orders and parental responsibility

Section 33(3) of the Children Act 1989 states that the local authority acquires parental responsibility by virtue of the care order and has 'the power (subject to the following provisions of this section) to determine the extent to which a parent or guardian of the child may meet his parental responsibility for him'.[226] So, on the making of a care order, the local authority acquires parental responsibility, but parents or guardians retain theirs. However, those who have parental responsibility by virtue of a residence order lose parental responsibility on the making of a care order. This is because a care order automatically brings to an end any residence order. Even though parents and guardians retain parental responsibility, they cannot exercise it in a way which is incompatible with the local authority's plans.[227] This means that, although parental responsibility is shared between parents and local authorities, in fact it is the local authority that very much controls what happens to the children in its care. However, that is not to say that local authorities are completely unrestrained in their use of parental responsibility and parents are powerless. The Children Act 1989 sets out a number of limitations on the exercise of a local authority's powers over children in its care, which protect the interests of parents. The list is interesting because it reflects those issues which the law regards as so fundamental to the concept of being a parent that the local authority should not be able to override the parents' wishes:

- Local authorities cannot permit the child to be brought up in a different religion from that which the parents intended for the child.[228]

- Local authorities do not have the right to consent (or refuse to consent) to the making of an application for adoption.[229] The consent of the parents is required before an adoption order is made.[230]

- Local authorities cannot appoint a guardian.[231]

- Local authorities cannot cause the child to be known by a different surname, unless they have the consent of all those with parental responsibility, or the leave of the court.[232]

---

[222] [1988] Fam 122.
[223] *St George's Healthcare NHS Trust v S* [1998] 2 FLR 728.
[224] *Re D (A Minor)* [1987] 1 FLR 422; *Re N (Leave to Withdraw Care Proceedings)* [2000] 1 FLR 134.
[225] [2013] EWHC 4036 (Fam).
[226] Although under CA 1989, s. 33(4) the local authority can only restrict a parent's parental authority if satisfied that to do so is necessary to safeguard or promote the child's welfare.
[227] CA 1989, s. 33(3).
[228] CA 1989, s. 33(6)(a).
[229] CA 1989, s. 33(6)(b)(i).
[230] See below, 'The consent of the parents'.
[231] CA 1989, s. 33(6)(b)(iii).
[232] CA 1989, s. 33(7).

An example of the kind of circumstances in which the court may be willing to give leave to change a surname is *Re M, T, P, K and B (Care: Change of Name)*,[233] where the children were in terror of their parents and had a pathological fear that their parents would remove them from their foster parents. Changing the children's name was seen as a means of preventing the parents from discovering the whereabouts of the children. However, if the parents refuse to register the birth or give a name, the local authority can use its parental responsibility to do so.[234]

- The child cannot be removed from the United Kingdom unless all those with parental responsibility consent or the court grants leave.[235]

- The mother of a child in care is at liberty to enter a parental responsibility agreement, thereby giving the father parental responsibility, despite the local authority's opposition.[236]

- The local authority cannot use their parental responsibility to authorise grave medical issues if the parents object.[237] A court order should be obtained. Routine vaccinations can be authorised by the local authority, even if parents object, unless there are particular issues relating to the child that make them serious.[238]

This list is incomplete. In *Re T (A Child: Care Order: Beyond Parental Control: Deprivation of Liberty: Authority to Administer Medication)*[239] Judge Howe QC explained that whenever the local authority was seeking to use their parental responsibility contrary to the wishes of the parent, an order of the court under the inherent jurisdiction would be required if there was a serious interference with the Article 8 rights of the parents.

The sharing of the parental responsibility between the parents and the local authority is highly controversial.[240] Some argue that it is inappropriate that parents who have appallingly abused their children, so that their children have been taken into care, retain parental responsibility. Others argue that the retention of parental responsibility by parents weakens the powers of local authorities.

A care order lasts until any of the following events occur:

- The child reaches the age of 18.

- The court discharges the care order.[241] The child, the local authority and anyone with parental responsibility may apply for the discharge of a care order.[242] It should be noted that unmarried fathers without parental responsibility, therefore, cannot apply for a discharge, although the father could apply for a residence order which, if granted, would

---

[233] [2000] 1 FLR 645.
[234] *Tower Hamlets LBC v T* [2019] EWHC 1572 (Fam).
[235] CA 1989, Sched. 2, para 19(3).
[236] *Re X (Parental Responsibility Agreement)* [2000] 1 FLR 517.
[237] [2017] EWFC B1. See also *Re SL (Permission to Vaccinate)* [2017] EWHC 125 (Fam).
[238] *Re H (A Child)(Parental Responsibility: Vaccination)* [2020] EWCA Civ 664.
[239] [2017] EWFC B1.
[240] Eekelaar (1991c: 43).
[241] A supervision order can be varied or discharged on the application of the child, any person with parental responsibility or the supervisor. Applications to discharge supervision orders are also governed by the welfare principle, although if the court wished to substitute a supervision order with a care order, this does necessitate proof of the significant harm test.
[242] CA 1989, s. 39(1). Variation of a care order is not permitted because there is nothing to vary apart from discharging it.

automatically discharge the care order.[243] According to *Re A (Care: Discharge Application by Child)*,[244] a child applying for discharge of a care order to which he or she is subject does not need leave. The welfare principle[245] governs applications to discharge care orders.[246] The court should focus on whether there were good reasons why the parent could not resume care of the child, rather than asking whether there were good reasons to disturb the current placement.[247] In some cases it may be appropriate to discharge a care order and replace it with a supervision order.[248] A care order in relation to a 15-year-old was discharged after the child ran away from authority care and the local authority was unable to return him to their care. The order was doing nothing and so there was no point in maintaining it.[249]

- If the court grants a residence order in respect of a child, this will bring to an end any care order relating to that child.
- An adoption order will bring to an end a care order.

D The effect and purpose of the supervision order

The supervision order aims to give the local authority some control over the child, without the degree of intervention involved in a care order.[250] Under a supervision order the child will remain at home, but will be under the watch of a designated officer of a local authority, or a probation officer.[251] Under s. 35(1) of the Children Act 1989 the supervisor has three duties:[252]

LEGISLATIVE PROVISION

Children Act 1989, section 35(1)

(a) to advise, assist and befriend the supervised child;

(b) to take such steps as are reasonably necessary to give effect to the order; and

where–

(i) the order is not wholly complied with; or

(ii) the supervisor considers that the order may no longer be necessary, to consider whether or not to apply to the court for its variation or discharge.

The making of the order does not alter the legal position of the parents: they retain full parental responsibility; the supervision order does not give parental responsibility to the local authority.

---

[243] CA 1989, s. 91(1).
[244] [1995] 1 FLR 599, [1995] 2 FCR 686, Thorpe J.
[245] CA 1989, s. 1.
[246] *Re T (Termination of Contact: Discharge of Order)* [1997] 1 FLR 517.
[247] *GM v Carmarthenshire CC* [2018] EWFC 36.
[248] E.g. *Re O (Care: Discharge of Care Order)* [1999] 2 FLR 119.
[249] *Re C (Care: Discharge of Care Order)* [2010] 1 FLR 774. The court made it clear that even if a care order was being ineffective there may be circumstances which made its retention useful.
[250] If the problems relate specifically to education, a special education supervision order is available.
[251] CA 1989, s. 31(1)(b).
[252] CA 1989, Sched. 3 sets out their duties in further detail.

The key element of a supervision order is that a supervisor advises, assists and befriends the child. As well as befriending the child, the supervisor can advise the parents and make recommendations about the upbringing of children. It is also possible to add specific conditions to a supervision order. Schedule 3 to the Children Act 1989[253] lists the conditions that a court can impose. These include requiring a child to live at a particular place, requiring the child to present him- or herself at a relevant place, or to participate in special activities. It is possible to impose conditions on a supervision order not listed in Sched. 3, but only with the parents' consent.[254]

The whole ethos of the supervision order is based on the parents' consent and cooperation. The supervision order does not give the supervisor the right to enter any property and remove a child. Nor does the supervisor have the power to direct the child to undergo medical or psychiatric examination or treatment. It is not even possible to force the parents to comply with the conditions in the order or the requests of the supervisor. Critics claim that supervision orders 'lack teeth' and are 'ineffective'.[255] However, the failure to comply with requests from the supervisor may lead to the supervisor applying for a care order or emergency protection order. As the threshold criteria for the making of a care and supervision order are the same, the court may well be convinced that it would be appropriate to make a care order if the parents are refusing to cooperate with the supervisor. This means that, although the supervision order is apparently based on partnership and voluntary cooperation between the local authority and the parents, the threat of having the children removed under a care order gives the supervision order a coercive edge. However, supervision orders appear to be unpopular with some social workers, who told researchers that the orders were 'a complete waste of time' and toothless.[256] A different kind of concern is indicated by research that children left with abusive parents are at risk of further abuse. In one study 40 per cent of children left with parents following local authority intervention suffered maltreatment in the 12 months following protective intervention. Fifteen per cent suffered serious maltreatment.[257] Another study[258] found that in 20 per cent of supervision orders there was a return to court within five years; including 10 per cent within the first year. This might be viewed as indicating the success of supervision orders: that in 80 per cent of cases they ensured no further court action was required. On the other hand, we might feel concerned that in 20 per cent of cases further intervention was needed, in which case, arguably all the supervision order achieved was to delay a longer-term solution.

A supervision order lasts for up to one year initially, although it can be made for a shorter period.[259] It is possible for the supervisor to apply for an extension for up to three years. The welfare principle will cover any application for an extension.[260] Any existing supervision order will be terminated if the court subsequently makes a care order.[261]

---

[253] For a judicial discussion see *Re v (Care or Supervision Order)* [1996] 1 FLR 776.
[254] CA 1989, Sched. 3, para 3(1).
[255] Harwin *et al.* (2016).
[256] Hunt and McLeod (1998: 237).
[257] Brandon (1999: 200–1).
[258] Harwin and Alrouh (2017).
[259] See, e.g., *M v Warwickshire* [1994] 2 FLR 593.
[260] *Re A (A Minor) (Supervision Extension)* [1995] 1 FLR 335.
[261] CA 1989, Sched. 3, para 10.

E Care or supervision order?

Where the threshold criteria (to be discussed shortly) have been made out, the local authority must decide whether a care order or a supervision order is more appropriate.[262]

The following factors are relevant:

1. If the local authority wishes to remove a child from the home, it must apply for a care order.[263] It is not possible to remove a child under a supervision order.[264] If the local authority decides that the child should stay with the family, either a care order or a supervision order can be made. If a care order is made, the child can be removed by the local authority at any time.[265] If a supervision order is made, the child can only be removed if a further application is made to the court, for an emergency protection order for example. The supervision order, combined with the power to apply for an emergency protection order, should be regarded as a 'strong package', especially as the supervision order gives instant access into the child's home.[266] However, where there is very serious harm or sexual abuse, the courts have suggested that a care order should be made.[267]

2. If the child is to be looked after by foster carers, a care order is normally appropriate.[268] Although a child can be placed with foster carers under a supervision order, with the consent of the parents, the parents would have the right in law to remove the child from the foster parents. If a long-term foster arrangement is proposed, a court may make an order under s. 91(14) of the Children Act 1989 so that the birth family can only apply with leave of the court.[269] That would give some security to the foster parents that they would not need to defend a baseless application from the birth family.

3. Hale J in *Re O (Care or Supervision Order)*[270] stated that a supervision order normally requires cooperation from the parents and is therefore appropriate only where there is at least a reasonable relationship between the parent and the local authority.[271]

4. Where the local authority wishes to acquire parental responsibility, a care order is appropriate.[272] *Re V (Care or Supervision Order)*[273] demonstrates this point well. There was a dispute between the parents and the local authority over what kind of education was appropriate for a disabled child. The local authority wanted to be able to make decisions relating to the child's education and so a care order was made, even though the child was to remain with the parents.

5. If a child was injured through an act of a parent that was thought to be out of character and so there was no future risk to the child, then a supervision order may be more appropriate than a care order.[274]

---

[262] For a useful summary of the relevant factors, see *Re D (Care or Supervision Order)* [2000] Fam Law 600.
[263] *Oxfordshire CC v L (Care or Supervision Order)* [1998] 1 FLR 70.
[264] Unless the child is voluntarily accommodated under CA 1989, s. 20.
[265] *Re T (A Child) (Care Order)* [2009] 2 FCR 367.
[266] *Re S (J) (A Minor) (Care or Supervision)* [1993] 2 FLR 919 at p. 947.
[267] *Re S (Care or Supervision Order)* [1996] 1 FLR 753.
[268] For a discussion of the current position of foster carers see Narey and Owers (2018).
[269] *A Mother v Dorset CC* [2019] EWFC B3.
[270] [1996] 2 FLR 755, [1997] 2 FCR 17.
[271] *Oxfordshire CC v L (Care or Supervision Order)* [1998] 1 FLR 70.
[272] *Re T (A Child) (Care Order)* [2009] 2 FCR 367.
[273] [1996] 1 FLR 776.
[274] *Manchester CC v B* [1996] 1 FLR 324.

6. If the parents would react very negatively to the making of a care order, but not to a super-vision order, this could be a significant factor, especially if the children are going to remain with the parents.[275]

In theory, a court could grant a care order even though the local authority only applied for a supervision order,[276] although this would require 'urgent and strong reasons'.[277]

9 Grounds for supervision and care orders: the threshold criteria

Learning objective 7

Analyse the threshold criteria

The grounds for a supervision or care order are set out in s. 31 of the Children Act 1989. Before a care order or a supervision order can be made, it is necessary to show four things:

1. The court must be satisfied that 'the child concerned is suffering, or is likely to suffer, sig-nificant harm'.[278]

2. '[T]hat the harm, or likelihood of harm, is attributable to: (i) the care given to the child, or likely to be given to him if the order were not made, not being what it would be reasonable to expect a parent to give him; or (ii) the child's being beyond parental control.'[279]

3. The making of the order would promote the welfare of the child.[280]

4. That making the order is better for the child than making no order at all.[281]

A The role of the threshold criteria

The first two requirements are commonly known as the 'threshold criteria'[282] and we shall focus on those in this section. It should be stressed that a care order or supervision order can-not be made simply on the basis that the child's parents agree that the child should be taken into care[283] or that it is in the welfare of the child to make a care order. As Lady Hale put it in *Re SB (Children)*:

> It is not enough that the social workers, the experts or the court think that a child would be better off living with another family. That would be social engineering of a kind which is not permitted in a democratic society.[284]

By contrast, simply because there is significant harm does not mean that an order must be made; it must also be shown that the making of the order will advance the child's welfare.[285]

---

[275] *Re B (Care Order or Supervision Order)* [1996] 2 FLR 693, [1997] 1 FCR 309.
[276] In *Re M (A Minor) (Care Order: Threshold Conditions)* [1994] 2 AC 424 the House of Lords made a care order even though the local authority wished to withdraw its application; see also *Re K (Care Order or Residence Order)* [1995] 1 FLR 675, [1996] 1 FCR 365, where a care order was made contrary to the local authority's wishes.
[277] *Oxfordshire CC v L (Care or Supervision Order)* [1998] 1 FLR 70.
[278] CA 1989, s. 31(2)(a).
[279] CA 1989, s. 31(2)(b).
[280] CA 1989, s. 1(1).
[281] CA 1989, s. 1(5). See *Redbridge LB v B, C and A* [2011] EWHC 517 (Fam).
[282] See Wilkinson (2009) for a critical assessment of these.
[283] *Re G (A Minor) (Care Proceedings)* [1994] 2 FLR 69.
[284] *Re SB (Children)* [2009] UKSC 17, para 7.
[285] *Humberside CC v B* [1993] 1 FLR 257, [1993] 1 FCR 613.

If there are several children involved, each child should be considered separately. For example, in **Re B (Care Proceedings: Interim Care Order)**[286] the evidence was that the parents cared for the daughter perfectly well, but treated their son very badly. The threshold criteria were only made out in respect of the son. A care order could not be made in relation to the daughter.

These two requirements of the threshold criteria will now be considered separately.

B 'Is suffering or is likely to suffer significant harm'

The following terms need to be examined.

(i) Harm

Harm is defined in s. 31(9) of the Children Act 1989 as 'ill-treatment or the impairment of health or development, including, for example, impairment suffered from seeing or hearing the ill-treatment of another'. This last clause covers, for example, the harm a child may suffer while witnessing the domestic violence of her mother.[287] 'Ill-treatment' includes 'sexual abuse and forms of ill-treatment which are not physical, including, for example, impairment suffered from seeing or hearing the ill-treatment of another'; 'development' is defined as 'physical, intellectual, emotional, social or behavioural development'; and 'health' means 'physical or mental health'.[288] Therefore, harm is not limited to physical abuse. For example, children can be harmed if their parents do not talk to them, or deprive them of opportunities of developing social skills. Similarly, not attending school[289] or not receiving adequate medical treatment[290] could amount to harm. In **Re C (A Child)**[291] it was confirmed that the child witnessing constant parental arguments could amount to harm. In **Re L (Interim Care Order: Extended Family)**[292] a suggestion that emotional harm should be seen as less serious than physical harm was firmly rejected. In **Re J (A Child)**[293] a mother who compelled her son to live as a girl was said to have caused him significant harm. Understandably this judgment has caused some alarm, although Hayden J made it very clear: 'This is not a case about gender dysphoria, rather it is about a mother who has developed a belief structure which she has imposed upon her child.' The mother 'had overborne his will and deprived him of his fundamental right to exercise his autonomy'. Nevertheless, the case does raise some complex issues: what does it mean exactly to raise a child as a boy or a girl? Was the judge right to find it reassuring that the child was now interested in football stickers and Power Rangers? In relation to broader issues, it shows that 'harm' in this context is clearly broader than physical and emotional harm.

The harm can be due to acts or omissions.[294] Of course, harm can be caused unintentionally. In **Re V (Care or Supervision Order)**[295] a mother, who was very protective of her son, sought to keep him at home rather than sending him to a special school (he suffered from cystic fibrosis). This was held as amounting to harm, even though she was acting from the best of motives.

---

[286] [2010] 1 FLR 1211.
[287] **Re R (Care: Rehabilitation in Context of Domestic Violence)** [2006] EWCA Civ 1638.
[288] CA 1989, s. 31(9).
[289] **Re O (A Minor) (Care Order: Education: Procedure)** [1992] 2 FLR 7, [1992] 1 FCR 489.
[290] **F v Suffolk CC** [1981] 2 FLR 208.
[291] [2011] EWCA Civ 918.
[292] [2013] EWCA Civ 179.
[293] [2016] EWHC 2430 (Fam).
[294] Bracewell J in **Re M (A Minor) (Care Order: Threshold Conditions)** [1994] Fam 95; approved [1994] 2 AC 424 HL
[295] [1996] 1 FLR 776.

There can be difficulties in defining harm. Imagine a child who is brought up by devoutly religious parents who require the child to spend two hours a day in prayer and memorising holy texts. Some may say this is providing the child with an invaluable spiritual basis for their life. Others may regard this as abuse, hindering the child's social development. Another, perhaps controversial, example of harm is the following case:

TOPICAL ISSUE

The 'miracle' baby case

In **London Borough of Haringey v Mrs E, Mr E**[296] a couple were caring for a child they claimed was theirs, produced as a result of a miracle following a prayer session with a religious leader. It was clear that the child was not biologically theirs and there were very strong suspicions that the child had been illegally brought into the country from overseas. It was held that the child was likely to suffer significant harm because the child was not Mr and Mrs E's and the child would be misled by them when he was older as to the origins of his birth. While it is understandable that authorities do not wish to encourage a practice which on one view of what happened amounted to 'baby selling', it is not obvious that this was a case where the child was suffering or was likely to suffer significant harm in the immediate future.[297]

(ii) Significant harm

Booth J in **Humberside CC v B**[298] suggested that 'significant' here meant 'considerable, noteworthy or important'. The Supreme Court in **Re B (Care Proceedings: Appeal)**,[299] while not disapproving of Booth's dicta, thought it was not helpful to seek to define the word significant. However, Lord Wilson quoted with approval Hale LJ (as she then was) in **Re C and B (Children) (Care Order: Future Harm)**:[300] 'a comparatively small risk of really serious harm can justify action, while even the virtual certainty of slight harm might not'. Significant harm can be the result of several minor harms. The court will readily assume that an abandoned child will be likely to suffer significant harm.[301] In the following case the Court of Appeal controversially found there was not a risk of significant harm.

CASE: Re MA (Care Threshold) [2009] EWCA CIV 853

The case involved a Pakistani family, who were illegally residing in the United Kingdom. They had three children of their own and a 'mystery' girl, aged 5. She was not their biological child and there was no information about her identity. She was kept secretly by the family and it was found that she was very badly treated. The children were accommodated by the local authority after the oldest child alleged physical abuse, although there was no evidence to support those allegations. The key issue in the case was whether the serious

---

[296] [2004] EWHC 2580 (Fam).
[297] The child was subsequently freed for adoption: *Haringey v Mr and Mrs E* [2006] EWHC 1620 (Fam).
[298] [1993] 1 FLR 257, [1993] 1 FCR 613.
[299] [2013] UKSC 33.
[300] [2000] 2 FCR 614.
[301] *Re M (Care Order: Parental Responsibility)* [1996] 2 FLR 84, [1996] 2 FLR 521.

abuse of the mystery girl could found the basis of a finding that the couple's own children would be likely to suffer significant harm. The judge decided not. The fact that they mistreated the mystery child was not evidence that they would treat their own children in the same way. The children's guardian appealed.

The Court of Appeal by a majority upheld the judge's ruling, which could not be said to be plainly wrong. To amount to significant harm, the harm had to be significant enough to justify the intervention of the state and justify an intervention in the family life of the parents, under Article 8 of the ECHR. The judge had been entitled to find that in this case there was not a sufficient risk to justify making an order. The court report noted that the children were 'well nourished, well cared for and with close attachments to their parents'. The court accepted that the position of the 'mystery child' was unclear and the judge was permitted to conclude that the way the parents had treated her was not sufficient evidence of a risk of serious harm to their natural children. Wilson LJ dissented, concluding that the way the mystery child had been treated was so 'grossly abnormal' she had suffered physical and emotional harm. This showed a capacity for cruelty and so gave rise to a real possibility that they would harm their own children.

The case shows how difficult it can be to determine whether harm is significant. There was evidence from one of the children that they had been hit and slapped by the parents. On this Hallett LJ commented:

> Reasonable physical chastisement of children by parents is not yet unlawful in this country. Slaps and even kicks vary enormously in their seriousness. A kick sounds particularly unpleasant, yet many a parent may have nudged their child's nappied bottom with their foot in gentle play, without committing an assault. Many a parent will have slapped their child on the hand to make the point that running out into a busy road is a dangerous thing to do. What M alleged, therefore, was not necessarily indicative of abuse. It will all depend on the circumstances.[302]

Not everyone would take such a sanguine view of the child's evidence, particularly in the light of the way the parents had treated the 'mystery girl'.[303] You might think that it was harmful for the children to see the 'mystery girl' treated in that way. Particularly concerning is the majority's argument that because the parents had not provided an explanation for the slaps and kicks it was better to assume they were innocuous. That appears to encourage parents not to provide an explanation for injuries.

In deciding whether the child is suffering significant harm, 'the child's health or development shall be compared with that which could reasonably be expected of a similar child'.[304] Lord Wilson explained in *Re B (Care Proceedings: Appeal)*[305] that 'whereas the concept of "ill-treatment" is absolute, the concept of "impairment of health or development" is relative to the health or development which could reasonably be expected of a similar child.' So, when considering health or development, the court must compare the child with a similar child. If the child has a learning difficulty one must compare their development with that expected of

---

[302] Paragraph 39.
[303] See the powerful analysis of Keating (2011) and Hayes, Hayes and Williams (2010) which is highly critical of the decision.
[304] CA 1989, s. 31(10).
[305] [2013] UKSC 33.

a child with that learning difficulty. However, the concept of ill treatment is the same, whatever the characteristics of the child. This might prevent a parent who, say, locks up a disabled child in a cupboard, from saying that although that would be ill treatment for other children, it would not for disabled children. There are three particularly controversial issues in considering the 'similar child' test:

1. There is particular controversy over the extent to which the cultural background of the child should be taken into account.[306] For example, if a particular religion or culture teaches that a teenage girl should not talk to anyone who is not related to her, and a local authority thought this was harming a girl's social development, should the girl be compared only with a girl brought up in the same culture?

   There are two main views on this. One is that 'Muslim children, Rastafarian children, the children of Hasidic Jews may be different and have different needs from children brought up in the indigenous white nominally Christian culture.'[307] This perspective would require the court to compare the child with a child from a similar culture or background. The other view is that there should be a minimum standard for all children; what is considered harmful to children should not depend on their cultural background. However, the fact that the harm was an aspect of cultural or religious practice may be very relevant in deciding whether making a care order would promote the welfare of the child.[308]

   In *Re D (Care: Threshold Criteria)*[309] the Court of Appeal adopted the second view, declaring that what amounts to significant harm should not depend on the child's cultural or ethnic background. This may be supported by the statement of Hughes LJ in *Re D (A Child) (Care Order: Evidence)*[310] that the standard of parenting expected in s. 31 was an objective standard. There is also some support for this in the approach of the law to female genital mutilation (FGM). This practice is illegal[311] and the President of the Family Division has suggested it is a 'gross breach of human rights' and will automatically satisfy the threshold criteria.[312] However, that very example raises the question, as the President noted, of how male circumcision is largely seen as acceptable, because it has long been an aspect of several major religions and cultures. The President accepted that male circumcision, unlike genital mutilation, did not automatically satisfy the threshold criteria. He noted that in 2015 the law was:

   > ... still prepared to tolerate non-therapeutic male circumcision performed for religious or even purely cultural or conventional reasons, while no longer being willing to tolerate FGM.

   The use of the word 'tolerate', and the difficulty the President had in justifying the law, leaves open the possibility this issue might be ripe for re-examination.[313]

2. To what extent are the characteristics or capabilities of the parents to be taken into account? If a child is brought up by a parent with a disability, should the child be considered only

---

[306] Freeman (1992a: 107). See also Brophy, Jhotti-Johal and Owen (2003).
[307] Freeman (1992a: 153). See also Freeman (1997a: ch. 7).
[308] CA 1989, s. 1(3)(d).
[309] [1998] Fam Law 656.
[310] [2010] EWCA Civ 1000, para 35.
[311] Female Genital Mutilation Act 2003. Schedule 2 of that Act allows a court to make a female genital mutilation order preventing a child from being taken to a place where FGM may occur (see *Re X (A Child) (Female Genital Mutilation Protection Order)* [2018] EWCA Civ 1825.
[312] *Re B and G (Care Proceedings: FGM) (No. 2)* [2015] EWFC 3.
[313] Fox and Thomson (2012).

in comparison with a similar child living with disabled parents?[314] Hughes LJ addressed the issue in *Re D (A Child) (Care Order: Evidence)*:[315]

> For the avoidance of doubt, the test under s. 31(2) is and has to be an objective one. If it were otherwise, and the 'care which it is reasonable to expect a parent to give' were to be judged by the standards of the parent with the characteristics of the particular parent in question, the protection afforded to children would be very limited indeed, if not entirely illusory.

3. What if the child has brought about the harm him- or herself? In *Re O (A Minor) (Care Order: Education: Procedure)*[316] it was suggested that in relation to a 15-year-old truant, the 'similar child' was 'a child of equivalent intellectual and social development who has gone to school and not merely an average child who may or may not be at school'. Crucially, the child was not to be compared with another truant child. The reason why truancy was not a relevant characteristic is not clear, but one interpretation of the decision is that factors that the child has brought upon him- or herself are not to be taken into account.

(iii) Is suffering

Section 31 requires proof on the balance of probability[317] that the child either is suffering or is likely to suffer significant harm. Notably, proof that the child has suffered harm in the past is insufficient, although harm in the past may be evidence that the child is likely to suffer harm in the future.

There has been much debate over what 'is' means in this context.[318] The leading case is now *Re M (A Minor) (Care Order: Threshold Conditions)*,[319] decided in the House of Lords.

CASE: *Re M (A Minor) (Care Order: Threshold Conditions)* [1994] 2 FLR 577, [1994] 2 FCR 871

The father murdered the mother in front of the children. The father was convicted of murder and given a life sentence, and there was a recommendation that he be deported on his release. Three of the four children were placed with W (the children's aunt). The remaining child, M, was initially placed with foster parents, but later joined her siblings with W. By the time the case came before the House of Lords it was agreed by everyone that M should live with W, but the local authority still wanted a care order just in case it became necessary in due course to remove M from W's house.

The crucial issue in the case was whether the phrase 'is suffering' meant that it had to be shown that the child was suffering at the time of the hearing before the court. This was important because, by the time the matter came to court, the child was safely with the foster parents and it could not have been found by the court that 'she is suffering significant harm'. Lord Mackay LC rejected such a reading. He stated that the date at which the child must be suffering significant harm was 'the date at which the local authority initiated

---

[314] See Freeman (1992a: 107).
[315] [2010] EWCA Civ 1000, para 35.
[316] [1992] 2 FLR 7, [1992] 1 FCR 489.
[317] *Re H (Minors) (Sexual Abuse: Standard of Proof)* [1996] AC 563. In *Re A (Children)* [2018] EWCA Civ 1718 the Court of Appeal said it was not helpful for the judge to seek to work out mathematically the probability of different events and use statistical assessments.
[318] Only lawyers . . . !
[319] [1994] 2 FLR 577, [1994] 2 FCR 871; discussed in Bainham (1994a).

the procedure for protection under the Act'. If the child was suffering significant harm at the time the local authority first intervened, and the social work continued to the date of the court hearing, then the child 'is suffering significant harm' for the purpose of the Act.

Applying this to the facts of the case in *Re M* it was clear that, at the time when the social work intervention started (i.e. just after the murder of the mother), it could have been said the child was suffering significant harm, and therefore a care order could be made. Lord Nolan explained:

> Parliament cannot have intended that temporary measures taken to protect the child from immediate harm should prevent the court from regarding the child as one who is suffering, or is likely to suffer, significant harm within the meaning of s. 31(2)(a), and should thus disqualify the court from making a more permanent order under the section. The focal point of the inquiry must be the situation which resulted in the temporary measures taken, and which has led to the application for a care or supervision order.[320]

The decision is clearly correct because, if it is necessary to show that at the time of a court hearing a child is suffering significant harm, then the local authority may have to delay taking measures to protect the child until there has been a court hearing.[321] Subsequently, the Court of Appeal in *Re G (Care Proceedings: Threshold Conditions)*[322] held that the local authority could rely on facts which subsequently came to light to demonstrate that at the time when the local authority first intervened the child was suffering significant harm, even if it did not know of those facts at that time.

(iv) Is likely to suffer significant harm

It is generally agreed that the state should be able to intervene and remove a child who is in real danger of suffering significant harm in the future, rather than wait until the harm occurs. However, removing a child on the basis of speculative harm, especially harm that may be a long way off, is controversial, because it is impossible to know whether or not the harm would materialise.

The simple words 'is likely to suffer significant harm' have proved highly problematic and have led to a string of decisions. The starting point is by the House of Lords in *Re H (Minors) (Sexual Abuse: Standard of Proof)*.[323] The case divided the House of Lords three to two and revealed the real problems at issue.

CASE: *Re H (Minors) (Sexual Abuse: Standard of Proof)* [1996] AC 563

A 15-year-old girl alleged that she had been sexually abused by her mother's cohabitant. The cohabitant was tried for rape but he was acquitted by a jury. The local authority was still concerned about the situation, especially because the cohabitant continued to live with the mother and her three younger children.[324] The local authority sought a care order

---

[320] [1994] 2 FCR 871 at para 32.
[321] Lord Templeman and Lord Nolan specifically took this point.
[322] [2001] FL 727.
[323] [1996] AC 563. A powerful criticism of the reasoning can be found in Freeman (2004a: 331–3).
[324] The 15-year-old child had moved to live elsewhere.

in respect of the three younger girls. It argued that, although it had not been proved beyond all reasonable doubt[325] that the older child had been abused, there was a substantial risk that the younger children could be abused. The judge at first instance accepted that there was 'a real possibility' that the older girl had been abused, but he felt that the 'high standard of proof' required for a care order had not been satisfied. He therefore dismissed the application for a care order. The House of Lords looked at five questions:

1. *What does 'likely' mean?* It was held unanimously that 'likely' meant that significant harm was a real possibility; that is, a possibility that could not sensibly be ignored. The Court of Appeal in *Re L-K (Children) (Non-Accidental Injuries: Fact Finding)*[326] added that the nature and gravity of the feared harm were relevant in deciding whether the risk was one that could not sensibly be ignored. The phrase 'likely' did not require the court to find that the harm was more likely than not to occur. This is a remarkably 'pro-child protection' stance of the law to take. A child can be taken away from parents, even though the child has not been harmed and it is not even more likely than not that the child will be, if it can be shown that there is a real possibility the child will suffer significant harm.

2. *When must the harm be likely?* It needs to be shown that the child was likely to be harmed at the time the local authority first intervened; in other words, the *Re M (A Minor) (Care Order: Threshold Conditions)*[327] approach to 'is' was also followed for 'is likely'. In *Re N (Leave to Withdraw Care Proceedings)*[328] Bracewell J stressed that the court was not restricted to looking at harm in the immediate future, but could also consider longer-term harms.

3. *What is the burden of proof?* It must be shown on the balance of probabilities that harm is likely. In other words, it must be more likely than not that there is a real possibility of harm.[329] In *A County Council v M and F*[330] it was emphasised that this meant that it would be wrong to suggest parents had the burden of proving that there was an innocent explanation for injuries. This was not controversial. However, the question has been made far more complex by the dicta of Lord Nicholls in *Re H (Minors) (Sexual Abuse: Standard of Proof)*,[331] who argued: 'the more serious the allegation the less likely it is that the event occurred and, hence, the stronger should be the evidence before the court concludes that the allegation is established on the balance of probability'.[332] That statement was interpreted by some to mean that in cases of more serious allegations more evidence was required to prove them than where less serious allegations were made. His statement was subsequently revised by the House of Lords in *Re B (Children) (Sexual Abuse: Standard of Proof)* (see below) which made it clear that in all cases the normal balance of probabilities test applies.

---

[325] The standard of proof in criminal proceedings.
[326] [2015] EWCA Civ 830.
[327] [1994] 2 FCR 871.
[328] [2000] 1 FLR 134.
[329] See, for an application of this, *A Local Authority v S, W and T* [2004] 2 FLR 129.
[330] [2011] EWHC 1804 (Fam).
[331] [1996] AC 563.
[332] [1996] AC 563 at p. 586; applied in *Re ET (Serious Injuries: Standard of Proof)* [2003] 2 FLR 1205.

4. *Who has to prove that the child is likely to suffer significant harm?* The House of Lords agreed that the local authority had to prove that the significant harm was likely to occur. The burden did not lie on the parents to show that it was not likely to occur.

5. *From what evidence can the risk of harm be established?* The majority argued that, in order to find that harm was likely, it was necessary first to find certain 'primary facts'. Each of these primary facts would have to be proved on the balance of probabilities. Then, looking at these primary facts, the court could consider whether they demonstrated that significant harm was likely (that is, that there was a real possibility of significant harm).[333] In *Re H*, because it had not been found on the balance of probabilities that the older child had been abused (there was only a strong suspicion that she had), there were no primary facts proved. Therefore, it could not be shown that the younger girls were likely to suffer significant harm. Suspicion itself was an insufficient basis on which to decide that there was a significant likelihood of abuse. One reason is that it would be unjustifiable for a parent to have his or her child removed (with the attendant shame and social exclusion which would probably follow) on the basis of a suspicion. Another reason is that, as Lord Nicholls explained subsequently in *Re O and N (Children) (Non-Accidental Injury)*,[334] otherwise a suspicion that a parent had harmed a child would not be sufficient to show that the child had suffered significant harm, but could be relied upon to show that the child was likely to suffer significant harm. That would be 'extraordinary', he suggested.[335]

The majority's approach in *Re H* has been subject to several criticisms:

(a) The minority argued that, looking at the case as a whole, there were sufficient worries (especially the fact that there was a strong suspicion that the cohabitant had abused the older girl) to justify the finding of likely harm. This, they thought, was sufficient to justify making the care order, and the approach of the majority over-complicated the issue.[336] This argument was particularly strong on the facts of that case because, if the older girl had been abused as she had alleged, there was a very serious danger facing the younger children.

(b) Mathematically, the majority's approach looks dubious. Imagine two cases: in case A there are ten alleged facts pointing to abuse and there is a 45 per cent chance that each alleged fact was true; in case B there is one alleged fact pointing to abuse for which there is a 60 per cent chance that it is true.[337] The approach of the majority would allow for a finding of likely harm only in case B. In case A, as none of the facts was proved on the balance of probabilities, an order could not be made. Yet, in statistical terms, case A would be a stronger case than case B. The approach of the minority, looking at the totality of the circumstances, would permit the making of a care order in case A.

---

[333] In *Lancashire County Council v R* [2010] 1 FLR 387 Ryder J held it to be wrong to assume that a person who engaged in domestic violence had a propensity to child abuse.

[334] [2003] 1 FCR 673. See the excellent discussion in Hayes (2004).

[335] [2003] 1 FCR 673 at para 16.

[336] The majority did admit that the totality of the evidence established a worrying number of circumstances, but, as no facts were proved, this belief was mere suspicion.

[337] Assuming that the ten facts, if true, would provide as good evidence that future harm was likely as the single fact, if true.

(c) The key underlying issue in the case has been explained by Hayes: 'The dilemma to be resolved is how the legal framework, and the legal process, can best reconcile safeguards for children suffering from significant harm with the obligation to respect parental autonomy and family privacy.'[338] There is an option of either threatening the parents' rights by removing the child from them without clear evidence, or threatening the child's rights by not providing protection even where there is a serious risk of danger. The House of Lords clearly preferred upholding parents' rights. Whether this is consistent with the welfare principle in s. 1 of the Children Act 1989 is open to debate.

(d) The question must be viewed in the light of the European Convention on Human Rights. A child must be protected from 'torture' and 'inhuman and degrading treatment'.[339] Yet, at the same time, the state is required to respect the private and family life of all the family members.[340] It is certainly arguable that the approach taken in *Re H* places more weight on the parents' right to respect for family life than on the child's right to respect for private life and to be protected from inhuman and degrading treatment.

Despite these criticisms, Lord Steyn's speech was confirmed as setting out the current law by the House of Lords in *Re B (Children) (Sexual Abuse: Standard of Proof)*[341] where their Lordships emphasised that the court had to rely on facts proved on the balance of probabilities to establish the threshold criteria. Unproven suspicions could not be used. Lady Hale justified that approach in this way:

> The threshold is there to protect both the children and their parents from unjustified intervention in their lives. It would provide no protection at all if it could be established on the basis of unsubstantiated suspicions: that is, where a judge cannot say that there is no real possibility that abuse took place, so concludes that there is a real possibility that it did not.[342]

Lady Hale went on to clarify the burden of proof:

> I . . . announce loud and clear that the standard of proof in finding the facts necessary to establish the threshold under s. 31(2) or the welfare considerations in s. 1 of the 1989 Act is the simple balance of probabilities, neither more nor less. Neither the seriousness of the allegation nor the seriousness of the consequences should make any difference to the standard of proof to be applied in determining the facts. The inherent probabilities are simply something to be taken into account, where relevant, in deciding where the truth lies.[343]

This makes it clear that for all issues the test is the balance of probabilities, but that some allegations were inherently unlikely and might be harder to prove on the balance of probabilities.[344] The error in Lord Nicholls's speech in *Re H* was to suggest that it was the severity of the allegation that indicated its unlikelihood. That was incorrect. It was permissible for the court to consider whether what was being alleged was particularly bizarre, or inherently unlikely. So, if a child claimed to have been abused by the Queen in 10 Downing Street, the court could start from the premise that was inherently unlikely and so would require quite a bit of evidence to be true. That must, however, be treated with care because a child's understanding of abuse might be limited. A child, for example, claiming to have been abused by an

---

[338] Hayes (1997: 1–2).
[339] Article 3.
[340] Article 8.
[341] [2008] 2 FCR 339.
[342] Paragraph 54.
[343] Paragraph 70.
[344] *Re S-B (Children)* [2009] UKSC 17, discussed in Bainham (2009b).

elephant might be struggling to put in terms they understand the abuse that occurred and a 'childish' explanation might even give credulity to their claim. Their Lordships' approach in *Re B* was later relied upon in *Re R (A Child)*[345] where a parent, whose care was normally exemplary, put their child into a bath of boiling water. It was said that given the history of excellent care it was inherently unlikely that the parent had deliberately sought to abuse the child. Clear evidence of that would be required.

Lady Hale in *Re B (Care Proceedings: Appeal)*[346] also made some pertinent observations about cases based on future harm:

> [T]he longer term the prospect of harm, the greater the degree of uncertainty about whether it will actually happen. The child's resilience or resistance, and the many protective influences at work in the community, whether from the wider family, their friends, their neighbourhoods, the health and social services and, perhaps above all, their schools, mean that it may never happen. The degree of likelihood must be such as to justify compulsory intervention *now*, for there is always the possibility of compulsory intervention later, should the 'real possibility' solidify.

The difficulty in the *Re H* approach was demonstrated in *Carmarthenshire CC v Y*.[347] The case concerned a child who was the daughter of Y, who since her teenage years had suffered serious mental ill health. Y was currently in hospital and the question was whether the child should be looked after by Y's parents or her sister. In her teenage years Y had alleged her father had repeatedly raped her. The problem was that Y was unable to give evidence and so these allegations were said by the court to be unproved and so the case had to continue on the basis there had been no abuse. Even though there was a 'ring of truth' about the allegations, the father had no opportunity to challenge them. Mostyn J appeared somewhat concerned about this outcome, but was able to rely on the fact that it was proved that Y had suffered severe trauma in childhood and the parents had failed to offer an adequate explanation for that. He refused to authorise a care plan that involved sending the child to Y's parents, although indicated that a plan that Y's sister would offer care could be approved.

It is important for a judge to consider all of the evidence in the round. In *Re B-T (A Child: Threshold Conditions)*[348] the Court of Appeal accepted that in relation to each proven incident looked at alone, it might not be said the child was at risk of suffering significant harm. However, when all the incidents were viewed together this created a convincing case for saying the child was likely to suffer significant harm.

C Harm attributable to the care given or likely to be given or the child's being beyond parental control

The court must be satisfied that the harm is attributable to the care of the child not being what it would be reasonable to expect a parent to give. In *Islington London Borough Council v Al Alas, Wray and Al Alas-Wray (Through Her Children's Guardian)*[349] the injuries to the child were the result of a medical condition and not the care of the parents. Therefore, of course, the threshold criteria were not made out. Similarly, in *Leicester City Council v AB*[350] the threshold criteria were held not to be made out where the mother had suffered a terminal illness and

---

[345] [2013] EWCA Civ 899.
[346] [2013] UKSC 33.
[347] [2017] EWFC 36.
[348] [2020] EWCA Civ 697.
[349] [2012] EWHC 865 (Fam).
[350] [2018] EWHC 1960 (Fam).

asked the local authority to provide accommodation for her children under s. 20 when she became too ill to care for them. Keehan J found she had behaved as a responsible, loving and caring mother and so it could not be said that any risk of harm was attributable to the parental care. The following case is another good example of this important point:

CASE: *Re X (Child with profound disability)* [2016] EWFC B100

A mother was struggling to care for a child (X) with profound disabilities. The mother asked for the local authority's help and the care was subsequently shared, with X spending time with her mother and alternating between two children's homes. The local authority sought a care order. Simon Woods QC declined to make one. He accepted that it was 'not ideal' that X lived in three homes but X did not appear to find it a problem. The fact the mother could not offer full-time care was the sheer exhaustion of the level of care required, and the fact she had a 14-year-old son to care for too. The local authority had relied on times when the mother had been unwell, overwhelmed or emotionally upset as evidence she was unable to provide the level of care required. However, the judge found these were the product of the exhausting nature of the care she had to provide. The threshold criteria were not made out.

The threshold criteria can be satisfied if the parent fails to protect the child from harm at the hands of another.[351] It is important to remember that, as Wall LJ stated in ***Re L (A Child) (Care Proceedings: Responsibility for Child's Injury)***,[352] 'a child may receive serious accidental injuries whilst in the care of his or her parents, even where those parents are both conscientious and competent'. The obvious point is that the fact a child has suffered a serious injury does not mean the child has not been given the care by her parents that she should have been. Similarly, a child's harm may result from the parenting, even though the parents are well motivated and doing their best[353] and cannot be blamed for their failings.[354]

(i) 'Diverse standards of parenting'

The Supreme Court in ***Re B (Care Proceedings: Appeal)***[355] emphasised that a court should be careful not to make a care order simply because they disapprove of the parents' character or beliefs. Only if a parent's behaviour causes the child harm or puts the child at risk of harm can it justify a care order. As Lady Hale put it:

We are all frail human beings, with our fair share of unattractive character traits, which sometimes manifest themselves in bad behaviours which may be copied by our children. But the state does not and cannot take away the children of all the people who commit crimes, who abuse alcohol or drugs, who suffer from physical or mental illnesses or disabilities, or who espouse anti-social political or religious beliefs.

---

[351] *A v Leeds City Council* [2011] EWCA Civ 1365.
[352] [2006] 1 FCR 285.
[353] *X v Liverpool City Council* [2005] EWCA Civ 1173.
[354] *Wandsworth London Borough Council v M (Rev. 2)* [2017] EWHC 2435 (Fam).
[355] [2013] UKSC 33.

She went on to approve the dicta of Hedley J in *Re L (Care: Threshold Criteria)*:[356]

> [S]ociety must be willing to tolerate very diverse standards of parenting, including the eccentric, the barely adequate and the inconsistent. It follows too that children will inevitably have both very different experiences of parenting and very unequal consequences flowing from it. It means that some children will experience disadvantage and harm, while others flourish in atmospheres of loving security and emotional stability. These are the consequences of our fallible humanity and it is not the provenance of the state to spare children all the consequences of defective parenting. In any event, it simply could not be done.[357]

That quote is now regularly cited by the courts and makes an important point. Simply because failing in parenthood can be identified and a judge might be readily persuaded that the parent does not deserve the 'Parent of the Year' award, does not mean that the threshold criteria is satisfied. As Aikens LJ put it in *Re J (A Child)*,[358] it is 'vital that local authorities, and, even more importantly, judges, bear in mind that nearly all parents will be imperfect in some way or other'. That is probably uncontroversial, but there is serious debate over how far 'diverse standards of parenting' should be accepted.

In *Re A (Application for Care and Placement Orders: Local Authority Failings)*[359] a mother was imprisoned, but the father was willing to look after the child. He was a member of the English Defence League;[360] had alleged drug and alcohol misuse; had not 'always been honest with professionals' and had early sexual experience.[361] Sir James Munby J held that although he was 'not the best of parents' nor the most 'suitable role model' that was not a reason for applying for a care order and seeking adoption. Perhaps more controversially His Honour Judge Jack in *North East Lincolnshire Council v G and L*[362] was considering a care order application in a case where there had been domestic violence between the parents and alcohol misuse. He stated:

> The reality is that in this country there must be tens of thousands of children who are cared for in homes where there is a degree of domestic violence (now very widely defined) and where parents on occasion drink more than they should. I am not condoning that for a moment, but the courts are not in the business of social engineering. The courts are not in the business of providing children with perfect homes. If we took into care and placed for adoption every child whose parents had had a domestic spat and every child whose parents on occasion had drunk too much then the care system would be overwhelmed and there would not be enough adoptive parents. So we have to have a degree of realism about prospective carers who come before the courts.

That case should certainly not be taken to suggest that domestic abuse cannot be used as the basis for a care order, as it is well established that it can.[363] Certainly there are grave concerns that victims of domestic abuse are thereby assumed to be unsuitable parents.[364] In one case authorising a care order it was said, 'The mother has repeatedly engaged in relationships characterised by violence and abuse, numerous incidents of which have been witnessed by the children.' This way of putting it can be seen to be blaming the mother for the abuse she has suffered and the impact on the children.

---

[356] [2007] 1 FLR 2050.
[357] Paragraph 50.
[358] [2015] EWCA 222, para 56.
[359] [2015] EWFC 11.
[360] A political group which many would regard as racist.
[361] See Flacks (2019) for a discussion of how parents with drug issues are treated in child protection proceedings.
[362] [2014] EWCC B77 (Fam).
[363] *Re T (Application to Revoke a Placement Order: Change in Circumstances)* [2014] EWCA Civ 1369.
[364] Thompson (2020).

(ii) Disabled parents

The courts have also considered cases where the parents have learning difficulties. There has been a shift in attitude in recent years and it is clear disabled parents should receive the support they need to be adequate parents. As Baker J put it in **Kent County Council v A Mother**:[365]

> The last thirty years have seen a radical reappraisal of the way in which people with a learning disability are treated in society. It is now recognised that they need to be supported and enabled to lead their lives as full members of the community, free from discrimination and prejudice . . . One consequence of this change in attitudes has been a wider acceptance that people with learning disability may, in many cases, with assistance, be able to bring up children successfully.

In **Wirrall BC v M**[366] Greensmith J explained:

> It is established that parents should be supported by The State to the extent that it is necessary to do so and such supports the welfare of the child; this has been referred to as 'supported parenting'.

In **Re D (Adoption) (No. 3)**[367] Munby J reluctantly accepted that even with support the parents with learning difficulties could not provide 'good enough' care for their child, because their child had complex needs they were unable to meet. In **Re G**[368] Dancey J held that although an effective package could be provided for the parents, the child's 'parenting would, in reality become parenting by his professional and other carers rather than by his parents, with all the adverse consequences for his emotional development and future welfare.'

(iii) Attributable to which parent's care?

A rather different issue concerning the 'attributable' condition has been raised by Andrew Bainham:

> Suppose that the parents separated when the children were very young and the threshold concerns relate exclusively to the mother and her later partners. There is nothing at all in the threshold relating to the father of the children (unless, as in some cases, the authority may wish to assert against him a failure to protect or that he has effectively abandoned the children). Why should the father not be able to argue at the final hearing that the court should need to be satisfied that the children would suffer significant harm or be at risk of it in his care, or, as it is commonly put, that he cannot provide 'good enough' care?[369]

His point with this hypothetical is that a care order could be made on the basis of the mother's lack of care, but that does not justify the order being made against the father. In such a case it might be thought that the welfare principle could be used to say the care order is not appropriate because the father can look after the child. However, that does not offer as strong a protection for the father, as is generally offered to parents by s. 31.

(iv) Lack of care by parent or another?

What happens if it is clear that the child had been harmed, but it is not clear who caused the harm? As a reminder, s. 31 states: '[T]hat the harm, or likelihood of harm, is attributable to: (i) the care given to the child, or likely to be given to him if the order were not made, not

---

[365] [2011] EWHC 402 (Fam).
[366] LV18C00700.
[367] [2016] EWFC 1.
[368] [2017] EWFC B94.
[369] Bainham (2019).

being what it would be reasonable to expect a parent to give him . . . ' Does that mean it must be shown the parent harmed the child?

The House of Lords in *Lancashire CC v B* examined this issue.[370]

CASE: *Lancashire CC v B* [2000] 1 FCR 509

The case involved child A, who was being cared for by a childminder while her parents were out at work. It became clear that A had suffered serious non-accidental head injuries, but it was impossible to establish whether these injuries were caused by the mother, the father or the childminder. The parents argued that s. 31(2)(b) required proof that it was the care of the parents (or primary carers) which was not of the standard expected of a reasonable parent and, as it was not clear that they had harmed the child, the care order should not be made. The local authority argued that all that needed to be shown was that the care given by someone who was caring for the child was below the standard expected of a reasonable parent. In other words, the reference to parents in s. 31(2)(b) was a reference to the standard of care expected and not a requirement that it was a parent whose care was less than the required standard.

The House of Lords acknowledged that there were difficulties with either interpretation. If the parents' argument was accepted, then a child might undoubtedly be suffering significant harm but, because it was not clear who had caused the harm, no protection could be offered. As Lord Nicholls maintained: '[s]uch an interpretation would mean that the child's future health, or even her life, would have to be hazarded on the chance that, after all, the non-parental carer rather than one of the parents inflicted the injuries.'[371] On the other hand, if the view of the local authority was accepted, a child could be taken into care even though the parents were blameless. The approach taken by the House of Lords steers a middle course between these views and holds that if it is clear that either of the parents or one of the primary carers caused the harm, the attributable condition has been made out.[372]

One difficulty with the House of Lords' decision is that it is far from clear who is 'a carer' in this context. In *Redbridge LB v B, C and A*[373] it was unclear if a child had been injured by a parent or a healthcare worker at the hospital. It was held that the threshold criteria were made out because the healthcare worker was a carer while the child was at the hospital. A wide interpretation was given in *Yorkshire County Council v SA*[374] where the term 'carer' was said to cover 'people with access to the child' but not 'anyone who had even a fleeting contact with the child in circumstances where there was the opportunity to cause injuries'. That seems to widen the concept of caring. A cleaner at the school would have access to the child, but would not normally be seen as a carer. A much narrower interpretation was given in *Re B (Children: Uncertain Perpetrator)*[375] where Peter Jackson LJ stated that the concept does not apply in a case of 'harm caused by someone outside the home or family unless it would have been reasonable

---

[370] [2000] 1 FCR 509, discussed in Bainham (2000a).
[371] *Lancashire CC v B* [2000] 1 All ER 97 at p. 103.
[372] See *Merton LBC v K* [2005] Fam Law 446 for an application of this approach.
[373] [2011] EWHC 517 (Fam).
[374] [2003] EWCA Civ 839, para 25. Comments approved in *Re B (Children: Uncertain Perpetrator)* [2019] EWCA Civ 575.
[375] [2019] EWCA Civ 575.

to expect a parent to have prevented it.' That approach has much to be said for it because it means the threshold criteria will apply where either the parent can be blamed for harming the child or failing to protect the child. However, it seems to be the approach rejected by the House of Lords in *Lancashire*.

The problem with the approach taken in *Lancashire* is that the House of Lords did not explain why it matters if the harm is from a carer or not. One can make a theoretically sound argument for saying either: (a) based on a child protection approach, if the child is facing harm it does not matter who is posing the risk, the child should be able to be taken into care; or (b) based on a parents' rights approach, only if the parents pose a risk to the child should the parents have their child removed. But saying, as their Lordships do, that if either a parent or carer harm the child the child can be taken into care, even if the parents are blameless, does not seem to make sense from either a child protection nor parental rights perspective. If a child should not be denied protection because it is unclear whether the harm is caused by a parent or childminder, why should he or she be denied protection if it is unclear whether the harm is caused by a parent or a non-carer (e.g. a bully at school)?

(v) Unknown perpetrators

The House of Lords in *Lancashire CC v B*[376] provided clear guidance on when the threshold criteria would be satisfied in a case where it was unclear if the risk to the child came from a parent or non-parent. Harder cases are those where it is not known whether the perpetrator of the abuse was one parent or the other and the parents have now separated. The problem is this: say the child was harmed while in the home but we do not know if it was the mother or the father. The couple have separated and the child now lives with the mother. Do we say, she may have abused the child and so there is a risk of harm and a care order can be made? Or do we say, it has not been proved she posed a risk of harm to the child and so a care order ought not to be made? The Supreme Court returned to that issue in three cases: *Re O and N (Children) (Non-Accidental Injury)*,[377] *Re S-B*[378] and *Re J (Children)*.[379] We will focus on the most recent of these, *Re J (Children)*, because that built on the earlier decisions and sets out the current law.

CASE: *Re J (Children)* [2013] UKSC 9

A couple had started a relationship in 2008. The mother had a child from a previous relationship (IJ) and the father had two children (HT and TJ). The three children all lived with the couple. The local authority became aware that the mother's first child had died and as a result another child had been taken into care. The investigations into the death found that the baby had died as a result of deliberate injuries, but were unable to establish who had caused the injuries. Both the mother and her ex-partner were in the 'pool of possible perpetrators'. Based on this history, the local authority brought care proceedings in relation to the child currently living with the mother. The key issue was whether the fact that the mother was in the pool of possible perpetrators in a previous case could be relied upon to establish that the child was at risk in relation to the current one.

---

[376] [2000] 1 All ER 97.
[377] [2003] 1 FCR 673, [2003] UKHL 18.
[378] Discussed in Keating (2009); Cobley and Lowe (2009).
[379] [2013] UKSC 9.

The Supreme Court determined that there were no proven facts which could be relied upon to make the care order. The fact the mother was in the pool of possible perpetrators was simply a finding there was a 'real possibility' she was involved in the death and not a finding of fact she was. A care order could not be based on the basis of reasonable suspicion. Lady Hale was clear:

> The judge found the threshold crossed in relation to [the child who had not been harmed] on the basis that there was a real possibility that the mother had injured [her other child]. That . . . is not a permissible approach to a finding of likelihood of future harm . . . a prediction of future harm has to be based upon findings of actual fact made on the balance of probabilities. It is only once those facts have been found that the degree of likelihood of future events becomes the 'real possibility' test adopted in *Re H*. It might have been open to the judge to find the threshold crossed in relation to [the unharmed child] on a different basis but she did not do so.

There had to be an objective factual basis from which the inference could be drawn that future harm was likely. In this case, had the local authority been able to find other facts this could have made out the case for the care order. For example, the local authority might have relied on the mother's attempts to disguise the injuries from medical professionals in the earlier cases, a fact which had been proved to be true. If there were other facts which led to the finding of a risk of harm, the fact the mother was in the pool of possible perpetrators could be taken into account in deciding what order to make (Lord Wilson dissented on that point, deciding that only facts proved could be used at all stages of the care proceedings).[380] That might include facts about the circumstances surrounding the original injury; the response of the parent to the injury; or any evidence of concealment or collusion surrounding the injury. For example, if the mother and father were possible perpetrators because it was not clear who had harmed the child, but it was established that the mother had failed to call for medical help when she discovered the injuries, that could be used to establish the threshold criteria.[381]

Lord Wilson (with whom Lord Sumption agreed) regarded this position as illogical because 'if, for the purpose of the requisite foundation, X's consignment to a pool has a value of zero on its own, it can, for this purpose, have no greater value in company'. Lord Hope most clearly articulated the flaw in this reasoning. In essence it involved an assumption that because something was not a sufficient fact it was also not a relevant fact.

The case law has been subjected to sustained criticism by Mary Hayes and other commentators.[382] At the heart of the objection is the complaint that the law means that children can be left with a parent who is a possible perpetrator of serious abuse, with no protection. Certainly, the current law can produce some strange distinctions. One scenario was put to the Court of Appeal:

> Take . . . a case of two parents who are consigned to a pool of possible perpetrators of non-accidental injuries to their child; and who then separate; and who each with other partners, produce a further child, who together become the subject of conjoined care proceedings.[383]

---

[380] *A Local Authority v A Mother* [2012] EWHC 2647 (Fam).
[381] *Re R (A Child)* [2013] EWCA Civ 1438; *LA v FM* [2013] EWHC 4671 (Fam); *Re S (A Child) (Care Proceedings: Non-accidental Injuries)* [2014] 1 FCR 128.
[382] Hayes (2014).
[383] *Re J (Children)* [2012] EWCA Civ 380.

Because in this scenario we do not know as a fact that either parent abused the child, the court cannot, without further evidence, make a care order in respect of either child, even though we know that one of the children is living with a person with a history of serious abuse, who must pose a risk to the child.

Not everyone will be disquieted with this outcome. It rests in part on a judgment: which is worse: to remove a child from an 'innocent' parent or to leave a child with an abusive one? The current law seems more concerned to avoid the former harm than the latter. If one wanted to support that view one could argue that just because a parent has abused in the past is no guarantee they will abuse again. Further that if the child is removed and alternative care is found we cannot guarantee that the alternative care will not be abusive.

Another odd consequence of the current state of the law is that if **Re M, Lancashire CC v A** and **Re J** are considered together, they can produce a result Mary Hayes describes:

> The impact of the Supreme Court's rulings now mean that where parents, two possible perpe-trators of significant harm to their child, are living together when the local authority first take protective action the threshold test will be applied at that point in time. The threshold can be crossed in relation to an unharmed sibling even though, as the case progresses, that child lives with just one parent, and the parents part shortly after the care proceedings commence. By con-trast, where parents separate before the local authority first take protective action, the threshold test cannot be crossed in relation to the unharmed child.

John Hayes[384] suggests that the correctness of the case depends on the perspective from which it is looked at:

> Those who believe that *Re J* . . . [was] rightly decided might counter by asking you to put yourself in the shoes of the innocent parent. Imagine, they argue, being faced with the risk of removal of your unharmed child in circumstances where the court has identified you not as an actual perpetrator but only as a possible perpetrator of harm to another child? Looked at purely from the perspective of that person, the argument appears to have some force. But what if you put yourself in the shoes of the child?

He suggests few people would choose to stay in a hotel run by a person who was one of two people who might have seriously assaulted hotel guests in the past.

Andrew Bainham[385] is much more supportive:

> [I]t is unacceptable in a democratic society that children should be removed in the longer term, as opposed to the interim, on the basis only of suspicion rather than proof. Otherwise, no parents under previous suspicion would ever feel able to have another child or rebuild their family lives without the spectre of local authority involvement hanging over them and their partners. Where, as will almost invariably be the case, there are present concerns relating to the current family situation, there is nothing in this decision which remotely prevents the appropriate protective action being taken. It is right that the state should demonstrate that it has real concerns which are not solely historical.

One result of the debates over the 'pool of perpetrators' cases is that more attention is being paid as to when it is suitable to place someone as a possible perpetrator. The court should do this when there is a real possibility that a person harmed the child. If it is clear on the balance

---

[384] Hayes (2014); Gilmore (2016).
[385] Bainham (2013).

of probabilities who is the perpetrator only that person should be listed. If it is unclear whether the injuries caused to the child have an innocent explanation or are the result of parental abuse it is not appropriate to use the 'possible perpetrator'.[386] So in *Re D (A Child)*[387] the oxygen supply to a child's ventilator stopped working while the mother and a student nurse were in the room. It was not appropriate to list the mother and student nurse as possible perpetrators as the evidence suggested it was a real possibility it was a malfunctioning of the machine. In *Re B (Children: Uncertain Perpetrator)*[388] the Court of Appeal emphasised it would be wrong to ask whether a person should be excluded from the pool of possible per- petrators. The correct approach was to ask whether the evidence showed on the balance of probabilities there was a real possibility that the person was a possible perpetrator. Peter Jackson LJ explained:

> The court should first consider whether there is a 'list' of people who had the opportunity to cause the injury. It should then consider whether it can identify the actual perpetrator on the balance of probability and should seek, but not strain, to do so . . . Only if it cannot identify the perpetrator to the civil standard of proof should it go on to ask in respect of those on the list: 'Is there a likelihood or real possibility that A or B or C was the perpetrator or a perpetrator of the inflicted injuries?' Only if there is should A or B or C be placed into the 'pool'.[389]

When the court comes to consider the welfare stage of the analysis, the strength of the evidence against a possible perpetrator will be taken into account.[390]

(vi) Beyond parental control

Subsection 31(2) of the Children Act 1989 also includes cases where the child is suffering harm or is likely to suffer harm because he or she is beyond parental control. The kind of situation here is where the child behaves in an uncontrolled manner. Commonly, it is used where the child is dependent upon illegal drugs. It does not matter if it is unclear whether the harm is caused by the parent or the child being beyond parental control. Ewbank J in *Re O (A Minor) (Care Order: Education: Procedure)*[391] suggested: '. . . where a child is suffering harm in not going to school and is living at home it will follow that either the child is beyond her parents' control or that they are not giving the child the care that it would be reasonable to expect a parent to give'. Where this ground is relied upon, it is not necessary to show that this is caused by the parenting of the child.[392] In *Re T (A Child: Care Order: Beyond Parental Control: Deprivation of Liberty: Authority to Administer Medication)*[393] the court considered a boy on the autism spectrum and with learning dif- ficulties who behaved in an extremely challenging way. Judge Howe QC found the 'beyond parental control' ground made out, describing it as a 'no fault' ground and saying it could be made out whether the source of the problem was the inabilities of the parents or the behaviour of the child.

---

[386] *A Local Authority v NB* [2013] EWHC 4100 (Fam).
[387] [2014] EWHC 121 (Fam).
[388] [2019] EWCA Civ 575.
[389] Para 49.
[390] *Re B (Children: Uncertain Perpetrator)* [2019] EWCA Civ 575.
[391] [1992] 2 FLR 7.
[392] *Re K (A Child: Post Adoption Placement Breakdown)* [2012] EWHC B9 (Fam).
[393] [2017] EWFC B1.

(vii) The role of the threshold criteria

One issue behind many of the cases interpreting s. 31 is the role of the threshold criteria. Here are three popular views:

1. According to Lord Nicholls in **Re O and N**,[394] the purpose of the threshold criteria is 'to protect families, both adults and children, from inappropriate interference in their lives by public authorities through the making of care and supervision orders'.
2. The threshold criteria are there to reinforce the welfare principle and to remind courts that children are normally best brought up by their parents and only where there is a real danger will it be in the child's welfare for a care order to be made.
3. The threshold criteria exist to protect parents' rights. The state in effect guarantees to parents that, unless they cause significant harm to their children, their children will not be removed.

Lady Hale in **Re J (Children)**[395] combined these theories in saying this:

> In a free society, it is a serious thing indeed for the state compulsorily to remove a child from his family of birth. Interference with the right to respect for family life, protected by article 8 of the European Convention on Human Rights, can only be justified by a pressing social need. Yet it is also a serious thing for the state to fail to safeguard its children from the neglect and ill-treatment which they may suffer in their own homes. This may even amount to a violation of their right not to be subjected to inhuman or degrading treatment, protected by Article 3 of the Convention. How then is the law to protect the family from unwarranted intrusion while at the same time protecting children from harm?

In England and Wales, the Children Act 1989 tries to balance these two objectives by setting a threshold which must be crossed before a court can consider what order, if any, should be made to enable the authorities to protect a child. The threshold is designed to restrict compulsory intervention to cases which genuinely warrant it, while enabling the court to make the order which will best promote the child's welfare once the threshold has been crossed.

D Grounds for supervision and care orders: the welfare test

The court must not reason that, because the threshold criteria are satisfied, the care or supervision order must be made. It is crucial for the court to consider whether the making of the order is in the child's welfare and whether the 'no order principle' is satisfied.[396] The court considers whether making the order is the best option for promoting the welfare of the child, considering the checklist of factors in s. 1(3) must be taken into account.[397] In considering the welfare of the child, the views of the child may be relevant.[398] Indeed in the case of older children they may dominate the assessment.[399]

(i) The welfare test and proportionality

When a local authority is applying for a care order, it must prepare a care plan.[400] This sets out what the local authority proposes should happen to the child while he or she is in care. It will

---

[394] [2003] 1 FCR 673 at para 14.
[395] [2013] UKSC 9.
[396] **Re O and N (Children) (Non-Accidental Injury)** [2003] 1 FCR 673 at para 23, *per* Lord Nicholls.
[397] CA 1989, s. 1(4)(b).
[398] **Re H (Care Order: Contact)** [2009] 2 FLR 55.
[399] **Wandsworth London Borough Council v M (Rev. 2)** [2017] EWHC 2435 (Fam).
[400] CA 1989, s. 31A; **Manchester City Council v F** [1993] 1 FLR 419, [1993] 1 FCR 1000.

suggest, for example, where the child should live; whether the authority intends to plan for adoption or special guardianship; and what contact there should be with the birth family. The court, when considering whether to make the care order, should take into account the care plan.[401] However, the court must consider any alternative possibilities. Those might include whether there are any relatives[402] (or perhaps even a family friend) who can look after the child.

In *Re B-S (Adoption: Application of s. 47(5))*[403] and *Re G (Care Proceedings: Welfare Evaluation)*[404] the Court of Appeal emphasised that if the threshold criteria are met the judge should look at all the realistic options in the round to determine which was the least interventionist order which would promote the welfare of the child.[405] So, if the local authority is seeking to have the child adopted, the court should consider whether a residence order in favour of a family relative would be more appropriate. Similarly, if a care order is sought the court will consider whether a supervision order might adequately protect the child. What the court should not do is simply ask whether the order sought by the local authority will promote the welfare of the child, without considering the alternatives.[406] However, the court only needs to consider the realistic options.[407] In *Re H (A Child) (Placement Order: Judge's Understanding of Earlier Proceedings)*[408] the Court of Appeal emphasised they were not saying there was a presumption in favour of the birth family,[409] but rather that all realistic options needed to be considered before deciding that removal from the birth family was the best option.

Lord Neuberger *in Re B (Care Proceedings: Appeal)*[410] emphasised that even if the threshold criteria are satisfied an adoption should only be made if it is necessary to make it. It should be a 'last resort' or as Lady Hale put it when 'nothing else will do'. However, in *Re DAM (Children)*[411] the Court of Appeal emphasised that these comments only apply in cases where the plan is for the child to be adopted. It does not apply where a care order is considered.

(ii) Section 1(5)

Section 1(5) requires the court to be persuaded that it is better for the child to make the care or supervision order than not to make an order at all. This provision was discussed in detail earlier in the text (see Chapter 10).

10 Interim care orders

It may be that, having heard all the evidence, the court still feels it is not in a position to make a final decision of whether to make a care order or supervision order, or no order at all.[412] In such cases an interim order is appropriate.[413] An interim care order can only be made if there

---

[401] CA 1989, s. 31(3A).
[402] *Re Al-Hilli* [2013] EWHC 2299 (Fam); *Re N-B and Others (Children) (Residence: Expert Evidence)* [2002] 3 FCR 259.
[403] [2013] EWCA Civ 1146.
[404] [2013] EWCA Civ 965.
[405] *Re T (Application to Revoke a Placement Order: Change in Circumstances)* [2014] EWCA Civ 1369.
[406] *Re J (Children)* [2019] EWCA Civ 2300.
[407] Although in *Re Y (Care Proceedings: Proportionality Evaluation)* [2014] EWCA Civ 1553 it was said the court would assume the child was best brought up by the birth family unless there was evidence to the contrary.
[408] [2015] EWCA Civ 1284.
[409] *Re MR (Welfare Hearing: No. 2)* [2013] EWHC 1156 (Fam).
[410] [2013] UKSC 33.
[411] [2018] EWCA Civ 386.
[412] *Re S, Re W (Children: Care Plan)* [2002] 1 FCR 577 at para 90.
[413] *Re CH (Care or Interim Care Order)* [1998] 1 FLR 402, [1998] 2 FCR 347.

are reasonable grounds for believing that the threshold and s. 1 criteria are met;[414] the making of the order will be in the welfare of the child; and that making an interim care order is proportionate to the risk faced by the child.[415] It should be used to regulate matters that cannot wait until the full hearing.[416] If, when hearing an application for a care order or supervision order, the court is not convinced that the child is in need of immediate local authority care, it may consider just making an interim residence order[417] in favour of a relative. However, it may do so only if the court is persuaded that the child will be adequately protected without an interim care order or supervision order.[418] The aim of an interim order should be to keep children safe until an application for a full care order can be heard.[419] Children should only be removed from their parents under an interim care order if that is necessary to protect them from an imminent risk to their safety and the order is a proportionate response.[420] Removal might be necessary so that a proper assessment of the parents can be made, which cannot safely be done while the children remain at home.[421] An application for an interim care order is, therefore, not the time to consider the long-term future of the child.[422] An interim supervision order may be appropriate in a case where the needs of the child are unclear and so the local authority are not in a position to determine whether a care order is an appropriate consideration.[423]

These interim orders provide a legal framework until a final order can be made. In *Re G (A Child) (Interim Care Order: Residential Assessment)*[424] Lord Scott explained:

> [A]n 'interim' care order is a temporary order, applied for and granted in care proceedings as an interim measure until sufficient information can be obtained about the child, the child's family, the child's circumstances and the child's need to enable a final decision in the care proceedings to be made.

It is important to stress that, as was made clear in *Re G (Minors) (Interim Care Order)*,[425] the fact that an interim order is made does not weigh on the court one way or the other in deciding the final order.[426] To make an interim supervision order or interim care order, the court must be satisfied that there are reasonable grounds for believing that the criteria under s. 31(2) of the Children Act 1989 (the threshold criteria) have been satisfied, but they do not have to prove the conditions exist.[427] Andrew Bainham claims that in practice this means it is very rare for a local authority to fail in an application for an interim care order.[428]

---

[414] CA 1989, s. 38(2), discussed in *Re B (Children)*, CA 16 August 2012..

[415] *Re G (Interim Care Order)* [2011] EWCA Civ 745; *Re GR (Interim Care Order)* [2010] EWCA Civ 871; *Re S (Interim Care Order)*, [2010] EWCA Civ 1383. See Bainham (2011) for an argument that the barrier is set too low for interim care orders.

[416] *Re C (A Child: Interim Separation)* [2020] EWCA Civ 257; *Re C (A Child) (Interim Separation)* [2019] EWCA Civ 1998.

[417] CA 1989, s. 1(1) and (5) would have to be satisfied.

[418] CA 1989, s. 38(3).

[419] *Re L (Interim Care Order: Prison Mother and Baby Unit)* [2013] EWCA Civ 489.

[420] *Re C (A Child: Interim Separation)* [2020] EWCA Civ 257; *Re L (Children: Interim Care Order)* [2016] EWCA Civ 1110.

[421] *Re B (Interim Care Order)* [2010] EWCA Civ 324.

[422] *Re L (Interim Care Order: Prison Mother and Baby Unit)* [2013] EWCA Civ 489.

[423] *Re L (Children: Interim Care Order)* [2016] EWCA Civ 1110.

[424] [2005] 3 FCR 621 at para 2.

[425] [1993] 2 FLR 839, [1993] 2 FCR 557.

[426] *Re B (Care Proceedings: Interim Care Order)* [2009] EWCA Civ 1254.

[427] *Re B (A Minor) (Care Order: Criteria)* [1993] 1 FLR 815, [1993] 1 FCR 565.

[428] Bainham (2014).

On the making of an interim care order, the local authority gains all the benefits and obligations of a care order: parental responsibility is placed on the local authority and the child is in the care of the local authority. However, the local authority should consult with the parents on all important issues relating to the child. If there is a dispute the matter should be brought to the court.[429]

While it is not possible for a court to attach a condition to a full care order, it can to an interim care order. There are two leading cases. The first is *Re C (Interim Care Order: Residential Assessment)*.[430] The House of Lords had to consider s. 38(6), which states:

> Where the court makes an interim care order, or interim supervision order, it may give such directions (if any) as it considers appropriate with regard to the medical or psychiatric examination or other assessment of the child . . . [431]

Their lordships held that this provision covered parents being assessed at a residential unit, so the court would have more evidence as to whether they posed a risk to the child. This was acceptable because it was necessary to enable the court to decide what order should be made.[432]

The decision in *Re C* does not sit easily with the general approach taken in the Children Act 1989 that the courts should not compel local authorities to spend their social services budget in a particular way.[433] In *Re C (Children) (Residential Assessment)*[434] the local authority argued that to be required to provide a residential assessment for the particular family would be to involve a disproportionate level of expenditure on one family, among all of those they had to care for. The Court of Appeal rejected this argument, but significantly on the basis that the local authority had not produced evidence to substantiate its claim. It was accepted that if such evidence had been forthcoming then the decision would have been different.

The second leading case on attaching conditions to an interim care order is *Re G (A Child) (Interim Care Order: Residential Assessment)*.[435] There a judge had attached a condition to an interim residence order requiring the local authority to fund an assessment of a mother, her new partner and their child at a hospital which specialised in multi-problem families. Their Lordships held that conditions attached through s. 38(6) had to have as their purpose the gathering of information. In this case the hospital would be engaged in providing treatment, advice and help for the family, as much as, if not more than, gathering information. Any assessment or examination must be for the purpose of gathering information and to provide treatment to the child or her parents. To use s. 38(6) as the judge had done was to contravene the 'cardinal principle' in the Children Act that the courts could not order local authorities to provide particular services to children in care. Similarly, in *Re Y (A Child)*[436] s. 38(6) could not be used to authorise a parent to attend a clinic that helped drug-dependent parents come off drugs. The clinic offered treatment, not assessment. Also, if the assessment was not actually going to help the court resolve the case that would be a strong reason not to order it.[437]

---

[429] *R (on the application of H) v Kingston Upon Hull CC* [2013] EWHC 388 (Admin).
[430] [1997] 1 FLR 1, [1997] 1 FCR 149.
[431] CA 1989, s. 38(7A) states that the assessment can be ordered only if the court is of the opinion that the examination or other assessment is necessary to assist the court to resolve the proceedings justly.
[432] *Re W (Care: Residential Assessment)* [2011] EWCA Civ 661.
[433] In *Re A (Residential Assessment)* [2009] EWHC 865 (Fam) it was confirmed that an assessment could be required, while the child lived with an aunt and great grandmother.
[434] [2001] 3 FCR 164.
[435] [2005] 3 FCR 621.
[436] [2018] EWCA Civ 992.
[437] *Re G (A Child: Section 38(6) Assessment)* [2020] EWCA Civ 282.

Section 38(6) states that children can refuse to participate in the assessment if they have sufficient understanding. Very controversially, in *South Glamorgan County Council v W and B*,[438] the court held that a court order under the inherent jurisdiction could override the refusal of a child. This seems to go against the normal position that an order under the inherent jurisdiction cannot run counter to a statutory provision. Here, s. 38(6) explicitly gives the child the right to refuse.

11 Care proceedings: procedural issues

Significant work has been done to improve the procedures behind care applications, developing a Public Law Outline which sets out requirements of good practice in preparing cases for care proceedings.[439] One study found that as a result of following the Public Law Outline nearly a quarter of children in their sample were diverted from the care proceedings, as a result of the recommended meetings with parents and interested parties, and early court hearings to determine what needs to be done to prepare the case for the full hearing.[440] There are, however, tensions here.[441] The more that is done in terms of preparatory meetings, the greater the risk of delay. The quicker the proceedings, the greater the risk that an alternative to care will be overlooked. The Children and Families Act imposes a 26-week time limit on care proceedings.[442] Notably, s. 14(3) provides for extensions to the time limit in eight-week increments only if there is 'special justification'. In *Re S (Parenting Assessment)*,[443] the first reported case on the extension provisions, Munby P quoted a comment of Pauffley J's: 'justice must never be sacrificed upon the altar of speed.' That said, he added, there needed to be strong reason to extend the permitted time period. There were three issues to consider. The first is whether there is evidence that the parent is committed to making the changes necessary to make a care order unnecessary. The second is whether there is evidence to believe that the parent will be able to maintain that commitment. The final question is whether there is evidence to believe the parent will be able to make such changes within the child's timescale.

The 26-week time limit has been criticised by Natasha Watson,[444] a lawyer specialising in childcare proceedings, who writes that the legal proceedings must be seen in the context of the broader response to child protection:

> From the perspective of the child 26 weeks is an artificial, lawyer-centric, construction. The journey for the child does not start or end with the court process. It starts from the time that the need for protection is identified. The bulk of child protection cases do not arise out of emergency applications. They rarely involve really deliberate child cruelty which has suddenly come to light. They are more usually a depressing collision of alcohol, drugs, mental health issues, domestic violence and poverty in every sense, including emotional.

---

[438] [1993] 1 FLR 574, [1993] 1 FCR 626.
[439] Children and Families Act 2014, ss. 13–15.
[440] Masson and Dickens (2013). See also Doughty (2014).
[441] Dickens (2014).
[442] Norgrave (2012).
[443] [2014] EWCC B44 (Fam).
[444] Watson (2014).

Faucet[445] expresses concerns that pressure to meet the deadlines has not prevented delay but that:

> the delay has simply been shifted from the proceedings stage to the period prior to proceedings. The need to ensure documents are ready and prepared, so as to enable local authorities to be confident the 26-week deadline will be met, places yet more pressure on already resource-stretched local authorities and consequently more delay at this earlier stage.

Another important procedural issue (raised in Chapter 2) is that legal aid restrictions have led to a growth in the number of litigants in person (LiPs) and difficulties in obtaining expert evidence. In *Re R (A Child)*[446] the difficulties of LiPs were acknowledged. It was said that local authorities will have to expect to assist LiPs in child protection cases.

12 Special guardianship

Learning objective 8

Explore the use of adoption and special guardianship

Now we turn to the long-term options for a local authority, if it believes the parents can no longer care for the child. One possibility is to apply for an adoption order, and we will explore that shortly. However, as we shall see, one of the major concerns over the nature of adoption in England and Wales is the way that it terminates the parental status of the birth parents. Those troubled by this have sought to replace adoption with a status which will provide security and an appropriate status for the new carer of the child, without ending completely the status of the birth parents.[447] Special guardianship seeks to do this. It was introduced in the Adoption and Children Act 2002.[448] This is not a replacement for adoption, but is an alternative to it. The White Paper mentions the kind of cases where special guardianship may be appropriate:

> Some older children do not wish to be legally separated from their birth families. Adoption may not be best for some children being cared for on a permanent basis by members of their wider birth family. Some minority ethnic communities have religious and cultural difficulties with adoption as it is set out in law. Unaccompanied asylum seeking children may also need secure, permanent homes, but have strong attachments to their families abroad.[449]

The Special Guardianship Guidance[450] lists some of the things special guardianship will do:

- Give the carer clear responsibility for all aspects of caring for the child and for taking the decisions to do with their upbringing. The child will no longer be looked after by a local authority.

- Provide a firm foundation on which to build a lifelong permanent relationship between the child and their carer.

- Be legally secure.

---

[445] Faucet (2019).
[446] [2014] EWCA Civ 597.
[447] Department of Health (2000: 248).
[448] See also Special Guardianship Regulations 2005 (SI 2005/1109) and Department for Education and Skills (2005c). Jordan and Lindley (2007) provide useful discussion of special guardianship.
[449] Department of Health (2000: para 5.9).
[450] Department for Education and Skills (2005a); Special Guardianship Regulations 2005 (SI 2005/1109).

- Preserve the basic link between the child and their birth family.
- Be accompanied by access to a full range of support services including, where appropriate, financial support.[451]

There were 3,830 special guardianship orders made in 2019 in relation to children being looked after by local authorities.[452] As we shall see, that is just slightly more than the number of adoptions. Typically, orders were made in favour of relatives with whom the child had been living for some time, particularly grandparents.[453] The children involved tend to be young, with the average age being of five years, seven months.[454]

A Who can apply for a special guardianship?

The following can apply for special guardianship:[455]

- any guardian of the child
- a local authority foster carer with whom the child has lived for one year immediately preceding the application
- anyone who holds a residence order with respect to the child, or who has the consent of all those in whose favour a residence order is in force
- anyone with whom the child has lived for three out of the last five years
- where the child is in the care of a local authority, any person who has the consent of the local authority
- anyone who has the consent of all those with parental responsibility for the child
- any person, including the child, who has the leave of the court to apply.

B The grounds for making a special guardianship order

A special guardianship order (SGO) can be made if it is in the welfare of the child to do so. The application is governed by s. 1 of the Children Act 1989. When considering an application for a special guardianship the court will, *inter alia,* take into account the applicant's connection with the child and (if the child is being looked after by a local authority) the local authority's plans for the child's future.[456]

Special guardianship is typically considered when the parents of the child cannot look after them and an alternative long-term carer is going to take on care. In such a case if adoption is not suitable, some kind of status is needed for that carer.[457] Special guardianship can give that form status and the security it brings.[458] A study of special guardianship found that the order gave the guardians a sense of security and a secure legal foundation.[459]

---

[451] A local authority scheme which paid special guardians at a reduced rate was found to be unlawful in *B v Lewisham BC* [2008] EWHC 738 (Admin).
[452] Office for National Statistics (2020).
[453] Ibid.
[454] Ibid.
[455] Children Act 1989, s. 14A
[456] CA 1989, s. 14A(12).
[457] *Northamptonshire County Council v M* [2017] EWHC 997 (Fam).
[458] *A Local Authority v Y, Z and Others* [2006] Fam Law 449.
[459] Wade, Dixon and Richards (2009).

In *Re M (Adoption or Residence Order)*[460] the child was strongly of the opinion that she did not want her links with her mother and siblings to be destroyed, even though she wished to live with the applicants in a permanent relationship. This is the kind of case where special guardianship will be considered.[461] In *Re F (Special Guardianship Order: Contact with Birth Family)*[462] it was decided the child should have contact with her great aunt so that the child's understanding of her cultural heritage could be retained. Given that links with the birth family were being retained it was held a special guardianship order was more sensible than adoption. The leading cases on when special guardianship is suitable are the following:

CASE: *Re S (A Child) (Adoption Order or Special Guardianship Order)* [2007] 1 FCR 271; *Re J (A Child) (Adoption Order or Special Guardianship Order)* [2007] 1 FCR 308; *Re M-J (A Child) (Adoption Order or Special Guardianship Order)* [2007] 1 FCR 329[463]

The cases all involved applicants who originally sought adoption, but for whom the local authority had proposed special guardianship. The courts made the following important points.

First, the court explained that there were fundamental differences between adoption and special guardianship. Of course, the most significant is that while adoption ends the parental status of the birth parents, special guardianship does not. The Court of Appeal was clear that these differences should be considered carefully when deciding between an adoption and special guardianship order.

Secondly, the court refused to accept that there were particular categories of cases where a special guardianship order was preferable to an adoption order or vice versa. In every case the question was simply one of asking what order would best promote the welfare of the child in question. In particular, there was no presumption that, where the child was to be raised within the wider family, a special guardianship was preferable to an adoption order. In *Re J* the argument that it would be confusing for a child to be raised under an adoption order by his uncle and aunt was rejected because the child knew the true family relationship. There was, therefore, no danger that the family relationships would be 'distorted' by an adoption order.

Thirdly, the court emphasised that, under the Human Rights Act 1998, the court must ensure that the intervention in family life was necessary and proportionate. As a special guardianship order was a less fundamental intervention than an adoption order, it should be preferred if it protects the welfare of the child to the same extent as an adoption order. In *Re S* it was held:

> In choosing between adoption and special guardianship, in most cases Article 8 is unlikely to add anything to the considerations contained in the respective welfare checklists. Under both statutes the welfare of the child is the court's paramount consideration, and the balancing exercise required by the statutes will be no different to that required by Article 8. However, in some cases, the fact that the welfare objective can be achieved with less disruption of existing family relationships can properly be regarded as helping to tip the balance.[464]

---

[460] [1998] 1 FLR 570.
[461] *Re K (Special Guardianship Order)* [2011] EWCA Civ 635.
[462] [2015] EWFC 25.
[463] For helpful discussions of these cases, see Bond (2007) and Bainham (2007).
[464] [2007] 1 FCR 271, para 49.

Fourthly, when considering whether to make a special guardianship order, it should be remembered that the child's parents will still be able to apply for section 8 orders. This is not true in the case of adoption. The special guardianship does not, therefore, provide the same permanency of protection as adoption. In a case (like *Re J*) where the carers and child needed an assurance that the placement could not be disturbed, then adoption may well be more appropriate. While it was true that, where a special guardianship order was made, a parent would need leave before making an application for a residence order, that did not provide the same level of security as an adoption order. A court could also make an order under s. 91(14) of the Children Act 1989 to require a parent seeking any section 8 order to obtain leave of the court first. Even then the level of security for special guardians would not match that available for adoption.

Fifthly, special guardianship orders can be made by the court on its own motion. In deciding whether to do so, the court must consider whether making the order against the wishes of the parties will promote the welfare interests of the child. A court can only make a guardianship order on its own motion when a report has been prepared by the local authority.[465]

In *Surrey County Council v Al-Hilli*[466] the children's parents were killed in tragic circumstances. The court ordered that a special guardianship order be made in favour of their aunt and uncle who had taken over their care. This gave them security with their new carers, while retaining the links with their deceased parents. That case can be contrasted with *N v B (Adoption by Grandmother)*[467] where adoption by a grandmother was appropriate after a father had murdered the mother and raped the aunt. This was better than special guardianship as the children needed to stay with the grandmother and the father's role in their life needed to be terminated.[468] The concern over the 'skewing' of relationship was of lesser concern as the children understood the position clearly. By contrast in *Cumbria CC v R*[469] it was held that children should be placed with the grandparents under an interim care order, rather than an SGO. The case was complex and the grandparents could receive the guidance, training and support under an interim care order which would not be available under an SGO.

C The effect of special guardianship

Special guardianship does not terminate the parental status of the birth parents, and special guardians are not treated as the parents of the child.[470] However, they are given many of the rights of a parent. They are able to make almost every decision about a child's upbringing. They can even change the child's name, with the consent of those with parental responsibility.[471]

---

[465] CA 1989, s. 14A(8).
[466] [2013] EWHC 3404.
[467] [2013] EWHC 820 (Fam).
[468] See also *Re T (A Child: Refusal of Adoption Order)* [2020] EWCA Civ 797.
[469] [2019] EWHC 2782 (Fam).
[470] Even where a special guardian has been appointed the birth parents will retain their rights in respect of adoption.
[471] CA 1989, s. 14C(3).

The status of special guardianship remains until revoked by an order of the court. It is, in a sense, a halfway house between a residence order and an adoption order.[472]

Often the court is choosing between special guardianship and adoption and so it is useful to consider their main differences:[473]

1. *The status of the carer.* The adopter becomes a parent for all purposes; the special guardian does not become a parent.

2. *The status of the birth family.* In adoption the child ceases to be a child of the birth family. That is not so in a case of special guardianship. In adoption the birth parents lose parental responsibility, while it is retained for birth parents in a case of special guardianship.[474] In a case of special guardianship, birth parents can seek contact orders, prohibited steps orders or specific issue orders without leave of the court. Special guardianship is, therefore, more suitable if there is to be an ongoing relationship with the birth family.[475]

3. *Duration.* An adoption order is life long[476] while a special guardianship order ceases on the child reaching age 18 or when it is revoked.

4. *Parental responsibility.* Adopters have full parental responsibility in the same way any other parent has. A special guardian's parental responsibility has limitations.[477] In particular:

   (i) Removal from the jurisdiction. A special guardian can remove a child from the country without leave for three months, but if they wish to remove the child for longer, they need the written consent of all those with parental responsibility or the leave of the court.

   (ii) Changing the name. Special guardians cannot change the child's surname without the written consent of all those with parental responsibility or an order of the court.

   (iii) Consent to adoption. The consent of both special guardians and birth parents is required before an adoption order can be made.

   (iv) Medical procedures. It may be that in the case of certain serious medical procedures (e.g. sterilisation) the consent of all those with parental responsibility will be required.

   (v) Voluntary accommodation. If a parent objects, it seems that a local authority cannot accommodate a child, even if the special guardians consent, without a court order.

5. *Death of the child.* Adopters have all the rights of a parent. Special guardians may not arrange for burials if the parents wish to undertake the arrangements.

6. *Revocation.* An adoption order is irrevocable, unless there are exceptional circumstances. Birth parents can apply for a special guardianship order to be revoked, with leave of the court.[478] Leave to apply for a revocation will only be granted if the application has a real prospect of showing there has been a significant change in circumstances.[479]

---

[472] Johnstone (2006: 116).
[473] See Schedule at the end of *Re AJ (A Child) (Adoption Order or Special Guardianship Order)* [2007] 1 FCR 308.
[474] CA 1989, s. 14C.
[475] *Re T (A Child: Adoption or Special Guardianship)* [2017] EWCA Civ 1797.
[476] ACA 2002, s. 67.
[477] CA 1989, s. 14C.
[478] CA 1989, s. 14D.
[479] *Re G (Special Guardianship Order)* [2010] EWCA Civ 300; *H v G (Adoption: Appeal)* [2013] EWHC 2136 (Fam).

7. *Financial support.* Following an adoption, birth parents cease to have any financial responsibilities for children. This is not so in a case of special guardianship. The guardians are entitled to a special guardianship allowance which is designed to cover the cost of caring for the child.[480]

8. *Intestacy.* If adopters die, their adopted children have rights of intestate succession. This is not so for children whose special guardians die.

D Variation and discharge of special guardianship

A special guardianship can be varied or discharged on the application of the following:[481]

(a) the special guardian;

(b) the child's birth parents or guardian, with the leave of the court;

(c) the child with the leave of the court;

(d) any individual who presently has the benefit of a residence order;

(e) any individual who had parental responsibility immediately before the making of the special guardianship order, with the leave of the court;

(f) the local authority, but only where a care order is made in respect of the child;

(g) the court on its own motion in any case where the welfare of the child arises.

Any application to revoke special guardianship must obtain the leave of the court.[482] Unless the application is by the local authority, the child or the special guardian him- or herself it needs to be shown that there has been a significant change in the circumstances from when the special guardianship order was made. This makes the special guardianship a little more secure than a residence order.[483]

E An assessment of special guardianship

The success of special guardianship flows from the fact that children and would-be adopters are satisfied it provides them with the sense of security and belonging together as a family which adoption has been said traditionally to provide.[484]

Another issue which is key to the success of a special guardianship is the relationship between the special guardian and the birth parents. The following case provides a vivid example of how special guardianship can produce tensions between the parents and special guardians.

> **CASE: *Re L (A Child) (Special Guardianship Order and Ancillary Orders)* [2007] 1 FCR 804**
>
> The parents of child L were drug addicts in a volatile relationship. When L was just three months old, she was placed with her grandparents, who were granted a residence order. Two years later, the grandparents sought an adoption order, but the judge made a special

---

[480] *R (Barrett) v Kirklees Metropolitan Council* [2010] 2 FCR 153. Although the local authority can determine the level of the award there need to be good reasons for it to be lower than the amounts paid to foster carers.

[481] CA 1989, s. 14D.

[482] One exception is where the child is applying (CA 1989, s. 14D(5)).

[483] Department of Health (2002: 50).

[484] It has been suggested that the practice of local authorities of paying a lower level of allowance to special guardians was making them unpopular. That practice may become less widespread following the court's criticism of it in *B v Lewisham BC* [2008] EWHC 738 (Admin).

guardianship order. On appeal to the Court of Appeal there were two key issues. First, was whether there should be contact with the parents. The trial judge had ordered that contact take place six times a year, away from the grandparents' house, supervised by the local authority. Further contact could be agreed between the mother and grandparents if approved by a social worker. Second, was whether the grandparents were entitled to change the surname of the child to their own. This, they explained, would mean that they would not need to explain the family history to everyone who came into contact with the child and queried the difference in surname. The trial judge had refused to grant this request, a conclusion the Court of Appeal agreed with.

At the heart of both of these issues was the extent to which special guardians are permitted to make decisions concerning the child. At the general level, the Court of Appeal explained that special guardianship did give guardians the right to exercise parental responsibility in the best interests of the child. However, that did not mean that there was no judicial control over the decisions of the guardians. Indeed, in the two issues under consideration, s. 14B of the Children Act 1989 required the court, when making a special guardianship order, to consider whether to make a contact order and enabled the court to give leave to change the surname. The response by the parents was:

> What real value . . . does the name tag have if it does not give the guardians the autonomy to bring up the child in a normal way without 'big brother', the social workers, exercising the real control which, absent a care order, the local authority does not have.[485]

The court's response was that:

> It is intended to promote and secure stability for the child cemented into this new family relationship. Links with the natural family are not severed as in adoption but the purpose undoubtedly is to give freedom to the special guardians to exercise parental responsibility in the best interests of the child. That, however, does not mean that the special guardians are free from the exercise of judicial oversight.[486]

On the surname issue, the court held that it was important that the child know of her background and live with the fact she is being brought up by her grandparents. However, given that the child was to have regular contact with her birth parents, it is not realistic to assume the child could be misled as to the relationship. As the court admitted:[487] 'In the scale of things in this child's life, her surname is a fact of little real significance.' With that in mind one might have thought that allowing the special guardians, who had undertaken, somewhat reluctantly, the enormous task of raising this troubled child, the liberty to change the name would be a minor concession. The court accepted 'that the care offered by the grandparents was exemplary' but the litigation and surrounding dispute had left them 'not far short from breaking point'.[488]

On the contact issue, the relationship between the grandparents and mother was volatile and so having them together at the time of the contact session was potentially harmful to the child. However, it was held that the requirement that a social worker approve of contact in excess of that ordered was unnecessary.

---

[485] Paragraph 30.
[486] Paragraph 33.
[487] Paragraph 40.
[488] Paragraph 22.

13 Adoption

Learning objective 9

Summarise the circumstances in which an adoption order will be made

The history of adoption reveals changes within our society.[489] Legal adoption started with the passing of the Adoption of Children Act 1926.[490] Before then informal adoption had taken place under the guise of wet-nursing, apprenticeship and informal arrangements for the care of a child. Traditionally, adoption was regarded as a convenient way of handing children born to an unmarried mother to a married infertile couple. It was seen as a blessing to all concerned: the unmarried mother could quietly and without embarrassment get rid of the child, who would otherwise be a public witness to her 'sin', and the married couple would be provided with the child they so longed for.

Nowadays adoption is seen as a service for children, rather than provision for infertile couples.[491] It is one of the ways in which the state may arrange care for children whose parents are unable or unwilling to care for them. Infertile couples are now more likely to turn to assisted reproduction than an adoption agency. Unmarried mothers are unlikely to feel that such is the stigma of extramarital birth that they should put up their children for adoption. Indeed, only about 50 mothers a year place their babies for adoption and this is usually because of the child's disability or their mother's personal circumstances.[492] Further, in recent years half of all adoptions have involved the mother and stepfather adopting the mother's child,[493] so that the stepfather can become the child's father in the eyes of the law.

Traditionally, adoption was based on the 'transplant' model, namely that children would be transplanted from one family and inserted into a new family. The child would cease to be a member of his or her 'old family' and would become a full member of the new family. Baroness Hale has explained:

> [A]n adoption order does far more than deprive the birth parents of their parental responsibility for bringing up the child and confer it upon her adoptive parents (provided for in Article 12 [of the ECHR]). It severs, irrevocably and for all time, the legal relationship between a child and her family of birth. It creates, irrevocably and for all time (unless the child is later adopted again into another family), a new legal relationship, not only between the child and her adoptive parents, but between the child and each of her adoptive parent's families.[494]

However, increasingly the transplant model is under challenge. It looks as if its primary focus is on meeting the concerns of would-be adopters, rather than focusing on what is best for the child. One of the significant changes in the nature of adoption is that the average age of children being adopted has risen. The older the child is, the more likely it is that they will be aware of who their biological parents are and that it will be appropriate for the adopted child to retain contact with their natural parents. In such cases the transplant model is unsuitable. Further, the skills required of a parent adopting a newborn baby are different from those for taking care of an older child with a troubled history. So, the kind of people who are adopting is changing too.[495]

---

[489] Douglas and Philpot (2003) and O'Halloran (2003) discuss the changing nature of adoption.
[490] Cretney (2003a: ch. 17) provides an excellent history of adoption.
[491] Lewis (2004). See Thoburn (2003) for a useful discussion of the effectiveness of adoption.
[492] Thoburn (2003).
[493] Lord Chancellor's Department (2003).
[494] In *Re G (Adoption: Unmarried Couple)* [2009] AC 173. See further *Uzbyakov v Russia* (App. No. 71160/13).
[495] *Re P* [2008] UKHL 38, para 91.

KEY STATISTICS

The following statistics relate to England for the year ending 31 March 2019.[496] They do not include children adopted by relatives.

- There were 3,570 adoptions, a notable fall from 5,360 adoptions in 2015; but a rise from 3,100 in 2011.
- 52% of children adopted were boys and 48% were girls.
- The average time between entering care and adoption was 1 year 11 months.
- The average age of children being adopted was 3 years and 1 month.
- 89% of children were adopted by couples and 12% by single adopters.
- 12% of children were adopted by same-sex couples.

At the turn of the century the number of adoptions had been in gradual decline and it had been forecast that adoption would become of little practical relevance for family lawyers. However, the Government indicated its desire to greatly increase the number of adoption orders being made and the law on adoption was significantly reformed by the Adoption and Children Act 2002. The Act was premised on the belief that adoption was underused by local authorities, was uncoordinated, and riddled with delays.[497] To improve the service the Act created a national register of people who wish to adopt a child and children who need to be adopted; required local authorities to maintain an adoption service;[498] and directed the Secretary of State to issued National Adoption Standards and other regulations which govern the way local authorities must perform their obligations concerning adoption.[499]

This enthusiasm among recent governments for adoption has surprised some, given that the adoption rate from care of children in the United Kingdom is already one of the highest in the world.[500] Initially the political intervention had little success in increasing adoption rates, but as the statistics in the box above show, the last few years have seen some notable increases. It should be noted though that adoption is still used for only a very small number of children looked after by local authorities. In 2018–19 there were 78,170 children being looked after in care, but only 3,570 were adopted.[501]

The Government is convinced that adoption benefits children. This could be supported on the basis of psychological evidence that children in care permanently placed with a family suffer less than children living in institutional children's homes.[502] Research on adopted children even indicates that there is no difference between the well-being of adopted children and children living with their biological parents.[503] Indeed, the majority of adopted children fare better on various indicia than children with comparable starts in life who live with their birth

---

[496] Office for National Statistics (2020i).
[497] Department of Health (2000).
[498] Adoption and Children Act 2002, s. 3. Further amendments were introduced by the Children and Families Act 2014.
[499] Department of Health (2014b).
[500] Tolson (2002).
[501] Adoption UK (2018).
[502] Quinton and Selwyn (2006a and b).
[503] Quinton and Selwyn (2006a and b).

parents.[504] Despite the widespread assumption that adoption benefits children, in fact there has been remarkably little research into the benefits of adoption. Those studies that have been carried out tend to suggest that adoption is beneficial, but the picture is not straightforward and much more research needs to be done before we can confidently assert that adoption is superior to long-term fostering.[505]

We will now explore some of the key issues relating to the law on adoption.

A Adoption and secret birth

There have been several cases where a mother has not wanted the wider family (including her parents) to be informed about the birth of a child and instead wishes the child to be adopted.[506] This has proved a controversial issue. Normally in child protection work the local authority will want to consider whether other members of the child's family can take on care of the child. There is now quite a body of law on what local authorities should do. The courts have taken into account the rights of the mother to anonymity. Holman J in *Z CC v R*[507] explained the importance of the right of the mother to anonymity:

> There is, in my judgment, a strong social need, if it is lawful, to continue to enable some mothers, such as this mother, to make discreet, dignified and humane arrangements for the birth and subsequent adoption of their babies, without their families knowing anything about it, if the mother, for good reason, so wishes.

In *Re C (Adoption: Father Unaware of Birth)*[508] the mother was herself a child and disclosure of the birth would have had a profound impact on her educational and social opportunities. This was sufficient reason not to notify the wider family.

The court will also take into account the desirability of the child being raised by the father or wider family. It is generally seen as preferable for a child to be cared for by their wider family if a parent cannot care for the child. It will be difficult to know if there are family members who can care for a child if they do not know the child exists.

The key case on how these factors can be balanced is the following:

CASE: *Re A, B and C (Adoption: Notification of Fathers and Relatives)* [2020] EWCA Civ 41

Three cases were heard together, all relating to mothers who concealed their pregnancies and did not want the father or wider family to know of the birth. Case A involved a student who was concerned about her history of depression, the father's mental health, and her wish not to be involved in the care of the child. Case B involved a homeless woman who had had an abusive childhood. She was scared of her family's reaction as they opposed sex outside marriage and feared violence from the father. Case C involved a married couple, with the wife saying the conception arose from marital rape. She had relinquished the baby at birth. She did not want the father or the wider family to know of the birth.

---

[504] Rushton (2002).
[505] Eekelaar (2003a); Warman and Roberts (2003).
[506] *Re R (A Child) (Adoption: Disclosure)* [2001] 1 FCR 238. See Marshall (2012 and 2018) for an excellent discussion of the issues. Contrast Sloan (2020).
[507] [2001] Fam Law 8.
[508] [2018] EWHC 3332.

It was held that the welfare principle did not apply to the decision whether a father or wider family should be informed. Child welfare was a central factor, but was not the paramount consideration. Court confirmation that it was appropriate not to involve the father and family was important to ensure the issue was not raised later in the proceedings. The court should consider the following factors:

- Did the father have parental responsibility?
- Did the father or family members have rights under Article 8?
- What was the substance of the relationships between the father/family members and the child?
- How likely was it that the father or family could offer an alternative to adoption?
- The impact on the physical, psychological and social well-being of the mother of notifications?
- Were there any relevant cultural and religious factors?
- Could the birth be kept confidential?
- Would notifying the father or family cause delay?
- Were there any other relevant factors?

In all the cases, applying these factors, it was determined that the family and/or father should be notified of the birth. In relation to Case A the Court of Appeal disagreed with the first instance judge who ordered the father and wider family should not be notified. The court was not satisfied there was evidence that the father could not be a potential carer of the child, apart from the opinion of the mother. The possibility of the child being raised by his birth family outweighed the concerns of the mother. In Case B the Court of Appeal agreed with the first instance judge that the potential for a family placement outweighed the concerns around the mother's vulnerability, the risk of violence and the cultural factors; and so the wider family should be notified. In relation to Case C, while the circumstances of the conception were distressing, the father had parental responsibility for the child and was the father/stepfather of the child's siblings. Not to notify him would have been 'an extremely strong course to take'.

This case seems to shift the balance towards notifying the father and wider family unless there are particularly compelling circumstances.[509] Indeed, the Court of Appeal said it would be exceptional to protect confidentiality in such cases. Of the cases considered, Case C seems particularly striking. That the perpetrator of rape might have a legitimate say in the care of his child is an astonishing claim. It will impose considerable extra stress for the mother and make public to her family the fact she has been raped, while ordinarily anonymity is promised for rape victims.

---

[509] In *Re L (Adoption: Identification of Possible Father)* [2020] EWCA Civ 577 it was held that the right to inform a man who may or may not have been the father was much weaker than a case where it was known for sure who the father was.

Jill Marshall[510] argues that these cases have placed too much weight on the child's right to identity, understood to mean that the child should know of their birth parents and family. However, she argues that a better understanding of identity would enable the law to respect a mother's right to a secret birth and the child's relational identity:

> Showing care and respect by listening to, and acting upon, a girl's or woman's choice to relinquish and to keep her pregnancy and birth secret can coincide with a child's best interests and identity rights by assisting the child to live in security and to be cared for by those who love, want, support, and are capable of looking after the child. Providing social conditions to improve care and belonging for both the child born secretly and the secret birth giver can be part of a process to bring about such freedom.

It should be emphasised that, as explained in *Re H (Care and Adoption: Assessment of Wider Family)*,[511] there is no positive duty on the local authority under Article 8 of the ECHR (the right to respect for family life) to inform the father or wider family. What *Re A, B and C (Adoption: Notification of Fathers and Relatives)*[512] was discussing was how a local authority ought to exercise its discretion. As discussed earlier in the text (see Chapter 8), it seems that for relatives, apart from a father, there needs to be an actual social relationship for there to be Article 8 rights and so that will not apply in these 'secret birth' cases. However, for fathers the case is different. At least if there is something more than a very casual relationship between the mother and the father, he may well have Article 8 rights.

B Who can adopt?

As part of the attempt to encourage an increase in the rate of adoption, the 2002 Act extends the category of those who can adopt. Now anyone can adopt, subject to the following restrictions:

1. An adoptive parent must be at least 21 years old. However, if a parent is adopting his or her own child then he or she need only be 18.[513]

2. If a couple wish to adopt together, they must be married, civil partners or 'living as partners in an enduring family relationship'.[514] If a couple are in a casual relationship, this would mean they could not adopt together, but one of them could adopt a child alone. In *Re CC (Adoption Application: Separated Applicants)*[515] a couple separated during the placement. The court approved a joint adoption order as the child had come to recognise both adults as her parents; and it was intended they would both play a full role in the child's life. It was accepted that it would be rare for the court to make a joint adoption for a separated couple.

3. A single person can adopt. But a married person can only adopt alone if he or she satisfies the court that his or her spouse cannot be found; or is incapable by reason of ill-health of applying for the adoption; or that the spouses have separated and it is likely to be a permanent separation.[516]

---

[510] Marshall (2012 and 2018).
[511] [2019] EWFC 10.
[512] [2020] EWCA Civ 41.
[513] Adoption and Children Act 2002 (hereafter ACA 2002), s. 50.
[514] ACA 2002, s. 144(4). See A Marshall (2003).
[515] [2013] EWHC 4815 (Fam).
[516] ACA 2002, s. 51.

4. There are complex rules which set out domicile or habitual residence requirements for would-be adopters.[517]

5. An adoption agency cannot place any child for adoption where a person over the age of 18 has been convicted or cautioned for a specified offence (e.g. child abuse).

At the time, one of the most controversial aspects of the 2002 Act was that it permitted adoption by a same-sex couple. Now there is such extensive evidence that same-sex couples can offer as good a quality of parenting as opposite-sex couples that it is uncontroversial.[518] Despite this, small-scale studies found same-sex couples were disadvantaged in the adoption process.[519]

C Who can be adopted?

Only a person under the age of 19 can be adopted, although the application must be made before that person's 18th birthday.[520] Although the child does not need to consent to the adoption, in the case of a child with sufficient understanding they should be consulted through the process and offered counselling. It is hard to imagine that an adoption agency would want to place a child for adoption who opposed it.

D The adoption procedures

Before setting out the procedures for matching adopters and children, we need to appreciate a tension in the law's goals here. A court will be willing to make an adoption order only if it is decided that there is no realistic hope of the child living with the birth family in the foreseeable future and that the adoption will promote the child's welfare. There are, therefore, difficulties in cases where the birth family objects to the adoption. When are their objections to be considered? If they are left to the end of the process, there could be a situation where the child has been placed with adopters for a trial period which has gone very well, with raised hopes of the adopters and perhaps the child, which are dashed when at the final hearing the judge decides that the birth parents are justifiably objecting to the proposed adoption. However, if the consent of the birth parents is dealt with as the first issue the judge is in the difficult position of having to decide whether to dispense with the parents' consent, without knowing whether or not the proposed adopters will be suitable. The solution adopted by the 2002 Act is that the consent issue should be dealt with early on in the process, at the stage of the placement. However, if there is a change in circumstances then at the final hearing the parents have a further chance to object.[521]

The road to adoption under the Adoption and Children Act 2002 involves the following stages:

1. *Planning for adoption.* The local authority should consider whether adoption is suitable for every child in its care. If it decides that the birth family are unable to meet a child's needs in the foreseeable future and that adoption is likely to provide the best means of doing so, then

---

[517] ACA 2002, s. 49(2), (3). See *Re A (Adoption: Removal)* [2009] 2 FLR 597.
[518] Golombok (2015).
[519] Hitchings and Sagar (2007) and Samuel (2010).
[520] ACA 2002, ss. 47(9) and 49(4). See *Re MW (Leave to Apply for Adoption)* [2014] EWHC 385 (Fam).
[521] It need hardly be said that this means a change in circumstances which makes the birth parent's opposition stronger: *Re T (Adoption)* [2012] EWCA Civ 191.

a plan for adoption should be drawn up.[522] In deciding whether to pursue adoption, the local authority must also consider the likelihood of finding appropriate adopters. In making the decision to consider adoption, a delicate balance has to be drawn. On the one hand, if the local authority believes that there is a hope of rehabilitation with the birth parents it will be reluctant to pursue an adoption. On the other hand, delaying adoption because of a faint hope of rehabilitation may mean the child has to spend years in limbo, making the chance of success of any later adoption more remote. Some local authorities use a process known as twin-tracking to deal with this difficulty: at the same time, work is done on the one hand with the family in an effort to pursue rehabilitation with the birth parent, while on the other hand preparations are made to find an alternative secure home for the child.[523] Such procedures can be difficult for all involved and require trust and commitment all round. There may also be concerns that such procedures may cause confusion for the child.

2. *Assessing would-be adopters.* When a couple or an individual approaches an adoption agency, wishing to be considered as an adopter, they will be assessed by the agency.[524] Many agencies take the view that the process should be as much about the agency deciding whether the couple are suitable to be adopters, as about assisting the couple to decide whether they wish to adopt. Applicants must be treated fairly, openly and with respect.[525] In the past there were concerns over the assessment of would-be adopters. In response, the Adoption Agency Regulations 2005 set out the grounds that should be taken into account.[526] This should at least ensure there is consistency in practice between the different agencies.

3. *The preparation of the report.* The adoption agency must interview and assess anyone who puts themselves forward as potential adopters and then prepare a detailed report for the agency's adoption panel.[527] The report might comment on the applicant's relationships, health and lifestyle, and will take up references. Attitudes to childcare, and the use of corporal punishment, will be considered too.[528]

4. *The adoption agency's decision on the applicant's suitability.* In the light of the report, the adoption agency will decide whether or not to approve the adopters. Although the report prepared by the panel will be taken into account, the decision is ultimately one for the agency. At present it appears that 95 per cent of applicants put before the agency are approved. This figure may seem very high, but it should be appreciated that most candidates thought unsuitable for adoption will have withdrawn from the process before the final report is placed before the panel.

   An applicant who was rejected as an adopter by a local authority could apply for judicial review of the local authority's decision. In *R (Johns and Johns) v Derby City Council (Equality and Human Rights Commission Intervening)*[529] a Christian couple wished to adopt. They strongly opposed all sexual behaviour outside marriage, including same-sex behaviour. These views were going to be taken into account in deciding they would be approved as fosters or adopters. A challenge to this assessment failed, with the court rejecting the argument that

---

[522] ACA 2002, s. 1.

[523] The courts have approved such schemes: e.g. *CM v Blackburn with Darwen Borough Council* [2014] EWCA Civ 1479.

[524] See Suitability of Adopters Regulations 2005 (SI 2005/1712) for the procedures which should be followed.

[525] Department for Education and Skills (2005c: standards B 1–7).

[526] See, further, Department for Education and Skills (2006b).

[527] This is required by the Department for Education and Skills (2006b).

[528] *R (A) v Newham London Borough Council* [2009] 1 FCR 545.

[529] [2011] EWHC 375 (Admin).

the approach amounted to improper discrimination on the grounds of religion. Importantly, the court noted that their views on sexual morality were only to be one factor to be considered. In *O v Coventry City Council (Adoption)*[530] the court upheld a decision not to consider as adopters a couple who had a history of financial insecurity and where one had failed to pay child support or be involved with children from a previous relationship.

5. *Matching the child and adopter.* If the adopter(s) is (or are) approved, the agency must then consider whether there are any children needing to be adopted who are an appropriate match. If there are, the applicants will be given brief details of the children. If the applicants are keen to proceed, the adoption panel will prepare a report for the adoption agency on the proposed match.

6. *The agency approves the match.* The adoption agency will need to approve the proposal that adoption between the child and would-be adopter should be pursued. It should be remembered that s. 1 of the Act applies to the agency. Thus the agency should approve the match if to do so would promote the child's welfare. Section 3 of the Children and Families Act 2014 has removed the specific requirement that the adoption agency give due consideration to the child's religious persuasion, racial origin and cultural and linguistic background, when placing the child for adoption. This is not to say that these factors are not to be considered, rather that they are part of the general welfare assessment. The requirement was removed because it was thought it elevated these factors to undue prominence in a welfare assessment.

TOPICAL ISSUE

Transracial adoption

The issue of transracial adoption is a controversial one.[531] At one extreme there are concerns that adoption can become a means of taking children away from deprived black families and giving them to infertile middle-class white couples. There is also conflicting evidence concerning whether children whose race differs from that of their primary carers suffer from confusions over their cultural identity. To others transracial adoption is to be encouraged as part of the creation of a racially and culturally diverse and mixed society.[532] The removal of the obligation in s. 1(5) of the Adoption and Children Act 2002 that requires the court when considering the placement of children to give 'due consideration' to the child's racial origin was designed to prevent a local authority avoiding an otherwise good matching, on the basis of racial differences between the adopters and child. In *Re A (Placement Orders: Cultural Heritage)*[533] the Court of Appeal approved the placement of children with adopters of a different ethnic and cultural background, as the would-be adopters were well placed to meet the children's other needs.[534] By contrast, in *Mander v Royal Borough of Windsor and Maidenhead*[535] a Sikh couple who were not approved as adopters, as nearly all the children the agency had available were white, were found to be the victims of unlawful race discrimination. In *R (Cornerstone) v The Office for Standards in Education, Children's Services and Skills*[536] it was found not to be lawful for an adoption agency to only accept heterosexual evangelical Christians as potential adopters.

[530] [2011] EWCA Civ 729 (Fam).
[531] See the discussions in Hayes and Hayes (2014) and Sargent (2015).
[532] Murphy (2000).
[533] [2015] EWCA Civ 1254.
[534] See also *Re CB (Adoption Order)* [2015] EWHC 3274 (Fam).
[535] Case No: C01RG184.
[536] [2020] EWHC 1679 (Admin).

7. *The adopters are provided with a full report on the child.* The would-be adopters at this stage will be provided with a full report on the child's health, needs and history.[537]

8. *Placement of the child with the would-be adopters.* The next stage will be the placement of the child with the adopters for what is, in effect, a trial period. To place a child, the agency must either have the consent of each parent with parental responsibility[538] or must have obtained a placement order from the court.[539] The issue of placement is complex and will be discussed in more detail shortly.

9. *The agency applies for an adoption order.* If the placement has worked well, the final stage will be for the adoption agency to apply for an adoption order. It is not possible to apply for an adoption order unless there has been a placement order or the parents are consenting to the adoption, with one exception: that is, foster carers who have looked after the child for at least 12 months, who can apply without satisfying any further requirements.[540] This will be discussed further shortly.

E Placement for adoption

As we have just seen, the placement of a child with potential adopters plays a crucial role in the process for adoption. Once placement takes place, the agency or the people with whom the child is placed acquire parental responsibility, but the birth parents do not lose it. However, the agency is entitled to restrict the way parents can exercise their parental responsibility. A placement order also prohibits the removal of the child from the adopters by anyone (including, most importantly, the birth parents) except the local authority.[541] To place a child, the agency must either have the consent of each parent with parental responsibility[542] or must have obtained a placement order from the court.[543] These two alternatives will now be considered:

1. *Placement by consent.* Parental consent can be specific (i.e. the parents consent to the child being placed with a particular person or people) or general (i.e. the parents consent to the child being placed with whomever the local authority believes to be appropriate). However, if at any time a parent withdraws his or her consent, the agency must apply for a placement order or return the child to the parents.[544]

2. *Placement by placement order.* The court can make a placement order only if all of the following are satisfied:

    (a) Either a care order has already been made in respect of the child or the court is satisfied that the significant harm test in s. 31 of the Children Act 1989 is satisfied.

---

[537] A local authority may be liable in tort if it fails to provide relevant information which, if disclosed, would have persuaded the adopters not to go ahead with the adoption: *A and B v Essex CC* [2002] EWHC 2709 (Fam).

[538] ACA 2002, s. 19(1), unless care proceedings are pending (s. 19(3)).

[539] ACA 2002, ss. 21(3), 52.

[540] ACA 2002, s. 47.

[541] ACA 2002, ss. 34(1), 47(4).

[542] ACA 2002, s. 19(1), unless care proceedings are pending (s. 19(3)).

[543] ACA 2002, ss. 21(3), 52.

[544] ACA 2002, ss. 22, 31 and 32. If the birth parent(s) do not wish to be involved any further in the process, they are entitled to ask that they not be informed of any application for adoption (s. 20(4)).

(b) Parental consent has been given or been dispensed with.[545] Dispensing with parental consent will be dealt with in more detail shortly, but in brief this can happen if to do so will promote the child's welfare.

(c) The court is persuaded that it is better to make the placement order than not to do so.[546]

The welfare principle applies when the court is making a placement order. The placement order can be made, even if it is foreseen that there may be difficulties in placing the child or even concerns that adoption may not be able to take place. In *NS-H v Kingston Upon Hull City Council and MC*[547] the Court of Appeal explained that placement was only suitable where 'the child is presently in a **condition** to be adopted and is **ready** to be adopted'. Proportionality will be a key matter: is the placement order a proportionate response to the risk the child is facing? In considering that, it was explained in *Re F (A Child) (Placement Order: Proportionality)*[548] there should be:

> an intense focus on the *type of risk* that is involved, *how likely* it is to happen and what the *likely consequences* might then be.

Before making a placement order, the court is required to consider the arrangements for contact between the child and birth family.[549] The placement order will terminate any existing contact order, but on making the placement order the court can make a new contact order. It can also authorise the agency to refuse contact between the child and any named person.[550] The placement order cannot be subject to conditions. So, a judge cannot set conditions on the kind of adopters a child can be placed with.[551] Nor can a court require a local authority to ensure that siblings are adopted together.[552]

It is illegal for anyone except an adoption agency to place a child for adoption with a person who is not a relative.[553] If parents wish to have their child adopted, they should contact an adoption agency. Only local authorities and adoption societies can run adoption services.[554] There are even criminal offences if an unauthorised person seeks to run an adoption service.[555] Where a couple have unlawfully brought a child to the United Kingdom, the court will not normally then allow the couple to adopt the child.[556]

F Revocation of a placement order by court order

A placement order can be revoked if it is decided that there is no plan for adoption.[557] That may be because the placement has not been a success. In rare cases there has been such an improvement in the position of the birth parents that they wish to be reconsidered as primary

---

[545] If consent has been given, the local authority is likely to go down the route of placement by consent.
[546] ACA 2002, s. 1(6).
[547] [2008] 2 FLR 918. See also *Re F (Appeal from Placement Order)* [2013] EWCA Civ 1277.
[548] [2018] EWCA Civ 2761.
[549] ACA 2002, ss. 26, 27(4).
[550] ACA 2002, s. 27.
[551] *Re A (Children) (Placement Orders: Conditions)* [2013] EWCA Civ 1611.
[552] *Re A, B, C, D and E (Children: Placement Orders)* [2018] EWFC B 11.
[553] ACA 2002, ss. 92, 93.
[554] ACA 2002, s. 92.
[555] ACA 2002, s. 93.
[556] *Northumberland County Council v Z* [2010] 1 FCR 494.
[557] The child is treated as placed for adoption when the child starts to live with the would-be adopters: *Coventry City Council v O (Adoption)* [2011] EWCA Civ 729.

carers of the child. Once the child has been placed,[558] birth parents cannot apply for revocation unless they have the leave of the court,[559] which will be granted only if it is in the welfare of the child to do so *and* there has been a change of circumstances of a nature and degree sufficient to justify reopening the issue.[560] It does not need to be shown that the change of circumstances was 'exceptional',[561] but they must have been unforeseen at the time the placement order was made.[562] The court will take into account the prospects of the applicant successfully resisting adoption and the impact on the child of there being a further hearing.[563] Only if the applicants 'have solid prospects, having regard to the paramount consideration of promoting the child's welfare throughout her life, of successfully opposing the adoption application' will leave be granted.[564] If the applicant had had an opportunity to challenge the placement order earlier but had not done so, then it is unlikely the court will give leave.[565] However, in *Re LG (Adoption: Leave to Oppose)*[566] the family of a very young father came to learn of the birth after the placement order had been made and were keen to help him raise the child. The court will take into account whether the change in circumstances is likely to continue.[567] If someone is not a parent with parental responsibility or a guardian and they wish to challenge a placement order they need to seek leave to apply for a child arrangements order under s. 8.[568]

If leave is granted, then whether or not the placement will be revoked will be considered on the basis of the welfare of the child.[569] Proportionality will play a dominant role.[570] The court will consider whether continuing with adoption is the option which will best promote the welfare of the child.

G Revocation by the local authority

A local authority can demand the return of the child within seven days under s. 35(2) of the Adoption and Children Act 2002 by way of a notice and then apply to the court under s. 35 to have the placement revoked. In *DL and ML v Newham LBC and Secretary of State for Education*[571] where a local authority became concerned about a child it had placed with a couple, they sought to revoke the placement under s. 35(2) of the Adoption and Children Act 2002. The prospective adopters sought judicial review of the decision to issue a section 35(2) notice. Charles J quashed the notice and directed the authority to reconsider whether the child should be returned to the applicants. He emphasised that a placement gave parental responsibility to the prospective adopters. This meant there was family life between the prospective adopters and the child for the purposes of Article 8. The local authority therefore had to ensure any interference in that family life was justified and complied with the Article 8 requirements for procedural fairness. The prospective adopters had not been given a proper opportunity to address the concerns.

---

[558] *Re S (Placement Order: Revocation)* [2009] 1 FLR 503.
[559] See *S-H v Kingston Upon Hull* [2008] EWCA Civ 493 for a case where the parent was granted leave to apply to revoke the placement order, because the child was not thriving during placement.
[560] *Re W (A Child: Leave to Oppose Adoption)* [2020] EWCA Civ 16; *Re A (Children)* [2019] EWCA Civ 609.
[561] *Re T (Application to Revoke a Placement Order: Change in Circumstances)* [2014] EWCA Civ 1369.
[562] *Prospective Adopters v London Borough of Tower Hamlets* [2020] EWFC 26.
[563] *Re W (A Child: Leave to Oppose Adoption)* [2020] EWCA Civ 16.
[564] *Prospective Adopters v London Borough of Tower Hamlets* [2020] EWFC 26.
[565] *Re A (Children)* [2019] EWCA Civ 609.
[566] [2015] EWFC 52.
[567] *Re G (A Child)* [2015] EWCA Civ 119.
[568] *Re G (Adoption: Leave to Oppose)* [2014] EWCA Civ 432.
[569] Adoption and Children Act 2002, s. 1.
[570] *Re T (Application to Revoke a Placement Order: Change in Circumstances)* [2014] EWCA Civ 1369.
[571] [2011] EWHC 1127 (Admin).

CASE: RCW v A Local Authority [2013] EWHC 235 (Fam)

The local authority sought to remove a child who had been placed with a young single woman, R, after she lost her sight. The placement had been going very well. It was held that the removal of a child from a prospective adopter was 'momentous'. It had to be welfare based and reached fairly. Here there had been little direct observation of how well R was able to care for the child; no assessment; no discussion with her friends and supporters; no proper understanding of her condition. She had not been invited to attend at meetings where the placement had been discussed. R had not been given an opportunity to address the local authority's concern. This breached the common law principle of fairness and her rights under Article 6 or 8. Strikingly the local authority admitted it did not even know if R's condition was permanent or temporary. It was emphasised that visual impairment did not disqualify someone from being a loving parent. She was awarded damages under s. 7 of the Human Rights Act 1998 for the interference in her rights.

In **RY v Southend Borough Council**[572] it was held that even though s. 35 did not include a requirement that the local authority prove the child was suffering significant harm before a revocation of a placement order was made, it should be read as if it did. This would ensure the Article 8 rights of the child and adopters were protected from interference. In **Borough of Poole v Mrs and Mr W**,[573] where the child was settled with the adopters and traumatised by an attempt to reintroduce her to her birth family, the court had no difficulty in refusing to revoke the placement. That case might be contrasted with the following controversial decision.

CASE: A and B v Rotherham Metropolitan Borough Council and Others [2014] EWFC 47 (Fam)

A child had been removed from the mother at birth. The mother untruthfully told the social workers that her partner was the father. Both the mother and partner were white, although the child was described as being of mixed race appearance. Despite this the mother's statements on paternity were accepted. A care order was made and the child placed for adoption, with what were described as 'perfect' adopters. The real genetic father then discovered the child's existence and although he had never seen the child wanted his sister (the child's aunt) to raise him. He emphasised that his family were Black African, while the adopters were white British (although they did seek to raise the child with an awareness of his African heritage). The case was seen as difficult because although had the father come forward before the placement the child would almost certainly have been placed with the aunt, the child was well settled into life with the adopters, who were providing an 'exemplary standard' of care. The social workers and psychologist favoured revoking the placement. Holman J agreed, concluding that the father coming forward was a change in circumstances and looking at the child's welfare during his whole life, the short-term disruption to his care was outweighed by the child living with the aunt who could be a 'bridge' to the birth family.

---

[572] [2015] EWHC 2509 (Fam).
[573] [2014] EWHC 1777 (Fam).

Undoubtedly people will disagree on the outcome here and Holman J admitted it was a finely balanced case. It seems a brave decision to move the child from what everyone agreed was a settled, attached and secure environment to a family the child had never met, but could offer the cultural heritage background. The child was aged 20 months and had lived with the adopters for 13 months. Certainly, other cases (*Re C (Adoption Proceedings: Change of Circumstances)*[574]) have placed considerable weight on the current security and happiness of a child if the placement is going well.

H The making of an adoption order

It is not possible for an adoption to occur without a court order. So, if a couple take into their home a child and raise him or her as their own child, this will not be an adoption. Before considering an adoption order, the court will have to be satisfied that the placement criteria have been met. The exact requirements depend on the nature of the applicants:

- If the adoption is arranged by an adoption agency, the child must have lived with the applicants for at least 10 weeks before the application is made.[575]

- If the adoption is a non-agency case and the applicant is a step-parent or partner of the parent, the minimum period is six months.

- If the adoption is a non-agency case and the applicant is a local authority foster carer, a continuous period of one year is required.

- If the adoption is a non-agency case and the applicant is a relative, the child must have lived with the applicant for a cumulative period of three years during the preceding five years.[576]

These requirements ensure that the child and would-be adopters have spent a sufficient amount of time together for the court to be able properly to assess whether the adoption is likely to benefit the child. If the placement criteria are satisfied[577] the court will go on to consider the two key crucial requirements for an adoption order:

- that the making of the adoption order is in the child's welfare; and

- that the birth parent consents to the adoption or that consent has been dispensed with.[578]

These requirements will be considered separately.

---

[574] [2013] EWCA Civ 431.

[575] 'Lived with' here requires the parties to share the same household. Being in regular electronic contact is insufficient.

[576] ACA 2002, s. 42. It is possible to apply for leave to allow adoption without this requirement being met: *Re MW (Leave to Apply for Adoption)* [2014] EWHC 385 (Fam).

[577] If they are not satisfied, the court must grant leave to apply for the order. In such a case the court will consider the child's welfare and the likelihood of the application succeeding: *Re A (A Child) (Adoption)* [2008] 1 FCR 55.

[578] See *Down Lisburn v H* [2006] UKHL 36 which highlights the problem with the 'reasonable person test' for dispensing with consent under the old law.

(i) That the making of the adoption order is in the child's welfare

In deciding whether or not an adoption order is in the welfare of the child, the court must consider the checklist in s. 1(4) of the Adoption and Children Act 2002:

LEGISLATIVE PROVISION

Adoption and Children Act 2002, section 1(4)

(a) the child's ascertainable wishes and feelings regarding the decisions (considered in the light of the child's age and understanding);

(b) the child's particular needs;

(c) the likely effect on the child (throughout his life) of having ceased to be a member of the original family and become an adopted person;

(d) the child's age, sex, background and any of the child's characteristics which the court or agency considers relevant;

(e) any harm (within the meaning of the Children Act 1989) which the child has suffered or is at risk of suffering;

(f) the relationship which the child has with relatives, and with any other person in relation to whom the court or agency considers the relationship to be relevant, including—

   (i)   the likelihood of any such relationship continuing and the value to the child of its doing so;

   (ii) the ability and willingness of any of the child's relatives, or of any such person, to provide the child with a secure environment in which the child can develop, and otherwise to meet the child's needs;

   (iii) the wishes and feelings of the child's relatives, or of any such person, regarding the child.

Four points in particular will be emphasised about this list.[579] First, it should be noted that the court must consider the child's welfare not only during the child's minority, but for the rest of his or her life.[580] Thus, a court may be persuaded that making an adoption order in favour of a child just short of his or her 18th birthday will promote his or her welfare, if doing so will give him or her British citizenship.[581] In *Re T (A Child)*[582] the child's parents were in prison. Although they could not offer immediate care, it was considered that they may be able to do so in the future. The possibility of future care by birth parents was therefore taken into account in deciding whether the child should be adopted.

Secondly, as usual, the child's own views about the proposed adoption are likely to be very important, if not crucial, to a determination of the child's welfare. At one time it was proposed that an adoption order could not be made in respect of a child over the age of 12 without his or her consent. This did not appear in the final Act. However, it is hard to imagine a case where a court will decide that an adoption, against the wishes of a teenager, will

---

[579] The list is similar, but not identical to, CA 1989, s. 1(3).
[580] For a general discussion see Sloan (2013).
[581] *FAS v Secretary of State for the Home Department and Anor* [2015] EWCA Civ 951.
[582] [2014] EWCA Civ 929.

promote his or her welfare.[583] However, in one case the views of a seven-year-old were of 'passing interest' but he lacked the maturity to make the decision.[584] As Pauffley J put it, it is one thing to ask 'if he would like fish fingers for tea and quite another to take account of and assent to his choice about where he should live'. In *Re M (Adoption or Residence Order)*[585] the views of a 12-year-old that she did not want to be regarded as no longer the sibling of her siblings were decisive in ordering a residence order in favour of the applicants, rather than an adoption. The Court of Appeal was brave in doing this because the applicants had stated that they would not be able to care for the child if only granted a residence order and threatened that if they were denied an adoption order they would return the child to the local authority. In the face of strong evidence that it was in the interests of the child to live with the applicants, the Court of Appeal trusted that the applicants would not carry through their threats. In addition to a residence order, it also made an order under s. 91(14) of the Children Act 1989, preventing the birth mother making an application for an order under that Act without the leave of the court. This would provide some limited protection to the applicants from concerns that the birth mother would be constantly seeking to interfere with the way they were raising the child.

Third, the Act requires the court specifically to consider the child's relationships with his or her birth family: not just his or her birth parents, but his or her wider family.[586] In particular, the court must consider whether the child's blood relatives are in a position to care for the child. In *Re C (Family Placement)*[587] the Court of Appeal preferred to make a residence order to a five-year-old's grandmother, rather than place the child for adoption with strangers, as the local authority wished to do. They referred to the law's preference that children be raised within their family. The grandmother's age was noted (she was 70), but the court believed other family members would rally round if the grandmother became unable to care for the child. Of course, in some cases where the child has been through a particularly traumatic time there may be a positive benefit in severing all ties so that a new start can be made.[588]

The fourth point is that, as mentioned earlier in this chapter, proportionality will play a key role in these cases. When considering an application for an adoption order the court must recall the alternative orders that it can make.[589]

This will mean the court should consider all the alternative carers for the child. Even if it is decided the child should live with the adopters the court must still consider as alternatives to adoption: (i) a child arrangements order in favour of the applicants;[590] (ii) a special guardianship; or (iii) no order. All of these options could lead to the child living with the applicants, but, unlike adoption, the birth parents would not lose their parental status. Also, significantly, the formal links between the child and his or her wider family (e.g. siblings, grandparents, etc.) would remain. The court will have to weigh up the benefits of retaining the broad links with the birth family with the benefits of security offered by an adoption. Holman J in *Re H*

---

[583] Adoption Agencies Regulations 2005 require the agency to counsel the child and ascertain his or her wishes and feelings and report on these to the adoption panel, if appropriate.
[584] *Re MM (Long Term Fostering: Placement with Family Members: Wishes and Feelings)* [2013] EWHC 2697 (Fam).
[585] [1998] 1 FLR 570.
[586] Parkinson (2003).
[587] [2009] 1 FLR 1425.
[588] *Birmingham City Council v AB and Others* [2014] EWHC 3090 (Fam).
[589] *Re P (Children) (Adoption: Parental Consent)* [2008] 2 FCR 185.
[590] The ACA 2002 has amended s. 12 of the Children Act 1989 so that a residence order can last until the child's 18th birthday.

(Adoption Non-patrial)[591] summarised the benefits of an adoption order over and above a residence order in favour of the would-be adopters:

> It is well recognised that adoption confers an extra and psychologically and emotionally important sense of 'belonging'. There is real benefit to the parent/child relationship in knowing that each is legally bound to the other and in knowing that the relationship thus created is as secure and free from interference by outsiders as the relationship between natural parents and their child.

To similar effect, in *Re V (Long-Term Fostering or Adoption)*[592] Black LJ emphasised the difference in 'feel' offered by the permanence of adoption.

When considering whether the adoption will promote the child's welfare, the court will be aware of potential rights under the Human Rights Act 1998.[593] The approach of the European Court of Human Rights towards adoption is rather ambiguous. In *Johansen v Norway*[594] the European Court considered the placement of the applicant's daughter in a foster home with a view to adoption. The court stated:

> These measures were particularly far-reaching in that they totally deprived the applicant of the family life with the child and were inconsistent with the aim of reuniting them. Such measures should only be applied in exceptional circumstances and could only be justified if they were motivated by an overriding requirement pertaining to the child's best interests.[595]

This statement, subsequently repeated in many cases, appears to suggest that adoption is only permissible in exceptional cases and only if there is a very strong case for it based on the child's interests, while some later cases (e.g. *Söderbck v Sweden*)[596] suggested a more positive attitude towards adoption. Recently the ECtHR has confirmed its restrictive approach in *R and H v UK*,[597] stating 'measures which deprive biological parents of the parental responsibilities and authorise adoption should only be applied in exceptional circumstances and can only be justified if they are motivated by an overriding requirement pertaining to the child's best interests'.

The approach of the courts to adoption is now dominated by the following important decision:

CASE: *Re B-S (Children) (Adoption: Leave to Oppose)* [2013] EWCA Civ 1146

Two children had been removed from a mother and made the subject of care and placement orders. The children were placed with prospective adopters and an application for adoption was brought. The mother applied under the Adoption and Children Act 2002, s. 47(5) for leave to oppose the making of the adoption order. The basis of her application was that her life had been turned around and she was now able to offer good care of the children. At first instance, while accepting the improvements in the mother's situation it was emphasised that the children needed stability and care. Even if returned to her, the mother might not be able to cope and there was still 'a long road to travel'. She was refused leave to appeal. The appeal failed but the Court gave essential guidance on such applications and generally on the law's approach to adoption.

---

[591] [1996] 1 FLR 717 at p. 726.
[592] [2013] EWCA Civ 913.
[593] *Re P (Children) (Adoption: Parental Consent)* [2008] 2 FCR 185.
[594] (1996) 23 EHRR 33.
[595] At para 78.
[596] [1999] 1 FLR 250.
[597] (App. No. 35348/06) [2011] ECHR 844, para 81.

The Court of Appeal emphasised that s. 47(5) was intended to give a parent a 'meaningful remedy'. It was also stressed that the remedy was for the benefit of the child, as well as of the parent. Earlier dicta that only in 'exceptionally rare circumstances' would leave to oppose be granted were disapproved. The Court should ask two questions when considering leave to oppose. First, if there had been a change in circumstances and, second if so, whether leave to oppose should be given. In considering the second question the court should consider all the circumstances and in particular the parent's ultimate prospect of success of an adoption order not being made. Second, the impact on the child of the decision whether to give leave. If the judge determined that there had been a change of circumstances and there were solid grounds for seeking leave, the judge had to consider very carefully whether the child's welfare necessitated a refusal of leave. The more positive the change in circumstances and the more solid the grounds for seeking leave, the more compelling the arguments based on welfare would need to be if leave was to be refused. The impact on granting of leave on the potential adopters and the disturbance to them of having to defend adoption proceedings was a factor, but not one to carry undue weight.

Overriding all these points however was that the child's welfare was paramount; it was important to remember that adoption was 'the last resort' and 'only permissible if nothing else would do'. The law was based on the belief that a child's 'interests included being brought up by its parents or wider family unless the overriding requirements of the child's welfare made that impossible'. The judge, in making decisions about adoption, had to consider all the options and the pros and cons of each option. Munby P expressed concern at the 'recurrent inadequacy of the analysis and reasoning put forward in support of the case for adoption'; it was, he said, 'time to call a halt to sloppy practice'.[598] It was wrong to take a 'linear' approach and consider each option individually, starting with the least interventionist. Rather the task of the judge was 'to evaluate all the options, undertaking a global, holistic and . . . multi-faceted evaluation of the child's welfare which takes into account all the negatives and positives, all the pros and cons of each option'.

This case picked up and developed the comments of Lord Neuberger in **Re B**[599] where he refers to:

> . . . the importance of emphasising the principle that adoption of a child against her parents' wishes should only be contemplated as a last resort – when all else fails. Although the child's interests in an adoption case are 'paramount' (in the UK legislation and under Article 21 of the United Nations Convention on the Rights of the Child 1989), a court must never lose sight of the fact that those interests include being brought up by her natural family, ideally her natural parents, or at least one of them.

He also notes that in assessing the abilities of parents to care for their children the court must consider the assistance and support available from local authorities to parents to help them perform their role. In this regard parents who had a history of failing to cooperate with local authorities or not being honest with them, may be less likely to succeed than parents who had shown a willingness to receive assistance and support.[600] In **Re E (A Child)**[601] the local

[598] For similar concerns see **Re v (Long Term Fostering or Adoption)** [2013] EWCA Civ 913.
[599] [2013] UKSC 33.
[600] **Re W (A Child)** [2012] EWCA Civ 1828.
[601] [2013] EWCA Civ 1614.

authority supported adoption as the mother had an unsuitable partner. However, the court noted it had provided the mother with no assistance in extricating herself from the relationship (e.g. by offering alternative accommodation) and so it could not be concluded that it had been shown adoption was the only option.

Further guidance on the rejection of the 'linear approach' has been helpfully provided in *Re G (Care Proceedings: Welfare Evaluation)*:[602]

> The judicial exercise should not be a linear process whereby each option, other than the most draconian, is looked at in isolation and then rejected because of internal deficits that may be identified, with the result that, at the end of the line, the only option left standing is the most draconian and that is therefore chosen without any particular consideration of whether there are internal deficits within that option.[603]

McFarlane LJ went on to say that judges must be wary of simply using phrases such as 'draconian order' to indicate that they appreciate the severity of the adoption order; they must genuinely consider whether the order is the only way of adequately promoting the welfare of the child.

One of the major implications of *Re B-S* is the emphasis on the argument that adoption is to be used if absolutely necessary.[604] In *Re S (A Child) (Care and Placement Orders: Proportionality)*[605] the making of a care order and a placement order, with a view to adoption, were said to be orders which:

> . . . are 'very extreme', only made when 'necessary' for the protection of the child's interests, which means when 'nothing else will do', 'when all else fails', that the court 'must never lose sight of the fact that [the child's] interests include being brought up by her natural family, ideally her natural parents, or at least one of them' and that adoption 'should only be contemplated as a last resort'.

KEY CASE: *Re R (Adoption)* [2014] EWCA 1625

A mother had a problem with 'binge drinking' and abusive relationships. The police had removed the child from her care. The local authority had investigated but found no alternative family carers. They successfully sought a care order, with a view to placing the child for adoption. The mother appealed on the basis that the judge had failed to follow the approach recommended in *Re B-S*, in particular by not exploring all the alternatives to a care order and adoption and finding that adoption was the only alternative. The Court of Appeal emphasised that *Re B-S* was not intended to change the law and where making a care order and planning for adoption is best for the child the local authority should not shy away from doing so. It was true that where there was opposition from parents a care order with a plan for adoption was only permissible where 'nothing else will do'. However, *Re B-S* was designed to amend the way judgments were structured, rather than change the law. It was not intended to erode or put a glass on the welfare test. It required the court to look at all realistic options, but only realistic options, to determine if nothing else but a care order and adoption would do. It was not meant to make it harder to obtain a care order or supervision order.

---

[602] [2013] EWCA Civ 965.
[603] Approved in *Re C (Appeal from Care and Placement Orders)* [2013] EWCA Civ 1257.
[604] *Prospective Adopters v IA and London Borough of Croydon* [2014] EWHC 331 (Fam).
[605] [2013] EWCA Civ 1073.

It should be added that in *Re JL and AO (Babies Relinquished for Adoption)*[606] and *Re M and N (Twins: Relinquished Babies: Parentage)*[607] it was held that the 'nothing else will do' approach did not apply in a case where a mother handed over a child at birth, wanting it kept secret from her family. In this kind of case the court will not require proof that the wider family cannot offer care for the child.

However, as mentioned in relation to care orders, it is clear that some courts and commentators read too much into *Re B-S*. As mentioned earlier the Court of Appeal in *Re R (Adoption)*[608] emphasised that the court should not be deterred from making an adoption order where doing so was in the child's best interests.[609] A good example of the current approach is *Borough of Poole* v *Mrs and Mr W*.[610] The case arose by way of an attempt to revoke placement and leave to defend an adoption. This was based on the fact that there had been significant improvements in the parents' position, including them undertaking university degrees. It was argued that adoption could no longer be said to be the only option. However, the child, who had particular needs, would have been traumatised by an attempt to reunite her with the parents. The court therefore decided to proceed with the adoption process. It was emphasised that the welfare of the child is key and the dicta on the importance of the birth family in *Re B-S* could not be used to justify the child suffering harm. Indeed, it is still very true that in many cases the security and permanence offered by an adoption, especially where the placement has been a success, will carry significant weight in a welfare assessment.[611] In *Re R (Adoption)* Munby P was clear:

> I wish to emphasise, with as much force as possible, that *Re B-S* was not intended to change and has not changed the law. Where adoption is in the child's best interests, local authorities must not shy away from seeking, nor courts from making, care orders with a plan for adoption, placement orders and adoption orders. The fact is that there are occasions when nothing but adoption will do, and it is essential in such cases that a child's welfare should not be compromised by keeping them within their family at all costs.[612]

So the current position seems to be as follows.[613] The court should consider all realistic options.[614] If adoption is the only one which will promote the welfare of the child, that should be chosen.[615] If there is an alternative to adoption which is better than or as good as adoption that should be chosen, because adoption is a 'last resort'.[616] Even if there is another acceptable alternative to adoption, if adoption is clearly better it should still be preferred.[617] The court must take into account the underlying preference for being raised with the birth family. That can include the importance of being raised in the child's culture.[618] The court will also take into account the relationship that has developed between a child and potential adopters during

---

[606] [2016] EWHC 440 (Fam), para 50.

[607] [2017] EWFC 31.

[608] [2014] EWCA 1625.

[609] A point emphasised by McFarlane LJ extra-judicially: McFarlane (2016).

[610] [2014] EWHC 1777 (Fam).

[611] *BC v IA* [2014] EWFC 1491; *Re MM (Long Term Fostering: Placement with Family Members: Wishes and Feelings)* [2013] EWHC 2697 (Fam).

[612] [2014] EWCA 1625, para 44.

[613] See Sloan (2015c) and Holt and Kelly (2015a) for a helpful discussion of the current position.

[614] *Re S (Care Proceedings: Evaluation of Grandmother)* [2015] EWCA Civ 325.

[615] *Re S (Care Proceedings: Evaluation of Grandmother)* [2015] EWCA Civ 325.

[616] *Re B-S* [2013] EWCA Civ 1146.

[617] *Re M-H (Placement Order: Correct Test to Dispense with Consent)* [2014] EWCA Civ 1396, [2015] 2 FLR 357.

[618] *Newcastle City Council v WM and Others* [2015] EWFC 42.

placement. Where a strong attachment has already been formed the court may take some persuading that the proposed adoption should not go ahead.[619]

(ii) The consent of the parents

Before an adoption order can be made, the court must have the consent of the parents or dispense with that consent.

(a) Who must consent?

The consent of all parents with parental responsibility and any guardians is required. The consent of an unmarried father without parental responsibility is not required. The 1996 draft Adoption Bill required the consent of children over the age of 12 to being adopted, but this is not required under the 2002 Act.[620] The British Agencies for Adoption and Fostering objected to the consent requirement on the basis that children may feel they are being asked actively to reject their birth parents by consenting to adoption.

(b) The unmarried father without parental responsibility

As just noted, it is not necessary to have the consent of a father without parental responsibility before the court makes an adoption order; but that does not mean that he can be ignored by the adoption agency. The adoption agency should normally notify the father of the adoption proceedings.[621] Where the father has family life for the purposes of Article 8, the courts have held that he must be notified of the proceedings and involved sufficiently to protect his interests. Not to do so might infringe his rights under Articles 8 and 6.[622] This human rights dimension now means that the father should be informed of the proposed adoption unless there are very good reasons for not involving him (e.g. where there is a concern that he will be violent towards the mother if he should learn of the child's birth and proposed adoption).[623]

An example of this approach can be found in *Re M (Notification of Step-parent Adoption)*[624] where it was determined a father should not be notified of a step-parent adoption. He had played no role in the child's life, nor had he attempted to. He, therefore, had no Article 6 or 8 rights in relation to the child.[625] In any event there was a real possibility he would be violent to the mother or child if he were to be informed of the proceedings, so even if he did have an Article 8 right, the child and mother's interests justified an interference in it.

(c) What is consent?

Consent must be given 'unconditionally and with full understanding of what is involved'.[626] It is therefore not possible for a birth parent to consent to an adoption only under certain circumstances (e.g. that the adopter is a Chelsea supporter!). The consent must be in writing on a form which sets out the effect of adoption and is witnessed by a CAFCASS officer. The intention of these requirements is that the consent be given freely and with full

---

[619] *Re M'P-P (Children) (Adoption: Status Quo)* [2015] EWCA Civ 58. See Nickols (2014) for difficulties in reuniting children and birth families after they have been removed.

[620] See Piper and Miakishev (2003) for support for this proposal.

[621] This includes anyone believed to be a father by the agency.

[622] *Re R (Adoption: Father's Involvement)* [2001] 1 FLR 302.

[623] *Re S (A Child) (Adoption Proceedings: Joinder of Father)* [2001] 1 FCR 158.

[624] [2014] EWHC 1128 (Fam).

[625] *Re C (A Child)* [2013] EWCA Civ 431.

[626] ACA 2002, s. 52(5); *Re CA (A Baby)* [2012] EWHC 2190 (Fam).

understanding.[627] This explains why a birth mother's consent to adoption is valid only if the child is at least six weeks old.[628] Until this time she may not have full understanding of the significance of the decision she is making. A birth mother could consent to placement immediately following birth, but then would need to provide later consent to adoption.[629]

In *Re S (Child as Parent: Adoption: Consent)*[630] the court had to determine whether a child under 16 who was a parent could consent to an adoption. It was held she could if she had sufficient capacity to make the decision. She would have to be able to understand the following key features of adoption:

    (i)   Your child will have new legal parents, and will no longer be your son or daughter in law;

    (ii)   Adoption is final, and non-reversible;

    (iii)   During the process, other people (including social workers from the adoption agency) will be making decisions for the child, including who can see the child, and with whom the child will live;

    (iv)   You may obtain legal advice if you wish before taking the decision;

    (v)   The child will live with a different family forever; you will (probably) not be able to choose the adopters;

    (vi)   You will have no right to see your child or have contact with your child; it is highly likely that direct contact with your child will cease, and any indirect contact will be limited;

    (vii)   The child may later trace you, but contact will only be re-established if the child wants this;

    (viii) There are generally two stages to adoption; the child being placed with another family for adoption, and being formally adopted;

    (ix)   For a limited period of time you may change your mind; once placed for adoption, your right to change your mind is limited, and is lost when an adoption order is made.[631]

She had to 'be of sufficient intelligence and maturity to weigh up the information and arrive at a decision'. It should be noted if the mother is found to be unable to consent then her consent can be dispensed with, as will be discussed shortly.

(d) Consent to what?

The consent to the adoption can be consent to adoption by a specific person or general consent for the child to be adopted by anyone. The consent can be given at the time of placement or subsequently. This reflects the variety of roles that the birth family may wish to play in an adoption case. It may be that the birth parents do not want any involvement in adoption and hand over the child to the adoption agency, happy for them to select an appropriate adopter. On the other hand, it may be that the birth family want a say in the selection of the adopter (particularly if the adoption is to be an open one), in which case they may prefer to consent to a particular adopter of whom they approve.

(e) Changes of mind

If the consent is given in advance of the adoption order, it can subsequently be withdrawn as long as an application for an adoption order has not been made. But, if a placement order has

---

[627] Although see *Re A (Adoption: Agreement: Procedure)* [2001] 2 FLR 455 where the consent of a 15-year-old Kosovan rape victim to a freeing order was revoked on the basis that she had not understood what she was signing.

[628] ACA 2002, s. 52(3).

[629] *A Local Authority v GC and Others* [2009] 1 FLR 299.

[630] [2017] EWHC 2729 (Fam).

[631] Paragraph 37.

been made, a parent cannot object to the making of the adoption order without the leave of the court.[632] The court, under s. 47(7), must be persuaded that there has been a change in circumstances, such that it would be appropriate to reopen the question.[633] We discussed this earlier.

In *Re SSM (A Child)*[634] a father sought leave to oppose making an adoption order. Mostyn J held that the change in circumstances needed to be 'unexpected'. So, if, when making the original placement order, the court had foreseen that the father might improve his situation, such an improvement would not be a change in circumstances. However, in *Re W (Adoption: Procedure: Conditions)*[635] the Court of Appeal held the judge had been in error in asking whether there had been a 'sea change' or 'significant' change in circumstances. As the court noted, the issue was simply whether or not leave to oppose the adoption should be granted; the court was not considering whether or not the application would succeed.

(iii) Dispensing with consent

If a parent whose consent is required does not give the consent, the court can dispense with the requirement, in two circumstances:

1. 'The parent or guardian cannot be found or is incapable of giving consent.'[636] This provision will be used in cases where the parent or guardian has disappeared or is unknown (e.g. if the baby was found abandoned outside a hospital and the mother has never been identified).[637] It is also used if the parent is suffering a mental disability which means she lacks capacity to consent.

2. 'The welfare of the child requires the consent to be dispensed with.'[638] Under the Adoption Act 1976, parents' objections to adoption could only be overridden if they were unreasonably withholding their consent to the adoption. Section 1 of the Adoption and Children Act 2002 makes clear that now the sole consideration for the court in dispensing with consent is the child's welfare. So, the rights of the parents and questions about whether or not the parents were reasonable in their objections are irrelevant. This has led to heavy criticism by some who fear that to permit the adoption of children against the wishes of parents simply on the basis that it would be better for the child rides roughshod over the importance attached to parental rights. Can any parent be particularly confident that it is impossible to find someone else who would be better at raising his or her child?[639] Such concerns, however, may be overblown. There are a number of ways in which, despite the wording of s. 52(1)(b), the interests of parents could be taken into account:

   (i) The subsection uses the word 'requires'. This might suggest that, if it is shown that adoption is only slightly in the interests of the child, this will be insufficient to *require* the consent to be dispensed with.[640] In *Re P (Placement Orders: Parental Consent)*[641]

---

[632] ACA 2002, s. 47(3).

[633] *Re W (Adoption Order: Set Aside and Leave to Oppose)* [2010] EWCA Civ 1535.

[634] [2015] EWHC 327 (Fam).

[635] [2015] EWCA Civ 403.

[636] ACA 2002, s. 52(1)(a). See *Haringey v Mr and Mrs E* [2006] EWHC 1620 (Fam) for such a case.

[637] In *Re K and Another v FY and Another* [2014] EWHC 3111 (Fam) the mother was treated as not being able to be found, even though the court accepted with 'vast resources' and many people engaged in detective work she might be found.

[638] ACA 2002, s. 52(1)(b).

[639] Barton (2001).

[640] Davis (2005).

[641] [2008] EWCA Civ 535.

the Court of Appeal held that the word 'requires' carries a connotation of being imperative: that dispensing with the consent is not just reasonable or desirable but required in the interests of the child. In *Re Q (A Child)*[642] it was suggested the word 'requires' implies the adoption is necessary. These cases seem in line with the general approach of the case law following *Re B-S*.

(ii) The Court of Appeal emphasised in *Re Q (A Child)*[643] that under the Human Rights Act 1998 this subsection must be read in a way which is compatible with the European Convention if at all possible.[644] Clearly an adoption order is a grave interference with the right to respect for family life between the parent and child.[645] Indeed, it is hard to think of a graver one. It must therefore be a proportionate intervention. Only a substantial benefit to the child of adoption might be thought sufficient to make adoption a proportionate response and therefore permissible under Article 8(2).[646]

It should be added that if the child has lived with the would-be adopters and has developed a close relationship with them it is arguable that the would-be adopters and child have developed family life which is also protected under Article 8 (*DL and ML v Newham LBC and Secretary of State for Education*).[647] Such an argument is likely to be strongest where the child has lived with the applicants for a considerable period of time.[648]

(iii) Although at the adoption order stage the welfare test applies, at the placement stage the s. 31 threshold criteria will have to be satisfied. Therefore, it will have to have been shown that the parenting of the child caused or risked the child significant harm before a child can be adopted against the parent's wishes. Further, since *Re B-S* adoption will only be approved as a 'last resort'.[649]

(iv) The court may determine to dispense with consent even though the parents cannot be blamed. In *Re W (A Child) (Adoption: Delay)*[650] the father was committed to the children and was caring well for his other children. The child in question had lived with the would-be adopters for the past three years and the relationship with them was the dominating relationship in the child's life. The child had no meaningful relationship with the birth family and returning the child at this point would cause serious long-lasting harm.

Despite such arguments, Bridge and Swindells argue that there is a change in the law in that: 'Whereas parents (under the former law) could take a different view of their child's welfare and not be unreasonable, the court will now be able to impose its view on them.'[651] The point is that under the 1976 Act if it would be reasonable to take the view both that the child should

---

[642] [2011] EWCA Civ 1610.
[643] [2011] EWCA Civ 1610.
[644] In *ML v ANS* [2012] UKSC 30, a Scottish case, the Supreme Court took this approach. Welbourne (2002) and Choudhry (2003) provide useful discussions on the potential impact of the Human Rights Act 1998 in this context.
[645] *P, C, S v UK* [2002] 2 FLR 631.
[646] *P, C, S v UK* [2002] 2 FLR 631 at para 118.
[647] [2011] EWHC 1127 (Admin).
[648] *Re B (A Child) (Adoption Order)* [2001] EWCA 347, [2001] 2 FCR 89.
[649] *Re M-H (Placement Order: Correct Test to Dispense with Consent)* [2014] EWCA Civ 1396.
[650] [2017] EWHC 829 (Fam).
[651] Bridge and Swindells (2003: 152).

be adopted and that the child should not (i.e. it was a borderline case) it would not be possible to dispense with the parent's consent. However, in such a case under the 2002 Act it would be open to the court to decide that an adoption was (just) in a child's welfare and therefore to dispense with parental consent. This is revealed in **Re R (Placement Order)**[652] where Sumner J dispensed with the consent of Muslim parents to adoption. They opposed adoption as being contrary to Muslim practice. The judge held that the children's welfare required adoption despite the objections of the parents.

I The effect of an adoption order

An adopted child is to be treated as the 'legitimate child of the adopter or adopters'.[653] This means that the adoption order will have the following effects:

1. Parental responsibility for the child is given to the adopters.[654]

2. Adoptive parents can make all decisions about the child which other parents can make, including appointing a guardian.[655]

3. An adoption order extinguishes the parental status and parental responsibility of any other person. There is one exception to this and that is where a step-parent adopts their partner's child, where their partner will retain parental responsibility and status.[656]

4. After the making of an adoption order, an adopted child no longer has any right to inherit their birth parent's property.

5. On the making of an adoption order, an adopted child who is not a British citizen will acquire British citizenship if the adopter is a British citizen.[657]

There are, however, some circumstances in which the adoption order does not treat the adopted child in exactly the same way as a natural child.

- An adopted person is deemed within the prohibited degrees of relations for the purpose of marrying his or her birth relations.[658] Therefore, for example, if an adopted man marries his birth sister, entirely innocently, the marriage will be void. However, he can marry his adoptive relatives, including an adoptive sister, but not his adoptive mother.

- A minor may retain the nationality he or she had acquired from his or her birth. However, a minor adopted in the UK court will be a British citizen if one of the adopters is a British citizen.[659]

- Adoptions do not affect the right to succeed to peerages.

- Section 69 of the Adoption and Children Act 2002 states that an adoption will not affect certain dispositions of property.

---

[652] [2007] EWHC 3031 (Fam).
[653] ACA 2002, s. 67(1)–(3).
[654] ACA 2002, s. 46(1).
[655] ACA 2002, s. 67.
[656] ACA 2002, ss. 51(2), 67(3)(d).
[657] British Nationality Act 1981, s. 1(5).
[658] ACA 2002, s. 74(1).
[659] British Nationality Act 1981, s. 1(5).

The European Convention on Human Rights, under Article 14, prohibits improper discrimination between adopted children and birth children.[660] Of course, the legal effects are only a small part of the significance of adoption. As Munby P put it in *Re X (A Child) (Parental Order: Time Limit)*:

> . . . an adoption order . . . has an effect extending far beyond the merely legal. It has the most profound personal, emotional, psychological, social and, it may be in some cases, cultural and religious, consequences. It creates what Thorpe LJ in *Re J (Adoption: Non-Patrial)*, referred to as 'the psychological relationship of parent and child with all its far-reaching manifestations and consequences'. Moreover, these consequences are lifelong and, for all practical purposes, irreversible . . . [661]

In *A Mother v Dorset CC*[662] emphasis was placed on the practical significances of adoption, as compared with long-term fostering.

(a) the children would be shut out from any prospect of reunification with their mother (as they would currently wish) in the future;

(b) the proposal for direct contact with the children in foster care would be once every 6 weeks, in open adoption once a year (with letterbox contact in the intervening 6 months);

(c) the children also have a good relationship with their maternal uncle whose contact would be similarly restricted;

(d) the children would lose their relationship with their current carers with whom they are forming attachments, although it is proposed that contact with them could be maintained;

(e) it is unlikely, as the social workers accepted in evidence, that local adoptive placements could be found and the children would probably therefore have to move area and schools and lose current friendships, all of which are important to them.

Often such practical points will be of much greater significance than the legal significance.

J Open adoption

As originally conceived, adoption was seen as a closed and secretive process.[663] Birth parents were not told who had adopted the child, adoptive parents were not told who the birth parents were, and the child was not told that he or she had been adopted. Even if the child did find out, this was a secret to be kept from the rest of the world.[664] This secrecy model changed with evidence that some adopted children needed detailed information of their birth background to establish a secure sense of who they were, and birth parents needed to know that their child had been successfully and happily adopted.[665]

These concerns have led to an increase in willingness for local authorities to encourage open adoption. These are adoptions where the child maintains links with the birth parents or wider family. This may be indirectly through e-mails, or directly through face-to-face meetings. Research suggests that open adoptions more often involve contact between the birth mother

---

[660] *Pla and Puncernau v Andorra* [2004] 2 FCR 630; *Hand v George* [2017] EWHC 533 (Ch).
[661] [2014] EWHC 3135 (Fam), para 54.
[662] [2019] EWFC B3.
[663] See Hasan (2019) for a rights-based argument for open adoption.
[664] Cretney (2003a: ch. 17).
[665] Howe and Feast (2000).

and her side of the family, rather than the birth father.[666] At present at least 70 per cent of children who have been adopted retain some kind of contact with their birth families.[667]

The Children and Families Act 2014 has add a new s. 51A(2) to the Adoption and Children Act 2002 allowing the court to make an order allowing contact when making an adoption order.[668] This can require the adoptive parents to allow contact with another person. In fact, it seems court orders are rare.[669] The argument the courts have accepted is that if the adopters are happy for there to be contact then there is no need for the court to make an order requiring it;[670] and if the adopters do not want there to be contact it would be wrong to force them to do so.[671] This means that trust between the birth families and adopters is key.[672]

KEY CASE: *Re B (A Child) (Post-Adoption Contact)* [2019] EWCA Civ 29

A child was born to parents who had intellectual disabilities. The child was taken into care after it was determined the parents could not be supported to look after the child and was placed with potential adopters. The care plan supported no direct contact and a 'final visit' with the parents took place. At the time of the adoption application the parents sought post-adoption contact. The adopters opposed on the basis that it was not appropriate for contact to take place now, although they were open to it as a possibility in the future. The parents' application was refused, a decision upheld on appeal before the Court of Appeal.

The Court of Appeal emphasised the views of adopters on contact should not be over-ridden unless there were extremely unusual circumstances. Section 51A did not authorise imposing contact upon adopters who were unwilling to agree to it. The only powers of the court acting on its own motion was to prohibit contact. Only in extremely unusual cases would the court order contact. Section 51A was designed to enhance the position of adopters, not the position of birth parents seeking contact. As McFarlane P put it: 'the ultimate decision as to what contact is to take place is for the adopters.'

In *P (Children) (Adoption: Parental Consent)*[673] it was held to be of fundamental importance that two siblings keep in contact.[674] The Court of Appeal held that in such a case the court should order contact, rather than leaving it to be dealt with informally by the local authorities and adopters.[675] The court, on adoption, can require a person not to contact the adopted child. That might be appropriate if there are fears that a birth relative will seek to disrupt adoption. In fact, in *Re S-F (A Child)*[676] the Court of Appeal said it was 'relatively rare' to find would-be adopters who would facilitate direct contact after adoption.

[666] Neil (2000).

[667] Department of Health (2002d: 15). Thoburn (2003: 394) says the figure is around 80 per cent.

[668] Sloan (2014). Generally, conditions cannot be attached to an adoption order: *Re W (Adoption: Procedure: Conditions)* [2015] EWCA Civ 403.

[669] *Re R (A Child) (Adoption: Contact)* [2007] 1 FCR 149. Although see *X and Y v A Local Authority (Adoption: Procedure)* [2009] 2 FLR 984.

[670] *Re T (Adoption: Contact)* [1995] 2 FLR 251.

[671] *Re T (Adoption: Contact)* [1995] 2 FLR 251.

[672] Smith (2005).

[673] [2008] 2 FCR 185.

[674] Normally siblings will be adopted together. For a rare case where it was appropriate for them not to be see *Re BT and GT (Children: Twins – Adoption)* [2018] EWFC 76.

[675] See also *Re B (Open Adoption)* [2011] EWCA Civ 509.

[676] [2017] EWCA Civ 964.

DEBATE

Is open adoption a good idea?

The issue of open adoption is controversial.[677] In favour it is said that openly adopted children will feel less of a sense of being rejected by their birth families;[678] it will provide them with a greater sense of security; and it might encourage birth families to be supportive of the adoption.[679] Indeed, one study interviewing adopted children found that many wanted greater contact with their birth families.[680] Against open adoption it must be recalled that some cases of adoption are those where the child has suffered or been at risk of significant harm because of the parenting they have received. Particularly where the birth family have abused the child, the benefits of contact may be questioned. Further, there are concerns that contact with the birth family might undermine the position of the adopters.[681] It may also deter some would-be adopters from going through with the adoption.[682]

Questions

1. What would happen if adoption were abolished? What could replace it?
2. Is there a case for amending the law on adoption so that the birth parents retain some status in respect of the child?

Further reading
See **Harris-Short** (2008) for a useful discussion of the law on adoption.

K Adoption by a parent

A parent may decide to adopt his or her own child. The reason for doing this is usually to eliminate the other parent from the picture. Nowadays this is very rare, but it sometimes arises.

In *Re B (Adoption by the Natural Parent to Exclusion of Other)*[683] very shortly after the birth of her child a mother decided to place her child for adoption. The father, by chance, discovered this and offered to raise his child. The mother agreed to the arrangement. She did not want to play any role in the child's upbringing and was therefore happy for her maternal role to be ended. The Official Solicitor was appointed and objected on the basis that it was not in the child's welfare to terminate the link with her mother. At first instance the adoption order was made but the Court of Appeal allowed an appeal. Hale LJ held that only exceptional circumstances (e.g. disappearance of a parent or anonymous sperm donation) could justify single-parent adoptions. The House of Lords, however, allowed a further appeal and restored the adoption. It held, controversially, that an order which was in the child's best interests could not breach the child's rights. The decision was reached under the Adoption Act 1976 under

---

[677] Smith and Logan (2002) and Neil (2003) provide useful discussions.
[678] In *Re G (Adoption: Contact)* [2003] Fam Law 9 the fear was expressed that without contact the children might view their birth families as 'ogres'.
[679] Smith and Logan (2002). *Re G (Child: Contact)* [2002] 3 FCR 377 acknowledges that research is generally in favour of open adoption.
[680] Thomas (2001).
[681] For an example see *Re C (Contempt: Committal)* [1995] 2 FLR 767.
[682] Lowe and Murch (2002: 62).
[683] [2002] 1 FLR 196.

which the child's welfare was the first, but not paramount, consideration in any decision. It was held that, as the mother did not want to have anything to do with the child, an adoption could not be said to interfere improperly with the human rights of the mother or child.[684]

L Adoption by parent and step-parent

Twenty-two per cent of all adoptions in 2005 involved step-parents.[685] More recent statistics are not available. Typically, such adoptions arise where a mother remarries and her new husband wishes to have formal recognition of his status. He could enter into an agreement with his wife in relation to the child which would grant him parental responsibility.[686] However, he might still want the formal label of father and/or he may be concerned that the birth father may seek to interfere with the way that the stepfamily will care for the child; he, therefore, may consider adoption. The stepfather might have two options:

1. The mother and her new husband adopt the mother's child. So, rather strangely, the mother adopts her own child. The purpose of doing this is that the birth father will lose entirely his parental status. The stepfather and birth mother will become the legal parents of the child. However, to some the attraction of adoption is that it means the stepfamily need no longer fear that the birth family will interfere with the way they raise the child.

2. The Adoption and Children Act 2002 enables the partner of a parent to adopt a child, without that affecting the parental status of the birth parents.[687] Thus a stepfather can adopt the child. He will become the father, but the mother will remain as the mother. Notably the procedure can be used not only by the spouse of a parent, but any partner (including a same-sex partner).

If there is an application for adoption involving a step-parent, the application will be governed by the principles already outlined. It must be shown that the adoption will promote the welfare of the child, and the necessary parental consents must be obtained or dispensed with. It should be emphasised that the court must be persuaded that it is better to make an adoption order than to make no order at all.[688]

Many take the view that step-parent adoptions should not be permitted. In particular, while it is understandable why the stepfather might want some kind of recognition of his position in the child's life, that should not mean that the birth father and his side of the family lose their status in respect of the child.

> ### CASE: *Re P (A Child)* [2014] EWCA 1174
>
> A Polish woman with three children had formed a relationship with an English man (F). The birth fathers of the children had minimal contact with them. When their relationship settled, F, with the consent of the mother, applied for an adoption order. The fathers did not consent and the judge refused to consent on the basis that adoption was not essential to their welfare and was not a last resort.

---

[684] See Bainham (2002b) and Harris-Short (2002) for criticism of this decision.
[685] Department of Constitutional Affairs (2006).
[686] CA 1989, s. 4A
[687] ACA 2002, s. 52(2).
[688] ACA 2002, s. 1(6).

It was held that the key issue in dispensing with consent was proportionality. There was a difference to be drawn between cases where step-parents were adopting a child with the children remaining with their birth mother and where the children were to be adopted outside their family. That was because there was less disruption in the child's rights to respect to family life in a step-parent adoption case. The making of a step-parent adoption was more likely to be proportionate where the non-consenting parent had not had care or undertaken responsibility for the child; had no or infrequent contact with the child; and where the step-parent had formed a well-established relationship with the parent with whom the child was living.

M Post-adoption support

Lowe has suggested that adoption has changed from the gift/donation model to a contract/ services model.[689] He points out that at one time a child being adopted was regarded as a gift to be handed over by an adoption agency to an infertile couple. Once the child was received by the couple, the local authority's role was at an end and the adopter would be treated in the same way as a birth parent. Nowadays adoption is seen as one of the ways of arranging the care of a child taken into care. As the age of adopted children has increased, and, as a result, children being adopted may present a range of emotional and physical problems, it has become necessary to rethink the assumption that the local authority carries no responsibility for adopted children. This has led to increased awareness of the importance of providing support to children who have been adopted.[690] The task of adopting a child who has been severely abused or suffers from complex physical disability may be beyond all but the most gifted of parents without the assistance, advice and support of a local authority. The offering of services may help to decrease the rate of adoption breakdown and may encourage prospective adopters to adopt 'difficult' children. A more cynical view is that these 'services' may in effect amount to regulation of and intervention in the family life of the adoptive family.[691]

The Adoption and Children Act 2002 now requires adoption agencies to provide for a wide range of adoption support services.[692] However, this does not create a strong right to such services. The Children and Families Act 2014 has added a new s. 4A into the 2002 Act which requires the local authority to provide adoptive parents with a personal budget, but only where the local authority decides to provide adoption support. The personal budget allows the adoptive parents to purchase services they need. Section 5A requires the local authority to provide information about the services that might be available. However, neither of these provisions gives a right to post-adoption support or services. Although adoptive parents and adopted children have the right to request that they be assessed for the provision of adoption support, the Act does not require the local authority to meet the need.[693] This would mean that the local authority may assess an adopted child to be in need of services, but then decide that it is

---

[689] Lowe (1997a).
[690] Lowe (1997a).
[691] Harris-Short (2008).
[692] ACA 2002, s. 4(7); Adoption Support Services (Local Authorities) (England) Regulations 2003 (SI 2003/1348).
[693] ACA 2002, s. 4.

unable to afford to provide them.[694] Special guardians do not even have the right to be assessed, although a local authority may, if it wishes, provide services to them.[695]

McFarlane P[696] writing extra-judicially referred to reports he had read of adoptive parents:

> They give an account of only having received partial and inadequate information as to the harm suffered by the young people prior to their placement, a lack of therapeutic support in the early months and years of the placement and, when problems erupt during the teenage years, the adopters typically feel viewed by social services in the same light as failing 'parents' in ordinary care proceedings.

N Revocation of an adoption order

The adoption order continues to have effect unless another adoption order is made. In particular, the adoption order does not come to an end when the child reaches the age of 18. As mentioned above, one of the main advantages of adoption is the security it creates. If adoption could be brought to an end it would undermine that benefit.[697] The court will only revoke an adoption order in 'highly exceptional' circumstances.[698] There are just three circumstances in which an adoption order can be overturned:[699]

1. If the child is adopted by his or her father, but his or her mother then marries the father. In such a case the father could apply under s. 55 of the Adoption and Children Act 2002 for the adoption to be revoked and the child would then in law be the child of his or her parents. This provision is very rarely invoked.

2. It is possible to appeal against the making of the adoption order, although it is necessary to show a flaw in the making of the order itself and demonstrate exceptional circumstances. The case law provides three examples of exceptional circumstances:

   (i) Where the consent of the parent to the adoption was given on the basis of a fundamental mistake. In *Re M (A Minor) (Adoption)*[700] a father agreed to the adoption of his children by his former wife and her new husband. Unknown to him, his ex-wife was terminally ill and she died shortly afterwards. The court allowed the appeal in what they regarded as a 'very exceptional case' on the basis that ignorance of the wife's condition negated his consent, which was based on a fundamental mistake.[701]

   (ii) Where the adoption procedures involved a fundamental defect in natural justice.[702] In *Re K (Adoption and Wardship)*[703] an English foster carer had adopted a Muslim baby, who had been found under a pile of bodies in the former Yugoslavia. Unfortunately, the adoption process had been deeply flawed. The adoption order was set aside due to

---

[694] See, by analogy, *R (On the Application of A) v Lambeth* [2003] 3 FCR 419.

[695] CA 1989, s. 14F(1), (?)

[696] McFarlane (2017).

[697] *Re B (Adoption: Setting Aside)* [1995] 1 FLR 1 at p. 7.

[698] *HX v A Local Authority (Application to Revoke Adoption Order)* [2020] EWHC 1287 (Fam).

[699] *Re B (Adoption: Jurisdiction to Set Aside)* [1995] 2 FLR 1, [1994] 2 FLR 1297.

[700] [1991] 1 FLR 458; [1990] FCR 993.

[701] In *Re O (Human Fertilisation and Embryology Act 2008)* [2016] EWHC 2273 (Fam) a clinic incorrectly told a female partner she was not a mother as the paperwork had been improperly completed and so the couple adopted the child. The adoption could be revoked as she could in fact have been declared the mother.

[702] In *Re J (A Minor) (Revocation of Adoption Order)* [2017] EWHC 2704 (Fam) an adoption order was revoked after 'a wholesale abandonment of correct procedure and guidance' in the making of the order.

[703] [1997] 2 FLR 221; [1997] 2 FLR 230.

the lack of protection for the birth family and the breach of natural justice caused by the faulty procedure. At the rehearing[704] for the adoption order it was decided that the child should be made a ward of court but that he remain with the foster carers who were required to bring him up with instruction in the Bosnian language and Muslim religion. Every three months they were required to report back to the Bosnian family. In *HX v A Local Authority (Application to Revoke Adoption Order)*[705] McDonald J held that a case might involve a serious injustice, but not amount to a fundamental breach of natural justice.

(iii) In *PK v Mr and Mrs K*[706] the child successfully sought revocation. She had been adopted at a young age but essentially abandoned by her adoptive parents. She had eventually made contact with her mother and birth grandparents and now aged 14 wanted to revoke the adoption and live with her mother. The court described the case as 'highly exceptional and very particular' and revoked the adoption under the inherent jurisdiction.

(iv) In *Re J (Adoption: Appeal)*[707] the mother and new husband adopted J (a child the mother had had with a previous partner). The couple had misled the social workers and court by saying they did not know who the father was. Cobb J authorised the revocation of the adoption order to allow the father to pursue a relationship with the child and because the original order had been unjust and based on false information. That decision could be regarded as somewhat generous. The father (who had no parental responsibility) had no right to be involved in the decision making. He had fathered the child as a teenager and not sought to be involved in J's life for ten years, partly as a result of depression. The revocation of the adoption order meant J lost legal ties with the man who had raised him for much of his life and his 'adoptive' sibling.[708] It must be questioned whether the somewhat speculative hope of a relationship with J's birth father was worth removing the legal ties to his 'adoptive' father and sibling.

3. If the child is adopted by a new set of parents, this will end (but not revoke) the original adoption.

In the absence of one of these three grounds, an adoption order cannot be set aside, however sympathetic the court may be to the application.[709] If the birth family are seeking to challenge an adoption order and are not able to overturn the adoption order, they could still apply for a residence order in respect of the child. It would be unlikely that such an application would succeed unless the adoption had completely broken down.[710]

---

[704] [1997] 2 FLR 230.
[705] [2020] EWHC 1287 (Fam).
[706] [2015] EWHC 2316 (Fam).
[707] [2018] EWFC 8.
[708] Fenton-Glynn (2018) who emphasises that in this case the child's day-to-day living arrangements would not be impacted by the revocation and that this might have made the courts more sympathetic to the application. See for further discussion Sloan (2018).
[709] *Re B (Adoption: Jurisdiction to Set Aside)* [1995] 2 FLR 1, [1994] 2 FLR 1297.
[710] *Re O (A Minor) (Wardship: Adopted Child)* [1978] Fam 196.

A dramatic example of the application of these principles was the following case:

CASE: *Webster v Norfolk CC* [2009] EWCA Civ 59

Mr and Mrs Webster had three children in three years, born between 2000 and 2003. In late 2003 their middle child, B, was taken to hospital suffering multiple fractures. The hospital and local authority assessed the injuries to be non-accidental and caused by his parents. The children were adopted by late 2005.

In 2006 Mrs Webster became pregnant again. In the course of care proceedings relating to the new baby, the Websters obtained fresh expert evidence in relation to B. The new report was powerfully of the opinion that the injuries to B were caused by scurvy and iron deficiency rather than abuse. At the time scurvy was considered as unknown in the West and had not been considered as an explanation for the injuries. As a result, the care proceedings in relation to the baby were discontinued. The parents then sought to set aside all the orders relating to their three younger children.

Wall LJ confirmed that 'only in highly exceptional and very particular circumstances' can adoption be set aside. Why? Wall LJ thought the answer lay in the dicta of Swinton Thomas LJ in *Re B (Adoption: Jurisdiction to Set Aside)*:[711]

> An adoption order has a quite different standing to almost every other order made by a court. It provides the status of the adopted child and of the adoptive parents. The effect of an adoption order is to extinguish any parental responsibility of the natural parents. Once an adoption order has been made, the adoptive parents stand to one another and the child in precisely the same relationship as if they were his legitimate parents, and the child stands in the same relationship to them as to legitimate parents. Once an adoption order has been made the adopted child ceases to be the child of his previous parents and becomes the child for all purposes of the adopters as though he were their legitimate child.

In the Websters' case there was nothing in the procedure that led to the making of the order which rendered the procedure flawed, and hence the adoption order could not be set aside. Wilson LJ emphasised that the children had been with the adopters for four years in an arrangement they had been told was permanent.

The decision has proved controversial.[712] The author has argued that the reasoning of the case failed to place appropriate weight on the human rights of the parties and the welfare of the children.[713] While the decision placed weight on the importance for adopters in having the security of knowing adoptions will not be set aside unless there are exceptional circumstances, it did not mention the importance for birth parents in feeling secure that their children will not be permanently removed without good cause.[714] Andrew Bainham goes further and suggests that the decision requires a reconsideration of whether adoption should be a preferred

---

[711] [1995] Fam 239, at 245C.
[712] It was followed in *Re PW (Adoption)* [2011] EWHC 3793 (Fam).
[713] Herring (2009h).
[714] Herring (2010g).

model for children in care.[715] Not everyone has objected to the decision. Caroline Bridge has described it as a 'model of clarity and common sense'.[716] It was followed in *Re PW (Adoption)*[717] where Mrs Justice Parker noted that if it was too easy to apply to set aside an adoption order on the grounds of procedural failures, adoptive parents might seek to do so, which she thought undesirable.

O   The breakdown of adoption

Surprisingly, there are no official statistics on the rate of breakdown of adoptions.[718] The best indication we have is that in 2019 there were 180 children who entered the care of the local authority from adoption.[719] One study found that 9 per cent of the placements studied broke down before an adoption order was made and 8 per cent broke down after the order was made.[720] A survey by Selwyn and Masson[721] found a 3.2 per cent disruption rate, which is much lower than previous studies. The strongest predictor of disruption was the child's age, with nearly two-thirds of disruptions taking place during the child's teenage years and more than five years after the order has been made. Children who were four years old or more at placement were 13 times more likely to leave their adoptive family compared to those who were placed as infants. As the authors point out, it is sometimes assumed that adoption support is needed in the first few years after the adoption but can then safely be ended, but this study suggests it can be years after the adoption, as the child becomes a teenager, that support is particularly needed.

What is also striking about their study is that adoption seems to have a lower disruption rate than special guardianship orders (which had a 5.6 per cent disruption rate) and residence orders (25 per cent). Most residence orders will be with family members and so there is a clear warning there about the assumption that care with family members is best for children. However, these figures pale in comparison with the disruption rate of 65 per cent for children removed from parents under a care order, but then returned to parents. The impact of a failed adoption on the child and adoptive parents can hardly be imagined. Indeed, it is possible that failed adoptions will cause the child more harm than would have been suffered by the child if the adoption had not been attempted. It is therefore important that the Government's attempts to increase the number of adoptions do not lead to an increase in the rate of adoption breakdown. Where an adoption does break down, it will normally be necessary to take the child back into care through a care order.[722]

P   Access to birth and adoption register

One study estimated that one-third of adopted people seek to obtain access to their birth records.[723] Of course, others may make less formal attempts to find the background to their births. Another study found that 75 per cent in their sample sought their birth mother and 38

---

[715] Bainham (2009a).
[716] Bridge (2009: 381).
[717] [2011] EWHC 3793 (Fam).
[718] Department of Health (2002b).
[719] Office for National Statistics (2020i).
[720] Parker (1999: 10).
[721] Selwyn and Masson (2014).
[722] *Re K (A Child: Post Adoption Placement Breakdown)* [2012] EWHC B9 (Fam).
[723] Rushbrooke (2001).

per cent their father.[724] An adopted person seeking to discover information about his or her birth family could seek access to the following:[725]

1. *Birth certificates.* The Registrar-General is required under s. 79 of the Adoption and Children Act 2002 to keep records to enable adopted people to trace their original birth registration. This would enable a person to discover the details of their birth, including the name of their mother. There is no absolute right to obtain a copy of the birth certificate. This is demonstrated by *R v Registrar-General, ex p. Smith*,[726] where the Court of Appeal held that the Registrar-General was entitled to restrict the access of Smith to his birth records. Smith was in prison in Broadmoor, having killed his cell-mate in the belief that he was killing his mother. It was held that he might use the knowledge of his birth mother to harm her and the court held that it was therefore proper for the Registrar to deny him access.

2. *Information from adoption agencies.* The Adoption and Children Act requires adoption agencies to provide details which would enable an adopted person to obtain their birth certificate. They will also be able to obtain information from the court which made the adoption order.[727] If the agency does not wish to disclose the information, it can obtain a court order permitting non-disclosure.[728] If it is 'protected information', in that it concerns private information about other people, then the agency can refuse to disclose it although they should also take reasonable steps to ascertain the views of the people involved.

3. *The Adoption Contact Register.* If birth families wish to contact adopted children, they can use the Adoption Contact Register. At 30 June 2001, there were 19,683 adoptees and 8,492 relatives on the Adoption Contact Register for England and Wales, and 539 successful matches had been made since the start of the Adoption Contact Register in 1991.[729]

These measures go some way towards recognising a person's rights to know about their genetic origins,[730] which has been held to be an important aspect of a person's right to private life, protected by article 8 of the European Convention on Human Rights.[731] It should be noted that, in fact, adopted children who seek information about their birth parents are particularly interested in finding out about their mothers. It is also important to appreciate that even where contact is made this does not usually lead to an ongoing relationship.[732]

In *FL v Registrar General*[733] the adult daughter of an adopted man wished to find out about her father's birth family and sought information from the Registrar-General. Under s. 79(4) of the Adoption and Children Act 2002 in exceptional circumstances the court could order the Registrar-General to give information to a person other than the adopted person. Roderick Wood J held that matters had to be looked at in the context of the wider public interest, the interests of society and the protection of potential third parties who might be profoundly affected by such disclosure, as well as in the matter of confidentiality. Even taking into account the possible mental illness of the father, which might be hereditary, and questions over

---

[724] Howe and Feast (2000).

[725] Disclosure of Adoption Information (Post Commencement Adoptions) Regulations 2005 (SI 2005/888).

[726] [1991] FLR 255, [1991] FCR 403.

[727] ACA 2002, s. 60(4).

[728] ACA 2002, s. 60(3).

[729] BAAF (2014). Up-to-date statistics are not recorded.

[730] Howe and Feast (2000).

[731] *MG v UK* [2002] 3 FCR 289.

[732] Howe and Feast (2000) report a study that only 51 per cent of adopted children who had found their birth mother had continued the contact. However, 97 per cent of adopted people who had located their birth parents had no regrets about doing so.

[733] [2010] EWHC 3520 (Fam).

whether his erratic behaviour was exacerbated by the adoption, the case was not exceptional and so the Registrar-General was not ordered to make the disclosure. By contrast, in *Re X (Adopted Child: Access to Court File)*[734] a woman sought information about her father. The application was made under 3.14.24 of the Family Proceedings Rules 2002 and the court granted access to the court file. The factors seemed to be that the adoptive parents, birth parents and adopted person were dead and so would not suffer distress, while the woman had a genuine reason for seeking the information.

Q Inter-country adoption

The limits on the number of children available for adoption has caused some people to turn to adoption of babies from overseas. This practice is governed by the Adoption (Inter-country Aspects) Act 1999 and the Adoption and Children Act 2002, which give effect to the Hague Conference on Private International Law's Convention on Intercountry Adoption. This topic is not covered in detail in this text.

14 The position of children in care

KEY STATISTICS

- For the year ending March 2019 there were 78,150 children being looked after by local authorities in England, a notable increase from March 2015, when the figure was 69,540. Indeed, the figure has been gradually increasing for the past ten years. The rate per 10,000 children under 18 in care in England has increased from 54 in 2009 to 65 in 2019.[735]

- The most common age group of looked after children were those aged ten and over (64%), while children under one year old were only 5% of the looked after population.

- The majority of looked after children are of white ethnicity (74%). 10% were of mixed ethnicity and 8% were of Black or Black British ethnicity.

- There are a range of reasons why a child is looked after:
  - as a result of or because they were at risk of abuse or neglect – 49,570 children – the most common reason identified
  - primarily due to living in a family where the parenting capacity is chronically inadequate (family dysfunction) – 11,310
  - due to living in a family that is going through a temporary crisis that diminishes the parental capacity to adequately meet some of the children's needs (family being in acute stress) – 6,050
  - due to there being no parents available to provide for the child – 5,410
  - due to the child's or parent's disability or illness – 4,580
  - due to low income or socially unacceptable behaviour – 1,230.

- 75% of children being looked after by a local authority were under a care order.

---

[734] [2014] EWFC 33.
[735] Department for Education (2020).

The history of state-organised childcare in England and Wales is bleak, with widespread evidence of abuse and mistreatment of children in children's homes.[736] Indeed, it is not difficult to find cases where the intervention of the state has made matters worse, not better, for children.[737] Claire Taylor states that her study of residential care for children in care paints an 'incredibly bleak and depressing picture' which is a 'national disgrace'.[738] The following statistics provide some insight into the issues:

KEY STATISTICS

- Almost one-third of children in care leave school with no GCSEs or vocational qualifications like GNVQs.

- Only 13.2% of children in care obtain five good GCSEs – compared with 57.9% of all children.

- Only 6% of care leavers go to university – compared with 38% of all young people.

- One-third of care leavers are not in education, employment or training – compared with 13% of all young people.

- 23% of the adult prison population has been in care and almost 40% of prisoners under 21 were in care as children (only 2% of the general population spend time in prison).

- A quarter of young women leaving care are pregnant or already mothers, and nearly half become mothers by the age of 24.[739]

Despite this gloomy picture, one study found the care system worked well for children where there was early intervention to protect them, a stable environment while they were in care, followed swiftly by allowing them to live an independent life.[740] The authors of the report criticise media representations suggesting that children in care are doomed to a life of disadvantage.[741] Rather, care can be a positive intervention for many children.[742] Indeed another study comparing children who were in care who were returned home and those who remained in care, found those who remained in care fared better.[743]

The basic position under the Children Act 1989 is that local authorities (rather than courts) are responsible for deciding how children taken into care should be cared for. This is partly because the law recognises that decisions on how to look after a child in care involve careful interaction between the local authority, the parents, alternative carers and maybe other charitable bodies. These relationships might require ongoing and flexible negotiations of a kind unsuitable for court supervision. However, local authorities do not have unlimited discretion on how to bring up the child. There are four particular restrictions on local authorities' powers. First, there are financial restrictions which may limit the resources available to a local

---

[736] Waterhouse (2000); (Social Services Inspectorate (2002 (Philpot (2001)).
[737] E.g. *Re F* [2002] 1 FLR 217.
[738] Taylor (2006: 175).
[739] These statistics are all taken from Who Cares? Trust (2014).
[740] Hannon *et al.* (2010); Stein (2009).
[741] See Morgan (2010) and CAFCASS (2010) for a discussion of the views of children in care.
[742] Hannon *et al.* (2010).
[743] Wade *et al.* (2012); Giovannini (2011).

authority.[744] Secondly, there are a few issues over which the courts retain some control. In particular, only a court can discharge a care order[745] and a court order is required to approve the termination of contact between the child in care and his or her parents.[746] Thirdly, parents retain parental responsibility (even when a child is taken into care) and will be encouraged to be involved in decisions relating to the way their child is brought up while in care. Fourthly, the children in care themselves play an important role in determining the way they are brought up under the care system.

A Duties imposed upon a local authority

The Children Act 1989 imposes upon local authorities a number of duties owed towards children who are looked after by them.[747] These duties are owed to children who are voluntarily accommodated by the local authority for more than 24 hours[748] and to those who are the subject of a care order.[749]

(i) The general duty

The general duty of the local authority is contained in s. 22(3):

LEGISLATIVE PROVISION

Children Act 1989, section 22(3)

It shall be the duty of a local authority looking after any child—

(a) to safeguard and promote his welfare; and

(b) to make such use of services available for children cared for by their own parents as appears to the authority reasonable in his case.

This duty is self-explanatory, but it should be noted that the local authority can owe duties to children even if the children are cared for by their parents.

(ii) The duty to decide where the child should live

The local authority must 'receive the child into their care and . . . keep him in their care while the order remains in force'.[750] So on the making of the care order the local authority becomes responsible for deciding where the child should live.

---

[744] E.g. *Re C (Children) (Residential Assessment)* [2001] 3 FCR 164.
[745] CA 1989, s. 39.
[746] CA 1989, s. 34.
[747] CA 1989, s. 22, inserted by Children and Young Persons Act 2008. See HM Government (2010c) for detailed guidance.
[748] CA 1989, s. 22(2).
[749] CA 1989, s. 22(1).
[750] CA 1989, s. 33(1).

(iii) The duty to consult

The Children Act 1989, s. 22(4) requires a local authority to consult with the child and his or her family:

LEGISLATIVE PROVISION

Children Act 1989, section 22(4)

Before making any decision with respect to a child whom they are looking after, or proposing to look after, a local authority shall, so far as is reasonably practicable, ascertain the wishes and feelings of—

(a) the child;

(b) his parents;

(c) any person who is not a parent of his but who has parental responsibility for him; and

(d) any other person whose wishes and feelings the authority consider to be relevant regarding the matter to be decided.

The local authority must then give 'due consideration' to these views. The views of the child are taken into account as would be appropriate given the age and understanding of the child.[751]

(iv) The duty to provide accommodation

The local authority has a duty to accommodate a child in care.[752] There is a specific duty to make arrangements for the child to live with his or her family or friends unless it is not reasonably practicable or consistent with his or her welfare.[753] There is also a duty to accommodate the child as close as possible to the parents' home and to any siblings accommodated by the local authority.[754]

It is a common misconception that children taken into care spend the rest of their childhood in children's homes. One study found that in less than half the cases where care proceedings were instigated were children removed from their parents.[755] In fact 30 per cent of children who leave care return home.[756] The NSPCC has expressed concern that around half of those returned home then suffer further abuse or neglect.[757] Indeed, it is becoming less common for children in care to be accommodated in children's homes, at least as a long-term solution. In part this is in response to a depressing procession of scandals about the physical and sexual abuse of children in children's homes. Foster carers are often seen as a preferable solution. In 2019, 72 per cent of looked after children lived with foster parents.[758]

---

[751] CA 1989, s. 22(5)(a) and (b).
[752] CA 1989, s. 22A
[753] CA 1989, s. 22C
[754] CA 1989, s. 22C(8).
[755] Hunt and Macleod (1998: 287).
[756] Department for Education (2020).
[757] NSPCC (2012).
[758] Department for Education (2020).

(v) The duty to maintain

There is a duty on the local authority to maintain a child, but in some circumstances it can recoup the cost by requiring a financial contribution to the child's maintenance from their parents or others, if reasonable to do so.[759]

(vi) The duty to promote contact

A local authority is under a positive obligation[760] to promote contact between children and parents, family or friends unless such contact is not reasonably practicable or is inconsistent with the child's welfare.[761] This is required under s. 34 of the Children Act 1989 and would be required under Article 8 of the European Convention.[762] Local authorities are also required to keep in touch with persons who have parental responsibility for the child and specifically to keep them informed of the child's whereabouts.

The issue of contact between the child in care and his or her family is one of the few issues concerning children in care where the court has a major say. If the local authority wishes to prohibit contact for a period longer than seven days, it must apply for an order under s. 34 of the Children Act 1989 permitting it to do so.[763] If such an application is made, the court must determine whether there is to be contact and, if there is, the frequency and place of contact.[764]

The welfare principle and the s. 1(3) checklist govern the discretion of the court.[765] However, in considering this there is a presumption in favour of there being contact between children in care and their parents. Simon Brown LJ in *Re E (A Minor) (Care Order: Contact)*[766] explained why:

> Even when the s. 31 criteria are satisfied, contact may well be of singular importance to the long-term welfare of the child: first in giving the child the security of knowing that his parents love him and are interested in his welfare; secondly, by avoiding any damaging sense of loss to the child in seeing himself abandoned by his parents; thirdly, by enabling the child to commit himself to the substitute family with the seal of approval of the natural parents; and fourthly, by giving the child the necessary sense of family and personal identity. Contact, if maintained, is capable of reinforcing and increasing the chances of a permanent placement, whether on a long-term fostering basis or by adoption.

The presumption can also be seen as part of the right to respect for family life under the Human Rights Act 1998.[767] To justify a termination of contact under the Act, it would have to be shown that it was necessary in the child's interests and that it was proportionate to the harm faced by the child.[768]

---

[759] CA 1989, s. 22B.

[760] CA 1989, Sched. 2, para 15.

[761] For a detailed discussion see Richardson, Boylan and Brammer (2017).

[762] *L v Finland* [2000] 2 FLR 118.

[763] In such a case there is no duty to promote contact with the parents: CA s. 34(6A).

[764] CA 1989, s. 34(3).

[765] *Re H (Children) (Termination of Contact)* [2005] 1 FCR 658.

[766] [1994] 1 FLR 146, [1994] 1 FCR 584.

[767] *R v UK* [1988] 2 FLR 445. Although it will be easier to justify ending contact with a father who has had little contact with the child, than with a mother who has formed a close bond to the child: *Söderbck v Sweden* [1999] 1 FLR 250.

[768] *S and G v Italy* [2000] 2 FLR 771.

When a local authority seeks to terminate contact, this is often because contact is inconsistent with its plans for the child: for example, it wishes to place the child for adoption. So, the plans of the local authority will be relevant too. The court should give respect to the plans of the local authority, but in the end the welfare principle governs the issue.[769] Another factor can be the wishes of the child, as confirmed in *L v L (Child Abuse: Access)*.[770] However, the weight placed on the child's wishes depends on the age of the child and circumstances of the case. There are dangers in placing weight on abused children's wishes because abuse can cause a complex psychological relationship between the child and an abuser.[771]

The Court of Appeal has held that the duty of the local authority to promote contact extends to 'any relative, friend or other person connected with him'.[772] However, it needs to be stressed that unlike parents, the local authority does not require the consent of the court to terminate contact with those not listed in s. 34. This means that if a local authority does not permit contact, these other relatives and friends need to apply for a contact order under s. 8 of the Children Act 1989.[773] The court would then need to determine whether the contact would promote the welfare of the child.[774] The Court of Appeal considered that grandparents do not have a right of contact with children in care and must show that contact would be in the interests of the child. The court may well be prepared to assume that it is good for a child in care to maintain links with as many family members as possible if they are willing to go to the effort of visiting him or her.[775]

The court has no power to force an adult to have contact with the child, according to Wilson J in *Re F (Contact: Child in Care)*.[776] The only person who can be forced to behave in a particular way by an order under s. 34 is the local authority, which can be required to allow the parents to have contact with the child.

(vii) Duty to review

The local authority is required to keep under review the long-term plans for each child in care. The local authority must review a child's case within four weeks of the child being first accommodated by the authority. A second review should be carried out within three months of the first and, thereafter, reviews every six months. The purpose of the review is to ensure that the child does not 'drift through care' and instead that the time in care is part of a coordinated programme designed to promote the child's welfare.[777] So it should be decided as early as possible whether the child is to be adopted and, if so, what steps should be put in place to enable that to take place. Parents and children should be included in the review, or at least consulted.[778] Following the Human Rights Act 1998, the review should constantly ensure that the children's and parents' rights to respect for family life be maintained to the greatest extent possible and that, where appropriate, the care plan progresses towards reuniting the child and the parent.[779]

---

[769] *Re S (Children) (Termination of Contact)* [2005] 1 FCR 489.
[770] [1989] 2 FLR 16, [1989] FCR 697.
[771] *Re G (A Child) (Domestic Violence. Direct Contact)* [2001] 2 FCR 134.
[772] CA 1989, Sched, 2, para 15(1)(c).
[773] CA 1989, s. 34(3)(b).
[774] *Re M (Care: Contact: Grandmother's Application for Leave)* [1995] 2 FLR 86, [1995] 3 FCR 550.
[775] *Re W (Care Proceedings: Leave to Apply)* [2004] EWHC 3342 (Fam).
[776] [1995] 1 FLR 510, [1994] 2 FCR 1354.
[777] For an appalling example of such drift, see *Re F, F v Lambeth LBC* [2002] Fam Law 8.
[778] Review of Children's Cases Regulations 1991 (SI 1991/895).
[779] *L v Finland* [2000] 2 FLR 118.

B Empowering children in care

A variety of provisions seek to protect the rights of children in care:

- Children's views must be given due consideration when making decisions about their time in care.[780]
- Children can apply to the court for an order authorising contact with another person.[781]
- Children can apply for a section 8 order.[782]
- The child can institute the complaints procedures.[783]
- The child can apply to discharge a care order.[784]

Despite these provisions, research suggests that children in care feel that their wishes are not being taken into account and that they are not listened to.[785] Some argue that the high levels of anti-social behaviour and running away among children in care is explained by the fact that they feel they are not being heard. There are particular concerns with the complaints procedure, which should be readily accessible to children in care. Some local authorities appoint a children's rights officer to promote good practice and to assist children to use the complaints procedure.[786]

15 Questioning local authority decisions about children in care

The Children Act 1989 is designed to prevent disputes between parents and local authorities arising in the first place. There are two main ways in which this is done. The first is through the concept of partnership: this is the idea that local authorities should work in partnership with the child's family and others interested in the child's welfare. The second is through regular reviews: local authorities are required periodically to review each child looked after by them and have a duty to establish procedures to hear complaints or representations.

Despite these attempts to avoid disputes, inevitably they do arise and there are a number of routes of appeal for those seeking to challenge local authority decisions.[787]

A Internal complaints procedures

The internal complaints procedure is primarily designed to work in cases where there is no dispute over what the facts are or the law is. The complaints procedure is most appropriate where the dispute is whether the local authority has misused its powers. *R v Kingston-upon-Thames RB, ex p. T*[788] suggested that the complaints procedure should be preferred to judicial review in most cases.

---

[780] CA 1989, s. 22(4)(a) and (5)(a).
[781] CA 1989, s. 34(2) and (4).
[782] See Chapter 9.
[783] CA 1989, s. 26(3)(a). Complaints procedures will be further discussed shortly.
[784] CA 1989, s. 39(1).
[785] Hunt, Waterhouse and Lutman (2010).
[786] CA 1989, Sched. 2A
[787] See Bailey-Harris and Harris (2002) for an excellent discussion.
[788] [1994] 1 FLR 798, [1994] 1 FCR 232.

B Human Rights Act 1998

Under s. 7 of the Human Rights Act 1998 an individual can bring a claim against a local authority which has infringed or is about to infringe that individual's rights under that Act. Section 8 provides that if the application is successful then the court can provide such relief or remedy as is appropriate. This could include requiring the local authority to pay damages[789] or reverse its decision and reconsider what should happen to the child.[790] Proceedings should only be brought under s. 8 if there are no ongoing care proceedings. If care proceedings are ongoing, human rights arguments should be made in the context of those proceedings.[791] In *C v Bury Metropolitan Borough Council*[792] a mother brought an action against a local authority under the Human Rights Act 1998 claiming that it had infringed her Article 8 rights and those of her son who was in care. The case centred on the decision by the local authority to move the son to a residential school 350 miles away from the mother. Although it was accepted that their Article 8 rights had been infringed, it was held that the infringement was lawful, being in the son's interests and a proportionate interference. Perhaps of significance was the fact that the mother did not have a settled lifestyle and moved around the United Kingdom, and the finding that the local authority had acted reasonably given its financial responsibilities to all the children in its care. The decision has led one commentator to speculate that the Human Rights Act remedies may rarely differ in outcome from judicial review.[793] That would be surprising, but time will tell.

C Judicial review

Judicial review is another court-based remedy when an individual is claiming that a local authority is acting illegally. Leave is required before an application for judicial review can be launched.[794] The court must be persuaded that the applicant has sufficient interest in the matter.[795] Clearly, a parent will have sufficient standing, as will other relatives if their relationship to the child was close enough. Before the court grants leave it will need to be satisfied that the applicant has a reasonable prospect of winning the case.[796] In *Re M; R (X and Y) v Gloucestershire CC*[797] Munby J held that judicial review was not an appropriate means of seeking to prevent a local authority from commencing emergency protection or care proceedings, unless there were exceptional circumstances.[798] In *A and S v Enfield London Borough Council*[799] Blair J suggested that it would be rare that judicial review should be used in the field of child protection. The purpose of judicial review is not to decide whether or not the decision was the right one but to decide whether the decision was reached in accordance with the law. So, even if the court thinks that the decision was the wrong one, it cannot overturn it unless the decision was outside the bounds of the law.

---

[789] Damages are to be ordered only if just and appropriate: Human Rights Act 1998, ss. 7 and 8. See *Re v (A Child) (Care: Pre-birth Actions)* [2006] 2 FCR 121; *GD v FD* [2016] EWHC 3312 (Fam).

[790] *Re M (Challenging Decisions by Local Authority)* [2001] 2 FLR 1300.

[791] *Re I. (Care Proceedings: Human Rights Claims)* [2004] 1 FCR 289; *Re v (Care Proceedings: Human Rights Claims)* [2004] Fam Law 238. The same is true if a claim is made in habeas corpus.

[792] [2002] 2 FLR 868.

[793] Bailey-Harris (2002).

[794] Rules of the Supreme Court, Order 53, r. 3.

[795] Clearly, parents and the child him- or herself will have sufficient interest but more remote relatives might have difficulty.

[796] *R v Lancashire CC, ex p. M* [1992] 1 FLR 109, [1992] FCR 283.

[797] [2003] Fam Law 444.

[798] See also *Re M (Care Proceedings: Judicial Review)* [2004] 1 FCR 302.

[799] [2008] 2 FLR 1945.

The following list indicates the kinds of complaints that have led to judicial review proceedings:

- removing a child from foster carers without consultation;[800]
- improperly removing a person from a list of approved adopters;[801]
- unjustifiably placing a child on a child protection register;[802]
- disclosing to third parties allegation of child abuse;[803]
- failing to take into account the views of a 15-year-old child in care about where she was to live.[804]

Even if a local authority is found to have acted illegally, the remedies after a successful claim for judicial review are limited. The court will declare the decision unlawful and require the local authority to reconsider the issue. The court does not normally have the power to compel the local authority to act in a particular way. The limited remedies available under judicial review indicate that it is best used when an applicant is attempting to challenge a general policy of a local authority. Where the complaint is about the way a particular individual was treated, an application under the Human Rights Act 1998 may be more appropriate. Munby J has described judicial review in this context as a 'singularly blunt and unsatisfactory tool' and 'a remedy of last resort'.[805]

D Secretary of State's default powers

The Secretary of State has the power to intervene in an extreme case. The Secretary of State will be reluctant to use this power in an individual complaint but may be persuaded to do so where a local authority has adopted what he or she regards as an undesirable policy. An example may be a local authority which has failed to set up a satisfactory complaints system.[806]

E The local government ombudsman

A complaint can be made to the relevant local government ombudsman if there is maladministration. Recourse to the local government ombudsman is only possible where there is no remedy by way of the internal complaints procedure or it would be unreasonable to use that procedure. The ombudsman will issue a report and can award an *ex gratia* payment.[807] However, the ombudsman has no power to order the local authority to act towards a child in a particular way.

F Civil actions

There have been in recent years several attempts by parents and children to sue local authorities under the law of tort for compensation for harms caused by local authorities when performing

---

[800] *R v Hereford and Worcester County Council, ex p. R* [1992] 1 FLR 448, [1992] FCR 497; *R v Lancashire CC, ex p. M* [1992] 1 FLR 109, [1992] FCR 283.
[801] *R v Wandsworth LBC, ex p. P* [1989] 1 FLR 387.
[802] E.g. *R v Hampshire CC, ex p. H* [1999] 2 FLR 359.
[803] *R v Devon CC, ex p. L* [1991] 2 FLR 541.
[804] *R (CD) v Isle of Anglesey CC* [2004] 3 FCR 171.
[805] *Re M (Care Proceedings: Judicial Review)* [2004] 1 FCR 302.
[806] *R v Brent LBC, ex p. S* [1994] 1 FLR 203.
[807] This is not enforceable.

their childcare obligations.[808] These claims are usually based on either the tort of negligence or the breach of statutory duty.[809] The cases involve some highly complex issues of tort law and so only a broad outline can be provided here. The position that the law has now reached is that each case depends on its facts. There is no blanket immunity that a local authority can rely upon when facing a claim of negligence. Instead a duty of care is owed where it is fair, just and reasonable. For example, in *W v Essex CC*[810] foster parents specifically told a local authority that they would not be willing to care for a child who was himself a known child abuser. Nevertheless, the local authority housed such a child with them and he abused the foster parents' own children. The House of Lords were willing to accept that, potentially, the local authority could be liable in tort for the harm caused to the foster parents and their children. In *Barrett v Enfield LBC*[811] a local authority was held liable for damages to a child whom it had taken into care but then unsatisfactorily placed with foster carers. It was held that the courts should be more ready to find a duty of care where the claim was that a child taken into care had been mistreated, than in cases where the argument was that the taking into care was improper.[812]

JD v East Berkshire Community Health NHS Trust[813] marked a noticeable shift in the approach of the law. The House of Lords held, in line with the cases outlined above, that parents could not sue doctors or social workers who had acted negligently in child protection work. However, they indicated that the children concerned did have a right of action. Lord Nicholls explained why parents could not sue:

> A doctor is obliged to act in the best interests of his patient. In these cases the child is his patient. The doctor is charged with the protection of the child, not with the protection of the parent. The best interests of a child and his parent normally march hand-in-hand. But when considering whether something does not feel 'quite right', a doctor must be able to act single-mindedly in the interests of the child. He ought not to have at the back of his mind an awareness that if his doubts about intentional injury or sexual abuse prove unfounded he may be exposed to claims by a distressed parent.[814]

In *B v A CC*[815] the Court of Appeal held that a county council owed a duty of care in negligence towards adoptive parents with whom it was placing a child. Doing so would be 'fair, just and reasonable'. The parents lost their case because they were unable to prove that the county council had revealed the adoptive parents' identity to the birth family, despite a guarantee not to, and that as a result the adoptive parents had suffered a campaign of harassment. Had they succeeded in proving those allegations damages may well have been awarded. In *Merthyr Tydfil County Borough Council v C*[816] a mother reported sexual abuse of her children by a neighbour. The local authority failed to deal with the complaint properly and later denied a complaint had been made. The mother suffered psychological harm and it was held that there was a

---

[808] See Palser (2009) for a helpful summary of the law.

[809] For the key decisions on the doctrine of vicarious liability in the childcare context, see *Lister v Hesley Hall Ltd* [2001] 2 FLR 307 and *Armes v Nottinghamshire County Council* [2017] UKSC 60.

[810] [2000] 1 FLR 657.

[811] [1999] 3 WLR 79.

[812] See further *Pierce v Doncaster Metropolitan Borough Council* [2009] 1 FLR 1189.

[813] [2005] 2 AC 373. The Court of Appeal in *Lawrence v Pembrokeshire CC* [2007] 2 FCR 329 confirmed that the case still stands even in the light of the Human Rights Act 1998. In *L v Reading BC* [2008] 1 FCR 295 it was confirmed that the same principles would bar a claim against the social workers individually.

[814] [2005] 2 AC 373, para 85.

[815] *B v A County Council* [2006] 3 FCR 568.

[816] [2010] 1 FLR 1640.

reasonable prospect of a later court finding that the local authority did owe her a duty of care, created by virtue of the fact she had reported the abuse.[817] In *Armes v Nottinghamshire County Council*[818] the local authority were found vicariously liable in the law of tort for abuse suffered by the claimants at the hands of foster carers.

The law involves a delicate balance. On the one hand, in favour of liability of the local authority under the law of tort are arguments that tort liability will encourage the local authority to see that it has in place procedures to ensure that negligent acts do not take place. Also in favour of liability are arguments that children or adults who suffer as a result of local authority intervention or non-intervention deserve compensation for their loss. Indeed, they may be entitled to a remedy under Article 6 of the European Convention on Human Rights. On the other hand, there are also arguments against tortious liability. Local authorities may become too 'litigation conscious' in carrying out the delicate task of child protection, leading to social workers always adopting the safest course of action, which may not be the course which is the best policy for the child. A further complexity is that sometimes the decision over the form of intervention to protect a child is essentially a political one, involving allocation of resources.[819] Such decisions, partly economic or political, are normally thought inappropriate for judicial review. Due to the difficulties in pursuing a tort action an applicant may prefer, where possible, to use the Human Rights Act 1998.[820]

G Private orders

An aggrieved parent or relative could use a section 8 order.[821] In *Re A (Minors) (Residence Orders: Leave to Apply)*[822] a foster mother sought to challenge a local authority's decision that she was no longer permitted to foster four children by applying for a residence order in respect of the children. The Court of Appeal took the view that, in considering whether to give leave, the authority's plans were very important.[823] The court was willing to assume that departure from the local authority's plan would not promote the child's welfare and therefore it declined to grant leave. This case indicates that it will be rare for a court to grant leave for a section 8 application which the local authority opposes. Whether a court will have to be more willing to grant leave, relying on Article 6 of the European Convention on Human Rights, is open to debate.

H Inherent jurisdiction

If a child is in need and no other route is open to protect the child's welfare, the court may be willing to use the inherent jurisdiction in exceptional cases. In *Re M (Care: Leave to Interview Child)*[824] a father successfully applied under the inherent jurisdiction for an order that he could have his child interviewed to assist in his defence to a rape charge. The court will only make an order under the inherent jurisdiction if persuaded that the order sought will promote

---

[817] For another horrific example, see *ABB, BBB, CBB and DBB v Milton Keynes Council* [2011] EWHC 2745 (QB).

[818] [2017] UKSC 60.

[819] See e.g. *CN v Poole BC* [2017] EWCA Civ 2185 where the court held there was no duty to ensure children were housed where they would not be exposed to harm from problem neighbours.

[820] *Lawrence v Pembrokeshire CC* [2007] 2 FCR 329. But see *MAK and RK v United Kingdom* [2010] ECHR 363.

[821] Non-parents may require the leave of the court (see Chapter 10).

[822] [1992] 2 FLR 154, [1992] 2 FCR 174.

[823] As required under CA 1989, s. 10(9)(d)(i).

[824] [1995] 1 FLR 825, [1995] 2 FCR 643.

the welfare of the child. The inherent jurisdiction cannot be used to compel a public authority to act in a particular way.[825]

In *Re AB (Medical Treatment: Care Proceedings)*[826] parents of a very sick child disagreed with the care offered by the hospital. The parents were said to be uncooperative and to be interfering with the care the child needed. The local authority applied for a care order. Munby J noted that cases involving disputes between parents and doctors needed careful handling. He added: 'Local authorities need to think long and hard before embarking upon care proceedings against otherwise unimpeachable parents who may justifiably resent recourse to what they are likely to see as an unnecessarily adversarial and punitive remedy.' He noted that the inherent jurisdiction could be used to resolve issues of specific dispute over medical treatment. He noted the care order might grant a local authority parental responsibility, but it did not remove the parents' parental responsibility and the local authority could not assume that it could use its parental responsibility to override the parents' refusal. He also raised the issue of whether a care order would be productive if there were no alternative carers for the child. His judgment certainly gives the impression that use of care orders to resolve cases where the primary issue was a dispute between parents and doctors is unlikely to be the best course of action.

16 The balance of power between courts and local authorities

Learning objective 10

Analyse the balance of power between courts and the local authority

A recurring theme through the past two sections of the text has been the delicate balance of power between the courts and local authorities.[827] Courts and local authorities have each complained that the other has exceeded its powers. In *Nottingham CC v P*[828] the court criticised the local authority for failing to apply for a care order, leaving the court powerless to help the child; while in *Re C (Interim Care Order: Residential Assessment)*[829] the local authority felt that the courts were exceeding their powers in ordering the local authority to assess the child at a specialist centre.

How does the Children Act 1989 balance the power between the courts and the local authority? At a simple level the answer is that the courts decide whether to make an order, but the local authority decides how to implement the order. The position has been summarised by the Court of Appeal in *Re R (Care Proceedings: Adjournment)*:[830]

> [T]he judge is not a rubber stamp. But if the threshold criteria have been met and there is no realistic alternative to a care order and to the specific plans proposed by the local authority, the court is likely to find itself in the position of being obliged to hand the responsibility for the future decisions about the child to the local authority . . . To make other than a full care order on the facts of this case was to trespass into the assumption by the court of a control over the local authority which was specifically disallowed by the passing of the Children Act.

---

[825] *Re L (Care Proceedings: Human Rights Claims)* [2004] 1 FCR 289 at para 12.
[826] [2018] EWFC 3.
[827] Hayes (1996).
[828] [1993] 2 FLR 134, [1994] 1 FCR 624.
[829] [1997] 1 FLR 1, [1997] 1 FCR 149.
[830] [1998] 2 FLR 390, [1998] 3 FCR 654.

However, it is more complex than that. Dewar[831] has suggested two models that could describe the way that the court operates:

1. The first is the adjudicative or umpire model. Here the court simply decides whether a local authority has made out the threshold criteria for an order and will make the order without involving itself in planning issues. In other words, once the court is persuaded that the grounds for an order are made out, the local authority takes over control of what should happen during the order.

2. The second is the active or participatory model. The court should decide not only whether or not there should be an order but also what should happen once the order is made.

There is support for both models in the Children Act 1989 and the case law. In favour of the adjudicative model being an accurate description of the role of the court in this area is the ethos of partnership, indicating that disputes over what should happen to the child in care should be resolved between the local authority, the parents and the child, without court intervention.[832] In particular, the local authority is required to set up a complaints procedure which is designed to resolve any disputes and avoid the need to refer issues to the court.[833] In favour of the participative model is the fact that the courts retain control over the contact arrangements, although it should be noted that the courts have the power only to require the local authority to ensure contact continues. The courts have no power to order a local authority to prevent contact.[834] The courts also have the power to revoke a care order, for example, by making a residence order.

There have been several cases revealing clashes between the courts and local authorities.[835] The leading case is the following:

CASE: Re S, Re W (Children: Care Plan) [2002] 1 FCR 577[836]

Here the House of Lords was required to consider the extent to which a court could require a local authority to carry out its care order. The Court of Appeal in that case clearly felt frustrated that a judge makes a care order on the basis of a particular care plan, but the local authority may then decide to do something completely different with a child, without having to return to the court.[837] An extreme example might be that the local authority in the care plan proposes keeping the child with the birth family, but providing them with services. The judge, approving of this, makes a care order but the local authority could then decide to place the child with fosterers, with a view ultimately to adoption: quite a different prospect from that foreseen by the judge who made the original care order.[838] It should

---

[831] Dewar (1992).
[832] Department for Children, Schools and Families (2008a).
[833] CA 1989, s. 26(3).
[834] *Re W (Section 34(2) Orders)* [2000] 1 FLR 512.
[835] For an extraordinary judicial expression of outrage at the 'disgraceful' conduct of an adoption agency, see *Re F (A Child) (Placement Order)* [2008] 2 FCR 93.
[836] Discussed in Herring (2002b); Miles (2002); Mole (2002); Smith (2002).
[837] In *Re O (Care: Discharge of Care Order)* [1999] 2 FLR 119 the care order was discharged because the care plan had been departed from so radically.
[838] A more realistic example may be that the child is placed with the birth parents under the care order but the promised services are not provided. For an example of a child 'lost in care' while a local authority failed to carry out a care plan, see *F v Lambeth LBC* [2001] 3 FCR 738.

be added that local authorities tend to depart from care plans not because of malice, but a shortage of funds. One study found that only 60 of the 100 children studied had their care plans fulfilled.[839] The same study suggests that where care plans are implemented this normally promotes the child's welfare better than where the plan is departed from.[840]

The Court of Appeal in *Re S, Re W* therefore came up with a scheme under which, on making the care order, the court could star various items on the care plan (e.g. where the child was to live, crucial services which the local authority was to provide). If subsequently the local authority wished to depart from one of the starred items the local authority should take the matter back to court and seek approval of the course of action. If they failed to do so the matter could be brought before the judge by the guardian.

It must be admitted that there were no sections in the Children Act 1989 which mentioned this starring system. However, the Court of Appeal justified its creation of it by reference to the Human Rights Act 1998. The argument was that on making a care order the state would, inevitably, be interfering in Article 8 rights of the child and family. The court would have to make sure that the interference was justified and that the extent of the intervention was proportionate. The only way the court could do this would be to approve the extent of the intervention as set out in the care plan, and require court approval for any further intervention. The House of Lords, however, felt that the Court of Appeal's approach was illegitimate. The Court of Appeal had crossed the line from using the Human Rights Act to interpret legislation, which was permissible, to amending legislation, which was not.[841] The House of Lords pointed out that there were no words in the Children Act which the Court of Appeal were 'interpreting' to produce their starred system; rather, in effect, a new section was being added to the legislation.

The House of Lords went further and claimed that the Court of Appeal's interpretation infringed a cardinal principle in the Children Act 1989. Lord Nicholls explained:

> The court operates as the gateway into care, and makes the necessary care order when the threshold conditions are satisfied and the court considers a care order would be in the best interests of the child. That is the responsibility of the court. Thereafter the court has no continuing role in relation to the care order. Then it is the responsibility of the local authority to decide how the child should be cared for.[842]

In other words, the court has the task of deciding whether or not to make a care order, but the local authority has the task of deciding what should happen to a child who has been taken into care.[843] As Lord Nicholls acknowledges, this principle is not without exception. A local authority cannot, for example, terminate contact between a child in care and his or her family, nor change the child's name or religion without the permission of the court. Indeed, supporters of the Court of Appeal's approach might even claim that the Children Act does leave the courts with control over crucial issues concerning the upbringing of a child in care and therefore the issue is not as straightforward as the House of Lords might have suggested. It is worth noting that Lord Nicholls was clearly not unsympathetic to

---

[839] Harwin and Owen (2003: 72).
[840] Harwin and Owen (2003: 78). See also Hunt and McLeod (1998: chs. 7–9).
[841] *Re S, Re W (Children: Care Plan)* [2002] 1 FCR 577 at para 39. This approach to the balance of power between the courts and local authorities was approved in *Kent CC v G* [2005] UKHL 68.
[842] *Re S, Re W (Children: Care Plan)* [2002] 1 FCR 577 at para 28.
[843] For criticism of this, see Herring (2002b).

what the Court of Appeal was doing. He described the Court of Appeal's approach as 'understandable'[844] and made it clear that his objection was that such an approach should be created by Parliament, not the courts.

Having decided that the Court of Appeal's use of the starring system was illegitimate, Lord Nicholls then held that the present law (whereby the local authority could decide how to bring up a child in its care free from court supervision) was not incompatible with the rights of the child and his or her family under Article 8. He explained that although the law gave the local authority the power to infringe the child's rights (e.g. by disproportionately interfering in his or her Article 8 rights) that did not mean that the law itself thereby infringed the child's rights. The fact that the Children Act provided only limited remedies where it was claimed that the local authority had interfered with the child's or his or her family's right to family life, did not thereby render the Act itself incompatible with the European Convention. This was because the absence of a provision in a statute could not render that statute incompatible with the European Convention.[845] In any event, as Lord Nicholls pointed out, whenever a local authority infringed a child's or his or her family's Article 8 rights, they could bring proceedings against the local authority under s. 7 of the Human Rights Act 1998. This also provided protection for an individual's Article 6 rights.[846] He accepted that relying on parents bringing proceedings to protect the rights of a child in care was not fail-proof. A parent may not want or be unable to litigate. In such a case (unless the child was particularly mature) there would be no one who could enforce the child's rights.

In some ways the lesson to be learned from this litigation is that all too often local authorities lack the resources to implement care plans and this might lead to the infringement of the human rights of children in care. Although the temptation may be to enable the court to compel a local authority to abide by care plans, to do so might mean that local authorities will have to withdraw funding from other children in their care. The fact that all too often insufficient funds are available to ensure that the human rights of children in care are protected should shame our society.[847]

In *Re S and W (Children) (Care Proceedings: Care Plan)*[848] the Court of Appeal felt it necessary to return to the issue of how the courts should deal with an unsatisfactory care plan. In that case there was no question but that a care order should be made in respect of three siblings and that they should be removed from their parents. There was, however, substantial dispute among the professionals involved over whether the children should be adopted by strangers or whether they should be fostered by a great-aunt and uncle or grandparents. In relation to one of the three children the local authority care plan was that the child be fostered by the great-uncle and aunt, but the judge clearly thought that plan inappropriate. He adjourned the application to enable the director of social services of the local authority to reconsider the care

---

[844] *Re S, Re W (Children: Care Plan)* [2002] 1 FCR 577 at para 35.
[845] *Re S, Re W (Children: Care Plan)* [2002] 1 FCR 577 at para 59.
[846] Theoretically, if a parent's parental rights were infringed in a way which did not constitute an infringement of their Article 8 rights, then it may be that the parent's Article 6 rights could be infringed, but, as Lord Nicholls said, it is hard to think of an instance where this would happen.
[847] Herring (2002b).
[848] [2007] EWCA Civ 232.

plan. On appeal it was argued that the judge was acting inappropriately in adjourning the case and asking the local authority to reconsider its plans. It was argued before the Court of Appeal that when a judge was faced with an application for a care order, supported by a care plan, the judge's role was to decide whether or not to make a care order, but not to interfere with the content of the care plan. That argument was fiercely rejected by the Court of Appeal. In fact, they held, the judge had to scrutinise the care plan rigorously and if the judge did not think it met the needs of the child, the court could refuse to make the care order.[849] There is nothing wrong in a court seeking to persuade a local authority to amend its care plan.[850]

In *Re W (A Child)*[851] the Court of Appeal said that although the details of the care plan were for the local authority to develop, it had to do so taking the facts as determined by the judge. If the local authority disagreed with the findings of fact of a judge, they had to appeal it. The local authority should set out the range of options based on the facts found by the judge and explain the services available to meet each. The court could then determine what order to make.

There is much to be said for the general approach of leaving day-to-day issues relating to the treatment of a child in care to the local authority. The first is a practical one and that is that the court cannot provide continuous guidance relating to children in care, responding to particular issues as they arise. Secondly, some issues relating to the care of abused children lie in the expertise of the local authority's social workers. Thirdly, the local authority will have to balance the needs of all children (and other vulnerable people) in their area with the resources they have available to spend. Although courts are adept in deciding specific issues relating to a particular child, court procedures are not suitable for formulating general policies in allocation of resources. Indeed, this may have been the key policy behind the House of Lords' decision in *Re S, Re W (Children: Care Plan)*.[852]

KEY CASE: *Re T (A child) (Placement order)* [2018] EWCA Civ 650

The local authority brought care proceedings concerning an 18-month-old child. The parents wanted the child to be raised by the grandmother, although the local authority wished to pursue adoption. The judge at first decided that it was best for the child to be raised by the grandmother as a foster carer. However, the local authority's fostering panel refused to approve her. In light of that the judge decided to make a placement order with a view to an adoption. On appeal the Court of Appeal thought the judge had underestimated her powers. Having assessed that the grandmother fostering was the best option, the court had an obligation to see its assessment through. The judge could have called the local authority to account and expected 'a high level of respect for its assessments of risk and welfare, leading . . . to those assessments being put into effect'. Indeed, Peter Jackson LJ noted that a local authority which ignored the views of the court could face a judicial review.[853]

---

[849] *Re H (Care Plan: Human Rights)* [2011] EWCA Civ 1009.
[850] *Re H (Care Proceedings: Delay)* [2018] EWFC 61.
[851] [2013] EWCA Civ 1227.
[852] [2002] 1 FCR 577.
[853] See also *Re T-S (Children: Care Proceedings)* [2019] EWCA Civ 742.

17 Conclusion

Lady Hale[854] has explained:

> Taking a child away from her family is a momentous step, not only for her, but for her whole family, and for the local authority which does so. In a totalitarian society, uniformity and conformity are valued. Hence the totalitarian state tries to separate the child from her family and mould her to its own design. Families in all their subversive variety are the breeding ground of diversity and individuality. In a free and democratic society we value diversity and individuality. Hence the family is given special protection in all the modern human rights instruments . . .

This chapter has considered the circumstances in which it is appropriate to take a child into care. This is a notoriously problematic and controversial issue. It is all too easy, with hindsight, to claim that the local authority was too interventionist or not interventionist enough, but making the decisions in some of these cases must be agonising. The practical problems increase with the shortage of appropriately trained social workers. The Children Act 1989 has given the local authority the powers to provide services which are designed to prevent the authority having to use its more interventionist powers. Although the Children Act 1989 set up the threshold criteria before significant intervention in family life could be permitted, the interpretation of the criteria, particularly by the House of Lords, has had the effect of lessening the hurdle that they represent. The Human Rights Act 1998, as applied in case law, will now play an important role, at least in formulating the language which will be used: it must be shown that the intervention in family life by the state is a necessary and proportionate response to the threat faced by the child.

In a recent report written by Paul Bywaters[855] it was found that children living in the most deprived ten small neighbourhoods were over ten times more likely to become looked after by the local authority than children in the wealthiest ten neighbourhoods. This is a powerful reminder that the issues discussed in this chapter cannot be reduced to simply a few 'wicked parents' or 'difficult children' but reflect deep inequalities in society.[856]

In 1983 Michael Freeman wrote about the child's 'right not to be in care', reflecting the view that only in the most compelling cases should children be taken into care.[857] Judith Masson[858] in 2015 called for recognition of a child's 'right to state care', emphasising that the state has special obligations to children who cannot be cared for by their parents. These two different ways of expressing the issue reveal changes in quality of care that the state can offer and an increased awareness of the harm that abuse can cause. What everyone agrees is that the issue is of fundamental importance. It involves the exercise by the state of one of its most coercive powers in order to fulfil its fundamental duties to protect the most vulnerable of its citizens.

---

[854] *Re B (Care Proceedings: Standard of Proof)* [2009] AC 11.
[855] Bywaters (2017).
[856] McFarlane (2017).
[857] Freeman (1983).
[858] Masson (2015a).

Further reading

Adoption UK (2018) *Statistics on Adoption,* London: Adoption UK.

Bainham, A. (2013) 'Private and public children law: an under-explored relationship', *Child and Family Law Quarterly* 25: 138.

Bainham, A. and Markham, H. (2014) 'Living with *Re B-S: Re S* and its implications for parents, local authorities and the courts', *Family Law* 44: 991.

Doughty, J. (2014) 'Care proceedings – is there a better way?' *Child and Family Law Quarterly* 113.

Doughty, J. (2015) 'Myths and misunderstanding in adoption law and policy', *Child and Family Law Quarterly* 331.

Fauset, D. (2020) 'The reforms to care proceedings – one step forward and two steps back? A critical evaluation of the new legal framework and its impact on the pre-proceedings stage', *Child and Family Quarterly* 13.

Featherstone, B., Gupta, A., Morris, K., and White, S. (2018) *Protecting Children. A Social Model,* Bristol: Policy Press

Fox Harding, L. (1996) *Family, State and Social Policy,* Basingstoke: Macmillan.

Gilmore, S. (2013) '*Re J (Care Proceedings: Past Possible Perpetrators in a New Family Unit)* [2013] UKSC 9: Bulwarks and logic – the blood which runs through the veins of law – but how much will be spilled in future?' *Child and Family Law Quarterly* 215.

Hansen, S. (2019) 'Birth relationships after adoption – is there a role for Article 8?' *Child and Family Law Quarterly* 211.

Harding, M. and Newnham, A. (2017) 'Section 8 orders on the public–private law divide', *Journal of Social Welfare and Family Law* 39: 83.

Harwin, J., Alrouh, B., Palmer, M., Broadhurst, K. and Swift, S. (2017) *A national study of the usage of supervision orders and special guardianship over time (2007–2016),* London: Nuffield Foundation.

Hayes, M. (1998) 'Child protection – from principles and policies to practice', *Child and Family Law Quarterly* 10: 119.

Hayes, M. (2004) 'Uncertain evidence and risk-taking in child protection cases', *Child and Family Law Quarterly* 16: 63.

Hayes, M. (2014) 'The Supreme Court's failure to protect vulnerable children: *Re J (Children)*', *Family Law* 43: 1.

Hedley, M. (2014) 'Family life and child protection: Cleveland, Baby P et al.', *Child and Family Law Quarterly* 26: 7.

Hoyano, L. and Keenan, C. (2007) *Child Abuse: Law and Policy Across Boundaries,* Oxford: OUP.

Kaganas, F. (2014b) 'Child protection and the modernized family justice system', in J. Wallbank and J. Herring (eds) *Vulnerabilities, Care and Family Law,* London: Routledge.

Lowe, N. and Cobley, C. (2011) 'The statutory "threshold" under Section 31 of the Children Act 1989 – time to take stock', *Law Quarterly Review* 127: 396.

Marshall, J. (2012) 'Concealed births, adoption and human rights law', *Cambridge Law Journal* 71: 325.

Marshall, J. (2018) 'Secrecy in births, identity rights, care and belonging', *Child and Family Law Quarterly* 30: 167.

Masson, J. (2005) 'Emergency intervention to protect children: using and avoiding legal controls', *Child and Family Law Quarterly* 17: 75.

Masson, J. (2007) 'Reforming care proceedings – time for a review', *Child and Family Law Quarterly* 19: 411.

Masson, J. (2008a) 'The state as parent: reluctant parent? The problem of parents of last resort', *Journal of Law and Society* 35: 52.

Masson, J. (2015a) 'Children's rights: preventing the use of state care and preventing care proceedings', in A. Diduck, N. Peleg and H. Reece (eds) *Law in Society,* Leiden: Brill.

Masson, J. (2015b) 'Third (or fourth) time lucky for care proceedings reform?' *Child and Family Law Quarterly* 27: 3.

Masson, J. and Dickens, J. (2019) 'Outcomes of care proceedings for children', *Family Law* 49: 159.

McFarlane, A. (2017) 'Holding the risk: the balance between child protection and the right to family life', *Family Law* 599.

Munro, E. (2011) *The Munro Review of Child Protection,* London: Department for Education.

NSPCC (2018) *Child protection plan and register statistics,* London: NSPCC.

Parton, N. (2008) 'The "Change for Children" Programme in England: towards the "preventive-surveillance state"', *Journal of Law and Society* 35: 208.

Quinton, D. and Selwyn, J. (2006b) 'Adoption: research, policy and practice', *Child and Family Law Quarterly* 19: 459.

Sargent, S. (2015) 'Transracial adoption in England: a critical race and systems theory analysis', *International Journal of Law in Context* 11: 412.

Sloan, B. (2013) 'Conflicting rights: English adoption law and the implementation of the UN Convention on the Rights of the Child', *Child and Family Law Quarterly* 25: 40.

Sloan, B. (2014) 'Post-adoption contact reform: compounding the state-ordered termination of parenthood?' *Cambridge Law Journal* 73: 378.

Sloan, B. (2015c) 'Adoption decisions in England: *Re B (A Child) (Care Proceedings: Appeal)* and beyond', *Journal of Social Welfare and Family Law* 37: 437.

Sloan, B. (2020) 'Article 5 of the Convention on the Rights of the Child and the Involvement of Fathers in Adoption Proceedings: A Comparative Analysis', *International Journal of Children's Rights* 28: 666.

Taylor R. (2018) 'Religion as harm? Radicalisation, extremism and child protection', *Child and Family Law Quarterly* 41.

Visit **go.pearson.com/uk/he/resources** to access **resources** specifically written to complement this text.

12

Families and older people

Learning objectives

When you finish reading this chapter you will be able to:

1. Discuss the statistics on older people
2. Debate whether adult children should be legally required to support their parents
3. Explain and evaluate the law on mental capacity
4. Summarise the broad issues around succession and intestacy
5. Describe how the law responds to elder abuse

1 Introduction

There is no legislative definition of 'older people'. It is most common to draw a definition in terms of the retirement age, or the age at which state pension becomes payable.[1] However defined, older people hardly constitute a homogeneous group.[2] As the catchphrase states: 'you are only as old as you feel'.[3] Certainly there are stereotypes attached to old age – frailty and failing mental capacities – but many older people are highly active in their communities. Some may argue that it makes more sense to distinguish people with or without mental capacity or employment, rather than by using the category of age.[4] Indeed, as we shall see later in relation to elder abuse, in more recent years government policy has focused on the abuse of vulnerable people, rather than specifically elder abuse.

In the family law context there are increasingly important questions about the extent to which families are and should be responsible for their older relatives.[5] This chapter will consider whether adult children should be liable to support their impoverished parents in their old age, and how to balance the interests of the old and young within society. It will also

---

[1] See the discussion in Herring (2009d: ch 1; 2014c; 2016c).
[2] Hence, this section of the text will use the phrase 'older people' rather than 'elderly people'.
[3] For a discussion of the biological process of ageing, see Grimley Evans (2003).
[4] For discussion of this issue, see Herring (2008e).
[5] Herring (2009g).

examine the complexities that surround the abuse of older people. The chapter will then outline what happens when older people are no longer able to look after themselves. Finally, the chapter will discuss what happens to the property of older people on their death. Before considering these issues it is necessary to quote some statistics which reveal something of the position of older people within our society.

2 Statistics on older people

A Number of older people

Learning objective 1

Discuss the statistics on older people

There has been much talk of a 'generational time bomb'. It has been claimed that there is an increasing number of older people and that a growing proportion of the population is older. Certainly, the statistics support this, although whether it is a 'bomb' and therefore something which should be a cause for concern is another issue.

KEY STATISTICS

- In 2018, there were 12 million people aged 65 or over in the United Kingdom.
- By 2030 it is estimated that 21.8% of the population will be over 65 and there will be 21,000 over 100.[6]
- Babies born in 2018 are (at birth) projected to have a period life expectancy of 79.9 years (males) and 83.4 years (females).

B Older people and their families

It has been estimated that there are 14 million grandparents in the United Kingdom.[7] Grandparents are now the single most important source of pre-school childcare after parents.[8] To replace their care would cost £7.7 billion per year. One survey found that 38 per cent of grandparents looked after their grandchildren at least two days a week, with 12 per cent looking after them every day.[9] Even if they are not taking part in childcare, it appears that most older people are able to keep in contact with family or friends. However, there is also evidence that older people, especially men, who divorce early on in life have weaker links with their families in old age. Society has yet to see the full consequences of the increased rate of divorce. The number of older people living alone has been increasing. Now 3.8 million people over the age of 65 live alone.[10] Eleven per cent of older people report they are in contact with family, friends and neighbours less than once a month. Twenty-four per cent of people aged 50+ living in England feel lonely some of the time, with 7 per cent (1.4 million people) feeling lonely often.[11]

---

[6] All the statistics in this box are taken from Age UK (2020).
[7] Age UK (2020).
[8] Spitz (2012).
[9] Age UK (2020).
[10] Age UK (2020).
[11] Age UK (2020).

Around 38 per cent of older people in England receive the help they need from family and friends. But it is often forgotten that older people are, themselves a significant source of care. It has been estimated that 2 million carers in the United Kingdom are over 65.[12]

Despite all of this, grandparents have a very limited set of rights in family law. This was discussed earlier in the text.[13] An emblematic case for their position is *Re K (A Child)*[14] where a mother handed over a baby to a grandmother shortly after the birth. The grandmother raised the child. The Supreme Court held this gave her 'inchoate rights' for the purposes of the Hague Convention on Child Abduction. The grandparent had undertaken the sole responsibility for the child and that had been accepted by a range of public bodies. Even if she did not have a formal legal status, she in effect had taken on the rights and responsibilities of the parental role. The difficulties this case found in recognising the legal position of the grandmother reveals the precarious position that grandparents find themselves in.

C Income

Poverty is endemic in old age. Two million (16 per cent) pensioners in the UK live in poverty on this definition; 1.1 million pensioners are in severe poverty (i.e. with an income less than the 50 per cent threshold of contemporary median income; 7 per cent of pensioners aged 65+ in the UK are materially deprived (800,000 individuals), that is, they do not have certain goods, services or experiences because of financial, health-related or social isolation barriers[15]. Age UK states that 2 million pensioners (16 per cent of them) live below the poverty line, that is, with incomes below 60 per cent of median household income after housing costs. Of these, 1.1 million older people are defined as living in severe poverty. Seven per cent suffer material deprivation, meaning they lack two or more basic utilities such as a washing machine, freezer, phone, microwave or television.[16] Poverty does not lie equally on gender or race lines.[17] There is a particular problem with poverty among divorced women, caused by the failure to ensure divorce settlements provide adequately for women on retirement. Not only are there an increasing number of pensioners below the poverty line, but the gap between the income of pensioners and employees has widened. One cause of this is the linking of pensions with the increase in the prices of goods rather than wages. There are further difficulties because many pensioners do not claim all of the credits and benefits to which they are entitled.

D Age discrimination

Much of the recent legal discussion concerning older people has centred on the concept of age discrimination.[18] The Equality Act 2010 outlaws discrimination on the ground of age generally. It covers both direct discrimination[19] (where the discrimination is blatantly on the grounds of age) and indirect discrimination[20] (where the discrimination does not refer explicitly to age, but to other grounds which in effect discriminate on the basis of age). The Act only applies to those over the age of 18. A child, therefore, cannot complain that they were

---

[12] Age UK (2020).
[13] See Chapter 8 and below, 'Do older people have rights?'
[14] [2014] UKSC 29.
[15] DWP (2019b).
[16] Age UK (2020).
[17] On gender see Burholt and Windle (2006). On race see Platt (2007).
[18] For an excellent discussion of age discrimination, see Fredman (2003). See also Herring (2009d).
[19] Section 13.
[20] Section 19.

discriminated against on the basis of their age. It applies to the provision of services.[21] However, unlike other forms of discrimination, age discrimination can be justified if it is a 'proportionate means of achieving a legitimate aim'.[22]

3 Do children have an obligation to support their parents?

Learning objective 2

Debate whether adult children should be legally required to support their parents

Some legal systems require adult children to support their aged parents.[23] In Britain such a legal obligation generally has not been accepted.[24] There is no equivalent of the Child Support Act which requires an adult child to support a parent in old age. Further, the social security system does not treat an adult child as a 'liable relative' of a parent, meaning that an adult child's resources are not taken into account when considering a parent's claim for income support. However, with the debate raging over how care for older people is to be financed, this question must be reconsidered. There is widespread feeling that there is at least a moral obligation on adult children to provide some support for their infirm parents; however, it is hard to find a convincing basis for this sense of obligation.[25] There are a number of ways that one could establish an obligation on adult children to support parents:

1. *Reciprocated duty.* It could be argued that an obligation to support parents is a reflection of the obligation on parents to support young children. In other words, because parents provided for children in their vulnerability, children should support parents when parents become infirm. Despite the initial attraction of such an argument, there are difficulties with it. First, although parents can be said to have caused the child to be born in his or her vulnerable state, the adult child cannot be said to have caused the vulnerable state of his or her parents. A similar point is that, although parents can be said to have chosen to have the child and so impliedly undertaken the obligation to care for the child, the same could not be said of children.[26] In the light of these objections, it is clear that there is not necessarily a straightforward link between the duty of parents to care for children and an adult child's obligation to care for parents.

2. *Relational support.* It could be argued that an obligation to support parents flows from the relationship of love that exists between parents and children. The difficulty is that clearly not all parents and children are in loving relationships. However, even where children and parents do not love each other, adult children may feel a sense of obligation to support their parents. This suggests that the obligation to support comes not so much from a relationship of mutual love, but from some other source. A further difficulty with the relational argument is that people do not feel an obligation to support all those with whom they are in a loving relationship. Most people would not feel obliged to support a good friend in his or her old age, even though they may choose to do so. It has been suggested that what distinguishes family relationships from friendships is the notion of intimacy. The argument

---

[21] Section 29.
[22] Section 13(2).
[23] See e.g. the discussion in Deech (2010a).
[24] Herring (2008d). See also Oldham (2001) for an excellent discussion of the English and French approaches to this issue.
[25] Mullin (2010).
[26] Daniels (1988).

here is that family life involves bonds of sharing and intimacy, unlike that in any other relationship.[27] Parents and children reveal to each other aspects of their lives that they show to no other person. However, whether this intimacy is unique to families may be questioned. Some people may feel that they are more open to their friends than to their families. All these points suggest that, although a loving relationship might form the basis of an obligation to support parents, there are other aspects that together complete a more complex picture of obligation.

3. *Implied contract.* It could be argued that there is an implied contract between parents and children that they will support each other. An obvious objection is that children are unable to consent to such a contract at birth. However, the law could assume that the child would have agreed to the contract at birth had he or she been competent to do so. This approach might carry some weight, especially if children were free to rescind the contract once they had reached sufficient maturity to decide whether to uphold it. Another objection to the contract approach is that to see the relationship between family members in terms of contract would not seem in accordance with the realities of family life. A family which regarded its relationships as governed by the terms of a formal contract would be rather unusual.

4. *Dependency.* Here the argument is that the obligation to support flows from the vulnerability of the parent. There is no doubt that some older people need care and financial help from someone. Our society would not accept that older people could be abandoned without any support. It is, then, a matter for society to decide who should provide that support. It could be argued that children are in the best position to give that care, and therefore society is entitled to require adult children to supply it.[28] This is a similar argument to the one used by Eekelaar to explain why parents are under a duty to care for their children.[29] Although children may be uniquely placed to provide emotional comfort for their older parents, whether the same is true for financial support is a different issue. This argument at its strongest could lead us to conclude that society would be entitled, if it wished, to require some kind of support of older parents by adult children. However, although there is widespread acceptance that the law is right to require parents to fulfil their parental duties, the idea that children must support their parents is much more controversial.[30]

A Moral obligations or legal obligations?

English[31] has argued that although there may be moral obligations to support older relatives, these should not give rise to legal obligations. She argues that the law does not generally enforce obligations that arise out of love or friendship. Family members do not add up all they have given and all they have received from a relative in order to work out whether they should help them. Parents do not change nappies out of a sense of legal obligation, but as part of sacrificial love. These are strong arguments, but they could be used equally well in relation to adults and young children. We do place legal obligations on parents to care for young children, even though their relationship is one based on love. The law sets out the minimum required of parents, while accepting that it is just part of what is morally required of them. However,

---

[27] English (1979).
[28] Kellet (2006).
[29] Eekelaar (1991b).
[30] See Oldham (2006) for an excellent discussion
[31] English (1979).

as we shall see, there is a fine line between legal obligations which compel people to provide care they may not wish to give, and the law encouraging and enabling people to give care and support voluntarily. So, before deciding what the law's response should be, it is necessary to consider what obligations family members actually feel towards older people.

B What obligations do people actually feel?

Despite the fact that it is difficult to pin down precisely *why* adult children owe a moral obligation to their parents, there is a widespread feeling that they do. However, such feelings of obligation are complex. Finch,[32] in her wide-ranging study of family obligations, distinguishes two kinds of moral obligation: a normative guideline; and a negotiated commitment. In basic terms, the normative guideline is an accepted standard that applies across the board to certain relationships: for example, that parents should care for their young children. The negotiated commitment is an agreement reached between two people which governs their behaviour: for example, the relationship between an elderly aunt and her nephew may develop over time to the stage where the nephew feels obliged to support his aunt even though, generally, nephews are not expected to support aunts. Finch found that, in deciding whether a person felt under an obligation to provide assistance to another, there were guidelines rather than strict rules in operation. Finch[33] suggests that people tend to ask two key questions: 'Who is this person?' (e.g. are they a relative?); and 'How well do I get on with this person?' She found that parent–child links were the strongest family ties. In parent–child relationships the second question ('How well do I get on with this person?') is less significant than the needs of the older person. So, an adult child may feel little responsibility for a spry elderly parent, even if their relationship is close; whereas an adult child might feel a burden of responsibility for an infirm parent, even if their relationship is not close. That said, Finch notes that most people do not think through in a rational way why they make the wills they do.

Further important aspects in the obligations that family members feel they owe to each other are gender and sexuality. Ungerson[34] found that women have a clearer sense of obligation to family members than men. As noted earlier, it is women who perform the majority of practical care for older relatives. Gay and lesbian people, especially in the past, struggled to use wills to pass on property to their lovers, in a way which was not open to legal challenge.[35]

C Integrating family and state care

If, then, there is a sense of moral obligation towards older parents, how should the law respond? There has been some debate over whether the provision of state aid for older people has weakened the feeling of responsibility of adult children to support their parents. Finch thinks not, arguing: 'If anything it has been the state's assuming some responsibility for individuals – such as the granting of old age pensions – which has freed people to develop closer and more supportive relationships with their kin.'[36] Indeed, the existence of state services for older people has not meant that relatives do not care for each other. A high level of acceptance

---

[32] Finch (1994).
[33] Finch (1994).
[34] Ungerson (1987).
[35] Westwood (2015).
[36] Finch (1994: 243).

that children should care for their older parents has also been found. Although Finch argues that the sense of family obligation has not lessened, she accepts that the circumstances of modern life (e.g. the fact that more women are working) mean that the way people carry out their obligations has changed.[37] Such changes may lead to the result that social services will be required to perform more day-to-day services for older people.

There is increasing acceptance that it is necessary to integrate state support for older people with the support of relatives. Tinker suggests the aim should be:

> . . . the interleaving of informal, usually family, care with statutory services that is so necessary but so difficult to achieve. What does seem evident is that without good basic statutory services, such as community nursing and help in the home, informal carers will not be able to support older people without cost to their mental and physical health. It is no use paying lip service to support for informal carers if help from professionals is not forthcoming.[38]

Not only can the role of the state be regarded as a necessary support for carers, there is also some evidence that older people perceive direct financial support from their children embarrassing and, in a sense, a lessening of their autonomy. There is evidence that older people find it difficult to be in relationships with their children where they are receiving rather than giving. Therefore, receiving money directly from the Government in the form of pensions, rather than from their children, may be regarded by many as a more acceptable form of financial assistance.

D Conclusion

A case can be made for imposing obligations on adult children. Starting with the vulnerability and needs of older people, and accepting that they should be met somehow, society *could* choose to require adult children to provide that care, as they are often best placed to provide it. Such an obligation appears to be reflected in the attitudes and practices of most adult children. However, there are good reasons why our society may prefer to support older people through taxation rather than require financial support from relatives. First, there is the evidence mentioned above that older people dislike feeling that they are a drain on their younger relatives. Enforcing financial support and practical care may therefore damage the family relationships which can be so important in old age. Secondly, such a system could work against the interests of those older people who have no children. Thirdly, as we shall see shortly, there is clear evidence of the strain often incurred by those caring for vulnerable older relatives, and such strain may be exacerbated with an explicit legal obligation. So, it is submitted, a better option is for the state to seek to enable and encourage caring among family members, rather than compel it.[39] As we shall now see, there is some attempt to do this in the present benefits system.

4 Financial support for older people and their carers

The state provides a wide selection of benefits to the retired.[40] Most obviously, there is the basic state pension, supplemented by the state earnings-related pension if paid into by the claimant during his or her employment. In addition to the state provision, the Government

---

[37] Finch (1994).
[38] Tinker (1997: 250).
[39] For further discussion, see Herring (2008d).
[40] See Herring (2013a) for detailed consideration.

in recent years has encouraged people to take out private pensions if their employers have not provided occupational pensions.

Despite these state provisions, as seen earlier, poverty is rife among older people. The problem in part is the low level of benefits and in part the low rate of take-up.[41]

The failure of support applies not just to older people, but also those who care for them, many of whom are family members.[42] There is ample evidence that carers suffer great strain, both emotional and financial. While there is increasing recognition of the work they do, the burden of the care is considerable.

Carers fail to receive sufficient support.[43] The Care Act 2014 has improved the position. For example, the local authority has the power to make special grants to enable carers to have breaks; and carers can be assessed for their own needs. Further, there are special benefits available for those who spend significant time caring for dependent relatives.[44] By offering these funds, the state is recognising the benefits that carers provide not only to their dependants, but also to the state through saving the state the cost of providing the care. Despite this, care can bring considerable disadvantages. Carers UK report that: 'of those caring more than 50 hours a week, almost half (49%) reported their finances had been negatively impacted, 52% had suffered poorer physical health and the vast majority (77%) were suffering from stress or anxiety as a result of missing out.'[45]

The details of these benefits are beyond the scope of this text, but three important points on a theoretical level can be made:

1. Parents who do not seek employment, and instead care for children, receive no special benefits in respect of their care, while those caring for an adult do.[46] So here the voluntary care by mothers (and especially lone mothers) of young children is not positively valued and encouraged by the state.[47] By contrast, the care of older people is supported and encouraged through the benefits system, although many argue that the support given to such carers is inadequate.[48] It may be that the Government feels that carers of older people need financial incentives to provide care, which the parents of children do not need.

2. There are grave concerns that carers are inadequately valued within society.[49] Social provision for frail and older people is predicated on the expectation that women provide the vast majority of the care at no fiscal cost to the state, and that the care the state does provide is subsidised by underpaid female care assistants. It has been claimed that the value of the care provided for older people and other dependent relatives is a staggering £57 billion per year, more than the spending on the NHS.[50] However, there is a dark side to care of older people at home. The majority of carers described themselves as 'extremely tired' and some were depressed.[51] Both the older people and carers were terrified about the possibility of having to move the older person into a nursing home. It should not be assumed that, once the older person is in residential care, their carers are then free from strain.

---

[41] Age UK (2014).
[42] For a detailed discussion, see Herring (2013a).
[43] Herring (2007a, 2008b and 2013).
[44] For the details, see Clements (2011).
[45] Carers UK (2020). See Herring (2019) for further discussion.
[46] Apart from child benefit, which is available in full to those households where neither parent's income exceeds £50,000.
[47] See the discussion at the start of the text (Chapter 1).
[48] See the campaigns of Carers UK
[49] Herring (2013a).
[50] ONS (2020j).
[51] Carers UK (2020).

3. What is the state's obligation towards an older person who is wealthy enough to pay for support him- or herself? To what extent can the National Health Service and social services be expected to provide free care for an older person? The current system is based on a fundamental distinction between healthcare which is paid for by Government and social care which is means tested and can be charged for. For a long time it has been accepted that this division is problematic and has led to serious inadequacies in the care provided. In an attempt to move the debate forward, the Government in 2010 set up a commission headed by the respected economist Andrew Dilnot to investigate the issue. The key proposals of the Dilnot Report are as follows:

- Individuals' lifetime contributions towards their social care costs – which are currently potentially unlimited – should be capped. After the cap is reached, individuals would be eligible for full state support. This cap should be between £25,000 and £50,000. We consider that £35,000 is the most appropriate and fair figure.

- The means-tested threshold, above which people are liable for their full care costs, should be increased from £23,250 to £100,000.

- National eligibility criteria and portable assessments should be introduced to ensure greater consistency.

- All those who enter adulthood with a care and support need should be eligible for free state support immediately rather than being subjected to a means test.

The Commission also sought a scheme whereby people in care homes could defer payment, meaning that they would not be required to sell their homes to pay for care,[52] although it may well be that on death their home would need to be sold to pay for the costs. The Commission estimates that its proposals – based on a cap of £35,000 – would cost the state around £1.7 billion per annum.[53]

The Dilnot Commission was clearly influenced by the political reality that an expensive scheme was unlikely to be supported by the Government. The cost of £1.7 billion, while considerable, was a feasible sum of money to deal with a major issue.

Sadly, the Governments since the Dilnot Report, while expressing determination to deal with the issue, have failed to enact an effective response.

In the 2017 election the Conservative Party indicated an intention to impose a levy to recoup up to £100,000 for care costs on a person's death. The outcry was considerable and it was described as a dementia tax. The plans were modified and effectively dropped. The political fallout from that indicates the dangers for politicians seeking to intervene in this area, but if they do not, the burden will fall on older people and those who care for them.

5 Intergenerational justice

At the heart of the Equality Act 2010 is the principle that discrimination on the grounds of age (and other characteristics) is prohibited. Too often older people are seen as a burden. This is implied with the hysterical reporting that can accompany reports that people are living longer and that we are an ageing population, rather than recognising that this is in fact good news![54]

---

[52] This issue is well discussed in Fox O'Mahony (2012).
[53] Dilnot (2011).
[54] See Herring (2009d) for a discussion of ageism

In the United States, in particular, there has been much discussion of intergenerational justice.[55] This is an ethos that there should be fairness between the older members of society and the younger. There are some who argue that older people receive a disproportionate level of society's resources. Although those over 65 constitute 20 per cent of the population in the United Kingdom, 41 per cent of hospital admissions were of those aged over 65.[56] However, it is worth noting that the statistics indicate that the majority of hospital admissions involve people below the age of 65. The idea that hospitals are full of older people is false. Some talk almost in terms of a battle between the older and younger generations, with the older generation calling for even greater health and pension provision for which the younger generation would have to pay through taxes. There is no easy way of avoiding the fact that a society which distributes resources on the basis of need may well prefer one age group over another.

The House of Lords in 2018 interestingly created a Select Committee on Intergenerational Fairness and Provision[57]. They define intergenerational fairness in this way:

> the idea that each cohort should retain a fair expectation of social improvement and can have a fulfilling life without being unduly harmed by the actions of a previous or subsequent cohort.[58]

They go to explain:

> Each generation contributes through the state and our communities, as well as having the opportunity to receive the benefits of state and community action. As the challenges faced by each generation change, the nature of this contribution and the benefits our collective institutions provide will necessarily change. But, to sustain a positive relationship between generations without animosity, there should be a broad equivalence, and a sense of equivalence, about what is contributed over a lifetime and what is received. This sense of fairness must also extend to generations just born, or about to be born, who have no voice to advocate for them. Policy based on the expectation that future generations will disproportionately pay for present or past consumption cannot be considered just or sustainable.[59]

Daniels[60] wishes to move away from the image of competition between generations. He proposes the 'lifespan approach', in which he suggests that society needs to consider whether the state should provide people with special resources in their young, middle or old age. The fact that the state might provide an especially high level of services in old age is not preferring the old to the young, because the young will receive the same benefits when older. Across each person's lifetime the state expenditure will be the same, Daniels argues. In other words, 'transfers between age groups are really transfers within lives'.[61] Although his approach has much to recommend it to society, medicine and technology are changing too quickly for his approach to provide a satisfactory solution. For example, when a person is born, social attitudes and medical advances may mean that society wishes to focus provision on children, but by the time the person is older, social advances may mean that there is no need to spend so much on the young, and those funds might be better spent on older people.

---

[55] E.g. G. Smith II (1997).
[56] Age UK (2018).
[57] House of Commons, Select Committee on Intergenerational Fairness and Provision (2019).
[58] Ibid, para 2.
[59] Ibid, Para 3.
[60] Daniels (1988: 5).
[61] Daniels (1988: 63).

6 Older people lacking capacity

A Do older people have rights?

Learning objective 3

Explain and evaluate the law on mental capacity

Clearly, old people who have mental capacity have rights. However, more difficult is the position of older people who through illness or old age lack capacity.[62] One in 14 people over the age of 65 (7 per cent of that age group) and 1 in 6 people over the age of 80 have dementia,[63] although not all those with dementia will necessarily have lost capacity.[64] When children's rights were discussed earlier in the text (Chapter 9), it was noted that there are some difficulties in claiming that children have rights because they cannot choose whether to exercise their rights. The approach propounded by Eekelaar was that children's basic, developmental and autonomy interests should be promoted so that once children were sufficiently mature they would be in a position to make life choices for themselves.[65] Such an approach is not possible for older people lacking capacity. Older people will already have developed their own style of life and values. Therefore, the law cannot take a neutral position and make decisions for older people that would enable them to make their own once competent; this is because, having lost competence, most older people will not regain it.

Goodin and Gibson suggest that, for these reasons, it is inappropriate to hold that an incompetent older person has rights and instead the law should move towards a different approach: 'A much more apt description of our duties and their due is couched in terms of a broader but in many ways more demanding notion of "right conduct" towards dependent others.'[66] So, rather than talking about the protection of interests, 'it is rather, that there are certain sorts of things that we must, and certain sorts of things that we must not, do to and for particular sorts of people'.[67] This view therefore says that we cannot talk about rights for the older person lacking capacity, because they cannot choose what they want, and the law cannot ascertain the interests that should be protected. However, this does not mean that older people should be unprotected because others are obliged to treat them with 'right conduct'. There is much to be said for such an approach, although talk of 'right conduct' lacks the punch of 'rights' in political rhetoric.[68]

B When does an older person lose capacity in the eyes of the law?

Section 1(2) of the Mental Capacity Act 2005 (MCA 2005) makes it clear it should be presumed that a patient has capacity, unless there is evidence that he or she has not.[69] If the case comes to court, the burden is on the doctor or whoever treated the patient in a particular way to demonstrate that the patient lacks capacity on the balance of probabilities.

---

[62] Goodin and Gibson (1997).
[63] Age UK (2018).
[64] For a discussion of legal responses to dementia see Foster, Herring and Doron (2014); Herring (2009f and 2011f).
[65] Eekelaar (1986).
[66] Goodin and Gibson (1997: 186).
[67] Goodin and Gibson (1997: 186).
[68] Poffé (2015).
[69] Mental Capacity Act 2005, s. 1. See Herring (2012b) for a discussion of the law.

But what exactly does it mean to say that the patient lacks capacity? Section 2(1) of the MCA 2005 states:

LEGISLATIVE PROVISION

Mental Capacity Act 2005, section 2(1)

. . . a person lacks capacity in relation to a matter if at the material time he is unable to make a decision for himself in relation to the matter because of an impairment of, or a disturbance in the functioning of, the mind or brain.

So, for a person to lack capacity, it must be shown that he or she is unable to make a decision for him- or herself. Section 3(1) explains:

LEGISLATIVE PROVISION

Mental Capacity Act 2005, section 3(1)

. . . a person is unable to make a decision for himself if he is unable—

(a) to understand the information relevant to the decision,

(b) to retain that information,

(c) to use or weigh that information as part of the process of making the decision, or

(d) to communicate his decision (whether by talking, using sign language or any other means).

As this indicates, there are a number of ways in which a person may be said to be unable to make a decision.[70] It may be a case of lack of comprehension: the person is not capable of understanding their condition or the proposed treatment or the consequences of not receiving treatment.[71] Also assessment of capacity is issue specific. A patient may be found to have sufficient understanding to be able to consent to a minor straightforward piece of medical treatment, but not have sufficient understanding to be able to consent to a far more complex procedure. The MCA 2005, however, emphasises that a patient should not be treated as lacking capacity 'unless all practical steps to help him' reach capacity 'have been taken without success'. That may involve their family or friends assisting them in making decisions. Further, under s. 2(2):

LEGISLATIVE PROVISION

Mental Capacity Act 2005, section 2(2)

A person is not to be regarded as unable to understand the information to a decision if he is able to understand an explanation of it given to him in a way that is appropriate to his circumstances (using simple language, visual aids or any other means).

---

[70] Harding, R (2012).
[71] MCA 2005, s. 2(4).

To have capacity, the patient must also be able to use the information: weigh it and be able to make a decision. This means that, even though a patient may fully understand the issues involved, if she is in such a panic that she is unable to process this knowledge to reach a decision then she will lack capacity. Section 1(3) of the MCA 2005 states that: 'A person is not to be treated as unable to make a decision merely because he makes an unwise decision.'[72] There is a careful line to be trodden between not allowing the line of reasoning: this decision is irrational, therefore the patient lacks capacity; but permitting the reasoning: this decision is irrational because the individual is not able to properly weigh up the different issues and therefore lacks capacity.

In order to show that a person lacks capacity under the MCA 2005, it is not enough just to show that they are unable to make a decision for themselves; it must be shown that this is as a result of an impairment of, or disturbance in the functioning of, the mind or the brain. The significance of this is that a patient has capacity if there is no mental impairment or disturbance, however impaired their reasoning process may have been. So, for example, a patient with no mental impairment who refuses all treatment because of her religious belief that God will cure her will not lack capacity, even if the doctors try to argue that she does not properly understand the reality of her situation.

A final point on capacity is that the MCA 2005 makes special provision to ensure that patients are not assessed as lacking capacity in a prejudicial way. Section 2(3) states:

LEGISLATIVE PROVISION

Mental Capacity Act 2005, section 2(3)

A lack of capacity cannot be established merely by reference to—

(a)   a person's age or appearance, or

(b)   a condition of his, or an aspect of his behaviour, which might lead others to make unjustified assumptions about his capacity.

This is designed to ensure that a patient who appears unkempt or disordered is not assessed as lacking capacity purely on that basis. The use of the word 'merely' is perhaps surprising because it suggests prejudicial attitudes can be a factor taken into account in assessing capacity.

The treatment of a patient lacking capacity is now governed by the Mental Capacity Act 2005. The Act applies only to those over the age of 16. It will be remembered that the Act makes it clear that a patient should be presumed to have capacity.[73] If it is found that the patient lacks capacity and a medical professional wishes to treat the patient, then the following questions must be considered:

1. Has the patient created an effective advance decision (sometimes called a 'living will') which refuses the treatment in question? If so, the advance decision must be respected.[74]

---

[72] Despite the clear statement of this principle, commentators have claimed that the judges have done exactly this to ensure patients receive the treatment they need: Montgomery (2000).

[73] MCA 2005, s. 1(2).

[74] MCA 2005, s. 24.

2. Has the patient effectively created a lasting power of attorney (LPA)? If so, the donee of the LPA may be able to make the decision.[75]

3. Has the court appointed a deputy? If so, the deputy in some cases can make the decision.[76]

4. If there is no effective advance decision and no LPA or deputy who can make the decision, then the question is whether the treatment is in the best interests of the patient.

We need to consider, therefore, the four scenarios separately.

C Advance decisions

An advance decision is defined in MCA 2005, s. 24(1) thus:

LEGISLATIVE PROVISION

Mental Capacity Act 2005, section 24(1)

'Advance Decision' means a decision made by a person ('P'), after he has reached 18 and when he has capacity to do so, that if—

(a) at a later time and in such circumstances as he may specify, a specified treatment is proposed to be carried out or continued by a person providing health care for him, and

(b) at that time he lacks capacity to consent to the carrying out or continuation of the treatment,

the specified treatment is not to be carried out or continued.

A number of points should be noted about this definition. First, the advance decision is only effective if, when it was made, P (the patient) was over 18 and competent. Secondly, the advance decision is only to be relevant if the patient lacks capacity to consent to the treatment. So, if a patient has signed an advance decision refusing to consent to a blood transfusion, but at the time is competent and consents, then the advance decision should be ignored.[77] Thirdly, the definition of advance decisions only allows 'negative' decisions; decisions to refuse treatment. An advance decision cannot be used to compel a medical professional to provide treatment. The definition of advance decision covers both treatment and the continuation of treatment. An advance decision, therefore, could indicate that P is willing to receive treatment, but only for a certain period of time. If the advance decision does reject life-saving treatment, it must be in writing and signed by P and witnessed by a third party.[78] Otherwise, the decision does not need to be in writing.

Section 25 explains how an advance decision may be invalid. This is where P, with capacity, has withdrawn the advance decision; where P has created an LPA after making the advance decision and given the LPA the power to make the decision in question; or where P has done anything else which is clearly inconsistent and to which the decision related.

---

[75] MCA 2005, s. 9.
[76] MCA 2005, s. 19.
[77] MCA 2005, s. 25(3).
[78] MCA 2005, s. 25(6).

Section 26(1) of the MCA 2005 explains:

LEGISLATIVE PROVISION

Mental Capacity Act 2005, section 26(1)

If P has made an advance decision which is—

(a) valid, and

(b) applicable to the treatment,

the decision has the effect as if he had made it, and had had capacity to make it, at the time when the question arises whether the treatment should be carried out or continued.

This means that if P has a valid and applicable advance decision which rejects treatment the medical professional should not provide it. If she or he does, then there is the potential for a criminal or tortious action. However, under s. 26(2): 'A person does not incur liability for carrying out or continuing the treatment unless, at the time, he is satisfied that an advance decision exists which is valid and applicable to the treatment.'

D Lasting powers of attorney

If a person wants someone else to make decisions on their behalf when they become incompetent, they can make a lasting power of attorney (LPA) under s. 9 of the MCA 2005. The donee or donees of the LPA can make decisions for general matters relating to someone's welfare, including some medical decisions. In order to execute an LPA the person (P) must be over 18 years old and have capacity to do so.[79] There are strict regulations as to the formalities surrounding the LPA and its registration. These are set out in Sched. 1 to the MCA 2005. If they are not complied with, the LPA will be ineffective.

The donee of the LPA must be over the age of 18. It is possible to appoint more than one LPA. Unless the LPA says so, where more than one donee is appointed they are to act jointly.[80] In other words, all of them must agree on the decision in question before using the LPA. An LPA can be revoked at any time if P has the capacity to do so.[81]

Where an LPA has been validly appointed and the donee has the power to make decisions about P's personal welfare, this can extend to consenting or refusing to the carrying out of healthcare. However, this is subject to an important restriction in that the donee must make the decision based on what would be in P's best interests, as described in s. 4 (which will be discussed below).

E Deputies

Under the MCA 2005, s. 16, if P lacks capacity in relation to a matter concerning her or his personal welfare (e.g. a health issue) then the court can make the decision on P's behalf or decide to appoint a deputy to make decisions on P's behalf. In deciding whether to appoint a

---

[79] MCA 2005, s. 9.
[80] MCA 2005, s. 9(5).
[81] MCA 2005, s. 13(2).

deputy the court should consider whether to do so would be in P's best interests (considering the factors in s. 4 which we shall be looking at shortly) and also the following principles:

(a) a decision by the court is to be preferred to the appointment of a deputy to make a decision; and

(b) the powers conferred on a deputy should be as limited in scope and duration as is reasonably practicable in the circumstances.

This suggests that where there is a 'one off' decision to be made about P, appointing a deputy is unlikely to be appropriate. Where decisions need to be made about P on a regular basis, a deputy may be more suitable. A deputy must be over the age of 18 and have consented to take on the role.[82] The court can appoint more than one deputy; and it can revoke the appointment of a deputy.[83]

F Court decision based on best interests

An application can be made to court in respect of any person who lacks capacity. The court can make a declaration as to the lawfulness of any act concerning the individual. The decision will be made based on what is in the best interests of the patient, as that is understood under MCA 2005, s. 4.

Section 1(6) emphasises that:

Before the act is done or decision is made, regard must be had to whether the purpose for which it is needed can be effectively achieved in a way that is less restrictive of the person's rights and freedom of action.

So, whenever a decision is being made about a patient lacking capacity, it is not enough just to show that the action is in P's best interests; it must be shown there is not an equally good way of promoting P's interests which is less invasive of his rights or freedom.

Section 4 of the MCA 2005 states that, in deciding what is in a patient's best interests, the court or deputy must consider all the relevant circumstances, including the following factors:

(i) '(a) whether it is likely that the person will at some time have capacity in relation to the matter in question, and (b) if it appears likely that he will, when that is likely to be'.[84] Clearly if the person is soon to regain capacity, it may be better, if possible, to postpone making a decision so she or he can make it for her- or himself.

(ii) The decision maker must 'so far as reasonably practicable, permit and encourage the person to participate, or to improve his ability to participate, as fully as possible in any act done for him and any decision affecting him'.[85] This is a recognition that even if it is not possible for the person to make a decision for him- or herself, he or she should still be involved to a reasonable extent in the decision-making process and their views listened to.

(iii) The decision maker must consider, so far as is reasonably ascertainable, '(a) the person's past and present wishes and feelings (and, in particular, any relevant written statement

[82] MCA 2005, s. 19.
[83] MCA 2005, s. 16(8).
[84] MCA 2005, s. 4(3).
[85] MCA 2005, s. 4(4). See Herring (2009f) for further discussion.

made by him when he had capacity), (b) the beliefs and values that would be likely to influence his decision if he had capacity, and (c) the other factors that he would be likely to consider if he were able to do so'.[86] It should be emphasised that the MCA 2005 does not adopt a substituted judgment test (see below). In other words, it does not require decision makers to make their decision based on what they guess the person would have decided if she or he had been competent. However, as this factor makes clear, the views of the person while competent, and assessment of what decision she or he would have made if competent, can be taken into account in deciding what are in her or his best interests.

(iv) The decision maker should, if practical and appropriate, consider the views of '(a) anyone named by the person as someone to be consulted on the matter in question or on matters of that kind, (b) anyone engaged in caring for the person or interested in his welfare, (c) any donee of a lasting power of attorney granted by the person, and (d) any deputy appointed for the person, by the court, as to what would be in the patient's best interests'. The decision maker may choose to consult a wider group of people than this, but is not required to do so.[87] It is unclear how much weight should be placed on the views of a family. If P's family are all Jehovah's Witnesses and oppose the required blood transfusion, should their views carry the day? Probably not; the views of family members are only one factor and in such a case it would be hard to see P's death as in P's best interests, as that term is generally understood in society. If the court decides that it is important that the relative has an ongoing relationship with P, then their views may be relevant to ensure that continues.[88]

There are two factors which the decision maker should not take into account:

(i) A decision as to what is in a person's best interests should not be made merely on the basis of '(a) the person's age or appearance, or (b) a condition of his, or an aspect of his behaviour, which might lead others to make unjustified assumptions about what might be in his best interests'. This might be most relevant in combating assumptions about older people and what is best for them.

(ii) Section 4(5) states: 'Where the determination relates to life-sustaining treatment [the decision maker], in considering whether the treatment is in the best interests of the person concerned, may not be motivated by a desire to bring about his death.'

Where a patient lacking capacity is being detained for treatment and there is a need for detention or restraint, the 'Liberty Protection Safeguards' must be complied with.[89] These are complex, but include a requirement that any deprivation of liberty be proportionate to the harm facing the person lacking capacity.[90]

The Mental Capacity Act 2005 has been widely welcomed for setting the law on a clear statutory footing; on providing an explicit legal authorisation for those caring for those lacking capacity to do so; and for protecting human rights. There are, however, some concerns for those family members or others caring for people lacking capacity. The first is that a decision

---

[86] MCA 2005, s. 4(6).
[87] Department of Constitutional Affairs (2004: para 4.23).
[88] *A Primary Care Trust and P v AH and A Local Authority* [2008] 2 FLR 1196.
[89] MCA 2005, s. 6.
[90] See Herring (2012d) for a detailed discussion of the law.

made by them about care might be said to be not in the person's best interests. This concern is dealt with by s. 5:

LEGISLATIVE PROVISION

Mental Capacity Act 2005, section 5

1. If a person ('D') does an act in connection with the care or treatment of another person ('P'), the act is one to which this section applies if—

    (a) before doing the act, D takes reasonable steps to establish whether P lacks capacity in relation to the matter in question, and

    (b) when doing the act, D reasonably believes—

        (i) that P lacks capacity in relation to the matter, and

        (ii) that it will be in P's best interests for the act to be done.

2. D does not incur any liability in relation to the act that he would not have incurred if P—

    (a) had had capacity to consent in relation to the matter, and

    (b) had consented to D's doing the act.

3. Nothing in this section excludes a person's civil liability for loss or damage, or his criminal liability, resulting from his negligence in doing the act.

This provides some protection from a carer who reasonably believes the person they are looking after lacks capacity and acts in what they think is in that person's best interests. Even if a court later decides they were mistaken, s. 5 offers them protection from legal challenge. However, this protection is somewhat limited by subsection 3.

A second concern is that at first blush the best interests test requires a family member to only consider P's interests and never their own when making decisions. Strictly interpreted this would put an unbearable burden on carers. However, the carer can take into account P's views when competent and presumably P would not want family members utterly overburdened, and so it might be legitimate for a carer to take their own interests into account in a limited way.[91]

Two cases will illustrate the way the Mental Capacity Act 2005 can be used in cases involving older people:

CASE: *Dorset CC v EH* [2009] EWHC 784 (Fam)

EH was aged 82 and had Alzheimer's disease. She lived alone in her home, supported by her brother, sister-in-law and a local community health team. She was struggling to care for herself, manage her food and medication. The local authority sought an order that she be moved to a nearby care home, something she resisted. She was assessed as lacking capacity because she did not understand the risks she faced at home. The court decided that in assessing her best interests it was necessary to weigh the benefits of the safety of the care home against the freedom of living in her own accommodation. Parker J concluded overall it was in her best interests to move into the home.

---

[91] See Herring (2008b and 2013a) for a detailed discussion.

CASE: *DL v A Local Authority* [2012] EWCA 253

A couple aged 85 and 90 lived with their son, who treated them badly. The local authority sought orders authorising their removal from their son. The couple opposed the intervention. They were assessed under the Mental Capacity Act 2005 and found to have capacity, but only just. Prior to this case it had been assumed that if someone was found to have capacity to make a decision, their views had to be respected. Controversially, however, the Court of Appeal held that in a case involving 'vulnerable adults' who were of borderline capacity the inherent jurisdiction could be used to protect them. The court justified the use of the jurisdiction by saying the couple were under the influence of their son and removing them would enable them to make a more autonomous decision.[92]

There is considerable complexity over the law on deprivation of liberty. In *P v Cheshire West and Chester Council*[93] the notion of deprivation of liberty was interpreted widely to cover any situation where a person was subject to continuous supervision and control and was not free to leave. Many care homes would fall under this definition. Indeed, it could apply to a person living at home if, for example, they had dementia and their family curtailed their freedom to move. In order to protect the right to protection from deprivation of liberty under Article 5 of the ECHR any deprivation must be authorised by law. This is now provided by the Liberty Protection Safeguards (LPS), which replaced the Deprivation of Liberty Safeguards (DoLS) in 2020. The DoLS set out a series of requirements in s. 4A and 4B of the MCA that had to be met if any deprivation of liberty was justified. There had been considerable dissatisfaction with the workings of the DoLS, which could be expensive and time consuming. The new LPS are designed to be easier to use and permit detention to be authorised in advance by a 'responsible body': a hospital manager, a clinical commissioning group and, in the case of deprivations taking place in a care home or the community, the local authority. It is too early to tell whether the new regime has been easier to use.

In recent years the courts have shown an increasing willingness to use the inherent jurisdiction to make orders in relation to those who are classified as vulnerable adults.[94] In *A Local Authority v DL*[95] the court confirmed the existence of this jurisdiction which can be used for those who have mental capacity but are restricted in their ability to make decisions for themselves because, for example, they are living in an oppressive relationship.[96] Under the inherent jurisdiction, orders can be made which will promote the best interests of the vulnerable adult.[97]

7 Succession and intestacy

Learning objective 4

Summarise the broad issues around succession and intestacy

We will now consider what happens to people's property on their death. What is particularly revealing is the law's acknowledgement that family members may have legally enforceable claims on the estate, even if there is no will. Before considering the law, the theoretical issues will be discussed.

---

[92] See Herring (2016d) and Lindsey (2020).
[93] [2014] UKSC 19.
[94] See Herring (2009g).
[95] [2012] EWCA 253.
[96] The case is discussed in detail in Chapter 7.
[97] *Al-Jeffery v Al-Jeffery (Vulnerable Adult: British Citizen)* [2016] EWHC 2151 (Fam).

A Theory

It is important to distinguish between two situations: first, where the deceased has left a will; and, secondly, where the deceased has not left a will or has left a will that does not deal with all of the deceased's property. These two scenarios give rise to quite different problems.

(i) Where there is a will

Where someone leaves a will, it might be thought that the issue is straightforward. Our society accepts that people should be free to dispose of their property in whatever ways they wish, however foolish others may think them to be. If during their lives people wish to spend all of their hard-earned money on gambling or purchasing law texts, they may, and unless they are mentally incompetent there is no way of stopping them. If this is true in life, should it not also be true in death? Not necessarily, because on divorce the law feels entitled to redistribute a spouse's property to achieve a fair result. If the law is willing to do this when a relationship is ended by divorce, should it not also be able to do so if the relationship is ended by death?

As we shall see, the law's response to these arguments is to seek a middle course. A person is permitted to make a will directing what should happen to his or her property on death, but if anyone feels that the will has not provided for them adequately then they are allowed to apply to the court for an order that they receive a payment out of the estate under the Inheritance (Provision for Family and Dependants) Act 1975. What is interesting is that the class of potential claimants is not restricted to spouses. Other relatives may claim that the deceased has not adequately provided for them in the will. The intervention of the law could be based on two grounds. First, it could be argued that even though the deceased had made a will, he or she could not really have intended not to provide for the claimant and the law is intervening to ensure that the will truly reflects the wishes of the deceased. Alternatively, the law could be explained as being a recognition that legal claims can be made on the deceased's income. Neither of these arguments is satisfactory. With the first there is the difficulty that an award can be made under the Act even if the evidence is clear that the deceased did not want the claimant to receive any of his or her money. The problem with the second is that, while a person is alive, the law does not recognise a liability to provide for other relatives apart from spouses.[98] There does not seem to be a strong reason to explain why these obligations suddenly spring into existence on the death of a person. It may be argued that, while alive, a person has the right to govern what happens to their property and this trumps the claims of other family members; however, once deceased, a person has no rights and so the law can give effect to the claims of other family members.

(ii) Where there is no will: intestacy

There are different issues where the deceased has left no will. Here there are two main possible approaches: the law could attempt to ascertain what the wishes of the deceased were, considering all the evidence available; or the law could decide objectively what would be a fair and just distribution of the property. The two approaches could be intermingled: we might presume that a deceased's intention would be a fair and just settlement, but there may be occasions when there is evidence that the deceased did not wish a fair distribution to be made.

In a way, the law on intestacy is easier to defend than the law where there is a will. The law makes it clear that if an individual does not make a will then the law will decide how the property will be distributed. If the deceased decides not to make a will, he or she can make no objection (were they able to!) about the distribution of the property. Given the difficulties and litigation

---

[98] Unless a legally binding contract has been entered into.

that would inevitably surround a law based on attempting to ascertain the deceased's wishes, the law has developed a set formula which operates in cases of intestacy. It has been estimated that about 40 per cent of people aged over 60 have not made a will[99] and so it is important that the formula is predictable and discourages litigation. However, because a formula is not appropriate in every case, English and Welsh law has established a procedure by which an application can be made to the court if the result of the statutory rules would produce injustice.

B The law in cases where there is a will

The starting point is that the will is enacted and property is distributed according to it. There are, of course, ways to challenge a will.[100] It can be argued that a will does not comply with the formalities in the Wills Act 1837,[101] or that the will was made by the deceased while of unsound mind or as a result of undue influence[102] or that the will has been revoked.[103] The detail of the law cannot be covered here,[104] but if the will is invalid for any of these reasons then the estate will be dealt with using the rules of intestacy. There may also be arguments that a particular piece of property does not belong (or does not wholly belong) to the deceased. For example, it may be argued that the house, although being in the name of the deceased, was in fact held on trust for the deceased and his wife under a constructive trust or proprietary estoppel.[104] In such a case, if the deceased purported in his will to give the house to his daughter, he would only be able to give her his share of the house.

If someone feels that they have not been adequately provided for under the will, they may be able to make a claim under the Inheritance (Provision for Family and Dependants) Act 1975, which will be discussed shortly.

C Intestacy

The rules that operate on intestacy apply where the deceased has not made a will or has made a will that does not dispose of his or her entire estate.[106] The rules are rather complex and depend on whether the deceased has a surviving spouse or any surviving issue (that is, children of the deceased, including adopted children and children born outside marriage).

(i) If there is a surviving spouse and children or grandchildren

If there is a surviving spouse[107] and issue, the surviving spouse is entitled to all of the personal chattels,[108] and £125,000 (known as the statutory legacy), if there is that much in the deceased's estate. If there is still money or property left in the estate after these transfers are made, the

---

[99] Law Commission Report 187 (1989).

[100] See *Marley v Rawlings* [2014] UKSC 2 on interpretation of wills.

[101] *Marley v Rawlings* [2014] UKSC 2.

[102] See Kerridge (2000) for concerns that the law may fail adequately to protect vulnerable testators.

[103] E.g. divorce will revoke a will.

[104] An excellent summary can be found in *Cattermole v Prisk* [2006] Fam Law 98.

[105] See Chapter 5.

[106] See Law Commission Consul Report 331 (2009) for proposals for reform of the law which would increase rights of cohabitants.

[107] It is necessary for the spouse to have survived the deceased by 28 days if he or she is to be seen as a surviving spouse: Administration of Estates Act 1925, s. 46. See *Official Solicitor to the Senior Courts v Yemoh and Others* [2010] EWHC 3727 (Ch) for a discussion of how to deal with cases where the deceased had entered polygamous marriages.

[108] In basic terms the furniture and personal objects of the parties. The term is defined in the Administration of Estates Act 1925, s. 55(1)(x).

spouse has a life interest in half the remainder. The balance of the estate (subject to the spouse's life interest) is held on statutory trust for the children. This will mean that the children will be entitled to maintenance until they are 18 and then they will be entitled to the capital.[109]

(ii) If there is a surviving spouse, no issue, but close relatives

If there is a surviving spouse and no children, but there are surviving parents, brothers or sisters,[110] the spouse is entitled to the personal chattels absolutely, £200,000 statutory legacy and half of the balance absolutely (rather than just a life interest). The parents, or if no parents then brothers or sisters (or their issue)[111], are entitled to the other half of the remainder.

(iii) If there is a surviving spouse, but no issue or close relatives

If there is a surviving spouse but no parents or brothers or sisters or issue of brothers and sisters, the spouse will take the intestate's estate absolutely.

(iv) If there is no surviving spouse

If there is no spouse, then there is a list of relatives who may be entitled to the estate in the following order. Whichever relatives are highest up the list will take the estate absolutely and those lower down the list will take nothing:

1. children of the deceased or grandchildren;
2. parents of the deceased;
3. brothers or sisters of the whole blood, or their issue;
4. brothers or sisters of the half blood, or their issue;
5. grandparents of the deceased;
6. aunts or uncles of the deceased, or their issue.

If there is more than one relative in a category, they will share the estate equally. If there is no one related to the deceased in this list, the estate will go to the Crown, *bona vacantia*. It is open to the Crown to give as a matter of grace some of the property to friends or others who fall outside the terms of the intestacy rules.[112] This power is most likely to be used in the case of cohabitants. Any person who is unhappy about the operation of the intestacy rules can apply to the court under the Inheritance (Provision for Family and Dependants) Act 1975.

As has been noted, a spouse is entitled to the personal chattels of the deceased: for example, the television, the bed, any pets, etc. This seems only sensible and is largely uncontroversial. In addition, the spouse is given absolutely a lump sum which he or she may use to purchase somewhere to live,[113] and a life interest in the rest of the estate which will provide him or her with an income. The rules do not mean that the spouse will automatically be able to live in the house. This may seem harsh but it is mitigated by two rules. The first is that if the family home is in the joint names of the deceased and the spouse then, on the deceased's death, under the rules of land law, the house will belong to the spouse absolutely and will not normally be

---

[109] The Law Commission Report 187 (1989) found that the majority of people thought the surviving spouse should receive everything on the death of a spouse.

[110] They must be of the whole blood.

[111] 'Issue' here means the children of the brother and sister. They will take their parent's share if the parent has died.

[112] See Williams, Potter and Douglas (2008) for evidence of support among the public for increased provision in the intestacy rules for cohabitants.

[113] The spouse is entitled to take the matrimonial home in lieu of his or her lump sum.

regarded as part of the deceased's estate. So, the spouse would have the house as well as the statutory legacy, and so should be well provided for. Secondly, even if the house is not in joint names then there are rules permitting the spouse to use his or her statutory legacy to purchase the house from the estate. Nevertheless, if the house is in the sole name of the deceased and is worth more than the statutory legacy, then the house may have to be sold. This has led some to argue that the spouse should be entitled to the entire estate of the deceased.[114] However, others argue that the present law is too generous to spouses. The circumstances in which it might appear too generous are where the deceased had remarried and the second spouse acquires the estate under the intestacy rules. The children of the deceased, especially if they do not get on well with their step-parent, may fear that the estate will ultimately be diverted to the step-parent's 'family' rather than the deceased's family. Another very important point about the intestacy rules is that they do not provide for unmarried cohabiting partners, nor good friends. The focus is very much on blood relations and spouses, not social relations. This is in contrast to other parts of the law[115] where social relationships are emphasised.

D The Inheritance (Provision for Family and Dependants) Act 1975

Where relatives or dependants feel that an inadequate sum has been left to them as a result of the deceased's will or the rules on intestacy, an application can be made to the court for an order. The burden of persuading the court to make the order rests on the applicant. There are no rights to property under the Act; the legislation simply gives the court a discretion to decide the appropriate amount, if any, to be paid to a claimant. The court is entitled to provide for someone who is not mentioned in the will or would not be entitled to money on intestacy. An individual can claim under the Act even if the deceased had made it quite plain that he or she did not wish the individual to receive any money on their death. The policy of the Act has been to ensure that a person who has become dependent upon the deceased does not suffer an injustice on the deceased's death.[116]

(i) Who can apply?

The following can apply under the Act:

1. The spouse or civil partner of the deceased.[117]

2. The former spouse or civil partner of the deceased, providing the applicant has not remarried or entered another civil partnership.[118]

3. A person who '. . . during the whole of the period of two years ending immediately before the date when the deceased died . . . was living – (a) in the same household as the deceased, and (b) as the husband or wife [or civil partner] of the deceased'.[119]

   This category would include many cohabiting couples.[120] The test to be applied is whether a reasonable person with normal powers of perception would say the couple was

---

[114] Law Commission Report 187 (1989).

[115] See Chapter 8, for example.

[116] *Jelley* v *Iliffe* [1981] Fam 128 CA

[117] Inheritance (Provision for Family and Dependants) Act 1975 (hereafter I(PFD)A 1975), s. 1(1)(a). This includes people who in good faith entered a void marriage with the deceased: I(PFD)A 1975, s. 25(4), but does not include former spouses.

[118] I(PFD)A 1975, s. 1(1)(b).

[119] I(PFD)A 1975, s. 1A This category of claimants is available only if the deceased died on or after 1 January 1996.

[120] See the reasoning in *Fitzpatrick* v *Sterling Housing Association Ltd* [2000] 1 FCR 21 HL; *Martin* v *Williams* [2017] EWHC 491 (Ch). See Sloan (2011) for a helpful discussion.

living together as husband and wife.[121] In using this test the reasonable person should be aware of the multifarious nature of marriages.[122] Therefore, in *Re Watson*[123] a couple in their fifties who started living together companionably without engaging in sexual relations could be said to be living as husband and wife. Indeed, Neuberger J noted that many married couples in their mid-fifties do not have sexual relations. In *Baynes v Hedger*[124] it was held that living as the deceased's civil partner or spouse required that the relationship was publicly acknowledged. A clandestine same-sex relationship could not be categorised as living as civil partners.[125] In *Lindop v Agus, Bass and Hedley*[126] the couple lived together, had a sexual relationship, shared finances and on occasions cared for children together. It was held that the woman could claim under the Act, even though she had retained a separate address for many formal purposes. In *Kaur v Dhaliwal*[127] the couple were treated as cohabitants when they had lived together, then separated, but regularly met up, including overnight visits. The requirement that the cohabitation last until 'immediately' before the death has to be interpreted sensibly. In *Re Watson*[128] the deceased spent the last few weeks of his life in hospital and that did not prevent the section applying. In *Gully v Dix*[129] the claimant and deceased had cohabited for over 25 years, but she left the house three months before his death, saying she would return when he stopped drinking. The Court of Appeal took the view that in light of the length of the relationship she was still living in the same household as the deceased, even if she had temporarily moved out. There had not been an irretrievable breakdown in relations. In *Churchill v Roach*[130] Judge Norris QC said that to live in the same household it was necessary to have 'elements of permanence, to involve a consideration of the frequency and intimacy of contact, to contain an element of mutual support, to require some consideration of the degree of voluntary restraint upon personal freedom which each party undertakes, and to involve an element of community of resources'.

4. Any child of the deceased, including posthumous, adopted and grown-up children.[131] An adopted child cannot claim under this ground against their biological parents, but can claim against their adopted parents.[132]

5. Any person 'treated by the deceased as a child of the family in relation to' a marriage or civil partnership.[133] This is similar to the concept of the 'child of the family' (see Chapter 8). It most commonly applies in relation to stepchildren.[134] It should be stressed that this category exists only in the context of a marriage or civil partnership. If the deceased cohabits with a woman and her child from a previous relationship, the child could not rely on this category.[135]

---

[121] *Re Watson* [1999] 1 FLR 878.
[122] See Chapter 1 for a discussion of the factors a court is likely to take into account in deciding whether there was cohabitation.
[123] [1999] 1 FLR 878.
[124] [2008] 3 FCR 151.
[125] It may be argued that this fails to take into account the prejudice that can be shown towards open same-sex couples. See Monk (2011).
[126] [2010] 1 FLR 631.
[127] [2014] EWHC 1991 (Ch).
[128] [1999] 1 FLR 878.
[129] [2004] 1 FCR 453.
[130] [2004] 3 FCR 744 at p. 761.
[131] I(PFD)A 1975, s. 1(1)(c).
[132] *Re Collins* [1990] Fam 56.
[133] I(PFD)A 1975, s. 1(1)(d).
[134] See *Re Leach* [1986] Ch 226 CA for an example of the potential breadth of the section.
[135] Although they may be able to rely on I(PFD)A 1975, s. 1(1)(e).

6. Any other person 'who immediately before the death of the deceased was being maintained, either wholly or partly, by the deceased'.[136] The phrase 'maintained' in this definition is clarified in s. 1(3):

> [A] person shall be treated as being maintained by the deceased, either wholly or partly, as the case may be, if the deceased, otherwise than for full valuable consideration, was making a substantial contribution in money or money's worth towards the reasonable needs of that person.

This could include unmarried cohabitees as well as two friends living together without a sexual relationship but with a degree of maintenance. A few points need to be stressed about fulfilling the definition of this category:

(a) The maintenance must be substantial. In *Rees v Newbery and the Institute of Cancer Research*[137] the deceased had provided the applicant (an actor) with a flat in London at a low rent. There was no cohabitation nor sexual or emotional relationship between them, but it was found that the applicant had been maintained by the deceased, by providing the flat. It does not need to be shown that but for the financial assistance the claimant would have been in dire poverty.[138]

(b) The contribution must be in 'money or money's worth'. There is some debate whether companionship and care could count as maintenance for 'money's worth'. As housework and nursing services and even 'companionship' can be bought, it is submitted that these can be regarded as being for money's worth.[139]

(c) It has to be shown that the maintenance was not paid for by valuable consideration.[140] This requirement has caused difficulties. Could it be said that, although a deceased cohabitant provided the claimant with free accommodation, this was in return for care and companionship and so the applicant was 'paid for' by valuable consideration? Although at one time it was suggested that it was necessary to weigh up the financial value of the maintenance provided by the deceased against the benefits to the deceased provided by the claimant, the courts no longer take such an approach. The courts will readily accept that one cohabitant was being maintained by the other. In *Bouette v Rose*[141] the Court of Appeal accepted that a mother was maintained by her disabled child. The child had been awarded a substantial sum of money as a result of her disability. The court took a practical approach and explained that the fund was used to support the lifestyle of both the mother and the child, and so the child was effectively maintaining the mother.

(d) The deceased must have been maintaining the claimant immediately before the death of the deceased. As *Re Watson*[142] makes clear, the fact that the deceased's last few weeks were spent in a hospital or a nursing home will not prevent the applicant's claim being accepted. However, if a couple clearly separate shortly before the death, a claim cannot be made. This is controversial: although the separation may indicate that the deceased would not have wanted to leave a former cohabitant any property, it does not necessarily mean that it would not be fair to make such an award.

---

[136] I(PFD)A 1975, s. 1(1)(e).
[137] [1998] 1 FLR 1041.
[138] *Churchill v Roach* [2004] 3 FCR 744.
[139] This seems to have been accepted in *Jelley v Illiffe* [1981] Fam 128.
[140] This, in simple terms, requires that the contribution had not been paid for.
[141] [2000] 1 FLR 363.
[142] [1999] 1 FLR 878.

(ii) What is reasonable financial provision?

The key question in deciding an order is whether reasonable financial provision was made for the claimant in the will. Rather strangely, the concept of reasonable provision depends on the exact relationship between the deceased and the claimant. If the claimant is the spouse, the question is simply whether the *provision* is 'reasonable'. This does not require a spouse to receive all of an estate.[143] For other cases, the question is whether the *maintenance* is reasonable. The emphasis on maintenance is important. A non-spouse applicant who is 'comfortably off' may have difficulty in persuading the court that they need to be maintained.[144] A spouse who is well off will more easily be able to argue that the provision was not reasonable. This is because a spouse may be entitled to a share in his or her spouse's property because of the length of the marriage, even though he or she may not need to be maintained.[145] Reasonable provision is not necessarily restricted to the minimum necessary to survive,[146] and can cover what is necessary to have a reasonable quality of life.[147] Under s. 3, in considering a claim, the court should consider:

LEGISLATIVE PROVISION

Inheritance (Provision for Family and Dependants) Act 1975, section 3

(a) the financial resources and financial needs which the applicant has or is likely to have in the foreseeable future;

(b) the financial resources and financial needs which any other applicant for an order . . . has or is likely to have in the foreseeable future;

(c) the financial resources and financial needs which any beneficiary of the estate of the deceased has or is likely to have in the foreseeable future;

(d) any obligations and responsibilities which the deceased had towards any applicant for an order . . . or towards any beneficiary of the estate of the deceased;

(e) the size and nature of the net estate of the deceased;

(f) any physical or mental disability of any applicant for an order . . . or any beneficiary of the estate of the deceased;

(g) any other matter, including the conduct of the applicant or any other person, which in the circumstances of the case the court may consider relevant.

These factors are largely self-explanatory. It should be noted that factors (b), (c), (d), (f) and (g) require the court to consider the position of all those who may be seeking money from the estate.[148] So, although a claimant may show a close relationship to the deceased and be in great need, his or her claim may fail if there are others interested in the estate who are of

---

[143] *Cowan v Foreman* [2019] EWHC 349 (Fam).
[144] *Re Jennings (Deceased)* [1994] Ch 256.
[145] I(PFD)A 1975, s. 1(2).
[146] *Re Coventry* [1990] Fam 561.
[147] *Lewis v Warner* [2016] EWHC 1787 (Ch).
[148] *Cattle v Evans* [2011] EWHC 945 (Ch).

greater need. Although it is not stated explicitly, the wishes of the deceased can be taken into account.[149] For example, in *Re Hancock (Deceased)*[150] there was a dramatic increase in the value of the estate (from £100,000 to £650,000) and the Court of Appeal accepted evidence that, had the deceased been aware that his estate would increase to this level, he would have provided for the applicant. There are some additional considerations that apply for specific kinds of applicants:

(a) Spouses

For a surviving spouse reasonable financial provision means 'such financial provision as it would be reasonable in all the circumstances of the case for a husband or wife to receive, whether or not that provision is required for his or her maintenance'.[151] When considering the appropriate level for a spouse, the court will have regard to the age of the applicant; the duration of the marriage; the applicant's contribution to the welfare of the family of the deceased; and the provision the applicant may reasonably have expected to receive if the marriage had been terminated by divorce rather than by death.[152] Miller[153] has suggested that the court should separate two elements of provision for spouses: first, the spouse's share of the 'family property', and, secondly, the proportion of the estate which would be necessary to provide the spouse with sufficient support.

This emphasis on the amount that might have been awarded on divorce reflects the argument that a spouse whose marriage is ended by death should not be worse off than if the marriage had been ended by divorce. However, death and divorce are distinguishable. On divorce, the crucial question is how to divide up the property fairly between the two parties. On death, there is no division required except between the spouse and the other relatives. It could be argued, therefore, that on death a spouse might expect a greater share than on divorce.[154] In *Lilleyman v Lilleyman*[155] it was held that the amount that would be awarded on divorce was neither a floor nor a ceiling, but rather a factor to be taken into account. There has been some dispute in the case law whether the divorce analogy should be seen as just one factor, or the guiding criterion. *Re Krubert*[156] preferred the view that the divorce analogy was only one factor to be taken into account. Applying this in *Fielden v Cunliffe*[157] the Court of Appeal suggested that the reasoning in *White v White*[158] could be used, with its yardstick of equality guideline, but only with caution.[159] This seems correct. First, as a matter of statutory interpretation – the divorce analogy relates to only one of several factors which should be taken into account. Secondly, as has already been mentioned, the two scenarios – death and divorce – are quite different. The Court of Appeal in *Fielden* indicated that the obligation to make reasonable provision is not the same as the goal of fairness emphasised in ancillary relief cases. In *P v G*[160] it was held that where a wealthy husband died after a lengthy marriage the wife

---

[149] According to I(PFD)A 1975, s. 21, a statement of the deceased is admissible evidence.
[150] [1998] 2 FLR 346.
[151] I(PFD)A 1975, s. 1(2)(a).
[152] I(PFD)A 1975, s. 3(2).
[153] Miller (1997).
[154] See, e.g., *Fielden v Cunliffe* [2005] 3 FCR 593 at p. 603, where it was said that the shortness of the marriage was a less critical factor in applications under the Act than in cases of divorce.
[155] [2012] EWHC 821 (Ch).
[156] [1997] Ch 97.
[157] [2005] 3 FCR 593. See Maguire and Frankland (2006) for a useful discussion
[158] [2001] 1 AC 596.
[159] See also *Baker v Baker* [2008] EWHC 977 (Ch).
[160] [2006] Fam Law 179.

might be entitled to more than the half share that a *White* v *White* approach might indicate in a divorce. This was because, unlike a divorce case, there was only the one spouse's needs and contributions to take into account; although Black J added that the court still needed to give due weight to the importance of testamentary freedom.

(b) Former spouses

A former spouse can only claim under the Act if he or she has not remarried.[161] It is rare for former spouses to claim under the Act because it is common on divorce for a court to order that an applicant cannot make a claim under the Act if the ex-spouse subsequently dies. If such an order is in place, an application cannot be made, whether or not the ex-spouse has remarried. Even if an ex-spouse is not prevented from bringing an application, the court may well take the view that it is reasonable provision for the deceased to leave a former spouse nothing in the will.[162]

(c) Child of the deceased

The court should have regard to the manner in which the child was being, or in which he or she might expect to be, educated or trained.[163] So if the intention was that the child be privately educated, money from the estate could be claimed to provide such education.

(d) Adult children

The courts are generally reluctant to allow adult children who have sufficient earning capacity to succeed in making a claim against their parents' estate.[164] The difficulty facing an employed adult child claimant is in showing that an award would be reasonable for his or her maintenance. The courts have usually required that an adult child establish a 'moral obligation' or some other special circumstances if the claim is to succeed. Examples of a moral obligation or special circumstances include a son who had worked on the family farm in the expectation that he would inherit it;[165] and an applicant whose father was left money by the applicant's mother on the understanding that he would leave the money in his will to the applicant but did not.[166] In *Re Hancock (Deceased)*[167] the Court of Appeal stressed that it would be wrong to say that an adult child can never succeed in an application unless there is a moral obligation or other special circumstances, but without those the application would be unlikely to succeed, especially if the applicant is in paid employment. In *Espinosa* v *Bourke*[168] the daughter had for a while cared for her father, but somewhat abandoned him when she ran off to Spain to live with a Spanish fisherman. Despite this being what some would regard as reprehensible conduct, she was entitled to an award based on her need, her doubtful earning capacity, and having no formal employment. Similarly, in *H* v *J's Personal Representatives, Blue Cross, RSPB and RSPCA*[169] a daughter failed in her claim against the estate of her mother who left her nothing after she had married a man the mother disapproved of. The court held that while many would not agree with the mother's actions, she was entitled to leave her money to animal charities if she wished. Similarly, in *Garland* v *Morris*[170] it was found to be reasonable for the

---

[161] I(PFD)A 1975, s. 1(1)(b).
[162] E.g. *Cameron* v *Treasury Solicitor* [1996] 2 FLR 716 CA; *Barrass* v *Harding* [2001] 1 FCR 297.
[163] I(PFD)A 1975, s. 3(3).
[164] *Ilott* v *Mitson and Others* [2011] EWCA Civ 346.
[165] *Re Pearce (Deceased)* [1998] 2 FLR 705.
[166] *Re Goodchild* [1996] 1 WLR 694.
[167] [1998] 2 FLR 346.
[168] [1999] 1 FLR 747.
[169] [2010] 1 FLR 1613.
[170] [2007] EWHC 2 (Ch).

deceased to make no provision given his daughter had not spoken to him for several years. These decisions stress that moral obligation is but one factor to be taken into account. It is generally thought that the following case has indicated a more generous approach will be taken in the future to adult children claimants.

CASE: *Ilott* v *Blue Cross* [2017] UKSC 17

The mother and daughter had been estranged for 26 years, after the daughter left home at the age of 17. The mother disapproved of the daughter's lifestyle. On her death the mother left the daughter nothing and left her estate of around £500,000 to animal charities. The deceased had not shown a particular interest in animals during her life, but a 'side letter' left with the will indicated she did not want her daughter to receive anything. The daughter claimed under the Inheritance (Provision for Family and Dependants) Act 1975.

The daughter was married with five children and renting property from a housing association and had an income of £20,000, primarily state benefits. The central issue under the legislation was whether or not no provision could be reasonable provision. The first instance judge took the view he was limited to awarding her enough to live at subsistence level and so made an award of £50,000. The Court of Appeal disagreed and increased the award to £143,000 (out of an estate of £486,000).

The Supreme Court upheld the award of £50,000 at first instance. It reiterated that reasonable financial provision for children under the 1975 Act is 'such provision as would be reasonable for the applicant to receive for maintenance only'. Maintenance is assessed on the facts of each case but is payment to 'enable the applicant in future to discharge the cost of his daily living at whatever standard of living is appropriate to him'. In this case that could include 'food and fuel', 'essential white goods, basic carpeting . . . and curtains' and replacement of, for example, a broken bed. The daughter also referred to costs connected to having a reliable car and a holiday. Lord Hughes approved previous case law in holding that maintenance could not 'extend to any or everything which it would be desirable for the claimant to have', but was not limited to 'subsistence' either.[171]

The court did not have an unrestricted right to amend a deceased's will and amendments should only be made in the limited circumstances provided for by the 1975 Act. The Supreme Court criticised the Court of Appeal for giving 'little if any weight' to the clear views of the deceased, and emphasised it is not for the court to make a moral judgement on the decision the testatrix had chosen to leave her estate. Lord Hughes stated 'it cannot be ignored that an award under the Act is at the expense of those whom the testator intended to benefit'. Indeed, he even suggested that it would have been legitimate for the judge to have concluded that it was entirely reasonable for no provision to be made at all in the will because of the estrangement. However, as the first instance judge had fixed on the figure of £50,000, he would stick with that. The flexibility over the outcome revealed what broad discretion judges have under the Act. Indeed, as Lady Hale pointed out in *Ilott*, our succession law 'has not, or not yet, recognised a public interest in expecting or

---

[171] Para 14 and 15.

obliging parents to support their adult children so as to save the public money'. Lady Hale highlighted that:

I have written this judgment only to demonstrate what, in my view, is the unsatisfactory state of the present law, giving as it does no guidance as to the factors to be taken into account in deciding whether an adult child is deserving or undeserving of reasonable maintenance. I regret that the Law Commission did not reconsider the fundamental principles underlying such claims when last they dealt with this topic in 2011.[172]

In *Re H (Deceased)*[173] Cohen J had to deal with a case of an adult daughter with considerable mental health issues. She had broken off contact with her father, for around six years prior to his death. She was awarded £138,918 out of his estate of £554,000. The award included money for psychiatric treatment and some money to make up for lost income. She sought £375,000–500,000 for a house but that failed. Notably, the award included sums to include payment for her solicitors employed on a contingency fee basis. The court awarded her much less than she sought, taking into account the fact that the relationship between the daughter and parents had broken down and the need to ensure that the widow's costs of living in a care home would be covered.

Wellesley v Wellesley[174] is an interesting application of the law on claims by adult children. It contained two striking features. First, the deceased's views were clear. He was the 7th Earl Cowley and from his estate of £1.3 million left his oldest daughter, Tara, a legacy of £20,000. He was said to believe in 'discipline, hard work and self-help' and had an 'abhorrence of drug use'. He saw Lady Tara, who had drunk heavily and used drugs in her youth and was currently unemployed, as a lost cause. They had been estranged for 30 years. Second, Lady Tara was in great need. She was unemployed and had suffered a troubled life. There were no other need claims on the estate. In awarding her nothing it was emphasised that 'need' alone was not sufficient to justify an award. Following *Ilott* the 'starting point' was that the deceased's views were to have respect. Here there was a lengthy estrangement and a clear expression of views, and these trumped the needs of the applicant. It was noted that he 'was not in any way vindictive, malicious or unfair towards Tara'. Maybe that suggests that in considering the deceased's views an assessment will be made as to whether they are unreasonable. It will be interesting to see if later cases pick up on that approach.

(e) Child of the deceased's family

When the court is considering a child who was not biologically the deceased's, but whom he or she treated as a child of the family, the court should consider whether the deceased had assumed responsibility for the child and whether, in assuming responsibility, the deceased knew that the applicant was not his or her own child. The liability of any other person to maintain the applicant should also be taken into account.

---

[172] Para 66.
[173] [2020] EWHC 1134 (Fam).
[174] [2019] EWHC 11.

(f) Dependants

In addition to the general factors, the court will consider 'the extent to which and the basis upon which the deceased assumed responsibility for the maintenance of the applicant, and . . . the length of time for which the deceased discharged that responsibility'.[175] Megarry V-C stressed that the deceased must have assumed responsibility for the applicant: that maintenance on its own would not be enough, if the deceased had not undertaken responsibility.[176] The Court of Appeal, however, has suggested that it is willing to infer assumption of responsibility from maintenance.[177] In determining the amount awarded to such claimants the court can take into account the lifestyle they enjoyed while being maintained by the deceased.[178]

(g) Cohabitants

If the claimant relies on s. 1A the following special factors apply:

(a) the age of the applicant and the [length of the period of cohabitation];

(b) the contribution made by the applicant to the welfare of the family of the deceased, including any contribution made by looking after the home or caring for the family.

However, a cohabitant cannot normally expect an award at a level which would enable him or her to retain the same standard of living as the couple had enjoyed together, even if it had been a lengthy relationship.[179] Nevertheless, the previous lifestyle was a factor to consider, as was the length of the relationships, whether there were any children and the needs of other claimants. In *Webster v Webster*[180] a woman who had cohabited with the deceased for 28 years and had two children with him was awarded the bulk of the estate. In *Re Watson*[181] the needs of the frail applicant were particularly significant.[182] Cohabitants are entitled to maintenance and that could include provision of property.[183]

In *Lewis v Warner*[184] the man had no expectation of inheriting from his partner and did not believe he had a moral claim against the estate. However, the Court of Appeal still awarded him the house (in return for a payment of the market price). They emphasised the fact he had no expectation did not detract from the fact he was being maintained. Further, they took account of the fact the man was old (over 90) and infirm and that the woman, when making her will, may not have imagined his condition at the time of her death. Although he believed he had no moral claim, that did not prevent the Court deciding he did. As with the other categories the wishes of the deceased will be considered. Therefore, in *Re Wynford Hodge*,[185] where the deceased did not want her partner's children to receive any of her money, the court granted her partner a life interest in the property which protected his need for a house, without benefiting his children.

---

[175] I(PFD)A 1975, s. 3(4).
[176] *Re Beaumont* [1980] Ch 444.
[177] *Jelley v Iliffe* [1981] Fam 128; *Bouette v Rose* [2000] 1 FLR 363, [2000] 1 FCR 385.
[178] *Negus v Bahouse* [2008] 1 FCR 768.
[179] *Graham v Murphy* [1997] 1 FLR 860.
[180] [2009] 1 FLR 1240.
[181] [1999] 1 FLR 878.
[182] *Musa v Holliday* [2012] EWCA Civ 1268.
[183] *Lewis v Warner* [2017] EWCA Civ 2182.
[184] [2017] EWCA Civ 2182.
[185] [2018] EWHC 688 (Ch).

8 Elder abuse

A Defining elder abuse

Learning objective 5

Describe how the law responds to elder abuse

The Law Commission has defined abuse in this context as the:

> . . . ill-treatment of that person (including sexual abuse and forms of ill-treatment that are not physical), the impairment of, or an avoidable deterioration in, the physical or mental health of that person or the impairment of his physical, intellectual, emotional, social or behavioural development.[186]

Notably, this definition includes abuse by omission (not providing the appropriate level of care) as well as abuse by act. It also makes it clear that abuse includes acts that were not intended to harm the dependent person. The most recent government publications have emphasised that elder abuse should be regarded as part of a wider problem of abuse of vulnerable people.[187]

Statistics on the level of abuse are hard to obtain, not least because much abuse goes unreported. We now have the benefit of a major recent study of elder abuse carried out for Comic Relief and the Department of Health.[188] It found that 2.6 per cent of people aged 66 or over who were living in their own private household reported mistreatment involving a family member, close friend or care worker in the past year. If the sample is an accurate reflection of the wider older population it would mean 227,000 people aged over 66 suffering mistreatment in a given year. The figures rise if the incidents involve neighbours or acquaintances to 4 per cent or 342,400 people.[189] Three-quarters of those interviewed said that the effect of mistreatment was either serious or very serious. The researchers believed these figures to be on the conservative side as they did not include care home residents in their survey and some of those most vulnerable to abuse lacked the capacity to take part. Also, even among those interviewed there may have been those who, for a variety of reasons, did not wish to disclose abuse.[190] A literature review looking at evidence of elder abuse around the world concluded that 6 per cent of older people had suffered significant abuse in the last month. A total of 5.6 per cent of older couples had experienced physical violence in their relationships and 25 per cent of older people had suffered significant psychological abuse.[191] Another meta-analysis found a pooled abuse rate of 15.7 per cent of older people.[192] There can be no doubt that elder abuse is prevalent and a major blight on the lives of many older people. Finding evidence on the levels of abuse in a residential setting is even harder. Professionals assert that, for example, 'the institutional abuse of older people is common'.[193] Although there is widespread anecdotal evidence to support this, there is little hard empirical evidence.[194]

---

[186] Law Commission Report 231 (1995: 9.8).
[187] Department of Health (2002f).
[188] O'Keeffe et al. (2008). See also Mowlam et al. (2008) and Cooper et al. (2008).
[189] O'Keeffe et al. (2008), 4.
[190] O'Keeffe et al. (2008), para 7.4
[191] Cooper et al. (2008).
[192] Yon et al. (2017).
[193] Garner and Evans (2002).
[194] Hussein et al. (2005).

B The law

The criminal law applies as it does with any other group of people. There is no equivalent of ageist-aggravated criminal offences, as there are with racially aggravated ones. The law provides a number of routes whereby an older person can obtain protection from abuse. Some of these remedies are the same as those available to cohabitants or spouses.

1. Non-molestation orders and occupation orders are available under the Family Law Act 1996.[195] To obtain a non-molestation order it is necessary to show that the older person is associated with the abuser. This can readily be established if the abuser is a relative. However, an older person who is living in a residential home will normally not be associated with a care assistant at the home.

2. Under the Mental Capacity Act 2005 the court can make orders based on what is in the best interests of a person lacking capacity. There have been cases where the court has restricted contact between such a person and others due to concerns that they pose a risk to them.[196] It is even possible to use the Act to remove the individual from an abusive house.[197] The Act can only be relied upon if the person has lost capacity. If they retain capacity, but are classified as vulnerable adults because they are unable to protect themselves, then orders under the inherent jurisdiction may be used (*A Local Authority* v *DL*[198]).

3. Older people are protected from abuse by the criminal law. However, this depends on the police being made aware of the abuse, which, given the private nature of abuse and the reluctance or inability of the older person to report the abuse, may mean that it is rare for the criminal law to be invoked. The Mental Capacity Act 2005 created an offence of ill-treating or neglecting a person without capacity,[199] but otherwise it will be rare that a failure to obtain care will amount to an offence.[200]

4. There is a limited power in s. 47 of the National Assistance Act 1948 to remove a person from care in a domestic setting. The application is on seven days' notice by a local authority to a magistrates' court. The main ground for such an application is that the person is living in unsanitary conditions and not receiving proper care and attention from other persons. The order initially lasts for three days. An emergency order can be applied for *ex parte* under the National Assistance (Amendment) Act 1951 for a maximum of three weeks. These powers are rarely used. This is in part because of the stigma that attaches to the phrase 'unsanitary conditions'.

The contrast with the protection available for children who are being abused is notable. In particular, there is no duty on a local authority to investigate a suspected case of abuse, as there is for children under s. 47 of the Children Act 1989. Also, there is no equivalent to a child being taken into care. Some commentators have argued that local authorities need to be given a similar set of powers and duties to protect vulnerable adults, as they are to protect children.[201]

[195] Discussed in detail in Chapter 7.
[196] *Re MM (An Adult)* [2009] 1 FLR 487.
[197] *G* v *E* [2010] EWCA Civ 822; *Re SK* [2008] EWHC 636 (Fam).
[198] [2012] EWCA Civ 253.
[199] Mental Capacity Act 2005, s. 44.
[200] Herring (2010a).
[201] E.g. Herring (2012g), who argues that human rights considerations require this.

The Law Commission[202] has called for a law which puts a duty on social services authorities to make enquiries where there is reason to believe a vulnerable adult in their area is suffering or is likely to suffer significant harm; a power to gain access to premises where it is believed a person at risk is living; the power to arrange a medical examination; the power to arrange the removal of the vulnerable person from the home; and the power to apply for temporary and long-term protection orders.[203] Currently none of these is available.

C Issues concerning elder abuse

The question of the abuse of older people gives rise to some complex issues, which might explain why the law has struggled to find an effective response. The following are some of the difficulties:

1. *Autonomy.* Normally, in a liberal democracy the state is not willing to remove adults from their homes, or to prevent them from seeing someone simply on the basis that it would not be good for them. We have seen when considering family violence that the law seeks to respect the autonomy of the victim, although there is a tension with other values that the law may seek to uphold. An example of the problem is that an older person may prefer to be cared for by a relative who is abusive, rather than being placed in a residential home. Should the state deprive the older person of that choice? One answer may be that it depends on whether the older person is competent to make that decision or not. However, there are real difficulties in deciding the level of competence of an older person, especially as the level of understanding may vary considerably from day to day. In any event, can we be sure that residential care is better for an older person than personal care by a loved one who is occasionally abusive? But does this last question reveal an attitude that would be regarded as unacceptable if we were talking about the care of a child?

2. *Definitions of self-neglect.* What might appear to be self-neglect to one person may be eccentricity to another. An older person who insists on sleeping all day and being awake at night might be exhibiting signs of self-neglect or neglect by carers, or might be eccentric. If older people are exhibiting eccentric behaviour, does this justify state intervention to protect them from themselves, or is this an unwarranted intrusion into the autonomy of older people?

3. *Problems in defining violence and neglect.* A carer who is rough in handling an older person or is irritable might be said to be abusive to the older person. But others might regard ill-temper as an inevitable part of the stresses involved in giving personal care.[204]

4. *Proof.* As always with issues of abuse, there are great problems in proving the abuse. One solution would be regular visits of social workers to older people who are perceived to be vulnerable. However, there is a widespread feeling among older people that visits of social workers are an infringement of privacy.

5. *Remedies.* If the abuse is taking place in the older person's home, there is the difficult question of remedy. Placing the older person in a residential home against his or her wishes could itself be seen as a form of abuse. Another issue is that, even if the carer has physically abused the older person, this may be due in part to the lack of provision of adequate resources by the social services.

---

[202] Law Commission Report 326 (2011).
[203] See also Action on Elder Abuse, *Consultation Paper on the Potential for Adult Protection Legislation in England, Wales and Northern Ireland* (Action on Elder Abuse, 2008).
[204] Although see Herring (2011e), which questions whether carers' stress explains elder abuse.

6. *Relationship of care-giver and care-receiver.* The relationship between the care-giver and care-receiver can be a complex one. The exhaustion and desperation that care-givers might feel could even be regarded as a form of abuse itself. Indeed, many cases of elder abuse are simply deeply sad stories that do not necessarily lead to blame of the kind that we place on the child abuser. Landau and Osmo[205] have pointed out that sometimes it is not clear who should be regarded as the social worker's client: the abused older person or the desperate carer.

9 Conclusion

The position of older people and their relatives is of increasing importance in family law. One key issue is the extent to which adult children should be required to provide financial support for older parents. Although there is widespread acceptance that there is a moral obligation owed by adult children to their parents, there are complex issues in the debate whether the obligation should become a legal one. The law on succession indicates that, at least once a person is dead, the law will give legal effect to moral obligations between a variety of relationships, including those between adult children and their parents. This chapter has also considered an issue which will become of increasing importance – intergenerational justice: how should society distribute its resources between the younger and older sections of society? The concluding discussion looked at the topic of abuse of older people and the complex issues that arise in protecting the rights, interests and dignity of the older person.

Further reading

Boyle, G. (2013) 'Facilitating decision-making by people with dementia: is spousal support gendered?' *Journal of Social Welfare and Family Law* 35: 227.

Clough, B. (2014) 'What about us? A case for legal recognition of interdependence in informal care relationships', *Journal of Social Welfare and Family Law* 36: 129.

Clough, B. and Herring, J. (2018) *Ageing, Gender and Family Law*, London: Routledge.

Foster, C., Herring, J. and Doron, I. (eds) (2014) *The Law and Ethics of Dementia*, Oxford: Hart.

Fredman, S. (2003) 'The Age of Equality', in S. Fredman and S. Spencer (eds) *Age as an Equality Issue*, Oxford: Hart.

Harding, R. (2012) 'Legal constructions of dementia: discourses of autonomy at the margins of capacity', *Journal of Social Welfare and Family Law* 34: 425.

Herring, J. (2008d) 'Together forever? The rights and responsibilities of adult children and their parents', in J. Bridgeman, H. Keating and C. Lind (eds) *Responsibility, Law and the Family*, London: Ashgate.

Herring, J. (2009d) *Older People in Law and Society*, Oxford: OUP.

Herring, J. (2012g) 'Elder Abuse: A Human Rights Agenda for the Future', in I. Doran and A. Soden (eds) *Beyond Elder Law*, Amsterdam: Springer.

---

[205] Landau and Osmo (2003).

Coventry University Library

Herring, J. (2016d) *Vulnerable Adults and the Law*, Oxford: OUP.

Herring, J. (2020a) 'Law and policy concerning older people', in J. Eekelaar and R. George (eds) *Routledge Handbook of Family Law and Policy*, Abingdon: Routledge.

Kellet, S. (2006) 'Four theories of filial duty', *The Philosophical Quarterly* 56: 254.

Monk, D. (2011) 'Sexuality and succession law: beyond formal equality', *Feminist Legal Studies* 19: 231.

Oldham, M. (2001) 'Financial obligations within the family – aspects of intergenerational maintenance and succession in England and France', *Cambridge Law Journal* 60: 128.

Oldham, M. (2006) 'Maintenance and the elderly: legal signalling kinship and the state', in F. Ebtehaj, B. Lindley and M. Richards (eds) *Kinship Matters,* Hart: Oxford.

Poffé, L. (2015) 'Towards a new United Nations Human Rights Convention for Older Persons?' *Human Rights Review* 15: 591.

Sloan, B. (2011) 'The concept of coupledom in succession law', *Cambridge Law Journal* 70: 623.

Spitz, L. (2012) 'Grandparents: their role in 21st century families', *Family Law* 42: 1254.

Stewart, A. (2007) 'Home or home: caring about and for elderly family members in a welfare state', in R. Probert (ed.) *Family Life and the Law,* Aldershot: Ashgate.

Williams, J. (2008) 'State responsibility and the abuse of vulnerable older people: is there a case for a public law to protect vulnerable older people from abuse?' in J. Bridgeman, H. Keating and C. Lind (eds) *Responsibility, Law and the Family,* London: Ashgate.

> Visit **go.pearson.com/uk/he/resources** to access **resources** specifically written to complement this text.

Bibliography and further reading

Abbs, P. *et al.* (2006) 'Modern life leads to more depression among children', Letter to *Daily Telegraph* 12 September.

Abrahams, H. (2010) *Rebuilding Lives after Domestic Violence: Understanding Long-Term Outcomes*, London: Jessica Kingsley.

Acker, A. van (2016) 'Disconnected relationship values and marriage policies in England', *Journal of Social Welfare and Family Law* 38: 36.

Action on Elder Abuse, *Consultation Paper on the Potential for Adult Protection Legislation in England, Wales and Northern Ireland* (Action on Elder Abuse, 2008).

Adams, L., McAndrew, F. and Winterbotham, M. (2005) *Pregnancy Discrimination at Work*, London: ECO.

Age UK (2020) *Statistics*, London: Age UK.

Aggarwal, S. (2019) 'Online divorce petitions', *Family Law* 49: 985.

Ahmed, F. (2010) 'Personal autonomy and the option of religious law', *International Journal of Law, Policy and the Family* 24: 222.

Ahmed, F. and Calderwood Norton, J. (2012) 'Religious tribunals, religious freedom, and concern for vulnerable women', *Child and Family Law Quarterly* 363.

Akhtar, R. (2016) 'Unregistered Muslim marriages', in J. Miles, R. Mody and R. Probert (eds) *Marriage Rites and Rights*, Oxford: Hart.

Akhtar, R. (2019) 'Plural approaches to faith-based dispute resolution by Britain's Muslim communities', *Child and Family Law Quarterly* 189.

Alderson, P. (2015) 'Michael Freeman's view of children's rights and some ideas arising from his views', in A. Diduck, N. Peleg and H. Reece (eds) *Law in Society*, Leiden: Brill.

Alderson, P. (2017) 'Common criticisms of children's rights and 25 years of the IJCR', *International Journal of Children's Rights* 25: 307.

Aldgate, J. and Jones, D. (2006) 'The place of attachment in children's development', in

J. Aldgate *et al.* (eds) *The Developing World of the Child*, London: Jessica Kingsley.

Alghrani, A. and Harris, J. (2006) 'Reproductive liberty: should the foundation of families be regulated?' *Child and Family Law Quarterly* 18: 191.

Alghrani, A. (2018) *Regulating Assisted Reproductive Technologies: New Horizons*, Cambridge: Cambridge University Press.

Ali, S. (2013) 'Authority and authenticity: Sharia councils, Muslim women's rights, and the English courts', *Child and Family Law Quarterly* 25: 133.

Allen, N. and Williams, H. (2009) 'The law and financial provision on the dissolution of civil partnerships', *Family Law* 39: 836.

Almack, K. (2006) 'Seeking sperm: accounts of lesbian couples reproductive decision-making and understanding of the needs of the child', *International Journal of Law, Policy and the Family* 20: 1.

Almond, B. (2006) *The Fragmenting Family*, Oxford: Oxford University Press.

Altman, S. (2003) 'A theory of child support', *International Journal of Law, Policy and the Family* 17: 173.

Altman, S, (2018a) 'Parental Control Rights', in E. Brake and L. Ferguson (eds) *Philosophical Foundations of Children's and Family Law*, Oxford: OUP.

Altman, S. (2018b) 'Reinterpreting the right to an open future: from autonomy to authenticity', *Law and Philosophy* 37: 415.

Amato, P. (2010) 'Research on divorce', *Journal of Marriage and the Family* 72: 650.

Ancliffe, S. (2019) 'Children arbitration: why we should all be encouraging it', *Family Law* 49: 821.

Andrews, R. and Johnston Miller, K. (2013) 'Representative bureaucracy, gender and policing', *Public Administration* 91: 998.

Archard, D. (2003) *Children, Family and the State*, Aldershot: Ashgate.

Archard, D. (2004a) 'Wrongful life', *Philosophy* 79: 403.

Archard, D. (2004b) *Children: Rights and Childhood*, London: Routledge.

Archard, D. (2010) *The Family: A Liberal Defence*, Basingstoke: Palgrave.

Archard, D. (2012) 'The future of the family', *Ethics and Social Welfare* 6: 132.

Archard, D. (2018) 'Family and family law', in E. Brake and L. Ferguson (eds) *Philosophical Foundations of Children's and Family Law*, Oxford: OUP.

Archard, D. and Macleod, M. (eds) (2002) *The Moral and Political Status of Children*, Oxford: OUP.

Archard, D. and Skivenes, M. (2009) 'Balancing a child's best interests and a child's views', *International Journal of Children's Rights* 17: 1–21.

Aris, R., Harrison, C. and Humphreys, C. (2002) *Safety and Child Contact*, London: LCD.

Arnold, W. (2000) 'Implementation of Part II: lessons learned', in Thorpe LJ and E. Clarke (eds) *No Fault or Flaw: The Future of the Family Law Act 1996*, Bristol: Jordans.

Auchmuty, R. (2004) 'Same-sex marriage revived: feminist critique and legal strategy', *Feminism and Psychology* 14: 101.

Auchmuty, R. (2008) 'What's so special about marriage? The impact of *Wilkinson v Kitzinger*', *Child and Family Law Quarterly* 20: 475.

Auchmuty, R. (2009) 'Beyond couples', *Feminist Legal Studies* 17: 205.

Auchmuty, R. (2012) 'Law and the power of feminism: how marriage lost its power to oppress women', *Feminist Legal Studies* 20: 71.

Auchmuty, R. (2016a): 'The experience of civil partnership dissolution: not "just like divorce"', *Journal of Social Welfare and Family Law* 38:152.

Auchmuty, R. (2016b) 'The limits of marriage protection in property allocation when a relationship ends', *Child and Family Law Quarterly* 303.

Auchmuty, R. (2016c) 'The limits of marriage protection: in defence of property law', *Oñati Socio-Legal Series* 6: 1196.

Auchmuty, R. (2020) 'Feminist Responses To Same Sex Relationship Recognition', in C. Ashford and A. Maine (eds) *Research Handbook on Gender, Sexuality and the Law*, Cheltenham: Edward Elgar.

Auckland, C. and Goold, I. (2018) 'Defining the limits of parental authority: Charlie Gard, best interests and risk of significant harm threshold', *Law Quarterly Review* 134: 37.

Auckland, C. and Goold, I. (2019) 'Parental Rights, Best Interests and Significant Harms: Who Should Have the Final Say Over A Child's Medical Care' *Cambridge Law Journal* 78: 287.

Baars, G. (2019) 'Queer Cases Unmake Gendered Law, Or, Fucking Law's Gendering Function', *Australian Feminist Law Journal* 45: 43.

Bailey-Harris, R. (2001) 'Same-sex partnerships in English family law', in R. Wintemute and M. Andenæs (eds) *Legal Recognition of Same-Sex Partnerships*, Oxford: Hart.

Bailey-Harris, R. (2001d) 'Contact – challenging conventional wisdom', *Child and Family Law Quarterly* 13: 361.

Bailey-Harris, R. (2002) 'Comment on *C v Bury MBC*', *Family Law* 32: 810.

Bailey-Harris, R. (2003) 'Comment on *GW v RW*', *Family Law* 33: 386.

Bailey-Harris, R. (2005) 'The paradoxes of principle and pragmatism: ancillary relief in England and Wales', *International Journal of Law, Policy and the Family* 19: 229.

Bailey-Harris, R. and Harris, M. (2002) 'Local authorities and child protection – the mosaic of accountability', *Child and Family Law Quarterly* 14: 117.

Bainham, A. (1989) 'When is a parent not a parent? Reflections on the unmarried father and his children in English law', *International Journal of Family Law* 3: 208.

Bainham, A. (1990) 'The privatisation of the public interest in children', *Modern Law Review* 53: 206.

Bainham, A. (1994a) 'The temporal dimension of care', *Cambridge Law Journal* 53: 458.

Bainham, A. (1994b) 'Non-Intervention and judicial paternalism', in P. Birks (ed.) *Frontiers of Liability*, Oxford: OUP.

Bainham, A. (1994c) 'Religion, human rights and the fitness of parents', *Cambridge Law Journal* 53: 39.

Bainham, A. (1995) 'Family law in a pluralistic society', *Journal of Law and Society* 23: 234.

Bainham, A. (1997) 'Do babies have rights?' *Cambridge Law Journal* 56: 48.

Bainham, A. (1998a) *Children: The Modern Law*, Bristol: Jordans.

Bainham, A. (1998b) 'Changing families and changing concepts: reforming the language of family law', *Child and Family Law Quarterly* 10: 1.

Bainham, A. (1998c) 'Honour thy father and thy mother: children's rights and children's duties', in G. Douglas and L. Sebba (eds) *Children's Rights and Traditional Values*, Aldershot: Dartmouth.

Bainham, A. (1999) 'Parentage, parenthood and parental responsibility: subtle, elusive yet important distinctions', in A. Bainham, S. Day Sclater and M. Richards (eds) *What is a Parent?* Oxford: Hart.

Bainham, A. (2000a) 'Attributing harm: child abuse and the unknown perpetrator', *Cambridge Law Journal* 59: 458.

Bainham, A. (2000b) 'Children law at the millennium', in S. Cretney (ed.) *Family Law – Essays for the New Millennium*, Bristol: Jordans.

Bainham, A. (2000c) 'Family rights in the next millennium', *Current Legal Problems* 53: 471.

Bainham, A. (2001a) 'Men and women behaving badly: is fault dead in English family law?' *Oxford Journal of Legal Studies* 21: 219.

Bainham, A. (2002a) 'Can we protect children and protect their rights?' *Family Law* 32: 279.

Bainham, A. (2002b) 'Unintentional parenthood: the case of the reluctant mother', *Cambridge Law Journal* 61: 288.

Bainham, A. (2002c) 'Sexualities, sexual relations and the law', in A. Bainham, S. Day Sclater and M. Richards (eds) *Body Lore and Laws*, Oxford: Hart.

Bainham, A. (2003a) 'Contact as a right and obligation', in A. Bainham, B. Lindley, M. Richards and L. Trinder (eds) *Children and Their Families*, Oxford: Hart.

Bainham, A. (2003b) 'International adoption from Romania – why the moratorium should not be ended', *Child and Family Law Quarterly* 15: 223.

Bainham, A. (2005) *Children: The Modern Law*, Bristol: Jordans.

Bainham, A. (2006a) 'Status anxiety? The Rush for family recognition', in F. Ebtehaj, B. Lindley and M. Richards (eds) *Kinship Matters*, Hart: Oxford.

Bainham, A. (2006b) 'The rights and obligations associated with the birth of a child', in J. Spencer and A. du Bois-Pedain, *Freedom and Responsibility in Reproductive Choice*, Oxford: Hart.

Bainham, A. (2007) 'Permanence for children: Special guardianship or adoption?' *Cambridge Law Journal* 66: 520.

Bainham, A. (2008a) 'Arguments about parentage', *Cambridge Law Journal* 67: 322.

Bainham, A. (2008b) 'Removing babies at birth: a more than questionable practice', *Cambridge Law Journal* 67: 260.

Bainham, A. (2008c) 'What is the point of birth registration?' *Child and Family Law Quarterly* 20: 449.

Bainham, A. (2009a) 'The peculiar finality of adoption', *Cambridge Law Journal* 68: 238.

Bainham, A. (2009b) 'Striking the balance in child protection', *Cambridge Law Journal* 68: 42.

Bainham, A. (2009c) 'Is legitimacy legitimate?' *Family Law* 39: 673.

Bainham, A. (2009d) 'Is anything now left of parental rights?' in R. Probert, S. Gilmore and J. Herring (eds) *Responsible Parents and Parental Responsibility*, Oxford: Hart.

Bainham, A. (2010) 'Rowing Back from *Re G*? Natural parents in the Supreme Court', *Family Law* 40: 394.

Bainham, A. (2011) 'Interim care orders: is the bar set too low?' *Family Law* 41: 374.

Bainham, A. (2013) 'Private and public children law: an under-explored relationship', *Child and Family Law Quarterly* 25: 138.

Bainham, A. (2016) 'Camberley to Carlisle: Where are we now on internal relocation?' *Family Law* 46: 458.

Bainham, A. (2017) 'Teenagers in care proceedings: welfare, rights and justice', *Family Law* 47: 505.

Bainham, A. (2019) 'Removing children from the family: some threshold issues', *Family Law* 49: 1290.

Bainham, A. and Gilmore, S. (2014) 'The English Children and Families Act 2014', *Victoria University Wellington Law Review* 627.

Bainham, A. and Gilmore, S. (2016) *Children: The Modern Law*, Bristol: Jordans.

Bainham, A. and Markham, H. (2014) Living with *Re B-S*: *Re S* and its implications for parents, local authorities and the courts', *Family Law* 44: 991.

Bainham, A., Lindley, B., Richards, M. and Trinder, L. (eds) (2003) *Children and Their Families*, Oxford: Hart.

Baker, H. (2009) 'New cohabitation law in Australia', *Family Law* 39: 1201.

Baker, H. (2012) 'Problematising the relationship between teenage boys and parent abuse: constructions of masculinity and violence', *Social Policy and Society* 11: 265.

Baker, K. (2004) 'Bargaining or biology? The history and future of paternity law and parental status', *Cornell Journal of Law and Public Policy* 14: 1.

Baksi, C. (2014) 'Take divorce out of judges' hands – Munby', *The Law Society Gazette* 24 April.

Bala, N. and Jaremko Bromwich, R. (2002) 'Context and inclusively in Canada's evolving definition of the family', *International Journal of Law, Policy and the Family* 16: 145.

Bamforth, N. (2001) 'Same-sex partnerships and arguments of justice', in R. Wintemute and M. Andenæs (eds) *Legal Recognition of Same-Sex Partnerships*, Oxford: Hart.

Banda, F. (2003) 'Global standards: local values', *International Journal of Law, Policy and the Family* 17: 1.

Banda, F. (2005) *Women, Law and Human Rights*, Oxford: Hart.

Bardasi, E. and Jenkins, S. (2002) *Work History and Income in Later Life*, York: Joseph Rowntree.

Barker, N. (2004) 'For better or worse?' *Journal of Social Welfare and Family Law* 26: 313.

Barker, N. (2006) 'Sex and the Civil Partnership Act: the future of (non) conjugality?' *Feminist Legal Studies* 14: 214.

Barker, N. (2012) *Not the Marrying Kind: A Feminist Critique of Same-Sex Marriage*, London: Macmillan.

Barker, N. (2014) 'Why care? "Deserving family members" and the conservative movement for broader family recognition', in J. Wallbank and J. Herring (eds) *Vulnerabilities, Care and Family Law*, London: Routledge.

Barker, N. and Monk, D. (eds) (2015) *From Civil Partnership to Same-sex Marriage. Interdisciplinary Reflections*, Abingdon: Routledge.

Barlow, A. (2009a) 'Legal rationality and family property', in J. Miles and R. Probert (eds) *Sharing Lives, Dividing Assets*, Oxford: Hart.

Barlow, A. (2009b) 'What does community of property have to offer English law?' in A. Bottomley and S. Wong (eds) *Changing Contours of Domestic Life, Family and Law*, Oxford: Hart.

Barlow, A. (2015) 'Solidarity, autonomy and equality: mixed messages for the family?' *Child and Family Law Quarterly* 223.

Barlow, A. (2017) 'Rising to the post-LASPO challenge: How should mediation respond?' *Journal of Social Welfare and Family Law* 39: 20.

Barlow, A. and Smithson, J. (2012) 'Is modern marriage a bargain? Exploring perceptions of pre-nuptial agreements in England and Wales', *Child and Family Law Quarterly* 24: 304.

Barlow, A., Burgoyne, C., Clery, E. and Smithson, J. (2008) 'Cohabitation and the law: myths, money and the media', in *British Social Attitudes Survey*, London: Sage.

Barlow, A., Callus, T. and Cooke, E. (2004) 'Community of property – a study for England and Wales', *Family Law* 34: 47.

Barlow, A., Duncan, S., James, G. and Park, A. (2003) *Family Affairs: Cohabitation, Marriage and the Law*, London: Nuffield Foundation.

Barlow, A., Duncan, S., James, G. and Park, A. (2005) *Cohabitation, Marriage and the Law*, Oxford: Hart.

Barlow, A., Hunter, R., Smithson, J. and Ewing, J. (2014) *Mapping Paths to Family Justice: Interim Results* (Exeter: University of Exeter).

Barlow, A., Hunter R., Smithson, J. and Ewing, J. (2017) *Mapping paths to family justice: resolving family disputes in neo-liberal times*, London: Palgrave.

Barnardo's (2004) *Domestic Violence*, London: Barnardo's.

Barnardo's (2008) *Don't Give Up On Us*, London: Barnardo's.

Barnes, R. and Donovan, C. (2019) 'Domestic violence in lesbian, gay, bisexual and/or transgender relationships', *Sexualities* 22: 741.

Barnett, A. (2009) 'The welfare of the child re-visited: in whose best interests? Part I', *Family Law* 39: 50 and 135.

Barnett, A. (2014a) 'Contact at all costs? Domestic violence and children's welfare', *Child and Family Law Quarterly* 439.

Barnett, A. (2014b) 'Like gold dust these days': domestic violence fact-finding hearings in child contact cases', *Feminist Legal Studies* 23: 47.

Barnett, A. (2017a) 'Family law without lawyers – A systems theory perspective', *Journal of Social Welfare and Family Law* 39: 22.

Barnett, A. (2017b) '"Greater than the mere sum of its parts": coercive control and the question of proof', *Child and Family Law Quarterly* 379.

Barnett, A. (2020) 'A genealogy of hostility: parental alienation in England and Wales', *Journal of Social Welfare and Family Law* 42: 1.

Barnett, S. (2000) 'Compatibility and religious rights', *Family Law* 30: 494.

Barrett, M. and MacIntosh, M. (1991) *The Anti-Social Family*, London: Verso.

Barrow, S. and Bartley, J. (2006) *What Future for Marriage?* London: Ekklesia.

Barry, K-A. (2019) 'McKenzie Friends and litigants in person: widening access to justice or foes in disguise?' *Child and Family Law Quarterly* 31.

Barton, C. (2001) 'Adoption and Children Bill 2001', *Family Law* 31: 431.

Barton, C. (2003) 'The mediator as midwife – a marketing opportunity', *Family Law* 33: 195.

Barton, C. (2004) 'Bigamy & marriage – horse & carriage', *Family Law* 34: 517.

Barton, C. (2008a) 'Domestic partnership contracts: sliced bread or a slice of the bread?' *Family Law* 38: 900.

Barton, C. (2008b) 'Hitting your children: common assault or common sense?' *Family Law* 38: 64.

Barton, C. (2009) 'Stepfathers, mothers' cohabitants and "uncles"', *Family Law* 39: 326.

Barton, C. (2018) 'Financial remedies today: "tools", "rules", "guidelines", "benchmarks", "yardsticks", "ordinary consequences" and "departure points"', *Family Law* 558.

Barton, C. and Bissett-Johnson, A. (2000) 'The declining number of ancillary relief orders', *Family Law* 30: 94.

Bates, L. and Hester, M. (2020) 'No longer a civil matter? The design and use of protection orders for domestic violence in England and Wales', *Journal of Social Welfare and Family Law* 42: 133.

BBC News Online (2005a) 'Girls reveal abuse by boyfriends', 21 March.

BBC News Online (2006a) 'Archbishop warns of child crisis', 18 September.

BBC News Online (2006b) 'Twenty-one-year-old father's seventh child', 2 July.

BBC News Online (2007a) 'Tories consider marriage tax help', 10 July.

BBC News Online (2007b) 'Sir Paul likens divorce to hell', 16 October.

BBC News Online (2007c) 'Call to stop children's drinking', 27 February.

BBC News Online (2007d) 'Sperm donor to pay child support', 3 December.

BBC News Online (2008a) 'Budget bride's basement bargains', 16 August.

BBC News Online (2008b) 'US "pregnant man" has baby girl', 3 July.

BBC News Online (2008c) 'Horses for divorces', 23 September.

BBC News Online (2008d) 'Unpaid child support at 1.8bn', 25 October.

BBC News Online (2009a) 'Vicar in "sham marriages" arrest', 1 July.

BBC News Online (2009b) 'Scientists claim sperm "first"', 7 July.

BBC News Online (2009c) 'Couples to test "intimacy" device', April 21.

BBC News Online (2009d) 'Fathers "cool on parental leave"', 18 May.

BBC News Online (2009e) 'Secret world of sperm donation', 18 September.

BBC News Online (2010a) 'Heart refusal girl back at school', 5 January 2010.

BBC News Online (2010b) 'Court says Dutch teenager Laura Dekker can set sail', 27 July.

BBC News Online (2010c) 'Reading men made £250,000 from sperm website', 13 September.

BBC News Online (2011) 'Children's screen habits revealed', 1 February.

BBC News Online (2014) 'More men face lonely old age says study', 14 October.

BBC News Online (2016) 'Time spent online "overtakes TV" among youngsters', 26 January.

BBC News Online (2020) 'Tafida Raqeeb: Brain-damaged girl in High Court case out of intensive care', 10 January 2020.

Bedford, D. and Herring, J. (eds) (2019) *Embracing Vulnerability* London: Routledge

Beaumont, P. (2017) Private international law concerning children in the UK after Brexit: comparing Hague Treaty law with EU Regulations', *Child and Family Law Quarterly* 213.

Beck, U. (2002) *Individualization*, London: Sage.

Beck, U. and Beck-Gernsheim, G. (1995) *The Normal Chaos of Love*, Cambridge: Polity Press.

Beesson, S. (2007) 'Enforcing the child's right to know her origins: contrasting approaches under the Convention on the Rights of the Child and the European Convention on Human Rights', *International Journal of Law, Policy and the Family* 21: 137.

Belhorn, S. (2005) 'Settling beyond the shadow of the law: how mediation can make the most of social norms', *Ohio State Journal on Dispute Resolution* 20: 981.

Bell, C. (2008) 'Domestic violence and contact', *Family Law* 38: 1139.

Bell, F., Cashmore, J., Parkinson, P. and Single, J. (2013) 'Outcomes of Child-Inclusive Mediation', *International Journal of Law, Policy and the Family* 27: 116.

Bellamy, C. and Lord, G. (2003) 'Reflections on Family Proceedings Rule 9.5', *Family Law* 33: 265.

Bendall, C. and Harding, R. (2018) 'Heteronormativity in dissolution proceedings', in E. Brake and L. Ferguson (eds) *Philosophical Foundations of Children's and Family Law*, Oxford: OUP.

Bennett, H. (2014) 'Family law finance arbitration: a new dawn', *Family Law* 44: 345.

Benson, H. (2009) *Married and Unmarried Family Breakdown*, Bristol: Community Family Trust.

Benson, H. (2013) *What is the divorce rate?* London: The Marriage Foundation.

Benson, H. (2015) *The Marriage Gap*, London: The Marriage Foundation.

Benson, H. (2016) *The Vanishing Divorce,* London: The Marriage Foundation.

Bernstein, A. (2003) 'For and against marriage: a revision', *Michigan Law Review* 102: 129.

Bernstein, A. (ed.) (2006) *Marriage Proposals: Questioning a Legal Status,* New York: New York University Press.

Bettle, J. and Herring, J. (2011) 'Shaken babies and care proceedings', *Family Law* 41: 1370.

Bettle, J. and Herring, J. (2014) 'With this diode I thee wed', www.familylawweek.co.uk/site. aspx?i=ed128544

Bevan, C. (2013) 'The role of intention in non-marriage cases post *Hudson v Leigh'*, *Child and Family Law Quarterly* 13: 80.

Bevan, G. and Davis, G. (1999) 'A preliminary exploration of the impact of family mediation on legal aid costs', *Child and Family Law Quarterly* 11: 411.

Billari, F. and Liefbroer, A. (2016) 'Why still marry? The role of feelings in the persistence of marriage as an institution' British Journal of Sociology 67: 516

Bindel, J. (2015) 'Beating your partner is a crime, not an illness', *The Guardian* 12 January.

Bingham, J. (2012) 'Britain Christians are being vilified, warns Lord Carey', *The Daily Telegraph* 13 April 2012.

Birchall, J. and Choudhry, S. (2018) *Domestic Abuse, Human Rights and The Family Court,* London: Women's Aid.

Bird, R. (2000) 'Pension sharing', *Family Law* 30: 455.

Bird, R. (2002) 'The reform of section 25', *Family Law* 32: 428.

Bishop, G., Kingston, S., Max, S. and Pressdee, P. (2011) 'Collab lite: no substitute for the real thing', *Family Law* 41: 1556.

Blacklaws, C. (2014) 'The impact of the LASPO changes to date in private family law and mediation', *Family Law* 44: 626.

Blacklaws, C. and Dowding, S. (2006) 'The representation of children: from aspiration to extinction', *Family Law* 36: 777.

Blackstone, W. (1770) *Commentaries on the Laws of England.*

Blakey, R. (2020) 'Cracking the code: the role of mediators and flexibility post-LASPO', *Child and Family Law Quarterly* 53.

Blyth, E. (2008) 'To be or not to be? A critical appraisal of the welfare of children conceived through new reproductive technologies', *International Journal of Children's Rights* 16: 505.

Blyth, E. and Frith, L. (2009) 'Donor-conceived people's access to genetic and biographical history', *International Journal of Law, Policy and the Family* 23: 174.

Blyth, E., Jones, C., Frith, L. and Speirs, J. (2009) 'The role of birth certificates in relation to access to biographical and genetic history in donor conception', *International Journal of Children's Rights* 17: 207.

Boele-Woelki, K., Ferrand, F., Beilfuss, C., Jantera-Jareborg, M., Lowe, N., Martiny, D. and Pintens, W. (2007) *Principles of European Family Law Regarding Parental Responsibilities,* Antwerp: Intersentia.

Bond, A. (2007) 'Special guardianship after *Re S, Re AJ* and *Re M-J'*, *Family Law* 37: 321.

Bonner, D., Fenwick, H. and Harris-Short, S. (2003) 'Judicial approaches to the Human Rights Act', *International and Comparative Law Quarterly* 52: 549.

Bonthuys, E. (2006) 'The best interests of children in the South African Constitution', *International Journal of Law, Policy and the Family* 20: 23.

Booth, P. (2004) 'Parental responsibility – what changes', *Family Law* 34: 353.

Booth, P. (2005) 'The punishment of children', *Family Law* 45: 33.

Booth, P. (2008) 'Judging Sharia', *Family Law* 38: 935.

Booth, R. and Mohdin, A. (2019) 'Revealed: the stark evidence of everyday racial bias in Britain' *The Guardian,* 2 December.

Borkowski, A. (2002) 'The presumption of marriage', *Child and Family Law Quarterly* 14: 250.

Bowcott, O. (2016) 'Family courts face "imminent crisis" over child custody cases', *The Guardian* 20 September.

Bowcott, O. (2017) 'Senior judge warns over shaming impact of legal aid cuts', *The Guardian* 13 October.

Bowcott, O. (2018a) 'Rise in deathbed weddings prompts call to protect cohabiting couples', *The Guardian* 18 August.

Bowcott, O. (2018b) 'Access to justice under threat in UK', *The Guardian* 26 September.

Bowcott, O. and Carroll, S. (2018) 'Civil partnership to be open to heterosexual couples', *The Guardian* 2 October.

Bowcott, O. and Steward, H. (2018) 'UK government to launch consultation on no-fault divorces', *The Guardian* 8 September.

Bowen, E., Brown, L. and Gilchrist, E. (2002) 'Evaluating probation-based offender programmes for domestic violence offenders', *Howard Journal of Criminal Justice* 41: 221.

Boyd, S. (1996) 'Is there an ideology of motherhood in (post) modern child custody law?' *Social and Legal Studies* 5: 495.

Boyd, S. (2008) 'Equality enough? Fathers' rights and women's rights', in R. Hunter (ed.) *Rethinking Equality Projects in Law*, Oxford: Hart.

Boyd, S. (2011) 'Relocation, indeterminacy, and burden of proof: lessons from Canada', *Child and Family Law Quarterly* 23: 155.

Boyd, S. (2016) 'Equality: an uncomfortable fit in parenting law', in R. Leckey (ed.) *After Legal Equality*, Abingdon: Routledge.

Boyd, S. and Young, C. (2003) 'From same-sex to no-sex?' *Seattle Journal for Social Justice* 1: 575.

Boyle, G. (2013) 'Facilitating decision-making by people with dementia: is spousal support gendered?' *Journal of Social Welfare and Family Law* 35: 227.

Bracken, L. (2020) 'Surrogacy and the genetic link', *Child and Family Law Quarterly* 303.

Bradley, D. (2001) 'Regulation of unmarried cohabitation in West-European jurisdictions – determinants of legal policy', *International Journal of Law, Policy and the Family* 15: 22.

Brake, E. (2005) 'Fatherhood and child support: do men have a right to choose?' *Journal of Applied Philosophy* 22: 56.

Brake, E. (2012) *Minimizing Marriage*, Oxford: OUP.

Brake, E. and Ferguson, L. (eds) (2018) *Philosophical Foundations of Children's and Family Law*, Oxford: OUP.

Bremner, P. (2017) 'Collaborative co-parenting and heteronormativity: recognising the interests of gay fathers', *Child and Family Law Quarterly* 293.

Bridge, C. (2000) 'Diversity, divorce and information meetings – ensuring access to justice', *Family Law* 30: 645.

Bridge, C. (2009) 'Comment', *Family Law* 39: 381.

Bridge, C. and Swindells, H. (2003) *Adoption: The Modern Law*, Bristol: Jordans.

Bridge, S. (2001) 'Marriage and divorce: the regulation of intimacy', in J. Herring (ed.) *Family Law – Issues, Debates, Policy*, Cullompton: Willan.

Bridge, S. (2007a) 'Financial relief for cohabitants: eligibility, opt out and provision on death', *Family Law* 37: 1076.

Bridge, S. (2007b) 'Financial relief for cohabitants: how the Law Commission's scheme would work', *Family Law* 37: 998.

Bridge, S. (2007c) 'Cohabitation: why legislative reform is necessary', *Family Law* 37: 911.

Bridgeman, J. (2007) *Parental Responsibility, Young Children and Healthcare Law*, Cambridge: CUP.

Bridgeman, J. (2010) 'Children with exceptional needs: welfare, rights and caring responsibilities', in J. Wallbank, S. Choudhry and J. Herring (eds) *Rights, Gender and Family Law*, Abingdon: Routledge.

Bridgeman, J. (2015) 'The right to responsible parents?' in A. Diduck, N. Peleg and H. Reece (eds) *Law in Society*, Leiden: Brill.

Bridgeman, J., Keating, H. and Lind, C. (2008) *Responsibility, Law and the Family*, London: Ashgate.

Bridges, S. and Disney, R. (2012) 'Household indebtedness and separation in Britain: evidence from the Families and Children Survey', *Child and Family Law Quarterly* 24: 24.

Brighouse, H. and Swift, A. (2014) *Family Values: The Ethics of Parent-Child Relationships*, Oxford: Princeton University Press.

Brinig, M. (2000) *From Contract to Covenant: Beyond the Law and Economics of the Family*, New York: Harvard University Press.

Brinig, M. (2010) *Family, Law and Community*, Chicago: Chicago University Press.

Brinig, M. (2015) 'Substantive parenting arrangements in the USA: unpacking the policy choices', *Child and Family Law Quarterly* 249.

Broadhurst, K., Shaw, M., Kerwhaw, S., Harwin, J., Alroug, B., Mason, C. and Pilling, M. (2015) 'Vulnerable birth mothers and repeat losses of infants to public care: is targeted reproductive health care ethically defensible?' *Journal of Social Welfare and Family Law* 37: 84.

Brophy, J. (2000) '"Race" and ethnicity in public law proceedings', *Family Law* 30: 740.

Brophy, J. (2008) 'Child maltreatment and diverse households', *Journal of Law and Society* 35: 75.

Brophy, J. (2014) 'Irreconcilable differences? Young people, safeguarding and the "next steps" in "transparency"', *Family Law* 1685.

Brophy, J. and Cover, M. (2012) 'Children, the recession and family courts', *Family Law* 42: 526.

Brophy, J., Jhotti-Johal, J. and Owen, C. (2003) *Significant Harm*, London: Department for Constitutional Affairs.

Brown, A. (2019) *What is the Family of Law?* Oxford: Hart.

Brown, B. (2020) 'Sex education and the war against marriage' *The Conservative Woman* 5 June 2020.

Browne, K. (2011) '"By partner we mean . . . ": alternative geographies of "gay marriage"', *Sexualities* 14: 100.

Bruckner, P. (2014) *Has Marriage for Love Failed?* London: Polity.

Brunner, K. (2001) 'Nullity in unconsummated marriages', *Family Law* 31: 837.

Brunning, L. (2018) 'The distinctiveness of polyamory', *Journal of Applied Philosophy* 35: 513.

Bryson, C., Ellman, I., McKay, S. and Miles, J. (2013) 'Child maintenance: how much should the state require fathers to pay when families separate?' *Family Law* 43: 1296.

Buchanan, A. and Hunt, J. (2003) 'Disputed contact cases in the courts', in A. Bainham, B. Lindley, M. Richards and L. Trinder (eds) *Children and Their Families*, Oxford: Hart.

Buchanan, A., Hunt, J., Bretherton, H. and Bream, V. (2001) *Families in Conflict*, Cambridge: Polity Press.

Bullock, K., Sarre, S., Tarling, R. and Wilkinson, M. (2010) *The Delivery of Domestic Abuse Programmes*, London: Ministry of Justice.

Bunting, L., Webb, M. and Healy, J. (2010) 'In two minds? – Parental attitudes toward physical punishment in the UK', *Children and Society* 24: 359.

Burch, R. and Gallup, G. (2004) 'Pregnancy as a stimulus for domestic violence', *Journal of Family Violence* 19: 243–7.

Burgoyne, C. and Sonnenberg, S. (2009) 'Financial practices in cohabiting heterosexual couples', in J. Miles and R. Probert (eds) *Sharing Lives, Dividing Assets*, Oxford: Hart.

Burgoyne, C., Clarke, V., Reibstein, J. and Edmunds, A. (2006) '"All my worldly goods I share with you"? Managing money at the transition to heterosexual marriage', *Sociological Review* 54: 619.

Burholt, V. and Windle, G. (2006) *The Material Resources and Well-Being of Older People*, York: Joseph Rowntree Foundation.

Burrows, L. (1998) *The Fight for the Family*, Oxford: Family Education Trust.

Burton, M. (2006) 'Judicial monitoring of compliance', *International Journal of Law, Policy and the Family* 20: 366.

Burton, M. (2008) *Legal Responses to Domestic Violence*, London: Routledge.

Burton, M. (2009) 'The civil law remedies for domestic violence: why are applications for non-molestation orders declining?' *Journal of Social Welfare and Family Law* 31: 109.

Burton, M. (2010) 'The human rights of victims of domestic violence: *Opuz v Turkey*', *Child and Family Law Quarterly* 22: 131.

Burton, M. (2015) 'Emergency barring orders in domestic violence cases: what can England and Wales learn from other European countries?' *Child and Family Law Quarterly* 25.

Burton, M. (2018) 'Specialist domestic violence courts for child arrangement cases: safer courtrooms and safer outcomes?' *Journal of Social Welfare and Family Law* 40: 533.

Butler, I., Robinson, M. and Scanlan, L. (2005) *Children and Decision Making*, York: Joseph Rowntree.

Butler-Sloss, E. (2003) *Are We Failing the Family? Human Rights, Children and the Meaning of Family in the 21st Century*, London: LCD.

Buzawa, E. and Buzawa, C. (2003) *Domestic Violence: The Criminal Justice Response*, 3rd edn, London: Sage.

Byrne, B. (2016) 'Do children still need to escape childhood?' *International Journal of Children's Rights* 24: 113.

Bywaters, P. (2017) *Identifying and Understanding Inequalities in Child Welfare Intervention Rates*, London: Nuffield Council.

CAFCASS (2010) *How It Looks To Me*, London: CAFCASS.

CAFCASS (2018a) *Domestic Abuse Perpetrator Programme*, London: CAFCASS.

CAFCASS (2018b) *Public Law Data*, London: CAFCASS.

Caffrey, L. (2013) 'Hearing the "voice of the child"? The role of child contact centres in the family justice system', *Child and Family Law Quarterly* 25: 357.

Cahn, N. and Carbone, J. (2010) *Red Families v Blue Families*, Oxford: OUP.

Cahn, N. and Collins, J. (2009) 'Eight is enough', *Wake Forest University Legal Studies Paper No. 1365975*.

Cain, R. (2011) 'The court of motherhood', in J. Bridgeman, H. Keating and C. Lind (eds) *Regulating Family Responsibilities*, Aldershot: Ashgate.

Caldwell, J. (2011) 'Common law judges and judicial interviewing', *Child and Family Law Quarterly* 23: 41.

Callus, T. (2008) 'First "designer babies", now à la carte parents', *Family Law* 38: 143.

Callus, T. (2012) 'A new parenthood paradigm for twenty-first century family law in England and Wales', *Legal Studies* 32: 347.

Callus, T. (2019) 'What's the point of parenthood? The agreed parenthood provisions under the HFE Act 2008 and inconsistency with intention', *Journal of Social Welfare and Family Law* 41: 389.

Cameron, G. (2015) 'Family justice reforms: how are they working in practice?' *Family Law* 1021.

Campbell, A., Carnevale, M., Jackson, S., Carnevale, F., Collin-Vézina, D. and Macdonald, M. (2011) 'Child citizenship and agency as shaped by legal obligations', *Child and Family Law Quarterly* 23: 489.

Campbell, T. (1992) 'The rights of the minor', in P. Alston, S. Parker and J. Seymour (eds) *Children, Rights and the Law*, Oxford: Clarendon Press.

Carbone, J. (2000) *From Partners to Parents*, New York: Columbia University Press.

Carbone, J. and Brinig, M. (1988) 'The reliance interest of marriage', *Tulane Law Review* 62: 855.

Carbone, J. and Brinig, M. (1991) 'Rethinking marriage', *Tulane Law Review* 65: 953.

Cardy, S. (2010) '"Care Matters" and the privatization of looked after children's services in England and Wales: Developing a critique of independent "social work practices"', *Critical Social Policy* 30: 430.

Carers UK (2020) *Facts About Carers*, London: Carers UK.

Carey, G. (2013) 'Love is not enough', in de Wall (ed.) *The Meaning of Matrimony*, London: Civitas.

Carruthers, J. and Crawford, E. (2017) 'Divorcing Europe: reflections from a Scottish perspective on the implications of Brexit for cross-border divorce proceedings', *Child and Family Law Quarterly* 233.

Casciani, D. (2014) 'Police fail domestic abuse victims – HMIC report', BBC News Online, 27 March.

Carline, A. and Easteal, P. (2016) *Shades of Grey – Domestic and Sexual Violence Against Women*, Abingdon: Routledge.

Case, M. A. (2010) 'What feminists have to lose in same-sex marriage litigation', *UCLA Law Review* 57: 1119.

Case, M. A. (2011) 'Feminist fundamentalism at the intersection of government and familial responsibility for children', in C. Lind, H. Keating and J. Bridgeman (eds) *Taking Responsibility, Law and the Changing Family*, Aldershot: Ashgate.

Cashmore, J. (2003) 'Children's participation in family law matters', in H. Hallet and A. Prout (eds) *Hearing the Voices of Children*, London: Routledge/Falmer.

Cassidy, C. (2009) *Thinking Children*, London: Continuum.

Cassidy, C. (2012) 'Children's status, children's rights and "dealing with" children', *International Journal of Children's Rights* 20: 57.

Cassidy, C., Conrad, S-J., Daniel, M-F., Figueroia-Rego, M., Kohan, W., Murris, K., Wu, X. and Zhelyazkova, T. (2017) 'Being children: children's voices on childhood', *International Journal of Children's Rights* 25: 698.

Cave, E. (2011) 'Maximisation of minors' capacity', *Child and Family Law Quarterly* 23: 431.

Cave, E. (2014a) 'Adolescent Refusal of MMR Inoculation: F (Mother) v F (Father)', *Modern Law Review* 77: 619.

Cave, E. (2014b) 'Goodbye *Gillick*? Identifying and resolving problems with the concept of child competence', *Legal Studies* 34: 103.

Cave, E. and Wallbank, J. (2012) 'Minors' capacity to refuse treatment: a reply to Gilmore and Herring', *Medical Law Review* 20(3) 423.

Cave, E. (2018) 'Liberalism, civil marriage, and amorous caregiving dyads', *Journal of Applied Philosophy*.

Centre for the Modern Family (2011) *Family*, London: Centre for the Modern Family.

Centre for Social Justice (2009) *Every Family Matters*, London: Centre for Social Justice.

Centre for Social Justice (2010) *Green Paper on the Family*, London: Centre for Social Justice.

Centre for Social Justice (2016) *Annual Fatherhood Survey*, London: Centre for Social Justice

Centre for Social Justice (2019) *A Review of the Family Test*, London: Centre for Social Justice.

Chambers, C. (2013) 'The marriage-free state', *Proceedings of the Aristotelian Society* 1.

Chambers, D. (2014) *A Sociology of Family Life*, Bristol: Polity.

Chambers, C. (2017) *Against Marriage*, Oxford: Oxford University Press.

Chan, W. (2013) 'Cohabitation, civil partnership, marriage and the equal sharing principle', *Legal Studies* 33: 1.

Chantler, K., Gangoli, G. and Hester, M. (2009) 'Forced marriage in the UK: religious, cultural, economic or state violence?' *Critical Social Policy* 29: 587.

Chau, P.-L. and Herring, J. (2002) 'Defining, assigning and designing sex', *International Journal of Law, Policy and the Family* 16: 327.

Chau, P.-L. and Herring, J. (2004) 'Men, women and people: the definition of sex', in B. Brooks-Gordon, L. Goldsthorpe, M. Johnson and A. Bainham (eds) *Sexuality Repositioned*, Oxford: Hart.

Chau, P.-L. and Herring, J. (2015) 'Three parents and a baby', *Family Law* 45: 912.

Cherkassky, L. (2015) 'The wrong harvest: the law on saviour siblings', *International Journal of Law, Policy and the Family* 29: 36.

Cherlin, A. (2005) 'American Marriage in the Early Twenty-First Century', *The Future of Children* 15: 33.

Cherney, I. (2010) 'Mothers', fathers', and their children's perceptions and reasoning about nurturance and self-determination rights', *International Journal of Children's Rights* 18: 79.

Chico, V. and Hagger, L. (2011) 'The Mental Capacity Act 2005 and mature minors: a missed opportunity?' *Journal of Social Welfare and Family Law* 33: 157.

Child Poverty Action Group (2020) *Child Poverty Facts*, London: CPAG.

Children Act Sub-Committee (2002a) *Making Contact Work*, London: LCD.

Children's Rights Alliance in England (2020) *State of Children's Rights in England*, London: CRAE.

Chokowry, K. and Skinner, K. (2011) 'The Forced Marriage (Civil Protection) Act 2007: two years on', *Family Law* 41: 76.

Choudhry, S. (2003) 'The Adoption and Children Act 2002, the welfare principle and the Human Rights Act 1998 – a missed opportunity', *Child and Family Law Quarterly* 15: 119.

Choudhry, S. (2009) 'Parental responsibility and corporal punishment', in R. Probert, S. Gilmore and J. Herring, *Responsible Parents and Parental Responsibility*, Oxford: Hart.

Choudhry, S. (2010) 'Mandatory prosecution and arrest as a form of compliance with due diligence duties in domestic violence – the gender implications', in J. Wallbank, S. Choudhry and J. Herring (eds) *Rights, Gender and Family Law*, Abingdon: Routledge.

Choudhry, S. (2012) 'Domestic violence, contact and the ECHR', in M. Freeman (ed.) *Law and Childhood Studies*, Oxford: OUP.

Choudhry, S. (2016) 'Towards a transformative conceptualisation of violence against women – a critical frame analysis of Council of Europe discourse on violence against women', *Modern Law Review* 79: 406.

Choudhry, S. (2019) 'When Women's Rights are *Not* Human Rights – the Non-Performativity of the Human Rights of Victims of Domestic Abuse within English Family Law', *Modern Law Review* 82: 1072.

Choudhry, S. and Fenwick, H. (2005) 'Taking the rights of parents and children seriously: confronting the welfare principle under the Human Rights Act', *Oxford Journal of Legal Studies* 25: 453.

Choudhry, S. and Herring, J. (2006a) 'Righting domestic violence', *International Journal of Law, Policy and the Family* 20: 95.

Choudhry, S. and Herring, J. (2006b) 'Domestic violence and the Human Rights Act 1998: a new means of legal intervention', *Public Law* 752.

Choudhry, S. and Herring, J. (2010) *European Human Rights and Family Law*, Oxford: Hart.

Choudhry, S. and Herring, J. (2017) 'A human right to legal aid? – The implications of changes to the legal aid scheme for victims of domestic abuse', *Journal of Social Welfare and Family Law* 39: 152.

Choudhry, S. and Herring, J. (eds) (2019) *Comparative Family Law*, Cambridge: Cambridge University Press.

Christian Institute (2002) *Counterfeit Marriage*, Newcastle-upon-Tyne: Christian Institute.

Christian Institute (2020) *No-fault divorce 'will lead to more broken families', warns pro-marriage group*. London: Christian Institute.

Churchill, H. (2008) 'Being a responsible mother', in J. Bridgeman, H. Keating and C. Lind (eds) *Responsibility, Law and the Family*, London: Ashgate.

Ciborowska, C. (2019) 'How to approach allegations of coercive and controlling behaviour in private law proceedings', *Family Law* 488.

Clark, B. (2011) 'Ante-nuptial contracts after *Radmacher*: an impermissible gloss?' *Journal of Social Welfare and Family Law* 33: 15.

Clark, B. (2017) 'Treading a tightrope: the fragility of family and religious minority rights in the jurisprudence of the European Court of Human Rights', *Child and Family Law Quarterly* 23.

Clark, V., Burgoyne, C. and Burns, M. (2006) 'Just a piece of paper? A qualitative exploration of same-sex couples' multiple conceptions of civil partnership and marriage', *Lesbian and Gay Psychology Review* 7: 141.

Clarkson, H. and Clarkson, D. (2007) 'Confusion and controversy in parental alienation', *Journal of Social Welfare and Family Law* 29: 265.

Clayton, M. (2006) *Justice and Legitimacy in Upbringing*, Oxford: OUP.

Cleary, A. (2004) 'Cohabitation – a word of caution', *Family Law* 34: 62.

Clements, L. (2011) *Carers and their Rights*, London: Carers UK.

Clifton, J. (2014) 'The long road to universal parental responsibility: some implications from research into marginal fathers', *Family Law* 44: 859.

Clough, B. (2014) 'What about us? A case for legal recognition of interdependence in informal care relationships', *Journal of Social Welfare and Family Law* 36: 129.

Clough, B. and Herring, J. (2018) *Ageing, Gender and Family Law*, London: Routledge.

Clucas, B. (2005) 'The Children's Commissioner for England: the way forward?' *Family Law* 35: 290.

Coalition for Marriage (2017) *Five reasons not to allow no fault divorce*, London: CfM.

Coalition for Marriage (2018) *The Revolution Never Stops*, London: CfM.

Cobb, S. (2013) 'Legal aid reform: its impact on family law', *Journal of Social Welfare and Family Law* 35: 3.

Cobb, S. (2015) 'Seen but not heard?' *Family Law* 45: 144.

Cobley, C. (2006) 'The quest for truth: substantiating allegations of physical abuse in criminal proceedings and care proceedings', *International Journal of Law, Policy and the Family* 20: 317.

Cohen, L. (2002) 'Marriage: the long-term contract', in A. Dnes and R. Rowthorn (eds) *The Law and Economics of Marriage and Divorce*, Cambridge: CUP.

Coleman, L. and Glenn, F. (2010) *When Couples Part: Understanding the Consequences for Adults and Children*, London: One plus One.

Coleridge, P. (2014) 'Lobbing a few pebbles in the pond; the funeral of a dead parrot', *Family Law* 16.

Collier, R. (2000) 'Anxious parenthood, the vulnerable child and the "good father"', in J. Bridgeman and D. Monk (eds) *Feminist Perspectives on Child Law*, London: Cavendish.

Collier, R. (2003) 'In search of the "good father"', in J. Dewar and S. Parker (eds) *Family Law Processes, Practices, Pressures*, Oxford: Hart.

Collier, R. (2005) 'Fathers 4 Justice, law and the new politics of fatherhood', *Child and Family Law Quarterly* 17: 511.

Collier, R. (2007) 'Feminist legal studies and the subject(s) of men', in A. Diduck and K. O'Donovan (eds) *Feminist Perspective on Family Law*, London: Routledge.

Collier, R. (2008) 'Engaging fathers? Responsibility, law and the "problem of fatherhood"', in J. Bridgeman, H. Keating and C. Lind (eds) *Responsibility, Law and the Family*, London: Ashgate.

Collier, R. (2009) 'Fathers' rights, gender and welfare: some questions for family law', *Journal of Social Welfare and Family Law* 31: 237.

Collier, R. (2010) *Men, Law and Gender*, London: Routledge.

Collier, R. (2016) 'Men, gender and fathers' rights after legal equality', in R. Leckey (ed.) *After Legal Equality*, Abingdon: Routledge.

Collier, R. and Sheldon, S. (2008) *Fragmenting Fatherhood*, Oxford: Hart.

Collins, J. (2014) 'The contours of 'vulnerability'', in Wallbank, J. and Herring, J. (2014) *Vulnerabilities, Care and Family Law*, London: Routledge.

Committee on the Rights of the Child (2016) *Concluding Observations on the Fifth Periodic Report of the United Kingdom of Great Britain and Northern Ireland*, Geneva: United Nations.

Conaghan, J. (2008) 'Intersectionality and the Feminist Project in Law', in D. Cooper (ed.) *Law, Power and the Politics of Subjectivity: Intersectionality and Beyond*, Routledge, Abingdon.

Conway, H (2018) 'Frozen corpses and feuding parents: *Re JS (Disposal of Body)*', *Modern Law Review* 81: 132.

Cook, R. (2002) 'Villain, hero or masked stranger: ambivalence in transaction with human gametes', in A. Bainham, S. Day Sclater and M. Richards (eds) *Body Lore and Laws*, Oxford: Hart.

Cook, R., Day Sclater, S. and Kaganas, F. (2003) *Surrogate Motherhood*, Oxford: Hart.

Cooke, E. (2007) '*Miller/McFarlane*: law in search of a definition', *Child and Family Law Quarterly* 19: 98.

Cookson, G. (2011) *Unintended Consequences: the cost of the Government's Legal Aid Reforms*, London: Law Society.

Cookson, G. (2013) 'Analysing the economic justification for the reforms to social welfare and family law legal aid', *Journal of Social Welfare and Family Law* 35: 21.

Cooper, C., Selwood, A. and Livingston, G. (2008) 'The prevalence of elder abuse and neglect: a systematic review', *Age and Ageing* 37: 151.

Coram Children's Legal Centre (2017) *Rights without remedies: Legal aid and access to justice for children*, London: CCLC.

Corker, M. and Davis, J. (2000) 'Disabled children: invisible under the law', in J. Cooper and S. Vernon (eds) *Disability and the Law*, London: Jessica Kingsley.

Cowan, D. (2004) 'On need and gatekeeping', *Child and Family Law Quarterly* 16: 331.

Cowan, S. (2014) 'Motivating Questions and Partial Answers: A Response to Prosecuting Domestic Violence by Michelle Madden Dempsey', *Criminal Law and Philosophy* (forthcoming).

Cowan, S. and Hodgson, J. (2007) 'Violence in the family context', in R. Probert (ed.) *Family Life and the Law*, Aldershot: Ashgate.

Cowden, M. (2012) '"No harm, no foul": a child's right to know their genetic parents', *International Journal of Law, Policy and the Family* 26: 102.

Coy, M. Scott, E., Tweedale, R. and Perks, K. (2015) '"It's like going through the abuse again": domestic violence and women and children's (un)safety in private law contact proceedings', *Journal of Social Welfare and Family Law* 37: 53.

Craig, P. (2007) 'Everybody's business: applications for contact orders by consent', *Family Law* 37: 26.

Crawford, S. and Pierce, J. (2010) 'Reporting proceedings', *Family Law* 40: 825.

Crawford, S. and Pierce, J. (2012) 'The highs and lows of shared parenting', *Family Law* 42: 1336.

Crawford, C., Goodman, A., Greaves, E. and Joyce, R. (2012) 'Cohabitation, marriage and child outcomes: an empirical analysis of the relationship between marital status and child outcomes in the UK using the Millennium Cohort Study', *Child and Family Law Quarterly* 24: 176.

Crawshaw, M. and Wallbank, J. (2014) 'Is the birth registration system fit for purpose? The rights of donor conceived adults', *Family Law* 44: 1154.

Cretney, S. (1996) 'Divorce reform in England: humbug and hypocrisy or a smooth transition?' in M. Freeman (ed.) *Divorce: Where Next?* Aldershot: Dartmouth.

Cretney, S. (2001) 'Black and white', *Family Law* 31: 3.

Cretney, S. (2003a) *Family Law in the Twentieth Century – a History*, Oxford: OUP.

Cretney, S. (2003b) 'Private ordering and divorce – how far can we go?' *Family Law* 33: 399.

Cretney, S. (2003c) 'A community of property system imposed by judicial decision', *Law Quarterly Review* 119: 349.

Cretney, S. (2006) *Same-sex Relationships*, Oxford: OUP.

Cretney, S., Masson, J. and Bailey-Harris, R. (2002) *Principles of Family Law*, London: Sweet & Maxwell.

Crompton, L. (2013a) 'Where's the sex in same sex marriage?' *Family Law* 564.

Crompton, L. (2013b) 'Domestic violence protection notices and orders: vulnerable to human rights challenge?' *Family Law* December.

Crompton, L. (2014) 'Domestic Violence Protection notices and orders: protecting victims or the public purse?' *Family Law* 44: 62.

Crompton, R. and Lyonette, C. (2008) 'Who does the housework? The division of labour within the home', in A. Park, J. Curtice, K. Thomson, M. Phillips and M. Johnson (eds) *British Social Attitudes: the 24th Report*, London: Sage.

Crook, H. (2001) '*Troxel et vir v Granville* – grandparent visitation rights in the United States Supreme Court', *Child and Family Law Quarterly* 13: 101.

Crown Prosecution Service (2007) *Reasonable Chastisement Research Report*, London: CPS.

Crown Prosecution Service (2009) *Policy for Prosecuting Cases of Domestic Violence*, London: CPS.

Crown Prosecution Service and Department of Constitutional Affairs (2004) *Specialist Domestic Violence Courts*, London: DCA.

Crisp, R. and Hunter, R. (2019) 'Domestic abuse in financial remedy applications', *Family Law* 49: 1440.

Cummings, T. (2020) 'Gendered dimensions and missed opportunities in *Akhter v Khan (Attorney-General and others intervening)*', *Child and Family Law Quarterly* 239.

Daly, M. and Scheiwe, K. (2010) 'Individualisation and personal obligations – social policy, family policy and law reform in Germany and the UK', *International Journal of Law, Policy and the Family* 24: 177.

Daly, A. (2018) 'No weight for "due weight"? A children's autonomy principle in best interest proceedings', *International Journal of Children's Rights* 26: 61.

Daniel, L. (2009) 'Australia's Family Law Amendment (Shared Responsibility) Act 2006: a policy critique', *Journal of Social Welfare and Family Law* 31: 147.

Daniels, C. (2006) *Exposing Men: The Science and Politics of Male Reproduction*, Oxford: OUP.

Daniels, N. (1988) *Am I My Brother's Keeper?* Oxford: OUP.

Dar, A. (2013) *Domestic Violence Statistics*, London: House of Commons Library.

Dauvergne, C. and Millbank, J. (2010) 'Forced marriage as a harm in domestic and international law', *Modern Law Review* 73: 57.

Davey, C. (2010) *Children' Participation in Decision-making*, London: Children's Commissioner.

Davies, L. and Krane, J. (2006) 'Collaborate with caution: protecting children, helping mothers', *Critical Social Policy* 26: 412.

Davis, G. (2000) *Monitoring Publicly Funded Family Mediation*, London: Legal Services Commission.

Davis, G. and Murch, M. (1988) *Grounds for Divorce*, Oxford: Clarendon Press.

Davis, G. and Wikeley, N. (2002) 'National survey of Child Support Agency clients – the relationship dimension', *Family Law* 32: 523.

Davis, G., Bevan, G., Clisby, S., Cumming, Z. *et al.* (2000) *Monitoring Publicly Funded Family Mediation*, London: Legal Services Commission.

Davis, G., Clisby, S., Cumming, Z. *et al.* (2003) *Monitoring Publicly Funded Family Mediation*, London: Legal Services Commission.

Davis, G., Cretney, S. and Collins, J. (1994) *Simple Quarrels*, Oxford: Clarendon Press.

Davis, G., Finch, S. and Fitzgerald, R. (2001) 'Mediation and legal services – the client speaks', *Family Law* 31: 110.

Davis, G., Pearce, J., Bird, R. *et al.* (2000) 'Ancillary relief outcomes', *Child and Family Law Quarterly* 12: 1243.

Davis, L. (2005) 'Adoption and Children Act 2002 – some concerns', *Family Law* 35: 294.

Davis, L. (2015) 'Neglect neglected', *Family Law* 45: 553.

Davis, S. (2008) 'Equal sharing: a judicial gloss too far?' *Family Law* 38: 429.

Day Sclater, S. (1999) *Divorce: A Psychological Study*, Aldershot: Dartmouth.

Day Sclater, S. and Kaganas, F. (2003) 'Contact: mothers, welfare rights', in A. Bainham, B. Lindley, M. Richards and L. Trinder (eds) *Children and Their Families*, Oxford: Hart.

Day Sclater, S. and Piper, C. (1999) *Undercurrents of Divorce*, Aldershot: Ashgate.

Dayton, J. (2003) 'The silencing of a woman's choice: mandatory arrest and no drop prosecution policies in domestic violence cases', *Cardozo Women's Law Journal* 9: 281.

De Campos, T. and Milo, C. (2018) 'Mitochondrial donations and the right to know and trace one's genetic origins: an ethical and legal challenge', *International Journal of Law, Policy and the Family* 32: 170.

Deech, R. (1990) 'Divorce law and empirical studies', *Law Quarterly Review* 106: 229.

Deech, R. (1993) 'The rights of fathers: social and biological concepts of parenthood', in J. Eekelaar and P. Sarcevic (eds) *Parenthood in Modern Society*, London: Martinus Nijhoff.

Deech, R. (1994) 'Comment: not just marriage breakdown', *Family Law* 24: 121.

Deech, R. (1996) 'Property and money matters', in M. Freeman (ed.) *Divorce: Where Next?* Aldershot: Dartmouth.

Deech, R. (2000) 'The legal regulation of infertility treatment in Britain', in S. Katz, J. Eekelaar and M. Maclean (eds) *Cross Currents*, Oxford: OUP.

Deech, R. (2009a) 'What's a woman worth?' *Family Law* 39: 1140.

Deech, R. (2009b) 'Divorce – a disaster?' *Family Law* 39: 1048.

Deech, R. (2010a) 'Sisters sisters – and other family members', *Family Law* 40: 375.

Deech, R. (2010b) 'Cousin marriage', *Family Law* 40: 619.

Deech, R. (2010c) 'Cohabitation', *Family Law* 40: 39.

Deech, R. (2010d) 'Same-sex unions and marriage: is there any difference?' *International Journal of Jurisprudence of the Family* 1.

Deech, R (2012) Getting married', *International Journal of Jurisprudence of the Family* 4: 1.

Delahunty, J. and Barnes, C. (2015) 'Radicalisation: cases in the Family Court', *Family Law* 1527.

Delphy, C. and Leonard, D. (1992) *Familiar Policy: A New Analysis of Marriage in Contemporary Western Societies*, Cambridge: Polity Press.

Dench, G. and Ogg, J. (2002) *Grandparenting in Britain*, London: Institute of Community Studies.

Dennison, G. (2010) 'Is mediation compatible with children's rights?' *Journal of Social Welfare and Family Law* 32: 169.

Den Otter, R. (2018) 'A perfectionist argument for legal recognition of polyamorous relationships', in E. Brake and L. Ferguson (eds) *Philosophical Foundations of Children's and Family Law*, Oxford: OUP.

Department for Children, Schools and Families (2008) *Children Act 1989: Guidance and Regulations*, London: DCSF.

Department for Culture, Media and Sport (2014) *Civil Partnership Review*, London: DCCS.

Department for Education (2014) *Children Looked After in England*, London: DfE.

Department for Education and Skills (2005a) *Special Guardianship Guidance*, London: DfES.

Department for Education and Skills (2005b) *Adoption Support Agencies: National Minimum Standards*, London: DfES.

Department for Education and Skills (2006) *Preparing and Assessing Prospective Adopters*, London: DfES.

Department for Education and Skills (2008) *Review Report: Reasonable Chastisement*, London: DfES.

Department of Education (2012) *Co-operative Parenting Following Family Separation*, London: DoE.

Department for Education (2020) *Children Looked After in England*, London: DoE.

Department for Work and Pensions (2006) *A Fresh Start: Child Support Redesign – the Government's response to Sir David Henshaw*, London: DWP.

Department for Work and Pensions (2012) *Supporting Separated Families: Securing Children's Futures*, London: The Stationery Office.

Department for Work and Pensions (2014a) *Sorting Out Separation: Web App Analysis of Management Information*, London: DWP.

Department for Work and Pensions (2014b) *Sorting Out Separation Web App: Evaluation of Effectiveness*, London: DWP.

Department for Work and Pensions (2014c) *The Families Test*, London: DWP.

Department of Constitutional Affairs (2004) *Mental Incapacity: Who Decides?* London: DCA.

Department of Constitutional Affairs (2006) *Judicial Statistics*, London: HMSO.

Department of Health (2000) *Protecting Children, Supporting Parents*, London: The Stationery Office.

Department of Health (2002) *Friends and Family Care*, London: DoH.

Department of Health (2002a) *Homelessness: Code of Guidance for Local Authorities*, London: DoH.

Department of Health (2002b) *Monitoring Adoption Disruption Rates Post Adoption Order*, London: DoH.

Department of Health (2002c) *Safeguarding Children*, London: DoH.

Department of Health (2002d) *Adoption and Permanence Taskforce Second Report*, London: DoH.

Department of Health (2002e) *Friends and Family Care (Kinship Care)*, London: DoH.

Department of Health (2002f) *No Secrets*, London: DoH.

Department of Health (2002g) *Adopter Preparation and Assessment and the Operation of Adoption Panels*, London: DoH.

Department of Health (2005) *Caring About Carers*, London: DoH.

Department of Health (2014a) *New Offences of Ill Treatment and Wilful Neglect*, London: DoH.

Department of Health (2014b) *Adoption National Minimum Standards*, London: DoH.

Department of Health (2018) *Department of Health response to the Law Commission's consultation on mental capacity and deprivation of liberty*, London: DoH.

Department of Social Security (2000) *Children's Rights and Parents' Responsibilities*, London: DSS.

Devereux, E. and George, R. (2015) '"Alas poor Payne, I knew him . . . ": an interpretation of the Court of Appeal's decision in *Re F (International Relocation Cases)*', *Family Law* 1232.

Dewar, J. (1992) *Law and the Family*, London: Butterworths.

Dewar, J. (1997) 'Reducing discretion in family law', *Australian Journal of Family Law* 11: 309.

Dewar, J. (2000a) 'Family law and its discontents', *International Journal of Law, Policy and the Family* 14: 59.

Dewar, J. (2000b) 'Making Family Law New?' in M. McLean (ed.) *Making Law for Families*, Oxford: Hart.

Dewar, J. (2010) 'Can the centre hold? Reflections on two decades of family law reform in Australia', *Child and Family Law Quarterly* 22: 377.

Dewar, J. and Parker, S. (2000) 'English family law since World War II: from status to chaos', in S. Katz, J. Eekelaar and M. Maclean (eds) *Cross Currents*, Oxford: OUP.

Dex, S., Ward, K. and Joshi, H. (2006) *Changes in Women's Occupations and Occupational Mobility over 25 Years*, London: Centre for Longitudinal Studies.

Dey, I. (2005) 'Adapting adoption: a case of closet politics', *International Journal of Law, Policy and the Family* 19: 289.

Dickens, J. (2014) 'Care proceedings in 26 weeks: justice, speed and thoroughness', *Family Law* 650.

Diduck, A. (2000) 'Solicitors and legal subjects', in J. Bridgeman and D. Monk (eds) *Feminist Perspectives on Child Law*, London: Cavendish.

Diduck, A. (2001a) 'A family by any other name . . . or Starbucks comes to England', *Journal of Law and Society* 28: 290.

Diduck, A. (2001b) 'Fairness and justice for all?' *Feminist Legal Studies* 9: 173.

Diduck, A. (2003) *Law's Families*, London: LexisNexis Butterworths.

Diduck, A. (2005) 'Shifting familiarity', in J. Holder and C. O'Cinneide (eds) *Current Legal Problems*, Oxford: OUP.

Diduck, A. (2007) 'If only we can find the appropriate terms to use the issue will be solved: law, identity and parenthood', *Child and Family Law Quarterly* 19: 458.

Diduck, A. (2008) 'Family law and family responsibility', in J. Bridgeman, H. Keating and C. Lind (eds) *Responsibility, Law and the Family*, London: Ashgate.

Diduck, A. (2011) 'What is family law for?' *Current Legal Problems* 64: 287.

Diduck, A. (2014a) 'Justice by ADR in private family matters: is it fair and is it possible?' *Family Law* 44: 616.

Diduck, A. (2014b) 'Autonomy and vulnerability in family law: the missing link', in J. Wallbank and J. Herring (eds) *Vulnerabilities, Care and Family Law*, London: Routledge.

Diduck, A. (2016) 'Consent, fraud and family law', *Journal of Social Welfare and Family Law* 38: 83.

Diduck, A (2018) 'Sharing loss on divorce — A commentary' *Australian Journal of Family Law* 32: 132.

Diduck, A. and Kaganas, F. (2004) 'Incomplete citizens: changing images of post-separation children', *Modern Law Review* 67: 959.

Diduck, A. and Kaganas, F. (2006) *Family Law Gender and the State*, Oxford: Hart.

Diduck, A. and O'Donovan, K. (2007) 'Feminism and families: Plus ça change?' in A. Diduck and K. O'Donovan (eds) *Feminist Perspectives on Family Law*, London: Routledge.

Diduck, A. and Orton, H. (1994) 'Equality and support for spouses', *Modern Law Review* 57: 681.

Dilnot, A. (2011) *Fairer Funding for All*, London: Department of Health.

Dingwall, R. (2010) 'Divorce mediation: should we change our mind?' *Journal of Social Welfare and Family Law* 32: 107.

Dingwall, R. and Greatbatch, D. (2001) 'Family mediators – what are they doing?' *Family Law* 31: 379.

Dixon, M. (2010) 'Confining and defining proprietary estoppel: the role of unconscionability', *Legal Studies* 30: 408.

Dixon, M. (2011) 'To sell or not to sell: that is the question of the irony of the Trusts of Land and Appointment of Trustees Act 1996', *Cambridge Law Journal* 70: 579.

Dnes, A. (2002) 'Cohabitation and marriage', in A. Dnes and R. Rowthorn (eds) *The Law and Economics of Marriage and Divorce*, Cambridge: CUP.

Dobash, R. and Dobash, R. (2000) 'Violence against women in the family', in S. Katz, J. Eekelaar and M. Maclean (eds) *Cross Currents*, Oxford: OUP.

Dobash, R. and Dobash, R. (2004) 'Women's violence to men in intimate relationships', *British Journal of Criminology* 44: 324.

Donovan, C. (2016) 'Tackling inequality in the intimate sphere', in R. Leckey (ed.) *After Legal Equality*, Abingdon: Routledge.

Donovan, C. and Hester, M. (2011) 'Seeking help from the enemy: help-seeking strategies of those in same-sex relationships who have experienced domestic abuse', *Child and Family Law Quarterly* 23: 26.

Doughty, J. (2008a) 'The "no order principle": a myth revived', *Family Law* 38: 561.

Doughty, J. (2008b) 'From court missionaries to conflict resolution: a century of family court welfare', *Child and Family Law Quarterly* 20: 131.

Doughty, J. (2009) 'Identity crisis in the family courts? Different approaches in England and Wales and Australia', *Journal of Social Welfare and Family Law* 31: 231.

Doughty, J. (2014) 'Care proceedings – is there a better way?' *Child and Family Law* 113.

Doughty, J. (2015) 'Myths and misunderstanding in adoption law and policy', *Child and Family Law Quarterly* 331.

Doughty, J. and Murch, M. (2012) 'Judicial independence and the restructuring of family courts and their support services', *Child and Family Law Quarterly* 23: 33.

Doughty, J., Maxwell, N. and Slater, T. (2020) 'Professional responses to 'parental alienation': research-informed practice', *Journal of Social Welfare and Family Law* 42: 68.

Douglas, G. (2000) 'Supporting families', in A. Bainham (ed.) *The International Survey of Family Law 2000 edition*, Bristol: Jordans.

Douglas, G. (2011) 'Bringing an end to the matrimonial post-mortem: *Wachtel v Wachtel* and its enduring significance for ancillary relief', in S. Gilmore, J. Herring and R. Probert (eds) *Landmark Cases in Family Law*, Oxford: Hart.

Douglas, G. (2005) *An Introduction to Family Law*, Oxford: OUP.

Douglas, G. (2015) 'Who regulates marriage? The case of religious marriage and divorce', in R. Sandberg (ed.) *Religion and Legal Pluralism*, Aldershot: Ashgate

Douglas, G. (2016) 'Towards an understanding of the basis of obligation and commitment in family law', *Legal Studies* 36: 1.

Douglas, G. and Ferguson, N. (2003) 'The role of grandparents in divorced families', *International Journal of Law, Policy and the Family* 17: 41.

Douglas, G. and Lowe, N. (1992) 'Becoming a parent in English Law', *Law Quarterly Review* 108: 414.

Douglas, G. and Murch, M. (2002) *The Role of Grandparents in Divorced Families*, Cardiff: Family Studies Research Centre, University of Wales.

Douglas, G. and Philpot, T. (eds) (2003) *Adoption: Changing Families: Changing Times*, London: Routledge.

Douglas, G., Doe, N., Gilliat-Ray, S., Sandberg, R. and Khan, A. (2012) 'The role of religious tribunals in regulating marriage and divorce', *Child and Family Law Quarterly* 24: 139.

Douglas, G., Murch, M., Miles, C. and Scanlan, L. (2006) *Research into the Operation of Rule 9.5 of the Family Proceedings Rules 1991*, London: DCA.

Douglas, G., Murch, M., Robinson, M. *et al.* (2001) 'Children's perspectives and experience of the divorce process', *Family Law* 31: 373.

Douglas, G., Murch, M., Scanlan, L. and Perry, A. (2000) 'Safeguarding children's welfare in non-contentious divorce: towards a new conception of the legal process', *Modern Law Review* 63: 177.

Douglas, G., Pearce, J. and Woodward, H. (2007) *A Failure of Trust: Resolving Property Issues on Cohabitation Breakdown*, Cardiff: Cardiff University.

Douglas, G., Pearce, J. and Woodward, H. (2008) 'The law commission's cohabitation proposals: applying them in practice', *Family Law* 38: 351.

Douglas, G., Pearce, J. and Woodward, H. (2009a) 'Money, property, cohabitation and separation', in J. Miles and R. Probert (eds) *Sharing Lives, Dividing Assets*, Oxford: Hart.

Douglas, G., Pearce, J. and Woodward, H. (2009b) 'Cohabitants, property and the law: a study of injustice', *Modern Law Review* 72: 24.

Downs, D. and Edwards, S. (2015) Brides and martyrs: protecting children from violent extremism', *Family Law* 45: 1073.

Draghici, C. (2017) 'Equal marriage, unequal civil partnership: a bizarre case of discrimination in Europe', *Child and Family Law Quarterly* 313.

Duckworth, P. (2002a) 'We are family. Really?' *Family Law* 32: 91.

Duckworth, P. (2002b) 'What is family? A personal view', *Family Law* 32: 367.

Duckworth, P. and Hodson, D. (2001) '*White* v *White* – bringing section 25 back to the people', *Family Law* 31: 24.

Dugan, E. (2017) 'Cutting legal aid to families has had the entirely opposite effect to the one the Government intended', *BuzzFeed* 31 October.

Duggan, M. and Grace, J. (2018) 'Assessing vulnerabilities in the Domestic Violence Disclosure Scheme', *Child and Family Law Quarterly* 145.

Duncan, S. and Phillips, M. (2010) 'People who live apart together (LATs) – how different are they?' *The Sociological Review* 58: 1.

Duncan, S., Carter, J., Roseneil, S. and Stoilova, M., (2012) 'Legal rights for people who "Live Apart Together"?' *Journal of Social Welfare and Family Law* 34: 443.

Dunn, G. (1999) 'A passion for sameness? Sexuality and gender accountability', in E. Silva and C. Smart (eds) *The New Family*, London: Sage.

Dunn, J. (2003) 'Contact and children's perspectives on parental relationships', in A. Bainham, B. Lindley, M. Richards and L. Trinder (eds) *Children and Their Families*, Oxford: Hart.

Dunn, J. and Deater-Deckard, K. (2001) *Children's Views of Their Changing Family*, London: YPS.

Dutta, A. (2017) 'Brexit and international family law from a continental perspective', *Child and Family Law Quarterly* 119.

Dutton, M (2003) 'Understanding Women's Response to Domestic Violence', *Hofstra Law Review* 21: 1191.

Dwyer, J. (2006) *The Relationship Rights of Children*, Cambridge: CUP.

Dwyer, J. (2018 'Regulating Child Rearing in a Culturally Diverse Society', in E. Brake and L. Ferguson (eds) *Philosophical Foundations of Children's and Family Law*, Oxford: OUP.

Dyer, C. (2000) 'Government drops plan for no-fault divorce', *The Guardian*, 2 September.

Dyson, Lord (2010) 'Mediation in the English legal order six years after *Halsey*', speech, October 2010.

Easteal, P., Young, L. and Carline, A. (2018) 'Domestic violence, property and family law in Australia', *International Journal of Law, Policy and the Family* 32: 204.

Easton, D. and Jarmain, S. (2016) 'Internal relocation', *Family Law* 175.

Edge, P. (2016) 'Let's talk about a divorce: religious and legal wedding', in J. Miles, R. Mody and R. Probert (eds) *Marriage Rites and Rights*, Oxford: Hart.

Edwards, L. (2004) *The Lever Fabergé Family Report 2004*, London: Lever Fabergé.

Edwards, R., Hadfield, L. and Mauthner, M. (2005) *Children's Understanding of Their Sibling Relationships*, York: Joseph Rowntree Foundation.

Edwards, S. (2000) *Briefing Note: Reducing Domestic Violence*, London: Home Office.

Edwards, S. (2004) 'Division of assets and fairness – "Brick Lane" – gender culture and ancillary relief on divorce', *Family Law* 34: 809.

Edwards, S. (2007) 'Imagining Islam . . . of meaning and metaphor symbolising and jilbab', *Child and Family Law Quarterly* 19: 247.

Edwards, R. and Gillies, B. (2012) 'Farewell to family? Notes on an argument for retaining the concept', *Families, Relationships and Societies* 1: 63.

Eekelaar, J. (1984) *Family Law and Social Policy*, London: Weidenfeld & Nicholson.

Eekelaar, J. (1986) 'The eclipse of parental rights', *Law Quarterly Review* 102: 4.

Eekelaar, J. (1987) 'Family law and social control', in J. Eekelaar and J. Bell (eds) *Oxford Essays in Jurisprudence*, Oxford: OUP.

Eekelaar, J. (1988) 'Equality and the purpose of maintenance', *Journal of Law and Society* 15: 188.

Eekelaar, J. (1990) 'Investigation under the Children Act 1989', *Family Law* 20: 486.

Eekelaar, J. (1991a) *Regulating Divorce*, Oxford: Clarendon Press.

Eekelaar, J. (1991b) 'Are parents morally obliged to care for their children?' *Oxford Journal of Legal Studies* 11: 51.

Eekelaar, J. (1991c) 'Parental responsibility: state of nature or nature of the state?' *Journal of Social Welfare and Family Law* 13: 37.

Eekelaar, J. (1992) 'The importance of thinking that children have rights', *International Journal of Law, Policy and the Family* 6: 221.

Eekelaar, J. (1994a) 'The interests of the child and the child's wishes: the role of dynamic self-determinism', *International Journal of Law and the Family* 8: 42.

Eekelaar, J. (1994b) 'Non-marital property', in P. Birks (ed.) *Frontiers of Liability*, Oxford: OUP.

Eekelaar, J. (1994c) 'Families and children', in C. McCrudden and D. Chambers (eds) *Individual Rights and the Law in Britain*, Oxford: OUP.

Eekelaar, J. (1995) 'Family justice: ideal or illusion? Family law and communitarian values', *Current Legal Problems* 48: 191.

Eekelaar, J. (1996) 'Parental responsibility – a new legal status?' *Law Quarterly Review* 112: 233.

Eekelaar, J. (1998) 'Do parents have a duty to consult?', *Law Quarterly Review* 114: 337.

Eekelaar, J. (1999) 'Family law: keeping us "on message"', *Child and Family Law Quarterly* 11: 387.

Eekelaar J. (2000a) 'Family law and the responsible citizen', in M. Maclean (ed.) *Making Law for Families*, Oxford: Hart.

Eekelaar, J. (2000b) 'Post-divorce financial obligations', in S. Katz, J. Eekelaar and M. Maclean (eds) *Cross Currents*, Oxford: OUP.

Eekelaar, J. (2001a) 'Asset distribution on divorce – the durational element', *Law Quarterly Review* 117: 24.

Eekelaar, J. (2001b) 'Rethinking parental responsibility', *Family Law* 31: 426.

Eekelaar, J. (2002a) 'Beyond the welfare principle', *Child and Family Law Quarterly* 14: 237.

Eekelaar, J. (2002b) 'Contact – over the limit', *Family Law* 32: 271.

Eekelaar, J. (2003a) 'Contact and the adoption reform', in A. Bainham, B. Lindley, M. Richards and L. Trinder (eds) *Children and Their Families*, Oxford: Hart.

Eekelaar, J. (2003b) 'Asset distribution on divorce – time and property', *Family Law* 33: 838.

Eekelaar, J. (2004) 'Children between cultures', *International Journal of Law, Policy and the Family* 18: 178.

Eekelaar, J. (2006a) 'Property and financial settlement on divorce – sharing and compensating', *Family Law* 36: 754.

Eekelaar, J. (2006b) *Family Life and Personal Life*, Oxford: OUP.

Eekelaar, J. (2007) 'Why people marry: the many faces of an institution', *Family Law Quarterly* 41: 413.

Eekelaar, J. (2009) 'Law, family and community', in G. Douglas and N. Lowe (eds) *The Continuing Evolution of Family Law*, Bristol: Family Law.

Eekelaar, J. (2010) 'Evaluating legal regulation of family behaviour', *International Journal of Jurisprudence of the Family* 1: 17.

Eekelaar, J. (2011a) 'The Arbitration and Mediation Services (Equality) Bill 2011', *Family Law* 41: 1209.

Eekelaar, J. (2011b): '"Not of the highest importance": family justice under threat', *Journal of Social Welfare and Family Law* 33: 317.

Eekelaar, J. (2011c) 'Naturalism or Pragmatism? Towards an Expansive View of Human Rights', *Journal of Human Rights* 10: 230.

Eekelaar, J. (2012a) 'Rights and obligations in the contemporary family: retheorizing individualism, families and the state', *Theoretical Inquiries in Law* 13: 75.

Eekelaar, J. (2013a) 'Marriage: a modest proposal', *Family Law* 43: 83.

Eekelaar, J. (2013b) 'Law and community practices', in M. Maclean and J. Eekelaar, *Managing Family Justice in Diverse Societies*, Oxford: Hart Publishing.

Eekelaar, J. (2014) 'Family justice on trial: Re A', *Family Law* 44: 543.

Eekelaar, J. (2015a) 'The role of the best interests principle in decisions affecting children and decisions about children', *International Journal of Children's Rights* 23: 3.

Eekelaar, J. (2015b) 'Law, values cultures', in A. Diduck, N. Peleg and H. Reece (eds) *Law in Society*, Leiden: Brill.

Eekelaar, J. (2018a) 'Family law and legal theory', in E. Brake and L. Ferguson (eds) *Philosophical Foundations of Children's and Family Law*, Oxford: OUP.

Eekelaar, J. (2018b) 'Welfare and discrimination: Re M', *Family Law* 393.

Eekelaar, J. and Clive, E. (1977) *Custody After Divorce*, Oxford: OUP.

Eekelaar, J. and Maclean, M. (1986) *Maintenance After Divorce*, Oxford: Clarendon Press.

Eekelaar, J. and Maclean, M. (1997) *The Parental Obligation*, Oxford: Hart.

Eekelaar, J. and Maclean, M. (2004) 'Marriage and the moral bases of personal relationships', *Journal of Law and Society* 4: 510.

Eekelaar, J. and Maclean, M. (2009) *Family Law Advocacy*, Oxford: Hart.

Eekelaar, J. and Maclean, M. (2013) *Family Justice: The Work of Family Judges in Uncertain Times*, Oxford: Hart.

Eekelaar, J. and Nhlapo, T. (1998) 'Introduction', in J. Eekelaar and T. Nhlapo (eds) *The Changing Family: International Perspectives on the Family and Family Law*, Oxford: Hart.

Eekelaar, J., Maclean, M. and Beinart, S. (2000) *Family Lawyers*, Oxford: Hart.

Eijkholt, M. (2010) 'The right to found a family as a stillborn right to procreate?', *Medical Law Review* 18: 127.

Ekaney, N. (2020) 'Equal family justice – its pursuit in a pandemic', *Family Law* 50: 959.

Elizabeth, V. (2017) 'Custody stalking: a mechanism of coercively controlling mothers following separation', *Feminist Legal Studies* 25: 185.

Elizabeth, V. (2019) 'It's an invisible wound': the disenfranchised grief of post-separation mothers who lose care time', *Journal of Social Welfare and Family Law* 41: 34.

Elizabeth, V. (2020) 'The affective burden of separated mothers in PA(S)inflected custody law systems: a New Zealand case study', *Journal of Social Welfare and Family Law* 42: 118.

Ellickson, R. (2010) *The Household: Informal Order Around the Hearth*, Princeton: Princeton University Press.

Ellison, L. (2002a) 'Responding to victim withdrawal in domestic violence prosecutions', *Criminal Law Review* 760.

Ellison, L. (2002b) 'Prosecuting domestic violence without victim participation', *Modern Law Review* 65: 834.

Ellman, I. (2000b) 'The misguided movement to revive fault divorce', in M. King White (ed.) *Marriage in America*, Lanham, MD: Rowman & Littlefield.

Ellman, I. (2005) 'Do Americans play football?', *International Journal of Law, Policy and the Family* 19: 257.

Ellman, I. (2007) 'Financial settlement on divorce: two steps forward, two to go', *Law Quarterly Review* 123: 2.

Ellman, I., McKay, S., Miles, J. and Bryson, C. (2014) 'Child support judgments: comparing public policy to the public's policy', *International Journal of Law Policy and the Family* 28: 274.

Elmalik, K. and Wheeler, R. (2007) 'Consent: luck or law?' *Annals of the Royal College of Surgeons England* 89: 627.

Elster, J. (1987) 'Solomonic judgments: against the best interests of the child', *University of Chicago Law Review* 54: 1.

Emens, E. (2004) 'Just monogamy?' in M. Lyndon Shanley (ed.) *Just Marriage*, Oxford: OUP.

Emmerson, D. and Platt, J. (2014) 'Legal Aid, Sentencing and Punishment of Offenders Act 2012: LASPO Reviewed', *Family Law* 44: 515.

Engles, F. (1978) *The Origin of the Family*, Pekling: Foreign Languages Press.

English, J. (1979) 'What do grown children owe their parents?' in O. O'Neill and W. Ruddick (eds) *Having Children*, New York: OUP.

Engster, D. (2018) 'Equal opportunity and the family: levelling up the Brighouse-Swift thesis', *Journal of Applied Philosophy*.

Equality and Human Rights Commission (2009) *Trans Research Review*, London: Equality and Human Rights Commission.

Equality and Human Rights Commission (2020) *Inclusive Justice, a system designed for all – Interim evidence report; Video hearings and their impact on effective participation* London: EHRC

Ermisch, J. and Francesconi, M. (2001) *The Effects of Parents' Employment on Children's Lives*, London and York: Family Policy Studies Centre and Joseph Rowntree Foundation.

Ermisch, J. and Francesconi, M. (2003) *Working Parents: The Impact on Kids*, London: Institute for Social and Economic Research.

Eskridge, W. and Spedale, D. (2006) *Gay marriage? For better or for worse?* Cambridge: Cambridge University Press.

Everett, K. and Yeatman, L. (2010) 'Are some parents more natural than others?' *Child and Family Law Quarterly* 22: 290.

Fahey, T. (2012) 'Small bang? The impact of divorce legislation on marital breakdown in Ireland', *International Journal of Law, Policy and the Family* 26: 242.

Fairburn, C. (2010) *Marriage and Cohabitation*, London: Hansard.

Fairburn, C. (2017) *No Fault Divorce*, London: Hansard.

Falconer, Lord (2004) *Domestic Violence*, London: DCA.

Family Lives (2012) *When Family Life Hurts: Family Experience of Aggression in Children*, London: Family Lives.

Family Matters Institute (2009) *Do Grandparents Matter?* London: Family Matters Institute.

Family Mediation Council (2010) *Code of Practice*, London: FMC.

Farmer, E. and Pollock, S. (1998) *Substitute Care for Sexually Abused and Abusing Children*, Chichester: John Wiley & Sons.

Farson, R. (1978) *Birthrights*, London: Penguin.

Fatherhood Institute (2008) *The Difference a Dad Makes*, London: Fatherhood Institute.

Faulkner, E. and Nyamutata, C. (2020) 'The Decolonisation of Children's Rights and the Colonial Contours of the Convention on the Rights of the Child', *International Journal of Children's Rights* 28: 66.

Fauset, D. (2020) 'The reforms to care proceedings – one step forward and two steps back? A critical evaluation of the new legal framework and its impact on the pre-proceedings stage', *Child and Family Quarterly* 13.

Fawcett Society (2010) *Keeping Mum*, London: Fawcett Society.

Featherstone, B. (2009) *Contemporary Fathering*, Bristol: Policy Press.

Featherstone, B. (2010) 'Gender, rights, responsibilities and social policy', in J. Wallbank, S. Choudhry and J. Herring (eds) *Rights, Gender and Family Law*, Abingdon: Routledge.

Featherstone, B., Gupta, A., Morris, K., and White, S. (2018) *Protecting Children. A Social Model*, Bristol: Policy Press

Federle, K. (2009) 'Rights, not wrongs', *International Journal of Children's Rights* 17: 321.

Fehlberg, B. (2004) 'Spousal maintenance in Australia', *International Journal of Law, Policy and the Family* 18: 1.

Fehlberg, B. (2005) '"With all my worldly goods I thee endow"?: the partnership theme in Australian matrimonial property law', *International Journal of Law, Policy and the Family* 19: 176.

Fehlberg, B. and Smyth, B. (2002) 'Binding pre-nuptial agreements in Australia: the first year', *International Journal of Law, Policy and the Family* 16: 127.

Fehlberg, B., Millward, C., Campo, M., Carson, R. (2013) 'Post-separation parenting and financial arrangements: exploring changes over time', *International Journal of Law Policy and the Family* 27: 359.

Fehlberg, B., Smyth, B., Maclean, M. and Roberts, C. (2011) *Caring for Children After Parental Separation*, Oxford: University of Oxford.

Fehlberg, B., Smyth, B. and Trinder, L. (2014) 'Parenting issues after separation: developments in common law countries', in J. Eekelaar and R. George (eds) *Routledge Handbook of Family Law and Policy*, Abingdon: Routledge.

Fenton, R. Heenan, S. and Rees, J. (2010) 'Finally fit for purpose? The Human Fertilisation and Embryology Act 2008', *Journal of Social Welfare and Family Law* 32: 275.

Fenton-Glynn, C. (2015) 'The regulation and recognition of surrogacy under English law: an overview of the case-law', *Child and Family Law Quarterly* 83.

Fenton-Glynn, C. (2016) 'Adoption targets', *Family Law* 148.

Fenton-Glynn, C. (2018a) 'Revoking adoption: *Re J (Adoption: Appeal)*', *Family Law* 372.

Fenton-Glynn, C. (2018b) 'The end of corporal punishment?' *Family Law* 954.

Fenton Glynn, C. (2018c) 'Civil partnerships in an era of human rights incompatibility: *Steinfeld and Keidan*', *Family Law* 944.

Fenton-Glynn, C. (2018) 'Why not civil partnerships for siblings?' *Family Law* 48: 1501.

Ferguson, E., Maughan, B. and Golding, J. (2008) 'Which children receive grandparental care and what effect does it have?' *Journal of Child Psychology and Psychiatry* 49: 161.

Ferguson, L. (2008) 'Family, social inequalities and the persuasive force of interpersonal obligation', *International Journal of Law, Policy and the Family* 22: 61.

Ferguson, L. (2013a) 'Arbitration in financial dispute resolution: the final step to reconstructing the default(s) and exception(s)?', *Journal of Social Welfare and Family Law* 35: 115.

Ferguson, L. (2013b) 'Not merely rights for children but children's rights: The theory gap and the assumption of the importance of children's rights', *International Journal of Children's Rights* 21: 177.

Ferguson, L. (2015a) 'Arbitral awards: a magnetic factor of determinative importance – yet not to be rubber-stamped?', *Journal of Social Welfare and Family Law* 37: 99.

Ferguson, L. (2015b) '*Wyatt v Vince*: the reality of individualised justice – financial orders, forensic delay, and access to justice', *Child and Family Law Quarterly* 195.

Ferguson, L. (2015c) 'The jurisprudence of making decisions affecting children: an argument to prefer duty to children's rights and welfare', in A. Diduck, N. Peleg and H. Reece (eds) *Law in Society*, Leiden: Brill.

Ferguson, L. (2016) 'The curious case of civil partnership: the extension of marriage to same-sex couples and the status-altering consequences of a wait-and-see approach', *Child and Family Law Quarterly* 347.

Ferguson, L. (2018) 'An argument for treating children as a "special case"', in E. Brake and L. Ferguson (eds) *Philosophical Foundations of Children's and Family Law*, Oxford: OUP.

Ferguson, L. and Brake, E. (2018) 'Introduction: the importance of theory to children's and family law', in E. Brake and L. Ferguson (eds) *Philosophical Foundations of Children's and Family Law*, Oxford: OUP.

Ferguson, N. (2004) *Grandparenting in Divorced Families*, Bristol: Policy Press.

Finch, J. (1994) 'The proper thing to do', in J. Eekelaar and M. Maclean (eds) *A Reader on Family Law*, Oxford: OUP.

Finch, J. (2007) 'Displaying families', *Sociology* 41: 65.

Fineman, M. (1988) 'Dominant discourse, professional language and legal change in child custody decision-making', *Harvard Law Review* 101: 727.

Fineman, M. (2002) 'Domestic violence, custody and visitation', *Family Law Quarterly* 36: 211.

Fineman, M. (2004) *The Autonomy Myth*, New York: The New Press.

Fineman, M. (2006) 'The meaning of marriage', in A. Bernstein (ed.) *Marriage Proposals*, New York: New York University Press.

Fineman, M. (2011) 'Responsibility, family and the limits of equality', in C. Lind, H. Keating and J. Bridgeman (eds) *Taking Responsibility, Law and the Changing Family*, Aldershot: Ashgate.

Fineman, M. (2018 'Melinda Cooper, family values', *Social and Legal Studies* 32: 781.

Fineman, M. and Grear A. (eds) (2013) *Vulnerability: Reflections on a New Ethical Foundation for Law and Politics*, Aldershot: Ashgate.

Fink, H. and Carbone, J. (2003) 'Between private ordering and public fiat: a new paradigm for family law decision-making', *Journal of Law and Family Studies* 5: 1.

Fisher, H. and Low, H. (2009) 'Who wins, who loses and who recovers from divorce?' in J. Miles and R. Probert (eds) *Sharing Lives, Dividing Assets*, Oxford: Hart.

Fisher, H. and Low, H. (2016) 'Recovery from divorce: comparing high and low income couples', *International Journal of Law, Policy and the Family* 30: 338.

Fisher, L. (2002) 'The unexpected impact of *White* – taking "equality" too far', *Family Law* 32: 108.

Fisher, M., Saleem, S. and Vora, V. (2018) 'Islamic Marriages: Given the independent review into the application of Sharia Law in England and Wales, what is the way forward?' *Family Law* 552.

Flacks, S. (2014) 'Is childhood a "disability"? Exploring the exclusion of children from age discrimination provisions in the Equality Act 2010', *Child and Family Law Quarterly* 421.

Flacks, S. (2019) 'Substance misuse and parenting: making drugs and gender in the family court', *International Journal of Law in Context* 15: 424.

Fleming, J. and McClain, L. (2013) *Ordered Liberty*, Harvard: Harvard University Press.

Forced Marriage Unit (2020) *Forced Marriage Unit Statistics 2017*, London: FMU.

Ford, M. and Morgan, D. (2003) 'Addressing a misconception', *Child and Family Law Quarterly* 15: 199.

Fortin, J. (1999) 'The HRA's impact on litigation involving children and their families', *Children and Family Law Quarterly* 11: 237.

Fortin, J. (2001) 'Children's rights and the use of physical force', *Child and Family Law Quarterly* 13: 243.

Fortin, J. (2002) 'Children's rights and the impact of two international conventions: the UNCRC and the ECHR', in Thorpe LJ and C. Cowton (eds) *Delight and Dole*, Bristol: Jordans.

Fortin, J. (2003) 'Children's rights and the use of force "in their own best interests"', in J. Dewar and S. Parker (eds) *Family Law Processes, Practices, Pressures*, Oxford: Hart.

Fortin, J. (2006a) 'Accommodating children's rights in a post Human Rights Act era', *Modern Law Review* 69: 299.

Fortin, J. (2006b) 'Children's rights – substance or spin?' *Family Law* 36: 759.

Fortin, J. (2009a) 'Children's right to know their origins – too far, too fast?' *Child and Family Law Quarterly* 21: 336.

Fortin, J. (2009b) *Children's Rights and the Developing Law*, London: Butterworths.

Fortin, J. (2011) 'The *Gillick* decision – not just a high-water mark', in S. Gilmore, J. Herring and R. Probert (eds) *Landmark Cases in Family Law*, Oxford: Hart.

Fortin, J. (2014) 'Children's rights – flattering to deceive?' *Child and Family Law Quarterly* 26: 51.

Fortin, J. (2015) 'Child contact: the longer perspective', *Family Law* 45: 945.

Fortin, J. Hunt, J. and Scanlan, L. (2012) *Taking a Longer View Of Contact: The Perspectives of Young Adults who Experienced Parental Separation in their Youth*, Brighton: Sussex Law School.

Foster, C., Herring, J. and Doron, I. (eds) (2014) *The Law and Ethics of Dementia*, Oxford: Hart.

Foster, H. and Freund, D. (1972) 'A Bill of Rights for children', *Family Law Quarterly* 6: 343.

Fovargue, S. (2013) 'Doctrinal incoherence or practical problem? Minor parents consenting to their offspring's medical treatment and involvement in research in England and Wales', *Child and Family Law Quarterly* 25: 1.

Fox, L. (2003) 'Reforming family property – comparisons, compromises and common dimensions', *Child and Family Law Quarterly* 15: 1.

Fox, L. (2005) 'Creditors and the concept of "family home": a functional analysis', *Legal Studies* 25: 201.

Fox, L. (2006) *Conceptualising Home: Theories, Law and Policies*, Oxford: Hart.

Fox O'Mahony, L. (2012) *Home Equity and Ageing Owners: Between Risk and Regulation*, Oxford: Hart.

Fox, M. and Thomson, M. (2005) 'Short changed? The law and ethics of male circumcision', *International Journal of Children's Rights* 13: 161.

Fox, M. and Thomson, M. (2012) 'The new politics of male circumcision', *Legal Studies* 32: 255.

Fox Harding, L. (1996) *Family, State and Social Policy*, Basingstoke: Macmillan.

Francis, N. (2006) 'If it's broken – fix it', *Family Law* 36: 104.

Franck, J.-U. (2009) '"So hedge therefore, who join forever": understanding the interrelation of no-fault divorce and premarital contracts', *International Journal of Law, Policy and the Family* 23: 235.

Francoz-Terminal, L. (2009) 'From same-sex couples to same-sex families? Current French legal issues', *Child and Family Law Quarterly* 21: 485.

Frantz, C. and Dagan, H. (2002) *On Marital Property: Research Paper 45*, New York University Law School.

Frantz, C. and Dagan, H. (2004) 'Properties of marriage', *Columbia Law Review* 104: 75.

Fredman, S. (2002) *Discrimination Law*, Oxford: OUP.

Fredman, S. (2003) 'The age of equality', in S. Fredman and S. Spencer (eds) *Age as an Equality Issue*, Oxford: Hart.

Freeman, M. (1983) *The Rights and Wrongs of Children*, London: Frances Pinter.

Freeman, M. (1992) *Children, Their Families and the Law*, Basingstoke: Macmillan.

Freeman, M. (1996) 'The new birth right?' *International Journal of Children's Rights* 4: 273.

Freeman, M. (1997) *The Moral Status of Children*, London: Martinus Nijhoff.

Freeman, M. (2000a) 'Disputing children', in S. Katz, J. Eekelaar and M. Maclean (eds) *Cross Currents*, Oxford: OUP.

Freeman, M. (2000b) 'The end of the century of the child?' *Current Legal Problems* 55: 505.

Freeman, M. (2000c) 'Images of child welfare in child abduction appeals', in J. Murphy (ed.) *Ethnic Minorities, Their Families and the Law*, Oxford: Hart.

Freeman, M. (2002a) *Human Rights*, Cambridge: Polity Press.

Freeman, M. (2002b) 'Human rights, children's rights and judgment', *International Journal of Children's Rights* 10: 345.

Freeman, M. (2003) 'The state, race and the family in England today', in J. Dewar and S. Parker (eds) *Family Law Processes, Practices, Pressures*, Oxford: Hart.

Freeman, M. (2004a) 'The sexual abuse of children', in B. Brooks-Gordon, L. Goldsthorpe, M. Johnson and A. Bainham (eds) *Sexuality Repositioned*, Oxford: Hart.

Freeman, M. (2004b) 'Introduction', in M. Freeman (ed.) *Children's Rights*, Dartmouth: Ashgate.

Freeman, M. (2005) 'Rethinking *Gillick*', *International Journal of Children's Rights* 13: 201.

Freeman, M. (2007) 'Why it remains important to take children's rights seriously', *International Journal of Children's Rights* 15: 5.

Freeman, M. (2008) 'The right to responsible parents', in J. Bridgeman, H. Keating and C. Lind (eds) *Responsibility, Law and the Family*, London: Ashgate.

Freeman, M. (2010) 'The human rights of children', *Current Legal Problems* 63: 1.

Freeman, T. and Richards, M. (2006) 'DNA testing and kinship', in F. Ebtehaj, B. Lindley and M. Richards (eds) *Kinship Matters*, Hart: Oxford.

Fretwell Wilson, R. (2002) 'Fractured families, fragile children – the sexual vulnerability of girls in the aftermath of divorce', *Child and Family Law Quarterly* 14: 1.

Future Foundation (1999) *Family Life*, London: Family Foundation.

Gaffney-Rhys, R. (2005) 'The relating to affinity after *B and L v UK*', *Family Law* 35: 955.

Gaffney-Rhys, R. (2006) '*Sheffield City Council v E and another* – capacity to marry and the rights and responsibilities of married couples', *Child and Family Law Quarterly* 18: 139.

Gaffney-Rhys, R. (2014) 'Same-sex marriage but not mixed-sex partnerships: should the Civil Partnership Act 2004 be extended to opposite-sex couples?' *Child and Family Law Quarterly* 134.

Gaffney-Rhys, R. (2015) 'The criminalisation of forced marriage in England and Wales: one year on', *Family Law* 45: 1378.

Gaffney-Rhys, R. (2016) 'Recent developments in the law relating to female genital mutilation', *Child and Family Law Quarterly* 87.

Gaffney-Rhys, R. (2017) 'Opposite-sex civil partnerships in England and Wales? Let's wait and see', *Family Law* 1216.

Gallagher, M. (2001) 'What is marriage for? The public purposes of marriage law', *Louisiana Law Review* 62: 1.

Gallagher, M. and Waite, L. (2001) *The Case for Marriage*, New York: Doubleday.

Galloway, K. (2019) 'The Role of Pateman's Sexual Contract in Beneficial Interests in Property', *Feminist Legal Studies* 27: 263.

Gangoli, G. and Chantler, K. (2009) 'Protecting victims of forced marriage: is age a protective factor?', *Feminist Legal Studies* 17: 267.

Gangoli, G., McCarry, M. and Razak, A. (2009) 'Child marriage or forced marriage? South Asian communities in North East England', *Children and Society* 23: 418.

Gardner, R., Sauber, R. and Lorandos, D. (2005) *The International Handbook of Parental Alienation Syndrome*, New York: Haworth Press.

Gardner, S. (1993) 'Rethinking family property', *Law Quarterly Review* 109: 263.

Gardner, S. (2004) 'Quantum in *Gissing v Gissing* constructive trusts', *Law Quarterly Review* 120: 541.

Gardner, S. (2006) 'The remedial element in proprietary estoppel – again', *Law Quarterly Review* 122: 492.

Gardner, S. (2008) 'Family property today', *Law Quarterly Review* 122: 422.

Gardner, S. (2013) 'Problems in family property', *Cambridge Law Journal* 72: 301.

Garner, J. and Evans, S. (2002) 'An ethical perspective on institutional abuse of older adults', *Psychiatric Bulletin* 26: 166.

Garrison, M. (2004) 'Is consent necessary? An evaluation of the emerging laws of cohabitant obligation', *UCLA Law Review* 52: 815.

Garrison, M. (2007) 'The decline of formal marriage: inevitable or reversible?' *Family Court Review* 41: 439.

Garrison, M. (2014) 'The changing face of marriage', in J. Eekelaar and R. George (eds) *Routledge Handbook of Family Law and Policy*, Abingdon: Routledge.

Garrison, M. (2015) 'Fostering family law norms through educational initiatives', *Child and Family Law* 261.

Gatrell, C. (2005) *Hard Labour*, Maidenhead: Open University Press.

Gavison, R. (1992) 'Feminism and the Public/Private Distinction', *Stanford Law Review* 45: 1.

Gay, O. (2014) *Domestic Violence*, London: House of Commons Library.

Geist, C. (2010) 'Men and women's reports about housework', in J. Trew and S. Drobnic (eds) *Dividing the Domestic*, Stanford: University of Stanford Press.

Geldof, B. (2003) 'The real love that dare not speak its name', in A. Bainham, B. Lindley, M. Richards and L. Trinder (eds) *Children and Their Families*, Oxford: Hart.

George, R. H. (2008b) 'Changing names, changing places: reconsidering s 13 of the Children Act 1989', *Family Law* 38: 1121.

George, R. H. (2011a) 'Practitioners' views on children's welfare in relocation disputes: comparing approaches in England and New Zealand', *Child and Family Law Quarterly* 22: 175.

George, R. H. (2011b) 'Reviewing relocation', *Child and Family Law Quarterly* 23: 793.

George, R. H. (2011c) 'Regulating responsibilities in relocation disputes', in J. Bridgeman, H. Keating and C. Lind (eds) *Regulating Family Responsibilities*, Aldershot: Ashgate.

George, R. H. (2012a) 'Cohabitants' property rights: when is fair fair?' *Cambridge Law Journal* 71: 394.

George, R. H. (2012b) *Ideas and Debates in Family Law*, Oxford: Hart.

George, R. H. (2012c) 'International relocation, care arrangements and case taxonomy', *Family Law* 42: 1478.

George, R. H. (2012d) 'The international relocation debate', *Journal of Social Welfare and Family Law* 34: 141.

George, R. H. (2013) *Relocation Disputes: Law and Practice in England and New Zealand*, Oxford: Hart.

George, R. (2015) 'How do judges decide international relocation cases?' *Child and Family Law Quarterly* 377.

George, R. H. and Cominetti, O. (2013) 'International relocation: key findings from the 2012 study', *Family Law* 43: 1430.

George, R. H. and Roberts, C. (2009) *The Media and the Family Courts*, Oxford: OXFLAP.

George, R. H., Harris, P. and Herring, J. (2009) 'Pre-nuptial agreements: for better or for worse?' *Family Law* 39: 934.

Gershoff, E. (2002) 'Corporal punishment by parents and associated child behaviours and experiences: a meta-analytic and theoretical review', *Psychological Bulletin* 128: 539.

Gheaus, A. (2018) 'Children's vulnerability and legitimate authority over children', *Journal of Applied Philosophy* 35: 60.

Gibson, C. (2000) 'Changing family patterns in England and Wales', in S. Katz *et al.* (eds) *Cross Currents*, Oxford: OUP.

Gibson, D. (1998) *Aged Care*, Cambridge: CUP.

Giddens, A. (1989) *Sociology*, Cambridge: Polity Press.

Giddens, A. (1992) *The Transformation of Intimacy*, Cambridge: Polity Press.

Giddens, A. (1998) *The Third Way: The Renewal of Social Democracy*, Cambridge: Polity Press.

Giesen, D. (1997) 'Artificial reproduction revisited: status problems and welfare of the child – a comparative view', in C. Bridge (ed.) *Family Law Towards the Millennium: Essays for PM Bromley*, London: Butterworths.

Gilbert, A. (2014) 'From "pretended family relationship" to "ultimate affirmation": British conservatism and the legal recognition of same-sex relationships', *Child and Family Law Quarterly* 26: 463.

Gill, A. and Anitha, S. (2009) 'The illusion of protection? An analysis of forced marriage legislation and policy in the UK', *Journal of Social Welfare and Family Law* 31: 257.

Gill, A. and Anitha, S. (eds) (2011) *Forced Marriage*, London: Zed Books.

Gilligan, C. (1982) *In a Different Voice*, London: Harvard University Press.

Gilmore, S. (2003a) 'Parental responsibility and the unmarried father – a new dimension to the debate', *Child and Family Law Quarterly* 15: 21.

Gilmore, S. (2003b) '*Bellinger v Bellinger* – not quite between the ears and between the legs – transsexualism and marriage in the Lords', *Child and Family Law Quarterly* 15: 295.

Gilmore, S. (2004a) 'Duration of marriage and seamless preceding cohabitation', *Family Law* 34: 205.

Gilmore, S. (2004b) 'The nature, scope and use of the specific issue order', *Child and Family Law Quarterly* 16: 367.

Gilmore, S. (2006a) 'Contact/shared residence and child well-being: research evidence and its decisions for legal decision-making', *International Journal of Law, Policy and the Family* 20: 344.

Gilmore, S. (2006b) 'Court decision-making in shared residence order cases: a critical examination', *Child and Family Law Quarterly* 18: 478.

Gilmore, S. (2007) 'Horses and carts: contact and child support', *Child and Family Law Quarterly* 19: 357.

Gilmore, S. (2008a) 'The assumption that contact is beneficial: challenging the "secure foundation"', *Family Law* 38: 1226.

Gilmore, S. (2008b) 'Disputing contact: challenging some assumptions', *Child and Family Law Quarterly* 20: 285.

Gilmore, S. (2009) 'The limits of parental responsibility', in R. Probert, S. Gilmore and J. Herring (eds) *Responsible Parents and Parental Responsibility*, Oxford: Hart.

Gilmore, S. (2011) 'Corbett v Corbett: once a man, always a man?' in S. Gilmore, J. Herring and R. Probert (eds) Landmark Cases in Family Law, Oxford: Hart.

Gilmore, S. (2012) 'Why should they cite us?' in R. Probert and C. Barton (eds) Fifty Years in Family Law, Amsterdam: Intersentia.

Gilmore, S. (2013) 'Re J (Care Proceedings: Past Possible Perpetrators in a New Family Unit) [2013] UKSC 9: bulwarks and logic – the blood which runs through the veins of law – but how much will be spilled in future?' Child and Family Law Quarterly 215.

Gilmore, S. (2015) 'Withdrawal of parental responsibility: lost authority and a lost op-portunity', Modern Law Review 78: 1042.

Gilmore, S. (2016) 'Less of the "P" discipline and more of the "H" word – putting Payne in its place! Re F (A Child) (International Relocation Cases) [2015] EWCA Civ 882', Journal of Social Welfare and Family Law 38: 87.

Gilmore, S. (2017) 'Use of the UNCRC in family law cases in England and Wales', International Journal of Children's Rights 25: 500.

Gilmore, S. (2020) 'Justice and implacable hostility to contact: parental beliefs, factual foundation and justification', Law Quarterly Review 136: 99.

Gilmore, S. and Glennon, L. (2012) 'Hayes and Williams', Family Law, Oxford: Oxford University Press.

Gilmore, S. and Herring, J. (2011a) '"No" is the hardest word: consent and children's autonomy', Child and Family Law Quarterly 23: 3.

Gilmore, S. and Herring, J. (2011b) 'Children's refusal of medical treatment: could Re W be distinguished?', Family Law 41: 715.

Gilmore, S. and Herring, J. (2012) 'Children's refusal of treatment: the debate continues', Family Law 42.

Gilmore, S. and Herring, J. (2014) 'Listening to children . . . whatever', Law Quarterly Review 139: 531.

Giovannini, E. (2011) Outcomes of Family Justice Children's Proceedings, London: Ministry of Justice.

Gingerbread (2016) Missing Maintenance, London: Gingerbread.

Gingerbread (2018) Children Deserve More, London: Gingerbread.

Gingerbread (2020) Maintenance Matters, London: Gingerbread.

Ginn, J. and Price, D. (2002) 'Do divorced women catch up in pension building?', Child and Family Law Quarterly 14: 157.

Girgis, S., George, R. and Anderson, T. (2010) 'What is marriage?' Harvard Journal of Law and Public Policy 34: 245.

Girlguiding (2013) Girls' Attitude Survey 2013, London: Girlguiding.

Girlguiding (2019) Girls' Attitude Survey 2019, London: Girlguiding.

Glendon, M. (1989) The Transformation of Family Law, Chicago: University of Chicago Press.

Glennon, L. (2000) 'Fitzpatrick v Sterling Housing Association Ltd – an endorsement of the functional family', International Journal of Law, Policy and the Family 14: 226.

Glennon, L. (2005) 'Displacing the "conjugal family" in legal policy – a progressive move?' Child and Family Law Quarterly 17: 141.

Glennon, L. (2006) 'Strategizing for the future through the Civil Partnership Act', Journal of Law and Society 33: 244.

Glennon, L. (2008) 'Obligations between adult partners: moving from form to function?' International Journal of Law, Policy and the Family 22: 22.

Glennon, L. (2010) 'The limitations of equality discourses on the contours of intimate obligations', in J. Wallbank, S. Choudhry and J. Herring (eds) Rights, Gender and Family Law, Abingdon: Routledge.

Goldscheid, J. (2014) 'Gender Neutrality and the "Violence against Women" Frame' CUNY Academic Works. http://academicworks.cuny.edu/cl_pubs/60

Goldstein, J., Solnit, A., Goldstein, S. and Freud, A. (1996) The Best Interests of the Child, New York: Free Press.

Golombok, S. (2015) Modern Families: Parents and Children in New Family Forms, Cambridge: CUP.

Golombok, S., MacCallum, F., Goodman, E. and Rutter, M. (2002) 'Families with children conceived by donor insemination', Child Development 73: 952.

Golynker, O. (2015) 'Family-friendly reform of employment law in the UK: an overstretched flexibility', Journal of Social Welfare and Family Law 37: 378.

Goodin, R. and Gibson, D. (1997) 'Rights, young and old', Oxford Journal of Legal Studies 17: 185.

Goodman, A. and Greaves, E. (2010a) Cohabitation, Marriage and Child Outcomes, London: Institute for Fiscal Studies.

Goodman, A. and Greaves, E. (2010b) Cohabitation, Marriage and Relationship Stability, London: Institute for Fiscal Studies.

Goodmark, L. (2009) 'Reframing Domestic Violence Law and Policy: An Anti-Essentialist Proposal', *Washington University Journal of Law and Policy* 39

Goody, J. (1983) *The Development of Marriage and the Family in Europe*, Cambridge: CUP.

Goold, I., Herring, J. and Auckland, C. (eds) (2020) *Parental Rights, Best Interests, and Significant Harm*, Oxford: Hart.

Goosey, S. (2019) 'Is age discrimination a less serious form of discrimination?' *Legal Studies* 39: 533.

Gordon-Bouvier, E. (2000) 'The open future: analysing the temporality of autonomy in family law', *Child and Family Law Quarterly* 75.

Gössl, S. and Völzmann, B. (2019) 'Legal Gender Beyond the Binary', *International Journal of Law Policy and the Family* 33: 403.

Grace, V. and Daniels, K. (2007) 'The (ir)relevance of genetics: engendering parallel worlds of procreation and reproduction', *Sociology of Health and Illness* 29: 692.

Grenfell, L. (2003) 'Making sex: law's narratives of sex, gender and identity', *Legal Studies* 23: 66.

Griffin, J. (2008) *On Human Rights*, Oxford: OUP.

Griffiths, K. (2019) 'From 'form' to function and back again: a new conceptual basis for developing frameworks for the legal recognition of adult relationships', *Child and Family Law Quarterly* 27: 227.

Grillo, R. (2014) *Muslim Families, Politics and the Law*, Aldershot: Ashgate.

Grimley Evans, J. (2003) 'Age discrimination: implications of the ageing process', in S. Fredman and S. Spencer (eds) *Age as an Equality Issue*, Oxford: Hart.

Gross, N. (2005) 'The detraditionalization of intimacy reconsidered', *Sociological Theory* 23: 286.

Gruber, A. (2007) 'The feminist war on crime', *Iowa Law Review* 92: 741.

Grundy, E. and Henretta, J. (2006) 'Between elderly parents and adult children: a new look at the intergenerational care provided by the "sandwich generation"', *Ageing and Society* 26: 707.

Guardian, The (1996) *ICM Poll*, 7 November 1996.

Guardian, The (2014) 'Report reveals "extensive" violence against women in EU', 5 March 2014.

Guggenheim, M. (2005) *What's Wrong with Children's Rights?* Cambridge, MA: Harvard University Press.

Guggenheim, M. (2006) 'Ratify the UN Convention on the Rights of the Child, but don't expect any miracles', *Emory International Law Review* 20: 43.

Gupta, S., Evertsson, M., Grunow, D., Nermo, M., Sayer, L. (2010) 'Economic inequality and housework', in J. Trew and S. Drobnic (eds) *Dividing the Domestic*, Stanford: University of Stanford Press.

Hague, G., Thiara, R. and Mullender, A. (2010) 'Disabled women, domestic violence and social care: the risk of isolation, vulnerability and neglect', *British Journal of Social Work* 40: 1.

Haldane, J. (1994) 'Children, families, autonomy and the state', in D. Morgan and G. Douglas (eds) *Constitution Families*, Stuttgart: Franz Steiner Verlag.

Hale, Baroness (2004) 'Unmarried couples in family law', *Family Law* 34: 419.

Hale, Baroness (2006) 'Understanding children's rights: theory and practice', *Family Court Review* 44: 350.

Hale, Baroness (2009) 'The future of marriage', in G. Douglas and N. Lowe (eds) *The Continuing Evolution of Family Law*, Bristol: Family Law.

Hale, Baroness (2011a) 'Equality and autonomy in family law', *Journal of Social Welfare and Family Law* 33: 3.

Hale, Baroness (2011b) 'Family responsibility: where are we now?', in C. Lind, H. Keating and J. Bridgeman (eds) *Taking Responsibility, Law and the Changing Family*, Aldershot: Ashgate.

Hale, Baroness (2016) 'Listening to children: are we nearly there yet?' *Family Law* 38: 320.

Hale, L. J. (1999) 'The view from Court 45', *Child and Family Law Quarterly* 11: 377.

Hale, L. J. (2000) 'The Family Law Act 1996 – dead duck or golden goose?' in S. Cretney (ed.) *Family Law – Essays for the New Millennium*, Bristol: Jordans.

Hamilton, C. (1995) *Family, Law and Religion*, London: Sweet & Maxwell.

Hanmer, J. (2000) 'Domestic violence and gender relations', in J. Hanmer and C. Itzin (eds) *Home Truths About Domestic Violence*, London: Routledge.

Hannon, C., Wood, C. and Bazalgett, L. (2010) *In Loco Parentis*, London: Demos.

Hansen, S. (2019) 'Birth relationships after adoption – is there a role for Article 8?' *Child and Family Law Quarterly* 211.

Harder, L. and Thomarat, M. (2012) 'Parentage law in Canada', *International Journal of Law, Policy and Family* 26: 62.

Hardesty, J. and Chung, G. (2006) 'Intimate partner violence, parental divorce, and child custody: directions for intervention and future research', *Family Relations* 55: 200.

Harding, M. and Newnham, A. (2014) Initial research findings: the typical levels of parental involvement where post-separation parenting is resolved by court order', *Family Law* 44: 672.

Harding, M. and Newnham, A. (2017) 'Section 8 orders on the public–private law divide', *Journal of Social Welfare and Family Law* 39: 83

Harding, R. (2007) 'Sir Mark Potter and the protection of the traditional family: why same sex marriage is (still) a feminist issue', *Feminist Legal Studies* 15: 223.

Harding, R. (2012) 'Legal constructions of dementia: discourses of autonomy at the margins of capacity', *Journal of Social Welfare and Family Law* 34: 425.

Harding, R. (2014) 'Re(inscribing) the heteronormative family', in R. Leckey (ed.) *After Legal Equality*, Abingdon: Routledge.

Harker, R. and Heath, R. (2014) *Children in Care in England: Statistics*, London: House of Commons Library.

Harkness, S. (2005) *Employment, Work Patterns and Unpaid Work*, London: ESRC.

Harne, L. and Radford, J. (2008) *Tackling Domestic Violence: Theories, Policies and Practice*, Maidenhead: Open University Press.

Harold, G. and Murch, M. (2005) 'Inter-parental conflict and children's adaptation to separation and divorce', *Child and Family Law Quarterly* 17: 185.

Harris, J. (2003) 'Assisted Reproductive Technological Blunders (ARTBs)', *Journal of Medical Ethics* 29: 205.

Harris, M. (2006) *President's Guidance No. 1*, London: Gender Recognition Panel.

Harris, N. (2005) 'Empowerment and state education', *Modern Law Review* 68: 925.

Harris, P. (2008) 'The Miller paradoxes', *Family Law* 38: 1096.

Harris, P. (2014) 'Article 8 of the European Convention and the welfare principle: a thesis of conflict resolution', *Family Law* 44: 331.

Harris, P. (2016) 'Meeting the challenge: family settlements not judgments', *Family Law* 36: 38.

Harris, P., George, R. H., Herring J. (2011) 'With this ring I thee wed (terms and conditions apply)', *Family Law* 41: 367.

Harris-Short, S. (2002) 'Putting the child at the heart of adoption?' *Child and Family Law Quarterly* 14: 325.

Harris-Short, S. (2005) 'Family law and the Human Rights Act 1998: judicial restraint or revolution?' *Child and Family Law Quarterly* 17: 329.

Harris-Short, S. (2008) 'Making and breaking family life: adoption, the state and human rights', *Journal of Law and Society* 35: 28.

Harris-Short, S. (2010) 'Resisting the march towards 50/50 shared residence: rights, welfare and equality in post-separation families', *Journal of Social Welfare and Family Law* 32: 257.

Harris-Short, S. (2011) 'Building a house upon sand: post-separation parenting, shared residence and equality – lessons from Sweden', *Child and Family Law Quarterly* 23: 344.

Harwin, J. and Alrouh, B. (2017) 'Supervision orders and special guardianship: how risky are they? Findings from a national study of supervision orders and special guardianship', *Family Law* 513.

Harwin, J., Alrouh, B., Palmer, M., Broadhurst, K. and Swift, S. (2016) 'Spotlight on supervision orders: what do we know and what do we need to know?' *Family Law* 365.

Harwin, J., Alrouh, B., Palmer, M., Broadhurst, K. and Swift, S. (2017) *A national study of the usage of supervision orders and special guardianship over time (2007–2016)*, London: Nuffield Foundation.

Harwin, J. and Owen, M. (2003) 'The implementation of care plans and its relationship to Children's Welfare', *Child and Family Law Quarterly* 15: 71.

Harwood, J. (2019) "We don't know what it is we don't know": how austerity has undermined the courts' access to information in child arrangements cases involving domestic abuse', *Child and Family Law Quarterly* 321.

Haskey, J. (2001) 'Demographic aspects of cohabitation in Great Britain', *International Journal of Law, Policy and the Family* 15: 51.

Haskey, J. (2016) 'Civil partnerships and same-sex marriages in England and Wales: a social and demographic perspective', *Family Law* 44: 46.

Haskey, J. (2018) 'Facts and figures: grounds for divorce since the 1969 Divorce Reform Act in England and Wales', *Family Law* 1006.

Haskey, J. (2019) 'Some scenarios on the numerical implications of the proposed new divorce reform legislation for England and Wales', *Family Law* 49: 1040.

Haskey, J. and Lewis, J. (2006) 'Living-apart-together in Britain: context and meaning', *International Journal of Law in Context* 2: 37.

Hasson, E. (2003) 'Divorce law and the Family Law Act 1996', *International Journal of Law, Policy and the Family* 17: 338.

Hasson, E. (2004) 'The street-level response to relationship breakdown: a lesson for national policy', *Journal of Social Welfare and Family Law* 26: 35.

Hauari, H. and Hollingworth, K. (2010) *Understanding Fatherhood: Masculinity, Diversity and Change*, York: JRF.

Hawthorne, J., Jessop, J., Pryor, J. and Richards, M. (2003) *Supporting Children Through Family Change*, York: Joseph Rowntree Foundation.

Hayes, J. (2014) 'The judge's dilemma: *Re J*', *Family Law* 44: 91.

Hayes, J., Hayes, M., and Williams, J. (2010) '"Shocking" abuse followed by a "staggering" ruling: *Re MA (Care Threshold)*', *Family Law* 40: 166.

Hayes, J. and Hayes, P. (2014) 'Adoption in England: the end of placements dictated by race, culture, religion and language', *Family Law* 1288.

Hayes, M. (1994) '"Cohabitation clauses" in financial provision and property adjustment orders – law, policy and justice', *Law Quarterly Review* 110: 124.

Hayes, M. (1996) 'The proper role of courts in child care cases', *Child and Family Law Quarterly* 8: 201.

Hayes, M. (1997) 'Reconciling protection of children with justice for parents in cases of alleged child abuse', *Legal Studies* 17: 1.

Hayes, M. (1998) 'Child protection – from principles and policies to practice', *Child and Family Law Quarterly* 10: 119.

Hayes, M. (2004) 'Uncertain evidence and risk taking in child protection cases', *Child and Family Law Quarterly* 16: 63.

Hayes, M. (2006) 'Relocation cases: is the court of appeal applying the correct principles?' *Child and Family Law Quarterly* 19: 351.

Hayes, M. (2014) 'The Supreme Court's failure to protect vulnerable children: *Re J (Children)*', *Family Law* 43: 1.

Hayward, A. (2012) '"Family property" and the process of "familialisation" of property law', *Child and Family Law Quarterly* 18: 284.

Hayward, A. (2015) 'Cohabitants, detriment and the potential of proprietary estoppel: *Southwell v Blackburn* [2014] EWCA Civ 1347', *Child and Family Law Quarterly* 303.

Hayward, J. (2019) 'The Steinfeld effect: equal civil partnerships and the construction of the cohabitant', *Child and Family Law Quarterly* 31: 283.

Hayward, A. and Fenwick, H, (2018) 'From same-sex marriage to equal civil partnerships:

on a path towards "perfecting" equality?' *Child and Family Law Quarterly* 30: 97.

Hayward, J. and Brandon, G. (2011) *Cohabitation: An Alternative to Marriage?* Cambridge: Jubilee Centre.

Hazan, E. (2013) 'Seen But Not Really Heard? Testamentary Guardianship and the Conceptualisation of Children in English Law and Practice', *International Journal of Law, Policy and the Family* 27: 216.

Healy, C. (2015) 'Dispute resolution through collaborative practice: a comparative analysis', *Child and Family Law Quarterly* 17: 173.

Hedley, J. (2009) 'Illusion and disillusion? Perceptions of children in the family justice system', *Family Law* 39: 118.

Hedley, M. (2014) 'Family life and child protection: Cleveland, Baby P *et al.*', *Child and Family Law Quarterly* 26: 7.

Heenan, A. (2018) 'Causal and temporal connections in financial remedy cases: the meaning of marriage', *Child and Family Law Quarterly* 30: 75.

Held, V. (2006) *The Ethics of Care*, Cambridge: CUP.

Henaghan, M. (2011) 'Relocation cases – the rhetoric and the reality of a child's best interests – a view from the bottom of the world', *Child and Family Law Quarterly* 23: 31.

Henaghan, M. (2015) 'Michael Freeman's contribution to childhood rights', in A. Diduck, N. Peleg, H. Reece (eds) *Law in Society*, Leiden: Brill.

Henricson, C. (2003) *Government and Parenting*, York: Joseph Rowntree Foundation.

Henricson, C. and Bainham, A. (2005) *The Child and Family Policy Divide*, York: Joseph Rowntree Foundation.

Henry, P. and Hamilton, K. (2012) 'The inclusion of children in family dispute resolution in Australia: balancing welfare versus rights principles', *International Journal of Children's Rights* 20(4) 584.

Herring, J. (1997) 'Children's abortion rights', *Medical Law Review* 5: 257.

Herring, J. (1998a) '"Name this child"', *Cambridge Law Journal* 57: 266.

Herring, J. (1998b) 'Book review', *Cambridge Law Journal* 57: 213.

Herring, J. (1999a) 'The welfare principle and the rights of parents', in A. Bainham, S. Day Sclater and M. Richards (eds) *What is a Parent?* Oxford: Hart.

Herring, J. (1999b) 'The Human Rights Act and the welfare principle in family law – conflicting or complementary?' *Child and Family Law Quarterly* 11: 223.

Herring, J. (2000a) 'The caesarean section cases and the supremacy of autonomy', in M. Freeman and A. Lewis (eds) *Law and Medicine*, Oxford: OUP.

Herring, J. (2000b) 'The suffering children of blameless parents', *Law Quarterly Review* 116: 550.

Herring, J. (2001) 'Parents and children', in J. Herring (ed.) *Family Law: Issues, Debates, Policy*, Cullompton: Willan.

Herring, J. (2002) 'The human rights of children in care', *Law Quarterly Review* 118: 534.

Herring, J. (2003a) 'Connecting contact', in A. Bainham, B. Lindley, M. Richards and L. Trinder (eds) *Children and Their Families*, Oxford: Hart.

Herring, J. (2003b) 'Children's rights for grown-ups', in S. Fredman and S. Spencer (eds) *Age as an Equality Issue*, Oxford: Hart.

Herring, J. (2005a) 'Why financial orders on divorce should be unfair', *International Journal of Law, Policy and the Family* 19: 218.

Herring, J. (2005b) 'Farewell welfare', *Journal of Social Welfare and Family Law* 27: 159.

Herring, J. (2007a) 'Where are the carers in healthcare law and ethics?' *Legal Studies* 27: 51.

Herring, J. (2007b) 'Familial homicide, failure to protect and domestic violence: who's the victim?' *Criminal Law Review* 923.

Herring, J. (2008a) 'Mum's not the word: an analysis of section 5, Domestic Violence, Crime and Victims Act 2004', in C. Clarkson and S. Cunningham, *Criminal Liability for Non-Aggressive Death*, Aldershot: Ashgate.

Herring, J. (2008b) 'The place of carers', in M. Freeman (ed.) *Law and Bioethics*, Oxford: OUP.

Herring, J. (2008c) 'Respecting family life', *Amicus Curiae* 75: 21.

Herring, J. (2008d) 'Together forever? The rights and responsibilities of adult children and their parents', in J. Bridgeman, H. Keating, and C. Lind (eds) *Responsibility, Law and the Family*, London: Ashgate.

Herring, J. (2008e) 'Older people and the law', in C. O'Cinneide and J. Holder (eds) *Current Legal Problems*, Oxford: OUP.

Herring, J. (2009a) 'Who decides on human rights?' *Law Quarterly Review* 125: 1.

Herring (2009b) *The Woman Who Tickled Too Much*, Harlow: Pearson.

Herring, J. (2009d) *Older People in Law and Society*, Oxford: OUP.

Herring, J. (2009e) 'Losing it? Losing what? The law and dementia', *Child and Family Law Quarterly* 21: 3.

Herring, J. (2009f) 'Protecting vulnerable adults: a critical review of recent case law', *Child and Family Law Quarterly* 21: 498.

Herring, J. (2009g) 'Revoking adoptions', *New Law Journal* 159: 379.

Herring, J. (2010a) 'The legal duties of carers', *Medical Law Review* 18: 248.

Herring, J. (2010b) 'Relational autonomy and family law', in J. Wallbank, S. Choudhry and J. Herring (eds) *Rights, Gender and Family Law*, London: Routledge.

Herring, J. (2010c) 'Sexless family law', *Lex Familiae* 11: 3.

Herring, J. (2010d) 'Seven ways of getting it wrong', *New Law Journal* 160: 715.

Herring, (2010e) 'Family law', in *All England Law Review 2009*, London: LexisNexis.

Herring, J. (2010f) '20:10:2010: the death knell of marriage', *New Law Journal* 1511.

Herring, J. (2011a) 'No more holding and having', in S. Gilmore, J. Herring and R. Probert (eds) *Landmark Cases in Family Law*, Oxford: Hart.

Herring, J. (2011b) 'The meaning of domestic violence', *Journal of Social Welfare and Family Law* 33: 297.

Herring, J. (2011c) 'Who's the daddy?' *New Law Journal* 1577.

Herring, J. (2011d) 'Elder abuse and stressing carers', in Bridgeman, J., Keating, H. and Lind, C. (2011) *Regulating Family Responsibilities*, Aldershot: Ashgate.

Herring, J. (2011e) 'Legal issues surrounding dementia', *Elder Law Journal* 1: 182.

Herring, J. (2012a) 'Divorce, internet hubs and Stephen Cretney', in R. Probert and C. Barton (eds) *Fifty Years in Family Law*, London: Intersentia.

Herring, J. (2012b) 'Breaking the chain', *New Law Journal* 705.

Herring J. (2012c) *Criminal Law: Text and Materials*, Oxford: OUP.

Herring, J. (2012e) 'Vulnerability, children and the law', in M. Freeman (ed.) *Law and Childhood Studies*, Oxford: OUP.

Herring, J. (2012f) 'What's wrong with kidnapping?' *Criminal Law Review* 343.

Herring, J. (2012g) 'Elder abuse: a human rights agenda for the future', in I. Doran and A. Soden (eds) *Beyond Elder Law*, Amsterdam: Springer.

Herring, J. (2012h) 'The power of naming: surnames, children, and spouses', in M. Freeman and F. Smith (eds) *Law and Language*, Oxford: OUP.

Herring, J. (2012i) 'Mental disability and capacity to consent to sex: *A Local Authority v H* [2012]

EWHC 49 (COP)', *Journal of Social Welfare and Family Law* 34:4.

Herring, J. (2013a) *Caring and the Law*, Oxford: Hart.

Herring, J. (2013b) 'An injection of sense', *New Law Journal* 8 November.

Herring, J. (2014a) 'Making family law less sexy and more careful', in R. Leckey (ed.) *After Legal Equality*, Abingdon: Routledge.

Herring, J. (2014b) 'The welfare principle and the Children Act: presumably it's about welfare?' *Journal of Social Welfare and Family Law* 36: 14.

Herring, J. (2014c) 'Law and policy concerning older people', in J. Eekelaar and R. George (eds) *Routledge Handbook of Family Law and Policy*, Abingdon: Routledge.

Herring, J. (2014d) *Family Law: A Very Short Introduction*, Oxford University Press: OUP.

Herring, J. (2014e) *Relational Autonomy and Family Law*, Amsterdam: Springer.

Herring, J. (2015) 'The abuse of parents by children', in A. Diduck, N. Peleg and H. Reece (eds) *Law in Society*, Leiden: Brill.

Herring, J. (2016a) 'Why marriage needs to be less sexy', in J. Miles, R. Mody and R. Probert (eds) *Marriage Rites and Rights*, Oxford: Hart.

Herring, J. (2016b) *Medical Law and Ethics*, Oxford: OUP.

Herring, J. (2016c) 'Family law and older people in a European perspective', in Scherpe, J. (ed.) *European Family Law*, London: Elgar.

Herring, J. (2016d) *Vulnerable Adults and the Law*, Oxford: OUP.

Herring, J. (2017) 'Parental responsibility; hyper-parenting and the role of technology', in R. Brownsword, E. Scotford and K. Yeung (eds) *Oxford Handbook on Law and Regulation of Technology*, Oxford: OUP.

Herring, J. (2017a) 'Compassion, ethics of care and legal rights', *International Journal of Law in Context* 13: 158.

Herring, J. (2017b) 'Is law too sexy?' *Modern Believing* 58: 361.

Herring, J. (2017c) 'Points of View', *New Law Journal* 17 February.

Herring, J. (2018a) 'The Istanbul Convention: Is domestic abuse violence against women?' in G. Douglas, M. Murch and V. Stephens (eds) *International and National Perspectives on Child and Family Law*, London: Intersentia.

Herring, J. (2018b) *Medical Law and Ethics* Oxford: OUP.

Herring, J. (2019a) Law and the Relational Self, Cambridge: CUP.

Herring, J. (2019b) 'Maternalism and Making Decisions for Children', in H. Willekens, K. Scheiwe, T. Richarz and E. Schumann (eds) *Motherhood and the Law*, University of Gottingen.

Herring, J. (2020a) 'Law and policy concerning older people', in J. Eekelaar and R. George (eds) *Routledge Handbook of Family Law and Policy*, Abingdon: Routledge.

Herring, J. (2020b) 'Disputes Over Medical Treatment for Children', in J. Dwyer (ed.) *Oxford Handbook of Children and the Law*, Oxford: OUP

Herring, J. (2020c) 'Vulnerability and Medical Decisions Concerning Children', in I. Goold, J. Herring and C. Auckland (eds) (2020) *Parental Rights, Best Interests, and Significant Harm*, Oxford: Hart.

Herring, J. (2021) *Law through the Life Course*, Bristol: BUP.

Herring, J. and Chau, P.-L. (2001) 'Assigning sex and intersexuals', *Family Law* 31: 762.

Herring, J. and Dunn, M. (2011) 'Safeguarding children and adults: much of a muchness? *A Local Authority v A and B* [2010] EWHC 978 (Fam)', *Child and Family Law Quarterly* 23: 659.

Herring, J. and Foster, C. (2011) '"Please don't tell me": the right not to know', *Cambridge Quarterly of Healthcare Ethics* 21: 1.

Herring, J. and Foster, C. (2012) 'Welfare means relationality, virtue and altruism', *Legal Studies* 32: 480.

Herring, J. and Powell, O. (2013) 'The rise and fall of presumptions surrounding the welfare principle', *Family Law* 43: 543.

Herring, J., Probert, R. and Gilmore, S. (2015) *Great Debates: Family Law*, Basingstoke: Palgrave.

Herring, J. and Taylor, R. (2006) 'Relocating relocation', *Child and Family Law Quarterly* 18: 517.

Herring, J. and Wall, J. (2013) 'Capacity to cohabit: hoping "everything turns out well in the end"', *Child and Family Law Quarterly* 25: 471.

Herring, J. and Wall, J. (2014a) 'Understanding capacity: "the heart may easily overrule the head"', *Elder Law Journal* 4: 190.

Herring, J. and Wall, J. (2014b) 'Capacity to consent to sex', *Medical Law Review* 254.

Hester, M. (2002) 'One step forward and three steps back? Children, abuse and parental contact in Denmark', *Child and Family Law Quarterly* 14: 267.

Hester, M. (2009) *Who Does What to Whom? Gender and Domestic Violence Perpetrators*, London: Northern Rock.

Hester, M. (2011) 'The three planet model: towards an understanding of contradictions in approaches to women and children's safety in contexts of domestic violence', *British Journal of Social Work* 41: 837.

Hester, M. (2012) 'Portrayal of women as intimate partner domestic violence perpetrators', *Violence Against Women* 18: 1067.

Hester, M. (2013) 'Who does what to whom? Gender and domestic violence perpetrators in English police records', *European Journal of Criminology* 10: 623.

Hester, M. and Westmarland, N. (2005) *Tackling Domestic Violence*, London: Home Office.

Hester, M., Westmarland, N., Pearce, J. and Williamson, E. (2008) *Early Evaluation of the Domestic Violence, Crime and Victims Act 2004*, London: Ministry of Justice.

Hetherington, M. and Kelly, J. (2002) *For Better or For Worse*, New York: WW Norton & Co.

Hewlett, P. (2003) *Baby Hunger*, New York: Atlantic Books.

Hibbs, M., Barton, C. and Beswick, J. (2001) 'Why marry? Perceptions of the affianced', *Family Law* 31: 197.

Hill, R. (2005) 'The Domestic Violence, Crime and Victim Act 2004', *Family Law* 35: 281.

Hitchings, E. (2005) 'A consequence of blurring the boundaries – less choice for victims of domestic violence', *Social Policy and Society* 5: 91.

Hitchings, E. (2008) 'Everyday cases in the post-White era', *Family Law* 38: 873.

Hitchings, E. (2009a) 'From pre-nups to post-nups: dealing with marital property agreements', *Family Law* 39: 1056.

Hitchings, E. (2009b) 'Chaos or consistency?' in J. Miles and R. Probert (eds) *Sharing Lives, Dividing Assets*, Oxford: Hart.

Hitchings, E. (2010) 'The impact of recent ancillary relief jurisprudence in the "everyday" ancillary relief case', *Child and Family Law Quarterly* 22: 93.

Hitchings, E. (2017) 'Official, operative and outsider justice: the ties that (may not) bind in family financial disputes', *Child and Family Law Quarterly* 29: 359.

Hitchings, E. and Miles, J. (2016) 'Mediation, financial remedies, information provision and legal advice: the post-LASPO conundrum', *Journal of Social Welfare and Family Law* 38(2) 175.

Hitchings, E. and Miles, J. (2018) 'Meal tickets for life? The need for evidence-based evaluation of financial remedies law', *Family Law* 993.

Hitchings, E. and Sagar, T. (2007) 'The Adoption and Children Act 2002: a level playing field for same-sex adopters', *Child and Family Law Quarterly* 19: 60.

HM Government (2004) *Parental Separation: Children's Needs and Parents' Responsibilities*, London: The Stationery Office.

HM Government (2009) *Handling Cases of Forced Marriage*, London: The Stationery Office.

HM Government (2010a) *State of the Nation Report*, London: The Stationery Office.

HM Government (2010b) *Government's Response to the Joint Committee on Human Rights' (JCHR) Report, Children's Rights*, London: Children's Rights.

HM Government (2010c) *Care Planning, Placement and Case Review*, London: The Stationery Office.

HM Government (2012a) *Caring For Our Future: Progress Report On Funding Reform*, London: The Stationery Office.

HM Government (2012b) *Social Justice: Transforming Lives*, London: The Stationery Office.

HM Government (2013) *Working Together to Safeguard Children*, London: The Stationery Office.

HM Government (2016a) *Using the Child Maintenance Service or Child Support Agency*, London: The Stationery Office.

HM Government (2016b) *Legal Aid Statistics*, London: The Stationery Office.

HM Government (2018a) *Transforming the Response to Domestic Abuse*, London: The Stationery Office.

HM Government (2020a) *Domestic Abuse Bill 2000: Statutory Definition of Domestic Abuse*, London: The Stationery Office.

HM Government (2020b) *Child Maintenance Statistics*, London: The Stationery Office.

HM Inspectorate of Court Administration (2005) *Safeguarding Children in Family Proceedings*, London: The Stationery Office.

HM Inspectorate of Court Administration (2007) *Assisting Families by Court Order*, London: The Stationery Office.

HMIC/CPSI (2004) *A Joint Inspection of the Investigation and Prosecution of Cases Involving Domestic Violence*, London: HMIC.

HMIC (2014) *Everyone's Business: Improving the Police Response to Domestic Abuse*, London: HMIC.

HMIC (2019) The Police Response to Domestic Abuse, London: HMIC.

Hobbs, T. (2002) 'Parental alienation syndrome and the UK family courts, Part 1', *Family Law* 32: 182.

Hochschild, A. (1996) 'The emotional geography of work and family life', in L. Morris and S. Lyons (eds) *Gender Relations in Public and Private: Changing Research Perspectives*, London: Macmillan.

Hodson, D. (2009) 'Report from the *Family Law Review* of the Centre for Social Justice: "Every Family Matters"', *Family Law* 39: 864.

Hodson, D., Green, M. and De Souza, N. (2003) '*Lambert* – shutting Pandora's box', *Family Law* 33: 37.

Hofferth, S. and Anderson, K. (2003) 'Are all dads equal? Biology versus marriage for a basis for parental investment', *Journal of Marriage and the Family* 65: 213.

Hoggett, B., Pearl, D., Cooke, E. and Bates, P. (2003) *Family Law and Society*, London: Butterworths.

Holehouse, M. (2014) 'Divorced and separated parents should be open to criticism, say Tory MPs', *Daily Telegraph*, 14 January.

Holgate, L. (2005) *Children's Rights, State Intervention, Custody and Divorce*, New York: Edwin Mellen Press.

Holt, A. (2011) 'The terrorist in my home': teenagers' violence towards parents – constructions of parent experiences in public online message boards', *Child and Family Social Work* 16: 454.

Holt, A. (2012) *Adolescent-to-Parent Abuse*, Bristol: Policy Press.

Holt, J. (1975) *Escape from Childhood*, London: Dutton.

Holt, K. (2013) 'Territory skirmishes with DIY advocacy: a Dickensian Misadventure', *Family Law* 43: 1150.

Holt, K. and Kelly, N. (2015a) 'Access to justice: the welfare of children and their families – lost in a target focused and cost driven system', *Family Law* 45: 167.

Holt, K and Kelly, N. (2015b) 'When adoption without parental consent breaches human rights: implications of *Re B-S (Children)* [2013] EWCA Civ 963 on decision making and permanency planning for children', *Journal of Social Welfare and Family Law* 37: 228.

Holt, S. (2018) 'A voice or a choice? Children's views on participating in decisions about post-separation contact with domestically abusive fathers', *Journal of Social Welfare and Family Law* 40: 459

Home Affairs Select Committee (2008) *Domestic Violence, Forced Marriage and 'Honour' Based Violence*, London: Hansard.

Home Office (1998) *Supporting Families*, London: The Stationery Office.

Home Office (1999) *Living Without Fear*, London: Home Office.

Home Office (2000a) *Report of the Interdepartmental Working Group on Transsexual People*, London: Home Office.

Home Office (2000b) *Setting the Boundaries*, London: Home Office.

Home Office (2000c) *A Choice By Right*, London: Home Office.

Home Office (2004) *Alcohol and Intimate Partner Violence*, London: Home Office.

Home Office (2006) *National Domestic Violence Delivery Plan*, London: Home Office.

Home Office (2015a) *Using Domestic Violence Protection Notices and Domestic Violence Protection Orders to Make Victims Safer*, London: Home Office.

Home Office (2015b) *Controlling or Coercive Behaviour in an Intimate or Family Relationship Statutory Guidance Framework*, London: Home Office.

Home Office (2016) *Forced Marriage Statistics*, London: Home Office.

Home Office (2018) *The Independent Review into the Application of Sharia Law in England and Wales*, London: Home Office.

Hood, A. and Waters, T. (2017) *Benefit cuts set to increase child poverty, with biggest rises likely in North East and Wales*, London: IFS.

Hood, H. (2009) 'The role of conduct in divorce suits and claims for ancillary relief', *Family Law* 39: 948.

Hope, G. (2019) 'Co-mediation – what is it and how can it help resolve disputes?' *Family Law* 49: 1332.

Horsey, K. (2006) 'Who are the UK sperm donors?', *Bionews*, 14 February.

Horsey, K. (2010) 'Challenging presumptions: legal parenthood and surrogacy arrangements', *Child and Family Law Quarterly* 22: 439.

Horsey, K. (2015) *Surrogacy in the UK: Myth Busting and Reform*: Surrogacy UK.

Horton, M. (2013) 'The variability of lump sum orders', *Family Law* 43: 411.

Horwath, J., Lees, J., Sidebotham, P., Higgins, J. and Imtiaz, A. (2008) *Religion, Beliefs and Parenting Practices*, York: JRF.

Hosie, R. (2018) 'Average UK wedding cost reaches all time high', *The Independent* 23 July.

House of Commons Home Affairs Select Committee (2008) *Domestic Violence, Forced Marriage and 'Honour-Based' Violence*, London: The Stationery Office.

House of Commons Justice Committee (2011) *Government's Proposed Reform of Legal Aid. Third Report of Session 2010–11, Vol. 1, HC 681–I*, London: The Stationery Office.

House of Commons Justice Committee (2012) *Pre-legislative Scrutiny of the Children and Families Bill Fourth Report of Session 2012–2013*, London: The Stationery Office.

House of Commons Public Accounts Committee (2007) *Legal Services Commission: Legal Aid and Mediation for People Involved in Family Breakdown*, London: The Stationery Office.

House of Commons, Select Committee on Intergenerational Fairness and Provision (2019) Report of Session 2017–19: *Tackling Intergenerational Unfairness*. London: Hansard.

House of Commons Women and Equalities Committee (2016) *Transgender Equality*, London: The Stationery Office.

House of Commons Work and Pensions Committee (2005) *The Performance of the Child Support Agency*, London: The Stationery Office.

Howard, M. and Wilmott, M. (2000) 'The networked family', in H. Wilkinson (ed.) *Family Business*, London: Demos.

Howarth, E., Stimpson, L., Baran, D. and Robinson, A. (2009) *Safety in Numbers*, London: Hestia Fund.

Howe, D. and Feast, J. (2000) *Adoption, Search and Reunion*, London: The Children's Society.

Hoyano, L. and Keenan, C. (2007) *Child Abuse: Law and Policy Across Boundaries*, Oxford: OUP.

Hoyle, C. and Sanders, A. (2000) 'Police responses to domestic violence: from victim choice to victim empowerment', *British Journal of Criminology* 40: 14.

Hughes, K. and Sloan, B. (2012) 'Post-adoption photographs: welfare, rights and judicial reasoning', *Child and Family Law Quarterly* 393.

Humphreys, C. (2001) 'The impact of domestic violence on children', in P. Foley, J. Roche and S. Tucker (eds) *Children in Society*, Buckingham: Open University Press.

Humphreys, C. and Harrison, C. (2003a) 'Squaring the circle – contact and domestic violence', *Family Law* 33: 419.

Humphreys, C. and Harrison, C. (2003b) 'Focusing on safety – domestic violence and the role of child contact centres', *Child and Family Law Quarterly* 15: 237.

Humphreys, C. and Thiara, R. (2002) *Routes to Safety*, Bristol: Women's Aid.

Humphreys, C. and Thiara, R. (2003) 'Neither justice nor protection; women's experiences of post-separation violence', *Journal of Social Welfare and Family Law* 25: 195.

Humphreys, C., Hester, M., Hague, G. *et al.* (2002) *From Good Intentions to Good Practice: Mapping Services Working with Families where there is Domestic Violence*, York: Policy Press.

Hunt, J. (2006a) 'Contact with non-resident parents after separation and divorce', in M. Thorpe and R. Budden, *Durable Solutions*, Bristol: Jordans.

Hunt, J. (2006b) 'Substitute care of children by members of their extended families and social networks', in F. Ebtehaj, B. Lindley and M. Richards (eds) *Kinship Matters*, Oxford: Hart.

Hunt, J. (2012) 'Through a glass darkly: the uncertain future of private law child contact litigation', *Journal of Social Welfare and Family Law* 33: 379.

Hunt, J. (2014) 'Shared parenting time: messages from research', *Family Law* 44: 676.

Hunt, J. and Macleod, A. (1998) *The Best-Laid Plans*, London: The Stationery Office.

Hunt, J. and Macleod, A. (2008) *Outcomes of Applications to Court for Contact Orders after Parental Separation or Divorce*, London: Ministry of Justice.

Hunt, J. and Trinder, L. (2011) *Chronically Litigated Contact Cases: How Many Are There and What Works?* London: Family Justice Council.

Hunt, J., Waterhouse, S. and Lutman, E. (2008) *Keeping Them in the Family: Outcomes for Abused and Neglected Children Placed with Family or Friends Carers through Care Proceedings*, London: BAAF.

Hunt, J., Waterhouse, S. and Lutman, E. (2010) 'Parental contact for children placed in kinship care through care proceedings', *Child and Family Law Quarterly* 22: 71.

Hunter, R. (2011) 'Doing violence to family law', *Journal of Social Welfare and Family Law* 33: 343.

Hunter, R. (2014a) 'Access to justice after LASPO', *Family Law* 44: 640.

Hunter, R. (2014b) 'Exploring the "LASPO Gap"', *Family Law* 44: 660.

Hunter, R (2014c) 'Domestic violence: a UK perspective', in J. Eekelaar and R. George (eds) *Routledge Handbook of Family Law and Policy*, Abingdon: Routledge.

Hunter, R. (2017) 'Inducing demand for family mediation – before and after LASPO', *Journal of Social Welfare and Family Law* 39: 189.

Hunter, R and Choudhry, S. (2018) 'Conclusion: international best practices', *Journal of Social Welfare and Family Law* 40: 548.

Huntington, C. (2014) *Failure to Flourish: How Law Undermines Family Relationships*, Oxford: OUP.

Hussein, S. Manthorpe, J. Penhale, B. (2005) *Public Perceptions of the Neglect and Mistreatment of Older People: Findings of a United Kingdom Survey*, London: King's College.

Huston, T. and Melz, H. (2004) 'The case for (promoting) marriage: the devil is in the detail', *Journal of Marriage and the Family* 66: 943.

ICM Poll (2004) *Generation Survey*, London: ICM.

Idriss, M. (2017) 'Not domestic violence or cultural tradition: is honour-based violence distinct from domestic violence?', *Journal of Social Welfare and Family Law* 39: 3.

Illman, J. (1996) *The Guardian*, 9 July.

Independent on Sunday (2000) 'Gay couple's twins to get right to stay', 9 January.

Instone-Brewer, D. (2002) *Divorce and Remarriage in the Bible*, Amsterdam: William B. Eerdmans.

Irvine, C. (2009) 'Mediation and social norms: a response to Dame Hazel Genn', *Family Law* 39: 351.

Jackson, E. (2002) 'Conception and the irrelevance of the welfare principle', *Modern Law Review* 65: 176.

Jackson, E. (2007a) 'Rethinking the pre-conception welfare principle', in K. Horsey and H. Biggs, *Human Fertilisation and Embryology: Reproducing Regulation*, London: Routledge.

Jackson, E. (2007b) 'Prisoners, their partners and the right to family life', *Child and Family Law Quarterly Review* 19: 239.

Jackson, E. (2014) 'Assisted concept and surrogacy in the UK', in J. Eekelaar and R. George (eds) *Routledge Handbook of Family Law and Policy*, Abingdon: Routledge.

Jackson, E., Wasoff, F., Maclean, M. and Dobash, R. (1993) 'Financial support on divorce: the right mixture of rules and discretion?' *International Journal of Law, Policy and the Family* 7: 230.

James, A. (2002) 'The Family Law Act 1996', in A. Carling, S. Duncan and R. Edwards, *Analysing Families*, London: Routledge.

James, A., James, A. and McNamee, S. (2003) 'Constructing children's welfare in family proceedings', *Family Law* 33: 889.

James, A., James, A. and McNamee, S. (2004) 'Turn down the volume? – not hearing children in family proceedings', *Child and Family Law Quarterly* 16: 189.

James, G. and Busby, N. (2011) *Families, Care-Giving and Paid Work*, London: Edward Elgar.

Jarrett, T. (2019) *Child Maintenance: The Multi-Billion Pound Write-Off Of Arrears On Child Support Agency Cases*, London: House of Commons Library.

Jeffries, S. (2016) 'In the Best Interests of the Abuser: Coercive Control, Child Custody Proceedings and the "Expert" Assessments That Guide Judicial Determinations', *Laws* 5: 14.

Jivraj, S. and Herman, D. (2009) '"It is difficult for a white judge to understand": orientalism, racialisation, and Christianity in English child welfare cases', *Child and Family Law Quarterly* 21: 283.

John, M. (2003) *Children's Rights and Power*, London: Jessica Kingsley.

Johnson, M. (1999) 'A biomedical perspective on parenthood', in A. Bainham, S. Day Sclater and M. Richards (eds) *What is a Parent?* Oxford: Hart.

Johnson, M., Derrington, R., Menard, A., Ooms, T. and Stanley, S. (2010) *Making Distinctions Between Different Kinds of Intimate Partner Violence*, Washington: National Healthy Marriage Resource Centre.

Johnson, P. (2015) 'Marriage, heteronormativity, and the European Court of Human Rights: a reappraisal', *International Journal of Law, Policy and the Family* 29: 56.

Johnson, S. (2013) Religion, children and the family courts', *Family Law* 43: 574.

Johnstone, A. (2006) 'Special Guardianship Orders: a guide', *Family Law* 26: 116.

Joint Committee on Human Rights (2014) *Annual Report: The Implications for Access to Justice of the Government's Proposals to Reform Legal Aid*, para 142.

Jones, C. (2007) *Why Donor Insemination Requires Developments in Family Law: The Need For New Definitions of Parenthood*, Lewiston: Edwin Mellen.

Jones, C. (2010) 'The identification of "parents" and "siblings"', in J. Wallbank, S. Choudhry and J. Herring (eds) *Rights, Gender and Family Law*, Abingdon: Routledge.

Jordan, A. (2009) '"Dads aren't Demons. Mums aren't Madonnas". Constructions of fatherhood and masculinities in the (real) Fathers 4 Justice campaign', *Journal of Social Welfare and Family Law* 31: 419.

Jordan, L. and Lindley, B. (2007) *Special Guardianship: What Does it Offer to Children who Cannot Live with their Parents?* London: Family Rights Group.

Jowett, A. and Peel, E. (2019) 'Reshaping relational scripts? Marriage and civil partnership proposals among same-gender couples', *Psychology & Sexuality* 10: 325–337,

Judd, F. and George, R. (2010) 'International relocation: do we stand alone?' *Family Law* 40: 63.

Judicial Working Group on Litigants in Person (2013) *Report,* London: Ministry of Justice.

Kaganas, F. (1995) 'Partnership under the Children Act 1989 – an overview', in F. Kaganas, M. King and C. Piper (eds) *Legislating for Harmony,* London: Jessica Kingsley.

Kaganas, F. (2002) 'Domestic homicide, gender and the expert', in A. Bainham, S. Day Sclater and M. Richards (eds) *Body Lore and Laws,* Oxford: Hart.

Kaganas, F. (2007a) 'Domestic violence, men's groups and the equivalence argument', in A. Diduck and K. O'Donovan (eds) *Feminist Perspectives on Family Law,* London: Routledge.

Kaganas, F. (2007b) 'Grandparents' rights and grandparents' campaigns', *Child and Family Law Quarterly* 19: 17.

Kaganas, F. (2010a) 'Child protection, gender and rights', in J. Wallbank, S. Choudhry and J. Herring (eds) *Rights, Gender and Family Law,* Abingdon: Routledge.

Kaganas, F. (2010b) 'When it comes to contact disputes, what are family courts for?' *Current Legal Problems* 63: 235.

Kaganas, F. (2014) 'Child protection and the modernized family justice system', in J. Wallbank and J. Herring (eds) *Vulnerabilities, Care and Family Law,* London: Routledge.

Kaganas, F. (2017) 'Justifying the LASPO Act: authenticity, necessity, suitability, responsibility and autonomy', *Journal of Social Welfare and Family Law* 39: 168.

Kaganas, F. (2018) 'Parental Involvement: A Discretionary Presumption' *Legal Studies* 38: 548

Kaganas, F. and Day Sclater, S. (2000) 'Contact and domestic violence – the winds of change?' *Family Law* 30: 630.

Kaganas, F. and Day Sclater, S. (2004) 'Contact disputes: narrative constructions of "good parents"', *Feminist Legal Studies* 12: 1.

Kaganas, F. and Murray, C. (2001) 'Law, women and the family: the question of polygamy in a new South Africa', *Acta Juridica* 116.

Kaganas, F. and Piper, C. (1994) 'Domestic violence and divorce mediation', *Journal of Social Welfare and Family Law* 16: 265.

Kaganas, F. and Piper, C. (1999) 'Divorce and domestic violence', in S. Day Sclater and C. Piper (eds) *Undercurrents of Divorce,* Aldershot: Ashgate.

Kaganas, F. and Piper, C. (2001) 'Grandparents and contact: "*rights* v *welfare*" revisited', *International Journal of Law, Policy and the Family* 15: 250.

Kaganas, F. and Piper, C. (2015) 'Michael Freeman and the rights and wrongs of resolving private law disputes', in A. Diduck, N. Peleg and H. Reece (eds) *Law in Society,* Leiden: Brill.

Kaganas, F. and Piper, C. (2020) 'Grandparent contact: another presumption?' *Journal of Social Welfare and Family Law* 42: 176.

Kan, M.-Y. and Laurie, H. (2016) *Gender, Ethnicity and Household Labour in Married and Cohabiting Couples in the UK,* London: ESRC.

Kapp, M. (1982) 'The father's lack of rights and responsibilities in the abortion decision', *Ohio University Law Review* 9: 370.

Katz, J. Holland, C., Peace, S. and Taylor, E. (2011) *A Better Life: What Older People With High Support Needs Value,* York: Joseph Rowntree Foundation.

Kavanagh, M. (2004) 'Rewriting the legal family: beyond exclusivity to a care-based standard', *Yale Journal of Law and Feminism* 16: 83.

Kaye, M., Stubbs, J. and Tolmie, J. (2003) 'Domestic violence and child contact arrangements', *Australian Journal of Family Law* 17: 1.

Kazez, J. (2017) *The philosophical parent: Asking the hard questions about having and raising children,* Oxford: OUP.

Keating, H. (2006) 'Protecting or punishing children: physical punishment, human rights and English law reform', *Legal Studies* 26: 394.

Keating, H. (2008) 'Being responsible, becoming responsible, and having responsibility thrust upon them: constructing the "responsibility" of children and parents', in J. Bridgeman, H. Keating and C. Lind (eds) *Responsibility, Law and the Family,* London: Ashgate.

Keating, H. (2009) 'Suspicions, sitting on the fence and standards of proof', *Child and Family Law Quarterly* 21: 230.

Keating, H. (2011) '*Re MA*: the significance of harm', *Child and Family Law Quarterly* 23: 15.

Keating, J. (2012) '"When the kissing has to stop": children, sexual behavior and the criminal law', in M. Freeman, *Law and Childhood Studies,* Oxford: OUP.

Keating, J. (2015) 'Children's rights and children's criminal responsibility', in A. Diduck, N. Peleg, H. Reece (eds) *Law in Society*, Leiden: Brill.

Kellet, S. (2006) 'Four theories of filial duty', *The Philosophical Quarterly* 56: 254.

Kelloggs, (2020) *A Lost Education*, London: Kelloggs.

Kelly, F. (2004) 'Nuclear norms or fluid families? Incorporating lesbian and gay parents and their children into Canadian family law', *Canadian Journal of Family Law* 21: 133.

Kelly, F. (2005) 'Conceptualising the child through an ethic of care: lessons for family law', *International Journal of Law in Context* 1: 375.

Kelly, J. (2003) 'Legal and education interventions for families in residence and contact Disputes', in J. Dewar and S. Parker (eds) *Family Law Processes, Practices, Pressures*, Oxford: Hart.

Kelly, J. and Johnson, M. (2008) 'Differentiation among types of intimate partner violence: research update and implications for interventions', *Family Court Review* 46: 476.

Kelly, L. and Lovett, J. (2005) *What a Waste*, London: Women's National Commission.

Kelly, L., Sharp, N. and Klein, R. (2013) *Finding the Costs of Freedom*, London: London Metropolitan University.

Kelly, L. and Westmarland, N. (2016) 'Naming and Defining "Domestic Violence": Lessons from Research with Violent Men', *Feminist Review* 113.

Kennett, W. (2016) 'It's arbitration, but not as we know it: reflections on family law dispute resolution', *International Journal of Law, Policy and the Family* 16: 1.

Kerridge, R. (2000) 'Wills made in suspicious circumstances: the problem of the vulnerable testator', *Cambridge Law Journal* 59: 310.

Khaliq, U. and Young, J. (2001) 'Cultural diversity, human rights and inconsistency in the English courts', *Legal Studies* 21: 192.

Kiernan, K. (2001) 'The rise of cohabitation and childbearing outside marriage in Western Europe', *International Journal of Law, Policy and the Family* 15. 1.

Kiernan, K. and Mensah, F. (2010) 'Partnership trajectories: parent and child wellbeing', in K. Hansen, H. Joshi and S. Dex (eds) *Children of the Twenty-first Century*, Bristol: Policy Press.

Kiernan, K., Barlow, A. and Merlo, R. (2006) 'Cohabitation law reform and its impact on marriage', *Family Law* 36: 1074.

Kiernan, K., Barlow, A. and Merlo, R. (2007) 'Cohabitation law reform and its impact on marriage: evidence from Australia and Europe', *International Family Law* 71.

Kilkelly, U. (2000) *The Child and the European Convention on Human Rights*, Aldershot: Ashgate.

King, E. (2017) 'Giving children a voice in litigation: are we there yet?', Family Law 289.

King, M. (2000) 'Future uncertainty as a challenge to law's programmes: the dilemma of parental disputes', *Modern Law Review* 63: 523.

King, M. and Piper, C. (1995) *How the Law Thinks About Children*, Aldershot: Arena.

King, T. and Jobling, M. (2009) 'What's in a name?', *Trends in Genetics* 25: 351.

Kitzmann, K., Gaylord, N., Holt, A. and Kenny, E. (2003) 'Child witnesses to domestic violence: a meta-analytic review', *Journal of Consultative Clinical Psychology* 71: 339.

Knight, C. (2012) 'Doing (linguistic) violence to prevent (domestic) violence? *Yemshaw v Hounslow LBC* in the Supreme Court', *Child and Family Law Quarterly* 24: 95.

Krause, H. (1994) 'Child support reassessed: limits of private responsibility and the public interest', in J. Eekelaar and M. Maclean (eds) *A Reader on Family Law*, Oxford: OUP.

Laming, Lord (2003) *The Victoria Climbié Report*, London: The Stationery Office.

Laming, Lord (2009) *The Protection of Children in England*, London: The Stationery Office.

Lamont, R. (2017) 'Not a European family: implications of "Brexit" for international family law', *Child and Family Law Quarterly* 267.

Lampard, R. (2014) 'Stated reasons for relationship dissolution in Britain: marriage and cohabitation compared', *European Sociological Review* 30: 315.

Landau, R. and Osmo, R. (2003) 'Professional and personal hierarchies of ethical principles', *International Journal of Social Work* 12: 42.

Lane, M. (2003) 'Ethical issues in surrogacy arrangements', in R. Cook, S. Day Sclater and F. Kaganas (eds) *Surrogate Motherhood*, Oxford: Hart.

Lansdown, G. (2001) 'Children's welfare and children's rights', in P. Foley, J. Roche and S. Tucker (eds) *Children in Society*, Buckingham: Open University Press.

Langdon-Down, G. (2019) 'The pension split: Unfair Shares', *New Law Journal* 7856.

Lasch, C. (1977) *Haven in a Heartless World*, New York: Basic Books.

Laufer-Ukeles, P. (2008) 'Selective recognition of gender difference in the law: revaluing the caretaker role', *Harvard Journal of Law and Gender* 31: 1.

Laurance, J. (2000) 'The booming baby market', *Independent on Sunday*, 7 April.

Law Commission Consultation Paper 179 (2006) *Cohabitation: The Financial Consequences of Relationship Breakdown*, London: The Stationery Office.

Law Commission Consultation Paper 208 (2012) *Matrimonial Property, Needs and Agreements*, London: The Stationery Office.

Law Commission of Canada (2002) *Beyond Conjugality*, Ottawa: Law Commission of Canada.

Law Commission Report 6 (1966) *Reform of the Grounds of Divorce*, London: HMSO.

Law Commission Report 33 (1970) *Report on Nullity of Marriage*, London: HMSO.

Law Commission Report 187 (1989) *Distribution on Intestacy*, London: HMSO

Law Commission Report 192 (1990) *Family Law: The Ground of Divorce*, London: HMSO.

Law Commission Report 207 (1992) *Family Law, Domestic Violence and Occupation of the Family Home*, London: Law Commission.

Law Commission Report 231 (1995) *Mental Incapacity*, London: HMSO.

Law Commission Report 278 (2002) *Sharing Homes*, London: The Stationery Office.

Law Commission Report 307 (2007) *Cohabitation: The Financial Consequences of Relationship Breakdown*, London: The Stationery Office.

Law Commission Report 326 (2011) *Adult Social Care*, London: The Stationery Office.

Law Commission Report 343 (2014) *Matrimonial Property, Needs and Agreements: The Future of Financial Orders on Divorce and Dissolution*, London: The Stationery Office.

Law Commission Scoping Paper (2015) *Getting Married*, London: The Stationery Office.

Law Society (2006) *Family Law Protocol*, London: Law Society.

Law Society (2017) *Access denied? LASPO four years on: a Law Society review*, London: Law Society.

Laws, J. (1998) 'The limitation of human rights', *Public Law* 254.

Leach, V. (2005) *Family Mediation: The Context*, London: Family Justice Council.

Leapman, B. (2007) 'Third of graduate women will be childless', *The Sunday Telegraph*, 22 April, p. 1.

Leckey, R. (2008) *Contextual Subjects*, Toronto: University of Toronto.

Leckey, R. (2013) 'Two mothers in law and fact', *Feminist Legal Studies* 21(1):1–19.

Leckey, R. (2014) 'Must equal mean identical? Same-sex couples and marriage', *International Journal of Law in Context* 10: 5.

Leckey, R. (2018a) 'Cohabitants, choice, and the public interest', in E. Brake, and L. Ferguson (eds) *Philosophical Foundations of Children's and Family Law*, Oxford: OUP.

Leckey, R. (2018b) 'Judging in marriage's shadow', *Feminist Legal Studies* 26: 25.

Leckey (2019) 'Cohabitation, female sacrifice, and judge-made law', *Journal of Social Welfare and Family Law* 41: 72.

Lee, E. (2004) 'Young women, pregnancy and abortion in Britain', *International Journal of Law, Policy and the Family* 18: 283.

Lees, J. and Horwath, J. (2009) '"Religious parents . . . just want the best for their kids": young people's perspectives on the influence of religious beliefs on parenting', *Children and Society* 23: 162.

Legal Aid Agency (2014) *The Legal Aid, Sentencing and Punishment of Offenders Act (LASPO) 2012 –Evidence Requirements for Private Family Law Matters*, London: Legal Aid Agency.

Lenard, D. (1980) *Sex and Generation: A Study of Courtship and Weddings*, London: Tavistock.

Lethem, C. (2014) 'Fair case management in family proceedings following LASPO', *Family Law* 44: 556.

Levin, I. (2004) 'Living apart together: a new family form', *Current Sociology* 52: 223.

Lewis, J. (2001a) 'Debates and issues regarding marriage and cohabitation in the English and American Literature', *International Journal of Law, Policy and the Family* 15: 159.

Lewis, J. (2001b) *The End of Marriage?* Cheltenham: Edward Elgar.

Lewis, J. (2004) 'Adoption: the Nature of policy shifts in England and Wales', *International Journal of Law, Policy and the Family* 18: 235.

Lewis, J. (2006) 'Repartnering and the management of risk', *International Journal of Law, Policy and the Family* 20: 151.

Lewis, J. (2009) *Work–Family Balance, Gender and Policy*, Cheltenham: Edward Elgar.

Lewis, J. and Campbell, M. (2007) 'Work/family balance policies in the UK since 1997: a new departure?', *Journal of Social Policy* 36: 365.

Lewis, J. and Welsh, E. (2006) 'Fathering practices in twenty-six intact families and the implications for child contact', *International Journal of Law in Context* 1: 81.

Lewis, J., Arthur, A., Fitzgerald, R. and Maclean, M. (2000) *Settling Up*, London: NCSR.

Lewis, M. (2005) *Unilever Family Report 2005: Home Alone*, London: Unilever.

Lim, H. and Roche, J. (2000) 'Feminism and children's rights', in J. Bridgeman and D. Monk (eds) *Feminist Perspectives on Child Law*, London: Cavendish.

Lind, C. (2011) 'Power and the taking of responsibility: shifting the legal family from marriage to friendship', in C. Lind, H. Keating and J. Bridgeman (eds) *Taking Responsibility, Law and the Changing Family*, Aldershot: Ashgate.

Lind, C. and Hewitt, T. (2009) 'Law and the complexities of parenting: parental status and parental function', *Journal of Social Welfare and Family Law* 31: 391.

Lind, C., Keating, H. and Bridgeman, J. (2011) *Taking Responsibility, Law and the Changing Family*, Aldershot: Ashgate.

Lindsey, J. (2020) 'Protecting vulnerable adults from abuse: under-protection and over-protection in adult safeguarding and mental capacity law' *Child and Family Law Quarterly* 157.

Lloyd, P. (2014) *Stand by Your Manhood*, London: Biteback.

Lombard, N. and Whiting, N. (2017) 'What's in a Name? The Scottish Government, Feminism and the Gendered Framing of Domestic Abuse', in N. Lombard (ed.) *Routledge Handbook of Gender and Violence*, Abingdon: Routledge.

Lord Chancellor's Department (1995) *Looking to the Future: Mediation and the Ground for Divorce*, London: HMSO.

Lord Chancellor's Department (1998) *Court Procedures for the Determination of Paternity*, London: HMSO.

Lord Chancellor's Department (2001) *Guidelines for Good Practice on Parental Contact in Cases where there is Domestic Violence*, London: LCD.

Lord Chancellor's Department (2002a) *Making Contact Work*, London: LCD.

Lord Chancellor's Department (2002b) *Scoping Study on Delay in Children Act Cases*, London: LCD.

Lord Chancellor's Department (2003) *Reducing Delays in Family Proceedings Courts*, London: LCD.

Long, R., Roberts, N., Loft, P. (2020) *Bullying in UK Schools*, London: House of Commons Library.

Lowe, N. (1997) 'The changing face of adoption – the gift/donation model versus the contract services model', *Child and Family Law Quarterly* 9: 371.

Lowe, N. (2011) 'J v C: Placing the child's welfare centre stage', in S. Gilmore, J. Herring and R. Probert (eds) *Landmark Cases in Family Law*, Oxford: Hart.

Lowe, N. (2012) 'Inherently disposed to protect children', in R. Probert and C. Barton (eds) *Fifty Years in Family Law*, Amsterdam: Intersentia.

Lowe, N. (2017) 'What are the implications of the Brexit vote for the law on international child abduction?' *Child and Family Law Quarterly* 253.

Lowe, N. and Cobley, C. (2011) 'The statutory "threshold" under section 31 of the Children Act 1989 – time to take stock', *Law Quarterly Review* 127: 396.

Lowe, N. and Douglas, N. (2007) *Bromley's Family Law*, London: Butterworths.

Lowe, N. and Murch, M. (2001) 'Children's participation in the family justice system – translating principles into practice', *Child and Family Law Quarterly* 13: 137.

Lowe, N. and Murch, M. (2002) *The Plan for the Child*, London: BAAF.

Lowe, N. and Murch, M. (2003) 'Translating principles into practice', in J. Dewar and S. Parker (eds) *Family Law: Processes, Practices, Pressures*, Oxford: OUP.

Lowenstein, A. and Daatland, S. (2006) 'Filial norms and family support in a comparative cross-national context: evidence from the OASIS study', *Ageing and Society* 26: 203.

Luk, S. (2012) 'How religious arbitration could enhance personal autonomy', *Oxford Journal of Legal Studies* 424.

Lwekowicz, M. and Phillimore, S. (2019) 'Indirect contact: on what basis do such orders promote the welfare of children?' *Family Law* 49: 465.

Lynch, C. (2018) 'Cooperation or coercion? Children coming into the care system under s. 20 voluntary arrangements', *Family Law* 191.

Lyndon Shanley, M. (2004) 'Just marriage', in M. Lyndon Shanley (ed.) *Just Marriage*, Oxford: OUP.

Lyon, C. (2000) 'Children's participation in private law proceedings', in Thorpe LJ and E. Clarke (eds) *No Fault or Flaw: The Future of the Family Law Act 1996*, Bristol: Family Law.

Lyon, C. (2007) 'Children's participation and the promotion of their rights', *Journal of Social Welfare and Family Law* 29: 99.

Lyonette, C. (2015) 'Part-time work, work–life balance and gender equality', *Journal of Social Welfare and Family Law* 37: 321.

Lyons, B. (2010) 'Dying to be responsible: adolescence, autonomy and responsibility', *Legal Studies* 30: 257.

McCall Smith, A. (1990) 'Is anything left of parental rights', in E. Sutherland and A. McCall Smith (eds) *Family Rights: Family Law and Medical Ethics*, Edinburgh: Edinburgh University Press.

McCandless, J. (2012) 'The role of sexual partnership in UK Family Law: The Case of Legal Parenthood', in D. Cutas and S. Chan (eds) *Families: Beyond the Nuclear Ideal*, London: Bloomsbury.

McCandless, J. and Sheldon, S. (2010a) 'The Human Fertilisation and Embryology Act (2008) and the tenacity of the sexual family form', *Modern Law Review* 73: 175.

McCandless, J. and Sheldon, S. (2010b) '"No father required"? Rewriting the family through the welfare clause of the HFE Act (2008)', in G. Haddow, M. Richards and C. Smart (eds) *Reproducing Parents and Kin: Assisted Reproduction and DNA Testing*, Basingstoke: Palgrave.

MacCormick, N. (1976) 'Children's rights: a test-case for theories of rights', *Archiv für Rechts und Sozialphilosophie* 62: 305.

Maccullum, F. and Golombok, S. (2004) 'Children raised in fatherless families from infancy', *Journal of Child Psychology and Psychiatry* 48: 5.

MacDonald, A. (2008) 'The voice of the child: still a faint cry', *Family Law* 38: 648.

MacDonald, A. (2009) 'Bringing rights home for children: arguing the UNCRC', *Family Law* 39: 1073.

Macdonald, G. (2013) *Domestic Violence and Private Family Court Proceedings: Promotion Child Welfare or Promoting Contact?* Bath: University of Bath.

MacDonald, P. (2020) *The Remote Access Family Court*, London: Ministry of Justice.

MacFarlane, J. (2002) 'Mediating ethically: the limits of codes of conduct and the potential of a reflective practice model', *Osgoode Hall Law Journal* 40: 49.

McDougal, R. (2007) 'Parental virtue: A new way of thinking about the morality of reproductive actions', *Bioethics* 21: 181.

McFarlane, A. (2016) 'Nothing else will do', *Family Law* 1403.

McFarlane, A. (2017) 'Holding the risk: the balance between child protection and the right to family life', *Family Law* 599.

McFarlane, A. (2018) 'Restoring confidence in family justice', *Family Law* 988.

MacFarlane, A. (2020) *The Road Ahead*, London: Ministry of Justice.

McFarlane, B. and Robertson, A. (2009) 'Apocalypse averted: proprietary estoppel in the House of Lords', *Law Quarterly Law Review* 125: 535.

McFarlane, LJ (2014) 'The Hershman Levy Memorial Lecture 2014' at www.judiciary.gov.uk/wp-content/uploads/2014/06/speech-by-rt-hon-sir-andrew-mcfarlane-memorial-lecture.pdf

McGee, C. (2000) 'Children's and mother's experiences of support and protection following domestic violence', in J. Hanmer and C. Itzin (eds) *Home Truths About Domestic Violence*, London: Routledge.

Mackay, Lord (2000) 'Family law reform', in S. Cretney (ed.) *Family Law – Essays for the New Millennium*, Bristol: Jordans.

McKie, L. and Callan, S. (2012) *Understanding Families*, London: Sage.

Mackinnon, C. (1987) *Feminism Unmodified*, Cambridge, MA: Harvard University Press.

Maclean, M. (ed.) (2007) *Parenting after Partnering*, Oxford: Hart.

Maclean, M. (2011) 'Family law in hard times', *Journal of Social Welfare and Family Law* 33: 309.

Maclean, M. (2014) 'The changing professional landscape', *Family Law* 44: 177.

Maclean, M. and Dijksterhuis, B. (eds) (2019) *Digital Family Justice: From Alternative Dispute Resolution to Online Dispute Resolution?* Oxford: Hart.

Maclean, M. and Eekelaar, J. (2005) 'The significance of marriage: contrasts between white British and ethnic minority groups in England', *Law and Policy* 27: 379.

Maclean, M. and Eekelaar, J. (2009) 'The perils of reforming family law and the increasing need for empirical research', in J. Miles and R. Probert (eds) *Sharing Lives, Dividing Assets*, Oxford: Hart.

Maclean, M. and Eekelaar, J. (2016) *Lawyers and Mediators*, Oxford: Hart.

Maclean, M. and Eekelaar, J. (2019) *Act the Act: Access to Family Justice after LASPO*, Oxford: Hart.

Maclean, S. and Maclean, M. (1996) 'Keeping secrets in assisted reproduction – the tension between donor anonymity and the need of the child for information', *Child and Family Law Quarterly* 8: 243.

Maclean, M. and Mueller-Johnson, K. (2003) 'Supporting cross-household parenting', in A. Bainham, B. Lindley, M. Richards and L. Trinder (eds) *Children and Their Families*, Oxford: Hart.

Maclean, M., Eekelaar, J., Lewis, J., Arthur, S. *et al.* (2002) 'When cohabiting parents separate – law and expectations', *Family Law* 32: 373.

Macleod, A. (2018) 'Are children's rights important?' in E. Brake and L. Ferguson (eds) *Philosophical Foundations of Children's and Family Law*, Oxford: OUP.

Madden Dempsey, M. (2006) 'What counts as domestic violence? A conceptual analysis', *William and Mary Journal of Women and the Law* 12: 301.

Madden Dempsey, M. (2007) 'Toward a feminist state: what does "effective" prosecution of domestic violence mean?' *Modern Law Review* 70: 908.

Madden Dempsey, M. (2009) *Prosecuting Domestic Violence*, Oxford: OUP.

Margaria, A. (2020) 'Trans men Giving birth and reflections on fatherhood: What to expect' *International Journal of Law, Policy and the Family* forthcoming.

Maguire, J. and Frankland, E. (2006) ''Til death do us part: inheritance claims and the short marriage', *Family Law* 36: 374.

Magrath, P. and Phillimore, S. (2015) 'The transparency paradox: open justice versus closed minds', *Family Law* 1237-1.

Mahmood, S. (2013) 'Cohabitation? I know it when I see it', *Family Law* 43: 77.

Maidment, S. (2001) 'Parental responsibility – is there a duty to consult?' *Family Law* 31: 518.

Malik, M. (2007) '"The branch on which we sit": multiculturism, minority women and family law', in A. Diduck and K. O'Donovan (eds) *Feminist Perspectives on Family Law*, London: Routledge.

Malik, M. (2014) 'Family law in diverse societies', in J. Eekelaar and R. George (eds) *Routledge Handbook of Family Law and Policy*, Abingdon: Routledge.

Mallender, P. and Rayson, J. (2006) *The Civil Partnership Act 2004*, Cambridge: CUP.

Mant, J. (2017) 'Neoliberalism, family law and the cost of access to justice', *Journal of Social Welfare and Family Law* 39: 246.

Mant, J. (2019) 'Litigants' experiences of the post-LASPO family court: key findings from recent research', *Family Law* 49: 300.

Mant, J. and Wallbank, J. (2018) 'The mysterious case of disappearing family law and the shrinking vulnerable subject: the shifting sands of family law's jurisdiction', *Social and Legal Studies* 26: 629.

Manthorpe, J. and Price, E. (2005) 'Lesbian carers: personal issues and policy responses', *Social Policy and Society* 5: 15.

Mantle, G. (2001) *Helping Families in Dispute*, Aldershot: Ashgate.

Marriage Foundation, The (2014c) *Unmarried Parents Account for One Fifth of Couples But Half of All Family Breakdown*, London: Marriage Foundation.

Marriage Foundation, The (2020a) *Family Breakdown Costs £50bn a year*, London: Marriage Foundation.

Marshall, A. (2003) 'Comedy of adoption – when is a parent not a parent?', *Family Law* 33: 840.

Marshall, J. (2008) 'Giving birth, but refusing motherhood', *International Journal of Law in Context* 4: 169.

Marshall, J. (2012) 'Concealed births, adoption and human rights law', *Cambridge Law Journal* 71: 325.

Marshall, J. (2018) 'Secrecy in births, identity rights, care and belonging', *Child and Family Law Quarterly* 30: 167.

Marshall, E., Henderson, K., Hawes, A. and Nicholson, J. (2014) 'The law relating to needs and spousal maintenance: one firm's view', *Family Law* 43: 423.

Masson, J. (1995) 'Partnership with parents: doing something together under the Children Act 1989', in F. Kaganas, M. King and C. Piper (eds) *Legislating for Harmony*, London: Jessica Kingsley.

Masson, J. (2000) 'Thinking about contact – a social or a legal problem?', *Child and Family Law Quarterly* 12: 15.

Masson, J. (2002) 'Securing human rights for children and young people in secure accommodation', *Child and Family Law Quarterly* 14: 77.

Masson, J. (2005) 'Emergency intervention to protect children: using and avoiding legal controls', *Child and Family Law Quarterly* 17: 75.

Masson, J. (2006a) 'Parenting by being; parenting by doing – in search of principles for founding families', in J. Spencer and A. du Bois-Pedain, *Freedom and Responsibility in Reproductive Choice*, Oxford: Hart.

Masson, J. (2006b) 'Consent orders in contact cases', *Family Law* 36: 1041.

Masson, J. (2007) 'Reforming care proceedings – time for a review', *Child and Family Law Quarterly* 19: 411.

Masson, J. (2008) 'The state as parent: reluctant parent? The problem of parents of last resort', *Journal of Law and Society* 35: 52.

Masson, J. (2015a) 'Children's rights: Preventing the use of state care and preventing care proceedings', in A. Diduck, N. Peleg and H. Reece (eds) *Law in Society*, Leiden: Brill.

Masson, J. (2015b) 'Third (or fourth) time lucky for care proceedings reform?' *Child and Family Law Quarterly* 27: 3.

Masson, J. and Dickens, J. (2013) 'Care proceedings reform: The future of the pre-proceedings process', *Family Law* 1414.

Masson, J. and Dickens, J. (2019) 'Outcomes of care proceedings for children', *Family Law* 49: 159.

Masson, J. and Humphreys, C. (2005) 'Facilitating and enforcing contact: the Bill and the ten per cent', *Family Law* 35: 548.

Masson, J. and Lindley, B. (2006) 'Recognising carers for what they do – legal problems and solutions for the kinship care of children', in F. Ebtehaj, B. Lindley and M. Richards (eds) *Kinship Matters*, Oxford: Hart.

Masson, J., McGovern, D., Pick, K. and Winn Oakley, M. (2007) *Protecting Powers: Emergency Intervention for Children's Protection*, Chichester: John Wiley.

Maushart, S. (2001) *Wifework*, London: Bloomsbury.

May, V. and Smart, C. (2004) 'Silence in court? – Hearing children in residence and contact disputes', *Child and Family Law Quarterly* 16: 305.

Mayall, B. (2000) 'The sociology of children in relation to children's rights', *International Journal of Children's Rights* 8: 243.

Mayall, B. (2002) *Towards a Sociology for Childhood*, Buckingham: Open University Press.

Mayhew, E., Finch, N., Beresford, B. and Keung, A. (2005) 'Children's time and space', in J. Bradshaw and E. Mayhew (eds) *The Well-being of Children in the UK*, London: Save the Children.

McGill, B. (2014) 'Fathering attitudes and father involvement'. *Journal of Family Issues* 35: 1089.

McLellan, D. (1996) 'Contract marriage – the way forward or dead end?', Journal of Law and Society 23: 234

McNeilly, K. (2014) 'Gendered Violence and International Human Rights: Thinking Non-discrimination Beyond the Sex Binary' (2014) 22 *Legal Studies* 263.

Mears, M. (1991) 'Getting it wrong again', *Family Law* 21: 231.

Mee, J. (1999) *The Property Rights of Cohabitees*, Oxford: Hart.

Mee, J. (2004) 'Property rights and personal relationships: reflections on reform', *Legal Studies* 24: 414.

Mee, J. (2009) 'The limits of proprietary estoppel: *Thorner v Major*', *Child and Family Law Quarterly* 21: 367.

Melville, A. and Laing, K. (2010) 'Closing the gate: family lawyers as gatekeepers to a holistic service', *International Journal of Law in Context* 6: 167.

Merrick, R. (2000) *Grandparents Suffering as Divorces Rise*, London: Family Policy Studies Centre.

Miccio, G. (2005) 'A house divided: mandatory arrest, domestic violence, and the conservatization of the battered women's movement', *Houston Law Review* 42: 237.

Miles, J. (2001) 'Domestic violence', in J. Herring (ed.) *Family Law: Issues, Debates, Policy*, Cullompton: Willan.

Miles, J. (2002) 'Mind the gap . . . : Child protection, statutory interpretation and the Human Rights Act', *Cambridge Law Journal* 61: 533.

Miles, J. (2003) 'Property law *v* family law: resolving the problems of family property', *Legal Studies* 23: 624.

Miles, J. (2005) 'Principle or pragmatism in ancillary relief: the virtues of flirting with academic theories and other jurisdictions', *International Journal of Law, Policy and the Family* 19: 242.

Miles, J. (2008) '*Charman v Charman* (No. 4) [2007] EWCA Civ 503 – making sense of need, compensation and equal sharing after *Miller; McFarlane*', *Child and Family Law Quarterly* 20: 378.

Miles, J. (2011a) 'Legal aid, Article 6 and "exceptional funding" under the Legal Aid etc. Bill 2011', *Family Law* 41: 1003.

Miles, J. (2011b) 'Marriage and divorce in the Supreme Court and the Law Commission: for love or money?' *Modern Law Review* 74: 430.

Miles, J. (2011c) 'Responsibility in family finance and property law', in J. Bridgeman, H. Keating and C. Lind (eds) *Regulating Family Responsibilities*, Aldershot: Ashgate.

Miles, J. (2019) 'Should the regime be discretionary or rules-based?' in J. Palmer *et al.* (eds) *Law and Policy in Modern Family Finance*, Cambridge: Intersentia.

Miles, J. and Probert, R. (eds) (2009) *Sharing Lives, Dividing Assets*, Oxford: Hart.

Miles, J., Balmer, N. and Smith, M. (2012) 'When exceptional is the rule: mental health, family problems and the reform of legal aid in England and Wales', *Child and Family Law Quarterly* 2 J.

Miles, J., Mody, P. and Probert, R. (eds) (2016) *Marriage Rites and Rights*, Oxford: Hart.

Miles, J., Pleasence, P. and Balmer, N. (2009) 'The experience of relationship breakdown and civil law problems by people in different forms of relationship', *Child and Family Law Quarterly* 21: 47.

Miles, J., Wasoff, F. and Mordaunt, E. (2011) 'Cohabitation: lessons from research north of the border?' *Child and Family Law Quarterly* 23: 256.

Millbank, J. (2008a) 'Unlikely fissures and uneasy resonances: lesbian co-mothers, surrogate parenthood and fathers' rights', *Feminist Legal Studies* 16: 141.

Millbank, J. (2008b) 'The role of "functional family" in same-sex family recognition trends', *Child and Family Law Quarterly* 20: 155.

Millbank, J. (2015) 'Responsive regulation of cross border assisted reproduction', *Journal of Law and Medicine* 22: 346.

Miller, G. (1997) 'Provision for a surviving spouse', *Conveyancer* 61: 442.

Mills, L. (2003) *Insult to Injury: Rethinking Our Responses to Intimate Abuse*, Princeton: Princeton University Press.

Mills, C. (2003) 'The child's right to an open future?', *Journal of Social Philosophy* 34: 499.

Mills and Reeve (2015) *The Changing Face of Divorce*, London: Mills and Reeve.

Mills and Reeve (2017) *Cohabitation: Pitfalls and Protection*, London: Mills and Reeve.

Millum, J. (2018) *The Moral Foundations of Parenthood*, Oxford: OUP.

Ministry of Justice (2010) *Proposals for the Reform of Legal Aid in England and Wales, Consultation Paper*, London: Ministry of Justice.

Ministry of Justice (2011) *Reform of Legal Aid in England and Wales: The Government Response*, London: Ministry of Justice.

Ministry of Justice (2012a) *Government Response to the Family Justice Review*, London: Ministry of Justice.

Ministry of Justice (2012b) *Family Matters Tables*, London: Ministry of Justice.

Ministry of Justice (2014a) *Divorce Myths to be Dispelled*, London: Ministry of Justice.

Ministry of Justice (2014b) *Child Arrangements Programme*, London: Ministry of Justice.

Ministry of Justice (2015a) *Written Ministerial Statement by Courts Minister Shailesh Vara on the HMCTS Estate*, London: Ministry of Justice.

Ministry of Justice (2015b) *Government Response to Voice of the Child: Dispute Resolution Advisory Group*, London: Ministry of Justice.

Ministry of Justice (2018) *Research on the domestic violence evidential requirements for legal aid*, London: MoJ.

Ministry of Justice (2019a) *Post-Implementation Review of LASPO*, London: MoJ

Ministry of Justice (2019b) *Legal Support: The Way Ahead*, London: MoJ.

Ministry of Justice (2020a) *Family Court Statistics*, London: MoJ.

Ministry of Justice (2020b) *Assessing Risk of Harm to Children and Parents in Private Law Children Cases*, London: MoJ.

Mintel (2004) *Mintel Housework Survey*, London: Mintel.

Mitchell, F. and Travis, M. (2018) 'Legislating intersex equality: building the resilience of intersex people through law', *Legal Studies* 38: 587.

Mnookin, R. (1975) 'Child custody adjudication', *Law and Contemporary Problems* 39: 226.

Mnookin, R. (1981) 'Thinking about children's rights – beyond kiddie libbers and child savers', *Stanford Lawyer* 1981: 24.

Mody, P. (2016) 'Forced Marriage: Rites and Rights', in J. Miles, R. Mody and R. Probert (eds) *Marriage Rites and Rights*, Oxford: Hart.

Moen, P. (2003) *It's About Time*, Ithaca, NY: Cornell University Press.

Mole, N. (2002) 'A note on the judgment from the perspective of the European Convention for the Protection of Human Rights and Fundamental Freedoms 1950', *Child and Family Law Quarterly* 14: 447.

Monk, D. (2011) 'Sexuality and succession law: beyond formal equality', *Feminist Legal Studies* 19: 231.

Monk, D. and Macvarish, J. (2019) 'Siblings, contact and the law: an overlooked relationship?' *Family Law* 49: 180.

Montgomery, J. (1988) 'Children as property', *Modern Law Review* 51: 323.

Montgomery, J. (2000) 'Time for a paradigm shift', *Current Legal Problems* 53: 363.

Mooney, J. (2000) 'Women's experiences of violence', in J. Hanmer and C. Itzin (eds) *Home Truths About Domestic Violence*, London: Routledge.

Morgan, D. (2011) *Rethinking Family Practices*, Basingstoke: Palgrave.

Morgan, P. (1999) *Farewell to the Family?* London: IEA.

Morgan, P. (2000) *Marriage-Lite*, London: Institute for the Study of Civil Society.

Morgan, P. (2007) *The War between the State and the Family*, London: IEA.

Morgan, R. (2010) *Children's Care Monitor 2009*, London: CAFCASS.

Morris, A. (2009) 'Selective treatment of irreversibly impaired infants: decision-making at the threshold', *Medical Law Review* 17: 347.

Morris, C. (2005) 'Divorce in a multi-faith society', *Family Law* 35: 727.

Morris, C. (2007) '*Evans v United Kingdom*: paradigms of parenting', *Modern Law Review* 70: 797.

Morris, P. (2013) 'Mediation, the Legal Aid, Sentencing and Punishment of Offenders Act of 2012 and the Mediation Information Assessment Meeting', *Journal of Social Welfare and Family Law* 35:4.

Moshiri, N. (2016) 'Rates of IVF treatment on NHS reach 12 year low', ITV News, 22 September.

Motro, S. (2010) 'The Prince of Pleasure', *Northwestern University Law Review* 104: 917.

Mount, F. (1982) *The Subversive Family*, London: Jonathan Cape.

Mourby, M. (2014) 'Overly exceptional funding: the LAA and Article 6', *Family Law* 44: 524.

Moylan, H.H.J. (2010) *What Have Human Rights Done for Family Justice?* London: Resolution.

Moylan, H. H. J. (2013) Custody, care and control to shared parental responsibility', *Family Law* 43: 1538.

Moynagh, M. and Worsley, R. (2000) *Tomorrow*, King's Lynn: Tomorrow Project.

Mullender, A. (2005) *Tackling Domestic Violence: Providing Support For Children Who Have Witnessed Domestic Violence*, London: Home Office.

Mullender, A. and Burton, S. (2000) *Domestic Violence. What Works? Perpetrator Programmes*, London: Home Office.

Mullender, A., Hague, G., Iman, U., Kieely, L., Malos, E. and Regan, L. (2002) *Children's Perspectives on Domestic Violence*, London: Sage.

Mullin, A. (2010) 'Filial responsibilities of dependent children', *Hypatia* 25: 157.

Munby, J. (2005) 'Access to and reporting of family proceedings', *Family Law* 35: 945.

Munby, J. (2015) 'Unheard voices: the involvement of children and vulnerable people in the family justice system', *Family Law* 44: 861.

Munby, J. (2018) 'Changing families: family law yesterday, today and tomorrow – a view from south of the Border', *Family Law* 538.

Munby, J. (2019) 'The family court in an era of austerity: problems and priorities', *Family Law* 49: 975.

Munro, E. (2011) *The Munro Review of Child Protection*, London: Department of Education.

Munro, V. (2007) *Law and Politics at the Perimeter: Re-evaluating Key Debates in Feminist Theory*, Oxford: Hart.

Munroe, A. and Tautz, W. (2020) 'Not remotely fair: an analysis of *Re P* and remote hearings in the family courts', *Family Law* 59: 643.

Murch, M. (2003) *The Voice of the Child in Private Family Law Proceedings*, Bristol: Family Law.

Murch, M., Douglas, G., Scanlon, I. *et al.* (1999) *Safeguarding Children's Welfare in Uncontentious Divorce*, Cardiff: Cardiff University.

Murphy, J. (2000) 'Child welfare in transracial adoption', in J. Murphy (ed.) *Ethnic Minorities, Their Families and the Law*, Oxford: Hart.

Murphy, J. (2005) *International Dimensions in Family Law*, Manchester: Manchester University Press.

Murray, A. (2013) 'Are our higher courts prejudiced against the role of the married woman? The need for reform', *Family Law* 43: 66.

Namy, S., Carlson, C., O'Hara, K. et al (2017) et al 'Towards a feminist understanding of intersecting violence against women and children in the family' (2017) 184 *Social Science and Medicine* 40.

Narey, M. and Owers, M. (2018) *Foster care in England*, London: TSO.

Natalia, K. (2018) 'State facilitated economic abuse: a structural analysis of men deliberately withholding child support', *Feminist Legal Studies* 26: 121.

National Centre for Social Research (2017) *British Social Attitudes Survey*, London: Sage.

National Centre for Social Research (2019) *British Social Attitudes Survey*, London: Sage.

National Centre for Social Research (2015) *Support for Same-Sex Marriage Continues to Rise*, London: NCSR.

NatCen Social Research (2018) *British Social Attitudes Survey*, London: Sage.

NHS (2020a) *Fruit and Vegetables*, London: NHS.

NHS (2020b) *Statistics on Obesity, Physical Activity and Diet*, London: NHS.

NICE (2010) *Fertility: Assessment and Management*, London: NICE.

Neale, B. (2004) *Young Children's Citizenship*, York: Joseph Rowntree Foundation.

Neale, B., Flowerdew, J. and Smart, C. (2003) 'Drifting towards shared residence?' *Family Law* 33: 904.

Neale, B. and Smart, C. (1997) 'Good and bad lawyers? Struggling in the shadow of the new law?' *Journal of Social Welfare and Family Law* 19: 377.

Neale, B. and Smart, C. (1999) *Agents or Dependants?* Leeds: Centre for Research on Family, Kinship and Childhood, Leeds University.

Nedelsky, J. (2011) *Law's Relations*, Oxford: OUP.

Neil, E. (2000) 'The reasons why young children are placed for adoption', *Child and Family Social Work* 11: 303.

Neil, E. (2003) 'Adoption and contact: a research review', in A. Bainham, B. Lindley, M. Richards and L. Trinder (eds) *Children and Their Families*, Oxford: Hart.

Newcastle Centre for Family Studies (2004) *Picking up the Pieces*, London: DCA.

Newell, P. (1989) *Children Are People Too*, London: Bedford Square Press.

Newnham, A. (2011) 'Shared residence: lessons from Sweden', *Child and Family Law Quarterly* 23: 251.

Newnham, A. (2013) 'Common intention constructive trusts: a way forward', *Family Law* 43: 718.

Newnham, A. (2015) 'Shared parenting, law and policy: considering power within the framework of autopoietic theory', *International Journal of Law in Context* 11: 426.

Nickols, D. (2014) 'Fostering for adoption: progress, an unjustifiable 'fait accompli' or something in-between?' *Family Law* 44: 54.

Nield, S. (2003) 'Constructive trusts and estoppel', *Legal Studies* 23: 311.

Nixon, J. and Humphreys, C. (2010) 'Marshalling the evidence: using intersectionality in the domestic violence frame', *Social Policy* 17: 137.

Noddings, N. (2003) *Caring*, Berkeley: University of California Press.

Nolan, A. (2011) *Children's Socio-Economic Rights*, Oxford: Hart.

Nordqvist, P. (2014) 'The drive for openness in donor conception: disclosure and the trouble with real life', *International Journal of Law, Policy and the Family* 28: 321.

Norgrave, D. (2012) *Family Justice Review*, London: Department of Education.

NSPCC (2012) *Returning Home from Care*, London: NSPCC.

NSPCC (2018) *Child protection plan and register statistics*, London: NSPCC.

Nuffield Council on Bioethics (2007) *Critical Care and Decisions in Fetal and Neonatal Medicine: Ethical Issues*, London: Nuffield Council.

O'Donnell, K. (2004) '*Re C (Welfare of Child: Immunisation)* – room to refuse? Immunisation,

welfare and the role of parental decision making', *Child and Family Law Quarterly* 16: 213.

O'Donovan, K. (1982) 'Should all maintenance of spouses be abolished?', *Modern Law Review* 45: 424.

O'Donovan, K. (1984) 'Legal marriage – who needs it?' *Modern Law Review* 47: 111.

O'Donovan, K. (1988) 'A right to know one's parentage', *International Journal of Law, Policy and the Family* 2: 27.

O'Donovan, K. (1993) *Family Law Matters*, London: Pluto.

O'Donovan, K. (2000) 'Constructions of maternity and motherhood in stories of lost children', in J. Bridgeman and D. Monk (eds) *Feminist Perspectives on Child Law*, London: Cavendish.

O'Donovan, K. (2005) 'Flirting with academic categorisations', *Child and Family Law Quarterly* 17: 415.

Office of the Children's Commissioner (2012) *Parliamentary Briefing on the Legal Aid, Sentencing and Punishment of Offenders Bill for House of Lords Report Stage (Legal Aid Provisions)*, London: OCC.

Office for National Statistics (2015) *Measuring National Well-being: Our Relationships*, London: ONS.

Office for National Statistics (2019) *Domestic Abuse*, London: ONS.

Office for National Statistics (2020a) *Households and Families*, London: ONS.

Office for National Statistics (2020b) *Child Poverty and Education Outcomes By Ethnicity*, London: ONS.

Office for National Statistics (2020c) *Legal Aid Statistics*, London: ONS.

Office for National Statistics (2020d) *Divorces in England and Wales*, London: ONS.

Office for National Statistics (2020e) *Marriages in England and Wales*, London: ONS.

Office for National Statistics (2020f) *Tribunal Statistics*, London: ONS.

Office for National Statistics (2020g) *Child Abuse and Neglect*, London: ONS.

Office for National Statistics (2020h) *Child Abuse: Nature and Extent*, London: ONS.

Office for National Statistics (2020i) *Looked After Children*, London: ONS.

Office for National Statistics (2020j) *Unpaid Carers*, London: ONS.

Office for National Statistics (2020k) *Gender Pay Gap 2019*. London: ONS.

Official Solicitor and Public Trustee (2011) *Annual Report*, London: HMSO.

Ofsted (2008) *Parents on Council Care*, London: The Stationery Office.

O'Grady, M. (2013) 'Shared parenting: keeping welfare paramount by learning from mistakes', *Family Law* 43: 448.

O'Halloran, K. (2003) 'Adoption – a public or private legal process?', in J. Dewar and S. Parker (eds) *Family Law: Processes, Practices, Pressures*, Oxford: Hart.

O'Keeffe, M., Hills, A., Doyle, M., McCreadie, C., Scholes, S., Constantine, R., Tinker, A., Manthorpe, J., Biggs, S. and Erens, B. (2008) *UK Study of Abuse and Neglect of Older People Prevalence Survey Report*, London: Department of Health.

Okin, S. (1992) *Justice, Gender and the Family*, New York: Basic Books.

Oldham, M. (2001) 'Financial obligations within the family – aspects of intergenerational maintenance and succession in England and France', *Cambridge Law Journal* 60: 128.

Oldham, M. (2006) 'Maintenance and the elderly: legal signalling, kinship and the state', in F. Ebtehaj, B. Lindley and M. Richards (eds) *Kinship Matters*, Hart: Oxford.

Olsen, F. (1992) 'Children's rights', in P. Alston, S. Parker and J. Seymour (eds) *Children, Rights and the Law*, Oxford: Oxford University Press.

Olsson, S. (2008) 'Children's suffrage: a critique of the importance of voters' knowledge for the well-being of democracy', *International Journal of Children's Rights* 16: 55.

O'Neill, B. (2013) 'A liberal critique of gay marriage', in A. de Waal (ed.) *The Meaning of Matrimony*, London: Civitas.

O'Neill, O. (1992) 'Children's rights and children's lives', *International Journal of Law and the Family* 6: 24.

O'Neill, O. (2002) *Autonomy and Trust in Bioethics*, Cambridge: CUP.

O' Reilly (2019) 'CMS and its reform' *Family Law* 49: 1242

Osborne, H. (2014) 'Cost of raising a child surges past £225,000', *The Guardian*, 14 January.

O'Sullivan, K. and Jackson, L. (2017) 'Muslim marriage (non) recognition: implications and possible solutions', *Journal of Social Welfare and Family Law* 39: 22.

Otto, D. (2013) 'International Human Rights Law: Towards Rethinking Sex/Gender Dualism and Asymmetry', M. Davies and V. Munro (eds) *A Research Companion to Feminist Legal Theory*, Aldershot: Ashgate.

Ouazzani, S. (2009) 'Ancillary relief and the public/private divide', *Family Law* 40: 842.

Ouazzani, S. (2013) 'Prenuptial agreements: The implications of gender', *Family Law* 43: 421.

Oxfam (2017) 'Women spend two days a month more than men on housework and childcare in UK, survey finds', at www.oxfam.org.uk/media-centre/press-releases/2016/03/women-spend-two-days-a-month-more-than-men-on-housework-and-childcare

Pahl, J. (1989) *Money and Marriage*, Basingstoke: Macmillan.

Pahl, J. (2004) *Ethics Review in Social Care Research*, London: Department of Health.

Pahl, J. (2005) 'Individualisation in couple's finances', *Social Policy and Society* 4: 4.

Palmer, E. (2010) 'The Child Poverty Act 2010: holding government to account for promises in a recessionary climate?' *European Human Rights Law Review* 17: 305.

Palmer, G. and Kenway, P. (2007) *Poverty Rates Among Ethnic Groups in Great Britain*. York: JRF.

Palmer, S. (2015) *Toxic Childhood*, London: Orion.

Palser, E. (2009) 'Shutting the door on negligence liability: *Lawrence v Pembrokeshire County Council* and *L v Reading Borough Council*', *Child and Family Law Quarterly* 21: 384.

Park, A., Phillips, M. and Johnson, M. (2004) *Young People in Britain: The Attitudes and Experiences of 12 to 19 Year Olds*, London: National Centre for Social Research.

Park, A., Bryson, C., Clery, E., Curtice, J. and Phillips, M. (2013) *British Social Attitudes Survey*, London: NatCen.

Parker, M. (2015) 'The draft Nuptial Agreements Bill and the abolition of the common law rule: 'swept away' or swept under the carpet?' *Child and Family Law Quarterly* 63.

Parker, R. (1999) *Adoption Now*, London: DoH.

Parker, S. (1991) 'Child support in Australia: children's rights or public interest?', *International Journal of Law and Family* 5: 24.

Parkes, A. (2009) 'The right of the child to be heard in family law proceedings: Article 12 UNCRC', *International Family Law Journal* 4: 238.

Parkinson, L. (2011) 'Family mediation: ideology or new discipline? Part I', *Family Law* 41: 88.

Parkinson, L. (2013) 'The Place of Mediation in the Family Justice System', *Child and Family Law Quarterly* 300.

Parkinson, P. (1996) 'Multiculturalism and the recognition of marital status in Australia', in G. Douglas and N. Lowe (eds) *Families Across Frontiers*, London: Kluwer.

Parkinson, P. (2003) 'Child protection, permanency planning and children's right to family life', *International Journal of Law, Policy and the Family* 17: 147.

Parkinson, P. (2005) 'The yardstick of equality: assessing contributions in Australia and England', *International Journal of Law, Policy and the Family* 19: 163.

Parkinson, P. (2006) 'Keeping in contact: the role of family relationship centres in Australia', *Child and Family Law Quarterly* 18: 157.

Parkinson, P. (2011) *Family Law and the Indissolubility of Parenthood*, Cambridge: Cambridge University Press.

Parkinson, P. (2012) 'About time we all cared more about marriage', *Sydney Morning Herald*, 24 August 2012.

Parkinson, P. and Cashmore, J. (2010) *The Voice of a Child in Family Law Disputes*, Oxford: OUP.

Parton, N. (1991) *Governing the Family*, London: Macmillan.

Parton, N. (2008) 'The "Change for Children" Programme in England: towards the "preventive-surveillance state"', *Journal of Law and Society* 35: 208.

Patel, H. (2009) 'Dowry abuse', *Family Law* 39: 1092.

Pawlowski, M. and Brown, J. (2012) 'Orders for sale: the creditor and the family home', *Family Law* 42: 62.

Peacey, V. and Rainford, L. (2004) *Attitudes Towards Child Support*, London: ONS.

Penington, E. (2020) *Fact Checking Claims about Child Poverty*, London: Children's Commissioner.

Pearce, N. (2013) 'AI v. MT [2013] EWHC 100 (Fam)', *Journal of Social Welfare and Family Law* 35: 259.

Peleg, N. (2009) *The Child's Right to Development*, Cambridge: CUP.

Pepper, J. (2019) 'Forced marriage: is enough being done?' *Family Law* 49: 1310.

Peroni, L. (2016) 'Violence against migrant women: the Istanbul Convention through a postcolonial feminist lens', *Feminist Legal Studies* 24: 49.

Perry, A. (2006) 'Safety first? Contact and family violence in New Zealand', *Child and Family Law Quarterly* 18: 1.

Perry, A. and Rainey, B. (2007) 'Supervised, supported and indirect contact orders: research findings', *International Journal of Law, Policy and the Family* 21: 21.

Perry, P., Douglas, G., Murch, M. et al. (2000) *How Parents Cope Financially on Marriage Breakdown*, London: Joseph Rowntree Foundation.

Phillimore, S. (2020) 'Credibility versus demeanour – the impact of remote court hearings', *Family Law* 50: 591.

Phillips, B. and Alderson, P. (2003) 'Beyond "anti-smacking": challenging violence and coercion in parent–child relationships', *International Journal of Children's Rights* 115: 175.

Phillips, C. (2003) 'Who's who in the pecking order?' *British Journal of Criminology* 43: 710.

Philpot, T. (2001) *A Very Private Practice*, London: BAAF.

Pickford, R. (1999) 'Unmarried fathers and the law', in A. Bainham, S. Day Sclater and M. Richards (eds) *What is a Parent?* Oxford: Hart.

Piper, C. (1996) 'Norms and negotiation in mediation and divorce', in M. Freeman (ed.) *Divorce: Where Next?* Aldershot: Dartmouth.

Piper, C. (2009) *Investing in Children: Policy, Law and Practice in Context*, Cullompton: Willan.

Piper, C. (2014) 'Mediation and vulnerable parents', in J. Wallbank and J. Herring (eds) (2014) *Vulnerabilities, Care and Family Law*, London: Routledge.

Piper, C. and Miakishev, A. (2003) 'A child's right to veto in England and Russia – another welfare ploy', *Child and Family Law Quarterly* 15: 57.

Place, M. (2013) 'Reducing the impact of early abuse and neglect: the emerging scale of the challenge', *Family Law* 43: 707.

Platt, J. (2008) 'The Domestic Violence, Crime and Victims Act 2004 Part 1: Is it working?', *Family Law* 38: 642.

Platt, J. and Emmerson, D. (2013) 'Legal aid for private law cases under s. 8 of the Children Act: is there any light at the end of the tunnel?' *Family Law* 43: 832.

Platt, L. (2007) *Poverty and Ethnicity in the UK*, York: Joseph Rowntree Foundation.

Pleasence, P., Balmer, N., Buck, A. et al. (2003) 'Family problems – what happens to whom', *Family Law* 33: 497.

Pleasence, P. and Balmer, N. (2012). 'On the rocks: recession-related life problems and relationship stability', *Child and Family Law Quarterly* 24: 39.

Ploubidis, G., Silberwood, R., DeStavola, B. and Grundy, E. (2015) 'Life-course partnership status and biomarkers in midlife: evidence from the 1958 British birth cohort', *American Journal of Public Health* 105: 1596.

Pontifical Council for the Family (2000) *Family, Marriage, and 'De Facto' Unions*, Rome: Pontifical Council for the Family.

Poffé, L. (2015) 'Towards a new United Nations Human Rights Convention for Older Persons?' *Human Rights Review* 15: 591.

Poole, E., Speight, S., O'Brien, M., Connolly, S. and Aldrich (2013) *What Do We Know About Non-Resident Fathers?* London: NatCen Social Research.

Poulter, S. (1987) 'Ethnic minority cultural customs, English law and human rights', *International and Comparative Law Quarterly* 36: 589.

Poulter, S. (1998) *Ethnicity, Law and Human Rights*, Oxford: OUP.

Poussin, E. and Martin-LeBrun, G. (2002) 'A French study of children's self-esteem after parental separation', *International Journal of Law, Policy and the Family* 16: 313.

Pressdee, P. (2008) 'Relocation, relocation, relocation: rigorous security revisited', *Family Law* 38: 220.

Price, D. (2006) 'The poverty of older people in the UK', *Journal of Social Work Practice* 20: 251.

Price, D. (2009) 'Pension accumulation and gendered household structures', in J. Miles and R. Probert (eds) *Sharing Lives, Dividing Assets*, Oxford: Hart.

Probert, R. (2002a) 'Sharing homes – a long-awaited paper', *Family Law* 32: 834.

Probert, R. (2002b) 'When are we married? Void, non-existent and presumed marriages', *Legal Studies* 22: 398.

Probert, R. (2003) 'Family law and property law: competing spheres in the regulation of the family home?' in A. Hudson (ed.) *New Perspectives on Family Law, Human Rights and the Home*, London: Cavendish Publishing.

Probert, R. (2004a) 'Families, assisted reproduction and the law', *Child and Family Law Quarterly* 16: 273.

Probert, R. (2004b) '*Sutton v Mischon de Reya and Gawor & Co* – cohabitation contracts and Swedish sex slaves', *Child and Family Law Quarterly* 16: 453.

Probert, R. (2005) 'How would *Corbett v Corbett* be decided today?' *Family Law* 35: 382.

Probert, R. (2007a) 'Cohabitants and joint ownership: the implications of *Stack v Dowden*', *Family Law* 37: 924.

Probert, R. (ed.) (2007b) *Family Life and the Law*, Aldershot: Ashgate.

Probert, R. (2007c) '*Hyde v Hyde*: defining or defending marriage?', *Child and Family Law Quarterly* 19: 322.

Probert, R. (2009a) *Marriage Law and Practice in the Long Eighteenth Century: A Reassessment*, Cambridge: CUP.

Probert, R. (2009b) 'Parental responsibility and children's partnership choices', in R. Probert, S. Gilmore and J. Herring (eds) *Responsible Parents and Parental Responsibility*, Oxford: Hart.

Probert, R. (2012a) 'Civil rites', in R. Probert and C. Barton (eds) *Fifty Years in Family Law*, Amsterdam: Intersentia.

Probert, R. (2012b) *The Changing Legal Regulation of Cohabitation*, Cambridge: Cambridge University Press.

Probert, R. (2013a) 'For better or for worse? Encouraging marriage through the tax system', *Family Law* 43: 285.

Probert, R. (2013b) 'The evolving concept of 'non-marriage', *Child and Family Law Quarterly* 314.

Probert, R. (2018a) '*Hayatleh v Modfy*: presuming the validity of a known ceremony of marriage', *Child and Family Law Quarterly* 61.

Probert, R. (2018b) 'Criminalising non-compliance with marriage formalities?', *Family Law* 48: 702

Probert, R., Gilmore, S. and Herring, J. (2009) *Responsible Parents and Parental Responsibility*, Oxford: Hart.

Proudman, C. (2012) 'The criminalisation of forced marriage', *Family Law* 42: 460.

Pryor, J. (2003) 'Children's contact with relatives', in A. Bainham, B. Lindley, M. Richards and L. Trinder (eds) *Children and Their Families*, Oxford: Hart.

Pryor, J. and Daly Peoples, R. (2001) 'Adolescent attitudes toward living arrangements after divorce', *Child and Family Law Quarterly* 13: 197.

Public Health England (2016) *Child Obesity*, London: PHE.

Purdy, L. (1994) 'Why children shouldn't have equal rights', *International Journal of Children's Rights* 2: 223.

Quinton, D. and Selwyn, J. (2006a) 'Adoption in the UK', in C. McAuley, P. Pecora and W. Rose (eds) *Enhancing the Well-Being of Children and Families through Effective Intervention*, London: Jessica Kingsley.

Quinton, D. and Selwyn, J. (2006b) 'Adoption: research, policy and practice', *Child and Family Law Quarterly* 19: 459.

Radford, L. and Hester, M. (2006) *Mothering through Domestic Violence*, London: Jessica Kingsley.

Ragoné, H. (2003) 'The gift of life', in R. Cook, S. Day Sclater and F. Kaganas (eds) *Surrogate Motherhood*, Oxford: Hart.

Rainey, S. (2017) 'In sickness and in health: cripping and queering marriage equality', *Hypatia* 32: 230.

Rao, R. (2003) 'Surrogacy law in the United States', in R. Cook, S. Day Sclater and F. Kaganas (eds) *Surrogate Motherhood*, Oxford: Hart.

Rasmusen, E. (2002) 'An economic approach to adultery law', in A. Dnes and R. Rowthorn (eds) *The Law and Economics of Marriage and Divorce*, Cambridge: CUP.

Raz, J. (1986) *The Morality of Freedom*, Oxford: OUP.

Raz, J. (1994) 'Multiculturalism: a liberal perspective', *Dissent* 1994: 67.

Readhead, P. (2006) *Same-Sex Couples Tie the Knot*, London: ESRC.

Reece, H. (1996) 'The paramountcy principle: consensus or construct?', *Current Legal Problems* 49: 267.

Reece, H. (2000) 'Divorcing the children', in J. Bridgeman and D. Monk (eds) *Feminist Perspectives on Child Law*, London: Cavendish.

Reece, H. (2003) *Divorcing Responsibly*, Oxford: Hart.

Reece, H. (2005) 'From parental responsibility to parenting responsibly', in M. Freeman (ed.) *Law and Sociology*, Oxford: OUP.

Reece, H. (2006a) 'The end of domestic violence', *Modern Law Review* 69: 770.

Reece, H. (2006b) 'UK women's groups' child contact campaign: "so long as it is safe"', *Child and Family Law Quarterly* 18: 538.

Reece, H. (2009a) 'Feminist anti-violence discourse as regulation', in E. Jackson, F. Ebtehaj, M. Richards and S. Day Sclater (eds) *Regulating Autonomy: Sex, Reproduction and Families*, Oxford: Hart.

Reece, H. (2009b) 'The degradation of parental responsibility', in R. Probert, S. Gilmore and J. Herring, *Responsible Parents and Parental Responsibility*, Oxford: Hart.

Reece, H. (2009c) 'Parental responsibility as therapy', *Family Law* 39: 1167.

Reece, H. (2010) 'Bright line rules may be appropriate in some cases, but not where the object is to promote the welfare of the child: barring in the best interests of the child?', *Child and Family Law Quarterly* 22: 678.

Reece, H. (2015) 'Michael Freeman and domestic violence', in A. Diduck, N. Peleg and H. Reece (eds) *Law in Society*, Leiden: Brill.

Reece, H, (2016) 'Leaping without looking', in R. Leckey (ed.) *After Legal Equality*, Abingdon: Routledge.

Reece, H. (2017) 'Was there, is there and should there be a presumption against deviant parents?' *Child and Family Law Quarterly* 9.

Regan, M. (1993) *Family Law and the Pursuit of Intimacy*, New York: New York University Press.

Regan, M. (1999) *Alone Together: Law and the Meaning of Marriage*, New York: OUP.

Regan, M. (2000) 'Morality, fault and divorce law', in M. King White (ed.) *Marriage in America*, Lanham, MD: Rowman & Littlefield.

Relationships Foundation (2020) *Cost of Family Failure Index*, London: Relationships Foundation.

Reid, V. (2009) 'ADR: an alternative to justice', *Family Law* 39: 981.

Reinhold, S. Kneip, T. and Bauer, G. (2013) 'The long run consequences of unilateral divorce laws on children-evidence from SHARELIFE', *Journal of Population Economics* 26: 1035.

Reshef, Y. (2013) 'Rethinking the value of families', *Critical Review of International Social and Political Philosophy* 16:1.

Resolution (2010) *Survey into attitudes on divorce and relationship breakdown*, London: Resolution.

Rhoades, H. (2002) 'The "no contact mother": reconstructions of motherhood in the era of the "new father"', *International Journal of Law, Policy and the Family* 16: 71.

Rhoades, H. (2003) 'Enforcing contact or supporting parents?', unpublished paper presented to the Oxford Centre for Family Law and Policy.

Rhoades, H. (2010a) 'Revising Australia's parenting laws: a plea for a relational approach to children's best interests', *Child and Family Law Quarterly* 22: 172.

Rhoades, H. (2010b) 'Concluding thoughts: the enduring chaos of family law', in J. Wallbank, S. Choudhry and J. Herring (eds) *Rights, Gender and Family Law*, Abingdon: Routledge.

Rhoades, H. (2012) 'Legislating to promote children's welfare and the quest for certainty', *Child and Family Law Quarterly* 24: 158.

Rhode, D. (2014) *What Women Want: An Agenda for the Women's Movement*, Oxford: OUP.

Ribbens McCarthy, J., Edwards, R. and Gillies, V. (2003) *Making Families*, Durham: Sociology Press.

Richards, C. (2001) 'Allowing blame and revenge into mediation', *Family Law* 31: 775.

Richards, C. (2005) 'Equal opportunities: who decides', *Family Law* 35: 389.

Richards, M. (1994) 'Divorcing children: roles for parents and the state', in M. Maclean and J. Kurczewski (eds) *Families, Politics and the Law*, Oxford: Oxford University Press.

Richards, M. (1995a) 'Private worlds and public intentions: the role of the state at divorce', in A. Bainham, D. Pearl and R. Pickford (eds) *Frontiers of Family Law*, London: John Wiley & Co.

Richards, M. (1995b) 'But what about the children? Some reflections on the Divorce White Paper', *Child and Family Law Quarterly* 4: 223.

Richards, M. (1996) 'Divorce and divorce legislation', *Family Law* 26: 151.

Richards, M. (1997) 'The interests of children at divorce', in M. Meulders-Klein (ed.) *Familles et Justice*, Brussels: Bruylant.

Richards, M. (2003) 'Assisted reproduction and parental relationships', in A. Bainham, B. Lindley, M. Richards and L. Trinder (eds) *Children and Their Families*, Oxford: Hart.

Richards, M. (2006) 'Genes, genealogies and paternity', in J. Spencer and A. du Bois-Pedain (eds) *Freedom and Responsibility in Reproductive Choice*, Oxford: Hart.

Richards, M. and Connell, J. (2000) 'Children and the Family Law Act', in Thorpe LJ and E. Clarke (eds) *No Fault or Flaw: The Future of the Family Law Act 1996*, Bristol: Jordans.

Richards, N. (2018) 'Raising a child with respect', *Journal of Applied Philosophy* forthcoming.

Richardson, V., Boylan, J. and Brammer, A. (2017) 'Contact, welfare and children in care: revisiting the significance of birth family relationships after finding significant harm', *Journal of Social Welfare and Family Law* 39: 67.

Richardson, K. and Speed, A. (2019) 'Restrictions on legal aid in family law cases in England and Wales: creating a necessary barrier to public funding or simply increasing the burden on the family courts?' *Journal of Social Welfare and Family Law* 41: 135.

Rights of Women (2004) *Response to the Home Office Consultation Paper Society and Justice*, London: Rights of Women.

Rivlini, R. (2013) 'The right to divorce: Its direction and why it matters', *International Journal of Jurisprudence of the Family* 4: 133.

Roberts, D. (2014) 'Child protection as surveillance of African American families', *Journal of Social Welfare and Family Law* 36: 426.

Roberts, L. (2010) 'Teenage Jehovah's Witness refuses blood transfusion and dies', *Daily Telegraph*, 18 May 2010.

Roberts, M. (2000) 'Children by donation: do they have a claim to their genetic parentage?', in J. Bridgeman and D. Monk (eds) *Feminist Perspectives on Child Law*, London: Cavendish.

Roberts, M. (2001) 'Childcare policy', in P. Foley, J. Roche and S. Tucker (eds) *Children in Society*, Buckingham: Open University Press.

Roberts, M. and Moscati, M. (eds) (2020) *Family Mediation: Contemporary Issues*, London: Bloomsbury.

Roberts, S. (1988) 'Three models of family mediation', in J. Eekelaar and R. Dingwall (eds) *Divorce, Mediation and the Legal Process*, Oxford: Clarendon.

Roberts, S. (2000) 'Family mediation in the new millennium', in S. Cretney (ed.) *Family Law – Essays for the New Millennium*, Bristol: Jordans.

Robinson, N. (2016) 'The power and potential of family mediation: a manifesto', *Family Law* 46: 762.

Roe, T. (2018) 'HMCTS reform divorce project', *Family Law* 48: 468.

Rogers, B. and Pryor, J. (1998) *Divorce and Separation*, York: Joseph Rowntree Foundation.

Roiser, A. (2015) 'No fault divorce: where next?' *Family Law* November.

Rolfe, A. and Peel, E. (2011) '"It's a double-edged thing": the paradox of civil partnership and why some couples are choosing not to have one', *Feminism and Psychology* 21: 317.

Rosettenstein, D. (2005) '"Big money" divorces and unequal distributions; value, risk, liquidity and other issues on the road to unfairness', *International Journal of Law, Policy and the Family* 19: 206.

Rothstein, M., Murray, T., Kaebnick, G. and Majumder, M. (2006) *Genetic Ties and the Family*, New York: Johns Hopkins University Press.

Rowland, A., Gerry, F. and Stanton, M. (2017) 'Time to end the defence of reasonable chastisement in UK, USA and Australia', *International Journal of Children's Rights* 26: 165.

Rowthorn, R. (1999) 'Marriage and trust', *Cambridge Journal of Economics* 23: 661.

Royal College of Pediatrics and Child Health (2019) *The Health Impacts of Screen Time*, London: RCPCH.

Ruegger, M. (2001) *Hearing the Voice of the Child*, Lyme Regis: Russell House.

Rushbrooke, R. (2001) *The Proportion of Adoptees who have Received their Birth Records*, London: ONS.

Rushton, P. (2002) *Adoption as a Placement Choice*, London: King's College London.

Ryan, K. (2019) 'More than a third of men and women in UK admit to being in a coercive relationship', *Family Law* 49: 723.

Ryan, M., Harker, L., Rothera, S. (2020) *Remote Hearings in the Family Justice System*, London: Nuffield Family Justice Observatory.

Salter, D. (2000) 'A practitioner's guide to pension sharing', *Family Law* 30: 489.

Salter, D. (2008) 'Pension transfer values: the new regime', *Family Law* 38: 1205.

Samad, Y. (2010) 'Forced marriage among men: an unrecognized problem', *Critical Social Policy* 30: 189.

Samet, I. (2015) 'Proprietary estoppel and responsibility for omissions', *Modern Law Review* 78: 85.

Samuel, Z. (2010) 'Adoption for gay and lesbian couples', *Family Law* 40: 1220.

Sandland, R. (2005) 'Feminism and the Gender Recognition Act 2004', *Feminist Legal Studies* 14: 43.

Sarajlic, E. (2018) 'The ethics and politics of child naming', *Journal of Applied Philosophy* 35: 121.

Sargent, S. (2015) 'Transracial adoption in England: a critical race and systems theory analysis', *International Journal of Law in Context* 11: 412.

Saunders, H. (2004) *Twenty-nine Child Homicides*, Bristol: Women's Aid.

Saunders, B. and Goddard, C. (2010) *Physical Punishment in Childhood: The Rights of the Child*, Chichester: Wiley-Blackwell.

Saunders, Z. (2011) 'In defence of Barder', *Family Law* 41: 1352.

Sawyer, C. (2000) 'Hitting people is wrong', *Family Law* 30: 654.

Sawyer, C. (2001) 'Applications by children: still seen but not heard?' *Law Quarterly Review* 117: 203.

Sawyer, C. (2004) 'Equity's children – constructive trusts for the new generation', *Child and Family Law Quarterly* 16: 31.

Sayer, L. (2010) 'Gender differences in the relationship between long employment hours and multitasking', in B. Ruben (ed.) *Research in the Sociology of Work*, Amsterdam: Elsevier.

Schaffer, L. (2007) 'Taking the gloves off', *Family Law* 37: 439.

Schapps, G. (2009) 'The IVF postcode lottery: don't promise what you can't deliver', *Bionews* 9 August 2009.

Scherpe, J. (2009) 'Establishing and ending parental responsibility: a comparative view', in R. Probert, S. Gilmore and J. Herring (eds) *Responsible Parents and Parental Responsibility*, Oxford: Hart.

Scherpe, J. (2010) 'Pre-nups, private autonomy and paternalism', *Cambridge Law Journal* 69: 35.

Scherpe, J. (2012) *Marital Agreements and Private Autonomy*, Oxford: Hart.

Scherpe, J. (2013) 'A comparative overview of the treatment of non-matrimonial assets, indexation and value increases', *Child and Family Law Quarterly* 61.

Scherpe, J. and Sloan, B. (2014) 'Contractualisation of Family Law in England and Wales', available at: http://ssrn.com/abstract=2481097

Scherpe, J. and Hayward, A. (2018) *The future of registered partnerships: family recognition beyond marriage?* Cambridge: Intersentia.

Schneider, E. (2000a) *Battered Women and Feminist Law Making*, New Haven: Yale University Press.

Schneider, E. (2000b) 'Law and violence against women in the family at century's end', in S. Katz, J. Eekelaar and M. MacLean (eds) *Cross Currents*, Oxford: OUP.

Schumm, R. and Abbotts, C. (2017) 'Spousal maintenance and gender inequality', *Family Law* 1116.

Schwartz, P. (2000) 'Peer marriages', in M. Whyte (ed.) *Marriage in America*, Lanham, MD: Rowman & Littlefield.

Scott, E. (2003) 'Marriage commitment and the legal regulation of divorce', in A. Dnes and R. Rowthorn (eds) *The Law and Economics of Marriage and Divorce*, Cambridge: CUP.

Scott, E. and Scott, R. (2014) 'From contract to status: collaboration and the evolution of novel family relationships', Columbia Public Law Research Paper No. 14–409; Columbia Law and Economics Working Paper. Available at SSRN: http://ssrn.com/abstract=2483430.

Scott, J. and Dex, S. (2009) 'Paid and unpaid work', in J. Miles and R. Probert (eds) *Sharing Lives, Dividing Assets*, Oxford: Hart.

Seden, J. (2001) 'Family Assistance Orders and the Children Act 1989: ambivalence about intervention or a means of safeguarding and promoting children's welfare?' *International Journal of Law, Policy and the Family* 15: 226.

Selwyn, J., and Masson, J. (2014) 'Adoption, special guardianship and residence orders: a comparison of disruption rates', *Family Law* 1709.

Sevenhuijsen, S. (2000) 'Caring in the third way', *Critical Social Policy* 20: 5.

Sevenhuijsen, S. (2002) 'An approach through the ethic of care', in A. Carling, S. Duncan and R. Edwards (eds) *Analysing Families*, London: Routledge.

Seymour, J. (2000) *Childbirth and the Law*, Oxford: OUP.

Shah, P. (2003) 'Attitudes to polygamy in English law', *International and Comparative Law Quarterly* 52: 369.

Sharpe, A. (2002) *Transgender Jurisprudence*, London: Cavendish.

Sharpe, A. (2007) 'Endless sex: the Gender Recognition Act 2004 and the persistence of a legal category', *Feminist Legal Studies* 15: 57.

Sharpe, A. (2012) 'Transgender marriage and the legal obligation to disclose gender', *Modern Law Review* 75: 33.

Shaw, M. (2002) 'When young people refuse treatment: balancing autonomy and protection', in Thorpe LJ and C. Cowton (eds) *Delight and Dole*, Bristol: Jordans.

Shaw Spaht, K. (2002) 'Louisiana's covenant marriage law', in A. Dnes and R. Rowthorn (eds) *The Law and Economics of Marriage and Divorce*, Cambridge: CUP.

Sheehy, E. and Boyd, S. (2020) 'Penalizing women's fear: intimate partner violence and parental alienation in Canadian child custody cases', *Journal of Social Welfare and Family Law* 42: 80.

Sheff, E (2013) *The Polyamorists Next Door: Inside Multi-Partner Relationships and Families*, New York: Rowman & Littlefield.

Sheldon, S. (2001a) '"Sperm bandits", birth control fraud and the battle of the sexes', *Legal Studies* 21: 460.

Sheldon, S. (2001b) 'Unmarried fathers and parental responsibility: a convincing case for reform?' *Feminist Legal Studies* 9: 93.

Sheldon, S. (2003) 'Unwilling fathers and abortion: terminating men's child support obligations', *Modern Law Review* 66: 175.

Sheldon, S. (2004) '*Evans v Amicus* – revealing cracks in the "twin pillars"', *Child and Family Law Quarterly* 16: 437.

Sheldon, S. (2005) 'Fragmenting fatherhood: the regulation of reproductive technologies', *Modern Law Review* 68: 523.

Sheldon, S. (2009) 'From "absent objects of blame" to "fathers who want to take responsibility": reforming birth registration law', *Journal of Social Welfare and Family Law* 31: 373.

Shepherd, N. (2009) 'Ending the blame game: getting no fault divorce back on the agenda', *Family Law* 39: 122.

Sifris, A. (2009) 'The legal recognition of lesbian-led families: justifications for change', *Child and Family Law Quarterly* 21: 197.

Sigle-Rushton, W. (2009) 'Great Britain: "Things can only get better . . . "', in H.-J. André and D. Hummelsheim (eds) *When Marriage Ends*, Cheltenham: Edward Elgar.

Silva, E. and Smart, C. (1999) *The New Family*, London: Sage.

Simmonds, C. (2012) 'Paramountcy and the ECHR: a conflict resolved?', *Cambridge Law Journal* 498.

Simmonds, C. (2013) 'An unbalanced scale: anonymous birth and the European Court of Human Rights', *Cambridge Law Journal* 72: 263.

Simon, T. (2000) 'United Nations Convention on Wrongs to the Child', *International Journal of Children's Rights* 8: 1.

Simpson, B., Jessop, J. and McCarthy, P. (2003) 'Fathers after divorce', in A. Bainham, B. Lindley, M. Richards and L. Trinder (eds) *Children and Their Families*, Oxford: Hart.

Singer, H. H. J. (2001) 'Sexual discrimination in ancillary relief', *Family Law* 31: 115.

Singer, P. (2012) 'Arbitration in family financial proceedings: the IFLA Scheme: Part 1', *Family Law* 42: 1353.

Singleton, M and Cover, G. (2016) 'Two thousand babies', *Family Law* 417.

Skinner, C. (2019) 'One lawyer acting for two clients: implications arising from an experimental practice model '"Family Matters", *Journal of Social Welfare and Family Law* 41: 265.

Slater and Gordon (2018) *Divorcing Couples Admit to 'Exaggerating' Foul Play*, London: Slater and Gordon.

Slaughter, M. (2002) 'Marital bargaining', in M. Maclean (ed.) *Making Law for Families*, Oxford: Hart.

Sloan, B. (2009) '*Re C (A Child) (Adoption: Duty of Local Authority)* – welfare and the rights of the birth family in "fast track" adoption cases', *Child and Family Law Quarterly* 21: 87.

Sloan, B. (2011) 'The concept of coupledom in succession law', *Cambridge Law Journal* 70: 623.

Sloan, B. (2013) Conflicting rights: English adoption law and the implementation of the UN Convention on the Rights of the Child', *Child and Family Law Quarterly* 25: 40.

Sloan, B. (2014) 'Post-Adoption contact reform: compounding the state-ordered termination of parenthood?', *Cambridge Law Journal* 73: 378.

Sloan, B. (2015a) 'Keeping up with the *Jones* case: establishing constructive trusts in "sole legal owner" scenarios', *Legal Studies* 35: 226.

Sloan, B. (2015b) 'A hippy-hippy clean break?' *Cambridge Law Journal* 74: 218.

Sloan, B. (2015c) 'Adoption decisions in England: *Re B (A Child) (Care Proceedings: Appeal)* and beyond', *Journal of Social Welfare and Family Law* 37: 437.

Sloan, B. (2018) Finality versus fathers: undoing adoption to recognise biological ties', *Cambridge Law Journal* 77: 258.

Sloan, B. (2020) 'Article 5 of the Convention on the Rights of the Child and the Involvement of Fathers in Adoption Proceedings: A Comparative Analysis', *International Journal of Children's Rights* 28: 666.

Smart, C. (1984) *The Ties that Bind*, London: Routledge.

Smart, C. (1989) *Feminism and the Power of Law*, London: Routledge.

Smart, C. (1991) 'The legal and moral ordering of child custody', *Journal of Law and Society* 19: 485.

Smart, C. (2000) 'Divorce in England 1950–2000: a moral tale', in S. Katz, J. Eekelaar and M. Maclean (eds) *Cross Currents*, Oxford: OUP.

Smart, C. (2002) 'From children's shoes to children's voices', *Family Court Review* 40: 307.

Smart, C. (2003) 'Children and the transformation of family law', in J. Dewar and S. Parker (eds) *Family Law: Processes, Practices, Pressures*, Oxford: Hart.

Smart, C. (2004) 'Equal shares? Rights for fathers or recognition for children?' *Critical Social Policy* 24: 484.

Smart, C. (2006) 'Parenting disputes, gender conflict and the courts', in M. Thorpe and R. Budden (eds) *Durable Solutions*, Bristol. Jordans.

Smart, C. (2007) *Personal Life*, Bristol: Polity.

Smart, C. (2009) 'Making kin: relationality and law', in A. Bottomley and S. Wong (eds) *Changing Contours of Domestic Life, Family and Law*, Oxford: Hart.

Smart, C. (2010) 'Law and the regulation of family secrets', *International Journal of Law, Policy and the Family* 24: 397.

Smart, C. (2014) 'Law and family life: insights from 25 years of empirical research', *Child and Family Law Quarterly* 26: 14.

Smart, C. and May, V. (2004a) 'Residence and contact disputes in court', *Family Law* 34: 36.

Smart, C. and Neale, B. (1997) 'Argument against virtue – must contact be enforced?', *Family Law* 27: 332.

Smart, C. and Neale, B. (1999a) *Family Fragments?* Cambridge: Polity Press.

Smart, C. and Neale, B. (1999b) '"I hadn't really thought about it": new identities/new fatherhoods', in J. Seymour and P. Bagguley (eds) *Relating Intimacies: Power and Resistance*, Basingstoke: Macmillan.

Smart, C. and Neale, B. (2000) '"It's my life too": children's perspectives on post-divorce parenting', *Family Law* 30: 163.

Smart, C. and Stevens, P. (2000) *Cohabitation Breakdown*, London: Joseph Rowntree Foundation.

Smart, C., Masson, J. and Shipman, B. (2006) *Gay and Lesbian 'Marriage'*, Manchester: Morgan Centre.

Smart, C., May, V., Wade, A. and Furniss, C. (2005) *Residence and Contact Disputes in Court Vol. 2*, London: DCA.

Smart, C., Neale, B. and Wade, A. (2001) *The Changing Experience of Childhood*, Cambridge: Polity Press.

Smeaton, D. (2006) *Dads and their Babies*, London: Policy Studies Institute.

Smith, C. (2002) 'Human rights and the Children Act 1989', *Child and Family Law Quarterly* 14: 427.

Smith, C. (2005) '*Trust v law*: promoting and safeguarding post-adoption contact', *Journal of Social Welfare and Family Law* 27: 315.

Smith, C. and Logan, J. (2002) 'Adoptive parenthood as a "legal fiction" – its consequences for direct post-adoption contact', *Child and Family Law Quarterly* 14: 281.

Smith, D. (2003) 'Making contact work in international cases: promoting contact whilst preventing international parental child abduction', in A. Bainham, B. Lindley, M. Richards and L. Trinder (eds) *Children and Their Families*, Oxford: Hart.

Smith II, G. (1997) *Legal and Healthcare Ethics for the Elderly*, Washington: Taylor and Francis.

Smith, L. (2007) '*Re G (Children) (Residence: Same-sex Partner)* [2006] UKHL 43, [2006] 1 WLR 2305', *Journal of Social Welfare and Family Law* 29: 307.

Smith, L. (2010) 'Clashing symbols? Reconciling support for fathers and fatherless families after the Human Fertilisation and Embryology Act 2008', *Child and Family Law Quarterly* 22: 46.

Smith, L. (2011) '*T v T (Shared Residence)* [2010] EWCA Civ 1366', *Journal of Social Welfare and Family Law* 33: 175.

Smith, L. (2013) 'Tangling the web of legal parenthood: legal responses to the use of known donors in lesbian parenting arrangements', *Legal Studies* 33: 355.

Smith, L., Hitchings, E. and Sefton, M. (2017) 'Fee-charging McKenzie Friends in private family law cases: key findings from the research report', *Family Law* 971.

Smith, L. and Trinder, L. (2012) 'Mind the gap: Parent education programmes and the family justice systems', *Child and Family Law Quarterly* 428.

Smith, M., Robertson, J., Dixon, J. and Quigley, M. (2001) *A Study of Step Children and Step Parenting*, London: Thomas Coram Research Unit.

Smith, M., Balmer, N., Miles, J., Denvir, C. and Patel, A. (2014) 'In scope but out of reach? Examining differences between publicly funded telephone and face-to-face family law advice', *Child and Family Law Quarterly* 253.

Smith, R. (2004) '"Hands-off parenting?" – towards a reform of the defence of reasonable chastisement in the UK', *Child and Family Law Quarterly* 16: 261.

Smithson, J., Barlow, A. and Hunter, R. and Ewing, J. (2015) 'The "child's best interests" as an argumentative resource in family mediation sessions', *Discourse Studies* 1.

Social and Community Planning Research (2000) *Women's Attitudes to Combining Paid Work and Family Life*, London: SCPR.

Social Services Inspectorate (2002) *Fostering for the Future*, London: DoH.

Solicitors Family Law Association (2003) *Protection Before Punishment*, London: SFLA.

Somerville, M. (2010) 'Children's human rights to natural biological origins and family structure', *International Journal of Jurisprudence of Family Law* 35: 35.

Spencer, J. and Pedain, A. (2006) *Freedom and Responsibility in Reproductive Choice*, Oxford: Hart.

Spitz, L. (2012) 'Grandparents: their role in 21st century families', *Family Law* 42: 1254.

Spon-Smith, R. (2002) 'The man is father of the child – or is he?' *Family Law* 32: 26.

Spon-Smith, R. (2005) 'Civil Partnership Act 2004', *Family Law* 35: 369.

Stalford, H. (2012) *Children and the European Union*, Oxford: Hart.

Stalford, H., Hollingsworth, K. and Gilmore, S. (eds) (2017) *Rewriting Children's Rights Judgments*, London: Bloomsbury.

Stalford, H. and Hollingsworth, K. (2020) '"This case is about you and your future": Towards Judgments for Children' *Modern Law Review* 83: 1030

Stanley, N., Miller, P., Richardson Foster, H. and Thomson, G. (2010b) *Children and Families Experiencing Domestic Violence: Police and Children's Social Services' Responses*, London: NSPCC.

Stark, B. (2005) *International Family Law*, Aldershot: Ashgate.

Stark, E. (2007) *Coercive Control: How Men Entrap Women in Personal Life*, Oxford: OUP.

Stark, E. (2012) 'Looking Beyond Domestic Violence: Policing Coercive Control', *Journal of Police Crisis Negotiations* 12: 199.

Starmer, K. (2012) *Prosecuting Violence Against Women and Girls – Improving Culture, Confidence and Convictions*, London: CPS.

Stein, M. (2009) *Quality Matters in Children's Services: Messages from research*, London: Jessica Kingsley.

Steinberg, L. (2013) 'Does recent research on adolescent brain development inform the mature minor doctrine?', *The Journal of Medicine and Philosophy* 38: 256.

Steinbock, B. (2005) 'Defining parenthood', *International Journal of Children's Rights* 13: 287.

Stepan, M. (2010) 'Mediation is moving on', *Family Law* 40: 545.

Sterling, V. (2009) 'DNA, paternity deceit and reliability of the birth certificate as a historical document', *Family Law* 39: 701.

Stevenson, M. (2012a) 'Cooperative parenting following family separation', *Family Law* 42: 1396.

Stevenson, M. (2012b) 'A participant's experience of mediation', *Family Law* 44: 1014.

Stevenson, M. (2013) 'Mediation: a distinctive approach to problem-solving', *Family Law* 43: 98.

Stevenson, M. *et al.* (2015) 'A mediator's compass', *Family Law* 47: 751.

Stewart, A. (2007) 'Home or home: caring about and for elderly family members in a welfare state', in R. Probert (ed.) *Family Life and the Law*, Aldershot: Ashgate.

Stewart, M. (2004) 'Judicial redefinition of marriage', *Canadian Journal of Family Law* 21: 11.

Stewart, M., Wilkes, L., Jackson, D. and Mannix, J. (2006) 'Child-to-mother violence: a pilot study', *Advances in Nursing and Interpersonal Violence* 29: 217.

Stone, J. (2016) 'New Child Support system is unsafe for domestic abuse survivors, charities warn', *The Independent,* 12 September.

Strauss, M. and Donnolly, P. (1993) 'Corporal punishment of adolescents by American parents', *Society* 24: 419.

Strong, S. (2000) 'Between the baby and the breast', *Cambridge Law Journal* 59: 259.

Sturge, C. and Glaser, D. (2000) 'Contact and domestic violence – the experts' court report', *Family Law* 30: 615.

Stylianou, K. (2011) 'Challenging facing family mediation', *Family Law* 41: 874.

Sugarman, S. (1990) 'Dividing financial interests on divorce', in S. Sugarman and H. Kay (eds) *Divorce Reform at the Crossroads,* New Haven: Yale University Press.

Suk, J. (2009) *At Home in the Law,* New Haven: Yale University Press.

Sullivan, O. (2013) 'What do we learn about gender by analyzing housework separately from child care?' *Journal of Family Theory and Review* 5: 72.

Suresh, S. (2020) 'Welfare assessment in radicalisation cases under the Children Act 1989: to what extent do race and gender influence judicial intervention in the family home? Part II', *Family Law* 50: 730.

Sutherland, E. (2003) '"Man not included" – single women, female couples and procreative freedom in the UK', *Child and Family Law Quarterly* 15: 155.

Tamanna, N. (2013) 'Recognition of "difference" in Shari'a: a feminist scrutiny through the lens of substantive equality', *Journal of Social Welfare and Family Law* 35: 329.

Taylor, A. (2008) 'Cousin marriage: a cause for concern?', *Bionews* 461: 1.

Taylor, C. (2006) *Young People in Care and Criminal Behaviour,* London: Jessica Kingsley.

Taylor, R. (2006) 'Children's privacy and press freedom in criminal cases', *Child and Family Law Quarterly* 18: 269.

Taylor, R. (2007) 'Reversing the retreat from *Gillick*?', *Child and Family Law Quarterly* 19: 81.

Taylor, R. (2009) 'Parental responsibility and religion', in R. Probert, S. Gilmore and J. Herring (2009) *Responsible Parents and Parental Responsibility,* Oxford: Hart.

Taylor, R. (2011) 'Poles apart: fixed principles and shifting values in relocation law', in S. Gilmore, J. Herring and R. Probert (eds) *Landmark Cases in Family Law,* Oxford: Hart.

Taylor, R. (2013) 'Secular values and sacred rights: *Re G (Education: Religious Upbringing)*', *Child and Family Law Quarterly* 25: 336.

Taylor, R. (2015) 'Responsibility for the soul of the child: the role of the state and parents in determining religious upbringing and education', *International Journal of Law, Policy and the Family* 29: 15.

Taylor, R. (2016) 'Putting children first? Children's interests as a primary consideration in public law', *Child and Family Law Quarterly* 45.

Taylor, R. (2017) 'Pensions on divorce: another witches' brew', *Family Law* 163.

Taylor, R. (2018) 'Religion as harm? Radicalisation, extremism and child protection', *Child and Family Law Quarterly* 41.

Taylor, R. (2019) 'Grandparents and grandchildren: relatedness, relationships and responsibility', in B. Clough and J. Herring (eds) *Ageing, Gender and Family Law,* London: Routledge.

Taylor, R. (2020) 'Parental decisions and court jurisdiction: best interests or significant harm?' *Child and Family Law Quarterly* 141.

Taylor, R. and Hoyano, L. (2012) Criminal child maltreatment: the case for reform', *Criminal Law Review* 817.

Taylor, T. (2015)'Apples or pears? Pension offsetting on divorce', *Family Law* 1429.

Taylor Sands, M. (2013) *Saviour Siblings,* Abingdon: Routledge.

Tee, L. (2001) 'Division of property upon relationship breakdown', in J. Herring (ed.) *Family Law: Issues, Debates, Policy,* Cullompton: Willan.

Thatcher, A. (2011) *God, Sex and Gender,* Bristol: Wiley.

Thatcher, M. (1995) *The Downing Street Years,* London: HarperCollins.

Thiara, R. and Gill, A. (2010) *Violence against Women in South Asian Communities: Issues for Policy and Practice,* London: Jessica Kingsley Publishers.

Thoburn, J. (2003) 'The risks and rewards of adoption for children in the public care', *Child and Family Law Quarterly* 15: 391.

Thomas, N. (2001) 'Listening to children', in P. Foley, J. Roche and S. Tucker (eds) *Children in Society,* Buckingham: Open University Press.

Thomas, N., Cook, M., Cook, J., France, H., Hillman, J., Jenkins, C., Pearson, T., Pugh-Dungey, R., Sawyers, B., Taylor, M. and

Crowley, A. (2010) 'Evaluating the Children's Commissioner for Wales', *International Journal of Children's Rights* 18: 19.

Thompson, G. (2010) *Domestic Violence Statistics*, London: Hansard.

Thompson, L. (2020) 'Impossible expectations? Abused mothers' experiences of the child protection and family court systems', *Child and Family Law Quarterly* 31.

Thompson, M., Vinter, L. and Young, V. (2005) *Dads and their Babies*, London: EOC.

Thompson, S. (2011) '*Radmacher (formerly Granatino) v Granatino* [2010] UKSC 42', *Journal of Social Welfare and Family Law* 33: 61.

Thompson, S. (2013) 'Collaborative law: success or failure?' *Family Law* 43: 604.

Thompson, S. (2015) *Prenuptial Agreements and the Presumption of Free Choice: Issues of Power in Theory and Practice*, Oxford: Hart.

Thornton, A., Azinn, W. and Xie, Y. (2007) *Cohabitation and Marriage*, Chicago: University of Chicago.

Thorpe, LJ (2000) 'Introduction', in Thorpe LJ and E. Clarke (eds) *No Fault or Flaw: The Future of the Family Law Act 1996*, Bristol: Jordans.

Tilley, J. (2000) 'Cultural relativism', *Human Rights Quarterly* 19: 461.

Tilley, S. (2007) 'Recognising gender differences in all issues mediation', *Family Law* 37: 352.

Tinker, A. (1997) *Older People in Modern Society*, Harlow: Longman.

Tisdall, K., Bray, R., Marshall, K. and Celeand, A. (2004) 'Children's participation in family law proceedings', *Journal of Social Welfare and Family Law* 26: 17.

Tobin, J. (2013) 'Justifying children's rights', *International Journal of Children's Rights* 22: 295.

Tobin, J. (2015) 'Taking children's rights seriously', in A. Diduck, N. Peleg and H. Reece (eds) *Law in Society*, Leiden: Brill.

Todd, R. (2006) 'The inevitable triumph of the ante-nuptial contract', *Family Law* 36: 539.

Tolley, T. (2013) 'When binding is not binding and when not binding, binds: an analysis of the procedural route of non-binding arbitration in *AI v MT*', *Child and Family Law Quarterly* 25: 447.

Tolley, T. (2014) 'Hands-off or hands-on?: deconstructing the "test-case" of *Re G* within a culture of children's rights', *Modern Law Review* 77: 110.

Tolson, R. (2002) 'Goals and the team's performance', *Family Law* 32: 491.

Toner, H. (2004) *Partnership Rights, Free Movement and EU Law*, Oxford: Hart.

Trades Union Congress (2015) *Pay and Parenthood*, London: TUC.

Trew, J. and Drobnic, S. (2010) *Dividing the Domestic*, Stanford: University of Stanford Press.

Trimmings, K. and Beaumont, P. (eds) (2013) *International Surrogacy Arrangements*, Oxford: Hart.

Trinder, L. (2003) 'Working and not working contact after divorce', in A. Bainham, B. Lindley, M. Richards and L. Trinder (eds) *Children and Their Families*, Oxford: Hart.

Trinder, L. (2005) *A Profile of Applicants and Respondents in Contact Cases in Essex*, London: DCA.

Trinder, L. (2010) 'Shared residence: a review of recent research evidence', *Child and Family Law Quarterly* 21: 151.

Trinder, L. (2014) 'Climate change? The multiple trajectories of shared care law, policy and social practices', *Child and Family Law Quarterly* 30.

Trinder, L. (2015) 'In anticipation of a temporary blip: would a change in the divorce law increase the divorce rate?', at www.findingfault. org.uk/.

Trinder, L. (2017a) 'Losing the particulars? Digital divorce and the potential for harm reduction', *Family Law* 17.

Trinder, L. (2017b) *Finding Fault? Divorce Law and Practice in England and Wales*, London: Nuffield Foundation.

Trinder, L. (2018a) *No Contest*. London: Nuffield Foundation.

Trinder, L., Beek, M. and Connolly, J. (2002) *Making Contact: How Parents and Children Negotiate and Experience Contact After Divorce*, York: Joseph Rowntree Foundation.

Trinder, L., Connolly, J., Kellett, J. and Notley, C. (2006) *Evaluation of Family Resolutions Pilot Project*, London: DfES.

Trinder, L., Firth, A., and Jenks, C. (2010) '"So presumably things have moved on since then?" The management of risk allegations in child contact dispute resolution', *International Journal of Law, Policy and the Family* 24: 29.

Trinder, L., Hunt, J., Macleod, A., Pearce, J. and Woodward, J. (2013) *Enforcing Contact Orders: problem-solving or punishment?* Exeter: University of Exeter.

Trinder, L., Hunter, R., Hitchings, E., Miles, J., Moorhead, R., Smith, L, Sefton, M., Hinchly, V., Bader, K. and Pearce, J. (2014) *Litigants in*

Person in Private Family Law Cases, London: Ministry of Justice.

Trinder, L., Jenks, C. and Firth, A. (2010) 'Talking children into being *in absentia*? Children as a strategic and contingent resource in family court dispute resolution', *Child and Family Law Quarterly* 22: 234.

Trinder, L. and Kellett, J. (2007) 'Fairness, efficiency and effectiveness in court-based dispute resolution schemes in England', *International Journal of Law, Policy and the Family* 21: 322.

Trotter, S. (2018) 'The child in European human rights law', *Modern Law Review* 81: 412.

Trust for London (2011) *Domestic Violence Costs £5.5bn a year in England*, London: Trust for London.

Turkmendag, I., Dingwall, R. and Murphy, T. (2008) 'The removal of donor anonymity in the UK: the silencing of claims by would-be parents', *International Journal of Law, Policy and the Family* 22: 283.

UK Children's Commissioners (2009) *Joint Position Statement on Progress on the 2008 United Nations Committee on the Rights of the Child's Concluding Observations*, London: 11 Million.

Ungerson, C. (1987) *Policy is Personal: Sex, Gender and Informal Care*, London: Tavistock.

UNICEF (2020) *Worlds of Influence: Understanding what shapes child well-being in rich countries*, Geneva: UNICEF.

United Kingdom College of Mediators (2000) *Code of Practice for Family Mediators*, London: UK College of Mediators.

United Nations Committee on the Rights of the Child (2008) *Concluding Observations: United Kingdom*, Geneva: United Nations.

United Nations Human Rights Committee (2008) *Report*, Geneva: United Nations.

Valentine, G. (2004) *Public Space and the Culture of Childhood*, Aldershot: Ashgate.

Van der Sloot, B. (2014) 'Between fact and fiction: an analysis of the case-law on Article 12 of the European Convention on Human Rights', *Child and Family Law Quarterly* 397.

Van Krieken, R. (2005) 'The "best interests of the child" on parental separation: on the "civilising of parents"', *Modern Law Review* 68: 25.

Vardag, A. and Miles, J. (2016) 'The rite that defines the right?' in J. Miles, R. Mody and R. Probert (eds) *Marriage Rites and Rights*, Oxford: Hart.

Voice of the Child Dispute Resolution Advisory Group (2015) *Final Report*, London: Ministry of Justice.

Vogler, C. (2009) 'Managing money in intimate relationships', in J. Miles and R. Probert (eds) *Sharing Lives, Dividing Assets*, Oxford: Hart.

Vonk, M. (2007) *Children and Their Parents*, Antwerp: Intersentia.

Vora, V. (2016) 'The problem of unregistered Muslim marriage: questions and solutions', *Family Law* 46: 95.

Vora, V. (2020) 'The Continuing Muslim Marriage Conundrum: The Law of England and Wales on Religious Marriage and Non-Marriage in the United Kingdom', *Journal of Muslim Minority Affairs* 40: 148.

Waal, de, A. (2008) *Second Thoughts on the Family*, London: Civitas.

Waal, de, A. (ed.) (2013) *The Meaning of Matrimony*, London: Civitas.

Waddington, W. (2000) 'Marriage: an institution in transition and redefinition', in S. Katz, J. Eekelaar and M. Maclean (eds) *Cross Currents*, Oxford: OUP.

Wade, J. Biehal, N., Farrelly, N. and Sinclair, I. (2012) *Returning Home from Care: What's Best for Children?* London: NSPCC.

Wade, J., Dixon, J. and Richards, A. (2009) *Implementing Special Guardianship*, London: Department for Children, Schools and Families.

Waite, L. (2000) 'Cohabitation: a communitarian perspective', in M. Whyte (ed.) *Marriage in America*, Lanham, Md.: Rowman & Littlefield.

Waite, L. and Gallagher, M. (2001) *The Case for Marriage*, New York: Broadway Books.

Waites, M. (2005) *The Age of Consent: Young People, Sexuality and Citizenship*, Basingstoke: Palgrave.

Walby, S. (2004) *The Cost of Domestic Violence*, London: Home Office.

Walby, S. and Allen, J. (2004) *Domestic Violence, Sexual Assault and Stalking*, London: Home Office.

Walker, J. (2000) 'Information meetings revisited', *Family Law* 30: 330.

Walker, J. (2001a) *Information Meetings and Associated Provisions within the Family Law Act 1996*, London: Lord Chancellor's Department.

Walker, J. (2001b) 'The information pilots – using and abusing evidence', *Family Law* 31: 817.

Walker, J. (2004) 'FAInS – a new approach for family lawyers', *Family Law* 34: 436.

Walker, J. (2013) 'How can we ensure that children's voices are heard in mediation?', *Family Law* 43: 191.

Walker, J. and Lake-Carroll, A. (2014) 'Hearing the voices of children and young people in dispute resolution processes: promoting a child-inclusive approach', *Family Law* 48: 1577.

Walker, J. and Lake-Carroll, A. (2015) 'Child-inclusive dispute resolution: time for change', *Family Law* 49: 692.

Walker, J. and McCarthy, P. (2004) 'Picking up the pieces', *Family Law* 34: 580.

Walker, L. and Shapiro, D. (2010) 'Parental Alienation Disorder: why label children with a mental diagnosis?' *Journal of Child Custody* 7: 266.

Wall, HHJ (1997) 'Domestic violence and contact', *Family Law* 27: 813.

Wall, LJ (2006) *A Report to the President of the Family Division*, London: DCA.

Wall, LJ (2009) 'Making contact work in 2009', *Family Law* 39: 590.

Wall, P. (2010) 'Revised protocol for referrals of families to supported child contact centres by judges and magistrates', *Family Law* 40: 858.

Wall, P. (2012) 'The President's resolution address 2012', *Family Law* 42: 742.

Wallbank, J. (1998) 'Castigating mothers: the judicial response to wilful women in cases concerning contact', *Journal of Social Welfare and Family Law* 20: 257.

Wallbank, J. (2002) 'Clause 106 of the Adoption and Children Bill: legislation for the "good" father?' *Legal Studies* 22: 276.

Wallbank, J. (2004a) 'Reconstructing the HFEA 1990: is blood really thicker than water?' *Child and Family Law Quarterly* 16: 387.

Wallbank, J. (2004b) 'The role of rights and utility in instituting a child's right to know her genetic history', *Social and Legal Studies* 13: 245.

Wallbank, J. (2007) 'Getting tough on mothers: regulating contact and residence', *Feminist Legal Studies* 15: 189.

Wallbank, J. (2009) '"Bodies in the shadows": joint birth registration, parental responsibility and social class', *Child and Family Law Quarterly* 21: 267.

Wallbank, J. (2009) '(En)Gendering the fusion of rights and responsibilities in the law of contact', in J. Wallbank, S. Choudhry and J. Herring (eds) *Rights, Gender and Family Law*, Abingdon: Routledge.

Wallbank, J. A. (2010) 'Channelling the messiness of diverse family lives: resisting the calls to order and de-centring the hetero-normative family', *Journal of Social Welfare and Family Law* 32: 353.

Wallbank, J. (2014) 'Universal norms, individualization and the need for recognition', in J. Wallbank and J. Herring (eds) *Vulnerabilities, Care and Family Law*, London: Routledge.

Wallbank, J. and Dietz, C. (2013) 'Lesbian mothers, fathers and other animals: is the political personal in multiple parent families?' *Child and Family Law Quarterly* 25: 452.

Wallbank, J., Choudhry, S. and Herring, J. (eds) (2009) *Rights, Gender and Family Law*, London: Routledge.

Wallbank, J. and Herring, J. (2014) *Vulnerabilities, Care and Family Law*, London: Routledge.

Walsh, E. (2010) 'Children's guardians', *Family Law* 40: 783.

Wardle, L. (2006) 'The "end" of marriage', *Family Court Review* 44: 45.

Warman, C. and Roberts, C. (2003) *Adoption and Looked After Children – an International Comparison*, Oxford: Oxford Centre for Family Law and Policy.

Warner, K. (2000) 'Sentencing in cases of marital rape: towards changing the male imagination', *Legal Studies* 20: 592.

Warnock Report (1984) *Report of the Committee of Inquiry into Human Fertilisation and Embryology*, London: HMSO.

Warnock, M. (2002) *Making Babies*, Oxford: OUP.

Warnock, M. (2006) 'The limits of rights-based discourse', in J. Spencer and A. du Bois-Pedain (eds) *Freedom and Responsibility in Reproductive Choice*, Oxford: Hart.

Warren, E. (2002) 'Bankrupt children', *Minnesota Law Review* 86: 1003.

Warshak, R. (2013) 'In a land far, far away: assessing children's best interests in international relocation cases', *Journal of Child Custody* 10: 332.

Waterhouse, R. (2000) *Lost in Care*, London: The Stationery Office.

Watkins, D. (2016) 'Where do I stand? Assessing children's capabilities under English law', *Child and Family Law Quarterly* 25.

Watson, N. (2014) 'Achieving justice in no more than 26 weeks: the role of the local authority', *Family Law* 829.

Watson-Lee, P. (2004) 'Financial provision on divorce: clarity and fairness', *Family Law* 34: 348.

Weeks, J. (2004) 'The rights and wrongs of sexuality', in B. Brooks-Gordon, L. Goldsthorpe, M. Johnson and A. Bainham (eds) *Sexuality Repositioned*, Oxford: Hart.

Weeks, J., Donovan, C. and Heaphy, B. (2001) *Same-Sex Intimacies: Families of Choice and Other Life Experiments*, London: Routledge.

Weiner, M. (2015) 'Caregiver payments and the obligation to give care or share', *Villanova Law Review* 59: 135.

Welbourne, P. (2002) 'Adoption and the rights of children in the UK', *International Journal of Children's Rights* 10: 269.

Welbourne, P. (2017) 'Parents' and children's rights and good practice: section 20', *Family Law* 47: 80.

Weldon-Johns, M. (2011) 'The Additional Paternity Leave Regulations 2010: a new dawn or more "sound-bite" legislation', *Journal of Social Welfare and Family Law* 33: 25.

Welsh, E., Buchanan, A., Flouri, E. and Lewis, J. (2004) *Involved Fathering and Child Well-being*, London: National Children's Bureau.

Welstead, M. and Edwards, S. (2006) *Family Law*, Oxford: OUP.

Welstead, M. (2012) 'The sharing of pre-matrimonial property on divorce: *K v L*', *Family Law* 169.

Welstead, M. (2015) 'The parenthood war: biological fathers, lesbian mothers and the best interests of their children', *Family Law* 45: 356.

Welstead, M. (2019) 'A New Pathway to Domestic Surrogacy (Building Families Through Surrogacy: A New Law: The Law Commission's Joint Consultation Paper)', *Family Law* 49: 1031.

Welstead, M. (2020) 'Parental alienation – whose judgment?' *Family Law* 50: 375.

Westendorp, I. and Wolleswinkel, R. (2005) *Violence in the Domestic Sphere*, Antwerp: Intersentia.

Westwood, S. (2015) 'Complicating kinship and inheritance: older lesbians' and gay men's will-writing in England', *Feminist Legal Studies* 23: 181.

White, M. (2010) 'Same-sex marriage: the irrelevance of the economic approach to law', *International Journal of Law in Context* 6: 139.

Whitehead, T. (2011) 'Divorce is easier than obtaining driving licence, warns judge', *Daily Telegraph*, 13 July.

Whittle, S. (2002) *Respect and Equality*, London: Cavendish.

Who Cares? Trust (2000) *Remember My Messages*, London: Who Cares? Trust.

Who Cares? Trust (2014) *Statistics*, London: Who Cares? Trust.

Wikeley, N. (2005) '*R (Kehoe)* v *Secretary of State*: no redress when the Child Support Agency fails to deliver', *Child and Family Law Quarterly* 16: 97.

Wikeley, N. (2006a) 'Child support – back to the drawing board', *Family Law* 36: 312.

Wikeley, N. (2006b) *Child Support: Law and Policy*, Oxford: Hart.

Wikeley, N. (2007) 'Child support reform – throwing the baby out with the bathwater', *Child and Family Law Quarterly* 19: 435.

Wikeley, N. (2008a) 'Child support: the brave new world', *Family Law* 38: 1024.

Wikeley, N. (2008b) 'Child support: carrots and sticks', *Family Law* 38: 1102.

Wikeley, N. (2009) 'Financial support for children after parental separation: parental responsibility and responsible parenting', in R. Probert, S. Gilmore and J. Herring (eds) *Responsible Parents and Parental Responsibility*, Oxford: Hart.

Wikeley, N. and Young, L. (2008) 'Secrets and lies: no deceit down under for paternity fraud', *Child and Family Law Quarterly* 20: 81.

Wikeley, N., Ireland, E., Bryson, C. and Smith, R. (2008) *Relationship separation and child support study*, DWP Research Report 503, London: DWP.

Wild, L. and Richards, M. (2003) 'Exploring parent and child perceptions of interparental conflict', *International Journal of Law, Policy and Family* 17: 366.

Wilhelms, E. and V. Reyna (2013) 'Fuzzy trace theory and medical decisions by minors: Differences in reasoning between adolescents and adults', *The Journal of Medicine and Philosophy* 38: 268–82.

Wilkinson, B. (2009) 'Child protection: the statutory failure', *Family Law* 39: 420.

Willbourne, C. and Stanley, G. (2002) 'Contact under the microscope', *Family Law* 32: 687.

Willems, J. (2007) *Developmental and Autonomy Rights of Children*, Antwerp: Intersentia.

Williams, C. (2002) 'The practical operation of the Children Act complaints procedure', *Child and Family Law Quarterly* 14: 25.

Williams, C., Potter, G. and Douglas, G. (2008) 'Cohabitation and intestacy: public opinion and law reform', *Child and Family Law Quarterly* 20: 499.

849

Williams, J. (2008) 'State responsibility and the abuse of vulnerable older people: is there a case for a public law to protect vulnerable older people from abuse?' in J. Bridgeman, H. Keating and C. Lind (eds) *Responsibility, Law and the Family*, London: Ashgate.

Williams, K. (2011) *Litigants in Person: A Literature Review*, London: Ministry of Justice.

Willitts, M., Anderson, T., Tait, C. and Williams, G. (2005) *Children in Britain*, London: DWP.

Wilson, B. (2004) 'Emotion, rationality and decision-making in mediation', *Family Law* 34: 682.

Wilson, B. (2009) 'ADR professionals: do mediators care?' *Family Law* 39: 201.

Wilson, J. (2007) 'The ears of the child in family proceeding', *Family Law* 37: 808.

Wilson, Lord (2017) 'Changes over the centuries in the financial consequences of divorce', *Family Law* 728.

Woelke, A. (2002) 'Family credo', *Family Law* 32: 475.

Women's Aid (2003) *Failure to Protect*, London: Women's Aid.

Women's Aid (2012) *Picking Up the Pieces: Domestic Violence and Child Contact*, London: Women's Aid.

Women's Aid (2014) *Evidencing Domestic Violence: A Year On*, London: Women's Aid.

Women's Aid (2016) *Annual Survey*, London: Women's Aid.

Women's Aid (2017) *Femicide Census*, London: Women's Aid.

Women's Aid and CAFCASS (2017) *Allegations of domestic abuse in child contact cases*, London: Women's Aid.

Wong, S. (2005) 'The Human Rights Act 1998 and the shared home: issues for cohabitants', *Journal of Social Welfare and Family Law* 27: 265.

Wong, S. (2006) 'Cohabitation and the Law Commission's Project', *Feminist Legal Studies* 14: 145.

Wong, S. (2009) 'Caring and sharing: interdependency as a basis for property redistribution', in A. Bottomley and S. Wong (eds) *Changing Contours of Domestic Life, Family and Law*, Oxford: Hart.

Wong, S. and Cain, R. (2019) 'The impact of cuts in legal aid funding of private family law cases', x*Journal of Social Welfare and Family Law* 41: 3.

Wood, M. Barter, C. and Berridge, D. (2011) *'Standing On My Own Two Feet': Disadvantaged Teenagers, Intimate Partner Violence and Coercive Control*, London: NSPCC.

Woodhouse, B. (2000) 'The status of children', in S. Katz, J. Eekelaar and M. Maclean (eds) *Cross Currents*, Oxford: OUP.

Woodhouse, B. (2008) *Hidden in Plain Sight*, Princeton: Princeton University Press.

Woodward, H. (2015) 'Everyday' financial remedy orders: do they achieve fair pension provision on divorce?' *Child and Family Law Quarterly* 151.

Woodward, H. and Sefton, M. (2014) *Pensions on Divorce: A Study on When and How they are Taken into Account*, Cardiff: Cardiff University.

World Health Organization (2017) *Violence against Women*, Geneva: WHO.

Worwood, A. and Hale, C. (2016) 'Internal Relocation and Proportionality', *Family Law* 369.

Wray, H. (2016) 'The "pure" relationship, sham marriages and immigration control', in J. Miles, R. Mody and R. Probert (eds) *Marriage Rites and Rights*, Oxford: Hart.

Wright, C. (2006) 'The divorce process: a view from the other side of the desk', *Child and Family Law Quarterly* 18: 93.

Wright, K. (2008) 'Competing interests in reproduction: the case of Natallie Evans', *King's College Law Journal* 19: 135.

Yon, Y. Mikton, C., Gassoumis, Z. and Wilber, K. (2017) 'Elder Abuse Prevalence in Community Settings: A Systematic Review and Meta-analysis' (2017) 5(2) *The Lancet Global Health* e147.

YouGov (2015) *1 in 2 young people say they are not 100% heterosexual*, London: YouGov.

Young, Baroness (1996) *Hansard* (HL) vol. 569, col. 1638, 29 February.

Young, L. (2011) 'Resolving relocation disputes: the "interventionist" approach in Australia', *Child and Family Law Quarterly* 23: 278.

Young, L. and Wikeley, N. (2015) 'Earning capacity and maintenance in Anglo-Australian family law: different paths, same destination?' *Child and Family Law Quarterly* 129.

Young Minds (2020) *Mental Health Statistics*, London: Young Minds.

Zanghellini, A. (2018) 'Children's welfare, religious freedom, LGBTQ rights, and state neutrality: a philosophical discussion, by reference to *J v B* and *Lee v McArthur*', *Child and Family Law Quarterly* 178.

Zee, M. (2016) *Choosing Sharia? Multiculturalism, Islamic fundamentalism and Sharia Councils*, London: Eleven International Publishing.

Index

Publisher's acknowledgements

Text Credit(s):

The Incorporated Council of Law Reporting: 1 *Huang v Secretary of State for the Home Department,* [2007] 2 AC 167; **5:** *Gammans v Ekins* [1950] 2 KB 328 at p.331; **82:** In *Re G (Adoption: Unmarried Couple)* [2009] AC 173; **83:** *Hyde v Hyde and Woodhouse* (1866) LR 1 PD 130 at p.133, per Lord Penzance; **83, 85:** *Ghaidan v Godin-Mendoza* [2004] 2 AC 557; **129:** In *Re G (Adoption: Unmarried Couple)* [2009] AC 173; **130:** *Ghaidan v Godin-Mendoza* [2004] 2 AC 557; **137:** *Midland Bank Trust Co Ltd v Green* (No. 3) [1982] Ch 529 at p. 538; **139:** *In Re G (Adoption: Unmarried Couple)* [2009] AC 173; **185:** *Lloyds Bank v Rosset* [1991] 1 AC 107; **190:** *Stack v Dowden* [2007] 2 AC 432; **190:** *Marr v Collie* [2018] AC 631; **194:** *Thorner v Major* [2009] 1 WLR 776; **243:** *Miller v McFarlane* [2006] 2 AC 618; **255:** *W v W* [1976] Fam 107 at 110; **421, 470, 593:** In *Re G (Children) (Residence: Same-Sex Partner)* [2006] 1 WLR 2305; **426:** *S v S, W v Official Solicitor* (or W) [1972] AC 24; **450:** *Gillick v W Norfolk and Wisbech AHA* [1986] AC 112 at p. 184, per Lord Scarman; **470:** *J v C* [1970] AC 668 at pp. 710–11; **562:** In *Re D (A Child) (Abduction: Rights of Custody)* [2007] 1 AC 619; **648:** *R (On the Application of G) v Barnet LBC* [2004] 2 AC 208; **680:** In *Re H (Minors) (Sexual Abuse: Standard of Proof)* [1996] AC 563 at p. 586; **704:** In *Re G (Adoption: Unmarried Couple)* [2009] AC 173; **735:** In *Re B (Adoption: Jurisdiction to Set Aside)* [1995] Fam 239, at 245C; **747:** *JD v East Berkshire Community Health NHS Trust* [2005] 2 AC 373, para 85; **754:** In *Re B (Care Proceedings: Standard of Proof)* [2009] AC 11.